Microsoft®
EXCEL® 2010
COMPREHENSIVE

Microsoft®
EXCEL® 2010
COMPREHENSIVE

Gary B. Shelly
Jeffrey J. Quasney
Steven M. Freund
Raymond E. Enger
Mali B. Jones

COURSE TECHNOLOGY
CENGAGE Learning™

SHELLY
CASHMAN
SERIES®

Australia • Brazil • Japan • Korea • Mexico • Singapore • Spain • United Kingdom • United States

COURSE TECHNOLOGY
CENGAGE Learning

Microsoft® Excel® 2010: Comprehensive
Gary B. Shelly, Jeffrey J. Quasney,
Steven M. Freund, Raymond E. Enger,
Mali B. Jones

Vice President, Publisher: Nicole Pinard

Executive Editor: Kathleen McMahon

Product Manager: Jon Farnham

Associate Product Manager: Aimee Poirier

Editorial Assistant: Angela Giannopoulos

Director of Marketing: Elisa Roberts

Marketing Manager: Tristen Kendall

Marketing Coordinator: Adrienne Fung

Print Buyer: Julio Esperas

Director of Production: Patty Stephan

Content Project Manager: Matthew Hutchinson

Development Editors: Jill Batistick and
Lisa Ruffolo

Copyeditor: Foxxe Editorial

Proofreader: Chris Clark

Indexer: Rich Carlson

QA Manuscript Reviewers: Chris Scriver,
John Freitas, Serge Palladino, Susan Pedicini,
Danielle Shaw

Art Director: Marissa Falco

Cover Designer: Lisa Kuhn, Curio Press, LLC

Cover Photo: Tom Kates Photography

Text Design: Joel Sadagursky

Compositor: PreMediaGlobal

Microsoft and the Office logo are either
registered trademarks or trademarks of
Microsoft Corporation in the United States
and/or other countries. Course Technology,
a part of Cengage Learning, is an independent
entity from the Microsoft Corporation, and
not affiliated with Microsoft in any manner.

Library of Congress Control Number: 2011920009

ISBN-13: 978-1-4390-7901-0

ISBN-10: 1-4390-7901-3

Course Technology
20 Channel Center Street
Boston, MA 02210
USA

Cengage Learning is a leading provider of customized learning solutions with
office locations around the globe, including Singapore, the United Kingdom,
Australia, Mexico, Brazil, and Japan. Locate your local office at:
international.cengage.com/region

Cengage Learning products are represented in Canada by Nelson Education, Ltd.

Visit our website **www.cengage.com/ct/shellycashman** to share and gain
ideas on our textbooks!

To learn more about Course Technology,
visit **www.cengage.com/coursetechnology**

Purchase any of our products at your local college store or at our preferred
online store **www.cengagebrain.com**

*We dedicate this book to the memory of James S. Quasney (1940 – 2009), who for 18 years co-authored
numerous books with Tom Cashman and Gary Shelly and provided extraordinary leadership to the Shelly
Cashman Series editorial team. As series editor, Jim skillfully coordinated, organized, and managed the
many aspects of our editorial development processes and provided unending direction, guidance, inspiration,
support, and advice to the Shelly Cashman Series authors and support team members. He was a trusted,
dependable, loyal, and well-respected leader, mentor, and friend. We are forever grateful to Jim for his faithful
devotion to our team and eternal contributions to our series.*

The Shelly Cashman Series Team

Printed in the United States of America
3 4 5 6 7 17 16 15 14 13 12

Microsoft® EXCEL® 2010 COMPREHENSIVE

Contents

Microsoft **Excel 2010**

Appendices

What is the Microsoft® Office Specialist Program?

The Microsoft Office Specialist Program enables candidates to show that they have something exceptional to offer – proven expertise in certain Microsoft programs. Recognized by businesses and schools around the world, over 4 million certifications have been obtained in over 100 different countries. The Microsoft Office Specialist Program is the only Microsoft-approved certification program of its kind.

What is the Microsoft Office Specialist Certification?

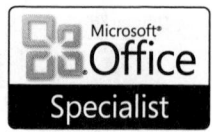 The Microsoft Office Specialist certification validates through the use of exams that you have obtained specific skill sets within the applicable Microsoft Office programs and other Microsoft programs included in the Microsoft Office Specialist Program. The candidate can choose which exam(s) they want to take according to which skills they want to validate.

The available Microsoft Office Specialist Program exams include*:
- Using Windows Vista®
- Using Microsoft® Office Word 2007
- Using Microsoft® Office Word 2007 - Expert
- Using Microsoft® Office Excel® 2007
- Using Microsoft® Office Excel® 2007 - Expert
- Using Microsoft® Office PowerPoint® 2007
- Using Microsoft® Office Access® 2007
- Using Microsoft® Office Outlook® 2007
- Using Microsoft SharePoint® 2007

The Microsoft Office Specialist Program 2010 exams will include*:
- Microsoft Word 2010
- Microsoft Word 2010 Expert
- Microsoft Excel® 2010
- Microsoft Excel® 2010 Expert
- Microsoft PowerPoint® 2010
- Microsoft Access® 2010
- Microsoft Outlook® 2010
- Microsoft SharePoint® 2010

What does the Microsoft Office Specialist Approved Courseware logo represent?

 The logo indicates that this courseware has been approved by Microsoft to cover the course objectives that will be included in the relevant exam. It also means that after utilizing this courseware, you may be better prepared to pass the exams required to become a certified Microsoft Office Specialist.

For more information:

To learn more about Microsoft Office Specialist exams, visit www.microsoft.com/learning/msbc

To learn about other Microsoft approved courseware from Cengage Learning, visit www.cengagebrain.com

*The availability of Microsoft Office Specialist certification exams varies by Microsoft program, program version and language. Visit www.microsoft.com/learning for exam availability.

Microsoft, Access, Excel, the Office Logo, Outlook, PowerPoint, SharePoint, and Windows Vista are either registered trademarks or trademarks of Microsoft Corporation in the United States and/or other countries. The Microsoft Office Specialist logo and the Microsoft Office Specialist Approved Courseware logo are used under license from Microsoft Corporation.

Preface

The Shelly Cashman Series® offers the finest textbooks in computer education. We are proud that since Mircosoft Office 4.3, our series of Microsoft Office textbooks have been the most widely used books in education. With each new edition of our Office books, we make significant improvements based on the software and comments made by instructors and students. For this Microsoft Excel 2010 text, the Shelly Cashman Series development team carefully reviewed our pedagogy and analyzed its effectiveness in teaching today's Office student. Students today read less, but need to retain more. They need not only to be able to perform skills, but to retain those skills and know how to apply them to different settings. Today's students need to be continually engaged and challenged to retain what they're learning.

   With this Microsoft Excel 2010 text, we continue our commitment to focusing on the user and how they learn best.

Objectives of This Textbook

Microsoft Excel 2010: Comprehensive is intended for a ten- to fifteen-week period in a course that teaches Excel 2010 as the primary component. No experience with a computer is assumed, and no mathematics beyond the high school freshman level is required. The objectives of this book are:

- To offer a comprehensive presentation of Microsoft Excel 2010

- To expose students to practical examples of the computer as a useful tool

- To acquaint students with the proper procedures to create worksheets suitable for coursework, professional purposes, and personal use

- To help students discover the underlying functionality of Excel 2010 so they can become more productive

- To develop an exercise-oriented approach that allows learning by doing

New to This Edition

Microsoft Excel 2010: Comprehensive offers a number of new features and approaches, which improve student understanding, retention, transference, and skill in using Excel 2010. The following enhancements will enrich the learning experience:

- Office 2010 and Windows 7: Essential Concepts and Skills chapter presents basic Office 2010 and Windows 7 skills.

- Streamlined first chapter allows the ability to cover more advanced skills earlier.

- Chapter topic redistribution offers concise chapters that ensure complete skill coverage.

- New pedagogical elements enrich material, creating an accessible and user-friendly approach.

  - Break Points, a new boxed element, identify logical stopping points and give students instructions regarding what they should do before taking a break.

  - Within step instructions, Tab | Group Identifiers, such as (Home tab | Bold button), help students more easily locate elements in the groups and on the tabs on the Ribbon.

  - Modified step-by-step instructions tell the student what to do and provide the generic reason why they are completing a specific task, which helps students easily transfer given skills to different settings.

The Shelly Cashman Approach

A Proven Pedagogy with an Emphasis on Project Planning

Each chapter presents a practical problem to be solved, within a project planning framework. The project orientation is strengthened by the use of Plan Ahead boxes, which encourage critical thinking about how to proceed at various points in the project. Step-by-step instructions with supporting screens guide students through the steps. Instructional steps are supported by the Q&A, Experimental Step, and BTW features.

A Visually Engaging Book that Maintains Student Interest

The step-by-step tasks, with supporting figures, provide a rich visual experience for the student. Call-outs on the screens that present both explanatory and navigational information provide students with information they need when they need to know it.

Supporting Reference Materials (Appendices, Quick Reference)

The appendices provide additional information about the Application at hand and include such topics as project planning guidelines and certification. With the Quick Reference, students can quickly look up information about a single task, such as keyboard shortcuts, and find page references of where in the book the task is illustrated.

Integration of the World Wide Web

The World Wide Web is integrated into the Excel 2010 learning experience by (1) BTW annotations; (2) BTW, Q&A, and Quick Reference Summary Web pages; and (3) the Learn It Online section for each chapter.

End-of-Chapter Student Activities

Extensive end-of-chapter activities provide a variety of reinforcement opportunities for students where they can apply and expand their skills.

Instructor Resources

The Instructor Resources include both teaching and testing aids and can be accessed via CD-ROM or at login.cengage.com.

Instructor's Manual Includes lecture notes summarizing the chapter sections, figures and boxed elements found in every chapter, teacher tips, classroom activities, lab activities, and quick quizzes in Microsoft Word files.

Syllabus Easily customizable sample syllabi that cover policies, assignments, exams, and other course information.

Figure Files Illustrations for every figure in the textbook in electronic form.

PowerPoint Presentations A multimedia lecture presentation system that provides slides for each chapter. Presentations are based on chapter objectives.

Solutions To Exercises Includes solutions for all end-of-chapter and chapter reinforcement exercises.

Test Bank & Test Engine Test Banks include 112 questions for every chapter, featuring objective-based and critical thinking question types, and including page number references and figure references, when appropriate. Also included is the test engine, ExamView, the ultimate tool for your objective-based testing needs.

Data Files for Students Includes all the files that are required by students to complete the exercises.

Additional Activities for Students Consists of Chapter Reinforcement Exercises, which are true/false, multiple-choice, and short answer questions that help students gain confidence in the material learned.

SAM: Skills Assessment Manager

SAM 2010 is designed to help bring students from the classroom to the real world. It allows students to train on and test important computer skills in an active, hands-on environment.

SAM's easy-to-use system includes powerful interactive exams, training, and projects on the most commonly used Microsoft Office applications. SAM simulates the Microsoft Office 2010 application environment, allowing students to demonstrate their knowledge and think through the skills by performing real-world tasks such as bolding word text or setting up slide transitions. Add in live-in-the-application projects, and students are on their way to truly learning and applying skills to business-centric documents.

Designed to be used with the Shelly Cashman Series, SAM includes handy page references so that students can print helpful study guides that match the Shelly Cashman textbooks used in class. For instructors, SAM also includes robust scheduling and reporting features.

Book Resources

🔒 Additional Faculty Files
🔒 Blackboard Testbank
🔒 Data Files
🔒 Instructor's Manual
🔒 Lecture Success System
🔒 PowerPoint Presentations
🔒 Solutions to Exercises
🔒 Syllabus
🔒 Test Bank and Test Engine
🔒 WebCT Testbank

Chapter Reinforcement Exercises

Student Downloads

Content for Online Learning

Course Technology has partnered with the leading distance learning solution providers and class-management platforms today. To access this material, instructors will visit our password-protected instructor resources available at login.cengage.com. Instructor resources include the following: additional case projects, sample syllabi, PowerPoint presentations per chapter, and more. For additional information or for an instructor user name and password, please contact your sales representative. For students to access this material, they must have purchased a WebTutor PIN-code specific to this title and your campus platform. The resources for students may include (based on instructor preferences), but are not limited to: topic review, review questions, and practice tests.

Course Notes

Course Technology's CourseNotes are six-panel quick reference cards that reinforce the most important and widely used features of a software application in a visual and user-friendly format. CourseNotes serve as a great reference tool during and after the student completes the course. CourseNotes are available for software applications such as Microsoft Office 2010, Word 2010, Excel 2010, Access 2010, PowerPoint 2010, and Windows 7. Topic-based CourseNotes are available for Best Practices in Social Networking, Hot Topics in Technology, and Web 2.0. Visit www.cengagebrain.com to learn more!

A Guided Tour

Add excitement and interactivity to your classroom with "*A Guided Tour*" product line. Play one of the brief mini-movies to spice up your lecture and spark classroom discussion. Or, assign a movie for homework and ask students to complete the correlated assignment that accompanies each topic. "*A Guided Tour*" product line takes the prep work out of providing your students with information about new technologies and applications and helps keep students engaged with content relevant to their lives; all in under an hour!

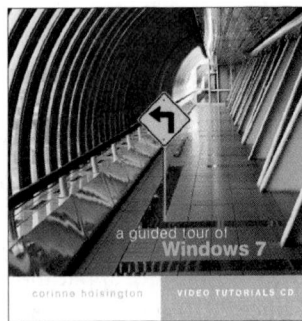

About Our Covers

The Shelly Cashman Series is continually updating our approach and content to reflect the way today's students learn and experience new technology. This focus on student success is reflected onour covers, which feature real students from University of Rhode Island using the Shelly Cashman Series in their courses, and reflect the varied ages and backgrounds of the students learning with our books. When you use the Shelly Cashman Series, you can be assured that you are learning computer skills using the most effective courseware available.

Textbook Walk-Through

The Shelly Cashman Series Pedagogy: Project-Based — Step-by-Step — Variety of Assessments

Plan Ahead boxes prepare students to create successful projects by encouraging them to think strategically about what they are trying to accomplish before they begin working.

Step-by-step instructions now provide a context beyond the point-and-click. Each step provides information on why students are performing each task, or what will occur as a result.

General Project Decisions

While creating an Excel worksheet, you need to make several decisions that will determine the appearance and characteristics of the finished worksheet. As you create the worksheet necessary to meet the requirements shown in Figure 2–2, you should follow these general guidelines:

1. **Plan the layout of the worksheet.** Rows typically contain items analogous to items in a list. A name could serve as an item in a list, and, therefore, each name could be placed in a row. As a list grows, such as a list of employees, the number of rows in the worksheet will increase. Information about each item in the list and associated calculations should appear in columns.

2. **Determine the necessary formulas and functions needed.** Calculations result from known values. Formulas for such calculations should be known in advance of creating a worksheet. Values such as the average, highest, and lowest values can be calculated using Excel functions as opposed to relying on complex formulas.

3. **Identify how to format various elements of the worksheet.** The appearance of the worksheet affects its ability to express information clearly. Numeric data should be formatted in generally accepted formats, such as using commas as thousands separators and parentheses for negative values.

4. **Establish rules for conditional formatting.** Conditional formatting allows you to format a cell based on the contents of the cell. Decide under which circumstances you would like a cell to stand out from related cells and determine in what way the cell will stand out.

5. **Specify how the hard copy of a worksheet should appear.** When it is possible that a person will want to create a hard copy of a worksheet, care should be taken in the development of the worksheet to ensure that the contents can be presented in a readable manner. Excel prints worksheets in landscape or portrait orientation, and margins can be adjusted to fit more or less data on each page. Headers and footers add an additional level of customization to the printed page.

When necessary, more specific details concerning the above guidelines are presented at appropriate points in the chapter. The chapter also will identify the actions performed and decisions made regarding these guidelines during the creation of the worksheet shown in Figure 2–1 on page EX 67.

Plan Ahead

In addition, using a sketch of the worksheet can help you visualize its design. The sketch for The Mobile Masses Store Biweekly Payroll Report worksheet includes a title, a subtitle, column and row headings, and the location of data values (Figure 2–3 on the following page). It also uses specific characters to define the desired formatting for the worksheet, as follows:

1. The row of Xs below the leftmost column defines the cell entries as text, such as employee names.

2. The rows of Zs and 9s with slashes, dollar signs, decimal points, commas, and percent signs in the remaining columns define the cell entries as numbers. The Zs indicate that the selected format should instruct Excel to suppress leading 0s. The 9s indicate that the selected format should instruct Excel to display any digits, including 0s.

3. The decimal point means that a decimal point should appear in the cell entry and indicates the number of decimal places to use.

4. The slashes in the second column identify the cell entry as a date.

5. The dollar signs that are not adjacent to the Zs in the first row below the column headings and in the total row signify a fixed dollar sign. The dollar signs that are adjacent to the Zs below the total row signify a floating dollar sign, or one that appears next to the first significant digit.

BTW

Aesthetics versus Function

The function, or purpose, of a worksheet is to provide a user with direct ways to accomplish tasks. In designing a worksheet, functional considerations should come before visual aesthetics. Avoid the temptation to use flashy or confusing visual elements within the worksheet. One exception to this guideline occurs when you may need to draw the user's attention to an area of a worksheet that will help the user more easily complete a task.

EX 86   Excel Chapter 2   Formulas, Functions, and Formatting

To Determine the Highest Number in a Range of Number

The next step is to select cell C15 and determine the highest (maximum
includes a function called the **MAX function** that displays the highest valu
the MAX function using the keyboard and Point mode as described in the p
to entering the function is to use the Insert Function box in the formula bar
Function box in the formula bar to enter the MAX function.

1

- Select the cell to contain the maximum number, cell C15 in this case.

- Click the Insert Function box in the formula bar to display the Insert Function dialog box.

- Click MAX in the 'Select a function' list (Insert Function dialog box) to select it (Figure 2–19). If the MAX function is not displayed in the 'Select a function' list, scroll the list until the function is displayed.

Figure 2–19

2

- Click the OK button (Insert Function dialog box) to display the Function Arguments dialog box.

- Type c4:c12 in the Number1 box (Function Arguments dialog box) to enter the first argument of the function (Figure 2–20).

Q&A Why did numbers appear in the Function Arguments dialog box?

As shown in Figure 2–20, Excel displays the value the MAX function will return to cell C15 in the Function Arguments dialog box. It also lists the first few numbers in the selected range, next to the Number1 box.

Figure 2–20

Explanatory callouts summarize what is happening on screen.

Navigational callouts in red show students where to click.

Break Points identify logical breaks in the chapter if students need to stop before completing the project.

Q&A boxes offer questions students may have when working through the steps and provide additional information about what they are doing right where they need it.

Experiment Steps within our step-by-step instructions, encourage students to explore, experiment, and take advantage of the features of the Excel 2010 user interface. These steps are not necessary to complete the projects, but are designed to increase the confidence with the software and build problem-solving skills.

To Save a Workbook Using the Same File Name

Earlier in this project, an intermediate version of the workbook was saved using the file name, The Mobile Masses Biweekly Payroll Report. The following step saves the workbook a second time, using the same file name.

1 Click the Save button on the Quick Access Toolbar to overwrite the previously saved file.

Break Point: If you wish to take a break, this is a good place to do so. You can quit Excel now. To resume at a later time, start Excel, open the file called Mobile Masses Biweekly Payroll Report, and continue following the steps from this location forward.

Verifying Formulas Using Range Finder

One of the more common mistakes made with Excel is to include a wrong cell reference in a formula. An easy way to verify that a formula references the cells you want it to reference is to use the Excel Range Finder. Use **Range Finder** to check which cells are referenced in the formula assigned to the active cell. Range Finder allows you to make immediate changes to the cells referenced in a formula.

To use Range Finder to verify that a formula contains the intended cell references, double-click the cell with the formula you want to check. Excel responds by highlighting the cells referenced in the formula so that you can check that the cell references are correct.

BTW

Entering Functions
You can drag the Function Arguments dialog box (Figure 2–20 on page EX 86) out of the way in order to select a range. You also can click the Collapse Dialog button to the right of the Number 1 box to hide the Function Arguments dialog box. The dialog box then collapses and the Collapse Dialog button becomes an Expand Dialog box button. After selecting the range, click the Expand Dialog to expand the dialog box.

To Verify a Formula Using Range Finder

The following steps use Range Finder to check the formula in cell J4.

1
• Double-click cell J4 to activate Range Finder

EX 96 Excel Chapter 2 Formulas, Functions, and Formatting

Q&A

What is the effect of clicking the Decrease Font Size button?

When you click the Decrease Font Size button, Excel assigns the next lowest font size in the Font Size gallery to the selected range. The Increase Font Size button works in a similar manner but causes Excel to assign the next highest font size in the Font Size gallery to the selected range.

BTW

Color Selection
Knowing how people perceive colors helps you emphasize parts of your worksheet. Warmer colors (red and orange) tend to reach toward the reader. Cooler colors (blue, green, and violet) tend to pull away from the reader. Bright colors jump out of a dark background and are easiest to see. White or yellow text on a dark blue, green, purple, or black background is ideal.

Figure 2–33

To Change the Background Color and Apply a Box Border to the Worksheet Title and Subtitle

The final formats assigned to the worksheet title and subtitle are the orange background color and thick box border (Figure 2–30b on page EX 92). The following steps complete the formatting of the worksheet titles.

1
• Select the range A1:A2 and then click the Fill Color button arrow (Home tab | Font group) to display the Fill Color gallery (Figure 2–34).

Experiment
• Point to a number of colors in the Fill Color gallery to display a live preview of the color in the range A1:A2.

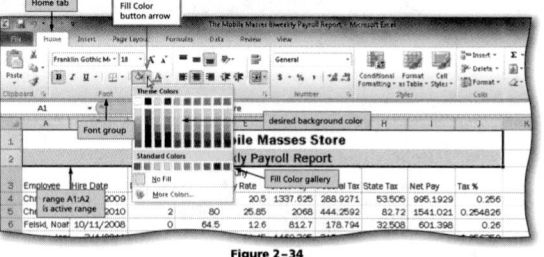

Figure 2–34

2
• Click Orange, Accent 1, Lighter 60% (column 5, row 3) in the Fill Color gallery to change the background color of the range of cells (Figure 2–35).

Figure 2–35

Textbook Walk-Through

Chapter Summary A concluding paragraph, followed by a listing of the tasks completed within a chapter together with the pages on which the step-by-step, screen-by-screen explanations appear.

4 Click the OK button (Page Setup dialog box) to set the print scaling to normal.

5 Display the Home tab.

Q&A What is the purpose of the Adjust to box in the Page Setup dialog box?

The Adjust to box allows you to specify the percentage of reduction or enlargement in the printout of a worksheet. The default percentage is 100%. When you click the Fit to option, this percentage automatically changes to the percentage required to fit the printout on one page.

BTW Quick Reference
For a table that lists how to complete the tasks covered in this book using the mouse, Ribbon, shortcut menu, and keyboard, see the Quick Reference Summary at the back of this book, or visit the Excel 2010 Quick Reference Web page (scsite.com/ex2010/qr).

To Save the Workbook and Quit Excel

With the workbook complete, the following steps save the workbook and quit Excel.

1 Click the Save button on the Quick Access Toolbar.

2 Click the Close button on the upper-right corner of the title bar.

Chapter Summary

In this chapter you have learned how to enter formulas, calculate an average, find the highest and lowest numbers in a range, verify formulas using Range Finder, added borders, align text, format numbers, change column widths and row heights, and add conditional formatting to a range of numbers. In addition, you learned to spell check a worksheet, print a section of a worksheet, and display and print the formulas version of the worksheet using the Fit to option. The items listed below include all the new Excel skills you have learned in this chapter.

1. Enter a Formula Using the Keyboard (EX 75)
2. Enter Formulas Using Point Mode (EX 77)
3. Copy Formulas Using the Fill Handle (EX 80)
4. Determine the Average of a Range of Numbers ~~... ~~ (EX 86)
   ~~...~~ nge of
   ~~...~~
   ~~...~~ nge of
   ~~...~~ to an
   ~~...~~ (EX 89)
   ~~...~~ (EX 91)
   ~~...~~ y a Box
   ~~...~~ tle (EX 96)
   ~~...~~ (EX 98)

12. Apply an Accounting Number Format and Comma Style Format Using the Ribbon (EX 100)
13. Apply a Currency Style Format with a Floating Dollar Sign Using the Format Cells Dialog Box (EX 102)
14. Apply a Percent Style Format and Use the Increase Decimal Button (EX 103)
15. Apply Conditional Formatting (EX 104)
16. Change the Widths of Columns (EX 107)
17. Change the Heights of Rows (EX 110)
18. Check Spelling on the Worksheet (EX 112)
19. Change the Worksheet's Margins, Header, and Orientation in Page Layout View (EX 114)
20. Print a Section of the Worksheet (EX 118)
21. Display the Formulas in the Worksheet and Fit the Printout on One Page (EX 119)

profile, your instructor may have assigned an autogradable
so, log into the SAM 2010 Web site at www.cengage.com/sam2010
and start files.

Learn It Online

Test your knowledge of chapter content and key terms.

Instructions: To complete the Learn It Online exercises, start your browser, click the Address bar, and then enter `scsite.com/ex2010/learn` as the Web address. When the Excel 2010 Learn It Online page is displayed, click the link for the exercise you want to complete and then read the instructions.

Chapter Reinforcement TF, MC, and SA
A series of true/false, multiple choice, and short answer questions that test your knowledge of the chapter content.

Flash Cards
An interactive learning environment where you identify chapter key terms associated with displayed definitions.

Practice Test
A series of multiple choice questions that test your knowledge of chapter content and key terms.

Who Wants To Be a Computer Genius?
An interactive game that challenges your knowledge of chapter content in the style of a television quiz show.

Wheel of Terms
An interactive game that challenges your knowledge of chapter key terms in the style of the television show *Wheel of Fortune*.

Crossword Puzzle Challenge
A crossword puzzle that challenges your knowledge of key terms presented in the chapter.

Apply Your Knowledge

Reinforce the skills and apply the concepts you learned in this chapter.

Profit Analysis Worksheet
Instructions: The purpose of this exercise is to open a partially completed workbook, enter formulas and functions, copy the formulas and functions, and then format the worksheet titles and numbers. As shown in Figure 2–73, the completed worksheet analyzes the costs associated with a police department's fleet of vehicles.

Vehicle ID	Miles Driven	Cost per Mile	Maintenance Cost	Mileage Cost	Total Cost	Total Cost per Mile
			Village of Scott Police Department			
			Monthly Vehicle Cost-per-Mile Summary			
670543	2,007	$ 0.49	$ 242.80	$ 983.43	$ 1,226.23	$ 0.61
979253	3,192	0.48	446.37	1,532.16	1,978.53	0.62
948173	3,802	0.65	472.47	2,471.30	2,943.77	0.77
837625	2,090	0.62	432.25	1,289.60	1,721.85	0.83
824664	2,475	0.56	369.88	1,386.00	1,755.88	0.71
655385	3,294	0.50	352.05	1,647.00	1,999.05	0.61
836417	3,640	0.70	417.80	2,548.00	2,965.80	0.81
993617	3,395	0.70	390.39	2,376.50	2,766.89	0.81
779468	4,075	0.55	442.17	2,241.25	2,683.42	0.66
Totals	**27,960**		**$ 3,566.18**	**$16,475.24**	**$20,041.42**	**$ 0.72**
Highest	4,075	$0.70	$472.47	$2,548.00	$2,965.80	$0.83
Lowest	2,007	$0.48	$242.80	$983.43	$1,226.23	$0.61
Average	3,107	$0.58	$396.24	$1,830.58	$2,226.82	$0.72

Figure 2–73

Learn It Online Every chapter features a Learn It Online section that is comprised of six exercises. These exercises include True/False, Multiple Choice, Short Answer, Flash Cards, Practice Test, and Learning Games.

Apply Your Knowledge This exercise usually requires students to open and manipulate a file from the Data Files that parallels the activities learned in the chapter. To obtain a copy of the Data Files for Students, follow the instructions on the inside back cover of this text.

Extend Your Knowledge

Extend the skills you learned in this chapter and experiment with new skills. You may need to use Help to complete the assignment.

Formatting a Worksheet and Adding Additional Charts

Instructions: Start Excel. Open the workbook Extend 1–1 Pack Right Moving Supplies. See the inside back cover of this book for instructions for downloading the Data Files for Students, or see your instructor for information on accessing the files required in this book. Perform the following tasks to format cells in the worksheet and to add two charts to the worksheet.

1. Use the commands in the Font group on the Home tab on the Ribbon to change the font of the title in cell A1 to 22-point Arial Black, green, bold, and the subtitle of the worksheet to 14-point Arial, red, bold.

2. Select the range A3:G8, click the Insert tab on the Ribbon, and then click the Dialog Box Launcher in the Charts group on the Ribbon to open the Insert Chart dialog box. If necessary, drag the lower-right corner of the Insert Chart dialog box to expand it (Figure 1–77).

Figure 1–77

3. Insert a Stacked Area in 3-D chart by clicking the Stack___ clicking the OK button. You may need to use the scroll ___ dialog box to view the Area charts in the gallery. Move ___ data in the worksheet. Click the Design tab and apply a ___

4. Deselect the chart and reselect the range A3:G8, and th___ Horizontal Cone chart in the worksheet. Move the cha___ that each chart does not overlap the Stacked Area in 3-___ the horizontal axis readable by expanding the size of th___ this chart than the one you selected for the Stacked Are___

> **Extend Your Knowledge** projects at the end of each chapter allow students to extend and expand on the skills learned within the chapter. Students use critical thinking to experiment with new skills to complete each project.

Make It Right

Analyze a workbook and correct all errors and/or improve the design.

Inserting Rows, Moving a Range, and Correcting Formulas in a Worksheet

Instructions: Start Excel. Open the workbook Make It Right 3-1 SpeedyOfficeSupply.com Annual Projected Net Income. See the inside back cover of this book for instructions for downloading the Data Files for Students, or see your instructor for information on accessing the files required for this book. Correct the following design and formula problems (Figure 3–86a) in the worksheet.

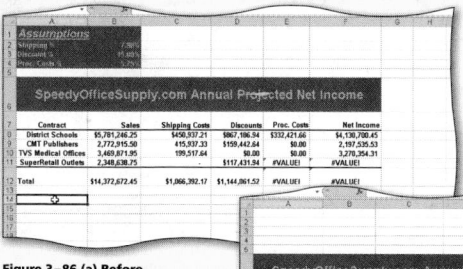

Figure 3–86 (a) Before

Figure 3–86 (b) After

1. The Shipping Cost in cell C8 is computed using the formula =B2*B8 (Shipping % × Sales). Similar formulas are used in cells C9, C10, and C11. The formula in cell C8 was entered and copied to cells C9, C10, and C11. Although the result in cell C8 is correct, the results in cells C9, C10, and C11 are incorrect. Edit the formula in cell C8 by changing cell B2 to an absolute cell reference. Copy the corrected formula in cell C8 to cells C9, C10, and C11. After completing the copy, click the Auto Fill Options button arrow that is displayed below and to the right of cell C11 and choose Fill Without Formatting.

2. The Discount amounts in cells D8, D9, D10, and D11 are computed using the IF function. The Discount amount should equal the amount in cell B3*B8 (Discount % × Sales) if the corresponding Sales in column B is greater than or equal to $2,500,000. If the corresponding Sales in column B is less than $2,500,000, then the Discount amount is 5%*B8 (5% × Sales). The IF function in cell D8

> **Make It Right** projects call on students to analyze a fi le, discover errors in it, and fix them using the skills they learned in the chapter.

Textbook Walk-Through

In the Lab

Lab 2: Analysis of Indirect Expense Allocations

Problem: Your classmate works part time as an advisor for the ReachOut Neighbors not-for-profit group. She has asked you to assist her in creating an indirect expense allocation worksheet (Figure 3–89) that will help the not-for-profit administration better evaluate the branch offices described in Table 3–11.

Figure 3–89

> **In the Lab** Three all new in-depth assignments per chapter require students to utilize the chapter concepts and techniques to solve problems on a computer.

Table 3–11 ReachOut Neighbor Worksheet Data

	Chicago Branch Office	Dallas Branch Office	Houston Branch Office	Jacksonville Branch Office
Total Donations	735356	98190	178435	212300
Distributed Goods and Services	529750	60891	135589	150895
Direct Expenses	57550	22530	14750	25300
Square Footage	15500	775	7550	8250

Instructions Part 1: Do the following to create the worksh
1. Apply the Solstice theme to the worksheet. Bold the e worksheet and using the Bold (Home tab | Font group
2. Change the following column widths: A = 30.00; B thr
3. Enter the worksheet titles in cells A1 and A2 and the sy 14-Mar-01 style.

> **Cases & Places** exercises call on students to create open-ended projects that reflect academic, personal, and business settings.

Cases and Places

Apply your creative thinking and problem solving skills to design and implement a solution.

1: Bachelor Degree Expense and Resource Projection

Academic

Attending college with limited resources can be a trying experience. One way to alleviate some of the financial stress is to plan ahead. Develop a worksheet following the general layout in Table 3–16 that shows the projected expenses and resources for four years of college. Use the formulas listed in Table 3–17 and the concepts and techniques presented in this chapter to create the worksheet.

Table 3–16 Bachelor Degree Expense and Resource Projection

Expenses	Freshman	Sophomore	Junior	Senior	Total
Room & Board	$12,550.00	Formula A ———————————→			—
Tuition & Books	16,450.00	Formula A ———————————→			—
Clothes	785.00	Formula A ———————————→			—
Entertainment	1,520.00	Formula A ———————————→			—
Miscellaneous	936.00	Formula A ———————————→			—
Total Expenses	—	—	—	—	—

Resources	Freshman	Sophomore	Junior	Senior	Total
Savings	Formula B ———————————→				—
Parents	Formula B ———————————→				—
Job	Formula B ———————————→				—
Loans	Formula B ———————————→				—
Scholarships	Formula B ———————————→				—

Assumptions	
Savings	10.00%
Parents	12.00%
Job	11.00%
Loans	35.00%
Scholarships	32.00%
Annual Rate Increase	8.25%

Table 3–17 Bachelor Degree Expense and Resource Projection Formulas

Formula A = Prior Year's Expense * (1 + Annual Rate Increase)

Formula B = Total Expenses for Year * Corresponding Assumption

After creating the worksheet: (a) perform what-if analysis by changing the percents of the resource assumptions; (b) perform a what-if analysis to determine the effect on the resources by increasing the Annual Rate Increase to 9.95% (answer = $149,520.41); and (c) with the original assumptions, goal seek to determine what the Annual Rate Increase would be for the total expenses to be $175,000 (answer = 20.77%). Submit the workbook and results of the what-if analysis as specified by your instructor.

Continued >

Microsoft®
EXCEL® 2010

COMPREHENSIVE

Office 2010 and Windows 7: Essential Concepts and Skills

Objectives

You will have mastered the material in this chapter when you can:

- Perform basic mouse operations
- Start Windows and log on to the computer
- Identify the objects on the Windows 7 desktop
- Identify the programs in and versions of Microsoft Office
- Start a program
- Identify the components of the Microsoft Office Ribbon

- Create folders
- Save files
- Change screen resolution
- Perform basic tasks in Microsoft Office programs
- Manage files
- Use Microsoft Office Help and Windows Help

Office 2010 and Windows 7: Essential Concepts and Skills

Office 2010 and Windows 7

This introductory chapter uses Excel 2010 to cover features and functions common to Office 2010 programs, as well as the basics of Windows 7.

Overview

As you read this chapter, you will learn how to perform basic tasks in Windows and Excel by performing these general activities:

- Start programs using Windows.
- Use features in Excel that are common across Office programs.
- Organize files and folders.
- Change screen resolution.
- Quit programs.

Introduction to the Windows 7 Operating System

Windows 7 is the newest version of Microsoft Windows, which is the most popular and widely used operating system. An **operating system** is a computer program (set of computer instructions) that coordinates all the activities of computer hardware such as memory, storage devices, and printers, and provides the capability for you to communicate with the computer.

The Windows 7 operating system simplifies the process of working with documents and programs by organizing the manner in which you interact with the computer. Windows 7 is used to run **application software**, which consists of programs designed to make users more productive and/or assist them with personal tasks, such as word processing.

Windows 7 has two interface variations, Windows 7 Basic and Windows 7 Aero. Computers with up to 1 GB of RAM display the Windows 7 Basic interface (Figure 1a). Computers with more than 1 GB of RAM also can display the Windows Aero interface (Figure 1b), which provides an enhanced visual appearance. The Windows 7 Professional, Windows 7 Enterprise, Windows 7 Home Premium, and Windows 7 Ultimate editions have the capability to use Windows Aero.

Using a Mouse

Windows users work with a mouse that has at least two buttons. For a right-handed user, the left button usually is the primary mouse button, and the right mouse button is the secondary mouse button. Left-handed people, however, can reverse the function of these buttons.

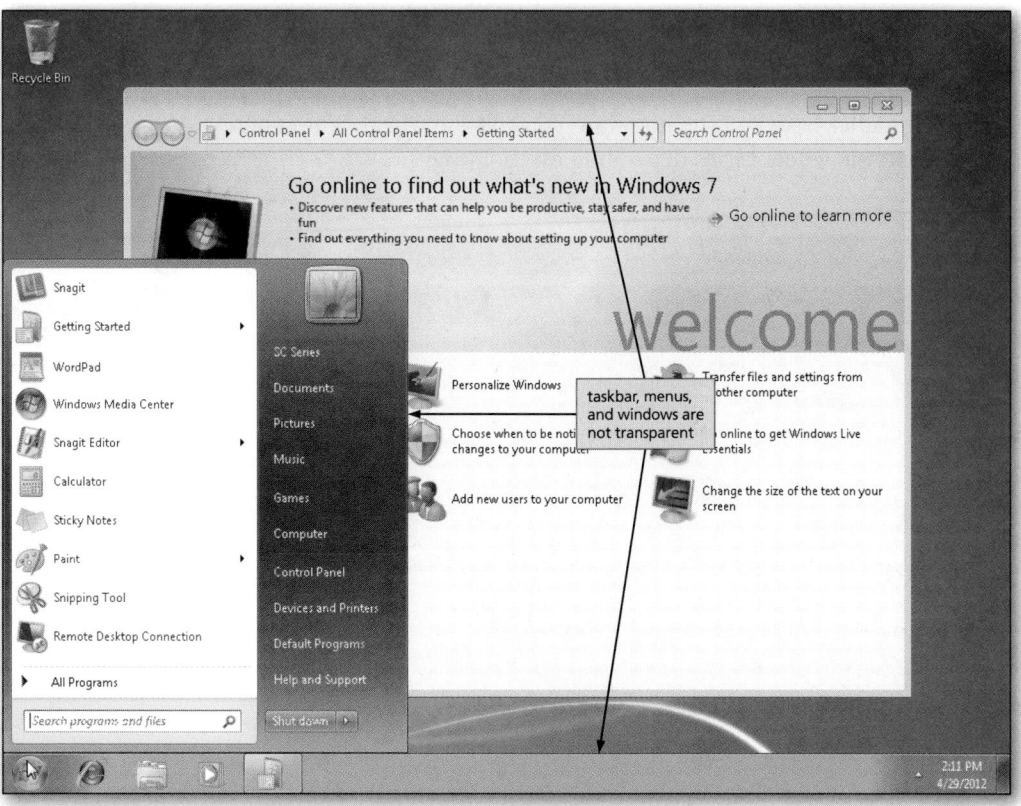

Figure 1(a) Windows 7 Basic interface

Figure 1(b) Windows 7 Aero interface

Table 1 explains how to perform a variety of mouse operations. Some programs also use keys in combination with the mouse to perform certain actions. For example, when you hold down the CTRL key while rolling the mouse wheel, text on the screen becomes larger or smaller based on the direction you roll the wheel. The function of the mouse buttons and the wheel varies depending on the program.

Table 1 Mouse Operations		
Operation	**Mouse Action**	**Example***
Point	Move the mouse until the pointer on the desktop is positioned on the item of choice.	Position the pointer on the screen.
Click	Press and release the primary mouse button, which usually is the left mouse button.	Select or deselect items on the screen or start a program or program feature.
Right-click	Press and release the secondary mouse button, which usually is the right mouse button.	Display a shortcut menu.
Double-click	Quickly press and release the left mouse button twice without moving the mouse.	Start a program or program feature.
Triple-click	Quickly press and release the left mouse button three times without moving the mouse.	Select a paragraph.
Drag	Point to an item, hold down the left mouse button, move the item to the desired location on the screen, and then release the left mouse button.	Move an object from one location to another or draw pictures.
Right-drag	Point to an item, hold down the right mouse button, move the item to the desired location on the screen, and then release the right mouse button.	Display a shortcut menu after moving an object from one location to another.
Rotate wheel	Roll the wheel forward or backward.	Scroll vertically (up and down).
Free-spin wheel	Whirl the wheel forward or backward so that it spins freely on its own.	Scroll through many pages in seconds.
Press wheel	Press the wheel button while moving the mouse.	Scroll continuously.
Tilt wheel	Press the wheel toward the right or left.	Scroll horizontally (left and right).
Press thumb button	Press the button on the side of the mouse with your thumb.	Move forward or backward through Web pages and/or control media, games, etc.

*Note: the examples presented in this column are discussed as they are demonstrated in this chapter.

Scrolling

Minimize Wrist Injury
Computer users frequently switch between the keyboard and the mouse while creating a workbook; such switching strains the wrist. To help prevent wrist injury, minimize switching. For instance, if your fingers already are on the keyboard, use keyboard keys to scroll. If your hand already is on the mouse, use the mouse to scroll.

A **scroll bar** is a horizontal or vertical bar that appears when the contents of an area may not be visible completely on the screen (Figure 2). A scroll bar contains **scroll arrows** and a **scroll box** that enable you to view areas that currently cannot be seen. Clicking the up and down scroll arrows moves the screen content up or down one line. You also can click above or below the scroll box to move up or down a section, or drag the scroll box up or down to move up or down to move to a specific location.

Shortcut Keys

In many cases, you can use the keyboard instead of the mouse to accomplish a task. To perform tasks using the keyboard, you press one or more keyboard keys, sometimes identified as

Figure 2

a **shortcut key** or **keyboard shortcut**. Some shortcut keys consist of a single key, such as the F1 key. For example, to obtain help about Windows 7, you can press the F1 key. Other shortcut keys consist of multiple keys, in which case a plus sign separates the key names, such as CTRL+ESC. This notation means to press and hold down the first key listed, press one or more additional keys, and then release all keys. For example, to display the Start menu, press CTRL+ESC, that is, hold down the CTRL key, press the ESC key, and then release both keys.

Starting Windows 7

It is not unusual for multiple people to use the same computer in a work, educational, recreational, or home setting. Windows 7 enables each user to establish a **user account**, which identifies to Windows 7 the resources, such as programs and storage locations, a user can access when working with a computer.

Each user account has a user name and may have a password and an icon, as well. A **user name** is a unique combination of letters or numbers that identifies a specific user to Windows 7. A **password** is a private combination of letters, numbers, and special characters associated with the user name that allows access to a user's account resources. A **user icon** is a picture associated with a user name.

When you turn on a computer, an introductory screen consisting of the Windows logo and copyright messages is displayed. The Windows logo is animated and glows as the Windows 7 operating system is loaded. After the Windows logo appears, depending on your computer's settings, you may or may not be required to log on to the computer. **Logging on** to a computer opens your user account and makes the computer available for use. If you are required to log on to the computer, the **Welcome screen** is displayed, which shows the user names of users on the computer (Figure 3). Clicking the user name or picture begins the process of logging on to the computer.

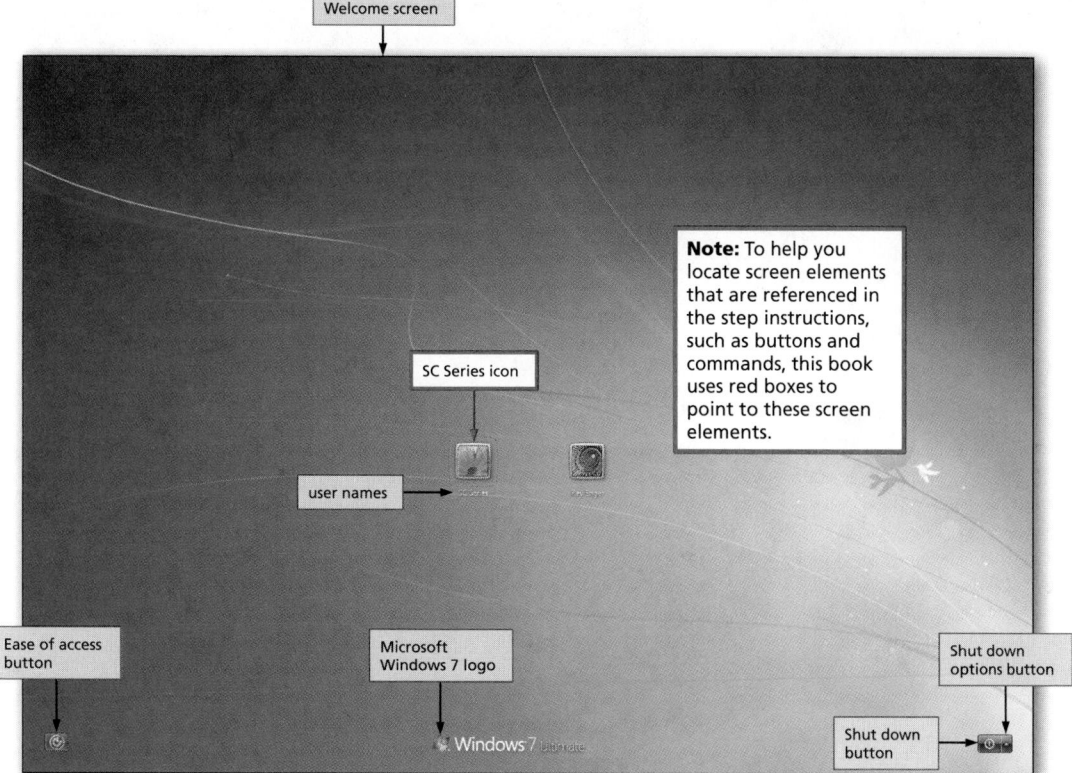

Figure 3

At the bottom of the Welcome screen is the 'Ease of access' button, Windows 7 logo, a Shut down button, and a 'Shut down options' button. The following list identifies the functions of the buttons and commands that typically appear on the Welcome screen:

- Clicking the 'Ease of access' button displays the Ease of Access Center, which provides tools to optimize your computer to accommodate the needs of the mobility, hearing, and vision impaired users.
- Clicking the Shut down button shuts down Windows 7 and the computer.
- Clicking the 'Shut down options' button, located to the right of the Shut down button, displays a menu containing commands that perform actions such as restarting the computer, placing the computer in a low-powered state, and shutting down the computer. The commands available on your computer may differ.
  - The **Restart command** closes open programs, shuts down Windows 7, and then restarts Windows 7 and displays the Welcome screen.
  - The **Sleep command** waits for Windows 7 to save your work and then turns off the computer fans and hard disk. To wake the computer from the Sleep state, press the power button or lift a notebook computer's cover, and log on to the computer.
  - The **Shut down command** shuts down and turns off the computer.

To Log On to the Computer

After starting Windows 7, you might need to log on to the computer. The following steps log on to the computer based on a typical installation. You may need to ask your instructor how to log on to your computer. This set of steps uses SC Series as the user name. The list of user names on your computer will be different.

- Click the user icon (SC Series, in this case) on the Welcome screen (shown in Figure 3 on the previous page); depending on settings, this either will display a password text box (Figure 4) or will log on to the computer and display the Windows 7 desktop.

Q&A Why do I not see a user icon?

Your computer may require you to type a user name instead of clicking an icon.

Q&A What is a text box?

A text box is a rectangular box in which you type text.

Q&A Why does my screen not show a password text box?

Your account does not require a password.

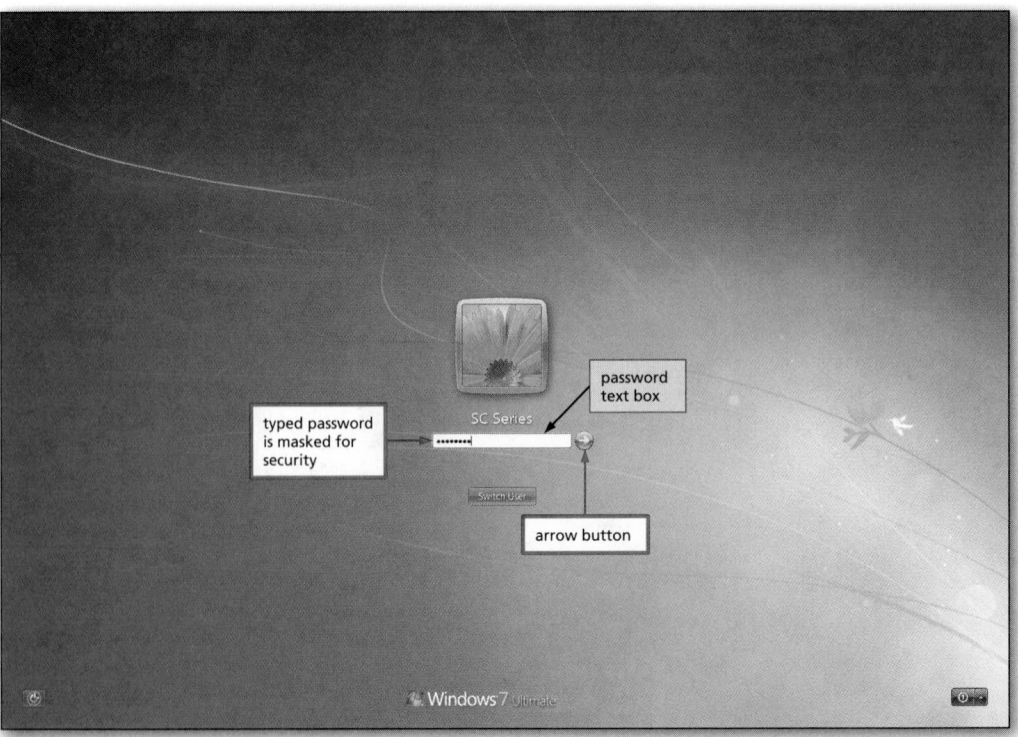

Figure 4

2

• If Windows 7 displays a password text box, type your password in the text box and then click the arrow button to log on to the computer and display the Windows 7 desktop (Figure 5).

Q&A

Why does my desktop look different from the one in Figure 5?

The Windows 7 desktop is customizable, and your school or employer may have modified the desktop to meet its needs. Also, your screen resolution, which affects the size of the elements on the screen, may differ from the screen resolution used in this book. Later in this chapter, you learn how to change screen resolution.

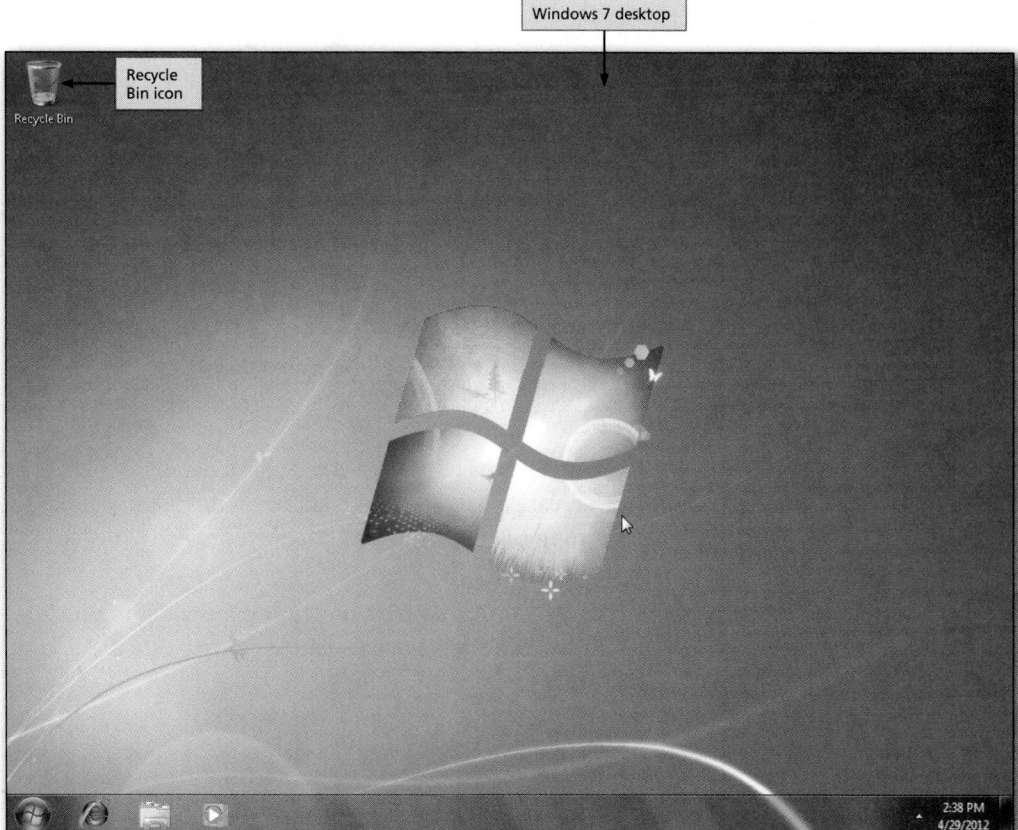

Figure 5

The Windows 7 Desktop

The Windows 7 desktop (Figure 5) and the objects on the desktop emulate a work area in an office. Think of the Windows desktop as an electronic version of the top of your desk. You can perform tasks such as placing objects on the desktop, moving the objects around the desktop, and removing items from the desktop.

When you start a program in Windows 7, it appears on the desktop. Some icons also may be displayed on the desktop. For instance, the icon for the **Recycle Bin**, the location of files that have been deleted, appears on the desktop by default. A **file** is a named unit of storage. Files can contain text, images, charts, and symbols. You can customize your desktop so that icons representing programs and files you use often appear on your desktop.

Introduction to Microsoft Office 2010

Microsoft Office 2010 is the newest version of Microsoft Office, offering features that provide users with better functionality and easier ways to work with the various files they create. These features include enhanced design tools, such as improved picture formatting tools and new themes, shared notebooks for working in groups, mobile versions of Office programs, broadcast presentation for the Web, and a digital notebook for managing and sharing multimedia information.

Microsoft Office 2010 Programs

Microsoft Office 2010 includes a wide variety of programs such as Word, PowerPoint, Excel, Access, Outlook, Publisher, OneNote, InfoPath, SharePoint Workspace, Communicator, and Web Apps:

- **Microsoft Word 2010**, or Word, is a full-featured word processing program that allows you to create professional-looking documents and revise them easily.
- **Microsoft PowerPoint 2010**, or PowerPoint, is a complete presentation program that allows you to produce professional-looking presentations.
- **Microsoft Excel 2010**, or Excel, is a powerful spreadsheet program that allows you to organize data, complete calculations, make decisions, graph data, develop professional-looking reports, publish organized data to the Web, and access real-time data from Web sites.
- **Microsoft Access 2010**, or Access, is a database management system that allows you to create a database; add, change, and delete data in the database; ask questions concerning the data in the database; and create forms and reports using the data in the database.
- **Microsoft Outlook 2010**, or Outlook, is a communications and scheduling program that allows you to manage e-mail accounts, calendars, contacts, and access to other Internet content.
- **Microsoft Publisher 2010**, or Publisher, is a desktop publishing program that helps you create professional-quality publications and marketing materials that can be shared easily.
- **Microsoft OneNote 2010**, or OneNote, is a note taking program that allows you to store and share information in notebooks with other people.
- **Microsoft InfoPath 2010**, or InfoPath, is a form development program that helps you create forms for use on the Web and gather data from these forms.
- **Microsoft SharePoint Workspace 2010**, or SharePoint, is collaboration software that allows you access and revise files stored on your computer from other locations.
- **Microsoft Communicator** is communications software that allows you to use different modes of communications such as instant messaging, video conferencing, and sharing files and programs.
- **Microsoft Web Apps** is a Web application that allows you to edit and share files on the Web using the familiar Office interface.

Microsoft Office 2010 Suites

A **suite** is a collection of individual programs available together as a unit. Microsoft offers a variety of Office suites. Table 2 lists the Office 2010 suites and their components.

Programs in a suite, such as Microsoft Office, typically use a similar interface and share features. In addition, Microsoft Office programs use **common dialog boxes** for performing actions such as opening and saving files. Once you are comfortable working with these elements and this interface and performing tasks in one program, the similarity can help you apply the knowledge and skills you have learned to another Office program(s). For example, the process for saving a file in Excel is the same in Word, PowerPoint, and the other Office programs. While briefly showing how to use Excel, this chapter illustrates some of the common functions across the Office programs and also identifies the characteristics unique to Excel.

Table 2 Microsoft Office 2010 Suites	Microsoft Office Professional Plus 2010	Microsoft Office Professional 2010	Microsoft Office Home and Business 2010	Microsoft Office Standard 2010	Microsoft Office Home and Student 2010
Microsoft Word 2010	✔	✔	✔	✔	✔
Microsoft PowerPoint 2010	✔	✔	✔	✔	✔
Microsoft Excel 2010	✔	✔	✔	✔	✔
Microsoft Access 2010	✔	✔	✗	✗	✗
Microsoft Outlook 2010	✔	✔	✔	✔	✗
Microsoft Publisher 2010	✔	✔	✗	✔	✗
Microsoft OneNote 2010	✔	✔	✔	✔	✔
Microsoft InfoPath 2010	✔	✗	✗	✗	✗
Microsoft SharePoint Workspace 2010	✔	✗	✗	✗	✗
Microsoft Communicator	✔	✗	✗	✗	✗

Starting and Using a Program

To use a program, such as Excel, you must instruct the operating system to start the program. Windows 7 provides many different ways to start a program, one of which is presented in this section (other ways to start a program are presented throughout this chapter). After starting a program, you can use it to perform a variety of tasks. The following pages use Excel to discuss some elements of the Office interface and to perform tasks that are common to other Office programs.

Excel

Excel is a powerful spreadsheet program that allows users to organize data, complete calculations, make decisions, graph data, develop professional-looking reports, publish organized data to the Web, and access real-time data from Web sites. The four major parts of Excel are:

- **Workbooks and Worksheets — A workbook** is like a notebook. Inside the workbook are sheets, each of which is called a **worksheet**. In other words, a workbook is a collection of worksheets. Worksheets allow users to enter, calculate, manipulate, and analyze data such as numbers and text. The terms worksheet and spreadsheet are interchangeable.

- **Charts** — Excel can draw a variety of charts.

- **Tables** — Tables organize and store data within worksheets. For example, once a user enters data into a worksheet, an Excel table can sort the data, search for specific data, and select data that satisfies defined criteria.

- **Web Support** — Web support allows users to save Excel worksheets or parts of a worksheet in HTML format, so that a user can view and manipulate the worksheet using a browser. Excel Web support also provides access to real-time data, such as stock quotes, using Web queries.

To Start a Program Using the Start Menu

Across the bottom of the Windows 7 desktop is the taskbar. The taskbar contains the **Start button**, which you use to access programs, files, folders, and settings on a computer. A **folder** is a named location on a storage medium that usually contains related files. The taskbar also displays a button for each program currently running on a computer.

Clicking the Start button displays the Start menu. The **Start menu** allows you to access programs, folders, and files on the computer and contains commands that allow you to start programs, store and search for files, customize the computer, and obtain help about thousands of topics. A **menu** is a list of related items, including folders, programs, and commands. Each **command** on a menu performs a specific action, such as saving a file or obtaining help.

The following steps, which assume Windows 7 is running, use the Start menu to start the Microsoft Excel 2010 program based on a typical installation. You may need to ask your instructor how to start Excel for your computer. Although the steps illustrate starting the Excel program, the steps to start any program are similar.

1

• Click the Start button on the Windows 7 taskbar to display the Start menu (Figure 6).

Q&A Why does my Start menu look different?

It may look different depending on your computer's configuration. The Start menu may be customized for several reasons, such as usage requirements or security restrictions.

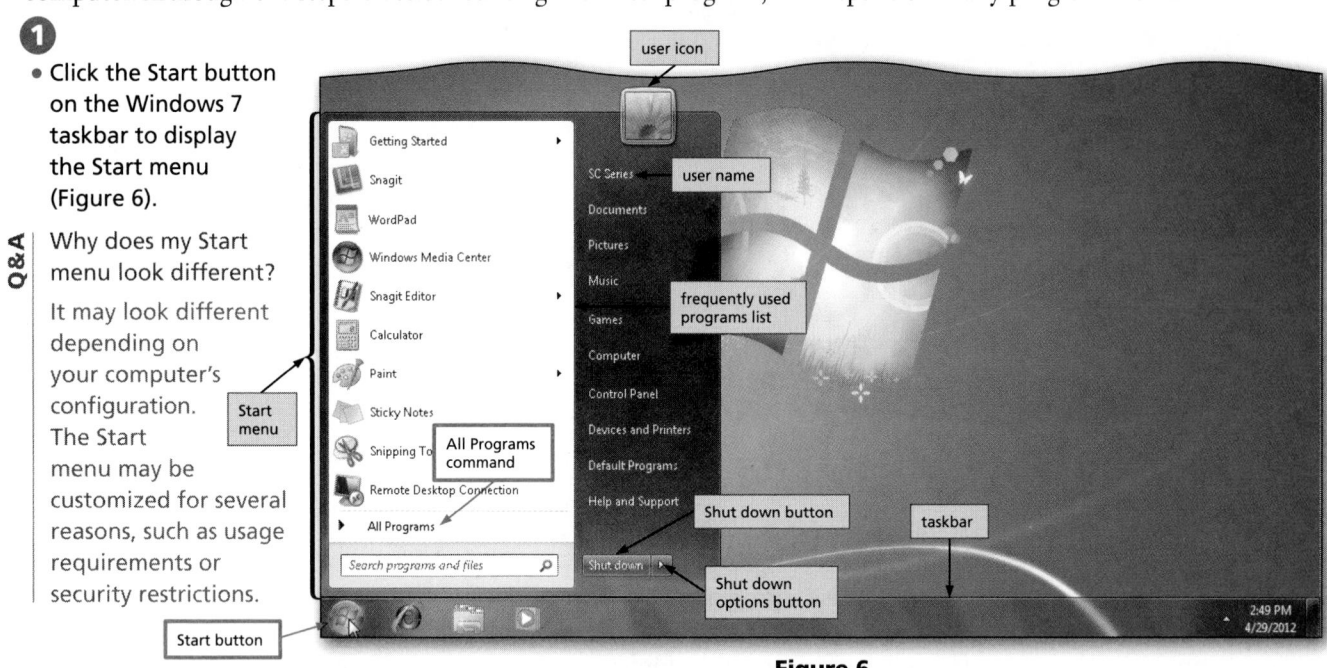

Figure 6

2

• Click All Programs at the bottom of the left pane on the Start menu to display the All Programs list (Figure 7).

Q&A What is a pane?

A **pane** is an area of a window that displays related content. For example, the left pane on the Start menu contains a list of frequently used programs, as well as the All Programs command.

Q&A Why might my All Programs list look different?

Most likely, the programs installed on your computer will differ from those shown in Figure 7. Your All Programs list will show the programs that are installed on your computer.

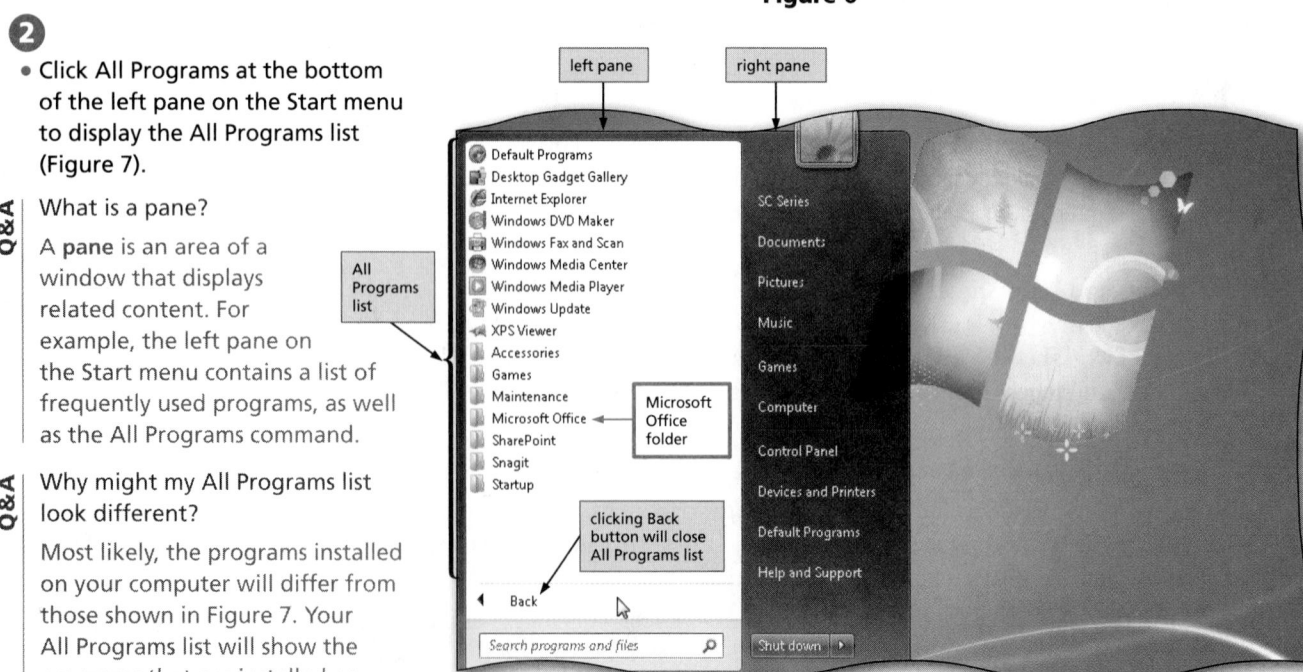

Figure 7

3

- If the program you want to start is located in a folder, click or scroll to and then click the folder (Microsoft Office, in this case) in the All Programs list to display a list of the folder's contents (Figure 8).

Q&A Why is the Microsoft Office folder on my computer?

During installation of Microsoft Office 2010, the Microsoft Office folder was added to the All Programs list.

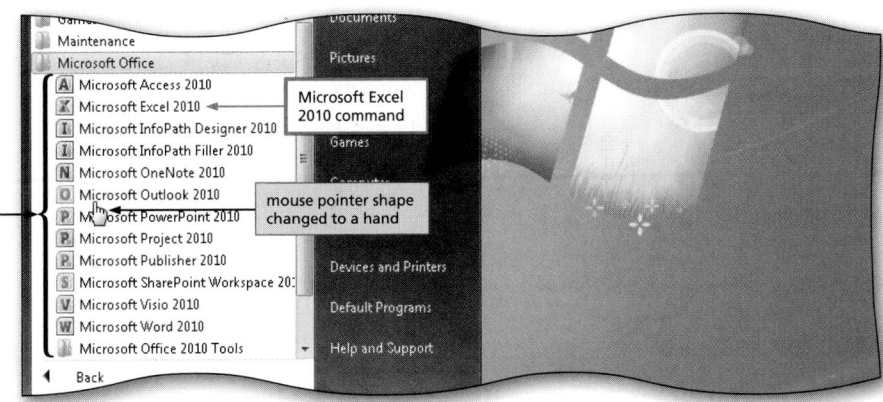

Figure 8

4

- Click, or scroll to and then click, the program name (Microsoft Excel 2010, in this case) in the list to start the selected program (Figure 9).

Q&A What happens when you start a program?

Many programs initially display a blank file in a program window, as shown in the Excel window in Figure 9; others provide a means for you to create a blank file. A **window** is a rectangular area that displays data and information. The top of a window has a **title bar**, which is a horizontal space that contains the window's name.

Figure 9

Q&A Why is my program window a different size?

The Excel window shown in Figure 9 is not maximized. Your Excel window already may be maximized. The steps on the next page maximize a window.

Other Ways

1. Double-click program icon on desktop, if one is present
2. Click program name in left pane of Start menu, if present
3. Display Start menu, type program name in search box, click program name
4. Double-click file created using program you want to start

To Maximize a Window

Sometimes content is not visible completely in a window. One method of displaying the entire contents of a window is to **maximize** it, or enlarge the window so that it fills the entire screen. The following step maximizes the Excel window; however, any Office program's window can be maximized using this step.

1

- If the program window is not maximized already, click the Maximize button (shown in Figure 9 on the previous page) next to the Close button on the window's title bar (the Excel window title bar, in this case) to maximize the window (Figure 10).

Q&A What happened to the Maximize button?

It changed to a Restore Down button, which you can use to return a window to its size and location before you maximized it.

Q&A How do I know whether a window is maximized?

A window is maximized if it fills the entire display area and the Restore Down button is displayed on the title bar.

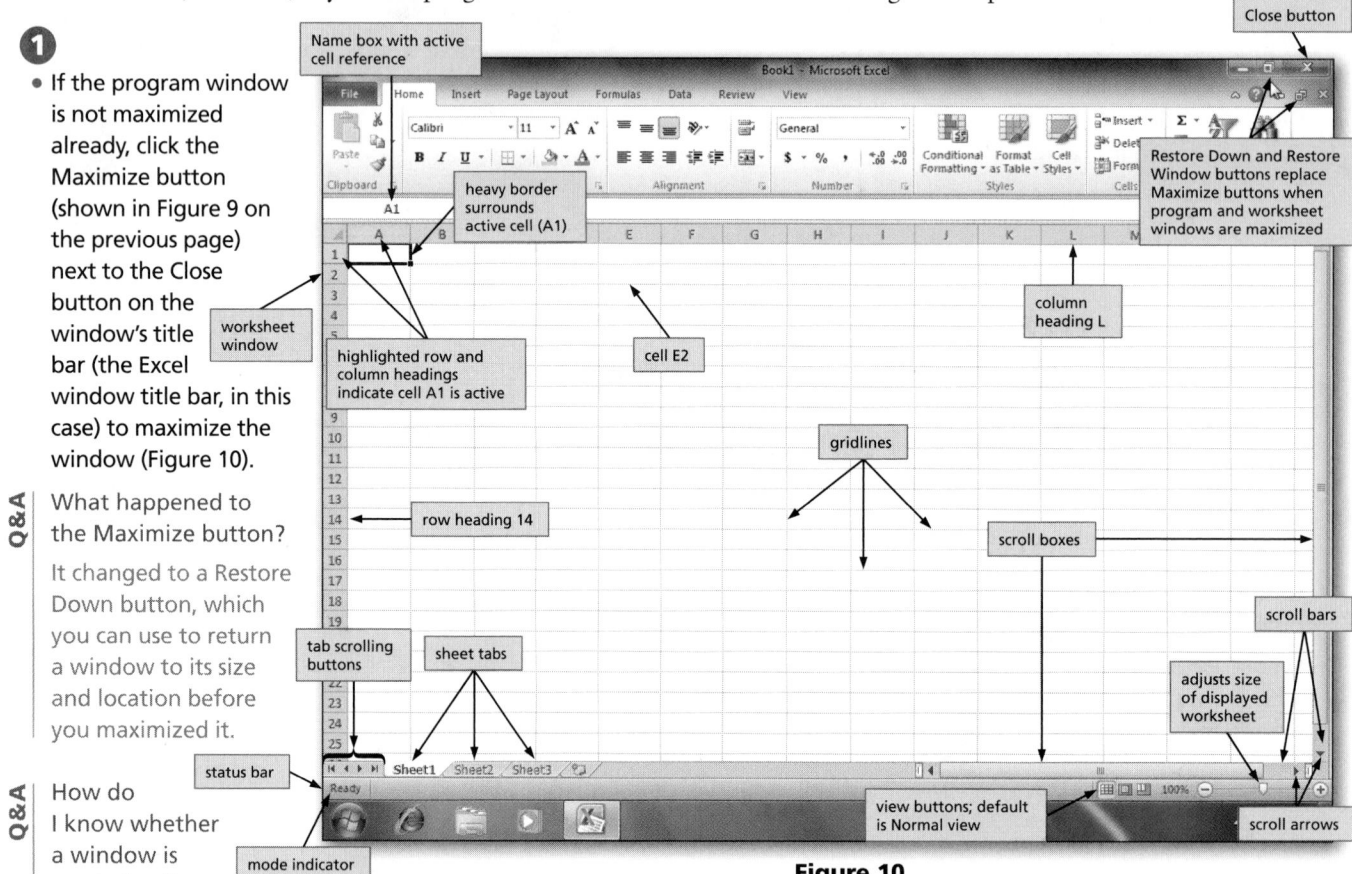

Figure 10

Other Ways

1. Double-click title bar
2. Drag title bar to top of screen

The Excel Worksheet Window, Ribbon, and Elements Common to Office Programs

The Excel window consists of a variety of components to make your work more efficient and worksheets more professional. These include the worksheet window, Ribbon, Mini toolbar, shortcut menus, and Quick Access Toolbar. Most of these components are common to other Microsoft Office 2010 programs; others are unique to Excel.

You view a portion of a worksheet on the screen through a **worksheet window** (Figure 11). The default (preset) view is **Normal Layout view**, which shows the worksheet in a continuous arrangement of rows and columns.

Scroll Bars You use a scroll bar to display different portions of a worksheet in the worksheet window. At the right edge of the worksheet window is a vertical scroll bar. A horizontal scroll bar also appears at the bottom of the worksheet window. On a scroll bar, the position of the scroll box reflects the location of the portion of the worksheet that is displayed in the worksheet window.

Figure 11

Status Bar   The **status bar**, located at the bottom of the worksheet window above the Windows 7 taskbar, presents information about the worksheet, the progress of current tasks, and the status of certain commands and keys; it also provides controls for viewing the worksheet. As you type text or perform certain tasks, various indicators and buttons may appear on the status bar.

In addition The left side of the status bar in Figure 11 shows the current progress of current tasks. The right side of the status bar includes buttons and controls you can use to change the view of a worksheet and adjust the size of the displayed worksheet.

Ribbon   The Ribbon, located near the top of the window below the title bar, is the control center in Excel and other Office programs (Figure 12). The Ribbon provides easy, central access to the tasks you perform while creating a workbook. The Ribbon consists of tabs, groups, and commands. Each **tab** contains a collection of groups, and each **group** contains related functions. When you start an Office program, such as Excel, it initially displays several main tabs, also called default tabs. All Office programs have a **Home tab**, which contains the more frequently used commands.

In addition to the main tabs, Office programs display **tool tabs**, also called contextual tabs (Figure 13), when you perform certain tasks or work with objects such as pictures or charts. If you insert a picture in an Excel worksheet, for example, the Picture Tools tab and its related subordinate Format tab appear, collectively referred to as the Picture Tools Format tab. When you are finished working with the picture, the Picture Tools Format tab disappears from the Ribbon. Excel and other Office programs determine when tool tabs should appear and disappear based on tasks you perform. Some tool tabs, such as the Chart Tools tab, have more than one related subordinate tab.

Items on the Ribbon include buttons, boxes (text boxes, check boxes, etc.), and tabs (Figure 12). Clicking a button on the Ribbon might display a gallery. A **gallery** is a set of choices, often graphical, arranged in a grid or in a list (Figure 13). You can scroll through choices in an in-Ribbon gallery by clicking the gallery's scroll arrows. Or, you can click a gallery's More button to view more gallery options on the screen at a time.

Figure 12

Some buttons and boxes have arrows that, when clicked, also display a gallery; others always cause a gallery to be displayed when clicked. Most galleries support **live preview**, which is a feature that allows you to point to a gallery choice and see its effect in the worksheet — without actually selecting the choice (Figure 13).

Some commands on the Ribbon display an image to help you remember their function. When you point to a command on the Ribbon, all or part of the command glows in shades of yellow and orange, and an Enhanced ScreenTip appears on the screen. An **Enhanced ScreenTip** is an on-screen note that provides the name of the command, available keyboard shortcut(s), a description of the command, and sometimes instructions for how to obtain help about the command (Figure 14). Enhanced ScreenTips are more detailed than a typical ScreenTip, which usually displays only the name of the command.

Some groups on the Ribbon have a small arrow in the lower-right corner, called a **Dialog Box Launcher**, that when clicked, displays a dialog box or a task pane with additional options for the group (Figure 15). When presented with a dialog box, you make selections and must close the dialog box before returning to the workbook. A **task pane**, in contrast to a dialog box, is a window that can remain open and visible while you work in the workbook.

Figure 13

Figure 14

Figure 15

Mini Toolbar   The **Mini toolbar**, which appears automatically based on tasks you perform, contains commands related to changing the appearance of text in a worksheet. All commands on the Mini toolbar also exist on the Ribbon. The purpose of the Mini toolbar is to minimize mouse movement.

When the Mini toolbar appears, it initially is transparent (Figure 16a). If you do not use the transparent Mini toolbar, it disappears from the screen. To use the Mini toolbar, move the mouse pointer into the toolbar, which causes the Mini toolbar to change from a transparent to bright appearance (Figure 16b). If you right-click an item in the worksheet window, Excel displays both the Mini toolbar and a shortcut menu, which is discussed in a later section in this chapter.

(a) transparent Mini toolbar   **(b) bright Mini toolbar**

Figure 16

BTW

Turning Off the Mini Toolbar
If you do not want the Mini toolbar to appear, click File on the Ribbon to open the Backstage view, click Options in the Backstage view, click General (Options dialog box), remove the check mark from the Show Mini Toolbar on selection check box, and then click the OK button.

Quick Access Toolbar   The **Quick Access Toolbar**, located initially (by default) above the Ribbon at the left edge of the title bar, provides convenient, one-click access to frequently used commands (Figure 14). The commands on the Quick Access Toolbar always are available, regardless of the task you are performing. The Quick Access Toolbar is discussed in more depth later in the chapter.

KeyTips   If you prefer using the keyboard instead of the mouse, you can press the ALT key on the keyboard to display **KeyTips**, or keyboard code icons, for certain commands

Figure 17

(Figure 17). To select a command using the keyboard, press the letter or number displayed in the KeyTip, which may cause additional KeyTips related to the selected command to appear. To remove KeyTips from the screen, press the ALT key or the ESC key until all KeyTips disappear, or click the mouse anywhere in the program window.

To Display a Different Tab on the Ribbon

When you start Excel, the Ribbon displays eight main tabs: File, Home, Insert, Page Layout, Formulas, Data, Review, and View. The tab currently displayed is called the **active tab**.

The following step displays the Insert tab, that is, makes it the active tab.

1

• Click Insert on the Ribbon to display the Insert tab (Figure 18).

🔍 **Experiment**

• Click the other tabs on the Ribbon to view their contents. When you are finished, click the Insert tab to redisplay the Insert tab.

Figure 18

Q&A | If I am working in a different Office program, such as PowerPoint or Access, how do I display a different tab on the Ribbon?

Follow this same procedure; that is, click the desired tab on the Ribbon.

To Minimize, Display, and Restore the Ribbon

To display more of a worksheet or other item in the window of an Office program, some users prefer to minimize the Ribbon, which hides the groups on the Ribbon and displays only the main tabs. Each time you start an Office program, such as Excel, the Ribbon appears the same way it did the last time you used that Office program. The chapters in this book, however, begin with the Ribbon appearing as it did at the initial installation of Excel.

The following steps minimize, display, and restore the Ribbon in Excel.

1

• Click the Minimize the Ribbon button on the Ribbon (shown in Figure 18) to minimize the Ribbon (Figure 19).

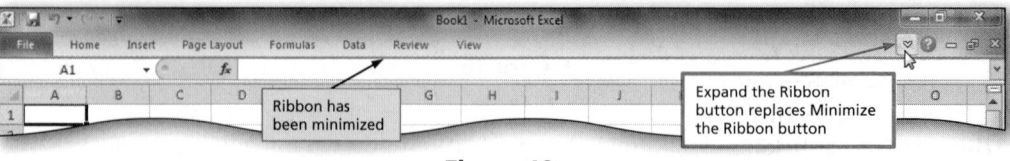

Figure 19

Q&A | What happened to the groups on the Ribbon?

When you minimize the Ribbon, the groups disappear so that the Ribbon does not take up as much space on the screen.

Q&A | What happened to the Minimize the Ribbon button?

The Expand the Ribbon button replaces the Minimize the Ribbon button when the Ribbon is minimized.

- Click Home on the Ribbon to display the Home tab (Figure 20).

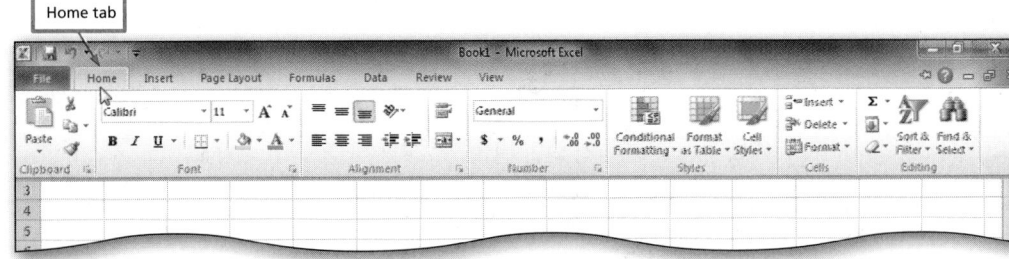

Figure 20

Q&A

Why would I click the Home tab?

If you want to use a command on a minimized Ribbon, click the main tab to display the groups for that tab. After you select a command on the Ribbon, the groups will be hidden once again. If you decide not to use a command on the Ribbon, you can hide the groups by clicking the same main tab or clicking in the program window.

- Click Home on the Ribbon to hide the groups again (shown in Figure 19).

- Click the Expand the Ribbon button on the Ribbon (shown in Figure 19) to restore the Ribbon.

Other Ways
1. Double-click Home on the Ribbon
2. Press CTRL+F1

To Display and Use a Shortcut Menu

When you right-click certain areas of the Excel and other program windows, a shortcut menu will appear. A **shortcut menu** is a list of frequently used commands that relate to the right-clicked object. When you right-click a scroll bar, for example, a shortcut menu appears with commands related to the scroll bar. When you right-click the Quick Access Toolbar, a shortcut menu appears with commands related to the Quick Access Toolbar. You can use shortcut menus to access common commands quickly. The following steps use a shortcut menu to move the Quick Access Toolbar, which by default is located on the title bar.

- Right-click the Quick Access Toolbar to display a shortcut menu that presents a list of commands related to the Quick Access Toolbar (Figure 21).

Figure 21

- Click Show Quick Access Toolbar Below the Ribbon on the shortcut menu to display the Quick Access Toolbar below the Ribbon (Figure 22).

Figure 22

3
• Right-click the Quick Access Toolbar to display a shortcut menu (Figure 23).

4
• Click Show Quick Access Toolbar Above the Ribbon on the shortcut menu to return the Quick Access Toolbar to its original position (shown in Figure 21 on the previous page).

Figure 23

To Customize the Quick Access Toolbar

The Quick Access Toolbar provides easy access to some of the more frequently used commands in Office programs. By default, the Quick Access Toolbar contains buttons for the Save, Undo, and Redo commands. You can customize the Quick Access Toolbar by changing its location in the window, as shown in the previous steps, and by adding more buttons to reflect commands you would like to access easily. The following steps add the Quick Print button to the Quick Access Toolbar in the Excel window.

1
• Click the Customize Quick Access Toolbar button to display the Customize Quick Access Toolbar menu (Figure 24).

Q&A Which commands are listed on the Customize Quick Access Toolbar menu?

It lists commands that commonly are added to the Quick Access Toolbar.

Q&A What do the check marks next to some commands signify?

Check marks appear next to commands that already are on the Quick Access Toolbar. When you add a button to the Quick Access Toolbar, a check mark will be displayed next to its command name.

Figure 24

2
• Click Quick Print on the Customize Quick Access Toolbar menu to add the Quick Print button to the Quick Access Toolbar (Figure 25).

Q&A How would I remove a button from the Quick Access Toolbar?

You would right-click the button you wish to remove and then click Remove from Quick Access Toolbar on the shortcut menu. If you want your screens to match the screens in the remaining chapters in this book, you would remove the Quick Print button from the Quick Access Toolbar.

Figure 25

To Enter Text in a Workbook

To enter data into a cell, you first must select it. The easiest way to select a cell (make it active) is to use the mouse to move the block plus sign mouse pointer to the cell and then click. An alternative method is to use the arrow keys that are located just to the right of the typewriter keys on the keyboard. An arrow key selects the cell adjacent to the active cell in the direction of the arrow on the key.

In Excel, any set of characters containing a letter, hyphen (as in a telephone number), or space is considered text. **Text** is used to place titles, such as worksheet titles, column titles, and row titles, on the worksheet. The following steps enter the worksheet title in cell A1.

- If it is not already the active cell, click cell A1 to make it the active cell (Figure 26).

Q&A
What if I make an error while typing?

You can press the BACKSPACE key until you have deleted the text in error and then retype the text correctly.

Figure 26

- Type Brain Busters Book Rentals in cell A1.

- Press the ENTER key to complete the entry and enter the worksheet title (Figure 27).

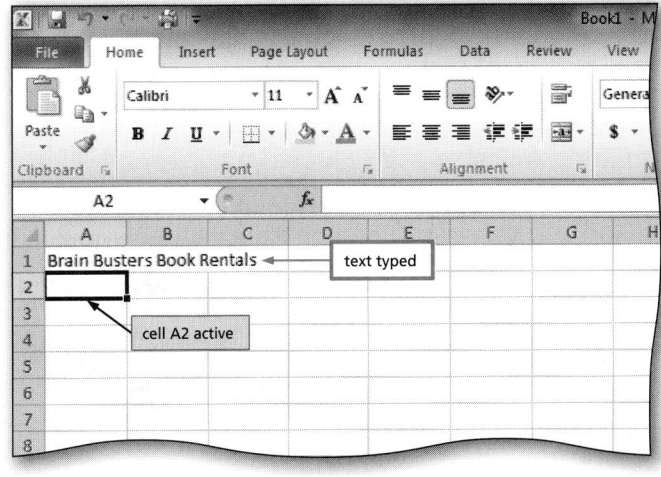

Figure 27

Saving and Organizing Files

While you are creating a workbook, the computer stores it in memory. When you save a workbook, the computer places it on a storage medium such as a hard disk, USB flash drive, or optical disc. A saved workbook is referred to as a file. A **file name** is the name assigned to a file when it is saved. It is important to save a workbook frequently for the following reasons:

- The workbook in memory might be lost if the computer is turned off or you lose electrical power while a program is running.
- If you run out of time before completing a project, you may finish it at a future time without starting over.

When saving files, you should organize them so that you easily can find them later. Windows 7 provides tools to help you organize files.

Organizing Files and Folders

A file contains data. This data can range from an inventory report to an accounting spreadsheet to an expense report. You should organize and store these files in folders to avoid misplacing a file and to help you find a file quickly.

If you are a freshman taking an introductory computer class (CIS 101, for example), you may want to design a series of folders for the different subjects covered in the class. To accomplish this, you can arrange the folders in a hierarchy for the class, as shown in Figure 28.

Figure 28

The hierarchy contains three levels. The first level contains the storage device, in this case a USB flash drive. Windows 7 identifies the storage device with a letter, and, in some cases, a name. In Figure 28, the USB flash drive is identified as REMOVABLE (E:). The second level contains the class folder (CIS 101, in this case), and the third level contains seven folders, one each for a different Office program that will be covered in the class (Word, PowerPoint, Excel, Access, Outlook, Publisher, and OneNote).

When the hierarchy in Figure 28 is created, the USB flash drive is said to contain the CIS 101 folder, and the CIS 101 folder is said to contain the separate Office folders (i.e., Word, PowerPoint, Excel, etc.). In addition, this hierarchy easily can be expanded to include folders from other classes taken during additional semesters.

The vertical and horizontal lines in Figure 28 form a pathway that allows you to navigate to a drive or folder on a computer or network. A **path** consists of a drive letter (preceded by a drive name when necessary) and colon, to identify the storage device, and one or more folder names. Each drive or folder in the hierarchy has a corresponding path.

Table 3 shows examples of paths and their corresponding drives and folders.

Table 3 Paths and Corresponding Drives and Folders	
Path	**Drive and Folder**
Computer ▶ REMOVABLE (E:)	Drive E (REMOVABLE (E:))
Computer ▶ REMOVABLE (E:) ▶ CIS 101	CIS 101 folder on drive E
Computer ▶ REMOVABLE (E:) ▶ CIS 101 ▶ Excel	Excel folder in CIS 101 folder on drive E

BTW

Saving Online
Instead of saving files on a USB flash drive, some people prefer to save them online so that they can access the files from any computer with an Internet connection. For more information, read Appendix C.

The following pages illustrate the steps to organize folders for a class and save a file in a folder:

1. Create a folder identifying your class.
2. Create an Excel folder in the folder identifying your class.
3. Save a file in the Excel folder.
4. Verify the location of the saved file.

To Create a Folder

When you create a folder, such as the CIS 101 folder shown in Figure 28, you must name the folder. A folder name should describe the folder and its contents. A folder name can contain spaces and any uppercase or lowercase characters, except a backslash (\), slash (/), colon (:), asterisk (*), question mark (?), quotation marks ("), less than symbol (<), greater than symbol (>), or vertical bar (|). Folder names cannot be CON, AUX, COM1, COM2, COM3, COM4, LPT1, LPT2, LPT3, PRN, or NUL. The same rules for naming folders also apply to naming files.

To store files and folders on a USB flash drive, you must connect the USB flash drive to an available USB port on a computer. The following steps create your class folder (CIS 101, in this case) on a USB flash drive.

1

• Connect the USB flash drive to an available USB port on the computer to open the AutoPlay window (Figure 29). (You may need to click the Windows Explorer program button on the taskbar to make the AutoPlay window visible.)

Q&A
Why does the AutoPlay window not open?

Some computers are not configured to open an AutoPlay window. Instead, they might display the contents of the USB flash drive automatically, or you might need to access contents of the USB flash drive using the Computer window. To use the Computer window to display the USB flash drive's contents, click the Start button, click Computer on the Start menu, and then click the icon representing the USB flash drive and then proceed to Step 3 on the next page.

Q&A
Why does the AutoPlay window look different from the one in Figure 29?

The AutoPlay window that opens on your computer might display different options. The type of USB flash drive, its contents, and the next available drive letter on your computer all will determine which options are displayed in the AutoPlay window.

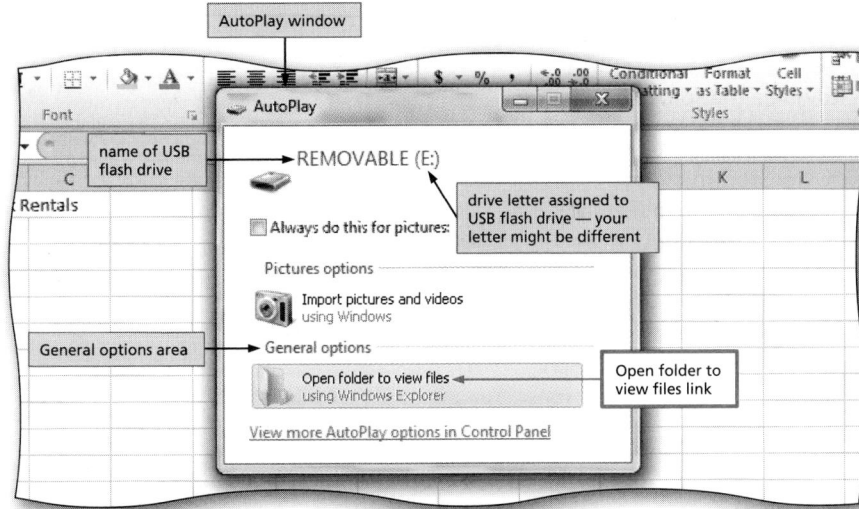

Figure 29

2

• Click the 'Open folder to view files' link in the AutoPlay window to open the USB flash drive window (Figure 30).

Q&A
Why does Figure 30 show REMOVABLE (E:) for the USB flash drive?

REMOVABLE is the name of the USB flash drive used to illustrate these steps. The (E:) refers to the drive letter assigned by Windows 7 to the USB flash drive. The name and drive letter of your USB flash drive probably will be different.

Figure 30

3

- Click the New folder button on the toolbar to display a new folder icon with the name, New folder, selected in a text box.

- Type **CIS 101** (or your class code) in the text box to name the folder.

- Press the ENTER key to create a folder identifying your class on the selected drive (Figure 31). If the CIS 101 folder does not appear in the navigation pane, double-click REMOVABLE (E:) in the navigation pane to display the folder just added.

Q&A What happens when I press the ENTER key?

The class folder (CIS 101, in this case) is displayed in the File list, which contains the folder name, date modified, type, and size.

Q&A Why is the folder icon displayed differently on my computer?

Windows might be configured to display contents differently on your computer.

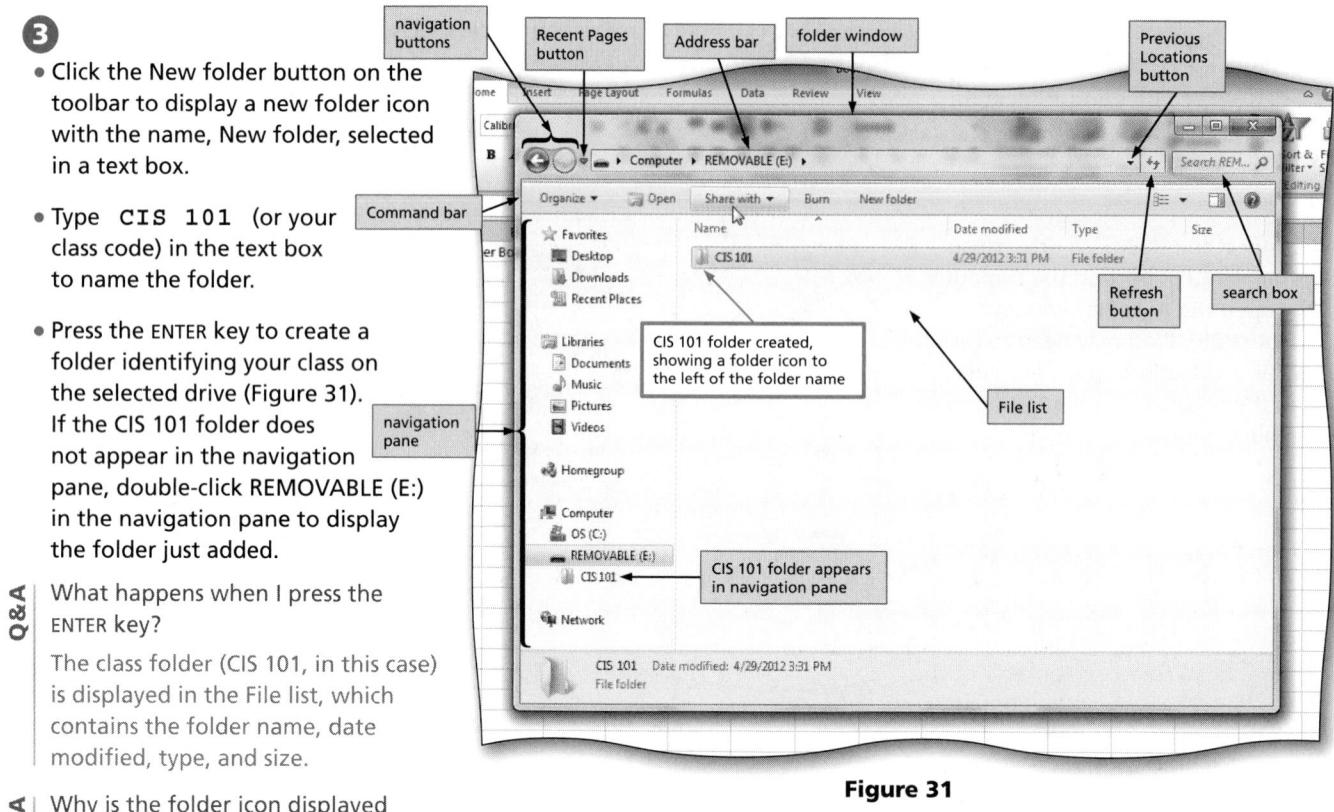

Figure 31

Folder Windows

The USB flash drive window (shown in Figure 31) is called a folder window. Recall that a folder is a specific named location on a storage medium that contains related files. Most users rely on **folder windows** for finding, viewing, and managing information on their computer. Folder windows have common design elements, including the following (Figure 31).

- The **Address bar** provides quick navigation options. The arrows on the Address bar allow you to visit different locations on the computer.
- The buttons to the left of the Address bar allow you to navigate the contents of the left pane and view recent pages. Other buttons allow you to specify the size of the window.
- The **Previous Locations button** saves the locations you have visited and displays the locations when clicked.
- The **Refresh button** on the right side of the Address bar refreshes the contents of the right pane of the folder window.
- The **search box** to the right of the Address bar contains the dimmed word, Search. You can type a term in the search box for a list of files, folders, shortcuts, and elements containing that term within the location you are searching. A **shortcut** is an icon on the desktop that provides a user with immediate access to a program or file.
- The **Command bar** contains five buttons used to accomplish various tasks on the computer related to organizing and managing the contents of the open window.
- The **navigation pane** on the left contains the Favorites area, Libraries area, Computer area, and Network area.

- The **Favorites area** contains links to your favorite locations. By default, this list contains only links to your Desktop, Downloads, and Recent Places.
- The **Libraries area** shows links to files and folders that have been included in a library.

A **library** helps you manage multiple folders and files stored in various locations on a computer. It does not store the files and folders; rather, it displays links to them so that you can access them quickly. For example, you can save pictures from a digital camera in any folder on any storage location on a computer. Normally, this would make organizing the different folders difficult; however, if you add the folders to a library, you can access all the pictures from one location regardless of where they are stored.

To Create a Folder within a Folder

With the class folder created, you can create folders that will store the files you create using Excel. The following steps create an Excel folder in the CIS 101 folder (or the folder identifying your class).

- Double-click the icon or folder name for the CIS 101 folder (or the folder identifying your class) in the File list to open the folder (Figure 32).

Figure 32

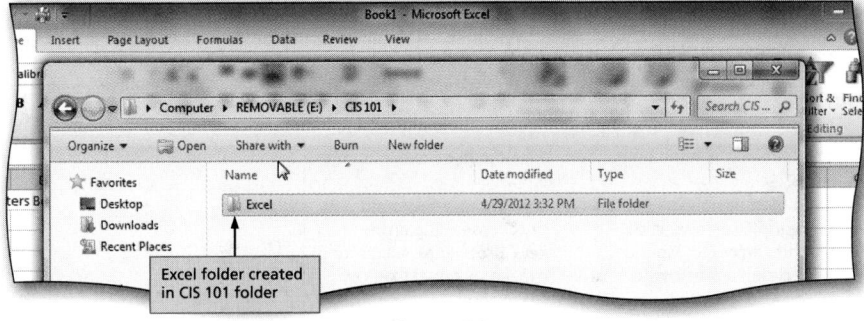

- Click the New folder button on the toolbar to display a new folder icon and text box for the folder.

- Type **Excel** in the text box to name the folder.

- Press the ENTER key to create the folder (Figure 33).

Figure 33

To Expand a Folder, Scroll through Folder Contents, and Collapse a Folder

Folder windows display the hierarchy of items and the contents of drives and folders in the right pane. You might want to expand a drive in the navigation pane to view its contents, scroll through its contents, and collapse it when you are finished viewing its contents. When a folder is expanded, it lists all the folders it contains. By contrast, a collapsed folder does not list the folders it contains. The steps on the next page expand, scroll through, and then collapse the folder identifying your class (CIS 101, in this case).

1

- Double-click the folder identifying your class (CIS 101, in this case) in the navigation pane, which expands the folder to display its contents and displays a black arrow to the left of the folder icon (Figure 34).

Q&A Why is the Excel folder indented below the CIS 101 folder in the navigation pane?

It shows that the folder is contained within the CIS 101 folder.

Q&A Why did a scroll bar appear in the navigation pane?

When all contents cannot fit in a window or pane, a scroll bar appears. As described earlier, you can view areas currently not visible by (1) clicking the scroll arrows, (2) clicking above or below the scroll bar, and (3) dragging the scroll box.

Experiment

- Click the down scroll arrow on the vertical scroll bar to display additional content at the bottom of the navigation pane.

- Click the scroll bar above the scroll box to move the scroll box to the top of the navigation pane.

- Drag the scroll box down the scroll bar until the scroll box is halfway down the scroll bar.

Figure 34

2

- Double-click the folder identifying your class (CIS 101, in this case) in the navigation pane to collapse the folder (Figure 35).

Figure 35

Other Ways	
1. Point in navigation pane to display arrows, click white arrow to expand or click black arrow to collapse	2. Select folder to expand or collapse using arrow keys, press RIGHT ARROW to expand; press LEFT ARROW to collapse

To Switch from One Program to Another

The next step is to save the Excel file containing the worksheet title you typed earlier. Excel, however, currently is not the active window. You can use the program button on the taskbar and live preview to switch to Excel and then save the workbook in the Excel window.

If Windows Aero is active on your computer, Windows displays a live preview window whenever you move your mouse on a button or click a button on the taskbar. If Aero is not supported or enabled on your computer, you will see a window title instead of a live preview. These steps use the Excel program; however, the steps are the same for any active Office program currently displayed as a program button on the taskbar.

The next steps switch to the Excel window.

1

- Point to the Excel program button on the taskbar to see a live preview of the open workbook(s) or the window title(s) of the open workbook(s), depending on your computer's configuration (Figure 36).

2

- Click the program button or the live preview to make the program associated with the program button the active window (shown in Figure 27 on page OFF 19).

Q&A What if multiple documents are open in a program?

If Aero is enabled on your computer, click the desired live preview. If Aero is not supported or not enabled, click the window title.

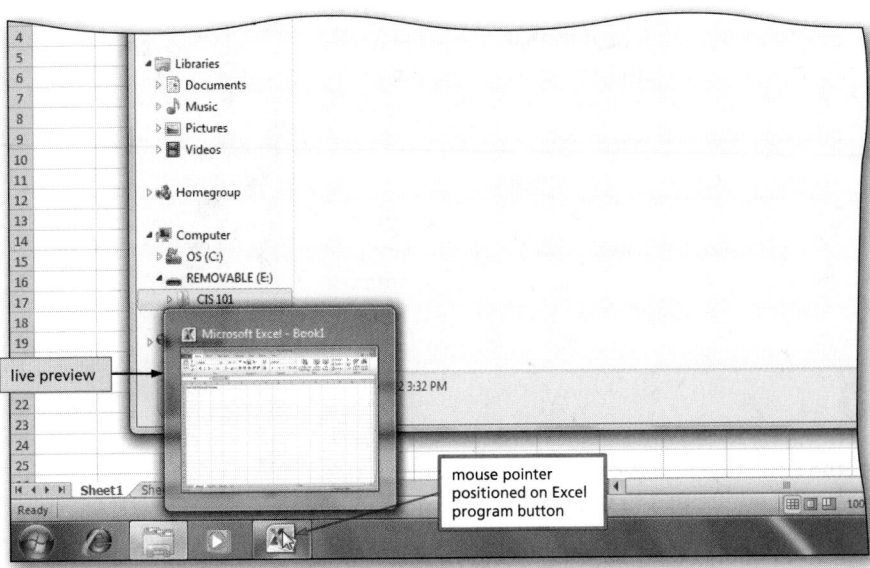

Figure 36

To Save a File in a Folder

Now that you have created the Excel folder for storing files, you can save the Excel workbook in that folder. The following steps save a file on a USB flash drive in the Excel folder contained in your class folder (CIS 101, in this case) using the file name, Brain Busters.

1

- With a USB flash drive connected to one of the computer's USB ports, click the Save button on the Quick Access Toolbar to display the Save As dialog box (Figure 37).

Figure 37

2

- Type **Brain Busters** in the File name text box (Save As dialog box) to change the file name. Do not press the ENTER key after typing the file name because you do not want to close the dialog box at this time (Figure 38).

Q&A What characters can I use in a file name?

The only invalid characters are the backslash (\), slash (/), colon (:), asterisk (*), question mark (?), quotation mark ("), less than symbol (<), greater than symbol (>), and vertical bar (|).

3

- Navigate to the desired save location (in this case, the Excel folder in the CIS 101 folder [or your class folder] on the USB flash drive) by performing the tasks in Steps 3a – 3c.

3a

- If the navigation pane is not displayed in the dialog box, click the Browse Folders button to expand the dialog box.
- If Computer is not displayed in the navigation pane, drag the navigation pane scroll bar until Computer appears.
- If Computer is not expanded in the navigation pane, double-click Computer to display a list of available storage devices in the navigation pane.
- If necessary, scroll through the dialog box until your USB flash drive appears in the list of available storage devices in the navigation pane (Figure 39).

3b

- If your USB flash drive is not expanded, double-click the USB flash drive in the list of available storage devices in the navigation pane to select that drive as the new save location and display its contents in the right pane.

3c

- If your class folder (CIS 101, in this case) is not expanded, double-click the CIS 101 folder to select the folder and display its contents in the right pane.

Q&A What if I do not want to save in a folder?

Although storing files in folders is an effective technique for organizing files, some users prefer not to store files in folders. If you prefer not to save this file in a folder, skip all instructions in Step 3c and proceed to Step 4.

- Click the Excel folder to select the folder and display its contents in the right pane (Figure 40).

Figure 38

Figure 39

Figure 40

4

- Click the Save button (Save As dialog box) to save the workbook in the selected folder on the selected drive with the entered file name (Figure 41).

Q&A

How do I know that the file is saved?

While an Office program such as Excel is saving a file, it briefly displays a message on the status bar indicating the amount of the file saved. In addition, the USB flash drive may have a light that flashes during the save process.

file name changed from Book1 to new file name, Brain Busters

Minimize button

saved workbook remains in memory and displayed on the screen

1 Brain Busters Book Rentals

Figure 41

Other Ways

1. Click File on Ribbon, click Save, type file name, navigate to desired save location, click Save button

2. Press CTRL+S or press SHIFT+F12, type file name, navigate to desired save location, click Save button

Navigating in Dialog Boxes

Navigating is the process of finding a location on a storage device. While saving the Brain Busters file, for example, Steps 3a – 3c in the previous set of steps navigated to the Excel folder located in the CIS 101 folder. When performing certain functions in Windows programs, such as saving a file, opening a file, or inserting a picture in an existing file, you most likely will have to navigate to the location where you want to save the file or to the folder containing the file you want to open or insert. Most dialog boxes in Windows programs requiring navigation follow a similar procedure; that is, the way you navigate to a folder in one dialog box, such as the Save As dialog box, is similar to how you might navigate in another dialog box, such as the Open dialog box. If you chose to navigate to a specific location in a dialog box, you would follow the instructions in Steps 3a – 3c on page OFF 26.

BTW

File Type
Depending on your Windows 7 settings, the file type .xlsx may be displayed immediately to the right of the file name after you save the file. The file type .xlsx is an Excel 2010 workbook.

To Minimize and Restore a Window

Before continuing, you can verify that the Excel file was saved properly. To do this, you will minimize the Excel window and then open the USB flash drive window so that you can verify the file is stored on the USB flash drive. A **minimized window** is an open window hidden from view but that can be displayed quickly by clicking the window's program button on the taskbar.

In the following example, Excel is used to illustrate minimizing and restoring windows; however, you would follow the same steps regardless of the Office program you are using.

The steps on the next page minimize the Excel window, verify that the file is saved, and then restore the minimized window.

1

- Click the Minimize button on the program's title bar (shown in Figure 41 on the previous page) to minimize the window.

Is the minimized window still available?

The minimized window, Excel in this case, remains available but no longer is the active window. It is minimized as a program button on the taskbar.

- If necessary, click the Windows Explorer program button on the taskbar to open the USB flash drive window (Figure 42).

Figure 42

2

- Double-click the Excel folder to select the folder and display its contents (Figure 43).

Why does the Windows Explorer button on the taskbar change?

The button changes to reflect the status of the folder window (in this case, the USB flash drive window). A selected button indicates that the folder window is active on the screen. When the button is not selected, the window is open but not active.

3

- After viewing the contents of the selected folder, click the Excel program button on the taskbar to restore the minimized window (as shown in Figure 41 on the previous page).

Other Ways

1. Right-click title bar, click Minimize on shortcut menu, click taskbar button in taskbar button area

2. Press WINDOWS+M, press WINDOWS+SHIFT+M

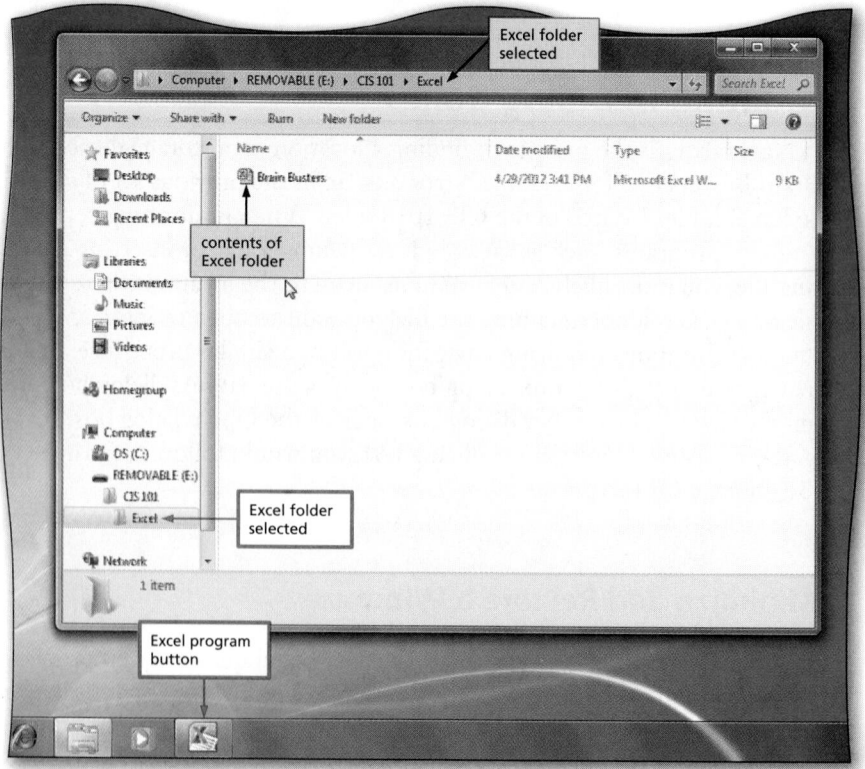

Figure 43

Screen Resolution

Screen resolution indicates the number of pixels (dots) that the computer uses to display the letters, numbers, graphics, and background you see on the screen. When you increase the screen resolution, Windows displays more information on the screen, but the information decreases in size. The reverse also is true: as you decrease the screen resolution, Windows displays less information on the screen, but the information increases in size.

Screen resolution usually is stated as the product of two numbers, such as 1024×768 (pronounced "ten twenty-four by seven sixty-eight"). A 1024×768 screen resolution results in a display of 1,024 distinct pixels on each of 768 lines, or about 786,432 pixels. Changing the screen resolution affects how the Ribbon appears in Office programs. Figure 44, for example, shows the Excel Ribbon at screen resolutions of 1024×768 and 1280×800. All of the same commands are available regardless of screen resolution. Excel, however, makes changes to the groups and the buttons within the groups to accommodate the various screen resolutions. The result is that certain commands may need to be accessed differently depending on the resolution chosen. A command that is visible on the Ribbon and available by clicking a button at one resolution may not be visible and may need to be accessed using its Dialog Box Launcher at a different resolution.

Comparing the two Ribbons in Figure 44, notice the changes in content and layout of the groups and galleries. In some cases, the content of a group is the same in each resolution, but the layout of the group differs. For example, the same gallery and buttons appear in the Cells groups in the two resolutions, but the layouts differ. In other cases, the content and layout are the same across the resolution, but the level of detail differs with the resolution. In the Clipboard group, when the resolution increases to 1280×800, the names of all the buttons in the group appear in addition to the buttons themselves. At the lower resolution, only the buttons appear.

Figure 44 (a) Ribbon at resolution of 1024 x 768

Figure 44 (b) Ribbon at resolution of 1280 x 800

To Change the Screen Resolution

If you are using a computer to step through the chapters in this book and you want your screen to match the figures, you may need to change your screen's resolution. The figures in this book use a screen resolution of 1024×768. The following steps change the screen resolution to 1024×768. Your computer already may be set to 1024×768 or some other resolution. Keep in mind that many computer labs prevent users from changing the screen resolution; in that case, read the following steps for illustration purposes.

- Click the Show desktop button on the taskbar to display the Windows 7 desktop.

- Right-click an empty area on the Windows 7 desktop to display a shortcut menu that displays a list of commands related to the desktop (Figure 45).

Q&A

Why does my shortcut menu display different commands?

Depending on your computer's hardware and configuration, different commands might appear on the shortcut menu.

Figure 45

- Click Screen resolution on the shortcut menu to open the Screen Resolution window (Figure 46).

Figure 46

3

- Click the Resolution button in the Screen Resolution window to display the resolution slider.

Q&A
What is a slider?

A **slider** is an object that allows users to choose from multiple predetermined options. In most cases, these options represent some type of numeric value. In most cases, one end of the slider (usually the left or bottom) represents the lowest of available values, and the opposite end (usually the right or top) represents the highest available value.

- If necessary, drag the resolution slider until the desired screen resolution (in this case, 1024 × 768) is selected (Figure 47).

Q&A
What if my computer does not support the 1024 × 768 resolution?

Some computers do not support the 1024 × 768 resolution. In this case, select a resolution that is close to the 1024 × 768 resolution.

Figure 47

4

- Click an empty area of the Screen Resolution window to close the resolution slider.

- Click the OK button to change the screen resolution and display the Display Settings dialog box (Figure 48).

5

- Click the Keep changes button (Display Settings dialog box) to accept the new screen resolution.

Figure 48

Q&A
Why is a message displayed stating that the image quality can be improved?

Some computer monitors are designed to display contents better at a certain screen resolution, sometimes referred to as an optimal resolution.

To Quit a Program with One File Open

When you quit an Office program, such as Excel, if you have made changes to a file since the last time the file was saved, the Office program displays a dialog box asking if you want save the changes you made to the file before it closes the program window. The dialog box contains three buttons with these resulting actions: the Save button saves the changes and then quits the Office program, the Don't Save button quits the Office program without saving changes, and the Cancel button closes the dialog box and redisplays the file without saving the changes.

If no changes have been made to an open file since the last time the file was saved, the Office program will close the window without displaying a dialog box.

The following steps quit Excel. You would follow similar steps in other Office programs.

- If necessary, click the Excel program button on the taskbar to display the Excel window on the desktop.

- Point to the Close button on the right side of the program's title bar, Excel in this case (Figure 49).

Figure 49

- Click the Close button to close the workbook and quit Excel.

Q&A What if I have more than one workbook open in Excel?

You would click the Close button for each open workbook. When you click the last open workbook's Close button, Excel also quits. As an alternative, you could click File on the Ribbon to open the Backstage view and then click Exit in the Backstage view to close all open workbooks and quit Excel.

Q&A What is the Backstage view?

The **Backstage view** contains a set of commands that enable you to manage files and data about the files. The Backstage view is discussed in more depth later in this chapter.

- If a Microsoft Excel dialog box appears, click the Save button to save any changes made to the workbook since the last save.

> **Other Ways**
>
> 1. Right-click the Office program button on Windows 7 taskbar, click Close window or 'Close all windows' on shortcut menu
>
> 2. Press ALT+F4

Break Point: If you wish to take a break, this is a good place to do so. To resume at a later time, continue to follow the steps from this location forward.

Additional Common Features of Office Programs

The previous section used Excel to illustrate common features of Office and some basic elements unique to Excel. The following sections continue to use Excel to present additional common features of Office.

In the following pages, you will learn how to do the following:

1. Start an Office program (Excel) using the search box.
2. Open a file in an Office program (Excel).
3. Save and close the file.
4. Reopen the file just closed.
5. Create a blank Office file from Windows Explorer and then open the file.
6. Save an Office file with a new file name.

To Start a Program Using the Search Box

The next steps, which assume Windows 7 is running, use the search box to start Excel based on a typical installation; however, you would follow similar steps to start any program. You may need to ask your instructor how to start programs for your computer.

- Click the Start button on the Windows 7 taskbar to display the Start menu.

- Type **Microsoft Excel** as the search text in the 'Search programs and files' text box and watch the search results appear on the Start menu (Figure 50).

Q&A

Do I need to type the complete program name or correct capitalization?

No, just enough of it for the program name to appear on the Start menu. For example, you may be able to type Excel or excel, instead of Microsoft Excel.

Figure 50

- Click the program name, Microsoft Excel 2010 in this case, in the search results on the Start menu to start Excel and display a new blank workbook in the Excel window.

- If the program window is not maximized, click the Maximize button on its title bar to maximize the window (Figure 51).

Figure 51

To Open an Existing File from the Backstage View

As discussed earlier, the Backstage view provides data about files and contains a set of commands that assist you with managing files. From the Backstage view in Excel, for example, you can create, open, print, and save workbooks. You also can share workbooks, manage versions, set permissions, and modify workbook properties.

Assume you wish to continue working on an existing file, that is, a file you previously saved. The following steps use the Backstage view to open a saved file, specifically the Brain Busters file, from the USB flash drive.

- With your USB flash drive connected to one of the computer's USB ports, if necessary, click File on the Ribbon to open the Backstage view (Figure 52).

Q&A

What is the purpose of the File tab?

The File tab is used to display the Backstage view for each Office program.

Figure 52

- Click Open in the Backstage view to display the Open dialog box (Figure 53).

- Navigate to the location of the file to be opened (in this case, the USB flash drive, then to the CIS 101 folder [or your class folder], and then to the Excel folder). For detailed steps about navigating, see Steps 3a – 3c on page OFF 26.

Q&A

What if I did not save my file in a folder?

If you did not save your file in a folder, the file you wish to open should be displayed in the Open dialog box before navigating to any folders.

- Click the file to be opened, Brain Busters in this case, to select the file (Figure 54).

Figure 53

- Click the Open button (Open dialog box) to open the selected file and display the opened file in the current program window (shown in Figure 41 on page OFF 27).

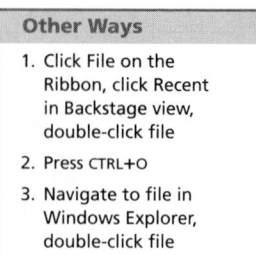

Other Ways

1. Click File on the Ribbon, click Recent in Backstage view, double-click file
2. Press CTRL+O
3. Navigate to file in Windows Explorer, double-click file

Figure 54

To Create a New Workbook from the Backstage View

You can create multiple files at the same time in an Office program, such as Excel. The following steps create a file, a blank workbook in this case, from the Backstage view.

1

- Click File on the Ribbon to open the Backstage view.

- Click the New tab in the Backstage view to display the New gallery (Figure 55).

Q&A

Can I create files through the Backstage view in other Office programs?

Yes. If the Office program has a New tab in the Backstage view, the New gallery displays various options for creating a new file.

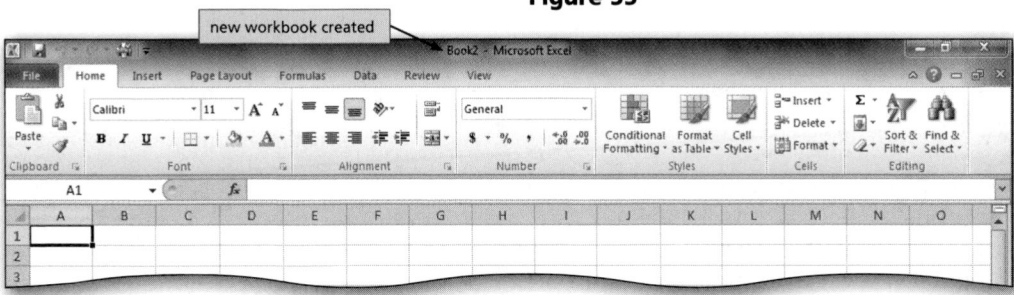

Figure 55

2

- Click the Create button in the New gallery to create a new workbook (Figure 56).

Figure 56

Other Ways
1. Press CTRL+N

To Enter Text in a Workbook

The next Excel workbook identifies the names of the Brain Busters sponsors. The following steps enter text in a workbook.

1 Type `List of Current Sponsors for the Brain Busters Event` and then press the ENTER key to enter the text and make cell A2 the active cell (Figure 57).

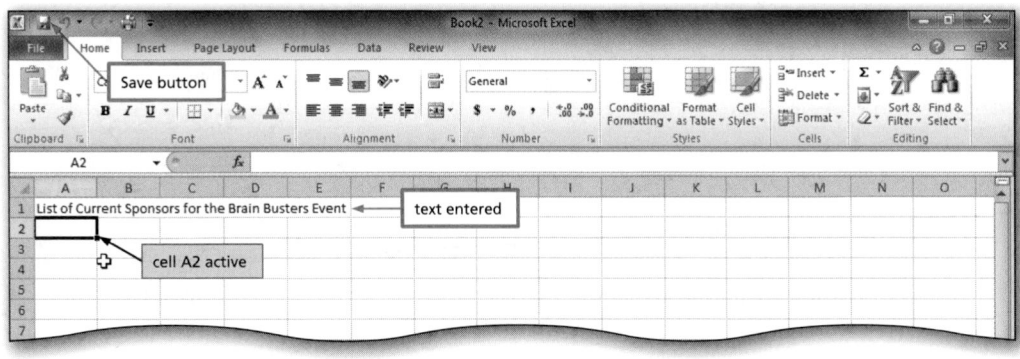

Figure 57

Customizing the Ribbon
In addition to customizing the Quick Access Toolbar, you can add items to and remove items from the Ribbon. To customize the Ribbon, click File on the Ribbon to open the Backstage view, click Options in the Backstage view, and then click Customize Ribbon in the left pane of the Options dialog box. More information about customizing the Ribbon is presented in a later chapter.

To Save a File in a Folder

The following steps save the second file in the Excel folder in the class folder (CIS 101, in this case) on a USB flash drive using the file name, Brain Busters Sponsors.

1 With a USB flash drive connected to one of the computer's USB ports, click the Save button on the Quick Access Toolbar to display the Save As dialog box.

2 Type `Brain Busters Sponsors` in the File name text box to change the file name. Do not press the ENTER key after typing the file name because you do not want to close the dialog box at this time.

3 If necessary, navigate to the desired save location (in this case, the Excel folder in the CIS 101 folder [or your class folder] on the USB flash drive).

4 Click the Save button (Save As dialog box) to save the file in the selected folder on the selected drive with the entered file name.

To Close a File Using the Backstage View

Sometimes, you may want to close an Office file, such as an Excel workbook, entirely and start over with a new file. You also may want to close a file when you are finished working with it so that you can begin a new file. The following steps close the current active Excel file (that is, the Brain Busters Sponsors workbook) without quitting the active program (Excel in this case).

- Click File on the Ribbon to open the Backstage view (Figure 58).

- Click Close in the Backstage view to close the open file (Brain Busters Sponsors, in this case) without quitting the active program.

What if Excel displays a dialog box about saving?

Click the Save button if you want to save the changes, click the Don't Save button if you want to ignore the changes since the last time you saved, and click the Cancel button if you do not want to close the file.

Q&A Can I use the Backstage view to close an open file in other Office programs, such as Word and PowerPoint?

Yes.

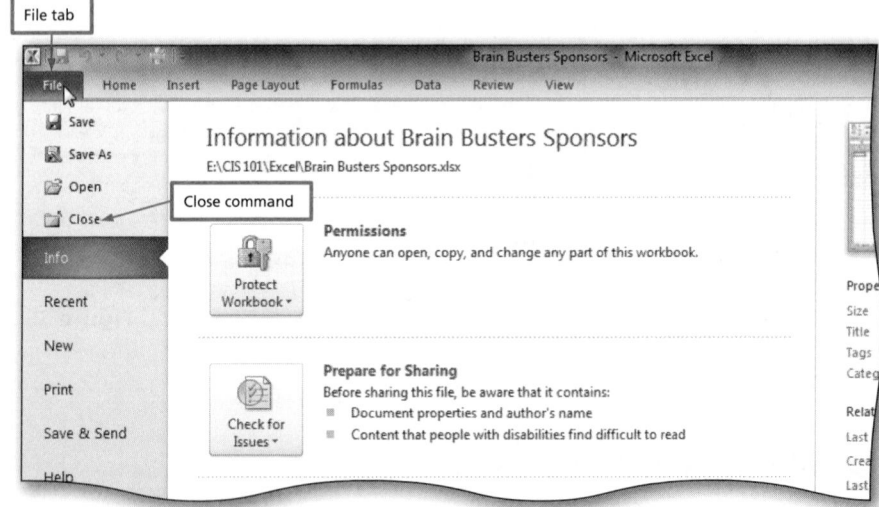

Figure 58

To Open a Recent File Using the Backstage View

You sometimes need to open a file that you recently modified. You may have more changes to make such as adding more content or correcting errors. The Backstage view allows you to access recent files easily. The next steps reopen the Brain Busters Sponsors file just closed.

1

- Click File on the Ribbon to open the Backstage view.

- Click the Recent tab in the Backstage view to display the Recent gallery (Figure 59).

2

- Click the desired file name in the Recent gallery, Brain Busters Sponsors in this case, to open the file (shown in Figure 57 on page OFF 35).

Q&A

Can I use the Backstage view to open a recent file when I am working in other Office programs, such as Word and PowerPoint?

Yes, as long as the file name appears in the list of recent files in the Recent gallery.

Figure 59

Other Ways

1. Click Start button, point to program name, click file name on submenu

2. Click File on Ribbon, click Open in Backstage view, navigate to file (Open dialog box), click Open button

To Create a New Blank Workbook from Windows Explorer

Windows Explorer provides a means to create a blank Office file without ever starting an Office program. The following steps use Windows Explorer to create a blank Excel workbook.

1

- Click the Windows Explorer program button on the taskbar to make the folder window the active window in Windows Explorer.

- If necessary, navigate to the desired location for the new file (in this case, the Excel folder in the CIS 101 folder [or your class folder] on the USB flash drive).

- With the Excel folder selected, right-click an open area in the right pane to display a shortcut menu.

- Point to New on the shortcut menu to display the New submenu (Figure 60).

Figure 60

- Click Microsoft Excel Worksheet on the New submenu to display an icon and text box for a new file in the current folder window (Figure 61).

Figure 61

- Type **Brain Busters Staff** in the text box and then press the ENTER key to assign a name to the new file in the current folder (Figure 62).

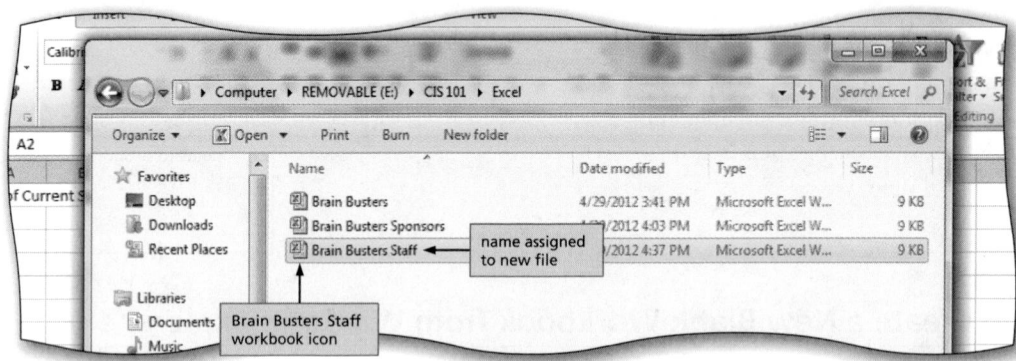

Figure 62

To Start a Program from Windows Explorer and Open a File

Previously, you learned how to start an Office program (Excel) using the Start menu and the search box. Another way to start an Office program is to open an existing file from Windows Explorer, which causes the program in which the file was created to start and then open the selected file. The following steps, which assume Windows 7 is running, use Windows Explorer to start Excel based on a typical installation. You may need to ask your instructor how to start Excel for your computer.

- If necessary, display the file to open in the folder window in Windows Explorer (shown in Figure 62).

- Right-click the file icon or file name (Brain Busters Staff, in this case) to display a shortcut menu (Figure 63).

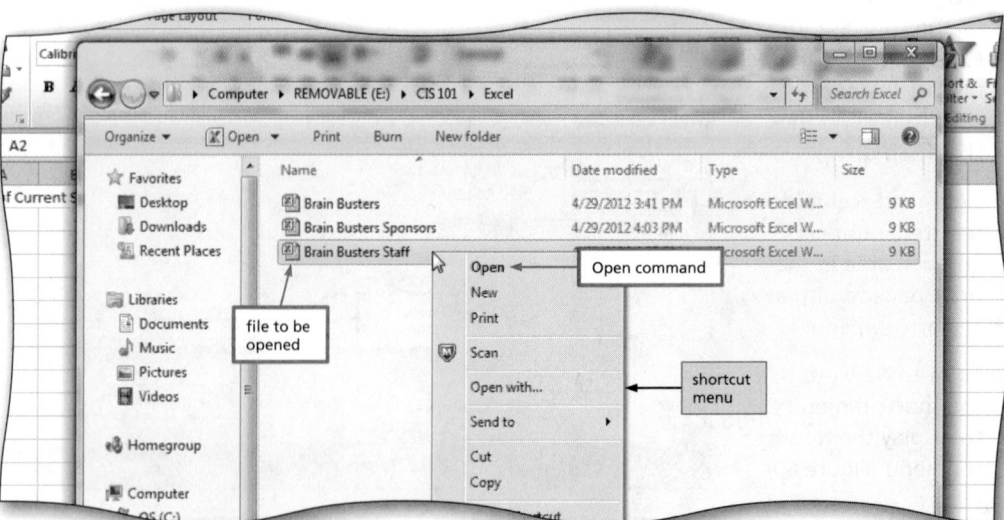

Figure 63

2

- Click Open on the shortcut menu to open the selected file in the program used to create the file, Microsoft Excel in this case.

- If the program window is not maximized, click the Maximize button on the title bar to maximize the window (Figure 64).

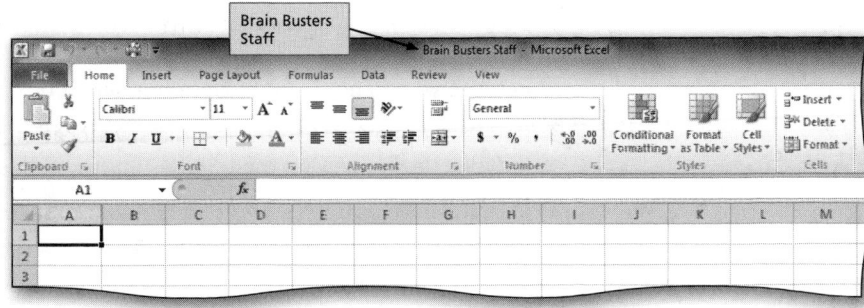

Figure 64

To Enter Text in a Workbook

The next step is to enter text in this blank Excel workbook. The following step enters text in a cell.

1 Type **Brain Busters Staff** and then press the ENTER key to enter the text and make cell A2 the active cell (shown in Figure 65).

To Save an Existing File with the Same File Name

Saving frequently cannot be overemphasized. You have made modifications to the file (workbook) since you created it. Thus, you should save again. Similarly, you should continue saving files frequently so that you do not lose your changes since the time you last saved the file. You can use the same file name, such as Brain Busters Staff, to save the changes made to the file. The following step saves a file again.

1

- Click the Save button on the Quick Access Toolbar to overwrite the previously saved file (Brain Busters Staff, in this case) on the USB flash drive (Figure 65).

Q&A Why did the Save As dialog box not appear?

Office programs, including Excel, overwrite the file using the setting specified the first time you saved the file.

Figure 65

<table>
<tr><td>**Other Ways**</td></tr>
<tr><td>1. Press CTRL+S or press SHIFT+F12</td></tr>
</table>

To Use Save As to Change the Name of a File

You might want to save a file with a different name and even to a different location. For example, you might start a homework assignment with a data file and then save it with a final file name for submitting to your instructor, saving it to a location designated by your instructor. The following steps save a file with a different file name.

1 With your USB flash drive connected to one of the computer's USB ports, click File on the Ribbon to open the Backstage view.

2 Click Save As in the Backstage view to display the Save As dialog box.

3 Type **Brain Busters Event Staff** in the File name text box (Save As dialog box) to change the file name. Do not press the ENTER key after typing the file name because you do not want to close the dialog box at this time.

4 If necessary, navigate to the desired save location (the Excel folder in the CIS 101 folder [or your class folder] on the USB flash drive, in this case).

5 Click the Save button (Save As dialog box) to save the file in the selected folder on the selected drive with the new file name.

To Quit an Office Program

You are finished using Excel. The following steps quit Excel. You would use similar steps to quit other Office programs.

1 Because you have multiple Excel workbooks open, click File on the Ribbon to open the Backstage view and then click Exit in the Backstage view to close all open workbooks and quit Excel.

2 If a dialog box appears, click the Save button to save any changes made to the file since the last save.

Moving, Renaming, and Deleting Files

Earlier in this chapter, you learned how to organize files in folders, which is part of a process known as **file management**. The following sections cover additional file management topics including renaming, moving, and deleting files.

To Rename a File

In some circumstances, you may want to change the name of, or rename, a file or a folder. For example, you may want to distinguish a file in one folder or drive from a copy of a similar file, or you may decide to rename a file to better identify its contents. The Excel folder shown in Figure 66 contains the Excel workbook, Brain Busters. The following steps change the name of the Brain Busters file in the Excel folder to Brain Busters Information.

1

• If necessary, click the Windows Explorer program button on the taskbar to display the folder window in Windows Explorer.

• If necessary, navigate to the location of the file to be renamed (in this case, the Excel folder in the CIS 101 [or your class folder] folder on the USB flash drive) to display the file(s) it contains in the right pane.

• Right-click the Brain Busters icon or file name in the right pane to select the Brain Busters file and display a shortcut menu that presents a list of commands related to files (Figure 66).

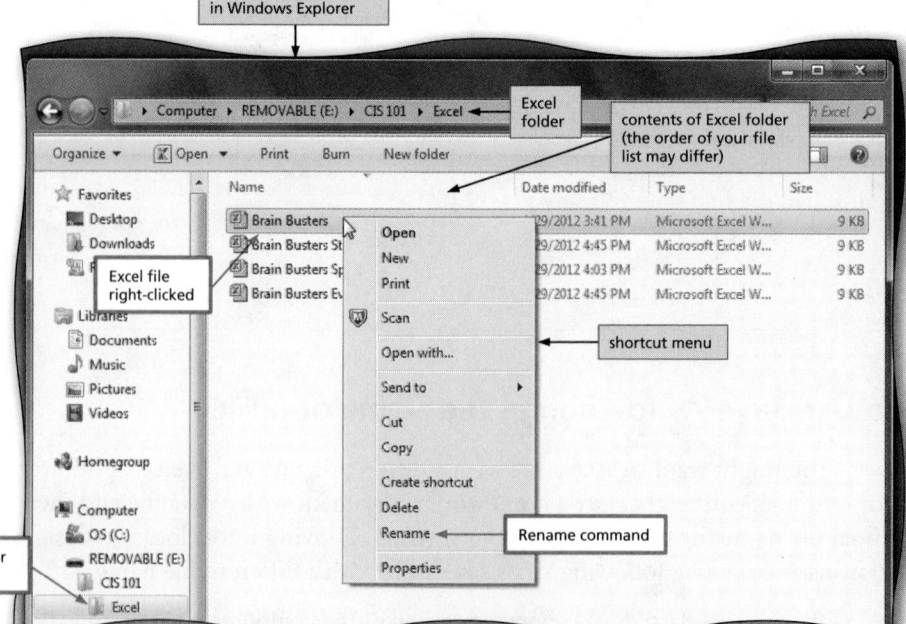

Figure 66

2

- Click Rename on the shortcut menu to place the current file name in a text box.

- Type **Brain Busters Information** in the text box and then press the ENTER key (Figure 67).

Q&A
Are any risks involved in renaming files that are located on a hard disk?

If you inadvertently rename a file that is associated with certain programs, the programs may not be able to find the file and, therefore, may not execute properly. Always use caution when renaming files.

Q&A
Can I rename a file when it is open?

No, a file must be closed to change the file name.

Figure 67

Other Ways

1. Select file, press F2, type new file name, press ENTER

To Move a File

At some time, you may want to move a file from one folder, called the source folder, to another, called the destination. When you move a file, it no longer appears in the original folder. If the destination and the source folders are on the same disk drive, you can move a file by dragging it. If the folders are on different disk drives, then you will need to right-drag the file. The following step moves the Brain Busters Staff file from the Excel folder to the CIS 101 folder.

1

- In Windows Explorer, if necessary, navigate to the location of the file to be moved (in this case, the Excel folder in the CIS 101 folder [or your class folder] on the USB flash drive).

- If necessary, click the Excel folder in the navigation pane to display the files it contains in the right pane.

- Drag the Brain Busters Staff file in the right pane to the CIS 101 folder in the navigation pane and notice the ScreenTip as you drag the mouse (Figure 68).

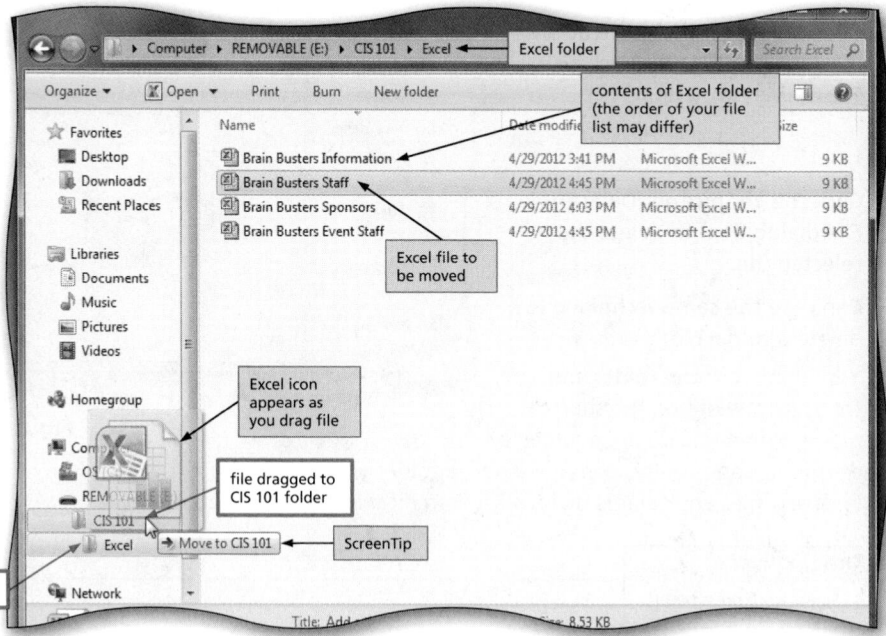

Figure 68

Other Ways

1. Right-click file, drag file to destination folder, click Move here

2. Right-click file to copy, click Cut on shortcut menu, right-click destination

folder, click Paste on shortcut menu

3. Select file to copy, press CTRL+X, select destination folder, press CTRL+V

To Delete a File

A final task you may want to perform is to delete a file. Exercise extreme caution when deleting a file or files. When you delete a file from a hard disk, the deleted file is stored in the Recycle Bin where you can recover it until you empty the Recycle Bin. If you delete a file from removable media, such as a USB flash drive, the file is deleted permanently. The next steps delete the Brain Busters Staff file from the CIS 101 folder.

- In Windows Explorer, navigate to the location of the file to be deleted (in this case, the CIS 101 folder [or your class folder] on the USB flash drive).

- If necessary, click the CIS 101 folder in the navigation pane to display the files it contains in the right pane.

- Right-click the Brain Busters Staff icon or file name in the right pane to select the file and display a shortcut menu (Figure 69).

Figure 69

- Click Delete on the shortcut menu to display the Delete File dialog box (Figure 70).

- Click the Yes button (Delete File dialog box) to delete the selected file.

Q&A

Can I use this same technique to delete a folder?

Yes. Right-click the folder and then click Delete on the shortcut menu. When you delete a folder, all of the files and folders contained in the folder you are deleting, together with any files and folders on lower hierarchical levels, are deleted as well.

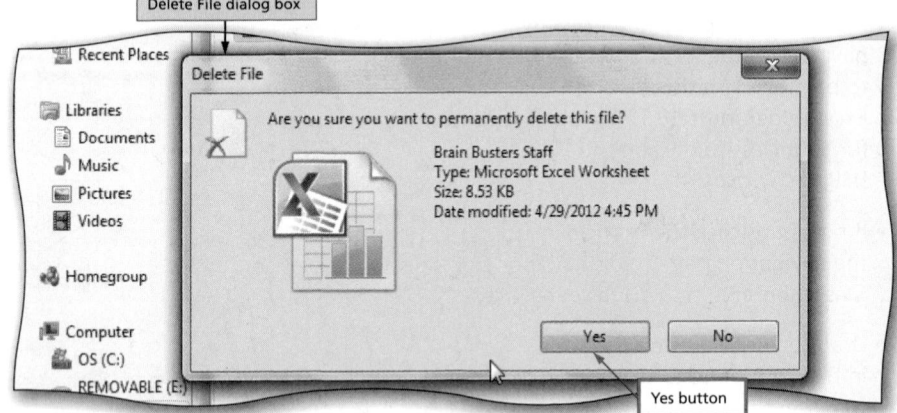

Figure 70

Other Ways

1. Select icon, press DELETE

Microsoft Office and Windows Help

At any time while you are using one of the Microsoft Office 2010 programs, such as Excel, you can use Office Help to display information about all topics associated with the program. This section illustrates the use of Excel Help. Help in other Office 2010 programs operates in a similar fashion.

In Office 2010, Help is presented in a window that has Web-browser-style navigation buttons. Each Office 2010 program has its own Help home page, which is the starting Help page that is displayed in the Help window. If your computer is connected to the Internet, the contents of the Help page reflect both the local help files installed on the computer and material from Microsoft's Web site.

To Open the Help Window in an Office Program

The following step opens the Excel Help window. The step to open a Help window in other Office programs is similar.

- Start Excel.

- Click the Microsoft Excel Help button near the upper-right corner of the program window to open the Excel Help window (Figure 71).

Q&A

What should I do if the Help table of contents is displayed when the Excel Help window opens?

Click the Hide Table of Contents button to close the table of contents.

Figure 71

Other Ways
1. Press F1

Moving and Resizing Windows

Up to this point, this chapter has used minimized and maximized windows. At times, however, it is useful, or even necessary, to have more than one window open and visible on the screen at the same time. You can resize and move these open windows so that you can view different areas of and elements in the window. In the case of the Help window, for example, it could be covering document text in the Excel window that you need to see.

To Move a Window by Dragging

You can move any open window that is not maximized to another location on the desktop by dragging the title bar of the window. The step on the next page drags the Excel Help window to the top left of the desktop.

1

• Drag the window title bar (the Excel Help window title bar, in this case) so that the window moves to the top left of the desktop, as shown in Figure 72.

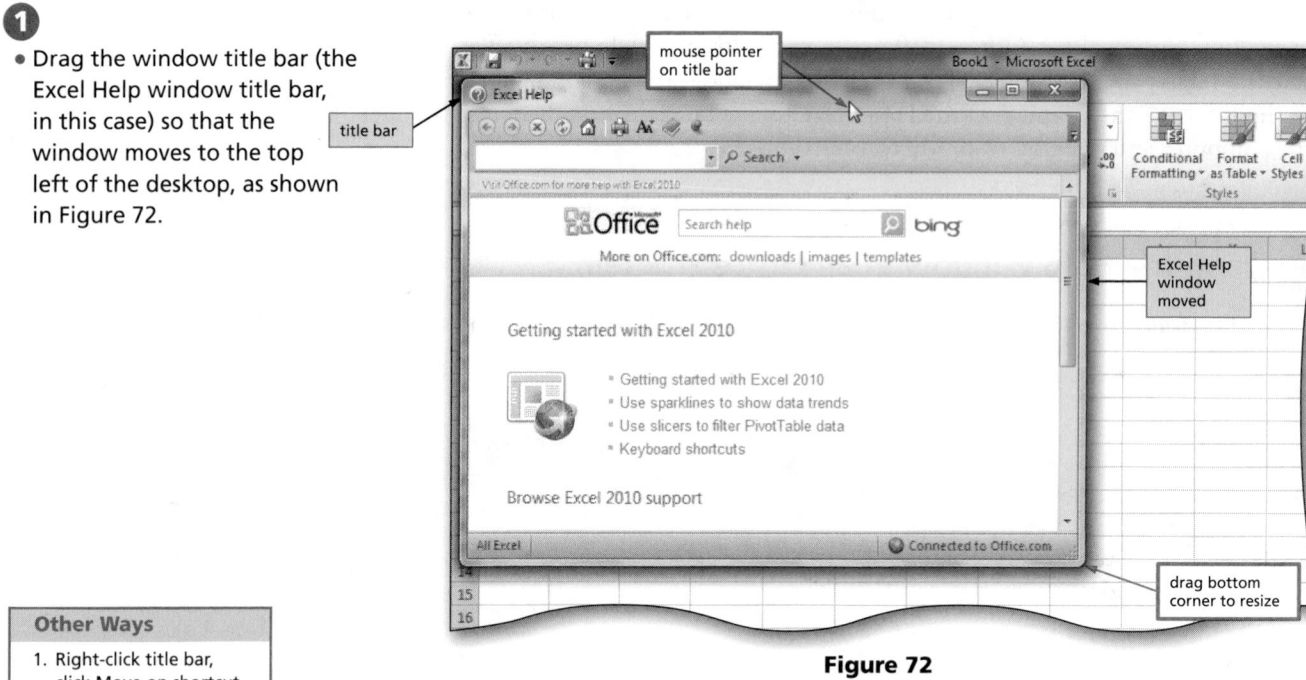

Figure 72

Other Ways

1. Right-click title bar, click Move on shortcut menu, drag window

To Resize a Window by Dragging

Sometimes, information is not visible completely in a window. A method used to change the size of the window is to drag the window borders. The following step changes the size of the Excel Help window by dragging its borders.

1

• Point to the lower-right corner of the window (the Excel Help window, in this case) until the mouse pointer changes to a two-headed arrow.

• Drag the bottom border downward to display more of the active window (Figure 73).

Q&A Can I drag other borders on the window to enlarge or shrink the window?

Yes, you can drag the left, right, and top borders and any window corner to resize a window.

Q&A Will Windows 7 remember the new size of the window after I close it?

Yes. When you reopen the window, Windows 7 will display it at the same size it was when you closed it.

Figure 73

Using Office Help

Once an Office program's Help window is open, several methods exist for navigating Help. You can search for help by using any of the three following methods from the Help window:

1. Enter search text in the 'Type words to search for' text box.
2. Click the links in the Help window.
3. Use the Table of Contents.

To Obtain Help Using the 'Type words to search for' Text Box

Assume for the following example that you want to know more about the Backstage view. The following steps use the 'Type words to search for' text box to obtain useful information about the Backstage view by entering the word, Backstage, as search text.

1

- Type **Backstage** in the 'Type words to search for' text box at the top of the Excel Help window to enter the search text.

- Click the Search button arrow to display the Search menu (Figure 74).

2

- If it is not selected already, click All Excel on the Search menu, so that Help performs the most complete search of the current program (Excel, in this case). If All Excel already is selected, click the Search button arrow again to close the Search menu.

Q&A

Why select All Excel on the Search menu?

Selecting All Excel on the Search menu ensures that Excel Help will search all possible sources for information about your search term. It will produce the most complete search results.

Figure 74

- Click the Search button to display the search results (Figure 75).

Why do my search results differ?

If you do not have an Internet connection, your results will reflect only the content of the Help files on your computer. When searching for help online, results also can change as material is added, deleted, and updated on the online Help Web pages maintained by Microsoft.

Why were my search results not very helpful?

When initiating a search, be sure to check the spelling of the search text; also, keep your search specific, with fewer than seven words, to return the most accurate results.

Figure 75

- Click the What and where is the Backstage view link to open the Help document associated with the selected topic (Figure 76).

Figure 76

4

- Click the Home button on the toolbar to clear the search results and redisplay the Help home page (Figure 77).

Figure 77

To Obtain Help Using the Help Links

If your topic of interest is listed in the Browse area of the Help window, you can click the link to begin browsing the Help categories instead of entering search text. You browse Help just as you would browse a Web site. If you know which category contains your Help information, you may wish to use these links. The following step finds the Worksheets Help information using the category links from the Excel Help home page.

1

- Click the Worksheets link on the Help home page (shown in Figure 77) to display the Worksheets page (Figure 78).

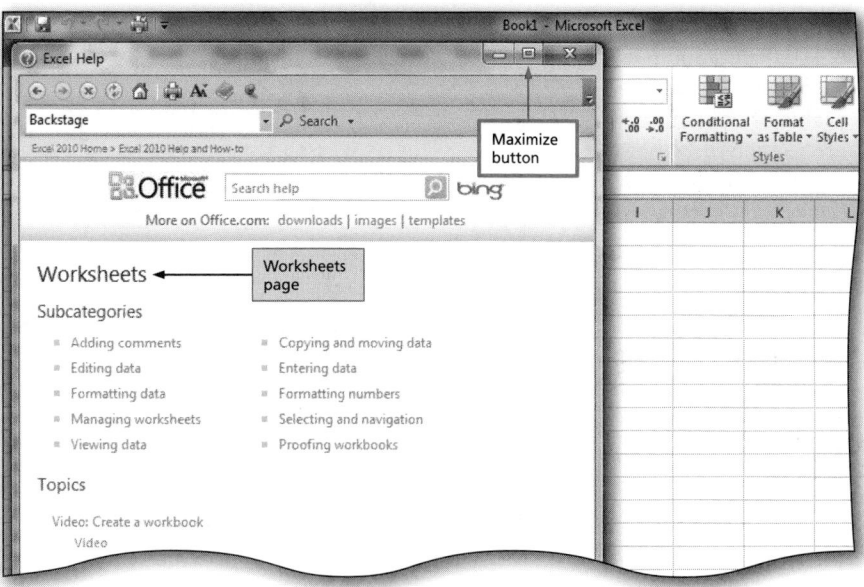

Figure 78

To Obtain Help Using the Help Table of Contents

A third way to find Help in Office programs is through the Help Table of Contents. You can browse through the Table of Contents to display information about a particular topic or to familiarize yourself with an Office program. The following steps access the Help information about themes by browsing through the Table of Contents.

1

- Click the Home button on the toolbar to display the Help home page.

- Click the Show Table of Contents button on the toolbar to display the Table of Contents pane on the left side of the Help window. If necessary, click the Maximize button on the Help title bar to maximize the window (Figure 79).

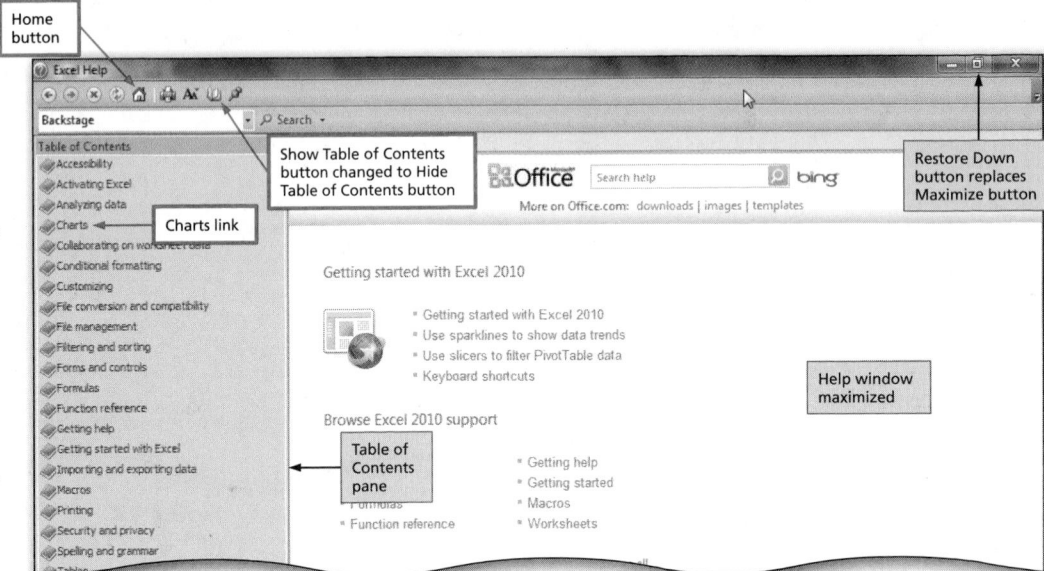

Figure 79

Why does the appearance of the Show Table of Contents button change?

When the Table of Contents is displayed in the Help window, the Hide Table of Contents button replaces the Show Table of Contents button.

2

- Click the Charts link in the Table of Contents pane to view a list of Help subtopics.

- Click the Creating charts link in the Table of Contents pane to expand the topic.

- Click the 'Create a chart from start to finish' link to view the selected Help document in the right pane (Figure 80).

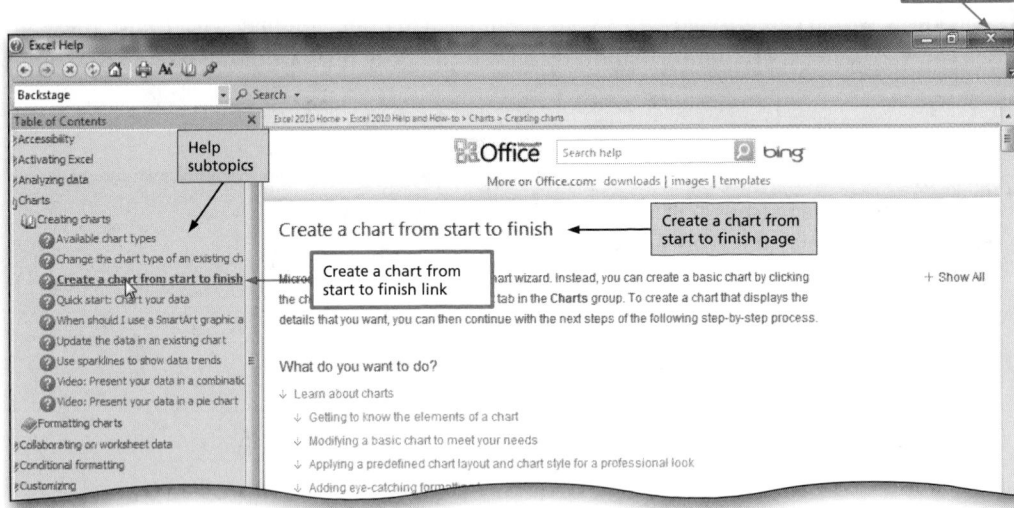

Figure 80

3

- After reviewing the page, click the Close button to quit Help.

- Click Excel's Close button to quit Excel.

How do I remove the Table of Contents pane when I am finished with it?

The Show Table of Contents button acts as a toggle. When the Table of Contents pane is visible, the button changes to Hide Table of Contents. Clicking it hides the Table of Contents pane and changes the button to Show Table of Contents.

Obtaining Help while Working in an Office Program

Help in Office programs, such as Excel, provides you with the ability to obtain help directly, without the need to open the Help window and initiate a search. For example, you may be unsure about how a particular command works, or you may be presented with a dialog box that you are not sure how to use.

Figure 81 shows one option for obtaining help while working in Excel. If you want to learn more about a command, point to the command button and wait for the Enhanced ScreenTip to appear. If the Help icon appears in the Enhanced ScreenTip, press the F1 key while pointing to the command to open the Help window associated with that command.

Figure 82 shows a dialog box that contains a Help button. Pressing the F1 key while the dialog box is displayed opens a Help window. The Help window contains help about that dialog box, if available. If no help file is available for that particular dialog box, then the main Help window opens.

Figure 81

Using Windows Help and Support

One of the more powerful Windows 7 features is Windows Help and Support. **Windows Help and Support** is available when using Windows 7 or when using any Microsoft program running under Windows 7. This feature is designed to assist you in using Windows 7 or the various programs. Table 4 describes the content found in the Help and Support Center. The same methods used for searching Microsoft Office Help can be used in Windows Help and Support. The difference is that Windows Help and Support displays help for Windows 7, instead of for Microsoft Office.

Figure 82

Table 4 Windows Help and Support Center Content Areas	
Area	**Function**
Find an answer quickly	This area contains instructions about how to do a quick search using the search box.
Not sure where to start?	This area displays three topics to help guide a user: How to get started with your computer, Learn about Windows Basics, and Browse Help topics. Clicking one of the options navigates to corresponding Help and Support pages.
More on the Windows Website	This area contains links to online content from the Windows Web site. Clicking the links navigates to the corresponding Web pages on the Web site.

To Start Windows Help and Support

The steps on the next page start Windows Help and Support and display the Windows Help and Support window, containing links to more information about Windows 7.

● Click the Start button on the taskbar to display the Start menu (Figure 83).

Q&A

Why are the programs that are displayed on the Start menu different?

Windows adds the programs you have used recently to the left pane on the Start menu. You have started Excel while performing the steps in this chapter, so that program now is displayed on the Start menu.

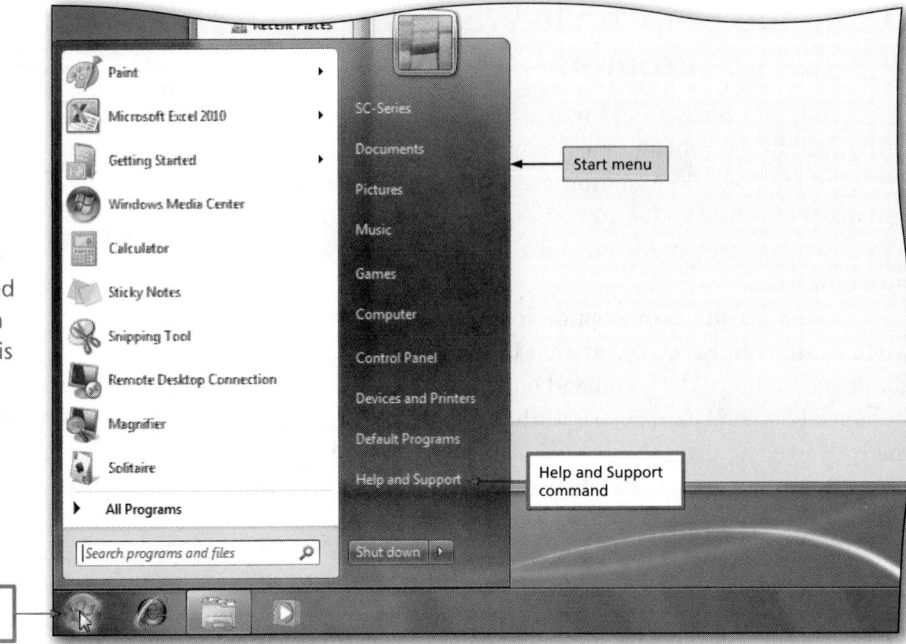

Figure 83

② ● Click Help and Support on the Start menu to open the Windows Help and Support window (Figure 84).

③ ● After reviewing the Windows Help and Support window, click the Close button to quit Windows Help and Support.

Other Ways

1. Press CTRL+ESC, press RIGHT ARROW, press UP ARROW, press ENTER
2. Press WINDOWS+F1

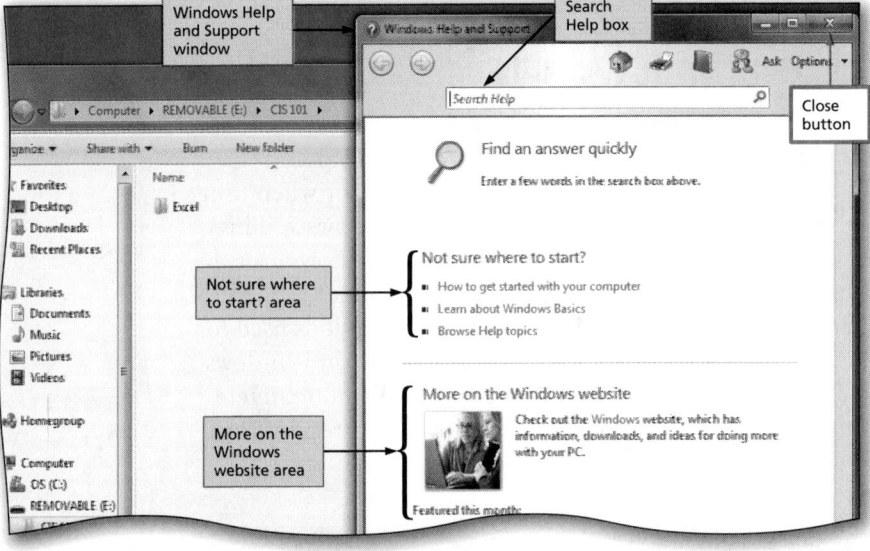

Figure 84

Chapter Summary

In this chapter, you learned about the Windows 7 interface. You started Windows 7, were introduced to the components of the desktop, and learned several mouse operations. You opened, closed, moved, resized, minimized, maximized, and scrolled a window. You used folder windows to expand and collapse drives and folders, display drive and folder contents, create folders, and rename and then delete a file.

You also learned some basic features of Microsoft Excel 2010. As part of this learning process, you discovered the common elements that exist among Microsoft Office programs.

Microsoft Office Help was demonstrated using Excel, and you learned how to use the Excel Help window. You were introduced to the Windows 7 Help and Support Center and learned how to use it to obtain more information about Windows 7.

The items listed below include all of the new Windows 7 and Excel 2010 skills you have learned in this chapter.

1. Log On to the Computer (OFF 6)
2. Start a Program Using the Start Menu (OFF 10)
3. Maximize a Window (OFF 12)
4. Display a Different Tab on the Ribbon (OFF 16)
5. Minimize, Display, and Restore the Ribbon (OFF 16)
6. Display and Use a Shortcut Menu (OFF 17)
7. Customize the Quick Access Toolbar (OFF 18)
8. Enter Text in a Workbook (OFF 19)
9. Create a Folder (OFF 20)
10. Create a Folder within a Folder (OFF 23)
11. Expand a Folder, Scroll through Folder Contents, and Collapse a Folder (OFF 23)
12. Switch from One Program to Another (OFF 24)
13. Save a File in a Folder (OFF 25)
14. Minimize and Restore a Window (OFF 27)
15. Change the Screen Resolution (OFF 30)
16. Quit a Program with One File Open (OFF 31)
17. Start a Program Using the Search Box (OFF 32)
18. Open an Existing File from the Backstage View (OFF 33)
19. Create a New Workbook from the Backstage View (OFF 35)
20. Close a File Using the Backstage View (OFF 36)
21. Open a Recent File Using the Backstage View (OFF 36)
22. Create a New Blank Workbook from Windows Explorer (OFF 37)
23. Start a Program from Windows Explorer and Open a File (OFF 38)
24. Save an Existing File with the Same File Name (OFF 39)
25. Rename a File (OFF 40)
26. Move a File (OFF 41)
27. Delete a File (OFF 42)
28. Open the Help Window in an Office Program (OFF 43)
29. Move a Window by Dragging (OFF 43)
30. Resize a Window by Dragging (OFF 44)
31. Obtain Help Using the 'Type words to search for' Text Box (OFF 45)
32. Obtain Help Using the Help Links (OFF 47)
33. Obtain Help Using the Help Table of Contents (OFF 48)
34. Start Windows Help and Support (OFF 49)

If you have a SAM 2010 user profile, your instructor may have assigned an autogradable version of this assignment. If so, log into the SAM 2010 Web site at www.cengage.com/sam2010 to download the instruction and start files.

Learn It Online

Test your knowledge of chapter content and key terms.

Instructions: To complete the Learn It Online exercises, start your browser, click the Address bar, and then enter the Web address **scsite.com/ex2010/learn**. When the Office 2010 Learn It Online page is displayed, click the link for the exercise you want to complete and then read the instructions.

Chapter Reinforcement TF, MC, and SA
A series of true/false, multiple choice, and short answer questions that test your knowledge of the chapter content.

Flash Cards
An interactive learning environment where you identify chapter key terms associated with displayed definitions.

Practice Test
A series of multiple choice questions that test your knowledge of chapter content and key terms.

Who Wants To Be a Computer Genius?
An interactive game that challenges your knowledge of chapter content in the style of a television quiz show.

Wheel of Terms
An interactive game that challenges your knowledge of chapter key terms in the style of the television show *Wheel of Fortune*.

Crossword Puzzle Challenge
A crossword puzzle that challenges your knowledge of key terms presented in the chapter.

Apply Your Knowledge

Reinforce the skills and apply the concepts you learned in this chapter.

Creating a Folder and a Document

Instructions: You will create an Excel folder and then create an Excel workbook and save it in the folder.

Perform the following tasks:

1. Connect a USB flash drive to an available USB port and then open the USB flash drive window.

2. Click the New folder button on the toolbar to display a new folder icon and text box for the folder name.

3. Type `Excel` in the text box to name the folder. Press the ENTER key to create the folder on the USB flash drive.

4. Start Excel.

5. Enter the text shown in Figure 85.

6. Click the Save button on the Quick Access Toolbar. Navigate to the Excel folder on the USB flash drive and then save the document using the file name, Apply 1 Class List.

7. If your Quick Access Toolbar does not show the Quick Print button, add the Quick Print button to the Quick Access Toolbar. Print the document using the Quick Print button on the Quick Access Toolbar. When you are finished printing, remove the Quick Print button from the Quick Access Toolbar.

8. Submit the printout to your instructor.

9. Quit Excel.

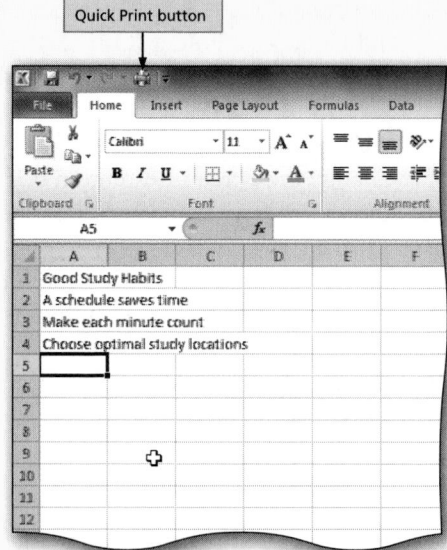

Figure 85

Extend Your Knowledge

Extend the skills you learned in this chapter and experiment with new skills. You will use Help to complete the assignment.

Using Help

Instructions: Use Excel Help to perform the following tasks.

Perform the following tasks:

1. Start Excel.

2. Click the Microsoft Excel Help button to open the Excel Help window (Figure 86).

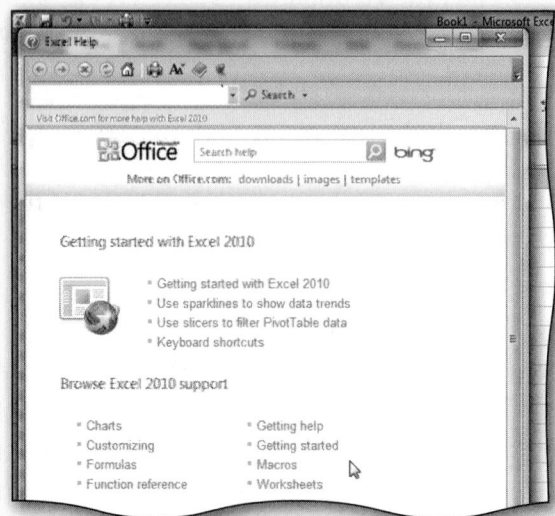

Figure 86

3. Search Excel Help to answer the following questions.

   a. What are three features new to Excel 2010?

   b. What training videos are available through Help?

   c. What are the steps to add a new group to the Ribbon?

   d. What are sparklines?

   e. What is a relative cell reference?

   f. What is a template?

   g. How do you print a workbook?

   h. What is a SmartArt graphic?

   i. What are five available chart types?

   j. What is the purpose of the Merge & Center command?

4. Submit the answers from your searches in the format specified by your instructor.

5. Quit Excel.

Make It Right

Analyze a file structure and correct all errors and/or improve the design.

Organizing Vacation Photos

Note: To complete this assignment, you will be required to use the Data Files for Students. See the inside back cover of this book for instructions on downloading the Data Files for Students, or contact your instructor for information about accessing the required files.

Instructions: Traditionally, you have stored photos from past vacations together in one folder. The photos are becoming difficult to manage, and you now want to store them in appropriate folders. You will create the folder structure shown in Figure 87. You then will move the photos to the folders so that they will be organized properly.

1. Connect a USB flash drive to an available USB port to open the USB flash drive window.

2. Create the hierarchical folder structure shown in Figure 87.

3. Move one photo to each folder in the folder structure you created in Step 2. The five photos are available on the Data Files for Students.

4. Submit your work in the format specified by your instructor.

Figure 87

In the Lab

Use the guidelines, concepts, and skills presented in this chapter to increase your knowledge of Windows 7 and Excel 2010. Labs are listed in order of increasing difficulty.

Lab 1: Using Windows Help and Support

Problem: You have a few questions about using Windows 7 and would like to answer these questions using Windows Help and Support.

Instructions: Use Windows Help and Support to perform the following tasks:

1. Display the Start menu and then click Help and Support to start Windows Help and Support.

2. Use the Help and Support Content page to answer the following questions.

   a. How do you reduce computer screen flicker?

   b. Which dialog box do you use to change the appearance of the mouse pointer?

   c. How do you minimize all windows?

   d. What is a VPN?

3. Use the Search Help text box in Windows Help and Support to answer the following questions.

   a. How can you minimize all open windows on the desktop?

   b. How do you start a program using the Run command?

   c. What are the steps to add a toolbar to the taskbar?

   d. What wizard do you use to remove unwanted desktop icons?

4. The tools to solve a problem while using Windows 7 are called **troubleshooters**. Use Windows Help and Support to find the list of troubleshooters (Figure 88), and answer the following questions.

   a. What problems does the HomeGroup troubleshooter allow you to resolve?

   b. List five Windows 7 troubleshooters that are not listed in Figure 88.

5. Use Windows Help and Support to obtain information about software licensing and product activation, and answer the following questions.

   a. What is genuine Windows?

   b. What is activation?

   c. What steps are required to activate Windows?

   d. What steps are required to read the Microsoft Software License Terms?

   e. Can you legally make a second copy of Windows 7 for use at home, work, or on a mobile computer or device?

   f. What is registration?

6. Close the Windows Help and Support window.

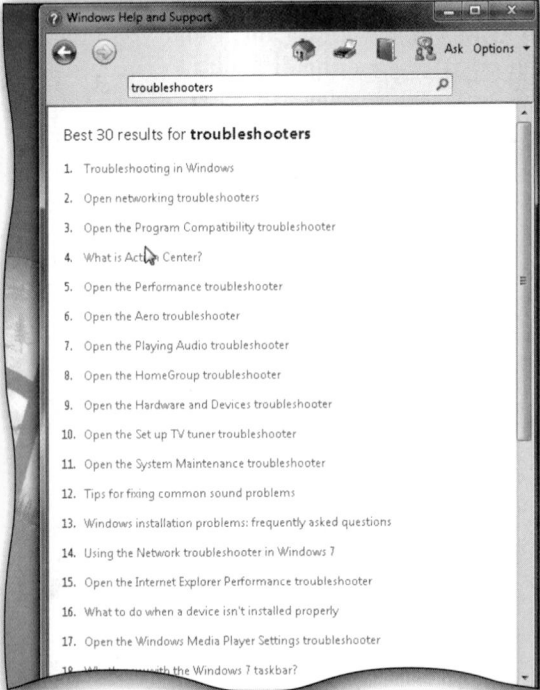

Figure 88

In the Lab

Lab 2: Creating Folders for a Pet Supply Store

Problem: Your friend works for Pete's Pet Supplies. He would like to organize his files in relation to the types of pets available in the store. He has five main categories: dogs, cats, fish, birds, and exotic. You are to create a folder structure similar to Figure 89.

Instructions: Perform the following tasks:

1. Connect a USB flash drive to an available USB port and then open the USB flash drive window.

2. Create the main folder for Pete's Pet Supplies.

3. Navigate to the Pete's Pet Supplies folder.

4. Within the Pete's Pet Supplies folder, create a folder for each of the following: Dogs, Cats, Fish, Birds, and Exotic.

5. Within the Exotic folder, create two additional folders, one for Primates and the second for Reptiles.

6. Submit the assignment in the format specified by your instructor.

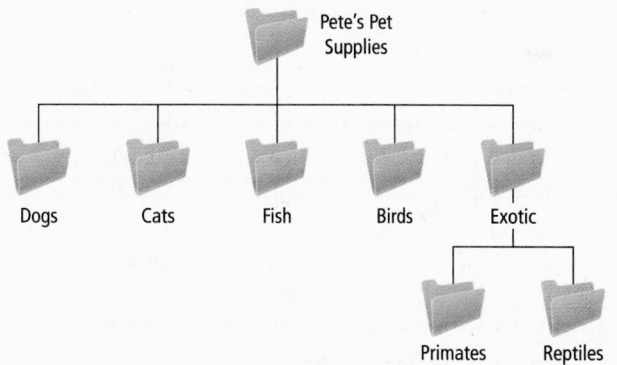

Figure 89

In the Lab

Lab 3: Creating Excel Workbooks and Saving Them in Appropriate Folders

Problem: You are taking a class that requires you to complete three Excel chapters. You will save the work completed in each chapter in a different folder (Figure 90).

Instructions: Create the folders shown in Figure 90. Then, using Excel, create three small files to save in each folder.

1. Connect a USB flash drive to an available USB port and then open the USB flash drive window.

2. Create the folder structure shown in Figure 90.

3. Navigate to the Chapter 1 folder.

4. Create an Excel Workbook containing the text, My Chapter 1 Excel Workbook, and then save it in the Chapter 1 folder using the file name, Excel Chapter 1 Workbook.

5. Navigate to the Chapter 2 folder.

6. Create another Excel workbook containing the text, My Chapter 2 Excel Workbook, and then save it in the Chapter 2 folder using the file name, Excel Chapter 2 Workbook.

7. Navigate to the Chapter 3 folder.

8. Create another Excel workbook containing the text, My Chapter 3 Excel Workbook, and then save it in the Chapter 3 folder using the file name, Excel Chapter 3 Workbook.

9. Quit Excel.

10. Submit the assignment in the format specified by your instructor.

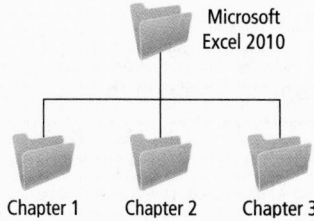

Figure 90

Cases and Places

Apply your creative thinking and problem solving skills to design and implement a solution.

Note: To complete these assignments, you may be required to use the Data Files for Students. See the inside back cover of this book for instructions on downloading the Data Files for Students, or contact your instructor for information about accessing the required files.

1: Creating Beginning Files for Classes

Academic

You are taking the following classes: Introduction to Engineering, Beginning Psychology, Introduction to Biology, and Accounting. Create folders for each of the classes. Use the following folder names: Engineering, Psychology, Biology, and Accounting, when creating the folder structure. In the Engineering folder, use Excel to create a workbook with the name of the class and the class meeting location and time (MW 10:30 – 11:45, Room 317). In the Psychology folder, use Excel to create a workbook containing the text, Behavioral Observations. In the Biology folder, use Excel to create a workbook with the title Research in the Biology folder. In the Accounting folder, create an Excel workbook with the text, Tax Information. Use the concepts and techniques presented in this chapter to create the folders and files.

2: Using Help

Personal

Your parents enjoy working and playing games on their home computers. Your mother uses a notebook computer downstairs, and your father uses a desktop computer upstairs. They expressed interest in sharing files between their computers and sharing a single printer, so you offered to research various home networking options. Start Windows Help and Support, and search Help using the keywords, home networking. Use the link for installing a printer on a home network. Start Excel and then type the main steps for installing a printer. Use the link for setting up a HomeGroup and then type the main steps for creating a HomeGroup in the Excel workbook. Use the concepts and techniques presented in this chapter to use Help and create the Excel workbook.

3: Creating Folders

Professional

Your boss at the bookstore where you work part-time has asked for help with organizing her files. After looking through the files, you decided upon a file structure for her to use, including the following folders: books, magazines, tapes, DVDs, and general merchandise. Within the books folder, create folders for hardback and paperback books. Within magazines, create folders for special issues and periodicals. In the tapes folder, create folders for celebrity and major release. In the DVDs folder, create a folder for book to DVD. In the general merchandise folder, create folders for novelties, posters, and games. Use the concepts and techniques presented in this chapter to create the folders.

1 | Creating a Worksheet and an Embedded Chart

Objectives

You will have mastered the material in this chapter when you can:

- Describe the Excel worksheet
- Enter text and numbers
- Use the Sum button to sum a range of cells
- Copy the contents of a cell to a range of cells using the fill handle
- Apply cell styles
- Format cells in a worksheet

- Create a Clustered Cylinder chart
- Change a worksheet name and worksheet tab color
- Change document properties
- Preview and print a worksheet
- Use the AutoCalculate area to display statistics
- Correct errors on a worksheet

1 | Creating a Worksheet and an Embedded Chart

Introduction

Almost any organization collects vast amounts of data. Often, data is consolidated into a summary so that people in the organization better understand the meaning of the data. An Excel worksheet allows data easily to be summarized and charted. A chart conveys a visual representation of data. In this chapter, you will create a worksheet that includes a chart. The data in the worksheet and chart includes data for donations made to a not-for-profit organization that operates in several cities.

Project Planning Guidelines

> The process of developing a worksheet that communicates specific information requires careful analysis and planning. As a starting point, establish why the worksheet is needed. Once the purpose is determined, analyze the intended users of the worksheet and their unique needs. Then, gather information about the topic and decide what to include in the worksheet. Finally, determine the worksheet design and style that will be most successful at delivering the message. Details of these guidelines are provided in Appendix A. In addition, each project developed in this book provides practical applications of these planning considerations.

Project — Worksheet with an Embedded Chart

The project in this chapter follows proper design guidelines and uses Excel to create the worksheet shown in Figure 1–1. The worksheet contains fundraising data for the Save Sable River Foundation. The Save Sable River Foundation raises funds to care for the environment and preserve the usability of a river that flows through six cities. The foundation raises funds by using five different fundraising activities. Through a concentrated marketing campaign and providing visible results to the communities, the Save Sable River Foundation quickly became a popular local institution. After several years of successful fundraising, senior management requested an easy-to-read worksheet that shows lifetime fundraising amounts for each fundraising technique by city. In addition, they asked for a chart showing lifetime fundraising amounts because the president of the foundation likes to have a graphical representation that allows him quickly to identify stronger and weaker fundraising activities by city.

Figure 1–1

The first step in creating an effective worksheet is to make sure you understand what is required. The person or persons requesting the worksheet should supply their requirements in a requirements document. A **requirements document** includes a needs statement, a source of data, a summary of calculations, and any other special requirements for the worksheet, such as charting and Web support. Figure 1–2 on the following page shows the requirements document for the new workbook to be created in this chapter.

BTW

Excel 2010 Features
With its what-if analysis tools, research capabilities, collaboration tools, streamlined user interface, smart tags, charting features, Web capabilities, hundreds of functions, and enhanced formatting capabilities, Excel 2010 is one of the easier and more powerful spreadsheet programs available. Its dynamic analytical features make it possible to answer complicated what-if questions and its Web capabilities allow you to create, publish, view, share, and analyze data on an intranet or the World Wide Web.

requirements document →

BTW

Worksheet Development Cycle
Spreadsheet specialists do not sit down and start entering text, formulas, and data into a blank Excel worksheet as soon as they have a spreadsheet assignment. Instead, they follow an organized plan, or methodology, that breaks the development cycle into a series of tasks. The recommended methodology for creating worksheets includes: (1) analyze requirements (supplied in a requirements document); (2) design solution; (3) validate design; (4) implement design; (5) test solution; and (6) document solution.

REQUEST FOR NEW WORKBOOK	
Date Submitted:	March 22, 2012
Submitted By:	Kevin Li
Worksheet Title:	Save Sable River Foundation Lifetime Fundraising Summary
Needs:	An easy-to-read worksheet that shows a summary of the Save Sable River Foundation's lifetime fundraising efforts for each city in which we operate (Allentown, Chamber City, Pattonsville, Sable Village, Strongville, and the Town of Cary). The worksheet also should include total funds raised for each city, total funds raised for each fundraising activity, and total lifetime funds raised.
Source of Data:	The data for the worksheet is available from the chief financial officer (CFO) of the Save Sable River Foundation.
Calculations:	The following calculations must be made for the worksheet: (a) total lifetime funds raised for each of the six cities; (b) total lifetime funds raised for each of the five fundraising activities; and (c) total lifetime funds raised for the organization.
Chart Requirements:	Below the data in the worksheet, construct a Clustered Cylinder chart that compares the total funds raised for each city within each type of fundraising activity.

Approvals

Approval Status:	X	Approved
		Rejected
Approved By:	Marsha Davis	
Date:	March 29, 2012	
Assigned To:	J. Quasney, Spreadsheet Specialist	

Figure 1–2

Overview

As you read this chapter, you will learn how to create the worksheet shown in Figure 1–1 on the previous page by performing these general tasks:

- Enter text in the worksheet
- Total data in the worksheet
- Format the text in the worksheet
- Insert a chart into the worksheet
- Identify the worksheet with a worksheet name
- Preview and print the worksheet

Plan Ahead

BTW

BTWs
For a complete list of the BTWs found in the margins of this book, visit the Excel 2010 BTW Web page (scsite.com/ex2010/btw).

General Project Guidelines
While creating an Excel worksheet, you need to make several decisions that will determine the appearance and characteristics of the finished worksheet. As you create the worksheet shown in Figure 1–1, you should follow these general guidelines:

1. **Select titles and subtitles for the worksheet.** Follow the *less is more* guideline. The less text in the titles and subtitles, the more impact the titles and subtitles will have. Use the fewest words possible to specify the information presented in the worksheet to the intended audience.

(continued)

(continued)

2. **Determine the contents for rows and columns.** Rows typically contain information that is analogous to items in a list, such as the fundraising techniques used by an organization. Columns typically contain descriptive information about items in rows or contain information that helps to group the data in the worksheet, such as the locations in which the organization operates. Row headings and column headings are usually placed in alphabetical sequence, unless an alternative order is recommended in the requirements document.

3. **Determine the calculations that are needed.** You can decide to total data in a variety of ways, such as across rows or in columns. You also can include a grand total.

4. **Determine where to save the workbook.** You can store a workbook permanently, or **save** it, on a variety of storage media including a hard disk, USB flash drive, CD, or DVD. You also can indicate a specific location on the storage media for saving the workbook.

5. **Identify how to format various elements of the worksheet.** The overall appearance of a worksheet significantly affects its ability to communicate clearly. Examples of how you can modify the appearance, or format, of text include changing its shape, size, color, and position on the worksheet.

6. **Decide on the type of chart needed.** Excel can create many different types of charts, such as cylinder charts and pie charts. Each type of chart relays a different message about the data in the worksheet. Choose a type of chart that relays the message that you want to convey.

7. **Establish where to position and how to format the chart.** The position and format of the chart should command the attention of the intended audience. If possible, position the chart so that it prints with the worksheet data on a single page.

8. **Choose a name for the worksheet.** Each worksheet in a workbook should be named to clarify its purpose. A good worksheet name is succinct, unique to the workbook, and meaningful to any user of the workbook.

9. **Determine the best method for distributing the workbook.** Workbooks and worksheets can be distributed on paper or electronically. The decision regarding how to distribute workbooks and worksheets greatly depends on your intended audience. For example, a worksheet may be printed for inclusion in a report, or a workbook may be distributed using e-mail if the recipient intends to update the workbook.

When necessary, more specific details concerning the above guidelines are presented at appropriate points in the chapter. The chapter also will identify the actions performed and decisions made regarding these guidelines during the creation of the worksheet shown in Figure 1–1 on page EX 3.

Plan Ahead

BTW

Worksheet Development
The key to developing a useful worksheet is careful planning. Careful planning can reduce your effort significantly and result in a worksheet that is accurate, easy to read, flexible, and useful. When analyzing a problem and designing a worksheet solution, you should follow these steps: (1) define the problem, including need, source of data, calculations, charting, and Web or special requirements; (2) design the worksheet; (3) enter the data and formulas; and (4) test the worksheet.

After carefully reviewing the requirements document (Figure 1–2) and making the necessary decisions, the next step is to design a solution or draw a sketch of the worksheet based on the requirements, including titles, column and row headings, the location of data values, and the Clustered Cylinder chart, as shown in Figure 1–3 on the following page. The dollar signs, 9s, and commas that you see in the sketch of the worksheet indicate formatted numeric values.

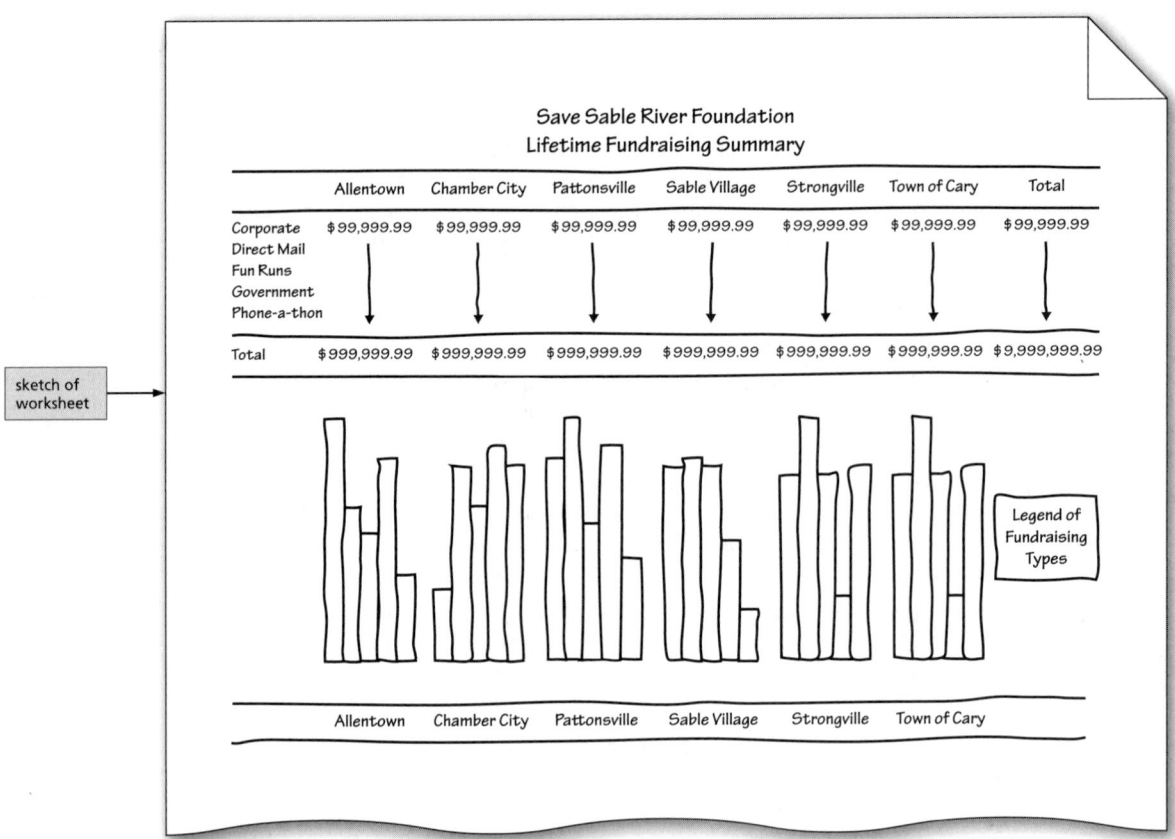

sketch of worksheet

Figure 1–3

BTW

The Ribbon and Screen Resolution
Excel may change how the groups and buttons within the groups appear on the Ribbon, depending on the computer's screen resolution. Thus, your Ribbon may look different from the ones in this book if you are using a screen resolution other than 1024 × 768.

With a good understanding of the requirements document, an understanding of the necessary decisions, and a sketch of the worksheet, the next step is to use Excel to create the worksheet and chart.

To Start Excel

If you are using a computer to step through the project in this chapter and you want your screens to match the figures in this book, you should change your screen's resolution to 1024 × 768. For information about how to change a computer's resolution, refer to the Office 2010 and Windows 7 chapter at the beginning of this book.

The following steps, which assume Windows 7 is running, start Excel based on a typical installation. You may need to ask your instructor how to start Excel for your computer. For a detailed example of the procedure summarized below, refer to the Office 2010 and Windows 7 chapter.

1 Click the Start button on the Windows 7 taskbar to display the Start menu.

2 Type `Microsoft Excel` as the search text in the 'Search programs and files' text box and watch the search results appear on the Start menu.

3 Click Microsoft Excel 2010 in the search results on the Start menu to start Excel and display a new blank workbook in the Excel window.

4 If the Excel window is not maximized, click the Maximize button next to the Close button on its title bar to maximize the window.

Selecting a Cell

To enter data into a cell, you first must select it. The easiest way **to select a cell** (make it active) is to use the mouse to move the block plus sign mouse pointer to the cell and then click.

An alternative method is to use the arrow keys that are located just to the right of the alphanumeric keys on a standard keyboard. An arrow key selects the cell adjacent to the active cell in the direction of the arrow on the key.

You know a cell is selected, or active, when a heavy border surrounds the cell and the active cell reference appears in the Name box on the left side of the formula bar. Excel also changes the active cell's column heading and row heading to a gold color.

Entering Text

In Excel, any set of characters containing a letter, hyphen (as in a telephone number), or space is considered text. **Text** is used to place titles, such as worksheet titles, column titles, and row titles, on the worksheet.

Select titles and subtitles for the worksheet.
Worksheet titles and subtitles should be as brief and meaningful as possible. A worksheet title could include the name of the organization, department, or a description of the content of the worksheet. A worksheet subtitle, if included, could include a more detailed description of the content of the worksheet. Examples of worksheet titles are December 2010 Payroll and Year 2011 Projected Budget, and examples of subtitles are Marketing Department and Rent and Utilities, respectively.

Plan Ahead

Determine the contents of rows and columns.
As shown in Figure 1–4, data in a worksheet often is identified by row and column titles so that the user of a worksheet easily can identify the meaning of the data. Rows typically contain information that is similar to items in a list. Columns typically contain descriptive information about items in rows or contain information that helps to group the data in the worksheet. Examples of row titles are Product and Total, and examples of column titles are Name and Address.

Plan Ahead

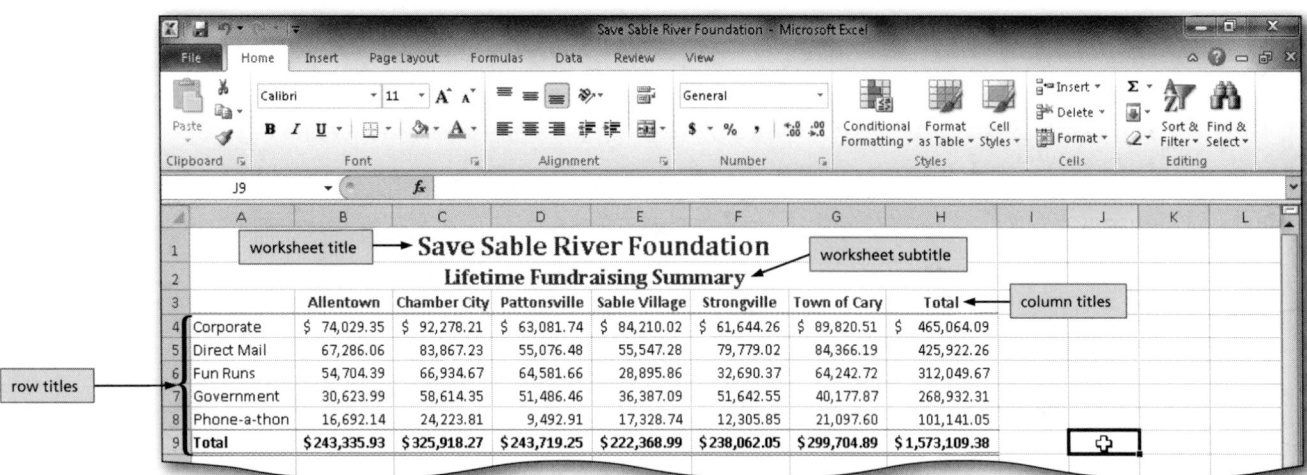

Figure 1–4

To Enter the Worksheet Titles

As shown in Figure 1–4 on the previous page, the worksheet title, Save Sable River Foundation, identifies the organization for which the worksheet is being created in Chapter 1. The worksheet subtitle, Lifetime Fundraising Summary, identifies the type of report.

The following steps enter the worksheet titles in cells A1 and A2. Later in this chapter, the worksheet titles will be formatted so they appear as shown in Figure 1–4.

1

• If necessary, click cell A1 to make cell A1 the active cell (Figure 1–5).

Q&A

What if I make a mistake while typing?

If you type the wrong letter and notice the error before clicking the Enter box or pressing the ENTER key, use the BACKSPACE key to delete all the characters back to and including the incorrect letter. To cancel the entire entry before entering it into the

Figure 1–5

cell, click the Cancel box in the formula bar or press the ESC key. If you see an error in a cell after entering the text, select the cell and retype the entry.

2

• Type **Save Sable River Foundation** in cell A1 and then point to the Enter box in the formula bar to prepare to enter text in the active cell (Figure 1–6).

Q&A

Why did the appearance of the formula bar change?

Excel displays the title in the formula bar and in cell A1. When you begin typing a cell entry, Excel displays two additional boxes in the formula bar:

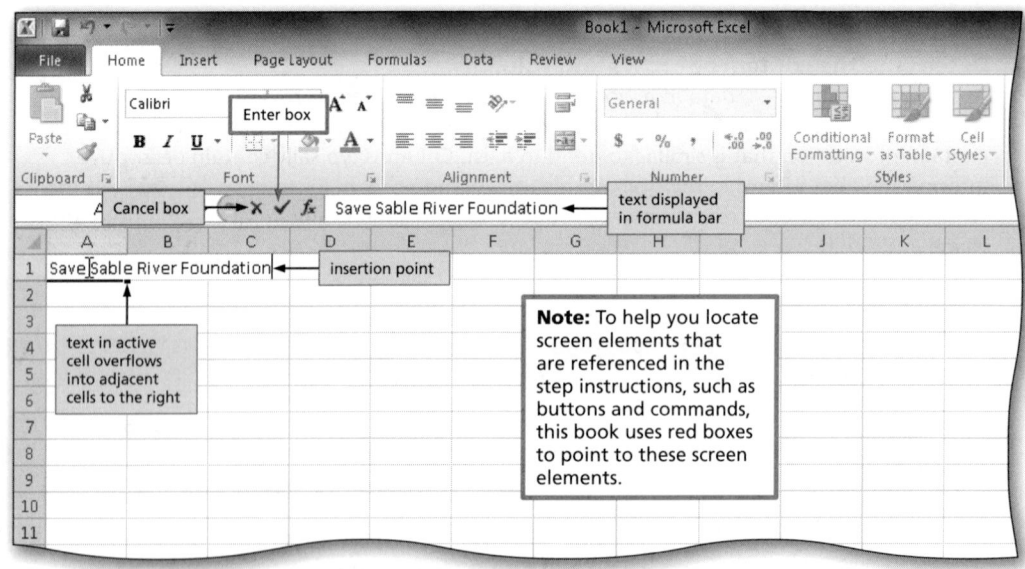

Figure 1–6

the Cancel box and the Enter box. Clicking the **Enter box** completes an entry. Clicking the **Cancel box** cancels an entry.

Q&A

What is the vertical line in cell A1?

The text in cell A1 is followed by the insertion point. The **insertion point** is a blinking vertical line that indicates where the next typed character will appear.

3

● Click the Enter box to complete the entry and enter a worksheet title (Figure 1–7).

Why does the entered text appear in three cells?

When the text is longer than the width of a column, Excel displays the overflow characters in adjacent cells to the right as long as those adjacent cells contain no data. If the adjacent cells contain data, Excel would hide the overflow characters. Excel displays the overflow characters in the formula bar whenever that cell is the active cell.

Figure 1–7

4

● Click cell A2 to select it.

● Type **Lifetime Fundraising Summary** as the cell entry.

● Click the Enter box to complete the entry and enter a worksheet subtitle (Figure 1–8).

What happens when I click the Enter box?

When you complete an entry by clicking the Enter box, the insertion point disappears and the cell in which the text is entered remains the active cell.

Figure 1–8

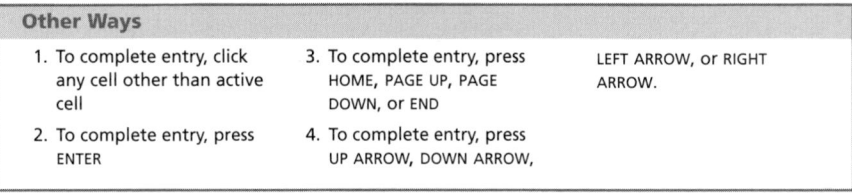

Other Ways
1. To complete entry, click any cell other than active cell   2. To complete entry, press ENTER   3. To complete entry, press HOME, PAGE UP, PAGE DOWN, or END   4. To complete entry, press UP ARROW, DOWN ARROW, LEFT ARROW, or RIGHT ARROW.

AutoCorrect

The **AutoCorrect feature** of Excel works behind the scenes, correcting common mistakes when you complete a text entry in a cell. AutoCorrect makes three types of corrections for you:

1. Corrects two initial capital letters by changing the second letter to lowercase.

2. Capitalizes the first letter in the names of days.

3. Replaces commonly misspelled words with their correct spelling. For example, it will change the misspelled word *recieve* to *receive* when you complete the entry. AutoCorrect will correct the spelling of hundreds of commonly misspelled words automatically.

To Enter Column Titles

The column titles in row 3 (Allentown, Chamber City, Pattonsville, Sable Village, Strongville, Town of Cary, and Total) identify the numbers in each column. In the case of the Save the Sable River Foundation data, the cities identify the funds raised using each fundraising type. The cities, therefore, are placed in columns. To enter the column titles in row 3, select the appropriate cell and then enter the text. The following steps enter the column titles in row 3.

1
- Click cell B3 to make it the active cell (Figure 1–9).

Figure 1–9

2
- Type **Allentown** to begin entry of a column title in the active cell (Figure 1–10).

Figure 1–10

3

- Press the RIGHT ARROW key to enter a column title and make the cell to the right the active cell (Figure 1–11).

Why is the RIGHT ARROW key used to complete the entry in the cell?

If the next entry you want to enter is in an adjacent cell, use the arrow keys to complete the entry in a cell. When you press an arrow key to complete an entry, the adjacent cell in the direction of the arrow (up, down, left, or right) becomes the active cell. If the next entry is in a nonadjacent cell, complete the current entry by clicking the next cell in which you plan to enter data. You also can click the Enter box or press the ENTER key and then click the appropriate cell for the next entry.

Figure 1–11

4

- Repeat Steps 2 and 3 to enter the remaining column titles; that is, enter **Chamber City** in cell C3, **Pattonsville** in cell D3, **Sable Village** in cell E3, **Strongville** in cell F3, **Town of Cary** in cell G3, and **Total** in cell H3 (complete the last entry in cell H3 by clicking the Enter box in the formula bar) (Figure 1–12).

Figure 1–12

To Enter Row Titles

The next step in developing the worksheet for this project is to enter the row titles in column A. For the Save Sable River Foundation data, the list of fundraising activities meets the criterion that information that identifies columns be in a list. It is more likely that in the future, the organization will add more fundraising activities as opposed to more cities. Each fundraising activity, therefore, should be placed in its own row. The row titles in column A (Corporate, Direct Mail, Fun Runs, Government, Phone-a-thon, and Total) identify the numbers in each row.

This process for entering row titles is similar to the process for entering column titles. The following steps enter the row titles in the worksheet.

1
- Click cell A4 to select it.

- Type **Corporate** and then press the DOWN ARROW key to enter a row title and to make the cell below the current cell the active cell (Figure 1–13).

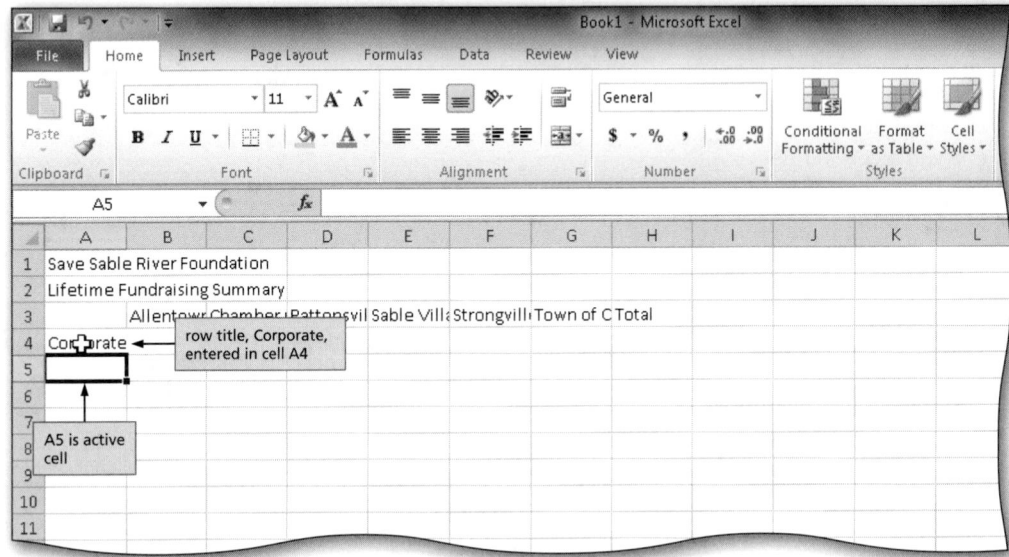

Figure 1–13

2
- Repeat Step 1 to enter the remaining row titles in column A; that is, enter **Direct Mail** in cell A5, **Fun Runs** in cell A6, **Government** in cell A7, **Phone-a-thon** in cell A8, and **Total** in cell A9 (Figure 1–14).

Q&A

Why is the text left-aligned in the cells?

When you enter text, Excel automatically left-aligns the text in the cell. Excel treats any combination of numbers, spaces, and nonnumeric characters as text. For example, Excel recognizes the following entries as text:

401AX21, 921–231, 619 321, 883XTY

You can change the text alignment in a cell by realigning it. Other alignment techniques are discussed later in this chapter.

Figure 1–14

Entering Numbers

In Excel, you can enter numbers into cells to represent amounts. A **number** can contain only the following characters:

0 1 2 3 4 5 6 7 8 9 + - ( ) , / . $ % E e

If a cell entry contains any other keyboard character (including spaces), Excel interprets the entry as text and treats it accordingly. The use of the special characters is explained when they are used in this book.

BTW

Numeric Limitations
In Excel, a number can be between approximately -1×10308 and 1×10308. This means it can be between a negative 1 followed by 308 zeros and a positive 1 followed by 308 zeros. To enter a number such as 6,000,000,000,000,000, you can type 6,000,000,000,000,000, or you can type 6E15, which translates to 6×1015.

To Enter Numbers

The Save Sable River Foundation Lifetime Fundraising Summary numbers used in Chapter 1 are summarized in Table 1–1. These numbers, which represent lifetime fundraising amounts for each of the fundraising activities and cities, must be entered in rows 4, 5, 6, 7, and 8.

Table 1–1 Save Sable River Foundation Lifetime Fundraising Summary						
	Allentown	**Chamber City**	**Pattonsville**	**Sable Village**	**Strongville**	**Town of Cary**
Corporate	74029.35	92278.21	63081.74	84210.02	61644.26	89820.51
Direct Mail	67286.06	83867.23	55076.48	55547.28	79779.02	84366.19
Fun Runs	54704.39	66934.67	64581.66	28895.86	32690.37	64242.72
Government	30623.99	58614.35	51486.46	36387.09	51642.55	40177.87
Phone-a-thon	16692.14	24223.81	9492.91	17328.74	12305.85	21097.60

The following steps enter the numbers in Table 1–1 one row at a time.

1

- Click cell B4 to select it.

- Type **74029.35** and then press the RIGHT ARROW key to enter the data in the selected cell and make the cell to the right the active cell (Figure 1–15).

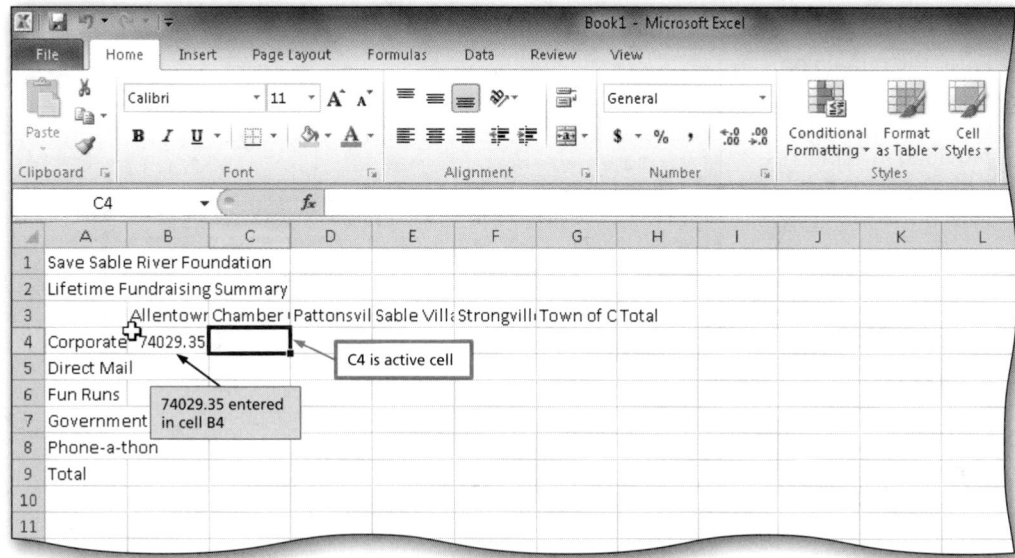

Figure 1–15

Q&A

Do I need to enter dollar signs, commas, or trailing zeros for the fundraising summary amounts?

You are not required to type dollar signs, commas, or trailing zeros. When you enter a dollar value that has cents, however, you must add the decimal point and the numbers representing the cents. Later in this chapter, the numbers will be formatted to use dollar signs, commas, and trailing zeros to improve the appearance and readability of the numbers.

2

• Enter `92278.21` in cell C4, `63081.74` in cell D4, `84210.02` in cell E4, `61644.26` in cell F4, and `89820.51` in cell G4 to complete the first row of numbers in the worksheet (Figure 1–16).

Q&A

Why are the numbers right-aligned?

When you enter numeric data in a cell, Excel recognizes the values as numbers and right-aligns the values in order to properly vertically align decimal and integer values. For example, values entered below those entered in this step automatically will be right-aligned as well so that the decimals of the values properly align.

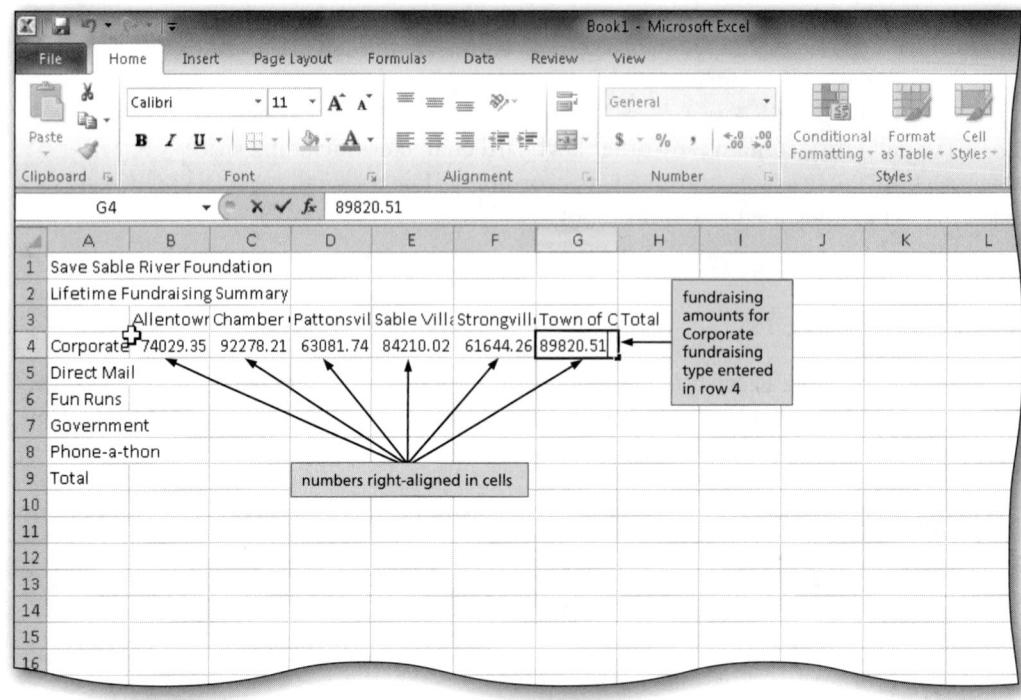

Figure 1–16

3

• Click cell B5 to select it and complete the entry in the previously selected cell.

• Enter the remaining lifetime fundraising summary numbers provided in Table 1–1 on page EX 13 for each of the four remaining fundraising activities in rows 5, 6, 7, and 8 to finish entering numbers in the worksheet (Figure 1–17).

Q&A

Why did clicking cell B5 complete the entry in cell G4?

Selecting another cell completes the entry in the previously selected cell in the same way as pressing the ENTER key, pressing an arrow key, or clicking the Enter box on the formula bar. In the next set of steps, the entry of the number in cell G4 will be completed by selecting another cell.

Figure 1–17

Calculating a Sum

The next step in creating the worksheet is to perform any necessary calculations, such as calculating the column and row totals.

To Sum a Column of Numbers

As stated in the requirements document in Figure 1–2 on page EX 4, totals are required for each city, each fundraising activity, and the organization. The first calculation is to determine the fundraising total for the fundraising activities in the city of Allentown in column B. To calculate this value in cell B9, Excel must add, or sum, the numbers in cells B4, B5, B6, B7, and B8. Excel's **SUM function**, which adds all of the numbers in a range of cells, provides a convenient means to accomplish this task.

A **range** is a series of two or more adjacent cells in a column or row or a rectangular group of cells. For example, the group of adjacent cells B4, B5, B6, B7, and B8 is called a range. Many Excel operations, such as summing numbers, take place on a range of cells.

After the total lifetime fundraising amount for the fundraising activities in the city of Allentown in column B is determined, the totals for the remaining cities and totals for each fundraising activity will be determined. The following steps sum the numbers in column B.

1
- Click cell B9 to make it the active cell and complete the entry in the previously selected cell.

- Click the Sum button (Home tab | Editing group) to display a formula in the formula bar and in the active cell (Figure 1–18).

Figure 1–18

Q&A
How does Excel know which cells to sum?

When you enter the SUM function using the Sum button, Excel automatically selects what it considers to be your choice of the range to sum. When proposing the range to sum, Excel first looks for a range of cells with numbers above the active cell and then to the left. If Excel proposes the wrong range, you can correct it by dragging through the correct range before pressing the ENTER key. You also can enter the correct range by typing the beginning cell reference, a colon (:), and the ending cell reference.

BTW
Calculating Sums
Excel calculates sums for a variety of data types. For example, Boolean values, such as TRUE and FALSE, can be summed. Excel treats the value of TRUE as 1 and the value of FALSE as 0. Times also can be summed. For example, Excel treats the sum of 1:15 and 2:45 as 4:00.

2

- Click the Enter box in the formula bar to enter a sum in the active cell (Figure 1–19).

Q&A

What is the purpose of the Sum button arrow?

If you click the Sum button arrow on the right side of the Sum button (Home tab | Editing group) (Figure 1–19), Excel displays a list of often used functions from which you can choose. The list includes functions that allow you to determine the average, the number of items in the selected range, the maximum value, or the minimum value of a range of numbers.

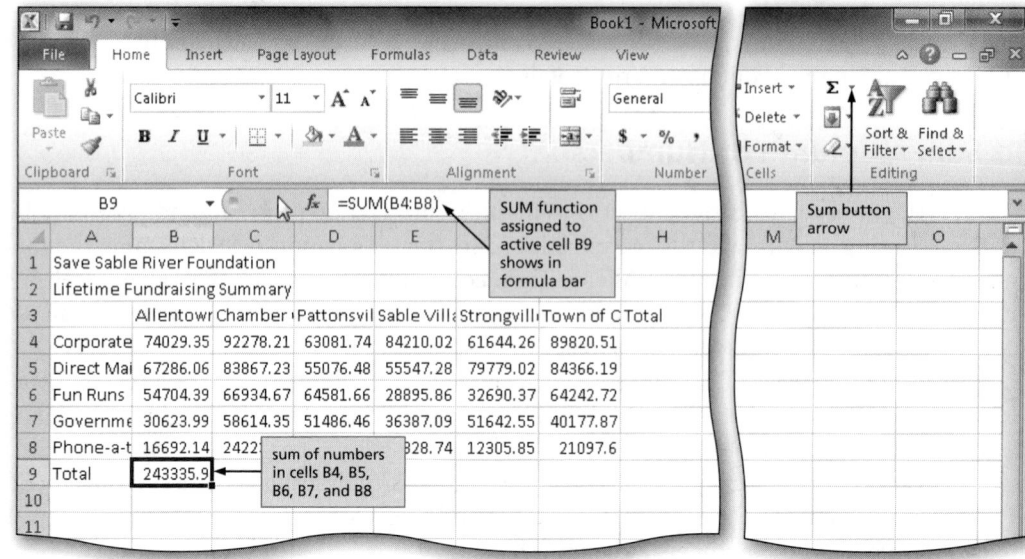

Figure 1–19

Other Ways

1. Click Insert Function button in the formula bar, select SUM in Select a function list, click OK button, select range, click OK button

2. Click Sum button arrow (Home tab | Editing group), click More Functions, select SUM (Insert Function dialog box), click OK button, select range, click OK button

3. Type = s in cell, select SUM from list, select range

4. Press ALT + EQUAL SIGN (=) twice

Using the Fill Handle to Copy a Cell to Adjacent Cells

Excel also must calculate the totals for Chamber City in cell C9, Pattonsville in cell D9, Sable Village in cell E9, Strongville in cell F9, and the Town of Cary in cell G9. Table 1–2 illustrates the similarities between the entry in cell B9 and the entries required to sum the totals in cells C9, D9, E9, F9 and G9.

Table 1–2 Sum Function Entries in Row 9		
Cell	**Sum Function Entries**	**Remark**
B9	=SUM(B4:B8)	Sums cells B4, B5, B6, B7, and B8
C9	=SUM(C4:C8)	Sums cells C4, C5, C6, C7, and C8
D9	=SUM(D4:D8)	Sums cells D4, D5, D6, D7, and D8
E9	=SUM(E4:E8)	Sums cells E4, E5, E6, E7, and E8
F9	=SUM(F4:F8)	Sums cells F4, F5, F6, F7, and F8
G9	=SUM(G4:G8)	Sums cells G4, G5, G6, G7, and G8

To place the SUM functions in cells C9, D9, E9, F9, and G9, you could follow the same steps shown previously in Figures 1–18 on page EX 15 and 1–19. A second, more efficient method, however, is to copy the SUM function from cell B9 to the range C9:G9. The cell being copied is called the **source area** or **copy area**. The range of cells receiving the copy is called the **destination area** or **paste area**.

Although the SUM function entries in Table 1–2 are similar, they are not exact copies. The range in each SUM function entry uses cell references that are one column to the right of the previous column. When you copy formulas that include cell references, Excel automatically adjusts them for each new position, resulting in the SUM function entries illustrated in Table 1–2. Each adjusted cell reference is called a **relative reference**.

To Copy a Cell to Adjacent Cells in a Row

The easiest way to copy the SUM formula from cell B9 to cells C9, D9, E9, F9, and G9 is to use the fill handle. The **fill handle** is the small black square located in the lower-right corner of the heavy border around the active cell. The following steps use the fill handle to copy cell B9 to the adjacent cells C9:G9.

1
- With cell B9 active, point to the fill handle to activate it (Figure 1–20).

Figure 1–20

2
- Drag the fill handle to select the destination area, range C9:G9, to display a shaded border around the source area and the destination area (Figure 1–21). Do not release the mouse button.

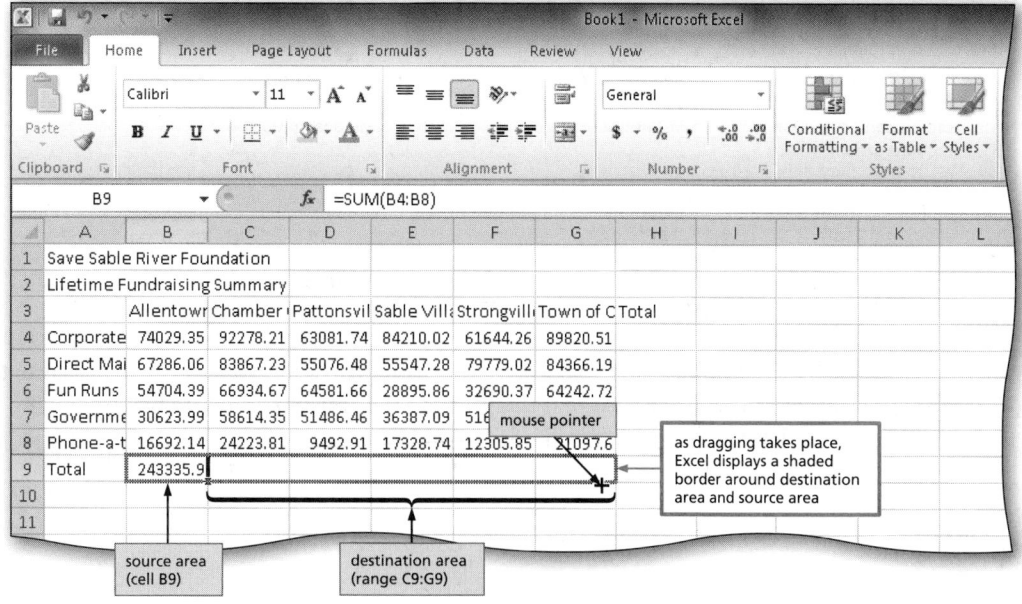

Figure 1–21

3

● Release the mouse button to copy the SUM function from the active cell to the destination area and calculate the sums (Figure 1–22).

Figure 1–22

Q&A

What is the purpose of the Auto Fill Options button?

When you copy one range to another, Excel displays an Auto Fill Options button (Figure 1–22). The Auto Fill Options button allows you to choose whether you want to copy the values from the source area to the destination area with formatting, do so without formatting, or copy only the format. To view the available fill options, click the Auto Fill Options button. The Auto Fill Options button disappears when you begin another activity in Excel, such as typing data in another cell or applying formatting to a cell or range of cells.

Other Ways

1. Select source area, click Copy button (Home tab | Clipboard group), select destination area, click Paste button (Home tab | Clipboard group)

2. Right-click source area, click Copy on shortcut menu, right-click destination area, click Paste on shortcut menu

3. Select source area and then point to border of range; while holding down CTRL, drag source area to destination area

To Determine Multiple Totals at the Same Time

The next step in building the worksheet is to determine the lifetime fundraising totals for each fundraising activity and total lifetime fundraising for the organization in column H. To calculate these totals, you can use the SUM function much as it was used to total the lifetime fundraising amounts by city in row 9. In this example, however, Excel will determine totals for all of the rows at the same time. The following steps sum multiple totals at once.

1

- Click cell H4 to make it the active cell (Figure 1–23).

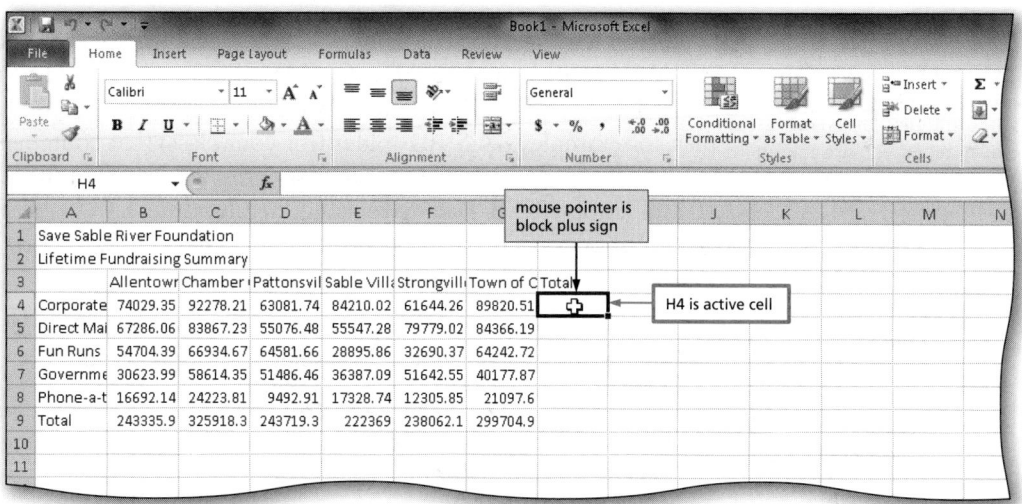

Figure 1–23

2

- With the mouse pointer in cell H4 and in the shape of a block plus sign, drag the mouse pointer down to cell H9 to highlight the range with a transparent view (Figure 1–24).

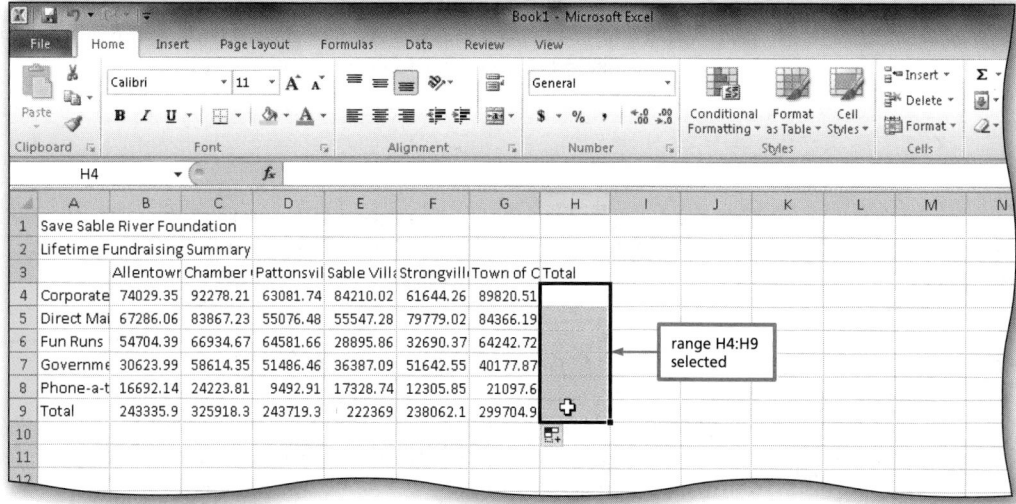

Figure 1–24

3

- Click the Sum button (Home tab | Editing group) to calculate and display the sums of the corresponding rows (Figure 1–25).

- Select cell A10 to deselect the selected range.

Q&A How does Excel create unique totals for each row?

If each cell in a selected range is next to a row of numbers, Excel assigns the SUM function to each cell when you click the Sum button.

Figure 1–25

BTW

Organizing Files and Folders
You should organize and store files in folders so that you easily can find the files later. For example, if you are taking an introductory computer class called CIS 101, a good practice would be to save all Excel files in an Excel folder in a CIS 101 folder. For a discussion of folders and detailed examples of creating folders, refer to the Office 2010 and Windows 7 chapter at the beginning of this book.

To Save a Workbook

You have performed many tasks while creating this workbook and do not want to risk losing work completed thus far. Accordingly, you should save the workbook.

The following steps assume you already have created folders for storing your files, for example, a CIS 101 folder (for your class) that contains an Excel folder (for your assignments). Thus, these steps save the workbook in the Excel folder in the CIS 101 folder on a USB flash drive using the file name, Save Sable River Foundation. For a detailed example of the procedure summarized below, refer to the Office 2010 and Windows 7 chapter at the beginning of this book.

1 With a USB flash drive connected to one of the computer's USB ports, click the Save button on the Quick Access Toolbar to display the Save As dialog box.

2 Type `Save Sable River Foundation` in the File name text box to change the file name. Do not press the ENTER key after typing the file name because you do not want to close the dialog box at this time.

3 Navigate to the desired save location (in this case, the Excel folder in the CIS 101 folder [or your class folder] on the USB flash drive).

4 Click the Save button (Save As dialog box) to save the document in the selected folder on the selected drive with the entered file name.

Break Point: If you wish to take a break, this is a good place to do so. You can quit Excel. To resume at a later time, start Excel, open the file called Save Sable River Foundation, and continue following the steps from this location forward.

BTW

AutoRecover
The AutoRecover feature of Excel, sometimes called AutoSave, allows you to specify how often and where Excel automatically saves workbooks. If your computer loses power, becomes unusable while you are interacting with a workbook, or you forget to save a workbook before closing it, Excel notifies you if there are workbooks that were automatically saved when one of these events occurred. You view and change AutoRecover options by clicking the Options button in the Backstage view and then clicking Save in the left panel of the Excel Options dialog box.

Formatting the Worksheet

The text, numeric entries, and functions for the worksheet now are complete. The next step is to format the worksheet. You **format** a worksheet to emphasize certain entries and make the worksheet easier to read and understand.

Figure 1–26a shows the worksheet before formatting. Figure 1–26b shows the worksheet after formatting. As you can see from the two figures, a worksheet that is formatted not only is easier to read but also looks more professional.

Plan Ahead

Identify how to format various elements of the worksheet.
By formatting the contents of the worksheet, you can improve its overall appearance. When formatting a worksheet, consider the following formatting suggestions:

- **Increase the font size of cells.** An increased font size gives more impact to the text in a cell. In order to indicate their relative importance, worksheet titles should have the largest font size, followed by worksheet subtitles, and then column and row headings.

- **Change the font color of cells.** Different cell colors help the reader of a worksheet quickly differentiate between the sections of a worksheet. Worksheet titles and subtitles easily should be identifiable from column and row headings. The overuse of too many colors, however, may be distracting to the reader of a worksheet.

- **Center the worksheet titles, subtitles, and column headings.** Centering text in worksheet titles and subtitles over the portion of the worksheet that they represent helps the reader of a worksheet quickly to identify the information that is of interest to them.

(continued)

(continued)

Plan
Ahead

- **Modify column widths to best fit text in cells.** Make certain that text in a cell does not overflow into another cell. A column's width should be adjusted to accommodate the largest amount of text used in a cell in the column. Columns that contain data that is similar in nature to other columns should share the same column width.

- **Change the font style of cells.** Use a bold font style to make worksheet titles, worksheet subtitles, column headings, row headings, and totals stand out. Use italics and underline font styles judiciously, as specific rules of grammar apply to their use.

Figure 1–26 (a) Before Formatting

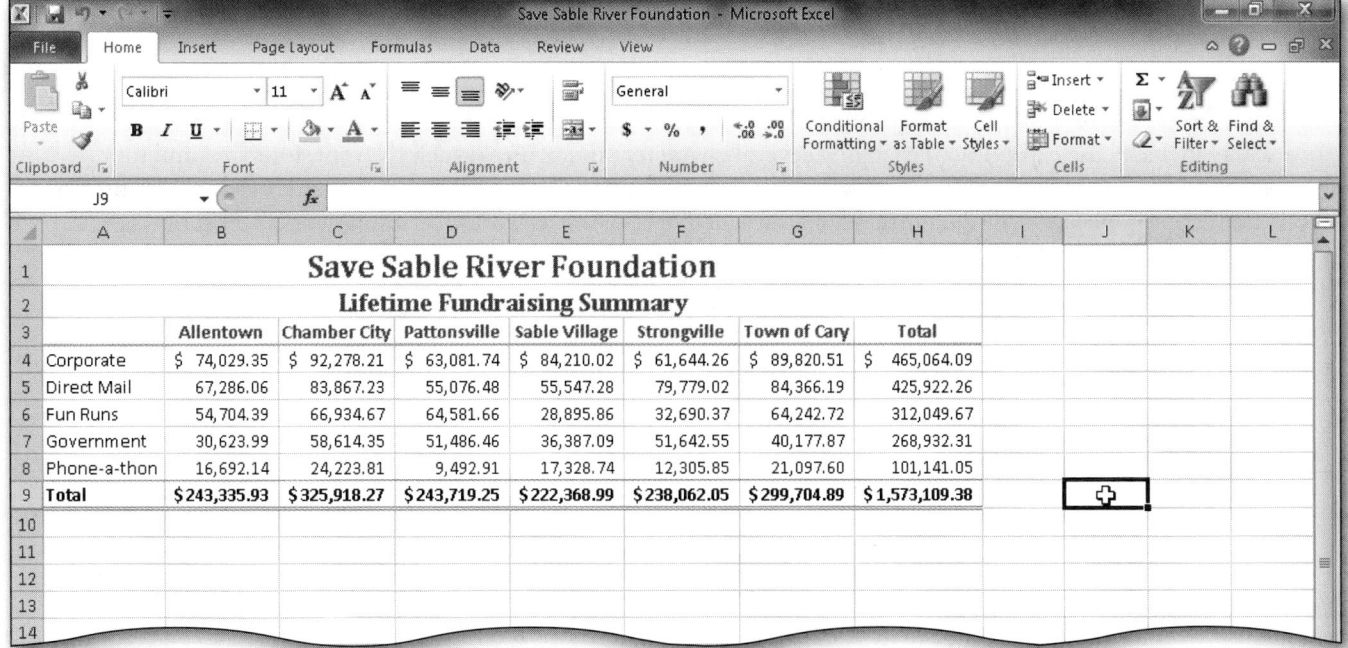

Figure 1–26 (b) After Formatting

To change the unformatted worksheet in Figure 1–26a on the previous page to the formatted worksheet in Figure 1–26b on the previous page, the following tasks must be completed:

1. Change the font, change the font style to bold, increase the font size, and change the font color of the worksheet titles in cells A1 and A2.

2. Center the worksheet titles in cells A1 and A2 across columns A through H.

3. Format the body of the worksheet. The body of the worksheet, range A3:H9, includes the column titles, row titles, and numbers. Formatting the body of the worksheet changes the numbers to use a dollars-and-cents format, with dollar signs in the first row (row 4) and the total row (row 9); adds underlining that emphasizes portions of the worksheet; and modifies the column widths to fit the text in the columns and make the text and numbers readable.

The remainder of this section explains the process required to format the worksheet. Although the formatting procedures are explained in the order described above, you should be aware that you could make these format changes in any order. Modifying the column widths, however, usually is done last because other formatting changes may affect the size of data in the cells in the column.

BTW

Fonts
In general, use no more than two font types in a worksheet because the use of more fonts can make a worksheet difficult to read.

BTW

Fonts and Themes
Excel uses default recommended fonts based on the workbook's theme. A theme is a collection of fonts and color schemes. The default theme is named Office, and the two default fonts for the Office theme are Calibri and Cambria. Excel, however, allows you to apply any font to a cell or range as long as the font is installed on your computer.

Font, Style, Size, and Color

The characters that Excel displays on the screen are a specific font, style, size, and color. The **font**, or font face, defines the appearance and shape of the letters, numbers, and special characters. Examples of fonts include Calibri, Cambria, Times New Roman, Arial, and Courier. **Font style** indicates how the characters are emphasized. Common font styles include regular, bold, underline, and italic. The **font size** specifies the size of the characters on the screen. Font size is gauged by a measurement system called points. A single point is about 1/72 of one inch in height. Thus, a character with a **point size** of 10 is about 10/72 of one inch in height. The **font color** defines the color of the characters. Excel can display characters in a wide variety of colors, including black, red, orange, and blue.

When Excel begins, the preset font for the entire workbook is Calibri, with a font size, font style, and font color of 11–point regular black. Excel allows you to change the font characteristics in a single cell, a range of cells, the entire worksheet, or the entire workbook.

To Change a Cell Style

Excel includes the capability of changing several characteristics of a cell, such the font, font size, and font color, all at once by assigning a predefined cell style to a cell. Using the predefined styles that Excel includes provides a consistent appearance to common portions of your worksheets, such as worksheet titles, worksheet subtitles, column headings, and total rows. The following steps assign the Title cell style to the worksheet title in cell A1.

1

- Click cell A1 to make cell A1 the active cell.

- Click the Cell Styles button (Home tab | Styles group) to display the Cell Styles gallery (Figure 1–27).

Figure 1–27

2

- Point to the Title cell style in the Titles and Headings area of the Cell Styles gallery to see a live preview of the cell style in the active cell (Figure 1–28).

🔎 **Experiment**

- Point to several other cell styles in the Cell Styles gallery to see a live preview of other cell styles in cell A1.

Figure 1–28

3

- Click the Title cell style to apply the cell style to the active cell (Figure 1–29).

Q&A

Why do several items in the Font group on the Ribbon change?

The changes to the Font box, Bold button, and Font Size box indicate the font changes applied to the active cell, cell A1, as a result of applying the Title cell style.

Figure 1–29

To Change the Font

Different fonts often are used in a worksheet to make it more appealing to the reader and to relate or distinguish data in the worksheet. The following steps change the worksheet subtitle's fonts from Calibri to Cambria.

1

• Click cell A2 to make it the active cell.

• Click the Font box arrow (Home tab | Font group) to display the Font gallery (Figure 1–30).

Q&A

Which fonts are displayed in the Font gallery?

Because many programs supply additional fonts beyond what comes with the Windows 7 operating system, the number of fonts available on your computer will depend on the programs installed. This book uses only fonts that come with the Windows 7 operating system and Microsoft Office 2010.

Figure 1–30

2

• Point to Cambria in the Theme Fonts area of the Font gallery to see a live preview of the selected font in the active cell (Figure 1–31).

🔍 **Experiment**

• Point to several other fonts in the Font gallery to see a live preview of other fonts in the selected cell.

Q&A

What is the Theme Fonts area?

Excel applies the same default theme to any new workbook that you start. A **theme** is a collection of cell styles and other styles that have common characteristics, such as a color scheme and font. The default theme for an Excel workbook is the Office theme. The Theme Fonts area of the Font gallery includes the fonts included in the default Office theme. Cambria is recommended for headings and Calibri is recommended by Microsoft for cells in the body of the worksheet (Figure 1–31).

Figure 1–31

3
- Click Cambria in the Theme Fonts area to change the font of the worksheet subtitle to Cambria (Figure 1–32).

Figure 1–32

To Bold a Cell

You **bold** an entry in a cell to emphasize it or make it stand out from the rest of the worksheet. The following step bolds the worksheet subtitle in cell A2.

1
- With cell A2 active, click the Bold button (Home tab | Font group) to change the font style of the active cell to bold (Figure 1–33).

Q&A
What if a cell already includes a bold style?

If the active cell is already bold, then Excel displays the Bold button with a transparent orange background.

Q&A
How do I remove the bold style from a cell?

Clicking the Bold button (Home tab | Font group) a second time removes the bold font style.

Figure 1–33

To Increase the Font Size of a Cell Entry

Increasing the font size is the next step in formatting the worksheet subtitle. You increase the font size of a cell so that the entry stands out and is easier to read. The following steps increase the font size of the worksheet subtitle in cell A2.

- With cell A2 selected, click the Font Size box arrow (Home tab | Font group) to display the Font Size list.

- Point to 14 in the Font Size list to see a live preview of the active cell with the selected font size (Figure 1–34).

Experiment

- Point to several other font sizes in the Font Size list to see a live preview of other font sizes in the selected cell.

Figure 1–34

- Click 14 in the Font Size list to change the font size in the active cell (Figure 1–35).

Q&A

Can I assign a font size that is not in the Font Size list?

Yes. An alternative to clicking a font size in the Font Size list is to click the Font Size box (Home tab | Font group), type the font size, and then press the ENTER key. This procedure allows you to assign a font size not available in the Font Size list to a selected cell entry.

Figure 1–35

Other Ways

1. Click Increase Font Size button (Home tab | Font group) or Decrease Font Size button (Home tab | Font group)

2. Click Font Size box arrow on Mini toolbar, click desired font size in Font Size gallery

3. Right-click cell, click Format Cells on shortcut menu, click Font tab (Format Cells dialog box), select font size in Size box, click OK button

To Change the Font Color of a Cell Entry

The next step is to change the color of the font in cell A2 from black to dark blue. The following steps change the font color of a cell entry.

1

- With cell A2 selected, click the Font Color button arrow (Home tab | Font group) to display the Font Color gallery.

- Point to Dark Blue, Text 2 (dark blue color in column 4, row 1) in the Theme Colors area of the Font Color gallery to see a live preview of the font color in the active cell (Figure 1–36).

 Experiment

- Point to several other colors in the Font Color gallery to see a live preview of other font colors in the active cell.

Q&A Which colors does Excel make available on the Font Color gallery?

You can choose from more than 60 different font colors on the Font Color gallery (Figure 1–36). Your Font Color gallery may have more or fewer colors, depending on color settings of your operating system. The Theme Colors area includes colors that are included in the current workbook's theme.

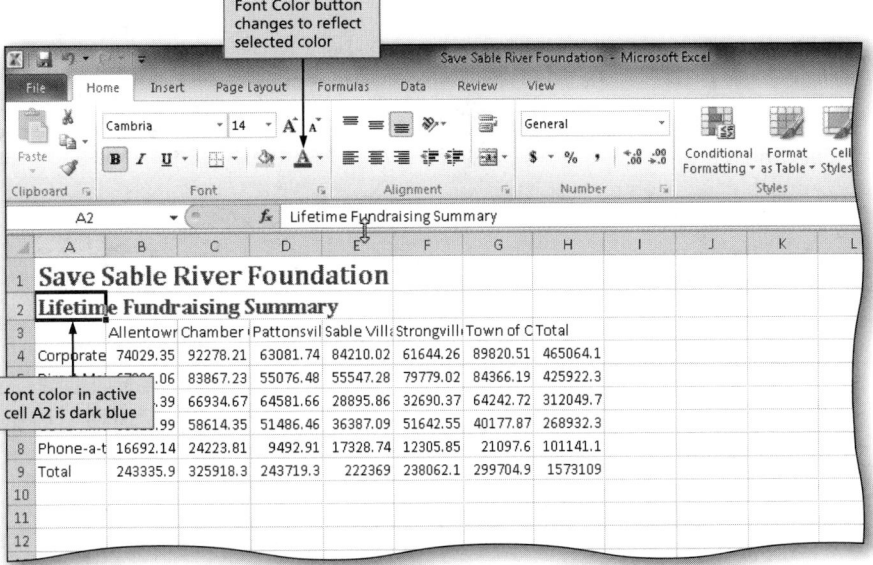

Figure 1–36

2

- Click Dark Blue, Text 2 (column 4, row 1) on the Font Color gallery to change the font of the worksheet subtitle in the active cell (Figure 1–37).

Q&A Why does the Font Color button change after I select the new font color?

When you choose a color on the Font Color gallery, Excel changes the Font Color button (Home tab | Font group) to the chosen color. Thus, to change the font color of the cell entry in another cell to the same color, you need only to select the cell and then click the Font Color button (Home tab | Font group).

Figure 1–37

Other Ways

1. Click Font Color box arrow on Mini toolbar, click desired font color in the Font Color gallery

2. Right-click cell, click Format Cells on shortcut menu, click Font tab (Format Cells dialog box), select color in Font Color gallery, click OK button

To Center Cell Entries Across Columns by Merging Cells

The final step in formatting the worksheet title and subtitle is to center them across columns A through H. Centering a title across the columns used in the body of the worksheet improves the worksheet's appearance. To do this, the eight cells in the range A1:H1 are combined, or merged, into a single cell that is the width of the columns in the body of the worksheet. The eight cells in the range A2:H2 are merged in a similar manner. **Merging cells** involves creating a single cell by combining two or more selected cells. The following steps center the worksheet title and subtitle across columns by merging cells.

1

• Select cell A1 and then drag to cell H1 to highlight the range to be merged and centered (Figure 1–38).

Q&A What if a cell in the range B1:H1 contains data?

For the Merge & Center button (Home tab | Alignment group) to work properly, all the cells except the leftmost cell in the selected range must be empty.

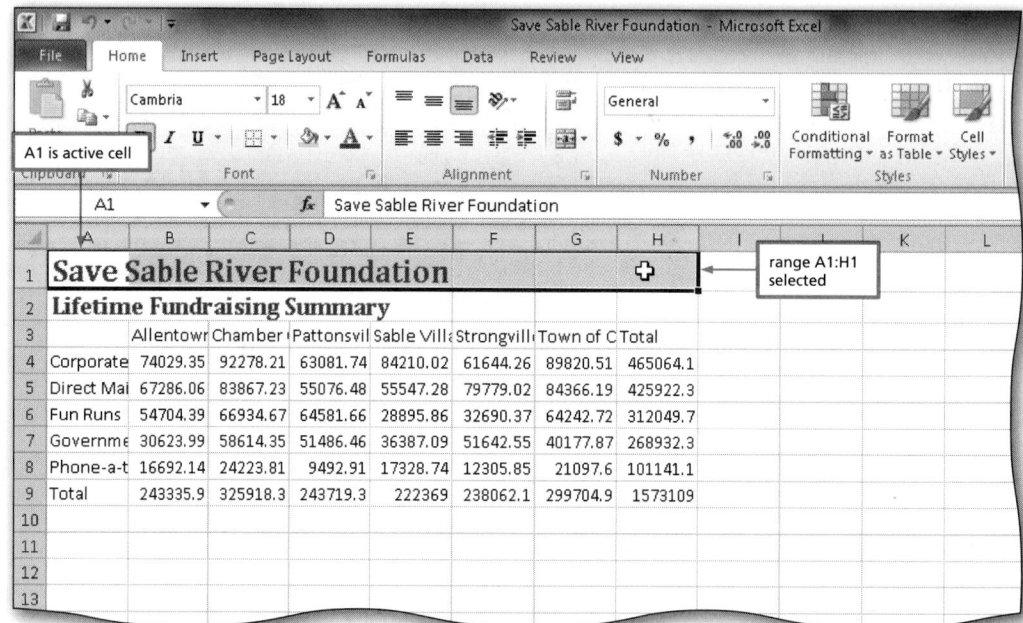

Figure 1–38

2

• Click the Merge & Center button (Home tab | Alignment group) to merge cells A1 through H1 and center the contents of the leftmost cell across the selected columns (Figure 1–39).

Q&A What happened to cells B1 through H1?

After the merge, cells B1 through H1 no longer exist. The new cell A1 now extends across columns A through H.

Figure 1–39

3

• Repeat Steps 1 and 2 to merge and center the worksheet subtitle across cells A2 through H2 (Figure 1–40).

Q&A Are cells B1 through H1 and B2 through H2 lost forever?

No. The opposite of merging cells is **splitting a merged cell**. After you have merged multiple cells to create one merged cell, you can unmerge, or split, the merged cell to display the original cells on the worksheet. You split a merged cell by selecting it and clicking the Merge & Center button. For example, if you click the Merge & Center button a second time in Step 2, it will split the merged cell A1 into cells A1, B1, C1, D1, E1, F1, G1, and H1.

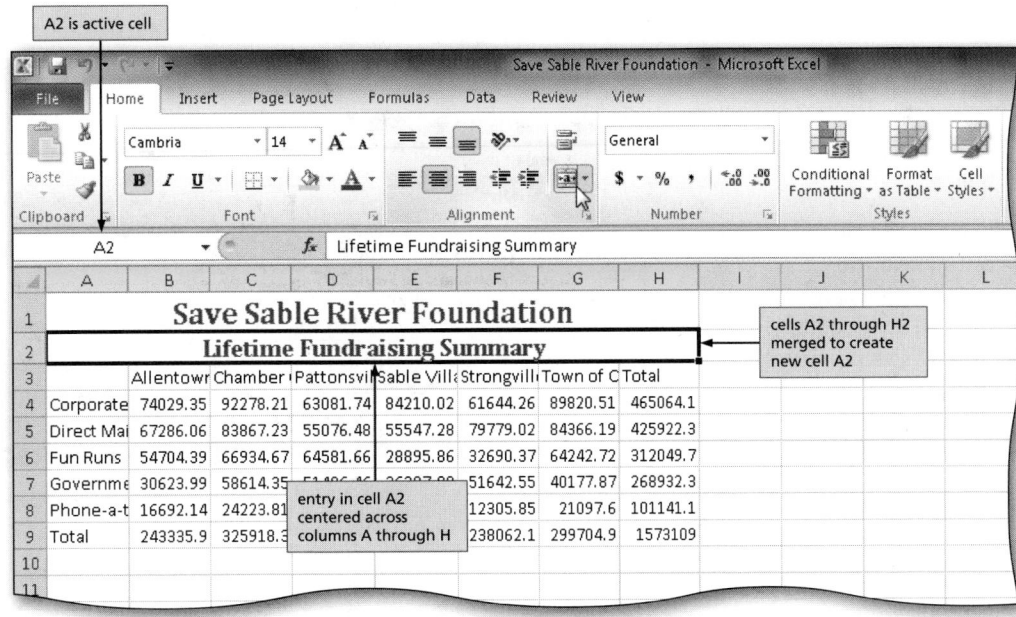

Figure 1–40

Other Ways

1. Right-click selection, click Merge & Center button on Mini toolbar
2. Right-click selection, click Format Cells on shortcut

menu, click Alignment tab (Format Cells dialog box), select Center Across Selection in Horizontal list, click OK button

To Format Column Titles and the Total Row

The next step to format the worksheet is to format the column titles in row 3 and the total values in row 9. Column titles and the total row should be formatted so anyone who views the worksheet quickly can distinguish the column titles and total row from the data in the body of the worksheet. The following steps format the column titles and total row using cell styles in the default worksheet theme.

1

• Click cell A3 and then drag the mouse pointer to cell H3 to select a range (Figure 1–41).

Q&A Why is cell A3 selected in the range for the column headings?

The style to be applied to the column headings includes an underline that will help to distinguish the column headings from the rest of the worksheet. Including cell A3 in the range ensures that the cell will include the underline, which is visually appealing and further helps to separate the data in the worksheet.

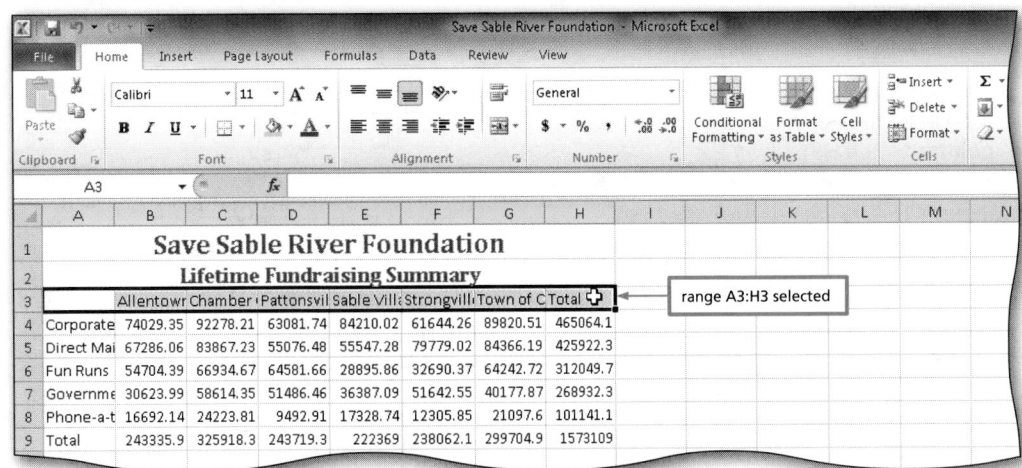

Figure 1–41

2

- Click the Cell Styles button (Home tab | Styles group) to display the Cell Styles gallery.

- Point to the Heading 3 cell style in the Titles and Headings area of the Cell Styles gallery to see a live preview of the cell style in the selected range (Figure 1–42).

Figure 1–42

 Experiment

- Point to other cell styles in the Titles and Headings area of the Cell Styles gallery to see a live preview of other cell styles in the selected range, A3:H3.

3

- Click the Heading 3 cell style to apply the cell style to the selected range.

- Click the Center button (Home tab | Alignment group) to center the column headings in the selected range.

- Click cell A9 and then drag the mouse pointer to cell H9 to select a range (Figure 1–43).

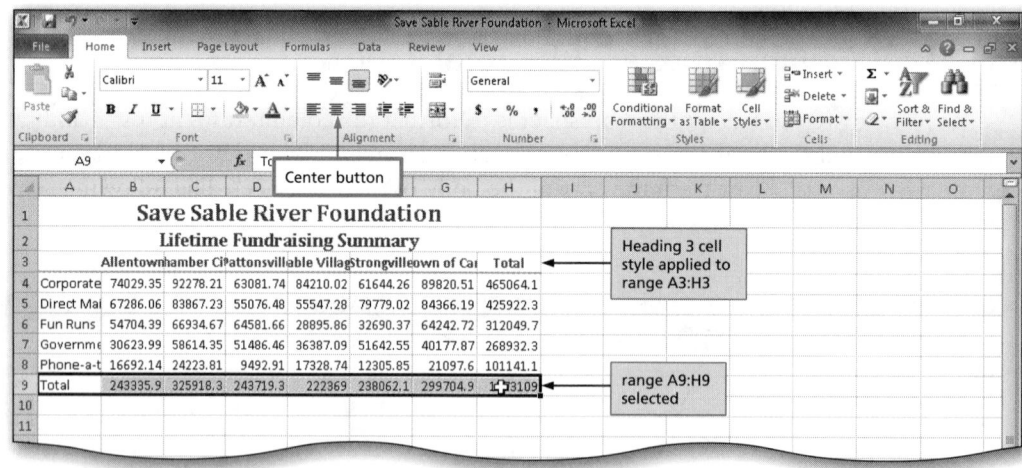

Figure 1–43

Q&A

Why should I choose Heading 3 instead of another heading cell style?

Excel includes many types of headings, such as Heading 1 and Heading 2, because worksheets often include many levels of headings above columns. In the case of the worksheet created for this project, the Heading 3 title includes formatting that makes the column titles' font size smaller than the title and subtitle and makes the column titles stand out from the data in the body of the worksheet.

4

- Click the Cell Styles button (Home tab | Styles group) to display the Cell Styles gallery and then click the Total cell style in the Titles and Headings area to apply the selected cell style to the cells in the selected range.

- Click cell A11 to select it (Figure 1–44).

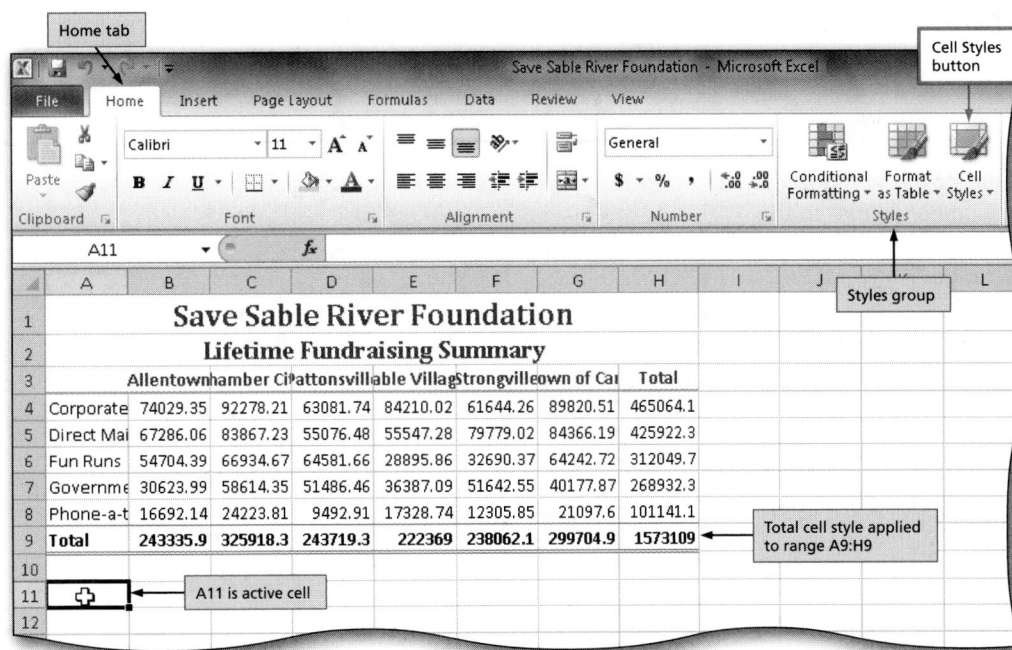

Figure 1–44

To Format Numbers in the Worksheet

As previously noted, the numbers in the worksheet should be formatted to use a dollar-and-cents format, with dollar signs in the first row (row 4) and the total row (row 9). Excel allows you to format numbers in a variety of ways, and these methods are discussed in other chapters in this book. The following steps use buttons on the Ribbon to format the numbers in the worksheet.

1

- Select cell B4 and drag the mouse pointer to cell H4 to select a range (Figure 1–45).

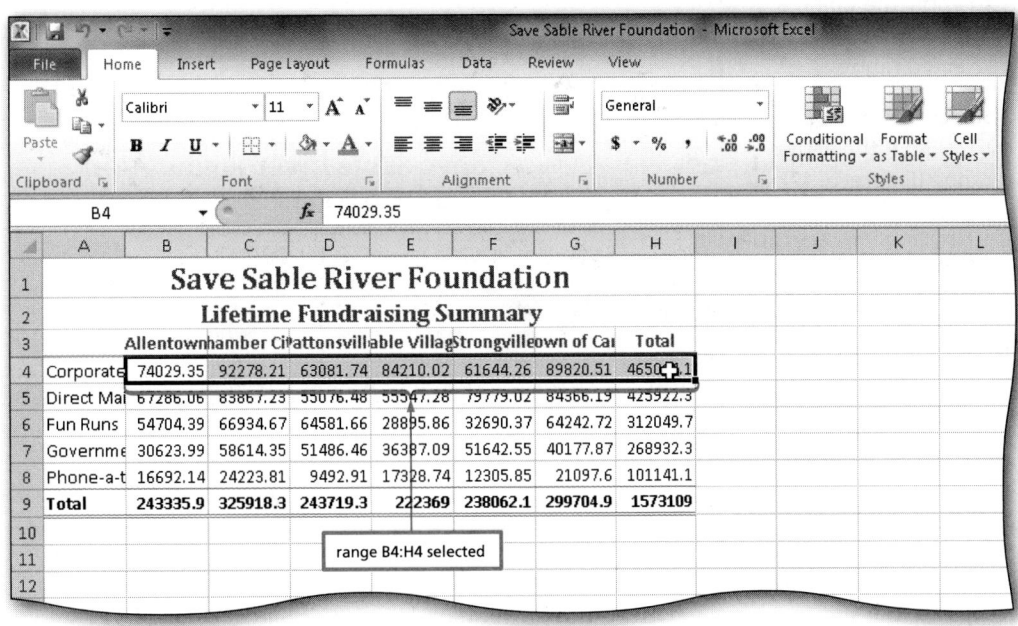

Figure 1–45

2

- Click the Accounting Number Format button (Home tab | Number group) to apply the Accounting Number format to the cells in the selected range.

- Select the range B5:H8 (Figure 1–46).

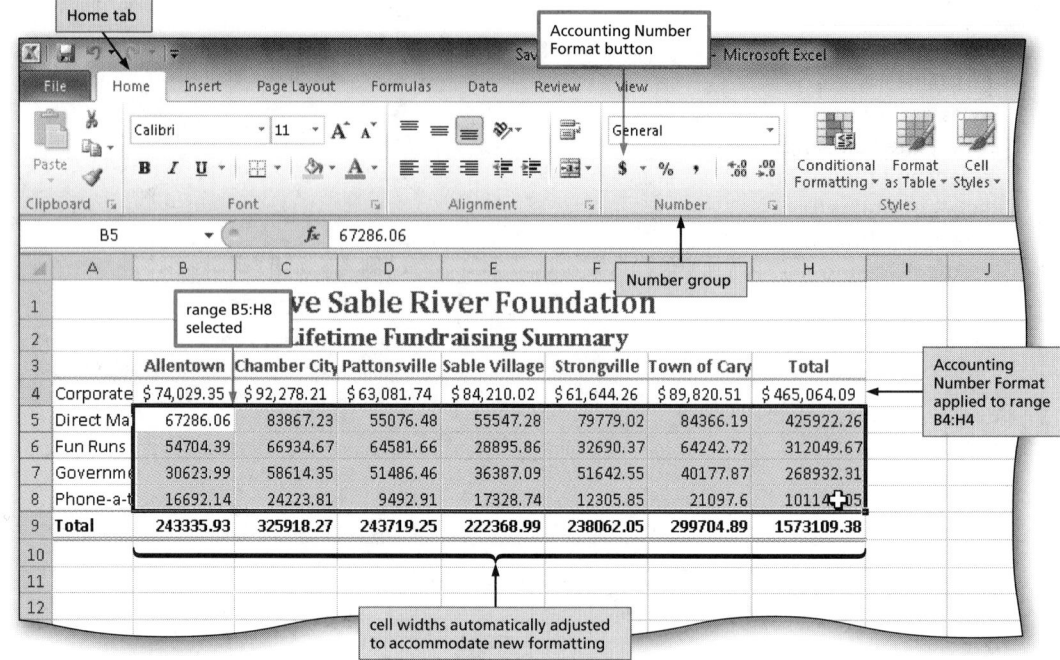

Figure 1–46

Q&A | What effect does the Accounting Number format have on the selected cells?

The Accounting Number format causes the cells to be displayed with two decimal places so that decimal places in cells below the selected cells align vertically. Cell widths are adjusted automatically to accommodate the new formatting.

3

- Click the Comma Style button (Home tab | Number group) to apply the Comma Style format to the selected range.

- Select the range B9:H9 to make it the active range (Figure 1–47).

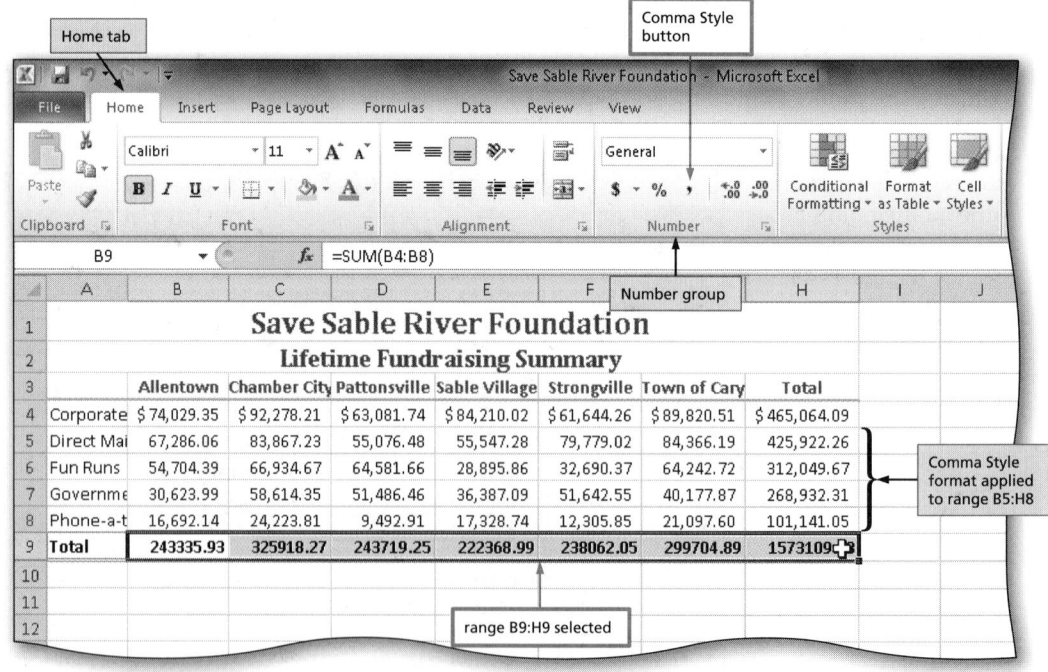

Figure 1–47

Q&A | What effect does the Comma Style format have on the selected cells?

The Comma Style format causes the cells to be displayed with two decimal places and commas as thousands separators.

4

- Click the Accounting Number Format button (Home tab | Number group) to apply the Accounting Number format to the cells in the selected range.

- Select cell A11 (Figure 1–48).

Q&A

Why did the column widths automatically adjust again?

Because the total row contains larger numbers, the Accounting Number format again causes the cell widths automatically to adjust to accommodate the new formatting just as occurred in Step 2.

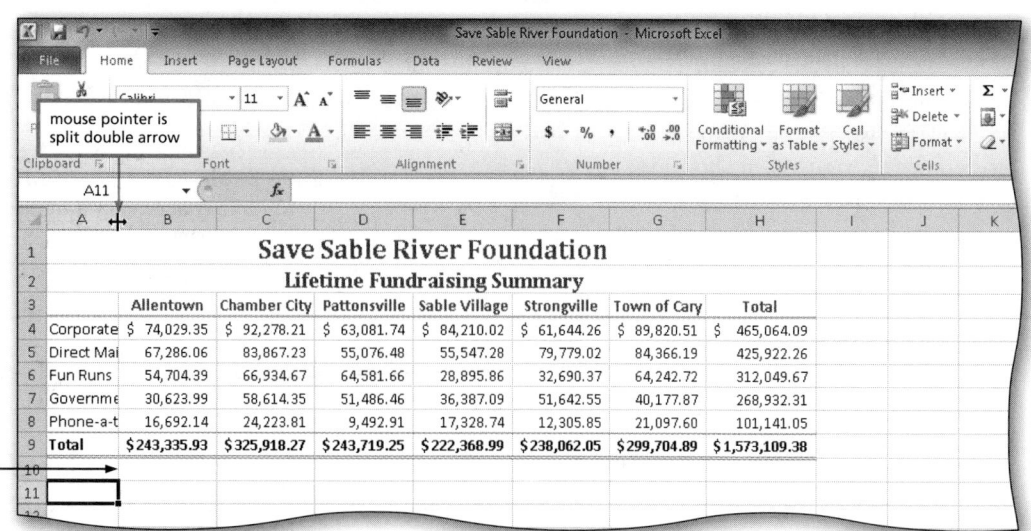

Figure 1–48

Other Ways
1. Click Accounting Number Format or Comma Style button on Mini toolbar	Number tab (Format Cells dialog box), select Accounting in Category list or select Number and click Use 1000 Separator, click OK button
2. Right-click selection, click Format Cells on the shortcut menu, click	

To Adjust the Column Width

The last step in formatting the worksheet is to adjust the width of column A so that the word Phone-a-thon in cell A8 is shown in its entirety in the cell. Excel includes several methods for adjusting cell widths and row heights, and these methods are discussed later in this book. The following steps adjust the width of column A so that the contents of cell A8 are displayed in the cell.

1

- Point to the boundary on the right side of the column A heading above row 1 to change the mouse pointer to a split double arrow (Figure 1–49).

Figure 1–49

2

- Double-click on the boundary to adjust the width of the column to the width of the largest item in the column (Figure 1–50).

Q&A

What if none of the items in column A extends through the entire width of the column?

If all of the items in column A were shorter in length than the width of the column when you double-click the right side of the column A heading, then Excel still would adjust the column width to the largest item in the column. That is, Excel would reduce the width of the column to the largest item.

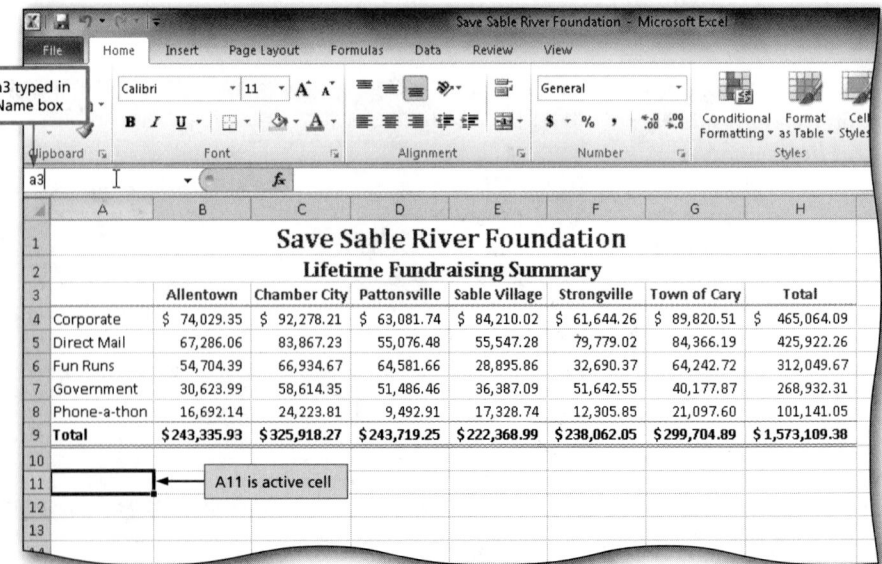

Figure 1–50

Using the Name Box to Select a Cell

The next step is to chart the lifetime fundraising amounts for the five fundraising activities used by the organization. To create the chart, you first must select the cell in the upper-left corner of the range to chart (cell A3). Rather than clicking cell A3 to select it, the next section describes how to use the Name box to select the cell.

To Use the Name Box to Select a Cell

The Name box is located on the left side of the formula bar. To select any cell, click the Name box and enter the cell reference of the cell you want to select. The following steps select cell A3 using the Name box.

1

- Click the Name box in the formula bar and then type **a3** as the cell you wish to select (Figure 1–51).

Q&A

Why is cell A11 still selected?

Even though cell A11 is the active cell, Excel displays the typed cell reference a3 in the Name box until you press the ENTER key.

Figure 1–51

2

- Press the ENTER key to change the active cell in the Name box (Figure 1–52).

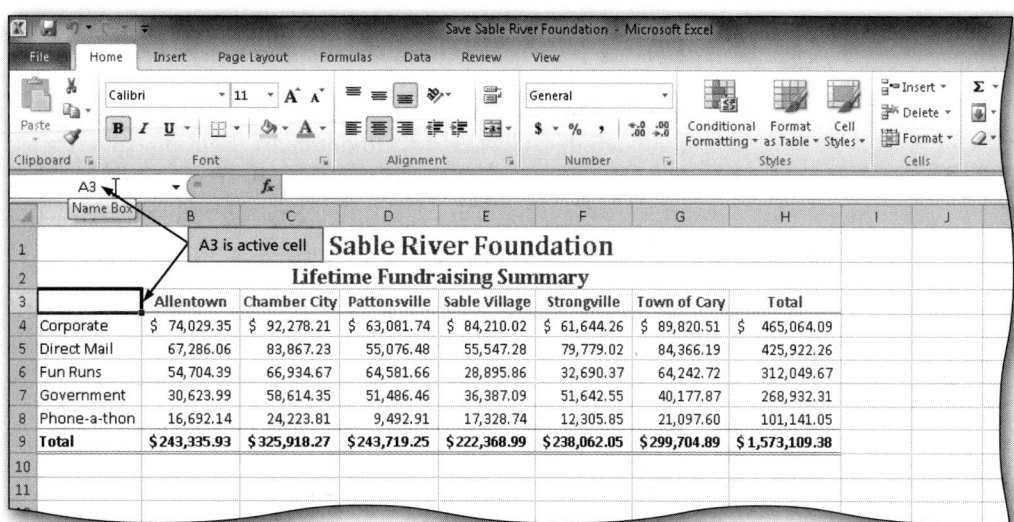

Figure 1–52

Other Ways to Select Cells

As you will see in later chapters, in addition to using the Name box to select any cell in a worksheet, you also can use it to assign names to a cell or range of cells. Excel supports several additional ways to select a cell, as summarized in Table 1–3.

Table 1–3 Selecting Cells in Excel	
Key, Box, or Command	**Function**
ALT+PAGE DOWN	Selects the cell one worksheet window to the right and moves the worksheet window accordingly.
ALT+PAGE UP	Selects the cell one worksheet window to the left and moves the worksheet window accordingly.
ARROW	Selects the adjacent cell in the direction of the arrow on the key.
CTRL+ARROW	Selects the border cell of the worksheet in combination with the arrow keys and moves the worksheet window accordingly. For example, to select the rightmost cell in the row that contains the active cell, press CTRL+RIGHT ARROW. You also can press the END key, release it, and then press the appropriate arrow key to accomplish the same task.
CTRL+HOME	Selects cell A1 or the cell one column and one row below and to the right of frozen titles and moves the worksheet window accordingly.
Find command on Find and Select menu or SHIFT+F5	Finds and selects a cell that contains specific contents that you enter in the Find and Replace dialog box. If necessary, Excel moves the worksheet window to display the cell. You also can press CTRL+F to display the Find dialog box.
Go To command on Find and Select menu or F5	Selects the cell that corresponds to the cell reference you enter in the Go To dialog box and moves the worksheet window accordingly. You also can press CTRL+G to display the Go To dialog box.
HOME	Selects the cell at the beginning of the row that contains the active cell and moves the worksheet window accordingly.
Name box	Selects the cell in the workbook that corresponds to the cell reference you enter in the Name box.
PAGE DOWN	Selects the cell down one worksheet window from the active cell and moves the worksheet window accordingly.
PAGE UP	Selects the cell up one worksheet window from the active cell and moves the worksheet window accordingly.

Break Point: If you wish to take a break, this is a good place to do so. Be sure to save the Save Sable River Foundation file again and then you can quit Excel. To resume at a later time, start Excel, open the file called Save Sable River Foundation, and continue following the steps from this location forward.

Adding a Clustered Cylinder Chart to the Worksheet

As outlined in the requirements document in Figure 1–2 on page EX 4, the worksheet should include a Clustered Cylinder chart to graphically represent the lifetime fundraising for each fundraising activity in which the organization engages. The Clustered Cylinder chart shown in Figure 1–53 is called an **embedded chart** because it is drawn on the same worksheet as the data.

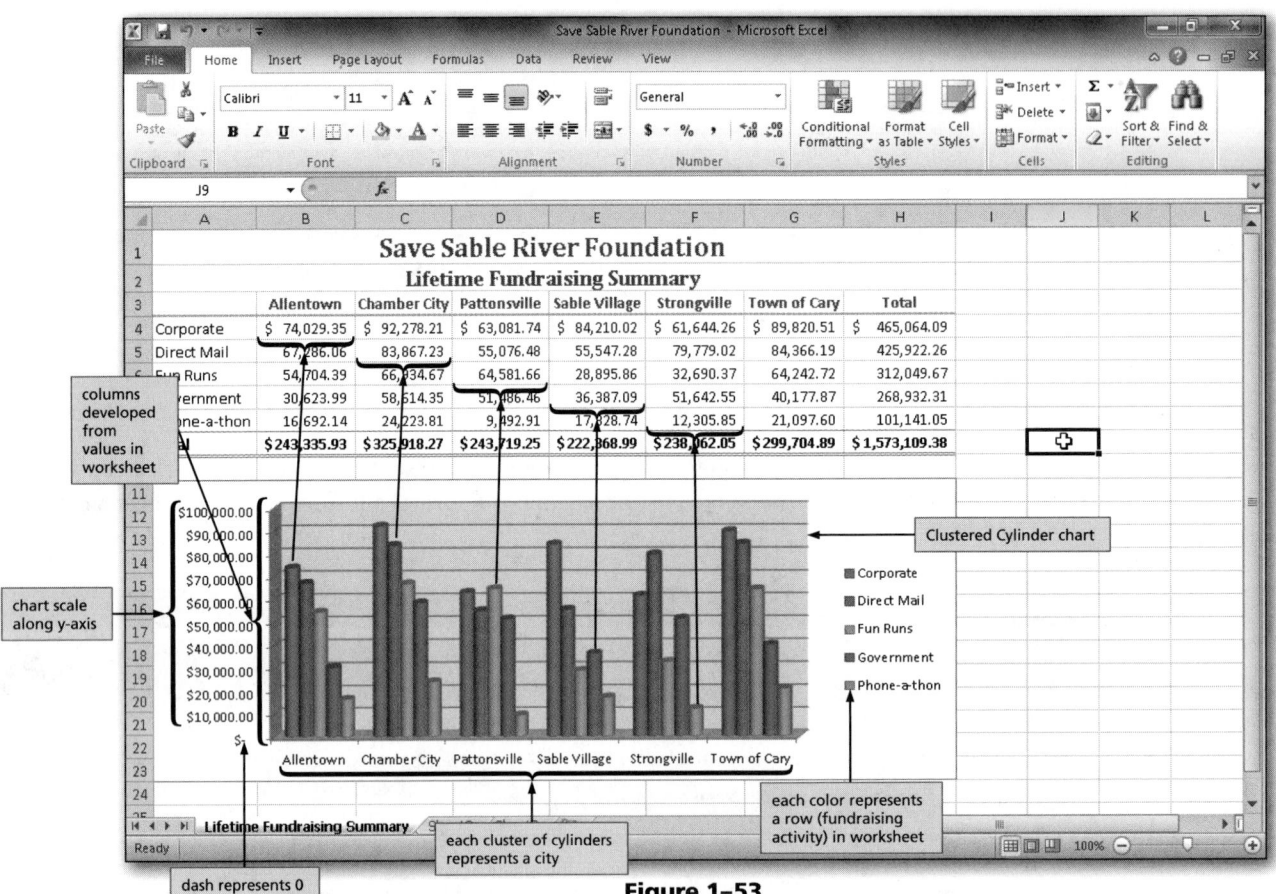

Figure 1–53

Plan Ahead

Decide on the type of chart needed.
Excel includes 11 chart types from which you can choose, including column, line, pie, bar, area, X Y (scatter), stock, surface, doughnut, bubble, and radar. The type of chart you choose depends on the type of data that you have, how much data you have, and the message you want to convey.

A line chart often is used to illustrate changes in data over time. Pie charts show the contribution of each piece of data to the whole, or total, of the data. Area charts, like line charts, illustrate changes over time, but often are used to compare more than one set of data and the area under the lines is filled in with a different color for each set of data. An X Y (scatter) chart is used much line a line chart, but each piece of data is represented by a dot and is not connected with a line. A stock chart provides a number of methods commonly

(continued)

(continued)

used in the financial industry to show stock market data. A surface chart compares data from three columns and/or rows in a three-dimensional manner. A doughnut chart is much like a pie chart, but a doughnut chart allows for comparing more than one set of data, resulting in a chart that looks like a doughnut, with each subsquent set of data surrounding the previous set. A bubble chart is much like an X Y (scatter) chart, but a third set of data results indicates how large each individual dot, or bubble, is on the chart. A radar chart can compare several sets of data in a manner that resembles a radar screen, with each set of data represented by a different color. A column or cylinder chart is a good way to compare values side by side. A Clustered Cylinder chart can go even further in comparing values across categories.

Establish where to position and how to format the chart.

- When possible, try to position charts so that both the data and chart appear on the screen on the worksheet together and so that the data and chart can be printed in the most readable manner possible.

- When choosing/selecting colors for a chart, consider the color scheme of the rest of the worksheet. The chart should not present colors that are in stark contrast to the rest of the worksheet. If the chart will be printed in color, minimize the amount of dark colors on the chart so that the chart both prints quickly and conserves ink.

Plan Ahead

BTW

Cell Values and Charting
When you change a cell value on which a chart is dependent, Excel redraws the chart instantaneously, unless automatic recalculation is disabled. If automatic recalculation is disabled, then you must press the F9 key to redraw the chart. To enable or disable automatic recalculation, click the Calculations Options button (Formulas tab | Calculation group).

In the case of the Save Sable River Foundation Lifetime Fundraising Summary, comparisons of fundraising activities within each city can be made side by side with a Clustered Cylinder chart. The chart uses differently colored cylinders to represent amounts raised for different fundraising activities. Each city uses the same color scheme for identifying fundraising activities, which allows for easy identification and comparison.

- For the city of Allentown, for example, the dark blue cylinder representing Corporate donations shows lifetime donations of $74,029.35

- For Chamber City, the maroon cylinder representing Direct Mail donations shows lifetime donations of $83,867.23

- For the city of Pattonsville, the lime green cylinder representing donations for Fun Runs shows lifetime donations of $64,581.66

- For Sable Village, the purple cylinder representing Government donations shows lifetime donations of $36,387.09

- For the city of Strongville, the light blue cylinder representing Phone-a-thon donations shows lifetime donations of $12,305.85

Because the same color scheme is used in each city to represent the five fundraising activities, you easily can compare funds raised by each fundraising activity among the cities. The totals from the worksheet are not represented, because the totals are not in the range specified for charting.

Excel derives the chart scale based on the values in the worksheet and then displays the scale along the vertical axis (also called the **y-axis** or **value axis**) of the chart. For example, no value in the range B4:G8 is less than 0 or greater than $100,000.00, so the scale ranges from 0 to $100,000.00. Excel also determines the $10,000.00 increments of the scale automatically. For the numbers along the y-axis, Excel uses a format that includes representing the 0 value with a dash (Figure 1–53).

BTW

Using Dual Axes on a Chart
Figure 1–53 shows a chart with a y-axis along the left side of the chart. If you have additional data to chart for each city, you can overlay a second chart with a different y-axis on top of the first chart. The second y-axis is displayed on the right side of the chart. In this case, the chart is said to have dual axes. Additionally, a different type of chart usually is laid over the first chart. For example, if a second y-axis were added to the chart shown in Figure 1–53, a good choice for the second chart would be a line chart. To add a second y-axis to a chart, click the data series to plot on the new axis, click Format Selection (Chart Tools Format tab | Current Selection group), click the Secondary Axis option button (Format Data Series dialog box), and then click the Close button.

To Add a Clustered Cylinder Chart to the Worksheet

The area on the worksheet where the chart appears is called the chart location. As shown in Figure 1–53 on page EX 36, the chart location in this worksheet is the range A11:G23; this range is immediately below the worksheet data. Placing the chart below the data on the Save Sable River Foundation Lifetime Fundraising Summary worksheet makes it easier to read the chart along with the data, and the chart and data easily can be printed on one sheet of paper.

The following steps draw a Clustered Cylinder chart that compares the funds raised by fundraising activity for the six cities.

1

• Click cell A3 and then drag the mouse pointer to cell G8 to select the range to be charted (Figure 1–54).

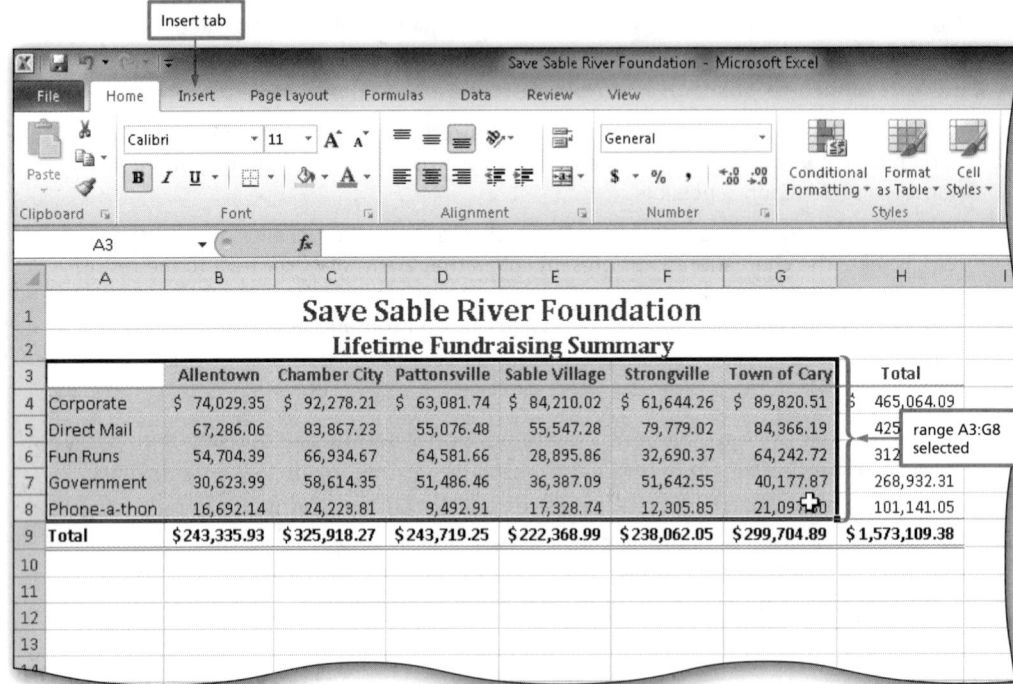

Figure 1–54

2

• Click Insert on the Ribbon to display the Insert tab (Figure 1–55).

Q&A

What tasks can I perform with the Insert tab?

The Insert tab includes commands that allow you to insert various objects, such as shapes, tables, illustrations, and charts, into a worksheet. These objects will be discussed as they are used throughout this book.

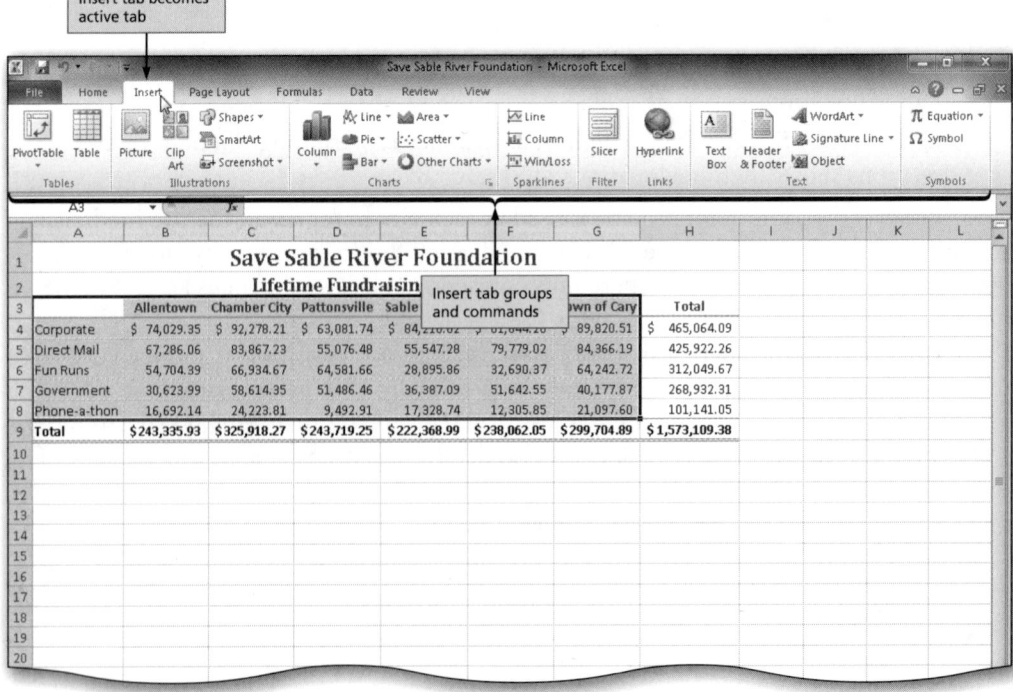

Figure 1–55

3
- Click the Column button (Insert tab | Charts group) to display the Column gallery (Figure 1–56).

Figure 1–56

4
- Click the Clustered Cylinder chart type in the Cylinder area of the Column gallery to add the selected chart type to the middle of the worksheet in a selection rectangle.

- Press and hold down the mouse button while pointing to the upper-right edge of the selection rectangle to change the mouse pointer to a double two-headed arrow (Figure 1–57).

Q&A

Why is a new tab displayed on the Ribbon?

When you select objects such as shapes or charts, Excel displays contextual tabs that include special commands that are used to work

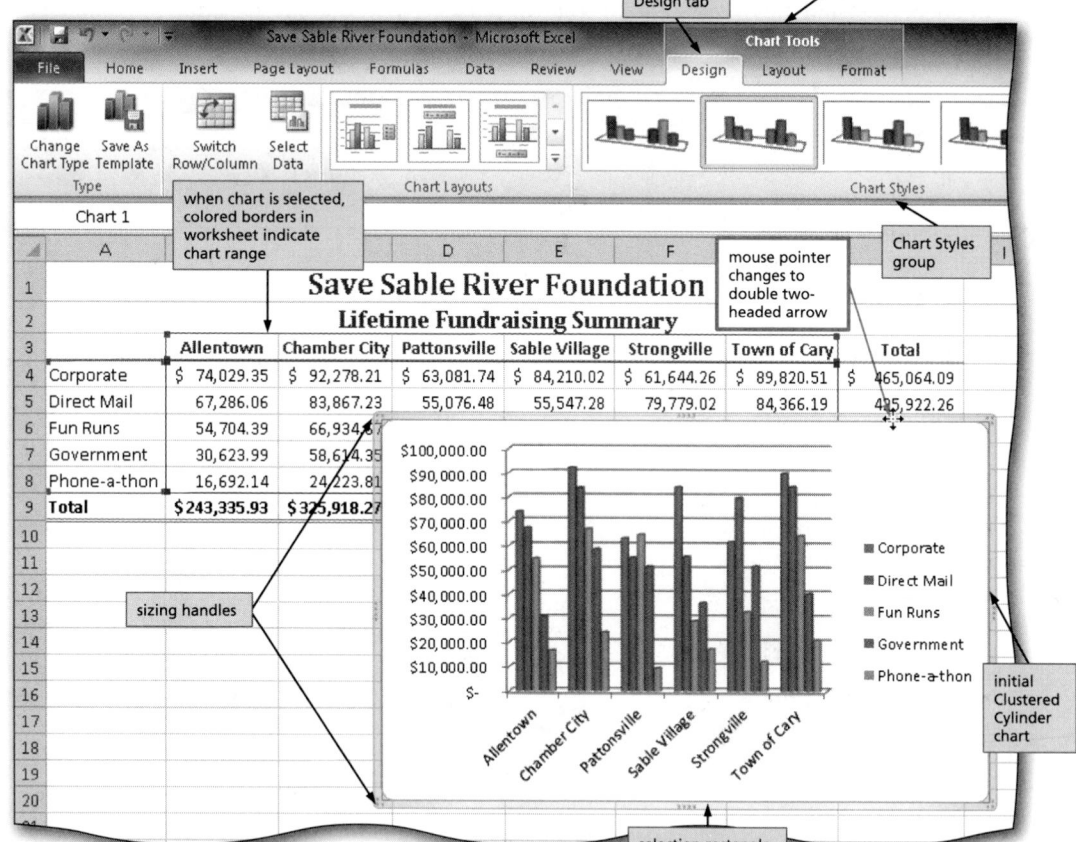

Figure 1–57

with the type of object selected. Because a chart is selected, Excel displays the Chart Tools contextual tab. The three tabs below the Chart Tools contextual tab, Design, Layout, and Format, are tabs that include commands to work with charts.

5

- Drag the chart down and to the left to position the upper-left corner of the dotted line rectangle over the upper-left corner of cell A11.

- Press and hold down the mouse button while pointing to the middle sizing handle on the right edge of the chart (Figure 1–58).

Q&A

How does Excel know which data to use to create the chart?

Excel automatically selects the entries in the topmost row of the chart range (row 3) as the titles for the horizontal axis (also called the **x-axis** or **category axis**) and draws a column for each of the 30 cells in the range containing numbers.

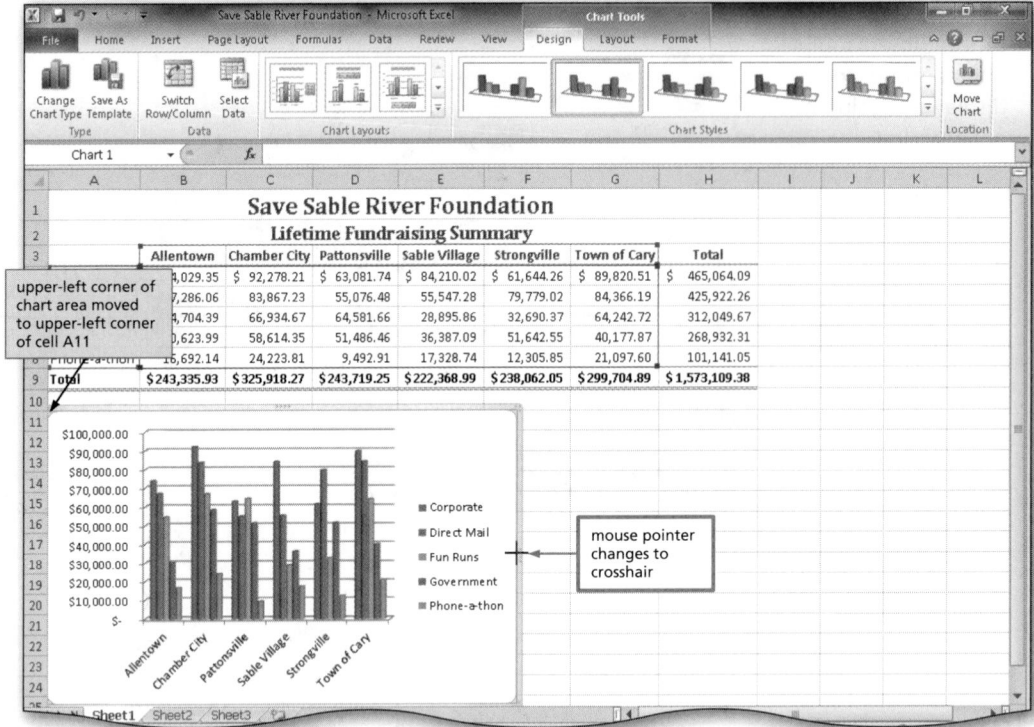

Figure 1–58

6

- While continuing to hold down the mouse button, press the ALT key and drag the right edge of the chart to the right edge of column H and then release the mouse button to resize the chart.

- Press and hold down the mouse button while pointing to the middle sizing handle on the bottom edge of the selection rectangle and do not release the mouse button (Figure 1–59).

Q&A

Why should I hold the ALT key down while I resize a chart?

Holding down the ALT key while you drag a chart **snaps** (aligns) the edge of the chart area to the worksheet gridlines. If you do not hold down the ALT key, then you can place an edge of a chart in the middle of a column or row.

Figure 1–59

7

- While continuing to hold down the mouse button, press the ALT key and drag the bottom edge of the chart up to the bottom edge of row 23 and then release the mouse button to resize the chart.

- If necessary, scroll the worksheet so that row 1 displays at the top of the worksheet.

- Click the More button in the Chart Styles gallery (Chart Tools Design tab | Chart Styles group) to expand the gallery (Figure 1–60).

Figure 1–60

8

- Click Style 34 in the Chart Styles gallery (column 2, row 5) to apply the chart style to the chart.

- Click cell J9 to deselect the chart and complete the worksheet (Figure 1–61).

Q&A

What is the purpose of the items on the right side of the chart?

The items to the right of the column chart in Figure 1–61 are the **legend**, which identifies the colors assigned to each bar in the chart. Excel automatically selects the entries in the leftmost column of the chart range (column A) as titles within the legend.

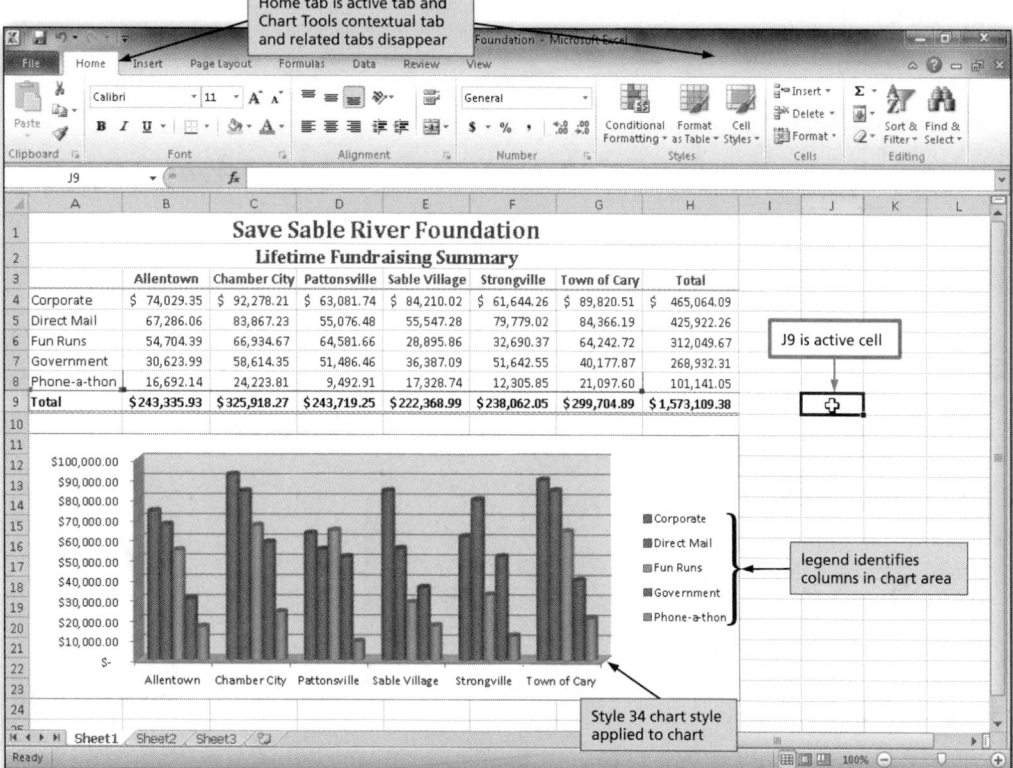

Figure 1–61

Changing the Worksheet Names

The sheet tabs at the bottom of the window allow you to view any worksheet in the workbook. You click the sheet tab of the worksheet you want to view in the Excel window. By default, Excel presets the names of the worksheets to Sheet1, Sheet2, and so on. The worksheet names become increasingly important as you move toward more sophisticated workbooks, especially workbooks in which you reference cells between worksheets.

Plan Ahead

Choose a name for the worksheet.
Use simple, meaningful names for each worksheet. Worksheet names often match the worksheet title. If a worksheet includes multiple titles in multiple sections of the worksheet, use a name that encompasses the meaning of all of the sections.

To Change the Worksheet Names

Lifetime Fundraising Summary is a meaningful name for the Save Sable River Foundation Lifetime Fundraising Summary worksheet. The following steps rename worksheets by double-clicking the sheet tabs.

1

- Double-click the sheet tab labeled Sheet1 in the lower-left corner of the window.

- Type **Lifetime Fundraising Summary** as the worksheet name and then press the ENTER key to display the new worksheet name on the sheet tab (Figure 1–62).

Q&A What is the maximum length for a worksheet tab?

Worksheet names can be up to 31 characters (including spaces) in length. Longer worksheet names, however, mean that fewer sheet tabs will show. To view more sheet tabs, you can drag the tab split box (Figure 1–62) to the right. This will reduce the size of the scroll bar at the bottom of the screen. Double-click the tab split box to reset it to its normal position.

Sheet1 name changed to Lifetime Fundraising Summary

tab split box

Figure 1–62

2

- Right-click the sheet tab labeled Lifetime Fundraising Summary in the lower-left corner of the window to display a shortcut menu.

- Point to Tab Color on the shortcut menu to display the color gallery (Figure 1–63).

Q&A How can I quickly move between worksheet tabs?

You can use the tab scrolling buttons to the left of the sheet tabs (Figure 1–63) to move between worksheets. The leftmost and rightmost scroll buttons move to the first or last worksheet in the workbook. The two middle scroll buttons move one worksheet to the left or right.

shortcut menu

desired color

Tab Color command

tab scrolling buttons

Figure 1–63

3

- Click Red, Accent 2 (column 6, row 1) in the Theme Colors area to change the color of the tab (Figure 1–64)

4

- If necessary, click Home on the Ribbon to display the Home tab.

Figure 1–64

Changing Document Properties

Excel helps you organize and identify your files by using **document properties**, which are the details about a file. Document properties, also known as **metadata**, can include information such as the project author, title, subject, and keywords. A **keyword** is a word or phrase that further describes the document. For example, a class name or document topic can describe the file's purpose or content.

Document properties are valuable for a variety of reasons:

- Users can save time locating a particular file because they can view a document's properties without opening the document.

- By creating consistent properties for files having similar content, users can better organize their documents.

- Some organizations require Excel users to add document properties so that other employees can view details about these files.

Five different types of document properties exist, but the more common ones used in this book are standard and automatically updated properties. **Standard properties** are associated with all Microsoft Office documents and include author, title, and subject. **Automatically updated properties** include file system properties, such as the date you create or change a file, and statistics, such as the file size.

To Change Document Properties

The **Document Information Panel** contains areas where you can view and enter document properties. You can view and change information in this panel at any time while you are creating a workbook. Before saving the workbook again, you want to add your name and course information as document properties. The following steps use the Document Information Panel to change document properties.

1

- Click File on the Ribbon to open the Backstage view. If necessary, click the Info tab in the Backstage view to display the Info gallery (Figure 1–65).

Q&A

How do I close the Backstage view?

Click File on the Ribbon or click the preview of the document in the Info gallery to return to the Excel document window.

Figure 1–65

- Click the Properties button in the right pane of the Info gallery to display the Properties menu (Figure 1–66).

Figure 1–66

- Click Show Document Panel on the Properties menu to close the Backstage view and display the Document Information Panel in the Excel workbook window (Figure 1–67).

Q&A

Why are some of the document properties in my Document Information Panel already filled in?

The person who installed Microsoft Office 2010 on your computer or network may have set or customized the properties.

Figure 1–67

- Click the Author text box, if necessary, and then type your name as the Author property. If a name already is displayed in the Author text box, delete it before typing your name.

- Click the Subject text box, if necessary delete any existing text, and then type your course and section as the Subject property.

- If an AutoComplete dialog box appears, click its Yes button.

- Click the Keywords text box, if necessary delete any existing text, and then type **Lifetime Fundraising Summary** as the Keywords property (Figure 1–68).

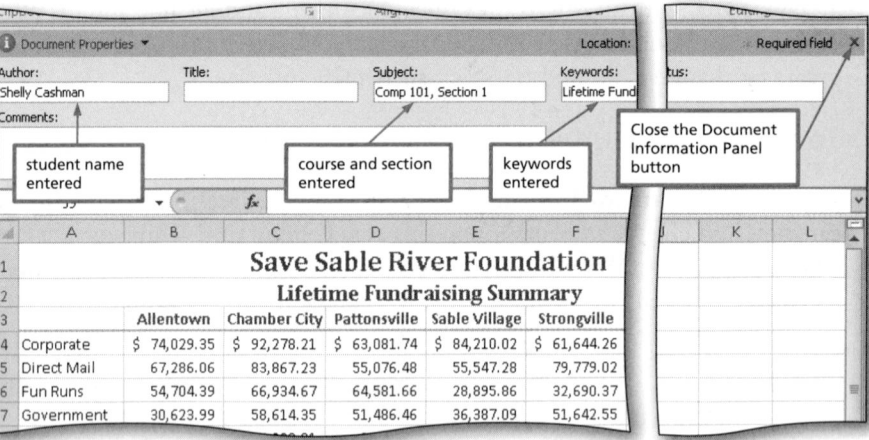

Figure 1–68

Q&A

What types of document properties does Excel collect automatically?

Excel records details such as time spent editing a workbook, the number of times a workbook has been revised, and the fonts and themes used in a workbook.

- Click the Close the Document Information Panel button so that the Document Information Panel no longer is displayed. If a dialog box is displayed, click the No button to close it.

Other Ways

1. Click File on Ribbon, click Info in the Backstage view, if necessary click Show All Properties link in Info gallery, click property to change and type new information, close the Backstage view

To Save an Existing Workbook with the Same File Name

You have made several modifications to the workbook since you last saved it. Thus, you should save it again. The following step saves the workbook again. For an example of the step listed below, refer to the Introduction to Office 2010 and Windows 7 chapter at the beginning of this book.

 Click the Save button on the Quick Access Toolbar to overwrite the previously saved file.

Previewing and Printing a Worksheet

After creating a worksheet, you may want to print it. Printing a worksheet enables you to distribute the worksheet to others in a form that can be read or viewed but typically not edited. It is a good practice to save a workbook before printing a worksheet, in the event you experience difficulties printing.

Determine the best method for distributing the worksheet.
The traditional method of distributing a worksheet uses a printer to produce a hard copy. A **hardcopy or printout** is information that exists on a physical medium such as paper. For users that can receive fax documents, you can elect to print a hard copy on a remote fax machine. Hard copies can be useful for the following reasons:

- Many people prefer proofreading a hard copy of a worksheet rather than viewing it on the screen to check for errors and readability.

- Hard copies can serve as reference material if your storage medium is lost or becomes corrupted and you need to re-create the worksheet.

Instead of distributing a hard copy of a worksheet, users can choose to distribute the worksheet as an electronic image that mirrors the original worksheet's appearance. The electronic image of the worksheet can be e-mailed, posted on a Web site, or copied to a portable storage medium such as a USB flash drive. Two popular electronic image formats, sometimes called fixed formats, are PDF by Adobe Systems and XPS by Microsoft. In Excel, you can create electronic image files through the Print tab in the Backstage view, the Save & Send tab in the Backstage view, and the Save As dialog box. Electronic images of worksheets, such as PDF and XPS, can be useful for the following reasons:

- Users can view electronic images of worksheets without the software that created the original worksheet (e.g., Excel). Specifically, to view a PDF file, you use a program called Acrobat Reader, which can be downloaded free from Adobe's Web site. Similarly, to view an XPS file, you use a program called an XPS Viewer, which is included in the latest versions of Windows and Internet Explorer.

- Sending electronic documents saves paper and printer supplies. Society encourages users to contribute to **green computing**, which involves reducing the environmental waste generated when using a computer.

BTW

Printing Document Properties
To print document properties, click File on the Ribbon to open the Backstage view, click the Print tab in the Backstage view to display the Print gallery, click the first button in the Settings area to display a list of options specifying what you can print, click Document Properties in the list to specify you want to print the document properties instead of the actual document, and then click the Print button in the Print gallery to print the document properties on the currently selected printer.

Plan Ahead

BTW

Conserving Ink and Toner
If you want to conserve ink or toner, you can instruct Excel to print draft quality documents by clicking File on the Ribbon to open the Backstage view, clicking Options in the Backstage view to display the Excel Options dialog box, clicking Advanced in the left pane (Excel Options dialog box), scrolling to the Print area in the right pane, placing a check mark in the 'Use draft quality' check box, and then clicking the OK button. Then, use the Backstage view to print the document as usual.

To Preview and Print a Worksheet in Landscape Orientation

With the completed workbook saved, you may want to print it. Because the worksheet is included in a report, you will print a hard copy on a printer. The following steps print a hard copy of the contents of the Save Sable River Foundation Lifetime Fundraising Summary worksheet.

1

• Click File on the Ribbon to open the Backstage view.

• Click the Print tab in the Backstage view to display the Print gallery (Figure 1–69).

Q&A How can I print multiple copies of my worksheet?

Increase the number in the Copies box in the Print gallery.

Q&A What if I decide not to print the worksheet at this time?

Click File on the Ribbon to close the Backstage view and return to the Excel workbook window.

Figure 1–69

2

• Verify the printer name that appears on the Printer Status button will print a hard copy of the document. If necessary, click the Printer Status button to display a list of available printer options and then click the desired printer to change the currently selected printer.

3

• Click the Portrait Orientation button in the Settings area and then select Landscape Orientation to change the orientation of the page to landscape and view the entire worksheet on one page (Figure 1–70).

Figure 1–70

4

- Click the Print button in the Print gallery to print the worksheet in landscape orientation on the currently selected printer.

- When the printer stops, retrieve the hard copy (Figure 1–71).

Q&A Do I have to wait until my worksheet is complete to print it?

No, you can follow these steps to print a document at any time while you are creating it.

Q&A What if I want to print an electronic image of a worksheet instead of a hard copy?

You would click the Printer Status button in the Print gallery and then select the desired electronic image option such as a Microsoft XPS Document Writer, which would create an XPS file.

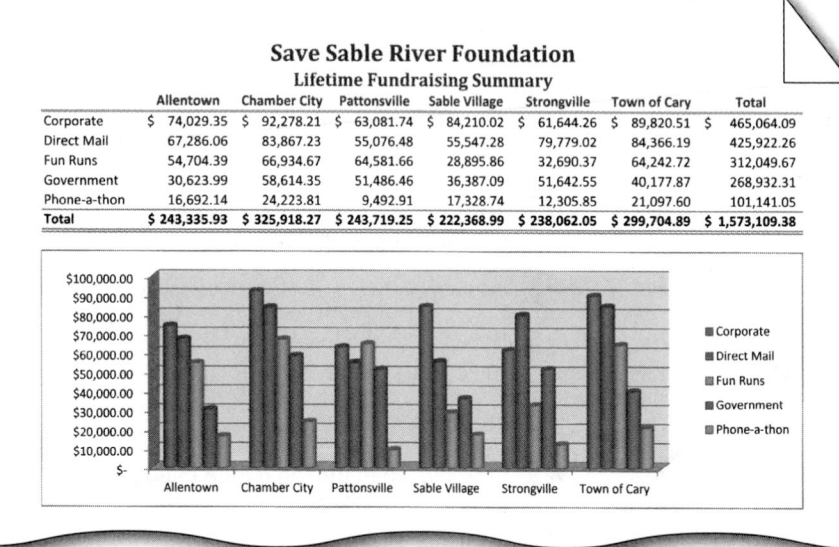

Figure 1–71

To Quit Excel

This Save Sable River Foundation workbook now is complete. The following steps quit Excel if only one workbook is open. For a detailed example of the procedure summarized below, refer to the Office 2010 and Windows 7 chapter at the beginning of this book.

1 If you have one Excel workbook open, click the Close button on the right side of the title bar to close the document and quit Excel; or if you have multiple Excel workbooks open, click File on the Ribbon to open the Backstage view and then click the Exit button to close all open workbooks and quit Excel.

2 If a Microsoft Office Excel dialog box appears, click the Save button to save any changes made to the workbook since the last save.

Starting Excel and Opening a Workbook

Once you have created and saved a workbook, you may need to retrieve it from your storage medium. For example, you might want to revise a worksheet or reprint it. Opening a workbook requires that Excel is running on your computer.

To Start Excel

1 Click the Start button on the Windows 7 taskbar to display the Start menu.

2 Type **Microsoft Excel** as the search text in the 'Search programs and files' text box and watch the search results appear on the Start menu.

3 Click Microsoft Excel 2010 in the search results on the Start menu to start Excel and display a new blank workbook in the Excel window.

4 If the Excel window is not maximized, click the Maximize button next to the Close button on its title bar to maximize the window.

BTW

Managing Versions
Excel automatically saves your work, even when you have not saved a file. If you inadvertently close a file without saving it, you can recover your work by clicking Info in the Backstage view and then clicking the Manage Versions button. On the Manage Versions list, click Recover Unsaved Workbooks to display the Open dialog box. Select the file you want to recover and then click the Open button (Open dialog box) to display the file. You also can click the file to recover in the Versions list next to the Manage Versions button. To delete recent copies of unsaved files, click Delete All Unsaved Workbooks on the Manage Versions list.

To Open a Workbook from Excel

Earlier in this chapter you saved your project on a USB flash drive using the file name, Save Sable River Foundation. The following steps open the Save Sable River Foundation file from the Excel folder in the CIS 101 folder on the USB flash drive. For a detailed example of the procedure summarized below, refer to page OFF 57 in the Office 2010 and Windows 7 chapter at the beginning of this book.

1 With your USB flash drive connected to one of the computer's USB ports, click File on the Ribbon to open the Backstage view.

2 Click Open in the Backstage view to display the Open dialog box.

3 Navigate to the location of the file to be opened (in this case, the USB flash drive, then to the CIS 101 folder [or your class folder], and then to the Excel folder).

4 Click Save Sable River Foundation to select the file to be opened.

5 Click the Open button (Open dialog box) to open the selected file and display the opened workbook in the Excel window.

AutoCalculate

BTW

AutoCalculate
Use the AutoCalculate area on the status bar to check your work as you enter data in a worksheet. If you enter large amounts of data, you select a range of data and then check the AutoCalculate area to provide insight into statistics about the data you entered. Often, you will have an intuitive feel for whether the numbers are accurate or if you may have made a mistake while entering the data.

You easily can obtain a total, an average, or other information about the numbers in a range by using the **AutoCalculate area** on the status bar. First, select the range of cells containing the numbers you want to check. Next, right-click the AutoCalculate area to display the Status Bar Configuration shortcut menu (Figure 1–72). The check mark to the left of the active functions (Average, Count, and Sum) indicates that the sum, count, and average of the selected range are displayed in the AutoCalculate area on the status bar. The functions of the AutoCalculate commands on the Status Bar Configuration shortcut menu are described in Table 1–4.

Table 1–4 AutoCalculate Shortcut Menu Commands	
Command	**Function**
Average	AutoCalculate area displays the average of the numbers in the selected range
Count	AutoCalculate area displays the number of nonblank cells in the selected range
Numerical Count	AutoCalculate area displays the number of cells containing numbers in the selected range
Minimum	AutoCalculate area displays the lowest value in the selected range
Maximum	AutoCalculate area displays the highest value in the selected range
Sum	AutoCalculate area displays the sum of the numbers in the selected range

To Use the AutoCalculate Area to Determine a Maximum

The following steps display the largest amounts of funds raised for any city for the Fun Runs fundraising activity.

1

- Select the range B6:G6 and then right-click the AutoCalculate area on the status bar to display the Customize Status Bar shortcut menu (Figure 1–72).

What is displayed on the Customize Status Bar shortcut menu?

This shortcut menu includes several commands that allow you to control the items displayed on the Customize Status Bar shortcut menu. The AutoCalculate area includes six commands as well as the result of the associated calculation on the right side of the menu.

Figure 1–72

2

- Click Maximum on the shortcut menu to display the Maximum value in the range B6:G6 in the AutoCalculate area of the status bar.

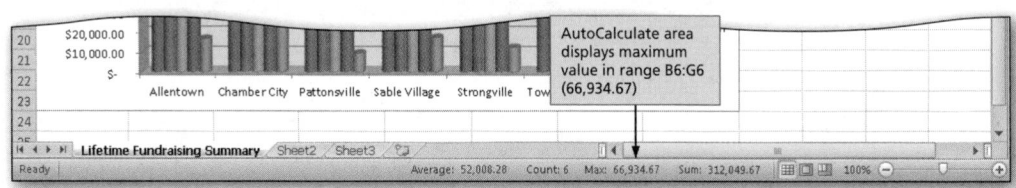

Figure 1–73

- Click anywhere on the worksheet to cause the shortcut menu to disappear (Figure 1–73).

3

- Right-click the AutoCalculate area and then click Maximum on the shortcut menu to cause the Maximum value to no longer appear in the AutoCalculate area.

- Click anywhere on the worksheet to cause the shortcut menu to disappear.

Correcting Errors

You can correct errors on a worksheet using one of several methods. The method you choose will depend on the extent of the error and whether you notice it while typing the data or after you have entered the incorrect data into the cell.

Correcting Errors While You Are Typing Data into a Cell

If you notice an error while you are typing data into a cell, press the BACKSPACE key to erase the incorrect characters and then type the correct characters. If the error is a major one, click the Cancel box in the formula bar or press the ESC key to erase the entire entry and then reenter the data from the beginning.

Correcting Errors After Entering Data into a Cell

If you find an error in the worksheet after entering the data, you can correct the error in one of two ways:

1. If the entry is short, select the cell, retype the entry correctly, and then click the Enter box or press the ENTER key. The new entry will replace the old entry.

2. If the entry in the cell is long and the errors are minor, using Edit mode may be a better choice than retyping the cell entry. Use the Edit mode as described below.

   a. Double-click the cell containing the error to switch Excel to Edit mode. In **Edit mode**, Excel displays the active cell entry in the formula bar and a flashing insertion point in the active cell (Figure 1–74). With Excel in Edit mode, you can edit the contents directly in the cell — a procedure called **in-cell editing**.

   b. Make changes using in-cell editing, as indicated below.

   (1) To insert new characters between two characters, place the insertion point between the two characters and begin typing. Excel inserts the new characters at the location of the insertion point.

   (2) To delete a character in the cell, move the insertion point to the left of the character you want to delete and then press the DELETE key or place the insertion point to the right of the character you want to delete and then press the BACKSPACE key. You also can use the mouse to drag through the character or adjacent characters you want to delete and then press the DELETE key or click the Cut button (Home tab | Clipboard group).

   (3) When you are finished editing an entry, click the Enter box or press the ENTER key.

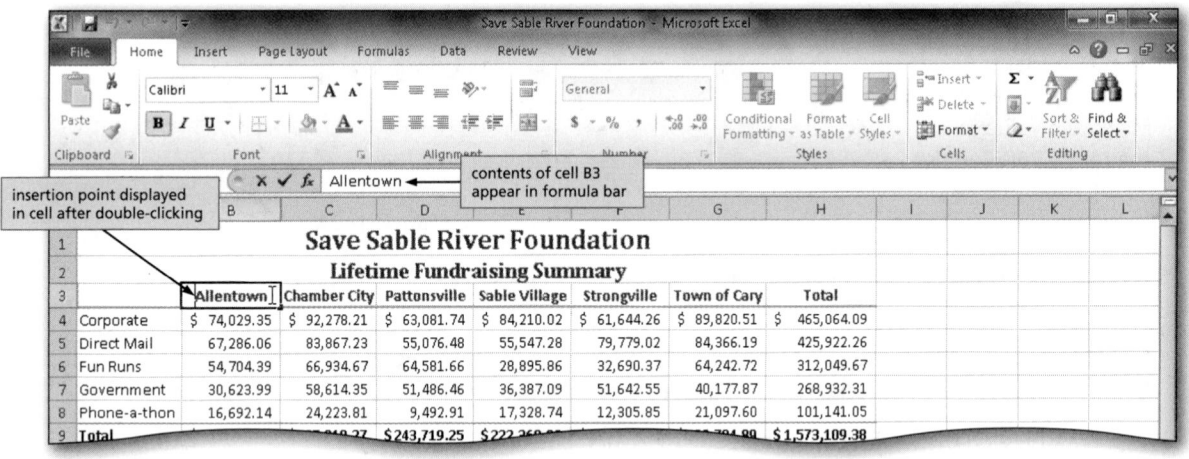

Figure 1–74

When Excel enters the Edit mode, the keyboard usually is in Insert mode. In **Insert mode**, as you type a character, Excel inserts the character and moves all characters to the right of the typed character one position to the right. You can change to Overtype mode by pressing the INSERT key. In **Overtype mode**, Excel overtypes, or replaces, the character to the right of the insertion point. The INSERT key toggles the keyboard between Insert mode and Overtype mode.

While in Edit mode, you may have reason to move the insertion point to various points in the cell, select portions of the data in the cell, or switch from inserting characters to overtyping characters. Table 1–5 summarizes the more common tasks performed during in-cell editing.

Table 1–5 Summary of In-Cell Editing Tasks

	Task	Mouse	Keyboard
1	Move the insertion point to the beginning of data in a cell.	Point to the left of the first character and click.	Press HOME
2	Move the insertion point to the end of data in a cell.	Point to the right of the last character and click.	Press END
3	Move the insertion point anywhere in a cell.	Point to the appropriate position and click the character.	Press RIGHT ARROW or LEFT ARROW
4	Highlight one or more adjacent characters.	Drag the mouse pointer through adjacent characters.	Press SHIFT+RIGHT ARROW or SHIFT+LEFT ARROW
5	Select all data in a cell.	Double-click the cell with the insertion point in the cell if there are no spaces in the data in the cell.	
6	Delete selected characters.	Click the Cut button (Home tab | Clipboard group)	Press DELETE
7	Delete characters to the left of the insertion point.		Press BACKSPACE
8	Delete characters to the right of the insertion point.		Press DELETE
9	Toggle between Insert and Overtype modes.		Press INSERT

BTW

Excel Help
At any time while using Excel, you can find answers to questions and display information about various topics through Excel Help. Used properly, this form of assistance can increase your productivity and reduce your frustrations by minimizing the time you spend learning how to use Excel. For instruction about Excel Help and exercises that will help you gain confidence in using it, read the Office 2010 and Windows 7 chapter at the beginning of this book.

Undoing the Last Cell Entry

Excel provides the Undo command on the Quick Access Toolbar (Figure 1–75), which allows you to erase recent cell entries. Thus, if you enter incorrect data in a cell and notice it immediately, click the Undo button and Excel changes the cell entry to what it was prior to the incorrect data entry.

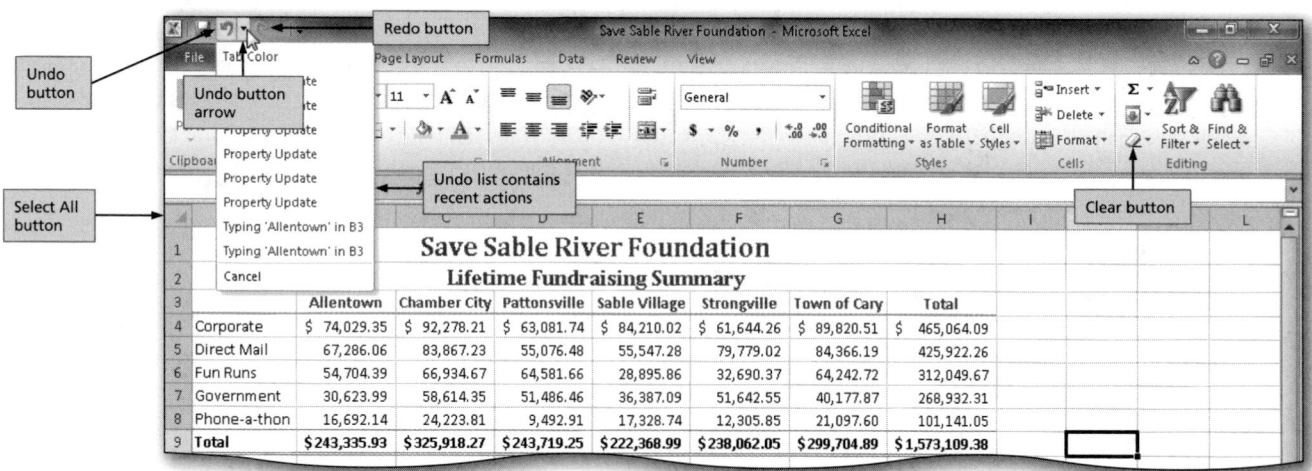

Figure 1–75

Excel remembers the last 100 actions you have completed. Thus, you can undo up to 100 previous actions by clicking the Undo button arrow to display the Undo list and then clicking the action to be undone (Figure 1–75). You can drag through several actions in the Undo list to undo all of them at once. If no actions are available for Excel to undo, then the Undo button is dimmed and inoperative.

The Redo button, next to the Undo button on the Quick Access Toolbar, allows you to repeat previous actions.

Clearing a Cell or Range of Cells

If you enter data into the wrong cell or range of cells, you can erase, or clear, the data using one of the first four methods listed below. The fifth method clears the formatting from the selected cells.

TO CLEAR CELL ENTRIES USING THE FILL HANDLE

1. Select the cell or range of cells and then point to the fill handle so the mouse pointer changes to a crosshair.
2. Drag the fill handle back into the selected cell or range until a shadow covers the cell or cells you want to erase. Release the mouse button.

TO CLEAR CELL ENTRIES USING THE SHORTCUT MENU

1. Select the cell or range of cells to be cleared.
2. Right-click the selection.
3. Click Clear Contents on the shortcut menu.

TO CLEAR CELL ENTRIES USING THE DELETE KEY

1. Select the cell or range of cells to be cleared.
2. Press the DELETE key.

TO CLEAR CELL ENTRIES AND FORMATTING USING THE CLEAR BUTTON

1. Select the cell or range of cells to be cleared.
2. Click the Clear button (Home tab | Editing group) (Figure 1–75 on the previous page).
3. Click Clear Contents on the menu.

TO CLEAR FORMATTING USING THE CELL STYLES BUTTON

1. Select the cell or range of cells from which you want to remove the formatting.
2. Click the Cell Styles button (Home tab | Styles group) and point to Normal.
3. Click Normal in the Cell Styles Gallery.

The Clear button (Home tab | Editing group) is the only command that clears both the cell entry and the cell formatting. As you are clearing cell entries, always remember that you should *never press the* SPACEBAR *to clear a cell*. Pressing the SPACEBAR enters a blank character. A blank character is text and is different from an empty cell, even though the cell may appear empty.

Clearing the Entire Worksheet

If the required worksheet edits are extremely extensive, you may want to clear the entire worksheet and start over. To clear the worksheet or delete an embedded chart, you would use the following steps.

TO CLEAR THE ENTIRE WORKSHEET

1. Click the Select All button on the worksheet (Figure 1–75).
2. Click the Clear button (Home tab | Editing group) and then click Clear All on the Clear menu to delete both the entries and formats.

The Select All button selects the entire worksheet. Instead of clicking the Select All button, you can press CTRL+A. To clear an unsaved workbook, click the workbook's Close Window button or click the Close button in the Backstage view. Click the No button if the Microsoft Excel dialog box asks if you want to save changes. To start a new, blank workbook, click the New button in the Backstage view.

To delete an embedded chart, you would complete the following steps.

TO DELETE AN EMBEDDED CHART

1. Click the chart to select it.
2. Press the DELETE key.

To Quit Excel

The project now is complete. The following steps quit Excel. For a detailed example of the procedure summarized below, refer to the Office 2010 and Windows 7 chapter at the beginning of this book.

1 If you have one Excel workbook open, click the Close button on the right side of the title bar to close the document and quit Excel; or if you have multiple Excel workbooks open, click File on the Ribbon to open the Backstage view and then click Exit in the Backstage view to close all open workbooks and quit Excel.

2 If a Microsoft Office Excel dialog box appears, click the Save button to save any changes made to the document since the last save.

BTW | **Quitting Excel**
Do not forget to remove your USB flash drive from the USB port after quitting Excel, especially if you are working in a laboratory environment. Nothing can be more frustrating than leaving all of your hard work behind on a USB flash drive for the next user.

Chapter Summary

In this chapter you have learned how to enter text and numbers to create a worksheet, how to select a range, how to use the Sum button, format cells, insert a chart, and preview and print a worksheet. The items listed below include all the new Excel skills you have learned in this chapter.

1. To Start Excel (EX 6)
2. Enter the Worksheet Titles (EX 8)
3. Enter Column Titles (EX 10)
4. Enter Row Titles (EX 12)
5. Enter Numbers (EX 13)
6. Sum a Column of Numbers (EX 15)
7. Copy a Cell to Adjacent Cells in a Row (EX 17)
8. Determine Multiple Totals at the Same Time (EX 18)
9. Save a Workbook (EX 20)
10. Change a Cell Style (EX 22)
11. Change the Font (EX 24)
12. Bold a Cell (EX 25)
13. Increase the Font Size of a Cell Entry (EX 26)
14. Change the Font Color of a Cell Entry (EX 27)
15. Center Cell Entries Across Columns by Merging Cells (EX 28)
16. Format Column Titles and the Total Row (EX 29)
17. Format Numbers in the Worksheet (EX 31)
18. Adjust the Column Width (EX 33)
19. Use the Name Box to Select a Cell (EX 34)
20. Add a Clustered Cylinder Chart to the Worksheet (EX 38)
21. Change the Worksheet Names (EX 42)
22. Change Document Properties (EX 43)
23. Save an Existing Workbook with the Same File Name (EX 45)
24. Preview and Print a Worksheet in Landscape Orientation (EX 46)
25. Quit Excel (EX 47)
26. Start Excel (EX 47)
27. Open a Workbook from Excel (EX 48)
28. Use the AutoCalculate Area to Determine a Maximum (EX 49)
29. Clear Cell Entries Using the Fill Handle (EX 52)
30. Clear Cell Entries Using the Shortcut Menu (EX 52)
31. Clear Cell Entries Using the DELETE Key (EX 52)
32. Clear Cell Entries and Formatting Using the Clear Button (EX 52)
33. Clear Formatting Using the Cell Styles Button (EX 52)
34. Clear the Entire Worksheet (EX 52)
35. Delete an Embedded Chart (EX 53)

If you have a SAM 2010 user profile, your instructor may have assigned an autogradable version of this assignment. If so, log into the SAM 2010 Web site at www.cengage.com/sam2010 to download the instruction and start files.

Learn It Online

Test your knowledge of chapter content and key terms.

Instructions: To complete the Learn It Online exercises, start your browser, click the Address bar, and then enter the Web address **scsite.com/ex2010/learn**. When the Excel 2010 Learn It Online page is displayed, click the link for the exercise you want to complete and then read the instructions.

Chapter Reinforcement TF, MC, and SA
A series of true/false, multiple choice, and short answer questions that test your knowledge of the chapter content.

Flash Cards
An interactive learning environment where you identify chapter key terms associated with displayed definitions.

Practice Test
A series of multiple choice questions that test your knowledge of chapter content and key terms.

Who Wants To Be a Computer Genius?
An interactive game that challenges your knowledge of chapter content in the style of a television quiz show.

Wheel of Terms
An interactive game that challenges your knowledge of chapter key terms in the style of the television show *Wheel of Fortune*.

Crossword Puzzle Challenge
A crossword puzzle that challenges your knowledge of key terms presented in the chapter.

Apply Your Knowledge

Reinforce the skills and apply the concepts you learned in this chapter.

Changing the Values in a Worksheet

Instructions: Start Excel. Open the workbook Apply 1–1 Clothes Campus Third Quarter Expenses (Figure 1–76a). See the inside back cover of this book for instructions for downloading the Data Files for Students, or see your instructor for information on accessing the files required in this book.

1. Make the changes to the worksheet described in Table 1–6 so that the worksheet appears as shown in Figure 1–76b. As you edit the values in the cells containing numeric data, watch the totals in row 7, the totals in column F, and the chart change.

2. Change the worksheet title in cell A1 to the Title cell style and then merge and center it across columns A through F. Use buttons in the Font group on the Home tab on the Ribbon to change the worksheet subtitle in cell A2 to 16-point Cambria red, bold font and then center it across columns A through F. Use the Red, Accent 2 theme color (column 6, row 1 on the Font gallery) for the red font color.

3. Apply the worksheet name, Third Quarter Expenses, to the sheet tab and apply the Red, Accent 2 theme color to the sheet tab.

4. Change the document properties as specified by your instructor. Save the workbook using the file name, Apply 1–1 Clothed for Campus Third Quarter Expenses. Submit the revised workbook as specified by your instructor.

Table 1–6 New Worksheet Data	
Cell	**Change Cell Contents To**
A1	Clothed for Campus
B4	7829.50
C4	19057.83
D5	24217.92
E5	25859.62
E6	35140.84

(a) Before

(b) After

Figure 1–76

Extend Your Knowledge

Extend the skills you learned in this chapter and experiment with new skills. You may need to use Help to complete the assignment.

Formatting a Worksheet and Adding Additional Charts

Instructions: Start Excel. Open the workbook Extend 1–1 Pack Right Moving Supplies. See the inside back cover of this book for instructions for downloading the Data Files for Students, or see your instructor for information on accessing the files required in this book. Perform the following tasks to format cells in the worksheet and to add two charts to the worksheet.

1. Use the commands in the Font group on the Home tab on the Ribbon to change the font of the title in cell A1 to 22-point Arial Black, green, bold, and the subtitle of the worksheet to 14-point Arial, red, bold.

2. Select the range A3:G8, click the Insert tab on the Ribbon, and then click the Dialog Box Launcher in the Charts group on the Ribbon to open the Insert Chart dialog box. If necessary, drag the lower-right corner of the Insert Chart dialog box to expand it (Figure 1–77).

Figure 1–77

3. Insert a Stacked Area in 3-D chart by clicking the Stacked Area in 3-D chart in the gallery and then clicking the OK button. You may need to use the scroll box on the right side of the Insert Chart dialog box to view the Area charts in the gallery. Move the chart either below or to the right of the data in the worksheet. Click the Design tab and apply a chart style of your choice to the chart.

4. Deselect the chart and reselect the range A3:G8, and then follow Step 3 above to insert a Clustered Horizontal Cone chart in the worksheet. Move the chart either below or to the right of the data so that each chart does not overlap the Stacked Area in 3-D chart. Make sure to make the values on the horizontal axis readable by expanding the size of the chart. Choose a different chart style for this chart than the one you selected for the Stacked Area in 3-D chart.

5. Resize each chart so that each snaps to the worksheet gridlines. You may need to scroll the worksheet to resize and view the charts. Preview the worksheet.

6. Apply a worksheet name to the sheet tab and apply a color of your choice to the sheet tab.

7. Change the document properties as specified by your instructor. Save the workbook using the file name, Extend 1–1 Pack Right Moving Supplies Charts. Submit the revised workbook as specified by your instructor.

Make It Right

Analyze a workbook and correct all errors and/or improve the design.

Fixing Formatting Problems and Data Errors in a Worksheet

Instructions: Start Excel. Open the workbook Make It Right 1–1 Pets. See the inside back cover of this book for instructions for downloading the Data Files for Students, or see your instructor for information on accessing the files required for this book. Correct the following formatting problems and data errors (Figure 1–78) in the worksheet, while keeping in mind the guidelines presented in this chapter.

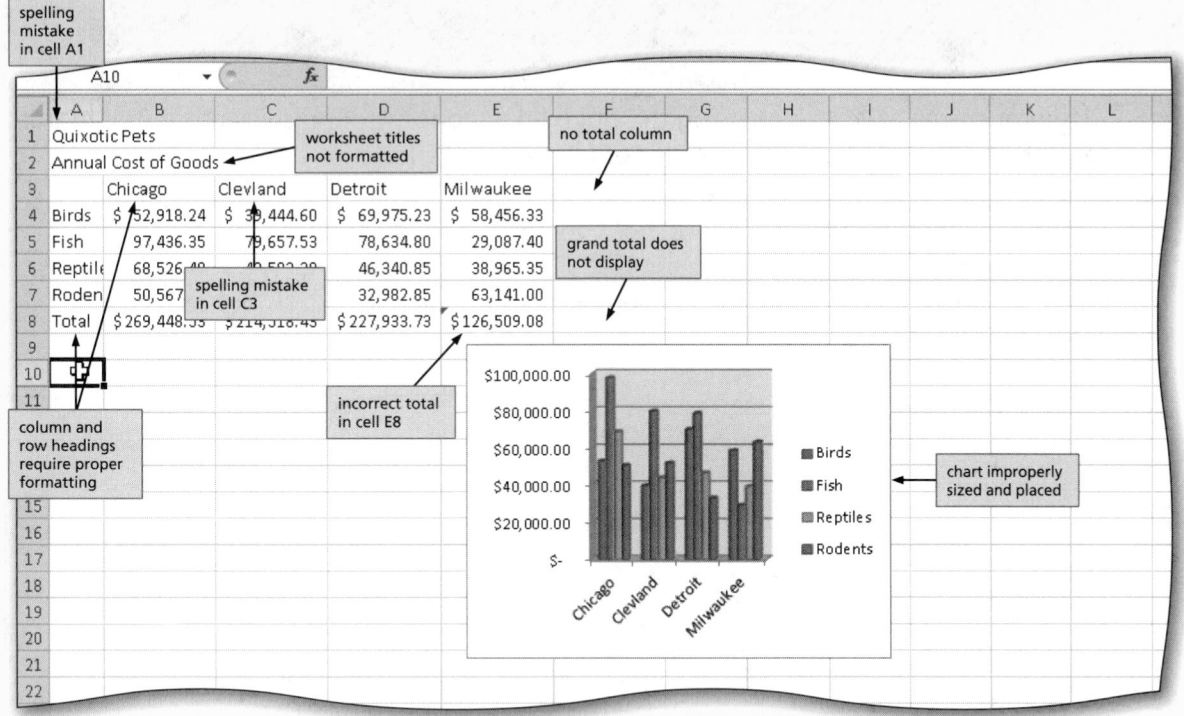

Figure 1–78

1. Merge and center the worksheet title and subtitle appropriately.

2. Format the worksheet title with a cell style appropriate for a worksheet title.

3. Format the subtitle using commands in the Font group on the Home tab on the Ribbon and apply the Red, Accent 2 color to the subtitle.

4. Correct the spelling mistake in cell A1 by changing Quixotic to Exotic. Correct the spelling mistake in cell C3 by changing Clevland to Cleveland.

Continued >

Make It Right *continued*

5. Add a column header for totals in column F, create the necessary totals in column E, and create the necessary totals in row 8 and column F.

6. Apply proper formatting to the column headers and total row, including centering the column headers.

7. Adjust the column sizes so that all data in each column is visible.

8. Create the grand total for the annual cost of goods.

9. The SUM function in cell E8 does not sum all of the numbers in the column. Correct this error by editing the range for the SUM function in the cell.

10. Resize and move the chart so that it is below the worksheet data and does not extend past the right edge of the worksheet data. Be certain to snap the chart to the worksheet gridlines by holding down the ALT key as you resize the chart to the right edge of column F and the bottom of row 22.

11. Apply a worksheet name to the sheet tab and apply the Aqua, Accent 5 color to the sheet tab.

12. Change the document properties as specified by your instructor. Save the workbook using the file name, Make It Right 1–1 Exotic Pets Annual Cost of Goods. Submit the revised workbook as specified by your instructor.

In the Lab

Design and/or create a workbook using the guidelines, concepts, and skills presented in this chapter. Labs 1, 2, and 3 are listed in order of increasing difficulty.

Lab 1: Annual Revenue Analysis Worksheet

Problem: You work as a spreadsheet specialist for A Healthy Body Shop, a high-end total fitness center franchise. Your manager has asked you to develop an annual revenue analysis worksheet similar to the one shown in Figure 1–79.

Figure 1–79

Instructions: Perform the following tasks.

1. Start Excel. Enter the worksheet title, A Healthy Body Shop, in cell A1 and the worksheet subtitle, Annual Revenue Analysis, in cell A2. Beginning in row 3, enter the franchise locations, fitness activities, and annual revenues shown in Table 1–7.

Table 1–7 A Healthy Body Shop Annual Revenues

	Atlanta	Boston	New York	Phoenix	Portland
Aquatics	72528.50	53461.85	88367.00	87288.00	65367.37
Cardiovascular	65371.00	92549.86	78345.85	91692.21	58936.63
Dance	53187.96	45493.24	72808.19	57019.34	70114.93
Weight Training	45910.25	85703.71	78719.20	88500.60	47105.30
Yoga & Stretching	58292.50	66884.85	74348.30	76219.00	57390.23

2. Create totals for each franchise location, fitness activity, and company grand total.

3. Format the worksheet title with the Title cell style. Center the title across columns A through G. Do not be concerned if the edges of the worksheet title are not displayed.

4. Format the worksheet subtitle to 14-point Constantia dark blue, bold font, and center it across columns A through G.

5. Use Cell Styles to format the range A3:G3 with the Heading 3 cell style, the range A4:G8 with the 40% - Accent 6 cell style, and the range A9:G9 with the Total cell style. Center the column headers in row 3. Apply the Accounting Number format to the range B4:G4 and the range B9:G9. Apply the Comma Style to the range B5:G8. Adjust any column widths to the widest text entry in each column.

6. Select the range A3:F8 and then insert a Clustered Cylinder chart. Apply the Style 26 chart style to the chart. Move and resize the chart so that it appears in the range A11:G24. If the labels along the horizontal axis (x-axis) do not appear as shown in Figure 1–79, then drag the right side of the chart so that it is displayed in the range A11:G24.

7. Apply the worksheet name, Annual Revenue Analysis, to the sheet tab and apply the Orange, Accent 6, Darker 25% color to the sheet tab. Change the document properties, as specified by your instructor.

8. Save the workbook using the file name Lab 1-1 A Healthy Body Shop Annual Revenue Analysis.

9. Preview and print the worksheet in landscape orientation.

10. Make the following two corrections to the sales amounts: 62,675.45 for New York Weight Training (cell D7), 67,238.56 for Portland Cardiovascular (cell F5). After you enter the corrections, the company totals in cell G9 should equal $1,723,864.05.

11. Preview and print the revised worksheet in landscape orientation. Close the workbook without saving the changes.

12. Submit the assignment as specified by your instructor.

In the Lab

Lab 2: Semiannual Sales Analysis Worksheet

Problem: As the chief accountant for Play 'em Again, a reseller of cell phones, DVDs, electronic games, MP3 players, and accessories, you have been asked by the vice president to create a worksheet to analyze the semiannual sales for the company by products across sales channels (Figure 1–80 on the following page). The sales channels and corresponding revenue by product for the year are shown in Table 1–8.

Continued >

In the Lab *continued*

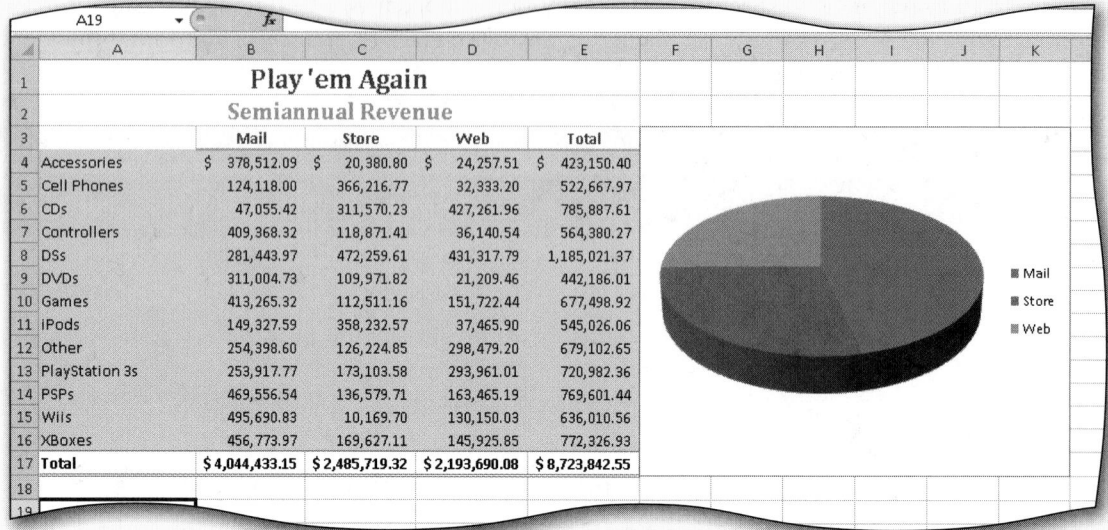

Figure 1–80

Instructions: Perform the following tasks.

1. Create the worksheet shown in Figure 1–80 using the data in Table 1–8.

2. Use the SUM function to determine total revenue for the three sales channels, the totals for each product, and the company total. Add column and row headings for the totals row and totals column, as appropriate.

Table 1–8 Play 'em Again Semiannual Revenue

	Mail	Store	Web
Accessories	378512.09	20380.80	24257.51
Cell Phones	124118.00	366216.77	32333.20
CDs	47055.42	311570.23	427261.96
Controllers	409368.32	118871.41	36140.54
DSs	281443.97	472259.61	431317.79
DVDs	311004.73	109971.82	21209.46
Games	413265.32	112511.16	151722.44
iPods	149327.59	358232.57	37465.90
Other	254398.60	126224.85	298479.20
PlayStation 3s	253917.77	173103.58	293961.01
PSPs	469556.54	136579.71	163465.19
Wiis	495690.83	10169.70	130150.03
XBoxes	456773.97	169627.11	145925.85

3. Format the worksheet title with the Title cell style and center it across columns A through E. Use the Font group on the Ribbon to format the worksheet subtitle to 16-point Cambria red, bold font. Center the title across columns A through E.

4. Format the range B3:E3 with the Heading 3 cell style and center the text in the cells. Format the range A4:E16 with the 20% - Accent 4 cell style, and the range B17:E17 with the Total cell style. Format cells B4:E4 and B17:E17 with the Accounting Number Format and cells B5:E16 with the Comma Style numeric format.

5. Create a pie chart that shows the revenue contributions of each sales channel. Chart the sales channel names (B3:D3) and corresponding totals (B17:D17). That is, select the range B3:D3, and then while holding down the CTRL key, select the range B17:D17. Insert the Pie in 3-D chart, as shown in Figure 1–80, by using the Pie button (Insert tab | Charts group). Use the chart location F3: K17.

6. Apply the worksheet name, Semiannual Revenue, to the sheet tab and apply the Purple, Accent 4, Lighter 80% color to the sheet tab. Change the document properties, as specified by your instructor.

7. Save the workbook using the file name, Lab 1-2 Play 'em Again Semiannual Revenue. Print the worksheet in landscape orientation.

8. Two corrections to the figures were sent in from the accounting department. The correct revenue is $118,124.45 for Cell Phones sold through the mail (cell B5) and $43,573.67 for iPods sold over the Web (cell D11). After you enter the two corrections, the company total in cell E17 should equal $8,723,956.77. Print the revised worksheet in landscape orientation.

9. Use the Undo button to change the worksheet back to the original numbers in Table 1–8. Use the Redo button to change the worksheet back to the revised state.

10. Close Excel without saving the latest changes. Start Excel and open the workbook saved in Step 7. Double-click cell C14 and use in-cell editing to change the Store PSPs revenue to $128,857.32. Write the company total in cell E17 at the top of the first printout. Click the Undo button.

11. Click cell A1 and then click the Merge & Center button on the Home tab on the Ribbon to split cell A1 into cells A1, B1, C1, D1, and E1. To merge the cells into one again, select the range A1:E1 and then click the Merge & Center button.

12. Close the workbook without saving the changes. Submit the assignment as specified by your instructor.

In the Lab

Lab 3: Projected College Cash Flow Analysis Worksheet

Problem: Attending college is an expensive proposition and your resources are limited. To plan for your four-year college career, you have decided to organize your anticipated resources and expenses in a worksheet. The data required to prepare your worksheet is shown in Table 1–9.

Table 1–9 College Cost and Resources

Resources	Freshman	Sophomore	Junior	Senior
529 Plans	2700.00	2889.00	3091.23	3307.62
Financial Aid	5250.00	5617.50	6010.73	6431.48
Job	3100.00	3317.00	3549.19	3797.63
Parents	3700.00	3959.00	4236.13	4532.66
Savings	4250.00	4547.50	4865.83	5206.43
Other	1100.00	1177.00	1259.39	1347.55
Expenses	**Freshman**	**Sophomore**	**Junior**	**Senior**
Activities Fee	500.00	535.00	572.45	612.52
Books	650.00	695.50	744.19	796.28
Clothes	750.00	802.50	858.68	918.78
Entertainment	1650.00	1765.50	1889.09	2021.32
Room & Board	7200.00	7704.00	8243.28	8820.31
Tuition	8250.00	8827.50	9445.43	10106.60
Miscellaneous	1100.00	1177.00	1259.39	1347.55

Continued >

In the Lab *continued*

Instructions Part 1: Using the numbers in Table 1–9, create the worksheet shown in columns A through F in Figure 1–81. Format the worksheet title as Calibri 24-point bold purple. Merge and center the worksheet title in cell A1 across columns A through F. Format the worksheet subtitles in cells A2 and A11 as Calibri 16-point bold red. Format the ranges A3:F3 and A12:F12 with the Heading 2 cell style and center the text in the cells. Format the ranges A4:F9 and A13:F19 with the 20% - Accent 2 cell style, and the ranges A10:F10 and A20:F20 with the Total cell style.

Change the name of the sheet tab and apply the Purple color from the Standard Colors area to the sheet tab. Update the document properties, including the addition of at least one keyword to the properties, and save the workbook using the file name, Lab 1-3 Part 1 College Resources and Expenses. Print the worksheet. Submit the assignment as specified by your instructor.

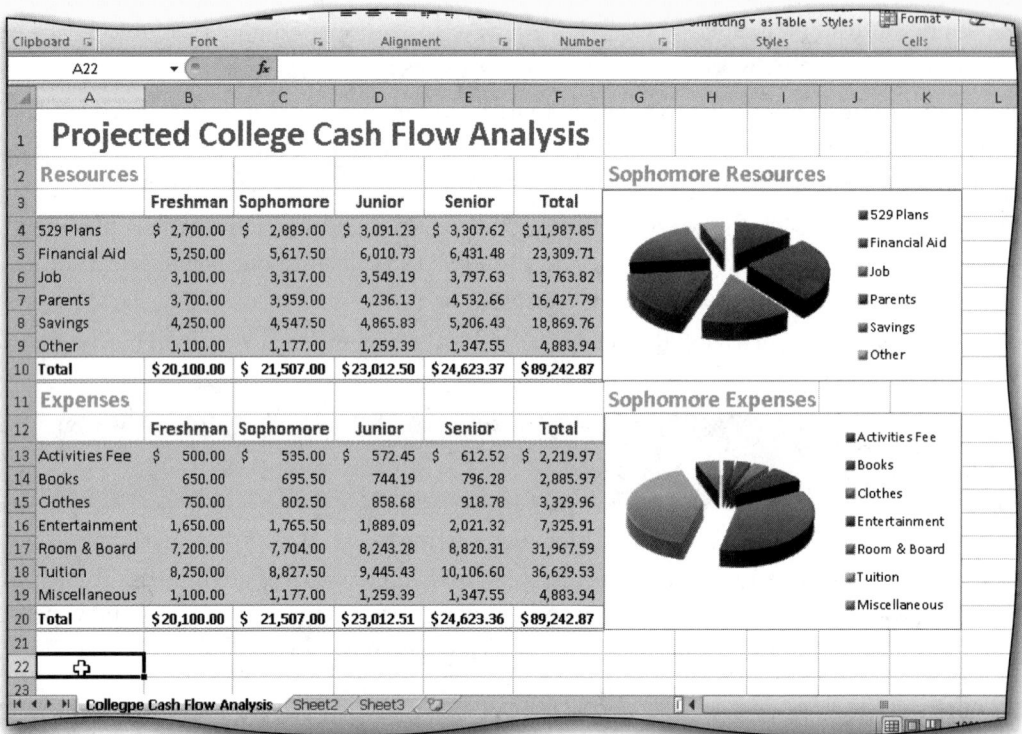

Figure 1–81

After reviewing the numbers, you realize you need to increase manually each of the Sophomore-year expenses in column C by $400, except for the Activities Fee. Change the Sophomore-year expenses to reflect this change. Manually change the Parents resources for the Sophomore year by the amount required to cover the increase in costs. The totals in cells F10 and F20 should equal $91,642.87. Print the worksheet. Close the workbook without saving changes.

Instructions Part 2: Open the workbook Lab 1-3 Part 1 College Resources and Expenses and then save the workbook using the file name, Lab 1-3 Part 2 College Resources and Expenses. Insert an Exploded pie in 3-D chart in the range G3:K10 to show the contribution of each category of resources for the Sophomore year. Chart the ranges A4:A9 and C4:C9 and apply the Style 26 chart style to the chart. Add the Pie chart title as shown in cell G2 in Figure 1–81. Insert an Exploded pie in 3-D chart in the range G12:K20 to show the contribution of each category of expenses for the Sophomore year. Chart the ranges A13:A19 and C13:C19 and apply the Style 26 chart style to the chart. Add the Pie chart title shown in cell G11 in Figure 1–81. Save the workbook. Print the worksheet in landscape orientation. Submit the assignment as specified by your instructor.

Instructions Part 3: Open the workbook Lab 1-3 Part 2 College Resources and Expenses and then save the workbook using the file name, Lab 1-3 Part 3 College Resources and Expenses. A close inspection of Table 1–9 shows that both cost and financial support figures increase 7% each year. Use Excel Help to learn how to enter the data for the last three years using a formula and the Copy and Paste buttons (Home tab | Clipboard group). For example, the formula to enter in cell C4 is =B4*1.07. Enter formulas to replace all the numbers in the range C4:E9 and C13:E19. If necessary, reformat the tables, as described in Part 1. The worksheet should appear as shown in Figure 1–81, except that some of the totals will be off by approximately 0.01 due to rounding errors. Save the workbook. Submit the assignment as specified by your instructor. Close the workbook without saving changes.

Cases and Places

Apply your creative thinking and problem solving skills to design and implement a solution.

1: Analyzing Quarterly Expenses

Academic

To estimate the funds needed by your school's Travel Club to make it through the upcoming quarter, you decide to create a report for the club itemizing the expected quarterly expenses. The anticipated expenses are listed in Table 1–10. Use the concepts and techniques presented in this chapter to create the worksheet and an embedded Clustered Cylinder chart. Be sure to use an appropriate chart style that compares the quarterly cost of each expense. Total each expense item and each quarter. Include a grand total for all of the expenses. Use the AutoCalculate area to determine the average amount spent per quarter on each expense. Manually insert the averages with appropriate titles in an appropriate area on the worksheet.

Table 1–10 Travel Club Quarterly Expenses				
	1st Quarter	2nd Quarter	3rd Quarter	4th Quarter
Copies and Supplies	75	50	80	150
Meeting Room Rent	400	425	400	425
Miscellaneous	150	100	175	70
Refreshments	130	155	150	225
Speaker Fees	200	200	400	500
Travel	450	375	500	375

2: Create an Exploded Pie in 3-D Chart to Summarize Property Values

Personal

Your wealthy Aunt Nicole owns several properties of varying value. She would like to see the values of the properties in a worksheet and chart that helps her to better understand her investments. She has asked you to develop a worksheet totaling the values of the properties and also to include other relevant statistics. The property values are: Property 1, $56,671.99; Property 2, $82,276.58; Property 3, $60,135.45; Property 4, $107,373.39; and Property 5, $87,512.82. Create an Exploded pie in 3-D chart to illustrate the relative property values. Use the AutoCalculate area to find the average, maximum, and minimum property values and manually enter them and their corresponding identifiers in an appropriate area of the worksheet. Use the Sum button to total the property values.

Continued >

Cases and Places *continued*

3: Analyzing Historical Yearly Sales

Business

You are working part-time for Noble's Mobile Services. Your manager has asked you to prepare a worksheet to help her analyze historical yearly sales by type of product (Table 1–11). Use the concepts and techniques presented in this chapter to create the worksheet and an embedded 3-D Clustered Column chart that includes proper numerical formatting, totaling, and formatting of the worksheet.

Table 1–11 Noble's Mobile Services Historical Yearly Sales				
	2008	2009	2010	2011
Camera Phones	92598	10487	136791	176785
Headsets	9035	8909	4886	6512
Music Phones	57942	44923	54590	67696
Other Accessories	27604	38793	24483	33095
Satellite Radios	17161	19293	30763	44367
Standard Mobile Phones	8549	9264	7600	6048
Wireless PDAs	57963	68059	103025	87367

2 | Formulas, Functions, and Formatting

Objectives

You will have mastered the material in this chapter when you can:

- Enter formulas using the keyboard
- Enter formulas using Point mode
- Apply the AVERAGE, MAX, and MIN functions
- Verify a formula using Range Finder
- Apply a theme to a workbook
- Apply a date format to a cell or range

- Add conditional formatting to cells
- Change column width and row height
- Check the spelling in a worksheet
- Set margins, headers, and footers in Page Layout view
- Preview and print versions of a worksheet

2 | Formulas, Functions, and Formatting

Introduction

In Chapter 1, you learned how to enter data, sum values, format a worksheet to make it easier to read, and draw a chart. This chapter continues to highlight these topics and presents some new ones.

The new topics covered in this chapter include using formulas and functions to create a worksheet. A **function** is a prewritten formula that is built into Excel. Other new topics include option buttons, verifying formulas, applying a theme to a worksheet, adding borders, formatting numbers and text, using conditional formatting, changing the widths of columns and heights of rows, spell checking, using alternative types of worksheet displays and printouts, and adding page headers and footers to a worksheet. One alternative worksheet display and printout shows the formulas in the worksheet instead of the values. When you display the formulas in the worksheet, you see exactly what text, data, formulas, and functions you have entered into it.

Project — Worksheet with Formulas and Functions

The project in this chapter follows proper design guidelines and uses Excel to create the worksheet shown in Figure 2–1. The Mobile Masses Store opened its doors when consumer demand for mobile devices, such as mobile phones and PDAs, had just begun. The store's owners pay each employee on a biweekly basis. Before the owners pay the employees, they summarize the hours worked, pay rate, and tax information for each employee to ensure that the business properly compensates its employees. This summary includes information such as the employee names, hire dates, number of dependents, hours worked, hourly pay rate, net pay, and tax information. As the complexity of the task of creating the summary increases, the owners want to use Excel to create a biweekly payroll report.

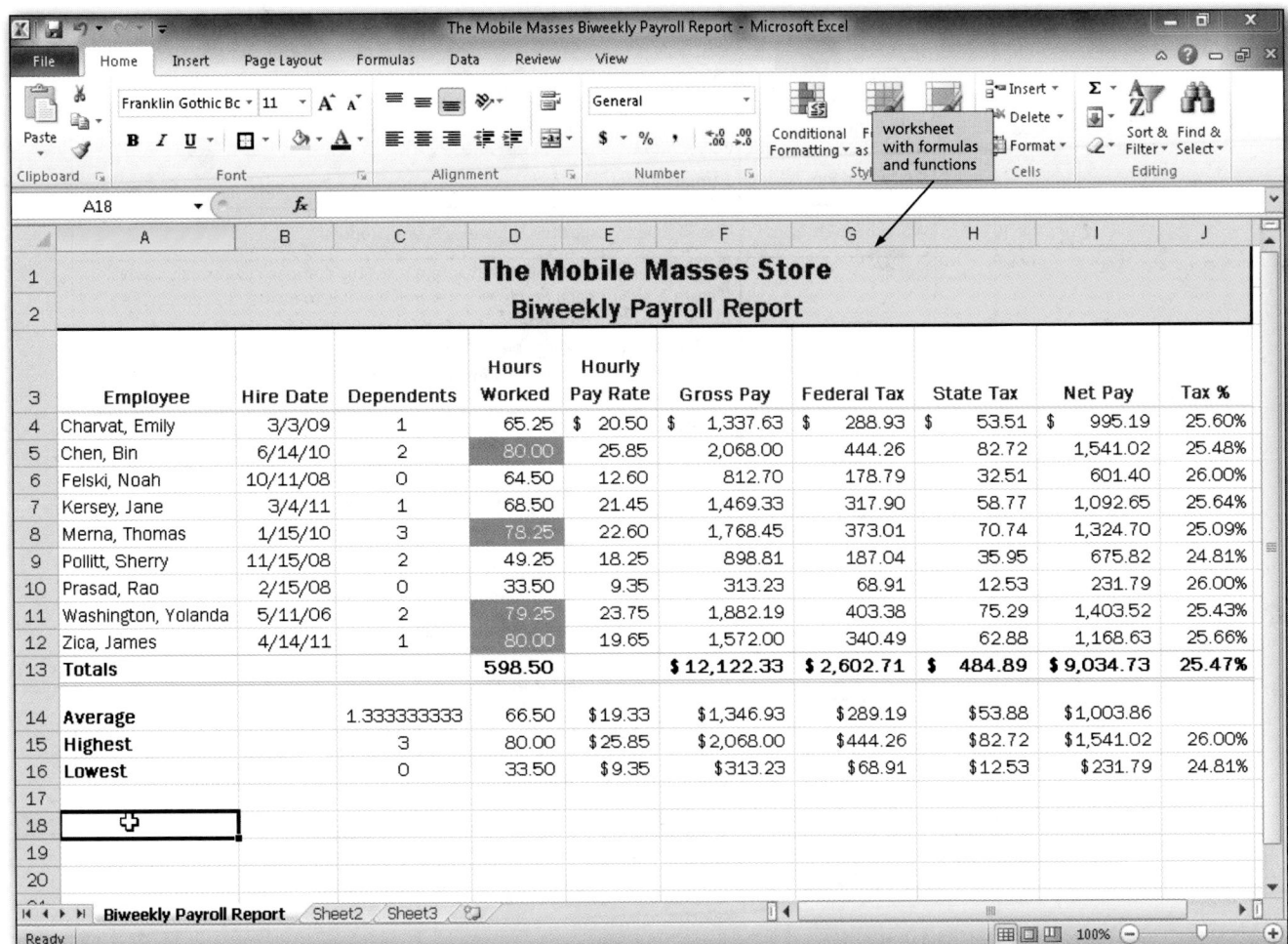

Figure 2 –1

Recall that the first step in creating an effective worksheet is to make sure you understand what is required. The people who will use the worksheet usually provide the requirements. The requirements document for The Mobile Masses Store Biweekly Payroll Report worksheet includes the following needs: source of data, summary of calculations, and other facts about its development (Figure 2 –2 on the following page).

REQUEST FOR NEW WORKSHEET

Date Submitted:	April 16, 2012
Submitted By:	Samuel Snyder
Worksheet Title:	The Mobile Masses Store Biweekly Payroll Report
Needs:	An easy-to-read worksheet that summarizes the company's biweekly payroll (Figure 2-3). For each employee, the worksheet is to include the employee's name, hire date, dependents, hours worked, hourly pay rate, gross pay, federal tax, state tax, net pay, and total tax percent. The worksheet also should include totals and the average, highest value, and lowest value for column of numbers specified below.
Source of Data:	The data supplied by Samuel includes the employee names, hire dates, hours worked, and hourly pay rates. This data is shown in Table 2-1 on page EX 72.
Calculations:	The following calculations must be made for each of the employees: 1. Gross Pay = Hours Worked × Hourly Pay Rate 2. Federal Tax = 0.22 × (Gross Pay – Dependents * 24.32) 3. State Tax = 0.04 × Gross Pay 4. Net Pay = Gross Pay – (Federal Tax + State Tax) 5. Tax % = (Federal Tax + State Tax) / Gross Pay 6. Compute the totals for hours worked, gross pay, federal tax, state tax, and net pay. 7. Compute the total tax percent. 8. Use the AVERAGE function to determine the average for dependents, hours worked, hourly pay rate, gross pay, federal tax, state tax, and net pay. 9. Use the MAX and MIN functions to determine the highest and lowest values for dependents, hours worked, hourly pay rate, gross pay, federal tax, state tax, net pay, and total tax percent.

Approvals

Approval Status:	X	Approved
		Rejected
Approved By:	Julie Adams	
Date:	April 23, 2012	
Assigned To:	J. Quasney, Spreadsheet Specialist	

Figure 2–2

Overview

As you read this chapter, you will learn how to create the worksheet shown in Figure 2–1 by performing these general tasks:

- Enter formulas and apply functions in the worksheet
- Add conditional formatting to the worksheet
- Apply a theme to the worksheet
- Set margins, and add headers and footers to a worksheet
- Work with the worksheet in Page Layout view
- Change margins on the worksheet
- Print a section of the worksheet

Formulas, Functions, and Formatting

Plan
Ahead

General Project Decisions
While creating an Excel worksheet, you need to make several decisions that will determine the appearance and characteristics of the finished worksheet. As you create the worksheet necessary to meet the requirements shown in Figure 2–2, you should follow these general guidelines:

1. **Plan the layout of the worksheet.** Rows typically contain items analogous to items in a list. A name could serve as an item in a list, and, therefore, each name could be placed in a row. As a list grows, such as a list of employees, the number of rows in the worksheet will increase. Information about each item in the list and associated calculations should appear in columns.

2. **Determine the necessary formulas and functions needed.** Calculations result from known values. Formulas for such calculations should be known in advance of creating a worksheet. Values such as the average, highest, and lowest values can be calculated using Excel functions as opposed to relying on complex formulas.

3. **Identify how to format various elements of the worksheet.** The appearance of the worksheet affects its ability to express information clearly. Numeric data should be formatted in generally accepted formats, such as using commas as thousands separators and parentheses for negative values.

4. **Establish rules for conditional formatting.** Conditional formatting allows you to format a cell based on the contents of the cell. Decide under which circumstances you would like a cell to stand out from related cells and determine in what way the cell will stand out.

5. **Specify how the hard copy of a worksheet should appear.** When it is possible that a person will want to create a hard copy of a worksheet, care should be taken in the development of the worksheet to ensure that the contents can be presented in a readable manner. Excel prints worksheets in landscape or portrait orientation, and margins can be adjusted to fit more or less data on each page. Headers and footers add an additional level of customization to the printed page.

When necessary, more specific details concerning the above guidelines are presented at appropriate points in the chapter. The chapter also will identify the actions performed and decisions made regarding these guidelines during the creation of the worksheet shown in Figure 2–1 on page EX 67.

In addition, using a sketch of the worksheet can help you visualize its design. The sketch for The Mobile Masses Store Biweekly Payroll Report worksheet includes a title, a subtitle, column and row headings, and the location of data values (Figure 2–3 on the following page). It also uses specific characters to define the desired formatting for the worksheet, as follows:

1. The row of Xs below the leftmost column defines the cell entries as text, such as employee names.
2. The rows of Zs and 9s with slashes, dollar signs, decimal points, commas, and percent signs in the remaining columns define the cell entries as numbers. The Zs indicate that the selected format should instruct Excel to suppress leading 0s. The 9s indicate that the selected format should instruct Excel to display any digits, including 0s.
3. The decimal point means that a decimal point should appear in the cell entry and indicates the number of decimal places to use.
4. The slashes in the second column identify the cell entry as a date.
5. The dollar signs that are not adjacent to the Zs in the first row below the column headings and in the total row signify a fixed dollar sign. The dollar signs that are adjacent to the Zs below the total row signify a floating dollar sign, or one that appears next to the first significant digit.

BTW

Aesthetics versus Function
The function, or purpose, of a worksheet is to provide a user with direct ways to accomplish tasks. In designing a worksheet, functional considerations should come before visual aesthetics. Avoid the temptation to use flashy or confusing visual elements within the worksheet. One exception to this guideline occurs when you may need to draw the user's attention to an area of a worksheet that will help the user more easily complete a task.

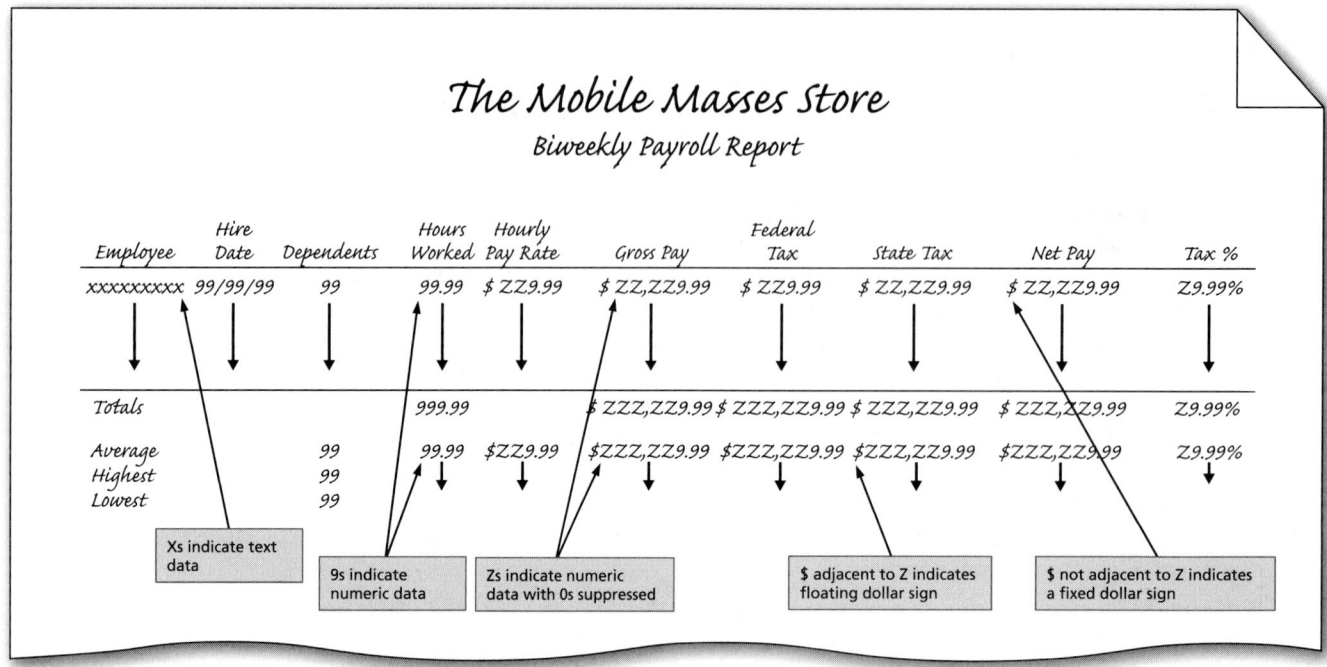

The Mobile Masses Store
Biweekly Payroll Report

Employee	Hire Date	Dependents	Hours Worked	Hourly Pay Rate	Gross Pay	Federal Tax	State Tax	Net Pay	Tax %
xxxxxxxxx	99/99/99	99	99.99	$ ZZ9.99	$ ZZ,ZZ9.99	$ ZZ9.99	$ ZZ,ZZ9.99	$ ZZ,ZZ9.99	Z9.99%
Totals			999.99		$ ZZZ,ZZ9.99	$ ZZZ,ZZ9.99	$ ZZZ,ZZ9.99	$ ZZZ,ZZ9.99	Z9.99%
Average		99	99.99	$ZZ9.99	$ZZZ,ZZ9.99	$ZZZ,ZZ9.99	$ZZZ,ZZ9.99	$ZZZ,ZZ9.99	Z9.99%
Highest		99							
Lowest		99							

Xs indicate text data

9s indicate numeric data

Zs indicate numeric data with 0s suppressed

$ adjacent to Z indicates floating dollar sign

$ not adjacent to Z indicates a fixed dollar sign

Figure 2–3

6. The commas indicate that the selected format should instruct Excel to display a comma separator only if the number has enough digits to the left of the decimal point.

7. The percent sign (%) in the far-right column indicates a percent sign should appear after the number.

With a good comprehension of the requirements document, an understanding of the necessary decisions, and a sketch of the worksheet, the next step is to use Excel to create the worksheet.

To Start Excel

For an introduction to Windows 7 and instruction about how to perform basic Windows 7 tasks, read the Office 2010 and Windows 7 chapter at the beginning of this book, where you can learn how to resize windows, change screen resolution, create folders, move and rename files, use Windows Help, and much more.

If you are using a computer to step through the project in this chapter and you want your screens to match the figures in this book, you should change your screen's resolution to 1024 × 768. For information about how to change a computer's resolution, refer to the Office 2010 and Windows 7 chapter at the beginning of this book.

The following steps, which assume Windows 7 is running, start Excel based on a typical installation. You may need to ask your instructor how to start Excel for your computer. For a detailed example of the procedure summarized below, refer to the Office 2010 and Windows 7 chapter.

1 Click the Start button on the Windows 7 taskbar to display the Start menu.

2 Type **Microsoft Excel** as the search text in the 'Search programs and files' text box, and watch the search results appear on the Start menu.

3 Click Microsoft Excel 2010 in the search results on the Start menu to start Excel and display a new blank workbook in the Excel window.

4 If the Excel window is not maximized, click the Maximize button next to the Close button on its title bar to maximize the window.

Entering the Titles and Numbers into the Worksheet

The first step in creating the worksheet is to enter the titles and numbers into the worksheet. The following sets of steps enter the worksheet title and subtitle and then the biweekly payroll report data shown in Table 2–1.

To Enter the Worksheet Title and Subtitle

The following steps enter the worksheet title and subtitle into cells A1 and A2.

1 If necessary, select cell A1. Type **The Mobile Masses Store** in the selected cell and then press the DOWN ARROW key to enter the worksheet title.

2 Type **Biweekly Payroll Report** in cell A2 and then press the DOWN ARROW key to enter the worksheet subtitle (Figure 2–4 on page 73).

The employee names and the row titles Totals, Average, Highest, and Lowest in the leftmost column begin in cell A4 and continue down to cell A16. The employee data is entered into rows 4 through 12 of the worksheet. The remainder of this section explains the steps required to enter the column titles, payroll data, and row titles, as shown in Figure 2–4, and then save the workbook.

To Enter the Column Titles

The column titles in row 3 begin in cell A3 and extend through cell J3. Some of the column titles in Figure 2–3 include multiple lines of text, such as Hours Worked in cell D3. To start a new line in a cell, press ALT+ENTER after each line, except for the last line, which is completed by clicking the Enter box, pressing the ENTER key, or pressing one of the arrow keys. When you see ALT+ENTER in a step, press the ENTER key while holding down the ALT key and then release both keys. The following steps enter the column titles.

1 With cell A3 selected, type **Employee** and then press the RIGHT ARROW key to enter the column heading.

2 Type **Hire Date** in cell B3 and then press the RIGHT ARROW key to enter the column heading.

3 Type **Dependents** and then press the RIGHT ARROW key to enter the column heading.

4 In cell D3, type **Hours** and then press ALT+ENTER to enter the first line of the column heading. Type **Worked** and then press the RIGHT ARROW key to enter the column heading.

5 Type **Hourly** and then press ALT+ENTER to begin a new line in the cell. Type **Pay Rate** and then press the RIGHT ARROW key to enter the column heading.

6 Type **Gross Pay** in cell F3 and then press the RIGHT ARROW key to enter the column heading.

7 Type **Federal Tax** in cell G3 and then press the RIGHT ARROW key to enter the column heading.

8 Type **State Tax** in cell H3 and then press the RIGHT ARROW key to enter the column heading.

9 Type **Net Pay** in cell I3 and then press the RIGHT ARROW key to enter the column heading.

10 Type **Tax %** in cell J3 to enter the column heading.

For an introduction to Office 2010 and instruction about how to perform basic tasks in Office 2010 programs, read the Office 2010 and Windows 7 chapter at the beginning of this book, where you can learn how to start a program, use the Ribbon, save a file, open a file, quit a program, use Help, and much more.

BTW

The Ribbon and Screen Resolution
Excel may change how the groups and buttons within the groups appear on the Ribbon, depending on the computer's screen resolution. Thus, your Ribbon may look different from the ones in this book if you are using a screen resolution other than 1024 × 768.

BTW

BTWs
For a complete list of the BTWs found in the margins of this book, visit the Excel 2010 BTW Web page (scsite.com/ex2010/btw).

To Enter the Biweekly Payroll Data

The biweekly payroll data in Table 2–1 includes a hire date for each employee. Excel considers a date to be a number and, therefore, it displays the date right-aligned in the cell. The following steps enter the data for each employee: name, hire date, dependents, hours worked, and hourly pay rate.

1 Select cell A4, type **Charvat, Emily**, and then press the RIGHT ARROW key to enter the employee name.

2 Type **3/3/09** in cell B4 and then press the RIGHT ARROW key to enter a date in the selected cell.

3 Type **1** in cell C4 and then press the RIGHT ARROW key to enter a number in the selected cell.

4 Type **65.25** in cell D4 and then press the RIGHT ARROW key to enter a number in the selected cell.

5 Type **20.50** in cell E4 and then click cell A5 to enter a number in the selected cell.

6 Enter the payroll data in Table 2–1 for the eight remaining employees in rows 5 through 12 (Figure 2–4).

Q&A

In step 2, why did the date that was entered change from 3/3/09 to 3/3/2009?

When Excel recognizes that you entered a date in mm/dd/yy format, it automatically formats the date as mm/dd/yyyy for you. Most professionals prefer to view dates in mm/dd/yyyy format as opposed to mm/dd/yy format because the latter can cause confusion regarding the intended year. For example, a date displayed as 3/3/50 could imply a date of 3/3/1950 or 3/3/2050. The use of a four-digit year eliminates this confusion.

Table 2–1 The Mobile Masses Store Biweekly Payroll Report Data				
Employee	**Hire Date**	**Dependents**	**Hours Worked**	**Hourly Pay Rate**
Charvat, Emily	3/3/09	1	65.25	20.50
Chen, Bin	6/14/10	2	80.00	25.85
Felski, Noah	10/11/08	0	64.50	12.60
Kersey, Jane	3/4/11	1	68.50	21.45
Merna, Thomas	1/15/10	3	78.25	22.60
Pollitt, Sherry	11/15/08	2	49.25	18.25
Prasad, Rao	2/15/08	0	33.50	9.35
Washington, Yolanda	5/11/06	2	79.25	23.75
Zica, James	4/14/11	1	80.00	19.65

To Enter the Row Titles

The following steps add row titles for the rows that will contain the totals, average, highest, and lowest amounts.

1 Select cell A13. Type **Totals** and then press the DOWN ARROW key to enter a row header.

2 Type **Average** in cell A14 and then press the DOWN ARROW key to enter a row header.

3 Type **Highest** in cell A15 and then press the DOWN ARROW key to enter a row header.

4 Type **Lowest** in cell A16 and then press the ENTER key to enter a row header. Select cell F4 to prepare to enter a formula in the cell (Figure 2–4).

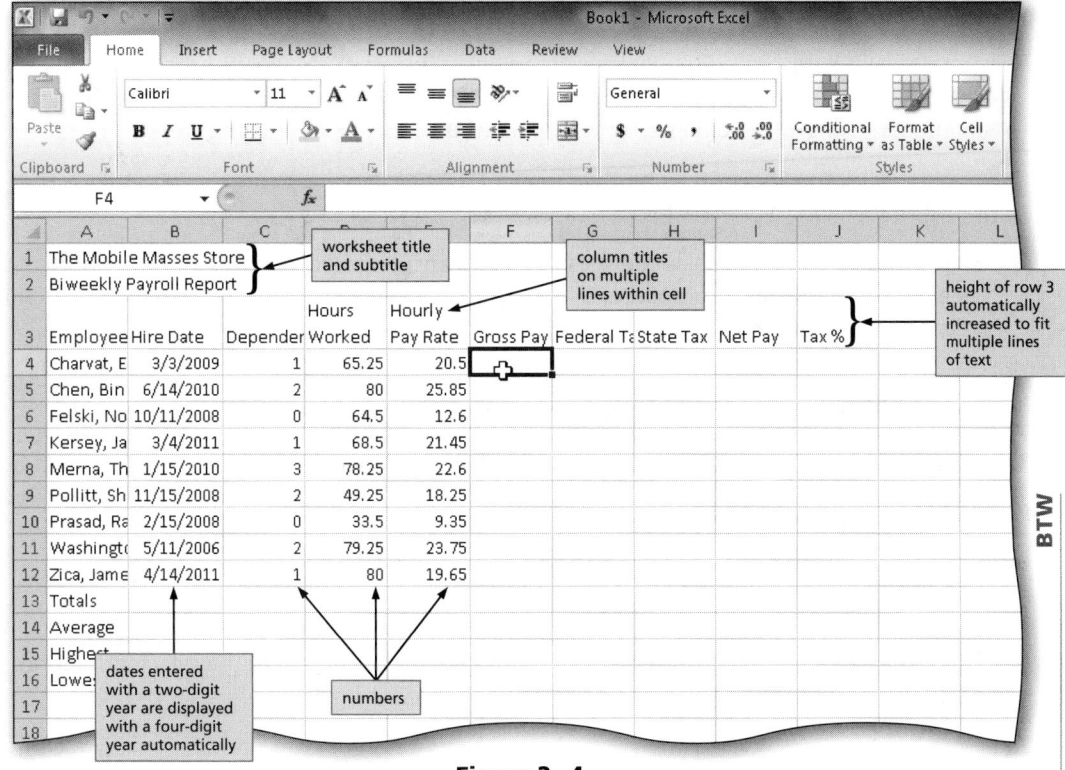

Figure 2–4

To Change Document Properties

As discussed in Chapter 1, the first time you save a workbook, you should change the document properties. The following steps change the document properties.

1 Click File on the Ribbon to open the Backstage view. If necessary, click the Info tab in the Backstage view to display the Info gallery.

2 Click the Properties button in the right pane of the Info gallery to display the Properties menu.

3 Click Show Document Panel on the Properties menu to close the Backstage view and display the Document Information Panel in the Excel workbook window.

4 Click the Author text box, if necessary, and then type your name as the Author property. If a name already is displayed in the Author text box, delete it before typing your name.

5 Click the Subject text box, if necessary delete any existing text, and then type your course and section as the Subject property.

6 If an AutoComplete dialog box appears, click its Yes button.

7 Click the Keywords text box, if necessary delete any existing text, and then type **Biweekly Payroll Report** as the Keywords property.

8 If an AutoComplete dialog box appears, click its Yes button.

9 Click the Close the Document Information Panel button so that the Document Information Panel no longer is displayed.

To Change the Sheet Name and Save the Workbook

The following steps change the sheet name to Biweekly Payroll Report, change the sheet tab color, and save the workbook on a USB flash drive in the Excel folder (for your assignments) using the file name, The Mobile Masses Biweekly Payroll Report.

1 Double-click the Sheet1 tab and then enter **Biweekly Payroll Report** as the sheet name and then press the ENTER key.

2 Right-click the tab to display the shortcut menu and then click Tab Color on the shortcut menu to display the Color gallery. Click Orange, Accent 1, Darker 25% (column 5, row 5) in the Theme Colors area to apply a new color to the sheet tab.

3 With a USB flash drive connected to one of the computer's USB ports, click the Save button on the Quick Access Toolbar to display the Save As dialog box.

4 Type **The Mobile Masses Biweekly Payroll Report** in the File name text box to change the file name. Do not press the ENTER key after typing the file name because you do not want to close the dialog box at this time.

5 Navigate to the desired save location (in this case, the Excel folder in the CIS 101 folder [or your class folder] on the USB flash drive).

6 Click the Save button (Save As dialog box) to save the document in the selected folder on the selected drive with the entered file name.

BTW

Entering Numbers in a Range
An efficient way to enter data into a range of cells is to select a range and then enter the first number in the upper-left cell of the range. Excel responds by accepting the value and moving the active cell selection down one cell. When you enter the last value in the first column, Excel moves the active cell selection to the top of the next column.

Entering Formulas

One of the reasons Excel is such a valuable tool is that you can assign a **formula** to a cell, and Excel will calculate the result. Consider, for example, what would happen if you had to multiply 65.25 by 20.5 and then manually enter the product for Gross Pay, 1,337.625, in cell F4. Every time the values in cells D4 or E4 changed, you would have to recalculate the product and enter the new value in cell F4. By contrast, if you enter a formula in cell F4 to multiply the values in cells D4 and E4, Excel recalculates the product whenever new values are entered into those cells and displays the result in cell F4.

Plan Ahead

Determine the formulas and functions needed.
As you have learned, formulas and functions simplify the creation and maintenance of worksheets because Excel performs calculations for you. When formulas and functions are used together properly, the amount of data that a user manually must enter in a worksheet greatly can be diminished:

- **Utilize proper algebraic notation.** Most Excel formulas are the result of algebraic calculations. A solid understanding of algebraic operators and the order of operations is important to writing sound formulas.

- **Utilize the fill handle and copy and paste operations to copy formulas.** The fill handle and the Excel copy and paste functionality help to minimize errors caused by retyping formulas. When possible, if a similar formula will be used repeatedly in a worksheet, avoid retyping the formula and instead use the fill handle.

- **Be careful about using invalid and circular cell references.** An invalid reference occurs when Excel does not understand a cell reference used in a formula, resulting in Excel displaying a #REF! error message in the cell.

(Continued)

(*Continued*)

A formula in a cell that contains a reference back to itself is called a **circular reference**. Excel often warns you when you create a circular reference. In almost all cases, circular references are the result of an incorrect formula. A circular reference can be direct or indirect. For example, placing the formula =A1 in cell A1 results in a direct circular reference. An indirect circular reference occurs when a formula in a cell refers to another cell or cells that include a formula that refers back to the original cell.

- **Employ the Excel built-in functions whenever possible.** Excel includes prewritten formulas called **functions** to help you compute a range of values and statistics. A function takes a value or values, performs an operation, and returns a result to the cell. The values that you use with a function are called **arguments**. All functions begin with an equal sign and include the arguments in parentheses after the function name. For example, in the function =AVERAGE(C4:C12), the function name is AVERAGE, and the argument is the range C4:C12. Become familiar with the extensive number of built-in functions. When you have the choice, always use built-in functions instead of writing and typing a formula version of your mathematical expression. Such a practice reduces the possibility of errors and simplifies the formula used in a cell, resulting in improved readability.

Plan Ahead

BTW

Automatic Recalculation
Every time you enter a value into a cell in the worksheet, Excel automatically recalculates all formulas. You can change to manual recalculation by clicking the Calculation Options button (Formulas tab | Calculation group) and then clicking Manual. In manual calculation mode, pressing the F9 key instructs Excel to recalculate all formulas.

To Enter a Formula Using the Keyboard

The formulas needed in the worksheet are noted in the requirements document as follows:

1. Gross Pay (column F) = Hours Worked × Hourly Pay Rate
2. Federal Tax (column G) = 0.22 × (Gross Pay − Dependents × 24.32)
3. State Tax (column H) = 0.04 × Gross Pay
4. Net Pay (column I) = Gross Pay − (Federal Tax + State Tax)
5. Tax% (column J) = (Federal Tax + State Tax) / Gross Pay

The gross pay for each employee, which appears in column F, is equal to hours worked in column D times hourly pay rate in column E. Thus, the gross pay for Emily Charvat in cell F4 is obtained by multiplying 65.25 (cell D4) by 20.50 (cell E4) or =D4*E4. The following steps enter the initial gross pay formula in cell F4 using the keyboard.

- With cell F4 selected, type **=d4*e4** in the cell to display the formula in the formula bar and in the current cell and to display colored borders around the cells referenced in the formula (Figure 2–5).

What occurs on the worksheet as I enter the formula?

The **equal sign** (=) preceding d4*e4 alerts Excel that you are entering a formula or function and not text. Because the most common error when entering a formula is to reference the wrong cell in a formula mistakenly, Excel colors the borders of the cells referenced in the formula. The coloring helps in the reviewing process to ensure the cell references are correct.

The **asterisk** (*) following d4 is the arithmetic operator that directs Excel to perform the multiplication operation.

Figure 2–5

2

- Press the RIGHT ARROW key to complete the arithmetic operation indicated by the formula, to display the result in the worksheet, and to select the cell to the right (Figure 2–6). The number of decimal places shown in cell F4 may be different, but these values will be adjusted later in this chapter.

Figure 2–6

Arithmetic Operations

Table 2–2 describes multiplication and other valid Excel arithmetic operators.

Table 2–2 Summary of Arithmetic Operators			
Arithmetic Operator	Meaning	Example of Usage	Meaning
−	Negation	−78	Negative 78
%	Percentage	=23%	Multiplies 23 by 0.01
^	Exponentiation	=3 ^ 4	Raises 3 to the fourth power
*	Multiplication	=61.5 * C5	Multiplies the contents of cell C5 by 61.5
/	Division	=H3 / H11	Divides the contents of cell H3 by the contents of cell H11
+	Addition	=11 + 9	Adds 11 and 9
−	Subtraction	=22 − F15	Subtracts the contents of cell F15 from 22

Order of Operations

When more than one arithmetic operator is involved in a formula, Excel follows the same basic order of operations that you use in algebra. Moving from left to right in a formula, the **order of operations** is as follows: first negation (–), then all percentages (%), then all exponentiations (^), then all multiplications (*) and divisions (/), and finally, all additions (+) and subtractions (–).

As in algebra, you can use parentheses to override the order of operations. For example, if Excel follows the order of operations, 8 * 3 + 2 equals 26. If you use parentheses, however, to change the formula to 8 * (3 + 2), the result is 40, because the parentheses instruct Excel to add 3 and 2 before multiplying by 8. Table 2–3 illustrates several examples of valid Excel formulas and explains the order of operations.

BTW

Troubling Formulas
If Excel does not accept a formula, remove the equal sign from the left side and complete the entry as text. Later, after you have entered additional data in the cells reliant on the formula or determined the error, reinsert the equal sign to change the text back to a formula and edit the formula as needed.

Table 2–3 Examples of Excel Formulas	
Formula	**Meaning**
=G15	Assigns the value in cell G15 to the active cell.
=2^4 + 7	Assigns the sum of 16 + 7 (or 23) to the active cell.
=100 + D2 or =D2 +100 or =(100 + D2)	Assigns 100 plus the contents of cell D2 to the active cell.
=25% * 40	Assigns the product of 0.25 times 40 (or 10) to the active cell.
– (K15 * X45)	Assigns the negative value of the product of the values contained in cells K15 and X45 to the active cell. You do not need to type an equal sign before an expression that begins with minus signs, which indicates a negation.
=(U8 – B8) * 6	Assigns the product of the difference between the values contained in cells U8 and B8 times 6 to the active cell.
=J7 / A5 + G9 * M6 – Z2 ^ L7	Completes the following operations, from left to right: exponentiation (Z2 ^ L7), then division (J7 / A5), then multiplication (G9 * M6), then addition (J7 / A5) + (G9 * M6), and finally subtraction (J7 / A5 + G9 * M6) – (Z2 ^ L7). If cells A5 = 6, G9 = 2, J7 = 6, L7 = 4, M6 = 5, and Z2 = 2, then Excel assigns the active cell the value –5; that is, 6 / 6 + 2 * 5 – 2 ^ 4 = –5.

To Enter Formulas Using Point Mode

The sketch of the worksheet in Figure 2–3 on page EX 70 calls for the federal tax, state tax, net pay, and tax % for each employee to appear in columns G, H, I, and J, respectively. All four of these values are calculated using formulas in row 4:

Federal Tax (cell G4) = 0.22 × (Gross Pay – Dependents × 24.32) or =0.22*(F4–C4*24.32)

State Tax (cell H4) = 0.04 × Gross Pay or = 0.04* F4

Net Pay (cell I4) = Gross Pay – (Federal Tax + State Tax) or =F4-(G4+H4)

Tax % (cell J4) = (Federal Tax + State Tax) / Gross Pay or =(G4+H4)/F4

An alternative to entering the formulas in cells G4, H4, I4, and J4 using the keyboard is to enter the formulas using the mouse and Point mode. **Point mode** allows you to select cells for use in a formula by using the mouse. The steps on the following pages enter formulas using Point mode.

- With cell G4 selected type =0.22*(to begin the formula and then click cell F4 to add a cell reference in the formula (Figure 2-7).

Figure 2-7

- Type – (minus sign) and then click cell C4 to add a subtraction operator and a reference to another cell to the formula.

- Type *24.32) to complete the formula (Figure 2-8).

Figure 2-8

3

• Click the Enter box in the formula bar and then select cell H4 to prepare to enter the next formula.

• Type =0.04* and then click cell F4 to add a cell reference to the formula (Figure 2–9).

Figure 2–9

Why should I use Point mode to enter formulas?

Using Point mode to enter formulas often is faster and more accurate than using the keyboard to type the entire formula when the cell you want to select does not require you to scroll. In many instances, as in these steps, you may want to use both the keyboard and mouse when entering a formula in a cell. You can use the keyboard to begin the formula, for example, and then use the mouse to select a range of cells.

4

• Click the Enter box in the formula bar and then select cell I4 to prepare to enter the next formula.

• Type = (equal sign) and then click cell F4 to begin the formula and add a cell reference to the formula.

• Type –((minus sign followed by an open parenthesis) and then click cell G4 to add a subtraction operator, open parenthesis, and cell reference to the formula.

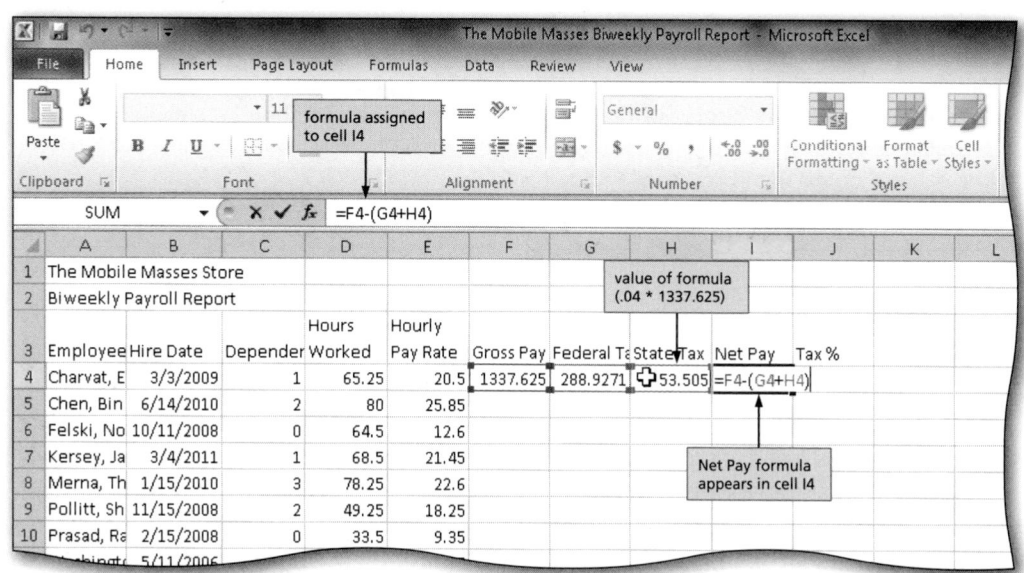

Figure 2–10

• Type + (plus sign) and then click cell H4 to add an addition operator and cell reference to the formula.

• Type) (close parenthesis) to complete the formula (Figure 2–10).

5

- Click the Enter box in the formula bar to enter the formula in cell I4.

- Select cell J4. Type = ((equal sign followed by an open parenthesis) and then click cell G4 to add a reference to the formula.

- Type + (plus sign) and then click cell H4 to add a cell reference to the formula.

- Type) / (close parenthesis followed by a forward slash), and then click cell F4 to add a cell reference to the formula.

- Click the Enter box in the formula bar to enter the formula in cell J4 (Figure 2–11).

Figure 2–11

Q&A Why do three decimal places show in cell J4?

The actual value assigned by Excel to cell J4 from the division operation in step 5 is 0.256000075. While not all the decimal places appear in Figure 2–11, Excel maintains all of them for computational purposes. Thus, if referencing cell J4 in a formula, the value used for computational purposes is 0.256000075, not 0.256. The cell formatting is set to display six digits after the decimal point, but the formatting also suppresses trailing zeroes. If the cell formatting were set to display six digits and show trailing zeroes, then Excel would display 0.256000 in cell J4. If you change the cell formatting of column J to display nine digits after the decimal point, then Excel displays the true value 0.256000075.

To Copy Formulas Using the Fill Handle

The five formulas for Emily Charvat in cells F4, G4, H4, I4, and J4 now are complete. You could enter the same five formulas one at a time for the eight remaining employees. A much easier method of entering the formulas, however, is to select the formulas in row 4 and then use the fill handle to copy them through row 12. When performing copying operations in Excel, the source area is the cell, or range, from which data or formulas are being copied. When a range is used as a source, sometimes it is called the source range. The destination area is the cell, or range, to which data or formulas are being copied. When a range is used as a destination, sometimes it is called the destination range. Recall from Chapter 1 that the fill handle is a small rectangle in the lower-right corner of the active cell or active range. The following steps copy the formulas using the fill handle.

1

- Select the source range, F4:J4 in this case, and then point to the fill handle.

- Drag the fill handle down through cell J12 and continue to hold the mouse button to select the destination range (Figure 2–12).

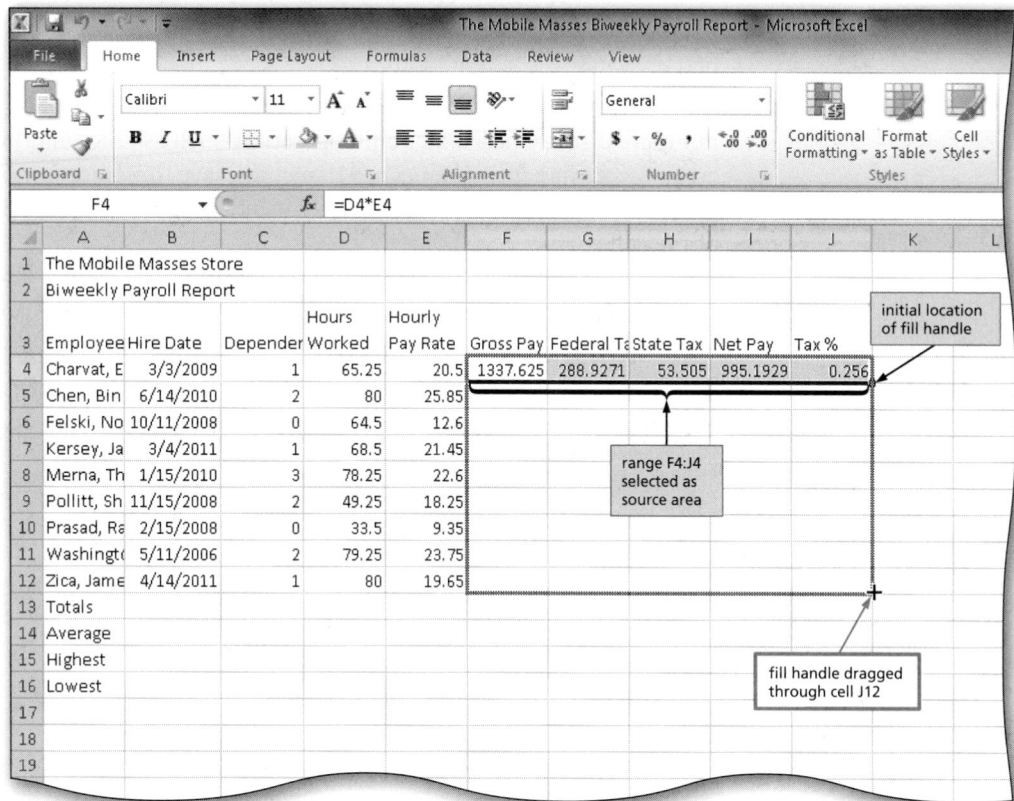

Figure 2–12

2

- Release the mouse button to copy the formulas to the destination range (Figure 2–13).

Q&A

How does Excel adjust the cell references in the formulas in the destination area?

Recall that when you copy a formula, Excel adjusts the cell references so that the new formulas contain references corresponding to the new location and perform calculations using the appropriate values. Thus, if you copy downward, Excel adjusts the row portion of cell references. If you copy across, then Excel adjusts the column portion of cell references. These cell references are called **relative cell references**.

	Hours	Hourly					
3	Employee Hire Date	Depender Worked	Pay Rate	Gross Pay	Federal Ta State Tax	Net Pay	Tax %
4	Charvat, E 3/3/2009	1 65.25	20.5	1337.625	288.9271 53.505	995.1929	0.256
5	Chen, Bin 6/14/2010	2 80	25.85	2068	444.2592 82.72	1541.021	0.254826
6	Felski, No 10/11/2008	12.6		812.7	178.794 32.508	601.398	0.26
7	Kersey, Ja 3/4/2011	21.45		1469.325	317.9011 58.773	1092.651	0.256359
8	Merna, Th 1/15/2010	22.6		1768.45	373.0078 70.738	1324.704	0.250924
9	Pollitt, Sh 11/15/2008	18.25		898.8125	187.038 35.9525	675.8221	0.248095
10	Prasad, Ra 2/15/2008	9.35		313.225	68.9095 12.529	231.7865	0.26
11	Washingt 5/11/2006	2 79.25	23.75	1882.188	403.3805 75.2875	1403.52	0.254315
12	Zica, Jame 4/14/2011	1 80	19.65	1572	340.4896 62.88	1168.63	0.256596
13	Totals						
14	Average						
15	Highest						

gross pay, federal tax, state tax, net pay, and tax % formulas in range F4:J4 copied to range F5:J12

Auto Fill Options button appears after copying the range F4:J4 to range F5:J12

Figure 2–13

Other Ways		
1. Select source area, click Copy button (Home tab | Clipboard group), select destination area, click Paste button (Home tab | Clipboard group)	2. Right-click source area, click Copy on shortcut menu, right-click destination area, click Paste icon on shortcut menu	3. Select source area and then point to border of range; while holding down CTRL, drag source area to destination area

Option Buttons

Excel displays Option buttons in a workbook while you are working on it to indicate that you can complete an operation using automatic features such as AutoCorrect, Auto Fill, error checking, and others. For example, the Auto Fill Options button shown in Figure 2–13 appears after a fill operation, such as dragging the fill handle. When an error occurs in a formula in a cell, Excel displays the Trace Error button next to the cell and identifies the cell with the error by placing a green triangle in the upper left of the cell.

Table 2–4 summarizes the Option buttons available in Excel. When one of these buttons appears on your worksheet, click the button arrow to produce the list of options for modifying the operation or to obtain additional information.

Table 2–4 Options Buttons in Excel

Button	Name	Menu Function
	Auto Fill Options	Gives options for how to fill cells following a fill operation, such as dragging the fill handle.
	AutoCorrect Options	Undoes an automatic correction, stops future automatic corrections of this type, or causes Excel to display the AutoCorrect Options dialog box.
	Insert Options	Lists formatting options following an insertion of cells, rows, or columns.
(Ctrl) ▾	Paste Options	Specifies how moved or pasted items should appear (for example, with original formatting, without formatting, or with different formatting).
	Trace Error	Lists error-checking options following the assignment of an invalid formula to a cell.

To Determine Totals Using the Sum Button

The next step is to determine the totals in row 13 for the hours worked in column D, gross pay in column F, federal tax in column G, state tax in column H, and net pay in column I. To determine the total hours worked in column D, the values in the range D4 through D12 must be summed. To do so, enter the function =sum(d4:d12) in cell D13 or select cell D13, click the Sum button (Home tab | Editing group), and then press the ENTER key. Recall that a function is a prewritten formula that is built into Excel. Similar SUM functions can be used in cells F13, G13, H13, and I13 to total gross pay, federal tax, state tax, and net pay, respectively. The following steps determine totals in cell D13 and the range F13:I13.

1 Select cell to contain the sum, cell D13 in this case. Click the Sum button (Home tab | Editing group) to sum the contents of the range D4:D12 in cell D13 and then click the Enter box to display a total in the selected cell.

2 Select the range to contain the sums, range F13:I13 in this case. Click the Sum button (Home tab | Editing group) to display totals in the selected range (Figure 2–14).

Figure 2–14

To Determine the Total Tax %

With the totals in row 13 determined, the next step is to copy the tax % formula in cell J12 to cell J13 as performed in the following steps.

1 Select the cell to be copied, J12 in this case, and then point to the fill handle.

2 Drag the fill handle down through cell J13 to copy the formula (Figure 2–15).

Q&A Why was the formula I13/F13 not copied to cell J13 earlier?

The formula, I13/F13, was not copied to cell J13 when cell J4 was copied to the range J5:J12 because both cells involved in the computation (I13 and F13) were blank, or zero, at the time. A **blank cell** in Excel has a numerical value of zero, which would have resulted in an error message in cell J13. Once the totals were determined, both cells I13 and F13 (especially F13, because it is the divisor) had nonzero numerical values.

ersey, Ja	3/4/2011	1	68.5	21.45	1469.325	317.9011	58.773	1092.651	0.256359
lerna, Th	1/15/2010	3	78.25	22.6	1768.45	373.0078	70	formula is =(G12+H12)/ F12	0.250924
ollitt, Sh	11/15/2008	2	49.25	18.25	898.8125	187.038	35.		0.248095
rasad, Ra	2/15/2008	0	33.5	9.35	313.225	68.9095	12		0.26
Vashingto	5/11/2006	2	79.25	23.75	1882.188	403.3805	75.2875	1403.52	0.254315
ca, Jame	4/14/2011	1	80	19.65	1572	340.489		1168.63	0.256596
otals			598.5		12122.33	2602.70	formula is =(G13+H13)/ F13	034.725	0.254704
verage									
ighest									

Auto Fill Options button appears after copying cell J12 to cell J13

Figure 2–15

Using the AVERAGE, MAX, and MIN Functions

The next step in creating The Mobile Masses Biweekly Payroll Report worksheet is to compute the average, highest value, and lowest value for the number of dependents listed in the range C4:C12 using the AVERAGE, MAX, and MIN functions in the range C14:C16. Once the values are determined for column C, the entries can be copied across to the other columns.

With Excel, you can enter functions using one of five methods: (1) the keyboard or mouse, (2) the Insert Function box in the formula bar, (3) the Sum menu, (4) the Sum command (Formulas tab | Function Library group), and (5) the Name box area in the formula bar (Figure 2–16). The method you choose will depend on your typing skills and whether you can recall the function name and required arguments.

In the following pages, each of the first three methods will be used. The keyboard and mouse method will be used to determine the average number of dependents (cell C14). The Insert Function button in the formula bar method will be used to determine the highest number of dependents (cell C15). The Sum menu method will be used to determine the lowest number of dependents (cell C16).

BTW

Statistical Functions
Excel usually considers a blank cell to be equal to 0. The statistical functions, however, ignore blank cells. Excel thus calculates the average of three cells with values of 10, blank, and 8 to be 9 [(10 + 8) / 2] and not 6 [(10 + 0 + 8) / 3].

To Determine the Average of a Range of Numbers Using the Keyboard and Mouse

The **AVERAGE function** sums the numbers in the specified range and then divides the sum by the number of cells with numeric values in the range. The following steps use the AVERAGE function to determine the average of the numbers in the range C4:C12.

1

- Select the cell to contain the average, cell C14 in this case.

- Type **=av** in the cell to display the Formula AutoComplete list. Press the DOWN ARROW key to highlight the required formula (Figure 2–16).

Q&A

What is happening as I type?

As you type the equal sign followed by the characters in the name of a function, Excel displays the Formula AutoComplete list. This list contains those functions that alphabetically match the letters you have typed. Because you typed =av, Excel displays all the functions that begin with the letters av.

Figure 2–16

2

- Double-click AVERAGE in the Formula AutoComplete list to select the function.

- Select the range to be averaged, C4:C12 in this case, to insert the range as the argument to the function (Figure 2–17).

 As I drag, why does the function in cell C14 change?

When you click cell C4, Excel appends cell C4 to the left parenthesis in the formula bar and surrounds cell C4 with a marquee. When you begin dragging, Excel appends to the argument a colon (:) and the cell reference of the cell where the mouse pointer is located.

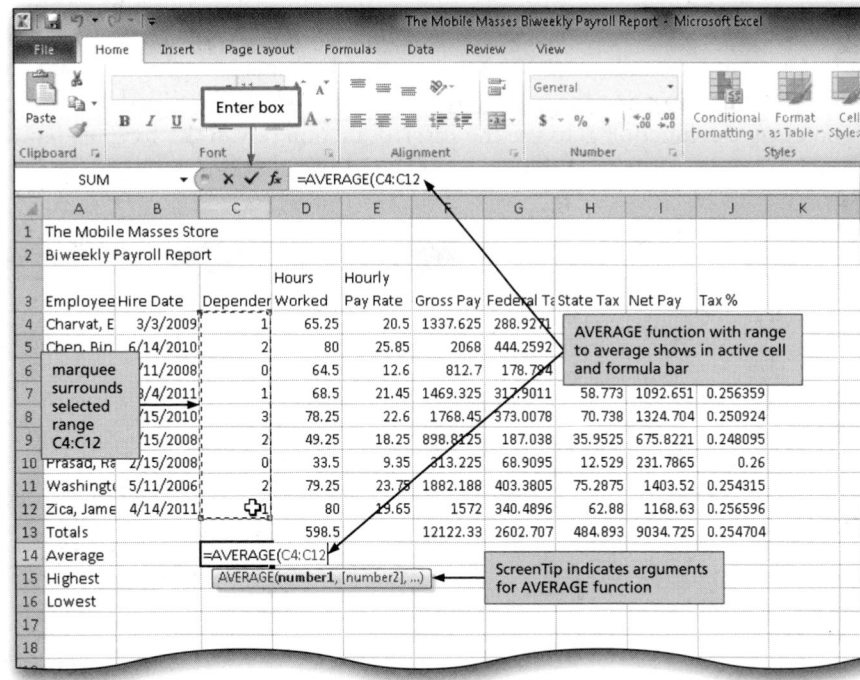

Figure 2–17

3

- Click the Enter box to compute the average of the numbers in the selected range and display the result in the selected cell (Figure 2–18).

Can I use the arrow keys to complete the entry instead?

No. When you use Point mode you cannot use the arrow keys to complete the entry. While in Point mode, the arrow keys change the selected cell reference in the range you are selecting.

What is the purpose of the parentheses in the function?

The AVERAGE function requires that the argument (in this case, the range C4:C12) be included within parentheses following the function name. Excel automatically appends the right parenthesis to complete the AVERAGE function when you click the Enter box or press the ENTER key.

Figure 2–18

Other Ways
1. Click Insert Function box in the formula bar, click AVERAGE	2. Click Sum button arrow (Home tab | Editing group), click Average	3. Click Sum button arrow (Formulas tab | Function Library group), click Average

To Determine the Highest Number in a Range of Numbers Using the Insert Function Box

The next step is to select cell C15 and determine the highest (maximum) number in the range C4:C12. Excel includes a function called the **MAX function** that displays the highest value in a range. Although you could enter the MAX function using the keyboard and Point mode as described in the previous steps, an alternative method to entering the function is to use the Insert Function box in the formula bar. The following steps use the Insert Function box in the formula bar to enter the MAX function.

- Select the cell to contain the maximum number, cell C15 in this case.
- Click the Insert Function box in the formula bar to display the Insert Function dialog box.
- Click MAX in the 'Select a function' list (Insert Function dialog box) to select it (Figure 2–19). If the MAX function is not displayed in the 'Select a function' list, scroll the list until the function is displayed.

Figure 2–19

- Click the OK button (Insert Function dialog box) to display the Function Arguments dialog box.
- Type c4:c12 in the Number1 box (Function Arguments dialog box) to enter the first argument of the function (Figure 2–20).

Q&A

Why did numbers appear in the Function Arguments dialog box?

As shown in Figure 2–20, Excel displays the value the MAX function will return to cell C15 in the Function Arguments dialog box. It also lists the first few numbers in the selected range, next to the Number1 box.

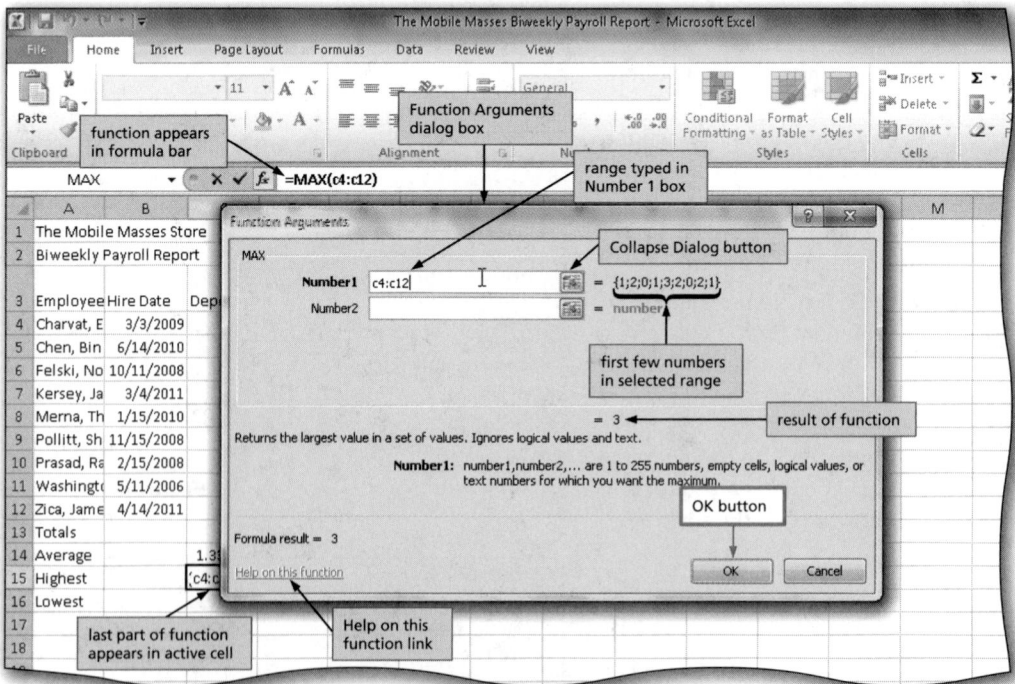

Figure 2–20

3

- Click the OK button (Function Arguments dialog box) to display the highest value in the chosen range in the selected cell (Figure 2–21).

Q&A

Why should I not just enter the highest value that I see in the range C4:C12 in cell C15?

In this example, rather than entering the MAX function, you visually could scan the range C4:C12,

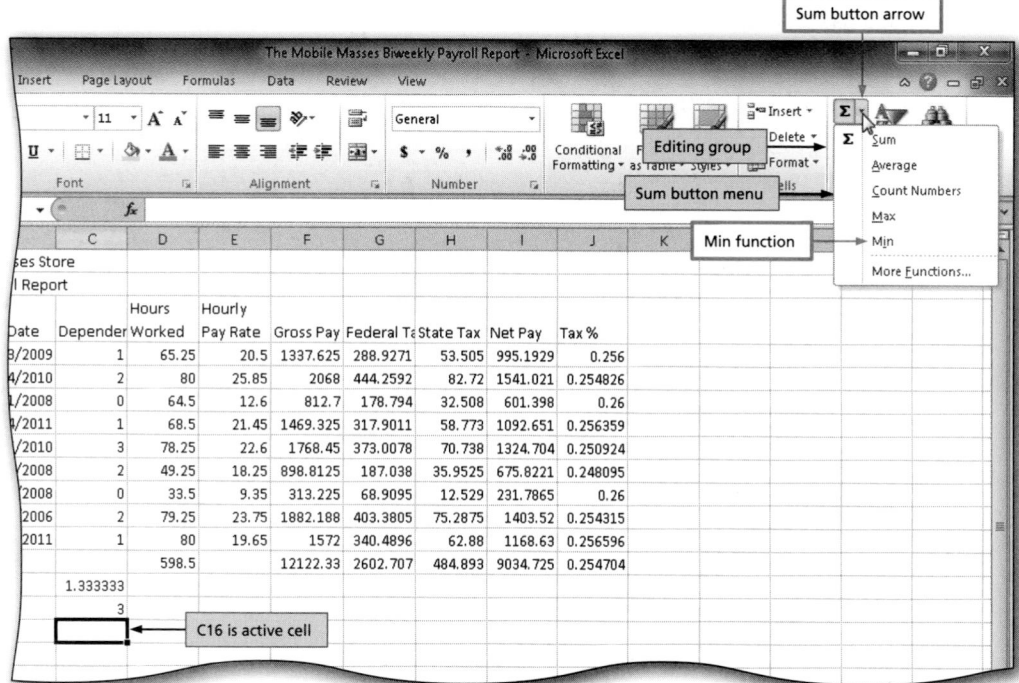

determine that the highest number of dependents is 3, and manually enter the number 3 as a constant in cell C15. Excel would display the number same as in Figure 2–21. Because it contains a constant, however, Excel will continue to display 3 in cell C15, even if the values in the range C4:C12 change. If you use the MAX function, Excel will recalculate the highest value in the range C4:C12 each time a new value is entered into the worksheet.

Other Ways

1. Click Sum button arrow (Home tab | Editing group), click Max
2. Click Sum button arrow (Formulas tab | Function Library group), click Max
3. Type **=MAX** in cell

To Determine the Lowest Number in a Range of Numbers Using the Sum Menu

The next step is to enter the **MIN function** in cell C16 to determine the lowest (minimum) number in the range C4:C12. Although you can enter the MIN function using either of the methods used to enter the AVERAGE and MAX functions, the following steps perform an alternative using the Sum button (Home tab | Editing group).

1

- Select cell C16 to prepare to enter the next function.

- Click the Sum button arrow (Home tab | Editing group) to display the Sum button menu (Figure 2–22).

Q&A

Why should I use the Sum button menu?

Using the Sum button menu allows you to enter one of five often-used functions easily into a cell, without having to memorize its name or the required arguments.

Figure 2–22

2

• Click Min to display the MIN function in the formula bar and in the active cell (Figure 2–23).

Q&A

Why does Excel select the range C14:C15?

The range C14:C15 automatically selected by Excel is not correct. Excel attempts to guess which cells you want to include in the function by looking for ranges that are adjacent to the selected cell and that contain numeric data.

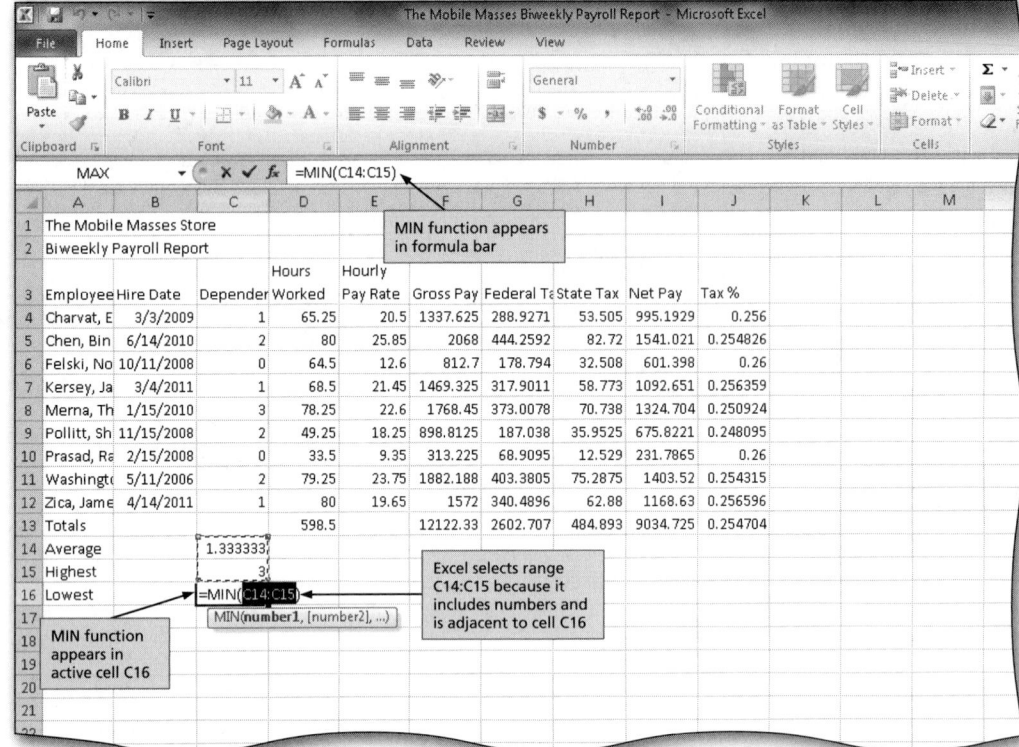

Figure 2–23

3

• Click cell C4 and then drag through cell C12 to display the function with the new range in the formula bar and in the selected cell (Figure 2–24).

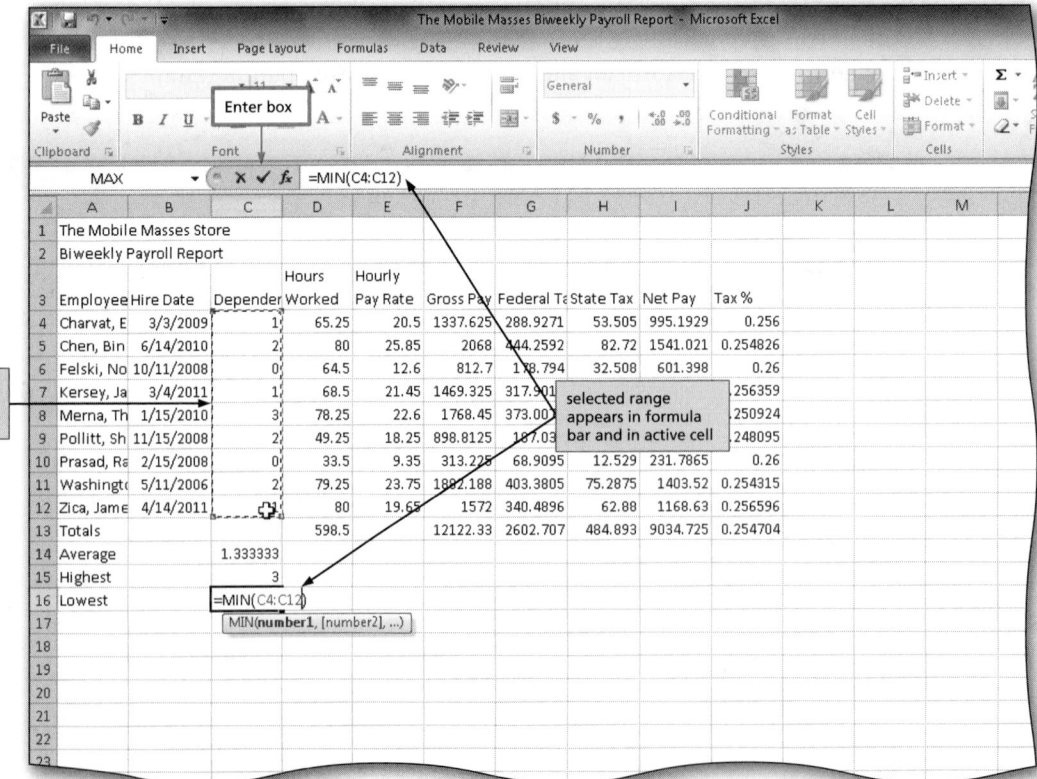

Figure 2–24

4

- Click the Enter box to determine the lowest value in the range C4:C12 and display the result in the formula bar and in the selected cell (Figure 2–25).

Q&A

How can I learn about other functions?

Excel has more than 400 additional functions that perform just about every type of calculation you can imagine. These functions are categorized in the Insert Function dialog box shown in Figure 2–19 on page EX 86. To view the categories, click the 'Or select a category' box arrow. To obtain a description of a selected function, select its name in the Insert Function dialog box. Excel displays the description of the function below the Select a function list in the dialog box.

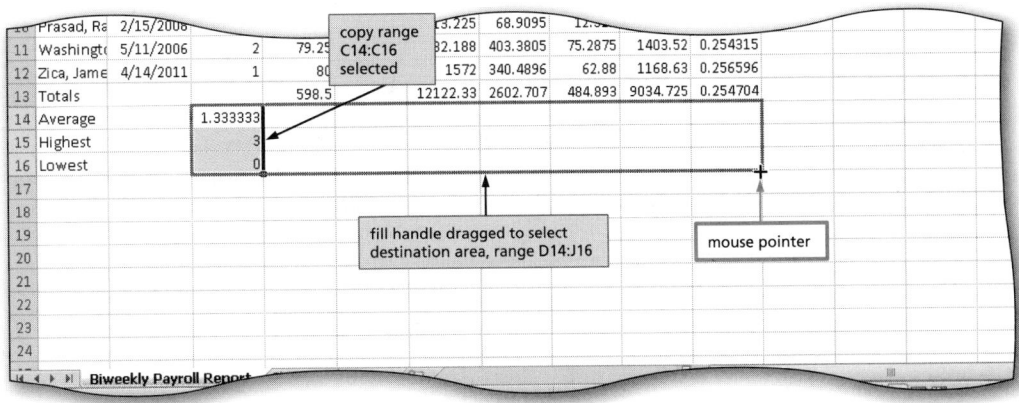

Figure 2–25

Other Ways

1. Click Insert Function box in the formula bar (if necessary, select Statistical category), click MIN
2. Click Sum button arrow (Formulas tab | Function Library group), click Min
3. Type =MIN in cell

To Copy a Range of Cells Across Columns to an Adjacent Range Using the Fill Handle

The next step is to copy the AVERAGE, MAX, and MIN functions in the range C14:C16 to the adjacent range D14:J16. The following steps use the fill handle to copy the functions.

1

- Select the source range from which to copy the functions, in this case C14:C16.

- Drag the fill handle in the lower-right corner of the selected range through cell J16 and continue to hold down the mouse button to begin a fill operation (Figure 2–26).

Figure 2–26

2

• Release the mouse button to copy the three functions to the selected range (Figure 2–27).

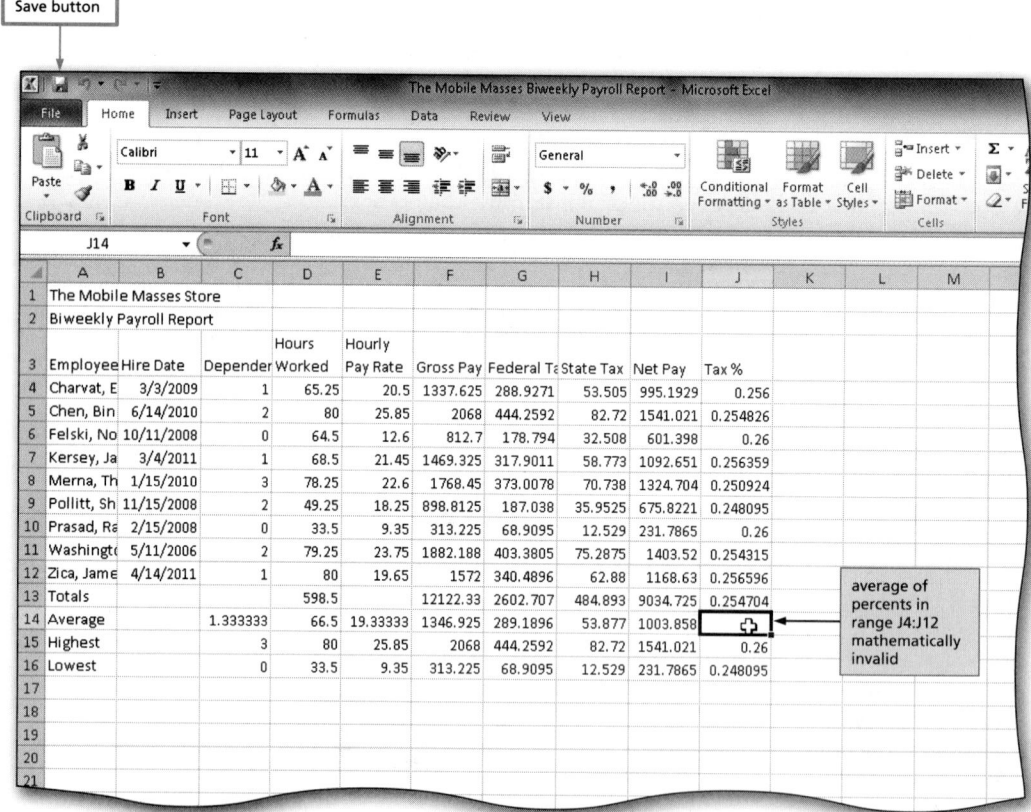

Figure 2–27

Q&A How can I be sure that the function arguments are proper for the cells in range D14:J16?

Remember that Excel adjusts the cell references in the copied functions so that each function refers to the range of numbers above it in the same column. Review the numbers in rows 14 through 16 in Figure 2–27. You should see that the functions in each column return the appropriate values, based on the numbers in rows 4 through 12 of that column.

3

• Select cell J14 and then press the DELETE key to delete the average of the tax % (Figure 2–28).

Q&A Why is the formula in cell J14 deleted?

The average of the tax % in cell J14 is deleted because an average of percentages of this type is mathematically invalid.

Figure 2–28

Other Ways

1. Select source area, click Copy button (Home tab | Clipboard group), select destination area, click Paste button (Home tab | Clipboard group)

2. Right-click source area, click Copy on shortcut menu, right-click destination area, click Paste icon on shortcut menu

3. Select source area and then point to border of

   range; while holding down CTRL, drag source area to destination area

4. Select source area, press CTRL+C, select destination area, press CTRL+V

To Save a Workbook Using the Same File Name

Earlier in this project, an intermediate version of the workbook was saved using the file name, The Mobile Masses Biweekly Payroll Report. The following step saves the workbook a second time, using the same file name.

1 Click the Save button on the Quick Access Toolbar to overwrite the previously saved file.

Break Point: If you wish to take a break, this is a good place to do so. You can quit Excel now. To resume at a later time, start Excel, open the file called The Mobile Masses Biweekly Payroll Report, and continue following the steps from this location forward.

Verifying Formulas Using Range Finder

One of the more common mistakes made with Excel is to include a wrong cell reference in a formula. An easy way to verify that a formula references the cells you want it to reference is to use the Excel Range Finder. Use **Range Finder** to check which cells are referenced in the formula assigned to the active cell. Range Finder allows you to make immediate changes to the cells referenced in a formula.

To use Range Finder to verify that a formula contains the intended cell references, double-click the cell with the formula you want to check. Excel responds by highlighting the cells referenced in the formula so that you can check that the cell references are correct.

BTW

Entering Functions
You can drag the Function Arguments dialog box (Figure 2–20 on page EX 86) out of the way in order to select a range. You also can click the Collapse Dialog button to the right of the Number 1 box to hide the Function Arguments dialog box. The dialog box then collapses and the Collapse Dialog button becomes an Expand Dialog box button. After selecting the range, click the Expand Dialog to expand the dialog box.

To Verify a Formula Using Range Finder

The following steps use Range Finder to check the formula in cell J4.

- Double-click cell J4 to activate Range Finder (Figure 2–29).

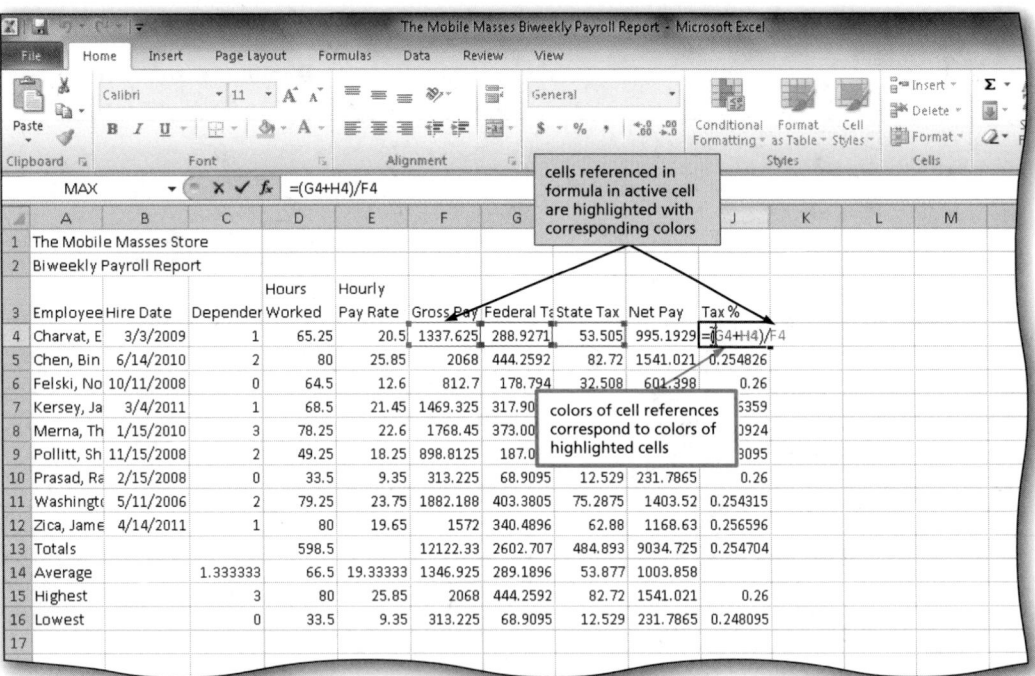

- Press the ESC key to quit Range Finder and then click anywhere in the worksheet, such as cell A18, to deselect the current cell.

Figure 2–29

Formatting the Worksheet

Although the worksheet contains the appropriate data, formulas, and functions, the text and numbers need to be formatted to improve their appearance and readability.

In Chapter 1, cell styles were used to format much of the worksheet. This section describes how to change the unformatted worksheet in Figure 2–30a to the formatted worksheet in Figure 2–30b using a theme and other commands on the Ribbon. The colors and fonts that are used in the worksheet shown in Figure 2–30b are those that are associated with the Trek theme.

(a) Unformatted Worksheet

(b) Formatted Worksheet

Figure 2–30

Plan
Ahead

Identify how to format various elements of the worksheet.
As you have learned, applying proper formatting to a worksheet improves its appeal and readability. The following list includes additional worksheet formatting considerations.

- **Consider using cell borders and fill colors for various portions of the worksheet.** Cell borders, or box borders, draw a border around a cell or range of cells to set the cell or range off from other portions of the worksheet. For example, worksheet titles often include cell borders. Similarly, the use of a fill color in a cell or range of cells sets off the cell or range from other portions of the worksheet and provides visual impact to draw the user's eye toward the cell or range.

- **Use good judgment when centering values in columns.** If a cell entry is short, such as the dependents in column C, centering the entries within their respective columns improves the appearance of the worksheet.

- **Consider the use of a different theme.** A **theme** is a predefined set of colors, fonts, chart styles, cell styles, and fill effects that can be applied to an entire workbook. Every new workbook that you create is assigned a default theme named Office. Excel, however, includes a variety of other themes that provide a range of visual effects for your workbooks.

- **Apply proper formatting for cells that include dates.** Excel provides a number of date formats so that date values can be formatted to meet your needs. How you decide to format a date depends on a number of factors. For example, dates that include years both before and after the year 2000 should be formatted with a four-digit year. Your organization or department may insist on the use of certain standard date formats. Industry standards also may indicate how you should format date values.

The following outlines the formatting suggested in the sketch of the worksheet in Figure 2–3 on page EX 70.

1. Workbook theme — Trek
2. Worksheet title and subtitle
   a. Alignment — center across columns A through J
   b. Cell style — Title
   c. Font size — title 18; subtitle 16
   d. Background color (range A1:J2) — Orange Accent 1, Lighter 60%
   e. Border — thick box border around range A1:J2
3. Column titles
   a. Cell style — Heading 3
   b. Alignment — center
4. Data
   a. Dates in column B — mm/dd/yy format
   b. Alignment — center data in range C4:C12
   c. Numbers in column D — Comma style and two decimal places; if a cell in range D4:D12 is greater than 70, then cell appears with background color of orange and a font color of white
   d. Numbers in top row (range E4:I4) — Accounting number format
   e. Numbers below top row (range E5:I12) — Comma style and decimal places
5. Total line
   a. Cell style — Total
   b. Numbers — Accounting number format

6. Average, highest, and lowest rows

    a. Font style of row titles in range A14:A16 — bold

    b. Numbers — Currency style with floating dollar sign in the range E14:I16

7. Percentages in column J

    a. Numbers — Percentage style with two decimal places

8. Column widths

    a. Columns A, B, and C — best fit

    b. Column H — 10.22 characters

    c. Column D, E, and J — 7.56 characters

9. Row heights

    a. Row 3 — 48.00 points

    b. Row 14 — 27.00 points

    c. Remaining rows — default

To Change the Workbook Theme

The Trek theme includes fonts and colors that provide the worksheet a professional and subtly colored appearance. The following steps change the workbook theme to the Trek theme.

1

- Display the Page Layout tab.

- Click the Themes button (Page Layout tab | Themes group) to display the Themes gallery.

- Scroll to the bottom of the gallery (Figure 2–31).

Experiment

- Point to several themes in the Themes gallery to see a live preview of the themes.

Q&A

Why should I change the theme of a workbook?

A company or department may standardize on a specific theme so that all of their documents have a similar appearance. Similarly, an individual may want to have a theme that sets his or her work apart from the work of others. Other Office programs, such as Word and PowerPoint, include the same themes included with Excel, meaning that all of your Microsoft Office documents can share a common theme.

Figure 2–31

2
- Click Trek in the Themes gallery to change the workbook theme (Figure 2–32).

Figure 2–32

Q&A

Why did the cells in the worksheet change?

The cells in the worksheet originally were formatted with the default font for the default Office theme. The default font for the Trek theme is different from that of the default font for the Office theme and, therefore, changed on the worksheet when you changed the theme. If you had modified the font for any of the cells, those cells would not receive the default font for the Trek theme.

To Format the Worksheet Titles

The following steps merge and center the worksheet titles, apply the Title cells style to the worksheet titles, and decrease the font of the worksheet subtitle.

1 Display the Home tab.

2 Select the range to be merged, A1:J1 in this case, and then click the Merge & Center button (Home tab | Alignment group) to merge and center the text in the selected range.

3 Select the range A2:J2 and then click the Merge & Center button (Home tab | Alignment group) to merge and center the text in the selected range.

4 Select the range to contain the Title cell style, in this case A1:A2, click the Cell Styles button (Home tab | Styles group) to display the cell styles gallery, and then click the Title cell style in the Cell Styles gallery to apply the Title cell style to the selected range.

5 Select cell A2 and then click the Decrease Font Size button (Home tab | Font group) to decrease the font size of the selected cell to the next lowest font size (Figure 2–33 on the following page).

What is the effect of clicking the Decrease Font Size button?

When you click the Decrease Font Size button, Excel assigns the next lowest font size in the Font Size gallery to the selected range. The Increase Font Size button works in a similar manner but causes Excel to assign the next highest font size in the Font Size gallery to the selected range.

Color Selection

Knowing how people perceive colors helps you emphasize parts of your worksheet. Warmer colors (red and orange) tend to reach toward the reader. Cooler colors (blue, green, and violet) tend to pull away from the reader. Bright colors jump out of a dark background and are easiest to see. White or yellow text on a dark blue, green, purple, or black background is ideal.

Figure 2–33

To Change the Background Color and Apply a Box Border to the Worksheet Title and Subtitle

The final formats assigned to the worksheet title and subtitle are the orange background color and thick box border (Figure 2–30b on page EX 92). The following steps complete the formatting of the worksheet titles.

- Select the range A1:A2 and then click the Fill Color button arrow (Home tab | Font group) to display the Fill Color gallery (Figure 2–34).

 Experiment

- Point to a number of colors in the Fill Color gallery to display a live preview of the color in the range A1:A2.

Figure 2–34

2

- Click Orange, Accent 1, Lighter 60% (column 5, row 3) in the Fill Color gallery to change the background color of the range of cells (Figure 2–35).

Figure 2–35

3

- Click the Borders button arrow (Home tab | Font group) to display the Borders list (Figure 2–36).

Figure 2–36

4

- Click Thick Box Border in the Borders list to display a thick box border around the selected range.

- Click anywhere in the worksheet, such as cell A18, to deselect the current range (Figure 2–37).

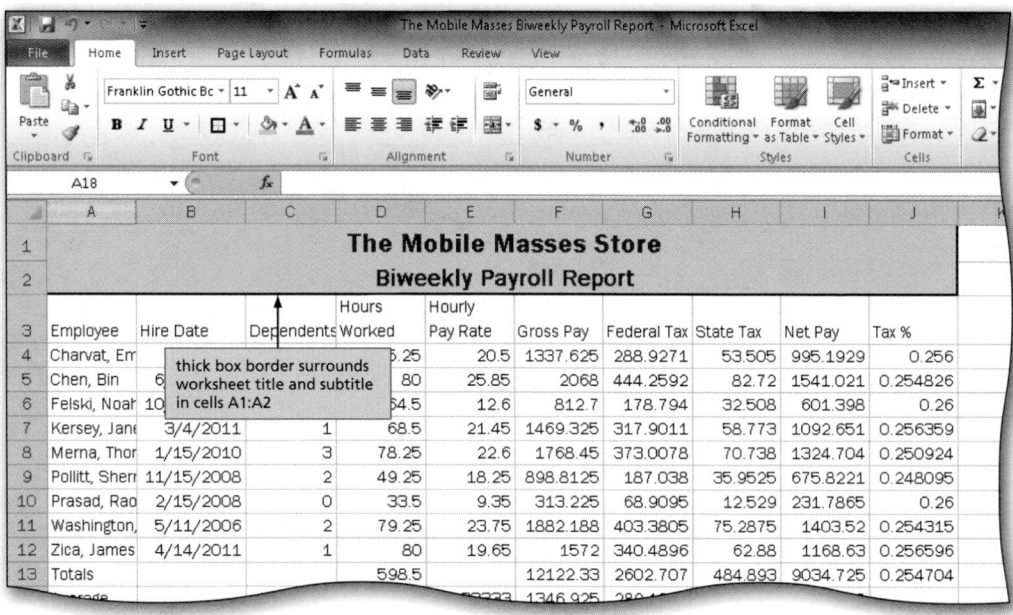

Figure 2–37

Other Ways

1. Click Format Cells Dialog Box Launcher (Home tab | Font group), click appropriate tab (Format Cells dialog box), click desired format, click OK button

2. Right-click range, click Format Cells on shortcut menu, click appropriate tab (Format Cells dialog box), click desired format, click OK button

3. Press CTRL+1, click appropriate tab (Format Cells dialog box), click desired format, click OK button

To Apply a Cell Style to the Column Headings and Format the Total Rows

As shown in Figure 2–30b on page EX 92, the column titles (row 3) should have the Heading 3 cell style and the totals row (row 13) should have the Total cell style. The summary information headings in the range A14:A16 should be bold. The following steps assign these styles and formats to row 3 and row 13 and the range A14:A16.

1 Select the range to be formatted, cells A3:J3 in this case.

2 Apply the Heading 3 cell style to the range A3:J3.

3 Click the Center button (Home tab | Alignment group) to center the column headings.

4 Apply the Total cell style to the range A13:J13.

5 Bold the range A14:A16 (Figure 2–38).

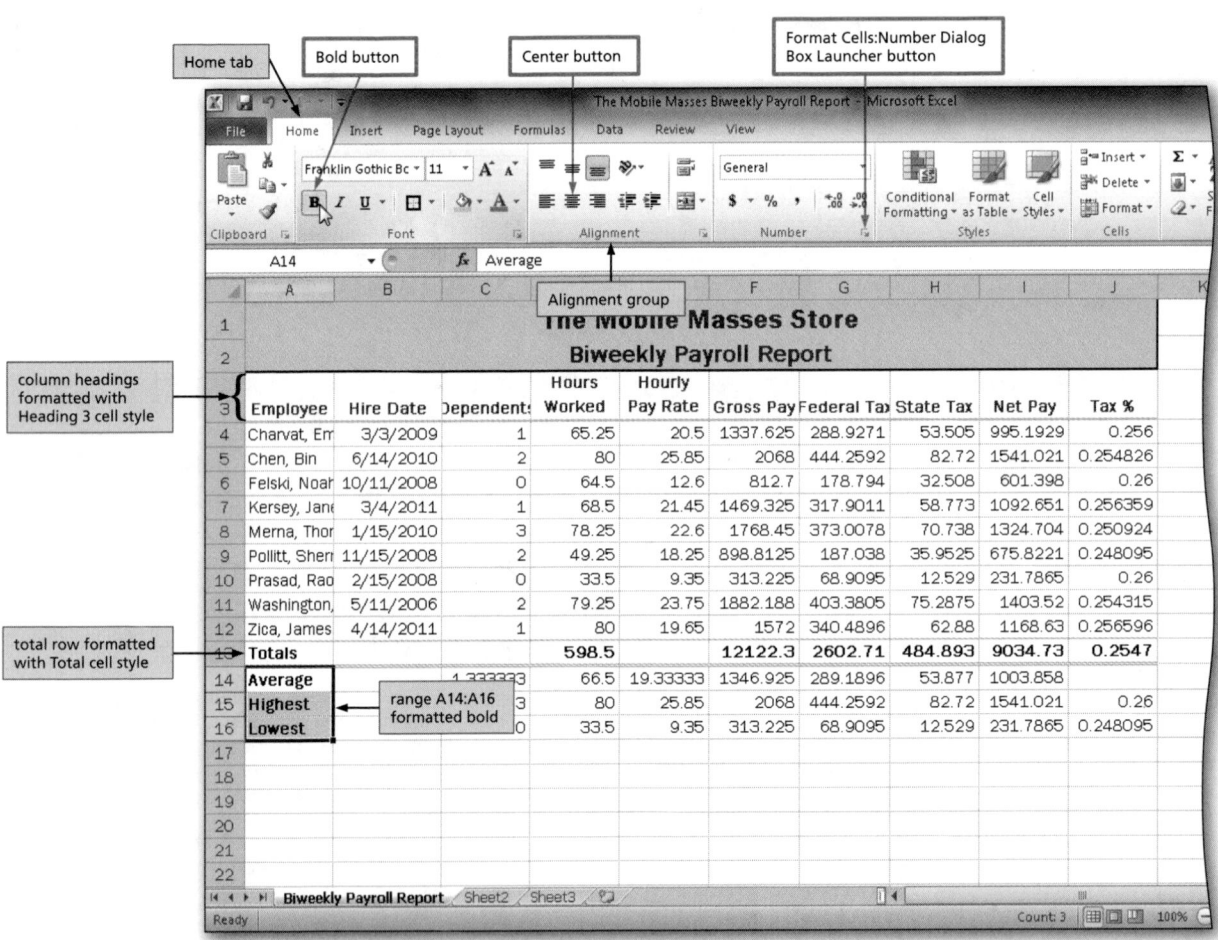

Figure 2–38

To Format Dates and Center Data in Cells

With the column titles and total rows formatted, the next step is to format the dates in column B and center the dependents in column C. The following steps format the dates in the range B4:B12 and center the data in the range C4:C12.

1

- Select the range to contain the new date format, cells B4:B12 in this case.

- Click the Format Cells: Number Dialog Box Launcher (Home tab | Number group) to display the Format Cells dialog box.

- If necessary, click the Number tab (Format Cells dialog box), click Date in the Category list, and then click 3/14/01 in the Type list to choose the format for the selected range (Figure 2–39).

Figure 2–39

2

- Click the OK button (Format Cells dialog box) to format the dates in the current column using the selected date format style.

3

- Select the range C4:C12 and then click the Center button (Home tab | Alignment group) to center the data in the selected range.

- Select cell E4 to deselect the selected range (Figure 2–40).

Figure 2–40

Q&A

Can I format an entire column at once?

Yes. Rather than selecting the range B4:B12 in Step 1, you could have clicked the column B heading immediately above cell B1, and then clicked the Center button (Home tab | Alignment group). In this case, all cells in column B down to the last cell in the worksheet would have been formatted to use center alignment. This same procedure could have been used to format the dependents in column C.

Other Ways

1. Right-click range, click Format Cells on shortcut menu, click appropriate tab (Format Cells dialog box), click desired format, click OK button

2. Press CTRL+1, click appropriate tab (Format Cells dialog box), click desired format, click OK button

Formatting Numbers Using the Ribbon

As shown in Figure 2–30b on page EX 92, the worksheet is formatted to resemble an accounting report. For example, in columns E through I, the numbers in the first row (row 4), the totals row (row 13), and the rows below the totals (rows 14 through 16) have dollar signs, while the remaining numbers (rows 5 through 12) in column E through column I do not.

Plan Ahead

Determine proper formatting for cells that include currency and other numeric amounts.

- To append a dollar sign to a number, you should use the Accounting number format. Excel displays numbers using the **Accounting number format** with a dollar sign to the left of the number, inserts a comma every three positions to the left of the decimal point, and displays numbers to the nearest cent (hundredths place). Clicking the Accounting Number Format button (Home tab | Number group) assigns the desired Accounting number format.

- When you use the Accounting Number Format button to assign the Accounting number format, Excel displays a **fixed dollar sign** to the far left in the cell, often with spaces between it and the first digit. To assign a **floating dollar sign** that appears immediately to the left of the first digit with no spaces, use the Currency style (Format Cells dialog box). Whether you use the Accounting number format or the Currency style format depends on a number of factors, including the preference of your organization, industry standards, and the aesthetics of the worksheet.

- The Comma style format is used to instruct Excel to display numbers with commas and no dollar signs. The **Comma style format**, which can be assigned to a range of cells by clicking the Comma Style button (Home tab | Number group), inserts a comma every three positions to the left of the decimal point and causes numbers to be displayed to the nearest hundredths.

To Apply an Accounting Number Format and Comma Style Format Using the Ribbon

The following steps assign formats using the Accounting Number Format button and the Comma Style button (Home tab | Number group). The Accounting Number format is applied to the currency amounts in rows 4 and 13. The Comma style is applied to the range E4:I12 and to column D (Hours Worked).

1

- Select the range to contain the Accounting Number Format, cells E4:I4 in this case.

- While holding down the CTRL key, select the range F13:I13 to select the nonadjacent range.

- Click the Accounting Number Format button (Home tab | Number group) to apply the Accounting number format with fixed dollar signs to the selected nonadjacent ranges (Figure 2–41).

Q&A

What is the effect of applying the Accounting number format?

The Accounting Number Format button assigns a fixed dollar sign to the numbers in the ranges E4:I4 and F13:I13. In each cell in these ranges, Excel displays the dollar sign to the far left with spaces between it and the first digit in the cell.

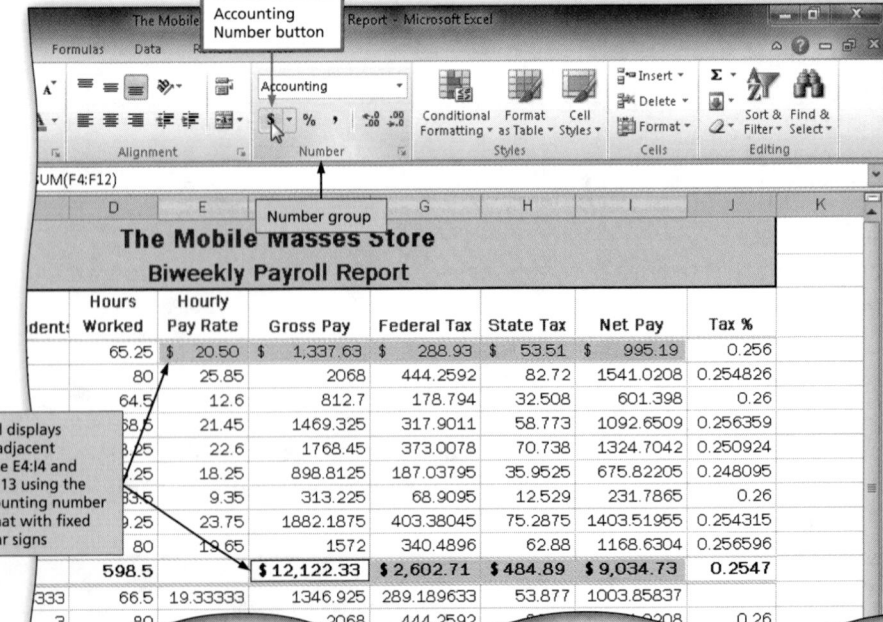

Figure 2–41

2

- Select the range to contain the Comma style format, cells E5:I12 in this case.

- Click the Comma Style button (Home tab | Number group) to assign the Comma style format to the selected range (Figure 2–42).

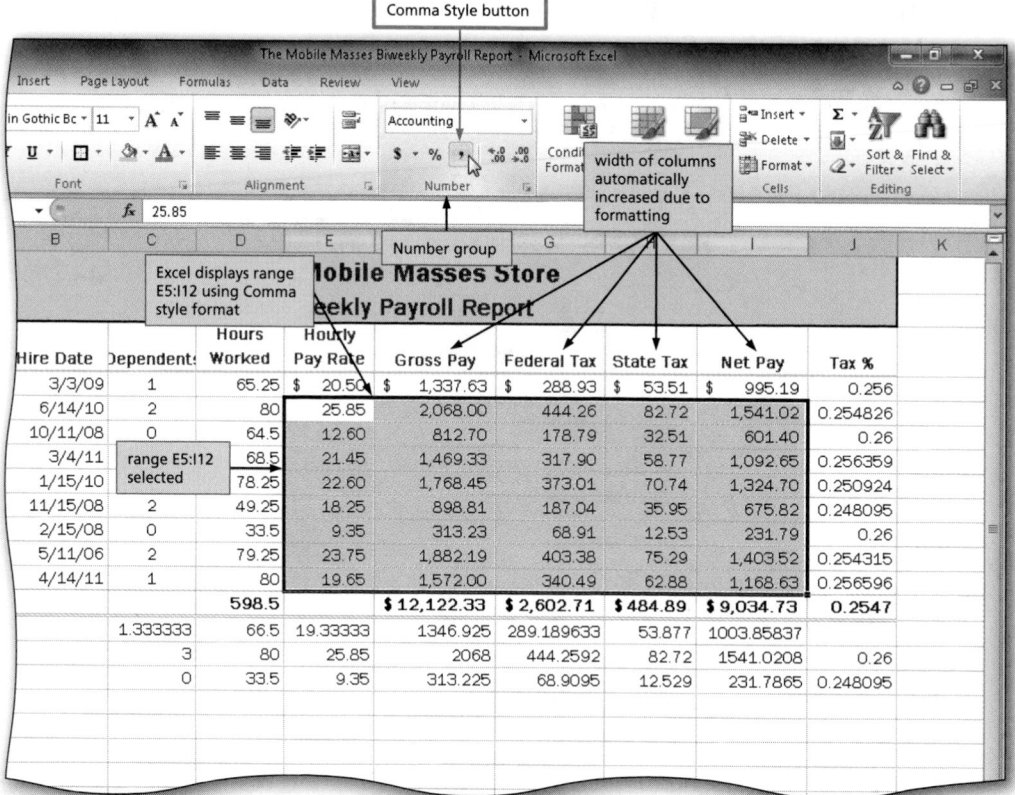

Figure 2–42

3

- Select the range to contain the Comma style format, cells D4:D16 in this case.

- Click the Comma Style button (Home tab | Number group) to assign the Comma style format to the selected range (Figure 2–43).

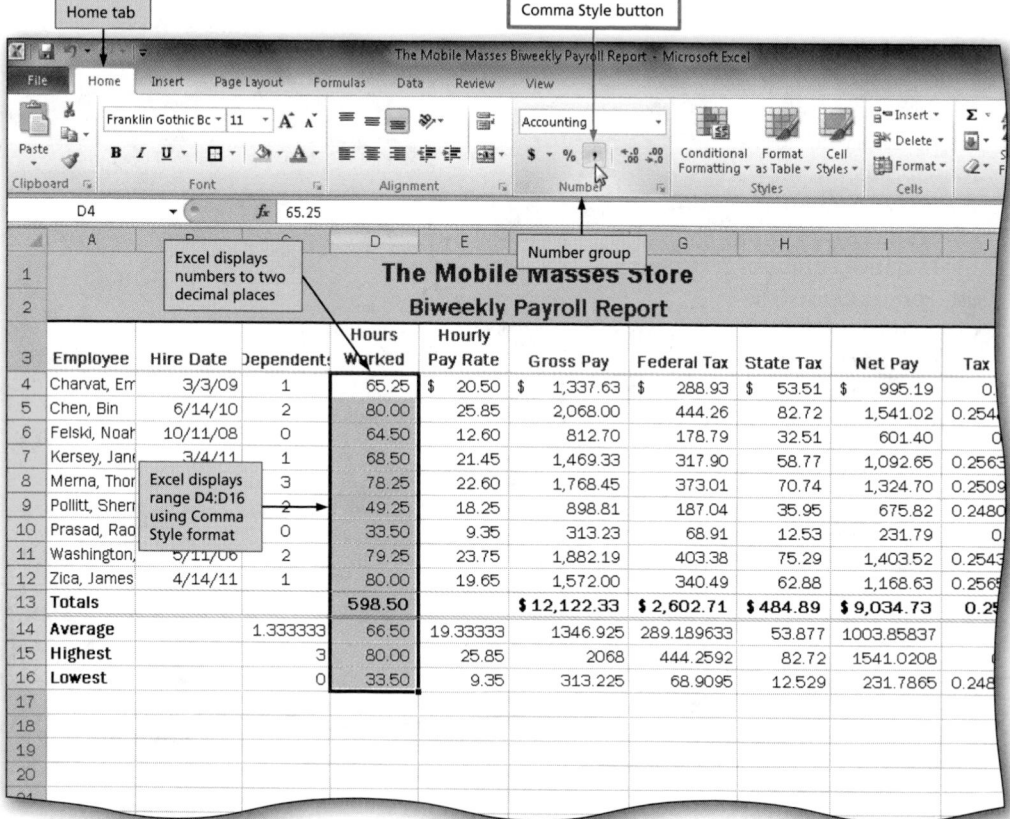

Figure 2–43

To Apply a Currency Style Format with a Floating Dollar Sign Using the Format Cells Dialog Box

The following steps use the Format Cells dialog box to apply the Currency style format with a floating dollar sign to the numbers in the range E14:I16.

1

- Select the range E14:I16 and then click the Format Cells: Number Dialog Box Launcher (Home tab | Number group) to display the Format Cells dialog box.

- If necessary, click the Number tab (Format Cells dialog box) to display the Number tab (Format Cells dialog box) (Figure 2–44).

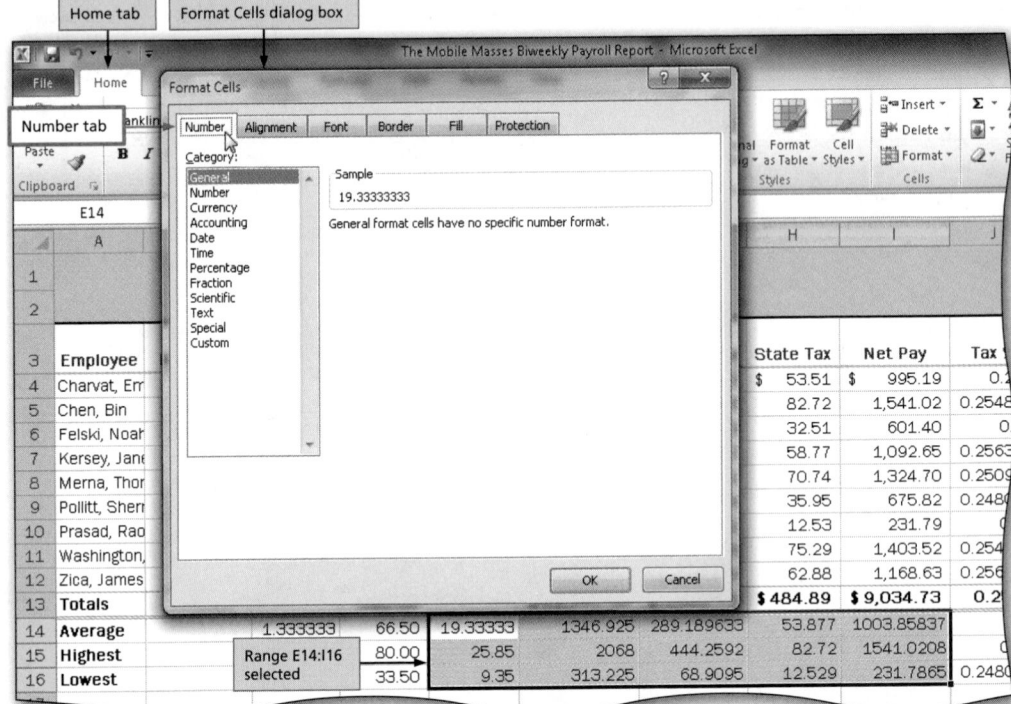

Figure 2–44

2

- Click Currency in the Category list to select the necessary number format category, and then click the third style ($1,234.10) in the Negative numbers list (Format Cells dialog box) to select the desired currency format for negative numbers (Figure 2–45).

Q&A How do I select the proper format?

You can choose from 12 categories of formats. Once you select a category, you can select the number of decimal places, whether or not a dollar sign should be displayed, and how negative numbers should appear. Selecting the appropriate negative numbers format is important, because doing so adds a space to the right of the number in order to align the numbers in the worksheet on the decimal points. Some of the available negative number formats do not align the numbers in the worksheet on the decimal points.

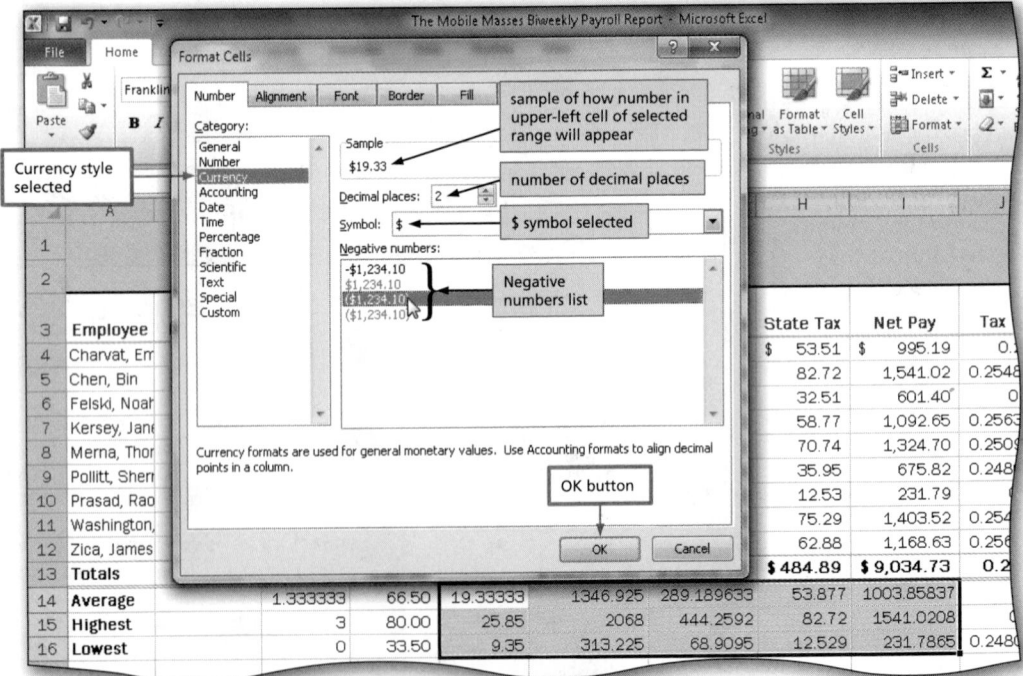

Figure 2–45

3

- Click the OK button (Format Cells dialog box) to assign the Currency style format with a floating dollar sign to the selected range (Figure 2–46).

Q&A What is the difference between using the Accounting Number style and Currency style?

When using the Accounting Number Style button, recall that a floating dollar sign always appears immediately to the left of the first digit, and the fixed dollar sign always appears on the left side of the cell. Cell E4, for example, has a fixed dollar sign, while cell E14 has a floating dollar sign. The Currency style was assigned to cell E14 using the Format Cells dialog box and the result is a floating dollar sign.

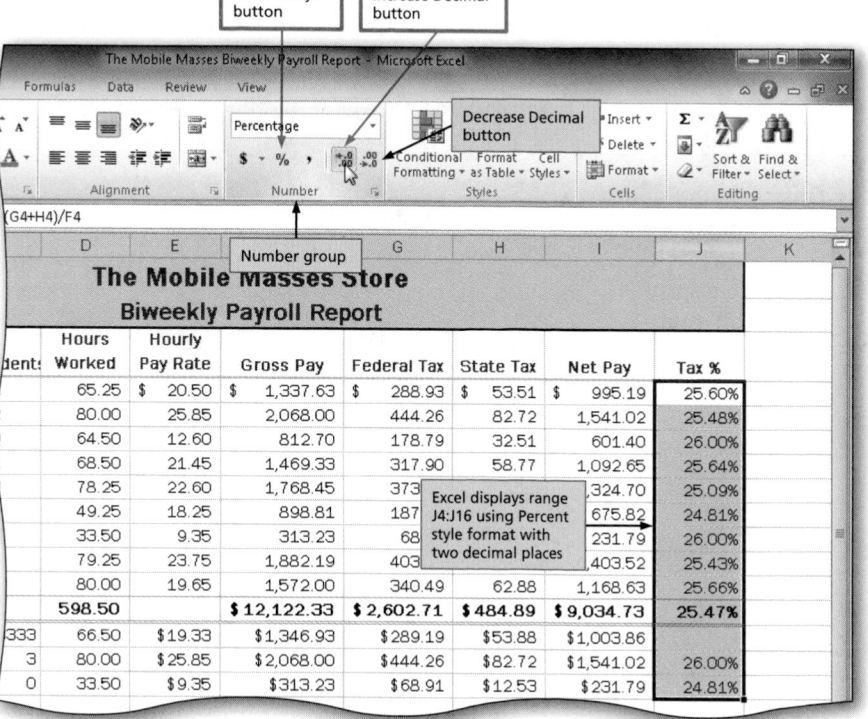

Figure 2–46

Other Ways

1. Press CTRL+1, click Number tab (Format Cells dialog box), click Currency

in Category list, select format, click OK button

2. Press CTRL+SHIFT+DOLLAR SIGN ($)

To Apply a Percent Style Format and Use the Increase Decimal Button

The next step is to format the tax % in column J. Currently, Excel displays the numbers in column J as a decimal fraction (for example, 0.256 in cell J4). The following steps format the range J4:J16 to the Percent style format with two decimal places.

1

- Select the range to format, cell J4:J16 in this case.

- Click the Percent Style button (Home tab | Number group) to display the numbers in the selected range as a rounded whole percent.

Q&A What is the result of clicking the Percent Style button?

The Percent Style button instructs Excel to display a value as a percentage, determined by multiplying the cell entry by 100, rounding the result to the nearest percent, and adding a percent sign. For example, when cell J4 is formatted using the Percent Style buttons, Excel displays the actual value 0.256 as 26%.

2

- Click the Increase Decimal button (Home tab | Number group) two times to display the numbers in the selected range with two decimal places (Figure 2–47).

Figure 2–47

Other Ways

1. Right-click range, click Format Cells on shortcut menu, click Number tab (Format Cells dialog box), click Percentage

in Category list, select format, click OK button

2. Press CTRL+1, click Number tab (Format Cells dialog box), click Percentage

in Category list, select format, click OK button

3. Press CTRL+SHIFT+ percent sign (%)

Conditional Formatting

The next step is to emphasize the values greater than 70 in column D by formatting them to appear with an orange background and white font color (Figure 2–48).

Plan Ahead

> **Establish rules for conditional formatting.**
>
> • Excel lets you apply formatting that appears only when the value in a cell meets conditions that you specify. This type of formatting is called **conditional formatting**. You can apply conditional formatting to a cell, a range of cells, the entire worksheet, or the entire workbook. Usually, you apply conditional formatting to a range of cells that contains values you want to highlight, if conditions warrant.
>
> • A **condition**, which is made up of two values and a relational operator, is true or false for each cell in the range. If the condition is true, then Excel applies the formatting. If the condition is false, then Excel suppresses the formatting. What makes conditional formatting so powerful is that the cell's appearance can change as you enter new values in the worksheet.
>
> • As with worksheet formatting, follow the less-is-more rule when considering conditional formatting. Use conditional formatting to make cells and ranges stand out and raise attention. Too much conditional formatting can result in confusion for the reader of the worksheet.

Conditional Formatting
You can assign any format to a cell, a range of cells, a worksheet, or an entire workbook conditionally. If the value of the cell changes and no longer meets the specified condition, Excel suppresses the conditional formatting.

To Apply Conditional Formatting

The following steps assign conditional formatting to the range D4:D12, so that any cell value greater than 70 will cause Excel to display the number in the cell with an orange background and a white font color.

1

• Select the range D4:D12.

• Click the Conditional Formatting button (Home tab | Styles group) to display the Conditional Formatting list (Figure 2–48).

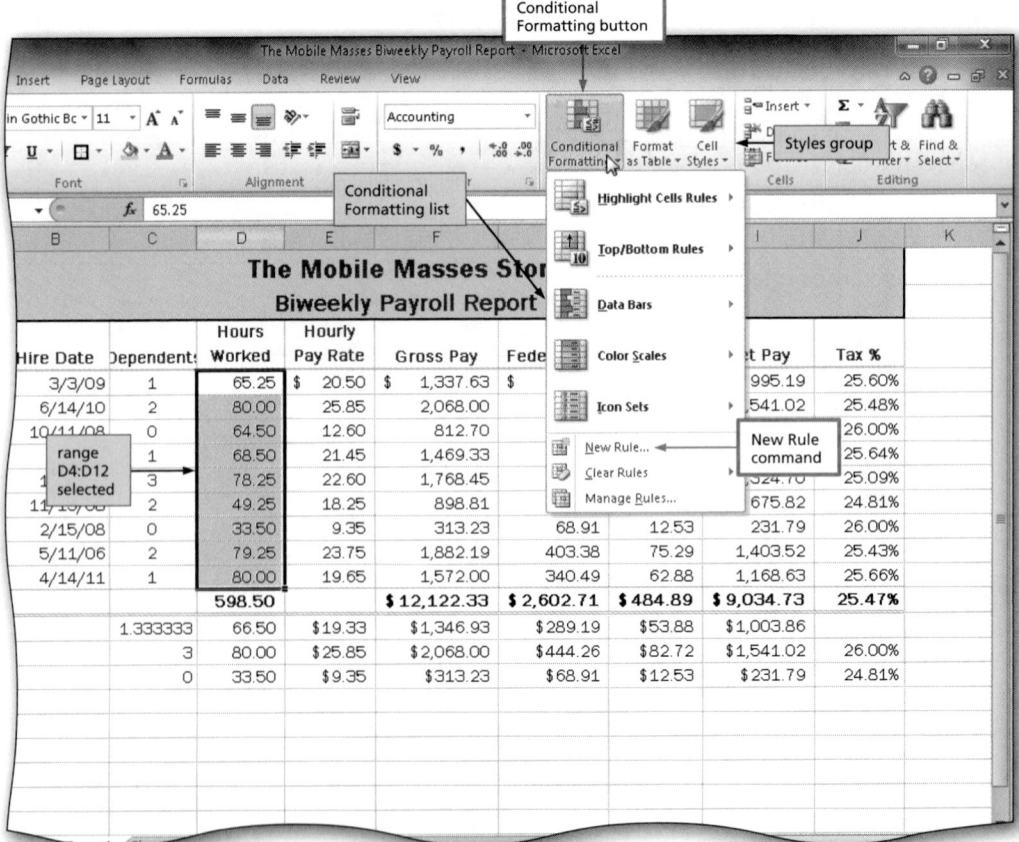

Figure 2–48

2

- Click New Rule in the Conditional Formatting list to display the New Formatting Rule dialog box.

- Click 'Format only cells that contain' in the Select a Rule Type area (New Formatting Rule dialog box) to change the 'Edit the Rule Description' area.

- In the 'Edit the Rule Description' area, click the box arrow in the relational operator box (second text box) to display a list of relational operators, and then select greater than to select the desired operator.

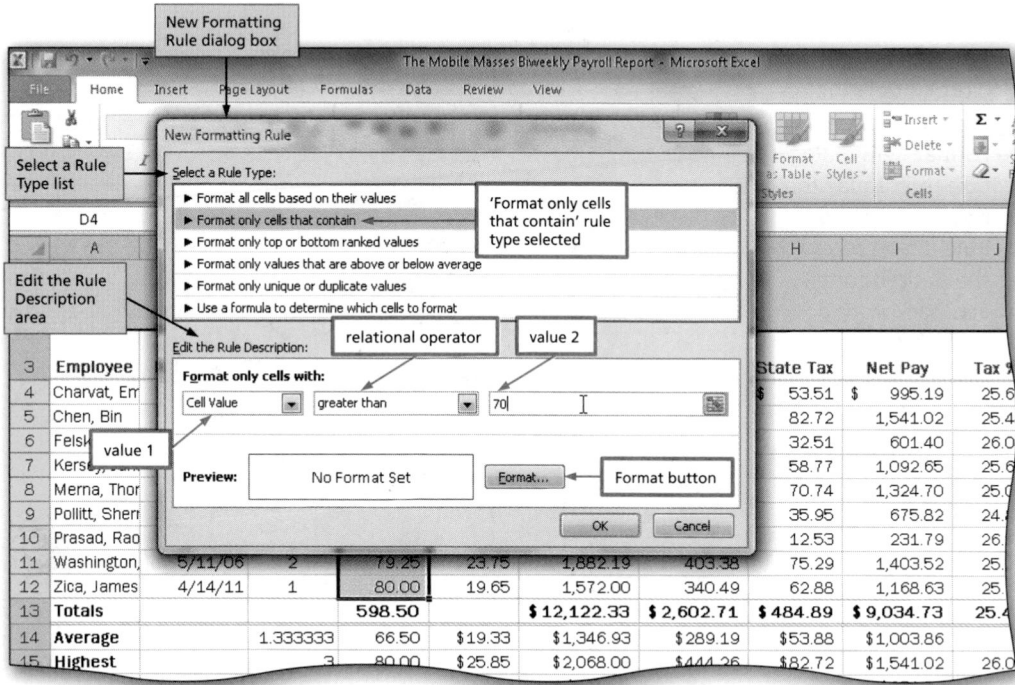

Figure 2–49

- Select the rightmost box, and then type   7 0   in the box in the 'Edit the Rule Description' area to enter the second value of the rule description (Figure 2–49).

Q&A

What do the changes in the 'Edit the Rule Description' indicate?

The 'Edit the Rule Description' area allows you to view and edit the rules for the conditional format. In this case, reading the area indicates that Excel should conditionally format only cells with cell values greater than 70.

3

- Click the Format button (New Formatting Rule dialog box) to display the Format Cells dialog box.

- If necessary, click the Font tab. Click the Color box arrow (Format Cells dialog box) to display the Color gallery and then click White, Background 1 (column 1, row 1) in the Color gallery to select the font color.

- Click the Fill tab (Format Cells dialog box) to display the Fill sheet and then click the orange color in column 5, row 5 to select the background color (Figure 2–50).

Figure 2–50

4

● Click the OK button (Format Cells dialog box) to close the Format Cells dialog box and display the New Formatting Rule dialog box with the desired font and background colors displayed in the Preview box (Figure 2–51).

Figure 2–51

5

● Click the OK button to assign the conditional format to the selected range.

● Click anywhere in the worksheet, such as cell A18, to deselect the current range (Figure 2–52).

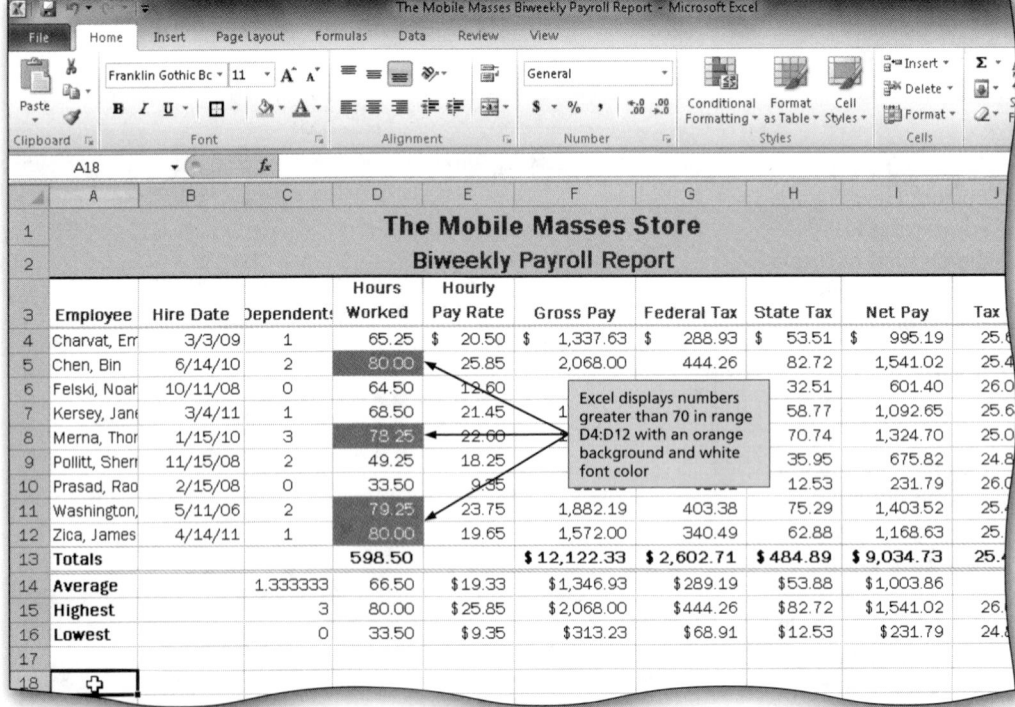

Figure 2–52

Conditional Formatting Operators

As shown in Figure 2–49 on page EX 105, the second text box in the New Formatting Rule dialog box allows you to select a relational operator, such as less than, to use in the condition. The eight different relational operators from which you can choose for conditional formatting in the New Formatting Rule dialog box are summarized in Table 2–5.

Table 2–5 Summary of Conditional Formatting Relational Operators

Relational Operator	Description
between	Cell value is between two numbers.
not between	Cell value is not between two numbers.
equal to	Cell value is equal to a number.
not equal to	Cell value is not equal to a number.
greater than	Cell value is greater than a number.
less than	Cell value is less than a number.
greater than or equal to	Cell value is greater than or equal to a number.
less than or equal to	Cell value is less than or equal to a number.

Changing the Widths of Columns and Heights of Rows

When Excel starts and displays a blank worksheet on the screen, all of the columns have a default width of 8.43 characters, or 64 pixels. These values may change depending on the theme applied to the workbook. For example, in this chapter, the Trek theme was applied to the workbook, resulting in columns having a default width of 8.11 characters. A character is defined as a letter, number, symbol, or punctuation mark in 11-point Calibri font, the default font used by Excel. An average of 8.43 characters in 11-point Calibri font will fit in a cell.

Another measure of the height and width of cells is pixels, which is short for picture element. A **pixel** is a dot on the screen that contains a color. The size of the dot is based on your screen's resolution. At the resolution of 1024 × 768 used in this book, 1024 pixels appear across the screen and 768 pixels appear down the screen for a total of 786,432 pixels. It is these 786,432 pixels that form the font and other items you see on the screen.

The default row height in a blank worksheet is 15 points (or 20 pixels). Recall from Chapter 1 that a point is equal to 1/72 of an inch. Thus, 15 points is equal to about 1/5 of an inch. You can change the width of the columns or height of the rows at any time to make the worksheet easier to read or to ensure that Excel displays an entry properly in a cell.

BTW

Hidden Rows and Columns
For some people, trying to unhide a range of columns using the mouse can be frustrating. An alternative is to use the keyboard: select the columns to the right and left of the hidden columns and then press CTRL+SHIFT+) (RIGHT PARENTHESIS). To use the keyboard to hide a range of columns, press CTRL+0 (ZERO). You also can use the keyboard to unhide a range of rows by selecting the rows immediately above and below the hidden rows and then pressing CTRL+SHIFT+((LEFT PARENTHESIS). To use the keyboard to hide a range of rows, press CTRL+9.

To Change the Widths of Columns

When changing the column width, you can set the width manually or you can instruct Excel to size the column to best fit. **Best fit** means that the width of the column will be increased or decreased so that the widest entry will fit in the column. Sometimes, you may prefer more or less white space in a column than best fit provides. To change the white space, Excel allows you to change column widths manually.

When the format you assign to a cell causes the entry to exceed the width of a column, Excel automatically changes the column width to best fit. If you do not assign a format to a cell or cells in a column, the column width will remain 8.43 characters. To set a column width to best fit, double-click the right boundary of the column heading above row 1.

The steps on the following pages change the column widths: column A, B, and C to best fit; column H to 10.22 characters; and columns D, E, and J to 7.56 characters.

1

- Drag through column headings A, B, and C above row 1 to select the columns.

- Point to the boundary on the right side of column heading C to cause the mouse pointer to become a split double arrow (Figure 2–53).

Q&A

What if I want to make a large change to the column width?

If you want to increase or decrease column width significantly, you can right-click a column heading and then use the Column Width command on the shortcut menu to change the column's width. To use this command, however, you must select one or more entire columns.

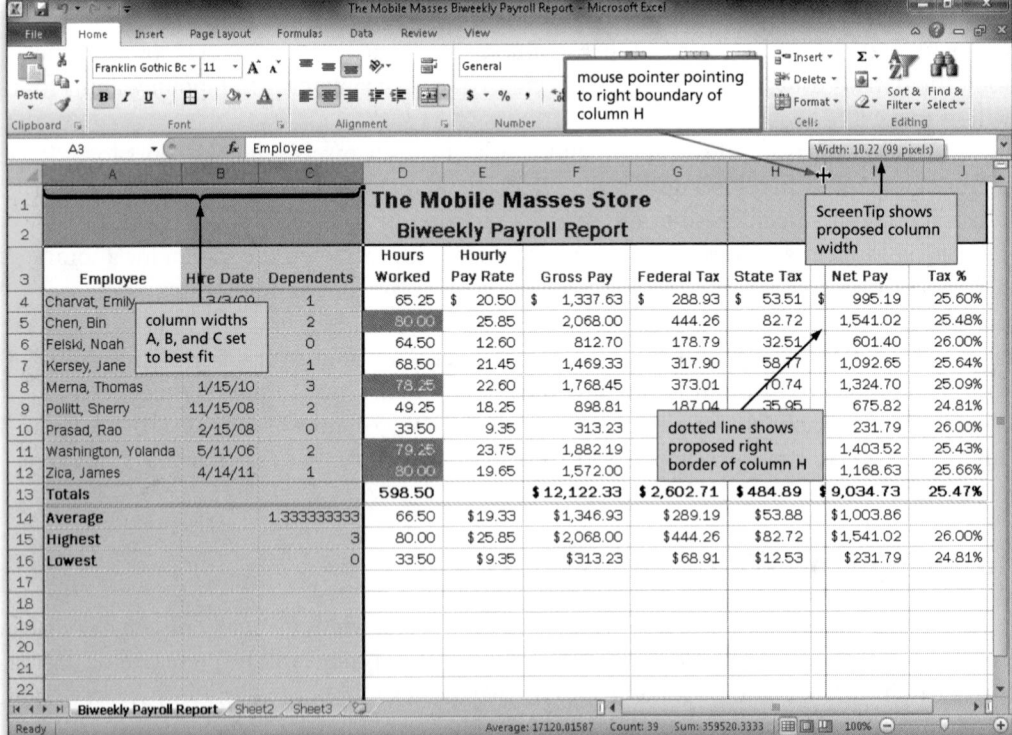

Figure 2–53

2

- Double-click the right boundary of column heading C to change the width of the selected columns to best fit.

- Point to the boundary on the right side of the column H heading above row 1.

- When the mouse pointer changes to a split double arrow, drag until the ScreenTip indicates Width: 10.22 (99 pixels). Do not release the mouse button (Figure 2–54).

Q&A

What happens if I change the column width to zero (0)?

If you decrease the column width to 0, the column is hidden. **Hiding cells** is a technique you can use to hide data that might not be relevant to a particular report or sensitive data that you do not want others to see. To instruct Excel to display a hidden column, position the mouse pointer to the right of the column heading boundary where the hidden column is located and then drag to the right.

Figure 2–54

3

- Release the mouse button to change the column width.

- Click the column D heading above row 1 to select the column.

- While holding down the CTRL key, click the column E heading and then the column J heading above row 1 so that nonadjacent columns are selected (Figure 2–55).

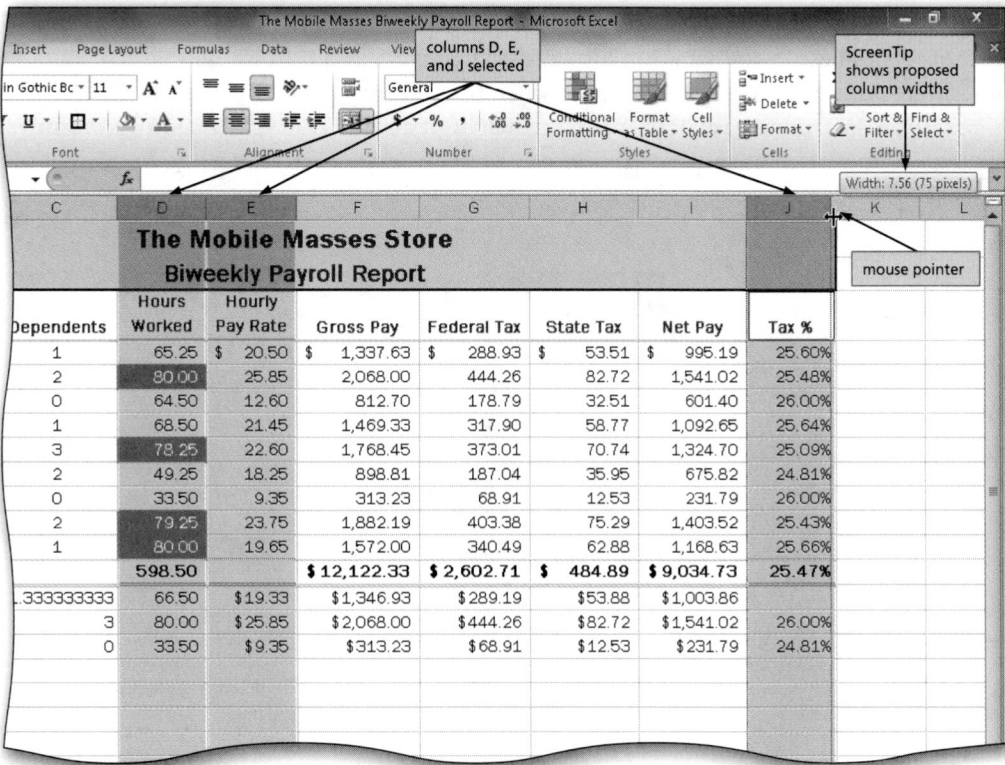

Figure 2–55

4

- If necessary, scroll the worksheet to the right so that the right border of column J is visible. Point to the boundary on the right side of the column J heading above row 1.

- Drag until the ScreenTip indicates Width: 7.56 (75 pixels). Do not release the mouse button (Figure 2–56).

Figure 2–56

5

- Release the mouse button to change the column widths.

- If necessary, scroll the worksheet to the left so that the left border of column A is visible.

- Click anywhere in the worksheet, such as cell A18, to deselect the columns (Figure 2–57).

Other Ways

1. Right-click column heading or drag through multiple column headings and right-click, click Column Width on shortcut menu, enter desired column width, click OK button

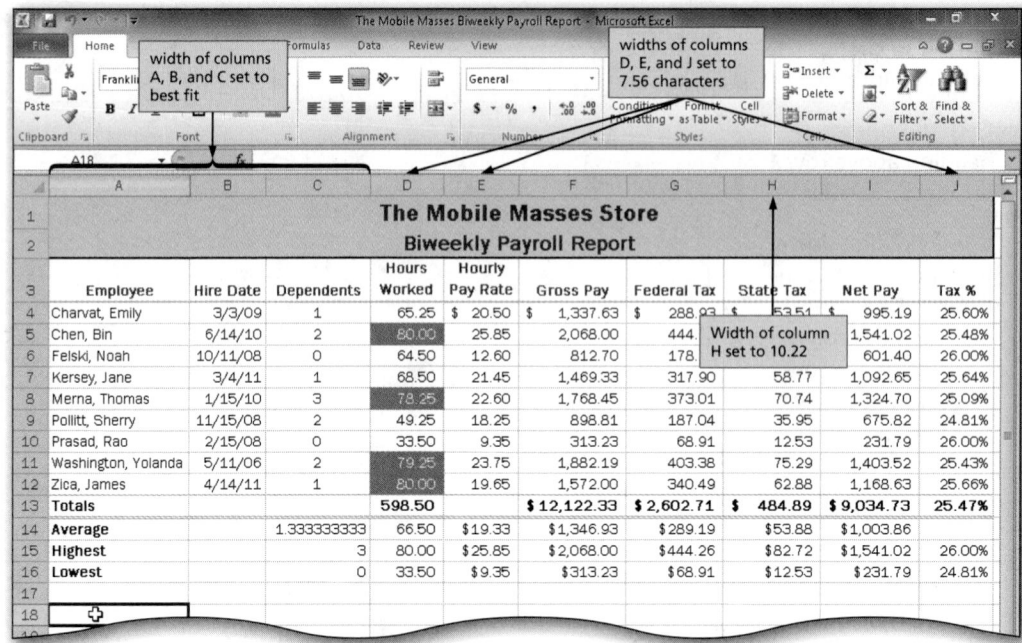

Figure 2–57

To Change the Heights of Rows

When you increase the font size of a cell entry, such as the title in cell A1, Excel automatically increases the row height to best fit so that it can display the characters properly. Recall that Excel did this earlier when multiple lines were entered in a cell in row 3, and when the cell style of the worksheet title and subtitle was changed.

You also can increase or decrease the height of a row manually to improve the appearance of the worksheet. The following steps improve the appearance of the worksheet by increasing the height of row 3 to 48.00 points and increasing the height of row 14 to 27.00 points.

1

- Point to the boundary below row heading 3.

- Drag down until the ScreenTip indicates Height: 48.00 (64 pixels). Do not release the mouse button (Figure 2–58).

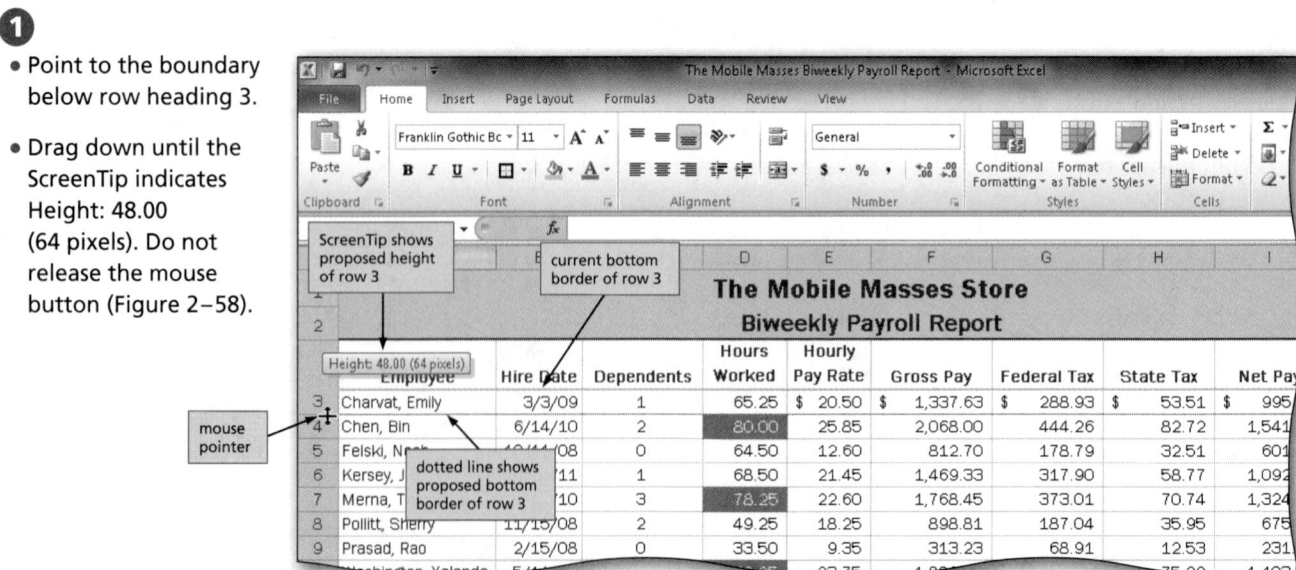

Figure 2–58

2

- Release the mouse button to change the row height.

- Point to the boundary below row heading 14.

- Drag down until the ScreenTip indicates Height: 27.00 (36 pixels). Do not release the mouse button (Figure 2–59).

Figure 2–59

3

- Release the mouse button to change the row height.

- Click anywhere in the worksheet, such as cell A18, to deselect the current cell (Figure 2–60).

Q&A Can I hide a row?

Yes. As with column widths, when you decrease the row height to 0, the row is hidden. To instruct Excel to display a hidden row, position the mouse pointer just below the row heading boundary where the row is hidden and then drag down. To set a row height to best fit, double-click the bottom boundary of the row heading.

Figure 2–60

Break Point: If you wish to take a break, this is a good place to do so. Be sure to save the The Mobile Masses Biweekly Payroll Report file again and then you can quit Excel. To resume at a later time, start Excel, open the file called The Mobile Masses Biweekly Payroll Report and continue following the steps from this location forward.

BTW

Spell Checking
While Excel's spell checker is a valuable tool, it is not infallible. You should proofread your workbook carefully by pointing to each word and saying it aloud as you point to it. Be mindful of misused words such as its and it's, through and though, and to and too. Nothing undermines a good impression more than a professional looking report with misspelled words.

Checking Spelling

Excel includes a **spell checker** you can use to check a worksheet for spelling errors. The spell checker looks for spelling errors by comparing words on the worksheet against words contained in its standard dictionary. If you often use specialized terms that are not in the standard dictionary, you may want to add them to a custom dictionary using the Spelling dialog box.

When the spell checker finds a word that is not in either dictionary, it displays the word in the Spelling dialog box. You then can correct it if it is misspelled.

To Check Spelling on the Worksheet

To illustrate how Excel responds to a misspelled word, the following steps misspell purposely the word, Employee, in cell A3 as the word, Empolyee, as shown in Figure 2–61.

1

- Click cell A3 and then type **Empolyee** to misspell the word Employee.

- Select cell A1 so that the spell checker begins checking at the selected cell.

- Click Review on the Ribbon to display the Review tab.

- Click the Spelling button (Review tab | Proofing group) to run the spell checker and display the misspelled word in the Spelling dialog box (Figure 2–61).

Figure 2–61

Q&A

What happens when the spell checker finds a misspelled word?

When the spell checker identifies that a cell contains a word not in its standard or custom dictionary, it selects that cell as the active cell and displays the Spelling dialog box. The Spelling dialog box lists the word not found in the dictionary and a list of suggested corrections (Figure 2–61).

②

- Click the Change button (Spelling dialog box) to change the misspelled word to the correct word (Figure 2–62).

- Click the Close button (Spelling dialog box) to close the Spelling dialog box.

- If the Microsoft Excel dialog box is displayed, click the OK button.

③

- Click anywhere in the worksheet, such as cell A18, to deselect the current cell.

- Display the Home tab.

- Click the Save button on the Quick Access Toolbar to save the workbook.

Figure 2–62

Q&A

What other actions can I take in the Spelling dialog box?

If one of the words in the Suggestions list is correct, click it and then click the Change button. If none of the suggestions is correct, type the correct word in the Not in Dictionary text box and then click the Change button. To change the word throughout the worksheet, click the Change All button instead of the Change button. To skip correcting the word, click the Ignore Once button. To have Excel ignore the word for the remainder of the worksheet, click the Ignore All button.

Other Ways
1. Press F7

Additional Spell Checker Considerations

Consider these additional guidelines when using the spell checker:

- To check the spelling of the text in a single cell, double-click the cell to make the formula bar active and then click the Spelling button (Review tab | Proofing group).

- If you select a single cell so that the formula bar is not active and then start the spell checker, Excel checks the remainder of the worksheet, including notes and embedded charts.

- If you select a cell other than cell A1 before you start the spell checker, Excel will display a dialog box when the spell checker reaches the end of the worksheet, asking if you want to continue checking at the beginning.

- If you select a range of cells before starting the spell checker, Excel checks the spelling of the words only in the selected range.

- To check the spelling of all the sheets in a workbook, right-click any sheet tab, click Select All Sheets on the sheet tab shortcut menu, and then start the spell checker.

- To add words to the dictionary such as your last name, click the Add to Dictionary button in the Spelling dialog box (Figure 2–61) when Excel identifies the word as not in the dictionary.

- Click the AutoCorrect button (Spelling dialog box) to add the misspelled word and the correct version of the word to the AutoCorrect list. For example, suppose that you misspell the word, do, as the word, dox. When the spell checker displays the Spelling dialog box with the correct word, do, in the Change to box, click the AutoCorrect button. Then, anytime in the future that you type the word dox, Excel automatically will change it to the word, do.

BTW

Error Checking
Always take the time to check the formulas of a worksheet before submitting it to your supervisor. You can check formulas by clicking the Error Checking button (Formulas tab | Formula Auditing group). You also should test the formulas by employing data that tests the limits of formulas. Experienced spreadsheet specialists spend as much time testing a workbook as they do creating it, and they do so before placing the workbook into production.

BTW

Changing the Header and Footer Size
To make a header or footer include more lines of text, change the top or bottom margin for the worksheet and then add the necessary lines of text to the header or footer. To make a header or footer wider, continue typing text in the header or footer area and the header or footer automatically will widen to accommodate the text. If text from adjacent header or footer areas overlaps, Excel displays the overlapped text, which will appear unreadable.

Preparing to Print the Worksheet

Excel allows for a great deal of customization in how a worksheet appears when printed. For example, the margins on the page can be adjusted. A header or footer can be added to each printed page as well. Excel also has the capability to work on the worksheet in Page Layout view. **Page Layout view** allows you to create or modify a worksheet while viewing how it will look in printed format. The default view that you have worked in up until this point in the book is called **Normal view**.

Plan Ahead

Specify how the printed worksheet should appear.

Before printing a worksheet, you should consider how the worksheet will appear when printed. In order to fit as much information on the printed page as possible, the margins of the worksheet should be set to a reasonably small width and height. While the current version of a worksheet may print on one page, you may add more data in the future that causes the worksheet to extend to multiple pages. It is, therefore, a good idea to add a page header to the worksheet that prints in the top margin of each page. A **header** is common content that prints on every page of a worksheet. Landscape orientation is a good choice for large worksheets because the printed worksheet's width is greater than its length.

To Change the Worksheet's Margins, Header, and Orientation in Page Layout View

The following steps change to Page Layout view, narrow the margins of the worksheet, change the header of the worksheet, and set the orientation of the worksheet to landscape. Often, you may want to reduce margins so that the printed worksheet better fits the page. **Margins** are those portions of a printed page outside the main body of the printed document and always are blank when printed. Recall that in Chapter 1, the worksheet was printed in landscape orientation. The current worksheet also is too wide for a single page and requires landscape orientation to fit on one page in a readable manner.

 1

- Click the Page Layout button on the status bar to view the worksheet in Page Layout view (Figure 2–63).

Q&A

What are some key features of Page Layout view?

Page Layout view shows the worksheet divided into pages. A gray background separates each page. The white areas surrounding each page indicate the print margins. The top of each page includes a Header area, and the bottom of each page includes a Footer area. Page Layout view also includes a ruler at the top of the page that assists you in placing objects on the page, such as charts and pictures.

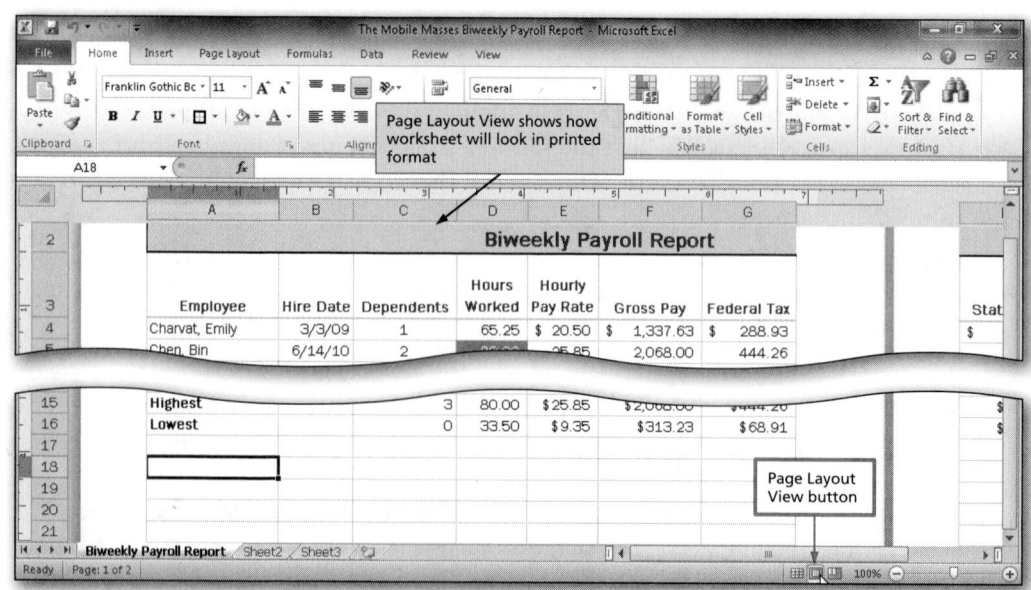

Figure 2–63

2

- Display the Page Layout tab.

- Click the Margins button (Page Layout tab | Page Setup group) to display the Margins gallery (Figure 2–64).

Figure 2–64

3

- Click Narrow in the Margins gallery to change the worksheet margins to the Narrow margin style.

- Drag the scroll bar on the right side of the worksheet to the top so that row 1 of the worksheet is displayed.

- Click above the worksheet title in cell A1 in the center area of the Header area.

- Type **Samuel Snyder** and then press the ENTER key. Type **Chief Financial Officer** to complete the worksheet header (Figure 2–65).

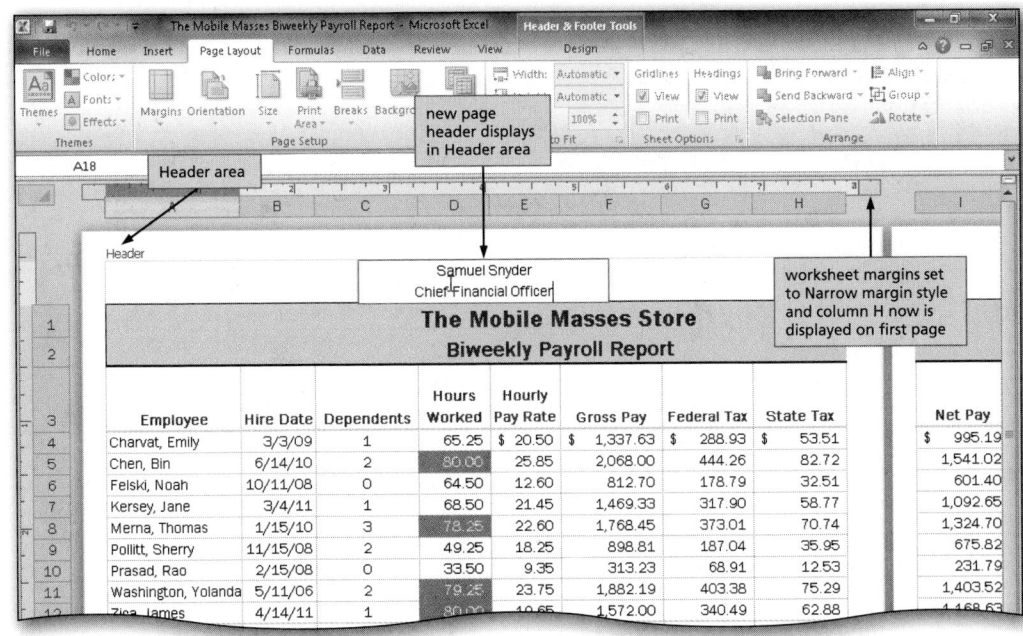

Figure 2–65

Q&A

What else can I place in a header?

You can add text, page number information, date and time information, the file path of the workbook, the file name of the workbook, the sheet name of the workbook, and pictures to a header.

4

- Select cell B16 to deselect the header. Click the Orientation button (Page Layout tab | Page Setup group) to display the Orientation gallery (Figure 2–66).

Q&A

Why do I need to deselect the header?

Excel disables almost all of the buttons on the Ribbon as you edit a header or footer. In addition to the commands on the Design tab (Figure 2–65 on the previous page), only a few commands remain available on the Home tab on the Ribbon. To continue working in Excel, therefore, you should select a cell in the worksheet so that all of the commands on the Ribbon are available for your use.

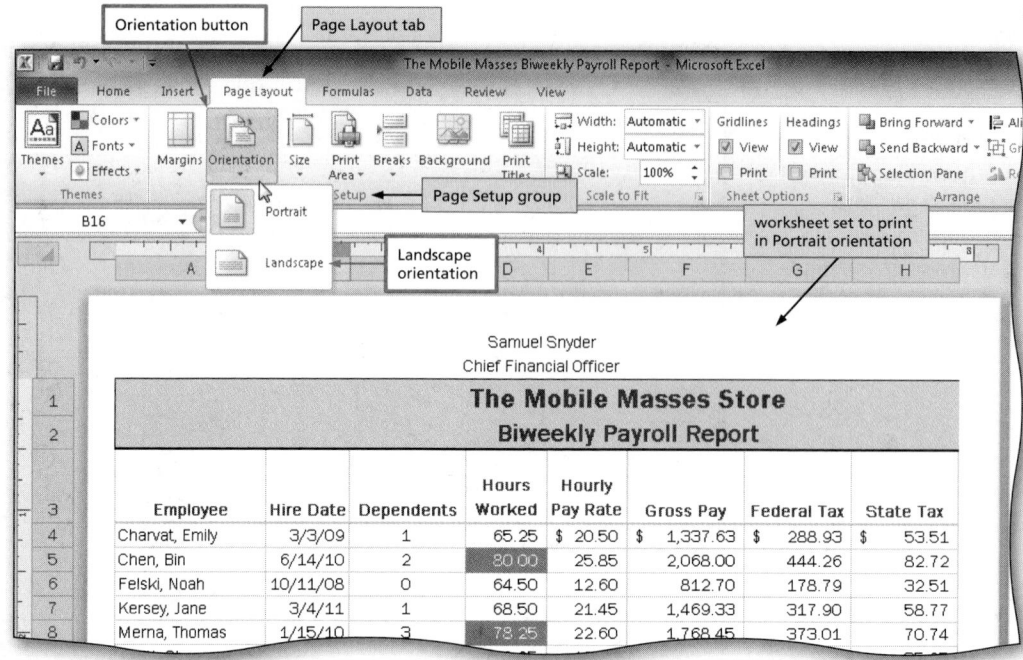

Figure 2–66

5

- Click Landscape in the Orientation gallery to change the worksheet's orientation to landscape (Figure 2–67).

Q&A

Do I need to change the orientation every time I want to print the worksheet?

No. Once you change the orientation and save the workbook, Excel will save the orientation setting for that workbook until you change it. When you open a new workbook, Excel sets the orientation to portrait.

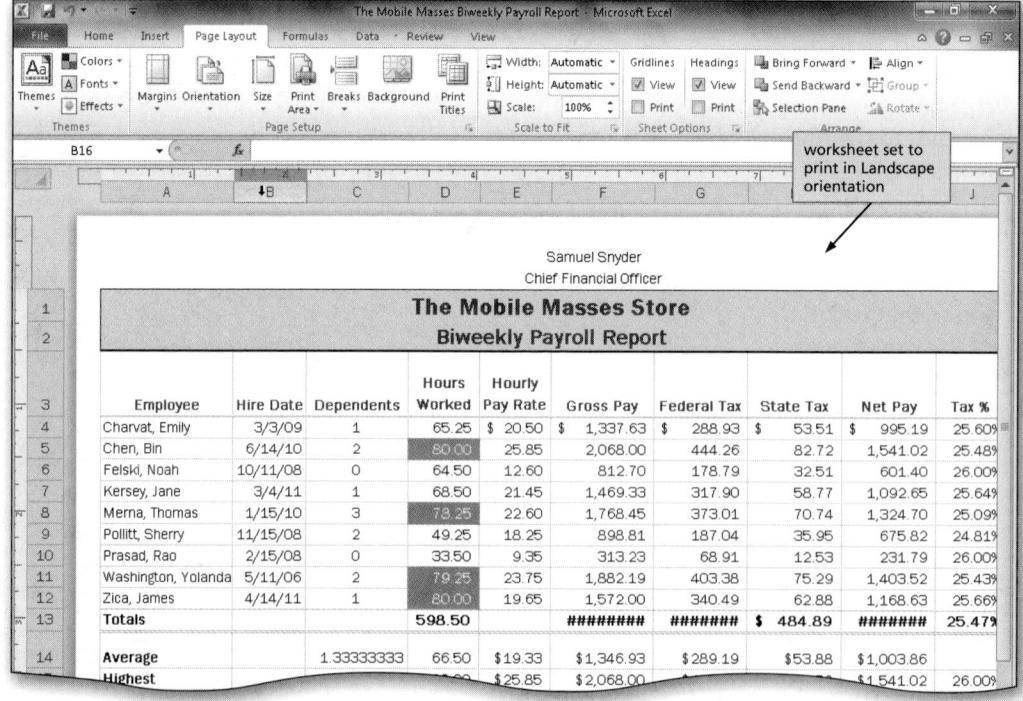

Figure 2–67

Other Ways
1. Click Page Setup Dialog Box Launcher (Page Layout tab | Page Setup group), click Page tab	(Page Setup dialog box), click Portrait or Landscape, click OK button

Printing the Worksheet

Excel provides other options for printing a worksheet. The following sections print the worksheet and print a section of the worksheet.

To Print a Worksheet

The following steps print the worksheet.

1 Click File on the Ribbon to open the Backstage view.

2 Click the Print tab in the Backstage view to display the Print gallery.

3 If necessary, click the Printer Status button in the Print gallery to display a list of available Printer options and then click the desired printer to change the currently selected printer.

4 Click the Print button in the Print gallery to print the worksheet in landscape orientation on the currently selected printer.

5 When the printer stops, retrieve the hard copy (Figure 2–68).

landscape orientation

Samuel Snyder
Chief Financial Officer

The Mobile Masses Store
Biweekly Payroll Report

Employee	Hire Date	Dependents	Hours Worked	Hourly Pay Rate	Gross Pay	Federal Tax	State Tax	Net Pay	Tax %
Charvat, Emily	3/3/09	1	65.25	$ 20.50	$ 1,337.63	$ 288.93	$ 53.51	$ 995.19	25.60%
Chen, Bin	6/14/10	2	80.00	25.85	2,068.00	444.26	82.72	1,541.02	25.48%
Felski, Noah	10/11/08	0	64.50	12.60	812.70	178.79	32.51	601.40	26.00%
Kersey, Jane	3/4/11	1	68.50	21.45	1,469.33	317.90	58.77	1,092.65	25.64%
Merna, Thomas	1/15/10	3	78.25	22.60	1,768.45	373.01	70.74	1,324.70	25.09%
Pollitt, Sherry	11/15/08	2	49.25	18.25	898.81	187.04	35.95	675.82	24.81%
Prasad, Rao	2/15/08	0	33.50	9.35	313.23	68.91	12.53	231.79	26.00%
Washington, Yolanda	5/11/06	2	79.25	23.75	1,882.19	403.38	75.29	1,403.52	25.43%
Zica, James	4/14/11	1	80.00	19.65	1,572.00	340.49	62.88	1,168.63	25.66%
Totals			598.50		$ 12,122.33	$ 2,602.71	$ 484.89	$ 9,034.73	25.47%
Average		1.333333333	66.50	$19.33	$1,346.93	$289.19	$53.88	$1,003.86	
Highest		3	80.00	$25.85	$2,068.00	$444.26	$82.72	$1,541.02	26.00%
Lowest		0	33.50	$9.35	$313.23	$68.91	$12.53	$231.79	24.81%

Figure 2–68

To Print a Section of the Worksheet

You might not always want to print the entire worksheet. You can print portions of the worksheet by selecting the range of cells to print and then clicking the Selection option button in the Print what area in the Print dialog box. The following steps print the range A3:F16.

• Select the range to print, cells A3:F16 in this case.

• Click File on the Ribbon to open the Backstage view.

• Click the Print tab to display the Print gallery.

• Click Print Active Sheets in the Settings area (Print tab | Print gallery) to display a list of options that determine what Excel should print (Figure 2–69).

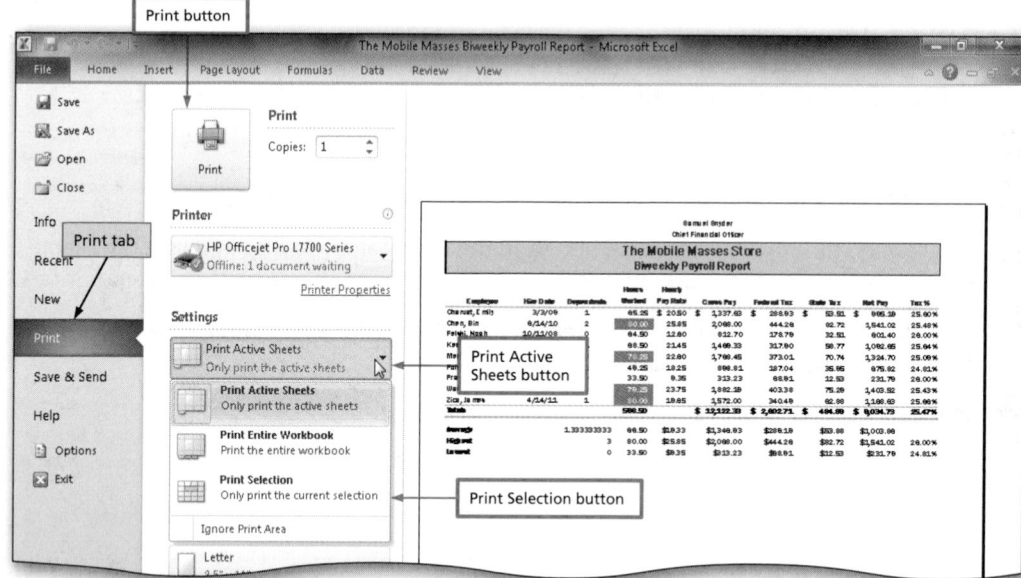

Figure 2–69

②

• Click Print Selection to instruct Excel to print only the selected range.

• Click the Print button in the Print gallery to print the selected range of the worksheet on the currently selected printer (Figure 2–70).

• Click the Normal button on the status bar to return to Normal view.

• Click cell A18 to deselect the range A3:F16.

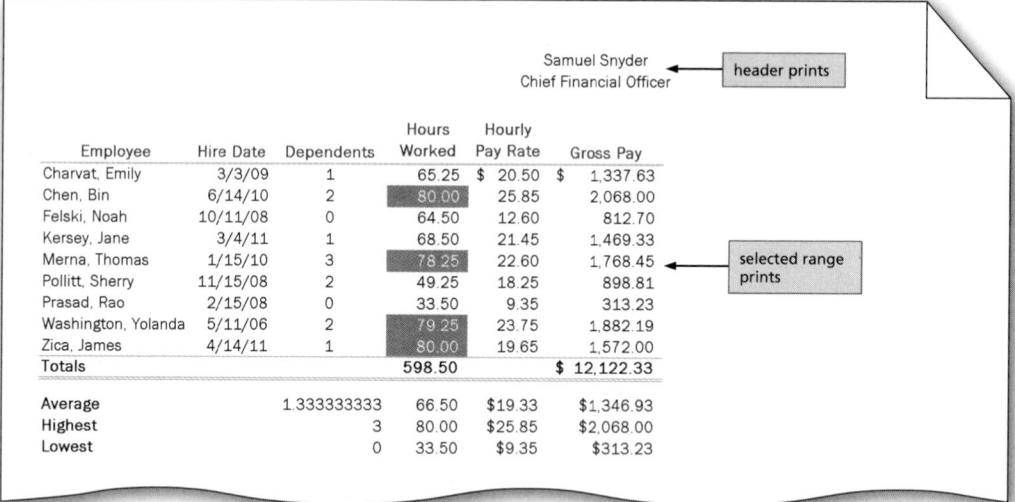

header prints

Employee	Hire Date	Dependents	Hours Worked	Hourly Pay Rate	Gross Pay
Charvat, Emily	3/3/09	1	65.25	$ 20.50	$ 1,337.63
Chen, Bin	6/14/10	2	80.00	25.85	2,068.00
Felski, Noah	10/11/08	0	64.50	12.60	812.70
Kersey, Jane	3/4/11	1	68.50	21.45	1,469.33
Merna, Thomas	1/15/10	3	78.25	22.60	1,768.45
Pollitt, Sherry	11/15/08	2	49.25	18.25	898.81
Prasad, Rao	2/15/08	0	33.50	9.35	313.23
Washington, Yolanda	5/11/06	2	79.25	23.75	1,882.19
Zica, James	4/14/11	1	80.00	19.65	1,572.00
Totals			598.50		$ 12,122.33
Average		1.333333333	66.50	$19.33	$1,346.93
Highest		3	80.00	$25.85	$2,068.00
Lowest		0	33.50	$9.35	$313.23

selected range prints

Figure 2–70

Q&A

What are my options for telling Excel what to print?

Excel includes three options to allow you to determine what should be printed (Figure 2–69). As shown in the previous steps, the Print Selection button instructs Excel to print the selected range. The Print Active Sheets button instructs Excel to print the active worksheet (the worksheet currently on the screen) or the selected worksheets. Finally, the Print Entire Workbook button instructs Excel to print all of the worksheets in the workbook.

Other Ways

1. Select range, click Print Area button (Page Layout tab | Page Setup group), click Set Print Area, click Quick Print button on Quick Access Toolbar, click Print Area, click Clear Print Area

2. Select range, click Print Area button (Page Layout tab | Page Setup group), click Set Print Area, click File tab to open Backstage view, click Print tab, click Print button

Displaying and Printing the Formulas Version of the Worksheet

BTW

Values versus Formulas
When completing class assignments, do not enter numbers in cells that require formulas. Most instructors will check both the values version and formulas version of your worksheets. The formulas version verifies that you entered formulas, rather than numbers, in formula-based cells.

Thus far, you have been working with the **values version** of the worksheet, which shows the results of the formulas you have entered, rather than the actual formulas. Excel also can display and print the **formulas version** of the worksheet, which shows the actual formulas you have entered, rather than the resulting values.

The formulas version is useful for debugging a worksheet. **Debugging** is the process of finding and correcting errors in the worksheet. Viewing and printing the formulas version instead of the values version makes it easier to see any mistakes in the formulas.

When you change from the values version to the formulas version, Excel increases the width of the columns so that the formulas and text do not overflow into adjacent cells on the right. The formulas version of the worksheet, thus, usually is significantly wider than the values version. To fit the wide printout on one page, you can use landscape orientation, which has already been selected for the workbook, and the Fit to option in the Page sheet in the Page Setup dialog box.

To Display the Formulas in the Worksheet and Fit the Printout on One Page

The following steps change the view of the worksheet from the values version to the formulas version of the worksheet and then print the formulas version on one page.

1
- Press CTRL+ACCENT MARK (`) to display the worksheet with formulas.
- Click the right horizontal scroll arrow until column J appears (Figure 2–71).

2
- Click the Page Setup Dialog Box Launcher (Page Layout tab | Page Setup group) to display the Page Setup dialog box.

Figure 2–71

3
- If necessary, click Landscape in the Orientation area to select it.
- If necessary, click Fit to in the Scaling area to select it.

4

- Click the Print button (Page Setup dialog box) to print the formulas in the worksheet on one page in landscape orientation (Figure 2–72). If necessary, in the Backstage view, select the Print Active Sheets option in the Settings area of the Print gallery.

- When Excel displays the Backstage view, click the Print button to print the worksheet.

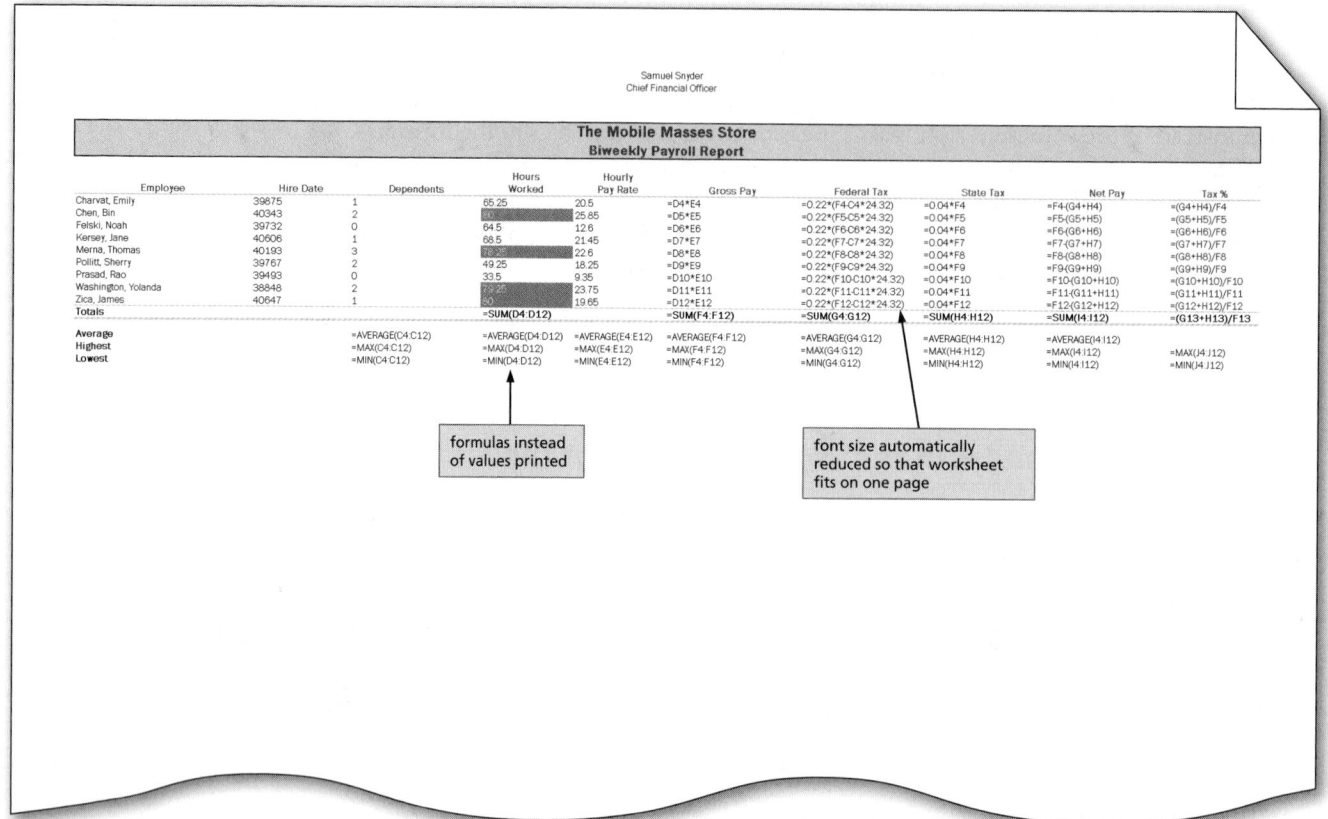

Figure 2–72

5

- After viewing and printing the formulas version, press CTRL+ACCENT MARK (`) to instruct Excel to display the values version.

- Click the left horizontal scroll arrow until column A appears.

Certification
The Microsoft Office Specialist (MOS) program provides an opportunity for you to obtain a valuable industry credential — proof that you have the Excel 2010 skills required by employers. For more information, visit the Excel 2010 Certification Web page (scsite.com/ex2010/cert).

To Change the Print Scaling Option Back to 100%

Depending on your printer, you may have to change the Print Scaling option back to 100% after using the Fit to option. Doing so will cause the worksheet to print at the default print scaling of 100%. The following steps reset the Print Scaling option so that future worksheets print at 100%, instead of being resized to print on one page.

1 If necessary, display the Page Layout tab and then click the Page Setup Dialog Box Launcher (Page Layout tab | Page Setup group) to display the Page Setup dialog box.

2 Click Adjust to in the Scaling area to select the Adjust to setting.

3 If necessary, type 100 in the Adjust to box to adjust the print scaling to a new percentage.

4 Click the OK button (Page Setup dialog box) to set the print scaling to normal.

5 Display the Home tab.

Q&A What is the purpose of the Adjust to box in the Page Setup dialog box?

The Adjust to box allows you to specify the percentage of reduction or enlargement in the printout of a worksheet. The default percentage is 100%. When you click the Fit to option, this percentage automatically changes to the percentage required to fit the printout on one page.

BTW **Quick Reference**
For a table that lists how to complete the tasks covered in this book using the mouse, Ribbon, shortcut menu, and keyboard, see the Quick Reference Summary at the back of this book, or visit the Excel 2010 Quick Reference Web page (scsite.com/ex2010/qr).

To Save the Workbook and Quit Excel

With the workbook complete, the following steps save the workbook and quit Excel.

1 Click the Save button on the Quick Access Toolbar.

2 Click the Close button on the upper-right corner of the title bar.

Chapter Summary

In this chapter you have learned how to enter formulas, calculate an average, find the highest and lowest numbers in a range, verify formulas using Range Finder, added borders, align text, format numbers, change column widths and row heights, and add conditional formatting to a range of numbers. In addition, you learned to spell check a worksheet, print a section of a worksheet, and display and print the formulas version of the worksheet using the Fit to option. The items listed below include all the new Excel skills you have learned in this chapter.

1. Enter a Formula Using the Keyboard (EX 75)
2. Enter Formulas Using Point Mode (EX 77)
3. Copy Formulas Using the Fill Handle (EX 80)
4. Determine the Average of a Range of Numbers Using the Keyboard and Mouse (EX 84)
5. Determine the Highest Number in a Range of Numbers Using the Insert Function Box (EX 86)
6. Determine the Lowest Number in a Range of Numbers Using the Sum Menu (EX 87)
7. Copy a Range of Cells Across Columns to an Adjacent Range Using the Fill Handle (EX 89)
8. Verify a Formula Using Range Finder (EX 91)
9. Change the Workbook Theme (EX 94)
10. Change the Background Color and Apply a Box Border to the Worksheet Title and Subtitle (EX 96)
11. Format Dates and Center Data in Cells (EX 98)
12. Apply an Accounting Number Format and Comma Style Format Using the Ribbon (EX 100)
13. Apply a Currency Style Format with a Floating Dollar Sign Using the Format Cells Dialog Box (EX 102)
14. Apply a Percent Style Format and Use the Increase Decimal Button (EX 103)
15. Apply Conditional Formatting (EX 104)
16. Change the Widths of Columns (EX 107)
17. Change the Heights of Rows (EX 110)
18. Check Spelling on the Worksheet (EX 112)
19. Change the Worksheet's Margins, Header, and Orientation in Page Layout View (EX 114)
20. Print a Section of the Worksheet (EX 118)
21. Display the Formulas in the Worksheet and Fit the Printout on One Page (EX 119)

 If you have a SAM 2010 user profile, your instructor may have assigned an autogradable version of this assignment. If so, log into the SAM 2010 Web site at www.cengage.com/sam2010 to download the instruction and start files.

Learn It Online

Test your knowledge of chapter content and key terms.

Instructions: To complete the Learn It Online exercises, start your browser, click the Address bar, and then enter **scsite.com/ex2010/learn** as the Web address. When the Excel 2010 Learn It Online page is displayed, click the link for the exercise you want to complete and then read the instructions.

Chapter Reinforcement TF, MC, and SA
A series of true/false, multiple choice, and short answer questions that test your knowledge of the chapter content.

Flash Cards
An interactive learning environment where you identify chapter key terms associated with displayed definitions.

Practice Test
A series of multiple choice questions that test your knowledge of chapter content and key terms.

Who Wants To Be a Computer Genius?
An interactive game that challenges your knowledge of chapter content in the style of a television quiz show.

Wheel of Terms
An interactive game that challenges your knowledge of chapter key terms in the style of the television show *Wheel of Fortune.*

Crossword Puzzle Challenge
A crossword puzzle that challenges your knowledge of key terms presented in the chapter.

Apply Your Knowledge

Reinforce the skills and apply the concepts you learned in this chapter.

Profit Analysis Worksheet
Instructions: The purpose of this exercise is to open a partially completed workbook, enter formulas and functions, copy the formulas and functions, and then format the worksheet titles and numbers. As shown in Figure 2–73, the completed worksheet analyzes the costs associated with a police department's fleet of vehicles.

	A	B	C	D	E	F	G	H	I	J	K
1		**Village of Scott Police Department**									
2		Monthly Vehicle Cost-per-Mile Summary									
3	Vehicle ID	Miles Driven	Cost per Mile	Maintenance Cost	Mileage Cost	Total Cost	Total Cost per Mile				
4	670543	2,007	$ 0.49	$ 242.80	$ 983.43	$ 1,226.23	$ 0.61				
5	979253	3,192	0.48	446.37	1,532.16	1,978.53	0.62				
6	948173	3,802	0.65	472.47	2,471.30	2,943.77	0.77				
7	837625	2,080	0.62	432.25	1,289.60	1,721.85	0.83				
8	824664	2,475	0.56	369.88	1,386.00	1,755.88	0.71				
9	655385	3,294	0.50	352.05	1,647.00	1,999.05	0.61				
10	836417	3,640	0.70	417.80	2,548.00	2,965.80	0.81				
11	993617	3,395	0.70	390.39	2,376.50	2,766.89	0.81				
12	779468	4,075	0.55	442.17	2,241.25	2,683.42	0.66				
13	**Totals**	**27,960**		$ 3,566.18	$ 16,475.24	$ 20,041.42	$ 0.72				
14	**Highest**	4,075	$0.70	$472.47	$2,548.00	$2,965.80	$0.83				
15	**Lowest**	2,007	$0.48	$242.80	$983.43	$1,226.23	$0.61				
16	**Average**	3,107	$0.58	$396.24	$1,830.58	$2,226.82	$0.72				
17											
18											
19											
20											

Figure 2–73

1. Start Excel. Open the workbook Apply 2-1 Village of Scott Police Department. See the inside back cover of this book for instructions for downloading the Data Files for Students or see your instructor for information on accessing the files required in this book.

2. Use the following formulas in cells E4, F4, and G4:

   Mileage Cost (cell E4) = Miles Driven * Cost per Mile or = B4 * C4

   Total Cost (cell F4) = Maintenance Cost + Mileage Cost or = D4 + E4

   Total Cost per Mile (cell G4) = Total Cost / Miles Driven or = F4 / B4

   Use the fill handle to copy the three formulas in the range E4:G4 to the range E5:G12.

3. Determine totals for the miles driven, maintenance cost, mileage cost, and total cost in row 13. Copy the formula in cell G12 to G13 to assign the formula in cell G12 to G13 in the total line. If necessary, reapply the Total cell style to cell G13.

4. In the range B14:B16, determine the highest value, lowest value, and average value, respectively, for the values in the range B4:B12. Use the fill handle to copy the three functions to the range C14:G16.

5. Format the worksheet as follows:

   a. change the workbook theme to Foundry by using the Themes button (Page Layout tab | Themes group)

   b. cell A1 — change to Title cell style

   c. cell A2 — change to a font size of 16

   d. cells A1:A2 — Rose background color and a thick box border

   e. cells C4:G4 and D13:G13 — Accounting number format with two decimal places and fixed dollar signs by using the Accounting Number Format button (Home tab | Number group)

   f. cells C5:G12 — Comma style format with two decimal places by using the Comma Style button (Home tab | Number group)

   g. cells B4:B16 — Comma style format with no decimal places

   h. cells C14:G16 — Currency style format with floating dollar signs by using the Format Cells: Number Dialog Box Launcher (Home tab | Number group)

   i. cells G4:G12 — apply conditional formatting so that cells with a value greater than 0.80 appear with a rose background color

6. Switch to Page Layout View and delete any current text in the Header area. Enter your name, course, laboratory assignment number, and any other information, as specified by your instructor, in the Header area. Preview and print the worksheet in landscape orientation. Change the document properties, as specified by your instructor. Save the workbook using the file name, Apply 2-1 Village of Scott Police Department Complete.

7. Use Range Finder to verify the formula in cell G13.

Continued >

Apply Your Knowledge *continued*

8. Print the range A3:D16. Press CTRL+ACCENT MARK (`) to change the display from the values version of the worksheet to the formulas version. Print the formulas version in landscape orientation on one page (Figure 2–74) by using the Fit to option in the Page sheet in the Page Setup dialog box. Press CTRL+ACCENT MARK (`) to change the display of the worksheet back to the values version. Close the workbook without saving it.

9. Submit the workbook and results as specified by your instructor.

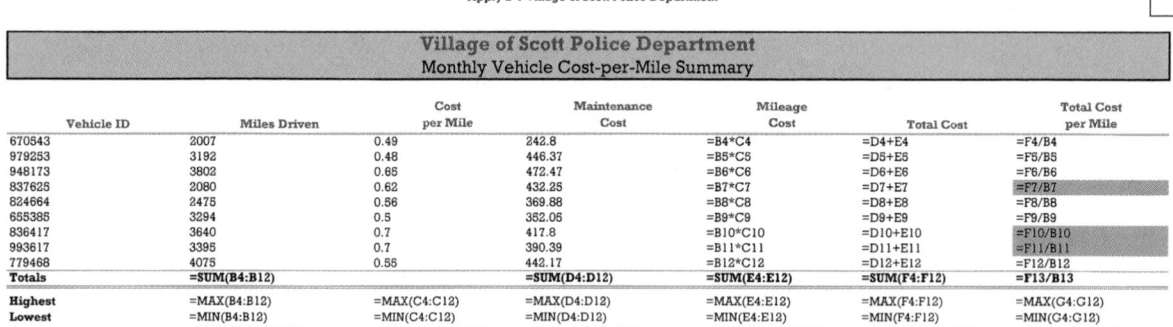

Jeff Quasney
Apply 2-1 Village of Scott Police Department

Village of Scott Police Department
Monthly Vehicle Cost-per-Mile Summary

Vehicle ID	Miles Driven	Cost per Mile	Maintenance Cost	Mileage Cost	Total Cost	Total Cost per Mile
670543	2007	0.49	242.8	=B4*C4	=D4+E4	=F4/B4
979253	3192	0.48	446.37	=B5*C5	=D5+E5	=F5/B5
948173	3802	0.65	472.47	=B6*C6	=D6+E6	=F6/B6
837625	2080	0.62	432.25	=B7*C7	=D7+E7	=F7/B7
824664	2475	0.56	369.88	=B8*C8	=D8+E8	=F8/B8
655385	3294	0.5	352.06	=B9*C9	=D9+E9	=F9/B9
836417	3640	0.7	417.8	=B10*C10	=D10+E10	=F10/B10
993617	3395	0.7	390.39	=B11*C11	=D11+E11	=F11/B11
779468	4075	0.55	442.17	=B12*C12	=D12+E12	=F12/B12
Totals	=SUM(B4:B12)		=SUM(D4:D12)	=SUM(E4:E12)	=SUM(F4:F12)	=F13/B13
Highest	=MAX(B4:B12)	=MAX(C4:C12)	=MAX(D4:D12)	=MAX(E4:E12)	=MAX(F4:F12)	=MAX(G4:G12)
Lowest	=MIN(B4:B12)	=MIN(C4:C12)	=MIN(D4:D12)	=MIN(E4:E12)	=MIN(F4:F12)	=MIN(G4:G12)
Average	=AVERAGE(B4:B12)	=AVERAGE(C4:C12)	=AVERAGE(D4:D12)	=AVERAGE(E4:E12)	=AVERAGE(F4:F12)	=AVERAGE(G4:G12)

Figure 2–74

Extend Your Knowledge

Extend the skills you learned in this chapter and experiment with new skills. You may need to use Help to complete the assignment.

Applying Conditional Formatting to Cells

Instructions: Start Excel. Open the workbook Extend 2-1 State Wildlife Department Employee Ratings. See the inside back cover of this book for instructions for downloading the Data Files for Students, or see your instructor for information on accessing the files required in this book. Perform the following tasks to apply three types of conditional formatting to cells in a worksheet:

1. Select the range C4:C18. Click the Conditional Formatting button (Home tab | Styles group) and then click New Rule in the Conditional Formatting list. Select 'Format only top or bottom ranked values' in the Select a Rule Type area (Conditional Formatting Rules Manager dialog box), as shown in Figure 2–75. Enter any value between 10 and 25 in the text box in the Edit the Rule Description (New Formatting Rule dialog box) area, and click the '% of the selected range' check box to select it. Click the Format button, and choose a blue background to assign this conditional format. Click the OK button in each dialog box and view the worksheet.

2. With range C4:C18 selected, apply a conditional format to the range that uses a green background color to highlight cells with scores that are below average.

3. With range D4:D18 selected, apply a conditional format to the range that uses an orange background to highlight cells that contain Exemplary or Exceeds Requirements.

4. With range B4:B18 selected, apply a conditional format to the range that uses a red background color to highlight cells with duplicate student names.

5. Change the document properties as specified by your instructor. Save the workbook using the file name, Extend 2-1 State Wildlife Department Employee Ratings Complete. Submit the revised workbook as specified by your instructor.

Figure 2–75

Make It Right

Analyze a workbook and correct all errors and/or improve the design.

Correcting Formatting, Functions, and Formulas in a Worksheet

Instructions: Start Excel. Open the workbook Make It Right 2-1 Dion Designwear Profit Analysis. See the inside back cover of this book for instructions for downloading the Data Files for Students, or see your instructor for information on accessing the files required for this book.

In this exercise you will learn how to correct formatting, functions, and formula problems in a worksheet (Figure 2–76).

	Product	Description	Cost	Profit	Units Sold	Total Sales	Total Profit	% Profit
						Dion Designwear		
						Profit Anaylsis		
4	4835	Coat	$247.63	$144.83	95,159	$37,346,101.14	$13,781,877.97	36.903%
5	7563	Custom	210.08	142.18	75,762	26,687,922.12	10,771,841.16	40.362%
6	8191	Dress	186.53	99.48	69,297	19,819,634.97	6,893,665.56	34.782%
7	8409	Hat	146.82	59.97	39,164	8,098,723.56	2,348,665.08	29.000%
8	5677	Jacket	140.68	85.63	38,261	8,658,846.91	3,276,289.43	37.837%
9	8985	Shirt	68.38	8.15	42,420	3,246,402.60	345,723.00	10.649%
10	5871	Slacks	144.54	30.44	68,536	11,992,429.28	2,086,235.84	17.396%
11	7796	Sleepwear	93.74	11.80	77,413	8,170,168.02	913,473.40	11.181%
12	7777	Suit	305.91	126.00	19,999	8,637,768.09	2,519,874.00	29.173%
13	8178	Sweater	112.21	9.24	61,257	7,439,662.65	566,014.68	7.608%
14	**Totals**				**587,268**	**$140,097,659.34**	**$43,503,660.12**	**31.052%**
15	Lowest		$68.38	$8.15	19,999	$3,246,402.60	$345,723.00	7.608%
16	Highest		$305.91	$144.83	95,159	$37,346,101.14	$13,781,877.97	40.362%
17	Average		$156.54	$71.77	54,679	$14,009,765.93	$3,302,420.24	25.489%

Figure 2–76

Continued >

Make It Right *continued*

Perform the following tasks:

1. Add a thick box border around the title and subtitle so that they appear more separated from the rest of the worksheet.

2. Adjust the width of column D to 8.11 pixels so that the word in the column header does not wrap. Adjust the column widths of columns F and G to best fit.

3. Spell check the worksheet and correct any spelling mistakes that are found, but ignore any spelling mistakes found with the worksheet title, document properties, and the product descriptions.

4. Center the values in the Product column.

5. The averages in several columns do not include the product in row 4. Adjust the functions in these cells so that all products are included in the calculation.

6. The total sales calculations should be:

   Total Sales = Units Sold * (Cost + Profit)

   Adjust the formulas in the range F4:F13 so that the correct formula is used.

7. The value for the lowest value in column E was entered as a number rather than as a function. Replace the value with the appropriate function.

8. The currency values in rows 4 and 14 should be formatted with the Accounting Number Format button (Home tab | Number group). They are currently formatted with the Currency format (floating dollar sign). The Accounting number format displays a fixed dollar sign.

9. Delete the function in the cell containing the average of % Profit because it is mathematically invalid.

10. Change the document properties as specified by your instructor. Save the workbook using the file name, Make It Right 2–1 Dion Designwear Profit Analysis Corrected. Submit the revised workbook as specified by your instructor.

In the Lab

Design and/or create a workbook using the guidelines, concepts, and skills presented in this chapter. Labs 1, 2, and 3 are listed in order of increasing difficulty.

Lab 1: Accounts Receivable Balance Worksheet

Problem: You are a part-time assistant in the accounting department at Aficionado Guitar Parts, a Chicago-based supplier of custom guitar parts. You have been asked to use Excel to generate a report that summarizes the monthly accounts receivable balance (Figure 2–77). A chart of the balances also is desired. The customer data in Table 2–6 is available for test purposes.

Table 2–6 Aficionado Guitar Parts Accounts Receivable Data				
Customer	**Beginning Balance**	**Credits**	**Payments**	**Purchases**
Cervantes, Katriel	803.01	56.92	277.02	207.94
Cummings, Trenton	285.05	87.41	182.11	218.22
Danielsson, Oliver	411.45	79.33	180.09	364.02
Kalinowski, Jadwiga	438.37	60.90	331.10	190.39
Lanctot, Royce	378.81	48.55	126.15	211.38
Raglow, Dora	710.99	55.62	231.37	274.71
Tuan, Lin	318.86	85.01	129.67	332.89

Instructions Part 1: Create a worksheet similar to the one shown in Figure 2–77. Include the five columns of customer data in Table 2–6 in the report, plus two additional columns to compute a service charge and a new balance for each customer. Assume no negative unpaid monthly balances.

	A	B	C	D	E	F	G
1			Aficionado Guitar Parts				
2			Monthy Accounts Receivable Balance Report				
3	Customer	Beginning Balance	Credits	Payments	Purchases	Service Charge	New Balance
4	Cervantes, Katriel	$803.01	$56.92	$277.02	$207.94	$15.24	$692.25
5	Cummings, Trenton	285.05	87.41	182.11	218.22	0.50	234.25
6	Danielsson, Oliver	411.45	79.33	180.09	364.02	4.94	520.99
7	Kalinowski, Jadwiga	438.37	60.90	331.10	190.39	1.51	238.27
8	Lanctot, Royce	378.81	48.55	126.15	211.38	6.63	422.12
9	Raglow, Dora	710.99	55.62	231.37	274.71	13.78	712.49
10	Tuan, Lin	318.86	85.01	129.67	332.89	3.39	440.46
11	Totals	$3,346.54	$473.74	$1,457.51	$1,799.55	$46.00	$3,260.84
12	Highest	$803.01	$87.41	$331.10	$364.02	$15.24	$712.49
13	Lowest	$285.05	$48.55	$126.15	$190.39	$0.50	$234.25
14	Average	$478.08	$67.68	$208.22	$257.08	$6.57	$465.83
15							
16							

Figure 2–77

Perform the following tasks:

1. Enter and format the worksheet title **Aficionado Guitar Parts** and worksheet subtitle **Monthly Accounts Receivable Balance Report** in cells A1 and A2. Change the theme of the worksheet to the Trek theme. Apply the Title cell style to cells A1 and A2. Change the font size in cell A1 to 28 points. Merge and center the worksheet title and subtitle across columns A through G. Change the background color of cells A1 and A2 to the Red standard color. Change the font color of cells A1 and A2 to the White theme color. Draw a thick box border around the range A1:A2.

2. Change the width of column A to 20.00 points. Change the widths of columns B through G to 12.00 points. Change the heights of row 3 to 36.00 points and row 12 to 30.00 points.

3. Enter the column titles in row 3 and row titles in the range A11:A14, as shown in Figure 2–77. Center the column titles in the range A3:G3. Apply the Heading 3 cell style to the range A3:G3. Apply the Total cell style to the range A11:G11. Bold the titles in the range A12:A14. Change the font size in the range A3:G14 to 12 points.

4. Enter the data in Table 2–6 in the range A4:E10.

5. Use the following formulas to determine the service charge in column F and the new balance in column G for the first customer. Copy the two formulas down through the remaining customers.

    a. Service Charge (cell F4) = 3.25% * (Beginning Balance – Payments – Credits)

    b. New Balance (G4) = Beginning Balance + Purchases – Credits – Payments + Service Charge

6. Determine the totals in row 11.

7. Determine the maximum, minimum, and average values in cells B12:B14 for the range B4:B10, and then copy the range B12:B14 to C12:G14.

Continued >

STUDENT ASSIGNMENTS

In the Lab continued

8. Format the numbers as follows: (a) assign the Currency style with a floating dollar sign to the cells containing numeric data in the ranges B4:G4 and B11:G14, and (b) assign a number style with two decimal places and a thousand's separator (currency with no dollar sign) to the range B5:G10.

9. Use conditional formatting to change the formatting to white font on a red background in any cell in the range F4:F10 that contains a value greater than 10.

10. Change the worksheet name from Sheet1 to Accounts Receivable and the sheet tab color to the Red standard color. Change the document properties, as specified by your instructor. Change the worksheet header with your name, course number, and other information as specified by your instructor.

11. Spell check the worksheet. Preview and then print the worksheet in landscape orientation. Save the workbook using the file name, Lab 2-1 Part 1 Aficionado Guitar Parts Accounts Receivable Balance Report.

12. Print the range A3:D14. Print the formulas version on another page. Close the workbook without saving the changes. Submit the assignment as specified by your instructor.

Instructions Part 2: In this part of the exercise, you will create a 3-D Bar chart on a new worksheet in the workbook (Figure 2–78). If necessary, use Excel Help to obtain information on inserting a chart on a separate sheet in the workbook.

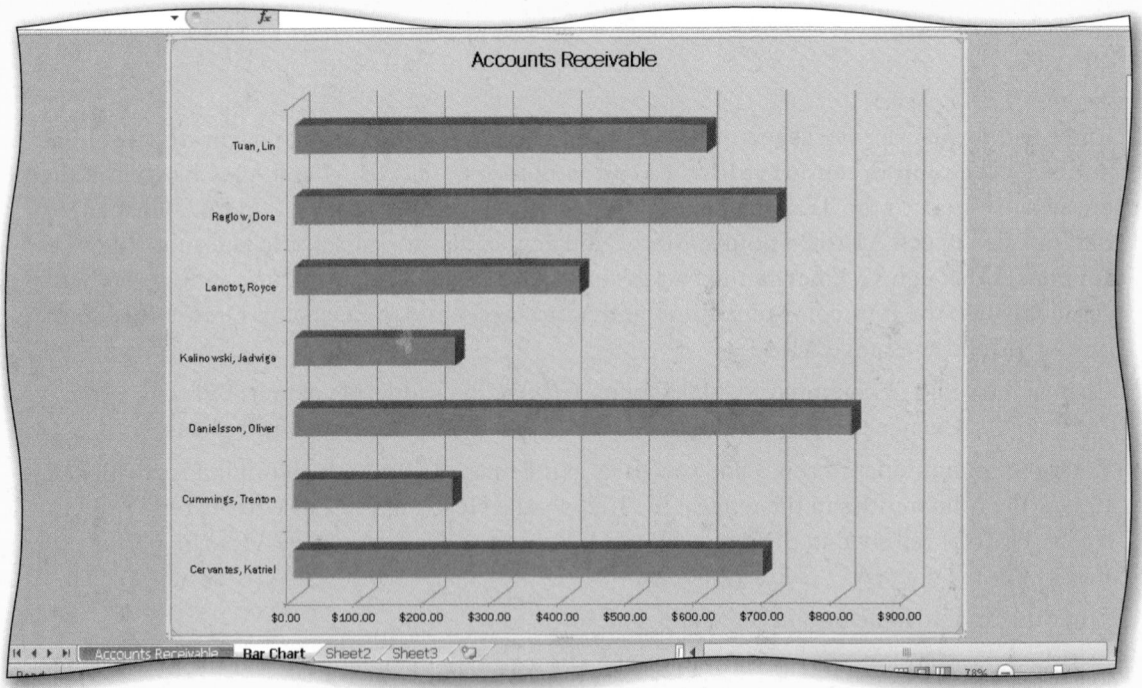

Figure 2–78

1. Open the workbook Lab 2-1 Part 1 Aficionado Guitar Parts Accounts Receivable Balance Report workbook created in Part 1. Save the workbook using the file name, Lab 2-1 Part 2 Aficionado Guitar Parts Accounts Receivable Balance Report.

2. Use the CTRL key and mouse to select the nonadjacent chart ranges A4:A10 and G4:G10. That is, select the range A4:A10 and while holding down the CTRL key, select the range G4:G10.

3. Click the Bar button (Insert tab | Charts group) and then select Clustered Bar in 3-D in the 3-D Bar area. When the chart is displayed on the worksheet, click the Move Chart button (Chart Tools Design tab | Location group). When the Move Chart dialog box appears, click New sheet and then type Bar Chart for the sheet name. Click the OK button (Move Chart dialog box). Change the sheet tab color to the Green standard color.

4. When the chart is displayed on the new worksheet, click the Series 1 series label and then press the DELETE key to delete it. Click the chart area, which is a blank area near the edge of the chart, click the Shape Fill button (Chart Tools Format tab | Shape Styles group), and then select Orange, Accent 1, Lighter 60% in the gallery (column 5, row 3). Click one of the bars in the chart. Click the Shape Fill button (Chart Tools Format tab | Shape Styles group) and then select the Green standard color. Click the Chart Title button (Chart Tools Layout tab | Labels group) and then select Above Chart in the Chart Title gallery. If necessary, use the scroll bar on the right side of the worksheet to scroll to the top of the chart. Click the edge of the chart title to select it and then type **Accounts Receivable** as the chart title.

5. Drag the Accounts Receivable tab at the bottom of the worksheet to the left of the Bar Chart tab to reorder the sheets in the workbook. Preview and print the chart.

6. Click the Accounts Receivable sheet tab. Change the following beginning balances: customer Oliver Danielsson to $702.13 and customer Lin Tuan to $482.74. The company also decided to change the service charge from 3.25% to 2.75% for all customers. After copying the adjusted formula in cell F4 to the range F5:F10, click the Auto Fill Options button and then click Fill without Formatting to maintain the original formatting in the range F5:F10. The total new balance in cell G11 should equal $3,720.82.

7. Select both sheets by holding down the SHIFT key and then clicking the Bar Chart tab. Preview and print the selected sheets. Save the workbook. Submit the assignment as specified by your instructor.

In the Lab

Lab 2: Sales Summary Worksheet

Problem: You have been asked to build a worksheet for a start-up company, Electry Auto, that analyzes the financing needs for the company's first six months in business. The company plans to begin operations in January with an initial investment of $500,000.00. The expected revenue and costs for the company's first six months are shown in Table 2–7. The desired worksheet is shown in Figure 2–79 on the following page. The initial investment is shown at the starting balance for January

Table 2–7 Electry Auto Start-Up Financing Needs Data		
Month	Revenue	Costs
January	105000	220000
February	82000	260000
March	200000	255000
April	250000	320000
May	325000	420000
June	510000	540000

(cell B4). The amount of financing required by the company is shown as the lowest ending balance (cell F12).

Continued >

In the Lab *continued*

Instructions Part 1:   Perform the following tasks to build the worksheet shown in Figure 2–79.

	A	B	C	D	E	F
1			**Electry Auto**			
2			**Start–Up Financing Needs**			
3	*Month*	*Starting Balance*	*Revenue*	*Costs*	*Net Income*	*Ending Balance*
4	January	$ 500,000.00	$ 105,000.00	$ 220,000.00	$ (115,000.00)	$ 385,000.00
5	February	385,000.00	82,000.00	260,000.00	(178,000.00)	207,000.00
6	March	207,000.00	200,000.00	255,000.00	(55,000.00)	152,000.00
7	April	152,000.00	250,000.00	320,000.00	(70,000.00)	82,000.00
8	May	82,000.00	325,000.00	420,000.00	(95,000.00)	(13,000.00)
9	June	(13,000.00)	510,000.00	540,000.00	(30,000.00)	(43,000.00)
10	*Average*	$218,833.33	$245,333.33	$335,833.33	($90,500.00)	$128,333.33
11	*Highest*	$500,000.00	$510,000.00	$540,000.00	($30,000.00)	$385,000.00
12	*Lowest*	($13,000.00)	$82,000.00	$220,000.00	($178,000.00)	($43,000.00)
13						
14						
15						
16						
17						
18						

Figure 2–79

1. Start Excel. Apply the Concourse theme to a new workbook.

2. Increase the width of column A to 10.00 and the width of columns B through F to 14.00.

3. Enter the worksheet title **Electry Auto** in cell A1 and the worksheet subtitle **Start-Up Financing Needs** in cell A2. Enter the column titles in row 3, as shown in Figure 2–79. In row 3, use ALT+ENTER to start a new line in a cell.

4. Enter the start-up financing needs data described in Table 2–7 in columns A, C, and D in rows 4 through 9. Enter the initial starting balance (cell B4) of 500000.00. Enter the row titles in the range A10:A12, as shown in Figure 2–79.

5. For the months of February through March, the starting balance is equal to the previous month's ending balance. Obtain the starting balance for February by setting the starting balance of February to the ending balance of January. Use a cell reference rather than typing in the data. Copy the formula for February to the remaining months.

6. Obtain the net income amounts in column E by subtracting the costs in column D from the revenues in column C. Enter the formula in cell E4 and copy it to the range E5:E9. Obtain the ending balance amounts in column F by adding the starting balance in column B to the net income in column E. Enter the formula in cell F4 and copy it to the range F5:F9.

7. In the range B10:B12, use the AVERAGE, MAX, and MIN functions to determine the average value, highest value, and lowest value in the range B4:B9. Copy the range B10:B12 to the range C10:F12.

8. One at a time, merge and center the worksheet title and subtitle across columns A through F. Select cells A1 and A2 and change the background color to light blue (column 7 in the Standard Colors area in the Fill Color gallery). Apply the Title cell style to cells A1 and A2. Change the worksheet title in cell A1 to 28-point white (column 1, row 1 on the Font Color gallery). Change the worksheet subtitle to the same color. Assign a thick box border to the range A1:A2.

9. Center the titles in row 3, columns A through F. Apply the Heading 3 cell style to the range A3:F3. Use the Italic button (Home tab | Font group) to italicize the column titles in row 3 and the row titles in the range A10:A12.

10. Assign a thick box border to the range A10:F12. Change the background and font color for cell F12 to the same colors applied to the worksheet title in Step 8.

11. Change the row heights of row 3 to 36.00 points and row 10 to 30.00 points.

12. Assign the Accounting number format to the range B4:F4. Assign the Comma style format to the range B5:F9. Assign a Currency format with a floating dollar sign to the range B10:F12.

13. Rename the sheet tab as Start-Up Financing Needs. Apply the Light Blue color to the sheet tab. Change the document properties, as specified by your instructor. Change the worksheet header with your name, course number, and other information as specified by your instructor. Save the workbook using the file name Lab 2-1 Part 1 Electry Auto Start-Up Financing Needs. Print the entire worksheet in landscape orientation. Next, print only the range A3:B9.

14. Display the formulas version by pressing CTRL+ACCENT MARK (`). Print the formulas version using the Fit to option button in the Scaling area on the Page tab in the Page Setup dialog box. After printing the worksheet, reset the Scaling option by selecting the Adjust to option button on the Page tab in the Page Setup dialog box and changing the percent value to 100%. Change the display from the formulas version to the values version by pressing CTRL+ACCENT MARK (`). Do not save the workbook.

15. Submit the revised workbook as requested by your instructor.

Instructions Part 2: In this part of the exercise, you will change the revenue amounts until the lowest ending balance is greater than zero, indicating that the company does not require financing in its first six months of operation. Open the workbook created in Part 1 and save the workbook as Lab 2-1 Part 2 Electry Auto Start-Up Financing Needs. Manually increment each of the six values in the revenue column by $1,000.00 until the lowest ending balance in cell F12 is greater than zero. The value of cell F12 should equal $5,000.00 All six values in column C must be incremented the same number of times. Update the worksheet header and save the workbook. Print the worksheet. Submit the assignment as specified by your instructor.

Instructions Part 3: In this part of the exercise, you will change the monthly costs until the lowest ending balance is greater than zero, indicating that the company does not require financing in its first six months of operation. Open the workbook created in Part 1 and then save the workbook as Lab 2–1 Part 3 Electry Auto Start-Up Financing Needs. Manually decrement each of the six values in the costs column by $1,000.00 until the lowest ending balance in cell F12 is greater than zero. Decrement all six values in column C the same number of times. Your worksheet is correct when the lowest ending balance in cell F12 is $5,000.00. Update the worksheet header and save the workbook. Print the worksheet. Submit the assignment as specified by your instructor.

In the Lab

Lab 3: Stock Club Investment Analysis

Problem: Several years ago, you and a large group of friends started a stock club. Each year every member invests more money per month. You have decided to create a portfolio worksheet (Figure 2–80) that summarizes the club's current stock holdings so that you can share the information with your group of friends. The club's portfolio is summarized in Table 2–8. Table 2–8 also shows the general layout of the worksheet to be created.

	A	B	C	D	E	F	G	H	I	J
	A18		f_x							
	A	B	C	D	E	F	G	H	I	J
1					**Sock-It-Away Stock Club**					
2					Summary of Investments					
3	Company	Stock Symbol	Purchase Date	Shares	Initial Price per Share	Initial Cost	Current Price per Share	Current Value	Gain/Loss	Percent Gain/Loss
4	Apple	AAPL	3/3/2007	250	$ 86.17	$ 21,542.50	$ 75.32	$ 18,830.00	$ (2,712.50)	-12.59%
5	Caterpillar	CAT	6/14/2008	200	81.74	16,348.00	69.02	13,804.00	(2,544.00)	-15.56%
6	Disney	DIS	10/11/2006	300	31.06	9,318.00	37.38	11,214.00	1,896.00	20.35%
7	General Electric	GE	3/4/2009	500	7.24	3,620.00	9.39	4,695.00	1,075.00	29.70%
8	MetLife	MET	1/15/2008	200	60.92	12,184.00	77.09	15,418.00	3,234.00	26.54%
9	Microsoft	MSFT	11/15/2006	500	29.20	14,600.00	36.30	18,150.00	3,550.00	24.32%
10	PepsiCo	PEP	2/15/2006	350	57.86	20,251.00	70.65	24,727.50	4,476.50	22.11%
11	Target	TGT	5/11/2004	450	44.11	19,849.50	44.02	19,809.00	(40.50)	-0.20%
12	Wal-Mart	WMT	4/14/2009	250	50.81	12,702.50	57.20	14,300.00	1,597.50	12.58%
13	Totals					$ 130,415.50		$ 140,947.50	$ 10,532.00	8.08%
14	Average			333.3333	$49.90	$14,490.61	$52.93	$15,660.83	$1,170.22	
15	Highest			500	$86.17	$21,542.50	$77.09	$24,727.50	$4,476.50	29.70%
16	Lowest			200	$7.24	$3,620.00	$9.39	$4,695.00	($2,712.50)	-15.56%
17										
18										
19										

Figure 2–80

Table 2–8 Sock-It-Away Stock Club

Company	Stock Symbol	Purchase Date	Shares	Initial Price per Share	Initial Cost	Current Price per Share	Current Value	Gain/ Loss	Percent Gain/ Loss
Apple	AAPL	3/3/2007	250	86.17	Formula A	75.32	Formula B	Formula C	Formula D
Caterpillar	CAT	6/14/2008	200	81.74		69.02			
Disney	DIS	10/11/2006	300	31.06		37.38			
General Electric	GE	3/4/2009	500	7.24		9.39			
MetLife	MET	1/15/2008	200	60.92		77.09			
Microsoft	MSFT	11/15/2006	500	29.20		36.30			
PepsiCo	PEP	2/15/2006	350	57.86		70.65			
Target	TGT	5/11/2004	450	44.11		44.02			
Wal-Mart	WMT	4/14/2009	250	50.81		57.20			
Totals			Formula E						
Average			Formula F						
Highest			Formula G						
Lowest			Formula H						

Instructions: Perform the following tasks:

1. Start Excel. Enter the worksheet titles Sock-It-Away Stock Club in cell A1 and Summary of Investments in cell A2.

2. Enter the column titles and data in Table 2–8 beginning in row 3.

3. Change the column widths and row heights as follows: column A — 11.78; column C — 10.00; columns E and G — 7.44; columns F, H, and I — 13.00; column J — 8.22; row 3 — 56.25 points; row 14 — 27.00 points.

4. Enter the following formulas in row 4 and then copy them down through row 12:

   a. Enter Formula A in cell F4: Initial Cost = Shares × Initial Price per Share

   b. Enter Formula B in cell H4: Current Value = Shares × Current Price Per Share

   c. Enter Formula C in cell I4: Gain/Loss = Current Value − Initial Cost

   d. Enter Formula D in cell J4: Percent Gain/Loss = Gain/Loss / Initial Cost

5. Compute the totals for initial cost, current value, gain/loss, and percent gain loss. For the percent gain/loss in cell J13, copy cell J12 to J13 using the fill handle.

6. In cells D14, D15, and D16, enter Formulas F, G, and H using the AVERAGE, MAX, and MIN functions. Copy the three functions across through the range E14:J16. Delete the invalid formula in cell J14.

7. Format the worksheet as follows:

   a. Apply the Trek theme to the worksheet.

   b. Format the worksheet title with Title cell style. Merge and center across columns A through J.

   c. Format the worksheet subtitle with Franklin Gothic Book font, 16 point font size, Black, Text 1 theme font color. Merge and Center across columns A through J.

   d. Format the worksheet title and subtitle background with Orange, Accent 1, Lighter 60% theme color and a thick box border.

   e. Format row 3 with the Heading 3 cell style and row 13 with the Total cell style.

   f. Format the data in rows 4 through 12: center data in column B; format dates in column C to the mm/dd/yyyy date format; range E4:I4 — Accounting number format style with fixed dollar sign; range E5:I12 — Comma style; range J4:J13 — Percent style with two decimal places; cells F13, H13, and I13 — Accounting Number format with fixed dollar sign.

   g. Format E14:I16 — Currency format with floating decimal places; J15:J16 — Percent style with two decimal places.

   h. Format J4:J12 — apply conditional formatting so that if a cell in range is less than 0, then cell appears with a pink background color.

8. Spell check the worksheet. Change the name of the sheet tab to Summary of Investments and apply the Orange, Accent 1, Darker 25% theme color to the sheet tab. Update the document properties, and save the workbook using the file name, Lab 2-3 Sock-It-Away Stock Club Summary of Investments. Print the worksheet in landscape orientation. Print the formulas version on one page. Close the workbook without saving changes. Submit the assignment as specified by your instructor.

Cases and Places

Apply your creative thinking and problem-solving skills to design and implement a solution.

1: Analyzing Emergency Student Loans

Academic

The Student Assistance office at your school provides emergency loans at simple interest. The data obtained from six types of loans and the desired report format are shown in Table 2–9. The required formulas are shown in Table 2–10. Use the concepts and techniques presented in this chapter to create and format the worksheet. Include total, average, maximum, and minimum values for Principal, Interest, and Amount Due.

Table 2–9 Emergency Student Loan Data and Worksheet Layout

Loan Type	Principal	Rate	Time in Years
Academic Supplies	$40,000	7.5%	.4
Medical Emergency	$25,500	12%	.33
Personal Emergency	$12,750	8.25%	.5
Room and Board	$27,000	6.5%	1
Travel Expenses	$4,550	12%	.5
Tuition Reimbursement	$107,000	6%	1

Table 2–10 Emergency Student Loan Formulas

Interest = Principal × Rate × Time
Amount Due = Principal + Interest
Average = AVERAGE function
Minimum = MIN function
Maximum = MAX function

2: Analyzing Energy Consumption

Personal

Your parents believe that your late night studying sessions and household appliance usage contribute to excessive electricity bills. You have decided to try to prove them wrong by analyzing your daily and monthly electricity consumption. You research the energy consumption of your personal items and appliance usage to obtain consumption costs per hour for each item. Table 2–11 contains the data and format for the report you want to create.

Use the concepts and techniques presented in this project to create and format the worksheet. Include an embedded 3-D Pie chart that shows the cost per month. Use Microsoft Excel Help to create a professional looking 3-D Pie chart with title and data labels.

Table 2–11 Appliance Electricity Usage Costs

Appliance	Cost per Hour	Hours Used Daily	Total Cost Per Day	Total Cost per Month (30 Days)
Clothes dryer	$0.325	1		
Computer	$0.02	6		
DVD player	$0.035	1		
Light bulbs	$0.043	8		
Refrigerator	$0.035	24		
Stereo	$0.02	5		
Television	$0.04	4		
Washing machine	$0.03	2		

3: Analyzing Profit Potential

Professional

You work for HumiCorp, an online retailer of home humidifiers. Your manager wants to know the profit potential of their inventory based on the items in inventory listed in Table 2–12. Table 2–12 contains the format of the desired report. The required formulas are shown in Table 2–13. Use the concepts and techniques developed in this chapter to create and format the worksheet. The company just received 67 additional desk-sized humidifiers and shipped out 48 room-sized humidifiers. Update the appropriate cells to reflect the change in inventory.

Table 2–12 HumiCorp Inventory Profit Potential Data and Worksheet Layout

Item	Units on Hand	Unit Cost	Total Cost	Unit Price	Total Value	Potential Profit
Desk	187	27.58	Formula A	Formula B	Formula C	Formula D
Filtered home-sized	42	324.14				
Filtered room-sized	118	86.55				
Home-sized	103	253.91				
Room-sized	97	53.69				
Total	—	—	—	—	—	—
Average	Formula E					
Lowest	Formula F					
Highest	Formula G					

Table 2–13 HumiCorp Inventory Profit Potential Formulas

Formula A = Units on Hand × Unit Cost
Formula B = Unit Cost × (1 / (1 − .66))
Formula C = Units on Hand × Unit Price
Formula D = Total Value − Total Cost
Formula E = AVERAGE function
Formula F = MIN function
Formula G = MAX function

3 | What-If Analysis, Charting, and Working with Large Worksheets

Objectives

You will have mastered the material in this chapter when you can:

- Rotate text in a cell
- Create a series of month names
- Copy, paste, insert, and delete cells
- Format numbers using format symbols
- Freeze and unfreeze rows and columns
- Show and format the system date
- Use absolute and mixed cell references in a formula
- Use the IF function to perform a logical test

- Create Sparkline charts
- Use the Format Painter button to format cells
- Create a 3-D Pie chart on a separate chart sheet
- Rearrange worksheet tabs
- Change the worksheet view
- Answer what-if questions
- Goal seek to answer what-if questions

3 | What-If Analysis, Charting, and Working with Large Worksheets

Introduction

Worksheets normally are much larger than those created in the previous chapters, often extending beyond the size of the Excel window. Because you cannot see the entire worksheet on the screen at one time, working with a large worksheet sometimes can be frustrating. This chapter introduces several Excel commands that allow you to control what is displayed on the screen so that you can view critical parts of a large worksheet at one time. One command allows you to freeze rows and columns so that Excel always displays them on the screen. Another command splits the worksheet into separate window-panes so that you can view different parts of a worksheet on the screen at one time.

When you set up a worksheet, you should use cell references in formulas whenever possible, rather than constant values. The use of a cell reference allows you to change a value in multiple formulas by changing the value in a single cell. The cell references in a formula are called assumptions. Assumptions are values in cells that you can change to determine new values for formulas. This chapter emphasizes the use of assumptions and shows how to use Excel to answer what-if questions, such as what happens to the six-month operating income if you decrease the marketing expenses assumption by 3 percent? Being able to analyze quickly the effect of changing values in a worksheet is an important skill in making business decisions.

This chapter also introduces you to techniques that will enhance your ability to create worksheets and draw charts. From your work in Chapter 1, you are aware of how easily you can create charts. This chapter covers additional charting techniques that allow you to convey a message in a dramatic pictorial fashion, such as Sparkline charts and an exploded 3-D pie chart. This chapter also covers other methods for entering values in cells, such as allowing Excel to enter values for you based on a pattern of values that you create, and formatting these values. In addition, you will learn how to use absolute cell references and how to use the IF function to assign a value to a cell based on a logical test.

Project — Financial Projection Worksheet with What-If Analysis and Chart

The project in the chapter follows proper design guidelines and uses Excel to create the worksheet and pie chart shown in Figures 3–1a and 3–1b. Modern Music Shops operates several stores that sell and service musical instruments. Each June and December, the director of finance and accounting submits a plan to the management team to show projected monthly sales revenues, costs of goods sold, gross margin, expenses, and operating income for the next six months. The director requires an easy-to-read worksheet that shows financial projections for the next six months. The worksheet should allow for quick analysis if projections for certain numbers change, such as the percentage of expenses allocated to marketing. In addition, a 3-D pie chart is required that shows the projected operating income contribution for each of the six months.

Figure 3–1 (a) Worksheet

Figure 3–1 (b) 3-D Pie Chart

Correctness
Studies have shown that more than 25 percent of all business worksheets have errors. You can ensure correctness in your formulas by carefully checking them using Range Finder. The Formula Auditing group on the Formulas tab on the Ribbon also can be helpful when verifying formulas.

    The requirements document for the Modern Music Shops Six-Month Financial Projection worksheet is shown in Figure 3–2. It includes the needs, source of data, summary of calculations, chart requirements, and other facts about its development.

REQUEST FOR NEW WORKBOOK

Date Submitted:	April 9, 2012
Submitted By:	Marcus Olek
Worksheet Title:	Modern Music Shops' Six-Month Financial Projection
Needs:	The needs are: (1) a worksheet (Figure 3-3a on page EX 142) that shows Modern Music Shops' projected monthly sales, cost of goods sold, gross margin, expenses, and operating income for a six-month period; and (2) a 3-D Pie chart (Figure 3-3b on page EX 142) that shows the projected contribution of each month's operating income to the six-month period operating income.
Source of Data:	The data supplied by the Finance department includes projections of the monthly sales and expenses (Table 3-1 on page EX 143) that are based on prior years. All the remaining numbers in the worksheet are determined from these 13 numbers using formulas.
Calculations:	The following calculations must be made for each month: 1. Cost of Goods Sold = Revenue − Revenue × Margin 2. Gross Margin = Revenue − Cost of Goods Sold 3. Bonus Expense = $200,000.00 if the Revenue exceeds the Revenue for Bonus; otherwise Bonus Expense = 0 4. Commission Expense = Commission Assumption × Revenue 5. Marketing Expense = Marketing Assumption × Revenue 6. Research and Development = Research and Development Assumption × Revenue 7. Support, General, and Administrative Expense = Support, General, and Administrative Assumption × Revenue 8. Total Expenses = Sum of Expenses 9. Operating Income = Gross Margin − Total Expenses
Chart Requirements:	Show Sparkline charts for Revenue and each of the items noted in the calculations area above. A 3-D Pie chart is required on a separate sheet (Figure 3-3b) to show the contribution of each month's operating income to the six-month period operating income. The chart should also emphasize the month with the greatest operating income.

Approvals

Approval Status:	X	Approved
		Rejected
Approved By:		Farah Qadir, CFO
Date:		April 16, 2012
Assigned To:		J. Quasney, Spreadsheet Specialist

Figure 3–2

Overview

As you read this chapter, you will learn how to create the worksheet shown in Figure 3–1 by performing these general tasks:

- Create a series of month names
- Use absolute cell references in a formula
- Use the IF function to perform a logical test
- Create Sparkline charts in a range of cells
- Use the Format Painter button to format cells
- Create a 3-D pie chart on a separate chart sheet
- Answer what-if questions
- Manipulate large worksheets

General Project Decisions

While creating an Excel worksheet, you need to make several decisions that will determine the appearance and characteristics of the finished worksheet. As you create the worksheet required to meet the requirements shown in Figure 3–2, you should follow these general guidelines:

1. **Plan the layout of the worksheet.** Worksheets that include financial data associated with time frames typically include dates, such as months, quarters, or years, as column headers. What-if assumptions should not clutter the worksheet, but placing them in an easily located portion of the worksheet allows for quicker creation of new projections.

2. **Determine the necessary formulas and functions needed.** Often, financial calculations rely on strict definitions and commonly accepted formulas for performing the calculations. Look for such situations and always use the accepted formulas. When using a what-if section on a worksheet, make certain to create formulas that use the what-if criteria. When a requirement necessitates a calculation only under a certain condition, a function can check for the condition and make the calculation when necessary.

3. **Specify how to best utilize Sparkline charts.** Sparkline charts allow worksheet users quickly to visualize information in a small chart within a cell. The use of multiple Sparkline charts in the worksheet will provide the user with a visual comparison of the various data items for each month. The user, therefore, can see trends for each line item over time and also compare relationships among various line items.

4. **Identify how to format various elements of the worksheet.** Format separate parts of a worksheet, such as what-if assumptions, in a manner that indicates that they are separate from the main area of the worksheet. Other financial items, such as sales revenue and expenses, are distinct categories of financial data and should be separated visually. Totals and subtotals should stand out to draw the reader's attention.

5. **Specify how charts should convey necessary information.** As you have learned, different chart types convey different messages and are appropriate in different situations. For example, a 3-D pie chart is a good way to compare visually a small set of numbers. Often one or two slices of a pie chart displays as exploded, meaning that the slice appears pulled away from the cart, in order to emphasize the slice to the user. Format chart data points so that the worksheet user's eye is drawn to important information.

6. **Perform what-if analysis and goal seeking using the best techniques.** What-if analysis allows you quickly to answer questions regarding various predictions. A what-if area of a worksheet allows users of the worksheet efficiently to ask questions. Goal seeking allows you automatically to modify values in a what-if area of a worksheet based on a goal that you have for another cell in the worksheet.

When necessary, more specific details concerning the above guidelines are presented at appropriate points in the chapter. The chapter also will identify the actions you perform and decisions made regarding these guidelines during the creation of the worksheet shown in Figure 3–1 on page EX 139.

Plan Ahead

Using a sketch of the worksheet can help you visualize its design. The sketch of the worksheet consists of titles, column and row headings, location of data values, calculations, and a rough idea of the desired formatting (Figure 3–3a). The sketch of the 3-D pie chart shows the expected contribution of each month's operating income to the six-month operating income (Figure 3–3b). The assumptions will be entered at the top of the worksheet (Figure 3–3a). The projected monthly sales revenue will be entered in row 13 of the worksheet. The projected monthly sales revenue and the assumptions shown in Table 3–1 will be used to calculate the remaining numbers in the worksheet.

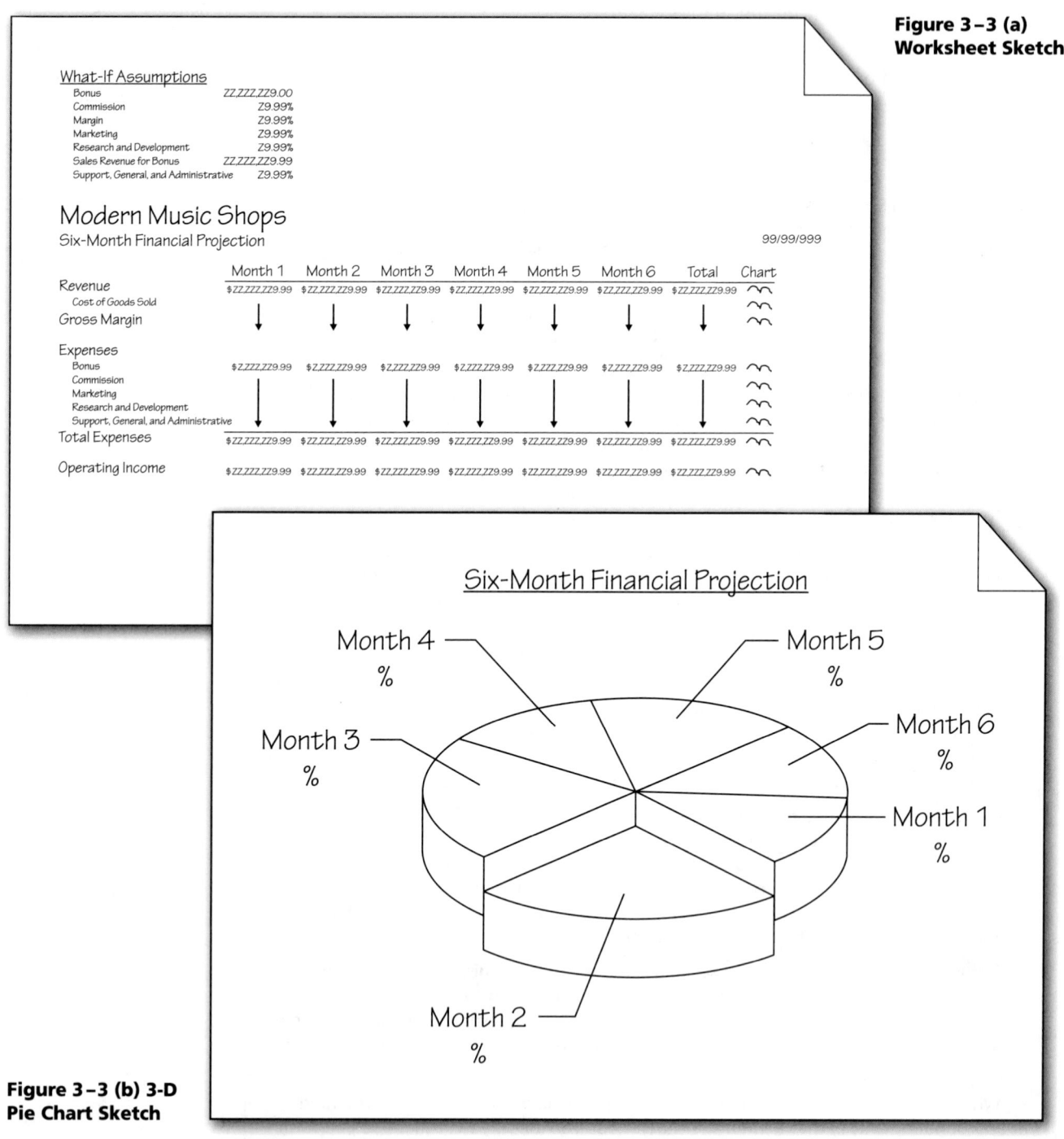

Figure 3–3 (a)
Worksheet Sketch

Figure 3–3 (b) 3-D
Pie Chart Sketch

With a solid understanding of the requirements document, an understanding of the necessary decisions, and a sketch of the worksheet, the next step is to use Excel to create the worksheet.

Table 3–1 Modern Music Shops Six-Month Financial Projections Data and What-If Assumptions	
Projected Monthly Total Sales Revenues	
July	$3,113,612.16
August	7,962,235.53
September	5,112,268.58
October	2,924,627.87
November	7,630,534.65
December	3,424,270.23
What-If Assumptions	
Bonus	$200,000.00
Commission	5.75%
Margin	57.50%
Marketing	15.00%
Research and Development	7.50%
Sales Revenue for Bonus	$3,500,000.00
Support, General, and Administrative	18.75%

To Start Excel

If you are using a computer to step through the project in this chapter and you want your screens to match the figures in this book, you should change your screen's resolution to 1024 × 768. For information about how to change a computer's resolution, refer to the Introduction to Office 2010 and Windows 7 chapter at the beginning of this book.

The following steps, which assume Windows 7 is running, start Excel based on a typical installation. You may need to ask your instructor how to start Excel for your computer. For a detailed example of the procedure summarized below, refer to the Office 2010 and Windows 7 chapter at the beginning of this book.

1 Click the Start button on the Windows 7 taskbar to display the Start menu.

2 Type `Microsoft Excel` as the search text in the 'Search programs and files' text box, and watch the search results appear on the Start menu.

3 Click Microsoft Excel 2010 in the search results on the Start menu to start Excel and display a new blank workbook in the Excel window.

4 If the Excel window is not maximized, click the Maximize button next to the Close button on its title bar to maximize the window.

For an introduction to Windows 7 and instruction about how to perform basic Windows 7 tasks, read the Office 2010 and Windows 7 chapter at the beginning of this book, where you can learn how to resize windows, change screen resolution, create folders, move and rename files, use Windows Help, and much more.

To Enter the Worksheet Titles, Change Document Properties, Apply a Theme, and Save the Workbook

The worksheet contains two titles, initially in cells A8 and A9. In the previous chapters, titles were centered across the worksheet. With large worksheets that extend beyond the size of a window, it is best to enter titles left-aligned as shown in the sketch of the worksheet in Figure 3–3a because the worksheet prints with the title on the first page if the worksheet requires multiple pages, and the user more easily finds the worksheet title when necessary. The following steps enter the worksheet titles, change the workbook theme to Opulent, change document properties, and then save the workbook.

1 Select cell A8 and then type **Modern Music Shops** as the worksheet title.

2 Select cell A9 and then type **Six-Month Financial Projection** as the worksheet subtitle and then press the ENTER key to enter the worksheet subtitle.

3 Change the document properties as specified by your instructor.

4 Apply the Opulent theme to the workbook.

5 With a USB flash drive connected to one of the computer's USB ports, click the Save button on the Quick Access Toolbar to display the Save As dialog box.

6 Type **Modern Music Shops Six-Month Financial Projection** in the File name text box to change the file name. Do not press the ENTER key after typing the file name because you do not want to close the dialog box at this time.

7 Navigate to the desired save location (in this case, the Excel folder in the CIS 101 folder [or your class folder] on the USB flash drive).

8 Click the Save button (Save As dialog box) to save the document in the selected folder on the selected drive with the entered file name.

Rotating Text and Using the Fill Handle to Create a Series

The data on the worksheet, including month names and the What-If Assumptions section, now can be added to the worksheet.

Plan Ahead

> **Plan the layout of the worksheet.**
> Excel allows you to rotate text in a cell. Rotated text often provides a strong visual appeal. Rotated text also allows you to fit more text into a smaller column width. Chapters 1 and 2 used the fill handle to copy a cell or a range of cells to adjacent cells. The fill handle also allows creation of a series of numbers, dates, or month names automatically. Using the fill handle in this way eliminates the need to type in such data, saving time and eliminating typographical errors.

To Rotate Text and Use the Fill Handle to Create a Series of Month Names

The design of the worksheet calls specifically for only six months of data. Because there always will be only six months of data in the worksheet, the months should be placed across the top of the worksheet as column headings rather than as row headings. The data for the worksheet includes more data items regarding each month than there are months, and, possibly, more expense categories could be added in the future. A proper layout, therefore, includes placing each month as column headings.

When you first enter text, its angle is zero degrees (0°), and it reads from left to right in a cell. Excel allows you to rotate text in a cell counterclockwise by entering a number between 1° and 90°.

The following steps enter the month name, July, in cell B10; format cell B10 (including rotating the text); and then use the fill handle to enter the remaining month names in the range C10:G10.

1

- If necessary, select the Home tab and then select cell B10 because this cell will include the first month name in the series of month names.

- Type `July` as the cell entry and then click the Enter box.

- Click the Format Cells: Alignment Dialog Box Launcher (Home tab | Alignment group) to display the Format Cells dialog box (Figure 3–4).

Figure 3–4

2

• Click the 45° point in the Orientation area (Format Cells dialog box) to move the Text hand in the Orientation area to the 45° point and to display a new orientation in the Degrees box (Figure 3–5).

Figure 3–5

3

• Click the OK button to rotate the text in the active cell and automatically increase the height of the current row to best fit the rotated text.

• Point to the fill handle on the lower-right corner of cell B10 to display the crosshair mouse pointer in preparation of filling the month series (Figure 3–6).

Figure 3–6

4
- Drag the fill handle to the right to select the range to fill, C10:G10 in this case. Do not release the mouse button (Figure 3–7).

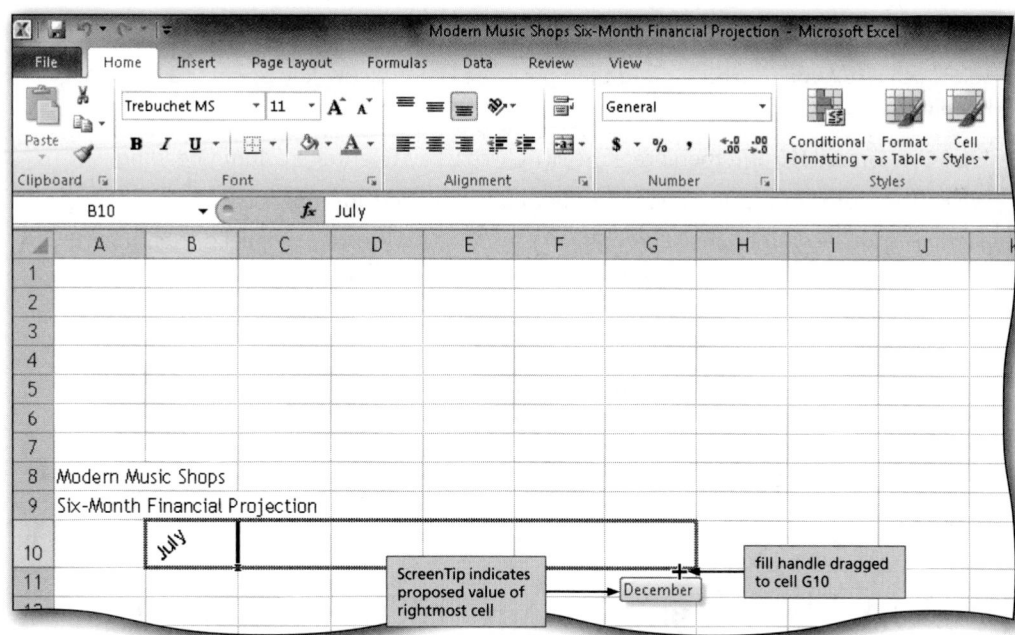

Figure 3–7

5
- Release the mouse button to create a month name series in the selected range and copy the format of the selected cell to the selected range.

- Click the Auto Fill Options button below the lower-right corner of the fill area to display the Auto Fill Options menu (Figure 3–8).

What if I do not want to copy the format of cell B10 during the auto fill operation?

In addition to creating a series of values, dragging the fill handle instructs Excel to copy the format of cell B10 to the range C10:G10. With some fill operations, you may not want to copy the formats of the

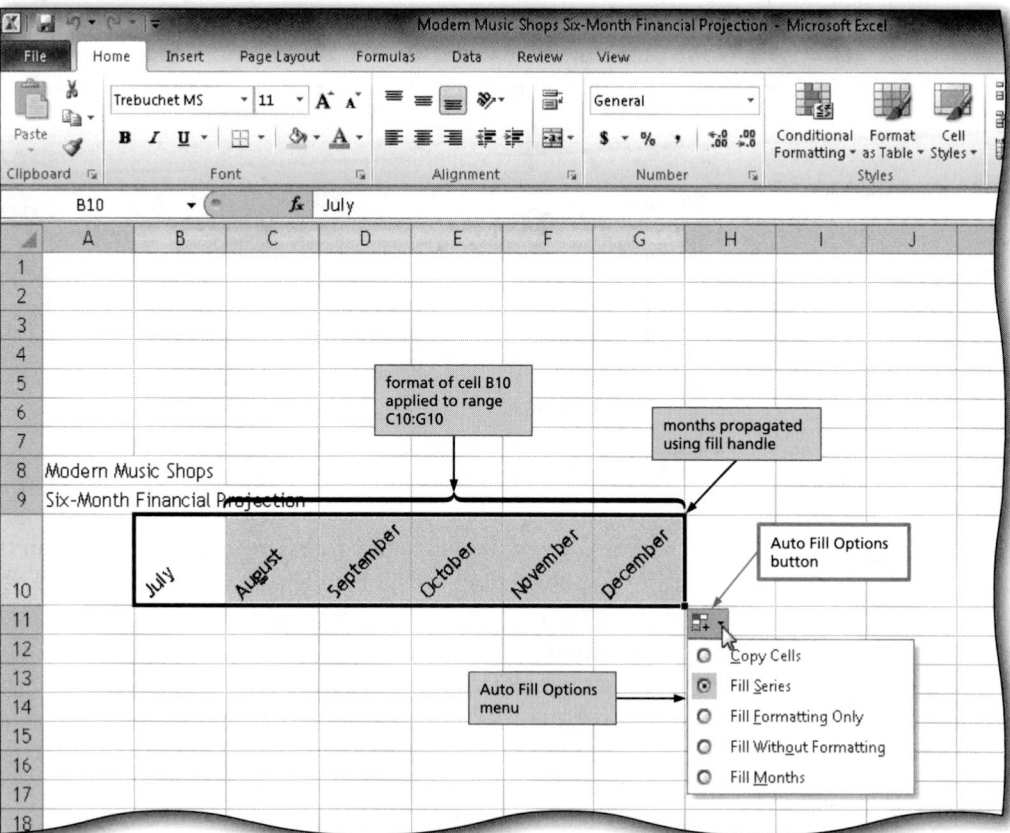

Figure 3–8

source cell or range to the destination cell or range. If this is the case, click the Auto Fill Options button after the range fills and then select the option you desire on the Auto Fill Options menu (Figure 3–8).

6

- Click the Auto Fill Options button to hide the Auto Fill Options menu.

- Select cell H10, type `Total,` and then press the RIGHT ARROW key to enter a column heading.

- Type Chart in cell I10 and then press the RIGHT ARROW key to enter a column heading.

Q&A | Why is the word Total automatically formatted with a 45° rotation?

Excel tries to save you time by automatically recognizing the adjacent cell format in cell G10 and applying it to cell H10. Such behavior also occurs when typing the column heading in cell I10.

Other Ways

1. Enter start month in cell, apply formatting, right-drag fill handle in direction to fill, click Fill Months on shortcut menu

2. Enter start month in cell, apply formatting, select range, click Fill button (Home tab | Editing group), click Series, click AutoFill

---

BTW

Rotating Text in a Cell
In Excel, you use the Alignment sheet of the Format Cells dialog box, as shown in Figure 3–5 on page 146, to position data in a cell by centering, left-aligning, or right-aligning; indenting; aligning at the top, bottom, or center; and rotating. If you enter 90 in the Degrees box in the Orientation area, the text will appear vertically and read from bottom to top in the cell.

Using the Auto Fill Options Menu

As shown in Figure 3–8 on the previous page, Fill Series is the default option that Excel uses to fill an area, which means it fills the destination area with a series, using the same formatting as the source area. If you choose another option on the Auto Fill Options menu, then Excel immediately changes the contents of the destination range. Following the use of the fill handle, the Auto Fill Options button remains active until you begin the next Excel operation. Table 3–2 summarizes the options on the Auto Fill Options menu.

Table 3–2 Options Available on the Auto Fill Options Menu	
Auto Fill Option	**Description**
Copy Cells	Fill destination area with contents using format of source area. Do not create a series.
Fill Series	Fill destination area with series using format of source area. This option is the default.
Fill Formatting Only	Fill destination area using format of source area. No content is copied unless fill is series.
Fill Without Formatting	Fill destination area with contents, without the formatting of source area.
Fill Months	Fill destination area with series of months using format of source area. Same as Fill Series and shows as an option only if source area contains a month.

BTW

The Mighty Fill Handle
If you drag the fill handle to the left or up, Excel will decrement the series rather than increment the series. To copy a word, such as January or Monday, which Excel might interpret as the start of a series, hold down the CTRL key while you drag the fill handle to a destination area. If you drag the fill handle back into the middle of a cell, Excel erases the contents of the cell.

You can use the fill handle to create a series longer than the one shown in Figure 3–8. If you drag the fill handle past cell G10 in Step 4, Excel continues to increment the months and logically will repeat July, August, and so on, if you extend the range far enough to the right.

You can create several different types of series using the fill handle. Table 3–3 illustrates several examples. Notice in examples 4 through 7, 9, and 11 that, if you use the fill handle to create a series of numbers or nonsequential months, you must enter the first item in the series in one cell and the second item in the series in an adjacent cell. Excel still creates the series, however, if the first two items are in a range and the cells between the items are empty. Next, select both cells and drag the fill handle through the destination area.

Table 3–3 Examples of Series Using the Fill Handle		
Example	Contents of Cell(s) Copied Using the Fill Handle	Next Three Values of Extended Series
1	4:00	5:00, 6:00, 7:00
2	Qtr2	Qtr3, Qtr4, Qtr1
3	Quarter 1	Quarter 2, Quarter 3, Quarter 4
4	22-Jul, 22-Sep	22-Nov, 22-Jan, 22-Mar
5	2012, 2013	2014, 2015, 2016
6	1, 2	3, 4, 5
7	625, 600	575, 550, 525
8	Mon	Tue, Wed, Thu
9	Sunday, Tuesday	Thursday, Saturday, Monday
10	4th Section	5th Section, 6th Section, 7th Section
11	−205, −208	−211, −214, −217

BTW

Custom Fill Sequences
You can create your own custom lists for use with the fill handle. For example, if you often type in the same list of products or names into Excel, you can create a custom fill sequence. You then can type the first product or name and then use the fill handle automatically to fill in the remaining products or names. To create a custom fill sequence, open the Excel Options dialog box by clicking the Options button in the Backstage view. Click the Advanced tab (Excel Options dialog box) and then click the Edit Custom Lists button (Excel Options dialog box).

To Increase Column Widths

In Chapter 2, you increased column widths after the values were entered into the worksheet. Sometimes, you may want to increase the column widths before you enter the values and, if necessary, adjust them later. The following steps increase the column widths.

- Move the mouse pointer to the boundary between column heading A and column heading B so that the mouse pointer changes to a split double arrow in preparation of adjusting the column widths.

- Drag the mouse pointer to the right until the ScreenTip displays the desired column width, Width: 36.00 (293 pixels) in this case. Do not release the mouse button (Figure 3–9).

Figure 3–9

- Release the mouse button to change the width of the column.

- Click column heading B to select the column and then drag through column heading G to select the range in which to change the widths.

- Move the mouse pointer to the boundary between column headings B and C in preparation of resizing column B, and then drag the mouse to the right until the ScreenTip displays the desired width, Width: 14.88 (124 pixels) in this case. Do not release the mouse button (Figure 3–10).

Figure 3–10

- Release the mouse button to change the width of the selected columns.

- If necessary, scroll the worksheet so that column H is visible and then use the technique described in Step 1 to increase the width of column H to 16.00.

To Enter Row Titles

Excel allows you to indent text in cells. Often, indentation sets off titles, such as row titles, from other titles to create a hierarchy, such as you may find in a table of contents in a book. The following steps enter the row titles in column A and indent several of the row titles.

- If necessary, scroll the worksheet so that column A and row 23 are visible and then enter the row titles in the range A11:A23 but without the indents (Figure 3–11).

- Select cell A12 and then click the Increase Indent button (Home tab | Alignment group) to increase the indentation of the text in the selected cell.

- Select the range A16:A20 and then click the Increase Indent button (Home tab | Alignment group) to increase the indentation of the text in the selected range (Figure 3–11).

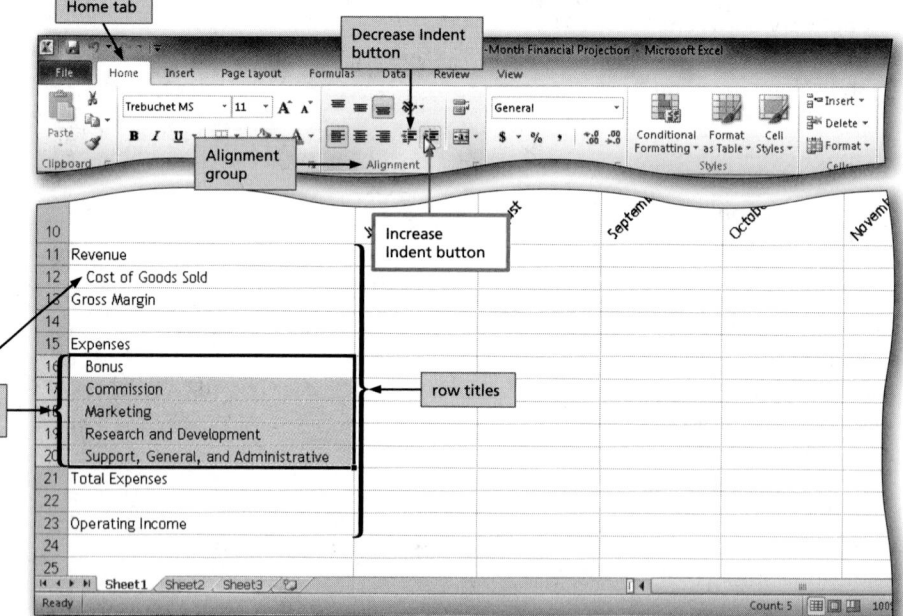

Figure 3–11

2

- Select cell A1 to finish entering the row titles and deselect the current cell.

Q&A

What happens when I click the Increase Indent button?

The Increase Indent button (Home tab | Alignment group) indents the contents of a cell to the right by three spaces each time you click it. The Decrease Indent button decreases the indent by three spaces each time you click it.

Other Ways		
1. To indent, right-click range, click Format Cells on shortcut menu, click Alignment tab (Format	Cells dialog box), click Left (Indent) in Horizontal list, type number of spaces to indent in Indent text box,	click OK button (Format Cells dialog box)

Copying a Range of Cells to a Nonadjacent Destination Area

The What-If Assumptions section should be placed in an area of the worksheet that is accessible easily yet does not impair the view of the main section of the worksheet. As shown in Figure 3–3a on page EX 142, the What-If Assumptions should be placed above the calculations in the worksheet. Additionally, the row titles in the Expenses area are the same as the row titles in the What-If Assumptions table, with the exception of the two additional entries in cells A4 (Margin) and A7 (Sales Revenue for Bonus). Hence, the What-If Assumptions table row titles can be created by copying the range A16:A20 to the range A2:A6 and then inserting two rows for the additional entries in cells A4 and A7. The source area (range A16:A20) is not adjacent to the destination area (range A2:A6). The first two chapters used the fill handle to copy a source area to an adjacent destination area. To copy a source area to a nonadjacent destination area, however, you cannot use the fill handle.

A more versatile method of copying a source area is to use the Copy button and Paste button (Home tab | Clipboard group). You can use these two buttons to copy a source area to an adjacent or nonadjacent destination area.

BTW

Fitting Entries in a Cell
An alternative to increasing column widths or row heights is to shrink the characters in a cell to fit the current width of the column. To shrink to fit, click Format Cells: Alignment Dialog Box Button Launcher (Home tab | Alignment group), and click Shrink to fit in the Text control area. After shrinking entries to fit in cells, consider using the Zoom slider on the status bar to make the entries more readable.

To Copy a Range of Cells to a Nonadjacent Destination Area

The Copy button copies the contents and format of the source area to the **Office Clipboard**, a reserved place in the computer's memory that allows you to collect text and graphics from an Office document and then paste them into almost any other type of document. The Paste button copies the item from the Office Clipboard to the destination area.

The following steps enter the what-if area row heading and use the Copy and Paste buttons to copy the range A16:A20 to the nonadjacent range A2:A6.

1

- With cell A1 selected, type **What-If Assumptions** as the new row title.

- Select the range A16:A20 and then click the Copy button (Home tab | Clipboard group) to copy the values and formats of the selected range, A16:A20 in this case, to the Office Clipboard.

- Select cell A2, the top cell in the destination area (Figure 3–12).

Q&A

Why do I not need to select the entire destination area?

You are not required to select the entire destination area (range A2:A6) before clicking the Paste button (Home tab | Clipboard group). Excel needs to know only the upper-left cell of the destination area. In the case of a single column range, such as A2:A6, the top cell of the destination area (cell A2) also is the upper-left cell of the destination area.

Figure 3–12

● Click the Paste button (Home tab | Clipboard group) to copy the values and formats of the last item placed on the Office Clipboard, range A16:A20 in this case, to the destination area, A2:A6 in this case (Figure 3–13).

Q&A

What if data already existed in the destination area?

When you complete a copy, the values and formats in the destination area are replaced with the values and formats of the source area. Any data contained in the destination area prior to the copy and paste is lost. If you accidentally delete valuable data, immediately click the Undo button on the Quick Access Toolbar.

3

● Press the ESC key to remove the marquee from the source area and disable the Paste button (Home tab | Clipboard group).

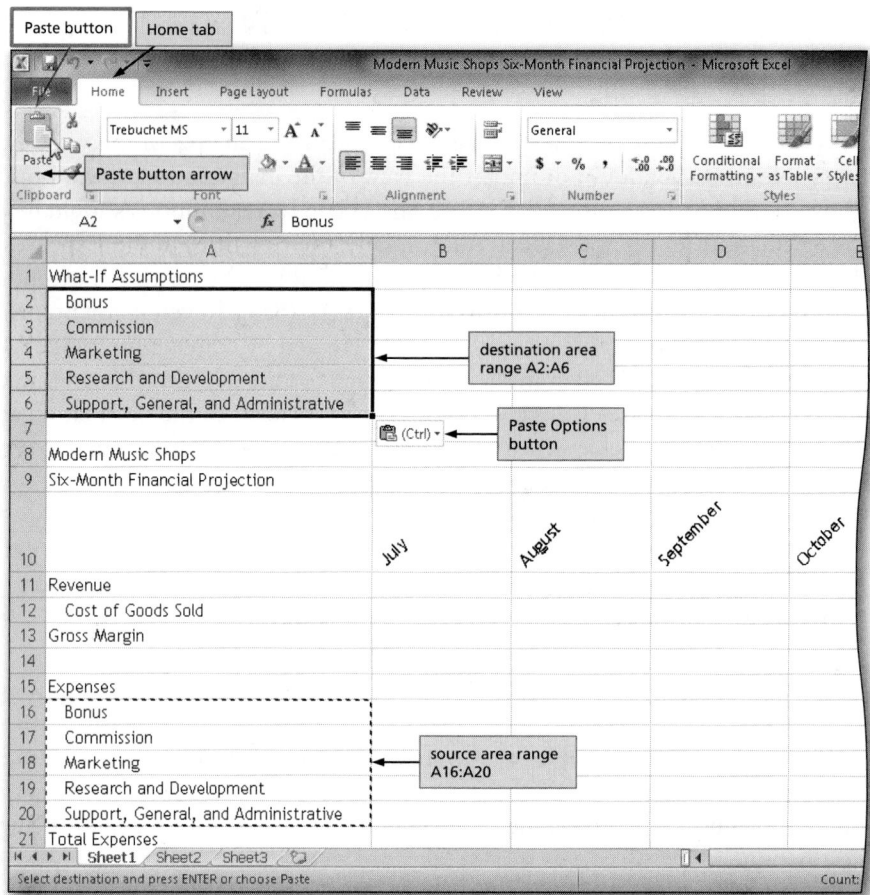

Figure 3–13

Other Ways

1. Right-click source area, click Copy on shortcut menu, right-click destination area, click Paste icon on shortcut menu

2. Select source area and point on border of range; while holding down CTRL key, drag source area to destination area

3. Select source area, press CTRL+C, select destination area, press CTRL+V

BTW

Q&As

For a complete list of the Q&As found in many of the step-by-step sequences in this book, visit the Excel 2010 Q&A Web page (scsite.com/ex2010/qa).

Using the Paste Options Menu

After you click the Paste button, Excel immediately displays the Paste Options button, as shown in Figure 3–13. If you click the Paste Options button arrow and select an option on the Paste Options gallery, Excel modifies the most recent paste operation based on your selection. Table 3–4 summarizes the options available on the Paste Options gallery. When the Paste Options button is visible, you can use shortcut keys to access the paste commands available in the Paste Options gallery. Additionally, you can use combinations of the options in the Paste Options gallery to customize your paste operation. That is, after clicking one of the icons in the Paste Options gallery, you can open the gallery again to further adjust your paste operation. The Paste button (Home tab | Clipboard group) includes an arrow that, when clicked, displays the same options as does the Paste Options button arrow.

Table 3–4 Options Available in the Paste Options Gallery

Paste Option Icon	Paste Option	Shortcut Key	Description
	Paste	CTRL+P	Copy contents and format of source area. This option is the default.
	Formulas	CTRL+F	Copy formulas from the source area, but not the contents and format.
	Formulas & Number Formatting	CTRL+O	Copy formulas and format for numbers and formulas of source area, but not the contents.
	Keep Source Formatting	CTRL+K	Copy contents, format, and styles of source area.
	No Borders	CTRL+B	Copy contents and format of source area, but not any borders.
	Keep Source Column Widths	CTRL+W	Copy contents and format of source area. Change destination column widths to source column widths.
	Transpose	CTRL+T	Copy the contents and format of the source area, but transpose, or swap, the rows and columns.
	Values	CTRL+V	Copy contents of source area, but not the formatting for formulas.
	Values & Number Formatting	CTRL+A	Copy contents and format of source area for numbers or formulas, but use format of destination area for text.
	Values & Source Formatting	CTRL+E	Copy contents and formatting of source area, but not the formula.
	Formatting	CTRL+R	Copy format of source area, but not the contents.
	Paste Link	CTRL+N	Copy contents and format and link cells so that a change to the cells in source area updates the corresponding cells in destination area.
	Picture	CTRL+U	Copy an image of the source area as a picture.
	Linked Pictures	CTRL+I	Copy an image of the source area as a picture so that a change to the cells in source area updates the picture in destination area.

BTW

Copying and Pasting from Other Programs
If you have data you need in Excel, but the data is stored in another program, copying and pasting likely will help you. You might need to experiment before you are successful because Excel might attempt to copy formatting or other information that you did not intend to paste from the other program. Using the various Paste buttons likely will solve most of such problems.

An alternative to clicking the Paste button is to press the ENTER key. The ENTER key completes the paste operation, removes the marquee from the source area, and disables the Paste button so that you cannot paste the copied source area to other destination areas. The ENTER key was not used in the previous set of steps so that the capabilities of the Paste Options button could be discussed. The Paste Options button does not appear on the screen when you use the ENTER key to complete the paste operation.

Using Drag and Drop to Move or Copy Cells

You also can use the mouse to move or copy cells. First, you select the source area and point to the border of the cell or range. You know you are pointing to the border of the cell or range when the mouse pointer changes to a block arrow. To move the selected cell or cells, drag the selection to the destination area. To copy a selection, hold down the CTRL key while dragging the selection to the destination area. You know Excel is in copy mode when a small plus sign appears next to the block arrow mouse pointer. Be sure to release the mouse button before you release the CTRL key. Using the mouse to move or copy cells is called **drag and drop**.

BTW

Move It or Copy It
Contrary to popular belief, move and copy operations are not the same. When you move a cell, the data in the original location is cleared and the format of the cell is reset to the default. When you copy a cell, the data and format of the copy area remains intact. In short, you should copy cells to duplicate entries and move cells to rearrange entries.

Using Cut and Paste to Move Cells

Another way to move cells is to select them, click the Cut button (Home tab | Clipboard group) (Figure 3–12 on page EX 151) to remove them from the worksheet and copy them to the Office Clipboard, select the destination area, and then click the Paste button (Home tab | Clipboard group) or press the ENTER key. You also can use the Cut command on the shortcut menu, instead of the Cut button.

Inserting and Deleting Cells in a Worksheet

At any time while the worksheet is on the screen, you can insert cells to enter new data or delete cells to remove unwanted data. You can insert or delete individual cells; a range of cells, rows, columns; or entire worksheets.

To Insert a Row

According to the sketch of the worksheet in Figure 3–3a on page EX 142, two rows must be inserted in the What-If Assumptions table, one between Commission and Marketing for the Margin assumption and another between Research and Development and Support, General, and Administrative for the Sales Revenue for Bonus assumption. The following steps insert the new rows into the worksheet.

1

- Right-click row heading 4, the row below where you want to insert a row, to display the shortcut menu and the Mini toolbar (Figure 3–14).

Figure 3–14

2

- Click Insert on the shortcut menu to insert a new row in the worksheet by shifting the selected row and all rows below it down one row.

- Select cell A4 in the new row and then enter **Margin** to enter a new row title (Figure 3–15).

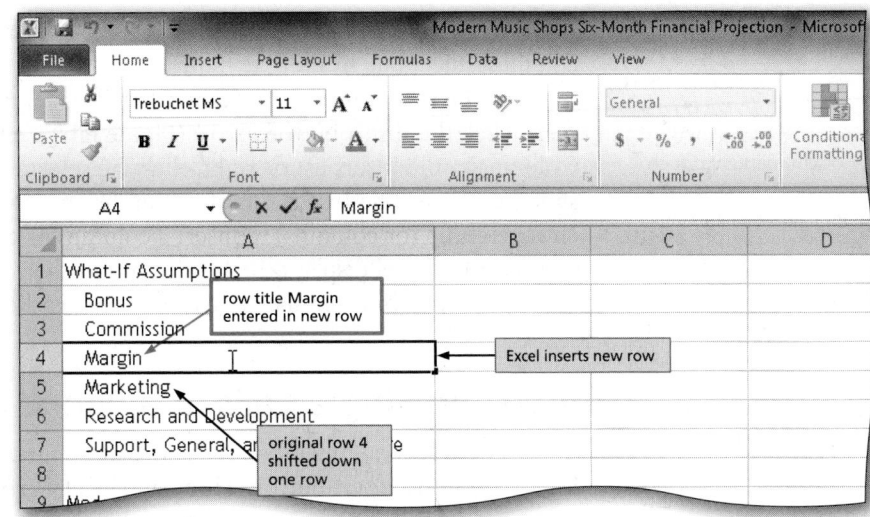

Q&A

What is the resulting format of the new row?

The cells in the new row inherit the formats of the cells in the row above them. You can change this behavior by clicking the Insert Options button that appears immediately below the inserted row. Following the insertion of a row, the Insert Options button allows you to select from the following options: (1) 'Format Same As Above'; (2) 'Format Same As Below'; and (3) Clear Formatting. The 'Format Same as Above' option is the default. The Insert Options button remains active until you begin the next Excel operation. Excel does not display the Insert Options button if the initial row does not contain any formatted data.

Figure 3–15

3

- Right-click row heading 7 to display a shortcut menu and then click Insert on the shortcut menu to insert a new row in the worksheet.

- Select cell A7 in the new row and then enter **Sales Revenue for Bonus** to enter a new row title (Figure 3–16).

Q&A

What would happen if cells in the shifted rows were included in formulas?

If the rows that shift down include cell references in formulas located in the worksheet, Excel automatically would adjust the cell references in the formulas to their new locations. Thus, in Step 2, if a formula in the worksheet references a cell in row 7 before the insert, then Excel adjusts the cell reference in the formula to row 8 after the insert.

Figure 3–16

Other Ways

1. Insert (Home tab | Cells group), click Insert Sheet Rows

2. Press CTRL + SHIFT + PLUS SIGN, click Entire row, click OK button

Inserting Columns

You insert columns into a worksheet in the same way you insert rows. To insert columns, select one or more columns immediately to the right of where you want Excel to insert the new column or columns. Select the number of columns you want to insert. Next, click the Insert button arrow (Home tab | Cells group) and then click Insert Sheet Columns in the Insert list or right-click the selected column(s), then click Insert on the shortcut menu. The Insert command on the shortcut menu requires that you select an entire column (or columns) to insert a column (or columns). Following the insertion of a column, Excel displays the Insert Options button, which allows you to modify the insertion in a fashion similar to that discussed earlier when inserting rows.

Inserting Single Cells or a Range of Cells

The Insert command on the shortcut menu or the Insert Cells command on the Insert list of the Insert button (Home tab | Cells group) allows you to insert a single cell or a range of cells. You should be aware that if you shift a single cell or a range of cells, however, it no longer lines up with its associated cells. To ensure that the values in the worksheet do not get out of order, spreadsheet experts recommend that you insert only entire rows or entire columns. When you insert a single cell or a range of cells, Excel displays the Insert Options button so that you can change the format of the inserted cell, using options similar to those for inserting rows and columns.

Deleting Columns and Rows

The Delete button (Home tab | Cells group) or the Delete command on the shortcut menu removes cells (including the data and format) from the worksheet. Deleting cells is not the same as clearing cells. The Clear command, described in Chapter 1 on page EX 52, clears the data from the cells, but the cells remain in the worksheet. The Delete command removes the cells from the worksheet and shifts the remaining rows up (when you delete rows) or shifts the remaining columns to the left (when you delete columns). If formulas located in other cells reference cells in the deleted row or column, Excel does not adjust these cell references. Excel displays the error message **#REF!** in those cells to indicate a cell reference error. For example, if cell A7 contains the formula =A4+A5 and you delete row 5, Excel assigns the formula =A4+#REF! to cell A6 (originally cell A7) and displays the error message #REF! in cell A6. Excel also displays an Error Options button when you select the cell containing the error message #REF!, which allows you to select options to determine the nature of the problem.

To Enter Numbers with Format Symbols

The next step in creating the Six-Month Financial Projection worksheet is to enter the what-if assumptions values in the range B2:B8. The numbers in the table can be entered and then formatted as in Chapters 1 and 2, or each one can be entered with format symbols. When a number is entered with a **format symbol**, Excel immediately displays it with the assigned format. Valid format symbols include the dollar sign ($), comma (,), and percent sign (%).

If you enter a whole number, it appears without any decimal places. If you enter a number with one or more decimal places and a format symbol, Excel displays the number with two decimal places. Table 3–5 illustrates several examples of numbers entered with format symbols. The number in parentheses in column 4 indicates the number of decimal places.

Table 3–5 Numbers Entered with Format Symbols			
Format Symbol	**Typed in Formula Bar**	**Displays in Cell**	**Comparable Format**
,	374, 149	374, 149	Comma(0)
	5,833.6	5,833.60	Comma(2)
$	$58917	$58,917	Currency(0)
	$842.51	$842.51	Currency(2)
	$63,574.9	$63,574.90	Currency(2)
%	85%	85%	Percent(0)
	12.80%	12.80%	Percent(2)
	68.4222%	68.4222%	Percent(4)

The following step enters the numbers in the What-If Assumptions table with format symbols.

1

- Enter `200,000.00` in cell B2, `5.75%` in cell B3, `57.50%` in cell B4, `15.00%` in cell B5, `7.50%` in cell B6, `3,500,000.00` in cell B7, and `18.75%` in cell B8 to display the entries using formats based on the format symbols entered with the numbers (Figure 3–17).

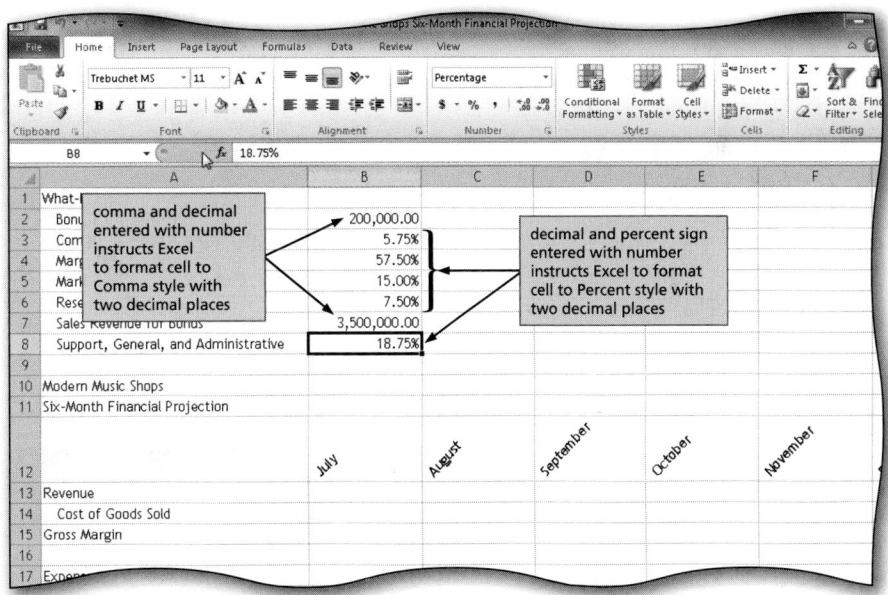

Figure 3–17

Other Ways
1. Right-click range, click Format Cells on shortcut menu, click Number tab (Format Cells dialog box), click category in Category list, [select desired format], click OK button (Format Cells dialog box) 2. Press CTRL + 1, click Number tab (Format Cells dialog box), click category in Category list, [select desired format], click OK button (Format Cells dialog box)

To Freeze Column and Row Titles

Freezing worksheet titles is a useful technique for viewing large worksheets that extend beyond the window. Normally, when you scroll down or to the right, the column titles in row 12 and the row titles in column A that define the numbers no longer appear on the screen. This makes it difficult to remember what the numbers in these rows and columns represent. To alleviate this problem, Excel allows you to **freeze the titles**, so that Excel displays the titles on the screen, no matter how far down or to the right you scroll.

The steps on the following page use the Freeze Panes button (View tab | Window group) to freeze the worksheet title and column titles in rows 10, 11, and 12, and the row titles in column A.

1

- Scroll the worksheet to ensure that Excel displays row 10 as the first row and column A on the screen.

- Select cell B13 to select the cell on which to freeze panes.

- Display the View tab and then click the Freeze Panes button (View tab | Window group) to display the Freeze Panes gallery (Figure 3–18).

Q&A

Why should I ensure that row 10 is the first row displayed?

Before freezing the titles, it is important that Excel display the first row that you want frozen as the first row displayed. For example, if cell B13 was selected while displaying row 1, then Excel would freeze the what-if assumptions and only show a few rows of data in the Six-Month Financial Project area of the worksheet. To ensure that you can view as much data as possible, always scroll to a row that maximizes the view of your important data before freezing panes.

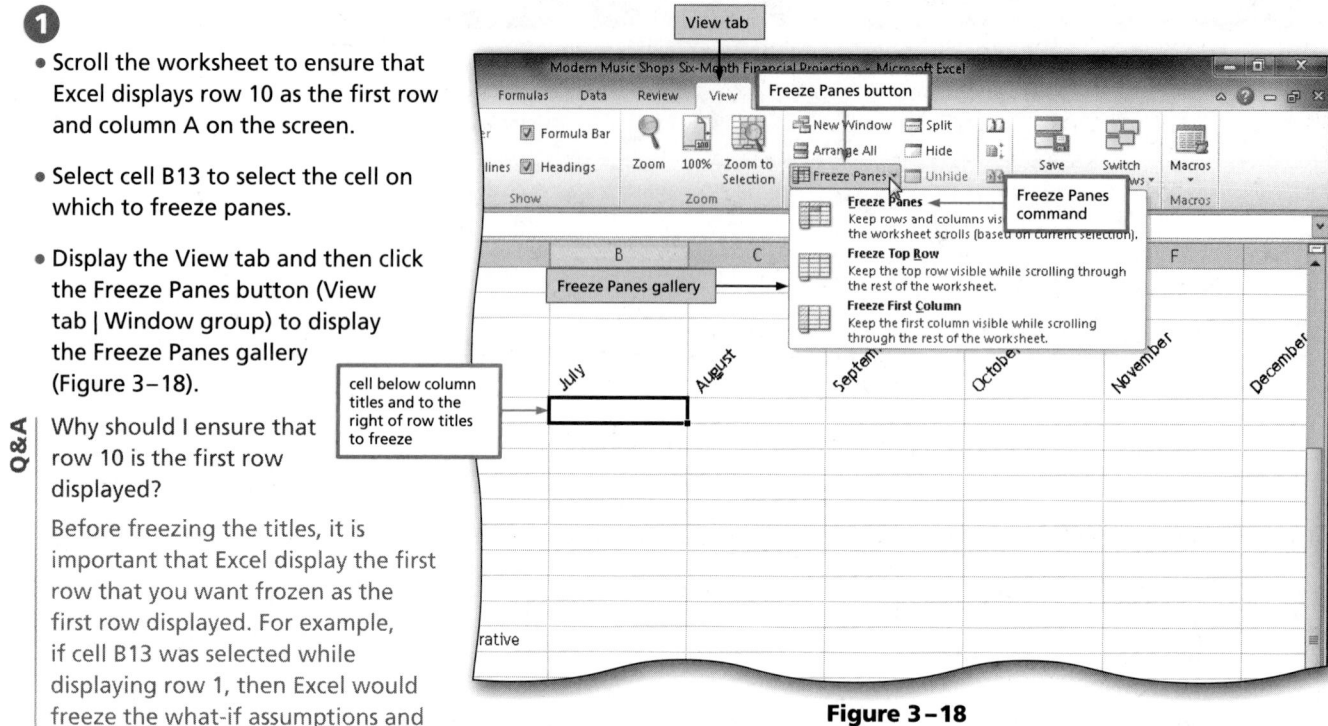

Figure 3–18

2

- Click Freeze Panes in the Freeze Panes gallery to freeze rows and columns to the left and above the selected cell, column A and rows 10 through 12 in this case (Figure 3–19).

Q&A

What happens after I click the Freeze Panes command?

Excel displays a thin black line on the right side of column A, indicating the split between the frozen row titles in column A and the rest of the worksheet. It also displays a thin black line below row 12, indicating the split between the frozen column titles in rows 10 through 12 and the rest of the worksheet (Figure 3–19).

Figure 3–19

To Enter the Projected Monthly Sales

The following steps enter the projected revenue, listed earlier in Table 3–1 on page EX 143, in row 13 and compute the projected six-month revenue in cell H13.

1 If necessary, display the Home tab.

2 Enter `3113612.16` in cell B13, `7962235.53` in cell C13, `5112268.58` in cell D13, `2924627.87` in cell E13, `7630534.65` in cell F13, and `3424270.23` in cell G13.

3 Select cell H13 and then click the Sum button (Home tab | Editing group) twice to create a sum in the selected cell (Figure 3–20).

BTW

Freezing Titles
If you want to freeze only column headings, select the appropriate cell in column A before you click the Freeze Panes button (View tab | Window group). If you want to freeze only row titles, select the appropriate cell in row 1 before you click the Freeze Panes button (View tab | Window group). To freeze both column headings and row titles, select the cell that is the intersection of the column and row titles before you click the Freeze Panes button (View tab | Window group).

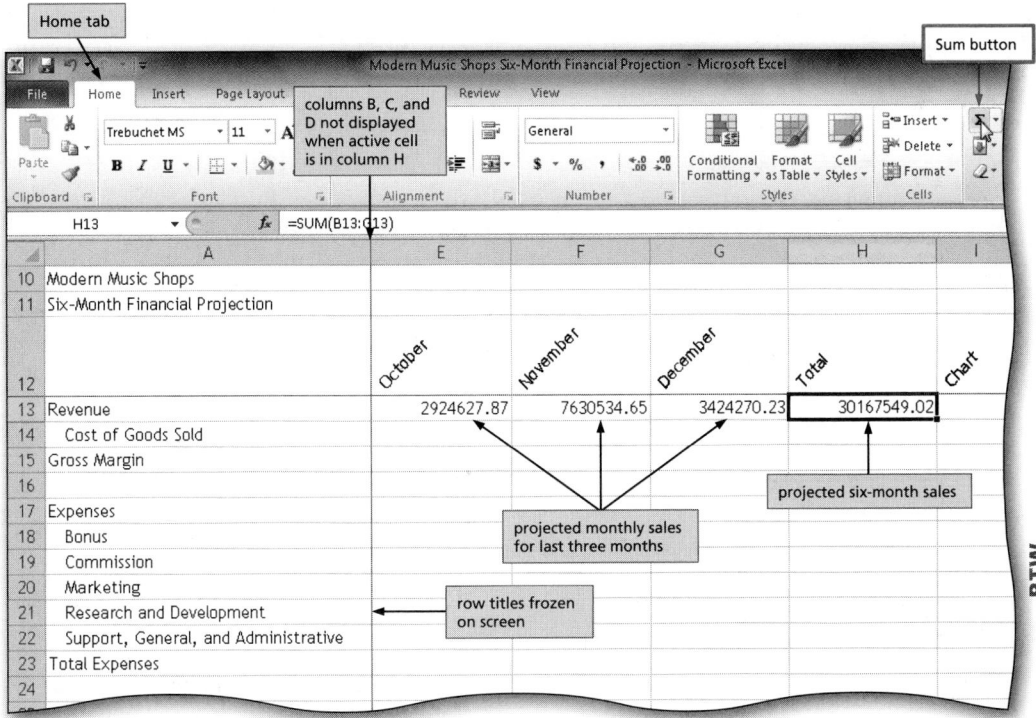

Figure 3–20

BTW

The Insert Options Button
When you insert columns or rows, Excel displays the Insert Options button only if formats are assigned to the leftmost column or top row of the selection.

To Enter and Format the System Date

The sketch of the worksheet in Figure 3–3a on page EX 142 includes a date stamp on the right side of the heading section. A **date stamp** shows the date a workbook, report, or other document was created or the period it represents. In business, a report often is meaningless without a date stamp. For example, if a printout of the worksheet in this chapter were distributed to the company's analysts, the date stamp would show when the six-month projections were made, as well as what period the report represents.

A simple way to create a date stamp is to use the NOW function to enter the system date tracked by your computer in a cell in the worksheet. The **NOW function** is one of 22 date and time functions available in Excel. When assigned to a cell, the NOW function returns a number that corresponds to the system date and time beginning with December 31, 1899. For example, January 1, 1900 equals 1, January 2, 1900 equals 2, and so on. Noon equals .5. Thus, noon on January 1, 1900 equals 1.5 and 6 P.M. on January 1, 1900 equals 1.75. If the computer's system date is set to the current date, which normally it is, then the date stamp is equivalent to the current date.

The steps on the following pages enter the NOW function and then change the format from mm/dd/yyyy hh:mm to mm/dd/yyyy.

1

- Select cell I11 and then click the Insert Function box in the formula bar to display the Insert Function dialog box.

- Click the 'Or select a category' box arrow (Insert Function dialog box) and then select Date & Time in the list to populate the 'Select a function' list with data and time functions.

- Scroll down in the 'Select a function list' and then click NOW to select the required function (Figure 3–21).

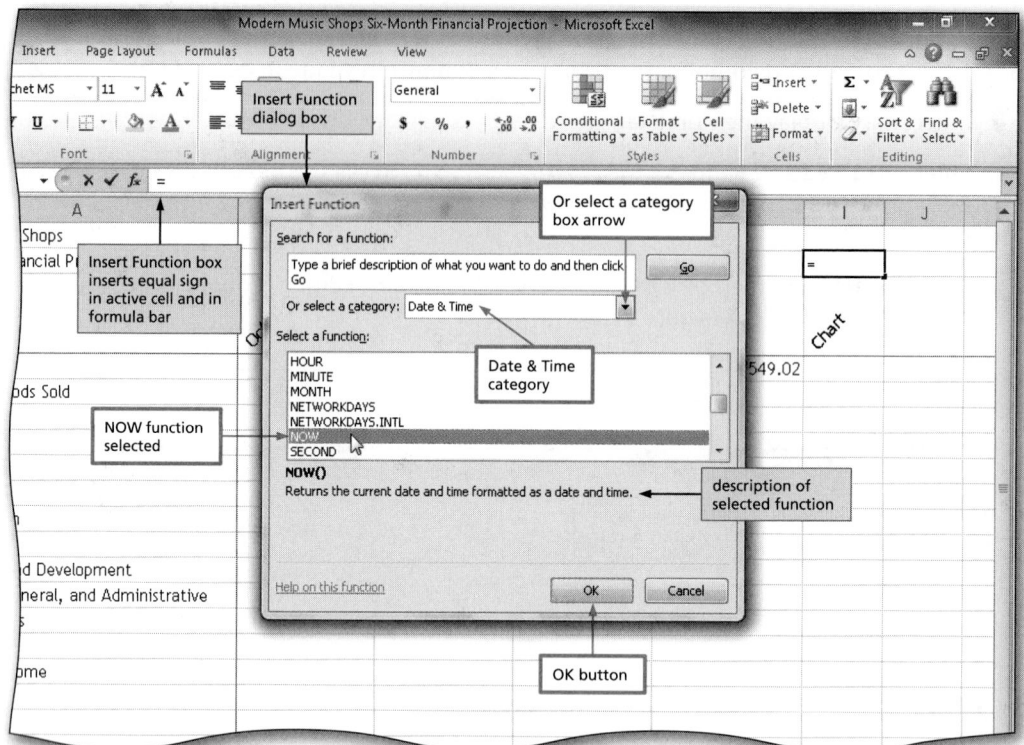

Figure 3–21

2

- Click the OK button (Insert Function dialog box) to close the Insert Function dialog box and display the Function Arguments dialog box.

- Click the OK button (Function Arguments dialog box) to display the system date and time in the selected cell, using the default date and time format mm/dd/yyyy hh:mm.

- Right-click cell I11 to display a shortcut menu and Mini toolbar (Figure 3–22).

Q&A

Why does the date appear with the mm/dd/yyyy hh:mm format?

Figure 3–22

Excel automatically formats the result of the NOW function as a date, using the date and time format, mm/dd/yyyy hh:mm, where the first mm is the month, dd is the day of the month, yyyy is the year, hh is the hour of the day, and mm is the minutes past the hour.

3

- Click Format Cells on the shortcut menu to display the Format Cells dialog box.

- If necessary, click the Number tab (Format Cells dialog box) to display the Number sheet.

- Click Date in the Category list (Format Cells dialog box) to display the types of date formats in the Type list. Scroll down in the Type list and then click 3/14/2001 to display a sample of the data in the active cell, I11 in this case, using the selected format in the Sample area (Figure 3–23).

 Why do the dates in the Type box show March 14, 2001 instead of the current date?

The date March 14, 2001 is used as a sample date in the Format cells dialog box.

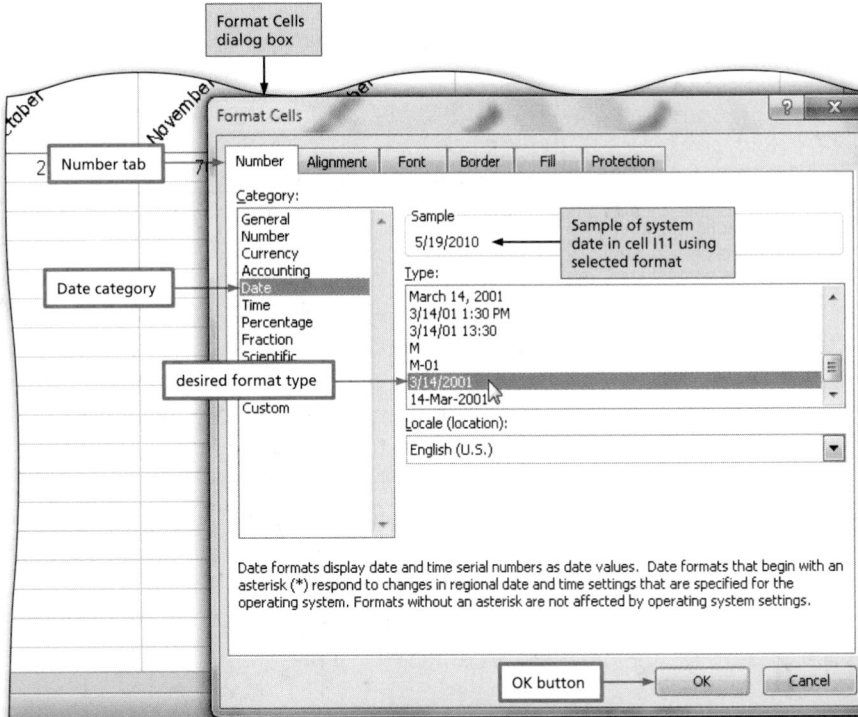

Figure 3–23

4

- Click the OK button (Format Cells dialog box) to display the system date in the format mm/dd/yyyy.

- Double-click the border between columns I and J to change the width of the column to best fit (Figure 3–24).

 How does Excel format a date?

In Figure 3–24, the date is displayed right-aligned in the cell because

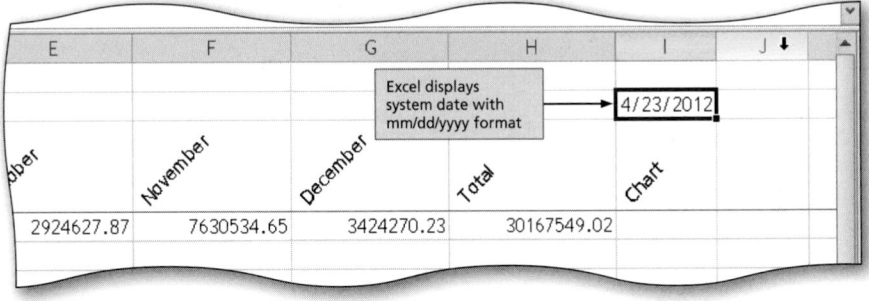

Figure 3–24

Excel treats a date as a number formatted to display as a date. If you assign the General format (Excel's default format for numbers) to a date in a cell, the date is displayed as a number with two decimal places. For example, if the system time and date is 9:00 AM on November 13, 2012 and the cell containing the NOW function is assigned the General format, then Excel displays the following number in the cell:

The whole number portion of the number (41226) represents the number of days since December 31, 1899. The decimal portion of the number (.375) represents 9:00 AM as the time of day, at which point 37.5% of the day is complete. To assign the General format to a cell, click General in the Category list in the Format Cells dialog box (Figure 3–23).

Other Ways

1. Click Date & Time (Formulas tab | Function Library group), click now

2. Press CTRL + SEMICOLON (not a volatile date)

3. Press CTRL + SHIFT + # to format date to day-month-year

Break Point: If you wish to stop working through the chapter at this point, you can quit Excel now and then resume the project at a later point in time by starting Excel, opening the file called Modern Music Shops Six-Month Financial Projection, and continuing to follow the steps from this location forward.

Absolute versus Relative Addressing

The next sections describe the formulas and functions needed to complete the calculations in the worksheet.

As you learned in Chapters 1 and 2, Excel modifies cell references when copying formulas. While copying formulas, however, sometimes you do not want Excel to change cell references. To keep a cell reference constant when copying a formula or function, Excel uses a technique called absolute cell referencing. To specify an absolute cell reference in a formula, enter a dollar sign ($) before any column letters or row numbers you want to keep constant in formulas you plan to copy. For example, $B$4 is an absolute cell reference, whereas B4 is a relative cell reference. Both reference the same cell. The difference becomes apparent when they are copied to a destination area. A formula using the **absolute cell reference** $B$4 instructs Excel to keep the cell reference B4 constant (absolute) in the formula as it copies it to the destination area. A formula using the **relative cell reference** B4 instructs Excel to adjust the cell reference as it copies it to the destination area. A cell reference with only one dollar sign before either the column or the row is called a **mixed cell reference**. When planning formulas, be aware of when you need to use absolute, relative, and mixed cell references. Table 3–6 gives some additional examples of each of these types of cell references.

Table 3–6 Examples of Absolute, Relative, and Mixed Cell References		
Cell Reference	**Type of Reference**	**Meaning**
$B$4	Absolute cell reference	Both column and row references remain the same when you copy this cell, because the cell references are absolute.
B$4	Mixed reference	This cell reference is mixed. The column reference changes when you copy this cell to another column because it is relative. The row reference does not change because it is absolute.
$B4	Mixed reference	This cell reference is mixed. The column reference does not change because it is absolute. The row reference changes when you copy this cell reference to another row because it is relative.
B4	Relative cell reference	Both column and row references are relative. When copied to another cell, both the column and row in the cell reference are adjusted to reflect the new location.

The next step is to enter the formulas that calculate the following values for July: cost of goods sold (cell B14), gross margin (cell B15), expenses (range B18:B22), total expenses (cell B23), and the operating income (cell B25). The formulas are based on the projected monthly revenue in cell B13 and the assumptions in the range B2:B8.

To Enter a Formula Containing Absolute Cell References

The formulas for each column (month) are the same, except for the reference to the projected monthly revenue in row 13, which varies according to the month (B13 for July, C13 for August, and so on). Thus, the formulas for July can be entered in column B and then copied to columns C through G. Table 3–7 shows the formulas for determining the July cost of goods sold, gross margin, expenses, total expenses, and operating income in column B.

Table 3–7 Formulas for Determining Cost of Goods Sold, Margin, Expenses, Total Expenses, and Operating Income for July

Cell	Row Title	Formula	Comment
B14	Cost of Goods Sold	=B13 * (1 – B4)	Revenue times (1 minus Margin %)
B15	Gross Margin	= B13 – B14	Revenue minus Cost of Goods Sold
B18	Bonus	=IF(B13 >= B7, B2, 0)	Bonus equals value in B2 or 0
B19	Commission	=B13 * B3	Revenue times Commission %
B20	Marketing	=B13 * B5	Revenue times Marketing %
B21	Research and Development	=B13 * B6	Revenue times Research and Development %
B22	Support, General, and Administrative	=B13 * B8	Revenue times Support, General, and Administrative %
B23	Total Expenses	=SUM(B18:B22)	Sum of July Expenses
B25	Operating Income	=B15 – B23	Gross Margin minus Total Expenses

As the formulas are entered as shown in Table 3–7 in column B for July and then copied to columns C through G (August through December) in the worksheet, Excel will adjust the cell references for each column automatically. Thus, after the copy, the August Commission expense in cell C19 would be =C13 * C3. While the cell reference C13 (August Revenue) is correct, the cell reference C3 references an empty cell. The formula for cell C19 should read =C13 * B3, rather than =C13 * C3, because B3 references the Commission % value in the What-If Assumptions table. In this instance, a way is needed to keep a cell reference in a formula the same, or constant, when it is copied.

The following steps enter the cost of goods formula = B13*(1 – $B$4) in cell B14 using Point mode. To enter an absolute cell reference, you can type the dollar sign ($) as part of the cell reference or enter it by pressing F4 with the insertion point in or to the right of the cell reference to change it to absolute.

1

- Press CTRL+HOME to select cell B13 and then click cell B14 to show cell B13 and to select the cell in which to enter the first formula.

- Type = (equal sign), select cell B13, type * (1–b4 to continue entering the formula, and then press F4 to change the most recently typed cell reference, in this case cell b4, from a relative cell reference to an absolute cell reference. Type) to complete the formula (Figure 3–25).

Q&A Is an absolute reference required in this formula?

No, because a mixed cell reference could have been used. The formula in cell B14 will be copied across columns, rather than down rows. So, the formula entered in cell B14 in Step 1 could have been entered as =B13*(1–$B4), rather than =B13*(1–$B$4). That is, the formula could have included the mixed cell reference $B4, rather than the absolute cell reference $B$4. When you copy a formula across columns, the row does not change anyway. The key is to ensure that column B remains constant as you copy the formula across columns. To change the absolute cell reference to a mixed cell reference, continue to press the F4 key until you achieve the desired cell reference.

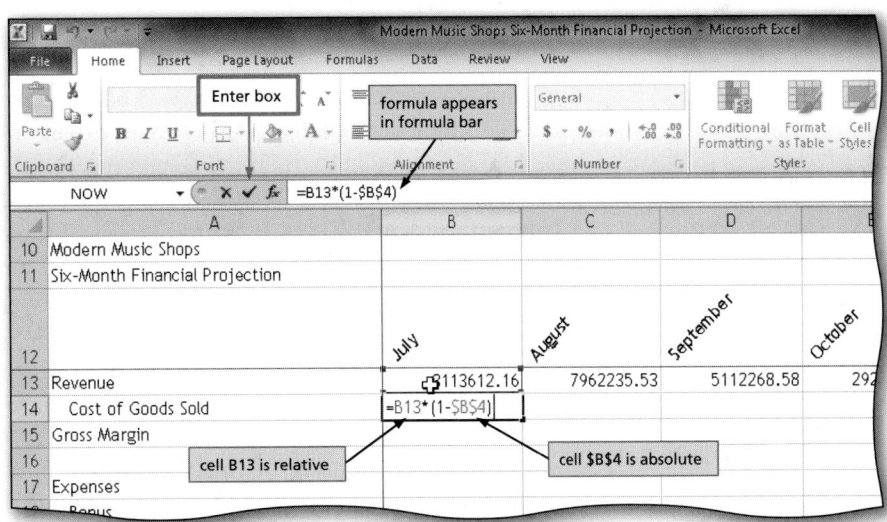

Figure 3–25

2

- Click the Enter box in the formula bar to display the result, 1323285.168, instead of the formula in B14 (Figure 3–26).

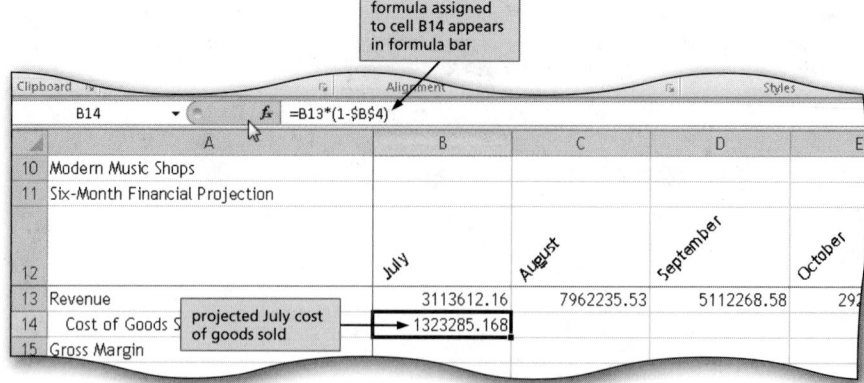

Figure 3–26

3

- Click cell B15 to select the cell in which to enter the next formula, type = (equal sign), click cell B13, type − (minus sign), and then click cell B14 to add a reference to the cell to the formula.

- Click the Enter box in the formula bar to display the result in the selected cell, in this case gross margin for July, 1790326.992, in cell B15 (Figure 3–27).

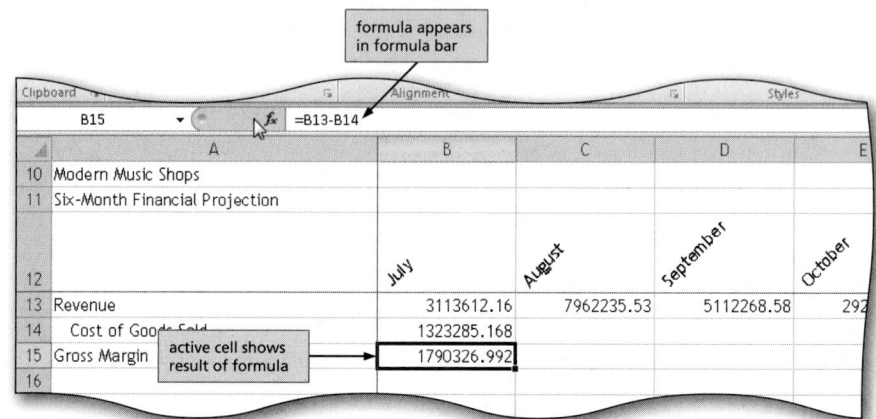

Figure 3–27

Making Decisions — The IF Function

Logical Operators in IF Functions
IF functions can use logical operators, such as AND, OR, and NOT. For example, the three IF functions =IF(AND(A1>C1, B1<C2), "OK", "Not OK") and =IF(OR(K5>J5, C3<K6), "OK", "Not OK") and =IF(NOT(B10<C10), "OK", "Not OK") use logical operators. In the first example, both logical tests must be true for the value_if_true OK to be assigned to the cell. In the second example, one or the other logical tests must be true for the value_if_true OK to be assigned to the cell. In the third example, the logical test B10<C10 must be false for the value_if_true OK to be assigned to the cell.

According to the Request for New Workbook in Figure 3–2 on page EX 140, if the projected July revenue in cell B13 is greater than or equal to the sales revenue for bonus in cell B7 (3,500,000.00), then the July bonus value in cell B18 is equal to the bonus value in cell B2 (200,000.00); otherwise, cell B18 is equal to 0. One way to assign the July bonus value in cell B18 is to check to see if the revenue in cell B13 equals or exceeds the sales revenue for the bonus amount in cell B7 and, if so, then to enter 200,000.00 in cell B18. You can use this manual process for all six months by checking the values for the corresponding months.

Because the data in the worksheet changes each time a report is prepared or the figures are adjusted, however, it is preferable to have Excel assign the monthly bonus to the entries in the appropriate cells automatically. To do so, cell B18 must include a formula or function that displays 200,000.00 or 0.00 (zero), depending on whether the projected July revenue in cell B13 is greater than, equal to, or less than the sales revenue for bonus value in cell B7.

The **IF function** is useful when you want to assign a value to a cell based on a logical test. For example, using the IF function, cell B18 can be assigned the following IF function:

$$=IF(B13>=\$B\$7, \$B\$2, 0)$$

logical_test   value_if_true   value_if_false

The IF function instructs Excel that, if the projected July revenue in cell B13 is greater than or equal to the sales revenue for bonus value in cell B7, then Excel should display the value 200000 in cell B2, in cell B18. If the projected July revenue in cell B13 is less than the sales revenue for bonus value in cell B7, then Excel displays a 0 (zero) in cell B18.

The general form of the IF function is:

=IF(logical_test, value_if_true, value_if_false)

The argument, logical_test, is made up of two expressions and a comparison operator. Each expression can be a cell reference, a number, text, a function, or a formula. Valid comparison operators, their meaning, and examples of their use in IF functions are shown in Table 3–8. The argument, value_if_true, is the value you want Excel to display in the cell when the logical test is true. The argument, value_if_false, is the value you want Excel to display in the cell when the logical test is false.

Table 3–8 Comparison Operators

Comparison Operator	Meaning	Example
=	Equal to	=IF(B12 = 200, F3 * H4, E10 + F3)
<	Less than	=IF(G56 * Q56 < D12, $M$10, B9 ^ 5)
>	Greater than	=IF(MIN(A12:A52) > 75, 0, 1)
>=	Greater than or equal to	=IF($T$9 >= B7, P3 - H12, 1000)
<=	Less than or equal to	=IF(C9 * G2 <= 99, $T35, 350 * C9)
<>	Not equal to	=IF(G15 <> 1, "No","Yes")

To Enter an IF Function

The following steps assign the IF function =IF(B13>=$B$7,$B$2,0) to cell B18. This IF function determines whether or not the worksheet assigns a bonus for July.

- Click cell B18 to select the cell for the next formula.

- Click the Insert Function box in the formula bar to display the Insert Function dialog box.

- Click the 'Or select a category' box arrow (Insert Function dialog box) and then select Logical in the list to populate the 'Select a function' list with logic functions.

- Click IF in the 'Select a function list' to select the required function (Figure 3–28).

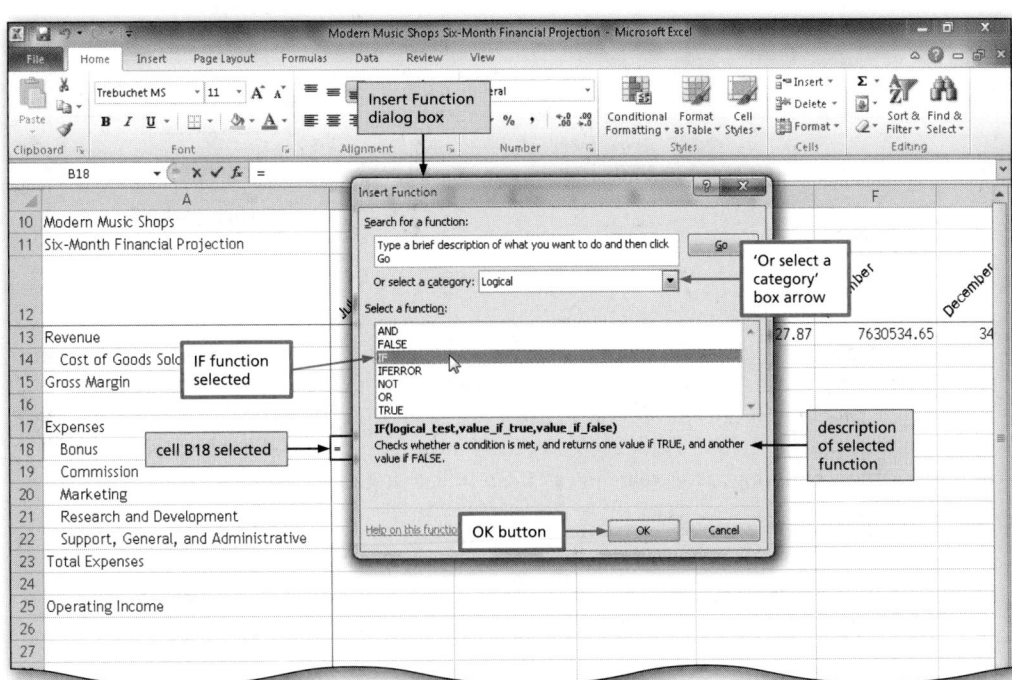

Figure 3–28

2

- Click the OK button (Insert Function dialog box) to display the Function Arguments dialog box.

- Type `b13>=$b$7` in the Logical test box to enter a logical test for the IF function.

- Type `$b$2` in the Value_if_true box to enter the result of the IF function if the logical test is true.

- Type `0` in the Value_if_false box to enter the result of the IF function if the logical test is false (Figure 3–29).

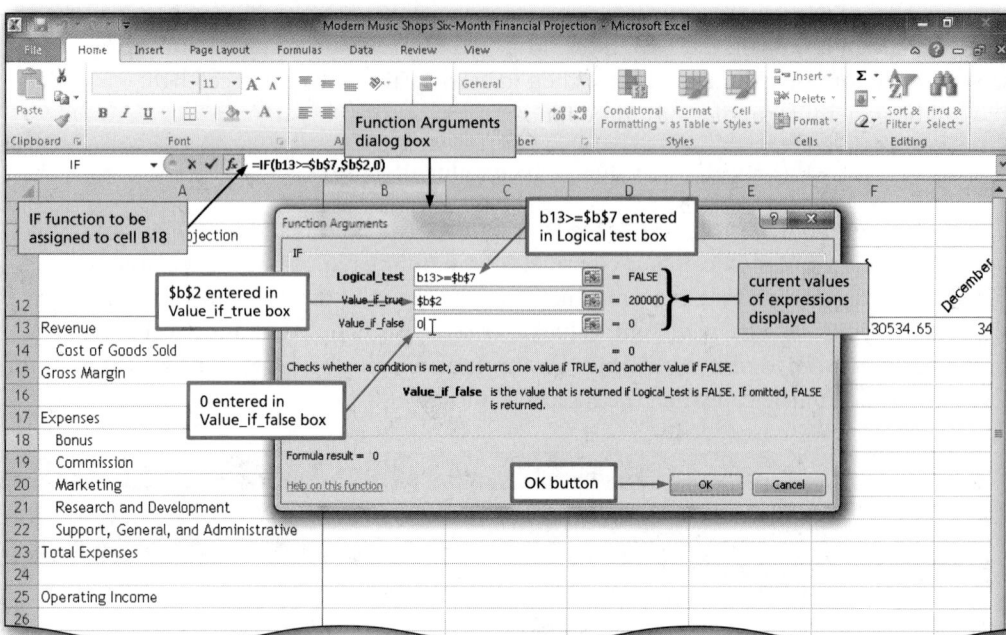

Figure 3–29

3

- Click the OK button (Function Arguments dialog box) to insert the IF function in the selected cell (Figure 3–30).

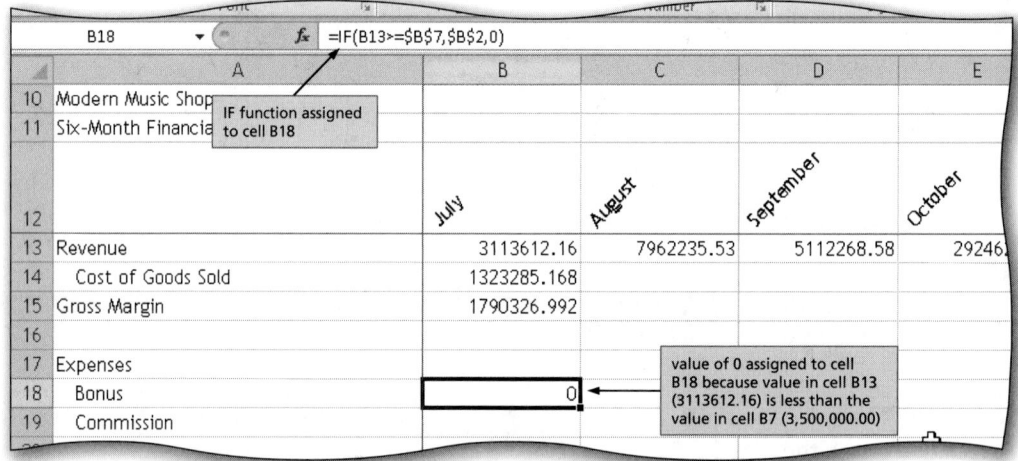

Figure 3–30

Q&A

Why is the value 0 displayed in cell B18?

The value that Excel displays in cell B18 depends on the values assigned to cells B13, B2, and B7. For example, if the value for July revenue in cell B13 is increased above 3,500,000.00, then the IF function in cell B18 will cause Excel to display 200,000.00. If you change the sales revenue for bonus in cell B7 from 3,500,000.00 to another number and the value in cell B13 is greater than or equal to the value in cell B7, it will change the results in cell B18 as well.

Other Ways

1. Click Logical button (Formulas tab | Function Library group), click IF

To Enter the Remaining July Formulas

The July commission expense in cell B19 is equal to the revenue in cell B13 times the commission assumption in cell B3 (5.75%). The July marketing expense in cell B20 is equal to the projected July revenue in cell B13 times the marketing assumption in cell B5 (15.00%). Similar formulas determine the remaining July expenses in cells B21 and B22.

The total expenses value in cell B23 is equal to the sum of the expenses in the range B18:B22. The operating income in cell B25 is equal to the gross margin in cell B15 minus the total expenses in cell B23. The formulas are short, and therefore, they are typed in the following steps, rather than entered using Point mode.

1 Select cell B19. Type `=b13*$b$3` and then press the DOWN ARROW key to enter the formula in the selected cell. Type `=b13*$b$5` and then press the DOWN ARROW key to enter the formula in the selected cell. Type `=b13*$b$6` and then press the DOWN ARROW key to enter the formula in the selected cell. Type `=b13*$b$8` and then press the DOWN ARROW key to enter the formula in the selected cell.

2 With cell B23 selected, click the Sum button (Home tab | Editing group) twice to insert a SUM function in the selected cell. Select cell B25 to prepare to enter the next formula. Type `=b15-b23` and then press the ENTER key to enter the formula in the selected cell.

3 Press CTRL+ACCENT MARK (`) to display the formulas version of the worksheet (Figure 3–31).

4 When you are finished viewing the formulas version, press CTRL+ACCENT MARK (`) to display the values version of the worksheet.

Q&A Why should I view the formulas version of the worksheet?

Viewing the formulas version (Figure 3–31) of the worksheet allows you to check the formulas assigned to the range B14:B25. Recall that formulas were entered in lowercase. You can see that Excel converts all the formulas from lowercase to uppercase.

BTW

Replacing a Formula with a Constant
By doing the following, you can replace a formula with its result so that the cell value remains constant: (1) click the cell with the formula; (2) press F2 or click in the formula bar; (3) press F9 to display the value in the formula bar; and (4) press the ENTER key.

Figure 3–31

To Copy Formulas with Absolute Cell References Using the Fill Handle

The following steps use the fill handle to copy the July formulas in column B to the other five months in columns C through G.

- Select the range B14:B25 and then point to the fill handle in the lower-right corner of the selected cell, B25 in this case, to display the crosshair mouse pointer (Figure 3–32).

Figure 3–32

- Drag the fill handle to the right to copy the formulas from the source area, B14:B25 in this case, to the destination area, C14:G25 in this case, and display the calculated amounts and Auto Fill Options button (Figure 3–33).

Q&A

What happens to the formulas after performing the copy operation?

Because the formulas in the range B14:B25 use absolute cell references, the formulas still refer to the current values in the Assumptions table when the formulas are copied to the range C14:G25.

Figure 3–33

Q&A

What happened to columns B, C, and D?

As shown in Figure 3–33, as the fill handle is dragged to the right, columns B, C, and D no longer appear on the screen because column A now acts just as the row numbers do in that columns scrolled off of the visible portion of the worksheet disappear behind column A. Column A, however, remains on the screen, because the row titles were frozen earlier in this chapter.

To Determine Row Totals in Nonadjacent Cells

BTW

Error Messages
When Excel cannot calculate a formula, it displays an error message in a cell. These error messages always begin with a number sign (#). The more commonly occurring error messages are as follows: #DIV/0! (tries to divide by zero); #NAME? (uses a name Excel does not recognize); #N/A (refers to a value not available); #NULL! (specifies an invalid intersection of two areas); #NUM! (uses a number incorrectly); #REF (refers to a cell that is not valid); #VALUE! (uses an incorrect argument or operand); and ##### (refers to cells not wide enough to display entire entry).

The following steps determine the row totals in column H. To determine the row totals using the Sum button, select only the cells in column H containing numbers in adjacent cells to the left. If, for example, you select the range H14:H25, Excel will display 0s as the sum of empty rows in cells H16, H17, and H24.

1. Select the range H14:H15. While holding down the CTRL key, select the range H18:H23 and cell H25, as shown in Figure 3–34.

2. Click the Sum button (Home tab | Editing group) to display the row totals in the selected ranges (Figure 3–34).

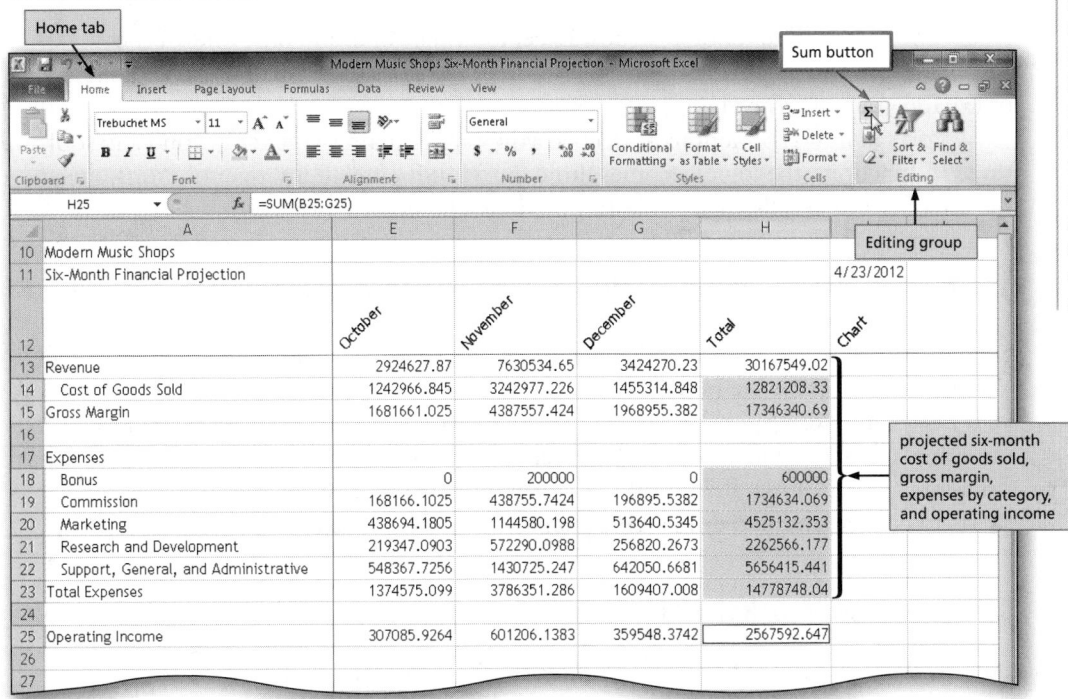

Figure 3–34

To Unfreeze the Worksheet Titles and Save the Workbook

All the text, data, and formulas have been entered into the worksheet. The following steps unfreeze the titles to allow you to work with the worksheet without frozen rows and columns, and save the workbook using its current file name, Modern Music Shops Six-Month Financial Projection.

1. Press CTRL+HOME to select cell B13 and view the upper-left corner of the screen.

2. Display the View tab and then click the Freeze Panes button (View tab | Window group) to display the Freeze Panes gallery.

3. Click Unfreeze Panes in the Freeze Panes gallery to unfreeze the frozen columns and rows.

4. Display the Home tab and then click the Save button on the Quick Access Toolbar to save the workbook.

Q&A

Why does pressing CTRL+HOME select cell B13?

When the titles are frozen and you press CTRL+HOME, Excel selects the upper-left cell of the unfrozen section of the worksheet. For example, in Step 1 of the previous steps, Excel selected cell B13. When the titles are unfrozen, pressing CTRL+HOME selects cell A1.

Nested Forms of the IF Function

BTW

Using IFERROR
Similar to the IF function, the IFERROR function checks a formula for correctness. For example, =IFERROR(formula, "Error Message") examines the formula argument. If an error appears (such as #N/A), Excel displays the Error Message text in the cell instead of the Excel #N/A error.

A **nested IF function** is one in which the action to be taken for the true or false case includes yet another IF function. The second IF function is considered to be nested, or layered, within the first. Study the nested IF function below, which determines the eligibility of a student to go on a field trip. The school permits the student to attend the field trip if the student's age is at least 14 and the student has provided a signed permission form. Assume the following in this example: (1) the nested IF function is assigned to cell L9, which instructs Excel to display one of three messages in the cell; (2) cell L7 contains a student's age; and (3) cell L8 contains a Y or N, based on whether the person provided a signed permission form.

=IF(L7>=14, IF(L8="Y","Allowed","Can Travel, but No Permission"),"Too Young to Travel")

The nested IF function instructs Excel to display one, and only one, of the following three messages in cell L9: (1) Allowed; or (2) Can Travel, but No Permission; or (3) Too Young to Travel.

You can nest IF functions as deep as you want, but after you get beyond a nest of three IF functions, the logic becomes difficult to follow and alternative solutions, such as the use of multiple cells and simple IF functions, should be considered.

Adding and Formatting Sparkline Charts

Sometimes you may want to condense a range of data into a small chart in order to show a trend or variation in the range. Excel's standard charts may be too large or extensive for your needs. An Excel **Sparkline chart** provides a simple way to show trends and variations in a range of data within a single cell. Excel includes three types of Sparkline charts: Line, Column, and Win/Loss. Because they exist in only one cell, you should use Sparkline charts to convey succinct, eye-catching summaries of the data they represent.

To Add a Sparkline Chart to the Worksheet

Each of the rows of monthly data, including those containing formulas, provides useful information easily summarized by a Line Sparkline chart. A Line Sparkline chart is a good choice because it shows trends over the six-month period for each row of data.

The following steps add a Line Sparkline chart to cell I13 and then use the fill handle to create Line Sparkline charts in the range I14:I25 that represent the monthly data in rows 13 through 25.

1
- Scroll the worksheet so that both columns B and I are displayed on the screen.

- Select cell I13 to prepare to insert a Sparkline chart in the cell.

- Display the Insert tab and then click Line (Insert tab | Sparklines group) to display the Create Sparklines dialog box (Figure 3–35).

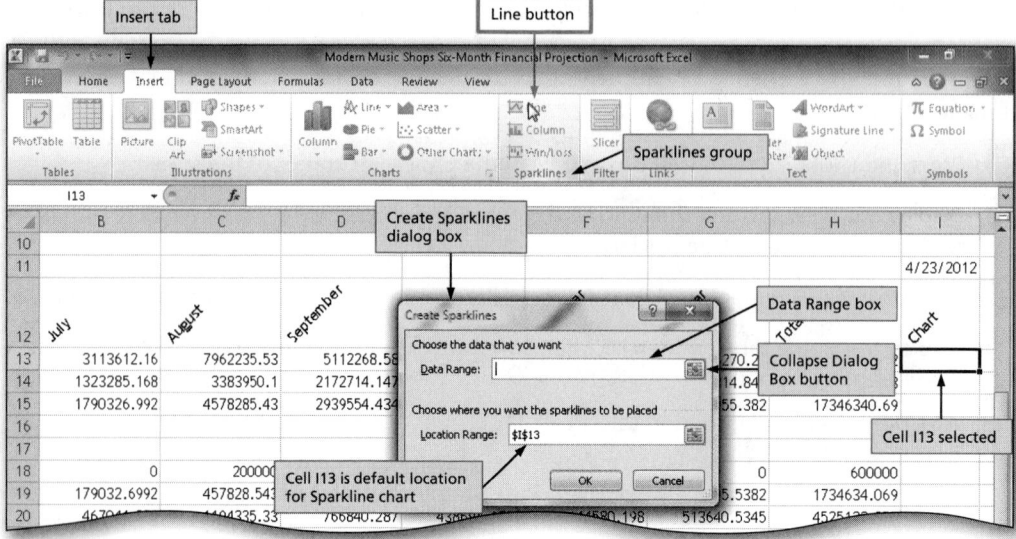

Figure 3–35

2

- Drag through the range B13:G13 to select the range. Do not release the mouse (Figure 3–36).

Q&A What happened to the Create Sparklines dialog box?

When a dialog box includes a Collapse Dialog Box button (Figure 3–35), selecting cells or a range collapses the dialog box so that only the current text box is displayed. Once the selection is made, the dialog box expands back to its original size. You also can click the Collapse Dialog Box button to make your selection and then click the Expand Dialog Box button (Figure 3–36) to expand the dialog box.

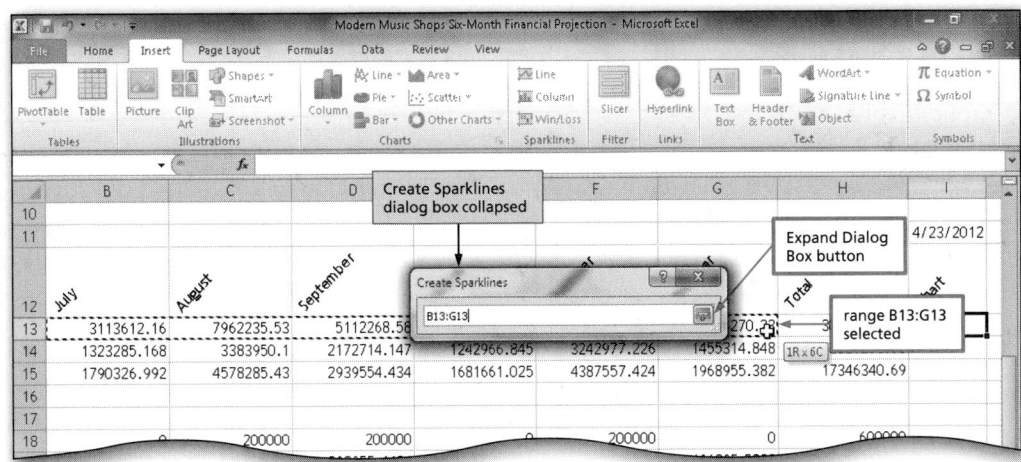

Figure 3–36

3

- Release the mouse button to insert the selected range, B13:G13 in this case, in the Data Range text box.

- Click the OK button (Create Sparklines dialog box) to insert a Line Sparkline chart in the selected cell and display the Sparkline Tools contextual tab (Figure 3–37).

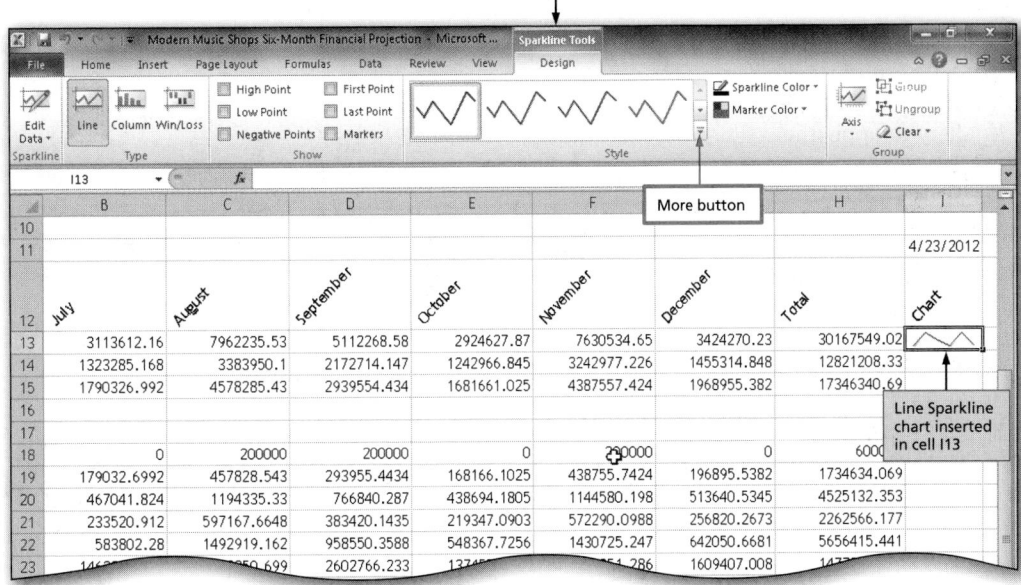

Figure 3–37

To Format and Copy the Sparkline Chart

Just as with standard charts, Excel provides formatting options for Sparkline charts. Sparkline chart formatting is restricted greatly as compared to standard charts. As shown in Figure 3–37, the Show group (Sparkline Tools Design tab) allows you to highlight various points in the chart. Markers provide a point on the chart for each cell represented in the chart. The Style group (Sparkline Tools Design tab) allows you to specify the style and color for the parts of a Sparkline chart.

The steps on the following page format the Sparkline chart in cell I13 using the Style 13 Sparkline chart style.

1

- Click the More button (Sparkline Tools Design tab | Style group) to display the Style gallery (Figure 3–38).

Figure 3–38

2

- Click Sparkline Style Accent 1, (no dark or light) in the Styles gallery to apply the style to the Sparkline chart in the selected cell, I13 in this case.

- Point to the fill handle in cell I13 and then drag through cell I25 to copy the Line Sparkline chart.

- Select cell I27 (Figure 3–39).

Q&A

Why do Sparkline charts not appear in cells I16, I17, and I24?

Excel does not draw Sparkline charts if the range for the Sparkline chart contains no data. In this case the ranges B16:G16, B17:G17, and B24:G24 do not contain data, so Excel draws no Sparkline chart. If you add data

	D	E	F	G	H	I
	September	October	November	December	Total	Chart
35.53	5112268.58	2924627.87	7630534.65	3424270.23	30167549.02	
8950.1	2172714.147	1242966.845	3242977.226	1455314.848	12821208.33	
285.43	2939554.434	1681661.025	4387557.424	1968955.382	17346340.69	
200000	200000	0	200000	0	600000	
28.543	293955.4434	168166.1025	438755.7424	196895.5	634.069	
335.33	766840.287	438694.1805	1144580.198	513640.5	132.353	
7.6648	383420.1435	219347.0903	572290.0988	256820.2673	2262566.177	
9.162	958550.3588	548367.7256	1430725.247	642050.6681	5656415.441	
0.699	2602766.233	1374575.099	3786351.286	1609407.008	14778748.04	
7306	336788.2009	307085.9264	601206.1383	359548.3742	2567592.647	

Line Sparkline chart copied to range I14:I25

Figure 3–39

to cells in those ranges, then Excel automatically would draw Line Sparkline charts for the rows to which you added data because the Sparkline charts were defined for cells I16, I17, and I24 by the drag operation.

Formatting the Worksheet

The worksheet created thus far shows the financial projections for the six-month period, from July to December. Its appearance is uninteresting, however, even though some minimal formatting (formatting assumptions numbers, changing the column widths, formatting the date, and formatting the Sparkline chart) was performed earlier. This section will complete the formatting of the worksheet to make the numbers easier to read and to emphasize the titles, assumptions, categories, and totals as shown in Figure 3–40.

Identify how to format various elements of the worksheet.

A worksheet, such as the one presented in this chapter, should be formatted in the following manner: (1) format the numbers; (2) format the worksheet title, column titles, row titles, and total rows; and (3) format an assumptions table. Numbers in heading rows and total rows should be formatted with a currency symbol. Other dollar amounts should be formatted with a Comma style. An assumptions table should be diminished in its formatting so that it does not distract from the main calculations and data in the worksheet. Assigning the data in an assumptions table a smaller font size would set it apart from other data formatted with a larger font size.

BTW

Customizing Sparkline Charts

You can customize sparkline charts in a number of ways on the Sparkline Chart Design tab. In the Show group (Sparkline Chart Design tab), you can specify values to show as markers on the chart, such as the highest value, lowest value, any negative numbers, the first point, and the last point. You can change the color of the sparkline and markers in the Style group (Sparkline Chart Design tab).

Plan Ahead

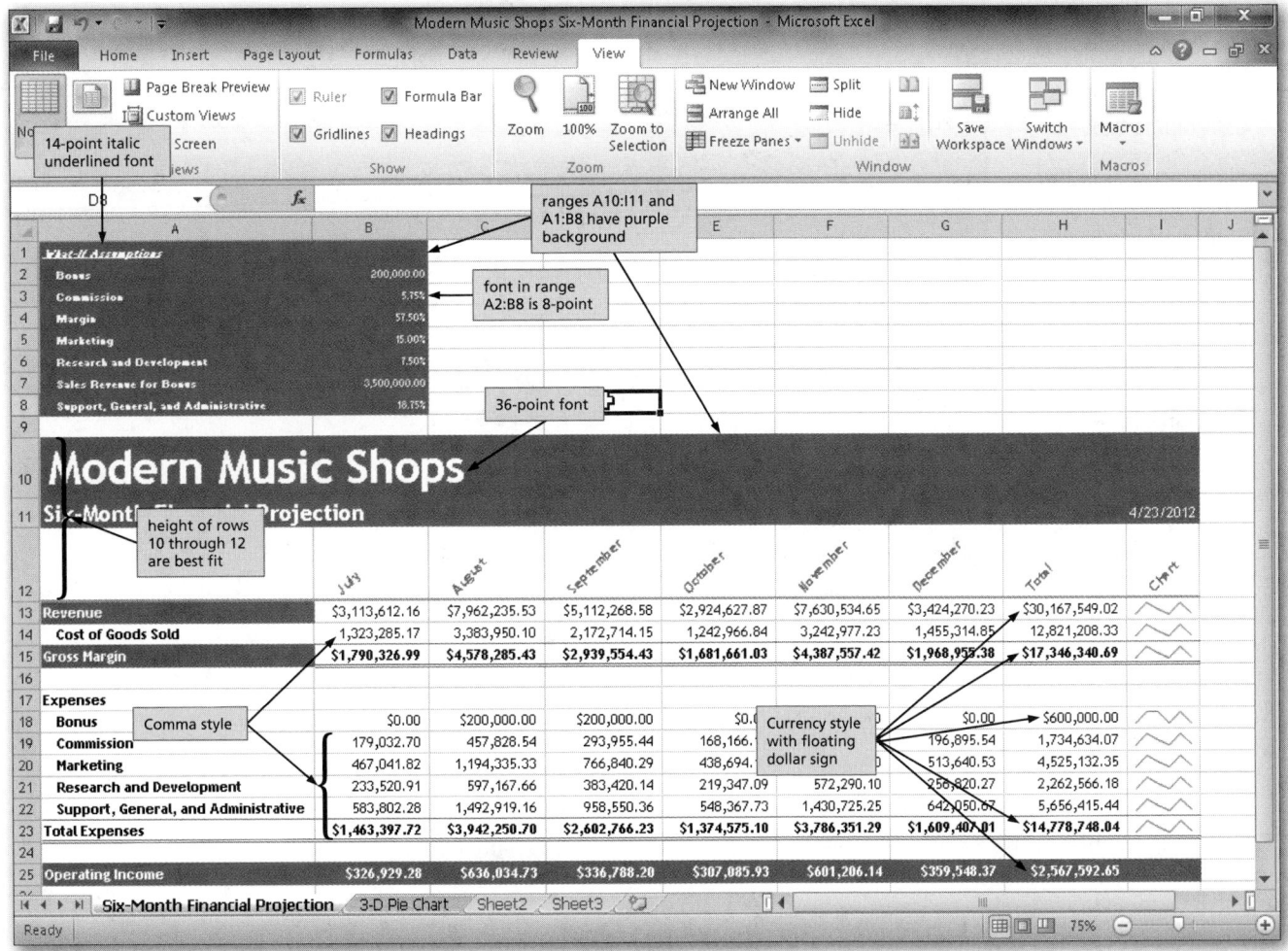

Figure 3–40

To Assign Formats to Nonadjacent Ranges

The numbers in the range B13:H25 are to be formatted as follows:

1. Assign the Currency style with a floating dollar sign to rows 13, 15, 18, 23, and 25.
2. Assign a Comma style to rows 14 and 19 through 22.

The following steps assign formats to the numbers in rows 13 through 25.

1

- Select the range B13:H13 as the first range to format.

- While holding down the CTRL key, select the nonadjacent ranges B15:H15, B18:H18, B23:H23, and B25:H25, and then release the CTRL key to select nonadjacent ranges.

- Click the Format Cells: Number Dialog Box Launcher (Home tab | Number group) to display the Format Cells dialog box.

- Click Currency in the Category list (Format Cells dialog box), if necessary select 2 in the Decimal places box, if necessary click $ in the Symbol list to ensure a dollar sign shows in the cells to be formatted, and

Figure 3–41

click the black font color ($1,234.10) in the Negative numbers list to prepare the desired Currency style for the selected ranges (Figure 3–41).

Q&A

Why was the particular style chosen for the negative numbers?

In accounting, negative numbers often are shown with parentheses surrounding the value rather than with a negative sign preceding the value. Thus, the format (1,234.10) in the Negative numbers list was clicked. The data being used in this chapter contains no negative numbers. You must select a format for negative numbers, however, and you must be consistent if you are choosing different formats in a column; otherwise, the decimal points may not line up.

Q&A

Why is the Format Cells dialog box used to create the format for the ranges in this step?

The requirements for this worksheet call for a floating dollar sign. To assign a Currency style with a floating dollar sign, use the Format Cells dialog box rather than the Accounting Style button (Home tab | Number group), which assigns a fixed dollar sign.

2

- Click the OK button (Format Cells dialog box) to close the Format Cells dialog box and apply the desired format to the selected ranges.

- Select the range B14:H14 as the next range to format.

- While holding down the CTRL key, select the range B19:H22, and then release the CTRL key to select nonadjacent ranges.

- Click the Format Cells: Number Dialog Box Launcher (Home tab | Number group) to display the Format Cells dialog box.

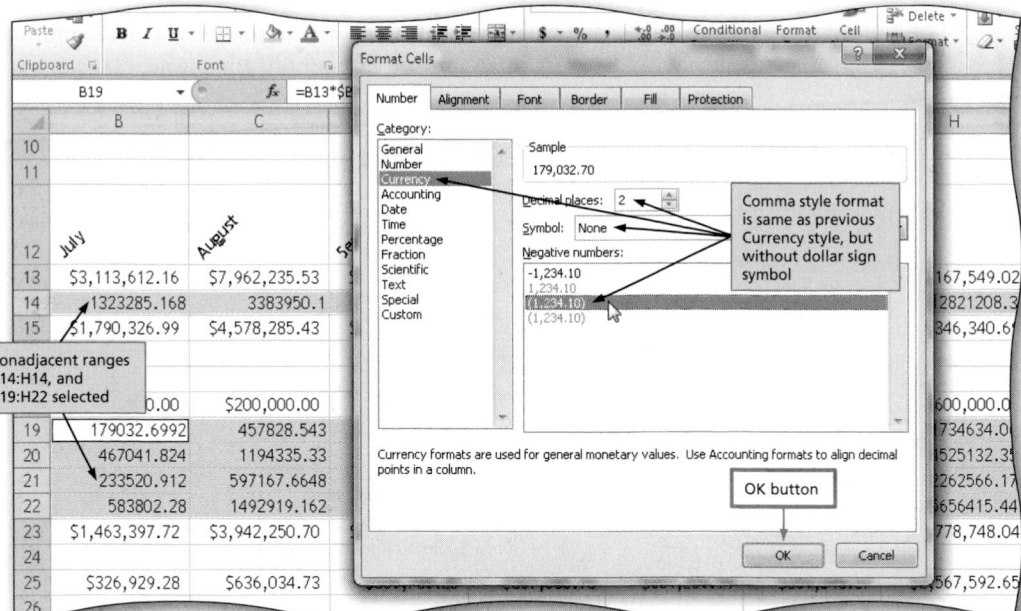

Figure 3–42

- Click Currency in the Category list (Format Cells dialog box), if necessary select 2 in the Decimal places box, click None in the Symbol list so a dollar sign does not show in the cells to be formatted, and click the black font color (1,234.10) in the Negative numbers list (Figure 3–42).

3

- Click the OK button (Format Cells dialog box) to close the Format Cells dialog box and apply the desired format to the selected ranges.

- Select cell B27 to select an empty cell and display the formatted numbers as shown in Figure 3–43.

	B	C					
12			Sep			De	
13	$3,113,612.16	$7,962,235.53	$5,112,268.58	$2,924,627.87	$7,630,534.65	$3,424,270.23	$30,167,549.02
14	1,323,285.17	3,383,950.10	2,172,714.15	1,242,966.84	3,242,977.23	1,455,314.85	12,821,208.33
15	$1,790,326.99	$4,578,285.43	$2,939,554.43	$1,681,661.03	$4,387,557.42	$1,968,955.38	$17,346,340.69
16							
18	$0.00	$200,000.00	$200,000.00	$0.00	$200,000.00	$0.00	$600,000.00
19	179,032.70	457,828.54	293,955.44	168,166.10	438,755.74	196,895.54	1,734,634.0
20	467,041.82	1,194,335.33	766,840.29	438,694.18	1,144,580.20	513,640.53	4,525,132.3
21	233,520.91	597,167.66	383,420.14	219,347.09	572,290.10	256,820.27	2,262,566.1
22	583,802.28	1,492,919.16	958,550.36	548,867.73	1,430,725.25	642,050.67	5,656,415.4
23	$1,463,397.72	$3,942,250.70	$2,602,766.23	$1,374,575.10	$3,786,351.29	$1,609,407.01	$14,778,748.04
24							
25	$326,929.28	$636,034.73	$336,788.20	$307,085.93	$601,206.14	$359,548.37	$2,567,592.65
26							
27							
28							

Figure 3–43

Q&A

Why is the Format Cells dialog box used to create the style for the ranges in Steps 2 and 3?

The Format Cells dialog box is used to assign the Comma style, because the Comma Style button (Home tab | Number group) assigns a format that displays a dash (–) when a cell has a value of 0. The specifications for this worksheet call for displaying a value of 0 as 0.00 (see cell B18 in Figure 3–40) rather than as a dash. To create a Comma style using the Format Cells dialog box, you can assign a Currency style with no dollar sign.

Other Ways

1. Right-click range, click Format Cells on shortcut menu, click Number tab (Format Cells dialog box), click category in Category list, select format, click OK button (Format Cells dialog box)

2. Press CTRL+1, click Number tab (Format Cells dialog box), click category in Category list, select format, click OK button (Format Cells dialog box)

To Format the Worksheet Titles

The following steps emphasize the worksheet titles in cells A10 and A11 by changing the font, size, and color. The steps also format all of the row headers in column A with a bold font style.

- Press CTRL+HOME to select cell A1 and then click the column A heading to select the column.

- Click the Bold button (Home tab | Font group) to bold all of the data in the selected column.

- Select cell A10, click the Font Size box arrow (Home tab | Font group), and then click 36 in the Font Size list to increase the font size of the selected cell.

- Select cell A11, click the Font Size box arrow, and then click 18 in the Font Size list to increase the font size of the selected cell (Figure 3–44).

Figure 3–44

- Select the range A10:I11 and then click the Fill Color button arrow (Home tab | Font group) to display the Fill Color gallery.

- Click Purple, Accent 2, Darker 25% (column 6, row 5) in the Fill Color gallery to add a background color to the selected range.

- Click the Font Color button arrow (Home tab | Font group) and then select White, Background 1 (column 1, row 1) in the Font Color gallery to change the font color of the selected range (Figure 3–45).

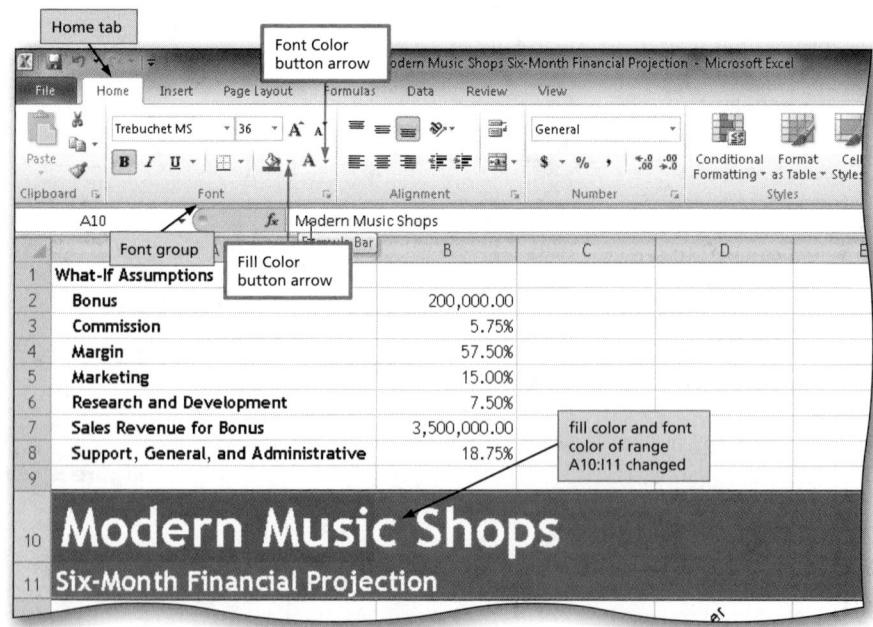

Figure 3–45

Other Ways

1. Right-click range, click Format Cells on shortcut menu, click Fill tab (Format Cells dialog box) to color background (or click Font tab to color font), click OK button

2. Press CTRL+1, click Fill tab (Format Cells dialog box) to color background (or click Font tab to color font), click OK button

To Assign Cell Styles to Nonadjacent Rows and Colors to a Cell

The next step to improving the appearance of the worksheet is to format the heading in row 12 and the totals in rows 15, 23, and 25. The following steps format the heading in row 13 with the Heading 3 cell style and the totals in rows 15, 23, and 25 with the Total cell style. Cell A13 also is formatted with a background color and font color.

1 Select the range A12:I12 and apply the Heading 3 cell style.

2 Select the range A15:I15 and while holding down the CTRL key, select the ranges A23:I23 and A25:I25.

3 Apply the Total cell style to the selected nonadjacent ranges.

4 Select cell A13, click the Fill Color button arrow (Home tab | Font group), and then click the Purple, Accent 2, Darker 25% color (column 6, row 5) in the Fill Color gallery.

5 Click the Font Color button arrow (Home tab | Font group) and then click the White, Background 1 color (column 1, row 1) in the Font Color gallery (Figure 3–46).

Figure 3–46

BTW

Toggle Commands
Many of the commands on the Ribbon, on the galleries, and the shortcut keys function as toggles. For example, if you click the Freeze Panes command on the Freeze Panes gallery, the command changes to Unfreeze Panes the next time you view the gallery. These types of commands work like on-off switches or toggles.

BTW

Work Days
Assume that you have two dates, one in cell A1 and the other in cell A2. Assume further that the date in cell A1 is your starting date and the date in cell A2 is the ending date. To calculate the work days between the two dates (excluding weekends), use the following formula: =NETWORKDAYS(A1, A2). For this function to work, make sure the Analysis ToolPak add-in is installed. You can install it on the Add-Ins page of the Excel Options dialog box.

BTW

The Fill and Font Color Buttons
You may have noticed that the color bar at the bottom of the Fill Color and Font Color buttons (Home tab | Font group) (Figure 3–45) changes to the most recently selected color. To apply this same color to a cell background or text, select a cell and then click the Fill Color button to use the color as a background or click the Font Color button to use the color as a font color.

To Copy a Cell's Format Using the Format Painter Button

Using the Format Painter, you can format a cell quickly by copying a cell's format to another cell or a range of cells. The following steps format cells A15 and the range A25:I25 using the Format Painter.

1

- If necessary, click cell A13 to select a source cell for the format to paint.

- Double-click the Format Painter button (Home tab | Clipboard group) and then move the mouse pointer onto the worksheet to cause the mouse pointer to change to a block plus sign with a paintbrush (Figure 3–47).

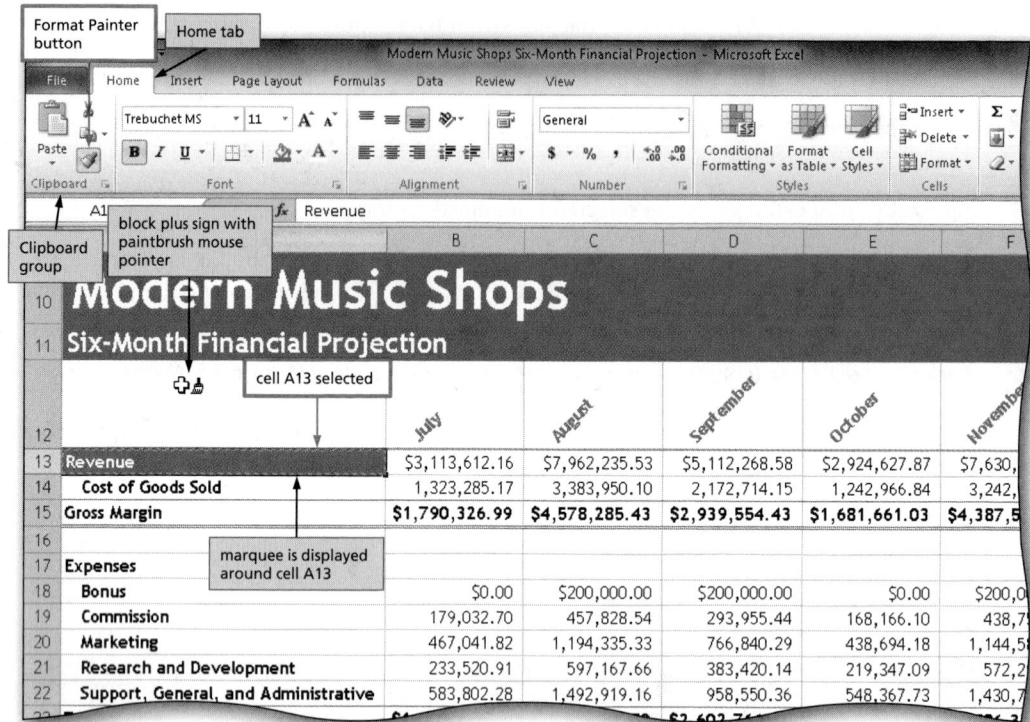

Figure 3–47

2

- Click cell A15 to assign the format of the source cell, A13 in this case, to the destination cell, A15 in this case (Figure 3–48).

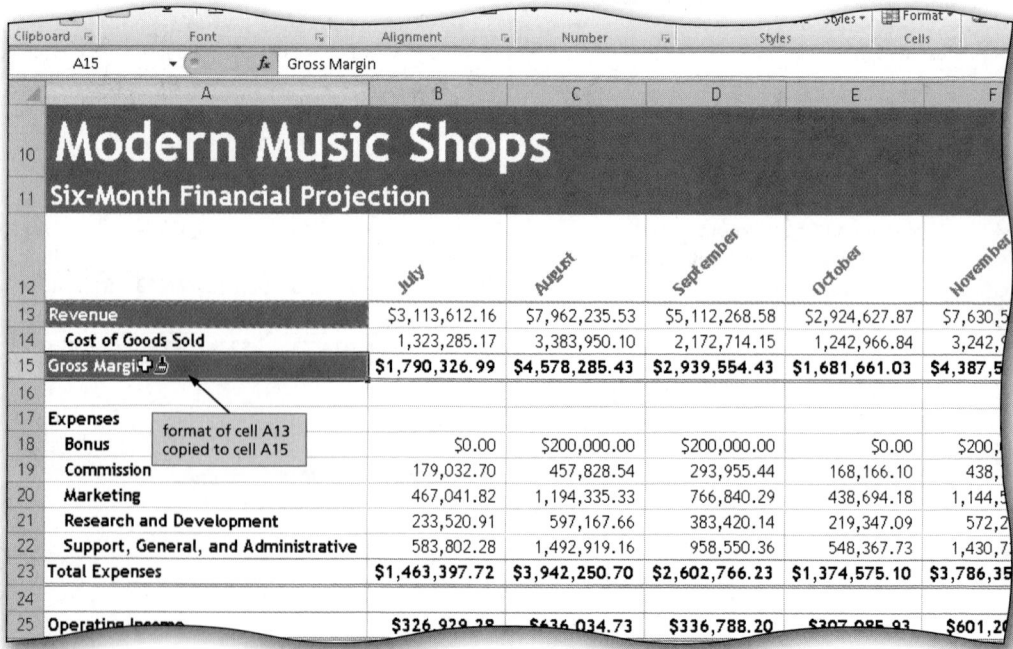

Figure 3–48

3

- With the mouse pointer still a block plus sign with a paintbrush, drag through the range A25:I25 to assign the format of the source cell, A13 in this case, to the destination range, A25:I25 in this case.

- Press the ESC key to stop the format painter.

- Apply the Currency style to the range B25:H25 to cause the cells in the range to appear with a floating dollar sign and two decimal places and then scroll the worksheet so that column A is displayed (Figure 3–49).

Figure 3–49

Q&A Why does the Currency style need to be reapplied to the range B25:H25?

Sometimes, the use of the format painter results in unintended outcomes. In this case, the changing of the background fill color and font color for the range B25:H25 resulted in the loss of the Currency style because the format being copied did not included the Currency style. Reapplying the Currency style to the range results in the proper number style, fill color, and font color.

Other Ways

1. Click Copy button (Home tab | Clipboard group), select cell, click Paste button arrow (Home tab | Clipboard group), click Formatting icon on Paste gallery

2. Right-click cell, click Copy, right-click cell, click Formatting icon on shortcut menu

To Format the What-If Assumptions Table and Save the Workbook

The last step to improving the appearance of the worksheet is to format the What-If Assumptions table in the range A1:B8. The specifications in Figure 3–40 on page EX 173 require an 8-point italic underlined font for the title in cell A1 and 8-point font in the range A2:B8. The following steps format the What-If Assumptions table.

1 Press CTRL+HOME to select cell A1.

2 Click the Font Size button arrow (Home tab | Font group) and then click 8 in the Font Size list to decrease the font size of the selected cell.

3 Click the Italic button (Home tab | Font Group) and then click the Underline button (Home tab | Font group) to italicize and underline the text in the selected cell.

4 Select the range A2:B8, click the Font Size button arrow (Home tab | Font group) and then click 8 in the Font Size list to apply a smaller font size to the selected range.

5 Select the range A1:B8 and then click the Fill Color button (Home tab | Font group) to apply the most recently used background color to the selected range.

BTW

Painting a Format to Nonadjacent Ranges
Double-click the Format Painter button (Home tab | Clipboard group) and then drag through the nonadjacent ranges to paint the formats to the ranges. Click the Format Painter button (Home tab | Clipboard group) to deactivate it.

BTW

Selecting Nonadjacent Ranges
One of the more difficult tasks to learn is selecting nonadjacent ranges. To complete this task, do not hold down the CTRL key when you select the first range because Excel will consider the current active cell to be the first selection, and you may not want the current active cell in the selection. Once the first range is selected, hold down the CTRL key and drag through the nonadjacent ranges. If a desired range is not visible in the window, use the scroll arrows to view the range. You need not hold down the CTRL key while you scroll.

6 Click the Font Color button (Home tab | Font group) to apply the most recently used font color to the selected range.

7 Click cell D8 to deselect the range A1:B8 and display the What-If Assumptions table, as shown in Figure 3–50.

8 Save the workbook.

Q&A

What happens when I click the Italic and Underline buttons?

Recall that when you assign the italic font style to a cell, Excel slants the characters slightly to the right, as shown in cell A1 in Figure 3–50. The **underline** format underlines only the characters in the cell, rather than the entire cell, as is the case when you assign a cell a bottom border.

Figure 3–50

Break Point: If you wish to stop working through the chapter at this point, you can quit Excel now and then resume the project at a later point in time by starting Excel, opening the file called Modern Music Shops Six-Month Financial Projection, and continuing to follow the steps from this location forward.

BTW

Charts
When you change a value on which a chart is dependent, Excel immediately redraws the chart based on the new value. With bar charts, you can drag the bar in the chart in one direction or another to change the corresponding value in the worksheet.

Adding a 3-D Pie Chart to the Workbook

The next step in the chapter is to draw the 3-D Pie chart on a separate sheet in the workbook, as shown in Figure 3–51. Use a **pie chart** to show the relationship or proportion of parts to a whole. Each slice (or wedge) of the pie shows what percent that slice contributes to the total (100%).

The 3-D Pie chart in Figure 3–51 shows the contribution of each month's projected operating income to the six-month projected operating income. The 3-D Pie chart makes it easy to evaluate the contribution of one month in comparison to the other months.

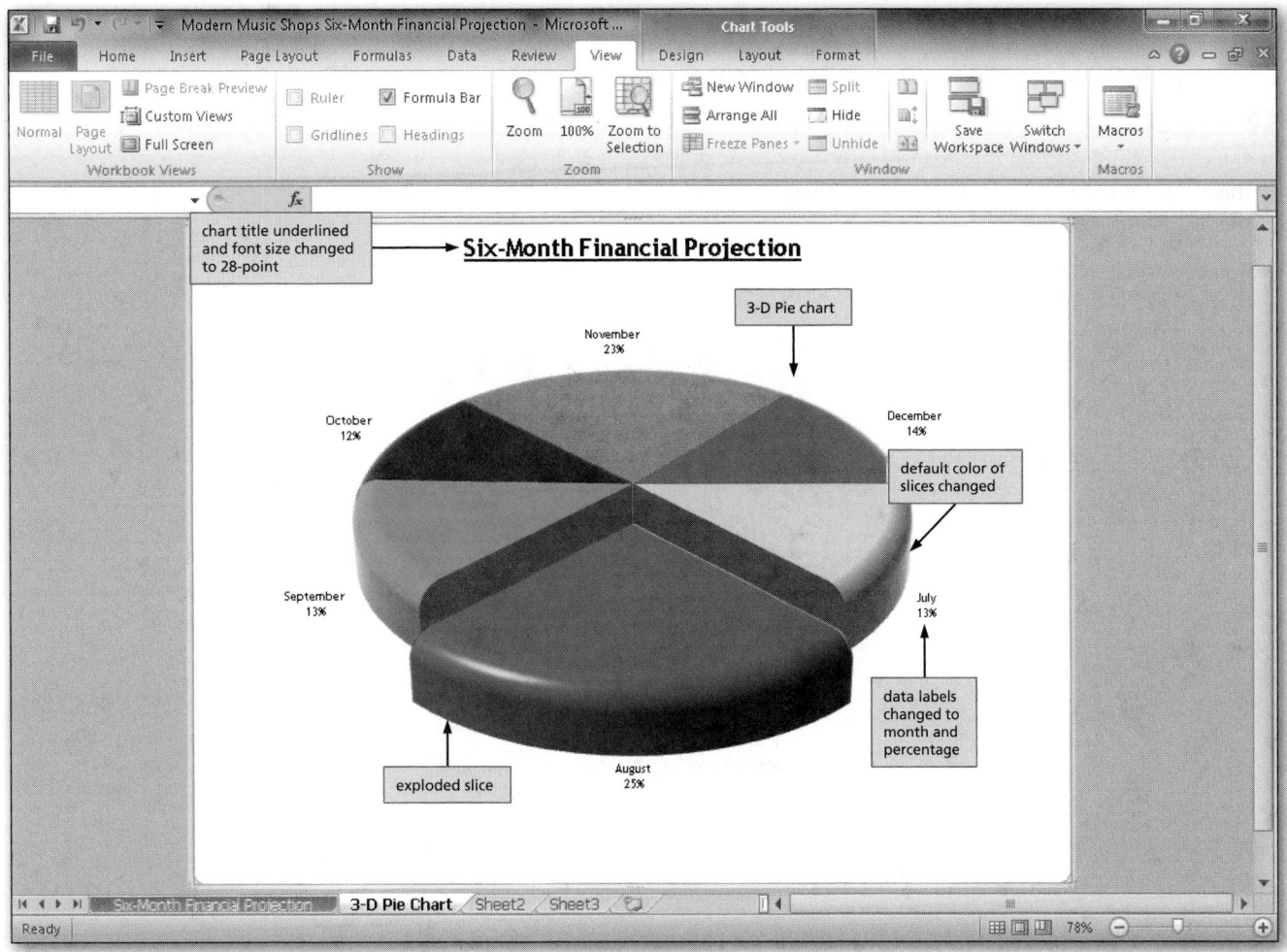

Figure 3–51

Unlike the 3-D Column chart created in Chapter 1, the 3-D Pie chart shown in Figure 3–51 is not embedded in the worksheet. Instead, the Pie chart resides on a separate sheet, called a **chart sheet**, which contains only the chart.

In this worksheet, the ranges to chart are the nonadjacent ranges B12:G12 (month names) and B25:G25 (monthly operating incomes). The month names in the range B12:G12 will identify the slices of the Pie chart; these entries are called **category names**. The range B25:G25 contains the data that determines the size of the slices in the pie; these entries are called the **data series**. Because six months are being charted, the 3-D Pie chart contains six slices.

The sketch of the 3-D Pie chart in Figure 3–3b on page EX 142 also calls for emphasizing the month of August by offsetting its slice from the main portion. A Pie chart with one or more slices offset is called an **exploded Pie chart**.

As shown in Figure 3–51, the default 3-D Pie chart also has been enhanced by rotating it, changing the colors of the slices, adding a bevel, and modifying the chart title and labels that identify the slices.

BTW

Chart Items
When you rest the mouse pointer over a chart item, such as a legend, bar, or axis, Excel displays a chart tip containing the name of the item.

BTW

Chart Templates
Once you create and format a chart to your liking, you may want to reuse the chart type and formatting for additional charts. Excel allows you to save your chart as a chart template by clicking the Save as Template button (Chart Tools Design tab | Type group). A chart template is saved in the Templates\Charts folder with a .crtx file extension. When you want to reuse the template, click the Templates folder in the Insert Chart dialog box and select your template.

To Draw a 3-D Pie Chart on a Separate Chart Sheet

The following steps draw the 3-D Pie chart on a separate chart sheet.

- Select the range B12:G12 to identify the range of the category name of the 3-D Pie Chart.

- If necessary, scroll the worksheet so that row 25 is displayed, and while holding down the CTRL key, select the range B25:G25.

- Display the Insert tab.

- Click the Pie button (Insert tab | Charts group) to display the Pie gallery (Figure 3–52).

Figure 3–52

- Click Pie in 3-D chart in the Pie gallery to select the desired chart type.

- When Excel draws the chart, click the Move Chart button (Chart Tools Design tab | Location group) to display the Move Chart dialog box (Figure 3–53).

Figure 3–53

- Click New sheet (Move Chart dialog box) and then type `3-D Pie Chart` in the 'New sheet name' text box to enter a sheet tab name for the chart sheet.

- Click the OK button (Move Chart dialog box) to move the chart to a new chart sheet with a new sheet name, 3-D Pie Chart in this case (Figure 3–54).

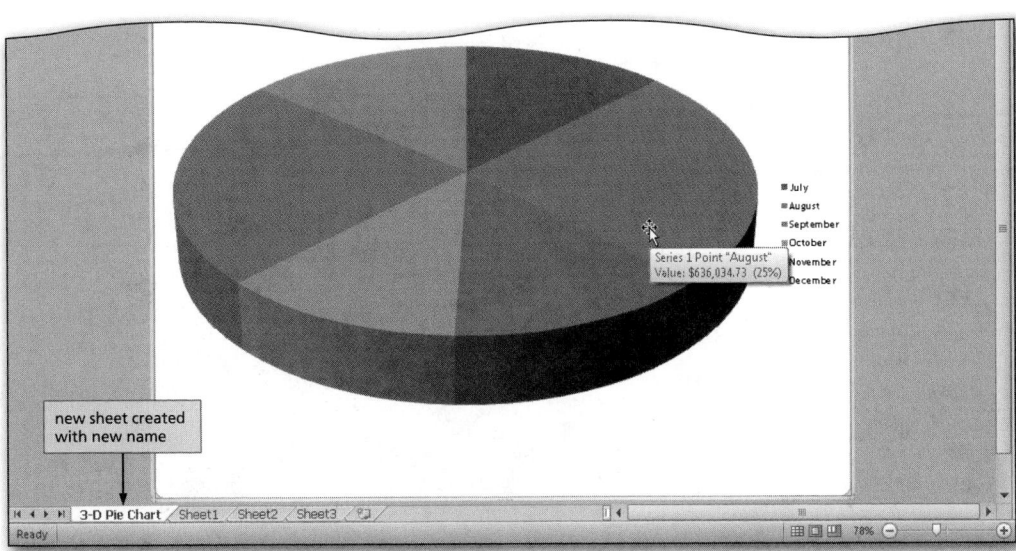

Figure 3–54

To Insert a Chart Title and Data Labels

The next step is to insert a chart title and labels that identify the slices. Before you can format a chart item, such as the chart title or data labels, you must select it. The following steps insert a chart title, remove the legend, and add data labels.

- Click anywhere in the chart area outside the chart to select the chart.

- Display the Chart Tools Layout tab and then click the Chart Title button (Chart Tools Layout tab | Labels group) to display the Chart Title gallery.

- Click the Centered Overlay Title command in the Chart Title gallery to add a chart title centered on top of the chart.

- Select the text in the chart title and then type `Six-Month Financial Projection` to add a new chart title (Figure 3–55).

Figure 3–55

- Select the text in the new title and then display the Home tab.

- Click the Underline button (Home tab | Font group) to assign an underline font style to the chart title (Figure 3–56).

Figure 3–56

- Display the Chart Tools Layout tab and then click the Legend button (Chart Tools Layout tab | Labels group) to display the Legend gallery (Figure 3–57).

Figure 3–57

- Click the None Legend option in the Legend gallery to turn off the legend on the chart.

- Click the Data Labels button (Layout tab | Labels group) and then click Outside End in the Data Labels gallery to display data labels outside the chart at the end of each slice (Figure 3–58).

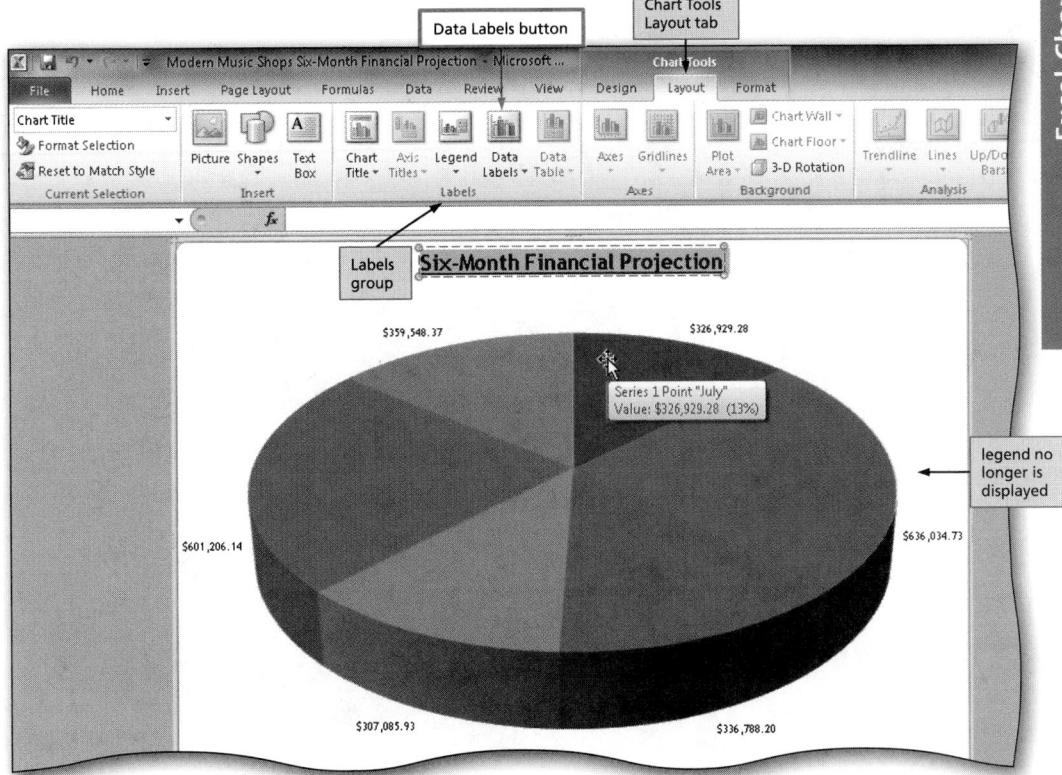

Figure 3–58

5

- If necessary, right-click any data label to select all of the data labels on the chart and to display a shortcut menu.

- Click the Format Data Labels command on the shortcut menu to display the Format Data Labels dialog box.

- If necessary, click the Series Name, Value, and Show Leader Lines check boxes to deselect them (Format Data Labels dialog box) and then click the Category Name and Percentage check boxes to cause the data labels to be displayed with category names and percent values, rather than currency values (Figure 3–59).

Figure 3–59

6
• Click the Close button
to close the Format
Data Labels dialog box
and display the chart
(Figure 3–60).

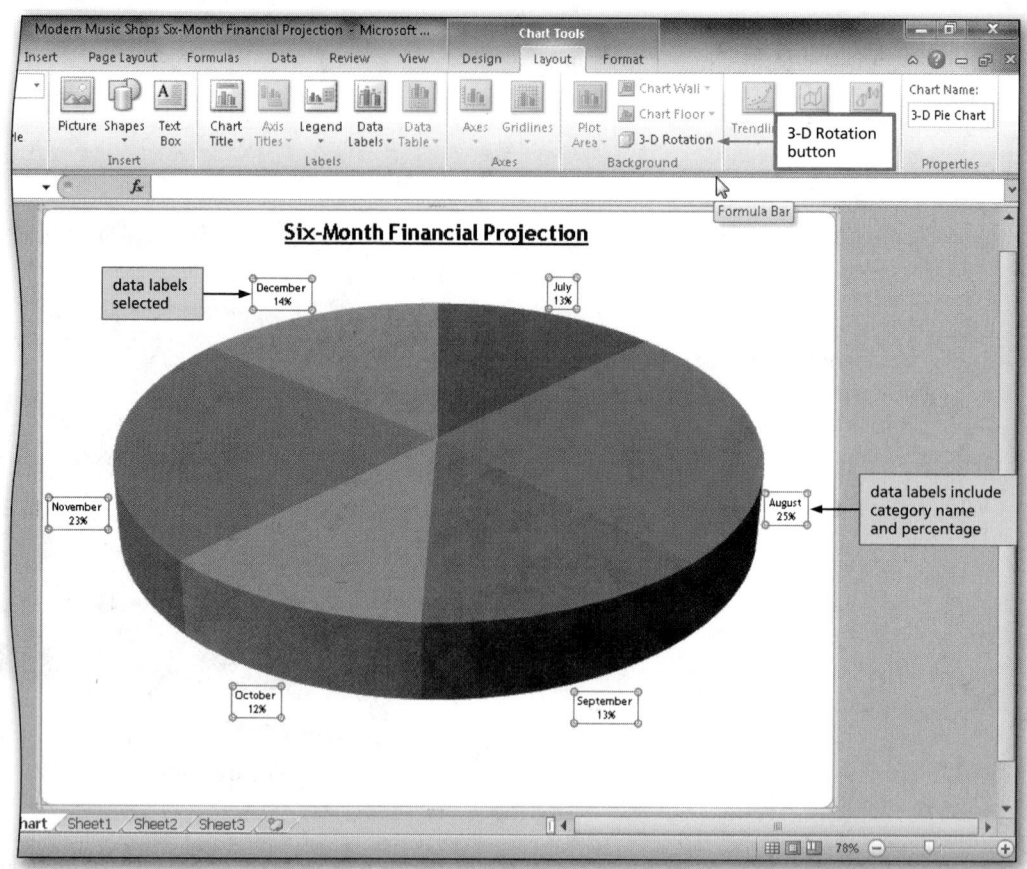

Figure 3–60

To Rotate the 3-D Pie Chart

With a three-dimensional chart, you can change the view to better show the section of the chart you are trying
to emphasize. Excel allows you to control the rotation angle, elevation, perspective, height, and angle of the axes.

When Excel initially draws a Pie chart, it always positions the chart so that one of the dividing lines between
two slices is a straight line pointing to 12 o'clock (or 0°). As shown in Figure 3–60, the line that divides the
December and July slices currently is set to 0°. This line defines the rotation angle of the 3-D Pie chart.

To obtain a better view of the offset August slice, the largest slice, the 3-D Pie chart can be rotated 90° to
the left. The following steps rotate the 3-D Pie chart.

Excel Chapter 3

1

• Click the 3-D Rotation button (Chart Tools Layout tab | Background group) to display the Format Chart Area dialog box.

• Click the Increase X Rotation button in the Rotation area of the Format Chart Area dialog box until the X rotation is at 90° to rotate the chart (Figure 3–61).

Q&A

What happens as I click the Increase X Rotation button?

Excel rotates the chart 10° in a clockwise direction each time you click the Increase X Rotation button. The Y box in the Rotation area allows you to control the tilt, or elevation, of the chart. You can tilt the chart towards or away from your view in order to enhance the view of the chart.

Figure 3–61

2

• Click the Close button (Format Chart Area dialog box) to close the dialog box and display the rotated chart (Figure 3–62).

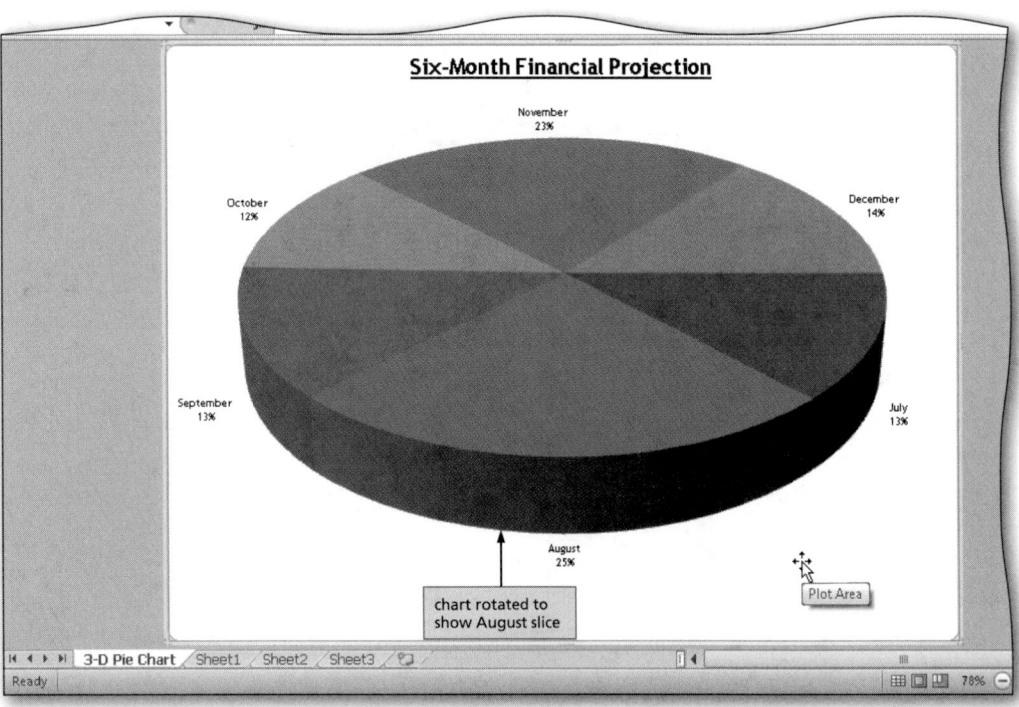

Figure 3–62

To Apply a 3-D Format to the Pie Chart

Excel allows you to apply dramatic 3-D visual effects to charts. The chart shown in Figure 3–62 could be enhanced with a bevel along the top edge. A bevel is a curve that is applied to soften the appearance of a straight edge. Excel also allows you to change the appearance of the material from which the surface of the chart appears to be constructed. The following steps apply a bevel to the chart and change the surface of the chart to a softer-looking material.

• Right-click the chart to display a shortcut menu and Mini toolbar (Figure 3–63).

Figure 3–63

2

• Click the Format Data Series command on the shortcut menu to display the Format Data Series dialog box and then click the 3-D Format category (Format Data Series dialog box) on the left side of the dialog box to display the 3-D Format panel.

• Click the Top button (Format Data Series dialog box) in the Bevel area to display the Bevel gallery (Figure 3–64).

Figure 3–64

3

- Click the Circle bevel button (column 1, row 1) in the Bevel gallery (Format Data Series dialog box) to add a bevel to the chart.

- Type **50 pt** in the uppermost Width box in the Bevel area (Format Data Series dialog box) and then type **50 pt** in the uppermost Height box in the Bevel area of the dialog box to increase the width and height of the bevel on the chart (Figure 3–65).

Figure 3–65

4

- Click the Material button in the Surface area (Format Data Series dialog box) to display the Material gallery (Figure 3–66).

Figure 3–66

• Click the Soft Edge
button (column 2,
row 2) in the Material
gallery and then click
the Close button
(Format Data Series
dialog box) to apply
the desired material
and close the Format
Data Series dialog box
(Figure 3–67).

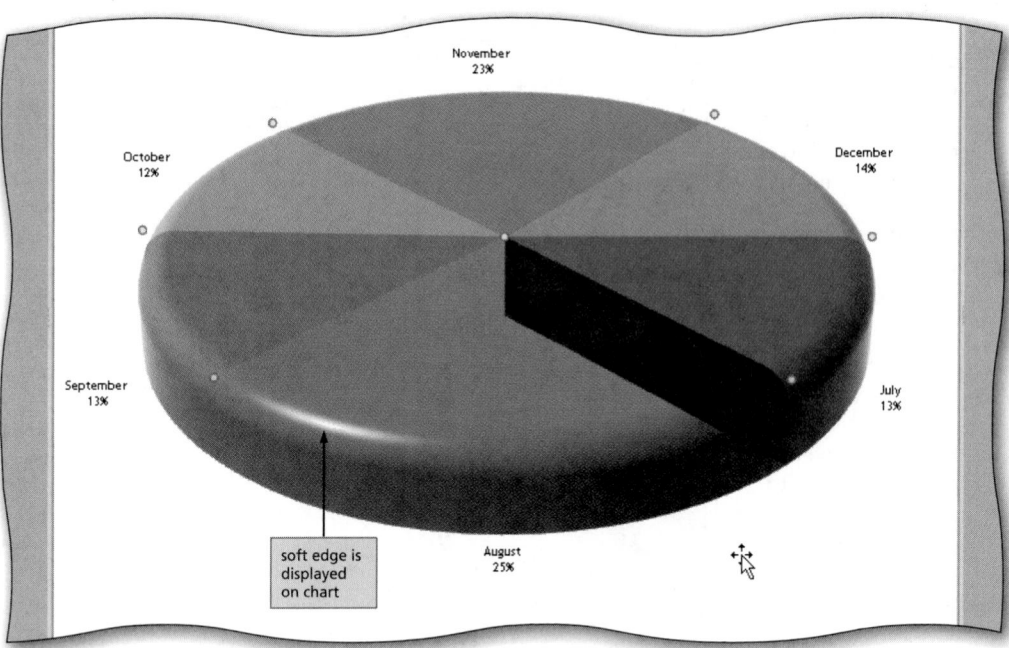

Figure 3–67

To Explode the 3-D Pie Chart and Change the Color of a Slice

The next step is to emphasize the slice representing August by offsetting, or exploding, it from the rest of the slices so that it stands out. The following steps explode the largest slice of the 3-D Pie chart and then change its color.

• Click the slice labeled
August twice (do
not double-click) to
select only one slice
of the 3-D Pie chart,
the August slice in
this case.

• Right-click the slice
labeled August to
display a shortcut
menu and Mini
toolbar (Figure 3–68).

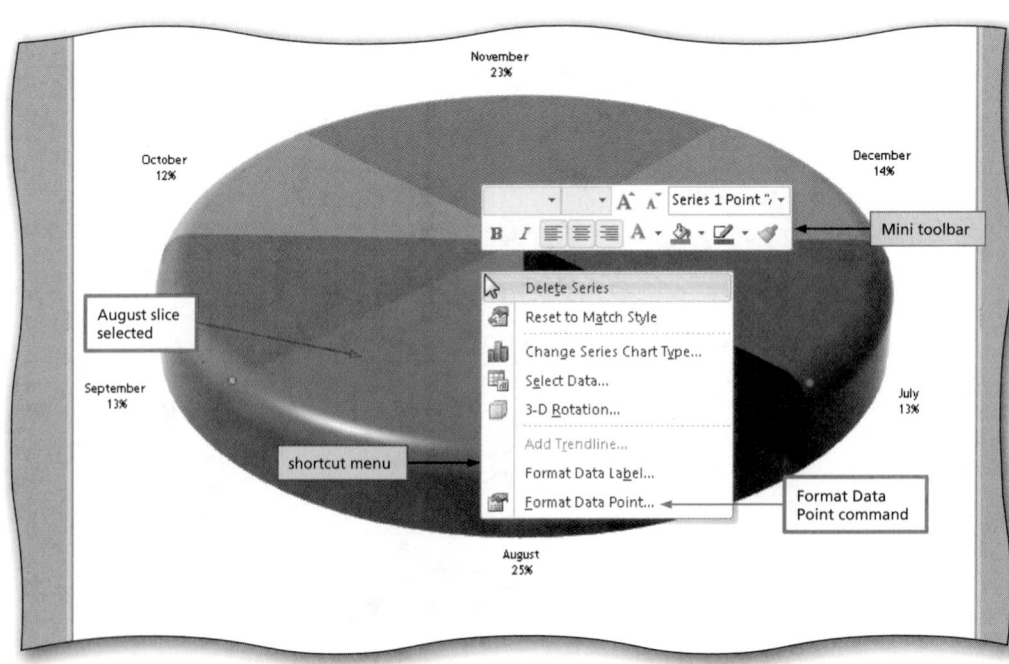

Figure 3–68

2

- Click Format Data Point on the shortcut menu to display the Format Data Point dialog box.

- Drag the Point Explosion slider (Format Data Point dialog box) to the right until the Point Explosion box reads 28% to set how far the slice in the 3-D Pie chart should be offset from the rest of the chart (Figure 3–69).

Q&A

Should I offset more slices?

You can offset as many slices as you want, but remember that the reason for offsetting a slice is to emphasize it. Offsetting multiple slices tends to reduce the impact on the reader and reduces the overall size of the Pie chart.

Figure 3–69

3

- Click the Fill category (Format Data Point dialog box) on the left side of the dialog box to display the Fill panel.

- Click Solid fill to display the Fill Color area and then click the Color button to display the Color gallery.

- Click the Blue color in the Standard Colors area of the color gallery and then click the Close button (Format Data Point dialog box) to change the color of the selected slice and close the dialog box (Figure 3–70).

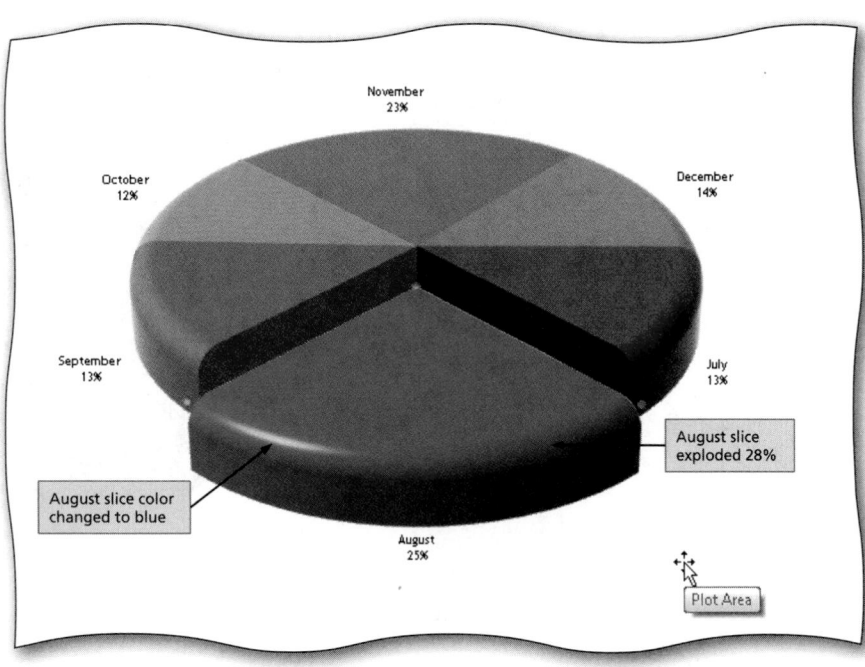

Figure 3–70

Other Ways

1. Right-click slice, click Shape Fill Color button arrow on Mini toolbar, select color

To Change the Colors of the Remaining Slices

BTW

Exploding a 3-D Pie Chart
If you click a 3-D Pie chart so that all of the slices are selected, you can drag one of the slices to explode all of the slices.

The colors of the remaining slices also can be changed to enhance the appeal of the chart. The following steps change the color of the remaining five chart slices.

1 Right-click the slice labeled July to select only the July slice, and display a shortcut menu and Mini toolbar.

2 Click the Shape Fill button arrow on the Mini toolbar to display the Color gallery.

3 Click the Yellow color in the Standard Colors area in the Color gallery to change the color of the slice.

4 Repeat Steps 1 through 3 for the remaining four slices. Assign the following colors in the Standard Colors area in the color gallery to each slice: September – Green; October – Dark Blue; November – Red; December – Purple.

5 Click anywhere outside the chart to deselect the December slice (Figure 3–71). The completed chart appears as shown in Figure 3–71.

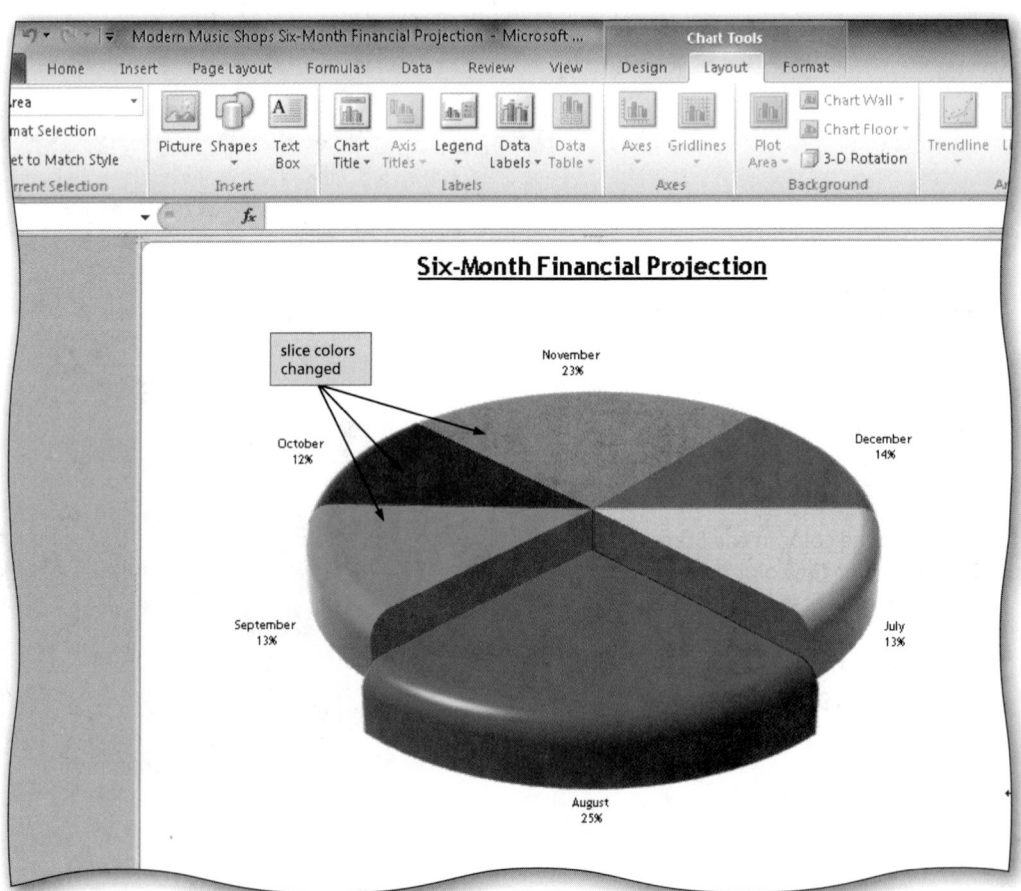

Figure 3–71

Renaming and Reordering the Sheets and Coloring their Tabs

The final step in creating the workbook is to reorder the sheets and modify the tabs at the bottom of the screen.

To Rename the Sheets and Color Their Tabs

The following steps rename the sheets and color the sheet tabs.

1 Change the sheet tab color of the 3-D Pie Chart sheet to Orange, Accent 6 (column 10, row 1).

2 Double-click the tab labeled Sheet1 at the bottom of the screen.

3 Type `Six-Month Financial Projection` as the new sheet name and then press the ENTER key.

4 Change the sheet tab color of the Six-Month Financial Projection sheet to Pink, Accent 1 (column 5, row 1) and then select cell D8 (Figure 3–72).

Figure 3–72

To Reorder the Sheet Tabs

Change the order sheets in a workbook so that they appear with the most important worksheets first. The following steps reorder the sheets so that the worksheet precedes the chart sheet in the workbook.

1

- Drag the Six-Month Financial Projection tab to the left in front of the 3-D Pie Chart tab to rearrange the sequence of the sheets (Figure 3–73).

Figure 3–73

Other Ways

1. To move sheet, right-click sheet tab, click Move or Copy on shortcut menu

To Check Spelling in Multiple Sheets

By default, the spell checker checks the spelling only in the selected sheets. It will check all the cells in the selected sheets, unless you select a range of two or more cells. Before checking the spelling, the following steps select both sheets in the workbook so that both worksheets in the workbook are checked for spelling errors.

BTW

Checking Spelling
Unless you first select a range of cells or an object before starting the spell checker, Excel checks the entire selected worksheet, including all cell values, cell comments, embedded charts, text boxes, buttons, and headers and footers.

1 With the Six-Month Financial Projection sheet active, press CTRL+HOME to select cell A1. Hold down the CTRL key and then click the 3-D Pie Chart tab to select multiple sheets.

2 Display the Review tab and then click the Spelling button (Review tab | Proofing group) to check spelling in the selected sheets.

3 Correct any errors and then click the OK button (Spelling dialog box or Microsoft Excel dialog box) when the spell check is complete.

4 Save the workbook.

To Preview and Print the Workbook

After checking the spelling, the next step is to preview and print the sheets. As with spelling, Excel previews and prints only the selected sheets. In addition, because the worksheet is too wide to print in portrait orientation, the orientation must be changed to landscape. The following steps adjust the orientation and scale, preview the workbook, and then print the workbook.

1 Ready the printer. If both sheets are not selected, hold down the CTRL key and then click the tab of the inactive sheet.

2 Click File on the Ribbon to open the Backstage view.

3 Click the Print tab in the Backstage view to display the Print gallery.

4 If necessary, click the Portrait Orientation button in the Settings area and then select Landscape Orientation to select the desired orientation.

5 If necessary, click the No Scaling button in the Settings area and then select 'Fit Sheet on One Page' to cause the workbook to print on one page.

6 If necessary, click the Printer Status button to display a list of available Printer options and then click the desired printer to change the currently selected printer.

7 Click the Print button in the Print gallery to print the worksheet in landscape orientation on the currently selected printer.

8 When the printer stops, retrieve the printed worksheet (Figure 3–74a and Figure 3–74b on the following page).

9 Right-click the Six-Month Financial Projection tab. Click Ungroup Sheets on the shortcut menu to deselect the 3-D Pie Chart tab.

10 Save the workbook.

Figure 3–74 (a) Worksheet

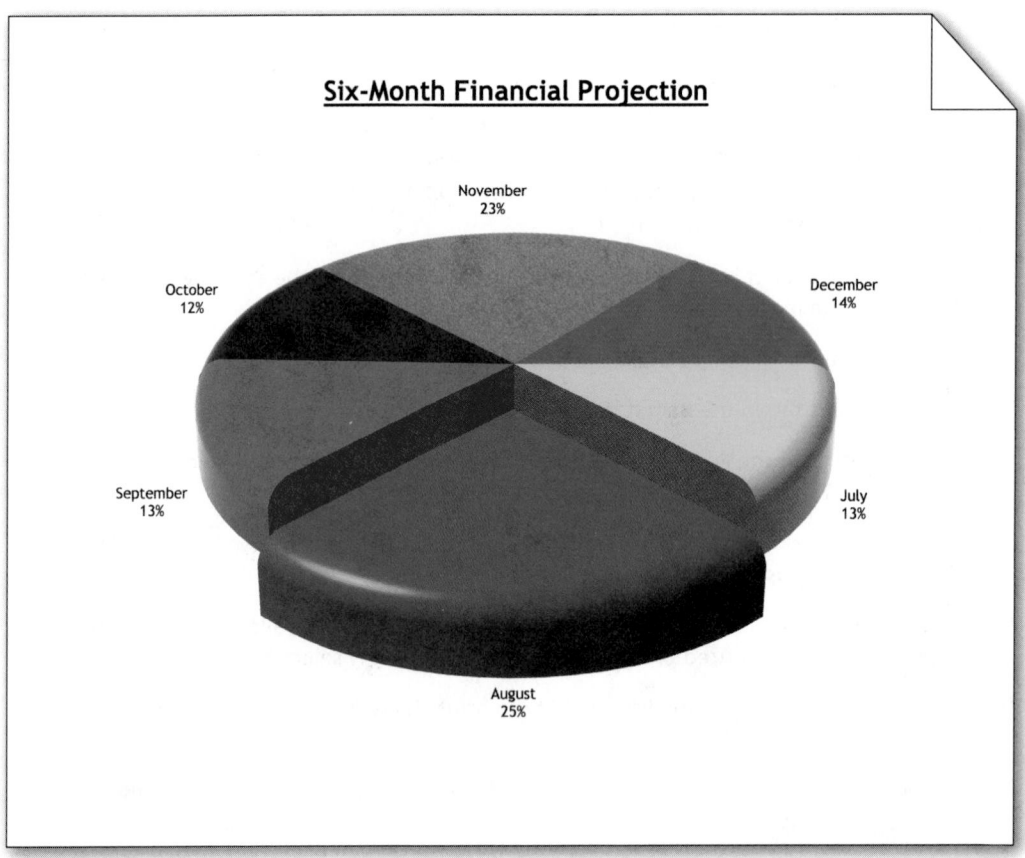

Figure 3–74 (b) 3-D Pie Chart

Changing the View of the Worksheet

With Excel, you easily can change the view of the worksheet. For example, you can magnify or shrink the worksheet on the screen. You also can view different parts of the worksheet through windowpanes.

To Shrink and Magnify the View of a Worksheet or Chart

You can magnify (zoom in) or shrink (zoom out) the appearance of a worksheet or chart by using the Zoom button (View tab | Zoom group). When you magnify a worksheet, Excel enlarges the view of the characters on the screen, but displays fewer columns and rows. Alternatively, when you shrink a worksheet, Excel is able to display more columns and rows. Magnifying or shrinking a worksheet affects only the view; it does not change the window size or printout of the worksheet or chart. The following steps shrink and magnify the view of the worksheet.

1

- If cell A1 is not active, press CTRL + HOME.

- Display the View tab and then click the Zoom button (View tab | Zoom group) to display a list of magnifications in the Zoom dialog box (Figure 3–75).

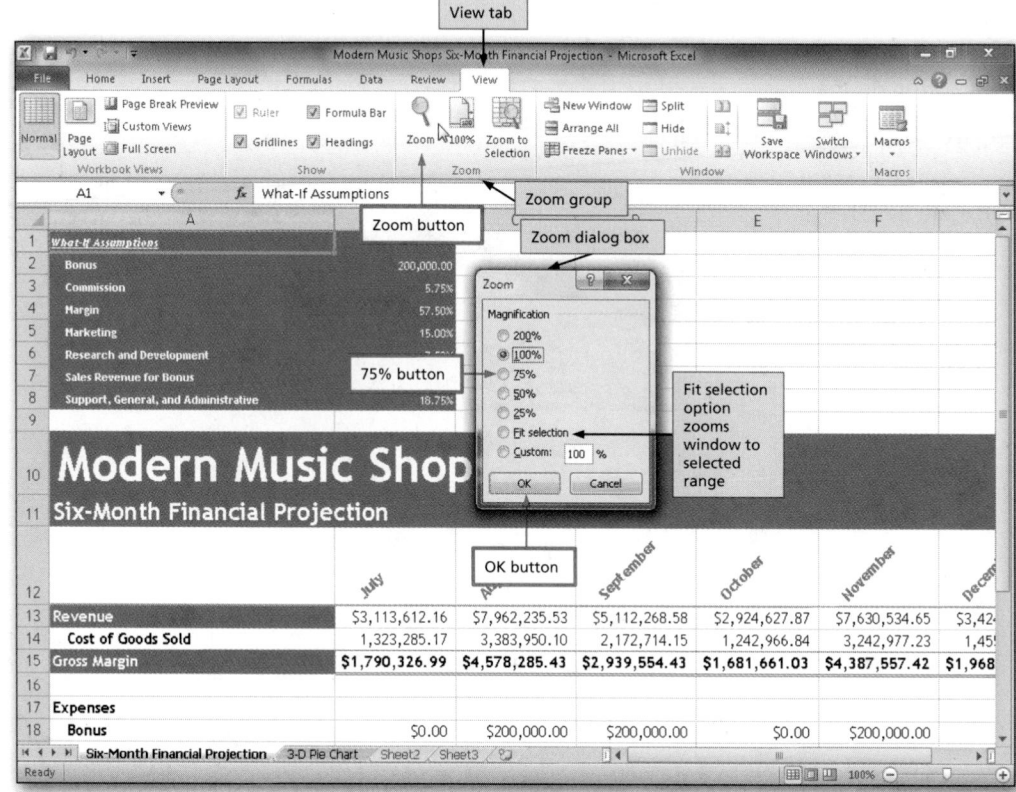

Figure 3–75

2

- Click 75% and then click the OK button (Zoom dialog box) to shrink the display of the worksheet (Figure 3–76).

Figure 3–76

3

- Click the Zoom In button on the status bar until the worksheet is displayed at 100% (Figure 3–77).

Figure 3–77

To Split a Window into Panes

When working with a large worksheet, you can split the window into two or four panes to view different parts of the worksheet at the same time. Splitting the Excel window into four panes at cell D13 allows you to view all four corners of the worksheet easily. The following steps split the Excel window into four panes.

1

- Select cell D13, the intersection of the four proposed panes, to select the cell at which to split the window.

- If necessary, display the View tab (Figure 3–78).

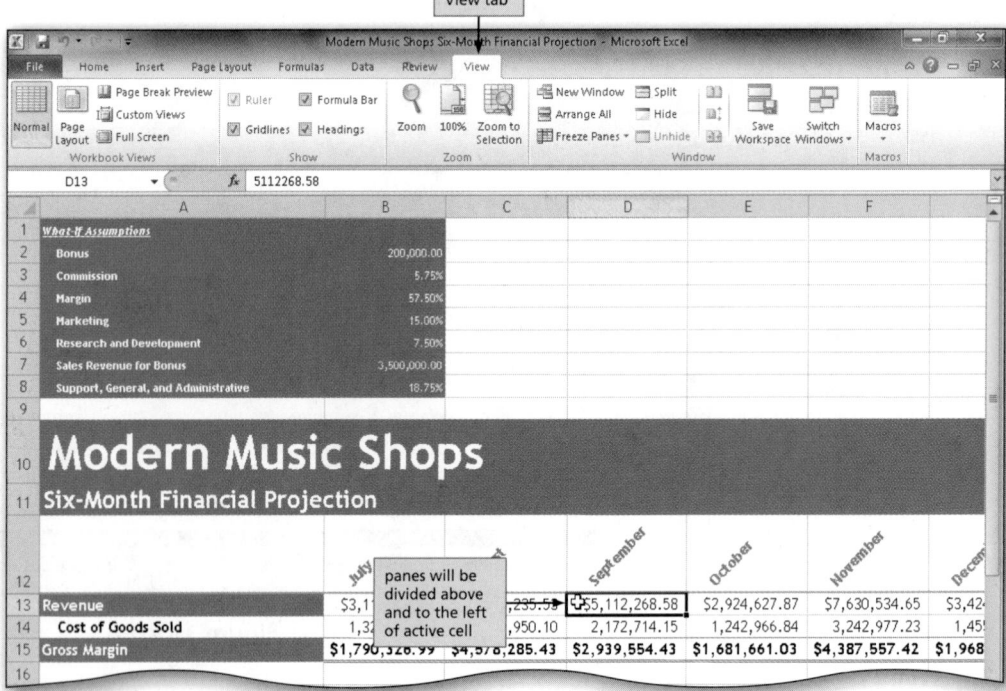

Figure 3–78

2

- Click the Split button (View tab | Window group) to divide the window into four panes.

- Use the scroll arrows to show the four corners of the worksheet at the same time (Figure 3–79).

Q&A

What is shown in the four panes?

The four panes in Figure 3–79 are used to show the following: (1) range A1:C12 in the upper-left pane; (2) range G1:I12 in the upper-right pane; (3) range A19:C24 in the lower-left pane; and (4) range G19:I24

Figure 3–79

in the lower-right pane. The vertical split bar is the vertical bar going up and down the middle of the window. The horizontal split bar is the horizontal bar going across the middle of the window. If you use the scroll bars below the window and to the right of the window to scroll the window, you will see that the panes split by the horizontal split bar scroll together vertically. The panes split by the vertical split bar scroll together horizontally. To resize the panes, drag either split bar to the desired location in the window.

To Remove the Panes from the Window

1 Position the mouse pointer at the intersection of the horizontal and vertical split bars.

2 When the mouse pointer changes to a four-headed arrow, double-click to remove the four panes from the window.

What-If Analysis

The automatic recalculation feature of Excel is a powerful tool that can be used to analyze worksheet data. Using Excel to scrutinize the impact of changing values in cells that are referenced by a formula in another cell is called what-if analysis or **sensitivity analysis**. When new data is entered, Excel not only recalculates all formulas in a worksheet but also redraws any associated charts.

In the workbook created in this chapter, many of the formulas are dependent on the assumptions in the range B2:B8. Thus, if you change any of the assumption values, Excel immediately recalculates all formulas. Excel redraws the 3-D Pie chart as well, because it is based on these numbers.

Other Ways

1. Drag horizontal split box and vertical split box to desired locations

BTW

Viewing Contents in a New Window
You can open a copy of the current workbook in a new window by clicking the New Window button (View tab | Windows group).

BTW

Zooming
You can use the Zoom in and Zoom out buttons on the status bar to zoom from 10% to 400% to reduce or enlarge the display of a worksheet.

To Analyze Data in a Worksheet by Changing Values

A what-if question for the worksheet in Chapter 3 might be *what* would happen to the six-month operating income in cell H25 *if* the Bonus, Commission, Support, General, and Administrative assumptions in the What-If Assumptions table were changed as follows: Bonus $200,000.00 to $150,000.00; Commission 5.75% to 4.00%; Support, General, and Administrative 18.75% to 15.75%? To answer a question like this, you need to change only the first, second, and seventh values in the What-If Assumptions table, as shown in the following steps. The steps also divide the window into two vertical panes. Excel instantaneously recalculates the formulas in the worksheet and redraws the 3-D Pie chart to answer the question.

- Press CTRL + HOME to select cell A1.

- Drag the vertical split box from the lower-right corner of the screen to the left so that the vertical split bar is positioned as shown in Figure 3–80 to split the screen vertically.

- Drag the horizontal split box from the upper-right corner of the screen down so that the horizontal split bar is positioned as shown in Figure 3–80 to split the screen horizontally.

- Use the scroll arrows in the lower-right pane to view the total operating income in column H in the lower-right pane.

Figure 3–80

- Enter `150000` in cell B2, `4%` in cell B3, and `15.75%` in cell B8 (Figure 3–80), which causes the six-month operating income in cell H25 to increase from $2,567,592.65 to $4,150,551.23.

To Goal Seek

If you know the result you want a formula to produce, you can use **goal seeking** to determine the value of a cell on which the formula depends. The following steps close and reopen the Modern Music Shops Six-Month Financial Projection workbook. They then use the Goal Seek command (Data tab | Data Tools group) to determine the Support, General, and Administrative percentage in cell B8 that will yield a six-month operating income of $3,000,000.00 in cell H25, rather than the original $2,567,592.65.

- Close the workbook without saving the changes and then reopen it.

- Drag the vertical split box from the lower-right corner of the screen to the left so that the vertical split bar is positioned as shown in Figure 3–81 to split the screen vertically.

- Drag the horizontal split box from the upper-right corner of the screen down so that the horizontal split bar is positioned as shown in Figure 3–81 to split the screen horizontally.

- Use the scroll arrows in the lower-right pane to view the total operating income in column H in the lower-right pane.

- Select cell H25, the cell that contains the six-month operating income.

- Display the Data tab and then click the What-If Analysis button (Data tab | Data Tools group) to display the What-If Analysis menu (Figure 3–81).

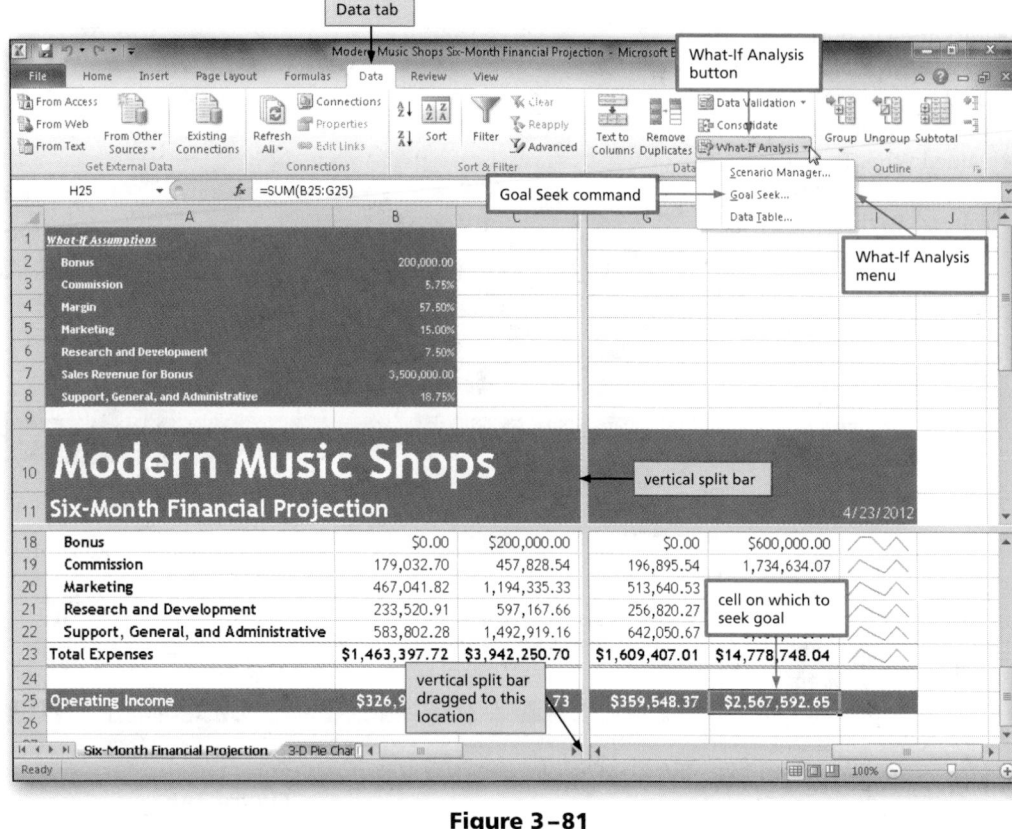

Figure 3–81

②
- Click Goal Seek to display the Goal Seek dialog box with the Set cell box set to the selected cell, H25 in this case.

- When Excel displays the Goal Seek dialog box, click the To value text box, type 3,000,000 and then click the 'By changing cell' box to select the 'By changing cell' box.

- Click cell B8 on the worksheet to assign the current cell, B8 in this case, to the 'By changing cell' box (Figure 3–82).

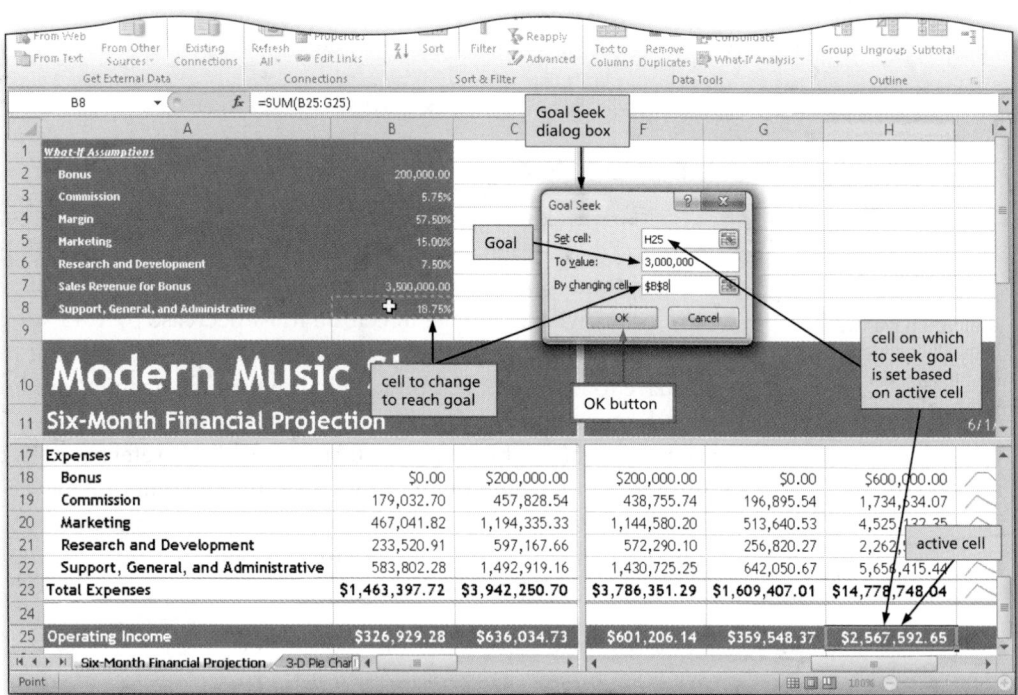

Figure 3–82

3

- Click the OK button (Goal Seek dialog box) to goal seek for the sought-after value in the 'To value' box, $3,000,000.00 in cell H25 in this case (Figure 3–83).

Q&A

What happens when I click the OK button?

Excel immediately changes cell H25 from $2,567,592.65 to the desired value of $3,000,000.00. More importantly, Excel changes the Support, General, and Administrative assumption in cell B8 from 18.75% to 17.32% (Figure 3–83). Excel also displays the Goal Seek Status dialog box. If you click the OK button, Excel keeps the new values in the worksheet. If you click the Cancel button, Excel redisplays the original values.

Figure 3–83

4

- Click the Cancel button in the Goal Seek Status dialog box to redisplay the original values in the worksheet.

Goal Seeking

Goal seeking assumes you can change the value of only one cell referenced directly or indirectly to reach a specific goal for a value in another cell. In this example, to change the six-month operating income in cell H25 to $3,000,000.00, the Support, General, and Administrative percentage in cell B8 must decrease by 1.43% from 18.75% to 17.32%.

You can see from this goal seeking example that the cell to change (cell B8) does not have to be referenced directly in the formula or function. For example, the six-month operating income in cell H25 is calculated by the function =SUM(B25:G25). Cell B8 is not referenced in this function. Instead, cell B8 is referenced in the formulas in rows 18 through 22, on which the monthly operating incomes in row 25 are based. Excel thus is capable of goal seeking on the six-month operating income by varying the value for the Support, General, and Administrative assumption.

To Quit Excel

With the workbook complete, the following steps quit Excel.

1 Click the Close button on the upper-right corner of the title bar.

2 If the Microsoft Excel dialog box is displayed, click the Don't Save button.

BTW

Quick Reference
For a table that lists how to complete the tasks covered in this book using the mouse, Ribbon, shortcut menu, and keyboard, see the Quick Reference Summary at the back of this book, or visit the Excel 2010 Quick Reference Web page (scsite.com/ex2010/qr).

Chapter Summary

In this chapter you learned how to work with large worksheets that extend beyond the window, how to use the fill handle to create a series, new formatting techniques, about the difference between absolute cell references and relative cell references, how to use the IF function, and how to rotate text in a cell, freeze titles, add Sparkline charts, change the magnification of the worksheet, show different parts of the worksheet at the same time through multiple panes, create a 3-D Pie chart, and improve the appearance of a 3-D Pie chart. This chapter also introduced you to using Excel to do what-if analysis by changing values in cells and goal seeking. The items listed below include all the new Excel skills you have learned in this chapter.

1. Rotate Text and Use the Fill Handle to Create a Series of Month Names (EX 145)
2. Increase Column Widths (EX 149)
3. Enter Row Titles (EX 150)
4. Copy a Range of Cells to a Nonadjacent Destination Area (EX 151)
5. Insert a Row (EX 154)
6. Enter Numbers with Format Symbols (EX 156)
7. Freeze Column and Row Titles (EX 157)
8. Enter and Format the System Date (EX 159)
9. Enter a Formula Containing Absolute Cell References (EX 162)
10. Enter an IF Function (EX 165)
11. Copy Formulas with Absolute Cell References Using the Fill Handle (EX 168)
12. Unfreeze the Worksheet Titles and Save the Workbook (EX 169)
13. Add a Sparkline Chart to the Worksheet (EX 170)
14. Format and Copy the Sparkline Chart (EX 171)
15. Assign Formats to Nonadjacent Ranges (EX 174)
16. Format the Worksheet Titles (EX 176)
17. Copy a Cell's Format Using the Format Painter Button (EX 178)
18. Draw a 3-D Pie Chart on a Separate Chart Sheet (EX 182)
19. Insert a Chart Title and Data Labels (EX 183)
20. Rotate the 3-D Pie Chart (EX 186)
21. Apply a 3-D Format to the Pie Chart (EX 188)
22. Explode the 3-D Pie Chart and Change the Color of a Slice (EX 190)
23. Reorder the Sheet Tabs (EX 194)
24. Check Spelling in Multiple Sheets (EX 194)
25. Shrink and Magnify the View of a Worksheet or Chart (EX 196)
26. Split a Window into Panes (EX 198)
27. Analyze Data in a Worksheet by Changing Values (EX 200)
28. Goal Seek (EX 200)

 If you have a SAM 2010 user profile, your instructor may have assigned an autogradable version of this assignment. If so, log into the SAM 2010 Web site at www.cengage.com/sam2010 to download the instruction and start files.

Learn It Online

Test your knowledge of chapter content and key terms.

Instructions: To complete the Learn It Online exercises, start your browser, click the Address bar, and then enter the Web address **scsite.com/ex2010/learn**. When the Excel 2010 Learn It Online page is displayed, click the link for the exercise you want to complete and then read the instructions.

Chapter Reinforcement TF, MC, and SA
A series of true/false, multiple choice, and short answer questions that test your knowledge of the chapter content.

Flash Cards
An interactive learning environment where you identify chapter key terms associated with displayed definitions.

Practice Test
A series of multiple choice questions that test your knowledge of chapter content and key terms.

Who Wants To Be a Computer Genius?
An interactive game that challenges your knowledge of chapter content in the style of a television quiz show.

Wheel of Terms
An interactive game that challenges your knowledge of chapter key terms in the style of the television show *Wheel of Fortune*.

Crossword Puzzle Challenge
A crossword puzzle that challenges your knowledge of key terms presented in the chapter.

Apply Your Knowledge

Reinforce the skills and apply the concepts you learned in this chapter.

Understanding Logical Tests and Absolute Cell Referencing
Instructions Part 1: Determine the truth value (true or false) of the following logical tests, given the following cell values: B4 = 30; W3 = 100; H5 = 32; L2 = 25; and M8 = 15. Enter true or false.

a. M8 > B4   Truth value: _____

b. W3 = L2   Truth value: _____

c. L2 + 15 * B4 / 10 <> W3   Truth value: _____

d. H5 – L2 < B4 / M8   Truth value: _____

e. (M8 + B4) * 2 <> W3 – (M8 / 3) * 2   Truth value: _____

f. M8 + 300 > B4 * H5 + 10   Truth value: _____

g. H5 * L2 >= 2 * (W3 + 25)   Truth value: _____

h. B4 = 10 * (M8 / 5)   Truth value: _____

Instructions Part 2: Write cell J49 as a relative reference, absolute reference, mixed reference with the column varying, and mixed reference with the row varying.

_____   _____   _____   _____

Instructions Part 3: Start Excel. Open the workbook Apply 3-1 Absolute Cell References. See the inside back cover of this book for instructions for downloading the Data Files for Students, or see your instructor for information on accessing the files required in this book. You will re-create the numerical grid pictured in Figure 3–84.

Perform the following tasks:

1. Enter a formula in cell C7 that multiplies the sum of cells C3 through C6 times cell C2. Write the formula so that when you copy it to cells D7 and E7, Excel adjusts all the cell references according to the destination cells. Verify your formula by checking it with the values found in cells C7, D7, and E7 in Figure 3–84.

2. Enter a formula in cell F3 that multiplies cell B3 times the sum of cells C3 through E3. Write the formula so that when you copy the formula to cells F4, F5, and F6, Excel adjusts all the cell references according to the destination cells. Verify your formula by checking it with the values found in cells F3, F4, F5, and F6 in Figure 3–84.

3. Enter a formula in cell C8 that multiplies the sum of cells C3 through C6 times cell C2. Write the formula so that when you copy the formula to cells D8 and E8, cell C2 remains absolute. Verify your formula by checking it with the values found in cells C8, D8, and E8 in Figure 3–84.

4. Enter a formula in cell G3 that multiplies the sum of cells C3, D3, and E3 times cell B3. Write the formula so that when you copy the formula to cells G4, G5, and G6, cell B3 remains absolute. Verify your formula by checking it with the values found in cells G3, G4, G5, and G6 in Figure 3–84.

5. Apply the worksheet name, Cell References, to the sheet tab and apply the Red, Accent 2 theme color to the sheet tab.

6. Change the document properties, as specified by your instructor. Change the worksheet header with your name, course number, and other information as specified by your instructor. Save the workbook using the file name, Apply 3-1 Absolute Cell References Complete, and submit the workbook as requested by your instructor.

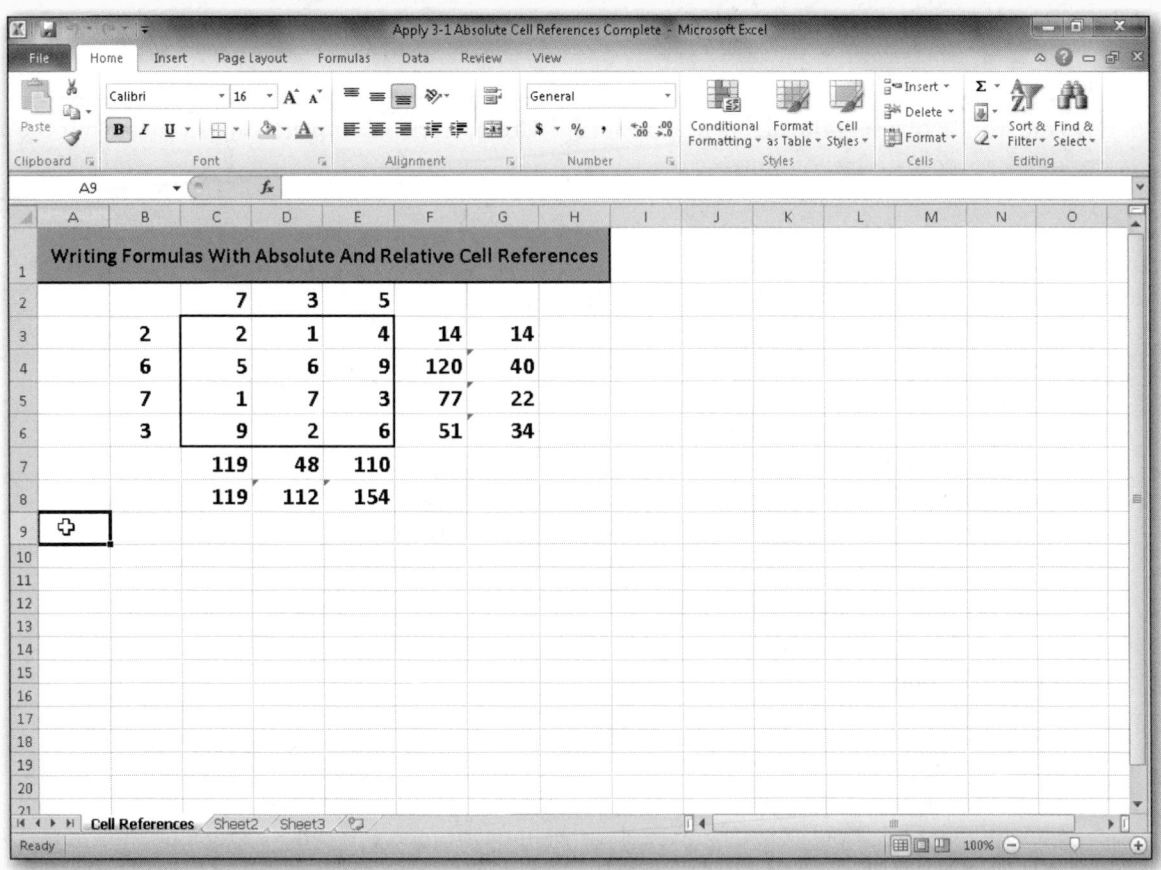

Figure 3–84

Extend Your Knowledge

Extend the skills you learned in this chapter and experiment with new skills. You may need to use Help to complete the assignment.

Nested IF Functions and More About the Fill Handle

Instructions Part 1:   Start Excel. You will use nested IF functions to determine values for sets of data.

1. Using the Insert Function dialog box, enter the following IF function in cell B1:

    IF(A1="TX", "Central", "Time Zone Error")

2. Select cell B1, select the text "Time Zone Error" in the Formula Bar, click the Logical button (Formulas tab | Function Library group), click IF, and enter the following IF function:

    IF(A1="OR", "Pacific", "Time Zone Error")

3. Select cell B1, select "Time Zone Error" in the Formula Bar, click Logical button (Formulas tab | Function Library group), click IF, and enter the following IF function:

    IF(A1="VA", "Eastern", "Time Zone Error")

4. Verify that the formula in cell B1 appears as follows:

    =IF(A1="TX","Central", IF(A1="OR","Pacific", IF(A1="VA","Eastern","Time Zone Error")))

5. Use the fill handle to copy the nested IF function down through cell B6. Enter the following data in the cells in the range A1:A6 and then write down the results that display in cells B1 through B6 for each set. Set 1: A1 = TX; A2 = NY; A3 = OR; A4 = MI; A5 = TX; A6 = VA. Set 2: A1= WI; A2 = OR; A3 = IL; A4 = VA; A5 = NJ; A6 = TX.

Set 1 Results: _____

Set 2 Results: _____

6. Save the workbook using the file name, Extend 3-1 Create Series Complete Part 1, and submit the workbook as specified by your instructor.

Instructions Part 2:   Start Excel. Open the workbook Extend 3-1 Create Series. See the inside back cover of this book for instructions for downloading the Data Files for Students, or see your instructor for information on accessing the files required in this book.

Perform the following tasks:

1. Use the fill handle on one column at a time to propagate the twelve series through row 14, as shown in Figure 3–85. For example, in column A, select cell A2 and drag the fill handle down to cell A14. In column C, hold down the CTRL key to repeat Saturday through cell C14. In column D, select the range D2:D3 and drag the fill handle down to cell D14. Likewise, in columns G through L, select the two adjacent cells in rows 2 and 3 before dragging the fill handle down to the corresponding cell in row 14.

2. Select cell D19. While holding down the CTRL key, one at a time drag the fill handle three cells to the right, to the left, up, and down to generate four series of numbers beginning with zero and incremented by one.

3. Select cell H19. Point to the cell border so that the mouse pointer changes to a plus sign with four arrows. Drag the mouse pointer down to cell H21 to move the contents of cell H19 to cell H21.

4. Select cell H21. Point to the cell border so that the mouse pointer changes to a plus sign with four arrows. While holding down the CTRL key, drag the mouse pointer to cell K21 to copy the contents of cell H21 to cell K21.

Figure 3–85

5. Select cell K19. Drag the fill handle in to the center of cell K19 so that the cell is shaded and the cell contents are deleted.

6. Apply a worksheet name to the sheet tab and apply a color of your choice to the sheet tab.

7. Select cell range H2:I14, click the Pie button (Insert tab | Charts group) to display the Pie gallery, click Pie in 3-D chart in the Pie gallery, click the Move Chart button (Chart Tools Design tab | Location group), click the New sheet option button (Move Chart dialog box), and then click the OK button (Move Chart dialog box) to move the 3-D Pie chart to a new worksheet.

8. Click the Chart Title button (Chart Tools Layout tab | Labels group), click Above Chart in the Chart Title gallery, select the title, and change the chart title to "Yearly Breakdown".

9. Click the Data Labels button (Chart Tools Layout tab | Labels group), click Outside End in the Data Labels gallery to add data points to the chart.

10. Apply a chart sheet name to the sheet tab and apply a color of your choice to the tab.

11. Change the document properties, as specified by your instructor. Change the worksheet header with your name, course number, and other information as specified by your instructor. Save the workbook using the file name, Extend 3-1 Create Series Complete Part 2, and submit the workbook as specified by your instructor.

Make It Right

Analyze a workbook and correct all errors and/or improve the design.

Inserting Rows, Moving a Range, and Correcting Formulas in a Worksheet

Instructions: Start Excel. Open the workbook Make It Right 3-1 SpeedyOfficeSupply.com Annual Projected Net Income. See the inside back cover of this book for instructions for downloading the Data Files for Students, or see your instructor for information on accessing the files required for this book. Correct the following design and formula problems (Figure 3–86a) in the worksheet.

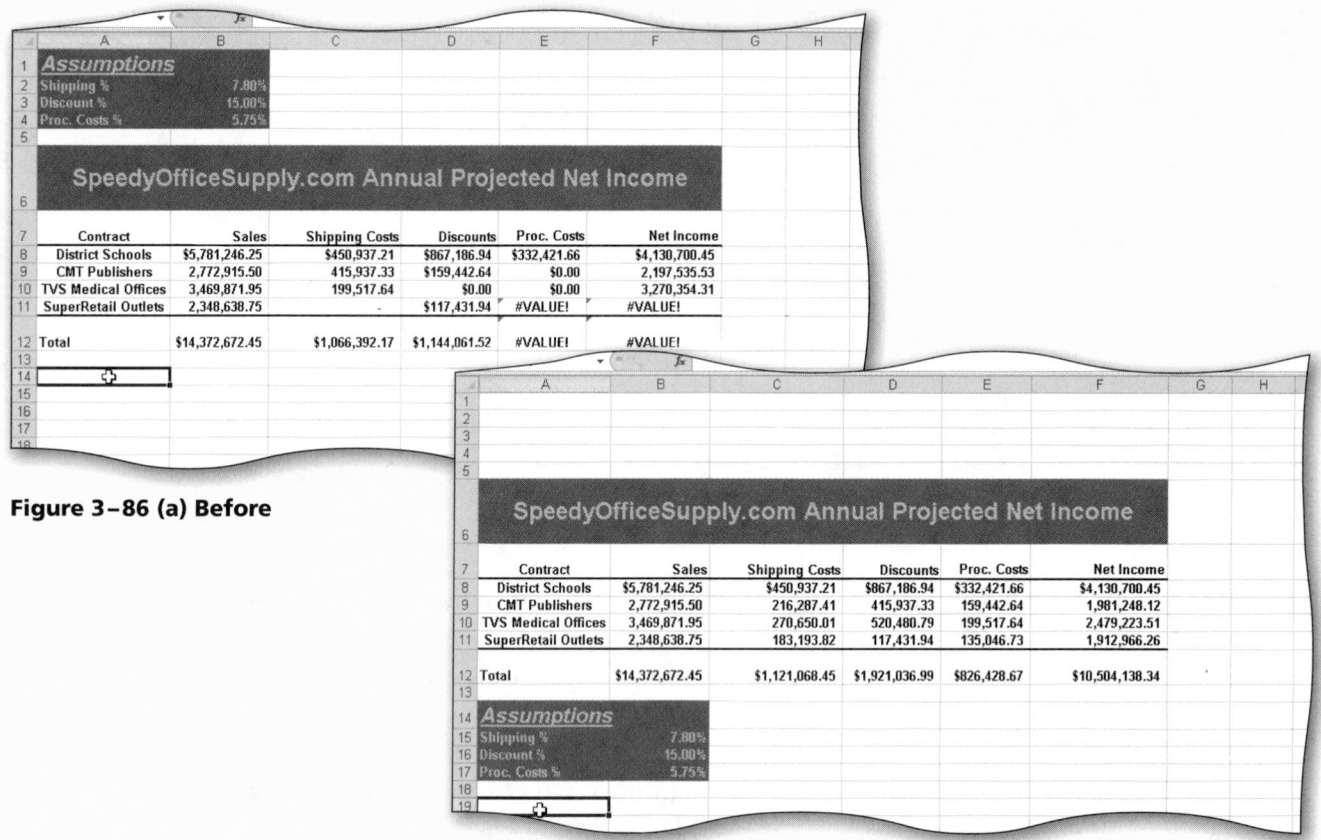

Figure 3–86 (a) Before

Figure 3–86 (b) After

1. The Shipping Cost in cell C8 is computed using the formula =B2*B8 (Shipping % × Sales). Similar formulas are used in cells C9, C10, and C11. The formula in cell C8 was entered and copied to cells C9, C10, and C11. Although the result in cell C8 is correct, the results in cells C9, C10, and C11 are incorrect. Edit the formula in cell C8 by changing cell B2 to an absolute cell reference. Copy the corrected formula in cell C8 to cells C9, C10, and C11. After completing the copy, click the Auto Fill Options button arrow that is displayed below and to the right of cell C11 and choose Fill Without Formatting.

2. The Discount amounts in cells D8, D9, D10, and D11 are computed using the IF function. The Discount amount should equal the amount in cell B3*B8 (Discount % × Sales) if the corresponding Sales in column B is greater than or equal to $2,500,000. If the corresponding Sales in column B is less than $2,500,000, then the Discount amount is 5%*B8 (5% × Sales). The IF function in cell D8

was entered and copied to cells D9, D10, and D11. The current IF functions in cells D8, D9, D10, and D11 are incorrect. Edit and correct the IF function in cell D8. Copy the corrected formula in cell D8 to cells D9, D10, and D11. After completing the copy, click the Auto Fill Options button arrow that is displayed below and to the right of cell D11 and choose Fill Without Formatting.

3. The Processing Costs in cell E8 is computed using the formula =B4*B8 (Proc. Costs % × Sales). The formula in cell E8 was entered and copied to cells E9, E10, and E11. Although the result in cell E8 is correct, the results in cells E9, E10, and E11 are incorrect. Edit and correct the formula in cell E8 by changing cell B4 to an absolute cell reference. Copy the corrected formula in cell E8 to cells E9, E10, and E11. After completing the copy, click the Auto Fill Options button arrow that displays below and to the right of cell E11 and choose Fill Without Formatting. Ensure that the range B9:E11 is formatted with the Accounting Number format.

4. Change the design of the worksheet by moving the Assumptions table in the range A1:B4 to the range A14:B17, as shown in Figure 3–86b. To complete the move drag the Assumptions table to the range A14:B17. Use Figure 3–86b to verify that Excel automatically adjusted the cell references based on the move. Use the Undo button and Redo button on the Quick Access Toolbar to move the Assumptions table back and forth while the results of the formulas remain the same.

5. Apply a worksheet name to the sheet tab and apply the Orange, Accent 3 color to the sheet tab.

6. Change the document properties, as specified by your instructor. Change the worksheet header with your name, course number, and other information as specified by your instructor. Save the workbook using the file name, Make It Right 3-1 SpeedyOfficeSupply.com Annual Projected Net Income Complete, and submit the revised workbook as specified by your instructor.

In the Lab

Create a workbook using the guidelines, concepts, and skills presented in this chapter. Labs are listed in order of increasing difficulty.

Lab 1: Six-Year Financial Projection

Problem: Your supervisor in the Finance department at Med Supply Online Warehouse has asked you to create a worksheet that will project the annual gross margin, expenses, total expenses, operating income, income taxes, and net income for the next six years based on the assumptions in Table 3–9. The desired worksheet is shown in Figure 3–87 on the following page. In Part 1 you will create the worksheet. In Part 2 you will create a chart to present the data, shown in Figure 3–88 on page EX 213. In Part 3 you will use Goal Seek to analyze three different sales scenarios.

Table 3–9 Med Supply Online Warehouse Financial Projection Assumptions	
Units Sold in Prior Year	1,589,712
Unit Cost	$59.50
Annual Sales Growth	4.50%
Annual Price Decrease	3.80%
Margin	38.80%

Continued >

In the Lab *continued*

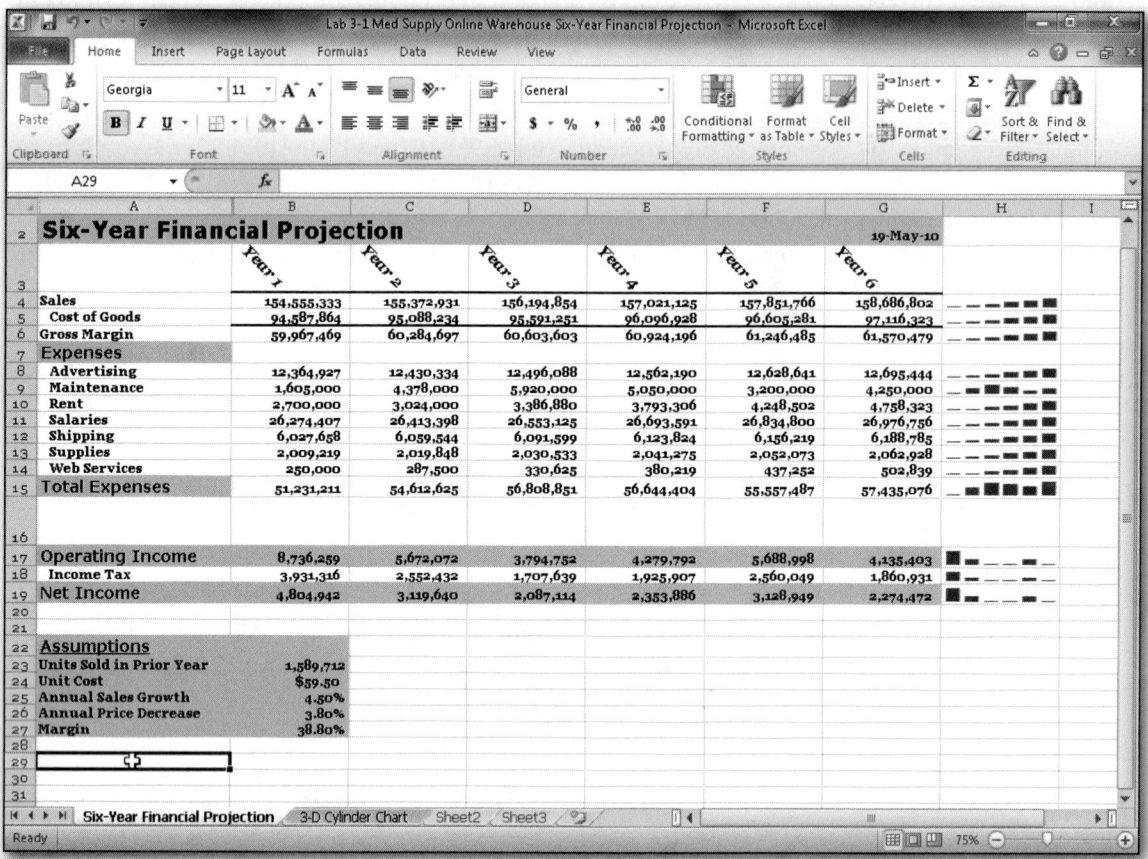

Figure 3–87

Instructions Part 1:

1. Start Excel. Apply the Civic theme to the worksheet by using the Themes button (Page Layout tab | Themes group). Bold the entire worksheet by selecting the entire worksheet and using the Bold button (Home tab | Font group).

2. Enter the worksheet title **Med Supply Online Warehouse** in cell A1 and the subtitle **Six-Year Financial Projection** in cell A2. Format the worksheet title in cell A1 to 36-point Copperplate Gothic Bold (or a similar font). Format the worksheet subtitle in cell A2 to 20-point Verdana (or a similar font). Enter the system date in cell G2 using the NOW function. Format the date to the 14-Mar-01 style.

3. Change the following column widths: A = 25.00 characters; B through H = 15.00 characters. Change the heights of rows 7, 15, 17, 19, and 22 to 18.00 points. Change the height of row 16 to 42.00 points.

4. Enter the six column titles Year 1 through Year 6 in the range B3:G3 by entering Year 1 in cell B3 and then dragging cell B3's fill handle through the range C3:G3. Format cell B3 as follows: (a) increase the font size to 14; (b) center and italicize it; and (c) angle its contents clockwise. Use the Format Painter button (Home tab | Clipboard group) to copy the format assigned to cell B3 to the range C3:G3.

5. Enter the row titles in the range A4:A19. Change the font in cells A7, A15, A17, and A19 to 14-point Verdana (or a similar font). Add thick bottom borders to the ranges B3:G3 and B5:G5. Use the Increase Indent button (Home tab | Alignment group) to increase the indent of the row titles in cell A5, the range A8:A14, and cell A18.

6. Enter the table title **Assumptions** in cell A22. Enter the assumptions in Table 3–9 on page EX 209 in the range A23:B27. Use format symbols when entering the numbers. Change the font size of the table title in cell A22 to 14-point Verdana and underline it.

7. Select the range B4:G19 and then click the Format Cells: Number Dialog Box Launcher (Home tab | Number group) to display the Format Cells dialog box. Use the Number category (Format Cells dialog box) to assign a comma style with no decimal places and negative numbers enclosed in parentheses to the range B4:G19.

8. Complete the following entries:

   a. Year 1 Sales (cell B4) = Units Sold in Prior Year * (Unit Cost / (1 – Margin)) or = B23*(B24/(1-B27))

   b. Year 2 Sales (cell C4) = Year 1 Sales * (1 + Annual Sales Growth) * (1 – Annual Price Decrease) or =B4*(1+$B$25)*(1-$B$26)

   c. Copy cell C4 to the range D4:G4.

   d. Year 1 Cost of Goods (cell B5) = Year 1 Sales * (1 – Margin) or =B4 * (1 - $B$27)

   e. Copy cell B5 to the range C5:G5.

   f. Gross Margin (cell B6) = Year 1 Sales - Year 1 Cost of Goods or =B4 – B5

   g. Copy cell B6 to the range C6:G6.

   h. Year 1 Advertising (cell B8) = 500 + 8% * Year 1 Sales or =500+8%*B4

   i. Copy cell B8 to the range C8:G8.

   j. Maintenance (row 9): Year 1 = 1,605,000; Year 2 = 4,378,000; Year 3 = 5,920,000; Year 4 = 5,050,000; Year 5 = 3,200,000; Year 6 = 4,250,000

   k. Year 1 Rent (cell B10) = 2,700,000

   l. Year 2 Rent (cell C10) = Year 1 Rent + (12% * Year 1 Rent) or =B10 + (12% * B14)

   m. Copy cell C10 to the range D10:G10.

   n. Year 1 Salaries (cell B11) = 17% * Year 1 Sales or =17%*B4

   o. Copy cell B11 to the range C11:G11.

   p. Year 1 Shipping (cell B12) = 3.9% * Year 1 Sales or =3.9%*B4

   q. Copy cell B12 to the range C12:G12.

   r. Year 1 Supplies (cell B13) = 1.3% * Year 1 Sales or =1.3%*B4

   s. Copy cell B13 to the range C13:G13.

   t. Year 1 Web Services (cell B14) = 250,000

   u. Year 2 Web Services (cell C14) = Year 1 Web Services + (15% * Year 1 Web Services) or =B14+ (15% * B14)

   v. Copy cell C14 to the range D14:G14.

   w. Year 1 Total Expenses (cell B15) = SUM(B8:B14)

   x. Copy cell B15 to the range C15:G15.

   y. Year 1 Operating Income (cell B17) = Year 1 Gross Margin - Year 1 Total Expenses or =B6-B15

   z. Copy cell B17 to the range C17:G17.

Continued >

In the Lab *continued*

    aa. Year 1 Income Taxes (cell B18): If Year 1 Operating Income is less than 0, then Year 1 Income Taxes equal 0; otherwise Year 1 Income Taxes equal 45% * Year 1 Operating Income or =IF(B17 < 0, 0, 45%*B17)

    bb. Copy cell B18 to the range C18:G18.

    cc. Year 1 Net Income (cell B19) = Year 1 Operating Income – Year 1 Income Taxes or = B17–B18

    dd. Copy cell B19 to the range C19:G19.

    ee. In cell H4, insert a Sparkline Column chart (Insert Tab | Sparklines group) for cell range B4:G4

    ff. Repeat step ee for the ranges H5:H6, H8:H15, and H17:H19

9. Change the background colors as shown in Figure 3–87. Use Teal, Accent 3, Lighter 40% for the background colors.

10. Zoom to: (a) 200%; (b) 75%; (c) 25%; and (d) 100%.

11. Change the document properties, as specified by your instructor. Change the worksheet header with your name, course number, and other information as specified by your instructor. Save the workbook using the file name, Lab 3-1 Med Supply Online Warehouse Six-Year Financial Projection.

12. Preview the worksheet. Use the Orientation button (Page Layout tab | Page Setup group) to fit the printout on one page in landscape orientation. Preview the formulas version (CTRL+`) of the worksheet in landscape orientation using the Fit to option. Press CTRL + ` to instruct Excel to display the values version of the worksheet. Save the workbook again and close the workbook.

13. Submit the workbook as specified by your instructor.

Instructions Part 2:

1. Start Excel. Open the workbook Lab 3-1 Med Supply Online Warehouse Six-Year Financial Projection.

2. Use the nonadjacent ranges B3:G3 and B19:G19 to create a 3-D Cylinder chart. Draw the chart by clicking the Column button (Insert tab | Charts group). When the Column gallery is displayed, click the Clustered Cylinder chart type (column 1, row 3). When the chart is displayed, click the Move Chart button to move the chart to a new sheet.

3. Select the legend on the right side of the chart and delete it. Add the chart title by clicking the Chart Titles button (Chart Tools Layout tab | Labels group). Click Above Chart in the Chart Title gallery. Format the chart title as shown in Figure 3–88.

4. To change the color of the cylinders, click one of the cylinders and use the Shape Fill button (Chart Tools Format tab | Shape Styles group). To change the color of the wall, click the wall behind the cylinders and use the Shape Fill button to change the chart wall color. Use the same procedure to change the color of the base of the wall.

5. Rename the sheet tabs Six-Year Financial Projection and 3-D Cylinder Chart. Rearrange the sheets so that the worksheet is leftmost and color their tabs as shown in Figure 3–88.

6. Click the Six-Year Financial Projection tab to display the worksheet. Save the workbook using the same file name (Lab 3-1 Med Supply Online Warehouse Six -Year Financial Projection) as defined in Part 1. Submit the workbook as requested by your instructor.

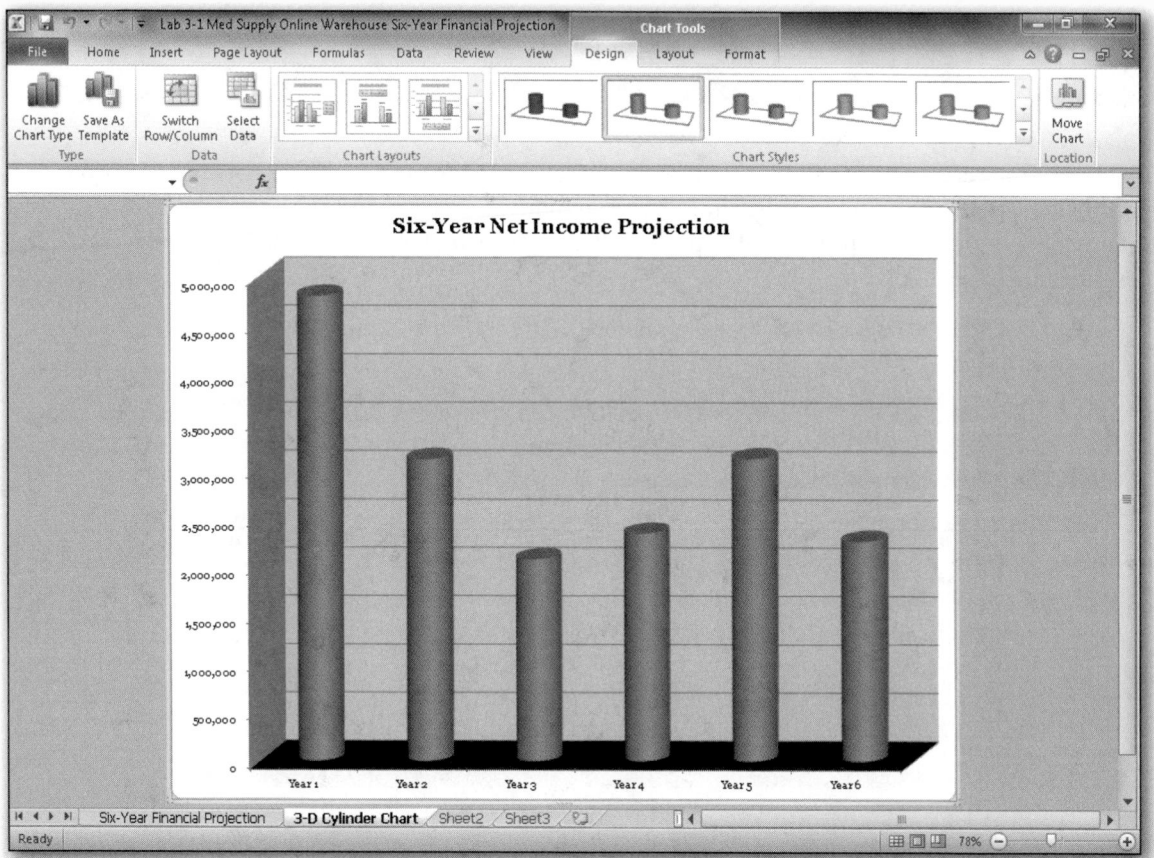

Figure 3–88

Instructions Part 3:

1. Start Excel. Open the workbook Lab 3-1 Med Supply Online Warehouse Six-Year Financial Projection. Do not save the workbook in this part of the In the Lab exercise. Divide the window into two panes by dragging the horizontal split box between rows 6 and 7. Use the scroll bars to show both the top and bottom of the worksheet. Using the numbers in columns 2 and 3 of Table 3–10, analyze the effect of changing the annual sales growth (cell B25) and annual price decrease (cell B26) on the net incomes in row 19. The resulting answers are in column 4 of Table 3–10. Submit the workbook or results of the what-if analysis for each case as requested by your instructor.

Table 3–10 Med Supply Online Warehouse Data to Analyze and Results			
Case	Annual Sales Growth	Annual Price Decrease	Year 6 Resulting Net Income in Cell G19
1	8.45%	5.75%	2,925,008
2	14.75%	23.00%	(2,353,532)
3	25.50%	2.65%	14,668,149

2. Close the workbook without saving it, and then reopen it. Use the What-If Analysis button (Data tab | Data Tools group) to goal seek. Determine a margin (cell B27) that would result in a Year 6 net income of $4,000,000 (cell G19). You should end up with a margin of 40.49% in cell B27. Submit the workbook with the new values or the results of the goal seek as requested by your instructor. Do not save the workbook with the latest changes.

In the Lab

Lab 2: Analysis of Indirect Expense Allocations

Problem: Your classmate works part time as an advisor for the ReachOut Neighbors not-for-profit group. She has asked you to assist her in creating an indirect expense allocation worksheet (Figure 3–89) that will help the not-for-profit administration better evaluate the branch offices described in Table 3–11.

Figure 3–89

Table 3–11 ReachOut Neighbor Worksheet Data

	Chicago Branch Office	Dallas Branch Office	Houston Branch Office	Jacksonville Branch Office	Los Angeles Branch Office	New York Branch Office	Reno Branch Office
Total Donations	735356	98190	178435	212300	175350	752900	1845230
Distributed Goods and Services	529750	60891	135589	150895	96050	589590	1629350
Direct Expenses	57550	22530	14750	25300	42670	58600	65000
Square Footage	15500	775	7550	8250	950	6275	8600

Instructions Part 1: Do the following to create the worksheet shown in Figure 3–89.

1. Apply the Foundry theme to the worksheet. Bold the entire worksheet by selecting the entire worksheet and using the Bold (Home tab | Font group).

2. Change the following column widths: A = 30.00; B through I = 13.00; J = 20.00.

3. Enter the worksheet titles in cells A1 and A2 and the system date in cell I2. Format the date to the 14-Mar-01 style.

4. Enter the column titles, row titles, and the first three rows of numbers in Table 3–11 in rows 3 through 6. Add the column heading Total to cell I3. Center and italicize the column headings in the range B3:I3. Add a thick bottom border to the range B3:I3. Sum the individual rows 4, 5, and 6 in the range I4:I6.

5. Enter the Square Footage row as shown in Table 3–11 with the comma format symbol in row 16. Sum row 16 in cell I16. Use the Format Painter button (Home tab | Clipboard group) to format cell I16. Change the height of row 16 to 42.00. Vertically center the range A16:I16 through the use of the Format Cells dialog box.

6. Enter the remaining row titles in the range A7:A17 as shown in Figure 3–89. Increase the font size in cells A7, A14, and A15 to 14 point and indent the text in the ranges A8:A13 and A18:A23.

7. Copy the row titles in range A8:A13 to the range A18:A23. Enter the numbers shown in the range B18:B23 of Figure 3–89 with format symbols.

8. The planned indirect expenses in the range B18:B23 are to be prorated across the branch office as follows: Administrative (row 8), Energy (row 10), and Marketing (row 13) on the basis of Total Donations (row 4); Depreciation (row 9), Insurance (row 11), and Maintenance (row 12) on the basis of Square Footage (row 16). Use the following formulas to accomplish the prorating:

   a. Chicago Branch Office Administrative (cell B8) = Administrative Expenses * Chicago Branch Office Total Donations / ReachOut Neighbors Total Donations or =$B$18*B4/$I$4

   b. Chicago Branch Office Depreciation (cell B9) = Depreciation Expenses * Chicago Branch Office Square Footage / Total Square Footage or =$B$19*B16/$I$16

   c. Chicago Branch Office Energy (cell B10) = Energy Expenses * Chicago Branch Office Total Donations / ReachOut Neighbor Total Donations or =$B$20*B4/$I$4

   d. Chicago Branch Office Insurance (cell B11) = Insurance Expenses * Chicago Branch Office Square Footage / Total Square Footage or =$B$21*B16 /$I$16

   e. Chicago Branch Office Maintenance (cell B12) = Maintenance Expenses * Chicago Branch Office Square Footage / Total Square Footage or =$B$22*B16/$I$16

   f. Chicago Branch Office Marketing (cell B13) = Marketing Expenses * Chicago Branch Office Total Donations / ReachOut Neighbor Total Donations or =$B$23*B4/$I$4

   g. Chicago Branch Office Total Indirect Expenses (cell B14) = SUM(B8:B13)

   h. Chicago Branch Office Net Income (cell B15) = Total Donations - (Distributed Goods and Services + Direct Expenses + Total Indirect Expenses) or =B4-(B5+B6+B14)

   i. Copy the range B8:B15 to the range C8:H15.

   j. Sum the individual rows 8 through 15 in the range I8:I15.

9. Add a thick bottom border to the range B13:I13. Assign the Currency style with two decimal places and show negative numbers in parentheses to the following ranges: B4:I4; B8:I8; and B14:I15. Assign the Comma style with two decimal places and show negative numbers in parentheses to the following ranges: B5:I6 and B9:I13.

10. Change the font in cell A1 to 48-point Britannic Bold (or a similar font). Change the font in cell A2 to 22-point Britannic Bold (or a similar font). Change the font in cell A17 to 18-point italic Britannic Bold.

11. Use the background color Green, Accent 1, Lighter 40% and the font color Tan, Background 2, Darker 75% for cell A7 and the ranges A1:I2; A15:I15; and A17:B23 as shown in Figure 3–89.

12. Insert a Sparkline Win/Loss chart for the range B8:H8 in cell J8. Copy the cell J8 to the cell range J9:J13.

Continued >

In the Lab *continued*

13. Rename the Sheet1 sheet as Indirect Expenses Analysis and color its tab green.

14. Update the document properties with your name, course number, and name for the workbook. Change the worksheet header with your name, course number, and other information as specified by your instructor. Save the workbook using the file name, Lab 3-2 ReachOut Neighbor Analysis of Indirect Expenses.

15. Preview the worksheet. Use the Orientation button (Page Layout tab | Page Setup group) to fit the printout on one page in landscape orientation using the Fit to option. Preview the formulas version (CTRL+`) of the worksheet in landscape orientation using the Fit to option. Press CTRL+` to instruct Excel to display the values version of the worksheet. Save the workbook again and close the workbook.

16. Divide the window into four panes and show the four corners of the worksheet. Remove the four panes. Close the workbook but do not save the workbook.

Instructions Part 2: Start Excel. Open Lab 3-2 ReachOut Neighbor Analysis of Indirect Expenses. Draw a 3-D Column Chart (Figure 3–90) on a separate sheet that shows the contribution of each category of indirect expense to the total indirect expenses. That is, chart the nonadjacent ranges A8:A13 (category names) and I8:I13 (data series). Show labels that include value of the column. Do not show the legend. Format the 3-D Column Chart as shown in Figure 3–90. Rename the chart sheet 3-D Column Chart and color the sheet tab red. Move the chart tab to the right of the worksheet tab. Save the workbook using the file name, Lab 3-2 ReachOut Neighbor Analysis of Indirect Expenses. Submit the workbook as specified by your instructor.

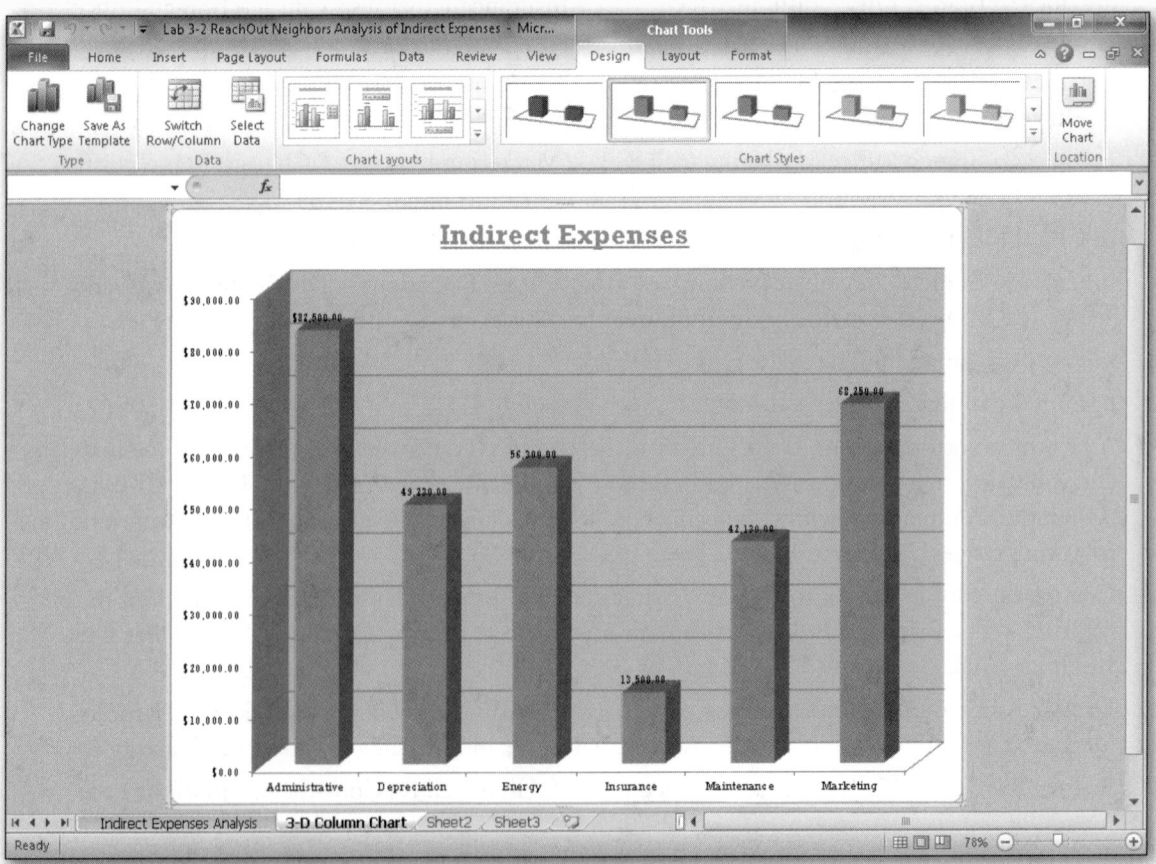

Figure 3–90

Instructions Part 3: Start Excel. Open Lab 3-2 ReachOut Neighbor Analysis of Indirect Expenses.

1. Using the numbers in Table 3–12, analyze the effect of changing the planned indirect expenses in the range B18:B23 on the net incomes for each branch office. You should end with the following totals in cell I15: Case 1 = $5,846.00 and Case 2 = $124,346.00. Close the workbook without saving the changes. Submit the workbook or results for each case as requested by your instructor.

2. Use the What-If Analysis button (Data tab | Data Tools group) to goal seek. Determine a planned indirect Marketing expense (cell B23) that would result in a total net income of $50,000 (cell I15). You should end up with a planned indirect Marketing expense of $225,586 in cell B23. Submit the workbook with the new values or the results of the goal seek as specified by your instructor.

Table 3–12 ReachOut Neighbor Indirect Expense Allocations What-If Data

	Case 1	Case 2
Administrative	124000	66500
Depreciation	156575	75000
Energy	72525	56000
Insurance	46300	67000
Maintenance	75000	48000
Marketing	39000	82400

In the Lab

Lab 3: Modifying a Weekly Inventory Worksheet

Problem: As a summer intern at Dinah's Candle Depot, you have been asked to modify the weekly inventory report shown in Figure 3–91a on the following page. The workbook, Lab 3-3 Dinah's Weekly Inventory Report, is included with the Data Files for Students. See the inside back cover of this book for instructions for downloading the Data Files for Students, or see your instructor for information on accessing the files required for this book.

The major modifications to the payroll report to be made in this exercise include: (1) reformatting the worksheet; (2) adding computations of quantity to order based on reorder level and weeks to arrive; (3) adding calculations to suggest changes in ordering; (4) adding current and last month sales for inventory items; (5) adding and deleting inventory items; and (6) changing inventory item information. The final inventory report is shown in Figure 3–91b on the following page.

Continued >

In the Lab *continued*

Figure 3–91 (a) Before

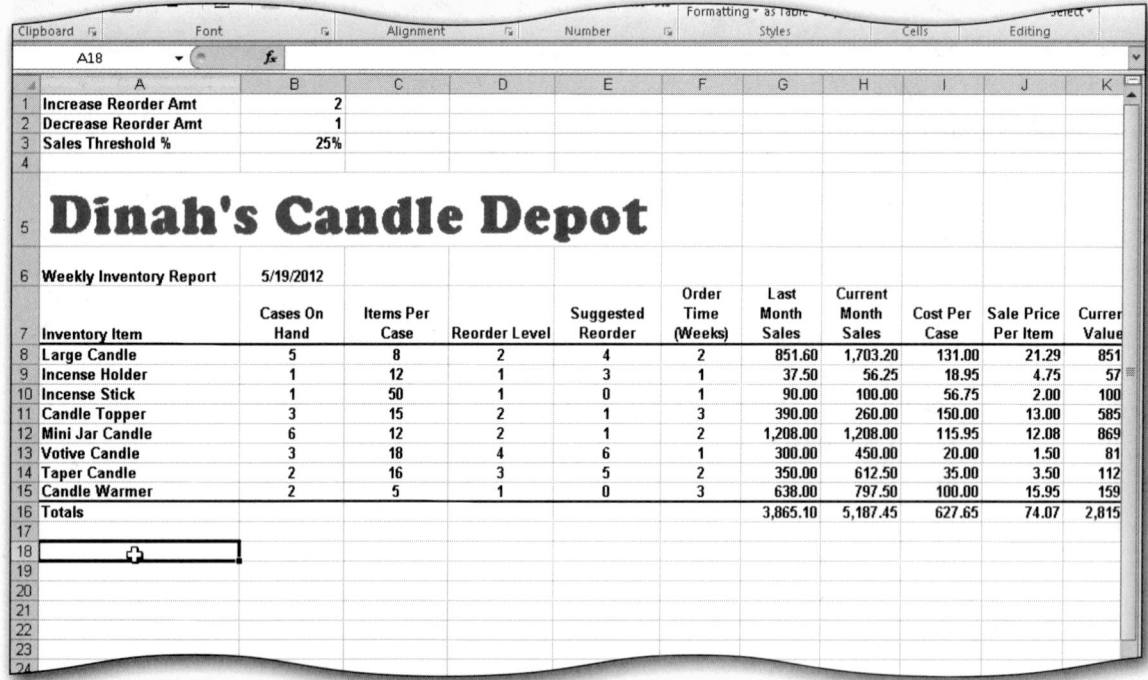

Figure 3–91 (b) After

Instructions Part 1:

1. Start Excel. Open the workbook, Lab 3-3 Dinah's Weekly Inventory Report and then save the workbook using the file name Lab 3-3 Dinah's Weekly Inventory Report Complete.

2. Select the worksheet by clicking the Select All button. Click the Clear button (Home tab | Editing group) and then click Clear Formats on the Clear menu to clear the formatting. Bold the entire worksheet.

3. Delete rows 11 through 13 to remove the statistics below the Totals row. Change all the row heights back to the default height (12.75).

4. Insert four rows above row 1 by selecting rows 1 through 4, right-clicking the selection, and clicking Insert on the shortcut menu.

5. Change the row heights as follows: row 5 = 48.00; row 6 = 25.50; and 7 = 38.25. For the range B7:I7, change the format so that the text wraps. Center the range B7:I7.

6. Delete column B by right-clicking the column heading and clicking Delete on the shortcut menu.

7. Insert a new column between columns D and E. Change the column widths as follows: A = 25.00; E = 13.00; and F through I = 9.71. Enter the new column E title **Suggested Reorder** in cell E7.

8. Insert two new columns between columns F and G. Enter the new column G title **Last Month Sales** in cell G7. Enter the new column H title **Current Month Sales** in cell H7.

9. Enhance the worksheet title in cell A5 by using a 36-point purple Cooper Black (or a similar font) font style as shown in Figure 3–91b.

10. Assign the NOW function to cell B6 and format it to the 3/14/2001 style.

11. Delete item Car Air Freshener (row 13). Change Mini Jar Candle's (row 12) cases on hand to 6. Change Large Candle's (row 8) items per case to 8 and cost per case to $131.00. Change Incense Stick's (row 10) sale price per item to $2.00 and Incense Holder's (row 9) sale price per item to $4.75.

12. Freeze column A and rows 1 through 7 by selecting cell B8, clicking the Freeze Panes button (View tab | Window group), and then clicking Freeze Panes on the Freeze Panes gallery.

13. In columns G and H, enter the current month and last month sales values listed in Table 3–13.

14. Insert three new rows immediately above the Totals row. Add the new items data as listed in Table 3–14.

Table 3–13 Dinah's Candle Depot Monthly Sales Values		
Inventory Item	Last Month Sales	Current Month Sales
Large Candle	851.6	1703.2
Incense Holder	37.5	56.25
Incense Stick	90	100
Candle Topper	390	260
Mini Jar Candle	1208	1208

Table 3–14 Dinah's Candle Depot New Items								
Inventory Item	Cases On Hand	Items Per Case	Reorder Level	Order Time (Weeks)	Last Month Sales	Current Month Sales	Cost Per Case	Sale Price Per Item
Votive Candle	3	18	4	1	300	450	20	1.5
Taper Candle	2	16	3	2	350	612.5	35	3.5
Candle Warmer	2	5	1	3	638	797.5	100	15.95

15. Center the range B8:F15. Use the Currency category in the Format Cells dialog box to assign a Comma style (no dollar signs) with two decimal places and negative numbers within parentheses to the range G8:K16. Draw a thick bottom border in the ranges A7:K7 and A15:K15.

16. As shown in Figure 3–91b, enter and format the Increase Reorder Amt (2), the Decrease Reorder Amt (1), and the Sales Threshold % (25%) information in the range A1:B3. Use format symbols where applicable.

Continued >

In the Lab *continued*

17. Remove any Totals in the range B16:F16. Update and add totals as necessary so that totals appear in the range G16:K16.

18. In cell E8, enter an IF function that applies the following logic and then copy it to the range E9:E15. If (Current Month Sales – Last Month Sales) / Current Month Sales >= Sales Threshold %, then Reorder Level + Increase Reorder Amt, otherwise Reorder Level – Decrease Reorder Amt or =IF((H8-G8)/H8 >= $B$3, D8+$B$1,D8-$B$2).

19. In cell L8, insert a Sparkline Line chart for range G8:H8. Copy cell L8 to the range L9:L16.

20. Unfreeze the worksheet by clicking the Freeze Panes button (View tab | Window group), and then clicking Unfreeze Panes on the Freeze Panes gallery.

21. Preview the worksheet. Use the Orientation button (Page Layout tab | Page Setup group) to fit the printout on one page in landscape orientation.

22. Change the document properties, as specified by your instructor. Change the worksheet header, adding your name, course number, and other information as specified by your instructor. Save the workbook.

23. Use the Zoom button (View tab | Zoom group) to change the view of the worksheet. One by one, select all the percents on the Zoom dialog box. When you are done, return the worksheet to 100% magnification.

24. Preview the formulas version (CTRL+`) in landscape orientation. Close the worksheet without saving the latest changes.

25. Submit the workbook as specified by your instructor.

Instructions Part 2:   Start Excel. Open Lab 3-3 Dinah's Weekly Inventory Report Complete. Do not save the workbook in this part. Using the numbers in Table 3–15, analyze the effect of changing the Sales Threshold in cell B3. The first case should result in a Suggested Reorder in cell E15 of 0. The second case should result in a Suggested Reorder in cell E15 of 3. Close the workbook without saving changes. Submit the results of the what-if analysis as specified by your instructor.

Table 3–15 The Dinah's Candle Depot's Sales Threshold Cases	
Case	Sales Threshold
1	30%
2	15%

Instructions Part 3:   Submit results for this part as requested by your instructor.

1. Start Excel. Open Lab 3-3 Dinah's Weekly Inventory Report Complete. Select cell E8. Write down the formula that Excel displays in the formula bar. Select the range D8:D15. Point to the border surrounding the range and drag the selection to the range E17:E24. Click cell E8, and write down the formula that Excel displays in the formula bar below the one you wrote down earlier. Compare the two formulas. What can you conclude about how Excel responds when you move cells involved in a formula? Click the Undo button on the Quick Access Toolbar.

2. Right-click the range D8:D15 and then click Delete on the shortcut menu. When Excel displays the Delete dialog box, click Shift cells left and then click the OK button. What does Excel display in cell D8? Click cell D8 and then point to the Trace Error button that is displayed to the left of the cell. Write down the ScreenTip that is displayed. Click the Undo button on the Quick Access Toolbar.

3. Right-click the range D8:D15 and then click Insert on the shortcut menu. When Excel displays the Insert dialog box, click 'Shift cells right' and then click the OK button. What does Excel display in the formula bar when you click cell F8? What can you conclude about how Excel responds when you insert cells next to cells involved in a formula? Close the workbook without saving the changes.

Cases and Places

Apply your creative thinking and problem solving skills to design and implement a solution.

1: Bachelor Degree Expense and Resource Projection

Academic

Attending college with limited resources can be a trying experience. One way to alleviate some of the financial stress is to plan ahead. Develop a worksheet following the general layout in Table 3–16 that shows the projected expenses and resources for four years of college. Use the formulas listed in Table 3–17 and the concepts and techniques presented in this chapter to create the worksheet.

Table 3–16 Bachelor Degree Expense and Resource Projection

Expenses	Freshman	Sophomore	Junior	Senior	Total
Room & Board	$12,550.00	Formula A ⟶			—
Tuition & Books	16,450.00	Formula A ⟶			—
Clothes	785.00	Formula A ⟶			—
Entertainment	1,520.00	Formula A ⟶			—
Miscellaneous	936.00	Formula A ⟶			—
Total Expenses	—	—	—	—	—
Resources	**Freshman**	**Sophomore**	**Junior**	**Senior**	**Total**
Savings	Formula B ⟶				
Parents	Formula B ⟶				—
Job	Formula B ⟶				—
Loans	Formula B ⟶				—
Scholarships	Formula B ⟶				—
Total Resources	—	—	—	—	—

Assumptions

Savings	10.00%
Parents	12.00%
Job	11.00%
Loans	35.00%
Scholarships	32.00%
Annual Rate Increase	8.25%

Table 3–17 Bachelor Degree Expense and Resource Projection Formulas

Formula A = Prior Year's Expense * (1 + Annual Rate Increase)

Formula B = Total Expenses for Year * Corresponding Assumption

After creating the worksheet: (a) perform what-if analysis by changing the percents of the resource assumptions; (b) perform a what-if analysis to determine the effect on the resources by increasing the Annual Rate Increase to 9.95% (answer = $149,520.41); and (c) with the original assumptions, goal seek to determine what the Annual Rate Increase would be for the total expenses to be $175,000 (answer = 20.77%). Submit the workbook and results of the what-if analysis as specified by your instructor.

Continued >

Cases and Places *continued*

2: Fuel Cost Analysis

Personal

You are thinking about buying a new vehicle, and you want to make sure that you get the most fuel savings you can find. You know that there are hybrid vehicles available and so you decide to research them as well as gas-only cars. Your friends also are interested in the results. Together, you decide to research the fuel costs associated with various types of vehicles. Research the gas mileage for six vehicles: three should run only on gas, and the others should be hybrid vehicles, combining gas and battery power. After you find the gas mileage for each vehicle, you will use formulas to calculate the fuel cost for 1 month, 1 year, and three years. Assume that in a typical month, you will drive 400 miles and that the average price of gas is $2.69 per gallon. Develop a worksheet following the general layout in Table 3–18 that shows the fuel cost analysis. Use the formulas listed in Table 3–19 and the concepts and techniques presented in this chapter to create the worksheet. Add a 3-D line chart showing the cost comparisons as an embedded chart.

Table 3–18 Fuel Cost Analysis				
Vehicle	Miles Per Gallon	1 Month	1 Year	3 Year
Ford Expedition	17	Formula A	Formula B	Formula C
Dodge RAM 1500	20	---	---	---
Honda Civic	31	---	---	---
Chevy Silverado Hybrid	21	---	---	---
Ford Fusion Hybrid	41	---	---	---
Honda Civic Hybrid	45	---	---	---
Assumptions				
Distance per Month	400			
Price of Gas	$2.69			

Table 3–19 Fuel Cost Analysis Formulas
Formula A = (Distance per Month / Miles per Gallon)*Price of Gas
Formula B = ((Distance per Month / Miles per Gallon)*Price of Gas)*12
Formula C = ((Distance Per Month / Miles per Gallon)*Price of Gas)*36

3: Quarterly Income Projections

Professional

Notable Web Site Design is one of the largest Web site design and Web site hosting companies in the Midwest. The company generates revenue from Web site design and selling Web site hosting space on their Web servers. A fixed percentage of the total net revenue is spent on administrative, equipment, marketing, payroll, and production expenses. A bonus is expensed if the total net revenue for the quarter exceeds $14,000,000. The company's projected receipts and expenditures for the next four quarters are shown in Table 3–20.

With this data, you have been asked to prepare a worksheet similar to Figure 3–87 on page EX 210 for the next management team meeting. The worksheet should show total net revenues, total expenditures, and operating income for each quarterly period. Include a 3-D Pie chart on a separate sheet that shows the quarterly income contributions to the annual operating income. Use the concepts and techniques presented in this chapter to create and format the worksheet and chart.

During the meeting, one manager lobbied to reduce marketing expenditures by 1.25% and payroll costs by 2.75%. Perform a what-if analysis reflecting the proposed changes in expenditures. The changes should result in an operating income of $22,425,581 for the year. Using the original assumptions shown in Table 3–20, another manager asked to what extent marketing would have to be reduced to generate an annual operating income of $21,000,000. Marketing would to be reduced from 13.50% by 1.92% to 11.58%.

Submit the workbook and results of the what-if analysis as specified by your instructor.

Table 3–20 Notable Website Design Operating Income Projection by Quarter				
Revenues	**Quarter 1**	**Quarter 2**	**Quarter 3**	**Quarter 4**
Site Design	12,247,999	15,234,813	16,567,102	10,619,201
Web Hosting	1,678,153	5,901,988	4,718,231	1,569,378
Expenditures				
Administrative	10.50%			
Bonus	250,000.00			
Equipment	17.75%			
Marketing	13.50%			
Payroll	22.50%			
Production	6.30%			
Revenue for Bonus	14,000,000.00			

4 Financial Functions, Data Tables, and Amortization Schedules

Objectives

You will have mastered the material in this chapter when you can:

- Control the color and thickness of outlines and borders

- Assign a name to a cell and refer to the cell in a formula using the assigned name

- Determine the monthly payment of a loan using the financial function PMT

- Use the financial functions PV (present value) and FV (future value)

- Create a data table to analyze data in a worksheet

- Add a pointer to a data table

- Create an amortization schedule

- Analyze worksheet data by changing values

- Use names and print sections of a worksheet

- Set print options

- Protect and unprotect cells in a worksheet

- Use the formula checking features of Excel

- Hide and unhide cell gridlines, rows, columns, sheets, and workbooks

4 | Financial Functions, Data Tables, and Amortization Schedules

Introduction

Two of the more powerful aspects of Excel are its wide array of functions and its capability of organizing answers to what-if questions. In this chapter, you will learn about financial functions such as the PMT function, which allows you to determine a monthly payment for a loan, and the PV function, which allows you to determine the present value of an investment.

In earlier chapters, you learned how to analyze data by using Excel's recalculation feature and goal seeking. This chapter introduces an additional what-if analysis tool, called data tables. You use a **data table** to automate data analyses and organize the answers returned by Excel. Another important loan analysis tool is an amortization schedule. An **amortization schedule** shows the beginning and ending balances and the amount of payment that is applied to the principal and interest over a period.

In previous chapters, you learned how to print in a variety of ways. In this chapter, you will learn additional methods of printing using range names and a print area.

Finally, this chapter introduces you to cell protection; hiding and unhiding rows, columns, sheets, and workbooks; and formula checking. **Cell protection** ensures that users do not change values inadvertently that are critical to the worksheet. **Hiding** portions of a workbook lets you show only the parts of the workbook that the user needs to see. The **formula checker** examines the formulas in a workbook in a manner similar to the way the spell checker examines a workbook for misspelled words.

Project — Loan Payment Calculator with Data Table and Amortization Schedule

The project in the chapter follows proper design guidelines and uses Excel to create the worksheet shown in Figure 4–1. FT Financial Services provides loans for homes and other types of property. The company's chief financial officer has asked for a workbook that calculates loan payment information, displays an amortization schedule, and displays a table that shows loan payments for varying interest rates. To ensure that the loan officers do not delete the formulas in the worksheet, she has asked that cells in the worksheet be protected so that they cannot be changed accidentally.

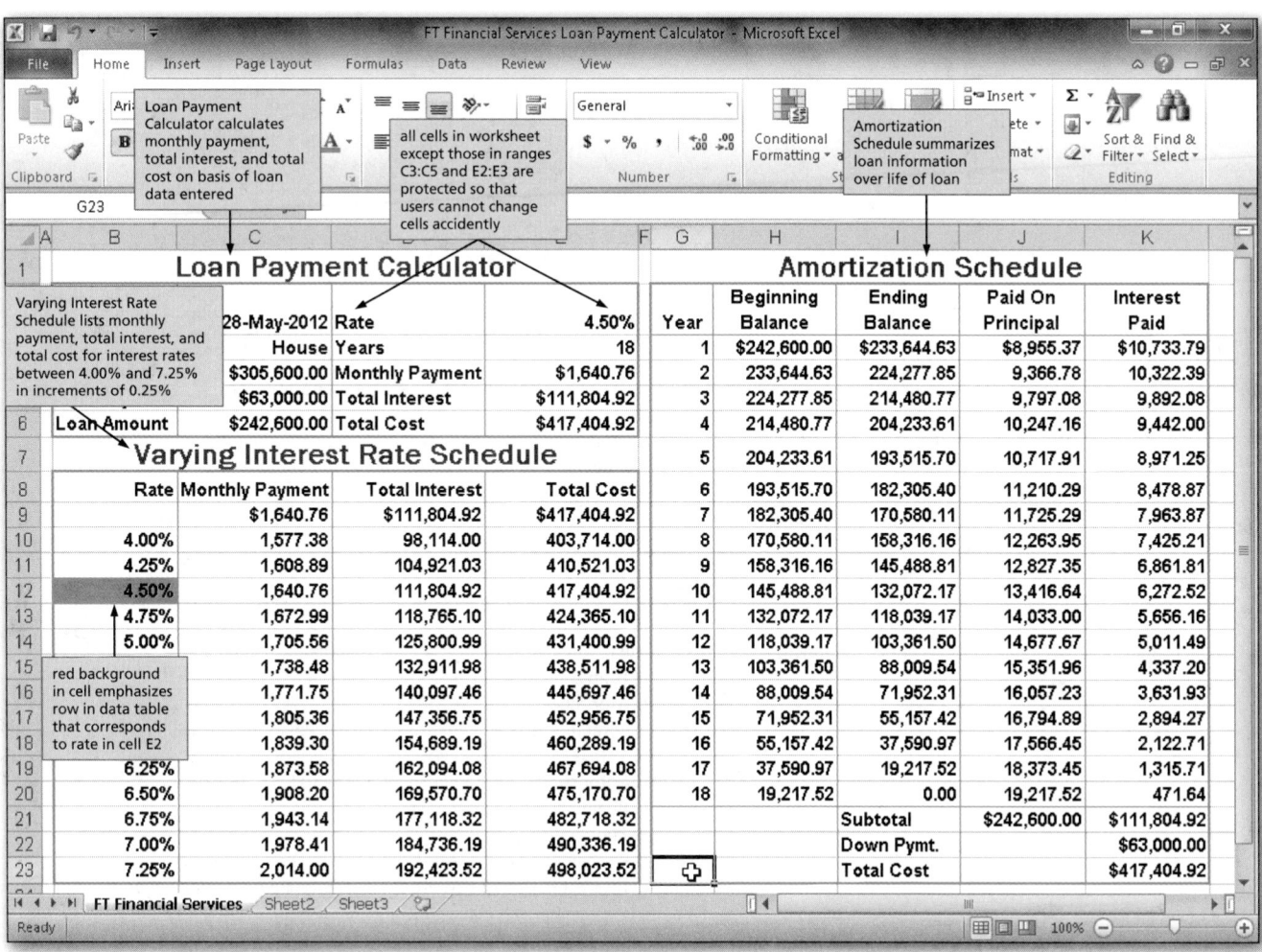

Figure 4–1

The requirements document for the FT Financial Services Loan Payment Calculator worksheet is shown in Figure 4–2 on the following page. It includes the needs, source of data, summary of calculations, special requirements, and other facts about its development.

REQUEST FOR NEW WORKBOOK

Date Submitted:	May 14, 2012
Submitted By:	Samuel Clewes, Jr.
Worksheet Title:	Loan Payment Calculator
Needs:	An easy-to-read worksheet (Figure 4-3 on page EX 230) that: 1. determines the monthly payment, total interest, and total cost for a loan; 2. shows a data table that answers what-if questions based on changing interest rates; 3. highlights the rate in the data table that matches the actual interest rate; 4. shows an amortization schedule that lists annual summaries.
Source of Data:	The data (item, price of the item, down payment, interest rate, and term of the loan in years) is determined by the loan officer and customer when they initially meet to review the loan. The Excel Data Table command creates the data table in the varying interest rate schedule.

Calculations:	1. The following calculations must be made for each loan:
	  a. Loan Amount = Price − Down Payment
	  b. Monthly Payment = PMT function
	  c. Total Interest = 12 × Years × Monthly Payment − Loan Amount
	  d. Total Cost = 12 × Years x Monthly Payment + Down Payment
	2. The amortization schedule involves the following calculations:
	  a. Beginning Balance = Loan Amount
	  b. Ending Balance = PV function or 0
	  c. Paid on Principal = Beginning Balance − Ending Balance
	  d. Interest Paid = 12 × Monthly Payment − Paid on Principal or 0
	  e. Paid on Principal Subtotal = SUM function
	  f. Interest Paid Subtotal = SUM function

Special Requirements	1. Assign names to the ranges of the three major sections of the worksheet and the worksheet itself, so that the names can be used to print each section separately. 2. Protect the worksheet in such a way that the loan officers cannot enter data into wrong cells mistakenly.

Approvals

Approval Status:	X	Approved
		Rejected
Approved By:	Donna Demers, Chief Information Officer	
Date:	May 21, 2012	
Assigned To:	J. Quasney, Spreadsheet Specialist	

Figure 4–2

Overview

As you read this chapter, you will learn how to create the worksheet shown in Figure 4–1 on page EX 227 by performing these general tasks:

- Create and format the Loan Payment Calculator section and use the payment function.
- Create and format a data table that includes the varying interest rate schedule.
- Create and format the amortization schedule and use the present value and future value functions.
- Create and test print areas in the worksheet.
- Protect cells in the worksheet.
- Check the formulas in the worksheet.

Plan Ahead

General Project Guidelines
While creating an Excel worksheet, the actions you perform and decisions you make will affect the appearance and characteristics of the finished worksheet. As you create the worksheet required to meet the requirements shown in Figure 4–2, you should follow these general guidelines:

1. **Create and format the data entry section of the worksheet.** A data entry section of a worksheet includes data items entered by a user of a worksheet. Place such data items in close proximity to each other on a worksheet so that the worksheet does not require the user to search for data items to enter. Format or delineate each section of a worksheet to make it distinct from the other sections of the worksheet. Cell borders help to set off sections of a worksheet.

2. **Create and format the data table section of the worksheet.** While Excel does not require that a data table have column or row headings, use them when possible in order to clarify the meaning of data in a data table. Cell borders or fill colors help to set off values computed in a data table.

3. **Create and format an amortization schedule in the worksheet.** Because an amortization schedule often includes complex formulas and functions, use descriptive column and row headings for the schedule. When possible, include subtotals and totals that allow a user of the worksheet quickly to find important results of what-if calculations.

4. **Specify and name print areas of the worksheet.** When users of the worksheet require the option to print the individual sections of the worksheet, name these sections and then print the sections by name. The ability of Excel to use range names to specify sections of a worksheet, such as a data table, makes printing easier for the user of the worksheet. Also, you quickly can modify range names when you add columns or rows to sections of the worksheet.

5. **Determine which cells to protect and unprotect in the worksheet.** When creating a workbook for use by others, the spreadsheet designer should consider which cells another user of the worksheet should be able to manipulate. Leave such cells unprotected. Protect all other cells in the worksheet from input by the user of the worksheet.

When necessary, more specific details concerning the above guidelines are presented at appropriate points in the chapter. The chapter also will identify the actions performed and decisions made regarding these guidelines during the creation of the worksheet shown in Figure 4–1 on page EX 227.

In addition, using a sketch of the worksheet can help you visualize its design. The sketch of the worksheet consists of titles, column and cell headings, the location of data values, and a general idea of the desired formatting (Figure 4–3).

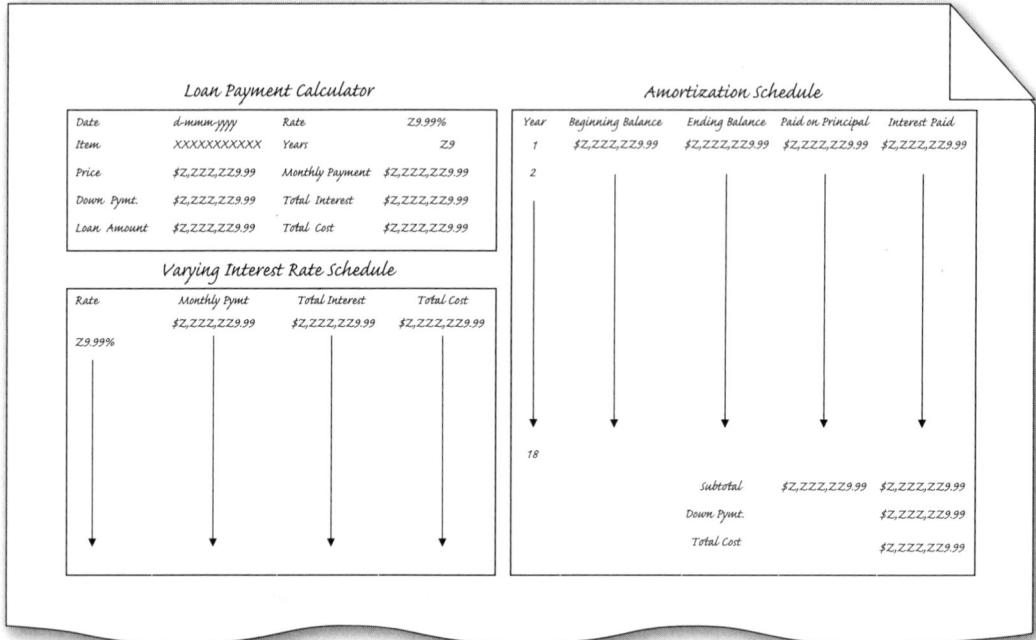

Figure 4–3

As shown in the worksheet sketch in Figure 4–3, the three basic sections of the worksheet are (1) the Loan Payment Calculator on the upper-left side, (2) the Varying Interest Rate Schedule data table on the lower-left side, and (3) the Amortization Schedule on the right side. The worksheet will be created in this order.

With a good understanding of the requirements document, an understanding of the necessary decisions, and a sketch of the worksheet, the next step is to use Excel to create the worksheet.

To Start Excel

If you are using a computer to step through the project in this chapter and you want your screens to match the figures in this book, you should change your screen's resolution to 1024 × 768. The following steps, which assume Windows 7 is running, start Excel based on a typical installation. You may need to ask your instructor how to start Excel for your computer.

1 Click the Start button on the Windows 7 taskbar to display the Start menu.

2 Type **Microsoft Excel** as the search text in the 'Search programs and files' text box, and watch the search results appear on the Start menu.

3 Click Microsoft Excel 2010 in the search results on the Start menu to start Excel and display a new blank workbook in the Excel window.

4 If the Excel window is not maximized, click the Maximize button next to the Close button on its title bar to maximize the window.

To Apply a Theme and Bold the Entire Worksheet

The following steps apply the Technic theme to the workbook and assign a bold format to the entire worksheet so that all entries will be emphasized.

1 Apply the Technic theme to the workbook.

2 Click the Select All button immediately above row heading 1 and to the left of column heading A to select the entire worksheet.

3 Click the Bold button (Home tab | Font group) to bold the entire worksheet.

BTW

Global Formatting
To assign formats to all the cells in all the worksheets in a workbook, click the Select All button, right-click a sheet tab, and click Select All Sheets on the shortcut menu. Next, assign the formats. To deselect the sheets, hold down the SHIFT key and click the Sheet1 tab. You also can select a cell or a range of cells and then select all sheets to assign formats to that cell or a range of cells on all sheets in a workbook.

To Enter the Section and Row Titles and System Date

The next step is to enter the Loan Payment Calculator section title, row titles, and system date. To make the worksheet easier to read, the width of column A will be decreased and used as a separator between the Loan Payment Calculator section and the row headings on the left. Using a column as a separator between sections on a worksheet is a common technique employed by spreadsheet specialists. The width of columns B through E will be increased so that the intended values fit. The height of row 1, which contains the title, will be increased so that it stands out. The Loan Payment Calculator section title also will be changed to the Title cell style and vertically middle-aligned.

The following steps enter the section title, row titles, and system date.

1 Select cell B1 and then type **Loan Payment Calculator** as the section title.

2 Select the range B1:E1 and then click the Merge & Center button (Home tab | Alignment group) to merge and center the section title in the selected range.

3 Click the Cell Styles button (Home tab | Styles group) and then click Title cell style in the Cell Styles gallery to apply the selected style to the active cell.

4 Click the Middle Align button (Home tab | Alignment group) to vertically center the text in the selected cell.

5 Position the mouse pointer on the bottom boundary of row heading 1 and then drag up until the ScreenTip indicates Height: 20.25 (27 pixels) to change the row height.

6 Position the mouse pointer on the bottom boundary of row heading 2 and then drag down until the ScreenTip indicates Height: 30.00 (40 pixels) to change the row height.

7 Select cell B2, Type **Date** as the row title, and then press the TAB key to complete the entry in the cell and select the cell to the right.

8 With cell C2 selected, type **=now()** and then click the Enter box to add a function to the cell that displays the system date.

9 Right–click cell C2 to open a shortcut menu and then click Format Cells on the shortcut menu to display the Format Cells dialog box. If necessary, click the Number tab to display the Number sheet, click Date in the Category list, scroll down in the Type list, and then click 14-Mar–2001 to select a date format.

10 Click the OK button (Format Cells dialog box) to close the Format Cells dialog box.

The Ribbon and Screen Resolution
Excel may change how the groups and buttons within the groups appear on the Ribbon, depending on the computer's screen resolution. Thus, your Ribbon may look different from the ones in this book if you are using a screen resolution other than 1024 x 768.

(11) Enter the following text in the indicated cells:

Cell	text	Cell	text
		D2	Rate
B3	Item	D3	Years
B4	Price	D4	Monthly Payment
B5	Down Pymt.	D5	Total Interest
B6	Loan Amount	D6	Total Cost

(12) Position the mouse pointer on the right boundary of column heading A and then drag to the left until the ScreenTip indicates Width: .77 (10 pixels) to change the column width.

(13) Position the mouse pointer on the right boundary of column heading B and then drag to the right until the ScreenTip indicates Width: 12.13 (102 pixels) to change the column width.

BTWs
For a complete list of the BTWs found in the margins of this book, visit the Excel 2010 BTW Web page (scsite.com/ex2010/btw).

(14) Click column heading C to select it and then drag through column headings D and E to select multiple columns. Position the mouse pointer on the right boundary of column heading C and then drag until the ScreenTip indicates Width: 15.00 (125 pixels) to change multiple column widths (Figure 4–4).

(15) Click cell B2 to deselect the selected columns.

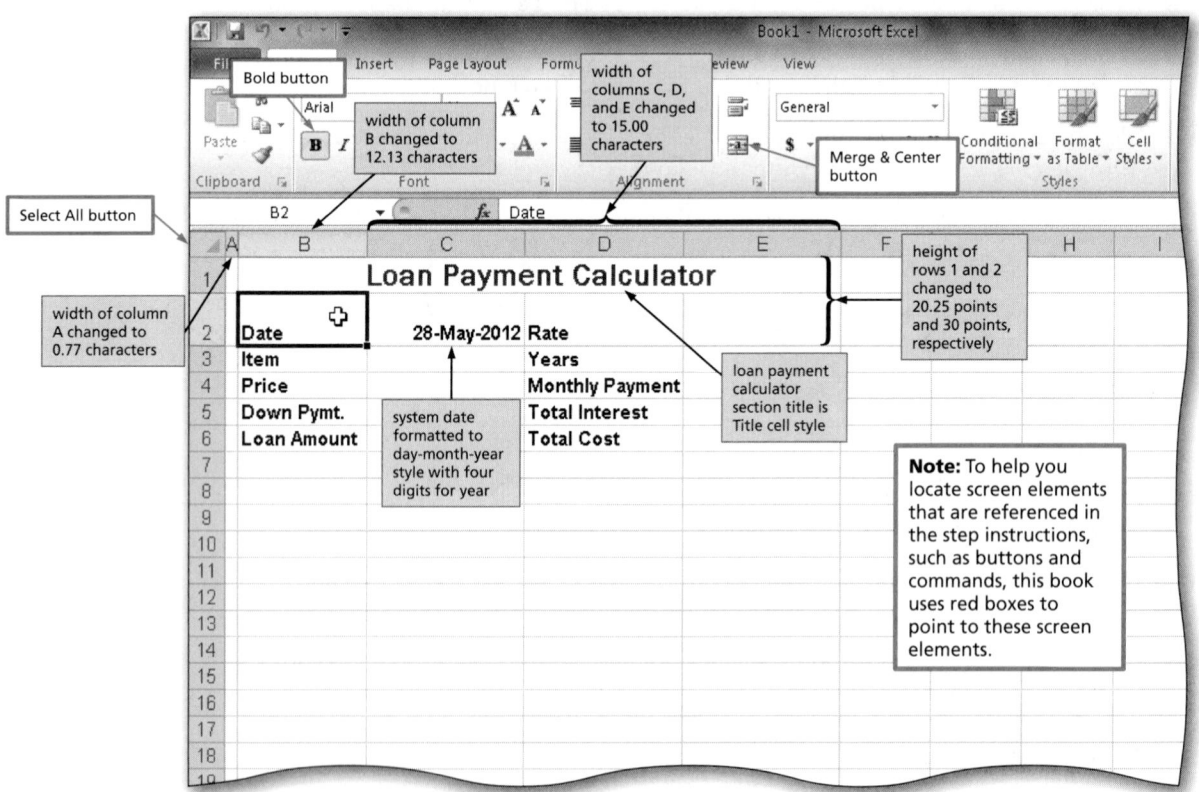

Figure 4–4

To Change the Sheet Name, Enter Document Properties, and Save the Workbook

The following steps change the Sheet1 name to a meaningful name, enter document properties, and then save the workbook.

1 Double-click the Sheet1 tab and then enter **FT Financial Services** as the sheet name.

2 Right-click the tab to display a shortcut menu and then point to Tab Color on the shortcut menu. Click Red (column 2, row 1) in the Standard Colors area to change the sheet tab color (Figure 4–5).

3 Change the document properties as specified by your instructor.

4 With a USB flash drive connected to one of the computer's USB ports, click the Save button on the Quick Access Toolbar to display the Save As dialog box.

5 Type **FT Financial Services Loan Payment Calculator** in the File name text box to change the file name. Do not press the ENTER key after typing the file name because you do not want to close the dialog box at this time.

6 Navigate to the desired save location (in this case, the Excel folder in the CIS 101 folder [or your class folder] on the USB flash drive).

7 Click the Save button (Save As dialog box) to save the document in the selected folder on the selected drive with the entered file name.

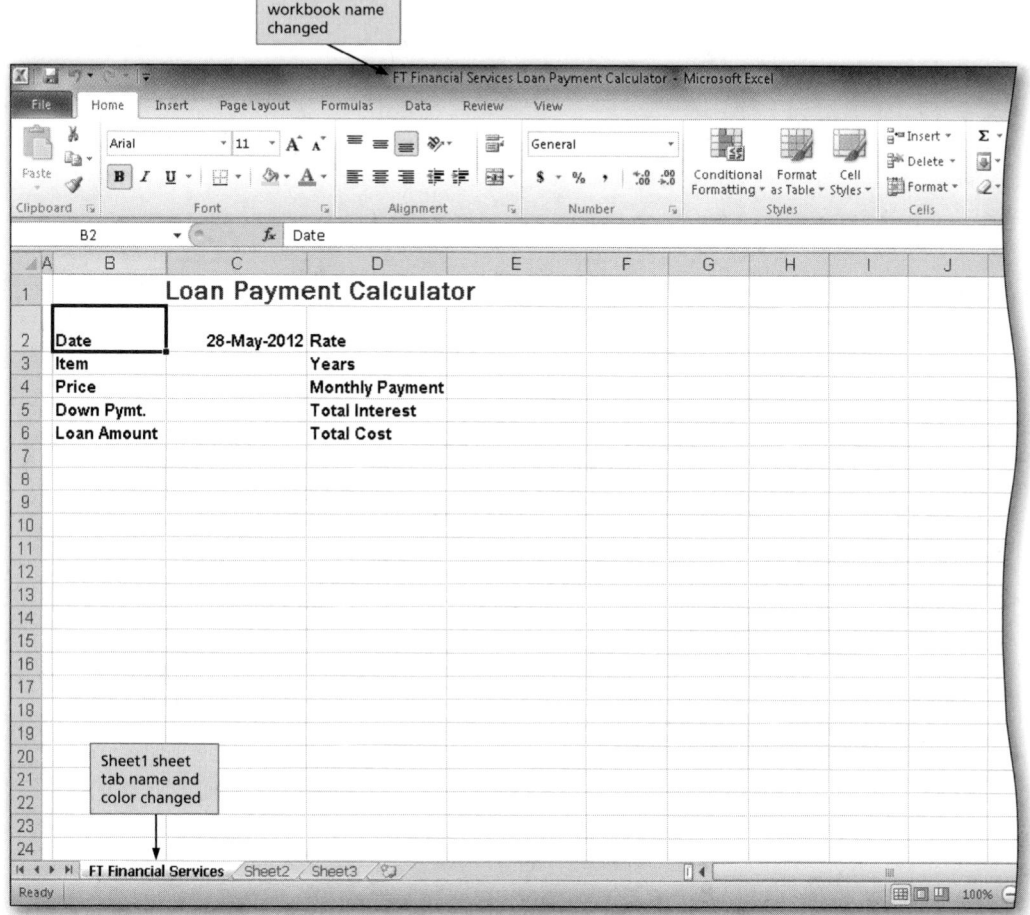

Figure 4–5

BTW

Cell References in Formulas

Are you tired of writing formulas that make no sense when you read them because of cell references? The Name Manager can help add clarity to your formulas by allowing you to assign names to cells. You then can use the names, such as Rate, rather than the cell reference, such as D2, in the formulas you create. To access the Name Manager, click the Name Manager button (Formulas tab | Defined Names).

Adding Custom Borders to a Range and Creating Cell Names

Previous chapters introduced you to outlining a range using cell borders or cell background colors to differentiate portions of a worksheet. The Borders button (Home tab | Font group), however, offers only a limited selection of border thicknesses. To control the color and thickness, Excel requires that you use the Border sheet in the Format Cells dialog box.

Worksheets often have column titles at the top of each column and row titles to the left of each row that describe the data within the worksheet. You can use these titles within formulas when you want to refer to the related data by name. A cell **name** often is created from column and row titles. You also can define descriptive names that are not column titles or row titles to represent cells, ranges of cells, formulas, or constants.

To Add Custom Borders to a Range

The following steps add a thick red border to the Loan Payment Calculator section. To subdivide the row titles and numbers further, light borders also are added within the section, as shown in Figure 4–1 on page EX 227.

1

- Select the range B2:E6 and then right–click to display a shortcut menu and Mini toolbar (Figure 4–6).

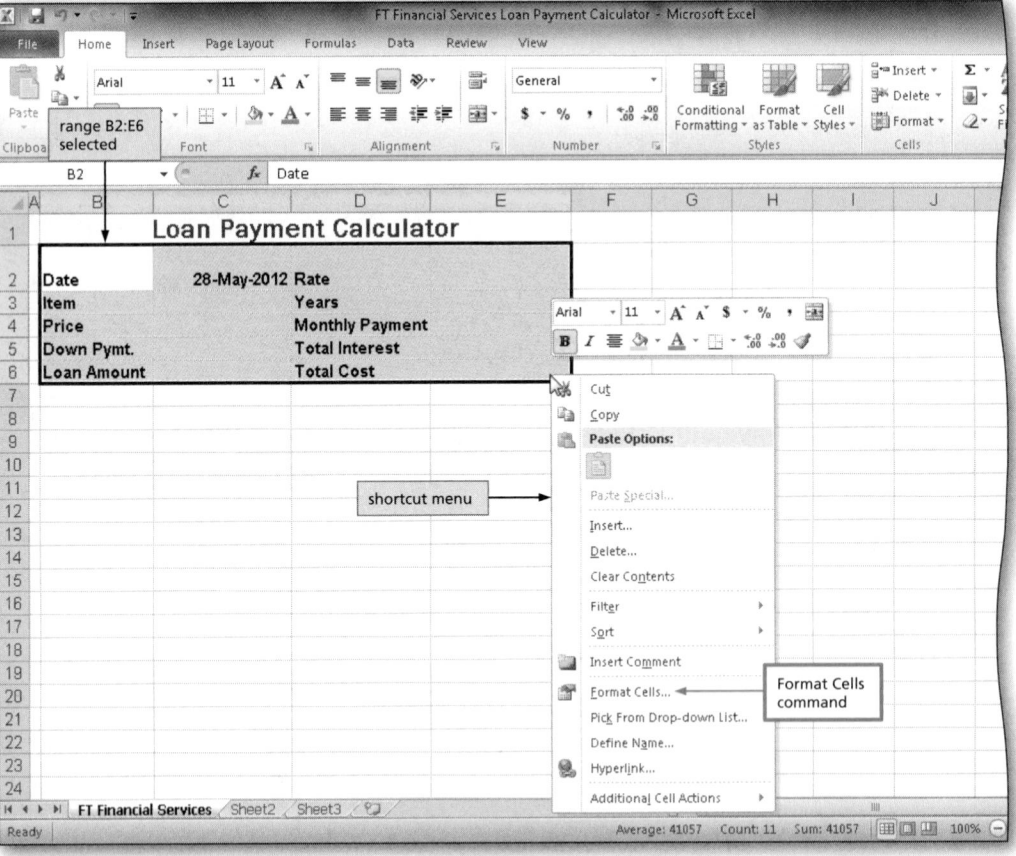

Figure 4–6

2

- Click Format Cells on the shortcut menu to display the Format Cells dialog box.

- Display the Border tab (Format Cells dialog box).

- Click the Color box arrow to display the Colors palette and then select the red color in the Standard Colors area.

- Click the medium border in the Style area (column 2, row 5) (Format Cells dialog box) to select the line style for the border.

- Click the Outline button in the Presets area (Format Cells dialog box) to display a preview of the outline border in the Border area (Figure 4–7).

Figure 4–7

3

- Click the light border in the Style area (column 1, row 7) (Format Cells dialog box) and then click the Vertical Line button in the Border area to preview the red vertical border in the Border area (Figure 4–8).

Q&A

How should I create my desired border?

As shown in Figure 4–8, you can add a variety of borders with different colors to a cell or range of cells to improve its appearance. It is important that you select border characteristics in the order specified in the steps; that is, (1) choose the border color, (2) choose the border line style, and (3) choose the border type. If you attempt to do these steps in any other order, you may not end up with the desired borders.

Figure 4–8

4

- Click the OK button (Format Cells dialog box) to add a red outline with vertical borders to the right side of each column in the selected range, B2:E6 in this case (Figure 4–9).

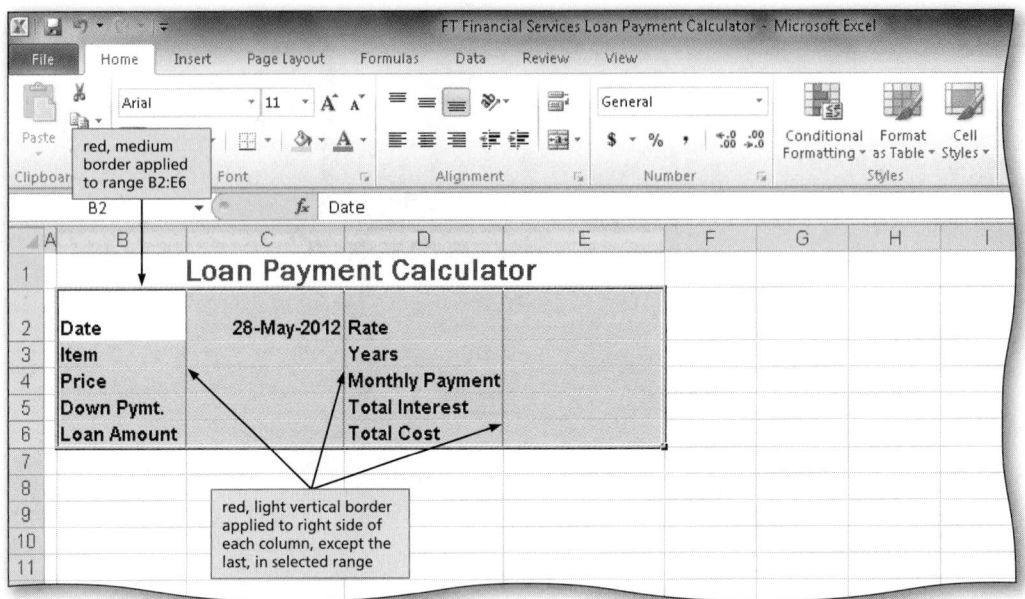

Figure 4–9

Other Ways

1. Select range, click Borders button arrow (Home tab | Font group), click border

2. Click Format Cells: Font Dialog Box Launcher (Home tab | Font group), click Border tab, click border

To Format Cells Before Entering Values

Q&As
For a complete list of the Q&As found in many of the step-by-step sequences in this book, visit the Excel 2010 Q&A Web page (scsite.com/ex2010/qa)

While usually you format cells after you enter values in cells, Excel also allows you to format cells before you enter the values. For example, at the beginning of this chapter, bold was applied to all the cells in the blank worksheet. The following steps assign the Currency style format with a floating dollar sign to the ranges C4:C6 and E4:E6 before the values are entered.

1 Select the range C4:C6 and, while holding down the CTRL key, select the nonadjacent range E4:E6.

2 Right-click one of the selected ranges to display a shortcut menu and then click Format Cells on the shortcut menu to display the Format Cells dialog box.

3 Click the Number tab (Format Cells dialog box) to display the Number sheet, select Currency in the Category list, and then select the second format, $1,234.10, in the Negative numbers list.

4 Click the OK button (Format Cells dialog box) to assign the Currency style format with a floating dollar sign to the selected ranges, C4:C6 and E4:E6 in this case.

When to Format
Excel lets you format (1) before you enter data; (2) when you enter data, through the use of format symbols; (3) incrementally after entering sections of data; and (4) after you enter all the data. Spreadsheet specialists usually format a worksheet in increments as they build the worksheet, but occasions do exist where it makes sense to format cells before you enter any data.

Q&A

What will happen when I enter values in the cells that were formatted in these steps?

As you enter numbers into these cells, Excel will display the numbers using the Currency style format. You also could have selected the range B4:E6 rather than the nonadjacent ranges and assigned the Currency style format to this range, which includes text. The Currency style format has no impact on text in a cell.

To Enter the Loan Data

As shown in the Source of Data section of the Request for New Workbook document in Figure 4–2 on page EX 228, five items make up the loan data in the worksheet: the item to be purchased, the price of the item, the down payment, the interest rate, and the number of years until the loan is paid back (also called the term of the loan). These items are entered into cells C3 through C5 and cells E2 and E3. The steps below enter the following loan data: Item — House; Price — $305,600.00; Down Pymt. — $63,000.00; Interest Rate — 4.50%; and Years — 18.

1 Select cell C3. Type **House** and then click the Enter box in the formula bar to enter text in the selected cell.

2 With cell C3 still active, click the Align Text Right button (Home tab | Alignment group) to right-align the text in the selected cell.

3 Select cell C4 and then enter **305600** for the price of the house.

4 Select cell C5 and then enter **63000** for the down payment.

5 Select cell E2 and then enter **4.50%** for the interest rate.

6 Select cell E3 and then enter **18** for the number of years.

7 Click the Enter box in the formula bar to complete the entry of data in the worksheet (Figure 4–10).

Q&A Why are the entered values already formatted?

The values in cells C4 and C5 in Figure 4–10 are formatted using the Currency style with two decimal places, because this format was assigned to the cells prior to entering the values. Excel also automatically formats the interest rate in cell E2 to the Percent style with two decimal places, because the percent sign (%) was appended to 4.50 when it was entered.

Q&A Do lenders provide 18-year loans?

While not as popular as 30-year, 20-year, or 15-year mortgages, many lending institutions offer 18-year loans. The reasons for choosing a particular length for a loan depend on several factors, including the goals of the recipient of the loan. A person who is wavering between a 15-year and 20-year loan may choose an 18-year loan as a preferable solution.

BTW

Entering Percents
When you format a cell to display percentages, Excel assumes that whatever you enter into that cell in the future will be a percentage. Thus, if you enter the number .5, Excel translates the value as 50%. A potential problem arises, however, when you start to enter numbers greater than or equal to one. For instance, if you enter the number 25, do you mean 25% or 2500%? If you want Excel to treat the number 25 as 25% instead of 2500% and Excel interprets the number 25 as 2500%, then click the Options in the Backstage View. When the Excel Options dialog box appears, click Advanced in the left pane, and make sure the 'Enable automatic percent entry' check box in the right pane is selected.

BTW

Entering Interest Rates
An alternative to requiring the user to enter an interest rate in percent form, such as 4.50%, is to allow the user to enter the interest rate as a number without an appended percent sign (4.50) and then divide the interest rate by 1200, rather than 12.

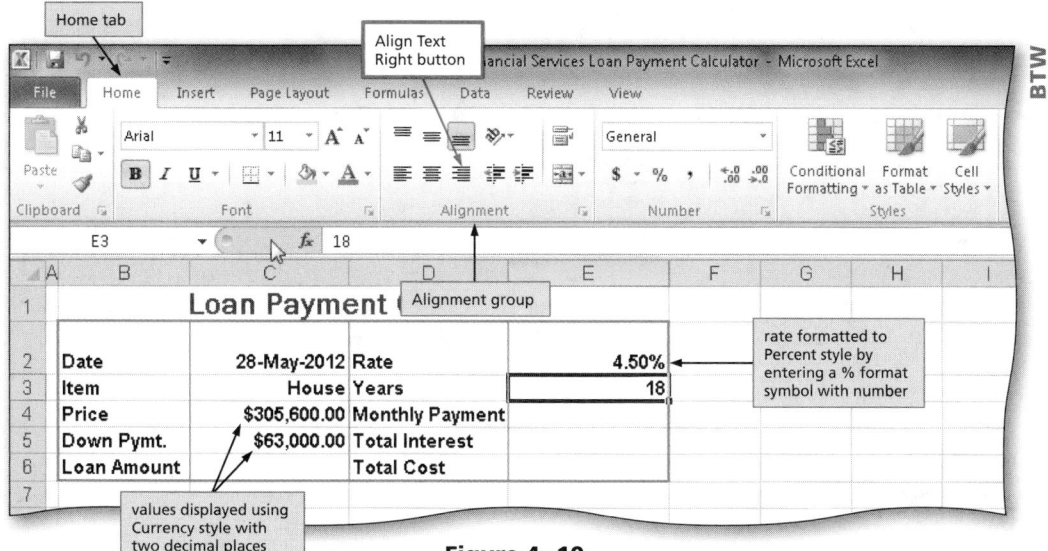

Figure 4–10

To Create Names Based on Row Titles

Naming a cell that you plan to reference in a formula helps make the formula easier to read and remember. For example, the loan amount in cell C6 is equal to the price in cell C4 minus the down payment in cell C5. According to what you learned in earlier projects, you can enter the loan amount formula in cell C6 as =C4 – C5. By naming cells C4 and C5 using the corresponding row titles in cells B4 and B5, however, you can enter the loan amount formula as =Price – Down_Pymt., which is clearer and easier to understand than =C4 – C5.

The following steps assign the row titles in the range B4:B6 to their adjacent cell in column C and assign the row titles in the range D2:D6 to their adjacent cell in column E.

1

- Select the range B4:C6.

- Display the Formulas tab (Figure 4–11).

Figure 4–11

2

- Click the Create from Selection button (Formulas tab | Defined Names group) to display the Create Names from Selection dialog box (Figure 4–12).

 How does Excel determine which option to select automatically in the Create Names from Selection dialog box?

Excel automatically selects the Left column check box in the 'Create names from values in the' area because the left column of the cells selected in Step 1 contains text.

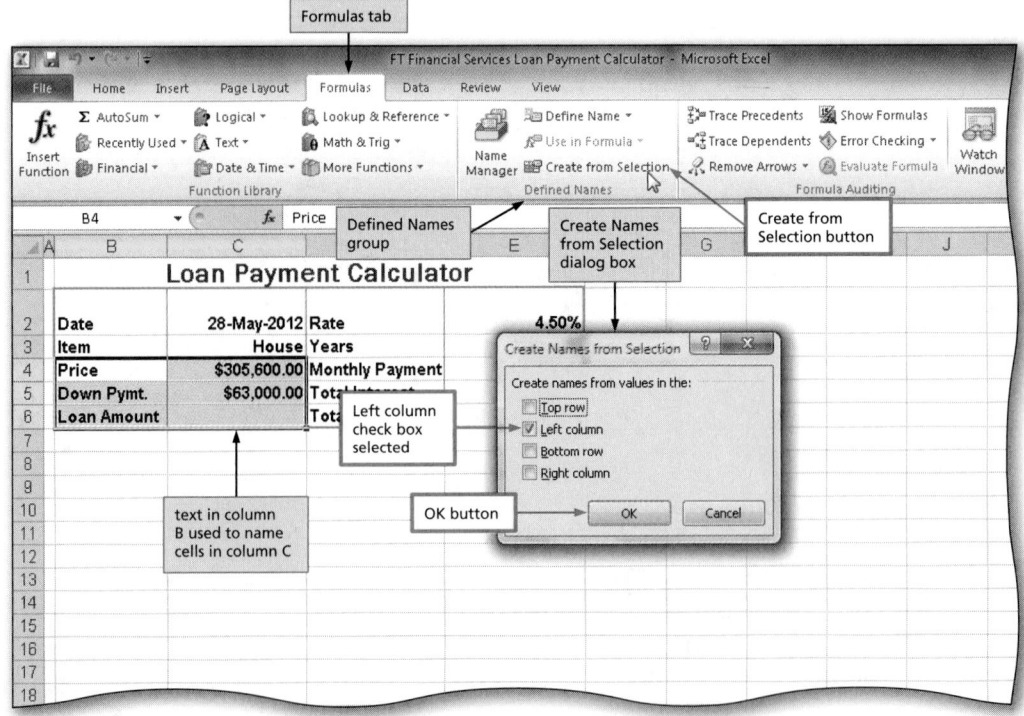

Figure 4–12

3

- Click the OK button (Create Names from Selection dialog box) to name the cells selected in the right column of the selection, C4:C6 in this case.

- Select the range D2:E6 and then click the Create from Selection button (Formulas tab | Defined Names group) to display the Create Names from Selection dialog box.

Figure 4–13 (a)

- Click the OK button (Create Names from Selection dialog box) to assign names to the cells selected in the right column of the selection, E2:E6 in this case.

- Click cell B8 to deselect the selected range and then click the Name box arrow in the formula bar to view the names created (Figure 4–13a).

Figure 4–13 (b)

Q&A How can the cell names be used?

You now can use the assigned names in formulas to reference cells in the ranges C4:C6 or E2:E6. Excel is not case sensitive with respect to names of cells. You, therefore, can enter the names of cells in formulas in uppercase or lowercase letters. To use a name that consists of two or more words in a formula, you should replace any space with the underscore character (_), as this is a commonly used standard for creating cell names. For example, the name, Down Pymt, is written as down_pymt. or Down_Pymt. when you want to reference the adjacent cell C5. The Name Manager dialog box appears when you click the Name Manager button (Figure 4–13b).

Q&A Is the period at the end of the Down_Pymt. cell name valid?

Yes. Periods and underscore characters are allowed in cell names. A cell name may not, however, begin with a period or an underscore.

Other Ways

1. Select cell or range, type name in Name box, press ENTER key

2. Select cell or range, click Define Name button (Formulas tab | Defined Names group), [type name], click OK button (New Name dialog box)

3. Select cell or range, click Name Manager button (Formulas tab | Defined Names group), click New (Name Manager dialog box), [type name], click OK button (New Name dialog box), click Close button (Name Manager dialog box)

Selecting Cells
If you double-click the top of the heavy black border surrounding an active cell, Excel will make the first nonblank cell in the column the active cell. If you double-click the left side of the heavy black border surrounding the active cell, Excel will make the first nonblank cell in the row the active cell. This procedure works in the same fashion for the right border and the bottom border of the active cell.

More about Cell Names

If you enter a formula using Point mode and click a cell that has an assigned name, then Excel will insert the name of the cell rather than the cell reference. Consider these additional points regarding the assignment of names to cells:

1. A name can be a minimum of 1 character to a maximum of 255 characters.

2. If you want to assign a name that is not a text item in an adjacent cell, use the Define Name button (Formulas tab | Defined Names group) (Figure 4–11 on page EX 238) or select the cell or range and then type the name in the Name box in the formula bar.

3. Names are absolute cell references. This is important to remember if you plan to copy formulas that contain names rather than cell references.

4. Excel displays the names in alphabetical order in the Name list when you click the Name box arrow and in the Name Manager dialog box when you click the Name Manager button (Formulas tab | Defined Names group) (Figures 4–13a and 4–13b on the previous page).

5. Names are **global** to the workbook. That is, a name assigned to a cell or cell range on one worksheet in a workbook can be used on other sheets in the same workbook to reference the named cell or range.

Spreadsheet specialists often assign names to a cell or range of cells so that they can select them quickly. If you want to select a cell or range of cells using the assigned name, you can click the Name box arrow (Figure 4–13a) and then click the name of the cell you want to select. This method is similar to using the F5 key to select a cell, but it is much quicker. When you select a name that references a range in the Name list, Excel highlights the range on the worksheet.

To Enter the Loan Amount Formula Using Names

To determine the loan amount in cell C6, subtract the down payment in cell C5 from the price in cell C4. As indicated earlier, this can be done by entering the formula =C4 – C5 or by entering the formula =Price – Down_ Pymt. in cell C6. The following steps enter the formula using Point mode.

- Select cell C6.

- Type = (equal sign), click cell C4, type – (minus sign), and then click cell C5 to display the formula in the selected cell, C6 in this case, and in the formula bar using the names of the cells rather than the cell references (Figure 4–14).

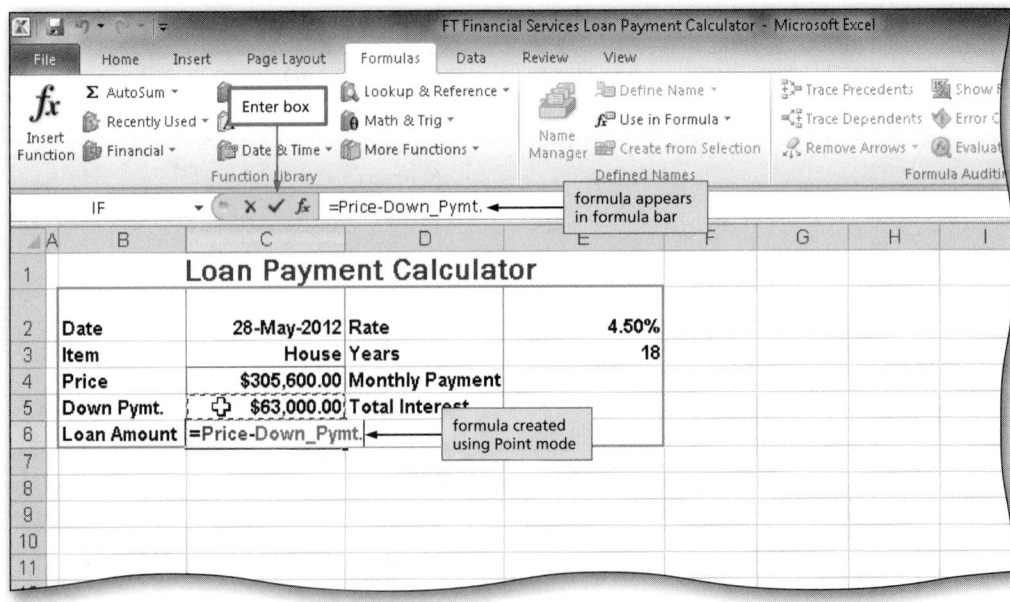

Figure 4–14

2

- Click the Enter box to assign the formula to the selected cell, =Price – Down_Pymt. to cell C6 in this case (Figure 4–15).

Figure 4–15

To Enter the PMT Function

The next step is to determine the monthly payment for the loan in cell E4. You can use Excel's PMT function to determine the monthly payment. The **PMT function** has three arguments: rate, payment, and loan amount. Its general form is as follows:

=PMT(rate, periods, loan amount)

where rate is the interest rate per payment period, periods is the number of payments, and loan amount is the amount of the loan.

In the worksheet shown in Figure 4–15, Excel displays the annual interest rate in cell E2. Financial institutions, however, calculate interest on a monthly basis. The rate value in the PMT function is, therefore, Rate / 12 (cell E2 divided by 12), rather than just Rate (cell E2). The periods (or number of payments) in the PMT function is 12 * Years (12 times cell E3) because each year includes 12 months, or 12 payments, per year.

Excel considers the value returned by the PMT function to be a debit and, therefore, returns a negative number as the monthly payment. To display the monthly payment as a positive number, begin the function with a negative sign instead of an equal sign. The PMT function for cell E4 is:

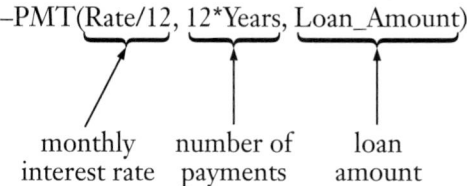

–PMT(Rate/12, 12*Years, Loan_Amount)

    monthly   number of   loan
  interest rate payments amount

The steps on the following page use the keyboard, rather than Point mode or the Insert Function dialog box, to enter the PMT function to determine the monthly payment in cell E4.

1

- Select cell E4.

- Type `-pmt(Rate/12, 12*Years, Loan_Amount` as the function to display the PMT function in the selected cell, E4 in this case, and in the formula bar (Figure 4–16).

Q&A

What happens as I enter the function?

The ScreenTip shows the general form of the PMT function. The arguments in brackets in the ScreenTip are optional and not required for the computation required in this project. The Formula AutoComplete list shows functions and cell names that match the letters that you type on the keyboard. You can type the complete cell name, such as Loan_Amount, or select the cell name from the list. Excel will add the closing parenthesis to the function automatically. Excel also may scroll the worksheet to the right in order to accommodate the display of the ScreenTip.

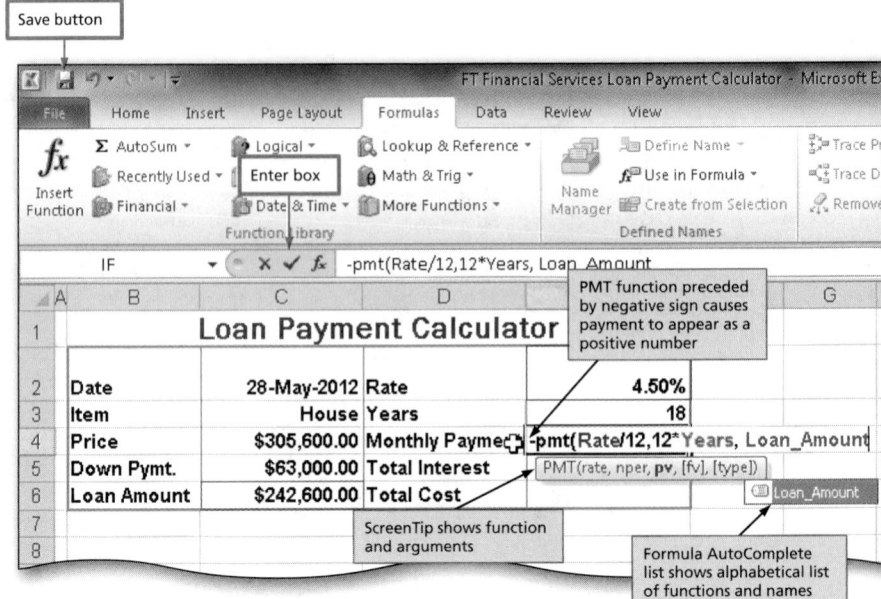

Figure 4–16

2

- If necessary, scroll the worksheet to the far left using the horizontal scroll bar to display column A.

- Click the Enter box in the formula bar to complete the function (Figure 4–17).

Q&A

What does Excel display after I click the Enter box?

Excel displays the monthly payment $1,640.76 in cell E4, based on a loan amount of $242,600.00 (Cell C6) with an annual interest rate of 4.50% (cell E2) for a term of 18 years (cell E3), as shown in Figure 4–17.

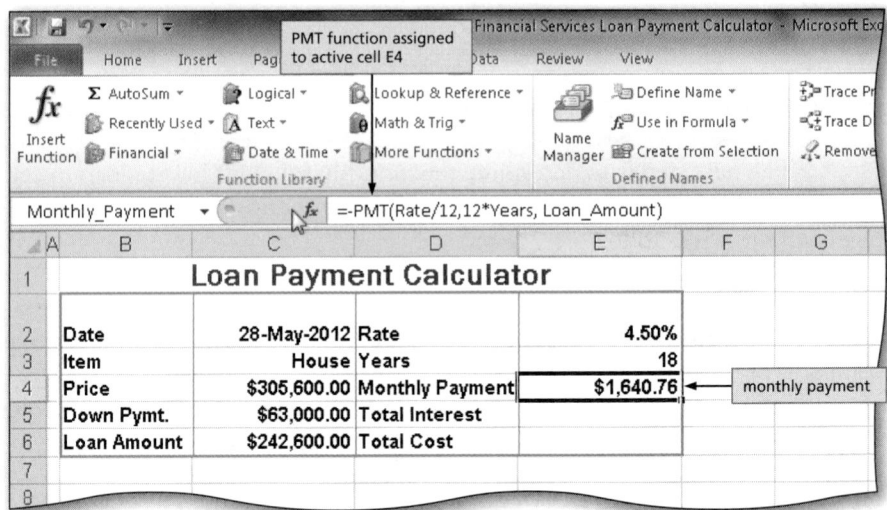

Figure 4–17

Other Ways

1. Click Financial button (Formulas tab | Function Library group), select PMT function, enter arguments, click OK button

2. Click Insert Function button in formula bar, select Financial category, select PMT function, click OK button, enter arguments, click OK button (Function Arguments dialog box)

Other Financial Functions

In addition to the PMT function, Excel provides more than 50 financial functions to help you solve the most complex finance problems. These functions save you from entering long, complicated formulas to obtain needed results. Table 4–1 summarizes three of the more frequently used financial functions.

Table 4–1 Frequently Used Financial Functions

Function	Description
FV (rate, periods, payment)	Returns the future value of an investment based on periodic, constant payments, and a constant interest rate.
PMT (rate, periods, loan amount)	Calculates the payment for a loan based on the loan amount, constant payments, and a constant interest rate.
PV (rate, periods, payment)	Returns the present value of an investment. The present value is the total amount that a series of future payments now is worth.

To Determine the Total Interest and Total Cost

The next step is to determine the total interest the borrower will pay on the loan (the lending institution's gross profit on the loan) and the total cost the borrower will pay for the item being purchased. The total interest (cell E5) is equal to the number of payments times the monthly payment, less the loan amount:

=12 * Years * Monthly_Payment – Loan_Amount

The total cost of the item to be purchased (cell E6) is equal to the price plus the total interest:

=Price + Total_Interest

The following steps enter formulas to determine the total interest and total cost using names.

1 Select cell E5 and then use Point mode and the keyboard to enter the formula `=12 * years * monthly_payment - loan_amount` to determine the total interest.

2 Select cell E6 and then use Point mode and the keyboard to enter the formula `=price + total_interest` to determine the total cost.

3 Select cell B8 (Figure 4–18).

4 Click the Save button on the Quick Access Toolbar to save the workbook using the file name, FT Financial Services Loan Payment Calculator.

Q&A

What are the new values displayed by Excel?

Excel displays a total interest (the lending institution's gross profit) of $111,804.92 in cell E5 and a total cost of $417,404.92 in cell E6, which is the total cost of the home to the borrower (Figure 4–18).

BTW

Range Finder
Remember to check all formulas carefully. You can double-click a cell with a formula and Excel will use Range Finder to highlight the cells that provide data for the formula. While Range Finder is active, you can drag the outlines from one cell to another to change the cells referenced in the formula, provided the cells have not been named.

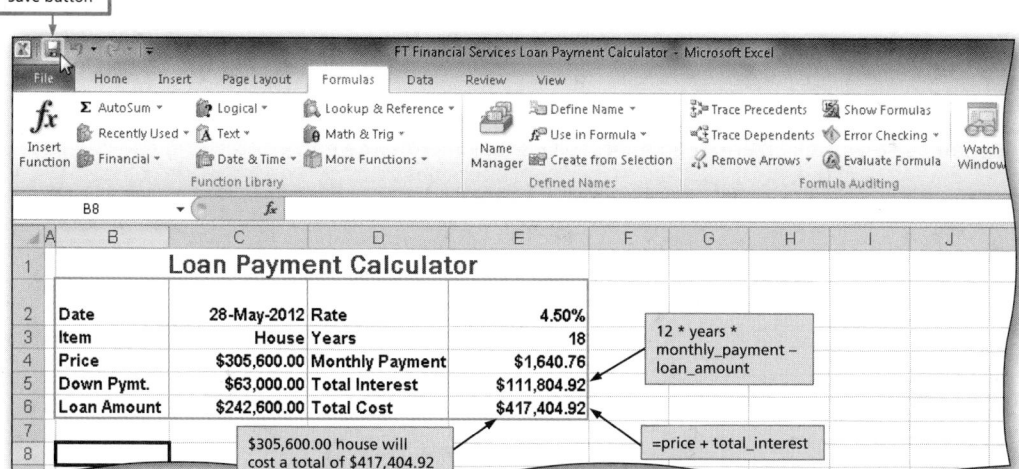

Figure 4–18

To Enter New Loan Data

Assume you want to purchase a condominium for $125,500.00. You have $32,000 for a down payment and you want the loan for a term of 10 years. FT Financial Services currently is charging 5.15% interest for a 10–year loan. The following steps enter the new loan data.

1 Enter `Condominium` in cell C3.

2 Enter `125500` in cell C4.

3 Enter `32000` in cell C5.

4 Enter `5.15%` in cell E2.

5 Enter `10` in cell E3 and then select cell B8 to recalculate the loan information in cells C6, E4, E5, and E6 (Figure 4–19).

Q&A What do the results of the new calculation mean?

As you can see from Figure 4–19, the monthly payment for the condominium is $998.58. By paying for the condominium over a 10–year period at an interest rate of 5.15%, you will pay total interest of $26,329.85 on the loan and pay a total cost of $151,829.85 for a $125,500.00 condominium.

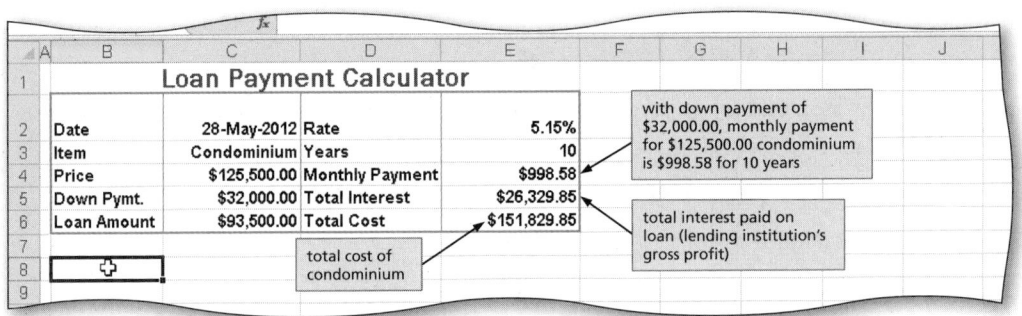

Figure 4–19

To Enter the Original Loan Data

The following steps reenter the original loan data.

1 Enter `House` in cell C3.

2 Enter `305600` in cell C4.

3 Enter `63000` in cell C5.

4 Enter `4.50` in cell E2.

5 Enter `18` in cell E3 and then select cell B8 to complete the entry of the original loan data.

Q&A What is happening on the worksheet as I enter the original data?

Excel instantaneously recalculates all formulas in the worksheet each time you enter a value. Excel displays the original loan information as shown in Figure 4–18.

Q&A Can the Undo button on the Quick Access Toolbar be used to change back to the original data?

Yes. The Undo button must be clicked five times, once for each data item. You also can click the Undo button arrow and drag through the first five entries in the Undo button arrow list.

Using a Data Table to Analyze Worksheet Data

You already have seen that if you change a value in a cell, Excel immediately recalculates and displays the new results of any formulas that reference the cell directly or indirectly. But what if you want to compare the results of the formula for several different values? Writing down or trying to remember all the answers to the what-if questions would be unwieldy. If you use a data table, however, Excel will organize the answers in the worksheet for you automatically.

A data table is a range of cells that shows the answers generated by formulas in which different values have been substituted. Data tables must be built in an unused area of the worksheet (in this case, the range B7:E23). Figure 4–20a illustrates the makeup of a one-input data table. With a **one-input data table**, you can vary the value in one cell (in this worksheet, cell E2, the interest rate). Excel then calculates the results of one or more formulas and fills the data table with the results.

An alternative to a one–input table is a two-input data table. A **two-input data table** allows you to vary the values in two cells, but you can apply a two-input data table to only one formula. A two-input data table example is illustrated in the Extend Your Knowledge exercise on page EX 283.

The interest rates that will be used to analyze the loan formulas in this project range from 4.00% to 7.25%, increasing in increments of 0.25%. The one–input data table shown in Figure 4–20b illustrates the impact of varying the interest rate on three formulas: the monthly payment (cell E4), total interest paid (cell E5), and the total cost of the item to be purchased (cell E6). The series of interest rates in column B are called **input values**.

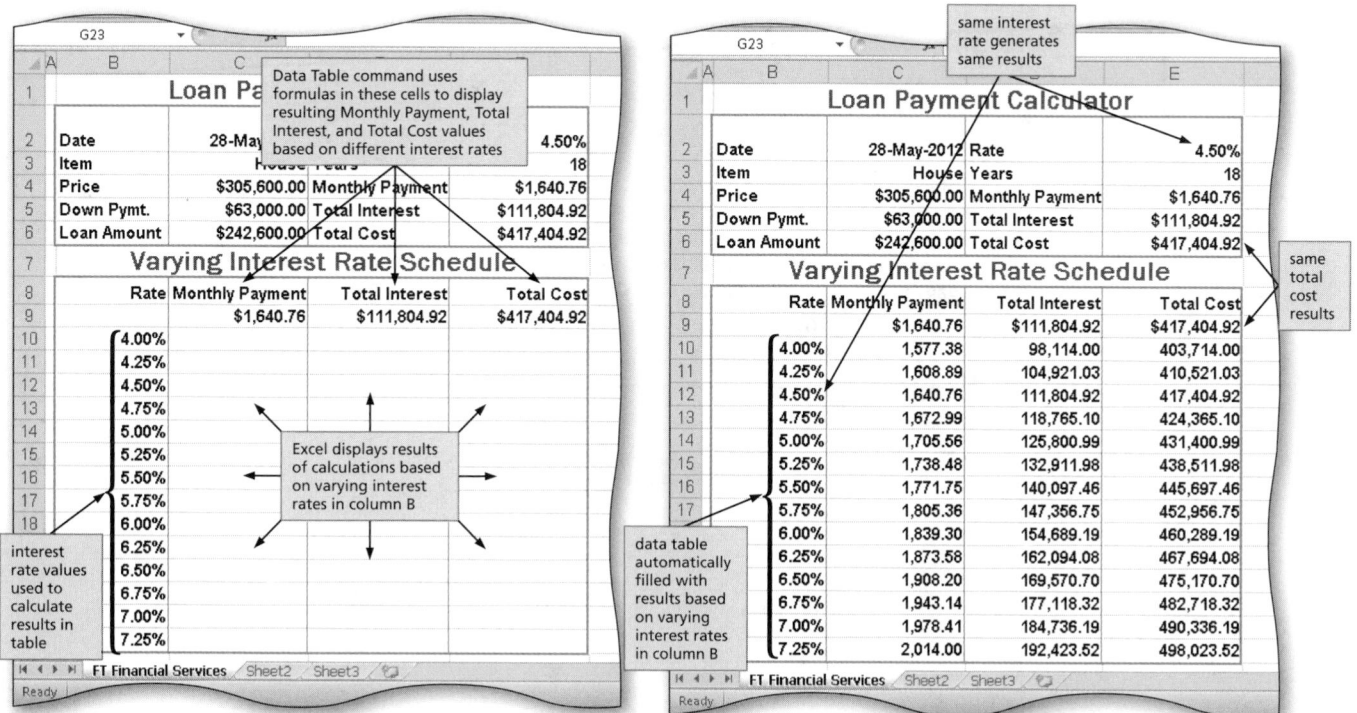

Figure 4–20 (a)   **Figure 4–20 (b)**

To Enter the Data Table Title and Column Titles

The first step in constructing the data table shown in Figure 4–20b is to enter the data table section title and column titles in the range B7:E8 and adjust the heights of rows 7 and 8.

1 Select cell B7 and then type `Varying Interest Rate Schedule` as the data table section title.

2 Select cell B1 and then click the Format Painter button (Home tab | Clipboard group) to copy the format of the cell. Click cell B7 to apply the copied format to the cell.

3 Enter the column titles in the range B8:E8, as shown in Figure 4–21, to create headers for the data table. Select the range B8:E8 and then click the Align Text Right button (Home tab | Alignment group) to right-align the column titles.

4 Position the mouse pointer on the bottom boundary of row heading 7 and then drag up until the ScreenTip indicates Height: 20.25 (27 pixels).

5 Position the mouse pointer on the bottom boundary of row heading 8 and then drag down until the ScreenTip indicates Height: 18.00 (24 pixels).

6 Click cell B10 to deselect the range B8:E8 (Figure 4–21).

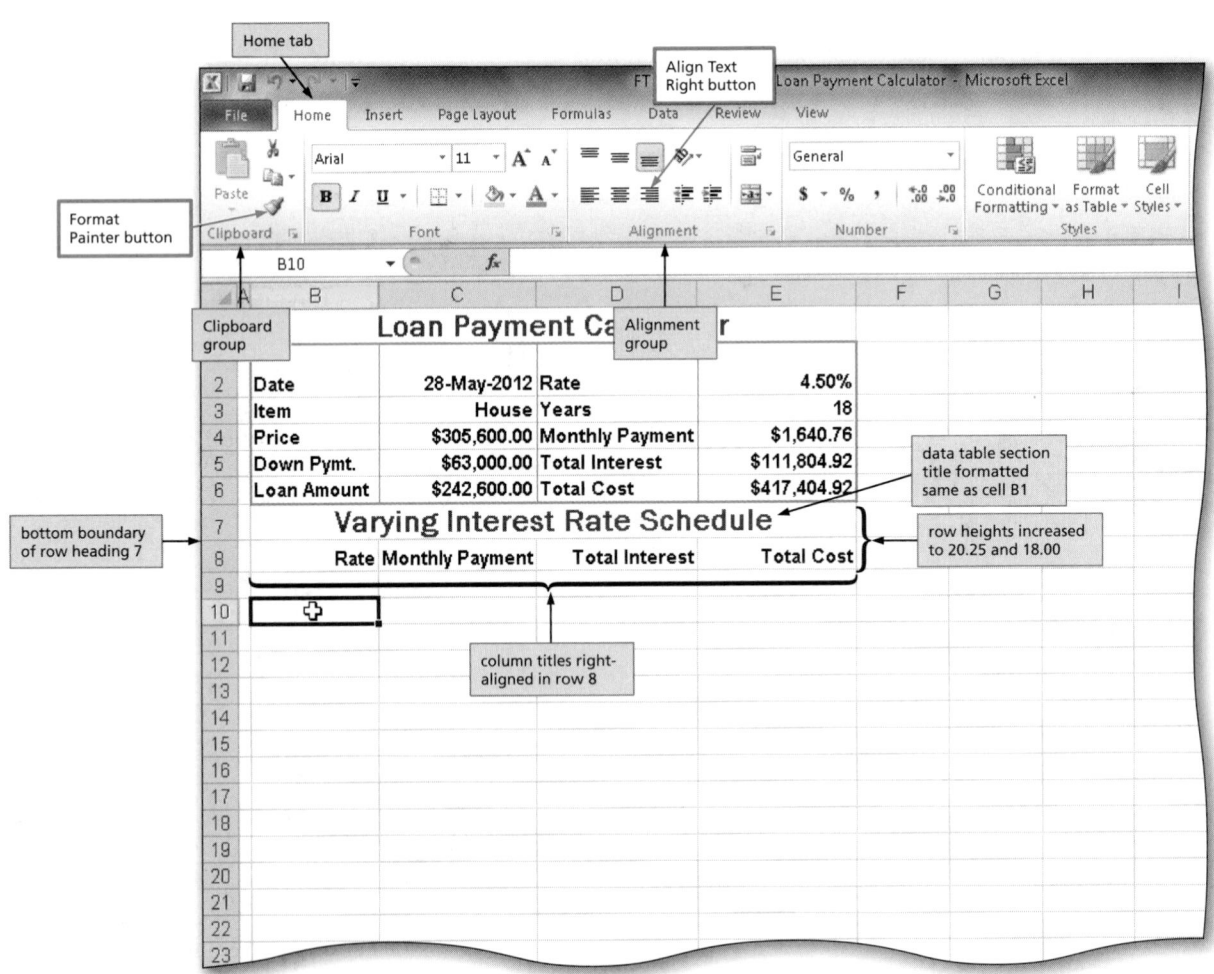

Figure 4–21

To Create a Percent Series Using the Fill Handle

The next step is to create the percent series in column B using the fill handle. These percent figures will serve as the input data for the data table.

1

• With cell B10 selected, type **4.00%** as the first number in the series.

• Select cell B11 and then type **4.25%** as the second number in the series.

• Select the range B10:B11.

• Drag the fill handle through cell B23 to create the border of the fill area as indicated by the shaded border (Figure 4–22). Do not release the mouse button.

Figure 4–22

2

• Release the mouse button to generate the percent series, in this case from 4.00% to 7.25%, and display the Auto Fill Options button.

• Click cell C9 to deselect the selected range, B10:B23 in this case (Figure 4–23).

Q&A

What is the purpose of the percent figures in column B?

Excel will use the percent figures in column B to calculate the formulas to be evaluated and entered at the top of the data table in row 9. This series begins in cell B10, not cell B9, because the cell immediately to the upper-left of the formulas in a one-input data table should not include an input value.

Figure 4–23

Other Ways
1. Right-drag fill handle in direction to fill, click Fill Series on shortcut menu
2. Select range, click Fill button (Home tab | Editing group), click Down

BTW

Formulas in Data Tables
Any experienced Excel user will tell you that to enter the formulas at the top of the data table, you should enter the cell reference or name of the cell preceded by an equal sign (Figure 4-24). This ensures that if you change the original formula in the worksheet, Excel automatically will change the corresponding formula in the data table. If you use a cell reference, Excel also copies the format to the cell. If you use a name, Excel does not copy the format to the cell.

To Enter the Formulas in the Data Table

The next step in creating the data table is to enter the three formulas at the top of the table in cells C9, D9, and E9. The three formulas are the same as the monthly payment formula in cell E4, the total interest formula in cell E5, and the total cost formula in cell E6. The number of formulas you place at the top of a one-input data table depends on the application. Some one-input data tables will have only one formula, while others might have several. In this case, three formulas are affected when the interest rate changes.

Excel provides four ways to enter these formulas in the data table: (1) retype the formulas in cells C9, D9, and E9; (2) copy cells E4, E5, and E6 to cells C9, D9, and E9, respectively; (3) enter the formulas =monthly_payment in cell C9, =total_interest in cell D9, and =total_cost in cell E9; or (4) enter the formulas =e4 in cell C9, =e5 in cell D9, and =e6 in cell E9.

The best alternative to define the formulas in the data table is the fourth alternative, which involves using the cell references preceded by an equal sign. This method is best because: (1) it is easier to enter the cell references; (2) if you change any of the formulas in the range E4:E6, the formulas at the top of the data table are updated automatically; and (3) Excel automatically assigns the format of the cell reference (Currency style format) to the cell. Using the third alternative, which involves using cell names, is nearly as good an alternative, but if you use cell names, Excel will not assign the format to the cells. The following steps enter the formulas of the data table in row 9.

1 With cell C9 active, type **=e4** and then press the RIGHT ARROW key to enter the first parameter of the function to be used in the data table.

2 Type **=e5** in cell D9 and then press the RIGHT ARROW key to enter the second parameter of the function to be used in the data table.

3 Type **=e6** in cell E9 and then click the Enter box to complete the assignment of the formulas and Currency style format to the selected range, C9:E9 in this case (Figure 4–24).

Q&A

Why are these cells assigned the values of cells in the Loan Payment Calculator area of the worksheet?

It is important to understand that the entries in the top row of the data table (row 9) refer to the formulas that the company wants to evaluate using the series of percentages in column B. Furthermore, recall that when you assign a formula to a cell, Excel applies the format of the first cell reference in the formula to the cell. Thus, Excel applies the Currency style format to cells C9, D9, and E9 because that is the format of cells E4, E5, and E6.

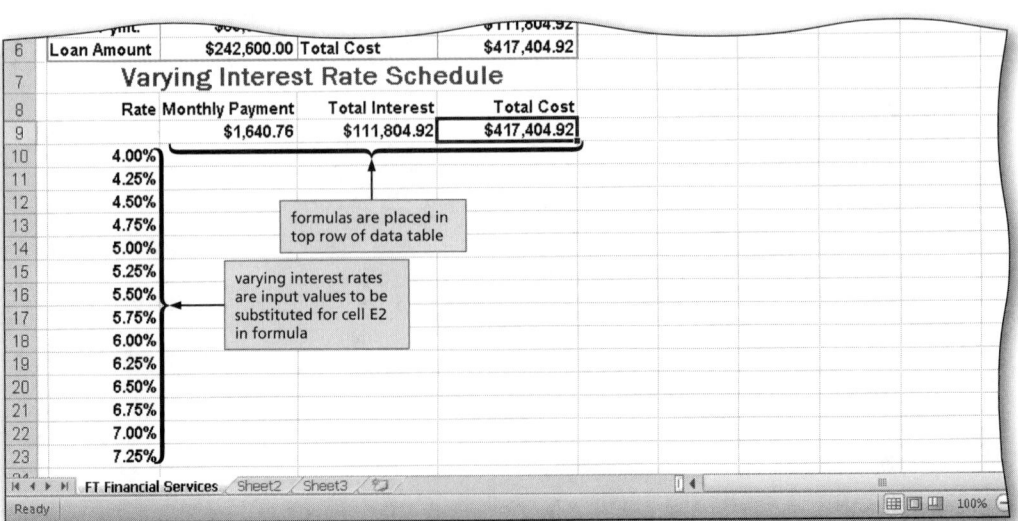

Figure 4–24

To Define a Range as a Data Table

After creating the interest rate series in column B and entering the formulas in row 9, the next step is to define the range B9:E23 as a data table. Cell E2 is the input cell for the data table, which means cell E2 is the cell in which values from column B in the data table are substituted in the formulas in row 9.

1

• Select the range B9:E23 as the range in which to create the data table.

• Display the Data tab and then click the What-If Analysis button (Data tab | Data tools) to display the What-IfAnalysis menu (Figure 4–25).

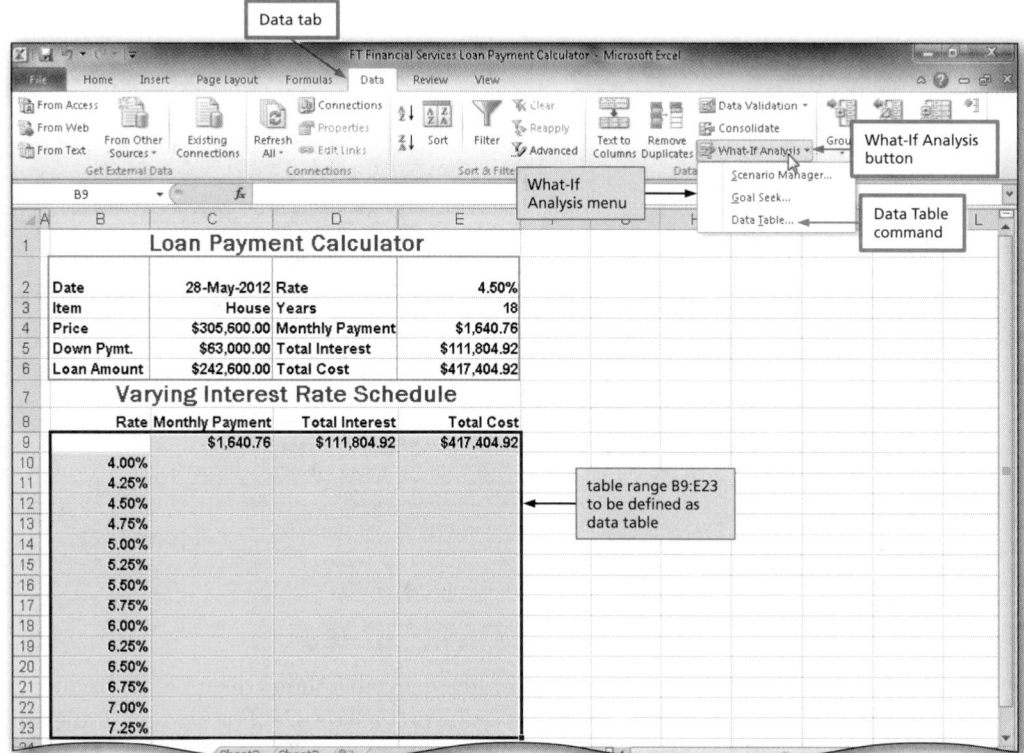

Figure 4–25

2

• Click Data Table on the What-If Analysis menu to display the Data Table dialog box.

• Click the 'Column input cell' box (Data Table dialog box) and then click cell E2 in the Loan Payment Calculator section of the spreadsheet to select the input cell for the data table (Figure 4–26).

Q&A

What is the purpose of clicking cell E2?

The purpose of clicking cell E2 is to select it for the Column input cell. A marquee surrounds the selected cell

Figure 4–26

E2, indicating it will be the input cell in which values from column B in the data table are substituted in the formulas in row 9. $E$2 now appears in the Column input cell box in the Data Table dialog box.

3

- Click the OK button (Data Table dialog box) to create the data table (Figure 4–27).

Q&A

How does Excel create the data table?

Excel calculates the results of the three formulas in row 9 for each interest rate in column B and immediately fills columns C, D, and E of the data table. The resulting values for each interest rate are displayed in the corresponding rows.

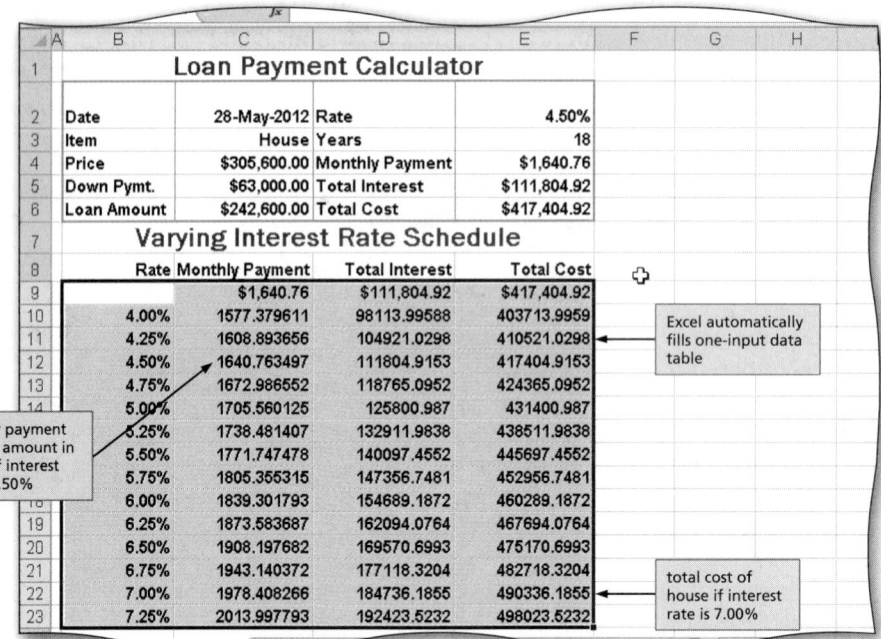

Figure 4–27

More about Data Tables

In Figure 4–27, the data table shows the monthly payment, total interest, and total cost for the interest rates in the range B10:B23. For example, if the interest rate is 4.50% (cell E2), the monthly payment is $1,640.76 (cell E4). If the interest rate is 7.00% (cell B22), however, the monthly payment is $1,978.41 rounded to the nearest cent (cell C22). If the interest rate is 5.75% (cell B17), then the total cost of the house is $452,956.75 rounded to the nearest cent (cell E17), rather than $417,404.92 (cell E6). Thus, a 1.25% increase from the interest rate of 4.50% to 5.75% results in a $35,551.83 increase in the total cost of the house.

The following list details important points you should know about data tables:

1. The formula(s) you are analyzing must include a cell reference to the input cell.

2. You can have as many active data tables in a worksheet as you want.

3. While only one value can vary in a one–input data table, the data table can analyze as many formulas as you want.

4. To include additional formulas in a one-input data table, enter them in adjacent cells in the same row as the current formulas (row 9 in Figure 4–27) and then define the entire new range as a data table by using the Data Table command on the What-If Analysis menu.

5. You delete a data table as you would delete any other item on a worksheet. That is, select the data table and then press the DELETE key.

To Format the Data Table

The following steps format the data table to improve its readability.

1 Select the range B8:E23. Right-click the selected range to display a shortcut menu and then click Format Cells on the shortcut menu to display the Format Cells dialog box.

2 Click the Border tab (Format Cells dialog box) to display the Border sheet. Click the Color box arrow to display the Colors palette and then click Red (column 2, row 1) in the Standard Colors area to change the border color.

3 Click the medium border in the Style area (column 2, row 5) to select the line style of the border. Click the Outline button in the Presets area to preview the border in the Border area.

4 Click the light border in the Style area (column 1, row 7) and then click the Vertical Line button in the Border area to preview the border in the Border area.

5 Click the OK button (Format Cells dialog box) to apply custom borders to the selected range.

6 Select the range C10:E23, right-click the selected range to display a shortcut menu, and then click Format Cells on the shortcut menu to display the Format Cells dialog box.

7 Click the Number tab (Format Cells dialog box) to display the Number sheet.

8 Click Currency in the Category list (Format Cells dialog box) to select a currency format and then click the Symbol box arrow to display the Symbol list. Click None to choose no currency symbol, and then click the second format, 1,234.10, in the Negative numbers list to assign a currency format to the selected range.

9 Click the OK button (Format Cells dialog box) to apply a currency format to the selected range and then select cell G23 to display the worksheet, as shown in Figure 4–28.

10 Click the Save button on the Quick Access Toolbar to save the workbook using the file name, FT Financial Services Loan Payment Calculator.

BTW

Undoing Formats
If you started to assign formats to a range and then realize you made a mistake and want to start over, select the range, click the Cell Styles button (Home tab | Styles group), and click Normal in the Cell Styles gallery.

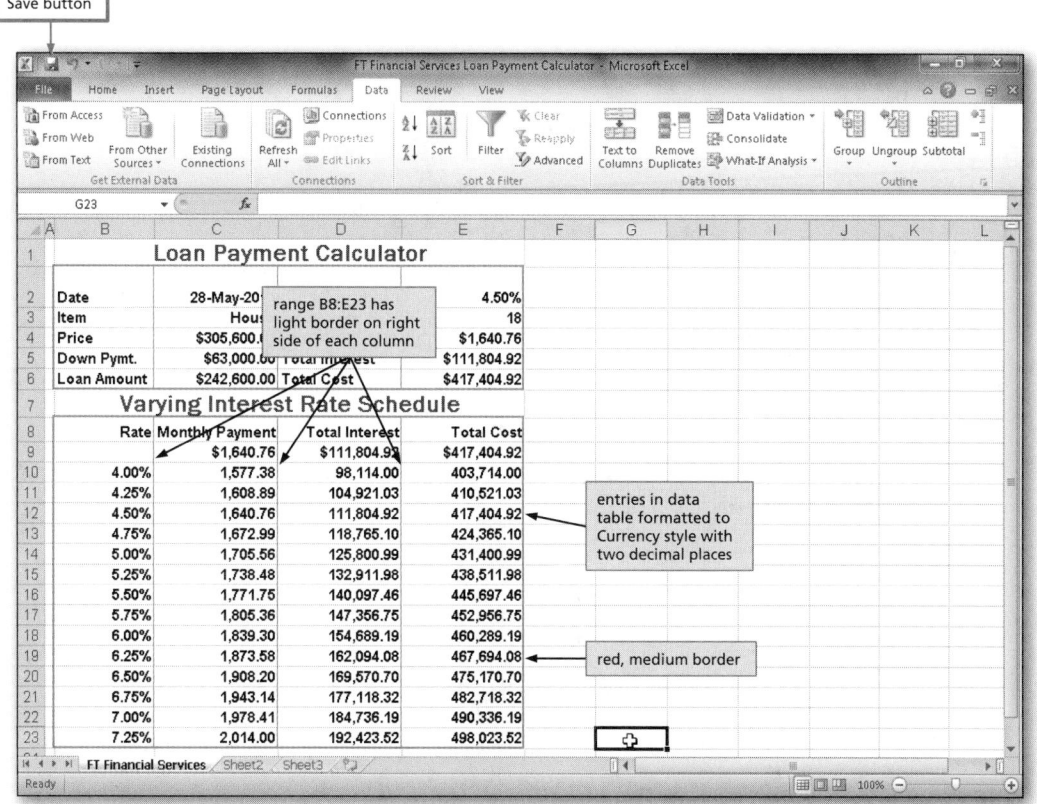

Figure 4–28

Break Point: If you wish to take a break, this is a good place to do so. You can quit Excel now. To resume at a later time, start Excel, open the file called FT Financial Services Loan Payment Calculator, and continue following the steps from this location forward.

BTW

Conditional Formatting
You can add as many conditional formats to a range as you like. After adding the first condition, click the Conditional Formatting button (Home tab | Styles group) and then click New Rule to add more conditions. If more than one condition is true for a cell, then Excel applies the formats of each condition, beginning with the first.

Adding a Pointer to the Data Table Using Conditional Formatting

If the interest rate in cell E2 is between 4.00% and 7.25% and its decimal portion is a multiple of 0.25 (such as 4.50%), then one of the rows in the data table agrees exactly with the monthly payment, interest paid, and total cost in the range E4:E6. For example, in Figure 4–28 on the previous page, row 12 (4.50%) in the data table agrees with the results in the range E4:E6, because the interest rate in cell B12 is the same as the interest rate in cell E2. Analysts often look for the row in the data table that agrees with the input cell results.

To Add a Pointer to the Data Table

To make the row stand out, you can add formatting that serves as a pointer to a row. To add a pointer, you can use conditional formatting to make the cell in column B that agrees with the input cell (cell E2) stand out. The following steps apply conditional formatting to column B in the data table.

- Select the range B10:B23 and then click the Conditional Formatting button (Home tab | Styles group) to display the Conditional Formatting list (Figure 4–29).

- Click New Rule on the Conditional Formatting list to display the New Formatting Rule dialog box.

- Click 'Format only cells that contain' in the Select a Rule Type box (New Formatting Rule dialog box) to select the type of rule to create.

- Select equal to in the second box from the left.

- Type =$E$2 in the right box to complete the condition for the rule based on a cell value.

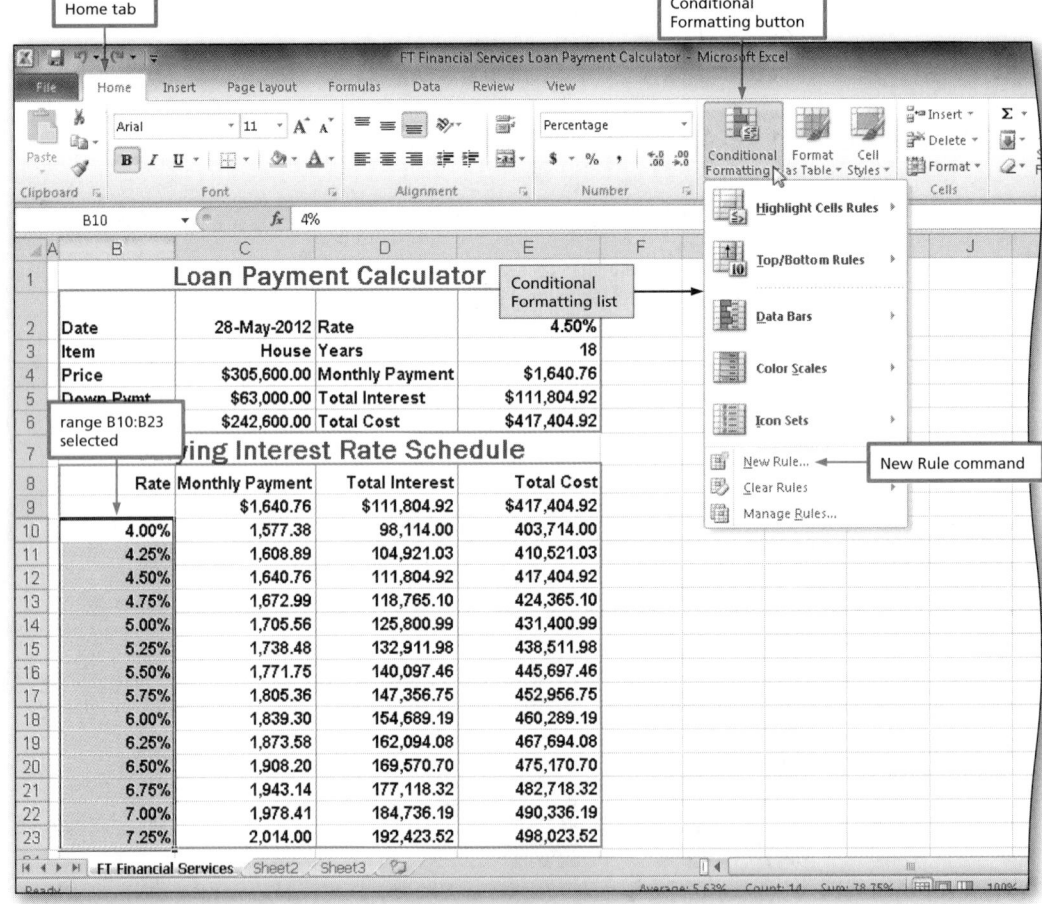

Figure 4–29

3

- Click the Format button (New Formatting Rule dialog box), click the Fill tab to display the Fill sheet, and then click Red (column 2, row 7) in the Background Color area to select a background color for the conditional format.

- Click the OK button (Format Cells dialog box) to display the New Formatting Rule dialog box with a preview of the conditional format (Figure 4–30).

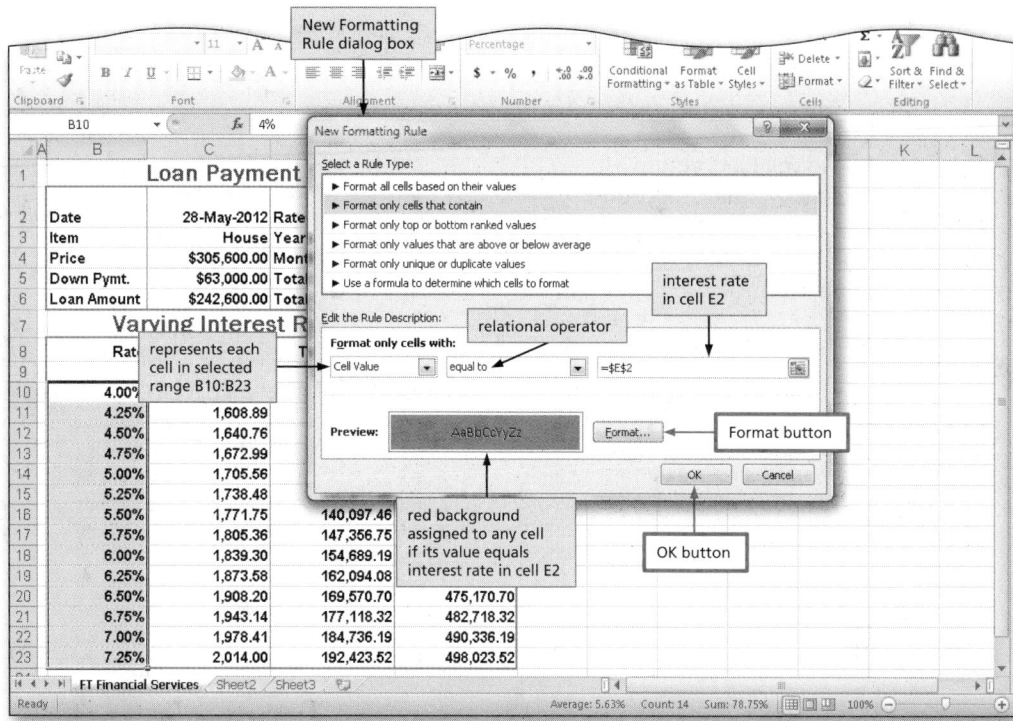

Figure 4–30

4

- Click the OK button (New Formatting Rule dialog box) to apply the conditional formatting rule.

- Click cell G23 to deselect the selected range, B10:B23 in this case (Figure 4–31).

Q&A

How does Excel apply the conditional formatting?

Cell B12 in the data table, which contains the value, 4.50%, appears with a red background, because the value 4.50% is the same as the interest rate value in cell E2.

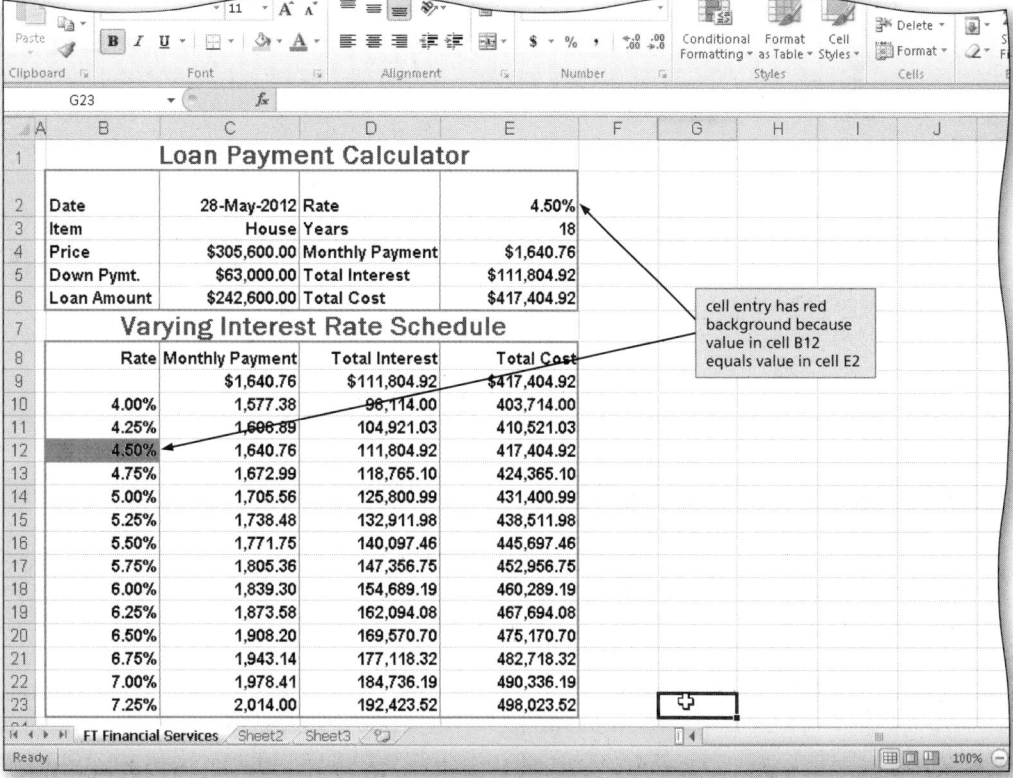

Figure 4–31

5

- Select cell E2 and then enter **7.25** as the interest rate (Figure 4–32).

6

- Enter **4.50** in cell E2 to return the Loan Payment Calculator section and Varying Interest Rate Schedule section to their original states, as shown in Figure 4–31.

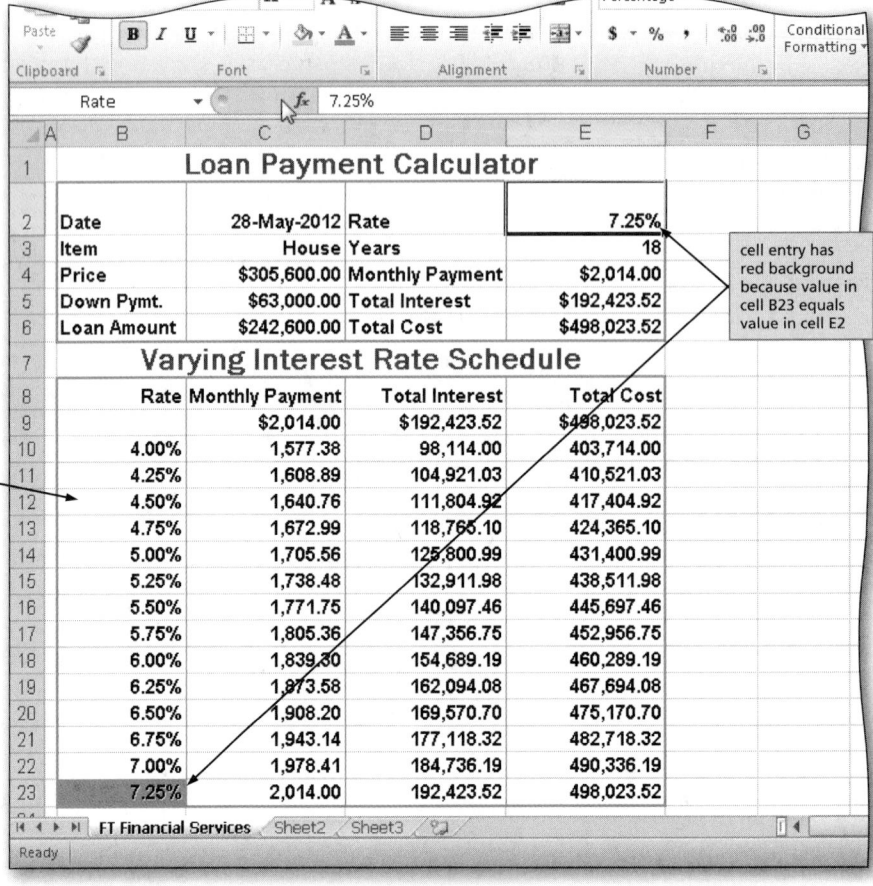

Figure 4–32

Q&A

What happens if I change the interest rate from 4.50% to something else?

Excel immediately displays the cell containing the new rate with a red background and displays cell B12 with a white background (Figure 4–32). Thus, the red background serves as a pointer in the data table to indicate the row that agrees with the input cell (cell E2). When the loan officer using this worksheet enters a different percent in cell E2, the pointer will move or disappear. It will disappear whenever the interest rate in cell E2 is outside the range of the data table or its decimal portion is not a multiple of 0.25, such as when the interest rate is 9.71% or 4.90%.

BTW

Amortization Schedules
Hundreds of Web sites offer amortization schedules. To find these Web sites, use a search engine, such as Google, and search using the keywords, amortization schedule.

Creating an Amortization Schedule

The next step in this project is to create the Amortization Schedule section on the right side of Figure 4–33. An amortization schedule shows the beginning and ending balances of a loan and the amount of payment that applies to the principal and interest for each year over the life of the loan. For example, if a customer wanted to pay off the loan after six years, the Amortization Schedule section would tell the loan officer what the payoff would be (cell I8 in Figure 4–33). The Amortization Schedule section shown in Figure 4–33 will work only for loans of up to 18 years. You, however, could extend the table to any number of years. The Amortization Schedule section also contains summaries in rows 21, 22, and 23. These summaries should agree exactly with the corresponding amounts in the Loan Payment Calculator section in the range B1:E6.

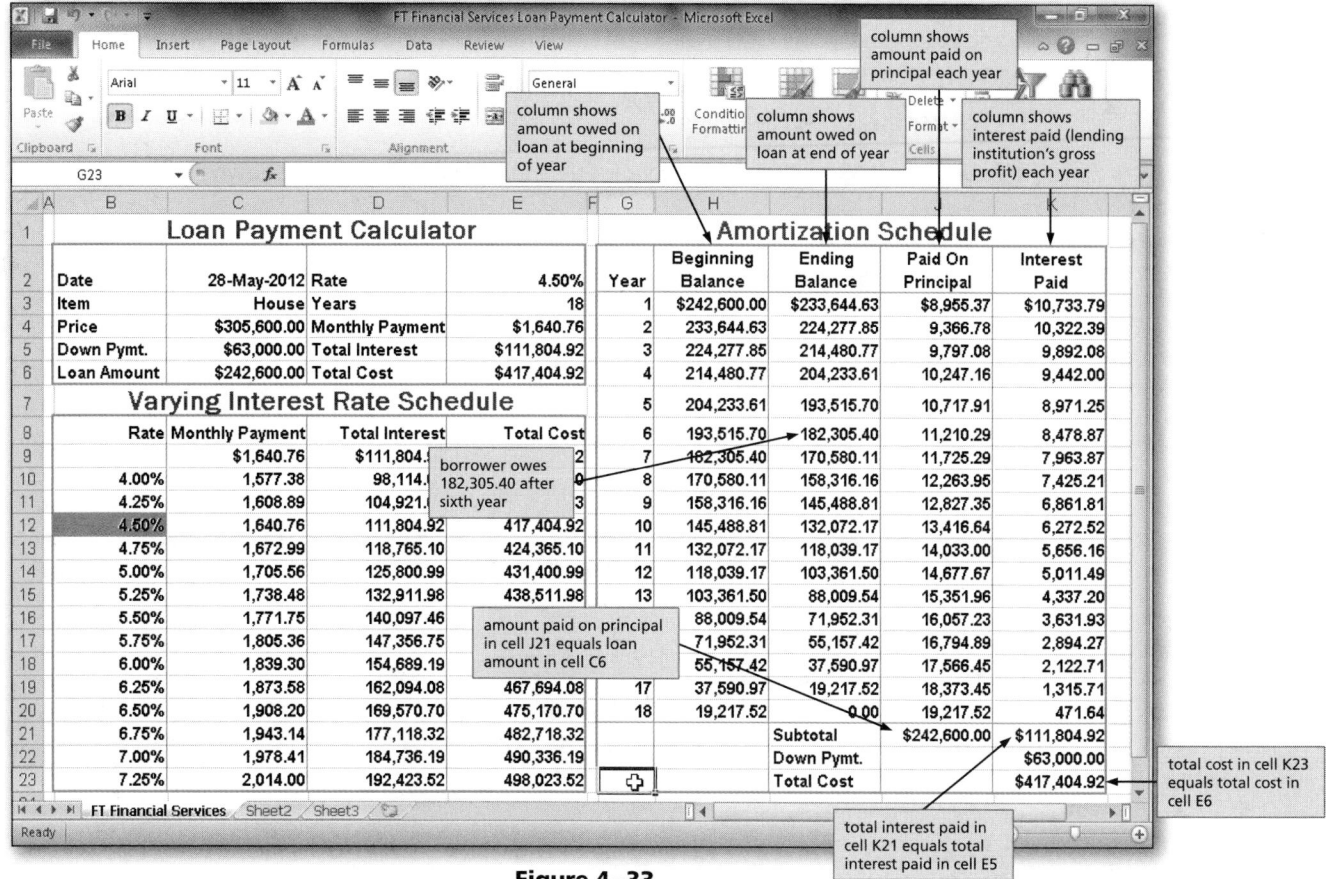

Figure 4–33

To Change Column Widths and Enter Titles

The first step in creating the Amortization Schedule section is to adjust the column widths and enter the Amortization Schedule section title and column titles. The following steps adjust column widths and enter column titles for the Amortization Schedule.

1 Position the mouse pointer on the right boundary of column heading F and then drag to the left until the ScreenTip shows Width: .77 (10 pixels) to change the column width.

2 Position the mouse pointer on the right boundary of column heading G and then drag to the left until the ScreenTip shows Width: 5.63 (50 pixels) to change the column width.

3 Drag through column headings H through K to select them. Position the mouse pointer on the right boundary of column heading K and then drag to the right until the ScreenTip shows Width: 12.13 (102 pixels) to change the column widths.

4 Select cell G1. Type `Amortization Schedule` and then press the ENTER key to enter the section title.

5 Select cell B1 and then click the Format Painter button (Home tab | Clipboard group) to start the format painter. Click cell G1 to copy the format of the selected cell, cell B1 in this case.

6 Click the Merge & Center button (Home tab | Alignment group) to split the selected cell, cell G1 in this case. Select the range G1:K1 and then click the Merge & Center button (Home tab | Alignment group) to merge and center the section title over the selected range.

BTW

Column Borders
In this chapter, columns A and F are used as column borders to divide sections of the worksheet from one another, as well as from the row headings. A column border is an unused column with a significantly reduced width. You also can use row borders to separate sections of a worksheet.

7 Enter the column headings in the range G2:K2, as shown in Figure 4–34. Where appropriate, press ALT+ENTER to enter the headings on two lines.

8 Select the range G2:K2 and then click the Center button (Home tab | Alignment group) to center the column headings.

9 Select cell G3 to display the section title and column headings, as shown in Figure 4–34.

Q&A

Why was cell G1 split in step 6?

After using the format painter, Excel attempted to apply to merge and center the text in cell G1 because the source of the format, cell B1, is merged and centered across four columns. The Amortization Schedule section, however, includes five columns. Splitting cell G1, therefore, changed cell G1 from including four columns to include one column. Next, the section heading was merged and centered across five rows as required by the design of the worksheet (Figure 4–3 on page EX 230).

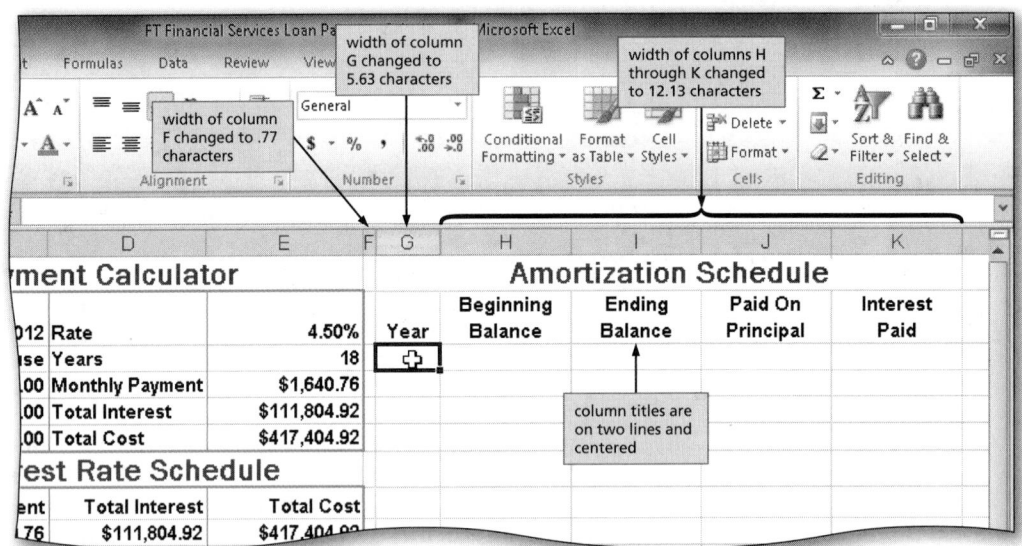

Figure 4–34

To Create a Series of Integers Using the Fill Handle

The next step is to create a series of numbers, using the fill handle, that represent the years during the life of the loan. The series begins with 1 (year 1) and ends with 18 (year 18). The following steps create a series of years in the range G3:G20.

1 With cell G3 active, type   1   as the initial year. Select cell G4 and then type   2   to represent the next year.

2 Select the range G3:G4 and then drag the fill handle through cell G20 to complete the creation of a series of integers, 1 through 18 in the range G3:G20 in this case (Figure 4–35).

Q&A

Why is year 5 of the amortization schedule larger than the other rows in the amortization schedule?

The design of the worksheet (Figure 4–3 on page EX 230) called for a large font size for the varying interest rate schedule section of the worksheet, which is in row 7 of the worksheet. To accommodate the larger font size, the height of row 7 was increased. Year 5 of the worksheet is in the taller row 7 and, therefore, is taller than the other years in the amortization schedule.

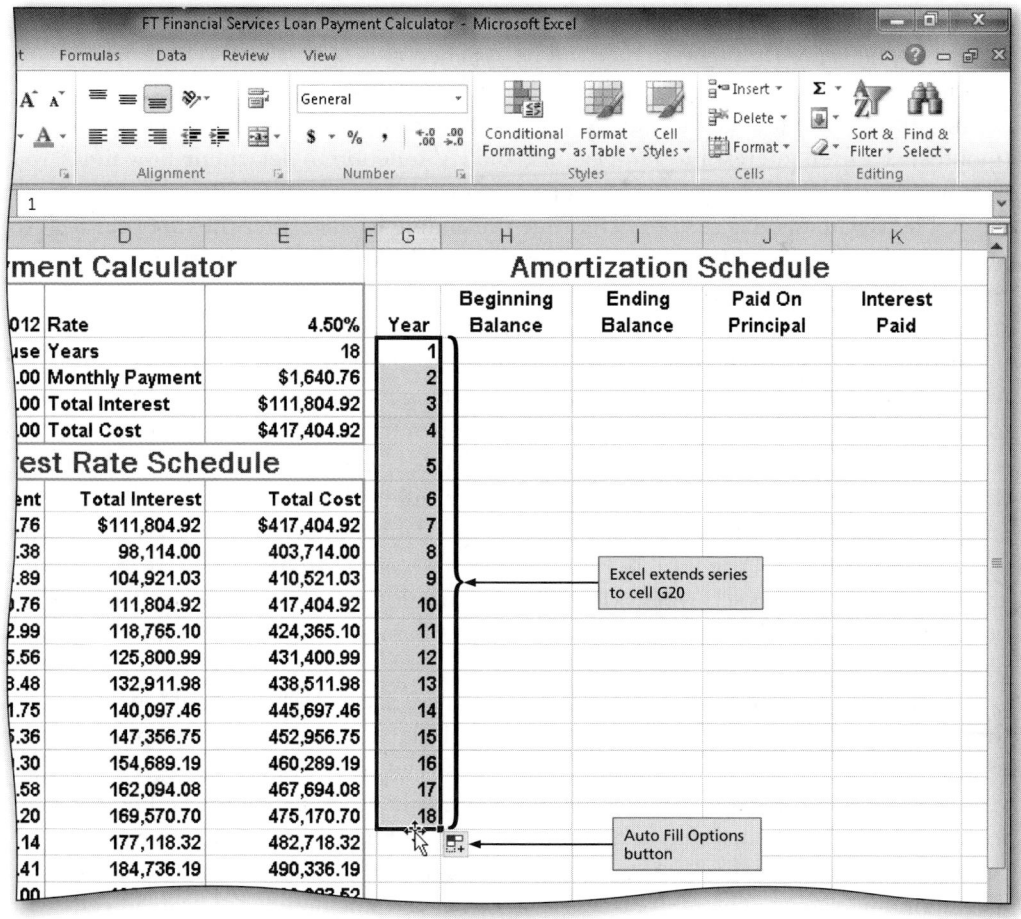

Figure 4–35

To Enter the Formulas in the Amortization Schedule

The next step is to enter the four formulas that form the basis of the amortization schedule in row 3. Later, these formulas will be copied through row 20. The formulas are summarized in Table 4–2.

Table 4–2 Formulas for the Amortization Schedule			
Cell	**Column heading**	**Formula**	**Example**
H3	Beginning Balance	=C6	The beginning balance (the balance at the end of a year) is the initial loan amount in cell C6.
I3	Ending Balance	=IF(G3<=$E$3, PV($E$2/12, 12*($E$3–G3), –$E$4), 0)	The ending balance (the balance at the end of a year) is equal to the present value of the payments paid over the remaining life of the loan.
J3	Paid on Principal	=H3–I3	The amount paid on the principal at the end of the year is equal to the beginning balance (cell H3) less the ending balance (cell I3).
K3	Interest Paid	=IF(H3>0, 12*$E$4–J3, 0)	The interest paid during the year is equal to 12 times the monthly payment (cell E4) less the amount paid on the principal (cell J3).

Of the four formulas in Table 4–2 on the previous page, perhaps the most difficult to understand is the PV function that will be assigned to cell I3. The **PV function** returns the present value of an annuity. An **annuity** is a series of fixed payments (such as the monthly payment in cell E4) made at the end of each of a fixed number of periods (months) at a fixed interest rate. You can use the PV function to determine how much the borrower of the loan still owes at the end of each year.

The PV function is used to determine the ending balance after the first year (cell I3) by using a term equal to the number of months for which the borrower still must make payments. For example, if the loan is for 18 years (216 months), then the borrower still owes 204 payments after the first year (216 months – 12 months). The number of payments outstanding can be determined from the formula 12 * (E3–G3) or 12*(18–1), which equals 204. Recall that column G contains integers that represent the years of the loan. After the second year, the number of payments remaining is 192, and so on.

If you assign the PV function as shown in Table 4–2 to cell I3 and then copy it to the range I4:I20, the ending balances for each year will be displayed properly. If the loan is for less than 18 years, however, then the ending balances displayed for the years beyond the time the loan is due are invalid. For example, if a loan is taken out for 5 years, then the rows representing years 6 through 18 in the amortization schedule should be 0. The PV function, however, will display negative numbers even though the loan already has been paid off.

To avoid the display of negative ending balances the worksheet should include a formula that assigns the PV function to the range I3:I20 as long as the corresponding year in column G is less than or equal to the number of years in cell E3. If the corresponding year in column G is greater than the number of years in cell E3, then the ending balance for that year and the remaining years should be 0. The following IF function causes the value of the PV function or 0 to be displayed in cell I3, depending on whether the corresponding value in column G is less than or equal to the number of years in cell E3. Recall that the dollar signs within the cell references indicate the cell references are absolute and, therefore, will not change as you copy the function downward.

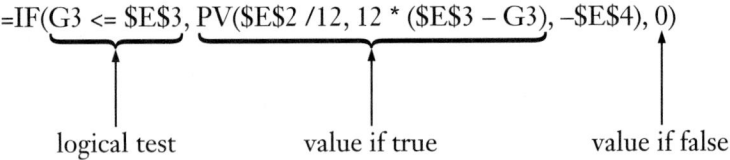

=IF(G3 <= $E$3, PV($E$2 /12, 12 * ($E$3 – G3), –$E$4), 0)

       logical test   value if true   value if false

In the preceding formula, the logical test determines if the year in column G is less than or equal to the term of the loan in cell E3. If the logical test is true, then the IF function assigns the PV function to the cell. If the logical test is false, then the IF function assigns zero (0) to the cell. You also could use two double-quote symbols (" ") to indicate to Excel to leave the cell blank if the logical test is false.

The PV function in the IF function includes absolute cell references (cell references with dollar signs) to ensure that the references to cells in column E do not change when the IF function later is copied down the column.

The following steps enter the four formulas shown in Table 4–2 into row 3. Row 3 represents year 1 of the loan.

1

- Select cell H3 and then enter =c6 as the beginning balance of the loan.

- Select cell I3 and then type =if(g3 <= e3, pv(e2 / 12, 12 * (e3 - g3), -e4), 0) as the entry (Figure 4–36).

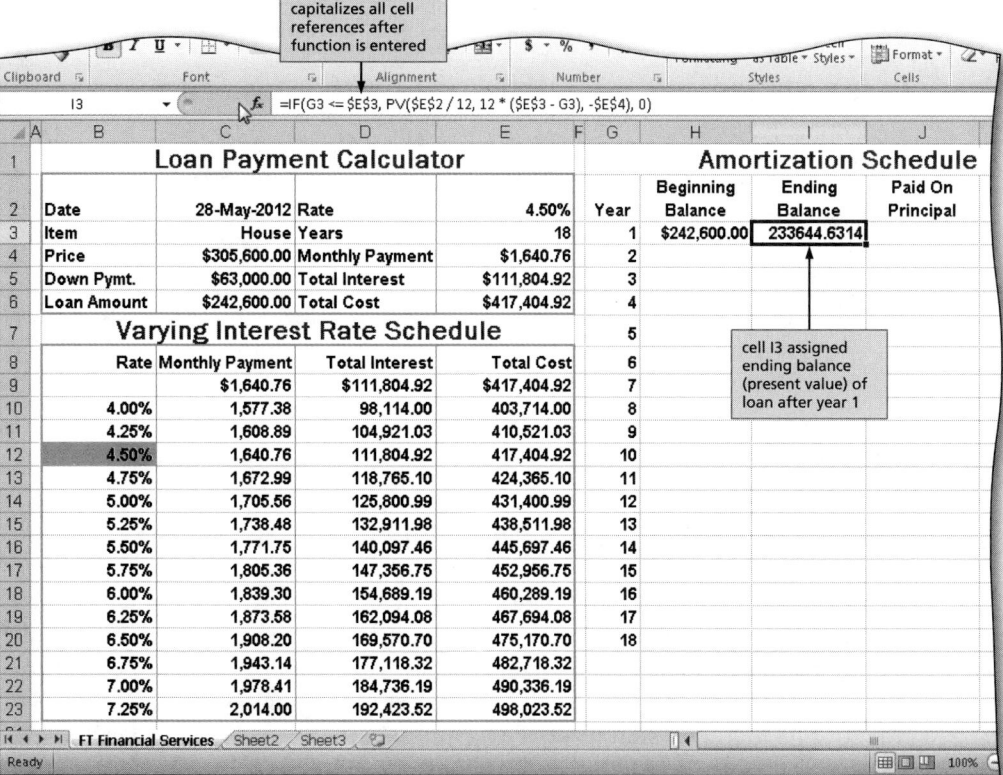

Figure 4–36

2

- Click the Enter box in the formula bar to insert the formula in the selected cell (Figure 4–37).

Q&A

What happens when the Enter box is clicked?

Excel evaluates the IF function in cell I3 and displays the result of the PV function (233644.6314) because the value in cell G3 (1) is less than or equal to the term of the loan in cell E3 (18). With cell I3 active, Excel also displays the formula in the formula bar. If the borrower wanted to pay off the loan after one year, the cost would be $233,644.63.

Figure 4–37

- Select cell J3. Enter the formula `=h3 - i3` and then press the RIGHT ARROW key to complete the entry.

- Select cell K3. Enter the formula `=if(h3 > 0, 12 * $e$4 - j3, 0)` (Figure 4–38).

Figure 4–38

- Click the Enter box in the formula bar to complete the entry of the formula (Figure 4–39).

Q&A What happens when the Enter box is clicked?

Excel displays the interest paid after 1 year (10733.79339) in cell K3. Thus, the lending company's gross profit for the first year of the loan is $10,733.79.

Q&A Why are some of the cells in the range H3:K3 formatted?

When you enter a formula in a cell, Excel assigns the cell the same format as the first cell reference in the formula. For example, when you enter =c6 in cell H3, Excel assigns the format in cell C6 to cell H3. The same applies to cell J3. Although this method of formatting also works for most functions, it does not work for the IF function. Thus, the results of the IF functions in cells I3 and K3 are displayed using the General style format, which is the format of all cells when you open a new workbook.

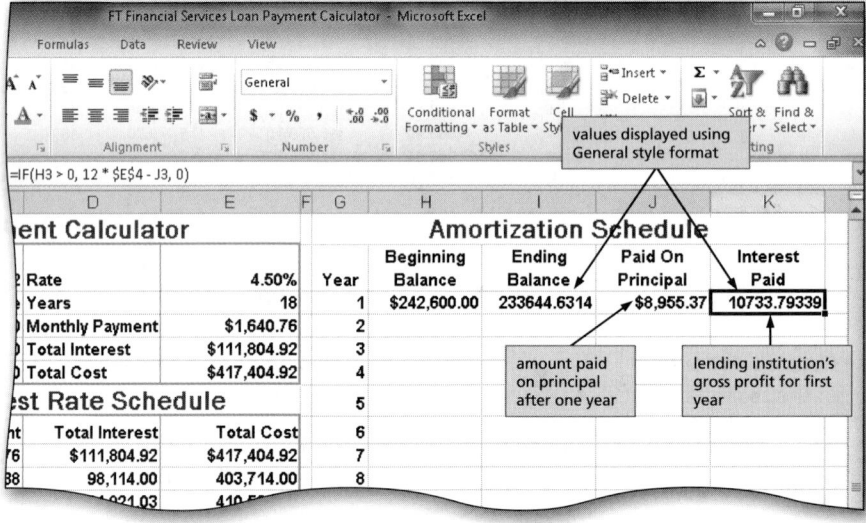

Figure 4–39

To Copy the Formulas to Fill the Amortization Schedule

With the formulas entered into the first row, the next step is to copy them to the remaining rows in the amortization schedule. The required copying is straightforward, except for the beginning balance column. To obtain the next year's beginning balance (cell H4), last year's ending balance (cell I3) must be used. After cell I3 (last year's ending balance) is copied to cell H4 (next year's beginning balance), then H4 can be copied to the range H5:H20. The following steps copy the formulas in the range I3:K3 and cell H4 through to the remainder of the amortization schedule.

1

- Select the range I3:K3 and then drag the fill handle down through row 20 to copy the formulas through the amortization schedule, I4:K20 in this case (Figure 4–40).

Q&A

Why do some of the numbers seem incorrect?

Many of the numbers displayed are incorrect because the cells in column H — except for cell H3 — do not yet contain beginning balances.

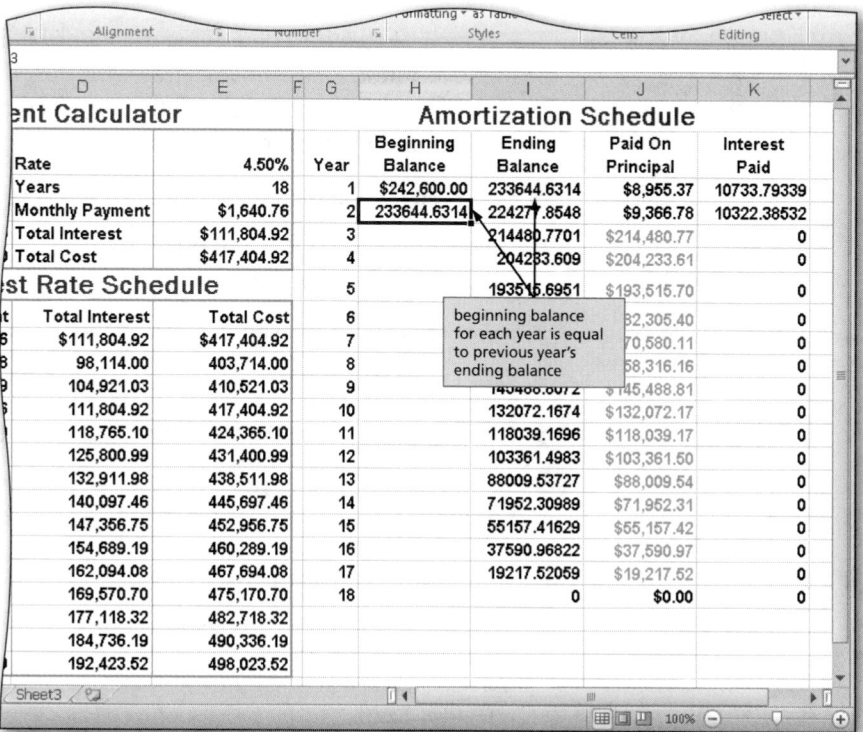

IF(G3 <= $E$3, PV($E$2 / 12, 12 * ($E$3 - G3), -$E$4), 0)

	D	E	F	G	H	I	J	K
	ent Calculator					Amortization Schedule		
				Year	Beginning Balance	Ending Balance	Paid On Principal	Interest Paid
	Rate	4.50%		1	$242,600.00	233644.6314	$8,955.37	10733.79339
	Years	18		2		224277.8548	$224,277.85	0
	Monthly Payment	$1,640.76		3		214480.7701	$214,480.77	0
	Total Interest	$111,804.92		4		204233.609	$204,233.61	0
	Total Cost	$417,404.92		5		193515.6951	$193,515.70	0
	st Rate Schedule			6		182305.4022	$182,305.40	0
	Total Interest	Total Cost		7		170580.1103	$170,580.11	0
6	$111,804.92	$417,404.92		8		158316.1606	$158,316.16	0
8	98,114.00	403,714.00				145488.8072	$145,488.81	0
9	104,921.03	410,				132072.1674	$132,072.17	0
6	111,804.92	417,				118039.1696	$118,039.17	0
9	118,765.10	424,365.10		11		103361.4983	$103,361.50	0
5	125,800.99	431,400.99		12		88009.53727	$88,009.54	0
	132,911.98	438,511.98		13		71952.30989	$71,952.31	0
	140,097.46	445,697.46		14		55157.41629	$55,157.42	0
	147,356.75	452,956.75		15		37590.96822	$37,590.97	0
	154,689.19	460,289.19		16		19217.52059	$19,217.52	0
	162,094.08	467,694.08		17		0	$0.00	0
	169,570.70	475,170.70		18				
	177,118.32	482,718.32						
	184,736.19	490,336.19						
	192,423.52	498,023.52						

range I3:K3 copied to range I4:K20

0s in column K are result of empty cells in column H

Sheet3

Average: 4691.366544   Count: 54   Sum: 253333.7934   100%

Auto Fill Options button

Figure 4–40

2

- Select cell H4, type =i3 as the cell entry, and then click the Enter box in the formula bar to display the ending balance (233644.6314) for year 1 as the beginning balance for year 2 (Figure 4–41).

	D	E	F	G	H	I	J	K
3								
	ent Calculator					Amortization Schedule		
				Year	Beginning Balance	Ending Balance	Paid On Principal	Interest Paid
	Rate	4.50%		1	$242,600.00	233644.6314	$8,955.37	10733.79339
	Years	18		2	233644.6314	224277.8548	$9,366.78	10322.38532
	Monthly Payment	$1,640.76		3		214480.7701	$214,480.77	0
	Total Interest	$111,804.92		4		204233.609	$204,233.61	0
	Total Cost	$417,404.92		5		193515.6951	$193,515.70	0
	st Rate Schedule			6			82,305.40	0
	Total Interest	Total Cost		7			70,580.11	0
6	$111,804.92	$417,404.92		8			58,316.16	0
8	98,114.00	403,714.00		9		145488.8072	$145,488.81	0
9	104,921.03	410,521.03		10		132072.1674	$132,072.17	0
5	111,804.92	417,404.92		11		118039.1696	$118,039.17	0
	118,765.10	424,365.10		12		103361.4983	$103,361.50	0
	125,800.99	431,400.99		13		88009.53727	$88,009.54	0
	132,911.98	438,511.98		14		71952.30989	$71,952.31	0
	140,097.46	445,697.46		15		55157.41629	$55,157.42	0
	147,356.75	452,956.75		16		37590.96822	$37,590.97	0
	154,689.19	460,289.19		17		19217.52059	$19,217.52	0
	162,094.08	467,694.08		18		0	$0.00	0
	169,570.70	475,170.70						
	177,118.32	482,718.32						
	184,736.19	490,336.19						
	192,423.52	498,023.52						

beginning balance for each year is equal to previous year's ending balance

Sheet3

100%

Figure 4–41

3

- With cell H4 active, drag the fill handle down through row 20 to copy the formula in the selected cell, cell H4 (=I3) to the range H5:H20 in this case (Figure 4–42).

Q&A

What happens after the fill operation is complete?

Because the cell reference I3 is relative, Excel adjusts the row portion of the cell reference as it is copied downward. Thus, each new beginning balance in column H is equal to the ending balance of the previous year.

	f_x	=I3						
	C	D		G	H	I	J	K
Loan Payment Calc		with beginning balances for each year calculated, remaining values in amortization schedule now are correct			**Amortization Schedule**			
28-May-2012	Rate			Year	Beginning Balance	Ending Balance	Paid On Principal	Interest Paid
	House	Years		1	$242,600.00	233644.6314	$8,955.37	10733.79339
$305,600.00	Monthly Payment	$1,640.76		2	233644.6314	224277.8548	$9,366.78	10322.38532
$63,000.00	Total Interest	$111,804.92		3	224277.8548	214480.7701	$9,797.08	9892.077244
$242,600.00	Total Cost	$417,404.92		4	214480.7701	204233.609	$10,247.16	9442.000886
rying Interest Rate Schedule				5	204233.609	193515.6951	$10,717.91	8971.248099
Monthly Payment	Total Interest	Total Cost		6	193515.6951	182305.4022	$11,210.29	8478.869012
$1,640.76	$111,804.92	$417,404.92		7	182305.4022	170580.1103	$11,725.29	7963.870115
1,577.38	98,1	cell H4 copied to range H5:H20	14.00	8	170580.1103	158316.1606	$12,263.95	7425.212259
1,608.89	104,9		21.03	9	158316.1606	145488.8072	$12,827.35	6861.808555
1,640.76	111,804.92	417,404.92		10	145488.8072	132072.1674	$13,416.64	6272.522184
1,672.99	118,765.10	424,365.10		11	132072.1674	118039.1696	$14,033.00	5656.1641
1,705.56	125,800.99	431,400.99		12	118039.1696	103361.4983	$14,677.67	5011.490633
1,738.48	132,911.98	438,511.98		13	103361.4983	88009.53727	$15,351.96	4337.20098
1,771.75	140,097.46	445,697.46		14	88009.53727	71952.30989	$16,057.23	3631.934579
1,805.36	147,356.75	452,956.75		15	71952.30989	55157.41629	$16,794.89	2894.268362
1,839.30	154,689.19	460,289.19		16	55157.41629	37590.96822	$17,566.45	2122.713889
1,873.58	162,094.08	467,694.08		17	37590.96822	19217.52059	$18,373.45	1315.714338
1,908.20	169,570.70	475,170.70		18	19217.52059	0	$19,217.52	471.6413684
1,943.14	177,118.32	482,718.32						
1,978.41	184,736.19	490,336.19						
2,014.00	192,423.52	498,023.52						

ending balance for year 18 is 0

Auto Fill Options button

al Services / Sheet2 / Sheet3

Average: 138367.2723   628   100%

Figure 4–42

To Enter the Total Formulas in the Amortization Schedule

The next step is to determine the amortization schedule totals in rows 21 through 23. These totals should agree with the corresponding totals in the Loan Payment Calculator section (range B1:E6). The following steps enter the total formulas in the amortization schedule.

1 Select cell I21 and then enter **Subtotal** as the row title.

2 Select the range J21:K21 and then click the Sum button (Home tab | Editing group) to sum the selected range.

3 Select cell I22 and then enter **Down Pymt.** as the row title.

4 Select cell K22 and then enter **=c5** to copy the down payment to the selected cell.

5 Select cell I23 and then enter **Total Cost** as the row title.

6 Select cell K23, type **=j21 + k21 + k22** as the total cost, and then click the Enter box in the formula bar to complete the amortization schedule totals (Figure 4–43).

Q&A

What was accomplished in the previous steps?

The formula assigned to cell K23 (=j21 + k21 + k22) sums the total amount paid on the principal (cell J21), the total interest paid (cell K21), and the down payment (cell K22). Excel assigns cell J21 the same format as cell J3, because cell J3 is the first cell reference in =SUM(J3:J20). Furthermore, because cell J21 was selected first when the range J21:K21 was selected to determine the sum, Excel assigned cell K21 the same format it assigned to cell J21. Finally, cell K22 was assigned the Currency style format, because cell K22 was assigned the formula =c5, and cell C5 has a Currency style format. For the same reason, the value in cell K23 appears in Currency style format.

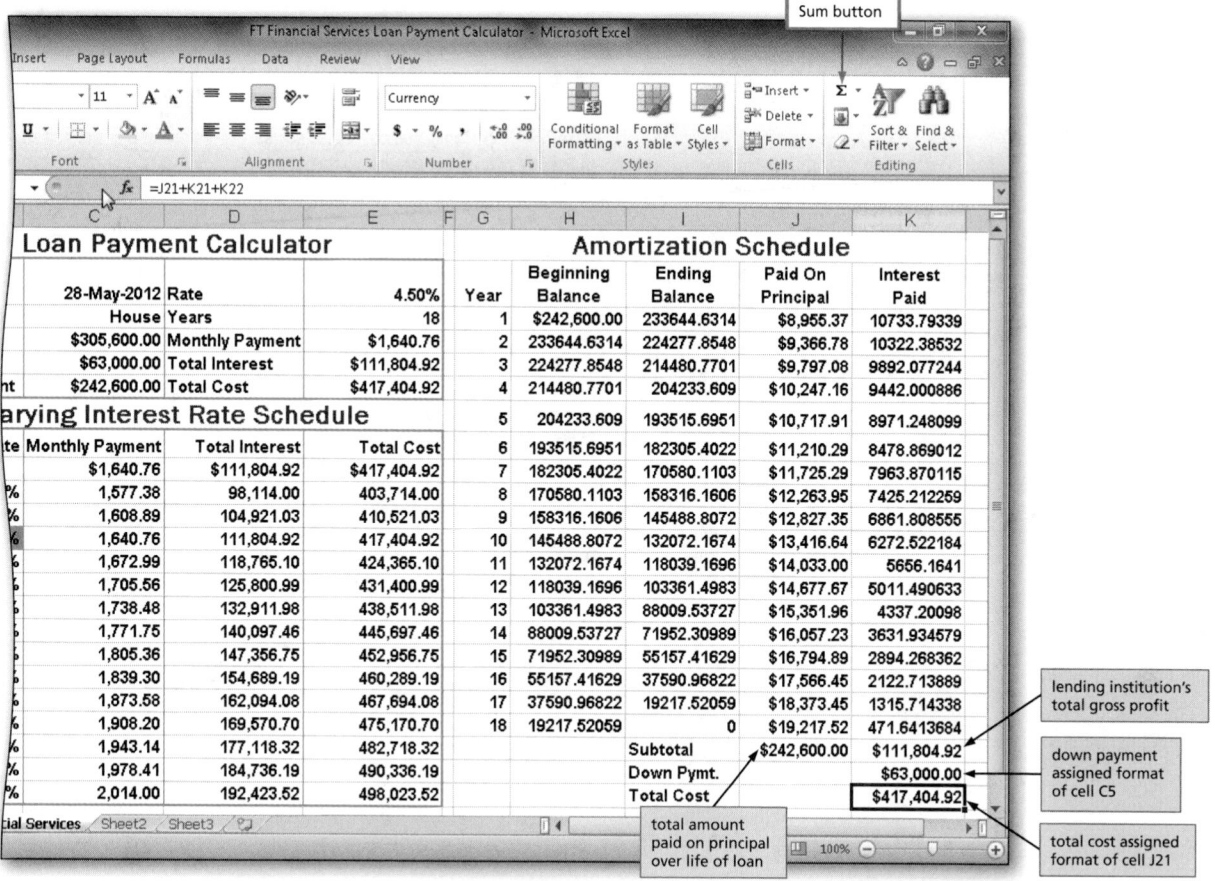

Figure 4–43

To Format the Numbers in the Amortization Schedule

The final step in creating the amortization schedule is to format it so that it is easier to read. The formatting is divided into two parts: (1) formatting the numbers and (2) adding borders.

When the beginning balance formula (=c6) was entered earlier into cell H3, Excel automatically copied the Currency style format along with the value from cell C6 to cell H3. The following steps copy the Currency style format from cell H3 to the range I3:K3. The Comma style then will be assigned to the range H4:K20.

① Select cell H3 and then click the Format Painter button (Home tab | Clipboard group) to start the format painter. Drag through the range I3:K3 to assign the Currency style format to the cells.

② Select the range H4:K20 and then right-click the selected range to display a shortcut menu. Click Format Cells on the shortcut menu to display the Format Cells dialog box and then, if necessary, click the Number tab (Format Cells dialog box) to display the Number sheet.

③ Click Currency in the Category list to select a currency format and then click the Symbol box arrow to display the Symbol list. Click None to choose no currency symbol, and then click the second format, 1,234.10, in the Negative numbers list to create a currency format.

④ Click the OK button (Format Cells dialog box) to apply the currency format to the selected range.

⑤ Select cell H21 to deselect the range H4:K20 and display the numbers in the amortization schedule, as shown in Figure 4–44 on the following page.

BTW

Round-Off Errors
If you manually add the numbers in column K (range K3:K20) and compare it to the sum in cell K21, you will notice that the total interest paid is $0.02 off. This round-off error is due to the fact that some of the numbers involved in the computations have additional decimal places that do not appear in the cells. You can use the ROUND function on the formula entered into cell K3 to ensure the total is exactly correct. For information on the ROUND function, click the Insert Function button in the formula bar, click Math & Trig in the 'Or select a category' list, scroll down in the 'Select a function' list, and then click ROUND.

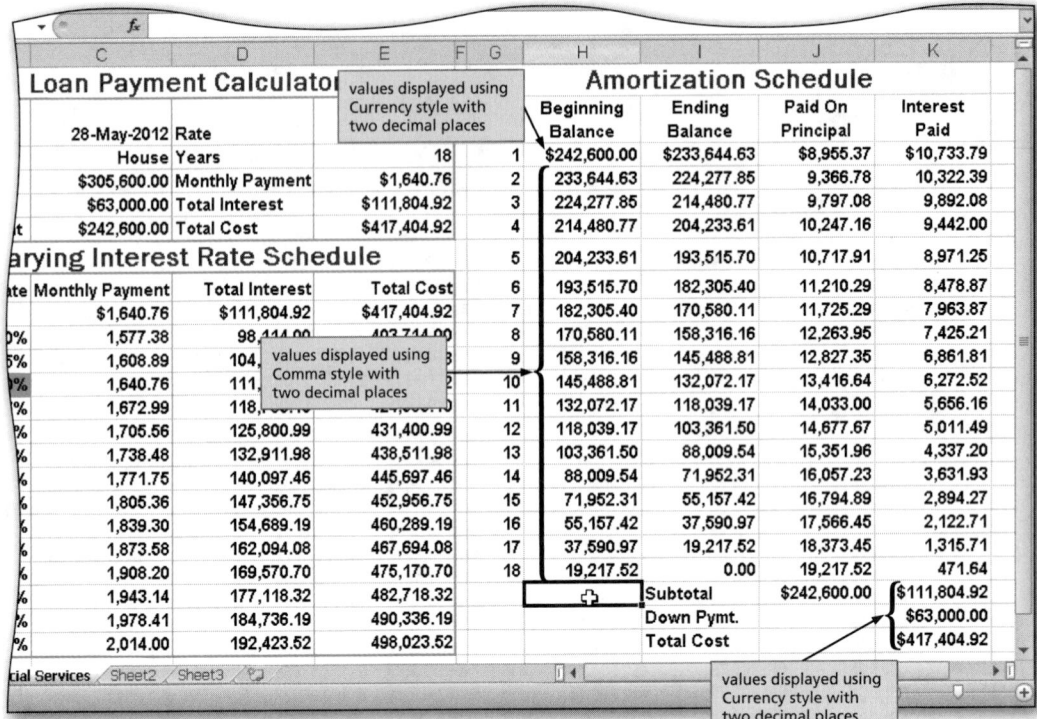

Figure 4–44

To Add Borders to the Amortization Schedule

The following steps add the borders to the amortization schedule.

1 Select the range G2:K23. Right-click the selected range to display a shortcut menu and then click Format Cells on the shortcut menu to display the Format Cells dialog box.

2 Click the Border tab (Format Cells dialog box) to display the Border sheet. Click the Color box arrow to display the Colors palette and then click Red (column 2, row 1) in the Standard Colors area to change the border color.

3 Click the medium border in the Style area (column 2, row 5). Click the Outline button in the Presets area to preview the border in the Border area.

4 Click the light border in the Style area (column 1, row 7). Click the Vertical Line button in the Border area to preview the border in the Border area.

5 Click the OK button (Format Cells dialog box) to apply custom borders to the selected range.

6 Select the range G2:K2 and then use the Format Cells dialog box to apply a red, light bottom border to the selected range.

7 Select the range G20:K20 and then use the Format Cells dialog box to apply a red, light bottom border to the selected range.

8 Select cell G23 to display the worksheet, as shown in Figure 4–45.

9 Click the Save button on the Quick Access Toolbar to save the workbook using the file name, FT Financial Services Loan Payment Calculator.

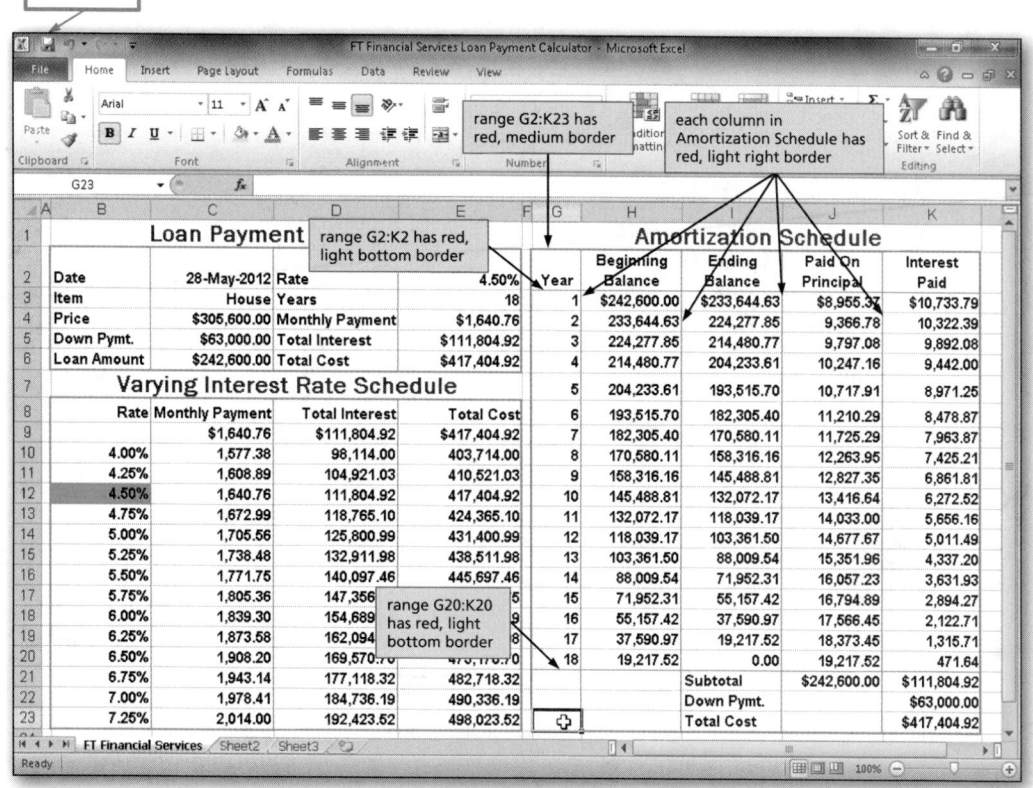

Figure 4–45

To Enter New Loan Data

With the Loan Payment Calculator, Varying Interest Rate Schedule, and Amortization Schedule sections of the worksheet complete, you can use them to generate new loan information. For example, assume you want to purchase land for $62,500.00. You have $9,000.00 for a down payment and want the loan for only 7 years. FT Financial Services currently is charging 7.25% interest for a 7–year loan on land. The following steps enter the new loan data.

1 Enter **Land** in cell C3.

2 Enter **62500** in cell C4.

3 Enter **9000** in cell C5.

4 Enter **7.25%** in cell E2.

5 Enter **7** in cell E3 and then press the DOWN ARROW key to calculate the loan data.

6 Select cell H22 to display the worksheet, as shown in Figure 4–46 on the following page.

Q&A

What happens on the worksheet when the new data is entered?

As shown in Figure 4–46, the monthly payment for the land is $814.01 (cell E4). The total interest is $14,877.04 (cell E5) and the total cost for the land is $77,377.04 (cell E6). Because the term of the loan is for 7 years, the rows for years 8 through 18 in the Amortization Schedule section display 0.00.

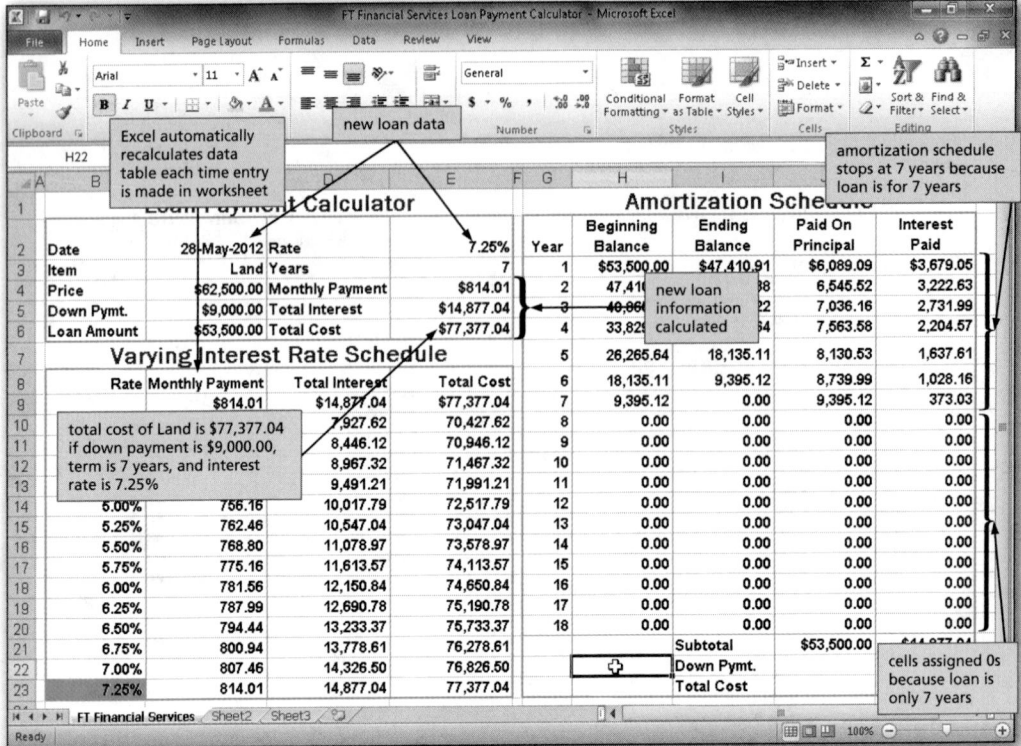

Figure 4–46

To Enter the Original Loan Data

The following steps reenter the original loan data.

BTW

Conserving Ink and Toner

If you want to conserve ink or toner, you can instruct Excel to print draft quality documents by clicking File on the Ribbon to open the Backstage view, clicking Options in the Backstage view to display the Excel Options dialog box, clicking Advanced in the left pane (Excel Options dialog box), scrolling to the Print area in the right pane, make sure that the 'High quality mode for graphics' button is unchecked and then clicking the OK button. Then, use the Backstage view to print the document as usual.

1 Enter **House** in cell C3.

2 Enter **305600** in cell C4.

3 Enter **63000** in cell C5.

4 Enter **4.50** in cell E2.

5 Enter **18** in cell E3 and then select cell H22.

Printing Sections of the Worksheet

In Chapter 2, you learned to print a section of a worksheet by selecting it and using the Selection option in the Print dialog box. If you find yourself continually selecting the same range in a worksheet to print, you can set a specific range to print each time you print the worksheet. When you set a range to print, Excel will continue to print only that range until you clear it.

To Set Up a Worksheet to Print

This section describes print options available in the Sheet tab in the Page Setup dialog box (Figure 4–47). These print options pertain to the way the worksheet will appear in the printed copy or when previewed. One important print option is the capability of printing in black and white, even when your printer is a color printer. Printing in black and white not only speeds up the printing process but also saves ink. The following steps ensure any printed copy fits on one page and prints in black and white.

1

- Display the Page Layout tab and then click the Page Setup Dialog Box Launcher (Page Layout tab | Page Setup group) to display the Page Setup dialog box.

- If necessary, click the Page tab (Page Setup dialog box) to display the Page sheet and then click Fit to in the Scaling area to set the worksheet to print on one page (Figure 4–47).

Figure 4–47

2

- Click the Sheet tab (Page Setup dialog box) to display the tab and then click 'Black and white' in the Print area to select the check box (Figure 4–48).

3

- Click the OK button (Page Setup dialog box) to close the Page Setup dialog box.

Figure 4–48

Naming Ranges
A name can be assigned to two or more nonadjacent ranges. After selecting the first range, hold down the CTRL key and drag through the additional ranges of cells to select them before entering the name in the Name box.

More about Print Options

Table 4–3 summarizes the print options available on the Sheet tab in the Page Setup dialog box.

Table 4–3 Print Options Available Using the Sheet Tab in the Page Setup Dialog Box	
Print Option	**Description**
Print area box	Excel prints from cell A1 to the last occupied cell in a worksheet unless you instruct it to print a selected area. You can select a range to print with the mouse, or you can enter a range or name of a range in the Print area box. Nonadjacent ranges will print on a separate page.
Print titles area	This area is used to instruct Excel to print row titles and column titles on each printed page of a worksheet. You must specify a range, even if you are designating one column (e.g., 1:4 means the first four rows).
Gridlines check box	A check mark in this check box instructs Excel to print gridlines.
Black and white check box	A check mark in this check box speeds up printing and saves colored ink if you have colors in a worksheet and a color printer.
Draft quality check box	A check mark in this check box speeds up printing by ignoring formatting and not printing most graphics.
Row and column headings check box	A check mark in this check box instructs Excel to include the column heading letters (A, B, C, etc.) and row heading numbers (1, 2, 3, etc.) in the printout.
Comments box	Indicates where comments are to be displayed on the printout.
Cell errors as box	Indicates how errors in cells should be displayed on the printout.
Page order area	Determines the order in which multipage worksheets will print.

To Set the Print Area

The following steps print only the Loan Payment Calculator section by setting the print area to the range B1:E6.

1

- Select the range B1:E6 and then click the Print Area button (Page Layout tab | Page Setup group) to display the Print Area menu (Figure 4–49).

Figure 4–49

- Click Set Print Area on the Print Area menu to set the range of the worksheet which Excel should print.

- Click File on the Ribbon to open the Backstage view and then click the Print tab in the Backstage view to display the Print gallery.

- Click the Print button in the Print gallery to print the selected area (Figure 4–50).

Figure 4–50

- Display the Page Layout tab.

- Click the Print Area button (Page Layout tab | Page Setup group) to display the Print Area list and then click the Clear Print Area command on the Print Area list to reset the print area to the entire worksheet.

Q&A

What happens when I set a print area?

Once you set a print area, Excel will continue to print the specified range, rather than the entire worksheet. If you save the workbook with the print area set, then Excel will remember the settings the next time you open the workbook and print only the specified range. To remove the print area so that the entire worksheet prints, click Clear Print Area on the Print Area menu as described in Step 3.

To Name and Print Sections of a Worksheet

With some spreadsheet applications, you will want to print several different areas of a worksheet, depending on the request. Rather than using the Set Print Area command or manually selecting the range each time you want to print, you can name the ranges using the Name box in the formula bar. You then can use one of the names to select an area before using the Set Print Area command or Selection option button. The following steps name the Loan Payment Calculator section, the Varying Interest Rate Schedule section, the Amortization Schedule section, and the entire worksheet, and then print each section.

- Click the Page Setup Dialog Box Launcher (Page Layout tab | Page Setup group) to display the Page Setup dialog box, click the Sheet tab to display the Sheet page, and, if necessary, click 'Black and white' to deselect the check box and ensure that Excel prints in color to color printers.

- Click the OK button (Page Setup dialog box) to close the Page Setup dialog box.

- If necessary, select the range B1:E6, click the Name box, and then type **Loan_Payment** as the name of the range to create a range name (Figure 4–51).

Figure 4–51

2

- Press the ENTER key to create a range name.

- Select the range B7:E23, click the Name box, type **Interest_ Schedule** as the name of the range, and then press the ENTER key to create a range name.

- Select the range G1:K23, click the Name box, type **Amortization_ Schedule** as the name of the range, and then press the ENTER key to create a range name.

- Select the range B1:K23, click the Name box, type **All_Sections** as the name of the range, and then press the ENTER key to create a range name.

- Select cell H22 and then click the Name box arrow in the formula bar to display the Name list with the new range names (Figure 4–52).

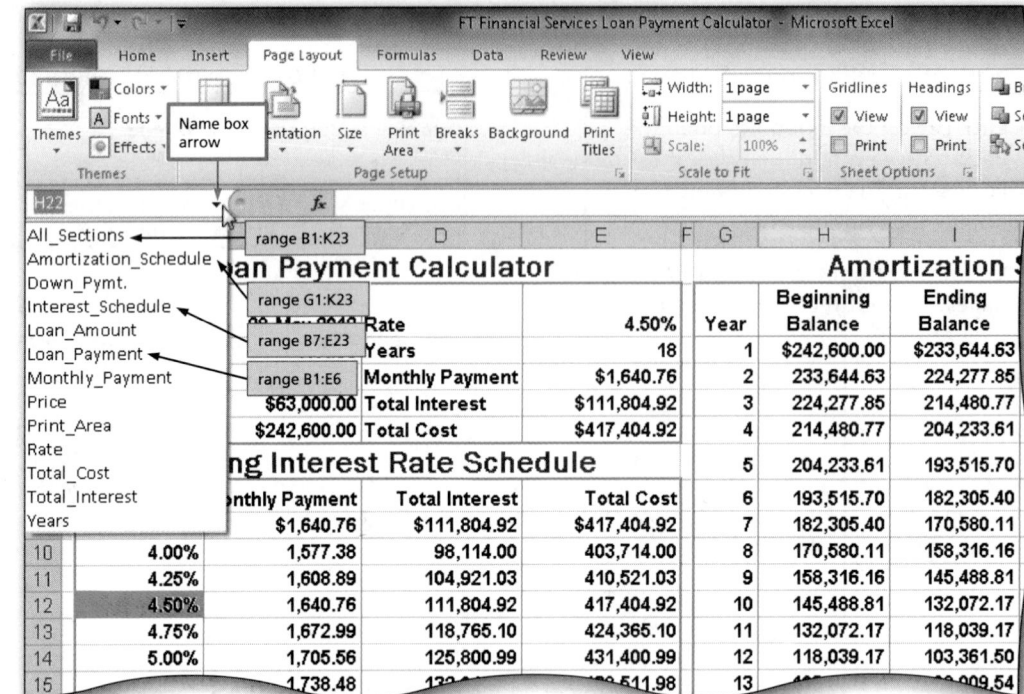

Figure 4–52

3

- Click Loan_Payment in the Name list to select the range associated with the name, B1:E6 in this case.

- Click File on the Ribbon to open the Backstage view and then click the Print tab in the Backstage view to display the Print gallery.

- If necessary, click the Print Active Sheets button in the Settings area and select Print Selection to select the desired item to print (Figure 4–53).

Figure 4–53

4

● Click the Print button in the Print gallery to print the selected named range, Loan_Payment in this case.

● One at a time, use the Name box to select the names Interest_Schedule, Amortization_ Schedule, and All_Sections, and then print them following the instructions in Step 3 to print the remaining named ranges (Figure 4–54).

5

● Click the Save button on the Quick Access Toolbar to save the workbook using the file name, FT Financial Services Loan Payment Calculator.

Q&A

Why does the All_Sections range print on one page?

Recall that the Fit to option was selected earlier (Figure 4–47 on page EX 267). This selection ensures that each of the printouts fits across the page in portrait orientation.

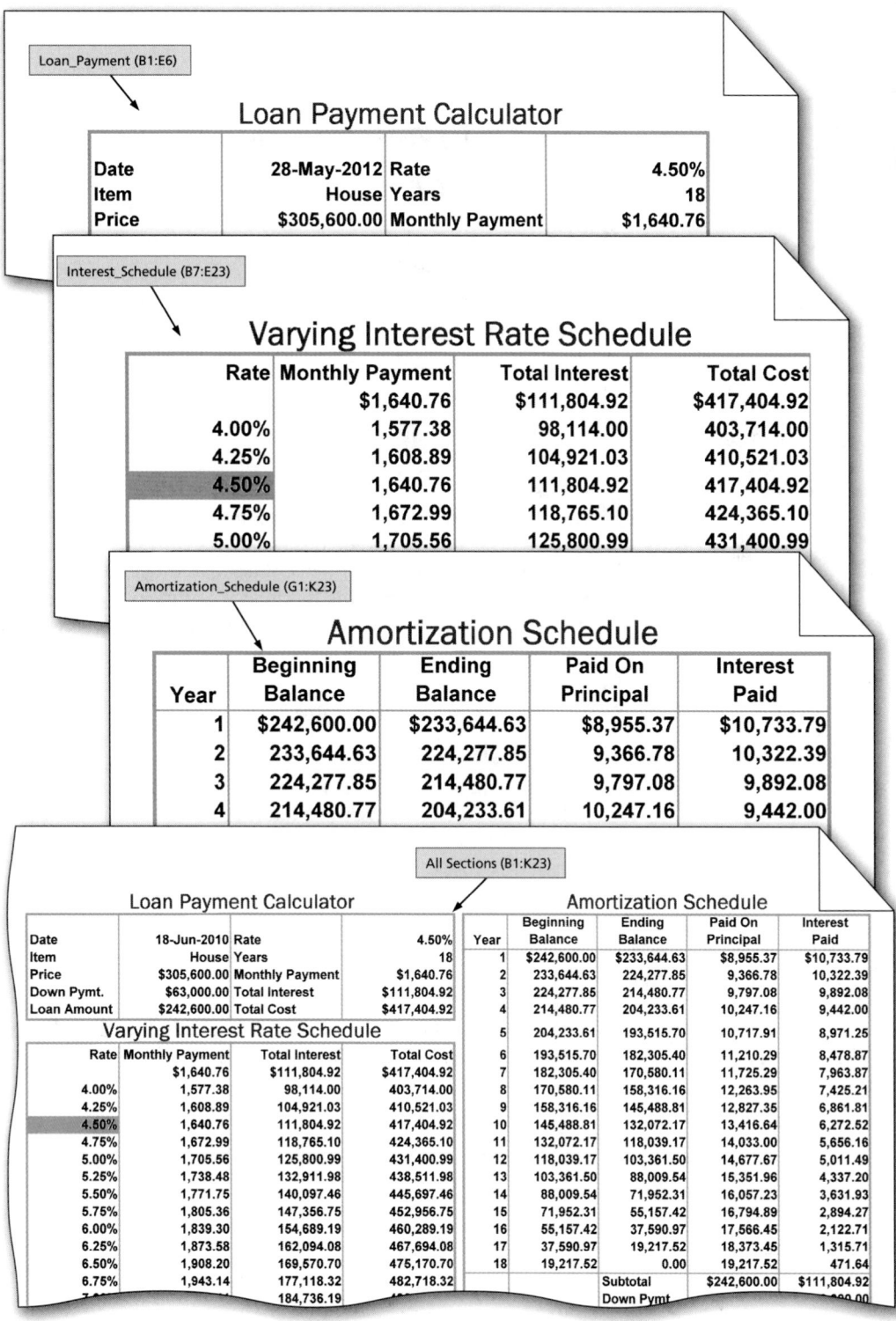

Figure 4–54

Other Ways
1. Select cell or range, click Define Name button (Formulas tab | Defined Names group), [type name], click OK button
2. Select cell or range, click Name Manager button (Formulas tab | Defined Names group), click New, [type name], click OK button, click Close button

Break Point: If you wish to take a break, this is a good place to do so. You can quit Excel now. To resume at a later time, start Excel, open the file called FT Financial Services Loan Payment Calculator, and continue following the steps from this location forward.

BTW

Hiding Worksheets
When sharing workbooks with others, you may not want them to see some of your worksheets. Hiding worksheets obscures the sheets from casual inspection; however, it is not only for hiding worksheets from others' eyes. Sometimes, you have several worksheets that include data that you rarely require or that you use only as a reference. To clean up the list of sheet tabs, you can hide worksheets that you usually do not need.

Protecting and Hiding Worksheets and Workbooks

When building a worksheet for novice users, you should protect the cells in the worksheet that you do not want changed, such as cells that contain text or formulas. Doing so prevents users from making ill-advised changes to text and formulas in cells.

When you create a new worksheet, all the cells are assigned a locked status, but the lock is not engaged, which leaves cells unprotected. **Unprotected cells** are cells whose values you can change at any time. **Protected cells** are cells that you cannot change.

Plan Ahead

> **Determine which cells to protect and unprotect in the worksheet.**
> In general, all cells should be protected except those that require an entry by the user of the worksheet. Any cells containing formulas should be protected so that a user of the worksheet cannot modify the formulas. You should protect cells only after the worksheet has been tested fully and the correct results appear. Protecting a worksheet is a two-step process:
>
> **1.** Select the cells you want to leave unprotected and then change their cell protection settings to an unlocked status.
>
> **2.** Protect the entire worksheet.
>
> At first glance, these steps may appear to be backwards. Once you protect the entire worksheet, however, you cannot change anything, including the locked status of individual cells.

To Protect a Worksheet

In the Loan Payment Calculator worksheet, the user should be able to make changes to only five cells: the item in cell C3, the price in cell C4, the down payment in cell C5, the interest rate in cell E2, and the years in cell E3 (Figure 4–55). These cells must remain unprotected so that users can enter the correct data. The remaining cells in the worksheet should be protected so that the user cannot change them.

The following steps protect the Loan Payment Calculator worksheet.

1

- Select the range C3:C5 and then, while holding down the CTRL key, select the nonadjacent range E2:E3 to select the ranges to unprotect.

- Right-click one of the selected ranges to display a shortcut menu and Mini toolbar (Figure 4–55).

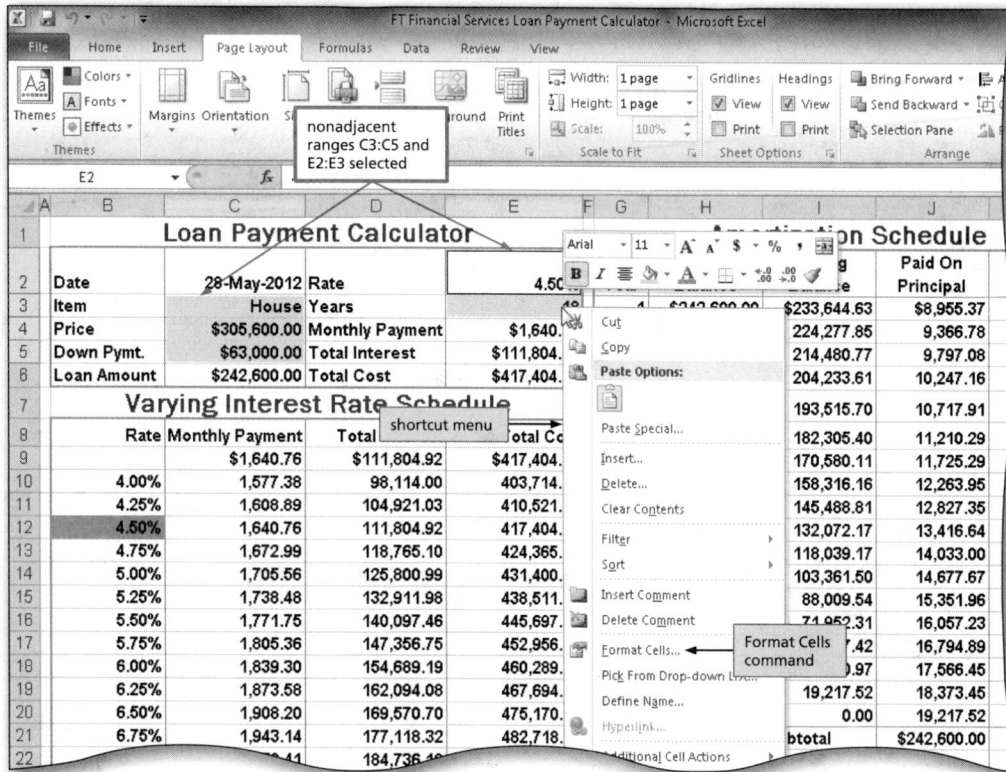

Figure 4–55

2

- Click Format Cells on the shortcut menu to display the Format Cells dialog box.

- Click the Protection tab (Format Cells dialog box) and then click Locked to remove the check mark (Figure 4–56).

Q&A

What is the meaning of the Locked check box?

Excel displays the Protection sheet in the Format Cells dialog box with the check mark removed from the Locked check box (Figure 4–56). This means the selected cells (C3:C5 and E2:E3) will not be protected when the Protect command is invoked later.

Figure 4–56

- Click the OK button to close the Format Cells dialog box.

- Select cell H22 to deselect the ranges, C3:C5 and E2:E3 in this case.

- Display the Review tab (Figure 4–57).

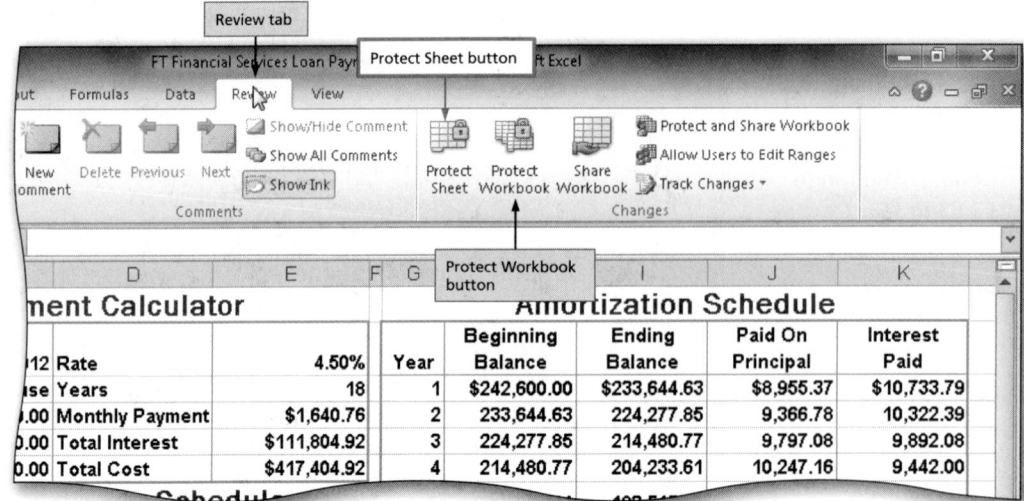

Figure 4–57

4

- Click the Protect Sheet button (Review tab | Changes group) to display the Protect Sheet dialog box.

- When Excel displays the Protect Sheet dialog box, ensure that the 'Protect worksheet and contents of locked cells' check box at the top of the dialog box and the first two check boxes in the list contain check marks so that the user of the worksheet can select both locked and unlocked cells (Figure 4–58).

Figure 4–58

Q&A

What do the three checked check boxes mean?

With all three check boxes selected, the worksheet (except for the cells left unlocked) is protected from changes to contents. The two check boxes in the list allow the user to select any cell on the worksheet, but the user can change only unlocked cells.

5

- Click the OK button (Protect Sheet dialog box) to close the Protect Sheet dialog box.

- Click the Save button on the Quick Access Toolbar to save the workbook.

Other Ways

1. Click Format Cells Dialog Box Launcher (Home tab | Font, Alignment, or Number group), click

   Protection tab, remove check mark from Locked check box, click OK button

More about Worksheet Protection

All the cells in the worksheet, except for the ranges C3:C5 and E2:E3, are protected, The Protect Sheet dialog box in Figure 4–58 enables you to enter a password that can be used to unprotect the sheet. You should create a **password** when you want to keep others from changing the worksheet from protected to unprotected. The check boxes in the list in the Protect Sheet dialog box also give you the option to modify the protection so that the user can make certain changes, such as formatting cells or inserting hyperlinks.

If you want to protect more than one sheet in a workbook, select each sheet before you begin the protection process or click the Protect Workbook button (Review tab | Changes group), instead of clicking the Protect Sheet button (Review tab | Changes group) (Figure 4–57). If you want to unlock cells for specific users, you can use the Allow Users to Edit Ranges button (Review tab | Changes group).

When this workbook is made available to users, they will be able to enter data in only the unprotected cells. If they try to change any protected cell, such as the monthly payment in cell E4, Excel displays a dialog box with an error message, as shown in Figure 4–59. An alternative to displaying this dialog box is to remove the check mark from the 'Select unlocked cells' check box in the Protect Sheet dialog box (Figure 4–58). With the check mark removed, the users cannot select a locked cell.

BTW

Using Protected Worksheets
You can move from one unprotected cell to another unprotected cell in a worksheet by using the TAB and SHIFT+TAB keys. This is especially useful when the cells are not adjacent to one another.

Figure 4–59

To unprotect the worksheet so that you can change all cells in the worksheet, unprotect the document by clicking the Unprotect Sheet button (Review tab | Changes group).

To Hide and Unhide a Sheet

You can hide rows, columns, and sheets that contain sensitive data. When you again need to access hidden rows, columns, and sheets, you can unhide them. You can use the mouse and keyboard to hide and unhide rows and columns by setting their heights and widths to zero. The following steps hide and then unhide a sheet.

- Right-click the FT Financial Services sheet tab to display a shortcut menu (Figure 4–60).

Q&A

Why is the Unhide command on the shortcut menu dimmed?

Excel dims the Unhide command when no sheets are hidden.

Figure 4–60

②

- Click Hide on the shortcut menu to hide the FT Financial Services sheet.

- Right-click any sheet tab to display a shortcut menu.

- Click Unhide on the shortcut menu to open the Unhide dialog box.

- When Excel displays the Unhide dialog box, if necessary, click FT Financial Services in the Unhide sheet list to select the sheet to unhide (Figure 4–61).

Q&A

When should I hide a sheet?

Hiding sheets in a workbook is common when working with complex workbooks that have one sheet with the results the user needs to see and one or more sheets with essential data that, while important to the functionality of the workbook, is unimportant to the user of the workbook and, thus, hidden from view. The data and formulas on the hidden sheets remain available for use on other sheets in the workbook. This same logic applies to hidden rows and columns.

Figure 4–61

③

- Click the OK button (Unhide dialog box) to unhide the hidden sheet.

To Hide and Unhide a Workbook

In addition to hiding worksheets, you also can hide an entire workbook. Some users apply this feature when they leave a workbook open on an unattended computer and do not want others to be able to see the workbook. This feature is also useful when you have several workbooks open simultaneously and want the user to be able to view only one of them. The following steps hide and unhide a workbook.

1
- Display the View tab (Figure 4–62).

Figure 4–62

2
- Click the Hide button (View tab | Window group) to hide the FT Financial Services Loan Payment Calculator workbook.

- Click the Unhide button (View tab | Window group) to display the Unhide dialog box.

- If necessary, click FT Financial Services Loan Payment Calculator in the Unhide workbook list to select a workbook to unhide (Figure 4–63).

Q&A
What else can I hide?

You can hide most window elements in order to display more rows of worksheet data. These window elements include the Ribbon, formula bar, and status bar. The Excel window elements can be hidden by using the Full Screen button (View tab | Workbook Views group) (Figure 4–62). These elements remain hidden only as long as the workbook is open. They are redisplayed when you close the workbook and open it again.

Figure 4–63

3
- Click the OK button (Unhide dialog box) to unhide the selected hidden workbook and display the workbook in the same state as it was in when it was hidden.

Formula Checking

Similar to the spell checker, Excel has a **formula checker** that checks formulas in a worksheet for rule violations. You invoke the formula checker by clicking the Error Checking button (Formulas tab | Formula Auditing group). Each time Excel encounters a cell with a formula that violates one of its rules, it displays a dialog box containing information about the formula and a suggestion about how to fix the formula. Table 4–4 lists Excel's error checking rules. You can choose which rules you want Excel to use by enabling and disabling them in the Formulas area in the Excel Options dialog box shown in Figure 4–64.

Table 4–4 Error Checking Rules		
Rule	**Name of Rule**	**Description**
1	Cells containing formulas that result in an error	The cell contains a formula that does not use the expected syntax, arguments, or data types.
2	Inconsistent calculated column formula in tables	The cell contains formulas or values that are inconsistent with the column formula or tables.
3	Cells containing years represented as 2 digits	The cell contains a text date with a two-digit year that can be misinterpreted as the wrong century.
4	Numbers formatted as text or preceded by an apostrophe	The cell contains numbers stored as text.
5	Formulas inconsistent with other formulas in the region	The cell contains a formula that does not match the pattern of the formulas around it.
6	Formulas which omit cells in a region	The cell contains a formula that does not include a correct cell or range reference.
7	Unlocked cells containing formulas	The cell with a formula is unlocked in a protected worksheet.
8	Formulas referring to empty cells	The cells referenced in a formula are empty.
9	Data entered in a table is invalid	The cell has a data validation error.

To Enable Background Formula Checking

Through the Excel Options dialog box, you can enable background formula checking. **Background formula checking** means that Excel continually will review the workbook for errors in formulas as you create or manipulate it. The following steps enable background formula checking.

1 Click the File on the Ribbon to open the Backstage view and then click the Options button to display the Excel Options dialog box.

2 Click the Formulas button (Excel Options dialog box) to display the Excel options related to formula calculation, performance, and error handling.

3 If necessary, click 'Enable background error checking' in the Error Checking area to select it.

4 Click any check box in the 'Error checking rules' area that does not contain a check mark to enable all error checking rules (Figure 4–64).

5 Click the OK button (Excel Options dialog box) to close the Excel Options dialog box.

Q&A

How can I decide which rules to have the background formula checker check?

You can decide which rules you want the background formula checker to highlight by adding and removing check marks from the check boxes in the 'Error checking rules' area (Figure 4–64). If you add or remove check marks, then you should click the Reset Ignored Errors button to reset error checking.

Figure 4–64

More about Background Formula Checking

When a formula fails to pass one of the rules and background formula checking is enabled, then Excel displays a small green triangle in the upper-left corner of the cell assigned the formula in question.

Assume, for example, that background formula checking is enabled and that cell E4, which contains the PMT function in the FT Financial Services Loan Payment Calculator workbook, is unlocked. Because rule 7 in Table 4–4 stipulates that a cell containing a formula must be locked, Excel displays a green triangle in the upper-left corner of cell E4.

When you select the cell with the green triangle, a Trace Error button appears next to the cell. If you click the Trace Error button, Excel displays the Trace Error menu (Figure 4–65). The first item in the menu identifies the error (Unprotected Formula). The remainder of the menu lists commands from which you can choose. The first

Figure 4–65

Certification
The Microsoft Office Specialist (MOS) program provides an opportunity for you to obtain a valuable industry credential — proof that you have the Excel 2010 skills required by employers. For more information, visit the Excel 2010 Certification Web page (scsite.com/ ex2010/cert).

Quick Reference
For a table that lists how to complete the tasks covered in this book using the mouse, Ribbon, shortcut menu, and keyboard, see the Quick Reference Summary at the back of this book, or visit the Excel 2010 Quick Reference Web page (scsite.com/ex2010/qr).

command locks the cell. Invoking the Lock Cell command fixes the problem so that the formula no longer violates the rule. The Error Checking Options command instructs Excel to display the Excel Options dialog box with the Formulas area active, as shown in Figure 4–65 on the previous page.

The background formula checker can become annoying when you are creating certain types of worksheets that may violate the formula rules until referenced cells contain data. You often may end up with green triangles in cells throughout your worksheet. If this is the case, then disable background formula checking by removing the check mark from the 'Enable background error checking' check box (Figure 4–64) and use the Error Checking button (Formulas tab | Formula Auditing group) to check your worksheet once you have finished creating it.

Use the background formula checking or the Error Checking button (Formulas tab | Formula Auditing group) during the testing phase to ensure the formulas in your workbook do not violate the rules listed in Table 4–4 on page EX 278.

To Quit Excel

With the workbook complete, the following steps quit Excel.

1 Click the Close button on the upper-right corner of the title bar.

2 If the Microsoft Excel dialog box is displayed, click the Don't Save button (Microsoft Excel dialog box).

Chapter Summary

In this chapter, you learned how to use names, rather than cell references, to enter formulas, use financial functions, such as the PMT and PV functions, analyze data by creating a data table and amortization schedule, set print options and print sections of a worksheet using names and the Set Print Area command, protect a worksheet or workbook, and hide and unhide rows, columns, sheets, and workbooks. The items listed below include all the new Excel skills you have learned in this chapter.

1. Add Custom Borders to a Range (EX 234)
2. Create Names Based on Row Titles (EX 238)
3. Enter the Loan Amount Formula Using Names (EX 240)
4. Enter the PMT Function (EX 241)
5. Create a Percent Series Using the Fill Handle (EX 247)
6. Define a Range as a Data Table (EX 249)
7. Add a Pointer to the Data Table (EX 252)
8. Enter the Formulas in the Amortization Schedule (EX 257)
9. Copy the Formulas to Fill the Amortization Schedule (EX 260)
10. Set Up a Worksheet to Print (EX 266)
11. Set the Print Area (EX 268)
12. Name and Print Sections of a Worksheet (EX 269)
13. Protect a Worksheet (EX 272)
14. Hide and Unhide a Sheet (EX 276)
15. Hide and Unhide a Workbook (EX 277)
16. Enable Background Formula Checking (EX 278)

Learn It Online

Test your knowledge of chapter content and key terms.

Instructions: To complete the Learn It Online exercises, start your browser, click the Address bar, and then enter the Web address `scsite.com/ex2010/learn`. When the Excel 2010 Learn It Online page is displayed, click the link for the exercise you want to complete and then read the instructions.

Chapter Reinforcement TF, MC, and SA

A series of true/false, multiple choice, and short answer questions that test your knowledge of the chapter content.

Flash Cards

An interactive learning environment where you identify chapter key terms associated with displayed definitions.

Practice Test

A series of multiple choice questions that test your knowledge of chapter content and key terms.

Who Wants To Be a Computer Genius?

An interactive game that challenges your knowledge of chapter content in the style of a television quiz show.

Wheel of Terms

An interactive game that challenges your knowledge of chapter key terms in the style of the television show *Wheel of Fortune*.

Crossword Puzzle Challenge

A crossword puzzle that challenges your knowledge of key terms presented in the chapter.

Apply Your Knowledge

Reinforce the skills and apply the concepts you learned in this chapter.

Loan Payment Calculator

Purpose: In this exercise, you will name cells, determine the monthly payment on a loan, create a data table, and protect a worksheet.

Instructions: Start Excel. Open the workbook Apply 4-1 Loan Payment Calculator from the Data Files for Students. See the inside back cover of this book for instructions for downloading the Data Files for Students or see your instructor for information on accessing the files required in this book.

Perform the following tasks:
1. Select the range B4:C9. Use the Create from Selection button (Formulas tab | Defined Names group) to create names for cells in the range C4:C9 using the row titles in the range B4:B9.
2. Enter the formulas shown in Table 4–5.

Table 4–5 Loan Payment Calculator and Interest Rate Schedule Formulas	
Cell	**Formula**
C8	= -PMT(Interest_Rate/12, 12 * Years, Loan_Amount)
C9	=Price – Down_Payment
F4	=C8
G4	=H4-C4
H4	=12 * C6 * C8 + C4

Continued >

Apply Your Knowledge *continued*

3. Change the document properties as specified by your instructor. Change the worksheet header with your name, course number, and other information as specified by your instructor. Save the workbook using the file name, Apply 4-1 Loan Payment Calculator Complete.

4. Use the Data Table button in the What-If Analysis gallery (Data tab | Data Tools group) to define the range E4:H19 as a one-input data table. Use cell C7 (interest rate) as the column input cell. Format the data table so that it appears as shown in Figure 4–66.

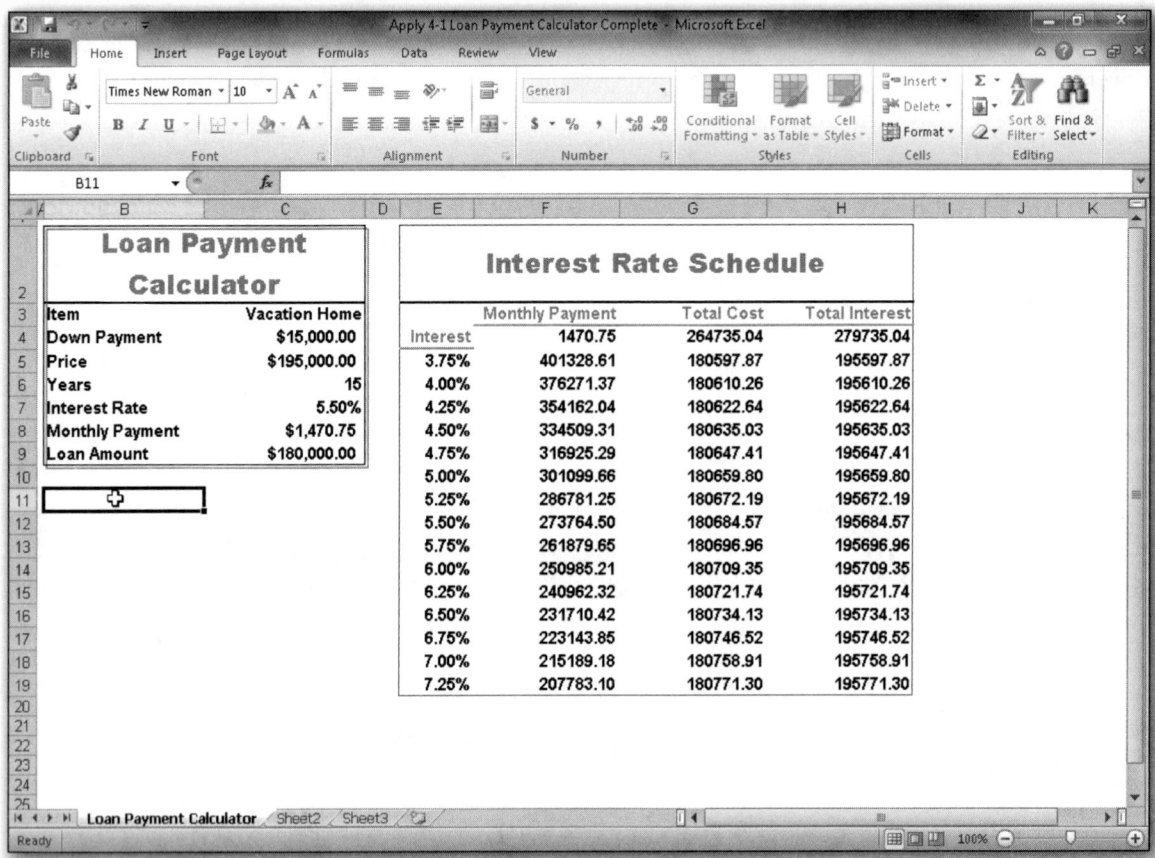

Figure 4–66

5. Use the Page Setup dialog box to select the Fit to and Black and white options. Select the range B2:C9 and then use the Set Print Area command to set a print area. Use the Print button in the Print gallery in the Backstage view to print the worksheet. Use the Clear Print Area command to clear the print area. Name the following ranges: B2:C9 – Calculator; E2:H19 – Rate_Schedule; and B2:H19 – All_Sections. Print each range by selecting the name in the Name box and using the Print Selection option on the Print tab in the Backstage view.

6. Unlock the range C3:C7. Protect the worksheet so that the user can select only unlocked cells.

7. Press CTRL+` and print the formulas version in landscape orientation. Press CTRL+` to display the values version.

8. Hide and then unhide the Loan Payment Calculator sheet. Hide and then unhide the workbook. Unprotect the worksheet and then hide columns E through H. Print the worksheet. Select columns D and I and unhide the hidden columns. Hide rows 11 through 19. Print the worksheet. Select rows 10 and 20 and unhide rows 11 through 19. Protect the worksheet.

9. Save the changes you have made to the workbook.

10. Determine the monthly payment and print the worksheet for each data set: (a) Item = Race Horse; Down Payment = $12,000.00; Price = $59,500.00; Years = 13; Interest Rate = 6.25%; (b) Item = Hybrid Car; Down Payment = $3,000.00; Price = $35,000.00; Years = 6; Interest Rate = 7.25%. You should get the following monthly payment results: (a) $445.50; (b) $549.42.

11. Submit the assignment as specified by your instructor.

Extend Your Knowledge

Extend the skills you learned in this chapter and experiment with new skills. You may need to use Help to complete the assignment.

Two-Input Data Table

Purpose: In this exercise you will use data from a 529C education savings account planning sheet (Figure 4–67a on the following page) to create a two-input data table (Figure 4–67b on the following page).

Instructions: Start Excel. Open the workbook Extend 4-1 529C Planning Sheet from the Data Files for Students. See the inside back cover of this book for instructions for downloading the Data Files for Students or see your instructor for information on accessing the files required in this book.

Perform the following tasks:

1. Enter the data table title and subtitle as shown in cells I1 and I3 in Figure 4–67b.

2. Change the document properties as specified by your instructor. Change the worksheet header with your name, course number, and other information as specified by your instructor. Save the workbook using the file name, Extend 4-1 529C Planning Sheet Complete.

3. Change the width of column H to 0.50 characters. Merge and center the titles over columns I through S. Format the titles as shown using the Title cell style for both the title and subtitle, a font size of 20 for the title, and a font size of 16 for the subtitle. Change the column widths of columns I through S to 11.71 characters.

4. For a two-input data table, the formula you are analyzing must be assigned to the upper-left cell in the range of the data table. Cell C14 contains the future value formula to be analyzed, therefore, enter =C14 in cell I4.

5. Use the fill handle to create two lists of percents: (a) 2.00% through 6.50% in increments of 0.25% in the range I5:I23; and (b) 2.00% through 11.00% in increments of 1.00% in the range J4:S4.

6. Select the range I4:S23. Click the What-If Analysis button (Data tab | Data Tools group). Click the Data Table command on the What-If Analysis menu. When Excel displays the Data Table dialog box, enter C8 (expected annual return) in the Row input cell box and C5 (employee percent invested) in the Column input cell box. Click the OK button to populate the table.

7. Format the two-input data table as shown in Figure 4–67b.

8. Use conditional formatting to change the format of the cell in the two-input data table that is equal to the future value in cell C14 to blue underlined font on a Purple, Accent 4, Lighter 80% background.

9. Protect the worksheet so that the user can select only unlocked cells (C3:C6 and C8:C9).

10. Change the print orientation to landscape. Print the worksheet using the Fit to option. Print the formulas version of the worksheet.

Continued >

11. Save your changes to the workbook.
12. Submit the assignment as requested by your instructor.

Figure 4–67 (a)

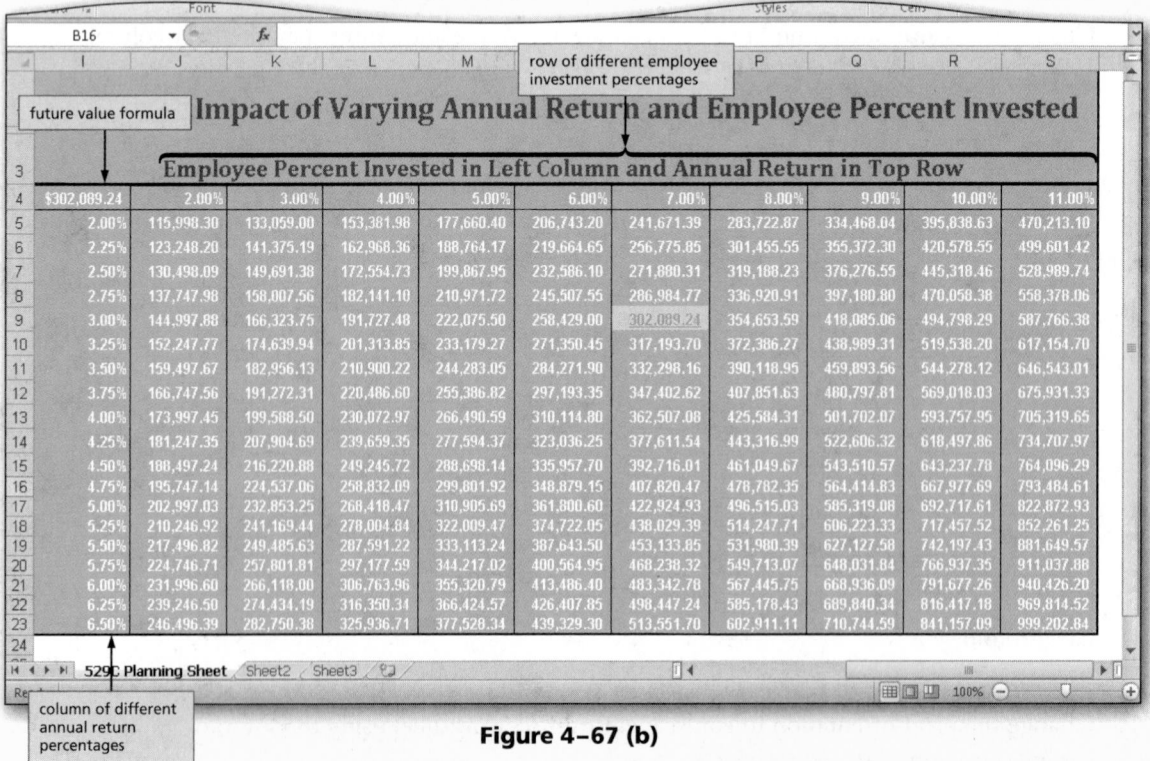

Figure 4–67 (b)

Make It Right

Analyze a workbook and correct all errors and/or improve the design.

Functions, Custom Borders, Cell Names, What-If Analysis, and Protection

Purpose: In this exercise, you will correct design and formula problems, complete what-if analysis, name cells, and protect the worksheet.

Instructions: Start Excel. Open the workbook Make It Right 4-1 Financial Calculator. See the inside back cover of this book for instructions for downloading the Data Files for Students, or see your instructor for information on accessing the files required for this book.

Perform the following tasks:

1. The worksheet is protected with no unprotected cells. Unprotect the worksheet so that the worksheet can be edited by clicking Unprotect Sheet (Review tab | Changes group).

2. Change the thick box border surrounding the range B2:C9 to a Dark Blue, Text 2 thick box border. Change the thick border separating columns B and C in the range B2:C9 to a Dark Blue, Text 2 light border.

3. Correct the Monthly Payment formula in cell C7 and the Total Interest formula in cell C8. The monthly payment should equal $2,050.00 and the total interest should equal $437,491.16. Use Goal Seek to change the down payment in cell C3 so that the monthly payment is $2,050.00, as shown in Figure 4–68.

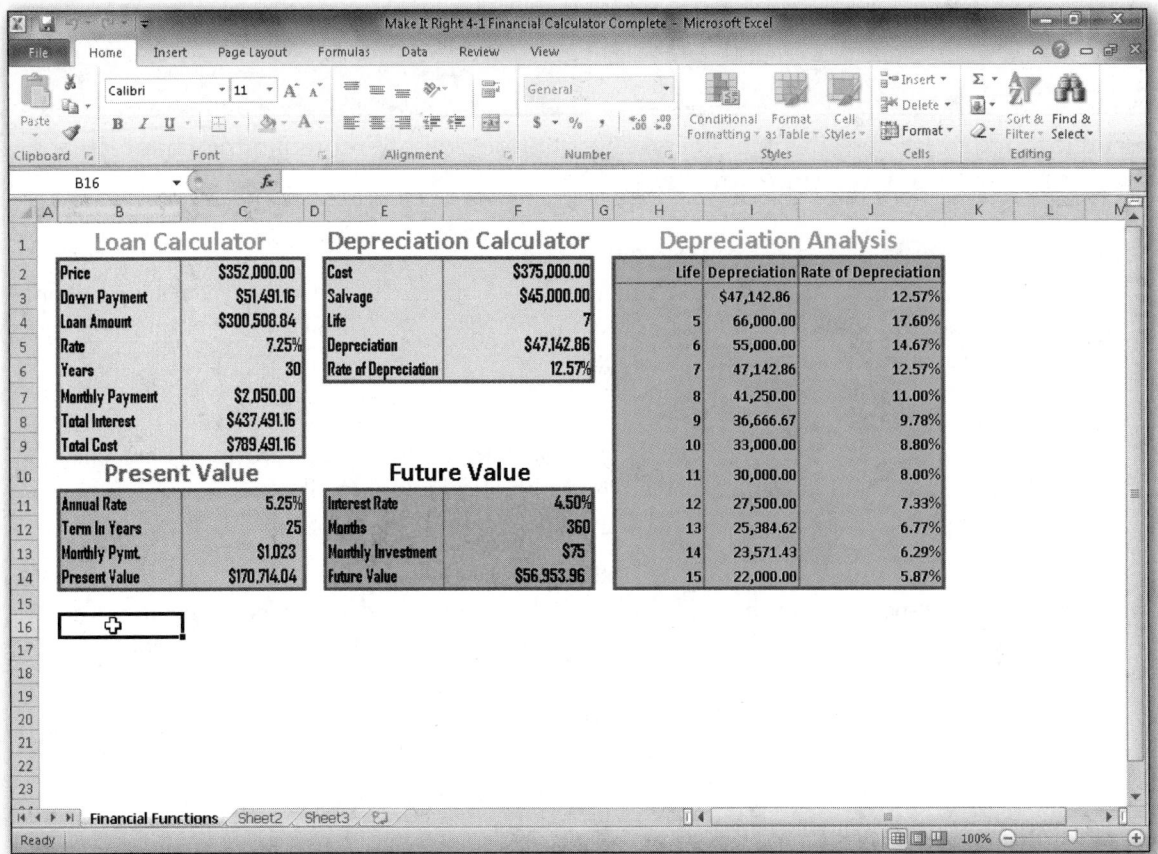

Figure 4–68

Continued >

Make It Right *continued*

4. Assign the name Loan_Calculator to the range B1:C9.

5. Assign the names in column E to the adjacent cells in column F for both the Depreciation Calculator and the Future Value. Edit the formulas in cells F5 and F6 and change the cell references to their corresponding names.

6. Correct the second argument in the Future Value function in cell F14 so that the number of months is not multiplied by 12. Correct the third argument in the Future Value function in cell F14. Display the future value as a positive number.

7. Correct the second and third arguments in the Present Value function in cell C14 so that the present value is displayed correctly as a positive number.

8. Complete the one–input data table in the range H3:J14 that determines the depreciation and rate of depreciation for varying years of life (cell F4). Format the numbers in the data table so that they appear as shown in Figure 4–68 on the previous page.

9. Change the document properties as specified by your instructor. Change the worksheet header so that it contains your name, course number, and other information as specified by your instructor.

10. Unlock the cells containing data (C2:C3, C5:C6, F2:F4, C11:C13, and F11:F13). Protect the worksheet so that the user can select only cells with data.

11. Save the workbook using the file name, Make It Right 4-1 Financial Calculator Complete.

12. Submit the revised workbook as requested by your instructor.

In the Lab

Create a workbook using the guidelines, concepts, and skills presented in this chapter. Labs are listed in order of increasing difficulty.

Lab 1: Mortgage Analysis and Amortization Schedule

Problem: The president of WeSavU National Bank has asked you to create a mortgage analysis worksheet including an amortization schedule as shown in Figure 4–69. He also wants you to demonstrate the goal seeking capabilities of Excel.

Instructions:

1. Start Excel. Apply the Foundry theme to a new worksheet. Bold the entire worksheet and change all the columns to a width of 17.00. Change the width of column A to .85.

2. Save the workbook using the file name Lab 4-1 WeSavU National Bank Loan Calculator.

3. Enter the worksheet title, WeSavU National Bank, in cell B1, apply the Title cell style, and change its font size to 28-point. Enter the worksheet subtitle, Subprime Loans for Everyone, in cell B2, and apply the Title cell style. One at a time, merge and center cells B1 and B2 across columns B through F.

4. Enter the row titles for the ranges B3:B5 and E3:E5 as shown in Figure 4–69. Use the Create from Selection button (Formulas tab | Defined Names group) to assign the row titles in the ranges B3:B5 and E3:E5 to the adjacent cells in ranges C3:C5 and F3:F5, respectively.

5. Enter 430000 (price) in cell C3, 110000 (down payment) in cell C4, 7.75% (interest rate) in cell F3, and 25 (years) in cell F4. Determine the loan amount by entering the formula =Price - Down_Payment in cell C5. Determine the monthly payment by entering the PMT function **−PMT(Rate / 12, 12 * Years, Loan_Amount)** in cell F5.

6. Create the amortization schedule in the range B6:F34 by assigning the first five formulas and functions in Table 4–6 to the cells indicated. Center the column headings. The years in column B starting at cell B7 should extend from 1 to 25 years centered. Use the fill handle to copy columns C, D, E and F of the amortization schedule down to the 25th year.

7. Enter the total titles in the range C32:E34 as shown in Figure 4–69. Enter the last four formulas in Table 4–6 on the following page.

8. Format the numbers in the amortization schedule as shown in Figure 4–69.

9. Change the colors and draw the borders as shown in Figure 4–69. Change the sheet tab name and color as shown in Figure 4–69.

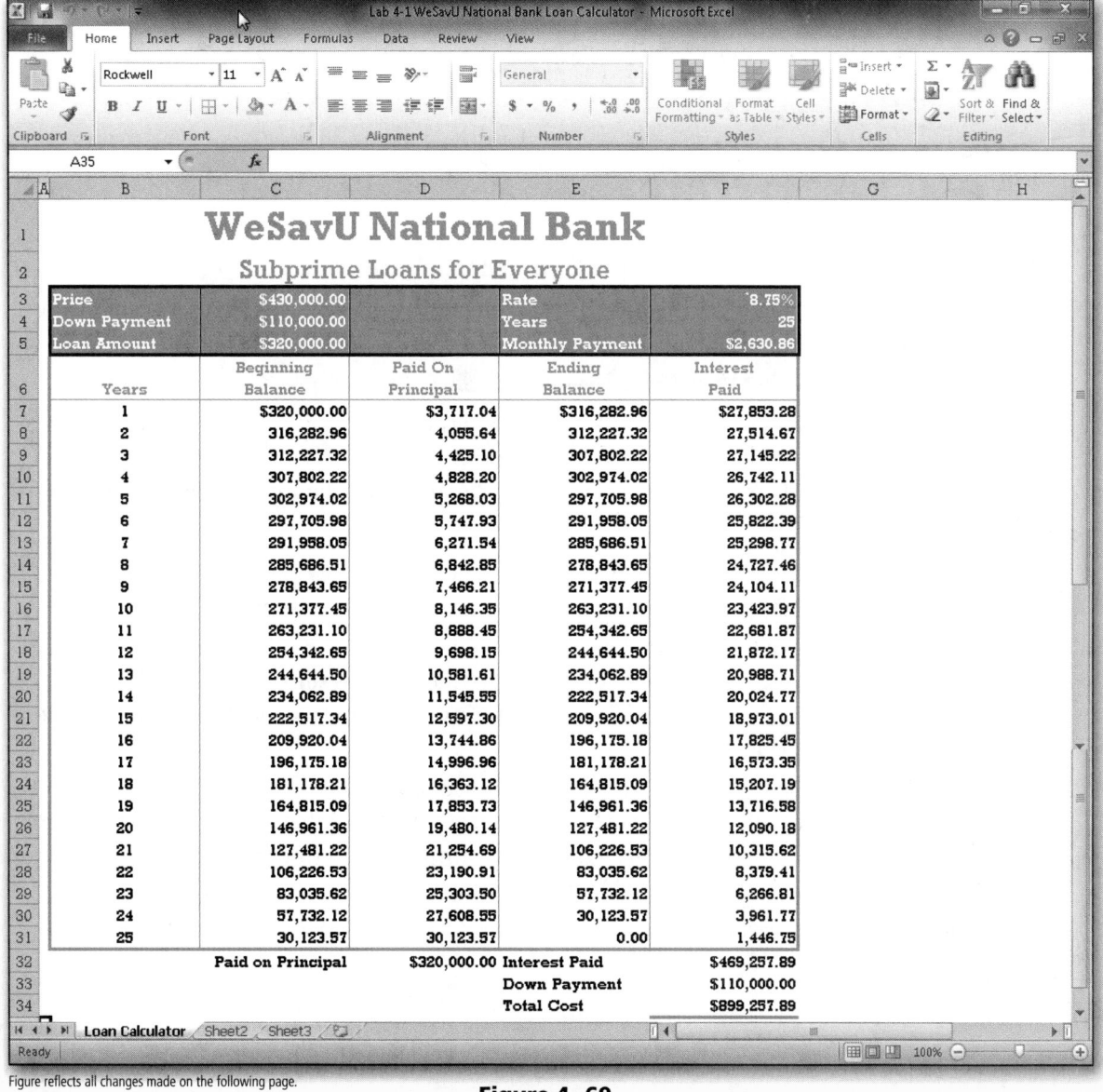

Figure reflects all changes made on the following page.

Figure 4–69

Continued >

In the Lab *continued*

10. Change the document properties as specified by your instructor. Change the worksheet header so that it contains your name, course number, and other information as specified by your instructor.

11. Spell check and formula check the worksheet. Use Range Finder (double–click cell) to check all formulas listed in Table 4–6.

Table 4–6 Cell Assignments	
Cell	**Formula or Function**
C7	=C5
D7	=C7–E7
E7	=IF(B7<= $F$4, PV($F$3/12, 12*($F$4–B7), –$F$5),0)
F7	=IF(C7>0, 12*$F$5–D7, 0)
C8	=E7
D32	=SUM(D7:D31)
F32	=SUM(F7:F31)
F33	=C4
F34	=D32+F32+F33

12. Use the Page Setup dialog box to select the Fit to and 'Black and white' options.

13. Unlock the cells in the ranges C3:C4 and F3:F4. Protect the worksheet so that users can select any cell in the worksheet, but can change only the unlocked cells.

14. Remove gridlines by clicking View (Page Layout tab | Sheet Options group).

15. WeSavU determined that a credit agency reduced the customer's credit score. WeSavU has decided, therefore, to raise the interest rate by 1% for the customer. Change the interest rate in F4 to 8.75%. The Monthly Payment should change to $2,630.86, and the Interest Paid should change to $469, 257.89.

16. Save your changes to the workbook.

17. Print the worksheet on one page. Print the formulas version of the worksheet.

18. Use Excel's goal seeking capabilities to determine the down payment required for the loan data if the monthly payment is set to $1,000.00. The down payment that results for a monthly payment of $1,000.00 is $308,336.75. Print the worksheet with the new monthly payment of $1,000.00. Close the workbook without saving changes.

19. Hide and then unhide the Loan Payment Calculator sheet. Hide and then unhide the workbook. Unprotect the worksheet and then hide columns D through F. Print the worksheet. Select columns C and G and unhide the hidden columns. Hide rows 6 through 34. Print the worksheet. Select rows 5 and 35 and unhide rows 6 through 34. Do not save the workbook.

20. Submit the assignment as requested by your instructor.

In the Lab

Lab 2: Analyzing Retirement Savings

Problem: You have been asked by the Employee Relations and Resource department to develop a retirement planning worksheet that will allow each current and prospective employee to see the effect (dollar accumulation) of investing a percent of his or her monthly salary over a period of years (Figure 4–70). The plan calls for the company to match an employee's investment, dollar for dollar, up to 2.50%. Thus, if an employee invests 5.00% of his or her annual salary, then the company matches the first 2.50%. If an employee invests only 1.75% of his or her annual salary, then the company matches the entire 1.75%. The Employee Relations and Resource department wants a one-input data table to show the future value of the investment for different years.

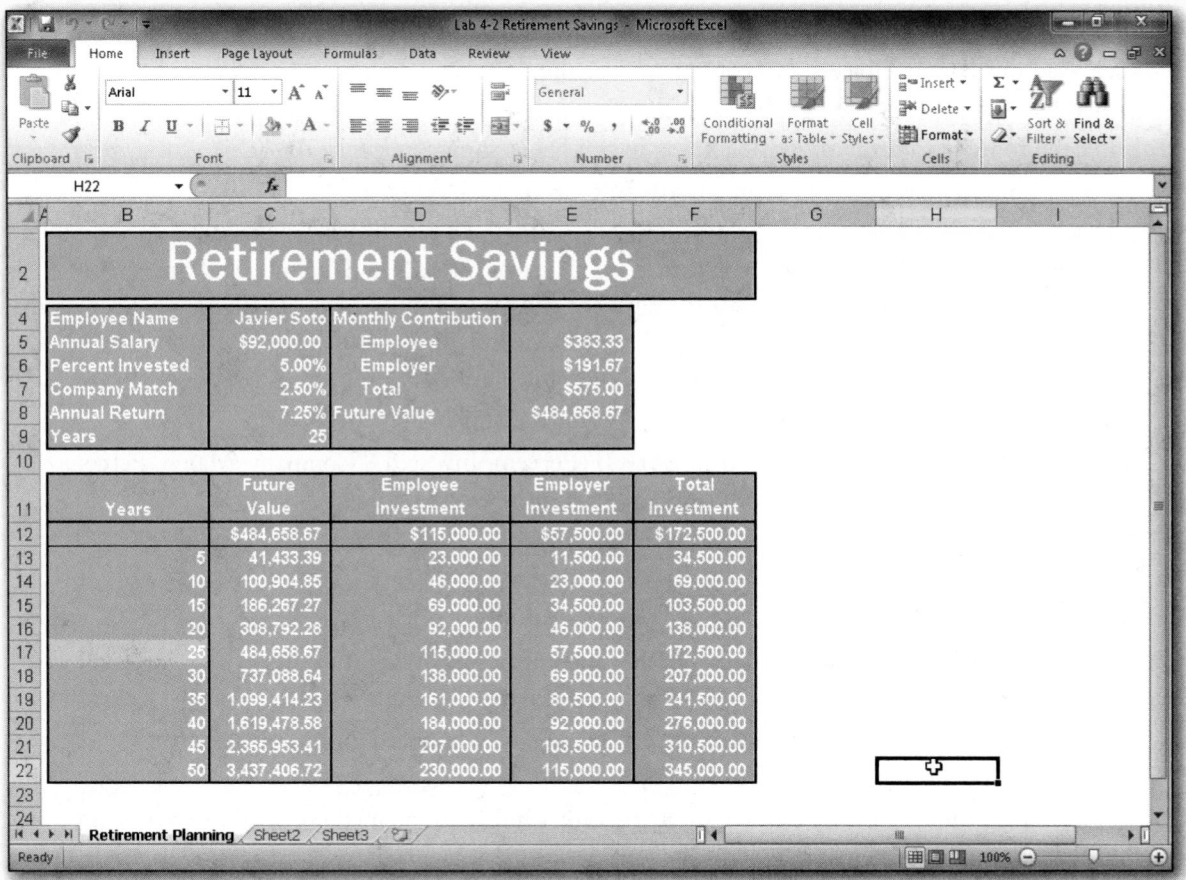

Figure 4–70

Instructions:

1. Start Excel. Apply the Technic theme to the worksheet and change the font of the entire worksheet to bold. Change the column widths to the following: A = 0.54; B = 17.00; C and F = 12.75; D=19.13. Change the heights of rows 1 and 3 to 4.50.

2. In cell B2, enter Retirement Savings as the worksheet title. Merge and center cell B2 across columns B through F. Apply the Title cell style to cell B2, and change the font size to 36 point. Change the background color of B2 to light green and change its font color to white. Draw a medium black border around cell B2.

Continued >

In the Lab *continued*

Table 4–7 Retirement Savings Employee Data	
Row Title	**Data**
Employee Name	Javier Soto
Annual Salary	$92,000.00
Percent Invested	5.00%
Company Match	2.50%
Annual Return	7.25%
Years	25

3. Enter the row titles in column B, beginning in cell B4 as shown in Figure 4–70 on the previous page. Add the data in Table 4–7 to column C. Use the dollar and percent signs format symbols to format the numbers in the range C5:C8.

4. Enter the row titles in column D, beginning in cell D4 as shown in Figure 4–70.

5. Save the workbook using the file name Lab 4-2 Retirement Savings.

6. Use the Create from Selection button (Formulas tab | Defined Names group) to assign the row titles in column B (range B4:B9) as cell names for the adjacent cells in column C and the row titles in column D (D5:D8) as cell names for the adjacent cells in column E5:E8. Use these newly created names to assign formulas to cells in the range E5:E8. Step 6e formats the displayed results of the formulas.

   a. Employee Monthly Contribution (cell E5) = Annual_Salary * Percent_Invested / 12

   b. Employer Monthly Contribution (cell E6) = IF(Percent_Invested < Company_Match, Percent_Invested * Annual_Salary / 12, Company_Match * Annual_Salary / 12)

   c. Total Monthly Contribution (cell E7) = SUM(E5:E6)

   d. Future Value (cell E8) = –FV(Annual_Return/12, 12 * Years, Total)

   The Future Value function (FV) in Step 6d returns to the cell the future value of the investment. The future value of an investment is its value at some point in the future based on a series of payments of equal amounts made over a number of periods earning a constant rate of return.

   e. If necessary, use the Format Painter button (Home tab | Clipboard group) to assign the Currency style format in cell C5 to the range E5:E8.

7. Add the background color light green, the font color white, and the medium borders to the range B4:E9, as shown in Figure 4–70.

8. Use the concepts and techniques developed in this chapter to add the data table in Figure 4–70 to the range B11:F22 as follows.

   a. Enter and format the table column titles in row 11.

   b. Use the fill handle to create the series of years beginning with 5 and ending with 50 in increments of 5 in column B, beginning in cell B13.

   c. In cell C12, enter `=E8` as the formula. In cell D12, enter `=12 * E5 * C9` as the formula (recall that using cell references in the formulas means Excel will copy the formats). In E12, enter `=12 * E6 * C9` as the formula. In F12, enter `=12 * E7 * C9` as the formula.

d. Use the Data Table command on the What-If Analysis gallery (Data tab | Data tools group) to define the range B12:F22 as a one-input data table. Use cell C9 as the column input cell.

e. Format the numbers in the range C13:F22 using the Comma style format. Underline rows 11 and 12 as shown in Figure 4–70 on page EX 289. Change the background color of the data table to light green and change its font color to white. Add borders to the range B11:F22, as shown in Figure 4–70.

9. Use the Conditional Formatting button (Home tab | Styles group) to add an orange pointer that shows the row that equates to the years in cell C9 to the Years column in the data table. Change the sheet tab name and color to light green as shown in Figure 4–70.

10. Remove gridlines by clicking View (Page Layout tab | Sheet Options group).

11. Change the document properties as specified by your instructor. Change the worksheet header with your name, course number, and other information as specified by your instructor.

12. Spell check and formula check the worksheet. Use Range Finder (double-click cell) to check all formulas.

13. Print the worksheet in landscape orientation. Print the formulas version of the worksheet.

14. Unlock the cells in the range C4:C9. Protect the worksheet. Allow users to select only unlocked cells.

15. Save your changes to the workbook.

16. Hide and then unhide the Retirement Planning Sheet worksheet. Hide and then unhide the workbook. Unprotect the worksheet and then hide rows 11 through 22. Print the worksheet. Select rows 10 and 23 and unhide the hidden rows. Hide rows 1 and 2. Print the worksheet. Click the Select All button and unhide rows 1 and 2.

17. Close the workbook without saving the changes.

18. Open the workbook Lab 4-2 Retirement Savings. Determine the future value for the data in Table 4–8. Print the worksheet for each data set. The following Future Value results should be displayed in cell E8: Data Set 1 = $395,756.16; Data Set 2 = $693,470.35; and Data Set 3 = $1,069,822.41. Quit Excel without saving the workbook.

Table 4–8 Future Value What-If Analysis Data			
	Data Set 1	Data Set 2	Data Set 3
Employee Name	John Roe	Dante Dacy	Janek Madhu
Annual Salary	$119,500.00	$65,000.00	$39,000.00
Percent Invested	2.50%	5.00%	6.00%
Company Match	2.50%	3.00%	2.00%
Annual Return	4.75%	6.50%	7.25%
Years	30	35	45

19. Submit the assignment as requested by your instructor.

In the Lab

Lab 3: Annual Income Statement and Break-Even Analysis

Problem: You are a summer intern at Telemobile, a company that sells the popular jPhone. Your area of expertise is cost-volume-profit or CVP (also called break-even analysis), which investigates the relationship among a product's expenses (cost), its volume (units sold), and the operating income (gross profit). Any money a company earns above the break-even point is called operating income, or gross profit (row 22 in the Break-Even Analysis table in Figure 4–71). You have been asked to prepare an annual income statement and a data table that shows revenue, expenses, and income for units sold between 140,000 and 220,000 in increments of 5,000.

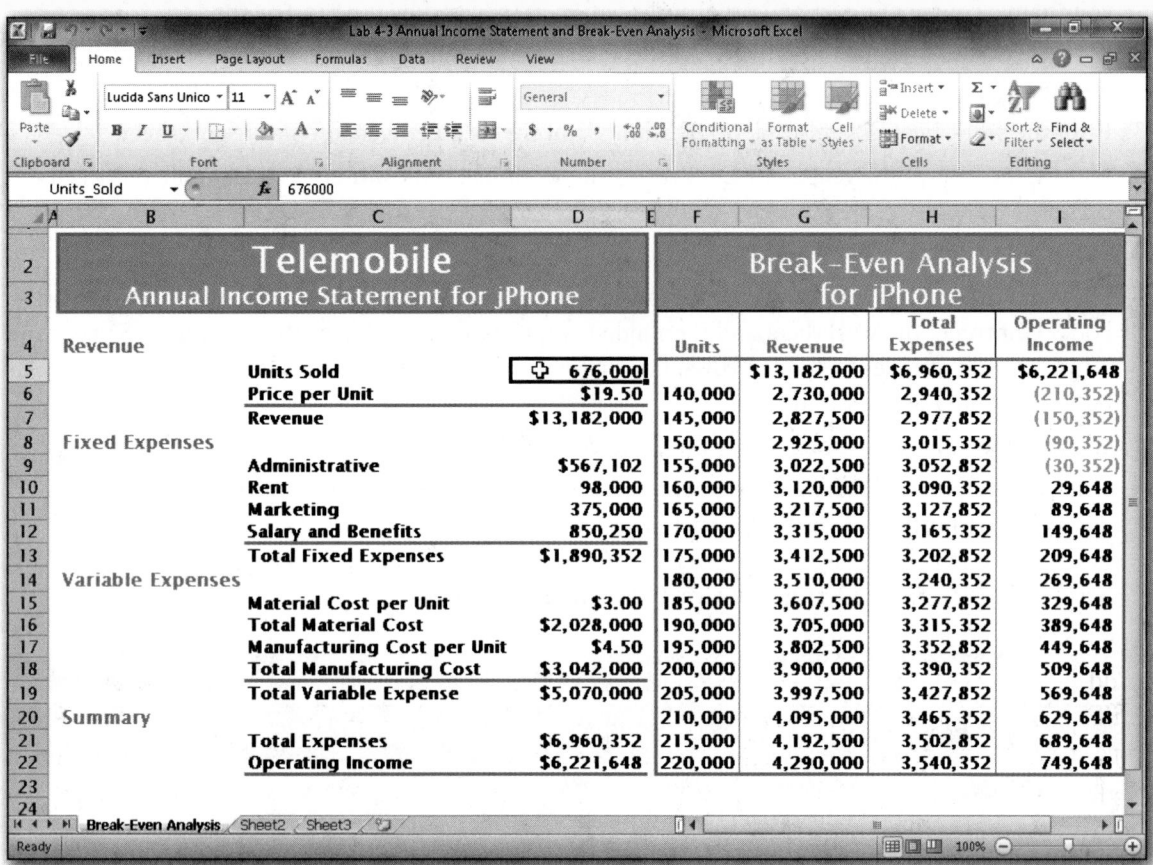

Figure 4–71

Instructions:

1. Start Excel. Apply the Concourse theme to the worksheet. Change the font of the entire worksheet to bold. Change the column widths to the following: A = 0.50; B = 18.00; C = 26.00; D = 12.78; E= 0.50; F = 7.44; and G through I = 12.00. Change the heights of rows 1 to 4.50; 2 to 30.75; and 3 to 19.50, respectively. Name the sheet tab Break–Even Analysis and color the tab blue.

2. Enter the worksheet titles: Telemobile in cell B2 and Annual Income Statement for jPhone in cell B3. Apply the Title cell style to both cells. Change the font sizes in cells B2 and B3 to 24 and 16, respectively. One at a time, merge and center cells B2 and B3 across columns B through D. Change the background color of cells B2 and B3 to Blue, Accent 4, Lighter 40%. Change the font color to white. Add a thick blue border to the range B2:B3.

3. Save the workbook using the file name, Lab 4-3 Annual Income Statement and Break-Even Analysis.

4. Enter the row titles in columns B and C as shown in Figure 4–71. Change the font size of the row titles in column B to 12–point and change the font color to blue. Add the data shown in Table 4–9 in column D. Format the numbers in column D as shown in Figure 4–71.

Table 4–9 Annual Income Statement Data		
Title	Column D Cell	Column D Data
Units Sold	D5	676000
Price per Unit	D6	19.50
Administrative	D9	567102
Rent	D10	98000
Marketing	D11	375000
Salary and Benefits	D12	850250
Material Cost per Unit	D15	3.00
Manufacturing Cost per Unit	D17	4.50

5. Assign the row titles in column C in the range C5:C22 to the adjacent cells in column D. Use these names to enter the following formulas in column D:

   a. Revenue (cell D7) = Units Sold * Price per Unit (or =D5 * D6)

   b. Fixed Expenses (cell D13) = SUM(D9:D12)

   c. Material Cost (cell D16) = Units Sold * Material Cost per Unit (or =D5 * D15)

   d. Total Manufacturing Cost (cell D18) = Units Sold * Manufacturing Cost per Unit (or =D5 * D17)

   e. Total Variable Expenses (cell D19) = Total Material Cost + Total Manufacturing Cost (or =D16 + D18)

   f. Total Expenses (cell D21) = Total Fixed Expenses + Total Variable Expense (or =D13 + D19)

   g. Operating Income (cell D22) = Revenue – Total Expenses (or =D7 – D21)

6. Assign the Currency style format in cell D9 to the unformatted dollar amounts in column D.

7. Add a thick blue bottom border to the ranges C6:D6, C12:D12, C18:D18, and C22:D22, as shown in Figure 4–71.

8. Use the concepts and techniques presented in this chapter to add the data table to the range F2:I22 as follows:

   a. Add the data table titles and format them as shown in Figure 4–71.

   b. Create the series in column F from 140,000 to 220,000 in increments of 5,000, beginning in cell F6.

   c. Enter the formula =D7 in cell G5. Enter the formula=D21 in cell H5. Enter the formula =D22 in cell I5. If necessary, adjust the column widths.

   d. Define the range F5:I22 as a one-input data table. Use cell D5 (Units_Sold) as the column input cell.

   e. Format the range F6:I22 to the Comma style format with no decimal places and negative numbers in red with parentheses. Add a medium outline border and light vertical borders to the range F2:I22.

9. Remove gridlines by clicking View (Page Layout tab | Sheet Options group).

10. Change the document properties as specified by your instructor. Change the worksheet header so that it contains your name, course number, and other information as specified by your instructor.

11. Spell check and formula check the worksheet. Use Range Finder to check all formulas.

Continued >

In the Lab *continued*

12. Select Landscape, the Fit to, and 'Black and white' printing options. Print the worksheet. Print the formulas version of the worksheet.

13. Unlock the following cells: D5, D6, D15, and D17. Protect the workbook.

14. Save your changes to the workbook.

15. Hide and then unhide the Break-Even Analysis sheet. Hide and then unhide the workbook. Unprotect the worksheet and then hide columns E through I. Print the worksheet. Select columns D and J and unhide the hidden columns. Hide rows 8 through 22. Print the worksheet. Select rows 7 and 23 and unhide rows 8 through 22. Close the workbook without saving the changes.

16. Open the workbook Lab 4-3 Annual Income Statement and Break-Even Analysis. Determine the operating income for the data sets in Table 4–10. Print the worksheet for each data set. You should get the following Income results in cell D22: Data Set 1 = $3,191,648; Data Set 2 = ($265,852); and Data Set 3 = $218,648. Quit Excel without saving the workbook.

Table 4–10 Operating Income Data

Title	Cell	Data Set 1	Data Set 2	Data Set 3
Units Sold	D5	484000	342000	228000
Price per Unit	D6	18.50	12.00	28.00
Material Cost per Unit	D15	5.50	2.75	11.00
Manufacturing Cost per Unit	D17	2.50	4.50	7.75

17. Submit the assignment as requested by your instructor.

Cases and Places

Apply your creative thinking and problem solving skills to design and implement a solution.

1: Future Value of a 529 College Savings Plan

Academic

Jacob and Sophia's dream for their recently born daughter, Emily, is that one day she will attend their alma mater, Purdue University. For the next 18 years, they plan to make monthly payment deposits to a 529 College Savings Plan at a local bank. The account pays 5.25% annual interest, compounded monthly. Create a worksheet for Jacob and Sophia that uses a financial function to show the future value (FV) of their investment and a formula to determine the percentage of the college's tuition saved. Jacob and Sophia have supplied the following information:

Out of State Annual Tuition = $52,000; Rate (per month) = 5.25% / 12; Nper (number of monthly payments) = years * 12; Pmt (monthly payment) = $425; and percentage of Tuition Saved = FV / Tuition for Four Years.

Jacob and Sophia are not sure how much they will be able to save each month. Use the concepts and techniques presented in this chapter to create a data table that shows the future value and percentage of tuition saved for monthly payments from $175 to $775, in $50 increments. Unlock the rate, monthly payment, and years. Protect the workbook so that the user can select only unlocked cells. Submit the workbook as requested by your instructor.

2: Saving for a Down Payment on Your First Car

Personal

Find a new car in your area that you would like to someday purchase. Based on the estimated current price of the car, determine how much money you need to save each month so that in three years, you have enough to make a down payment of 20% of the current estimated value. Assume that you can save the money in an account that is getting a 4.50% return. Create a worksheet that determines how much you have to save each month so that in three years the value of the account is 20% of the current estimated value. (*Hint:* Use the FV function with a monthly savings of $300.) Then use the Goal Seek command to determine the monthly savings amount needed for the car of your choice. Unlock cells that include data. Protect the worksheet. Submit the workbook as requested by your instructor.

3: Determining the Break-Even Point

Professional

You have been hired by Julio Quatorze, owner of Shrub and Trees Landscape Inc., to create a data table that analyzes the break-even point for a new shrub for prices between $3.00 and $9.25 in increments of $0.25. You can calculate the number of units you must sell to break even (break-even point) if you know the fixed expenses, the price per unit, and the expense (cost) per unit. The following formula determines the break-even point:

Break-Even Point = Fixed Expenses / (Price per Unit – Expense per Unit)

Assume Fixed Expenses = $300,000; Price per Unit = $7.50; and Expense per Unit = $2.10. Use the concepts and techniques presented in this chapter to determine the break-even point and then create the data table. Use the Price per Unit as the input cell and the break-even value as the result. For a price per unit of $8.00, the data table should show a break-even point of 50,847 units. Protect the worksheet so that only cells with data can be selected. Submit the workbook as requested by your instructor.

5 | Creating, Sorting, and Querying a Table

Objectives

You will have mastered the material in this chapter when you can:

- Create and manipulate a table
- Delete sheets in a workbook
- Add calculated columns to a table
- Use icon sets with conditional formatting
- Use the VLOOKUP function to look up a value in a table
- Print a table
- Add and delete records and change field values in a table

- Sort a table on one field or multiple fields
- Query a table
- Apply database functions, the SUMIF function, and the COUNTIF function
- Use the MATCH and INDEX functions to look up a value in a table
- Display automatic subtotals
- Use Group and Outline features to hide and unhide data

5 | Creating, Sorting, and Querying a Table

Introduction

A **table**, also called a **database**, is an organized collection of data. For example, a list of friends, a list of students registered for a class, a club membership roster, and an instructor's grade book all can be arranged as tables in a worksheet. In these cases, the data related to each person is called a record, and the individual data items that make up a record are called **fields**. For example, in a table of fundraisers, each fundraiser would have a separate record; each record might include several fields, such as name, experience, hire date, region, and fundraising quota.

A record in a table also can include fields (columns) that contain formulas and functions. A field, or column, that contains formulas or functions is called a **calculated column**. A calculated column displays results based on other columns in the table.

A worksheet's row-and-column structure can be used to organize and store a table. Each row of a worksheet can store a record, and each column can store one field for each record. Additionally, a row of column headings at the top of the worksheet can store field names that identify each field.

After you enter a table onto a worksheet, you can use Excel to (1) add and delete records; (2) change the values of fields in records; (3) sort the records so that Excel displays them in a different order; (4) determine subtotals for numeric fields; (5) display records that meet comparison criteria; and (6) analyze data using database functions. This chapter illustrates all six of these table capabilities.

Project — Kenson College Scholarship Fundraiser Table

The project in the chapter follows proper design guidelines and uses Excel to create the worksheet shown in Figures 5–1a and 5–1b. Kenson College raises funds for its scholarship program in several regions in the United States. The college's development director has asked for a workbook that summarizes key information about fundraisers and their performance. The data in the workbook should be easy to summarize, sort, edit, and query.

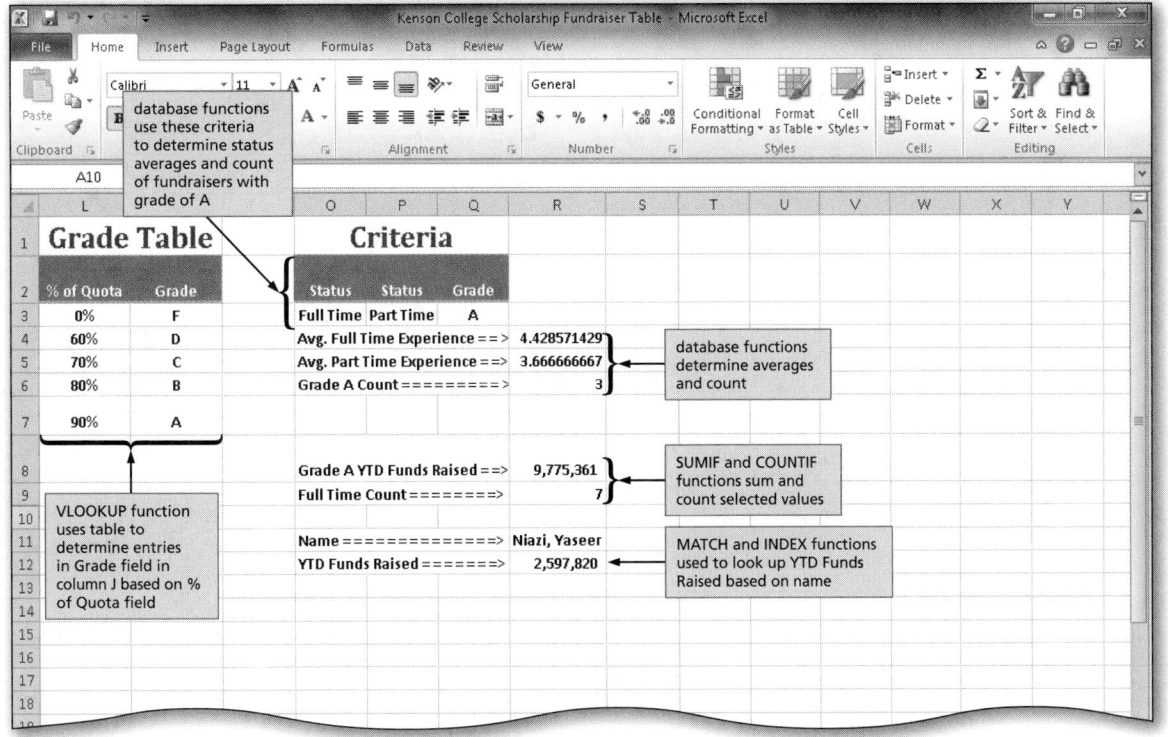

Figure 5–1 (a) Table

Figure 5–1 (b) Grade Table, Criteria, Statistics, and Look Up

The requirements document for the Kenson College Scholarship Fundraiser table is shown in Figure 5–2. It includes the needs, source of data, calculations, special requirements, and other facts about its development.

Table 5–1 describes the field names, columns, types of data, and column widths to use when creating the table.

REQUEST FOR NEW WORKBOOK	
Date Submitted:	June 4, 2012
Submitted By:	Larry Chao
Worksheet Title:	Kenson College Scholarship Fundraiser Table
Needs:	Create a fundraiser table (Figure 5-3a on page EX 302) that can be sorted, queried, maintained, and printed to obtain meaningful information. Using the data in the table, compute statistics that include the average experience of full-time fundraisers, average experience of part-time fundraisers, grade A count, sum of YTD Funds Raised for those with grade A, and the count of the full-time fundraisers, as shown in Figure 5-3b on page EX 302. The table field names, columns, types of data, and column widths are described in Table 5-1. Because Larry will use the table online as he travels among the offices, it is important that it be readable and visible on the screen. Some of the column widths listed in Table 5-1, therefore, are set based on the number of characters in the field names and not the maximum length of the data. The last two fields (located in columns I and J) use a formula and function to determine values based on data within each fundraiser record.
Source of Data:	Larry will supply the fundraiser data required for the table.
Calculations:	Include the following calculations and look up: 1. % of Quota field in table = YTD Funds Raised / Quota 2. Grade field in table = VLOOKUP function that uses the Grade table in Figure 5-3b 3. Average Full-Time Experience = AVERAGE function that uses the Criteria table in Figure 5-3b 4. Average Part-Time Experience = AVERAGE function that uses the Criteria table in Figure 5-3b 5. Grade A Count = DCOUNT function that uses the Criteria table in Figure 5-3b 6. Grade A YTD Funds Raised Sum = SUMIF function 7. Full-Time Count = COUNTIF function 8. Look up YTD Funds Raised given the name of a fundraiser
Special Requirements:	1. Delete unused sheets. 2. A Criteria area will be created above the table, in rows 1 through 6, to store criteria for use in a query. An Extract area will be created below the table, beginnning in row 25, to receive records that meet a criteria.

Approvals

Approval Status:	X	Approved
		Rejected
Approved By:	Terrell Knox	
Date:	June 18, 2012	
Assigned To:	J. Quasney, Spreadsheet Specialist	

Figure 5–2

Column Headings (Field Names)	Column in Worksheet	Type of Data	Column Width	Description As It Pertains to a Fundraiser
Name	A	Text	16.43	Last name and first name
Status	B	Text	10.29	Full-time or part-time
Experience	C	Numeric	14.71	Fundraising experience in years
Hire Date	D	Date	13.14	Date hired
Region	E	Text	11.00	Fundraising territory
Type	F	Text	14.00	Inside or outside fundraising
Quota	G	Numeric	13.29	Annual fundraising quota
YTD Funds Raised	H	Numeric	13.29	Year-to-date funds raised
% of Quota	I	Numeric calculation (YTD Funds Raised / Quota)	14.57	Percent of annual quota met
Grade	J	Text calculation (VLOOKUP function)	10.29	Grade that indicates how much of quota has been met

Table 5–1 Column Information for Kenson College Scholarship Fundraiser Table

Overview

As you read this chapter, you will learn how to create the worksheet shown in Figure 5–1 on page EX 299 by performing these general tasks:

- Create and format the fundraiser table.
- Sort the fundraiser table.
- Obtain answers to questions about the fundraisers using a variety of methods to query the fundraiser table.
- Extract records from the table based on given criteria.
- Display subtotals by grouping the fundraisers.

Plan Ahead

General Project Decisions

While creating an Excel worksheet, you need to make decisions that will determine the appearance and characteristics of the finished worksheet. As you create the worksheet required to meet the requirements shown in Figure 5–2, you should follow these general guidelines:

1. **Create and format the table.** A table should be formatted so that the records are easily distinguished. The data in the worksheet should start several rows from the top in order to leave room for the criteria area. Using banded rows (background colors varying between rows) to format the table provides greater readability. Some columns require calculations that can be created by using the table column headings within formulas. In some cases, calculated columns in tables require looking up values outside of the table. Excel's special lookup functions can be used in such cases. Totals also can be added to the table for averages, sums, and other types of calculations.

2. **Sort the table.** The user of the worksheet should be able to sort the table in a variety of manners and sort using multiple fields at the same time. Excel includes simple and advanced methods for sorting tables.

3. **Obtain answers to questions about the data in the table using a variety of methods to query the table.** A query can include filters, the use of which results in the table displaying only those records that meet certain criteria. Or, a query can include a calculation based on data in the table that then is displayed outside of the table but within the same worksheet.

4. **Extract records from the table based on given criteria.** A criteria area and extract area can be created on the worksheet. The **criteria area** can be used to enter rules regarding which records to extract, such as all full-time fundraisers with a grade of A. The **extract**

(continued)

(continued)

area can be used to store the records that meet the criteria. The column headings from the table should be used as column headings in both the criteria and extract areas of the worksheet, as this is required by Excel when working with criteria and extract areas.

5. **Display subtotals by grouping data in the table.** The user of the worksheet should be able to create subtotals of groups of records after sorting the table. Excel's grouping features provide for subtotaling.

When necessary, more specific details concerning the above guidelines are presented at appropriate points in the chapter. The chapter also will identify the actions you perform and decisions made regarding these guidelines during the creation of the worksheet shown in Figure 5–1 on page EX 299.

The fundraiser table should include the data provided in Table 5–1 on the previous page. Using a sketch of the worksheet can help you visualize its design. The sketch of the worksheet consists of the title, column headings, location of data values, and an idea of the desired formatting (Figure 5–3a). The sketch does not show the criteria area above the table and the extract area below the table, which are included as requirements in the requirements document (Figure 5–2 on page EX 300). The general layout of the grade table, criteria area, and required statistics and query are shown in Figure 5–3b.

Kenson College Scholarship Fundraiser Table

Name	Status	Experience	Hire Date	Region	Type	Quota	YTD Funds Raised	% of Quota	Grade
XXXXXXXX	XXXXX	99	99/99/99	XX	XXXXXXX	9,999,999	9,999,999	999.99%	X

Figure 5–3 (a) Table

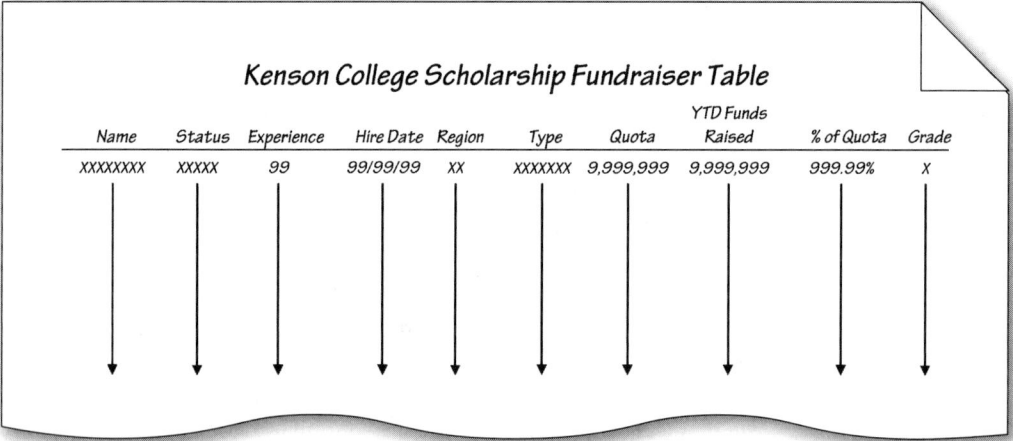

Grade Table			Criteria			
% of Quota	Grade		Status	Status	Grade	
0%	F		Full Time	Part Time	A	
60%	D		Aug. Full Time Experience ======➜			99.99
70%	C		Aug. Part Time Experience ======➜			99.99
80%	B		Grade A Count ===========➜			99
90%	A					
			Grade A YTD Funds Raised =====➜			99,999,999
			Full Time Count ==========➜			99
			Name ===============➜			XXXXXXX
			YTD Funds Raised =========➜			99,999,999

Figure 5–3 (b) Grade Table, Criteria, and Statistics

With a good understanding of the requirements document, an understanding of the necessary decisions, and a sketch of the worksheet, the next step is to use Excel to create the worksheet.

To Start Excel

If you are using a computer to step through the project in this chapter and you want your screens to match the figures in this book, you should change your screen's resolution to 1024 × 768. The following steps, which assume Windows 7 is running, start Excel based on a typical installation. You may need to ask your instructor how to start Excel for your computer.

1 Click the Start button on the Windows 7 taskbar to display the Start menu.

2 Type `Microsoft Excel` as the search text in the 'Search programs and files' text box, and watch the search results appear on the Start menu.

3 Click Microsoft Excel 2010 in the search results on the Start menu to start Excel and display a new blank workbook in the Excel window.

4 If the Excel window is not maximized, click the Maximize button next to the Close button on its title bar to maximize the window.

BTW

Starting Excel
If you plan to open an existing workbook, you can start Excel and open the workbook at the same time by double-clicking the workbook file name in Windows Explorer.

Create and format the table.
One way to create a table in Excel is to follow these four steps: (1) Enter the column headings (field names); (2) Define a range as a table using the Format as Table button (Home tab | Styles group); (3) Format the row immediately below the column headings; and (4) Enter records into the table.

Although Excel does not require a table title to be entered, it is a good practice to include one on the worksheet to show where the table begins. With Excel, you usually enter the table several rows below the first row in the worksheet. These blank rows later can be used as a criteria area to store criteria for use in a query.

Plan Ahead

When you create a table in Excel, you should follow some basic guidelines, as listed in Table 5–2.

Table 5–2 Guidelines for Creating a Table in Excel
Table Size and Workbook Location
1. Do not enter more than one table per worksheet.
2. Maintain at least one blank row between a table and other worksheet entries.
3. A table can have a maximum of 16,384 fields and 1,048,576 records on a worksheet.
Column Headings (Field Names)
1. Place column headings (field names) in the first row of the table.
2. Do not use blank rows or rows with repeating characters, such as dashes or underscores, to separate the column headings (field names) from the data.
3. Apply a different format to the column headings than to the data. For example, bold the column headings and format the data below the column headings using a regular style. Most quick table styles follow these guidelines.
4. Column headings (field names) can be up to 32,767 characters in length. The column headings should be meaningful.
Contents of Table
1. Each cell in any given column should have similar data. For example, Hire Date should be in the same column for all fundraisers.
2. Format the data to improve readability, but do not vary the format of the data within the cells of a column.

BTW

Setting Up a Table
When creating a table, leave several rows empty above the table on the worksheet to set up a criteria area for querying the table. Some spreadsheet specialists also leave several columns empty to the left of the table, beginning with column A, for additional worksheet activities. A range of blank rows or columns on the side of a table is called a *moat* of cells.

To Enter the Column Headings for a Table

The following steps change the column widths to those specified in Table 5–1, enter the table title, and enter and format the column headings. These steps also change the name of Sheet1 to Fundraiser Table, delete the unused sheets in the workbook, and save the workbook using the file name, Kenson College Scholarship Fundraiser Table.

Note: The majority of tasks involved in entering and formatting the table title and column headings of a list are similar to what you have done in previous chapters. Thus, if you plan to complete this chapter on your computer and want to skip the set of steps below, open the workbook Kenson College Scholarship Fundraiser Table from the Data Files for Students.

BTW

Merging and Centering Across a Selection
You merge and center across a selection when you want to treat the range of cells over which you center as a single cell. You center (but do not merge) across a selection when you want the selected range of cells to be independent of one another. With most workbooks, it makes little difference whether you center using one technique or the other. Thus, most spreadsheet specialists use the merge and center technique because the procedure easily is available by using the Merge & Center button (Home tab | Alignment group).

① Use the mouse to change the column widths as follows: A = 16.43, B = 10.29, C = 14.71, D = 13.14, E = 11.00, F = 14.00, G = 13.29, H = 13.29, I = 14.57, and J = 10.29.

② Enter `Kenson College Scholarship Fundraiser Table` as the table title in cell A7.

③ Select the range A7:H7. Right-click the selected range and then click Format Cells on a shortcut menu to display the Format Cells dialog box.

④ If necessary, click the Alignment tab (Format Cells dialog box) and then click the Horizontal box arrow in the Text alignment area to display a list of horizontal alignments.

⑤ Click Center Across Selection in the Horizontal list (Format Cells dialog box) to select the option to center the title through the selection, and then click the OK button (Format Cells dialog box) to close the Format Cells dialog box.

⑥ Apply the Title style to cell A7 and then change the font size to 20.

⑦ Enter the column headings in row 8 as shown in Figure 5–4. Center the column headings in the range B8:H8.

⑧ Apply the Heading 3 cell style to the range A8:H8 and then select cell A10.

⑨ Enter `Fundraiser Table` as the sheet name and then apply the Red, Accent 2 (column 6, row 1) color to the sheet tab.

⑩ Click the Sheet2 tab, hold down the CTRL key, and then click the Sheet3 tab to select both tabs.

⑪ Right-click the selected sheet tabs and then click Delete on a shortcut menu to delete the selected sheets from the workbook.

⑫ Update the document properties with your name and any other relevant information as specified by your instructor. Change the worksheet header by adding your name, course number, and other information as specified by your instructor.

⑬ With a USB flash drive connected to one of the computer's USB ports, click the Save button on the Quick Access Toolbar. Save the workbook using the file name, Kenson College Scholarship Fundraiser Table, on the USB flash drive (Figure 5–4).

Q&A

What is the difference between the Center Across Selection alignment and the Merge & Center button (Home tab | Alignment group)?

In Step 5, the Center Across Selection horizontal alignment was used to center the table title in row 7 horizontally across the range A7:H7. In earlier chapters, the Merge & Center button (Home tab | Alignment group) was used to center text across a range. The major difference between the Center Across Selection horizontal alignment and the Merge & Center button is that, unlike the Merge & Center button, the Center Across Selection horizontal alignment does not merge the selected cell range into one cell.

BTW

Q&As
For a complete list of the Q&As found in many of the step-by-step sequences in this book, visit the Excel 2010 Q&A Web page (scsite.com/ex2010/qa).

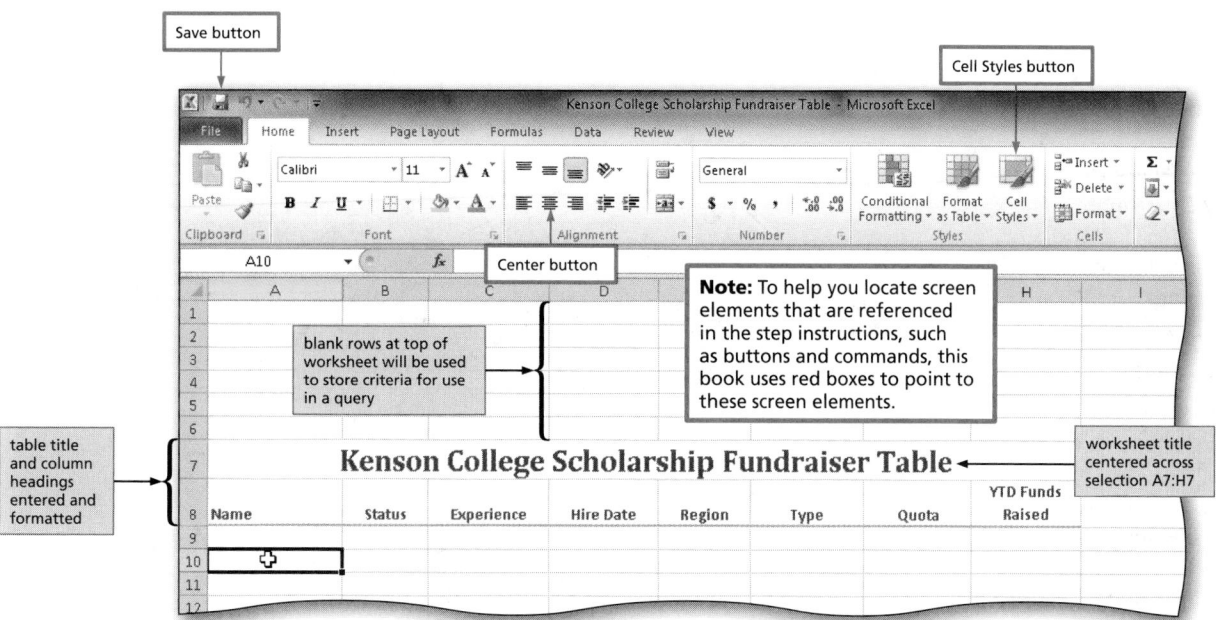

Figure 5–4

To Format a Range as a Table

The following steps define the range A8:H8 as a table by applying a table quick style to the range. Excel allows you to enter data in a range either before defining it as a table or after defining it as a table.

1

- Select the range A8:H8.

- Click the Format as Table button (Home tab | Styles group) to display the Format as Table gallery (Figure 5–5).

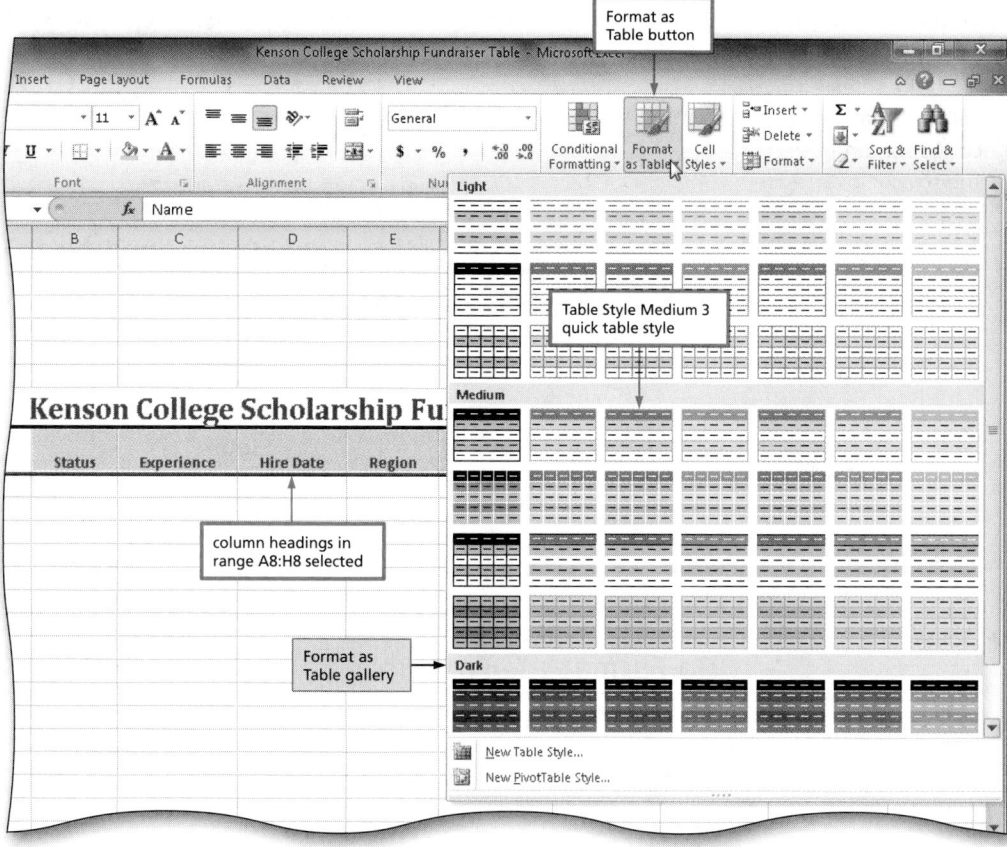

Figure 5–5

2

- Click the Table Style Medium 3 quick table style in the Format as Table gallery to display a marquee around the selected range and display the Format As Table dialog box.

- If necessary, click the 'My table has headers' check box to select the option to format the table with headers (Figure 5–6).

🔍 **Experiment**

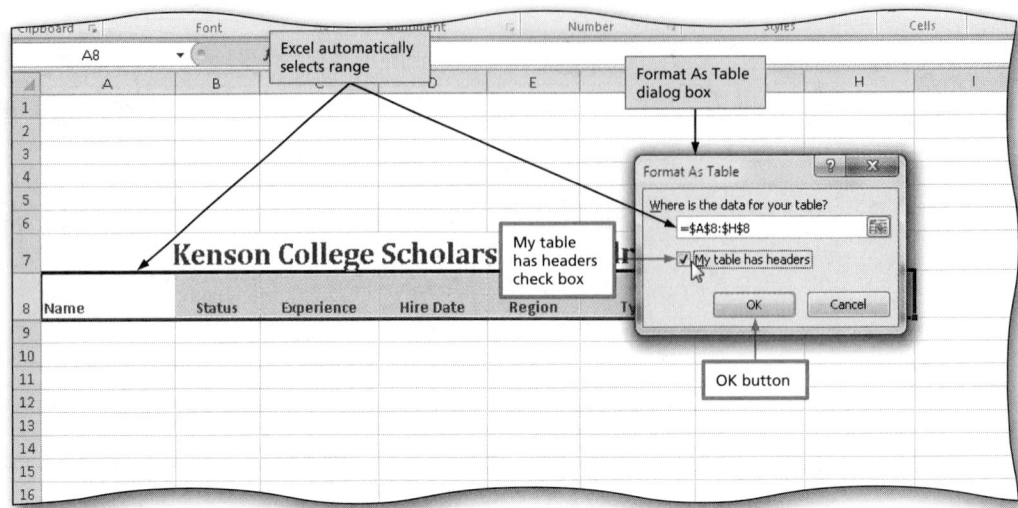

Figure 5–6

- Point to a number of table quick styles in the Format as Table gallery to preview them on the worksheet.

Q&A Why is the range A8:H8 already selected in the Format As Table dialog box?

Because the range A8:H8 was selected before clicking the Format as Table button, Excel automatically selects this range for the 'Where is the data for your table?' box.

3

- Click the OK button to create a table from the selected column headings and corresponding cells in the row below it.

- Scroll down until row 7 is at the top of the worksheet window (Figure 5–7).

Q&A Why does Excel indicate that the cells in row 9 are in the table?

Excel automatically creates an empty row in the table so that you are ready to enter the first record in the table.

Figure 5–7

Other Ways

1. Select range, click Table (Insert tab | Tables group), click OK button

To Format the First Row in an Empty Table

If the table contains no data, as in Figure 5–7, then Excel sets the format of the cells in the first row to the default associated with the table quick style chosen when the table was created. Further, if you create an empty table and require that the records be formatted in a manner that is different from the manner associated with the selected table quick style, format the first row after you create the table, not before. Otherwise, the formatting will disappear when you create the table. The following steps format the first row of the table.

① Select the range B9:H9 and then click the Center button (Home tab | Alignment group) to apply a center format to the range.

② Right-click cell D9 to display a shortcut menu. Click Format Cells on the shortcut menu to display the Format Cells dialog box.

③ Click the Number tab (Format Cells dialog box), click Date in the Category list, click 03/14/01 in the Type list, and then click the OK button to apply a MM/DD/YY date format to the selected cell.

④ Apply the comma style to the range G9:H9. Click the Decrease Decimal button (Home tab | Number group) twice so that data in the selected columns is displayed as whole numbers.

Q&A

Why are no changes apparent on the worksheet?

No visible changes appear on the worksheet because the table contains no records. As you enter records into the table, Excel applies the assigned formats to subsequent rows, even as you add more rows to the table.

To Modify a Table Quick Style

Before entering records in the table, the quick style used to create the table should be modified to make the table more readable. A bold font style with a black font color for the table's entries makes them more readable. The following steps create a new table quick style by copying the Table Style Medium 3 quick style and then modifying it so that a bold font style and black font color are applied to the entire table.

①

• If necessary, click cell A9 to activate the table.

• Click the Format as Table button (Home tab | Styles group) to display the Format as Table gallery and then right-click the Table Style Medium 3 quick table style to display a shortcut menu (Figure 5–8).

Figure 5–8

2

- Click Duplicate on the shortcut menu to display the Modify Table Quick Style dialog box.

- Type **TableStyleMedium3 – Custom** in the Name text box (Modify Table Quick Style dialog box) to name the new style (Figure 5–9).

Q&A What elements of a table can I customize?

The Table Element list in the Modify Table Quick Style dialog box allows you to choose almost any aspect of a table to modify. You can change the formatting for each element listed in the Table Element list by clicking the element and then clicking the Format button to display the Format Cells dialog box.

Figure 5–9

3

- With Whole Table selected in the Table Element list, click the Format button to display the Format Cells dialog box.

- If necessary, display the Font tab and then click Bold in the Font style list.

- Click the Color box arrow and then click the Black, Text 1 color (column 2, row 1) to select a font color for the new style (Figure 5–10).

4

- Click the OK button (Format Cells dialog box) to close the Format Cells dialog box.

- Click the OK button (Modify Table Quick Style dialog box) to close the Modify Table Quick Style dialog box.

- Apply the TableStyleMedium3 – Custom table style to the table.

- Select the range A8:H8 and then apply the White, Background 1 (column 1, row 1) font color to the range.

Figure 5–10

Q&A Why should the font color of the header row be changed to white?

The white font color allows the text in the header rows to stand out against the background color of the header row.

To Enter Records into a Table

The next step is to enter the fundraisers' records into the table. As indicated earlier, the computational fields in columns I and J will be added after the data is in the table. The following steps enter records into the table.

1

- If necessary, click cell A9 to activate the table.

- Type the fundraiser information for row 9, as shown in Figure 5–11. After typing the data for a field, press the RIGHT ARROW key to move to the next field. After you type the YTD Funds Raised, press the TAB key to start a new record.

Name	Status	Experience	Hire Date	Region	Type	Quota	YTD Funds Raised
Sprindys, Del	Full Time	2	09/27/02	North	Inside	2,112,696	1,780,578
Hennip, Beth	Full Time	5	10/30/02	Midwest	Outside	2,119,656	2,074,903

first two rows of table entered

cell A12 selected

table sizing handle

Figure 5–11

- Type the fundraiser information for row 10, as shown in Figure 5–11. After typing the data for a field, press the RIGHT ARROW key to move to the next field. After you type the YTD Funds Raised, click cell A12 to select it (Figure 5–11).

Q&A Is row 10 now part of the table?

Yes. Pressing the TAB key when a cell in the last column in a table is selected adds the next row below the table to the table. Row 10 now is part of the fundraiser table.

2

- Drag the table sizing handle to the top of cell H12 to add another row to the table (Figure 5–12).

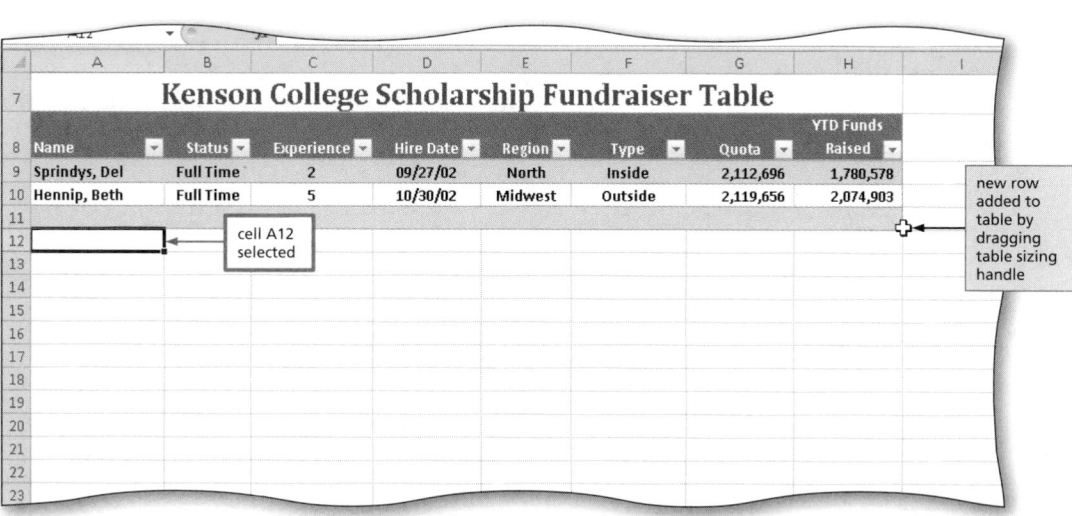

cell A12 selected

new row added to table by dragging table sizing handle

Figure 5–12

Q&A Why does row 11 have a different background color than row 10?

The quick style used to create the table includes a type of formatting called row banding. **Row banding** causes adjacent rows to have different formatting so that each row in the table is distinguished from surrounding rows.

3

- Enter the fundraiser record for the third fundraiser, as shown in Figure 5–13, and then select cell A12.

- Drag the table sizing handle to cell H21 to add 10 new rows to the table (Figure 5–13).

Q&A

Why were all of the rows not added to the table in Step 1?

Steps 1 through 3 demonstrate three different methods of adding rows to a

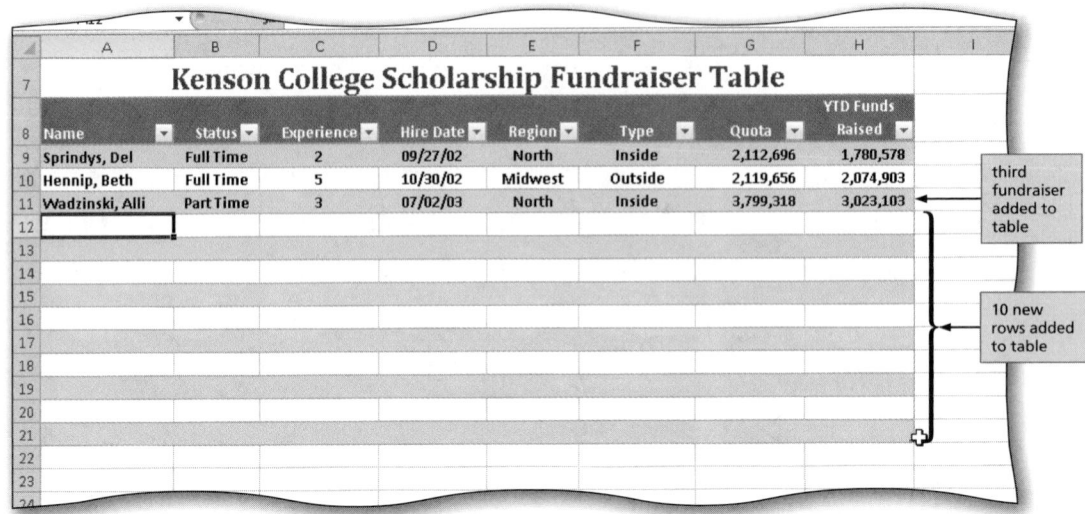

Figure 5–13

table. The first method can be used when you are adding a number of rows to the table and do not know how many rows you are going to add. Use the second method when you need to add one additional row to a table that you previously created. The third method can be used when you know exactly how many rows you need in a table.

Q&A

Why was cell A12 selected?

Cell A12 was selected after the first part of Step 3. A selected cell displays the fill handle instead of the table sizing handle. A different cell must be selected in order to display the table sizing handle in cell H11.

4

- Enter the remaining fundraisers' records as shown in Figure 5–14.

- Click cell A23 to deselect the table.

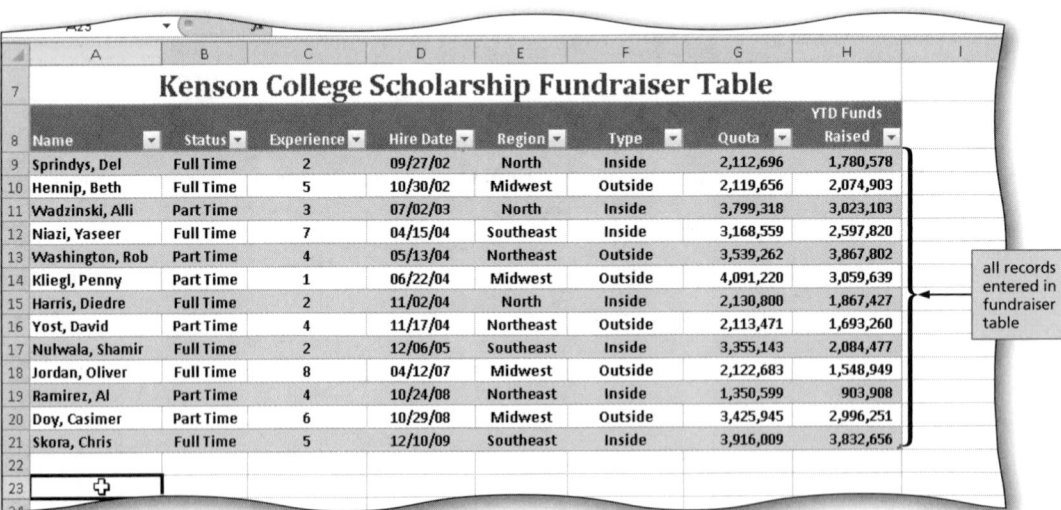

Figure 5–14

Break Point: If you wish to take a break, this is a good place to do so. Be sure to save the file again and then you can quit Excel. To resume at a later time, start Excel, open the file called Kenson College Scholarship Fundraiser Table, and continue following the steps from this location forward.

Adding Computational Fields to the Table

BTW

BTWs
For a complete list of the BTWs found in the margins of this book, visit the Excel 2010 BTW Web page (scsite.com/ex2010/btw).

The next step is to add the computational fields '% of Quota' in column I and Grade in column J. The first computational field involves dividing the YTD Funds Raised in column H by the Quota in column G. The second computational field involves a table lookup to determine a grade based upon the '% of Quota' in column I.

To Add New Fields to a Table

Adding new fields to a table in a worksheet illustrates another of Excel's powerful table capabilities. As shown in the following steps, if you add a new column heading in a column adjacent to the current column headings in the table, Excel automatically adds the adjacent column to the table's range and copies the format of the existing table heading to the new column heading. Adding a new row to a table works in a similar manner.

The first step in adding the two new fields is to enter the two column headings, or field names, in cells I8 and J8, enter the first '% of Quota' formula in cell I9, and then reformat the two cells immediately below the new column headings. The formula for the '% of Quota' in cell I9 is YTD FundsRaised / Quota. Rather than using cell references in the formula, Excel allows you to refer to the column headings in formulas by placing the column heading in brackets and adding the at symbol, or @, to the beginning of the column name. For example, the formula for cell I9 is =[@[YTD FundsRaised]] / [@Quota]. The column heading YTD Funds Raised must be between an open square bracket and a closed square bracket because the column heading includes spaces. Using this notation makes formulas easier to read, and the same formula could be used for all records in the table.

After you enter the formula in cell I9, Excel automatically copies the formula to the range I10:I21. When you enter a formula in the first row of a field, Excel creates a calculated column. A **calculated column** is a column in a table in which each row uses a common formula that references other fields in the table.

1

- Select cell I8 and type **% of Quota** as the new column heading.

- Select cell J8 and type **Grade** as the new column heading.

- Select cell I9, enter **= [@ [YTD FundsRaised]] / [@Quota]** as the formula and then click the Enter box on the formula bar to create a calculated column (Figure 5–15).

Figure 5–15

- Select the range I9:I21 and then click the Percent Style button (Home tab | Number group) to apply the percent style to the range.

- Click the Increase Decimal button (Home tab | Alignment group) twice to force numbers in the selected range to display two decimal places.

- Click the Center button (Home tab | Alignment group) to center the selected range (Figure 5–16).

Percent Style button

Increase Decimal button

Center button

column headings added adjacent to column headings in table are appended to the table automatically

=[@[YTD Funds Raised]] / [@Quota]

=[@[YTD Funds

Kenson College Scholarship Fundraiser Table

calculated column populated automatically when formula entered in first row

Status	Experience	Hire Date	Region	Type	Quota	YTD Funds Raised	% of Quota	Grade
Full Time	2	09/27/02	North	Inside	2,112,696	1,780,57	84.28%	
Full Time	5	10/30/02	Midwest	Outside	2,119,656	2,074,90	97.89%	
Part Time	3	07/02/03	North	Inside	3,799,318	3,023,10	79.57%	
Full Time	7	04/15/04	Southeast	Inside	3,168,559	2,597,82	81.99%	
Part Time	4	05/13/04	Northeast			3,867,80	109.28%	
Part Time	1	06/22/04	Midwest			3,059,63	74.79%	
Full Time	2	11/02/04	North			1,867,42	87.64%	
Part Time	4	11/17/04	Northeast	Outside	2,113,471	1,693,26	80.12%	
Full Time	2	12/06/05	Southeast	Inside	3,355,143	2,084,47	62.13%	
Full Time	8	04/12/07	Midwest	Outside	2,122,683	1,548,94	72.97%	
Part Time	4	10/24/08	Northeast	Inside	1,350,599	903,90	66.93%	
Part Time	6	10/29/08	Midwest	Outside	3,425,945	2,996,25	87.46%	
Full Time	5	12/10/09	Southeast	Inside	3,916,009	3,832,65	97.87%	

Figure 5–16

- Select the range A7:J7, right-click the selected range, click Format Cells on a shortcut menu, and then click the Alignment tab (Format Cells dialog box) to display the Alignment tab in the Format Cells dialog box.

- Click the Horizontal box arrow (Format Cells dialog box), click Center Across Selection, and then click the OK button to center the table heading and close the Format Cells dialog box.

- Select the range J9:J21 and then click the Center button (Home tab | Alignment group) to apply the center alignment to the range.

- Click cell J9 to deselect the range J9:J21.

BTW

Tables
To change an active table back to a normal range of cells, right-click the range, point to Table on a shortcut menu, and then click Convert to Range on the Table submenu.

Adding a Lookup Table

The entries in the % of Quota column give the user an immediate evaluation of where each fundraiser's total YTD Funds Raised stands in relation to his or her annual quota. Many people, however, dislike numbers as an evaluation tool. Most prefer simple letter grades, which, when used properly, group the fundraisers in the same way an instructor groups students by letter grades. Excel contains functions that allow you to assign letter grades based on a table.

Excel has several lookup functions that are useful for looking up values in tables such as tax tables, discount tables, parts tables, and grade tables. The two most widely used lookup functions are the HLOOKUP and VLOOKUP. Both functions look up a value in a table and return a corresponding value from the table to the cell containing the function. The **HLOOKUP function** is used when the table direction is horizontal, or across the worksheet. The **VLOOKUP function** is used when a table direction is vertical, or down the worksheet. The VLOOKUP function is by far the most often used because most tables are vertical, as is the table in this chapter.

To Create a Lookup Table

The grading scale in this chapter (Table 5–3) resembles the one that an instructor might use to determine your letter grade. As shown in Table 5–3, any score greater than or equal to 90% equates to a letter grade of A. Excel assigns scores greater than or equal to 80 and less than or equal to 89 a letter grade of B, and so on.

The VLOOKUP function requires that the table indicate only the lowest score for a letter grade. Furthermore, the table entries must be in sequence from lowest score to highest score. Thus, the entries in Table 5–3 must be resequenced for use with the VLOOKUP function so that they appear as shown in Table 5–4.

The general form of the VLOOKUP function is:

=VLOOKUP(lookup_value, table_array, col_index_num)

Table 5–3 Typical Grade Table

% of Quota	Grade
90% and higher	A
80% to 89%	B
70% to 79%	C
60% to 69%	D
0 to 59%	F

Table 5–4 Typical Grade Table Modified for the VLOOKUP Function

% of Quota	Grade
0	F
60%	D
70%	C
80%	B
90%	A

The VLOOKUP function searches the far-left column of the **table array**. The far-left column of the table_array contains what are called the **table arguments**. In this example, the table arguments include percentages (see Table 5–4). The VLOOKUP function uses the % of Quota value (called the lookup_value) in the record of a fundraiser to search the far-left column of the table array for a particular value. It then returns the corresponding **table value** from the column indicated by the col_index_num value. In this example, the grades are in the second, or far-right, column.

For the VLOOKUP function to work correctly, the table arguments must be in ascending sequence, because the VLOOKUP function will return a table value based on the lookup_value being less than or equal to the table arguments. Thus, if the % of Quota value is 79.57% (third record in Kenson College Scholarship Fundraiser table), then the VLOOKUP function returns a grade of C, because 79.57% is greater than or equal to 70 and is less than 80.

BTW

Sensitive Information in a Table

If you have a table with one or more columns of sensitive information, such as salary information, you can hide the columns by selecting them and then pressing CTRL+0. Next, password protect the worksheet. To view the hidden columns, unprotect the worksheet, select the columns adjacent to the hidden columns, and then press CTRL+SHIFT+RIGHT PARENTHESIS.

The following steps create the grade table in the range L1:M7.

1 Change the width of columns L and M to 11.00 (82 pixels).

2 Select cell L1 and then enter `Grade Table` as the table title.

3 If necessary, scroll the worksheet to the left and click cell A7 to select it. Scroll the worksheet to the right so that cell L1 is visible.

4 Click the Format Painter button (Home tab | Clipboard group) and then click cell L1 to copy the format of the selected cell to another cell.

5 Drag through cell M1 and then click the Merge & Center button (Home tab | Alignment group) to merge and center the data in the selected cell.

6 Select the range I8:J8. While holding down the CTRL key, point to the border of the range I8:J8 and drag to the range L2:M2 to copy the column headings in the selected range. Make sure that the source cells in the marquee are directly over the destination range before releasing the mouse button.

7 Enter the table entries in Table 5–4 on the previous page in the range L3:M7. Select the range L3:M7 and then click the Bold button (Home tab | Font group) to bold the entries in the selected range.

8 Click the Center button (Home tab | Alignment group) to center the values in the selected range.

9 Format the range L3:L7 with the percent style format. Click cell J9 to deselect the range L3:M7 (Figure 5–17).

Using HLOOKUP

HLOOKUP uses the same arguments as VLOOKUP, but it searches rows of information instead of columns. HLOOKUP also uses the row_index_num argument instead of the col_index_num argument, as shown in Figure 5–18. When using HLOOKUP, be sure to sort the values in the first row of the table_array in ascending order to find an approximate match. Otherwise, specify FALSE as the range_lookup argument to find an exact match.

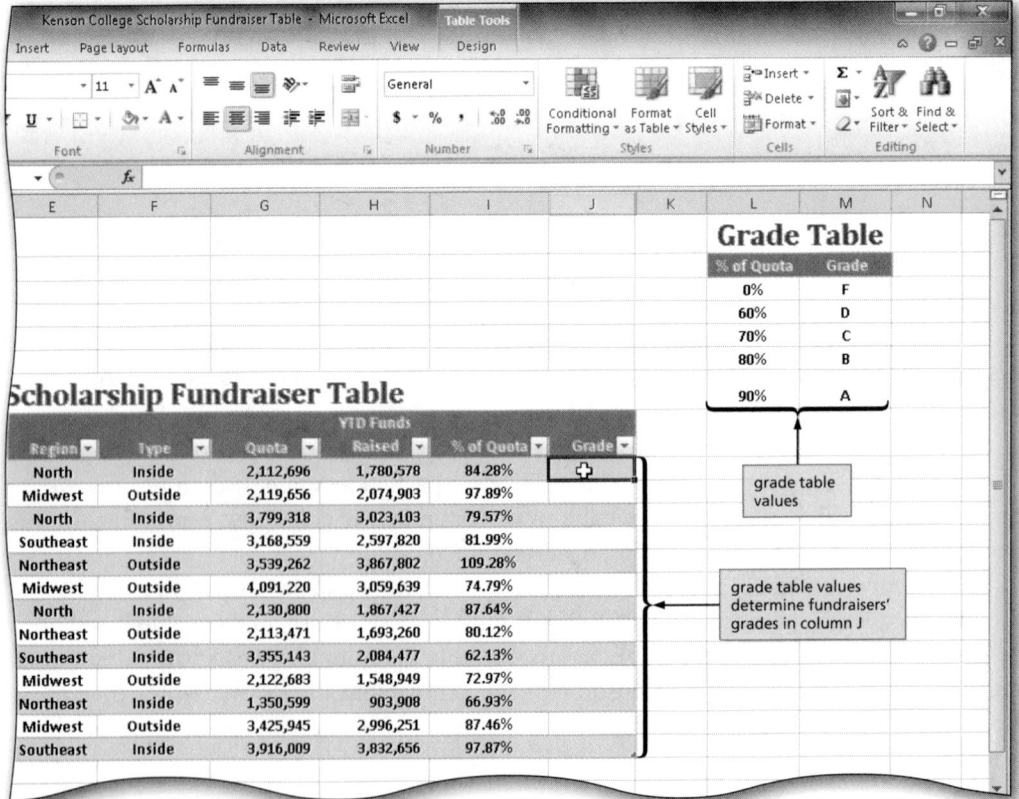

Figure 5–17

To Use the VLOOKUP Function to Determine Letter Grades

The following steps use the VLOOKUP function and the grade table to determine the letter grade for each fundraiser based on the fundraiser's % of Quota value. In this case, cell I9 is the lookup_value, $L$3:$M$7 is the table_array, and 2 is the col_index_num in the table_array.

1

• With cell J9 selected, type =vlookup(i9, l3:m7, 2 as the cell entry (Figure 5–18).

Q&A

Why are absolute cell references used in the function?

You need to use absolute cell references ($) for the table_array ($l$3:$m$7) in the VLOOKUP function so that Excel will not adjust the cell references when it creates the calculated column in the next step of this step sequence. If Excel adjusts the cell references, you will see unexpected results in column J.

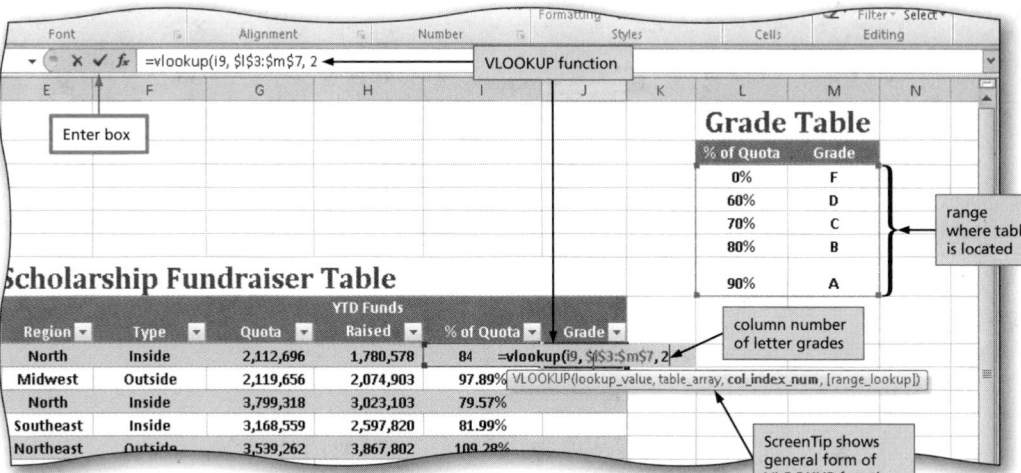

Figure 5–18

2

• Click the Enter box to create a calculated column for the selected field, the Grade field in this case (Figure 5–19).

Q&A

What happens when the Enter box is clicked?

Because cell I9 is the first record in a table, Excel creates a calculated column in column I by copying the VLOOKUP function through row 21. As shown in Figure 5–19, any % of Quota value below 60 in column I returns a grade of F in column J. The seventh record (Harris in row 15) receives a grade of B because its % of Quota value is 87.64%. A % of Quota value of 90% is required to move up to the next letter grade. The ninth record (Nulwala) receives a grade of D because his % of Quota value is 62.13%, which is less than 70% but greater than 60%.

=VLOOKUP(I9, $L$3:$M$7, 2) ← VLOOKUP function assigned to calculated column

Grade Table

% of Quota	Grade
0%	F
60%	D
70%	C
80%	B
90%	A

Scholarship Fundraiser Table

Region	Type	Quota	YTD Funds Raised	% of Quota	Grade
North	Inside	2,112,696	1,780,578	84.28%	B
Midwest	Outside	2,119,656	2,074,903	97.89%	A
North	Inside	3,799,318	3,023,103	79.57%	C
Southeast	Inside	3,168,559	2,597,820	81.99%	B
Northeast	Outside	3,539,262	3,867,802	109.28%	A
Midwest	Outside	4,091,220	3,059,639	74.79%	C
North	Inside	2,130,800	1,867,427	87.64%	B
Northeast	Outside	2,113,471	1,693,260	80.12%	B
Southeast	Inside	3,355,143	2,084,477	62.13%	D
Midwest	Outside	2,122,683	1,548,949	72.97%	C
Northeast	Inside	1,350,599	903,908	66.93%	D
Midwest	Outside	3,425,945	2,996,251	87.46%	B
Southeast	Inside	3,916,009	3,832,656	97.87%	A

VLOOKUP function returned grades and all grades automatically determined in calculated column

Figure 5–19

3

- Scroll the worksheet so that row 7 is the top row and then click cell A23 to show the completed table (Figure 5–20).

Q&A

How is the VLOOKUP function determining the grades?

From column J, you can see that the VLOOKUP function is not searching for a table argument that matches the lookup_value exactly.

The VLOOKUP function begins the search at the top of the table and works downward. As soon as it finds the first table argument greater than the lookup_value, the function returns the corresponding value from column M. The letter grade of F is returned for any value greater than or equal to 0 (zero) and less than 60. A score less than 0 returns an error message (#N/A) to the cell assigned the VLOOKUP function.

Kenson College Scholarship Fundraiser Table

Name	Status	Experience	Hire Date	Region	Type	Quota	YTD Funds Raised	% of Quota	Grade
Sprindys, Del	Full Time	2	09/27/02	North	Inside	2,112,696	1,780,578	84.28%	B
Hennip, Beth	Full Time	5	10/30/02	Midwest	Outside	2,119,656	2,074,903	97.89%	A
Wadzinski, Alli	Part Time	3	07/02/03	North	Inside	3,799,318	3,023,103	79.57%	C
Niazi, Yaseer	Full Time	7	04/15/04	Southeast	Inside	3,168,559	2,597,820	81.99%	B
Washington, Rob	Part Time	4	05/13/04	Northeast	Outside	3,539,262	3,867,802	109.28%	A
Kliegl, Penny	Part Time	1	06/22/04	Midwest	Outside	4,091,220	3,059,639	74.79%	C
Harris, Diedre	Full Time	2	11/02/04	North	Inside	2,130,800	1,867,427	87.64%	B
Yost, David	Part Time	4	11/17/04	Northeast	Outside	2,113,471	1,693,260	80.12%	B
Nulwala, Shamir	Part Time	2	12/06/05	Southeast	Inside	3,355,143	2,084,477	62.13%	D
Jordan, Oliver	Full Time	8	04/12/07	Midwest	Outside	2,122,683	1,548,949	72.97%	C
Ramirez, Al	Part Time	4	10/24/08	Northeast	Inside	1,350,599	903,908	66.93%	D
Doy, Casimer	Part Time	6	10/29/08	Midwest	Outside	3,425,945	2,996,251	87.46%	B
Skora, Chris	Full Time	5	12/10/09	Southeast	Inside	3,916,009	3,832,656	97.87%	A

table is complete

Figure 5–20

Other Ways

1. Click Insert Function box in formula bar, click 'Or select a category' box arrow, click Lookup & Reference, click VLOOKUP in 'Select a function' list

2. Click Lookup & Reference button (Formulas tab | Function Library group), click VLOOKUP

BTW

Conditional Formatting with the IF Function
You can apply conditional formatting based on the value of any IF function you specify. To create a conditional format based on a function or formula, select a range and then click the Conditional Formatting button (Home tab | Styles group). Click New Rule in the Conditional Formatting list to display the New Formatting Rule dialog box. Click Use a formula to determine which cells to format and then enter the desired IF function, or other formula, in the 'Format values where the formula is true' box.

Conditional Formatting

Conditional formatting allows you to create rules that change the formatting of a cell or range of cells based on the value of a particular cell. Excel includes five types of conditional formats: highlight, top and bottom rules, data bars, color scales, and icon sets. Excel allows you to combine different types of formats on any cell or range. For example, based on a cell's value, you can format it to include both an icon and a specific background color. You also can apply multiple conditional formatting rules to a cell or range.

The Conditional Formatting Rules Manager dialog box allows you to view all of the rules for the current selection or for an entire worksheet. The dialog box also allows you to view and change the order in which the rules are applied to a cell or range. You also can stop the application of subsequent rules after one rule is found to be true. For example, if the first rule specifies that a negative value in the cell results in a red background color being applied to the cell, then you may not want to apply any other conditional formats to the cell. In this case, put a check mark in the Stop If True column for the rule in the Conditional Formatting Rules Manager dialog box.

The project in this chapter uses an icon set as a type of conditional format. The exercises at the end of this chapter include instructions regarding the use of other types of conditional formats.

To Add a Conditional Formatting Rule with an Icon Set

The Grade field was added to the table in order to provide succinct information to the user of the worksheet regarding each fundraiser's performance. Another method to succinctly present information regarding each fundraiser's performance is to display an icon next to the % of Quota percentage for each fundraiser. Conditional formatting provides a number of icons, including icons with the appearance of traffic signals, flags, bars, and arrows. Icon sets include sets of three, four, or five icons. You use an icon set depending on how many ways you need to group your data. For example, in the case of grades for the fundraisers, there are five different grades and, therefore, an icon set that includes five icons should be used. You define rules for the conditions under which each icon of the five is displayed in a cell. The following steps add a conditional format to the % of Quota field in the Fundraiser table.

1

- Select the range I9:I21 and then click the Conditional Formatting button (Home tab | Styles group) to display the Conditional Formatting list.

- Click New Rule in the Conditional Formatting list to display the New Formatting Rule dialog box.

- Click the Format Style box arrow (New Formatting Rule dialog box) to display the Format Style list (Figure 5–21).

Figure 5–21

2

- Click Icon Sets in the Format Style list (New Formatting Rule dialog box) to display the Icon area in the Edit the Rule Description area.

- Click the Icon Style box arrow to display the Icon Style list and then scroll until 5 Arrows (Colored) appears in the list (Figure 5–22).

🔍 Experiment

- Click a variety of icon styles in the Icon Styles list to view the options in the Edit the Rule Description area for each option.

Figure 5–22

3

- Click 5 Arrows (Colored) in the Icon Style list (New Formatting Rule dialog box) to select an icon style that includes five different colored arrows.

- Click the top Type box arrow and then click Number in the list to select a numeric value for the Type rather than a percent value.

- Change the Type to Number for the remaining Type boxes.

- Type 0.9 in the first Value box, 0.8 in the second Value box, and 0.7 in the third Value box to assign ranges of values to each of the first three arrow colors.

- Type 0.6 in the final Value box and then press the TAB key to complete the conditions (Figure 5–23).

Figure 5–23

Q&A Why do the numbers next to each icon change as I type?

The area below the word Icon models the current conditional formatting rule. Excel automatically updates this area as you change the conditions on the right side of the Edit the Rule Description area. Use this area as an easy-to-read status of the conditions that you are creating.

4

- Click the OK button (New Formatting Rule dialog box) to display icons in each row of the table in the % of Quota field.

- Click cell A23 to deselect the table (Figure 5–24).

Q&A What do the icons represent?

In addition to the Grade field, the conditional formatting icons provide a visual representation of the fundraisers' progress on attaining their fundraising quotas. The green arrow and its direction represent a grade of A, the red arrow and its direction a grade of F, and the three different yellow arrows and their directions represent the B, C, and D levels. None of the fundraisers received a grade of F.

Figure 5–24

Working with Tables in Excel

When a table is active, the Design tab on the Ribbon provides powerful commands that allow you to alter the appearance and contents of a table quickly. For example, you quickly can add and remove header and total rows in a table. This section describes the use of these commands.

To Use the Total Row Check Box

The Total Row check box on the Design tab allows you to insert a **total row** at the bottom of the table. The total row sums the values that are in the far-right column of the table, if the values are numeric. If the values in the far-right column of the table are textual, then Excel counts the number of records and puts the number in the total row. For example, in Figure 5–26, the 13 in cell J22 on the right side of the total row is a count of the number of fundraiser records. Excel provides additional computations for the total row, as shown in the following steps.

1

- Click cell A9 to make the table active and then display the Table Tools Design tab (Figure 5–25).

🔑 **Experiment**

- Select a variety of combinations of check boxes in the Table Style Options group on the Table Tools Design tab. When finished, make sure that the check boxes are set as shown in Figure 5–25.

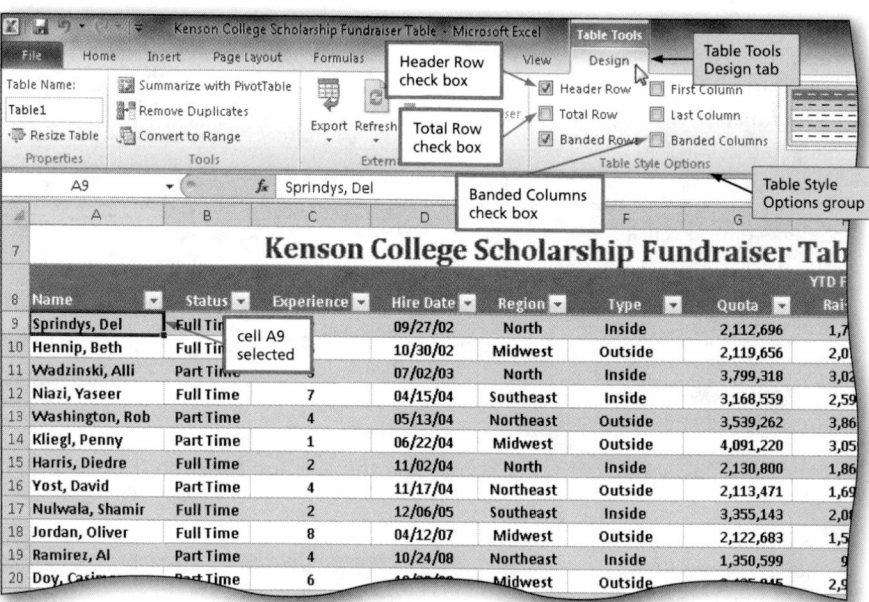

Figure 5–25

2

- Click the Total Row check box (Table Tools Design tab | Table Style Options group) to add the total row and display the record count in the far-right column of the table, cell J22 in this case.

- Select cell H22.

- Click the arrow on the right side of the cell to display a list of available statistical functions (Figure 5–26).

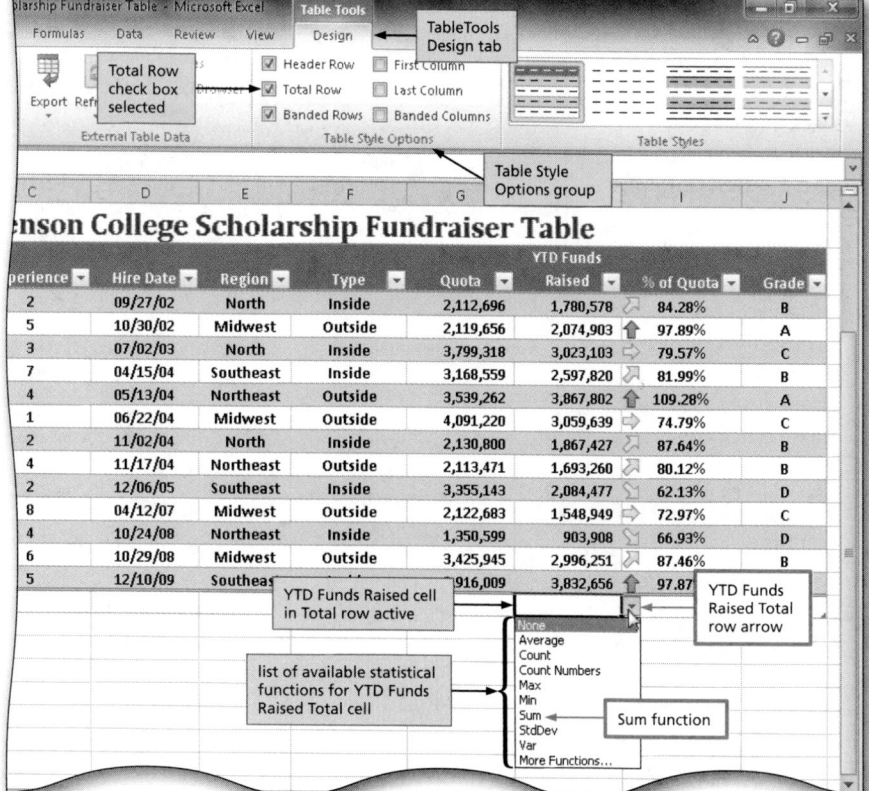

Figure 5–26

3

- Click Sum in the list to select the Sum function for the selected cell in the total row.

- Select cell G22, click the arrow on the right side of the cell, and then click Sum in the list to select the Sum function for the selected cell in the total row.

- Select cell C22, click the arrow on the right side of the cell, and then click Average in the list to select the Average function for the selected cell in the total row.

- Click cell A9 to deselect the cell containing the average function (Figure 5–27).

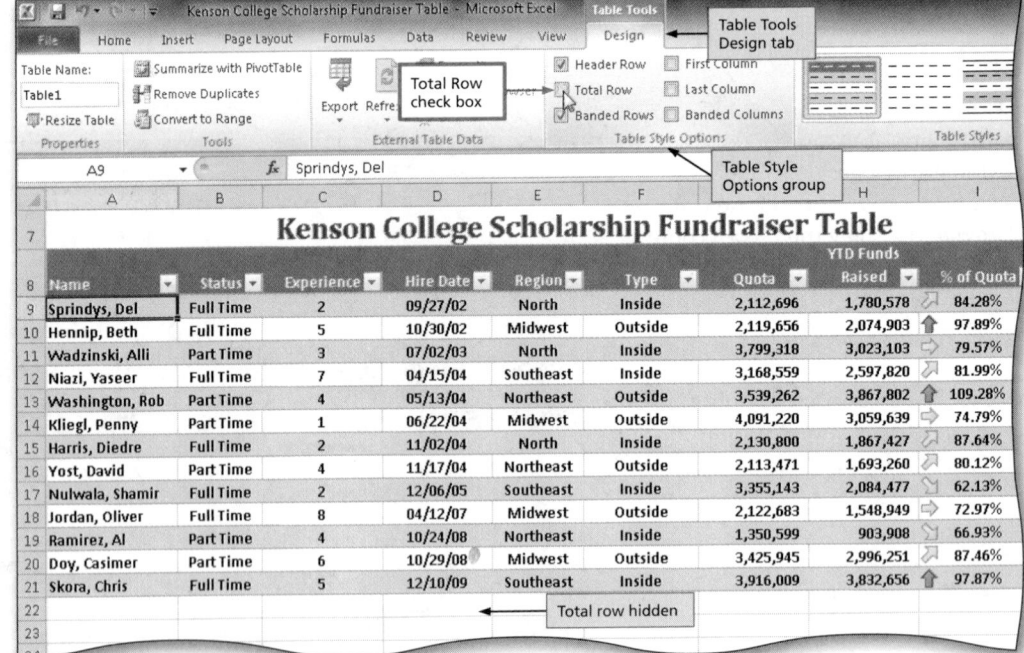

Figure 5–27

4

- Click the Total Row check box (Table Tools Design tab | Table Style Options group) to hide the total row (Figure 5–28).

Experiment

- Click the Header Row, Banded Rows, and Banded Columns check boxes (Table Tools Design tab | Table Style Options). When you are finished viewing the formatting caused by checking these check boxes, click the check boxes.

Q&A

What are banded columns?

As you have learned, banded rows include alternating colors every other row. Similarly, banded columns provide alternating colors every other column. You also can include a different color for the first and/or last column in a table. The quick style that you choose for a table must have these colors defined in the quick style. The quick style used in this chapter does not include special formatting for the first and last columns.

Figure 5–28

To Print the Table

When a table is selected and you display the Print tab in the Backstage view, an option in the Settings area allows you to print the contents of just the active table. The following steps print the table in landscape orientation using the Fit Sheet on One Page option.

- If necessary, click cell A9 to make the table active and then click File on the Ribbon to open the Backstage view.

- Click the Print tab to display the Print gallery.

- Click the Print Active Sheets in the Settings area to display a list of parts of the workbook to print.

- Select Print Selected Table to choose to print only the selected table.

- In the Settings area, select the options to print the table in landscape orientation using the Fit Sheet on One Page option (Figure 5–29).

Figure 5–29

- Click the Print button to print the table (Figure 5–30).

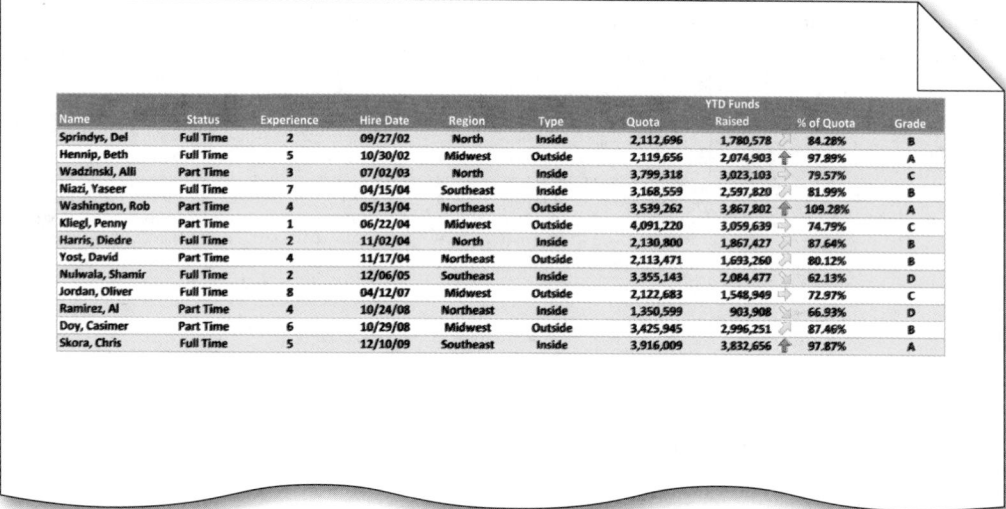

Name	Status	Experience	Hire Date	Region	Type	Quota	YTD Funds Raised	% of Quota	Grade
Sprindys, Del	Full Time	2	09/27/02	North	Inside	2,112,696	1,780,578	84.28%	B
Hennip, Beth	Full Time	5	10/30/02	Midwest	Outside	2,119,656	2,074,903	97.89%	A
Wadzinski, Alli	Part Time	3	07/02/03	North	Inside	3,799,318	3,023,103	79.57%	C
Niazi, Yaseer	Full Time	7	04/15/04	Southeast	Inside	3,168,559	2,597,820	81.99%	B
Washington, Rob	Part Time	4	05/13/04	Northeast	Outside	3,539,262	3,867,802	109.28%	A
Kliegl, Penny	Part Time	1	06/22/04	Midwest	Outside	4,091,220	3,059,639	74.79%	C
Harris, Diedre	Full Time	2	11/02/04	North	Inside	2,130,800	1,867,427	87.64%	B
Yost, David	Part Time	4	11/17/04	Northeast	Outside	2,113,471	1,693,260	80.12%	B
Nulwala, Shamir	Full Time	2	12/06/05	Southeast	Inside	3,355,143	2,084,477	62.13%	D
Jordan, Oliver	Full Time	8	04/12/07	Midwest	Outside	2,122,683	1,548,949	72.97%	C
Ramirez, Al	Part Time	4	10/24/08	Northeast	Inside	1,350,599	903,908	66.93%	D
Doy, Casimer	Part Time	6	10/29/08	Midwest	Outside	3,425,945	2,996,251	87.46%	B
Skora, Chris	Full Time	5	12/10/09	Southeast	Inside	3,916,009	3,832,656	97.87%	A

Figure 5–30

Sorting a Table

The data in a table is easier to work with and more meaningful if the records are arranged sequentially based on one or more fields. Arranging records in a specific sequence is called **sorting**. Data is in **ascending sequence** if it is in order from lowest to highest, earliest to most recent, or alphabetically from A to Z. Data is in **descending sequence** if it is sorted from highest to lowest, most recent to earliest, or alphabetically from Z to A. The field or fields you select to sort the records are called **sort keys**.

You can sort data in a table by using one of the following techniques:

1. Select a cell in the field on which to sort, click the Sort & Filter button (Home tab | Editing group), and then click one of the sorting options on the Sort & Filter menu.
2. With the table active, click the column heading arrow in the column on which to sort and then click one of the sorting options in the table.
3. Use the Sort button (Data tab | Sort & Filter group).
4. Right-click anywhere in a table and then point to Sort on a shortcut menu to display the Sort submenu.

To Sort a Table in Ascending Sequence by Name Using the Sort & Filter Button

The following steps sort the table in ascending sequence by the Name field using the Sort & Filter button (Home tab | Editing group).

1

- If necessary, display the Home tab.

- Click cell A9, if necessary, and then click the Sort & Filter button (Home tab | Editing group) to display the Sort & Filter menu (Figure 5–31).

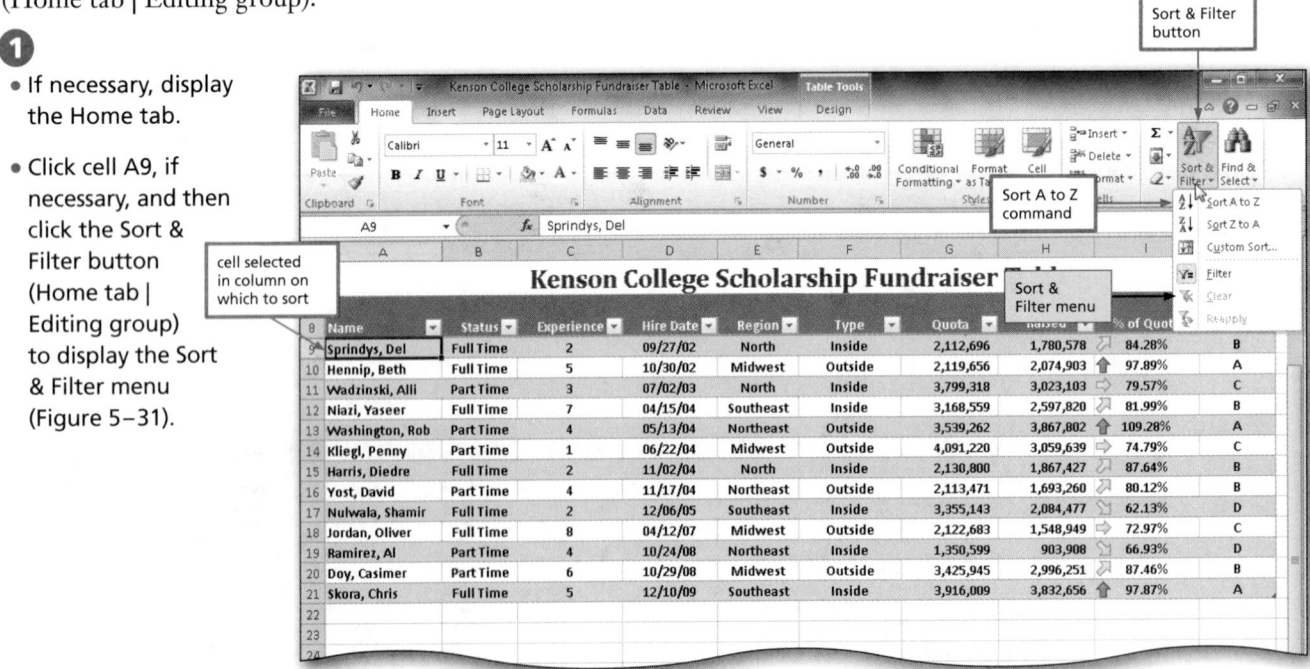

Figure 5–31

What if the column I choose includes numeric or date data?

If the column you choose includes numeric data, then the Sort & Filter menu would show the Sort Smallest to Largest and Sort Largest to Smallest commands instead of the Sort A to Z and Sort Z to A commands. If the column you choose includes date data, then the Sort & Filter menu would show the Sort Oldest to Newest and Sort Newest to Oldest commands instead of the Sort A to Z and Sort Z to A commands.

2

- Click the Sort A to Z command to sort the table in ascending sequence by the selected field, Name in this case (Figure 5–32).

Experiment

- Select other fields in the table and use the same procedure to sort on the fields you choose. When you are finished, remove any sorting, select cell A9, and repeat the two steps above.

Name	Status	Experience	Hire Date	Region	Type	Quota	YTD Fu Raise
Doy, Casimer	Part Time	6	10/29/08	Midwest	Outside	3,425,945	2,99
Harris, Diedre	Full Time	2	11/02/04	North	Inside	2,130,800	1,86
Hennip, Beth	Full Time	5	10/30/02	Midwest	Outside	2,119,656	2,02
Jordan, Oliver	Full Time	8	04/12/07	Midwest	Outside	2,122,683	1,5
Kliegl, Penny	Part Time	1	06/22/04	Midwest	Outside	4,091,220	3,0
Niazi, Yaseer	Full Time	7	04/15/04	Southeast	Inside	3,168,559	2,
Nulwala, Shamir	Full Time	2	12/06/05	Southeast	Inside	3,355,143	2,8
Ramirez, Al	Part Time	4	10/24/08	Northeast	Inside	1,350,599	9
Skora, Chris	Full Time	5	12/10/09	Southeast	Inside	3,916,009	3,8
Sprindys, Del	Full Time	2	09/27/02	North	Inside	2,112,696	1,7
Wadzinski, Alli	Part Time	3	07/02/03	North	Inside	3,799,318	3,02
Washington, Rob	Part Time	4	05/13/04	Northeast	Outside	3,539,262	3,86
Yost, David	Part Time	4	11/17/04	Northeast	Outside	2,113,471	1,69

records sorted in ascending sequence by name

Figure 5–32

Other Ways

1. Select field in table, click Sort A to Z button (Data tab | Sort & Filter group)

2. Click column heading arrow of field on which to sort, click Sort A to Z

3. Right-click column to sort, point to Sort on shortcut menu, click Sort A to Z

To Sort a Table in Descending Sequence by Name Using the Sort Z to A Button on the Data Tab

The following steps sort the records in descending sequence by name.

1 If necessary, click cell A9 to select the table.

2 Display the Data tab.

3 Click the Sort Z to A button (Data tab | Sort & Filter group) to sort the table in descending sequence by the selected field, Name in this case (Figure 5–33).

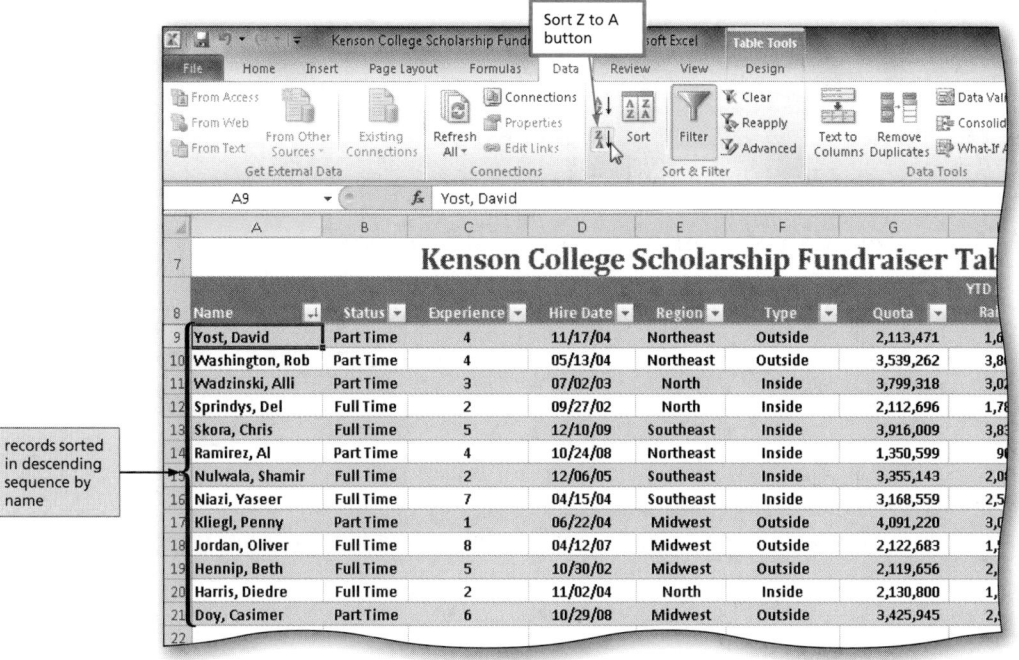

Name	Status	Experience	Hire Date	Region	Type	Quota	YTD Rai
Yost, David	Part Time	4	11/17/04	Northeast	Outside	2,113,471	1,6
Washington, Rob	Part Time	4	05/13/04	Northeast	Outside	3,539,262	3,8
Wadzinski, Alli	Part Time	3	07/02/03	North	Inside	3,799,318	3,02
Sprindys, Del	Full Time	2	09/27/02	North	Inside	2,112,696	1,78
Skora, Chris	Full Time	5	12/10/09	Southeast	Inside	3,916,009	3,83
Ramirez, Al	Part Time	4	10/24/08	Northeast	Inside	1,350,599	9
Nulwala, Shamir	Full Time	2	12/06/05	Southeast	Inside	3,355,143	2,0
Niazi, Yaseer	Full Time	7	04/15/04	Southeast	Inside	3,168,559	2,5
Kliegl, Penny	Part Time	1	06/22/04	Midwest	Outside	4,091,220	3,0
Jordan, Oliver	Full Time	8	04/12/07	Midwest	Outside	2,122,683	1,
Hennip, Beth	Full Time	5	10/30/02	Midwest	Outside	2,119,656	2,
Harris, Diedre	Full Time	2	11/02/04	North	Inside	2,130,800	1,
Doy, Casimer	Part Time	6	10/29/08	Midwest	Outside	3,425,945	2,

records sorted in descending sequence by name

Figure 5–33

To Sort a Table Using the Sort Command on an AutoFilter Menu

The following step sorts the table by Hire Date using the Sort Ascending command on an AutoFilter menu.

- Display the Home tab.

- Click the Hire Date AutoFilter arrow to display the AutoFilter menu for the selected field, Hire Date in this case (Figure 5–34).

- Click Sort Oldest to Newest in the Hire Date AutoFilter menu to sort the table in ascending sequence by the selected field.

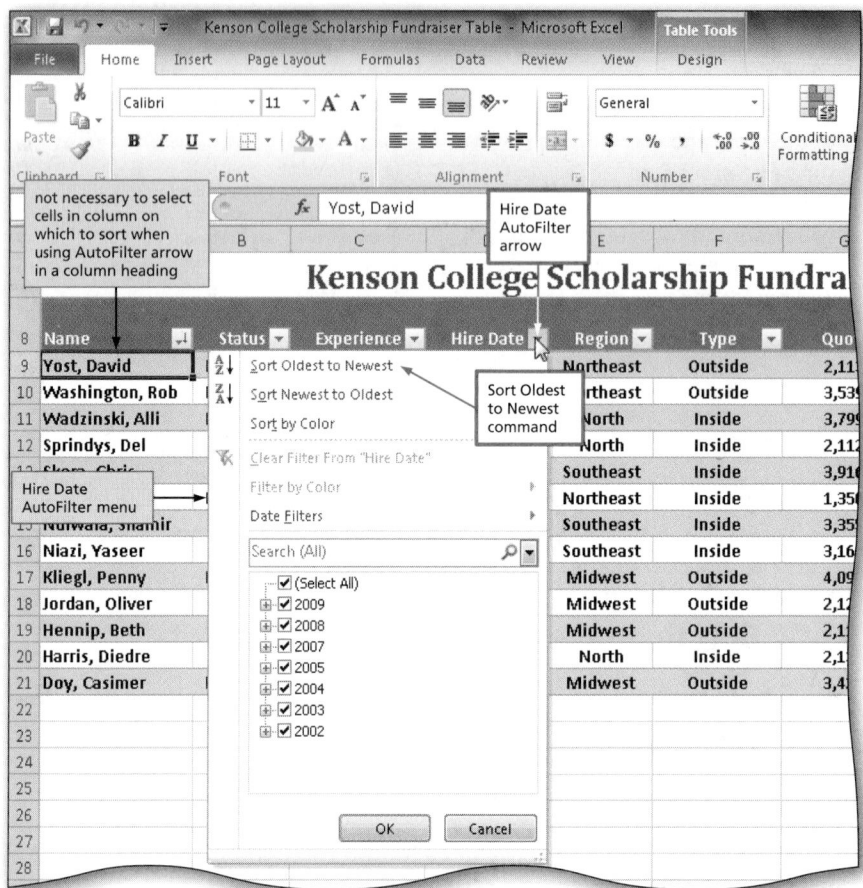

Figure 5–34

Other Ways
1. Select field in table, click Sort Oldest to Newest button (Data tab | Sort & Filter group)   2. Right-click column to sort, point to Sort on shortcut menu, click Sort Oldest to Newest

To Sort a Table on Multiple Fields Using the Custom Sort Command

Excel allows you to sort on a maximum of 256 fields in a single sort operation. For instance, the sort example in this part of the chapter uses the Custom Sort command on the Sort & Filter menu to sort the Kenson College Scholarship Fundraiser table by quota (column G) within status (column B) within type (column F). The Type and Status fields will be sorted in ascending sequence; the Quota field will be sorted in descending sequence.

The phrase, sort by quota within status within type, means that the records in the table first are arranged in ascending sequence by Type (Inside and Outside). Within Type, the records are arranged in ascending sequence by Status (Full Time or Part Time). Within Status, the records are arranged in descending sequence by the fundraiser's Quota. In this case, Type is the **major sort key** (Sort by field), Status is the **intermediate sort key** (first Then by field), and Quota is the **minor sort key** (second Then by field). The following steps sort the fundraiser table on multiple fields using the Custom Sort command.

1

- With a cell in the table active, click the Sort & Filter button (Home tab | Editing group) to display the Sort & Filter menu (Figure 5–35).

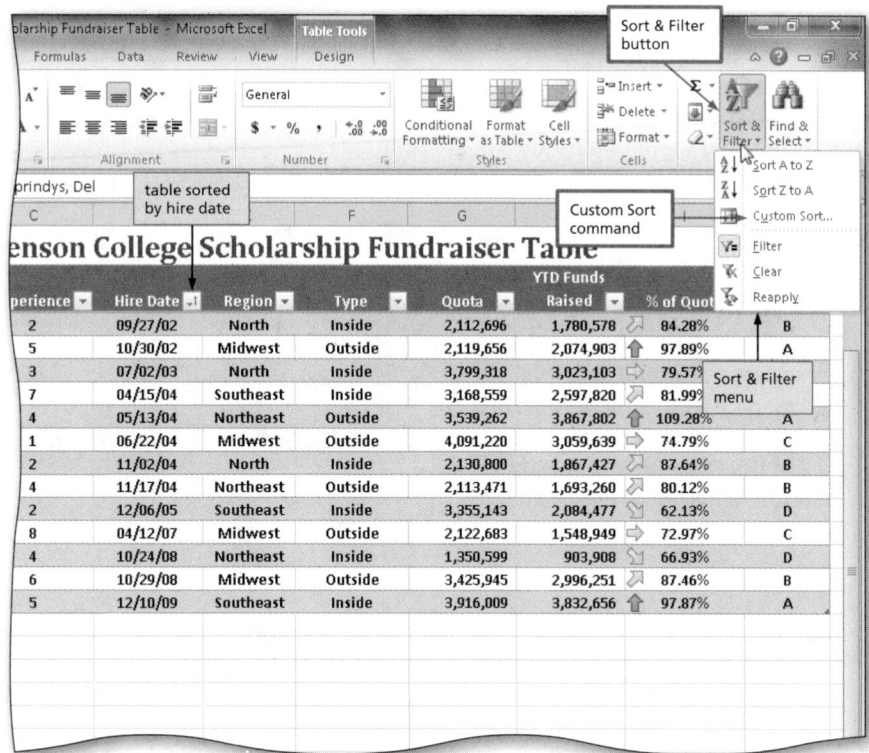

Figure 5–35

2

- Click Custom Sort on the Sort & Filter menu to display the Sort dialog box.

- Click the Sort by box arrow (Sort dialog box) to display the field names in the table (Figure 5–36).

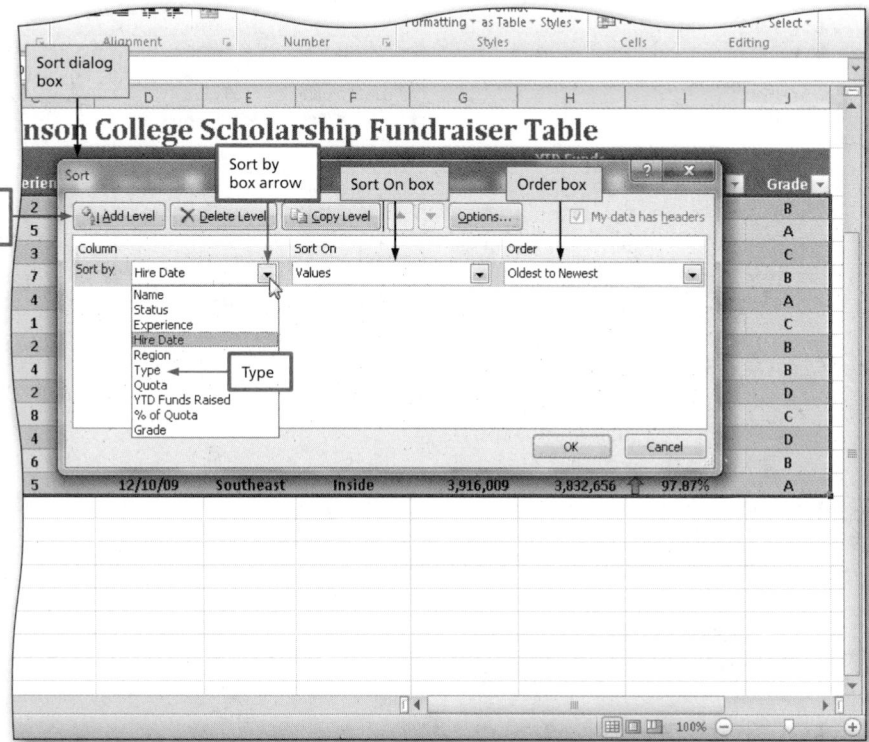

Figure 5–36

3

- Click Type to select the first sort level. If necessary, select Values in the Sort On box. If necessary, select A to Z in the Order box to specify that the field should be sorted alphabetically.

- Click the Add Level button to add a new sort level.

- Click the Then by box arrow and then click Status in the Then by list to select a second sort level. If necessary, select Values in the Sort On box and, if necessary, select A to Z in the Order box to specify that the field should be sorted alphabetically.

Figure 5–37

- Click the Add Level button to add a new sort level.

- Click the second Then by box arrow and then click Quota in the Then by list to select a third sort level. If necessary, select Values in the Sort On box. Select Largest to Smallest in the Order box to specify that the field should be sorted in reverse order (Figure 5–37).

4

- Click the OK button to sort the table, in this case by quota within status within type (Figure 5–38).

Q&A

How are the records sorted?

As shown in Figure 5–38, Excel sorts the records in ascending sequence by type in column F. Within each type, the records are sorted in ascending sequence by status in column B. Finally, within status, the records are sorted in descending sequence by the quotas in column G. Remember, if you make a mistake in a sort operation, you can return the records to their original order by clicking the Undo button on the Quick Access Toolbar or by sorting the table by hire date, which is the order in which the data was entered.

Name	Status	Experience	Hire Date	Region	Type	Quota	Rai
Skora, Chris	Full Time	5	12/10/09	Southeast	Inside	3,916,009	3,8
Nulwala, Shamir	Full Time	2	12/06/05	Southeast	Inside	3,355,143	2,0
Niazi, Yaseer	Full Time	7	04/15/04	Southeast	Inside	3,168,559	2,5
Harris, Diedre	Full Time	2	11/02/04	North	Inside	2,130,800	1,86
Sprindys, Del	Full Time	2	09/27/02	North	Inside	2,112,696	1,78
Wadzinski, Alli	Part Time	3	07/02/03	North	Inside	3,799,318	3,02
Ramirez, Al	Part Time	4	10/24/08	Northeast	Inside	1,350,599	90
Jordan, Oliver	Full Time	8	04/12/07	Midwest	Outside	2,122,683	1,54
Hennip, Beth	Full Time	5	10/30/02	Midwest	Outside	2,119,656	2,07
Kliegl, Penny	Part Time	1	06/22/04	Midwest	Outside	4,091,220	3,05
Washington, Rob	Part Time	4	05/13/04	Northeast	Outside	3,539,262	3,86
Doy, Casimer	Part Time	6	10/29/08	Midwest	Outside	3,425,945	2,9
Yost, David	Part Time	4	11/17/04	Northeast	Outside	2,113,471	1,6

Figure 5–38

Other Ways

1. Click minor field column heading arrow, click Sort Z to A button (Data tab | Sort & Filter group), click intermediate field column heading arrow, click Sort A to Z button (Data tab | Sort & Filter group), click major field column heading arrow, click Sort A to Z button (Data tab | Sort & Filter group)

Break Point: If you wish to take a break, this is a good place to do so. Be sure to save the file again and then you can quit Excel. To resume at a later time, start Excel, open the file called Kenson College Scholarship Fundraiser Table, and continue following the steps from this location forward.

Querying a Table Using AutoFilter

When you first create a table, Excel automatically enables AutoFilter; the column heading arrows thus appear to the right of the column headings. You can hide the arrows so that they do not show by toggling the Filter button (Data tab | Sort & Filter group) or the Filter command on the Sort & Filter menu (Home tab | Editing group). Clicking an arrow reveals the AutoFilter menu for the column heading. The query technique that uses the column heading arrows is called **AutoFilter**.

AutoFilter displays all records that meet the criteria as a subset of the table by hiding records that do not pass the test. Clicking a column heading arrow causes Excel to display commands and a list of all the items in the field (column) in an AutoFilter menu, which are all preselected. If you deselect an item from the AutoFilter menu, Excel immediately hides records that contain the item. The item you deselect from the AutoFilter menu is called the **filter criterion**. If you select a filter criterion from a second column heading while the first is still active, then Excel displays a subset of the first subset. The AutoFilter menu allows you to search for items in the column by typing in a Search box that appears above the list of items. The process of filtering activity based on one or more filter criteria is called a **query**.

To Sort a Table Using an AutoFilter Menu

The following steps sort the Kenson College Scholarship Fundraiser table into its previous sort order, sorted in ascending sequence by hire date.

1 Click cell A9 (or any cell in the table) to make the table active.

2 Click the Hire Date arrow and then click Sort Oldest to Newest in the Hire Date AutoFilter menu to sort the table in ascending sequence, in this case by hire date.

To Query a Table Using AutoFilter

The following steps query the Kenson College Scholarship Fundraiser table using AutoFilter, so that the table displays only those records that pass the following test:

Status = Full time AND Type = Inside

1

- Click the Status arrow in cell B8 to display the AutoFilter menu for the selected column (Figure 5–39).

Q&A

What is displayed below the Text Filters command on the AutoFilter menu?

The list below the Text Filters command is a list of all of the values that occur in the selected column. The check mark in the top item, (Select All), indicates that all values for this field currently are displayed in the table.

Figure 5–39

• Click Part Time in the Status list to remove the check mark and cause Excel to hide all records representing part-time fundraisers, so that only records representing full-time fundraisers appear.

• Click the OK button to apply the AutoFilter criterion.

• Click the Type arrow in row 8 to display the AutoFilter menu for the selected column (Figure 5–40).

3

• Click Outside in the Type list to remove the check mark and hide all records that do not match the AutoFilter criterion, in this case those that represent part-time fundraisers who are not inside fundraisers.

4

• Click the OK button to apply the AutoFilter criterion (Figure 5–41).

Q&A Why are the row headings of some rows displayed in blue?

Excel displays row headings in blue to indicate that these rows are the result of a filtering process.

Q&A Are both filters now applied to the table?

Yes. When you select a second filter criterion, Excel adds it to the first. Hence, in the previous steps, each record must pass two tests to appear as part of the final subset of the table.

Figure 5–40

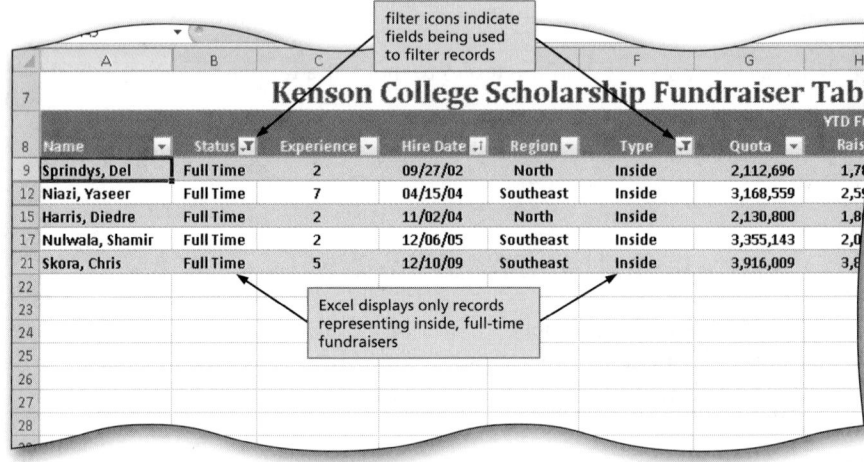

Figure 5–41

Other Ways

1. Click column heading AutoFilter arrow, type in Search box in AutoFilter menu, click OK button

More about AutoFilter

Other important points regarding AutoFilter include the following:

1. When you enable AutoFilter and records are hidden, Excel displays a filter icon in the table column heading arrows used to establish the filter. Excel also displays the row headings of the selected records in blue.

2. If the column heading arrows do not show, then you must manually enable AutoFilter by clicking the Filter command on the Sort & Filter menu (Home tab | Editing group). The Filter button also is on the Data tab.

3. To remove a filter criterion for a single field, select the Select All option from the column heading AutoFilter menu for that field.

4. When you create a formula in the total row of a table, the formula automatically recalculates the values even when you filter the list. For example, the results shown

in the total row in Figure 5–27 on page EX 320 are updated automatically if you apply a filter to the table.

5. You can filter and sort a column by color or conditional formatting using the Sort by Color and Filter by Color commands on the AutoFilter menu (Figure 5–39 on page EX 327).

To Show All Records in a Table

The following steps show all records in the table after a query hid some of the records.

1
- Display the Data tab.

2
- Click the Filter button (Data tab | Sort & Filter group) to display all of the records in the table (Figure 5–42).

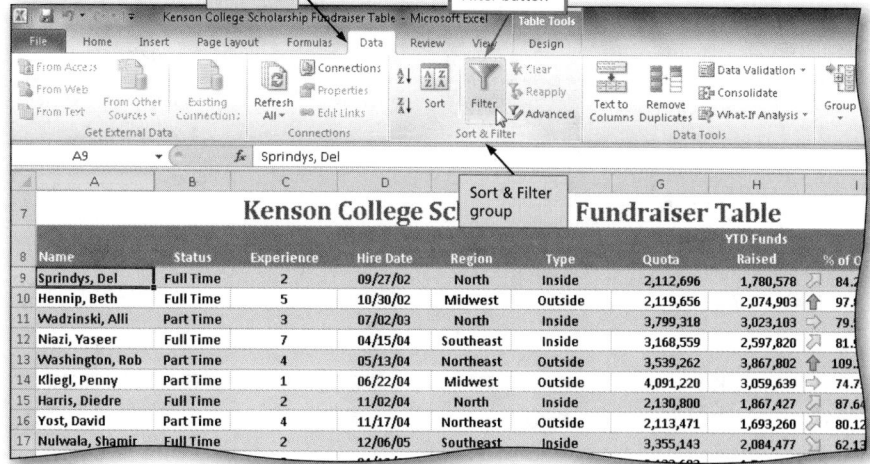

Figure 5–42

To Enter Custom Criteria Using AutoFilter

One of the commands available in all AutoFilter menus is Custom Filter. The Custom Filter command allows you to enter custom criteria, such as multiple options or ranges of numbers. The following steps enter custom criteria to show records in the table that represent fundraisers whose experience is between 3 and 5 years, inclusive; that is, their experience is greater than or equal to 3 and less than or equal to 5 (3 ≤ Experience ≤ 5).

1
- Click the Filter button (Data tab | Sort & Filter group) to display the AutoFilter arrows in the table.

- With the table active, click the Experience arrow in cell C8 to display the AutoFilter menu for the selected column.

- Point to Number Filters to display the Number Filters submenu (Figure 5–43).

Figure 5–43

2

- Click Custom Filter to display the Custom AutoFilter dialog box.

- Click the top-left box arrow (Custom AutoFilter dialog box), click 'is greater than or equal to' in the list, and then type 3 in the top-right box.

- Click the bottom-left box arrow, click 'is less than or equal to' in the list, and then type 5 in the bottom-right box (Figure 5–44).

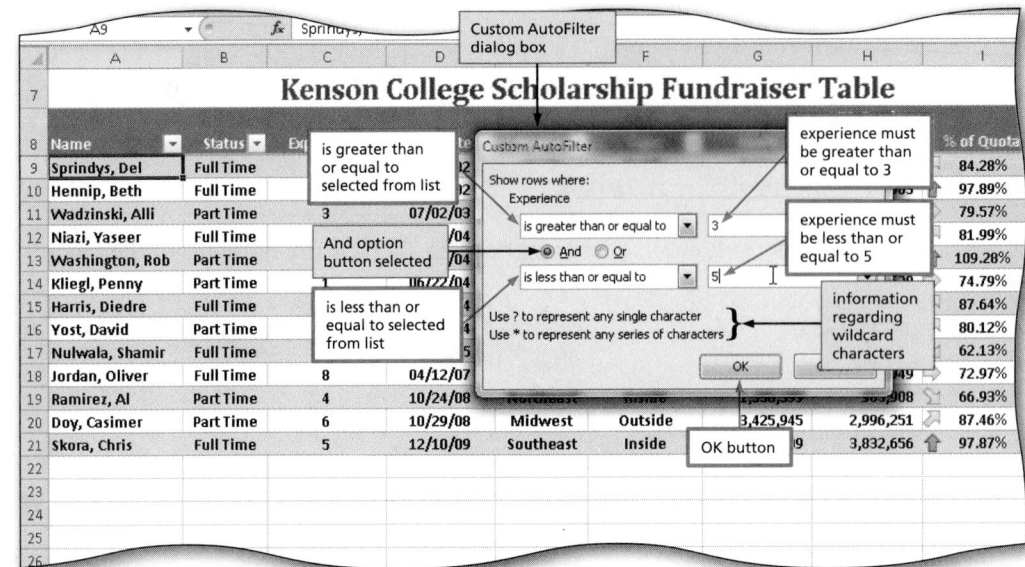

Figure 5–44

3

- Click the OK button (Custom AutoFilter dialog box) to display records in the table that match the customer AutoFilter criteria, in this case, fundraisers whose experience is between 3 and 5 inclusive (Figure 5–45).

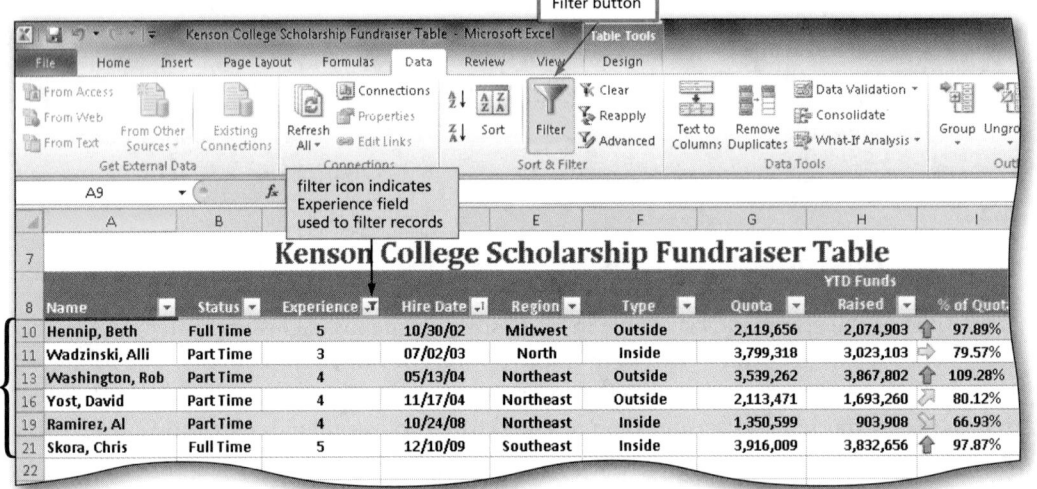

Figure 5–45

4

- After viewing the records that meet the custom criteria, click the Filter button (Data tab | Sort & Filter group) to remove the custom filter from the table.

 Experiment

- Create filters on other fields in the table, such as Type and Region. When you are finished, click the Filter button and then repeat the steps above so that the worksheet appears as it does in Figure 5–45.

Q&A

How are the And and Or option buttons used?

You can click the And option button or the Or option button to select the AND operator or the OR operator. The AND operator indicates that both parts of the criteria must be true; the OR operator indicates that only one of the two must be true. Use the AND operator when the custom criteria is continuous over a range of values, such as ($3 \leq$ Experience ≤ 5). Use the OR operator when the custom criteria is not continuous, such as Experience less than or equal to 3 OR greater than or equal to 5 ($3 \leq$ Experience ≥ 5).

Using a Criteria Range on the Worksheet

BTW

The AND and OR Operators
AND means each and every one of the comparison criteria must be true. OR means only one of the comparison criteria must be true.

You can set up a **criteria range** on the worksheet and use it to manipulate records that pass the comparison criteria. Using a criteria range on the worksheet involves two steps:

1. Create the criteria range and name it Criteria.
2. Use the Advanced button on the Data tab.

To Create a Criteria Range on the Worksheet

To set up a criteria range, first copy the column headings in the table to another area of the worksheet. If possible, copy the column headings to rows above the table. You should do this in case the table is expanded downward or to the right in the future; such an expansion can cause problems with references to contents of the table in formulas in the worksheet. Next, enter the comparison criteria in the row immediately below the field names you just copied to the criteria range. Then use the Name box in the formula bar to name the criteria range, Criteria.

The following step creates a criteria range in the range A2:J3 to find records that pass the test:

Status = Part Time AND Experience > 3 AND Grade > B

A grade greater than B alphabetically means that only fundraisers with grades of C, D, and F pass the test.

1

- Display the Home tab.

- Select the range A7:J8 and then click the Copy button (Home tab | Clipboard group).

- Select cell A1 and then press the ENTER key to paste the contents on the Office Clipboard to the destination area A1:J2.

- Select the range A2:J2 and apply the Red Accent 2 Fill color to the range so that the text is displayed in the range.

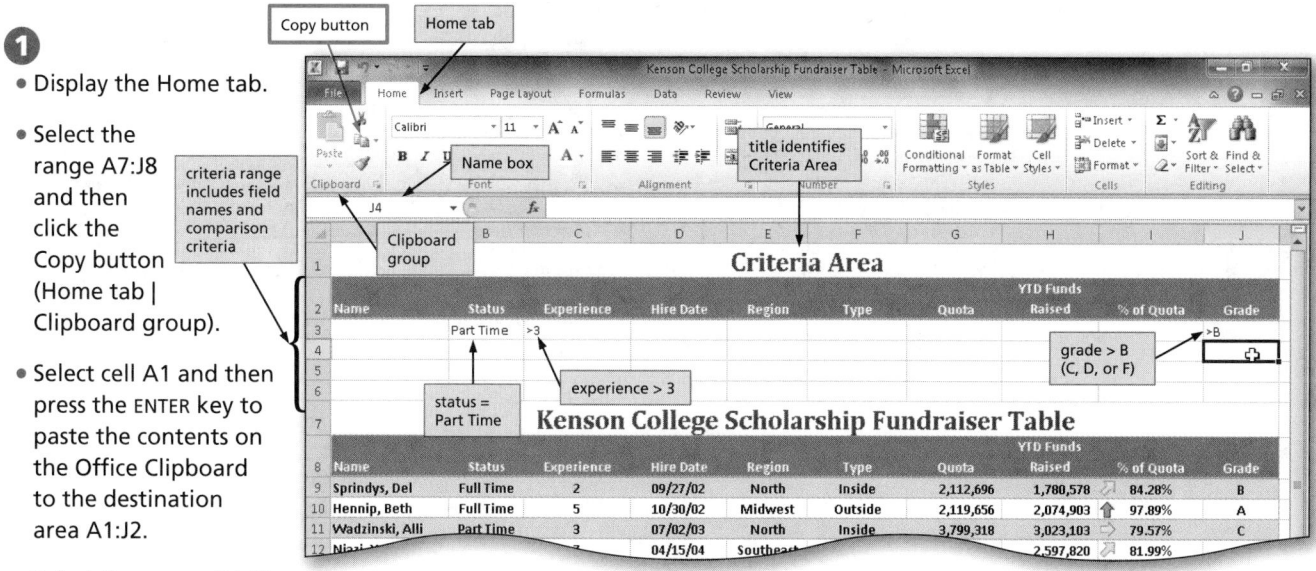

Figure 5–46

- Change the title to `Criteria Area` in cell A1, enter `Part Time` in cell B3, enter `>3` in cell C3, and then enter `>B` in cell J3.

- Select the range A2:J3, click the Name box in the formula bar, type `Criteria` as the range name, press the ENTER key, and then select cell J4 (Figure 5–46).

Q&A

Must the text in the column headings in the criteria range match those in the table exactly?

Yes. To ensure the column headings in the criteria range are spelled exactly the same as the column headings in the table, copy and paste the column headings in the table to the criteria range as shown in the previous set of steps.

To Query a Table Using the Advanced Filter Dialog Box

Using the Advanced Filter dialog box is similar to using the AutoFilter query technique, except that it does not filter records based on comparison criteria you select from a table. Instead, this technique uses the comparison criteria set up in a criteria range (A2:J3) on the worksheet.

The following steps use the Advanced Filter dialog box to query a table and show only the records that pass the test established in the criteria range in Figure 5–46 on the previous page (Status = Part Time AND Experience > 3 AND Grade > B).

1

- Click cell A9 to activate the table.

- Display the Data tab and then click the Advanced button (Data tab | Sort & Filter group) to display the Advanced Filter dialog box (Figure 5–47).

Q&A

What is displayed already in the Advanced Filter dialog box?

In the Action area, the 'Filter the list, in-place' option button is selected automatically. Excel automatically selects the table (range $A$8:$J$21) in the List range box. Excel also automatically selects the criteria range ($A$2:$J$3) in the Criteria range box, because the name Criteria was assigned to the range A2:J3 earlier.

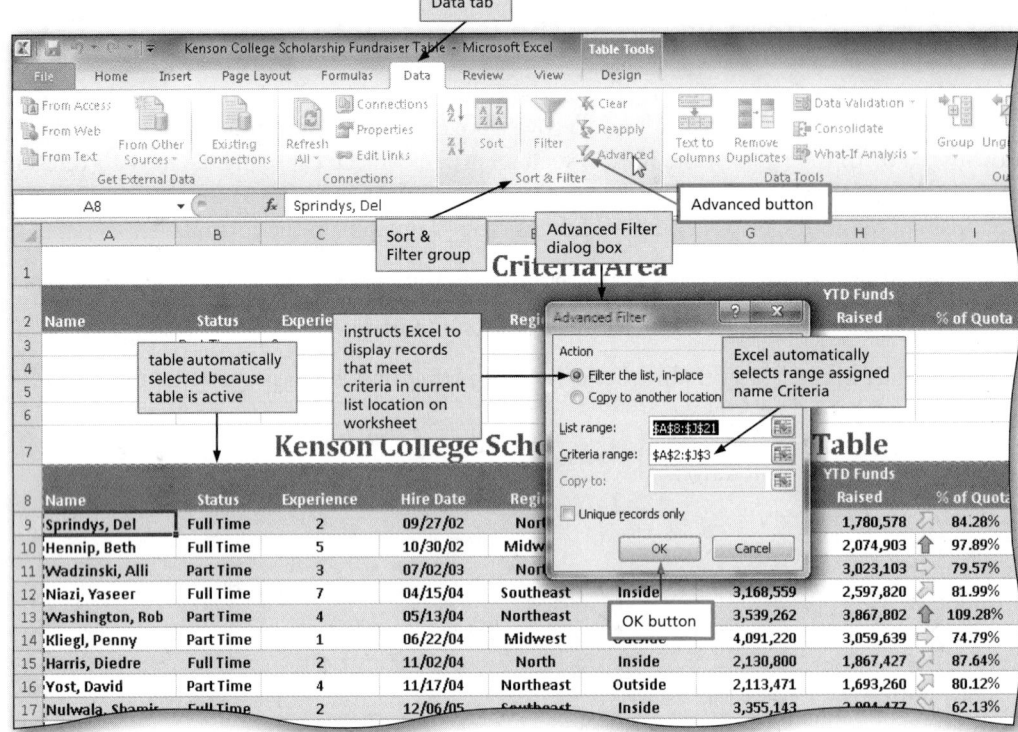

Figure 5–47

2

- Click the OK button (Advanced Filter dialog box) to hide all records that do not meet the comparison criteria (Figure 5–48).

Q&A

What is the main difference between using the AutoFilter query technique and using the Advanced Filter dialog box?

Like the AutoFilter query technique, the Advanced Filter command displays a subset of the table. The primary difference between the two is that the Advanced Filter command allows you to create more complex comparison criteria, because the criteria range can be as many rows long as necessary, allowing for many sets of comparison criteria.

Figure 5–48

To Show All Records in a Table

The following step shows all records in the table.

1 Click the Filter button (Data tab | Sort & Filter group).

Q&A Why was AutoFilter turned off?

When the Advanced Filter command is invoked, Excel disables the AutoFilter command, thus hiding the column heading arrows in the active table, as shown in Figure 5–48.

BTW

Setting Up the Extract Range
When setting up the extract range, all of the column headings do not have to be copied in the table to the proposed extract range. Instead, copy only those column headings you want, in any order. You also can type the column headings rather than copy them, although this method is not recommended because it increases the likelihood of misspellings or other typographical errors.

Extracting Records

If you select the 'Copy to another location' option button in the Action area of the Advanced Filter dialog box (Figure 5 – 49), Excel copies the records that meet the comparison criteria in the criteria range to another part of the worksheet, rather than displaying them as a subset of the table. The location to where the records are copied is called the **extract range**.

Plan
Ahead

> **Extract records from the table based on given criteria.**
> Extracting records allows you to pull data from a table so that you can analyze or manipulate the data further. For example, you may want to know which customers are delinquent on their payments. Extracting records that meet this criterion allows you to then use the records to create a mailing to such customers.
>
> Creating an extract range requires steps similar to those used to create a criteria range earlier in this chapter. Once the records that meet the comparison criteria in the criteria range are extracted (copied to the extract range), you can create a new table or manipulate the extracted records. To create an extract range, copy the field names of the table and then paste them to an area on the worksheet, preferably well below the table range. Next, name the pasted range Extract by using the Name box in the formula bar. Finally, use the Advanced Filter dialog box to extract the records.

To Create an Extract Range and Extract Records

The following steps create an extract range below the Kenson College Scholarship Fundraiser table and then extract records that meet the following criteria, as entered earlier in the Criteria range:

Status = Part Time AND Experience > 3 AND Grade > B

- Display the Home tab.

- Select range A7:J8, click the Copy button (Home tab | Clipboard group), select cell A25, and then press the ENTER key to paste the contents of the Office Clipboard to the destination area, A25:J26 in this case.

- Select the range A26:J26 and apply the Red Accent 2 Fill color to the range so that the text displays in the range with a red fill color.

- Click cell A25 and then enter **Extract Area** to title the extract area.

- Select the range A26:J26, enter the name **Extract** in the Name box in the formula bar, and then press the ENTER key to name the extract range.

2

- Click cell A9 to activate the table and then display the Data tab.

- Click the Advanced button (Data tab | Sort & Filter group) to display the Advanced Filter dialog box.

- Click 'Copy to another location' in the Action area (Advanced Filter dialog box) to cause the records that meet the criteria to be copied to a different location on the worksheet (Figure 5–49).

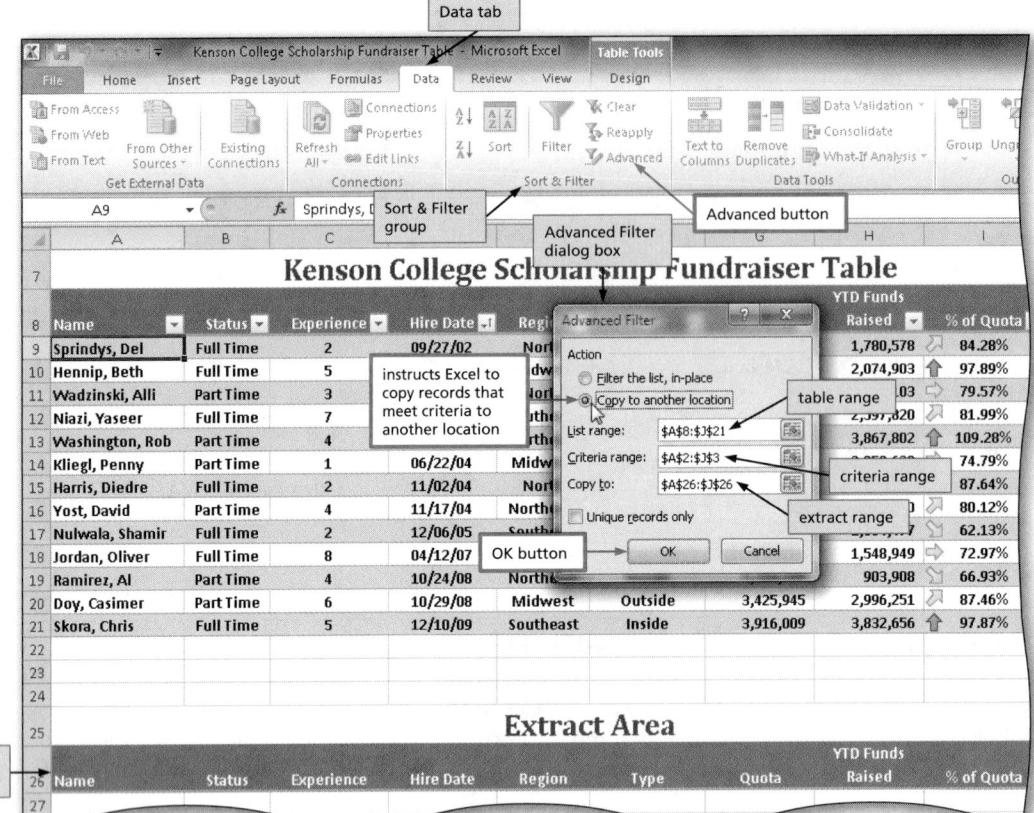

Figure 5–49

3

- Click the OK button to copy any records that meet the comparison criteria in the criteria range from the table to the extract range (Figure 5–50).

Q&A

What happens to the rows in the extract range if I perform another advanced filter operation?

Each time the Advanced Filter dialog box is used and the 'Copy to another location' option button is selected, Excel clears cells below the field names in the extract range. Hence, if you change the comparison criteria in the criteria range and then use the Advanced Filter dialog box a second time, Excel clears the previously extracted records before it copies a new set of records that pass the new test.

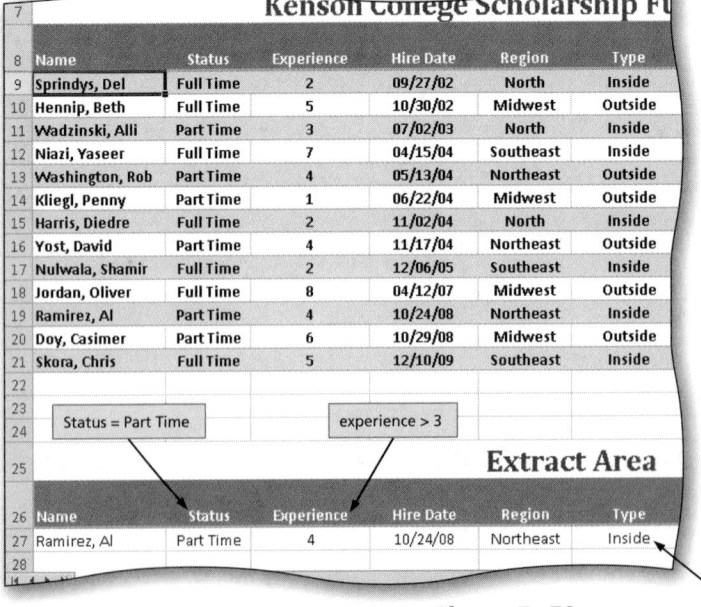

Figure 5–50

To Enable AutoFilter

As indicated earlier, when the Advanced Filter dialog box is used, Excel disables AutoFilter, thus hiding the column heading arrows in an active table. The following steps enable AutoFilter.

1 Click the Filter button (Data tab | Sort & Filter group) to display the column heading arrows in the table.

2 Display the Home tab.

More about the Criteria Range

The comparison criteria in the criteria range determine the records that will pass the test when the Advanced Filter dialog box is used. This section describes examples of different comparison criteria.

A Blank Row in the Criteria Range

If the criteria range contains a blank row, it means that no comparison criteria have been defined. Thus, all records in the table pass the test. For example, the blank row in the criteria range shown in Figure 5–51 means that all records will pass the test.

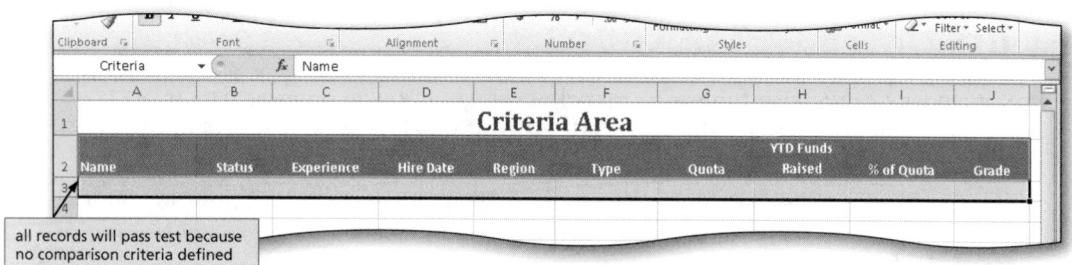

Figure 5–51

Using Multiple Comparison Criteria with the Same Field

If the criteria range contains two or more entries below the same field name, then records that pass either comparison criterion pass the test. For example, based on the criteria range shown in Figure 5–52, all records that represent fundraisers with a Region value of North or Midwest will pass the test.

If an AND operator applies to the same field name (Experience > 3 AND Experience < 5), then you must duplicate the field name (Experience) in the criteria range. That is, add the field name Experience in cell K2 to the right of Grade and then adjust the range assigned to the name Criteria by using the Define Name command (Formulas tab | Defined Name group).

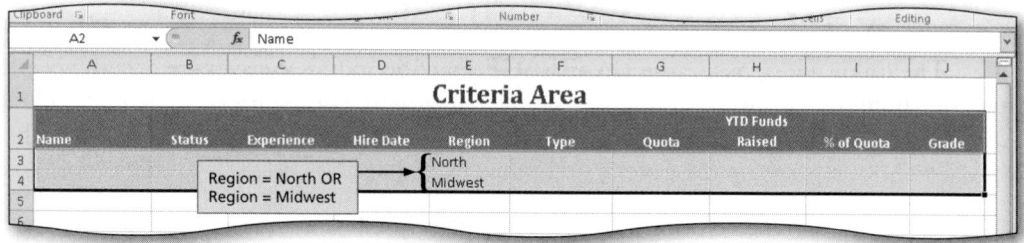

Figure 5–52

Comparison Criteria in Different Rows and Below Different Fields

When the comparison criteria below different field names are in the same row, then records pass the test only if they pass all the comparison criteria. If the comparison criteria for the field names are in different rows, then the records must pass only one of the tests. For example, in the criteria range shown in Figure 5–53, Full Time fundraisers OR Outside fundraisers pass the test.

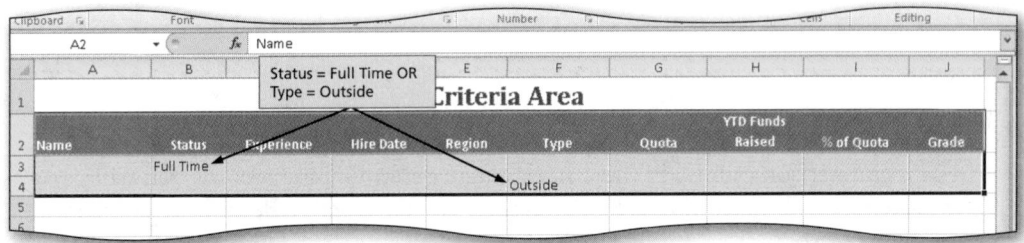

Figure 5–53

Break Point: If you wish to take a break, this is a good place to do so. Be sure to save the file again and then you can quit Excel. To resume at a later time, start Excel, open the file called Kenson College Scholarship Fundraiser Table, and continue following the steps from this location forward.

Using Database Functions

Excel includes 12 **database functions** that allow you to evaluate numeric data in a table. One of the functions is called the DAVERAGE function. As the name implies, the **DAVERAGE function** is used to find the average of numbers in a table field that pass a test. This function serves as an alternative to finding an average using the Subtotal button (Data tab | Outline group), which is described later in this chapter. The general form of the DAVERAGE function is:

=DAVERAGE(table range, "field name", criteria range)

where table range is the range of the table, field name is the name of the field in the table, and criteria range is the comparison criteria or test to pass.

Another often-used table function is the DCOUNT function. The **DCOUNT function** will count the number of numeric entries in a table field that pass a test. The general form of the DCOUNT function is:

=DCOUNT(table range, "field name", criteria range)

where table range is the range of the table, field name is the name of the field in the table, and criteria range is the comparison criteria or test to pass.

To Use the DAVERAGE and DCOUNT Database Functions

The following steps use the DAVERAGE function to find the average experience of full-time fundraisers and the average experience of part-time fundraisers in the table. The DCOUNT function is used to count the number of fundraisers' records that have a grade of A. The first step sets up the criteria areas that are required by these two functions.

1 Select cell O1 and then type **Criteria** to enter a criteria area title. Select cell L1, click the Format Painter button (Home tab | Clipboard group), and then click cell O1 to copy the format of one cell to another. Center the title, Criteria, across the range O1:Q1.

2 Select cell O2 and then type **Status** to enter a field name. Select cell P2 and, again, type **Status** to enter a field name. Select cell Q2 and then type **Grade** to enter a field name.

3 Select cell L2. Click the Format Painter button (Home tab | Clipboard group) and then drag through the range O2:Q2 to copy the format of a cell to a range.

4 Enter **Full Time** in cell O3 as the Type code for full-time fundraisers. Enter **Part Time** in cell P3 as the Type code for part-time fundraisers.

5 Enter **A** in cell Q3 as the Grade value. Select M3, click the Format Painter button (Home tab | Clipboard group), and then drag through the range O3:Q3 to copy the format of a cell to a range.

6 Enter **Avg. Full Time Experience = = >** in cell O4. Enter **Avg. Part Time Experience = =>** in cell O5. Enter **Grade A Count = = = = = = = = = >** in cell O6. If necessary, increase the width of column O so that the text does not extend into column R.

7 Select cell R4 and then type **=daverage(a8:j21, "Experience", o2:o3)** to enter a database function.

8 Select cell R5 and then type **=daverage(a8:j21, "Experience", p2:p3)** to enter a database function.

9 Click cell R6 and then type **=dcount(a8:j21, "Experience", q2:q3)** to enter a database function.

10 Apply the bold style to the range O4:R6 and then select cell O8 (Figure 5–54).

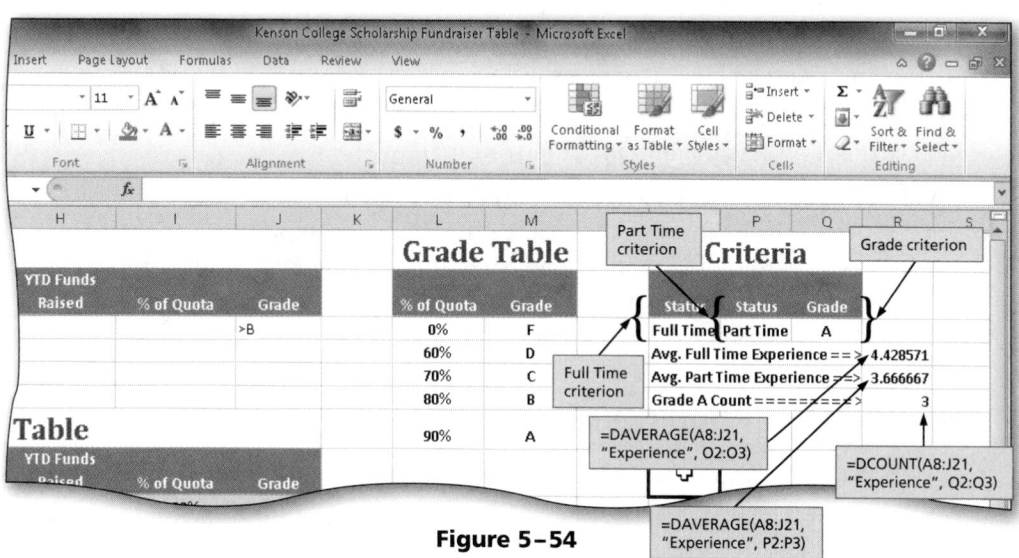

Figure 5–54

More about Using Database Functions

In Figure 5–54, the first value in the DCOUNT function, A8:J21, refers to the table range defined earlier in this chapter (range A8:J21). Instead of using the cell range, you can name the table using the Name box in the formula bar and then use the table name as the first argument in the database functions. Database is the name most often assigned to a table. If the table were named Database, then the DCOUNT function would be entered as:

=DCOUNT(Database, "Experience", Q2:Q3)

Excel uses the criteria range Q2:Q3 to select the records in the range Database where the Grade is A; it then counts the numeric Experience field in these records to determine the number of records that pass the criteria. Excel requires that you surround the field name Experience with quotation marks unless the field has been assigned a name through the Name box in the formula bar.

The third value, Q2:Q3, is the criteria range for the grade count. In the case of the DCOUNT function, you must select a numeric field to count even though the value of the numeric field itself is not used.

Other Database Functions

Other database functions that are similar to the functions described in previous chapters include the DMAX, DMIN, and DSUM functions. For a complete list of the database functions available for use with a table, click the Insert Function box in the formula bar. When Excel displays the Insert Function dialog box, select Database in the 'Or select a category' list. The 'Select a function' box displays the database functions. If you click a database function name, Excel displays a description of the function above the OK button in the Insert Function dialog box.

BTW

Quick Reference
For a table that lists how to complete the tasks covered in this book using the mouse, Ribbon, shortcut menu, and keyboard, see the Quick Reference Summary at the back of this book, or visit the Excel 2010 Quick Reference Web page (scsite.com/ex2010/qr).

Using the SUMIF, COUNTIF, MATCH, and INDEX Functions

The following list describes the reasons to use the SUMIF, COUNTIF, MATCH, and INDEX functions.

- The SUMIF and COUNTIF functions are useful when you want to sum values in a range or count values in a range only if they meet a criteria.
- Excel's MATCH function tells you the relative position of an item in a range or table that matches a specified value in a specified order.
- The INDEX function returns the value or reference of the cell at the intersection of a particular row and column in a table or range.

When used together, the MATCH and INDEX function provide the ability to look up a particular value in a table for some criteria. For example, you can combine the functions to look up the YTD funds raised based on the name of the fundraiser. The range for any of these functions need not be a table. The following sections use these four functions with the Kenson College Scholarship Fundraiser table.

To Use the SUMIF and COUNTIF Functions

Assume you want to know the sum of the YTD funds raised for the fundraisers that have a grade of A. Or, assume you want to know the number of full-time fundraisers. The first query can be answered by using the SUMIF function as follows:

=SUMIF(J9:J21, "A",H9:H21)

where the first argument J9:J21 is the range containing the cells with which to compare the criteria, the second argument "A" is the criteria, and the third argument H9:H21 is the range containing the numbers to add.

The second query can be answered by using the COUNTIF function as follows:

=COUNTIF(B9:B21,"Full Time")

where the first argument B9:B21 is the range containing the cells with which to compare the criteria.

The following steps enter identifiers and these two functions in the range O8:R9.

1 Enter `Grade A YTD Funds Raised = =>` in cell O8.

2 Enter `Full Time Count = = = = = = = =>` in cell O9.

3 Select cell R8 and then type `=SUMIF(j9:j21,"A",h9:h21)` to enter a function.

4 Select cell R9 and then type `=COUNTIF(b9:b21,"Full Time")` to enter a function.

5 Apply the bold style to the range O8:R9.

6 Apply the comma style to cell R8 and then click the Decrease Decimal button (Home tab | Number group) twice to decrease the number of decimal places to zero in the selected cell.

7 Double-click the right border of column heading R to change the width of column R to best fit (Figure 5–55).

Q&A Are there any differences when using these functions on a range?

Yes. The COUNTIF, SUMIF, and database functions will work on any range. The difference between using these functions on a range and table is that if the function references a table, then Excel automatically adjusts the first argument as a table grows or shrinks. The same cannot be said if the function's first argument is a range reference that is not defined as a table.

BTW

Using SUMIFS, COUNTIFS, and AVERAGEIFS Functions
SUMIF is designed to work with a single criterion, but the SUMIFS function lets you add two or more ranges and criteria. For example, =SUMIF(C1:C6,"<10") adds the values in C1:C6 that are less than 10. The formula =SUMIFS(C1:C6, D1:D6, "<10", D1:D6, ">5") sums the values in C1:C6 where the amounts in D1:D6 are between 5 and 10. COUNTIFS and AVERAGEIFS work the same way in relation to COUNTIF and AVERAGEIF respectively.

Figure 5–55

To Use the MATCH and INDEX Functions

Assume you want to look up the YTD funds raised for any fundraisers by name. The MATCH and INDEX functions can be placed in a formula together. The MATCH function can be used to find the row number given a name as follows:

=MATCH(R11, A9:A21, 0)

where the first argument R11 is the cell containing the name to look up, the second argument A9:A21 is the range in which the MATCH function should look for the name, and the third argument 0 informs the MATCH function to match a value exactly as given in the first argument.

BTW

Finding the Last Entry in a Range
Suppose you had a large range with many rows of data. You might want to find the last entry in the range that contains data in a particular column. For example, if a worksheet includes millions of order numbers in column A, you might like to find the last order number in column A so that you can add the next order. You can use the MATCH function to search column A by asking the function to search for the first million rows for the last entry by using the function =MATCH ("*", A1:A1000000, "−1").

The result of the MATCH function can be placed in the INDEX function to tell the INDEX function the row number of the table in which to look. The INDEX function returns a value in a table given a row and column. The INDEX function can be used to find the YTD funds raised for a given fundraiser's name as follows:

=INDEX(A9:J21, MATCH(R11, A9:A21, 0), 8)

range in which to look   MATCH function   column in which to look

where the first argument A9:J21 is the range in which the INDEX function looks. The second argument is the row of the table, in this case the result of the MATCH function, and the third argument is the column of the table in which the MATCH function should look. The following steps enter identifiers, the lookup value, and formula containing the MATCH and INDEX functions in the range O11:R12.

1 Enter `Name = = = = = = = = = = = = = =>` in cell O11.

2 Enter `YTD Funds Raised = = = = = = =>` in cell O12.

3 Select cell R11 and then type `Niazi, Yaseer` to enter a lookup value.

4 Select cell R12 and then type `=INDEX(A9:J21, MATCH(R11, A9:A21, 0), 8)` to enter a function.

5 Apply the bold style to the range O11:R12.

6 Apply the comma style to cell R12 and then click the Decrease Decimal button (Home tab | Number group) twice to decrease the number of decimal places to zero in the selected cell.

7 Double-click the right border of column heading R to change the width of column R to best fit and then select cell O14 (Figure 5–56).

BTW

The INDEX Function
The Index function can search for values in multiple ranges at the same time. To use the Index function to search noncontiguous ranges at the same time, enclose each range in parentheses in the first argument of the INDEX function.

Q&A

How else can I use the MATCH and INDEX functions?

The MATCH and INDEX functions provide greater flexibility than with the VLOOKUP and HLOOKUP functions. While the MATCH and INDEX functions can be used independently of each other, they are most productive when used together. As noted above, providing the third argument to the MATCH function with a value of zero resulted in an exact lookup of a name. This value also can be 1 or -1. A value of 1 matches the largest value that is less than or equal to the lookup value. A value of -1 finds the smallest value that is greater than or equal to the lookup value. In the first case, the values in the range must be sorted in ascending order. In the second case, the values in the range must be sorted in descending order.

Figure 5–56

To Print the Worksheet and Save the Workbook

The following steps print the worksheet on one page and save the workbook.

1 Ready the printer.

2 Click File on the Ribbon to open the Backstage view.

3 Click the Print tab in the Backstage view to display the Print gallery.

4 If necessary, click the Portrait Orientation button in the Settings area and then select Landscape Orientation to select the desired orientation.

5 If necessary, click the No Scaling button in the Settings area and then select 'Fit Sheet on One Page' to cause the workbook to print on one page.

6 If necessary, click the Printer Status button in the Print gallery to display a list of available printer options and then click the desired printer to change the currently selected printer.

7 Click the Print button in the Print gallery to print the worksheet in landscape orientation on the currently selected printer.

8 When the printer stops, retrieve the printed worksheet (Figure 5–57).

9 Save the workbook.

BTW

Printing Document Properties
To print document properties, click the File on the Ribbon to open the Backstage view, click the Print tab in the Backstage view to display the Print gallery, click the first button in the Settings area to display a list of options specifying what you can print, click Document Properties in the list to specify you want to print the document properties instead of the actual document, and then click the Print button in the Print gallery to print the document properties on the currently selected printer.

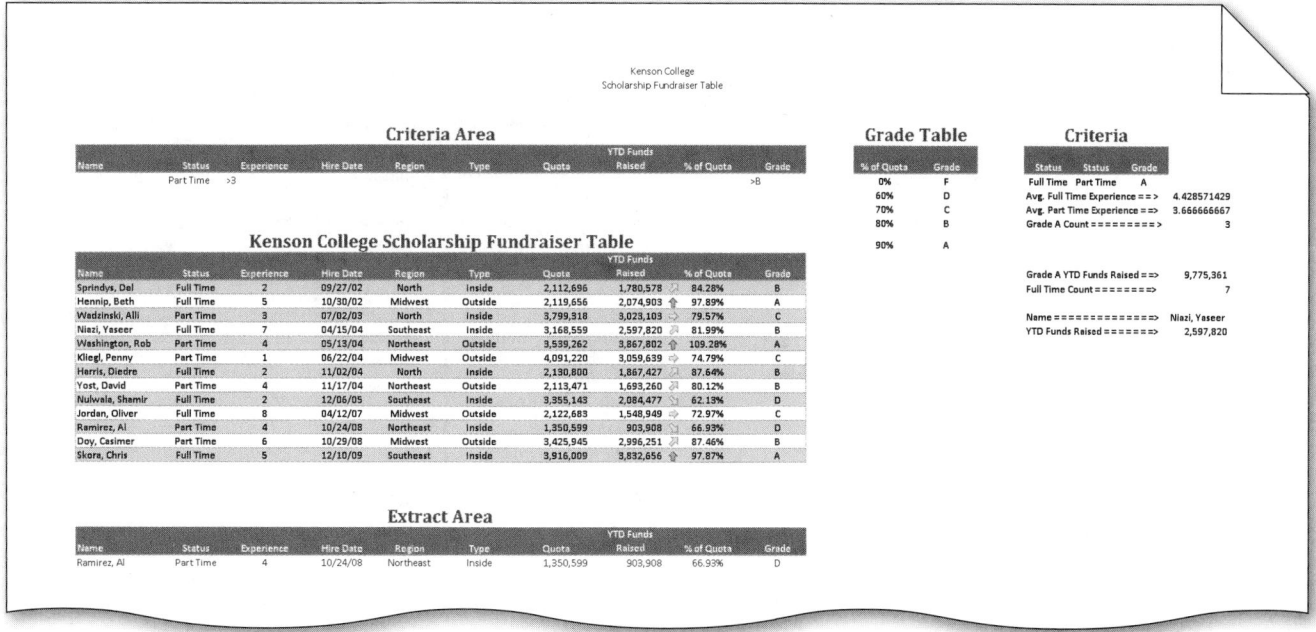

Figure 5–57

Displaying Automatic Subtotals in a Table

Displaying **automatic subtotals** is a powerful tool for summarizing data in a table. To display automatic subtotals, Excel requires that you sort the table on the field on which the subtotals will be based, convert the table to a range, and then use the Subtotal button (Data tab | Outline group).

The field on which you sort prior to clicking the Subtotal button is called the **control field**. When the control field changes, Excel displays a subtotal for the numeric fields selected in the Subtotal dialog box. For example, if you sort on the Region field and

BTW

Printing
To print individual sections of the worksheet, click the Name box in the formula bar, click the name of the section (Criteria or Extract) you want to print, and then click Print on the Office Button menu. When Excel displays the Print dialog box, click Selection in the Print what area and then click the OK button.

request subtotals for the Quota and YTD Funds Raised fields, then Excel recalculates the subtotal and grand total each time the Region field changes. The most common subtotal used with the Subtotals command is the SUM function, which causes Excel to display a sum each time the control field changes.

Plan Ahead

BTW

Certification
The Microsoft Office Specialist (MOS) program provides an opportunity for you to obtain a valuable industry credential – proof that you have the Excel 2010 skills required by employers. For more information, visit the Excel 2010 Certification Web page (scsite.com/ex2010/cert).

Display subtotals by grouping data in the table.

In general, the process for grouping data in a table involves four steps:

1. Convert the table back to a range.

2. Determine which field you will use as a control field and then sort the data using this field

3. Determine which fields will include calculations when the control field changes

4. Decide on the calculations that you want to perform on the fields that include calculations

   When possible, create a sketch of your plan for grouping data before beginning your work in Excel.

To Display Automatic Subtotals in a Table

The following steps display subtotals for the Quota field and YTD Funds Raised field by region.

1

- If necessary, display the Home tab and then scroll the worksheet so that column A is displayed and row 7 is the top row displayed.

- If necessary, select cell A9 and then enable AutoFilter. Click the Region arrow in cell E8 and then click Sort A to Z in the Region AutoFilter menu to sort the table in ascending order by the selected column, in this case Region.

- With cell A9 active, right-click anywhere in the table and then point to the Table command on the shortcut menu to display the Table submenu (Figure 5–58).

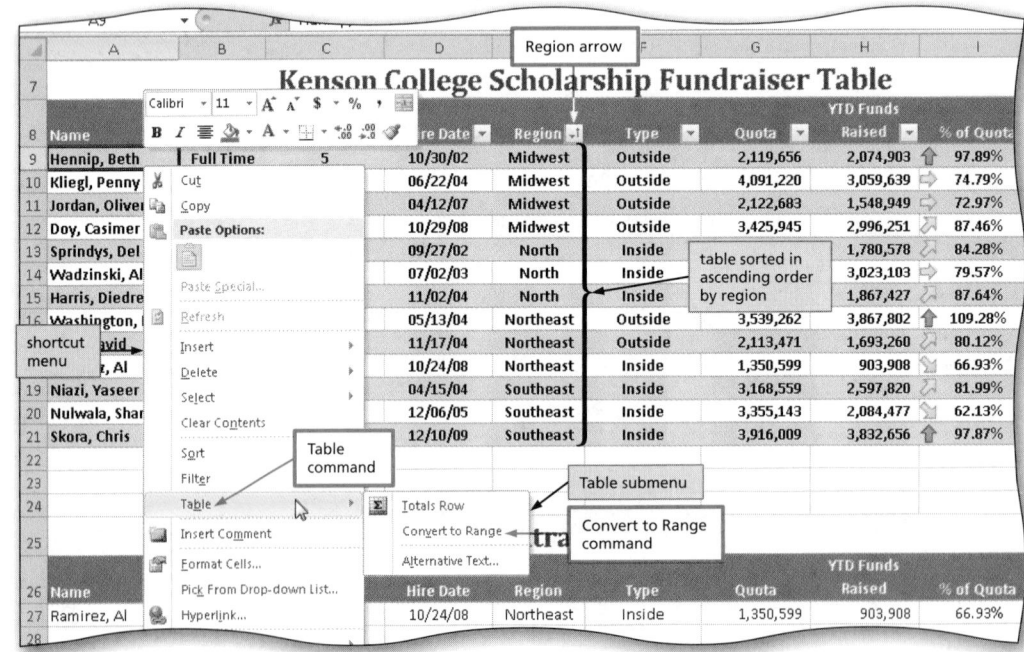

Figure 5–58

Q&A

Why does the table need to be converted to a range?

It is most important that you convert the table to a range before attempting to click the Subtotal button. If the table is not converted to a range, then the Subtotal button (Data tab | Outline group) is dimmed (not available).

Q&A

Why are the rows no longer banded?

When performing some sort operations, Excel may lose the row banding formatting. If you want to see the row banding, change the table style to a different style, and then reapply the desired table style.

2

- Click Convert to Range on the Table submenu to display a Microsoft Excel dialog box.

- Click the Yes button (Microsoft Excel dialog box) to convert a table to a range.

- Display the Data tab and then click the Subtotal button (Data tab | Outline group) to display the Subtotal dialog box.

- Click the 'At each change in' box arrow (Subtotal dialog box) and then click Region to select a column heading on which to create subtotals.

- If necessary, select Sum in the Use function list.

Figure 5–59

- In the 'Add subtotal to' list (Subtotal dialog box), click Grade to clear it and then click Quota and YTD FundsRaised to select values to subtotal (Figure 5–59).

3

- Click the OK button to add subtotals to the range (Figure 5–60).

Q&A

What changes does Excel make to the worksheet?

As shown in Figure 5–60, Excel adds four subtotal rows and one grand total row to the table, including one subtotal for each different region and one grand total row for the entire table. The names for each subtotal row are derived from the region names and appear in bold. Thus, the text, Midwest Total, in cell E13 identifies the subtotal row that contains Quota and YTD Funds Raised totals for the Midwest.

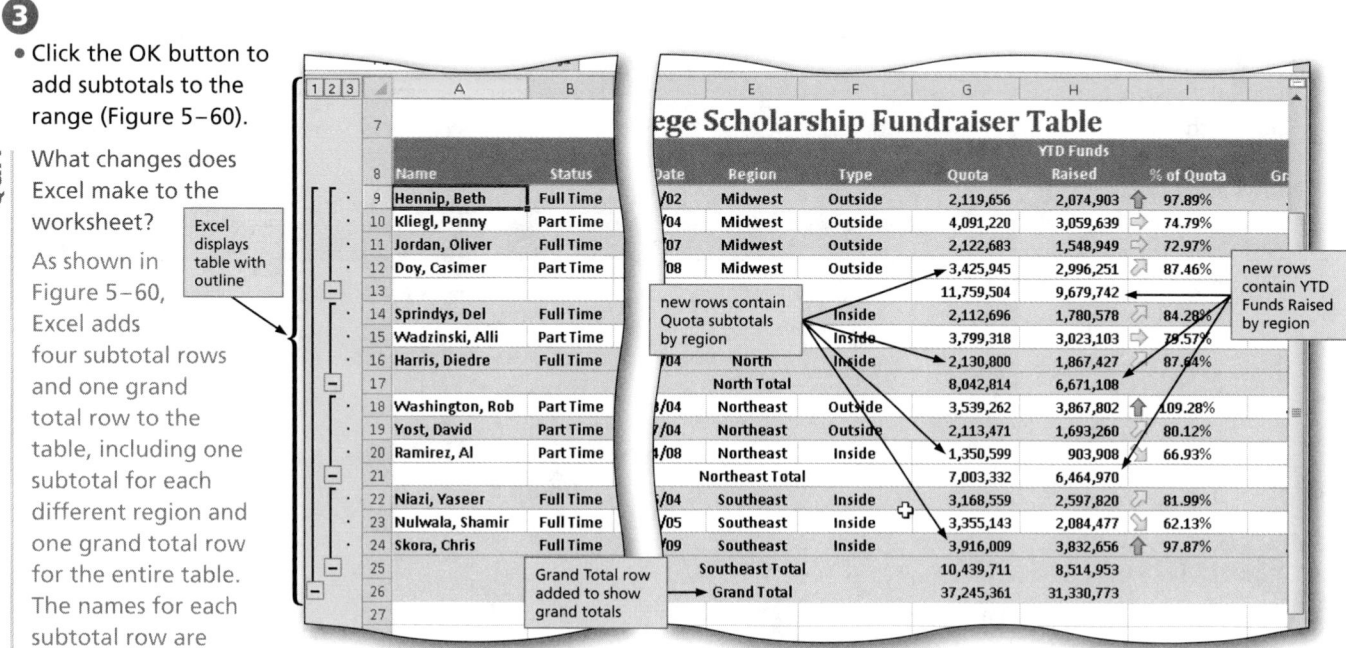

Figure 5–60

To Zoom Out on a Subtotaled Table and Use the Outline Feature

The following steps use the Zoom Out button on the status bar to reduce the magnification of the worksheet so that the table is more readable. The steps also use the outline features of Excel to hide and unhide data and totals.

1

• Click the Zoom Out button on the status bar once to reduce the zoom percent to 90% (Figure 5–61).

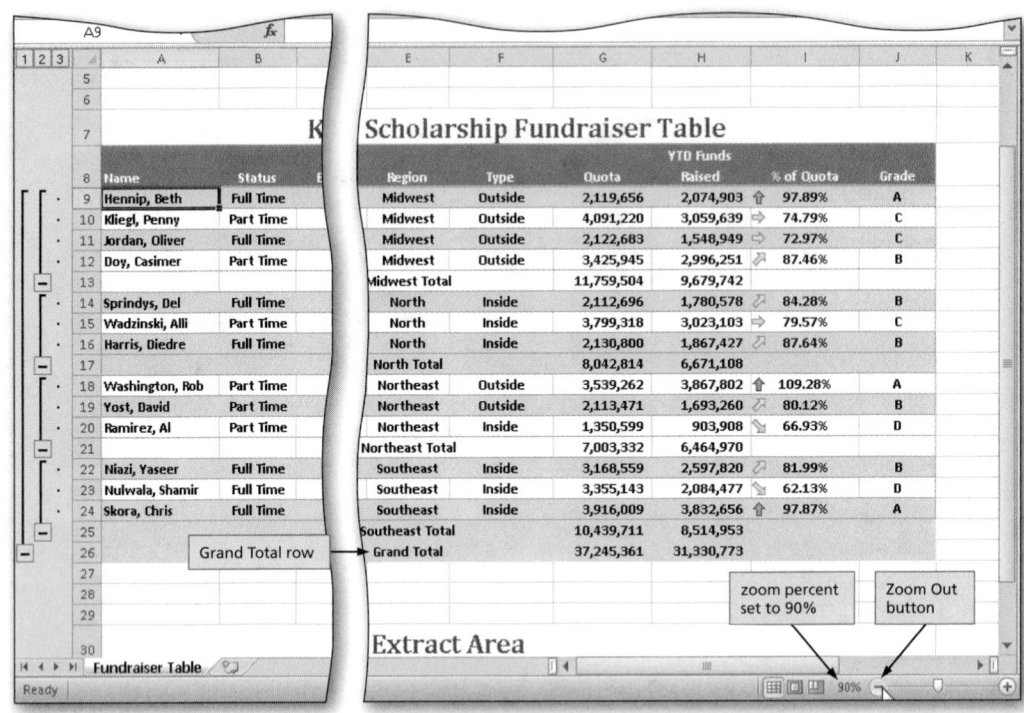

Figure 5–61

2

• Click the row level symbol 2 on the left side of the window to hide all detail rows and display only the subtotal and grand total rows (Figure 5–62).

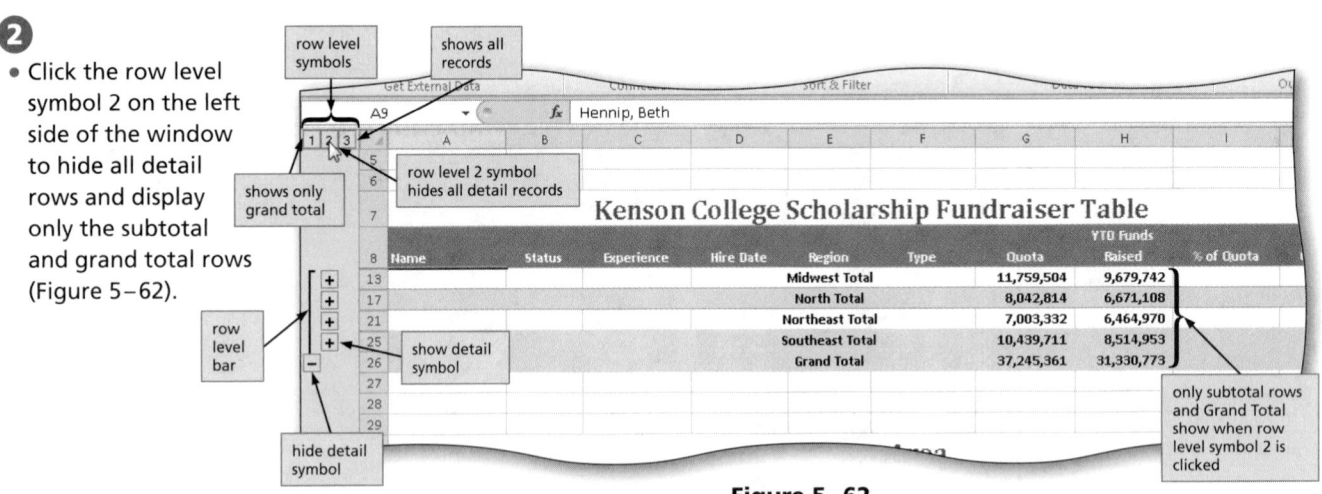

Figure 5–62

Q&A

How can I use the outlining features?

By utilizing the **outlining features** of Excel, you quickly can hide and show detail rows. You can click the **row level symbols** to expand or collapse rows in the worksheet. Row level symbol 1, immediately below the Name box, hides all rows except the Grand Total row. Row level symbol 2 hides the detail records so the subtotal rows and Grand Total row appear as shown in Figure 5–62. Row level symbol 3 shows all rows.

3

- Click each of the lower two show detail symbols (+) on the left side of the window to display detail records, in this case for the Northeast and Southeast regions, and change the show detail symbols to hide detail symbols (Figure 5–63).

4

- Click the row level symbol 3 on the left side of the window to show all detail rows.

- Click the Zoom In button on the status bar once to change the zoom percent back to 100%.

Q&A Can I group and outline without subtotals?

Yes. You do not have to use the Subtotals button to outline a worksheet. You can outline a worksheet by using the Group button (Data tab | Outline group). Usually, however, the Group button is useful only when you already have total lines in a worksheet.

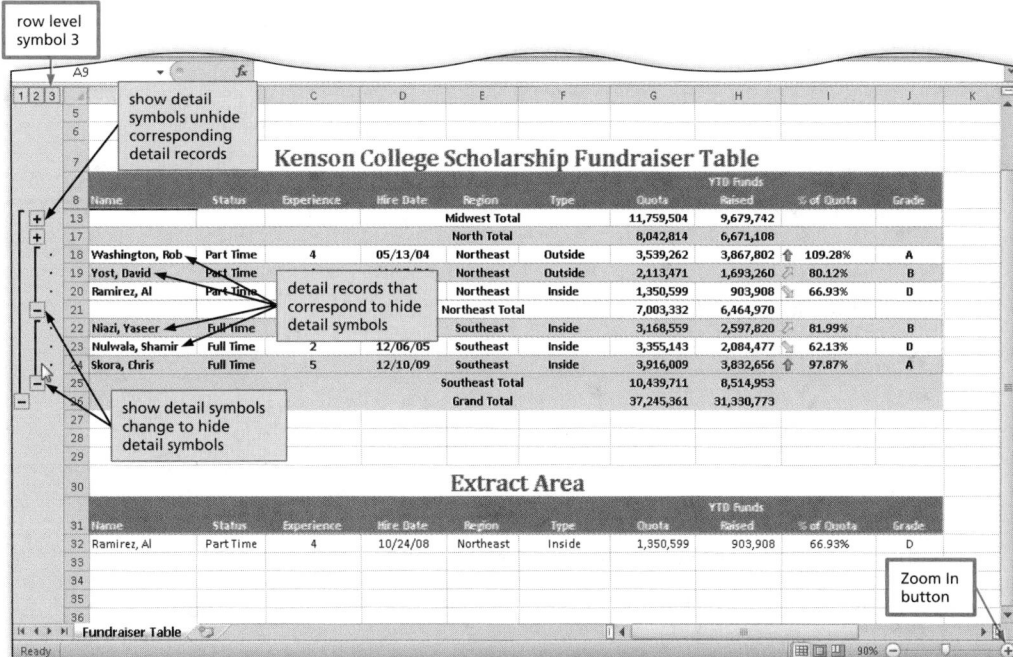

Figure 5–63

Other Ways

1. To group and outline, click Group button (Data tab | Outline group), click Group (Group dialog box)

2. To zoom, hold CTRL key while scrolling mouse wheel towards you

3. To zoom, click Zoom button (View tab | Zoom group), select magnification

To Remove Automatic Subtotals from a Table

The following steps remove the subtotals and convert the range back to a table.

1

- Click the Subtotal button (Data tab | Outline group) to display the Subtotal dialog box (Figure 5–64).

2

- Click the Remove All button (Subtotal dialog box) to remove all subtotals and close the Subtotal dialog box.

Figure 5–64

- Select the range A8:J21 and then display the Home tab.

- Click the Format as Table button (Home tab | Styles group) and then click the Custom quick style in the Format as Table gallery to apply the quick style to the selected range.

- When Excel displays the Format As Table dialog box, click the OK button to close the Format As Table dialog box.

4

- Save the workbook.

To Quit Excel

The following steps quit Excel.

1 Click the Close button on the right side of the title bar.

2 If the Microsoft Office Excel dialog box is displayed, click the Don't Save button.

Chapter Summary

In this chapter, you learned how to create, sort, and filter a table (also called a database); create subtotals; and use database functions such as SUMIF, COUNTIF, MATCH, and INDEX. The items listed below include all the new Excel skills you have learned in this chapter.

1. Format a Range as a Table (EX 305)
2. Modify a Table Quick Style (EX 307)
3. Enter Records in a Table (EX 309)
4. Add New Fields to a Table (EX 311)
5. Create a Lookup Table (EX 313)
6. Use the VLOOKUP Function to Determine Letter Grades (EX 315)
7. Add a Conditional Formatting Rule with an Icon Set (EX 316)
8. Use the Total Row Check Box (EX 319)
9. Print the Table (EX 321)
10. Sort a Table in Ascending Sequence by Name Using the Sort & Filter Button (EX 322)
11. Sort a Table in Descending Sequence by Name Using the Sort Z to A Button on the Data Tab (EX 323)
12. Sort a Table Using the Sort Command on an AutoFilter Menu (EX 324)
13. Sort a Table on Multiple Fields Using the Custom Sort Command (EX 324)
14. Query a Table Using AutoFilter (EX 327)
15. Show All Records in a Table (EX 329)
16. Enter Custom Criteria Using AutoFilter (EX 329)
17. Create a Criteria Range on the Worksheet (EX 331)
18. Query a Table Using the Advanced Filter Dialog Box (EX 332)
19. Create an Extract Range and Extract Records (EX 333)
20. Use the DAVERAGE and DCOUNT Database Functions (EX 336)
21. Use the SUMIF and COUNTIF Functions (EX 338)
22. Use the MATCH and INDEX Functions (EX 339)
23. Display Automatic Subtotals in a Table (EX 342)
24. Zoom Out on a Subtotaled Table and Use the Outline Feature (EX 344)
25. Remove Automatic Subtotals from a Table (EX 345)

If you have a SAM 2010 user profile, your instructor may have assigned an autogradable version of this assignment. If so, log into the SAM 2010 Web site at www.cengage.com/sam2010 to download the instruction and start files.

Learn It Online

Test your knowledge of chapter content and key terms.

Instructions: To complete the Learn It Online exercises, start your browser, click the Address bar, and then enter the Web address `scsite.com/ex2010/learn`. When the Excel 2010 Learn It Online page is displayed, click the link for the exercise you want to complete and then read the instructions.

Chapter Reinforcement TF, MC, and SA
A series of true/false, multiple choice, and short answer questions that test your knowledge of the chapter content.

Flash Cards
An interactive learning environment where you identify chapter key terms associated with displayed definitions.

Practice Test
A series of multiple choice questions that test your knowledge of chapter content and key terms.

Who Wants To Be a Computer Genius?
An interactive game that challenges your knowledge of chapter content in the style of a television quiz show.

Wheel of Terms
An interactive game that challenges your knowledge of chapter key terms in the style of the television show *Wheel of Fortune*.

Crossword Puzzle Challenge
A crossword puzzle that challenges your knowledge of key terms presented in the chapter.

Apply Your Knowledge

Reinforce the skills and apply the concepts you learned in this chapter.

Querying a List
Instructions: Assume that the figures that accompany each of the following six problems make up the criteria range for the College Textbook Sales Representative List shown in Figure 5–65. Fill in the comparison criteria to select records from the list to solve each of these six problems. So that you understand better what is required for this assignment, the answer is given for the first problem. You can open the workbook Apply 5-1 College Textbook Sales Representative List from the Data Files for Students and use the Filter button to verify your answers. See the inside back cover of this book for instructions for downloading the Data Files for Students or see your instructor for information on accessing the files required in this book.

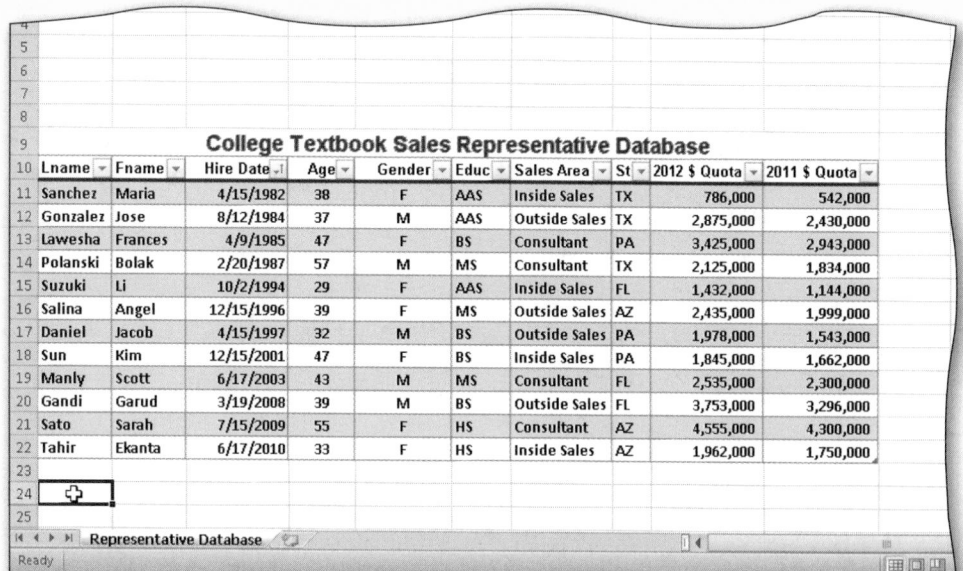

Lname	Fname	Hire Date	Age	Gender	Educ	Sales Area	St	2012 $ Quota	2011 $ Quota
Sanchez	Maria	4/15/1982	38	F	AAS	Inside Sales	TX	786,000	542,000
Gonzalez	Jose	8/12/1984	37	M	AAS	Outside Sales	TX	2,875,000	2,430,000
Lawesha	Frances	4/9/1985	47	F	BS	Consultant	PA	3,425,000	2,943,000
Polanski	Bolak	2/20/1987	57	M	MS	Consultant	TX	2,125,000	1,834,000
Suzuki	Li	10/2/1994	29	F	AAS	Inside Sales	FL	1,432,000	1,144,000
Salina	Angel	12/15/1996	39	F	MS	Outside Sales	AZ	2,435,000	1,999,000
Daniel	Jacob	4/15/1997	32	M	BS	Outside Sales	PA	1,978,000	1,543,000
Sun	Kim	12/15/2001	47	F	BS	Inside Sales	PA	1,845,000	1,662,000
Manly	Scott	6/17/2003	43	M	MS	Consultant	FL	2,535,000	2,300,000
Gandi	Garud	3/19/2008	39	M	BS	Outside Sales	FL	3,753,000	3,296,000
Sato	Sarah	7/15/2009	55	F	HS	Consultant	AZ	4,555,000	4,300,000
Tahir	Ekanta	6/17/2010	33	F	HS	Inside Sales	AZ	1,962,000	1,750,000

College Textbook Sales Representative Database

Representative Database

Ready

Figure 5–65

Continued >

Apply Your Knowledge *continued*

1. Select records that represent sales representatives who are less than 40 years old and hold an AAS degree.

Lname	Fname	Hire Date	Age	Gender	Educ	Sales Area	St	2012 $ Quota	2011 $ Quota
			<40		AAS				

2. Select records that represent sales representatives who cover the states of TX or AZ.

Lname	Fname	Hire Date	Age	Gender	Educ	Sales Area	St	2012 $ Quota	2011 $ Quota

3. Select records that represent females whose last names begin with the letter S and who are greater than 35 years old.

Lname	Fname	Hire Date	Age	Gender	Educ	Sales Area	St	2012 $ Quota	2011 $ Quota

4. Select records that represent males who are at least 40 years old and have an MS degree.

Lname	Fname	Hire Date	Age	Gender	Educ	Sales Area	St	2012 $ Quota	2011 $ Quota

5. Select records that represent females whose hire date was after 1995 or work Inside Sales.

Lname	Fname	Hire Date	Age	Gender	Educ	Sales Area	St	2012 $ Quota	2011 $ Quota

6. Select records that represent sales representatives who are less than 35 years old or greater than 50 years old.

Lname	Fname	Hire Date	Age	Gender	Educ	Sales Area	St	2012 $ Quota	2011 $ Quota

Extend Your Knowledge

Extend the skills you learned in this chapter and experiment with new skills. You may need to use Help to complete the assignment.

More Conditional Formatting

Instructions: Start Excel. Open the workbook Extend 5-1 Rommel's Auto Parts Six-Year Financial Projection from the Data Files for Students. See the inside back cover of this book for instructions for downloading the Data Files for Students or see your instructor for information on accessing the files required in this book. You have been asked to add conditional formatting to highlight the lowest and highest maintenance expenses, to add conditional formatting to show data bars for income taxes that are greater than zero, and add conditional formatting to show a three-icon set for net income (Figure 5–66). Complete the following tasks to add and manage conditional formatting rules in the worksheet.

Figure 5–66

1. Save the workbook using the file name, Extend 5-1 Rommel's Auto Parts Six-Year Financial Projection Complete.

2. Select the range B16:G16. Click the Conditional Formatting button (Home tab | Styles group) and then click New Rule. When Excel displays the New Formatting Rule dialog box, select 'Format only top or bottom ranked values' in the Select a Rule Type list. In the 'Format values that rank in the' area, type   1   in the center text box. Click the Format button in the Preview area. When Excel displays the Format Cells dialog box, click the Fill tab, click the dark red color (column 1, row 7) in the Background Color area, and then click the OK button. Click the OK button in the New Formatting Rule dialog box.

Continued >

Extend Your Knowledge *continued*

3. With the range B16:G16 selected, add a second rule to the range following the procedure from Step 2. When creating the new rule, select Bottom in the 'Format values that rank in the' list and type **1** in the center text box. Click the Format button and then select the yellow color (column 4, row 7) in the Background Color area. Click the OK button in the Format Cells dialog box and then click the OK button in the New Formatting Rule dialog box.

4. With the range B16:G16 selected, click the Conditional Formatting button (Home tab | Styles group) and then click Manage Rules to view the rules for the range. Click the Close button in the Conditional Formatting Rules Manager dialog box.

5. Select the range B23:G23. Add a new conditional formatting rule to format all cells based on their values. Select the Data Bar format style. Select Olive Green, Accent 2, Darker 25% (column 6, row 5) in the Bar Color palette. Select Gradient Fill as the Bar Appearance Fill and then close the New Formatting Rule dialog box.

6. With range B23:G23 selected, add a new conditional formatting rule. Select 'Format only cells that contain' as the rule type. Format only cells with a cell value less than or equal to zero. Do not select a format using the Format button. Make sure that the Preview area indicates that no format is set and then click the OK button to add the rule.

7. With the range B23:G23 selected, click the Conditional Formatting button (Home tab | Styles group) and then click Manage Rules to view the rules for the range. Click the Stop If True check box for the first rule in the dialog box to ensure that the second rule is not applied to negative values in the range (Figure 5–66 on the previous page). Click the OK button to close the Conditional Formatting Rules Manager dialog box.

8. With the range B24:G24 selected, add a new conditional formatting rule to format all cells based on their values. Select the Icon Sets format style. Select 3 Traffic Lights (Rimmed) in the Icon Styles and then close the New Formatting Rule dialog box.

9. Change the document properties as specified by your instructor. Change the worksheet header with your name, course number, and other information as specified by your instructor. Print the worksheet in landscape orientation using the 'Fit Sheet on One Page' option. Save the workbook.

10. Select the range B15:G19. Click the Conditional Formatting button (Home tab | Styles group), point to Color Scales on the Conditional Formatting menu, and then click Green – Yellow – Red Color Scale in the Color Scales gallery. Print the worksheet in landscape orientation using the 'Fit Sheet on One Page' option. Do not save the workbook.

11. Submit the assignment as requested by your instructor.

Make It Right

Analyze a workbook and correct all errors and/or improve the design.

Tables, Conditional Formatting, and Database Functions

Instructions: Start Excel. Open the workbook Make It Right 5-1 Kenson College Scholarship Fundraiser Table and then save the file using the file name, Make It Right 5-1 Kenson College Scholarship Fundraiser Table Complete. See the inside back cover of this book for instructions for downloading the Data Files for Students, or see your instructor for information on accessing the files required for this book. Correct the following table, conditional formatting, and database function problems so that the worksheet appears as shown in Figure 5–67.

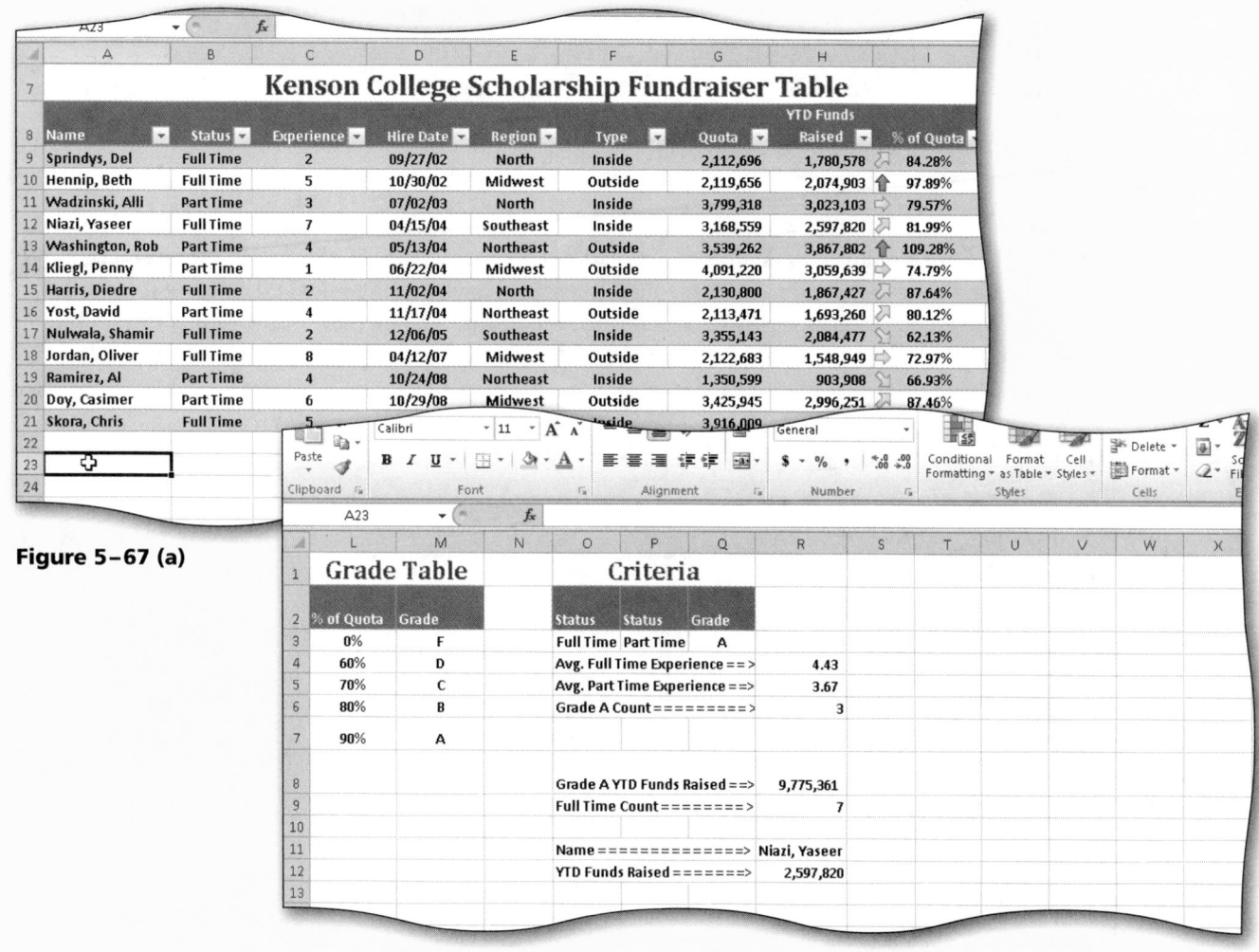

Figure 5–67 (a)

Figure 5–67 (b)

1. Use the Table Style Options group on the Design tab to make certain that the table in the worksheet includes banded rows.

2. The table does not show all of the records because the Experience field is filtered. Ensure that all records in the table are displayed.

3. The conditional formatting for the % of Quota field uses only four icons in the rule instead of five. Change the icon style of the rule to use 5 Arrows (Colored).

4. The values used by the conditional formatting rule to choose each arrow style are incorrect and should be based on the values listed in the grade table. Edit the conditional formatting rule so that the values in the grade table are reflected in the rules.

5. Correct the third argument in the DAVERAGE function used to calculate the average part-time experience.

6. Correct the second and third arguments in the SUMIF function used to calculate the grade A YTD Funds sum.

7. Change the formula for % of Quota to use [@Column_title] for YTD Funds Raised and Quota.

8. Change the document properties as specified by your instructor. Change the worksheet header with your name, course number, and other information as specified by your instructor.

9. Save the workbook and submit the revised workbook as requested by your instructor.

In the Lab

Create a workbook using the guidelines, concepts, and skills presented in this chapter. Labs are listed in order of increasing difficulty.

Lab 1: Creating, Filtering, and Sorting a Table and Determining Subtotals

Problem: You are employed by Anderson Scholastic, a company that markets books for several school types. The employees are assigned to each department and have varying sales and commissions by Dept. The three departments are K-12, Higher Ed, and Trade. The director of the Human Resources department has asked you to create an employee table (Figure 5–68), run queries against the table, generate various sorted reports, and generate subtotal information.

	Dept	Lname	Fname	Age	Gender	Sales	Commission
6			Anderson Scholastic Employees				
8	K-12	Day	Janice	32	F	▽ 1,075,800	80,685
9	Higher Ed	Angston	Lee	27	M	═ 5,500,400	412,530
10	K-12	Wyler	Deshanet	56	F	▽ 1,589,000	119,175
11	Trade	Cole	Arlene	30	F	▲ 11,500,000	977,500
12	K-12	Ruiz	Jorge	39	M	═ 5,347,500	401,063
13	Higher Ed	Grazier	Kim	25	F	▽ 3,005,000	225,375
14	K-12	Lipes	Jim	57	M	▽ 2,300,500	172,538
15	K-12	Steinberg	Josh	28	M	▽ 2,500,000	187,500
16	K-12	Beam	Saul	34	M	═ 5,500,000	412,500
17	Trade	Yenkle	Lisa	33	F	▽ 3,200,000	272,000
18	Trade	Wyler	Len	38	M	▲ 10,900,000	926,500
19	Higher Ed	Stavish	Napoleon	47	M	═ 5,890,000	441,750
20	Higher Ed	Goldberg	Joan	62	F	▽ 3,000,000	225,000
21	Total			39.07692308	13	61,308,200	4,854,115

25	Dept	Rate
26	K-12	6.50%
27	Higher Ed	7.50%
28	Trade	8.50%

Anderson Scholastic Employees

Ready

Figure 5–68

Instructions Part 1: Create the table shown in Figure 5–68 using the techniques learned in this chapter and following the instructions below.

1. Bold the entire worksheet.

2. Enter the table title in row 6 and apply the Title cell style. Enter and format the field names in row 7.

3. Use the Format as Table button (Home tab | Styles group) to create a table using data from the range A7:G7. Use Table Style Medium 7 to format the table. Format the first row below the field names and then enter the rows of data shown in rows 8 through 20 of Figure 5–68. Change the Sheet1 tab name to Anderson Scholastic Employees and delete Sheet2 and Sheet3. Enter the column data except for the commission column.

4. Copy the formatting from cell A7 to the range A25:B25. Enter the data shown in Figure 5–68 in A26:B28.

5. Enter a formula for commission that calculates the commission based upon multiplying Sales times the appropriate commission from the data in A26:B28. Use [@Column_title] referencing and the INDEX and MATCH functions for looking up data in the A26:B28 cell range.

6. With a cell in the employee table active, display the Design tab and then click the Total Row check box in the Table Style Options group. Show the record count in the Gender column, the average age in the Age column, and sums in the Sales and Commission columns, as shown in Figure 5–68.

7. Add the icon set 3 triangles using conditional formatting to the Sales column (F8:F20): Sales >=70; 70>Sales>=40; Sales<40, as shown in Figure 5–68. To add the conditional formatting, select the range F8:F20, click the Conditional Formatting button (Home tab | Styles group), and click the New Rule command. When Excel displays the New Formatting Rule dialog box, click the Icon Style box arrow, scroll up and click 3 Triangles. Click the Value box and enter the Sales limits described earlier.

8. Change the document properties as specified by your instructor. Change the worksheet header with your name, course number, and other information as specified by your instructor.

9. Print the worksheet in landscape orientation using the 'Fit Sheet on One Page' option. Save the workbook using the file name, Lab 5-1 Anderson Scholastic Employees. Submit the assignment as requested by your instructor.

Instructions Part 2:   Open the workbook Lab 5-1 Anderson Scholastic Employees created in Part 1. Do not save the workbook in this part. Step through each query exercise in Table 5–5 and print (or write down for submission to your instructor) the results for each. To complete a filter exercise, use the AutoFilter technique. If the arrows are not showing to the right of the column headings when the table is active, then click the Filter button (Data tab | Sort & Filter group). Select the appropriate arrow(s) to the right of the field names and option(s) on the corresponding menus. Use the Custom Filter option on the Number Filters list for field names that do not contain appropriate selections. For the filters that require it, use the Search box on the AutoFilter menu to query the table. Following each query, print the worksheet and then click the Filter button (Data tab | Sort & Filter group) twice to clear the query and reactivate the arrows in the field names. You should end up with the following number of records for Filters 1 through 12: 1 = 3; 2 = 4; 3 = 2; 4 = 1; 5 = 4; 6 = 5; 7 = 2; 8 = 3; 9 = 2; 10 = 2; 11 = 1; and 12 = 13. When you are finished querying the table, close the workbook without saving changes. Submit the assignment as requested by your instructor.

Table 5–5 Anderson Scholastic Employees Filter Criteria							
Filter	Dept	Lname	Fname	Age	Gender	Sales	Commission
1	Trade						
2	K-12				M		
3					F		> 250000
4	Higher Ed				M	5890000	
5				<40	F		
6				>30 and <40			
7		Wyler				>1500000	
8	Higher Ed					>3000000	
9						<=2500000	<150000
10			Begins with L				<600000
11	K-12			>50	F		
12	All	All	All	All	All	All	All

Instructions Part 3:   Open the workbook Lab 5-1 Anderson Scholastic Employees created in Part 1. Do not save the workbook in this part. Sort the table according to the following six sort problems. Print the table for each sort in landscape orientation using the 'Fit Sheet on One Page' option (or write down the last name in the first record for submission to your instructor). Begin problems 2 through 6 by sorting the Dept. field in descending sequence to sort the table back into its original order.

Continued >

In the Lab *continued*

1. Sort the table in descending sequence by Dept.
2. Sort the table by first name within last name within department. All three sort keys are to be in ascending sequence.
3. Sort the table by gender within dept. Both sort keys are to be in ascending sequence.
4. Sort the table by first name within last name within age within department. All four sort keys are to be in descending sequence.
5. Sort the table in ascending sequence by commission.
6. Sort the table by commission within sales within department. All three sort keys are to be in descending sequence.
7. Hide columns F and G by selecting them and pressing CTRL+0 (zero). Print the table. Press CTRL+A to select the entire table. In the Cells group on the Home tab, click the Format button. Point to Hide & Unhide and then click Unhide Columns. Close the Lab 5-1 Anderson Scholastic Employees workbook without saving changes. Submit the assignment as requested by your instructor.

Instructions Part 4: Open the Lab 5-1 Anderson Scholastic Employees workbook created in Part 1 and complete the following tasks. Do not save the workbook in this part.

1. Click a cell in the table to activate the table. Display the Design tab and then click the Total Row check box to remove the total row. Sort the table by sales within department. Select ascending sequence for both sort keys.
2. Select cell A8. Right-click anywhere in the table, point to the Table command on the shortcut menu, and then click the Convert to Range command on the Table submenu. When Excel displays the Microsoft Office Excel dialog box, click the Yes button to convert the table to a range. Display the Data tab and then click the Subtotal button (Data tab | Outline group). When Excel displays the Subtotal dialog box, click the 'At each change in' box arrow and then click Dept. If necessary, select Sum in the Use function list. In the 'Add subtotal to' list, click Sales and Commission to select them and then click the OK button. Print the table. Click row level symbol 1 and print the table. Click row level symbol 2 and print the table. Click the Subtotal button (Data tab | Outline group) and then click the Remove All button in the Subtotal dialog box to remove all subtotals. Close the workbook without saving changes. Submit the assignment as requested by your instructor.

In the Lab

Lab 2: Sorting, Finding, and Advanced Filtering

Problem: Cornelli's Inc. has many stores across the nation. Depending on the store classification, there are different departments available at the location; however, they do not have to have all the same departments. The company uses a table (Figure 5–69) that shows what departments are at each location as well as the store classification.

The CEO, Juniper Alvarez, has asked you to sort, query, and determine some statistics from the table. Carefully label each required printout by using the part number and step. If a step results in multiple printouts, label them a, b, c, and so on.

Instructions Part 1: Start Excel and perform the following tasks.

1. Open the workbook Lab 5-2 Cornelli's Department Availability Table from the Data Files for Students. See the inside back cover of this book for instructions for downloading the Data Files for Students or see your instructor for information on accessing the files required in this book. Do not save the workbook in this part.

Cornelli's Department Availability Table												
Location	Classification	Auto	Bath	Clothing	Electronics	Furniture	Grocery	Jewelry	Kitchen	Home	Pharmacy	Count
Orlando, FL	Superstore	Y	Y	Y	Y	Y	Y	Y	Y	Y	Y	10
Little Rock, AR	Home Store	N	Y	N	Y	Y	N	N	Y	Y	N	5
San Antonio, TX	Home Store	N	Y	N	Y	Y	N	N	Y	Y	N	5
Philadelphia, PA	Department	Y	Y	Y	Y	N	N	Y	Y	Y	N	7
Jacksonville, FL	Automotive	Y	N	N	N	N	N	N	N	N	N	1
Los Angeles, CA	Automotive	Y	N	N	N	N	N	N	N	N	N	1
New York, NY	Superstore	Y	Y	Y	Y	Y	Y	Y	Y	Y	Y	10
Austin, TX	Drugstore	N	N	N	Y	N	Y	Y	N	N	Y	4
Memphis, TN	Wholesale	N	Y	Y	Y	Y	Y	N	Y	N	Y	7
Baltimore, MD	MiniMart	Y	Y	N	N	N	Y	N	N	N	N	3
San Francisco, CA	Automotive	Y	N	N	N	N	N	N	N	N	N	1
Columbus, OH	Department	Y	Y	Y	Y	N	N	Y	Y	Y	N	7
San Jose, CA	Automotive	Y	N	N	N	N	N	N	N	N	N	1
Dallas, TX	Wholesale	Y	Y	N	Y	Y	Y	Y	Y	Y	N	8
Denver, CO	MiniMart	Y	Y	N	N	N	Y	N	N	N	N	3
Nashville, TN	Department	N	Y	Y	Y	N	N	Y	Y	Y	N	6
Boston, MA	Superstore	N	Y	Y	Y	Y	Y	Y	Y	Y	Y	9
El Paso, TX	MiniMart	Y	Y	N	N	N	Y	N	N	N	N	3
Fort Smith, AR	Drugstore	N	N	N	Y	N	Y	N	N	N	Y	4
Seattle, WA	Wholesale	Y	N	Y	Y	Y	Y	Y	Y	N	N	7

Figure 5–69

2. Complete the following tasks:

a. Sort the records in the table into ascending sequence by location. Austin, TX should appear first in the table. Seattle, WA should appear last. Print the table. Undo the sort.

b. Sort the records in the table by Location within Classification. Select descending sequence for the Location and ascending sequence for Classification. Dallas, TX (Wholesale) should be the first record. Print the table. Undo the sort.

c. Sort the table first by Auto, then Bath, then Furniture, and finally Home. Apply descending sort order for all four fields. The locations with all four departments will rise to the top of the table. Dallas, TX should be the first record. Print the table. Close the workbook without saving it. Submit the assignment as requested by your instructor.

Instructions Part 2:   Open the workbook Lab 5-2 Cornelli's Department Availability Table from the Data Files for Students. Do not save the workbook in this part. Select a cell within the table. If the column heading arrows do not appear, then click the Filter button (Data tab | Sort & Filter group). Use the column heading arrows to find the records that meet the criteria in items 1 through 4 below. Use the Clear Filter command on the column heading filter menu for each currently filtered column before starting items 2, 3, and 4. Print the table for each query. You should end up with the following number of records for items 1 through 4: item 1 should have 6; item 2 should have 3; item 3 should have 4; and item 4 should have 1. Close the workbook without saving the changes. Submit the assignment as requested by your instructor.

1. Find all records that have a pharmacy and a grocery department.

2. Find all records that represent locations with more than 7 departments that have a pharmacy and a clothing department.

3. Find all records that have a location in TX using search.

4. Find all records that have a location in CA using search and that are drugstores.

Instructions Part 3:   Open the workbook Lab 5-2 Cornelli's Department Availability Table from the Data Files for Students and then save the workbook using the file name, Lab 5-2 Cornelli's Department Availability Table Final. Perform the following tasks:

1. Add a criteria range by copying the table title and field names (range A9:M10) to the range A2:M3 (Figure 5–70 on the following page). Change cell A2 to Criteria Area and then color the title area as shown in Figure 5–70. Use the Name box in the formula bar to name the criteria range (A3:M4) Criteria.

Continued >

In the Lab *continued*

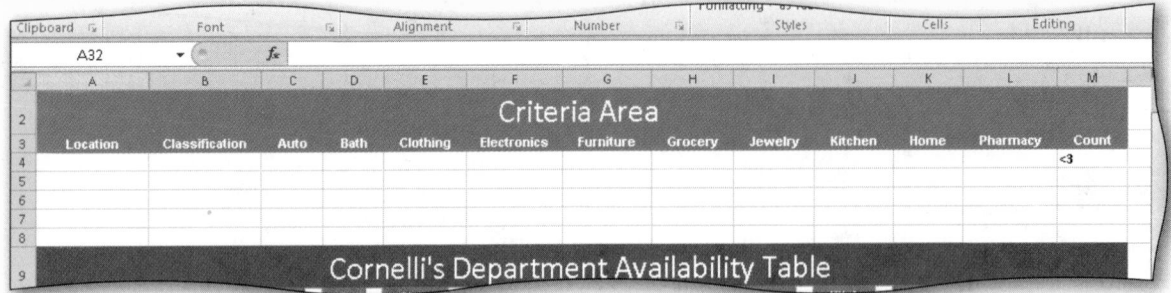

Figure 5–70

2. Add an extract range by copying the table title and field names (range A9:M10) to the range A34:M35 (Figure 5–71). Change cell A34 to Extract Area and then color the title area as shown in Figure 5–71. Use the Name box in the formula bar to name the extract range (range A35:M35) Extract.

Figure 5–71

3. With the table active, use the Advanced button (Data tab | Sort & Filter group) to extract records that pass the tests listed below in a through d. Print the worksheet in landscape orientation using the 'Fit Sheet on One Page' option for each extract.

   a. Extract the records that represent locations that have all of the departments. You should extract two records.

   b. Extract the records that represent superstores that have a pharmacy but not an auto department. You should extract one record.

   c. Extract the records that represent locations that have an auto department and have less than 7 departments total. The field Count in column M uses the COUNTIF function to count the number of Ys in a record. A count of 4 means the record represents a location with four departments. You should extract seven records.

   d. Extract the records that represent locations with less than three departments. You should extract 4 records.

4. Change the document properties as specified by your instructor. Change the worksheet header with your name, course number, and other information as specified by your instructor. Save the workbook using the current file name. Close the workbook. Submit the assignment as requested by your instructor.

Instructions Part 4:   Open the workbook Lab 5-2 Cornelli's Department Availability Table Final created in Part 3. If you did not complete Part 3, then open Lab 5-2 Cornelli's Department Availability Table from the Data Files for Students. Perform the following tasks:

1. Scroll to the right to display cell J1 in the upper-left corner of the window. Enter the criteria in the range O2:Q4 as shown in Figure 5–72. Enter the row titles in cells O7:O12 as shown in Figure 5–72.

Figure 5–72

2. Use the database function DAVERAGE and the appropriate criteria in the range O3:O4 and P3:P4 to determine the average number of departments of the Wholesale and Department stores in the range. Use the table function DCOUNT and the appropriate criteria in the range O3:O4 to determine the record count of those locations that have a Home department. The DCOUNT function requires that you choose a numeric field in the table to count, such as Count.

3. Use the SUMIF function to determine the Grocery N Sum Count in cell R11. That is, sum the Count field for all records containing an N in the Grocery column. Use the COUNTIF function to determine the Electronics Y Count in cell R12.

4. Print the worksheet in landscape orientation using the 'Fit Sheet on One Page' option. Save the workbook using the file name, Lab 5-2 Cornelli's Department Availability Table Final. Submit the assignment as requested by your instructor.

In the Lab

Lab 3: Creating a Table with a Lookup Function

Problem: You are a member of the Mega SaveMart, a grocery store chain in the Midwest. The produce manager wants you to create a table to help him manage the shelf life of his produce (Figure 5–73 on the following page). You decide it is a great opportunity to show your Excel skills. In addition to including the number of days of shelf life left for the product, the manager also would like a grade assigned to each based on the days left. Produce with a grade lower than C is ready to be rotated off the shelf.

Continued >

In the Lab *continued*

	A	B	C	D	E	F	G	H	I	J	K	L
6					*Mega SaveMart*					**Grade Table**		
7	Product ID	Produce	Type	Stock Date	Sell By Date	Shelf Life	Days Left	Grade		**Days left**	**Grade**	
8	369718	Potatoes	Vegetable	2/8/2012	2/26/2012	18	17	A		0	F	
9	471829	Apples	Fruit	2/5/2012	2/24/2012	19	15	A		3	D	
10	558129	Carrots	Vegetable	2/5/2012	2/19/2012	14	10	B		7	C	
11	716281	Grapes	Fruit	2/3/2012	2/13/2012	10	4	D		9	B	
12	895241	Oranges	Fruit	2/9/2012	2/19/2012	10	10	B		14	A	
13	638192	Lettuce	Vegetable	2/6/2012	2/19/2012	13	10	B				
14	721890	Tomatoes	Vegetable	2/2/2012	2/10/2012	8	1	F				
15	987456	Peaches	Fruit	2/4/2012	2/14/2012	10	5	D				
16	526891	Green Beans	Vegetable	2/4/2012	2/14/2012	10	5	D				
17	821928	Bananas	Fruit	2/9/2012	2/16/2012	7	7	C				
18	835570	Strawberries	Fruit	2/5/2012	2/10/2012	5	1	F				
19	557812	Mushrooms	Vegetable	2/7/2012	2/17/2012	10	8	C				
20	491526	Onions	Vegetable	2/3/2012	2/10/2012	7	1	F				
21	Total					19	17	13				
22												
23	Grade A Count		2		Current Date ==>	2/9/2012						
24	Grade B Count		3									
25	Grade C Count		2									
26	Vegetable Count		7									
27	Fruit Count		6									
28												

Figure 5–73

Instructions Part 1: Perform the following tasks to create the table shown in the range A7:20 in Figure 5–73.

1. Create a new workbook and then bold the entire Sheet1 worksheet. Create the table shown in Figure 5–73 using the techniques learned in this chapter. Assign appropriate formats to row 8, the row immediately below the field names. Rename the Sheet1 tab and delete Sheet2 and Sheet3.

2. Enter the data shown in the range A8:E20 and in E23:F23.

3. Calculate the Shelf Life in F8 by subtracting the Stock Date from the Sell By Date. Copy the function in cell F8 to range F9:F20.

4. Calculate the Days Left in G8 by subtracting the Current Date (F23) from the Sell By Date. Copy the function in cell G8 to range G9:G20.

5. Enter the Grade table in the range J6:K12. In cell H8, enter the function `=vlookup(G8, $J$8:$K$12, 2)` to determine the letter grade that corresponds to the Days Left in cell G8. Copy the function in cell H8 to the range H9:H20.

6. Select the Total Row option on the Design tab to determine the maximum shelf life, the maximum days left, and the record count in the Grade column in row 21.

7. Enter the total row headings in the range A23:A27. Use the COUNTIF functions to determine the totals in the range C23:C27.

8. Change the document properties as specified by your instructor. Change the worksheet header so that it contains your name, course number, and other information as specified by your instructor.

9. Save the workbook using the file name, Lab 5-3 Mega SaveMart Table. Print the worksheet in landscape orientation using the 'Fit Sheet on One Page' option. At the bottom of the printout, explain why the dollar signs ($) are necessary in the VLOOKUP function in Step 3. Submit the assignment as requested by your instructor.

Instructions Part 2: Open the workbook Lab 5-3 Mega SaveMart Table. Do not save the workbook in this part. Sort the table as follows. Print the table after each sort. After completing the third sort, close the workbook without saving the changes.

1. Sort the table in ascending sequence by the Stock Date.

2. Sort the table by Shelf Life within Type. Use ascending sequence for both fields.

3. Sort the table by Days Left within Type. Use descending sequence for both fields.

Instructions Part 3: Open the workbook Lab 5-3 Mega SaveMart Table. Use the concepts and techniques presented in this chapter to search the table using the AutoFilter search box. After completing each search, print the worksheet. After the last search, close the workbook without saving the changes.

1. Search for produce that was stocked on the 5th (three records).

2. Days left of 1 (three records).

3. Vegetables with shelf life of 10 (two records).

4. Fruit with grade of F (one record).

5. Submit the assignment as requested by your instructor.

Cases and Places

Apply your creative thinking and problem solving skills to design and implement a solution.

1: Inventory Level Priority

Academic

Create an Intro to Biology grade table from the data in Table 5–6. Also include a Final % field and a Grade field. Both are calculated columns. Final % is calculated with each quiz being worth 10% and each test being worth 35%. Create a Grade table in the range J6:K20 using the data shown in Table 5–7. Use the VLOOKUP function to determine the grade to assign to each record. Add the total row to the table. Show the averages of each quiz and test. In cell range A19:B19 show Mark Kennedy's grade using the MATCH and INDEX functions. Print the worksheet in landscape orientation using the 'Fit Sheet on One Page' option. Save the workbook.

Table 5–6 Intro to Biology Grades					
Name	Quiz 1	Quiz 2	Quiz 3	Test 1	Test 2
Cyrus, Hannah	85	88	78	90	87
Settle, Lee	58	49	43	50	49
Barnett, Betty	93	80	82	81	72
Kennedy, Mark	82	48	59	68	64
Francisco, Steven	60	58	64	57	56
Frye, Janice	73	84	88	87	89
Savage, Hector	79	75	72	72	70
Kidinger, Robert	97	100	85	85	100

Table 5–7 Grade Table			
Final %	Grade	Final %	Grade
0%	F	70%	B-
50%	D-	74%	B
54%	D	77%	B+
57%	D+	80%	A-
60%	C-	85%	A
64%	C	90%	A+
67%	C+		

Continued >

Cases and Places *continued*

2: Using Database Functions to Analyze Expenses

Personal

You want to create an expense log to show your expenses for the past six months (Jan–Jun). You have compiled your data together (as shown in Table 5–8). Create a household expense log using the data in Table 5–8. Name your table Database. Use the database functions you learned in this chapter to determine the minimum and maximum payments for food, cell phone, and travel. Indicate how much was spent for clothing in March. Finally, display a count of the total number of months in the expense log.

Table 5–8 Household Expense Log

Month	Rent	Food	Utilities	Cell Phone	Car Payments	Insurance	Clothing	Internet	Travel
Jan	680.00	601.89	225.00	75.00	275.41	149.50	350.89	81.99	190.00
Feb	680.00	582.89	210.00	80.00	275.41	149.50	101.55	81.99	120.00
Mar	680.00	451.88	175.00	75.00	275.41	149.50	55.75	81.99	150.00
April	680.00	515.45	165.00	95.00	275.41	149.50	75.69	95.85	450.00
May	680.00	632.85	120.00	75.00	275.41	149.50	259.86	81.99	120.00
Jun	680.00	650.11	135.00	75.00	275.41	149.50	180.00	87.00	180.00

3: Creating a Table of Companies

Professional

You have gathered information about companies at which you may want to work in your next job. Create a company info table using the data in Table 5–9. The information includes company name, state, city, miles from your current residence, and a rating for each company between 1 and 4, with 4 being the most preferred. Save the file as Case 5-3 Company Info Table. Complete the following sorts, print each sorted version of the table, and then undo the sorts in preparation for the next sort: (a) alphabetically (A to Z) by state, and (b) descending (smallest to largest) by miles from home. Filter the list for records with a rating greater than 2. Print the table and then show all of the records. Use the search filter to show which records are from Texas. Print the table and then show all of the records. Group the records by state, using the Average function in the Use function list in the Subtotal dialog box. Print the worksheet.

Table 5–9 Company Info

Company Name	State	City	Distance	Rating
GameTech	Florida	Orlando	960	4
CompIT Inc.	Arkansas	Little Rock	730	1
InfoSolutions	Pennsylvania	Philadelphia	480	3
Cyber Intelligence	New York	New York	560	3
Games InDesign	Texas	El Paso	590	4
Web Kings, Inc.	Maryland	Baltimore	430	2
BeachBiz IT Design	California	San Francisco	2430	4
HighTech Masters	Texas	Dallas	1050	2
Mountain Lightning IT	Colorado	Denver	1240	3
ALTSolutions	Washington	Seattle	2350	1

6 | Working with Multiple Worksheets and Workbooks

Objectives

You will have mastered the material in this chapter when you can:

- Use the ROUND function
- Use custom format codes
- Define, apply, and remove a style
- Add a worksheet to a workbook
- Create formulas that use 3-D cell references
- Add data to multiple worksheets at the same time

- Add a header or footer and change margins
- Insert and move a page break
- Save a workbook as a PDF or XPS file
- Create a workspace file
- Consolidate data by linking workbooks

6 | Working with Multiple Worksheets and Workbooks

Introduction

An organization may keep data from various departments or regions in different worksheets. If you enter each department's data on a worksheet in a workbook, you can click the sheet tabs at the bottom of the Excel window to move from worksheet to worksheet, or department to department. Note, however, that many business applications require data from several worksheets to be summarized on one worksheet. To facilitate this summarization, on a separate worksheet, you can enter formulas that reference cells on the other worksheets. This type of referencing allows you to summarize workbook data. The process of summarizing data included on multiple worksheets on one worksheet is called **consolidation**.

Another important concept presented in this chapter is the use of custom format codes. **Custom format codes** allow you to specify how a cell entry assigned a format will appear. You can customize a format code in a cell entry to specify how positive numbers, negative numbers, zeros, and text are displayed in a cell.

Project — Consolidated Expenditures Worksheet

The project in the chapter follows proper design guidelines and uses Excel to create the worksheets shown in Figure 6–1. The City of Calhoun's government organization includes three departments, Public Works, Police and Fire, and Parks and Recreation, as shown in Figure 6–1. Each department incurs five types of expenditures that are common to each department in a budget year, including payroll, pension, equipment, contractors, and administrative. The worksheet shown in Figure 6–1 shows the expenditures that were budgeted for the past budget year, 2011; those for the current budget year, 2012; and the proposed expenditures for the next budget year, 2013. The city manager would like to know the consolidated expenditures for the three departments. She also would like to see the individual department expenditures on separate worksheets. Additionally, she would like to see the consolidated and individual percent increases or decreases for each expenditure.

(a) Public Works Worksheet

(b) Police and Fire Worksheet

(c) Parks and Recreation Worksheet

(d) Consolidated Worksheet

Figure 6–1

The requirements document for the City of Calhoun Consolidated Expenditures workbook is shown in Figure 6–2. It includes the needs, source of data, summary of calculations, special requirements, and other facts about its development.

REQUEST FOR NEW WORKBOOK

Date Submitted:	July 3, 2012
Submitted By:	Dana Gatz
Worksheet Title:	City of Calhoun Consolidated Expenditures
Needs:	The needs are as follows: 1. A workbook containing three worksheets for the three major city departments and one worksheet to consolidate the city expenditure data. 2. Each worksheet should be identical in structure and allow for display of the previous, current, and next year's expenditures. 3. The worksheets should print with a common header and footer and meet the city's standards for worksheet printouts.
Source of Data:	The data will be collected and organized by the city manager, Dana Gatz.
Calculations:	Include the following formulas in each worksheet: 1. 2012 Expenditure = 2011 Expenditure + 2011 Expenditure × 2012 % Change in Expenditure 2. 2013 Expenditure = 2012 Expenditure + 2012 Expenditure × 2013 % Change in Expenditure 3. Average % Change in Expenditure = (2012 % Change in Expenditure + Expected 2013 % Change in Expenditure) / 2 4. Use the SUM function to determine totals. **Note:** Use dummy data in the consolidated worksheet to verify the formulas. Round the Average % Change to the nearest one-tenth of a percent.
Special Requirements:	Investigate a way the city can consolidate data from multiple workbooks into another workbook.

Approvals

Approval Status:	X	Approved
		Rejected
Approved By:	Brandon Stevens	
Date:	July 10, 2012	
Assigned To:	J. Quasney, Spreadsheet Specialist	

Figure 6–2

Overview

As you read this chapter, you will learn how to create the worksheets shown in Figure 6–1 by performing these general tasks:

- Add a worksheet to the workbook.
- Create and apply a custom format.
- Reference data on other worksheets.
- Add data to multiple worksheets at the same time.
- Print the worksheets with proper headers, footers, margins, and page breaks.
- Create a workspace and consolidate data by linking workbooks.

General Project Decisions

Plan Ahead

While creating an Excel worksheet, you need to make several decisions that will determine the appearance and characteristics of the finished worksheet. As you create the worksheets to meet the requirements shown in Figure 6–2, you should follow these general guidelines:

1. **Design the consolidated worksheet and plan the formatting.** When a workbook contains multiple worksheets with the same layout, spreadsheet specialists often create **sample data**—that is, sample data used in place of actual data to verify the formulas in the worksheet—and formatting on one worksheet and then copy that worksheet to additional worksheets. This practice avoids the need to format multiple worksheets separately.

2. **Identify additional worksheets needed in the workbook.** After the initial worksheet is created using sample data and the required formulas and then saved, it should be copied to the other worksheets. Actual data for the three other worksheets will replace the copied sample data. The data from the additional worksheets then can be consolidated onto the initial worksheet.

3. **Plan the layout and location of the required custom format codes.** Some organizations require that certain types of data be formatted in a specific manner. If the specific type of format is not included in Excel's list of formats, such as Currency or Accounting, then you must create a custom format code that meets the requirement and then apply the custom format code to the necessary cells.

4. **Examine the options, including headers, margins, and page breaks, that you have for printing worksheets.** When working with multiple worksheets, using properly formatted page headers and footers is important. Excel allows you to print page numbers and the sheet name of each sheet. In addition, margins and page breaks also can be adjusted to provide professional-looking printed worksheets.

5. **Identify workbooks to be consolidated into a workspace and then linked to create a consolidated workbook of the initial workbooks.** The special requirement for the project listed in the requirements document asks that methods to combine workbooks be investigated (Figure 6–2). Excel allows you to work with separate workbooks in a workspace and then link the workbooks to provide a consolidated view of the data in the workbooks.

When necessary, more specific details concerning the above guidelines are presented at appropriate points in the chapter. The chapter also will identify the actions you perform and decisions made regarding these guidelines during the creation of the worksheets shown in Figure 6–1 on page EX 363.

In addition, using a sketch of the worksheet can help you visualize its design. The sketch of the consolidated worksheet consists of titles, column and row headings, the location of data values, and a general idea of the desired formatting (Figure 6–3 on the following page).

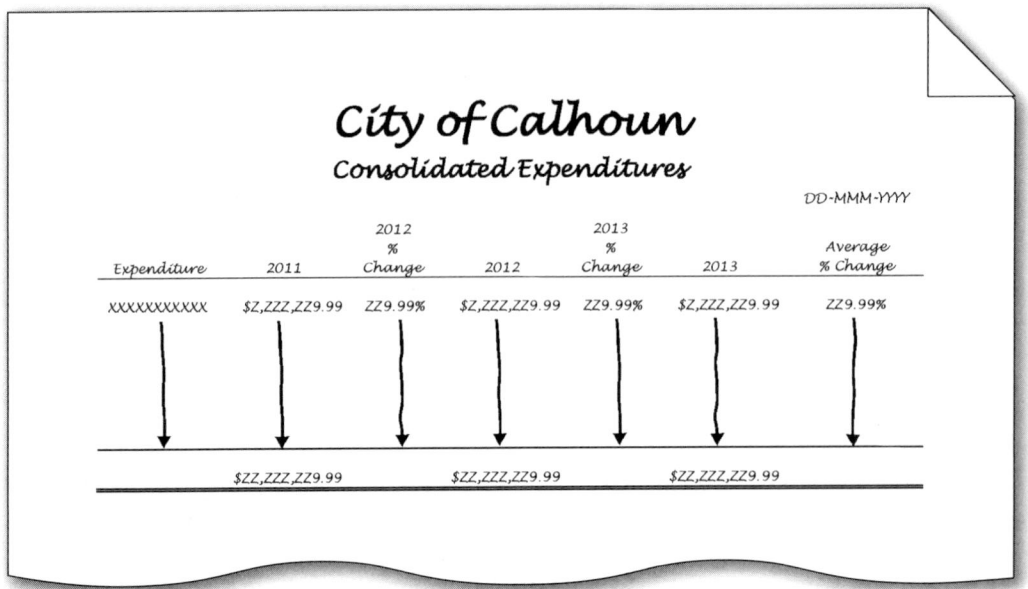

Figure 6–3

With a solid understanding of the requirements document, an understanding of the necessary decisions, and a sketch of the consolidated worksheet, the next step is to use Excel to create the consolidated worksheet.

To Start Excel

If you are using a computer to step through the project in this chapter and you want your screens to match the figures in this book, you should change your screen's resolution to 1024 × 768. The following steps start Excel.

1 Start Excel.

2 If the Excel window is not maximized, click the Maximize button next to the Close button on its title bar to maximize the window.

Creating the Consolidated Worksheet

The first step in building the workbook is to create and save a workbook that includes the consolidated worksheet that contains the titles, column and row headings, formulas, and formats used on each of the departments' sheets.

Plan Ahead

Design the consolidated worksheet and plan the formatting.
The consolidated worksheet will be used to create a number of other worksheets. Thus, it is important to consider the layout, cell formatting, and contents of the worksheet.

- **Set row heights and column widths.** Row heights and column widths should be set to sizes large enough to accommodate future needs.

- **Use placeholders for data when possible.** Placeholders often are used when creating an initial consolidated worksheet to guide users of the worksheet regarding what type of data to enter in cells. For example, the word Department could be used in a subtitle to indicate to a user of the worksheet to place the department name in the subtitle.

(continued)

(continued)

Plan Ahead

- **Use sample data to verify formulas.** When an initial consolidated worksheet is created, sample data should be used in place of actual data to verify the formulas in the worksheet. Selecting simple numbers such as 1, 2, and 3 allows you to check quickly to see if the formulas are generating the proper results. In consolidated worksheets with more complex formulas, you may want to use numbers that test the extreme boundaries of valid data.

- **Format cells in the worksheet.** Formatting that can be modified for each worksheet should be applied to titles and subtitles to provide cues to users of the worksheets. For example, by using a fill color for the title and subtitle, the fill color for additional worksheets can be changed after the consolidated worksheet is copied to subsequent worksheets. All numeric cell entry placeholders—sample data—should be formatted properly for unit numbers and currency amounts.

The first step in creating the workbook is to create the consolidated expenditures worksheet, shown in Figure 6–4. The consolidated worksheet then will be copied to three other worksheets. Each worksheet will contain expenditures for one of three departments.

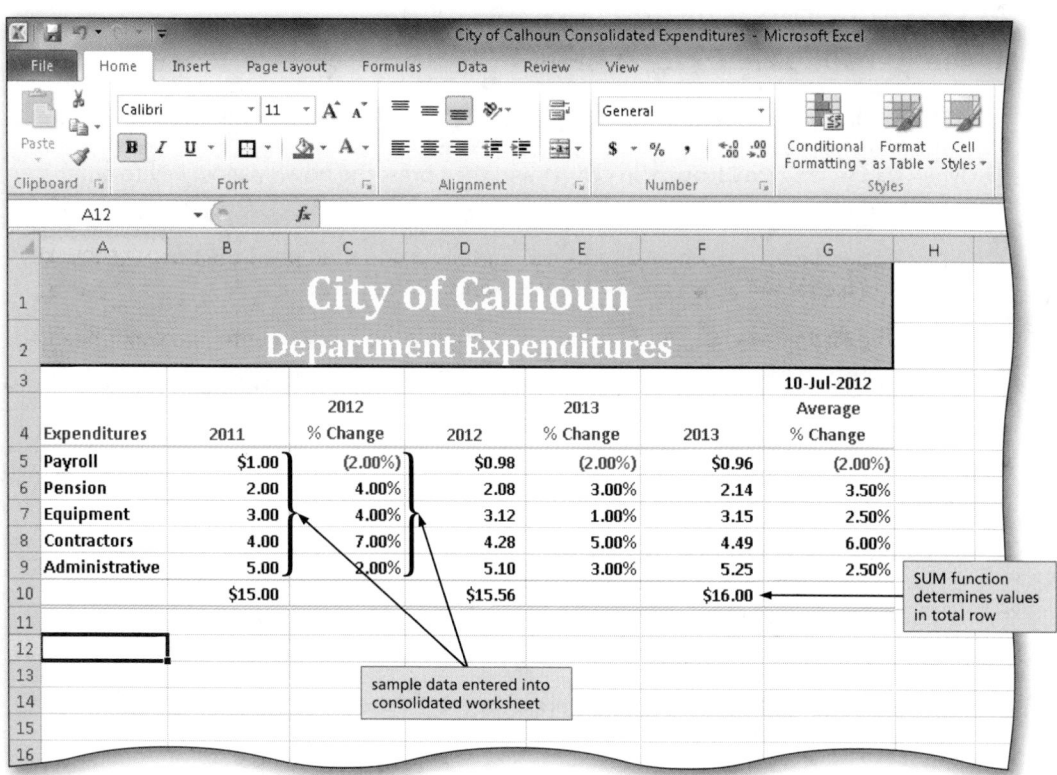

Figure 6–4

To Change the Font Style to Bold and Adjust the Row Heights and Column Widths of the Consolidated Worksheet

The first step in creating the consolidated worksheet with sample data is to change the font style to bold and adjust the height of row 4 to 30.75 points and column widths of column A to 13.57 characters; B, D, and F to 12.86 characters; C and E to 12.14 characters; and G to 14.14 characters. The row heights and column widths need to be changed to accommodate the data in the worksheet. The following steps change the font style to bold and adjust the row heights and column widths of the consolidated worksheet.

BTW

Selecting a Range of Cells
You can select any range of cells with entries surrounded by blank cells by clicking a cell in the range and pressing CTRL+SHIFT+ASTERISK (*).

BTW

Q&As
For a complete list of the Q&As found in many of the step-by-step sequences in this book, visit the Excel 2010 Q&A Web page (scsite.com/ex2010/qa).

1   Click the Select All button immediately above row heading 1 and to the left of column heading A and then click the Bold button (Home tab | Font group) to bold the entire worksheet. Select cell A1 to deselect the worksheet.

2   Drag the bottom boundary of row heading 4 down until the row height is 30.75 (41 pixels) to change the row height.

3   Drag the right boundary of column heading A to the right until the column width is 13.57 (100 pixels) to change the column width.

4   Select columns B, D, and F, and then drag the right boundary of column heading F right until the column width is 12.86 (95 pixels) to change several column widths at the same time.

5   Select columns C and E, and then drag the right boundary of column heading E right until the column width is 12.14 (90 pixels) to change several column widths at the same time.

6   Select column G, and then drag the right boundary of the column heading right until the column width is 14.14 (104 pixels) to change the column width. Select cell A1 to deselect column G.

BTW

Displaying Future Dates
You can display a future date, such as tomorrow's date, in a cell by adding a number to the NOW or TODAY function. For example, =NOW()+1 displays tomorrow's date in a cell and =NOW()+14 displays a date two weeks in the future. The function =NOW()–1 displays yesterday's date.

To Enter the Title, Subtitle, and Row Titles in the Consolidated Worksheet

The following steps enter the titles in cells A1 and A2 and the row titles in column A.

1   Type `City of Calhoun` in cell A1 and then press the DOWN ARROW key to enter a worksheet title.

2   Type `Department Expenditures` in cell A2 and then press the DOWN ARROW key twice to make cell A4 active and to enter a worksheet subtitle.

3   Type `Expenditures` and then press the DOWN ARROW key to enter a column heading.

4   With cell A5 active, enter the remaining row titles in column A, as shown in Figure 6–5.

To Enter Column Titles and the System Date in the Consolidated Worksheet

The next step is to enter the column titles in row 4 and the system date in cell G3. The following steps enter column titles and the system date in the consolidated worksheet.

BTW

Manipulating Dates
You can use the DATE function to change a year, month, and day to a serial number that automatically is formatted to mm/dd/yyyy. For example, if cell A1 equals the year 2012, cell A2 equals the month 2, cell A3 equals day 10, and cell A4 is assigned the function =DATE (A1, A2, A3), then 2/10/2012 appears in cell A4. The DATE function is most useful in formulas where year, month, and day are formulas, not constants.

1   Select cell B4. Type `2011` and then press the RIGHT ARROW key to enter a column heading.

2   Type `2012` and then press ALT+ENTER to begin a new line of text in the selected cell. Type `% Change` and then press the RIGHT ARROW key to enter a column heading.

3   With cell D4 active, enter the remaining column titles in row 4 as shown in Figure 6–5.

4   Select cell G3. Type `=now()` and then press the ENTER key to enter the system date.

5   Right-click cell G3 to display a shortcut menu and then click Format Cells on the shortcut menu.

6   When Excel displays the Format Cells dialog box, click Date in the Category list and then click 3/14/01 13:30 in the Type list to format a date with a 2-digit year and a time.

7   Click the OK button (Format Cells dialog box) to close the dialog box.

8   Select cell A12 to deselect cell G3.

Q&A

Why was the date not formatted as it appears in Figure 6–4?

The format assigned to the system date in cell G3 is temporary. For now, it ensures that the system date will appear properly, rather than as a series of number signs (#). The system date will be assigned a permanent format later in this chapter. The date might be displayed as a series of number signs if the date, as initially formatted by Excel, does not fit in the width of the cell.

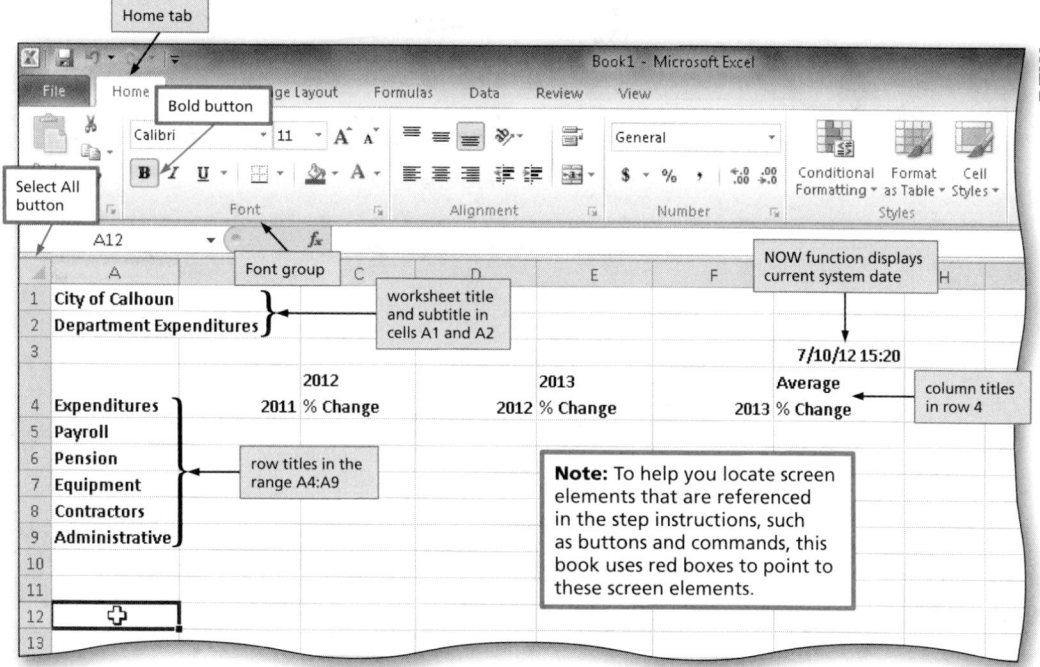

Figure 6–5

BTW

Sample Data
As you develop more sophisticated workbooks, it will become increasingly important that you create good test data to ensure your workbooks are free of errors. The more you test a workbook, the more confident you will be in the results generated. Always take the time to select test data that tests the limits of the formulas.

To Enter Sample Data in the Consolidated Worksheet Using the Fill Handle

While creating the consolidated worksheet in this chapter, sample data is used for the 2011 expenditure values in the range B5:B9 and the 2012 % Change values in the range C5:C9. The sample data is entered by using the fill handle to create a series of numbers in columns B and C. The series in column B begins with 1 and increments by 1; the series in column C begins with 2 and increments by 2. Recall that you must enter the first two numbers in a series so that Excel can determine the increment amount. If the cell to the right of the start value is empty and you want to increment by 1, however, you can create a series by entering only one number. The following steps enter sample data in the consolidated worksheet using the fill handle.

- Select cell B5.

- Type 1 and then press the ENTER key to enter the first value in the series.

- Select the range B5:C5.

- Drag the fill handle through cells B9 and C9 to begin a fill series operation. Do not release the mouse button (Figure 6–6).

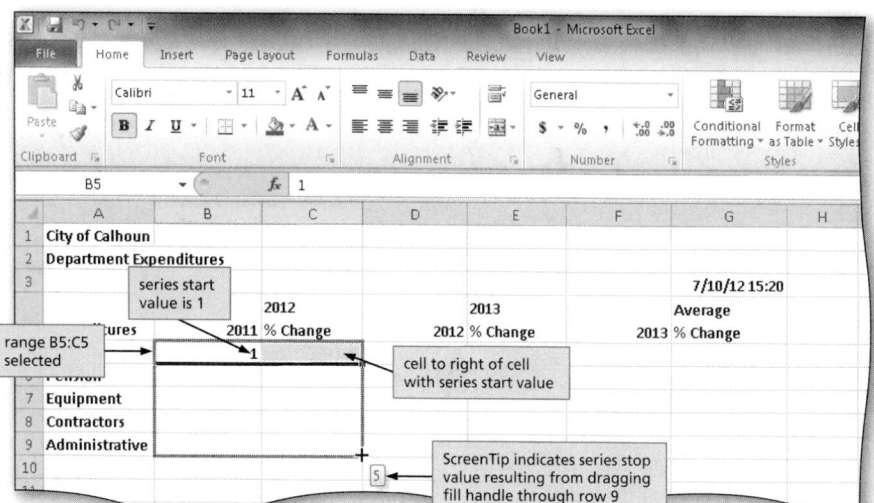

Figure 6–6

2

- Release the mouse button to create the series, 1 through 5 in this case, in increments of 1 in the first column of the selected range (Figure 6–7).

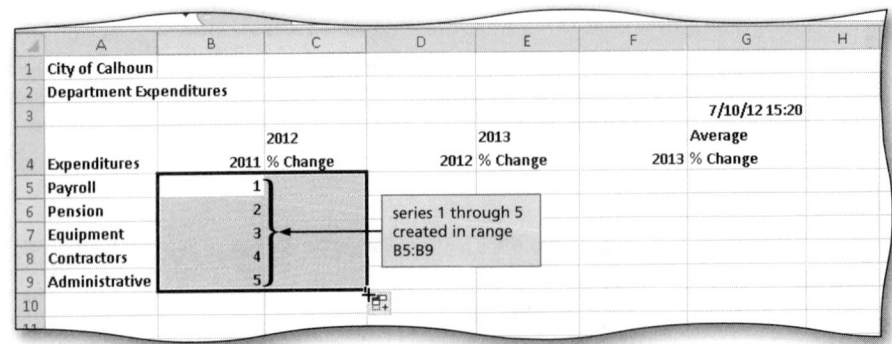

Figure 6–7

3

- Enter **2** in cell C5.

- Enter **4** in cell C6.

- Select the range C5:C6. Drag the fill handle through cell C9 to create a series in increments of 2 in the selected range, C5:C9 in this case (Figure 6–8).

Q&A

What other types of series can I create?

Excel allows you to create many types of series, including a **date series** (Jan, Feb, Mar, etc.), an **auto fill series** (1, 1, 1, etc.), and a **linear series** (1, 2, 3, etc. or 2, 4, 6, etc.), which was created in the previous steps. A fourth type of series is a growth series. A **growth series** multiplies values by a constant factor. You can create a growth series by entering an initial value in the first cell, selecting the range to fill, clicking the Fill button (Home tab | Editing group), clicking Series, clicking Growth in the type area, and then entering a constant factor in the Step value box.

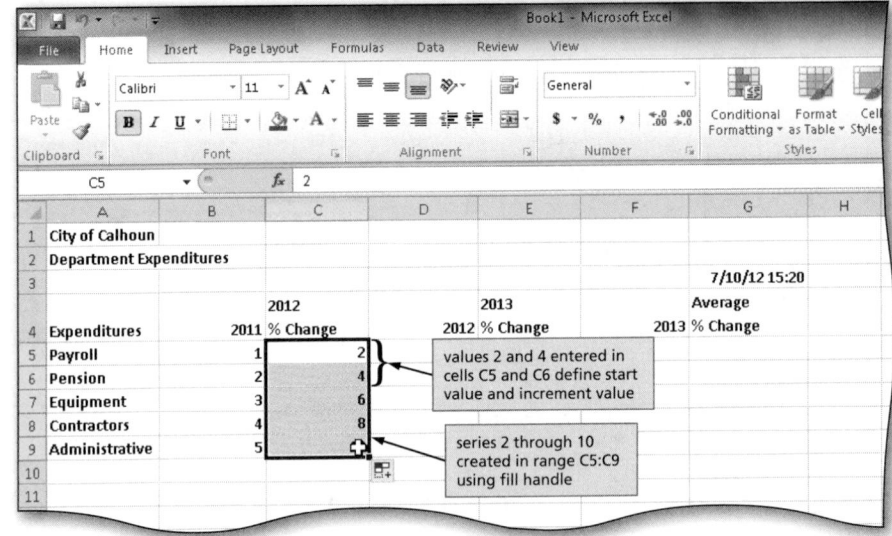

Figure 6–8

4

- Repeat Step 3 to create a series in increments of 2 starting at 2 in the range E5:E9.

Other Ways

1. Enter first number; click fill handle; while holding down CTRL key, drag through range
2. Enter start value, select range, click Fill button (Home tab | Editing group), click Series, enter parameters (Series dialog box), click OK button

The ROUND Function and Entering Formulas in the Template

BTW

Accuracy
The result of an arithmetic operation, such as multiplication or division, is accurate to the factor with the least number of decimal places.

The next step is to enter the three formulas for the first expenditure, Payroll, in cells D5, F5, and G5. When you multiply or divide decimal numbers that result in an answer with more decimal places than the format allows, you run the risk of the column totals being off by a penny or so because, for example, resulting values of calculations could include fractions of a penny beyond the two decimal places that currency formats usually display. For example, as shown in the worksheet sketch in Figure 6–3 on page EX 366, columns B, D, and F use the Currency and Comma style formats with two decimal places. And yet, the formulas used to calculate values for these columns result in several additional decimal places that Excel maintains for computation purposes. For this reason, it is recommended that you use the **ROUND function** on formulas that potentially can result in more decimal places than the applied format displays in a given cell. The general form of the ROUND function is

=ROUND (number, number of digits)

where the number argument can be a number, a cell reference that contains a number, or a formula that results in a number; and the number of digits argument can be any positive or negative number used to determine the number of places to which the number will be rounded.

The following is true about the ROUND function:

1. If the number of digits argument is greater than 0 (zero), then the number is rounded to the specified number of digits to the right of the decimal point.
2. If the number of digits argument is equal to 0 (zero), then the number is rounded to the nearest integer.
3. If the number of digits argument is less than 0 (zero), then the number is rounded to the specified number of digits to the left of the decimal point.

BTW

Fractions
The forward slash (/) has multiple uses. For example, dates often are entered using the slash. In formulas, the slash represents division. What about fractions? To enter a fraction, such as ½, type .5 or 0 1/2 (i.e., type zero, followed by a space, followed by the number 1, followed by a slash, followed by the number 2). If you type 1/2 without the preceding zero, Excel will store the value in the cell as the date January 2.

To Enter Formulas and Determine Totals in the Consolidated Worksheet

Table 6–1 shows the three formulas to enter in the consolidated worksheet in cells D5, F5, and G5. The ROUND function is used to round the values resulting from the formulas assigned to the cells to two decimal places.

Table 6–1 Formulas Used to Determine Expenditures and an Average			
Cell	Description	Formula	Entry
D5	2012	ROUND(2011 Expenditure + 2011 Expenditure × 2012 % Change, 4)	= ROUND(B5 + B5 * C5, 4)
F5	2013	ROUND(2012 Expenditure + 2012 Expenditure × 2013 % Change, 4)	= ROUND(D5 + D5 * E5, 4)
G5	Average % Change	ROUND((2012 % Change + 2013 % Change) / 2, 4)	= ROUND((C5 + E5) / 2, 4)

The following steps enter the three formulas in Table 6–1 in cells D5, F5, and G5. After the formulas are entered for Payroll in row 5, the formulas will be copied for the remaining four expenditures. The Sum button then is used to determine the totals in row 10. The following steps enter formulas and determine totals in the consolidated worksheet.

- Select cell D5. Type
  `=round(b5+b5*c5,4)` and then click the Enter box in the formula bar to display the formula in the formula bar and the resulting value in the select cell, in this case 3 in cell D5 (Figure 6–9).

Why does the formula result in a value of 3 rather than a percent change from cell A5?

Because the values in column C have not been entered or formatted as percentages, the values are treated as whole numbers in the calculation. Once the values in column C are entered and formatted as percentages, the resulting values in column D will display as expected, which is a percent change from column B.

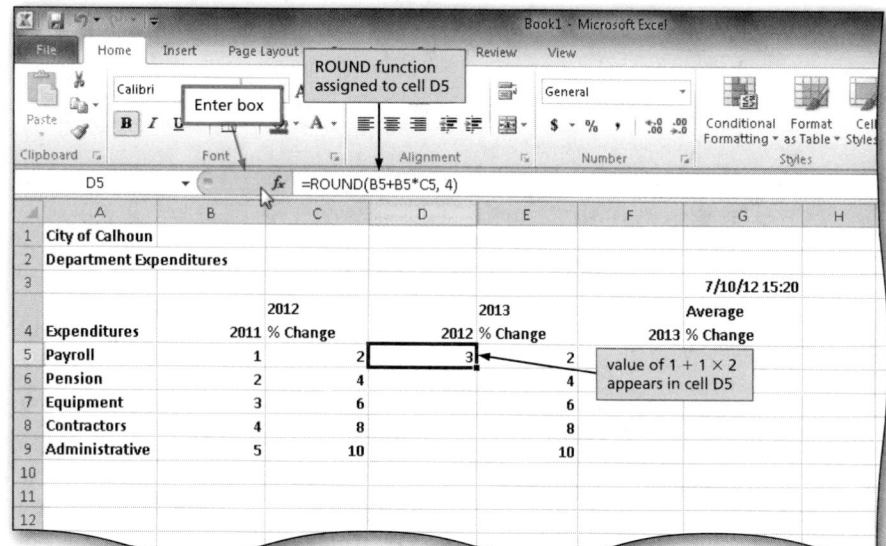

Figure 6–9

2

- Select cell F5. Type
  `=round(d5+d5*e5,4)` and
  then click the Enter box in the
  formula bar to display the formula
  in the formula bar and the resulting
  value in the select cell, in this case 9
  in cell F5 (Figure 6–10).

Figure 6–10

3

- Select cell G5. Type
  `=round((c5+e5)/2,4)` and
  then click the Enter box in the
  formula bar to display the formula
  in the formula bar and the resulting
  value in the select cell, in this case 2
  in cell G5 (Figure 6–11).

Figure 6–11

4

- Select cell D5, point to the fill
  handle, and then drag down
  through cell D9 to copy the formula
  in the selected cell through the
  selected range, D6:D9 in this case.

- Select the range F5:G5 and then
  point to the fill handle to begin
  a fill operation (Figure 6–12).

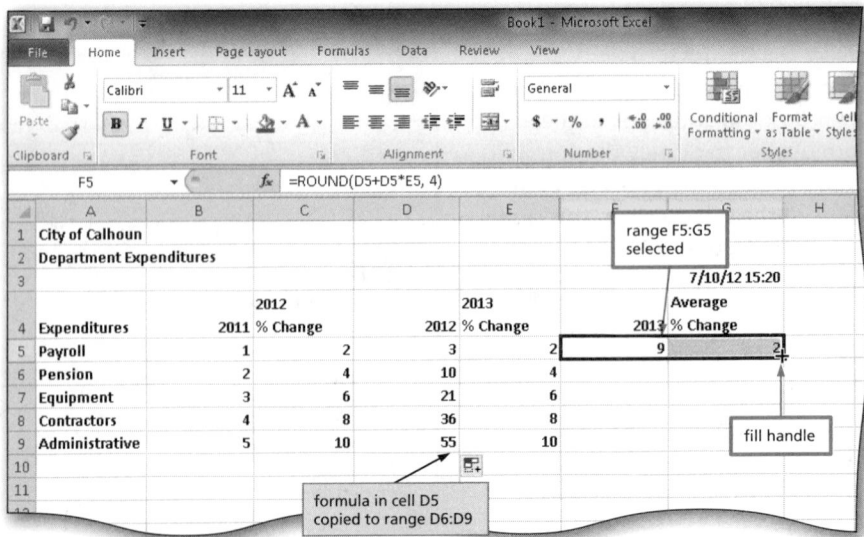

Figure 6–12

5

- Drag down through the range F6:G9 to copy the formulas in the selected range, F5:G5 in this case, to the selected range, F6:G9 in this case (Figure 6–13).

6

- Select cell B10 and then click the Sum button (Home tab | Editing group), select the range B5:B9, and then press the ENTER key to add a SUM function to the selected cell.

- If the Trace Error button is displayed, click it and then click Ignore Error on the Trace Error menu to ignore an error that Excel mistakenly reported.

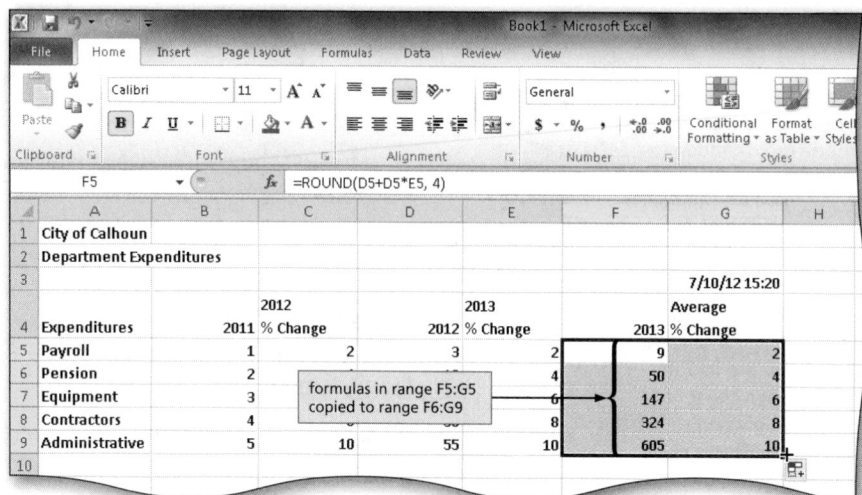

Figure 6–13

- Select cell D10, click the Sum button (Home tab | Editing group), select the range D5:D9, and then press the ENTER key to add a SUM function to the selected cell.

- Select cell F10, click the Sum button (Home tab | Editing group), select the range F5:F9, and then press the ENTER key to add a SUM function to the selected cell.

- Select cell A12 to deselect the selected cell and display the values based on the sample data entered earlier (Figure 6–14).

Figure 6–14

To Save the Worksheet

The following steps save the consolidated worksheet on a USB drive in drive E using the file name, City of Calhoun Consolidated Expenditures.

1 Update the document properties with your name and any other relevant information as specified by your instructor.

2 With a USB flash drive connected to one of the computer's USB ports, click the Save button on the Quick Access Toolbar. Save the workbook using the file name, City of Calhoun Consolidated Expenditures, on the USB flash drive.

Note: If you wish to take a break, this is a good place to do so. You can quit Excel now. To resume at a later time, start Excel, open the file called City of Calhoun Consolidated Expenditures, and continue following the steps from this location forward.

Changing Modes
You change from Enter mode or Edit mode to Point mode by typing the EQUAL SIGN (=) followed by clicking a cell or clicking the Insert Function box on the formula bar, selecting a function, and then clicking a cell. You know you are in Point mode when the word Point appears on the left side of the status bar at the bottom of the Excel window.

Formatting the Consolidated Worksheet

The next step is to format the consolidated worksheet so that it appears as shown in Figure 6–15. The following list summarizes the steps required to format the consolidated worksheet.

1. Format the titles in cells A1 and A2.
2. Format the column titles and total rows.
3. Assign the Currency style format with a floating dollar sign to cells B5, D5, F5, B10, D10, and F10.
4. Assign a Custom style format to the ranges C5:C9, E5:E9, and G5:G9.
5. Assign a Comma style format to the range B6:B9, D6:D9, and F6:F9.
6. Create a format style and assign it to the date in cell G3.

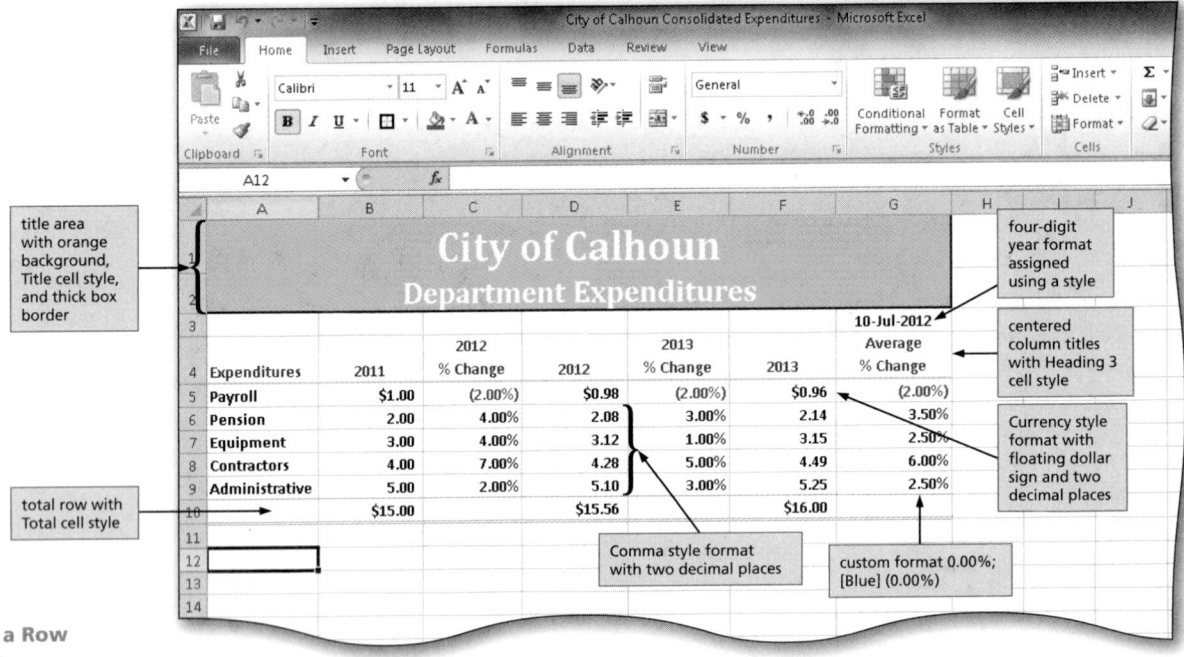

Figure 6–15

Summing a Row or Column
You can reference an entire column or an entire row in a function argument by listing only the column or only the row. For example, =sum(a:a) sums all the values in all the cells in column A, and =sum(1:1) sums all the values in all the cells in row 1. You can verify this by entering =sum(a:a) in cell C1 and then begin entering numbers in a few of the cells in column A. Excel will respond by showing the sum of the numbers in cell C1.

To Format the Consolidated Worksheet's Title and Subtitle

The steps used to format the consolidated worksheet's title and subtitle include changing cell A1 to 28-point with the Title cell style, changing cell A2 to 20-point with the Title cell style, centering both titles across columns A through G, changing the title background color to orange and the title font to white, and drawing a thick box border around the title area. The color scheme associated with the default Office template also will be changed to a new color scheme. One reason to change the color scheme is to add variety to the look of the worksheet that you create. The following steps format the title and subtitle.

1 Display the Page Layout tab. Click the Colors button (Page Layout tab | Themes group) to display the Colors gallery and then click Austin in the Colors gallery to apply a new color scheme to the workbook.

2 Select the range A1:A2. Display the Home tab and apply the Title cell style to the range. Change the font size of cell A1 to 28.

3 Select the range A1:G1. Click the Merge & Center button (Home tab | Alignment group) to merge and center the text in the selected range.

4 Change the font size of cell A2 to 20. Select the range A2:G2.

5 Click the Merge & Center button (Home tab | Alignment group) to merge and center the text in the selected range.

6 Select the range A1:A2, click the Fill Color button arrow (Home tab | Font group) to display the Fill Color gallery, and then click Orange, Accent 6 (column 10, row 1) on the Fill Color gallery to change the fill color of the cells in the selected range.

7 Click the Font Color button arrow (Home tab | Font group) to display the Font Color gallery and then click White, Background 1 (column 1, row 1) on the Font Color gallery to change the font color of the cells in the selected range.

8 Click the Borders button arrow (Home tab | Font group) to display the Borders menu and then click Thick Box Border in the Borders list to apply a border to the selected range.

9 Select cell A12 to deselect the range A1:A2.

BTW

Copying
To copy the contents of a cell to the cell directly below it, click in the target cell and press CTRL+D.

To Format the Column Titles and Total Row

The following steps center and underline the column titles and draw a top and double bottom border on the total row in row 10.

1 Select the range B4:G4 and then click the Center button (Home tab | Alignment group) to center the text in the cells of the selected range.

2 Hold down the CTRL key, click cell A4 to add it to the selection, and then apply the Heading 3 cell style to the range.

3 Select the range A10:G10, assign the Total cell style to the range, and then select cell A12 (Figure 6–16).

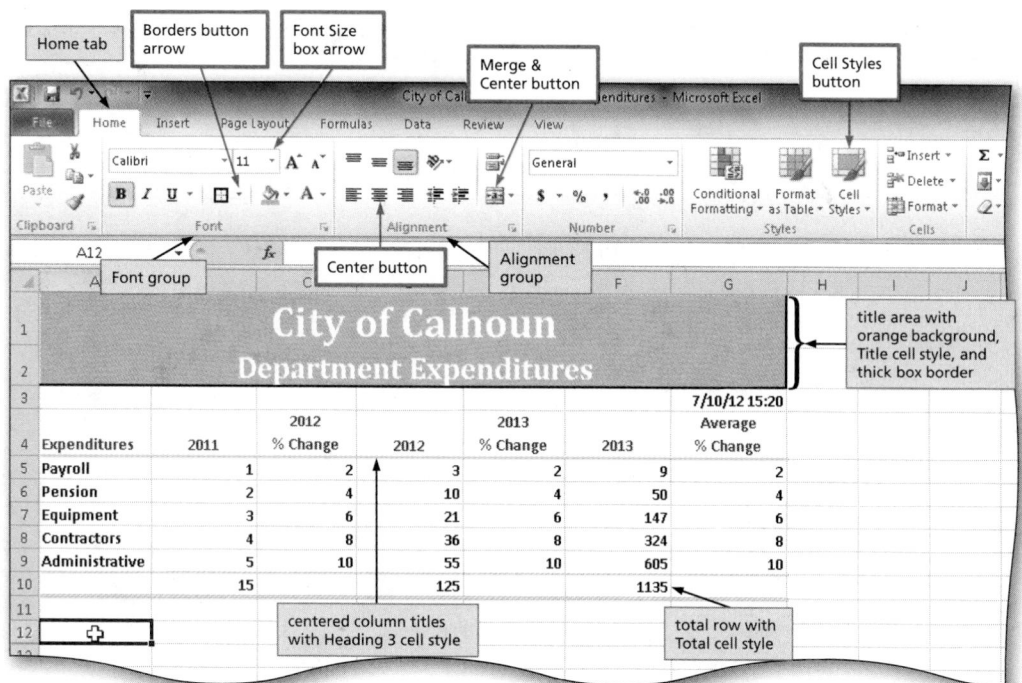

Figure 6–16

To Assign a Currency Style Using the Format Cells Dialog Box

As shown in Figure 6–15 on page EX 374, the consolidated worksheet for this chapter follows the **standard accounting format** for a table of numbers; that is, it contains floating dollar signs in the first row of numbers (row 5) and the totals row (row 10). Recall that while a fixed dollar sign always appears in the same position in a cell (regardless of the number of significant digits), a floating dollar sign always appears immediately to the left of the first significant digit in the cell. To assign a fixed dollar sign to rows 5 and 10, select the range and then click the Accounting Number Format button (Home tab | Number group). Assigning a floating dollar sign, by contrast, requires you to select the desired format in the Format Cells dialog box.

The following steps use the Format Cells dialog box to assign a Currency style with a floating dollar sign and two decimal places to cells B5, D5, F5, B10, D10, and F10.

1

- Select cell B5.

- While holding down the CTRL key, select the nonadjacent cells D5, F5, B10, D10, and F10 and then right-click any selected cell to highlight the nonadjacent ranges and display a shortcut menu and a Mini toolbar (Figure 6–17).

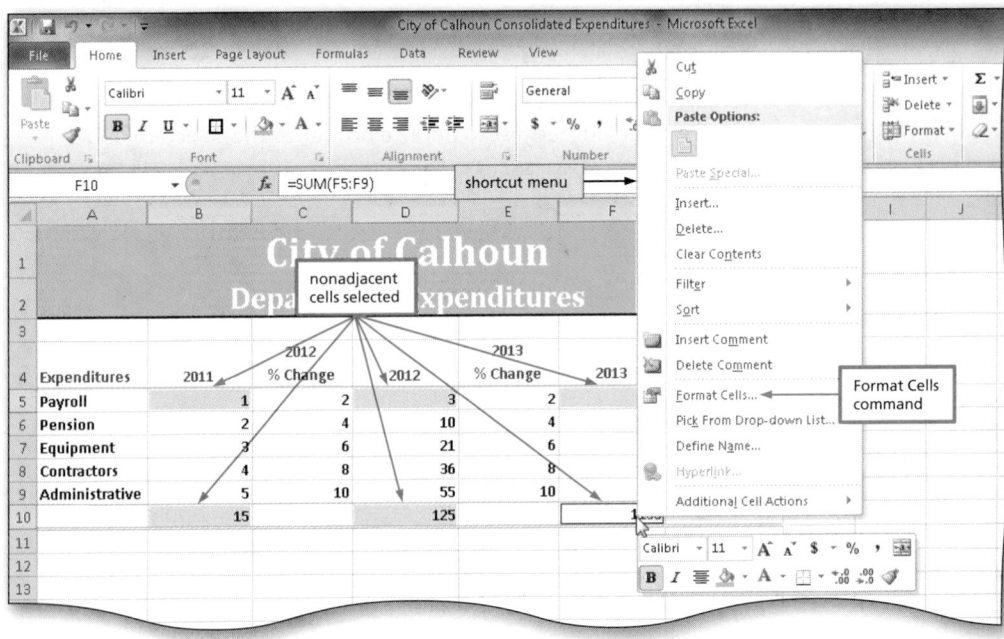

Figure 6–17

2

- Click Format Cells on the shortcut menu to display the Format Cells dialog box.

- If necessary, click the Number tab (Format Cells dialog box) to display the Number tab, click Currency in the Category list to select the type of format to apply, and then click the red ($1,234.10) in the Negative numbers list to select a currency format that displays negative numbers in red with parentheses (Figure 6–18).

Figure 6–18

3

- Click the OK button (Format Cells dialog box) to assign the Currency style with a floating dollar sign and two decimal places to the selected cells. Select cell A12 to deselect the nonadjacent cells (Figure 6–19).

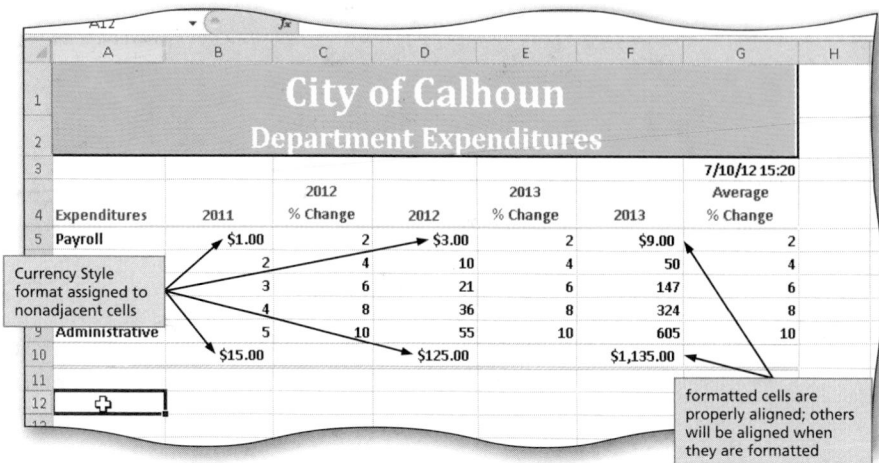

Figure 6–19

Other Ways

1. Press CTRL+1, click Number tab (Format Cells dialog box), select format, click OK button

Format Codes

Excel assigns a format code to every format style listed in the Category list in the Number sheet in the Format Cells dialog box. As shown in Table 6–2, a **format code** is a series of format symbols that defines how a cell entry assigned a format will appear. To view the entire list of format codes that come with Excel, select Custom in the Category list (Figure 6–18).

BTW

Creating Customized Formats
Each format symbol within the format code has special meaning. Table 6–2 summarizes the more frequently used format symbols and their meanings.

Table 6–2 Format Symbols in Format Codes		
Format Symbol	**Example of Symbol in Code**	**Description**
# (number sign)	###.##	Serves as a digit placeholder. If the value in a cell has more digits to the right of the decimal point than number signs in the format, Excel rounds the number. Extra digits to the left of the decimal point are displayed.
0 (zero)	0.00	Works like a number sign (#), except that if the number is less than 1, Excel displays a 0 in the one's place.
. (period)	#0.00	Ensures Excel will display a decimal point in the number. The placement of period symbols determines how many digits appear to the left and right of the decimal point.
% (percent)	0.00%	Displays numbers as percentages of 100. Excel multiplies the value of the cell by 100 and displays a percent sign after the number.
, (comma)	#,##0.00	Displays a comma as a thousand's separator.
( )	#0.00;(#0.00)	Displays parentheses around negative numbers.
$ or + or −	$#,##0.00; ($#,##0.00)	Displays a floating sign ($, +, or −).
* (asterisk)	$*##0.00	Displays a fixed sign ($, +, or −) to the left, followed by spaces until the first significant digit.
[color]	#.##;[Red]#.##	Displays the characters in the cell in the designated color. In the example, positive numbers appear in the default color, and negative numbers appear in red.
" " (quotation marks)	$0.00 "Surplus"; $-0.00 "Shortage"	Displays text along with numbers entered in a cell.
_ (underscore)	(#,##0.00_)	Skips the width of the character that follows the underscore.

Before creating custom format codes or modifying an existing custom format code, you should understand their makeup. As shown below, a format code can have up to four sections: positive numbers, negative numbers, zeros, and text. Each section is divided by a semicolon.

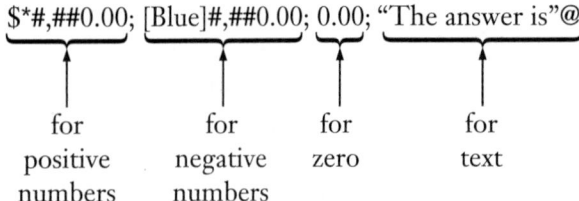

$*#,##0.00; [Blue]#,##0.00; 0.00; "The answer is"@

for positive numbers | for negative numbers | for zero | for text

A format code need not have all four sections. For most applications, a format code will have only a positive section and possibly a negative section.

To Create and Assign a Custom Format Code and a Comma Style Format

The next step is to create and assign a custom format code to the ranges that contain percentages: C5:C9, E5:E9, and G5:G9. The format code will display percentages with two decimal places to the right of the decimal point and also display negative percent values in blue with parentheses. The following steps create and assign a custom format code to percent values and then apply a comma style format to unformatted currency values.

- Select the ranges C5:C9, E5:E9, and G5:G9, right-click any of the selected ranges to display a shortcut menu, and then click Format Cells on the shortcut menu to display the Format Cells dialog box.

- If necessary, click the Number tab (Format Cells dialog box) to display the Number tab and then click Custom in the Category list to begin creating a custom format code.

- Delete the word General in the Type box (Format Cells dialog box) and then type `0.00%;[Blue] (0.00%)` to enter a custom format code (Figure 6–20).

Figure 6–20

What does the custom format mean?

The custom format has been modified to show percent values with two decimal places and to show negative percent values in blue with parentheses. In the Sample area, Excel displays a sample of the custom format assigned to the first number in the selected ranges.

2

- Click the OK button (Format Cells dialog box) to display the numbers in the ranges C5:C9, E5:E9, and G5:G9 using the custom format code created in Step 1.

- Select the ranges B6:B9, D6:D9, and F6:F9.

- Click the Comma Style button (Home tab | Number group) to display the numbers in the selected ranges using the Comma style format (Figure 6–21).

- Select cell A12.

Q&A Can I reuse the custom format code?

Yes. When you create a new custom format code, Excel adds it to the bottom of the Type list in the Number sheet in the Format Cells dialog box to make it available for future use.

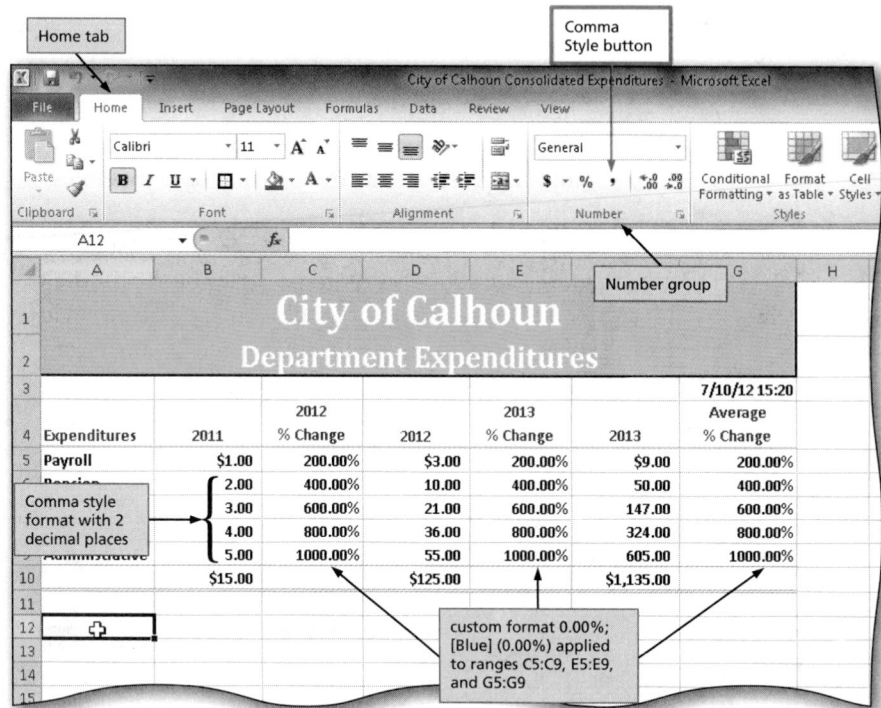

Figure 6–21

Q&A Why is the Comma style format used for numbers that are not large enough to display commas?

The Comma style allows the values in the cells to align properly with the values in rows 5 and 10, which are formatted with the Currency style with floating dollar signs and parentheses for negative numbers.

Cell Styles

A **style** is a group of format specifications that are assigned to a style name. Most of the cell styles in the Cell Styles gallery that are displayed when you click the Cell Styles button (Home tab | Styles group) include formatting only of visual characteristics, such as font name, font size, font color, and fill color. A cell style, however, also can contain information regarding nonvisual characteristics, such as cell protection.

Excel makes several general styles available with all workbooks and themes, as described in Table 6–3. You can apply these existing styles to a cell or cells in a worksheet, modify an existing style, or create an entirely new style.

Style Name	Description
Table 6–3 Styles Available with All Workbooks via the Cell Styles Button on the Home Tab	
Normal	Number = General; Alignment = General, Bottom Aligned; Font = Arial 10; Border = No Borders; Patterns = No Shading; Protection = Locked
Comma	Number = (*#,##0.00);_(*(#,##0.00);_(*"-"_);_(@_)
Comma(0)	Number = (*#,##0_);_(*(#,##0);_(*"-"_);_(@_)
Currency	Number = ($#,##0.00_);_($*(#,##0.00);_($*"-"??_);_(@_)
Currency(0)	Number = ($#,##0_);_($*(#,##0);_($*"-"_);_(@_)
Percent	Number = 0%

You can create and then assign a style to a cell, a range of cells, a worksheet, or a workbook in the same way you assign a format using the buttons on the Home tab on the Ribbon. In fact, the Comma Style button, Currency Style button, and Percent Style button assign the Comma, Currency, and Percent styles in Table 6–3, respectively. Excel automatically assigns the Normal style in Table 6–3 to all cells when you open a new workbook.

By right-clicking styles in the Cell Styles gallery, you also can delete, modify, and duplicate styles. The Merge Styles button in the Cell Styles gallery allows you to merge styles from other workbooks. You add a new style to a workbook or merge styles when you plan to use a group of format specifications over and over.

To Create a New Style

The following steps create a new style called Four-Digit Year by modifying the existing Normal style and assigning the style to cell G3, which contains the system date. The new style will include the following formats: Number = 14-Mar-2001 and Alignment = Horizontal Center and Bottom Aligned.

1
- Click the Cell Styles button (Home tab | Styles group) to display the Cell Styles gallery (Figure 6–22).

Figure 6–22

2
- Click the New Cell Style button in the Cell Styles gallery to display the Style dialog box.

- Type **Four-Digit Year** to name a new style (Figure 6–23).

Figure 6–23

• Click the Format button (Style dialog box) to display the Format Cells dialog box.

• If necessary, click the Number tab (Format Cells dialog box) to display the Number tab, click Date in the Category list to display the list of date formats, and then click 14-Mar-2001 in the Type list to define the new style as a date style (Figure 6–24).

Figure 6–24

• Click the Alignment tab (Format Cells dialog box) to display the Alignment tab, click the Horizontal box arrow to display the Horizontal list, and then click Center in the Horizontal list to define the alignment of a new style.

• Click the OK button (Format Cells dialog box) to close the Format Cells dialog box.

• When the Style dialog box becomes active, click Font, Border, Fill, and Protection to clear the check boxes, indicating that the new style does not use these characteristics (Figure 6–25).

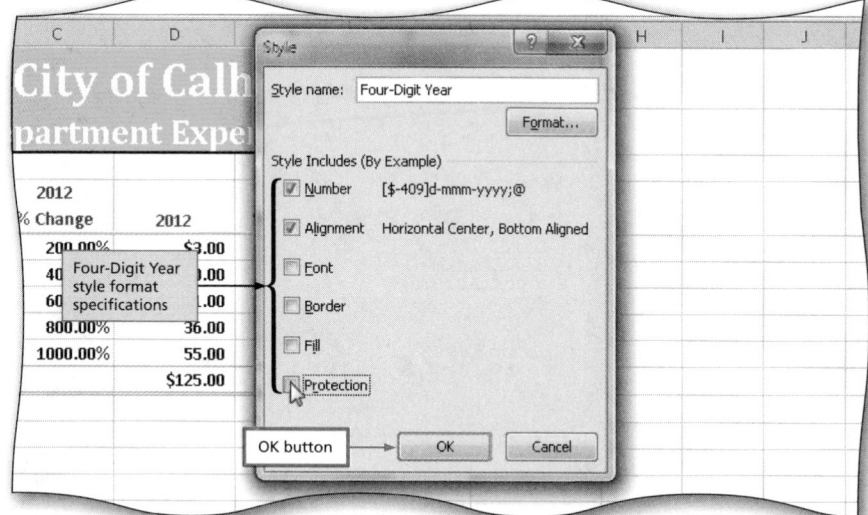

Figure 6–25

Q&A

What is the purpose of the Font, Border, Fill, and Protection settings?

When one of these settings is selected, the cell style will include that setting's formatting attributes. When not selected, as with the cell style created in this set of steps, the cell style does not include any information about these formatting attributes. When the cell style is applied, therefore, no information about the font, borders, fill color, or protection is applied to the cell or range.

• Click the OK button (Style dialog box) to add the new style, Four-Digit Year style in this case, to the list of styles available with the current workbook in the Cell Styles gallery.

To Apply a New Style

In earlier steps, cell G3 was assigned the system date using the NOW() function. The following steps assign cell G3 the Four-Digit Year style, which centers the content of the cell and assigns it the date format dd-mmm-yyyy.

1

- Select cell G3 and then click the Cell Styles button (Home tab | Styles group) to display the Cell Styles gallery (Figure 6–26).

Figure 6–26

2

- Click the Four-Digit Year style to assign the style to the selected cell, cell G3 in this case (Figure 6–27).

Figure 6–27

More About Using Styles

Keep in mind the following additional points concerning styles:

1. A style affects the format of a cell or range of cells only if the corresponding check box is selected in the Style Includes area in the Style dialog box (Figure 6–25 on page EX 381). For example, if the Font check box is not selected in the Style dialog box, then the cell assigned the style maintains the font format it had before the style was assigned.

2. If you assign two different styles to a range of cells, Excel adds the second style to the first, rather than replacing it. If the two cell styles include different settings for an attribute, such as fill color, then Excel applies the setting for the second style.

3. You can merge styles from another workbook into the active workbook by using the Merge Styles button in the Cell Styles gallery. You must, however, open the workbook that contains the desired styles before you use the Merge Styles button.

4. The six check boxes in the Style dialog box are identical to the six tabs in the Format Cells dialog box (Figure 6–24 on page EX 381).

BTW

Opening a Workbook at Startup
You can instruct Windows to open a workbook (or template) automatically when you turn on your computer by adding the workbook (or template) to the Startup folder. Use Windows Explorer to copy the file to the Startup folder. The Startup folder is in the All Programs list.

To Spell Check, Save, and Print the Consolidated Worksheet

With the formatting complete, the next step is to spell check the worksheet, save it, and then print it.

1 Select cell A1. Click the Review tab, and then click the Spelling button (Review tab | Proofing group) to spell check the workbook. Correct any misspelled words.

2 Click the Save button on the Quick Access Toolbar to save the workbook.

3 Print the workbook.

Note: If you wish to take a break, this is a good place to do so. You can quit Excel now. To resume at a later time, start Excel, open the file called City of Calhoun Consolidated Expenditures, and continue following the steps from this location forward.

Working with Multiple Worksheets

A workbook contains three worksheets by default. Excel limits the number of worksheets you can have in a workbook based upon the amount of memory in your computer. When working with multiple worksheets, you should name and color the sheet tabs so that you easily can identify them. With the consolidated worksheet complete, the next steps in completing the project are to add a worksheet to the workbook, copy the data in the consolidated worksheet to the department worksheets, and adjust the formatting and values in the department worksheets.

Identify additional worksheets needed in the workbook.
Excel provides three basic choices when you consider how to use Excel to organize data. Use a single worksheet when the data is tightly related. In this case you may want to analyze the data in a table and use a column, such as Department, Region, or Quarter, to identify groups of data. Use multiple worksheets when data is related but can stand alone on its own. For example, each region, department, or quarter may contain enough detailed information that you may want to analyze the data in separate worksheets. Use multiple workbooks when data is loosely coupled, or when workbooks come from multiple sources or must be gathered from multiple sources.

Plan Ahead

To Add a Worksheet to a Workbook

The City of Calhoun Consolidated Expenditures workbook requires four worksheets—one for each of the three departments and one for the consolidated totals. Thus, a worksheet must be added to the workbook. When you add a worksheet, Excel places the new sheet tab to the left of the active tab. To keep the worksheet with the sample data shown in Figure 6–27 on page EX 382 on top—that is, to keep its tab (Sheet1) to the far left—spreadsheet specialists often add a new worksheet between Sheet1 and Sheet2, rather than to the left of Sheet1. The following steps select Sheet2 before adding a worksheet to the workbook.

- Click the Sheet2 tab at the bottom of the window and then click the Insert Cells button arrow (Home tab | Cells group) to display the Insert Cells menu (Figure 6–28).

Can I start a new workbook with more sheets?

Yes. An alternative to adding worksheets is to change the default number of worksheets before you open a new workbook. To change the default number of worksheets in a blank workbook, click the Excel Options button in the Backstage view, and then change the number in the 'Include this many sheets' box in the 'When creating new workbooks' area of the Excel Options dialog box. Recall from Chapter 4 that you can delete a worksheet by right-clicking the sheet tab of the worksheet you want to delete and then clicking Delete on the shortcut menu.

Figure 6–28

- Click Insert Sheet on the Insert Cells menu to add a new worksheet to a workbook, in this case a sheet named Sheet 4 between Sheet 1 and Sheet 2 (Figure 6–29).

Can I insert more than one worksheet at a time?

Yes. You can insert as many worksheets at once as there are tabs in the current workbook. To insert multiple worksheets, select multiple tabs corresponding to the number of sheets you want to insert, and then select Insert Sheet on the Insert Cells menu.

Figure 6–29

Other Ways
1. Right-click tab, click Insert on shortcut menu

To Copy the Contents of a Worksheet to Other Worksheets in a Workbook

With four worksheets in the workbook, the next step is to copy the contents of Sheet1 to Sheet4, Sheet2, and Sheet3. Sheet1 eventually will be used as the Consolidated worksheet with the consolidated data. Sheet4, Sheet2, and Sheet3 will be used for the three department worksheets.

1

- Click the Sheet1 tab to display the worksheet on the sheet tab.

- Click the Select All button to select the entire worksheet and then click the Copy button (Home tab | Clipboard group) to copy the contents of the worksheet (Figure 6–30).

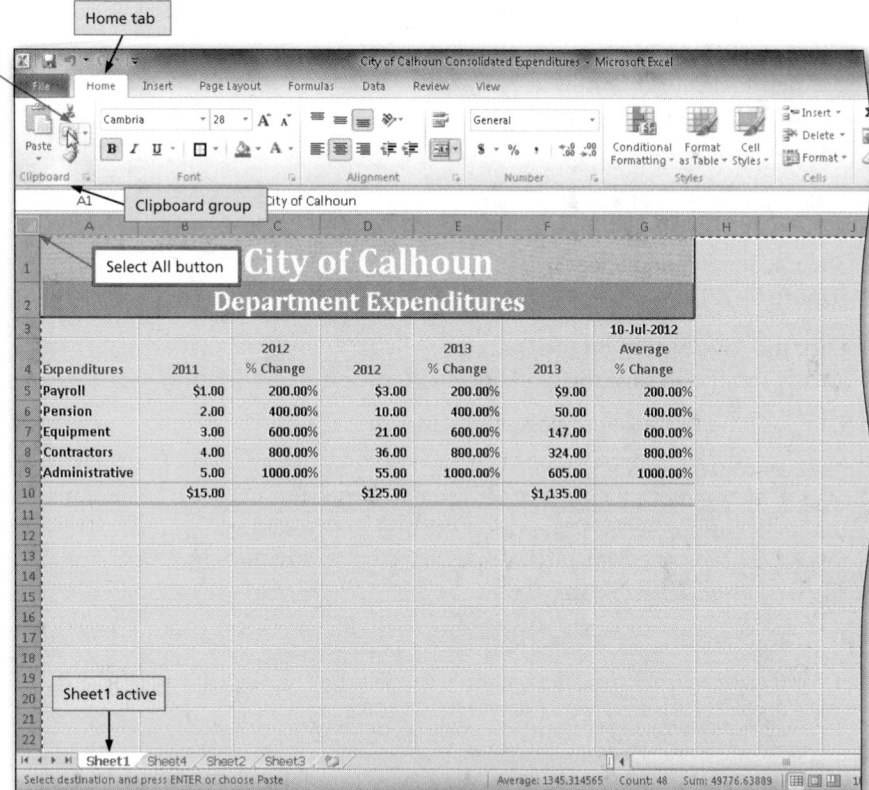

Figure 6–30

2

- Click the Sheet4 tab to display the worksheet on the sheet tab.

- While holding down the SHIFT key, click the Sheet3 tab to select all three blank worksheets in the workbook.

- Click the Paste button (Home tab | Clipboard group) to copy the data on the Office Clipboard to all of the selected sheets (Figure 6–31).

Q&A

Why does the word Group appear on the title bar?

The term [Group] following the workbook name on the title bar indicates that multiple worksheets are selected.

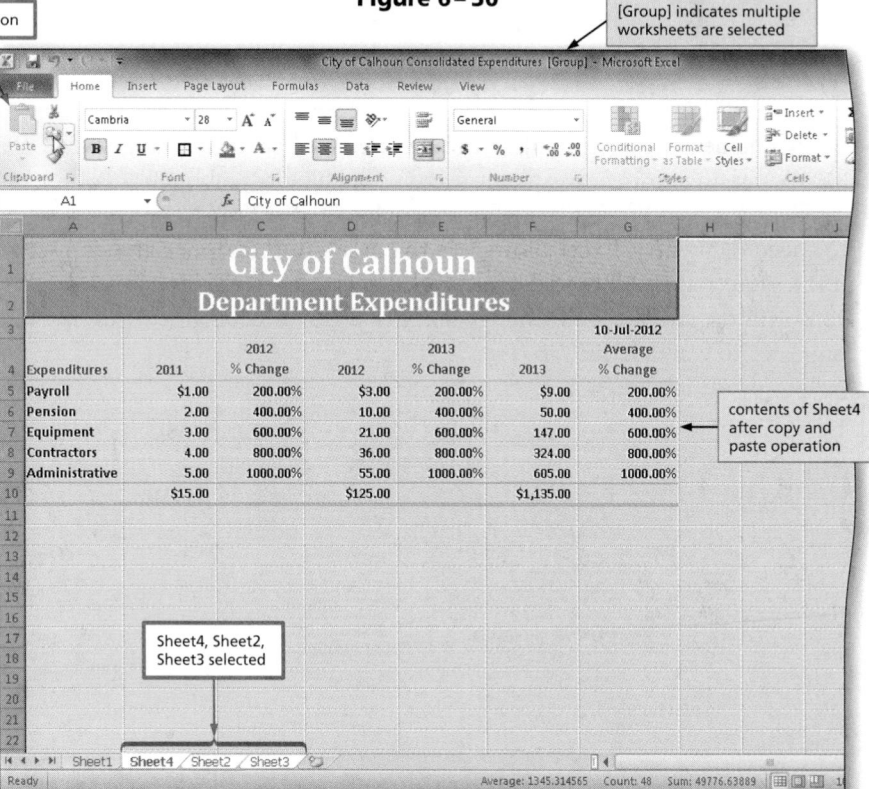

Figure 6–31

3

- Click the Sheet1 tab to display the worksheet on the sheet tab and then press the ESC key to remove the marquee surrounding the selection.

- Hold down the SHIFT key, click the Sheet3 tab to display the worksheet on the sheet tab, and then select cell A12 to select the same cell in multiple sheets.

- Hold down the SHIFT key and then click the Sheet1 tab to deselect Sheet4, Sheet2, and Sheet3 (Figure 6–32).

- Click the Save button on the Quick Access Toolbar to save the workbook.

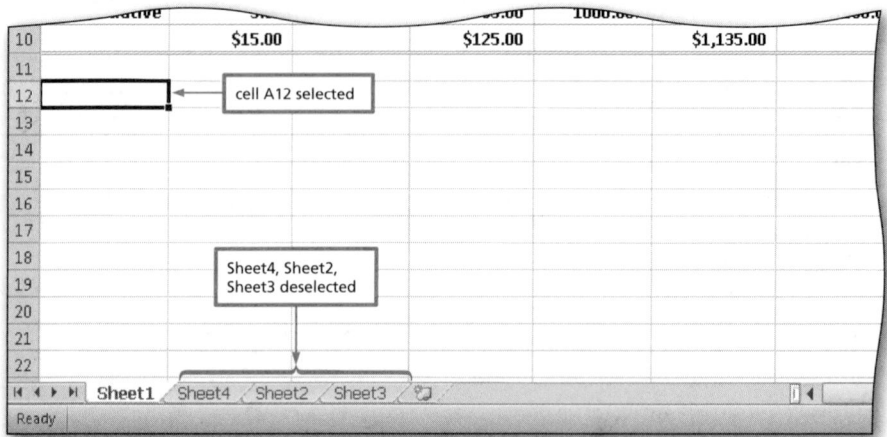

Figure 6–32

Q&A

Can I use the ENTER key to paste the data?

Yes. The ENTER key could have been used rather than the Paste button (Home tab | Clipboard group) to complete the paste operation in Step 2. Recall that if you complete a paste operation using the ENTER key, then the marquee disappears and the Office Clipboard no longer contains the copied data following the action. Because the Paste button was used, the ESC key was used in Step 3 to clear the marquee and Office Clipboard of the copied data.

Other Ways

1. Select source area, click Copy button (Home tab | Editing group), select worksheets, click Paste button (Home tab | Editing group)

2. Right-click source area, click Copy on shortcut menu, select worksheets, click Paste on shortcut menu

3. Select source area, press CTRL+C, select worksheets, press CTRL+V

To Drill an Entry through Worksheets

The next step is to replace the sample numbers in the ranges C5:C9 and E5:E9 with the 2012 % Change and 2013 % Change for each expenditure type (Table 6–4). The 2012 % Change and 2013 % Change for expenditures are identical on all four sheets. For example, the 2012 % Change for Payroll in cell C5 is -2.00% on all four sheets. To speed data entry, Excel allows you to enter a number once and copy it through worksheets so that it is entered in the same cell on all the selected worksheets. This technique is referred to as **drilling an entry**. The following steps drill the five 2012 % Change and five 2013 % Change entries in Table 6–4 through all four worksheets in the ranges C5:C9 and E5:E9.

Table 6–4 2012 % Change and 2013 % Change Values			
Cell	**2012 % Change**	**Cell**	**2013 % Change**
C5	−2.00	E5	−2.00
C6	4.00	E6	3.00
C7	4.00	E7	1.00
C8	7.00	E8	5.00
C9	2.00	E9	3.00

1

- With Sheet1 active, hold down the SHIFT key and then click the Sheet3 tab to select all four tabs at the bottom of the window.

- Select cell C5. Type −2.00 and then press the DOWN ARROW key to change sample data in the selected cell to a proper value.

- Enter the nine remaining 2012 % Change and 2013 % Change values in Table 6–4 in the ranges C6:C9 and E5:E9 to display the proper values.

- Select cell A12 to select the same cell in all of the selected worksheets (Figure 6–33).

4	Expenditures	2011	2012 % Change	2012	2013 % Change	2013	Average % Change
5	Payroll	$1.00	(2.00%)	$0.98	(2.00%)	$0.96	(2.00%)
6	Pension	2.00	4.00%			2.14	3.50%
7	Equipment	3.00	4.00%			3.15	2.50%
8	Contractors	4.00	7.00%			4.49	6.00%
9	Administrative	5.00	2.00%	5.10	3.00%	5.25	2.50%
10		$15.00		$15.56		$16.00	

Excel drills 2012 % Change values entered on Sheet1 through to same cells on Sheet4, Sheet2, and Sheet3

Sheet1, Sheet4, Sheet2, Sheet3 selected

Sheet1 / Sheet4 / Sheet2 / Sheet3

Ready

Figure 6–33

2

- Hold down the SHIFT key and then click the Sheet1 tab to deselect multiple sheets.

- One at a time, click the Sheet4 tab, the Sheet2 tab, and the Sheet3 tab to verify that all four sheets are identical (Figure 6–34).

Q&A What is the benefit of drilling data through worksheets?

In the previous set of steps, ten new numbers were entered on one worksheet. As shown in Figure 6–34, by drilling the entries through the three other worksheets, 40 new numbers now appear, ten on each of the four worksheets. Excel's capability of drilling data through worksheets is an efficient way to enter data that is common among worksheets.

same 2012 % Change and 2013 % Change values appear on all four sheets

Home tab

Font group

Sheet1

Sheet4

Sheet2

Sheet3

Figure 6–34

BTW

Drilling an Entry
Besides drilling a
number down through
a workbook, you can drill
a format, a function, or a
formula down through
a workbook.

To Modify the Public Works Sheet

With the outline of the City of Calhoun Consolidated Expenditures workbook created, the next step is to modify the individual sheets. The following steps modify the Public Works sheet (Sheet 4) by changing the sheet name, tab color, and worksheet subtitle; changing the color of the title area; and entering the 2011 expenditures in column B.

1 Double-click the Sheet4 tab to begin editing the sheet name. Type **Public Works** and then press the ENTER key to change the sheet name.

2 Right-click the Public Works tab to display a shortcut menu, point to Tab Color on the shortcut menu, and then click Brown, Accent 2 (column 6, row 1 in the Theme Colors area) on the Color palette to change the tab color.

3 Double-click cell A2 to begin editing text in a cell, drag through the words Department Expenditures to select the text, and then type **Public Works** to change the worksheet subtitle.

4 Select the range A1:A2, click the Fill Color button arrow (Home tab | Font group) to display the Fill Color gallery, and then click Brown, Accent 2 (column 6, row 1 in the Standard Colors area) on the Fill Color gallery to change the fill color of the selected range.

5 Enter the data listed in Table 6–5 in the range B5:B9 (Figure 6–35).

6 Select cell A12 and then click the Save button on the Quick Access Toolbar to save the workbook.

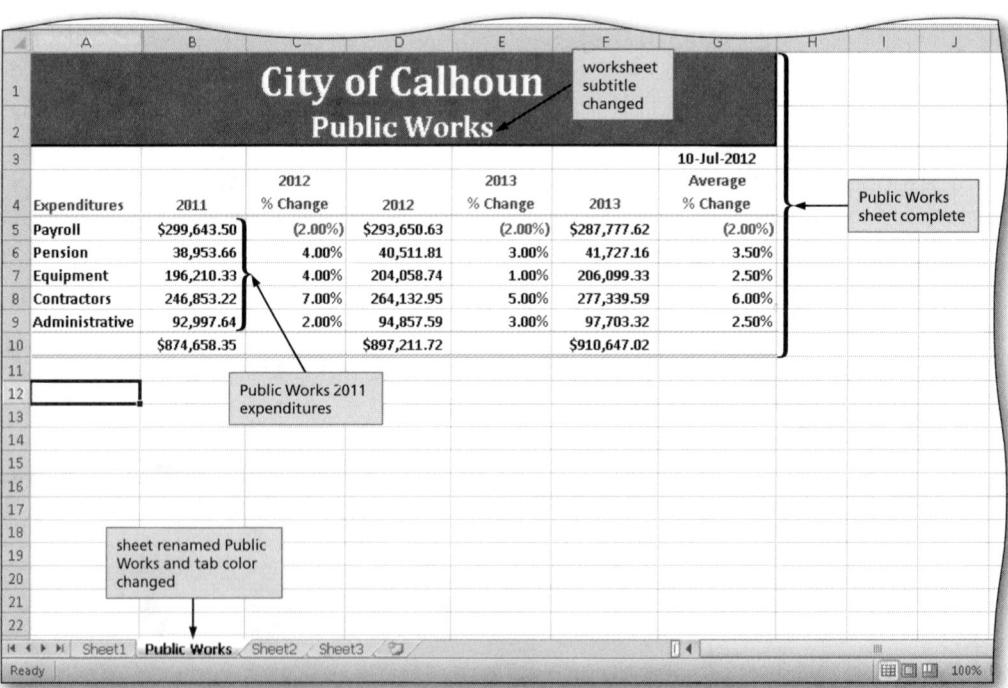

Figure 6–35

Table 6–5 Public Works 2011 Expenditures	
Cell	**2011 Expenditures**
B5	299643.50
B6	38953.66
B7	196210.33
B8	246853.22
B9	92997.64

To Modify the Police and Fire Sheet

The following steps modify the Police and Fire sheet (Sheet2).

1 Double-click the Sheet2 tab. Type `Police and Fire` and then press the ENTER key to change the sheet name.

2 Right-click the Police and Fire tab, point to Tab Color on the shortcut menu, and then click Green, Accent 1 (column 5, row 1 in the Theme Colors area) on the Color palette to change the tab color.

3 Double-click cell A2, drag through the words, Department Expenditures, and then type `Police and Fire` to change the worksheet subtitle.

4 Select the range A1:A2, click the Fill Color button arrow on the Ribbon, and then click Green, Accent 1 (column 5, row 1 in the Theme Colors area) in the Fill Color gallery.

5 Enter the data listed in Table 6–6 in the range B5:B9 (Figure 6–36).

6 Select cell A12 and then click the Save button on the Quick Access Toolbar.

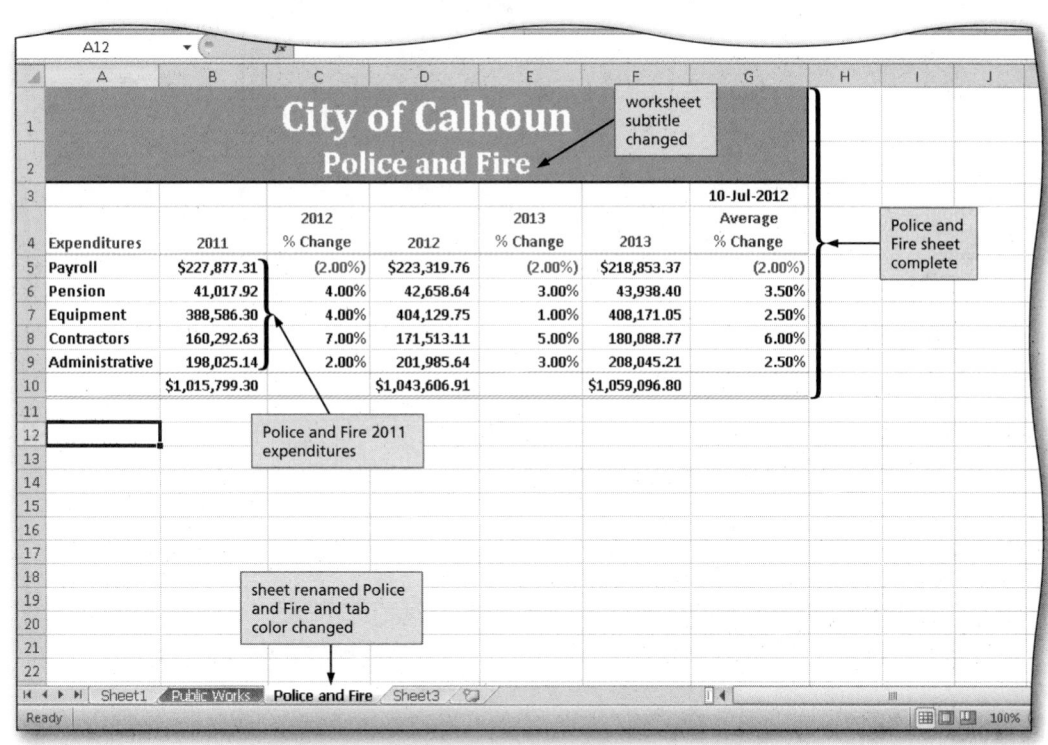

Figure 6–36

Table 6–6 Police and Fire 2011 Expenditures	
Cell	2011 Expenditures
B5	227877.31
B6	41017.92
B7	388586.30
B8	160292.63
B9	198025.14

To Modify the Parks and Recreation Sheet

As with the Public Works and Police and Fire sheets, the sheet name, tab color, worksheet subtitle, data, and background colors must be changed on the Parks and Recreation sheet. The following steps modify the Parks and Recreation sheet.

BTW

Importing Data
Expenditures, such as those entered into the range B5:B9, often are maintained in another workbook, a file, or a database. If the expenditures are maintained elsewhere, ways exist to link to a workbook or import data from a file or database into a workbook. Linking to a workbook is discussed later in this chapter. For information on importing data, see the From Other Sources button (Data tab | Get External Data group).

1 Double-click the Sheet3 tab. Type `Parks and Recreation` and then press the ENTER key to change the sheet name.

2 Right-click the Parks and Recreation tab, point to Tab Color on the shortcut menu, and then click Orange, Accent 3 (column 7, row 1 in the Standard Colors area) on the Color palette to change the tab color.

3 Double-click cell A2, drag through the words, Department Expenditures, and then type `Parks and Recreation` to change the worksheet subtitle.

4 Select the range A1:A2, click the Fill Color button arrow on the Ribbon, and then click Orange, Accent 3 (column 7, row 1 in the Standard Colors area) on the Fill Color gallery to change the fill color of the selected cell.

5 Enter the data listed in Table 6–7 in the range B5:B9 (Figure 6–37).

6 Select cell A12 and then click the Save button on the Quick Access Toolbar.

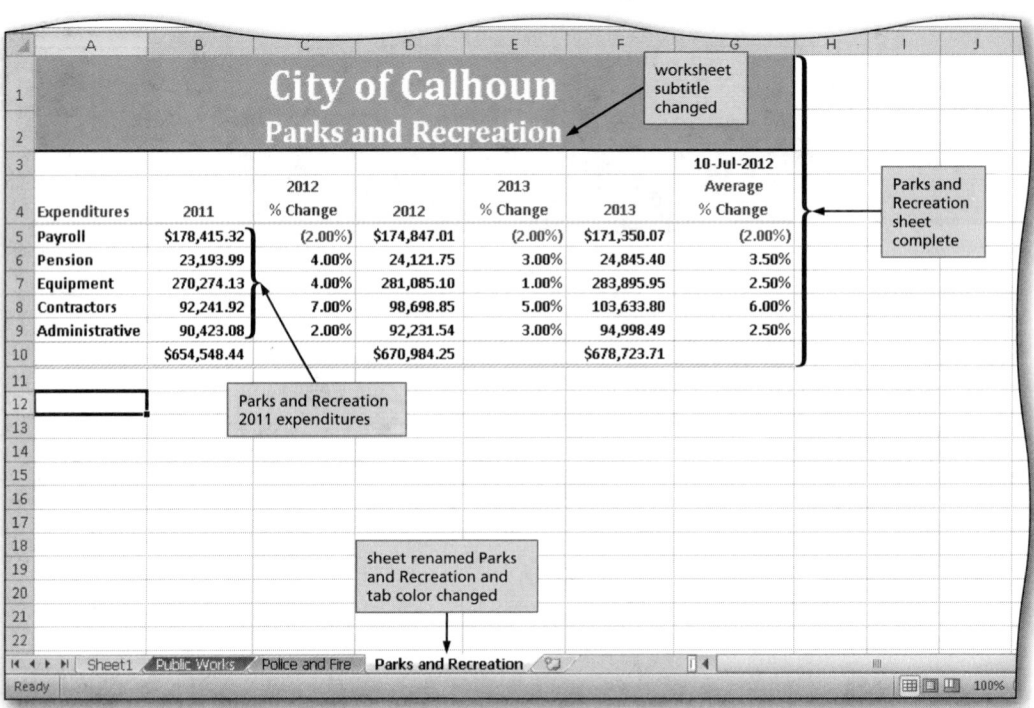

Figure 6–37

Table 6–7 Parks and Recreation 2011 Expenditures	
Cell	**2011 Expenditures**
B5	178415.32
B6	23193.99
B7	270274.13
B8	92241.92
B9	90423.08

Referencing Cells in Other Sheets in a Workbook

With the three region sheets complete, the next step is to modify Sheet1, which will serve as the consolidation worksheet containing totals of the data on the Public Works, Police and Fire, and Parks and Recreation sheets. Because this sheet contains totals of the data, you need to understand how to reference cells in other sheets in a workbook before modifying Sheet1.

To reference cells in other sheets in a workbook, you use the sheet name, which serves as the **sheet reference**, and the cell reference. For example, you refer to cell B5 on the Public Works sheet as shown below. The sheet name must be included in single quotation marks when the sheet name contains a space character.

='Public Work's!B5'

BTW | **Circular References**
A circular reference is a formula that depends on its own value. The most common type is a formula that contains a reference to the same cell in which the formula resides.

Using this method, you can sum cell B5 from each of the three department sheets by selecting cell B5 on the Sheet1 sheet and then entering:

='Public Works'!B5 + 'Police and Fire'!B5 + 'Parks and Recreation'!B5

A much quicker way to total the three cells is to use the SUM function as follows:

=SUM('Public Works':'Parks and Recreation'!B5)

The SUM argument ('Public Works:Parks and Recreation'!B5) instructs Excel to sum cell B5 on each of the three sheets (Public Works, Police and Fire, and Parks and Recreation). The colon (:) between the first sheet name and the last sheet name instructs Excel to include these sheets and all sheets in between, just as it does with a range of cells on a sheet. A range that spans two or more sheets in a workbook, such as 'Public Works:Parks and Recreation'!B5, is called a **3-D range**. The reference to this range is a **3-D reference**.

A sheet reference such as 'Public Works'! always is absolute. Thus, the sheet reference remains constant when you copy formulas.

To Modify the Consolidated Sheet

This section modifies the Consolidated sheet by changing the sheet name, tab color, and subtitle and then entering the SUM function in cells B5:F5. The SUM functions will determine the total expenditures for each year, by expenditure type. Cell B5 on the Consolidated sheet, for instance, will contain the sum of the Payroll expenditures, which are located in Public Works!B5, Police and Fire!B5, and Parks and Recreation!B5. Before determining the totals, the following steps change the sheet name from Sheet1 to Consolidated, color the tab, and change the subtitle to Consolidated Expenditures.

1 Double-click the Sheet1 sheet tab to display the worksheet. Type `Consolidated` and then press the ENTER key to rename the sheet.

2 Right-click the Consolidated tab to display the worksheet, point to Tab Color on the shortcut menu, and then click Orange, Accent 6 (column 10, row 1 in the Standard Colors area) on the Color palette to change the tab color.

3 Double-click cell A2 to begin editing a cell, drag through the words Department Expenditures to select the words in the cell, and then type `Consolidated` as the worksheet subtitle. Press the ENTER key to complete the change of the subtitle.

BTW | **3-D References**
If you are summing numbers on noncontiguous sheets, hold down the CTRL key rather than the SHIFT key when selecting the sheets.

To Enter and Copy 3-D References Using the Paste Gallery

You can enter a sheet reference in a cell by typing the sheet reference or by clicking the appropriate sheet tab while in Point mode. When you click the sheet tab, Excel activates the sheet and automatically adds the sheet name and an exclamation point after the insertion point in the formula bar. Next, select or drag through the cells you want to reference on the sheet.

If the range of cells to be referenced is located on several worksheets (as when selecting a 3-D range), click the first sheet tab and then select the cell or drag through the range of cells. Next, while holding down the SHIFT key, click the sheet tab of the last sheet you want to reference. Excel will include the cell(s) on the first sheet, the last sheet, and any sheets in between.

The following steps enter the 3-D references used to determine the total 2011 expenditures for each of the five types of expenditures. In these steps, the Formulas button on the Paste gallery is used to complete the paste operation. When the Formulas button is used, the paste operation pastes only the formulas, leaving the formats of the destination area unchanged.

- Select cell B5 and then click the Sum button (Home tab | Editing group) to display the SUM function and ScreenTip (Figure 6–38).

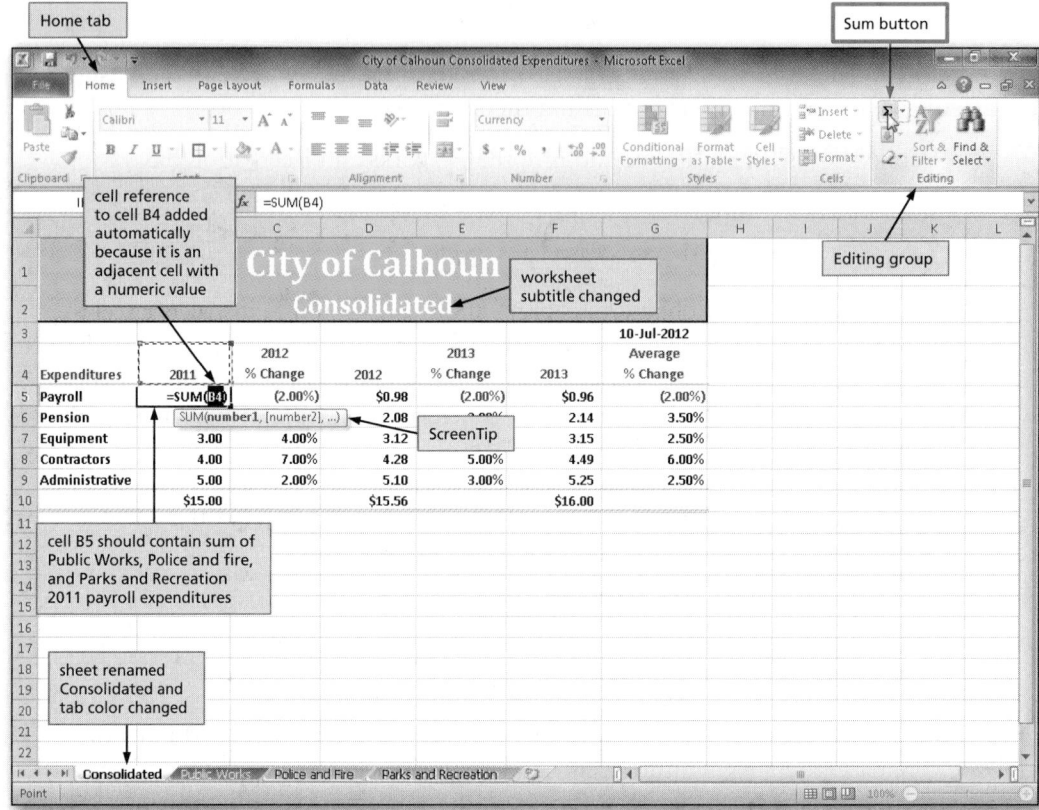

Figure 6–38

- Click the Public Works tab to display the worksheet and then click cell B5 to select the first portion of the argument for the SUM function.

- While holding down the SHIFT key, click the Parks and Recreation tab to select the ending range of the argument for the SUM function (Figure 6–39).

Figure 6–39

- Click the Enter box in the formula bar to enter the SUM function with the 3-D references in the selected cell, in this case Consolidated!B5 (Figure 6–40).

Figure 6–40

- With cell B5 active, click the Copy button (Home tab | Clipboard group) to copy the SUM function and the formats assigned to the selected cell to the Office Clipboard (Figure 6–41).

Figure 6–41

5

• Select the range B6:B9 and then click the Paste button arrow (Home tab | Clipboard group) to display the Paste gallery (Figure 6–42).

Figure 6–42

6

• Click the Formulas button on the Paste gallery to copy the SUM function in cell B5 to the range B6:B9 and automatically adjust the cell references in the SUM function to reference the corresponding cells on the three sheets in the workbook.

• Press the ESC key to clear the marquee surrounding the source cell, B5 in this case, and then select cell A12 to deselect the destination range, B6:B9 in this case.

• Click the Save button on the Quick Access Toolbar to save the workbook (Figure 6–43).

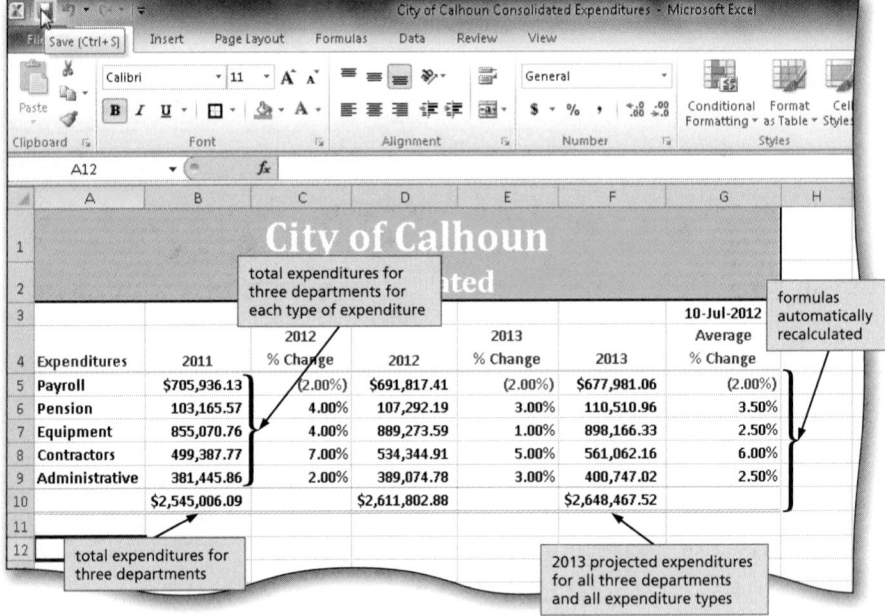

Figure 6–43

More About Pasting

If you click the Paste button (Home tab | Clipboard group) to complete the paste operation, rather than using the Formulas button as shown in Figure 6–42, any formats assigned to cell B5 also will be copied to the range B6:B9. Completing the paste operation by using the fill handle or by pressing the ENTER key also will copy any formats from the source area to the destination area. Oftentimes, as in the steps shown above, the formats of the source area and destination area differ; when you use the Formulas button on the Paste gallery, Excel copies the SUM function, but not the format, assigned to the source area. The Paste gallery, thus, is a useful option to complete the copy and paste operation without copying the formatting of the source area. Table 6–8 summarizes the commands available on the Paste gallery, as shown in Figure 6–42 on the next page.

Table 6–8 Paste Gallery Commands

Paste Option Icon	Paste Option	Shortcut Key	Description
	Paste	CTRL+P	Copy contents and format of source area. This option is the default.
	Formulas	CTRL+F	Copy formulas from the source area, but not the contents and format.
	Formulas & Number Formatting	CTRL+O	Copy formulas and format for numbers and formulas of source area, but not the contents.
	Keep Source Formatting	CTRL+K	Copy contents, format, and styles of source area.
	No Borders	CTRL+B	Copy contents and format of source area, but not any borders.
	Keep Source Column Widths	CTRL+W	Copy contents and format of source area. Change destination column widths to source column widths.
	Transpose	CTRL+T	Copy the contents and format of the source area, but transpose, or swap, the rows and columns.
	Values	CTRL+V	Copy contents of source area but not the formatting for formulas.
	Values & Number Formatting	CTRL+A	Copy contents and format of source area for numbers or formulas, but use format of destination area for text.
	Values & Source Formatting	CTRL+E	Copy contents and formatting of source area but not the formula.
	Formatting	CTRL+R	Copy format of source area but not the contents.
	Paste Link	CTRL+N	Copy contents and format and link cells so that a change to the cells in source area updates the corresponding cells in destination area.
	Picture	CTRL+U	Copy an image of the source area as a picture.
	Linked Picture	CTRL+I	Copy an image of the source area as a picture so that a change to the cells in source area updates the picture in destination area.

Note: If you wish to take a break, this is a good place to do so. You can quit Excel now. To resume at a later time, start Excel, open the file called City of Calhoun Consolidated Expenditures, and continue following the steps from this location forward.

Adding a Header and Footer, Changing the Margins, and Printing the Workbook

Before printing a workbook, consider the **page setup**, which defines the appearance and format of a printed worksheet. You can add a **header**, which appears at the top of every printed page, and a **footer**, which appears at the bottom of every printed page. You also can change the **margins** to increase or decrease the white space surrounding the printed worksheet or chart.

<table>
<tr><td>Plan
Ahead</td><td>**Examine the options, including headers, margins, and page breaks, that you have for printing worksheets.**
If you plan to distribute printed copies of worksheets, decide whether to select page setup options before printing.

• **Add headers and footers.** By default, both the header and footer are blank. You can change either so that information, such as the workbook author, date, page number, or tab name, prints at the top or bottom of each page. The headers and footers for chart sheets must be assigned separately.

• **Change the margins.** The default margins in Excel for both portrait and landscape orientation are set to the following: Top = .75 inch; Bottom = .75 inch; Left = .7 inch; Right = .7 inch. The header and footer are set at .3 inches from the top and bottom, respectively. Change these settings to provide more or less white space on the printed page.

• **Apply other page setup options.** Display the Page Layout tab to specify page setup options, such as setting the location of page breaks or centering a printout horizontally and vertically. Be sure to select all the sheets you want to modify before you change page setup options.</td></tr>
</table>

To Change Margins and Center the Printout Horizontally

As you modify the page setup, remember that Excel does not copy page setup characteristics when one sheet is copied to another. Thus, even if you assigned page setup characteristics to the consolidated worksheet before copying it to each department's worksheet, the page setup characteristics would not be copied to the new sheet. The following steps use the Page Setup dialog box to change the margins and center the printout of each department's worksheet horizontally.

• With the Consolidated sheet active, if necessary, scroll to the top of the worksheet.

• While holding down the SHIFT key, click the Parks and Recreation sheet tab to select the four worksheet tabs.

• Display the Page Layout tab (Figure 6–44).

Figure 6–44

• Click the Page Setup Dialog Box Launcher (Page Layout tab | Page Setup group) to display the Page Setup dialog box.

• When Excel displays the Page Setup dialog box, if necessary, click the Margins tab.

• Double-click the Top box and then type **1.5** to change the top margin.

• Enter **.5** in both the Left box and Right box to change the left and right margins.

• Click the Horizontally check box in the 'Center on page' area to center the worksheet on the printed page horizontally (Figure 6–45).

❸

• Click the OK button (Page Setup dialog box) to close the Page Setup dialog box.

Figure 6–45

Other Ways

1. In Backstage view, click Normal Margins button (Print tab | Settings area), click Custom Margins

To Add a Header and Footer

The following steps use Page Layout view to change the headers and footers of the worksheets.

❶

• Click the Page Layout button on the status bar to display the worksheet in Page Layout view (Figure 6–46).

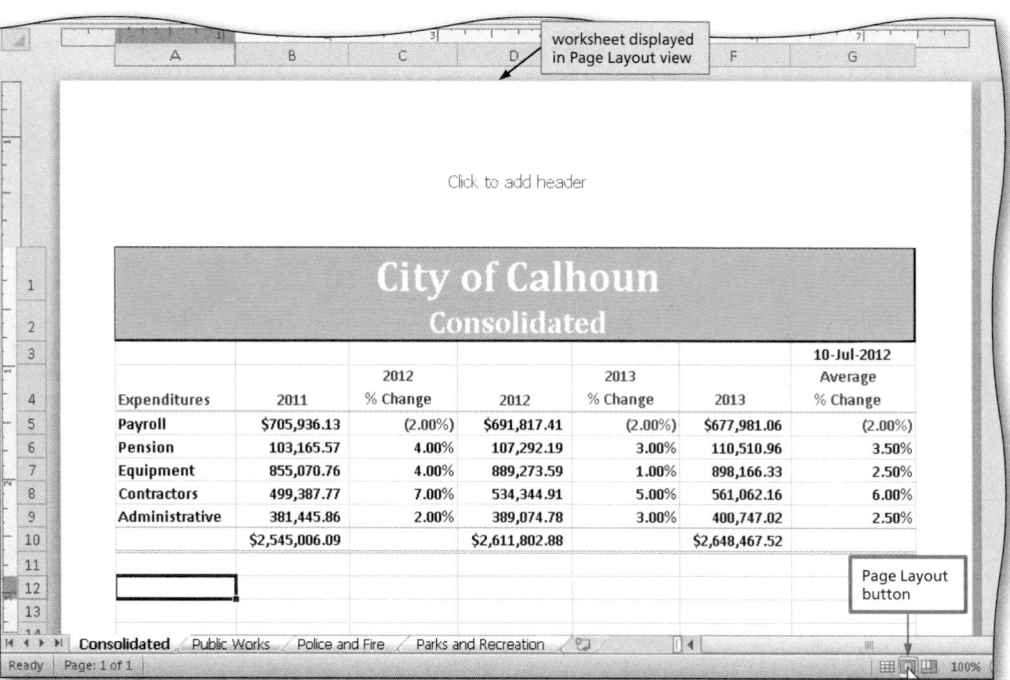

Figure 6–46

2

- If necessary, scroll the worksheet up until the Header area is displayed. Click the left Header box to select the left Header box as the area for a header and type `Shelly Cashman` (or your name) to enter a page header in the left Header box.

- Click the center Header box to select the center Header box as the area for a header and then type `City of Calhoun`. Press the ENTER key to begin a new line.

- Click the Sheet Name button (Header & Footer Tools Design tab | Header & Footer Elements group) to instruct Excel to insert the sheet name that appears on the sheet tab as part of the header.

- Click the right Header box to select the right Header box as the area for a header, click the Current Date button (Header & Footer Tools Design tab | Header & Footer Elements group) to insert the current date.

- Press the COMMA key and, then click the Current Time button (Header & Footer Tools Design tab | Header & Footer Elements group) to insert the date and time in the Header (Figure 6–47).

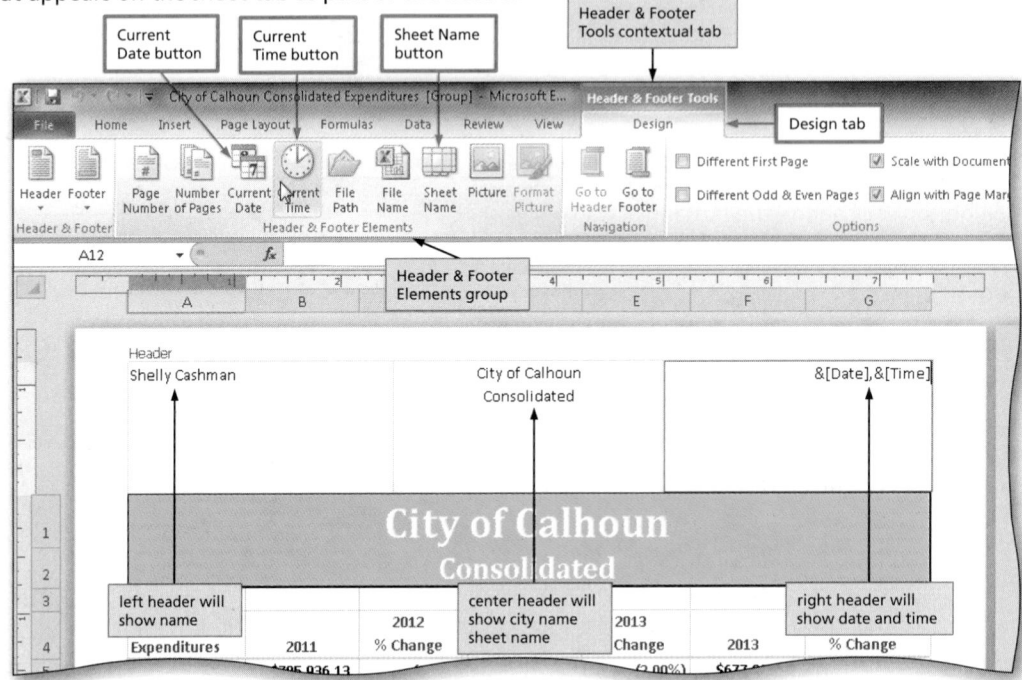

Figure 6–47

3

- Scroll the workbook down to view the Footer area.

- Click the middle Footer box to select the middle section box as the area for a footer and then type `Page`. Press the SPACEBAR, click the Page Number button (Header & Footer Tools Design tab | Header & Footer Elements group) to insert the page number, press the SPACEBAR, and then type `of` followed by the SPACEBAR.

- Click the Number of Pages button (Header & Footer Tools Design tab | Header & Footer Elements group) to add the number of pages to the footer (Figure 6–48).

Figure 6–48

Experiment

- Click the left Footer box, and then click other buttons in the Header & Footer Elements group on the Header & Footer Tools Design tab.

- Click the right Footer box to display the results, and then delete the contents of the left Footer box.

Q&A

What does Excel insert when I click a button in the Header & Footer Tools group on the Ribbon?

Excel enters a code (similar to a format code) into the active header or footer section. A code such as &[Page] instructs Excel to insert the page number.

4

- Click anywhere on the worksheet to deselect the page footer.

- Click the Normal view button on the status bar to return to Normal view and then select cell A12.

- Display the Page Layout tab and then click the Page Setup Dialog Box Launcher (Page Layout tab | Page Setup group) to display the Page Setup dialog box.

- Click the Print Preview button (Page Setup dialog box) to preview the current sheet in the Backstage view (Figure 6–49).

Figure 6–49

5

- Click the Next Page button and Previous Page buttons below the preview to preview the other pages.

- After previewing the printout, display the Home tab.

To Print All Worksheets in a Workbook

The following steps print all four sheets in the workbook.

1 Ready the printer.

2 Open the Backstage view, click the Print tab in the Backstage view to display the Print gallery, and then click the Print button to print the workbook as shown in Figure 6–50.

3 Hold down the SHIFT key and then click the Consolidated sheet tab to deselect all sheets but the Consolidated sheet.

Figure 6–50

To Print Nonadjacent Sheets in a Workbook

In some situations, nonadjacent sheets in a workbook may need to be printed. To select nonadjacent sheets, select the first sheet and then hold down the CTRL key and click the nonadjacent sheets. The following steps print the nonadjacent Consolidated and Parks and Recreation sheets.

1 With the Consolidated sheet active, hold down the CTRL key, and then click the Parks and Recreation sheet tab.

2 Open the Backstage view, click the Print tab in the Backstage view to display the Print gallery, and then click the Print button to print the nonadjacent worksheets.

3 Hold down the SHIFT key and click the Consolidated sheet tab to deselect the Parks and Recreation sheet.

Selecting and Deselecting Sheets

Beginning Excel users sometimes have difficulty trying to select and deselect sheets. Table 6–9 summarizes how to select and deselect sheets.

Table 6–9 Summary of How to Select and Deselect Sheets	
Task	**How to Carry Out the Task**
Select adjacent sheets	Select the first sheet by clicking its tab and then hold down the SHIFT key and click the sheet tab at the other end of the list of adjacent sheet tabs.
Select nonadjacent sheets	Select the first sheet by clicking its tab and then hold down the CTRL key and click the sheet tabs of the remaining sheets you want to select.
Multiple sheets are selected and you want to select a sheet that is selected, but not active (sheet tab name not in bold)	Click the sheet tab you want to select.
Multiple sheets are selected and you want to select the active sheet (sheet tab name in bold)	Hold down the SHIFT key and then click the sheet tab of the active sheet.

To Insert and Remove a Page Break

When you print a worksheet or use the Page Setup dialog box, Excel inserts **page breaks** that show the boundaries of what will print on each page. These page breaks are based upon the margins selected in the Margins sheet in the Page Setup dialog box and the type of printer you are using. If the Page breaks option is selected, Excel displays dotted lines on the worksheet to show the boundaries of each page. For example, the dotted line in Figure 6–52 shows the right boundary of the first page. If the dotted line does not show on your screen, then click the Options button in the Backstage view. When Excel displays the Excel Options dialog box, click the Advanced command to display Advanced Excel options. Scroll the window until the 'Display options for this worksheet' area appears. Click the Show page breaks check box (Figure 6–53 on page EX 403).

You can insert both horizontal and vertical page breaks in a worksheet. Manual page breaks are useful if you have a worksheet that is several pages long and you want certain parts of the worksheet to print on separate pages. For example, say you had a worksheet that comprised ten departments in sequence and each department had many rows of information. If you wanted each department to begin on a new page, then inserting page breaks would satisfy the requirement.

The following steps insert both a horizontal and vertical page break.

1

- With the Consolidated sheet active, select cell B10 and then display the Page Layout tab.

- Click the Breaks button (Page Layout tab | Page Setup group) to display the Breaks menu and then click Insert Page Break on the Breaks menu to insert a page break (Figure 6–51).

Q&A What appears on the worksheet?

Excel inserts a dotted line above row 10 indicating a horizontal page break and inserts a dotted line to the left of column B indicating a vertical page break (Figure 6–51). Excel displays a dotted line between pages.

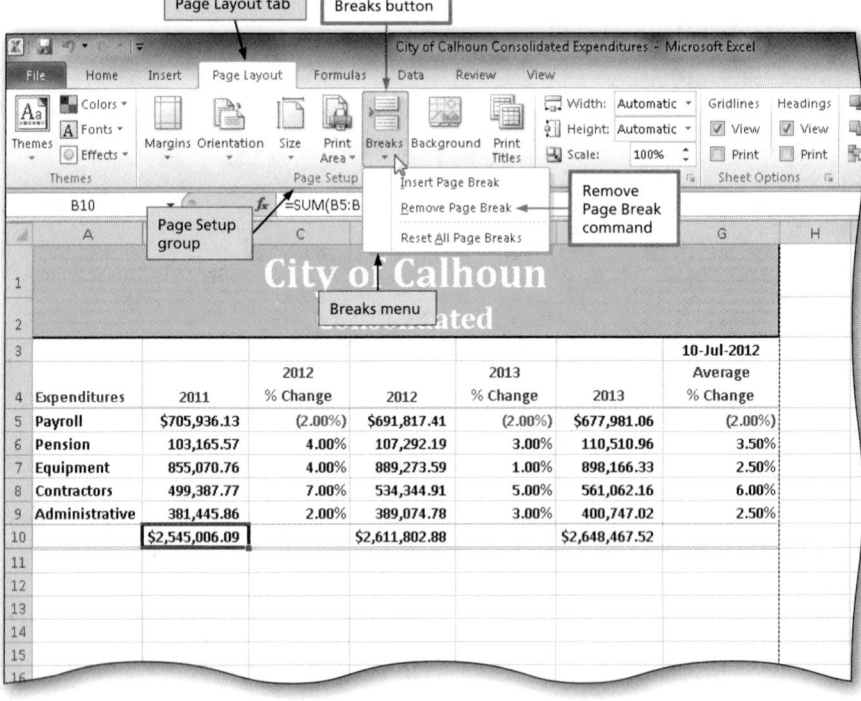

Figure 6–51

2

- With cell B10 active, click the Breaks button (Page Layout tab | Page Setup group) to display the Breaks menu (Figure 6–52).

3

- Click Remove Page Break on the Breaks menu to remove the page breaks.

Q&A Is there a way to move page breaks?

Yes. An alternative to using the Breaks button on the Page Layout tab to insert page breaks is to click the Page Break Preview button on the status bar. When the Page Break preview appears, you can drag the blue boundaries, which represent page breaks, to new locations.

Figure 6–52

Other Ways

1. Click Page Break Preview button on status bar, click OK button (Welcome to Page Break Preview dialog box), drag page breaks

To Hide Page Breaks

When working with a workbook, page breaks can be an unnecessary distraction, especially to users who have no interest in where pages break. The following steps hide the dotted lines that represent page breaks.

- Open the Backstage view.

- Click the Options button in the Backstage view to display the Excel Options dialog box.

- Click the Advanced button (Excel Options dialog box) to display Advanced Excel options.

- Scroll the window until the 'Display options for this worksheet' area appears.

- Click the 'Show page breaks' check box to clear the check box (Figure 6–53).

Figure 6–53

2

- Click the OK button to close the Excel Options dialog box and hide the page breaks (Figure 6–54).

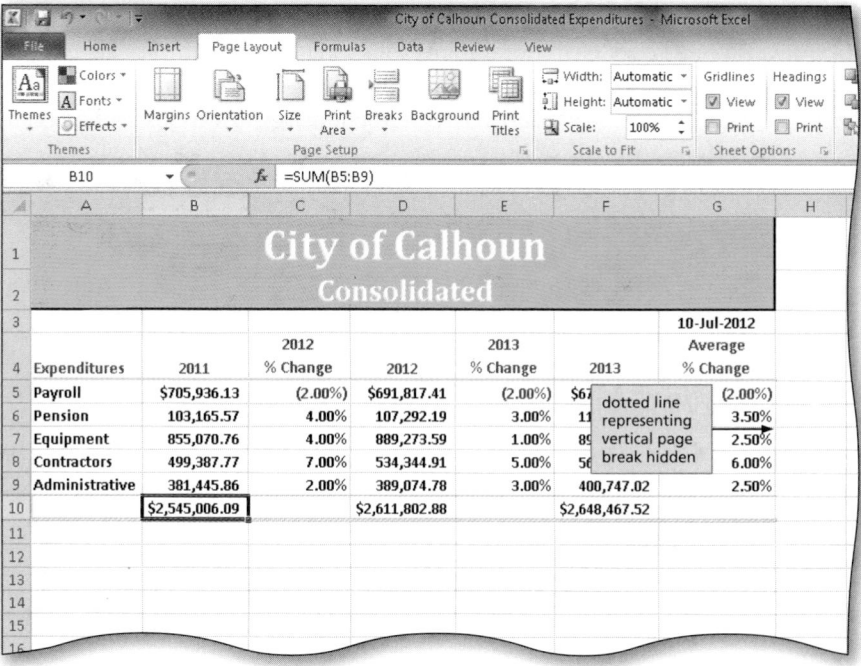

Figure 6–54

To Quit Excel

With the workbook complete, the following steps quit Excel.

1 Click the Close button on the upper-right corner of the title bar.

2 If the Microsoft Excel dialog box is displayed, click the Don't Save button so that any changes made to the workbook are not saved (Microsoft Excel dialog box).

BTW

Consolidation
You also can consolidate data across different workbooks using the Consolidate button (Data tab | Data Tools group), rather than by entering formulas. For more information on the Consolidate button, type consolidate in the Search box in the Excel Help dialog box, and then click the 'Consolidate data in multiple worksheets' link in the Results list.

Consolidating Data by Linking Workbooks

Earlier in this chapter, the data from three worksheets was consolidated into a fourth worksheet in the same workbook using 3-D references. An alternative to this method is to consolidate data from worksheets that are in other workbooks. Consolidating data from other workbooks also is referred to as linking. A **link** is a reference to a cell or range of cells in another workbook. In the case below, the 3-D reference also includes a workbook name. For example, the following 3-D reference pertains to cell B5 on the Public Works sheet in the workbook City of Calhoun Consolidated Expenditures located on drive E.

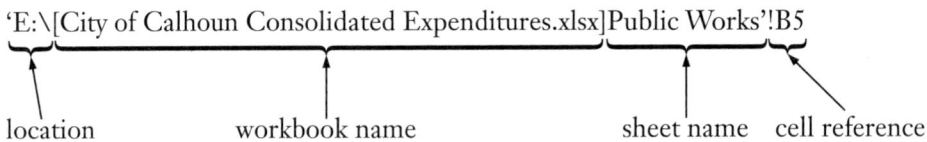

'E:\[City of Calhoun Consolidated Expenditures.xlsx]Public Works'!B5

        location   workbook name   sheet name   cell reference

The single quotation marks surrounding the location, workbook name, and sheet name are required if any of the three names contain spaces. If the workbook to which you are referring is in the same folder as the active workbook, the location (in this case, E:\) is not necessary. The brackets surrounding the workbook name are required.

To illustrate linking cells between workbooks, the Consolidated, Public Works, Police and Fire, and Parks and Recreation worksheets from the workbook created earlier in this chapter are on the Data Files for Students in separate workbooks as described in Table 6–10. The department workbooks contain the department data, but the Calhoun Consolidated Expenditures workbook does not include any consolidated data. The consolidation of data from the three department workbooks into the Calhoun Consolidated Expenditures workbook will be completed later in this section.

BTW

Quick Reference
For a table that lists how to complete the tasks covered in this book using the mouse, Ribbon, shortcut menu, and keyboard, see the Quick Reference Summary at the back of this book, or visit the Excel 2010 Quick Reference Web page (scsite.com/ex2010/qr).

Table 6–10 Workbook Names	
Worksheet in Calhoun Consolidated Expenditures Workbook Using the Workbook Name	**Saved on the Data Files for Students As**
Consolidated	Calhoun Consolidated Expenditures
Public Works	Calhoun Public Works Expenditures
Police and Fire	Calhoun Police and Fire Expenditures
Parks and Recreation	Calhoun Parks and Recreation Expenditures

The remaining sections of this chapter demonstrate how to search for the four workbooks in Table 6–10 on a USB flash drive, how to create a workspace from the four workbooks, and finally how to link the three department workbooks to consolidate the data into the Calhoun Consolidated Expenditures workbook.

To Search for and Open Workbooks

Excel has a powerful search tool that you can use to locate workbooks (or any file) stored on disk. You search for files using the Search text box in the Open dialog box. If you view files on the Data Files for Students, then you will see the four workbooks listed in the right column of Table 6–10. The following steps, however, search for workbooks and often are used when you cannot remember exactly the name of the file or its location. In this example, the search text Calhoun will be used to locate the workbooks. The located workbooks then are opened and **arranged** so that each one appears in its own window.

- Start Excel.

- Open the Backstage view.

- Click the Open button to display the Open dialog box and then select the drive for your USB port, Removable (E:) in this case, in the Address bar to select a drive to search.

- Type **Calhoun** in the Search box as the search text (Figure 6–55).

Figure 6–55

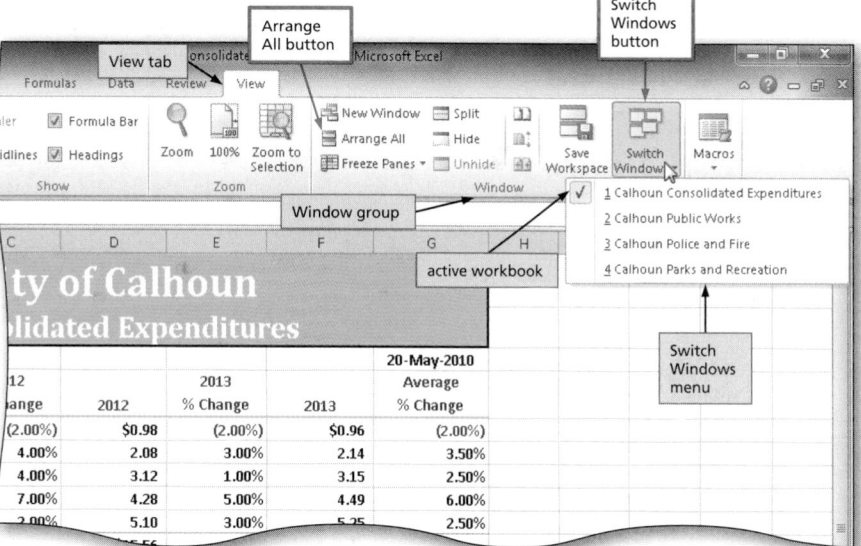

- In the File list, while holding down the CTRL key, click each of the three department workbook names one at a time and then click the Calhoun Consolidated Expenditures workbook name to select several workbooks to open.

- Click the Open button (Open dialog box) to open the selected workbooks.

- Display the View tab and then click the Switch Windows button (View tab | Window group) to display the names of the workbooks with a check mark to the left of the active workbook (Figure 6–56).

Figure 6–56

- Click the Arrange All button (View tab | Window group) to display the Arrange Windows dialog box.

- Click Vertical (Arrange Windows dialog box) to arrange the windows vertically, and then, if necessary, click the 'Windows of active workbook' check box to clear it (Figure 6–57).

Q&A

How can I arrange workbooks in the Excel window?

As shown in Figure 6–57, multiple opened workbooks can be arranged in

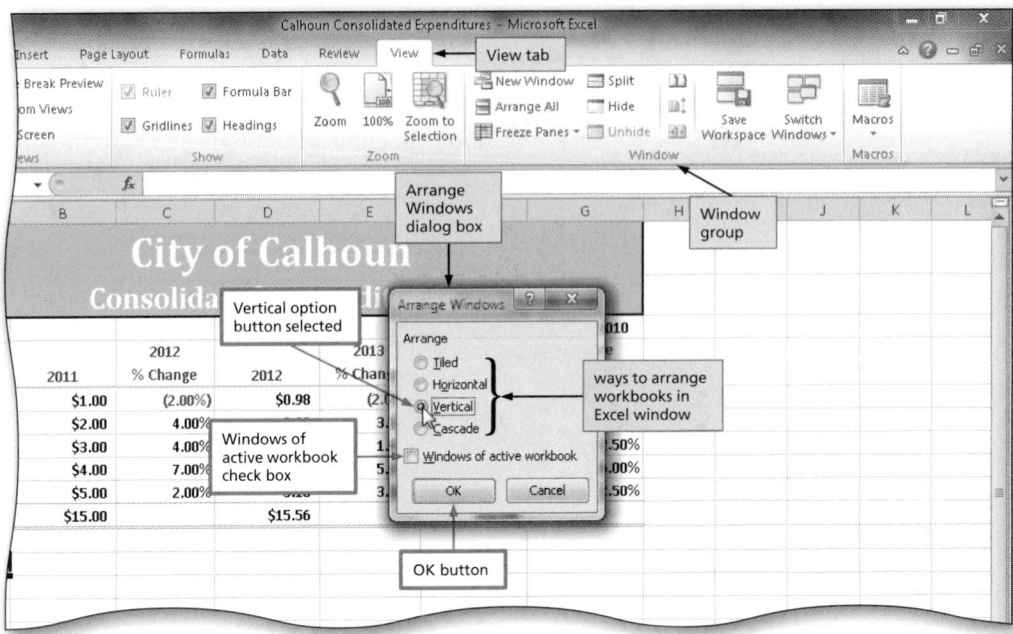

Figure 6–57

four ways. The option name in the Arrange Windows dialog box identifies the resulting window's configuration. You can modify any of the arranged workbooks by clicking within its window to activate it. To return to showing one workbook, double-click its title bar as described in Step 5.

- Click the OK button (Arrange Windows dialog box) to display the opened workbooks arranged vertically (Figure 6–58).

Q&A

Why do the windows display horizontally across the screen, yet the screens were tiled vertically?

The tiling effect determines the change on an individual window, not the group of windows. When

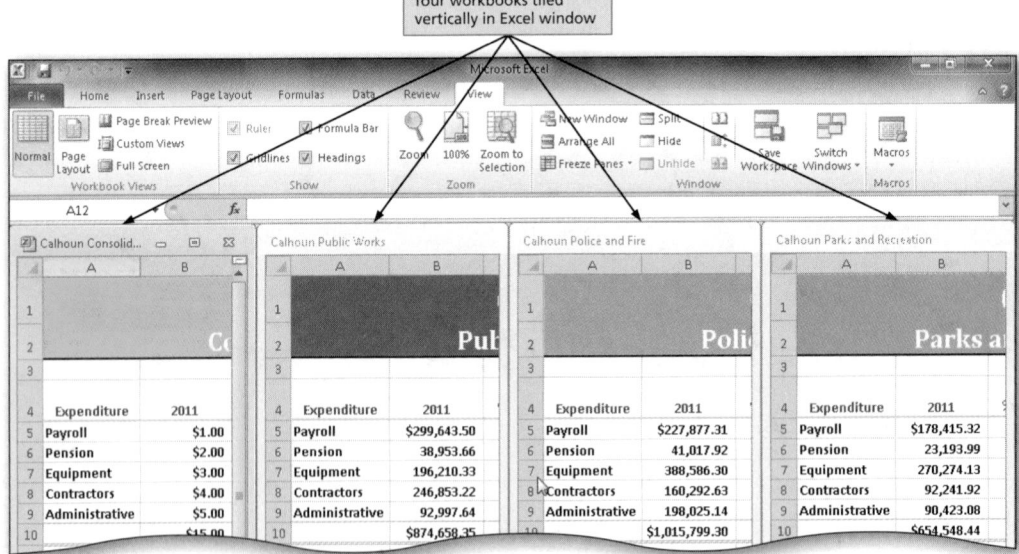

Figure 6–58

tiling windows vertically, therefore, each individual window appears vertically as tall as possible. When tiling windows horizontally, the windows appear as wide as possible.

- Double-click the Calhoun Consolidated Expenditures title bar to maximize the window and hide the other opened workbooks.

To Create a Workspace File

If you plan to consolidate data from other workbooks, it is recommended that you first bind the workbooks together using a workspace file. A **workspace file** saves information about all the workbooks that are open. The workspace file does not contain the actual workbooks; rather, it stores information required to open the files associated with the workspace file, including file names, which file was active at the time of the save, and other display settings. After you create and save a workspace file, you can open all of the associated files by opening the workspace. The following steps create a workspace file from the files opened in the previous set of steps.

1

- With the four workbooks opened and the Calhoun Consolidated Expenditures workbook active, if necessary, display the View tab (Figure 6–59).

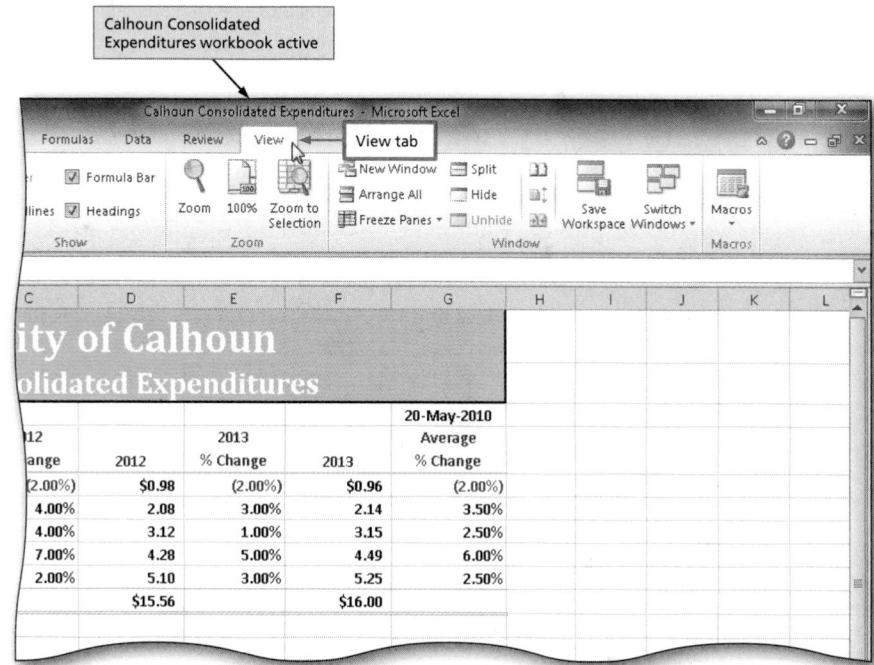

Figure 6–59

2

- Click the Save Workspace button (View tab | Window group) to display the Save Workspace dialog box.

- Select the drive for your USB port, Removable (E:) in this case, in the Address bar (Save Workspace dialog box).

- Navigate to the desired save location (in this case, the Excel folder in the CIS 101 folder [or your class folder] on the USB flash drive).

- Type **Calhoun Workspace** in the File name box to enter a name of a workspace to save (Figure 6–60).

Q&A Can I still open the workbooks separately or must I always open the workspace?

Figure 6–60

After the workspace is saved to disk, you can open the workbooks one at a time as you did in the past, or you can open all of the associated workbooks by opening the workspace. When you invoke the Open command, workspace file names appear in the Open dialog box, the same as any workbook file name.

- Click the Save button (Save Workspace dialog box) to save the file names of the workbooks open, of the workbooks displaying, and other display settings.

- If the Microsoft Excel dialog box is displayed for any of the workbooks, click the Don't Save button to ensure that any changes inadvertently made to the workbooks do not get saved.

- Open the Backstage view and then click the Exit button to quit Excel.

- If the Microsoft Excel dialog box is displayed for any workbooks that remain open, click the Don't Save button to ensure that any changes inadvertently made to the workbooks are not saved.

To Consolidate Data by Linking Workbooks

The following steps open the workspace file Calhoun Workspace and consolidate the data from the three department workbooks into the Calhoun Consolidated Expenditures workbook.

- Start Excel. Open the Backstage view and then click the Open button to display the Open dialog box.

- Navigate to the desired open location (in this case, the Excel folder in the CIS 101 folder [or your class folder] on the USB flash drive).

- Double-click Calhoun Workspace to open the four workbooks saved in the workspace.

- Make Calhoun Consolidated Expenditures the active worksheet. If necessary, double-click the Calhoun Consolidated Expenditures window title bar to maximize it.

2

- Select cell B5 and then click the Sum button (Home tab | Editing group) to begin a SUM function entry.

- Display the View tab and then click the Switch Windows button (View tab | Window group) to display the Switch Windows menu.

- Click Calhoun Public Works on the Switch Windows menu to select a worksheet to reference. Click cell B5 and then delete the dollar signs ($) in the reference to cell B5 in the formula bar so that the reference is not absolute. Click immediately after B5 in the formula bar and then press the COMMA key.

3

- Click the Switch Windows button (View tab | Window group) to display the Switch Windows menu and then click Calhoun Police and Fire workbook name to display the workbook.

- Select cell B5 as the next argument in the SUM function.

4

- Delete the dollar signs ($) in the reference to cell B5 in the formula bar so that the reference is not absolute. Click immediately after B5 in the formula bar and then press the COMMA key.

5

- Click the Switch Windows button (View tab | Window group) to display the Switch Windows menu and then click Calhoun Parks and Recreation to select the final workbook to reference in the SUM function.

- Select cell B5. Delete the dollar signs ($) in the reference to cell B5 in the formula bar so that the reference is not absolute.

- Click the Enter box to complete the SUM function.

Q&A

Why did the formulas need to be edited for each workbook?

As you link workbooks, remember that the cell reference inserted by Excel each time you click a cell in a workbook is an absolute cell reference ($B$5). You must edit the formula and change these to relative cell references because the SUM function later is copied to the range B6:B9. If the cell references are left as absolute, then the copied function always would refer to cell B5 in the three workbooks no matter where you copy the SUM function.

- With cell B5 active in the Calhoun Consolidated Expenditures workbook, drag the cell's fill handle through cell B9, and then select cell B5 (Figure 6–61).

7

- Click the Save button on the Quick Access Toolbar to save the workbook. If Excel displays a dialog box, select Overwrite changes.

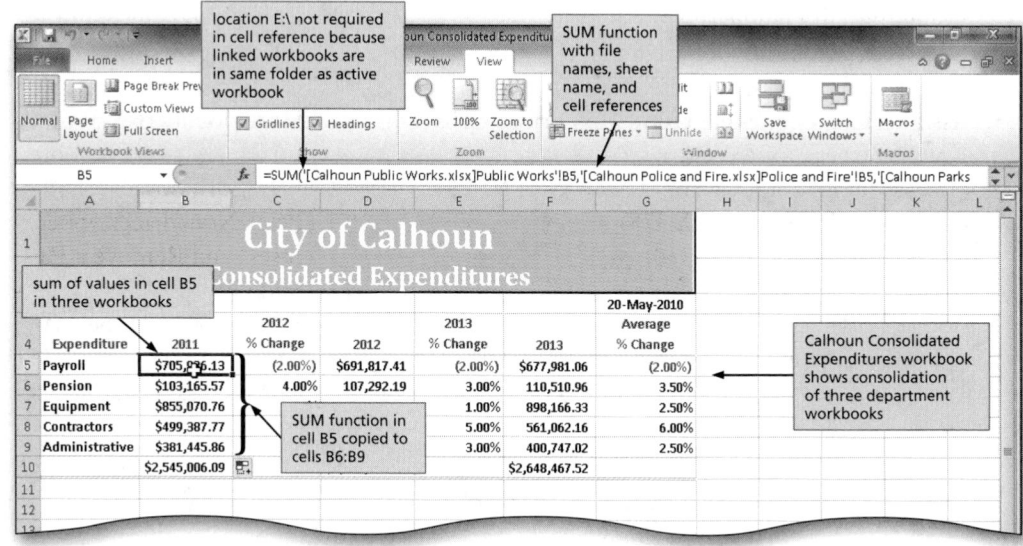

Figure 6–61

- If necessary, click the OK button (Microsoft Excel dialog box) to save the workbook.

- Print the worksheet.

Updating Links

Later, if you open the Calhoun Consolidated Expenditures workbook by itself, also called the **dependent workbook**, and if the linked workbooks are open, Excel automatically reads the data in the linked workbooks and recalculates formulas in the dependent workbook. The linked workbooks are called the **source workbooks**.

If the linked workbooks are not open, then Excel displays a security warning in a pane below the Ribbon. If you click the Enable Content button in the warning pane, Excel reads the data in the source workbooks and recalculates the formulas in the dependent workbook, but it does not open the source workbooks. If the three source workbooks are open along with the dependent workbook, as in the previous set of steps, Excel automatically updates the links (recalculates) in the Calhoun Consolidated Expenditures workbook when a value changes in any one of the source workbooks.

To Close All Workbooks at One Time and Quit Excel

To close all four workbooks at one time and quit Excel, complete the following steps.

1 Open the Backstage view and then click the Exit button to quit Excel.

2 If Excel displays the Microsoft Excel dialog box, click the Don't Save button.

BTW

Workspace Files
A workspace file saves display information about open workbooks, such as window sizes, print areas, screen magnification, and display settings. Workspace files do not contain the workbooks themselves.

BTW

Certification
The Microsoft Office Specialist (MOS) program provides an opportunity for you to obtain a valuable industry credential — proof that you have the Excel 2010 skills required by employers. For more information, visit the Excel 2010 Certification Web page (scsite.com/ex2010/cert).

Chapter Summary

In this chapter, you learned how to create and use a consolidated worksheet, customize formats, create styles, use 3-D reference to reference cells in other sheets and workbooks, add, remove, and change pages breaks, and create a workspace file. The items listed below include all the new Excel skills you have learned in this chapter.

1. Enter Sample Data in the Consolidated Worksheet Using the Fill Handle (EX 369)
2. Enter Formulas and Determine Totals in the Consolidated Worksheet (EX 371)
3. Assign a Currency Style Using the Format Cells Dialog Box (EX 376)
4. Create and Assign a Custom Format Code and a Comma Style Format (EX 378)
5. Create a New Style (EX 380)
6. Apply a New Style (EX 382)
7. Add a Worksheet to a Workbook (EX 384)
8. Copy the Contents of a Worksheet to Other Worksheets in a Workbook (EX 385)
9. Drill an Entry through Worksheets (EX 386)
10. Enter and Copy 3-D References Using the Paste Button Gallery (EX 391)
11. Change Margins and Center the Printout Horizontally (EX 396)
12. Add a Header and Footer (EX 397)
13. Print All Worksheets in a Workbook (EX 399)
14. Print Nonadjacent Sheets in a Workbook (EX 401)
15. Insert and Remove a Page Break (EX 401)
16. Hide Page Breaks (EX 403)
17. Search for and Open Workbooks (EX 405)
18. Create a Workspace File (EX 407)
19. Consolidate Data by Linking Workbooks (EX 408)

 If you have a SAM 2010 user profile, your instructor may have assigned an autogradable version of this assignment. If so, log into the SAM 2010 Web site at www.cengage.com/sam2010 to download the instruction and start files.

Learn It Online

Test your knowledge of chapter content and key terms.

Instructions: To complete the Learn It Online exercises, start your browser, click the Address bar, and then enter the Web address `scsite.com/ex2010/learn`. When the Excel 2010 Learn It Online page is displayed, click the link for the exercise you want to complete and then read the instructions.

Chapter Reinforcement TF, MC, and SA
A series of true/false, multiple choice, and short answer questions that test your knowledge of the chapter content.

Flash Cards
An interactive learning environment where you identify chapter key terms associated with displayed definitions.

Practice Test
A series of multiple choice questions that test your knowledge of chapter content and key terms.

Who Wants To Be a Computer Genius?
An interactive game that challenges your knowledge of chapter content in the style of a television quiz show.

Wheel of Terms
An interactive game that challenges your knowledge of chapter key terms in the style of the television show *Wheel of Fortune*.

Crossword Puzzle Challenge
A crossword puzzle that challenges your knowledge of key terms presented in the chapter.

Apply Your Knowledge

Reinforce the skills and apply the concepts you learned in this chapter.

Consolidating Data in a Workbook

Note: To complete this assignment, you will be required to use the Data Files for Students. See the inside back cover of this book for instructions on downloading the Data Files for Students, or contact your instructor for information about accessing the required files.

Instructions: Follow the steps below to consolidate the four quarterly mileage cost sheets on the Yearly Costs sheet in the workbook Apply 6-1 Yearly Mileage Costs (Figure 6–62). At the conclusion of the instructions, the Yearly Mileage Costs sheet be should displayed as shown in the lower screen in Figure 6–62.

Figure 6–62

Continued >

Apply Your Knowledge *continued*

Perform the following tasks:

1. Start Excel. Open the workbook Apply 6-1 Yearly Mileage Costs from the Data Files for Students and then save the workbook as Apply 6-1 Yearly Mileage Costs Complete. One by one, click the first four tabs and review the quarterly payroll totals. Click the Yearly Mileage Costs sheet tab.

2. Determine the miles driven totals on the Yearly Mileage Costs sheet by using the SUM function and 3-D references to sum the miles driven on the four quarterly sheets in cell B5. Do the same to determine the yearly mileage cost in cell C5. Copy the range B5:C5 to the range B6:C9 by using the Copy button (Home tab | Clipboard group) and the Formulas command on the Paste gallery (Home tab | Clipboard group).

3. Change the document properties as specified by your instructor. Select all five worksheets. Add a worksheet header with your name, course number, and other information as specified by your instructor. Add the page number and total number of pages to the footer. Center all worksheets horizontally on the page and print without gridlines. Preview and print the five worksheets. Click the Yearly Mileage Costs sheet tab to select the sheet.

4. Save the workbook with the new page setup. Close the workbook.

5. Submit the assignment as requested by your instructor.

Extend Your Knowledge

Extend the skills you learned in this chapter and experiment with new skills. You may need to use Help to complete the assignment.

Creating Custom Format Codes

Note: To complete this assignment, you will be required to use the Data Files for Students. See the inside back cover of this book for instructions on downloading the Data Files for Students, or contact your instructor for information about accessing the required files.

Instructions: Complete the following tasks.

1. Start Excel. Open the workbook Extend 6-1 Custom Format Codes from the Data Files for Students and then save the workbook as Extend 6-1 Custom Format Codes Complete. When completed, the Custom Formats sheet should appear as shown in Figure 6–63.

	A	B	C	D	E	F
1	Custom Format Codes					
2						
3						
4	10-digit phone number	(321) 787-4955				
5	6-digit number with text	PID 025831				
6	dollars and cents	110 dollars and .95 cents				
7	negative number with text	150.00 loss				
8	4-digit year with text	The year is 2012				
9	day followed by date	Thursday - 8/9/2012				
10	day and month with text	Day 4 of June				
11	negative % with parenthesis	(-80%)				
12	% and text	75% of work completed				
13	hours and minutes	11 hours and 30 minutes				
14	military time with text	1700 hours				
15						
16						

Figure 6–63

2. Select cell B4. Right-click the selected cell and click Format Cells on the shortcut menu to display the Format Cells dialog box. Click Custom in the Category list. Enter the format code for cell B4 as shown in Table 6–11.

Table 6–11 Format Codes	
Cell	**Format Code**
B4	(000) 000–0000
B5	"PID" 000000
B6	0 "dollars and" .00 "cents"
B7	#,##0.00; #,##0.00 "loss"
B8	"The year is " yyyy
B9	dddd "-" m/d/yyyy
B10	"Day " d "of" mmmm
B11	0%;(–0%)
B12	0% " of work completed"
B13	h "hours and " mm "minutes"
B14	hhmm "hours"

3. Using Table 6–11, select each cell in range B5:B14 and create the corresponding custom format code for each cell using the Format Cells dialog box.

4. Change the document properties as specified by your instructor. Change the worksheet header with your name, course number, and other information as specified by your instructor. Print the worksheet. Save the workbook.

5. Submit the assignment as requested by your instructor.

Make It Right

Analyze a workbook and correct all errors and/or improve the design.

Using Custom Formats, Rounding Totals, and Correcting 3-D Cell References

Note: To complete this assignment, you will be required to use the Data Files for Students. See the inside back cover of this book for instructions on downloading the Data Files for Students, or contact your instructor for information about accessing the required files.

Instructions: Start Excel. Open the workbook Make It Right 6-1 Maxwell Books and then save the workbook as Make It Right 6-1 Maxwell Books Complete. Correct the following design and formula problems so that the Sales Totals sheet appears as shown in Figure 6–64 on the following page.

Continued >

Make It Right *continued*

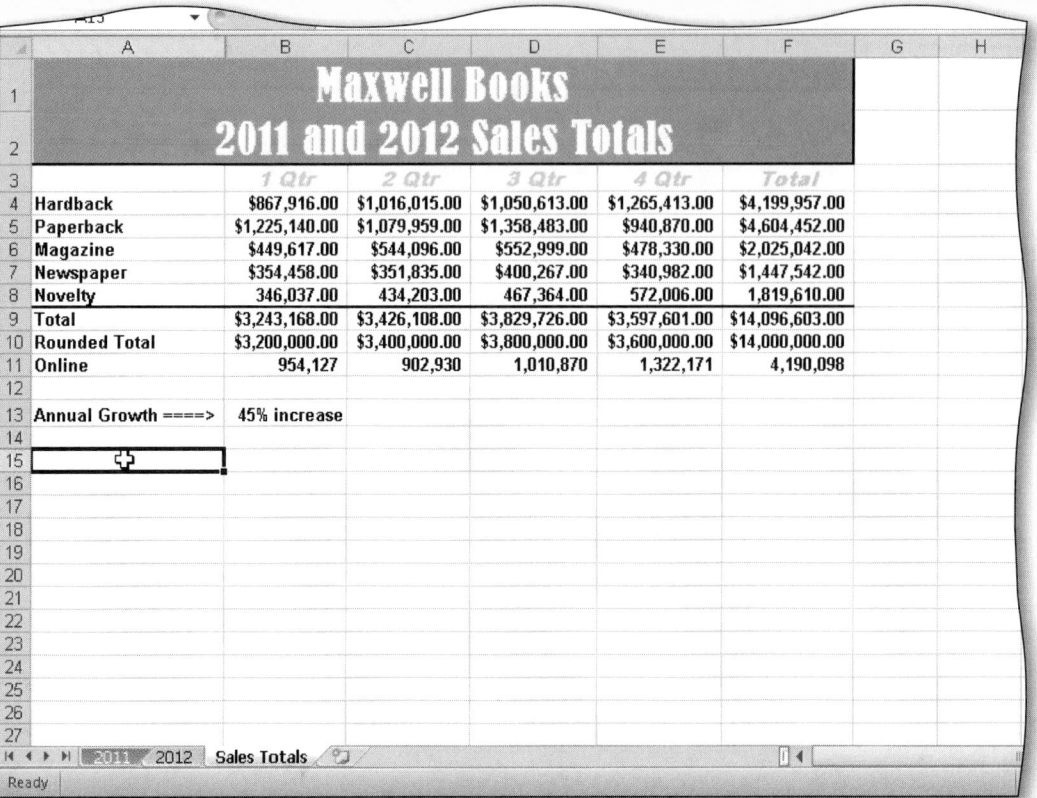

The worksheet shows:

	A	B	C	D	E	F
1			Maxwell Books			
2			2011 and 2012 Sales Totals			
3		*1 Qtr*	*2 Qtr*	*3 Qtr*	*4 Qtr*	*Total*
4	Hardback	$867,916.00	$1,016,015.00	$1,050,613.00	$1,265,413.00	$4,199,957.00
5	Paperback	$1,225,140.00	$1,079,959.00	$1,358,483.00	$940,870.00	$4,604,452.00
6	Magazine	$449,617.00	$544,096.00	$552,999.00	$478,330.00	$2,025,042.00
7	Newspaper	$354,458.00	$351,835.00	$400,267.00	$340,982.00	$1,447,542.00
8	Novelty	346,037.00	434,203.00	467,364.00	572,006.00	1,819,610.00
9	Total	$3,243,168.00	$3,426,108.00	$3,829,726.00	$3,597,601.00	$14,096,603.00
10	Rounded Total	$3,200,000.00	$3,400,000.00	$3,800,000.00	$3,600,000.00	$14,000,000.00
11	Online	954,127	902,930	1,010,870	1,322,171	4,190,098
12						
13	Annual Growth ====>	45% increase				

Sheet tabs: 2011 / 2012 / Sales Totals

Figure 6–64

Perform the following tasks:

1. Edit the header for the worksheet and change the fixed date to the current date using the Current Date header element.

2. Select the cell range B3:E3. Change the custom format code by using the Format Cells Dialog box to change the format to show a number followed by the text "Qtr".

3. Select cell B4, the supposed sum of cell B4 on the 2011 and 2012 sheets. Note that the SUM function is not referencing cell B4 on the 2011 sheet. Reenter the SUM function and select the appropriate range to sum. Do the same for cells B5, B6, B7, and B8. Copy the range B4:B8 to the range C4:E8.

4. Select cell B11, the supposed sum of cell B10 on the 2011 and 2012 sheets. Note that the SUM function is not referencing cell B10 on the 2011 and 2012 sheet. Reenter the SUM function and select the appropriate range to sum. Copy the cell B11 to the range C11:E11.

5. Select Cell B10, the supposed rounded value of B9 to the nearest 100,000 value. Note that the value is rounding to the nearest 100 value. Reenter the ROUND function to round to the nearest 100,000 value. Copy the cell B10 to the range C10:E10.

6. Select cell B13. Change the custom format code by using the Format Cells Dialog box to change the format to show the percent followed by the text "increase".

7. Change the document properties as specified by your instructor. Change the three worksheet headers to include your name, course number, and other information as specified by your instructor.

8. Save the workbook, and submit the revised workbook as requested by your instructor.

In the Lab

Create a workbook using the guidelines, concepts, and skills presented in this chapter. Labs are listed in order of increasing difficulty.

Lab 1: Using a Master Sheet to Create a Multiple-Sheet Workbook

Note: To complete this assignment, you will be required to use the Data Files for Students. See the inside back cover of this book for instructions on downloading the Data Files for Students, or contact your instructor for information about accessing the required files.

Problem: AtHome Blu-Ray is a company that specializes in home Blu-Ray players. The company has three stores in Chicago, New York, and Seattle. Their corporate office is in Los Angeles. The corporate officers in Los Angeles use a master sheet to create a profit potential analysis workbook. The workbook contains four sheets, one for each of the three stores and one sheet to consolidate data and determine the company totals. The Consolidated sheet appears as shown in Figure 6–65.

AtHome Blu-Ray
Company Profit Potential

						May 20	
Company	Units On Hand	Store Discount	Average Cost	Total Cost	Average Unit Price	Total Value	Profit Potential
Memorex	371	$40.00	$98.75	$36,636.25	$105.22	$39,036.62	$2,400.37
Phillips	355	10.00	127.45	45,244.75	177.43	62,987.65	17,742.90
Pioneer	633	26.67	118.75	75,168.75	147.96	93,660.79	18,492.04
Samsung	485	15.00	101.48	49,217.80	134.24	65,106.40	15,888.60
Sony	555	28.33	135.27	75,074.85	170.60	94,681.15	19,606.30
Sylvania	679	30.00	165.80	112,578.20	213.82	145,183.78	32,605.58
Vizio	685	55.00	110.25	75,521.25	107.13	73,384.05	(2,137.20)
	3,763 Units			$469,441.85		$574,040.44	$104,598.59

Consolidated Chicago New York Seattle

Figure 6–65

The master sheet used to create the profit potential analysis workbook is part of the Data Files for Students. Alice Stewart, the company's accountant, has asked you to use the master sheet to create the profit potential analysis workbook.

Instructions Part 1: *Perform the following tasks.*

1. Open the workbook Lab 6-1 AtHome Blu-Ray Master from the Data Files for Students. Save the workbook as a workbook using the file name, Lab 6-1 AtHome Blu-Ray Profit Potential Analysis.

2. Add a worksheet to the workbook between Sheet1 and Sheet2 and then paste the contents of Sheet1 to the three empty sheets.

Continued >

In the Lab *continued*

3. From left to right, rename the sheet tabs Consolidated, Chicago, New York, and Seattle. Color the tabs as shown in Figure 6–65. (The Consolidated tab uses the Tan, Accent 1 color.) On each of the three store sheets, change the subtitle in cell A2 to match the sheet tab name. Change the title style for each title area in the range A1:A2 to match the sheet tab color. Enter the data in Table 6–12 into the three store sheets.

Table 6–12 AtHome Blu-Ray Units on Hand and Store Discounts		Units on Hand	Store Discounts
Chicago	Memorex	100	$35.00
	Phillips	119	0.00
	Pioneer	135	15.00
	Samsung	180	35.00
	Sony	255	60.00
	Sylvania	179	10.00
	Vizio	201	50.00
New York	Memorex	75	$35.00
	Phillips	135	15.00
	Pioneer	200	30.00
	Samsung	146	10.00
	Sony	90	0.00
	Sylvania	175	25.00
	Vizio	225	60.00
Seattle	Memorex	196	$50.00
	Phillips	101	15.00
	Pioneer	298	35.00
	Samsung	159	0.00
	Sony	210	25.00
	Sylvania	325	55.00
	Vizio	259	55.00

4. On the Consolidated worksheet, use the SUM and AVERAGE functions, 3-D references, and copy and paste capabilities of Excel to total the corresponding cells on the three store sheets. First, compute the sum in cell B5 and then compute the average in cell C5. Copy the range B5:C5 to the range B6:C11. The Consolidated sheet should resemble Figure 6–65.

5. Change the document properties as specified by your instructor. Select all four sheets. Add a worksheet header with your name, course number, and other information as specified by your instructor. Add the page number and total number of pages to the footer. Change the left and right margins to .5.

6. With the four sheets selected, preview and then print the workbook in landscape orientation and use the Black and white option.

7. Save the workbook with the new page setup characteristics. Close the workbook.

8. Submit the assignment as requested by your instructor.

Instructions Part 2:   Complete the following tasks.

1. Start Excel. Open the workbook Lab 6-1 AtHome Blu-Ray Profit Potential Analysis.

2. Select the range D6:H11 on the Consolidated worksheet. Select all the worksheets.

3. Use the Format Cells dialog box to apply a custom format of #,##0.00; [Green](#,##0.00).

4. Select the cell B12 on the Consolidated worksheet. Select all the worksheets.

5. Use the Format Cells dialog box to apply a custom format of #,##0 "Units". Widen Column B so that contents of cell B12 are visible.

6. Save the workbook and then close the workbook.

7. Submit the assignment as requested by your instructor.

Instructions Part 3:   Complete the following tasks.

1. Start Excel. Open the workbook Lab 6-1 AtHome Blu-Ray Profit Potential Analysis.

2. Use the Cell Styles button (Home tab | Styles group) to create the following new cell styles:

   a. Name this style Month and Day. Use the Format button in the Cell Styles gallery to create a format using the Format Cells dialog box. Use the Number tab (Format Cells dialog box) to create a custom format using the format code mmmm d. Check only the Number and Alignment check boxes in the Style dialog box.

   b. Name this style My Title. Use the Format button to create a format using the Format Cells dialog box. Use the Font tab (Format Cells dialog box) to select the Broadway font. Check only the Alignment and Font check boxes in the Style dialog box.

   c. Name this style Grand Totals. Use the Format button in the Cell Styles gallery to create a format using the Format Cells dialog box. Use the Number tab (Format Cells dialog box) to create a custom currency style that colors negative numbers blue. Check only the Number and Alignment check boxes in the Style dialog box.

3. Select the cell H3 on the Consolidated worksheet. Select all the worksheets. Apply the Month and Day style to the cell.

4. Select the cell A1 on the Consolidated worksheet. Select all the worksheets. Apply the My Title style to the cell.

5. Select the cells E12, G12, and H12 on the Consolidated worksheet. Select all the worksheets. Apply the Grand Totals style to the cells.

6. Save the workbook and then close the workbook.

7. Submit the assignment as requested by your instructor.

In the Lab

Lab 2: Consolidating Data and Linking to a Workbook

Note: To complete this assignment, you will be required to use the Data Files for Students. See the inside back cover of this book for instructions on downloading the Data Files for Students, or contact your instructor for information about accessing the required files.

Problem: SciMat Containment is a company that manages three radioactive isotope containment facilities in the Western, Central, and Southern regions. Some agency watchdogs are concerned about containment costs while the material still is radioactive. The agency director has asked your group to prepare a workbook showing the amount of radioactive material remaining, containment costs, estimated agency appropriations, and the percentage of appropriations that will be spent on

Continued >

In the Lab *continued*

containment every year for the next decade. You have been given a master sheet to use to create your workbook as well as a workbook with the containment assumptions. The workbook you create will contain four sheets, one for each of the three regions and one sheet to consolidate data and determine the agency totals. The consolidated sheet, named Overall Costs, appears as shown in Figure 6–66.

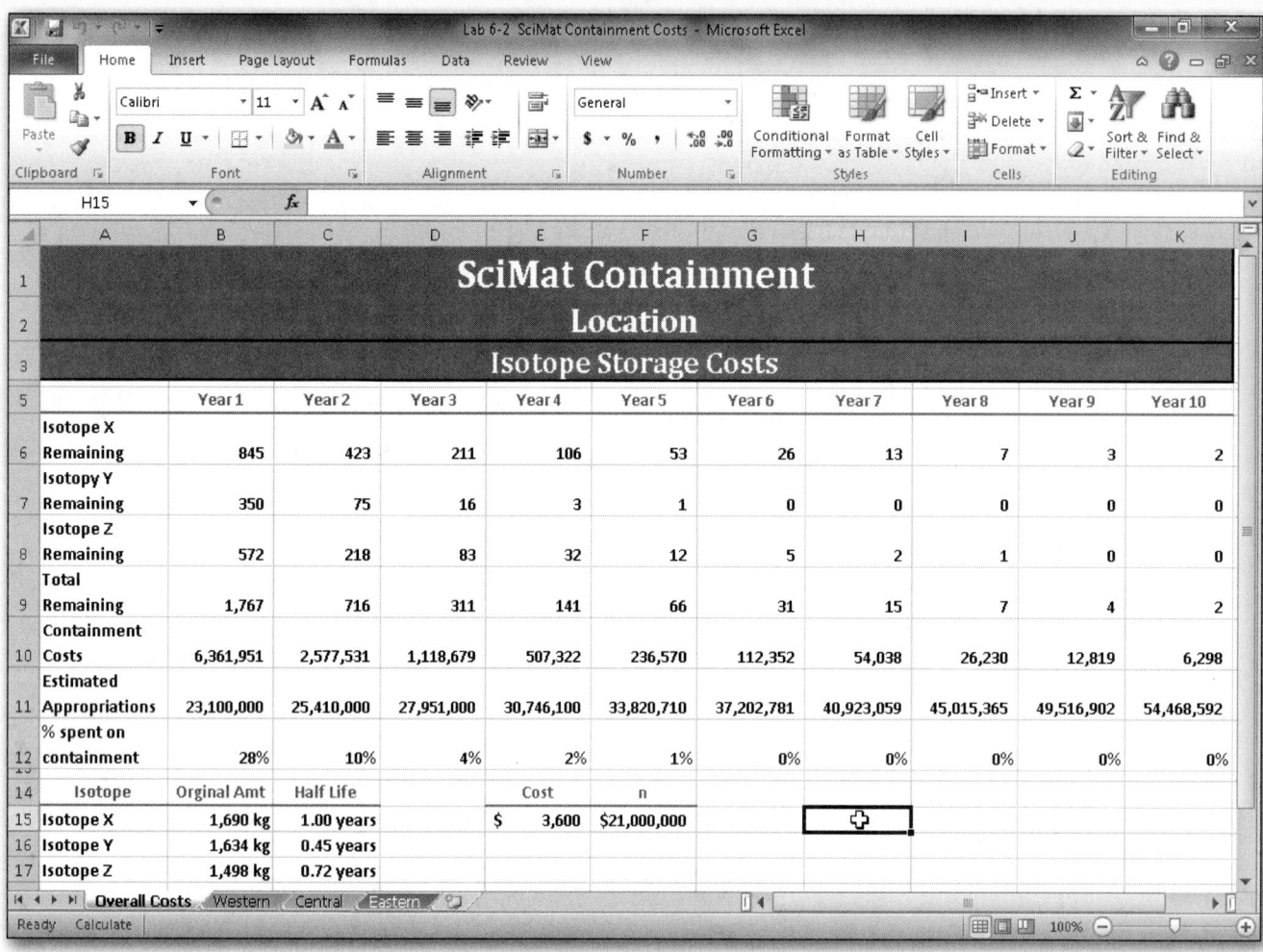

Figure 6–66

The master sheet and containment assumptions used to create the containment analysis workbook are part of the Data Files for Students.

Instructions Part 1: Perform the following tasks.

1. Open the workbook Lab 6-2 Containment Assumptions from the Data Files for Students.

2. Open the workbook Lab 6-2 SciMat Containment Master from the Data Files for Students. Save the workbook as a workbook using the file name, Lab 6-2 SciMat Containment Costs.

3. Add a worksheet to the workbook between Sheet1 and Sheet2 and then paste the contents of Sheet1 to the three empty sheets.

4. From left to right, rename the sheet tabs Overall Costs, Western, Central, and Eastern. Color the tabs as shown in Figure 6–66. (The Overall Costs tab uses the Tan, Accent 1, Darker 50% color.) On each of the three region sheets, change the subtitle in cell A2 to match the tab name.

Change the title style for each title area in the range A1:A3 to match the tab color. Enter the data in Table 6–13 into the three region sheets.

Table 6–13 SciMat Containment Isotope Starting Amounts		Original AMT
Western	Isotope X	300
	Isotope Y	750
	Isotope Z	500
Central	Isotope X	580
	Isotope Y	425
	Isotope Z	600
Eastern	Isotope X	810
	Isotope Y	459
	Isotope Z	398

5. On the Western worksheet, select cell E15 and select all worksheets except the Overall Costs sheet. Type '='. Click the Switch Windows button (View tab | Window group), and then click Lab 6-2 Containment Assumptions and then select cell B7 and press ENTER.

6. On the Western worksheet, select cell F15, select all worksheets except the Overall Costs sheet. Type '='. Click the Switch Windows button (View tab | Window group), and then click Lab 6-2 Containment Assumptions and then select cell B8 and press ENTER.

7. On the Overall Costs worksheet, select cell C15 and select all worksheets. Type '='. Click the Switch Windows button (View tab | Window group), and then click Lab 6-2 Containment Assumptions and then select cell B4 and press ENTER.

8. On the Overall Costs worksheet, select cell C16 and select all worksheets. Type '='. Click the Switch Windows button (View tab | Window group), and then click Lab 6-2 Containment Assumptions and then select cell B5 and press ENTER.

9. On the Overall Costs worksheet, select cell C17, select all worksheets. Type '='. Click the Switch Windows button (View tab | Window group), and then click Lab 6-2 Containment Assumptions and then select cell B6 and press ENTER.

10. On the Overall Costs worksheet, use the SUM function, 3-D references, and copy and paste capabilities of Excel to total the corresponding cells on the three region sheets. First, compute the sum in cell B15. Copy the cell B15 to the range B16:B17. Next, compute the sum in cell E15, and finally, compute the sum in cell F15. The Overall Costs sheet should resemble the one shown in Figure 6–66.

11. Change the document properties as specified by your instructor. Select all four sheets. Add a worksheet header with your name, course number, and other information as specified by your instructor. Add the page number and total number of pages to the footer. Change the left and right margins to .5.

12. With the four sheets selected, preview and then print the workbook in landscape orientation and use the Black and white option.

13. Save the workbook with the new page setup characteristics. Close the open workbooks.

14. Submit the assignment as requested by your instructor.

Continued >

In the Lab *continued*

Instructions Part 2: Complete the following tasks.

1. Start Excel. Open the workbook Lab 6-2 SciMat Containment Costs.
2. Select the range B5:K5 on the Overall Costs worksheet. Select all the worksheets.
3. Use the Format Cells dialog box to apply a custom format of "Year" 0.
4. Select the range B15:B17 on the Overall Costs worksheet. Select all the worksheets.
5. Use the Format Cells dialog box to apply a custom format of #,##0 "kg".
6. Select the range C15:C17 on the Overall Costs worksheet. Select all the worksheets.
7. Use the Format Cells dialog box to apply a custom format of 0.00 "years".
8. Save the workbook and then close the workbook.
9. Submit the assignment as requested by your instructor.

In the Lab

Lab 3: Consolidating Data by Linking Workbooks

Note: To complete this assignment, you will be required to use the Data Files for Students. See the inside back cover of this book for instructions on downloading the Data Files for Students, or contact your instructor for information about accessing the required files.

Problem: The Apply Your Knowledge exercise in this chapter calls for consolidating the Miles Driven and Mileage Cost from four worksheets on a fifth worksheet in the same workbook (see Figure 6–62 on page EX 411). This exercise takes the same data stored in four separate workbooks and consolidates the Qty on Hand and Total Value by linking to a fifth workbook.

Instructions Part 1: Perform the following tasks.

1. Start Excel. Open the following five files from the Data Files for Students. You can open them one at a time or you can open them all at one time by selecting the five files and then clicking the Open button.

   • Lab 6-3 Audio Ace Annual Inventory Totals
   • Lab 6-3 Audio Ace Quarter 1 Inventory Totals
   • Lab 6-3 Audio Ace Quarter 2 Inventory Totals
   • Lab 6-3 Audio Ace Quarter 3 Inventory Totals
   • Lab 6-3 Audio Ace Quarter 4 Inventory Totals

2. Click the Switch Windows button (View tab | Window group) and then click Lab 6-3 Audio Ace Annual Inventory Totals.

3. Click the Save Workspace button (View tab | Window group). When the Save Workspace dialog box is displayed, save the workspace using the file name, Lab 6-3 Audio Ace Inventory Workspace.

4. Close all the open workbooks. Open the workspace Lab 6-3 Audio Ace Inventory Workspace. When the Lab 6-3 Audio Ace Annual Inventory Totals window is displayed, click the Maximize button in the upper-right corner to maximize the window. Save the workbook using the file name, Lab 6-3 Part 1 Audio Ace Annual Inventory Totals.

5. Consolidate the data in the four quarterly inventory workbooks into the range B11:C14 in the workbook Lab 6-3 Part 1 Audio Ace Annual Inventory Totals by doing the following:

   a. Click cell B11. Display the Home tab and then click Sum button (Home tab | Editing group).

   b. Click the Switch Windows button (View tab | Window group) and then click Lab 6-3 Audio Ace Quarter 1 Inventory Totals. When the workbook is displayed, click cell C11, click the Switch Windows button (View tab | Window group), and then click Lab 6-3 Part 1 Audio Ace Annual Inventory Totals. Change the absolute cell reference $C$11 in the formula bar to the relative cell reference C11 by deleting the dollar signs. Click immediately after C11 in the formula bar and then press the COMMA key.

c. Click the Switch Windows button (View tab | Window group) and then click Lab 6-3 Audio Ace Quarter 2 Inventory Totals. When the workbook is displayed, click cell C11, click the Switch Windows button (View tab | Window group), and then click Lab 6-3 Part 1 Audio Ace Annual Inventory Totals. Change the absolute cell reference $C$11 in the formula bar to the relative cell reference C11 by deleting the dollar signs. Click immediately after C11 in the formula bar and then press the COMMA key.

d. Click the Switch Windows button (View tab | Window group) and then click Lab 6-3 Audio Ace Quarter 3 Inventory Totals. When the workbook is displayed, click cell C11, click the Switch Windows button (View tab | Window group), and then click Lab 6-3 Part 1 Audio Ace Annual Inventory Totals. Change the absolute cell reference $C$11 in the formula bar to the relative cell reference C11 by deleting the dollar signs. Click immediately after C11 in the formula bar and then press the COMMA key.

e. Click the Switch Windows button (View tab | Window group) and then click Lab 6-3 Audio Ace Quarter 4 Inventory Totals. When the workbook is displayed, click cell C11, click the Switch Windows button (View tab | Window group), and then click Lab 6-3 Part 1 Audio Ace Annual Inventory Totals. Change the absolute cell reference $C$11 in the formula bar to the relative cell reference C11 by deleting the dollar signs. Press the ENTER key to sum the four quarter hours worked. You should end up with an annual total of 777 quantity on hand in cell B11.

f. With the workbook Lab 6-3 Part 1 Audio Ace Annual Inventory Totals window active, select cell B11. Drag the fill handle through cell C11 to display the annual total value in cell C11. Select the range B11:C11. Drag the fill handle down to cell C14. When the Auto Fill Options button is displayed next to cell C14, click the Auto Fill Options button and then click the Fill Without Formatting option.

6. Change the document properties as specified by your instructor. Change the worksheet header with your name, course number, and other information as specified by your instructor. Preview and print the annual inventory totals. Save the workbook using the file name, Lab 6-3 Part 1 Audio Ace Annual Inventory Totals. Close all workbooks. Submit the assignment as requested by your instructor.

Instructions Part 2: Perform the following tasks to update the hours worked for Quarter 2 and Quarter 4.

1. Start Excel. Open Lab 6-3 Audio Ace Quarter 1 Inventory Totals from the Data Files for Students. Change the quantity on hand for item no. TZ3919 in row 12 from 145 to 219. Save the workbook using the file name, Lab 6-3 Audio Ace Quarter 1 Inventory Totals. Close the workbook.

2. Open Lab 6-3 Audio Ace Quarter 3 Inventory Totals. Change the quantity on hand for item no. LG6527 in row 14 from 160 to 145. Save the workbook using the file name, Lab 6-3 Audio Ace Quarter 3 Inventory Totals. Close the workbook.

3. Open Lab 6-3 Part 1 Audio Ace Annual Inventory Totals workbook saved earlier in Part 1 of this exercise. Save the workbook using the file name, Lab 6-3 Part 2 Audio Ace Annual Inventory Totals. Display the Data tab. Click the Edit Links button (Data tab | Connections group). Select each file in the Edit Links dialog box and then click the Update Values button to instruct Excel to apply the current values in the four source workbooks to the consolidated workbook (Figure 6–67).

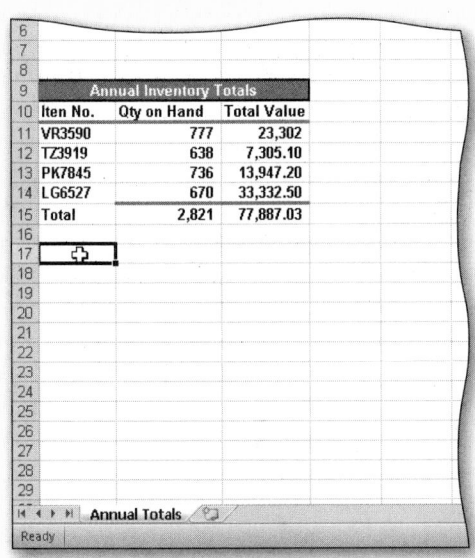

4. Insert a page break on Row 8. Preview and print the consolidated workbook. Remove the page break Save the workbook. Submit the assignment as requested by your instructor.

Figure 6–67

Cases and Places

Apply your creative thinking and problem solving skills to design and implement a solution.

1: Analyzing Annual College Expenses and Resources

Academic

College expenses are skyrocketing and your resources are limited. To plan for the upcoming year, you have decided to organize your anticipated expenses and resources in a workbook. The data required to prepare the workbook is shown in Table 6–14.

Create a workbook and add a worksheet for the consolidated data called Academic Year with the data for the first semester in Table 6–14 in mind. Sum both the expenses and resources for the semester. Copy the worksheet to create three more worksheets for each of the three semesters. Enter the data from Table 6–14 in each of the semester worksheets. Use 3-D cell references to consolidate the data on the Academic Year worksheet in the workbook. Use the concepts and techniques described in this chapter to format the workbook.

Table 6–14 Next Year's Anticipated College Expenses and Resources			
Expenses	**1st Semester**	**2nd Semester**	**Summer**
Rent	6,350.00	5,750.00	2,612.00
Car	1,500.00	1,500.00	900.00
Tuition	11,420.00	11,420.00	3,806.00
Books	1,350.00	1,450.00	230.00
Clothing	475.00	350.00	150.00
Personal Expenses	600.00	500.00	200.00
Miscellaneous	359.00	350.00	175.00
Resources	**1st Semester**	**2nd Semester**	**Summer**
Savings	3,500.00	3,500.00	600.00
Parents	5,300.00	8,200.00	2,120.00
Part-time job	1,540.00	1,295.00	785.00
Student Loan	8,000.00	8,000.00	4,205.00
Scholarship	2,500.00	2,500.00	500.00

2: Consolidating a Yearly Personal Budget

Personal

You want to create a workbook to help you analyze your personal budget. You have budgeted amounts and calculations of what you actually will pay for each month. You will include these in columns as well as a column to calculate the difference between the budgeted amounts and what you actually paid each month. Table 6–15 shows the data for the first four months.

Table 6–15 First 4 Months of Yearly Personal Expenses

		Budgeted Amount	Actual Amount
Jan	Rent	680.00	680.00
	Food	450.00	450.00
	Utilities	225.00	225.00
	Cell Phone	75.00	90.00
	Car Payments	275.41	275.41
	Insurance	149.50	149.50
	Clothing	250.00	100.00
	Internet	69.99	69.90
	Travel	110.00	250.00
Feb	Rent	680.00	680.00
	Food	450.00	450.00
	Utilities	225.00	225.00
	Cell Phone	75.00	90.00
	Car Payments	275.41	275.41
	Insurance	149.50	149.50
	Clothing	250.00	100.00
	Internet	69.99	69.90
	Travel	110.00	250.00
Mar	Rent	680.00	680.00
	Food	450.00	500.00
	Utilities	225.00	215.00
	Cell Phone	75.00	75.00
	Car Payments	275.41	275.41
	Insurance	149.50	149.50
	Clothing	250.00	230.00
	Internet	69.99	75.00
	Travel	110.00	100.00
Apr	Rent	680.00	680.00
	Food	450.00	450.00
	Utilities	225.00	225.00
	Cell Phone	75.00	90.00
	Car Payments	275.41	275.41
	Insurance	149.50	149.50
	Clothing	250.00	100.00
	Internet	69.99	69.90
	Travel	110.00	250.00

Continued >

Cases and Places *continued*

Create an annual worksheet based on the first month's personal expenses. Be sure to include a difference column that calculates the difference between the budgeted and actual amounts. Also include a total for the difference column. Using the annual worksheet, create worksheets for the 12 months. Enter the data for the first four months from Table 6–15. The rest of the 12 months follow the same pattern so you can use the data in Table 6–15 to fill in the remaining months.

Consolidate the budgeted and actual amounts on the annual worksheet using 3-D references. Using the techniques from the book, format the worksheet and add a custom format to the difference column so that it shows negative numbers as blue.

3: Analyzing Company Profits by Category

Professional

Starling Electronics sells various electronic devices and support materials ranging from HD TVs to wall mounts for the TVs. Merchandise is divided into six categories based on profit margin: TV & video (25%), cameras & camcorders (15%), audio (11%), game systems (20%), gadgets (9%), and support hardware (20%). Last year's sales data has been collected for the Philadelphia and Cincinnati Stores as shown in Table 6–16.

Develop a worksheet that can be used to determine marketing strategies for next year. Include sales, profit margins, profits (sales × profit margin), total sales, total profits, and functions to determine the most and least sales, profit margins, and profits. Create a custom style for the title of your worksheet.

Use the worksheet to create a workbook for each store and a consolidated workbook. Consolidate the data from the two stores into the consolidated workbook by applying techniques from the chapter regarding linking workbooks.

Table 6–16 Last Year's Sales for Philadelphia and Cincinnati Stores		
	Philadelphia	Cincinnatti
TV & Video	345,215.00	822,156.00
Cameras & Camcorders	140,135.00	255,812.00
Audio	75,912.00	72,345.00
Game Systems	46,125.00	58,012.00
Gadgets	8,532.00	12,589.00
Support Hardware	15,235.00	34,921.00

7 | Creating Templates, Importing Data, and Working with SmartArt, Images, and Screen Shots

Objectives

You will have mastered the material in this chapter when you can:

- Create and use a template

- Import data from a text file, an Access database, a Web page, and a Word document

- Transpose data while pasting it

- Convert text to columns

- Use Find and Replace commands

- Draw a Clustered Cone chart

- Use WordArt to create a title and to create and modify shapes

- Insert and modify an image

- Insert and modify a SmartArt graphic

- Insert a screen shot

7 | Creating Templates, Importing Data, and Working with SmartArt, Images, and Screen Shots

BTW

XML
XML can describe any type of data. Banks use it to transfer financial information among various systems, and graphic artists use it to share multimedia data. The versatility of XML is matched by its simplicity. XML also is being used to make queries over the Web using a common set of rules available to any user. For example, a user can send an XML query to a travel Web site and receive the current information for a specific flight in XML format.

BTW

BTWs
For a complete list of the BTWs found in the margins of this book, visit the Excel 2010 BTW Web page (scsite.com/ex2010/btw).

Introduction

In today's business environment, you often find that you need to create multiple worksheets or workbooks that follow the same basic format. A **template** is a special workbook you can create and then use as a pattern to create new, similar workbooks or worksheets. A template usually consists of a general format (worksheet title, column and row titles, and numeric format) and formulas that are common to all the worksheets. One efficient way to create the workbook is first to create a template, save the template, and then copy the template to a workbook as many times as necessary.

Another important concept is the ability to use and analyze data from a wide variety of sources. In this chapter, you will learn how to import, or bring in, data from various external sources into an Excel worksheet and then analyze that data. Excel allows you to import data from a number of types of sources, including text files, Web pages, database tables, data stored in Word documents, and XML files.

Finally, a chart, a graphic, image, or screen shot often conveys information or an idea better than words or numbers. You insert and modify graphics, images, and screen shots in order to enhance the visual appeal of an Excel workbook and illustrate its contents. Many of the skills you learn when working with graphics, screen shots, and images in Excel will be similar when working in other Office programs, such as Word, PowerPoint, or Outlook.

Project — YouBuild Computers Sales Analysis

The project in the chapter follows proper design guidelines and uses Excel to create the workbook shown in Figure 7–1. YouBuild Computers provides computer parts to local businesses to sell for those who want to build their own computers. The company provides parts in four regions. The company owner has requested that the sales results for the last two years be compared among the four regions. One of the regions provides the requested data in text format (Figure 7–1a) rather than in an Excel workbook. To make use of that data in Excel, the data must be imported before it can be formatted and manipulated. The same is true of other formats in which the offices in various regions store data, such as Microsoft Access tables (Figure 7–1b), Web pages (Figure 7–1c), or Word documents (Figure 7–1d). Excel provides the tools necessary to import and manipulate the data from these sources into a worksheet (Figure 7–1e and Figure 7–1f). Using the data from the worksheet, you can create the Clustered Cone chart (Figure 7–1g).

You then can add SmartArt graphics to create the SmartArt, (Figure 7–1h) along with images. Finally, you can add a screen shot to support your work (Figure 7–1i).

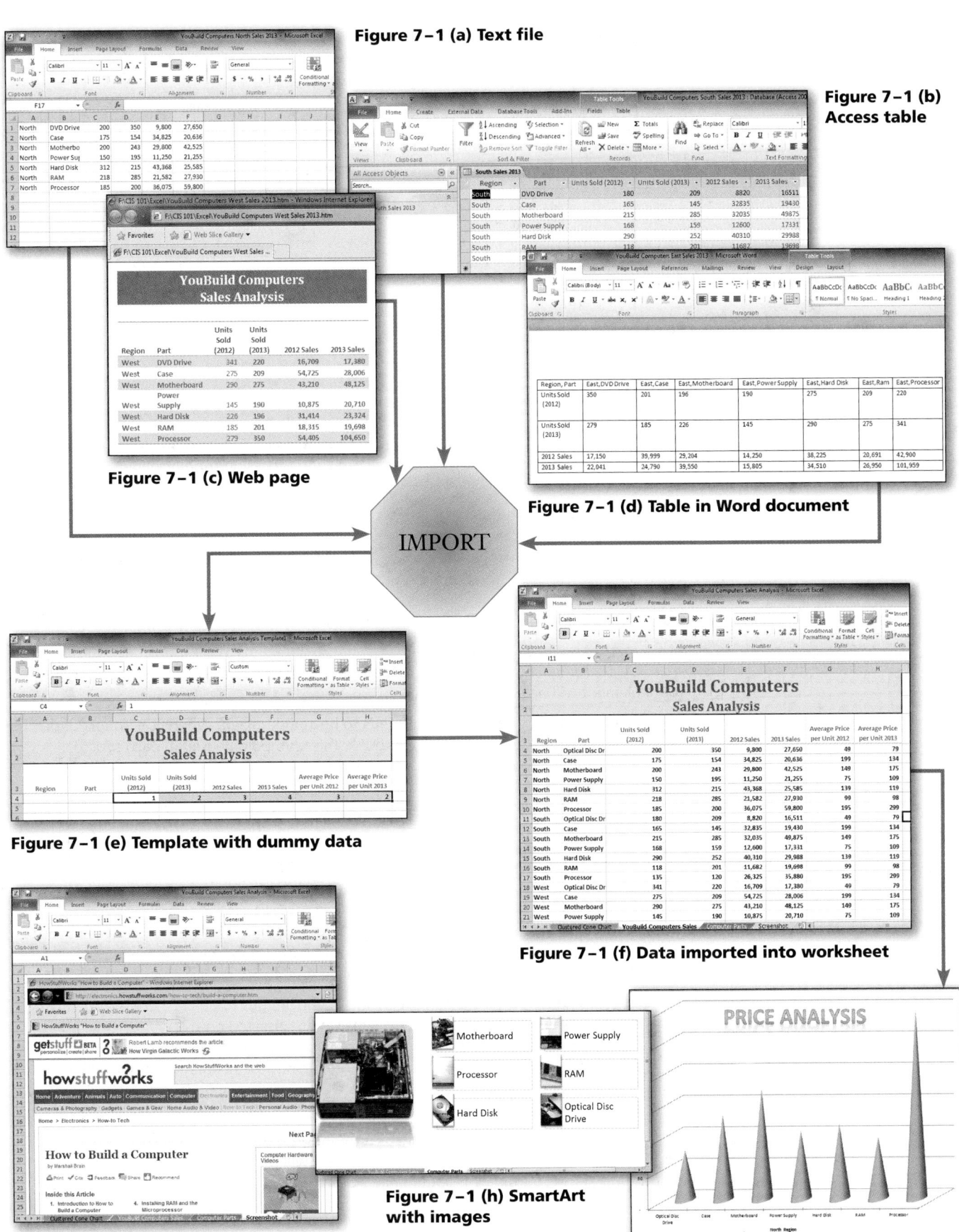

Figure 7–1 (a) Text file

Figure 7–1 (b) Access table

Figure 7–1 (c) Web page

Figure 7–1 (d) Table in Word document

IMPORT

Figure 7–1 (e) Template with dummy data

Figure 7–1 (f) Data imported into worksheet

Figure 7–1 (h) SmartArt with images

Figure 7–1 (i) Screen shot inserted in worksheet

Figure 7–1 (g) Clustered Cone chart

Overview

As you read this chapter, you will learn how to create the workbook shown in Figure 7–1 on the previous page by performing these general tasks:

- Create a template.
- Import data to an Excel worksheet from a text file, an Access database, a Web page, and a Word document.
- Insert WordArt on a chart.
- Insert and modify a SmartArt graphic.
- Add effects to a SmartArt graphic.
- Insert and modify an image.
- Add a screen shot to a worksheet.

Plan Ahead

General Project Guidelines

When creating templates, importing data, customizing charts, and modifying graphics, images, and screen shots, such as those shown in Figure 7–1, you should follow these general guidelines:

1. **Design the template and plan the formatting.** Templates help speed and simplify work because Excel users often work with the same types of problems repeatedly. Using a template allows you to begin your work with a preformatted worksheet. In the case of YouBuild Computers, the template saves the work of formatting the sales analysis worksheet. The formatting is done once in the template, and then that formatting is carried over to the new worksheet automatically.

2. **Analyze the existing workbook and the formats of the data to be imported.** You should have a good understanding of the layout of the data you want to import and how each data element will be arranged in the worksheet.

3. **Determine whether data you import needs to be standardized.** When you import data from multiple sources into a single workbook, the terminology used in each source might vary slightly. To make the terminology consistent, it may be necessary to find and replace text.

4. **Plan the layout and location of the required chart.** The chart may require additional artwork, including WordArt and, therefore, would be more suited for placement on a new worksheet. A Clustered Cone chart type is a proper choice for the YouBuild Computers chart because data from a few sales regions is compared. The tapering of the cones allows space for additional elements without any overlapping.

5. **Choose the type of SmartArt graphics to add.** Consider what you want to convey in your SmartArt. For example, for the components used in building a computer, the Picture Strips works best for displaying the different components and their names.

6. **Obtain the images to be used in the worksheet.** The images to be used are included with the Data Files for Students. Once the images are inserted on the worksheet, the image files no longer are needed because copies of the images become part of the worksheet. When obtaining an image, you must use only those images for which you have permission. Several sources provide royalty-free images, meaning that you do not have to pay to use them.

When necessary, more specific details concerning the above guidelines are presented at appropriate points in the chapter. The chapter also will identify the actions performed and decisions made regarding these guidelines during the creation of the workbook shown in Figure 7–1.

Figure 7–2 illustrates the requirements document for the YouBuild Computers Sales Analysis worksheet. It includes the needs, source of data, calculations, and other facts about the worksheet's development.

REQUEST FOR NEW WORKBOOK

Date Submitted:	January 1, 2013
Submitted By:	Carla Francis
Worksheet Title:	YouBuild Computers Sales Analysis
Needs:	The needs are as follows: 1. A template (Figure 7-1e) that can be used to create similar worksheets. 2. A workbook made from the template containing a worksheet (Figure 7-1f) that combines data imported from the four sales regions (Figures 7-1a, 7-1b, 7-1c, 7-1d). 3. A chart (Figure 7-1g) that compares the unit prices for the different computer parts in inventory for the North region. The chart should be placed on a separate sheet.
Source of Data:	The four sales managers for YouBuild Computers will submit data from their respective regions via a text file (North), an Access database (South), a Web page (West), and a Word document (East).
Calculations:	Include the following formulas in the template for each item: 1. Avg . Price per Unit 2012 = IF(Units Sold (2012) > 0, 2012 Sales / Units Sold (2012), 0) 2. Avg . Price per Unit 2013 = IF(Units Sold (2013) > 0, 2013 Sales / Units Sold (2013), 0)
Chart Requirements:	Create a Clustered Cone chart to compare the average price per unit for the North region. Use WordArt to create a title for the chart to enhance its appearance.

Approvals

Approval Status:	X	Approved
		Rejected
Approved By:	Juan Gutierrez	
Date:	January 10, 2013	
Assigned To:	S. Freund, Spreadsheet Specialist	

Figure 7–2

BTW

Workbook Survival
For workbooks to be successful and survive their expected life cycle in a business environment, they must be well documented and easy to understand. You document a workbook by adding comments to cells that contain complex formulas or to cells containing content that may not be understood easily. The documentation also should serve those who will maintain the workbook. You create easy-to-understand workbooks by reviewing alternative designs prior to creating the workbook. The more time you spend documenting and designing a workbook, the easier it will be for users and spreadsheet maintenance specialists to understand.

To Start Excel

If you are using a computer to step through the project in this chapter and you want your screens to match the figures in this book, you should change your screen's resolution to 1024 × 768. The following steps start Excel.

1 Start Excel.

2 If the Excel window is not maximized, click the Maximize button next to the Close button on its title bar to maximize the window.

Creating Templates

The first step in building the workbook is to create and save a template that contains the titles, column and row headings, formulas, and formats used on each of the worksheets.

Plan Ahead

Design the template and plan the formatting.
As mentioned earlier, a template is workbook that you use to create other similar workbooks. A template usually contains data and formatting that appears in every workbook created from that template. On Microsoft Office Online, Microsoft provides templates you can download and use as the basis for workbooks. You also can develop custom templates by creating a workbook and then saving it as a template. Because the template will be used to create a number of other worksheets, make sure you consider the layout, cell formatting, and contents of the workbook as you design the template.

- **Set row heights and column widths.** Row heights and column widths should be set to sizes large enough to accommodate future needs.

- **Use placeholders for data when possible.** Placeholders can guide users of the template regarding what type of data to enter in cells. For example, the words Sales Analysis should be used in the subtitle to indicate to a user of the template that the worksheet is included for sales analysis.

- **Use dummy data to verify formulas.** When a template is created, **dummy data** — that is, sample data used in place of actual data to verify the formulas in the template — should be used in place of actual data to verify the formulas in the template. Selecting simple numbers such as 1, 2, and 3 allows you to check quickly to see if the formulas are generating the proper results. In templates with more complex formulas, you may want to use numbers that test the extreme boundaries of valid data.

- **Format cells in the template.** Formatting should be applied to titles and subtitles that can be changed to provide cues to worksheet users. For example, using a fill color for the title and subtitle makes the text more noticeable. All numeric cell entry placeholders — dummy data — should be properly formatted for unit numbers and currency amounts.

BTW

Templates
Templates are most helpful when you need to create several similar or identical workbooks. They help reduce work and ensure consistency. Templates can contain: (1) text and graphics, such as a company name and logo; (2) formats and page layouts; and (3) formulas or macros.

After the template is saved, it can be used every time a similar workbook is developed. Because templates help speed and simplify their work, many Excel users create a template for each project on which they work. Templates can be simple — possibly using a special font or worksheet title, or they can be more complex — perhaps using specific formulas and format styles, such as the template for the YouBuild Computers Sales Analysis workbook.

Creating a template, such as the one shown in Figure 7–3, follows the same basic steps used to create a workbook. The only difference between developing a workbook and a template is the file type used to save the template.

Figure 7–3

To Bold the Font and Adjust the Row Heights and Column Widths of the Template

The first step in creating the template is to format the cells. The following steps change the font style to bold and adjust the height of row 3 to 45.75 points, the column widths of columns A through F to 13.00 characters, and the column widths of columns G and H to 14.00 characters.

1 Click the Select All button immediately above row heading 1 and to the left of column heading A and then click the Bold button (Home tab | Font group) to bold the cells. Select cell A1 to deselect the worksheet.

2 Drag the bottom boundary of row heading 3 down until the ScreenTip, Height 45.75 (61 pixels), appears, to change the height of the row.

3 Click column heading A, drag through to column heading F, and then drag the right boundary of column heading F right until the ScreenTip, Width: 13.00 (96 pixels), appears, to change the width of the selected columns.

4 Click column heading G, drag through to column heading H, and then drag the right boundary of column heading H right until the ScreenTip, Width: 14.00 (103 pixels), appears, to change the width of the selected columns. Select cell A1 to deselect columns G through H.

To Enter the Title and Subtitle in the Template

The following steps enter the titles in cells A1 and A2.

1 Type `YouBuild Computers` in cell A1 and then press the DOWN ARROW key to enter the worksheet title.

2 Type `Sales Analysis` in cell A2 and then press the DOWN ARROW key to enter the worksheet subtitle.

To Enter Column Titles in the Template

The following steps enter the column titles in row 3.

1 In cell A3, type **Region** and then press the RIGHT ARROW key to enter the title for column A.

2 In cell B3, type **Part** and then press the RIGHT ARROW key to enter the title for column B.

3 In cell C3, type **Units Sold** and then press ALT+ENTER. Type **(2012)** and then press the RIGHT ARROW key to enter the title for column C on two lines.

4 With cell D3 active, enter the remaining column titles in row 3 (shown in Figure 7–4).

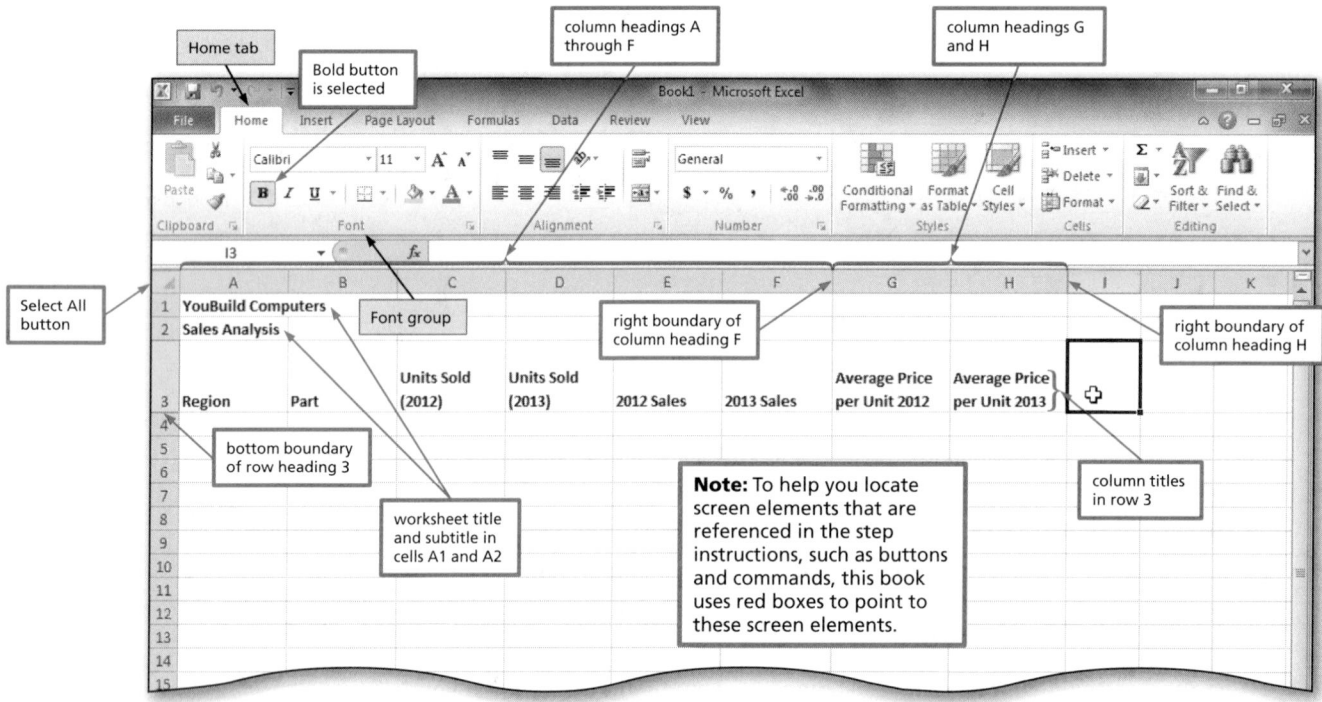

Figure 7–4

To Enter Sample Data in the Template Using the Fill Handle

While creating the YouBuild Computers template in this chapter, sample data is used for the Region, Part, Units Sold (2012), Units Sold (2013), 2012 Sales, and 2013 Sales (range A4:F4). Enter the sample data in cells C4 and D4 as instructed. Enter the rest of the data by selecting C4:D4 and then dragging the fill handle through the range E4:F4. The series in row 4 begins with 1 and increments by 1. Recall that you must enter the first two numbers in a series so that Excel can determine the increment amount as illustrated in the following steps.

1 Select cell C4. Type **1** and then press the RIGHT ARROW key to enter the first number in the series.

2 Type **2** and then press the ENTER key to enter the second number in the series.

3 Select the range C4:D4. Drag the fill handle through cell F4 to create the series 1 through 4 in increments of 1 in the range C4:F4 (Figure 7–5).

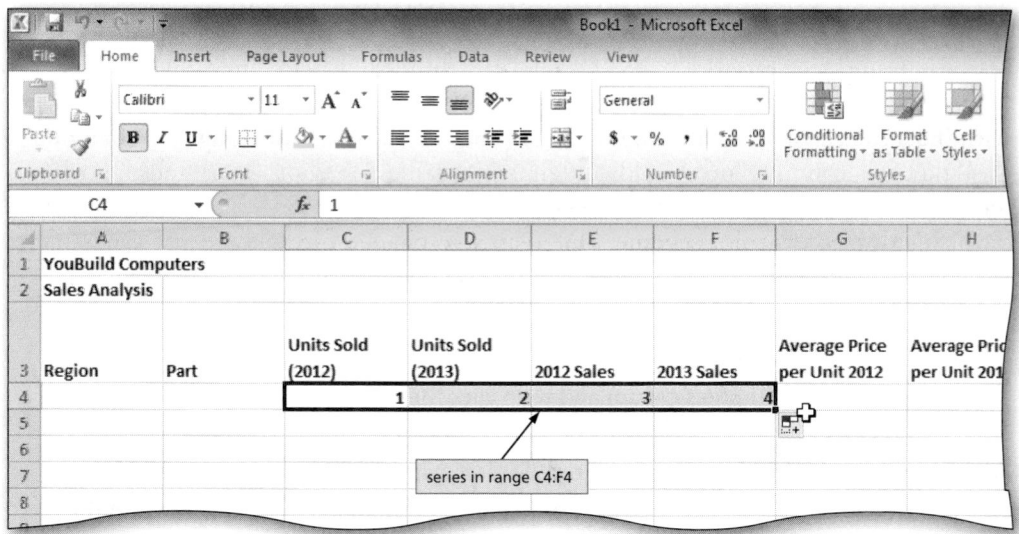

Figure 7–5

To Enter an IF Function

The following steps use the IF function to enter formulas to calculate the average price per unit for 2012 and 2013.

1 Select cell G4. Type `=IF(C4>0, E4/C4, 0)` as the formula for calculating the average price per unit for 2012, and then press the RIGHT ARROW key to select cell H4.

2 Type `=IF(D4>0, F4/D4, 0)` and then press the ENTER key to enter the formula for calculating the average price per unit for 2013 in cell H4 (Figure 7–6).

Figure 7–6

To Format the Template Title and Subtitle

The steps used to format the template title and subtitle include changing the text in cell A1 to 28-point with the Title cell style; changing the text in cell A2 to 22-point with the Title cell style; centering both titles across columns A through G; changing the title background color to gold; and drawing a thick box border around the title area (cells A1 and A2). The color scheme associated with the default Office template also will be changed to a new color scheme. One reason to change the color scheme is to add variety to the look of the worksheet that you create. The following steps format the title and subtitle.

1 Click Page Layout on the Ribbon to display the Page Layout tab. Click the Colors button (Page Layout tab | Themes group) and then click Metro in the Colors gallery to apply the Metro colors to the worksheet.

2 Select the range A1:A2. Display the Home tab, and then apply the Title cell style to the range. Select cell A1. Click the Font Size box arrow (Home tab | Font group) and then click 28 in the Font Size list to change the font size of cell A1. Select the range A1:H1. Click the Merge & Center button (Home tab | Alignment group) to merge and center the selected cells.

3 Select cell A2, click the Font Size box arrow (Home tab | Font group), and then click 22 in the Font Size list to change the font size of cell A2. Select the range A2:H2. Click the Merge & Center button (Home tab | Alignment group) to merge and center the selected cells.

4 Select the range A1:A2, click the Fill Color button arrow (Home tab | Font group), and then click Gold, Accent 3, Lighter 60% (column 7, row 3) on the Fill Color palette to set the fill color for the range.

5 Click the Borders button arrow (Home tab | Font group), and then click Thick Box Border in the Borders gallery to apply a border to the range.

6 Select cell A3 to deselect the range A1:A2.

To Format the Column Titles

The following steps format the column titles in row 3.

1 Select the range A3:H3, click the Center button (Home tab | Alignment group), and then apply the Heading 3 cell style to the range.

To Format the Table Data

The following steps format the cells in row 4 to use the Comma style.

1 Select the range C4:H4.

2 Apply the Comma style to the range.

3 Decrease the decimal of C4:H4 twice to not show any decimal places (Figure 7–7).

BTW

Summing a Row or Column
You can reference an entire column or row in a function argument by listing only the column or only the row. For example, =SUM(a:a) sums all the values in all the cells in column A, and =SUM(1:1) sums all the values in all the cells in row 1. You can verify this by entering =SUM(a:a) in cell C1 and then begin entering numbers in a few of the cells in column A. Excel will respond by showing the sum of the numbers in cell C1.

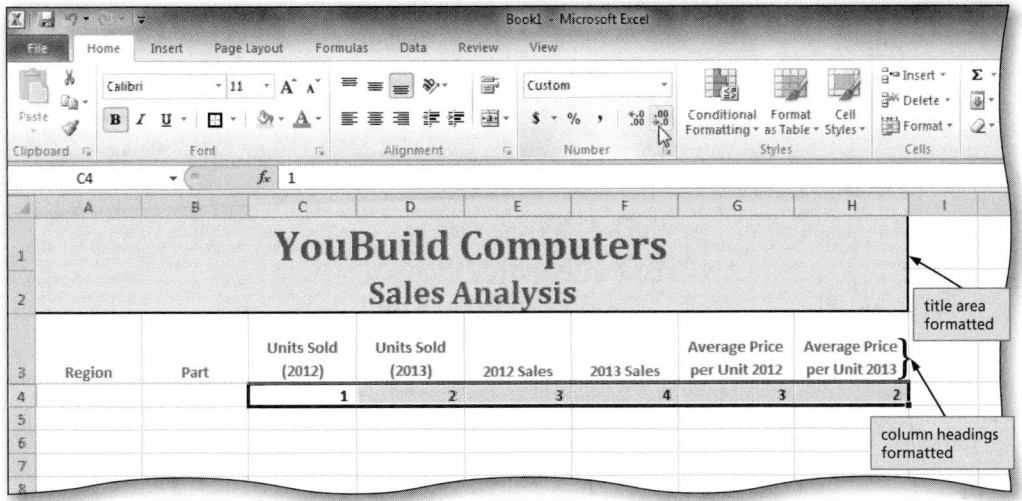

Figure 7–7

To Save the Template

Saving a template is similar to saving a workbook, except that the file type, Excel Template, is selected in the 'Save as type' box in the Save As dialog box. The following steps save the template on a USB flash drive in drive F using the file name, YouBuild Computers Sales Analysis Template.

1

- Update the document properties with your name and any other relevant information as specified by your instructor to identify your workbook.

- Change the sheet name to YouBuild Computers Sales to provide a descriptive name for the worksheet.

- Change the tab color to red to format the tab.

- Click the Save button on the Quick Access Toolbar to display the Save As dialog box (Figure 7–8).

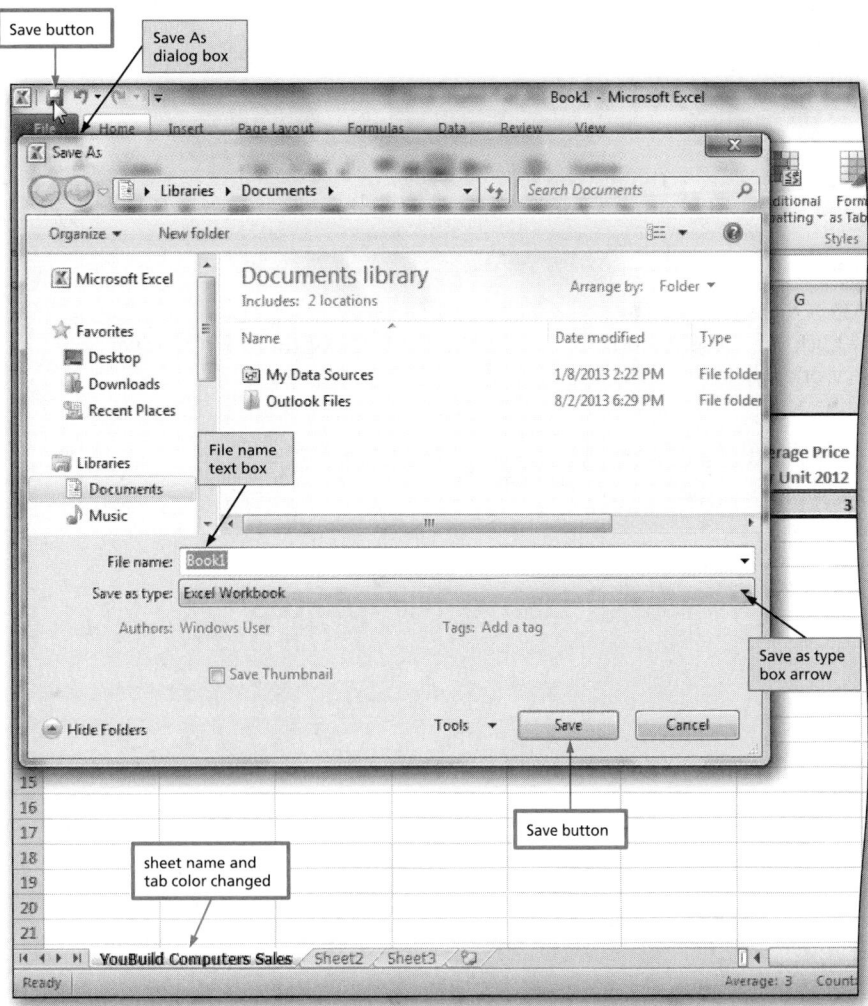

Figure 7–8

2

- Type **YouBuild Computers Sales Analysis Template** in the File name text box to enter a name for the file.

- Click the 'Save as type' box arrow and then click Excel Template in the list to specify that this workbook is saved as a template.

- Navigate to the location of the file to be saved (in this case, the Excel folder in the CIS 101 folder [or your class folder] on the USB flash drive).

- Click the Save button (Save As dialog box) to save the template on the USB flash drive and display the file name, YouBuild Computers Sales Analysis Template, on the title bar (Figure 7–9).

Figure 7–9

Q&A Why does Excel change the folder name when the Excel Template file type is chosen?

When the Excel Template file type is chosen in the 'Save as type' box, Excel automatically changes the contents of the Save in box to the Templates folder created when Office 2010 was installed. In a production environment — that is, when you are creating a template for a business, school, or personal application — the template typically would be saved in the Templates folder, not on the USB flash drive.

3

- Click the Close Window button on the right side of the worksheet window to close the workbook and leave Excel open.

Other Ways

1. Press CTRL+S, type file name, select Excel Template in 'Save as type' box, select drive or folder, click Save button (Save As dialog box)

Using Templates

Before using the template to create the YouBuild Computers Sales Analysis workbook, you should be aware of how templates are used and their importance. If you click the New tab in the Backstage view, the New gallery appears (Figure 7–10). The New gallery includes a My templates link in the Available Templates list, which you can click to view a list of Excel templates that you have saved on your computer.

Recall that Excel automatically chose Templates as the Save in folder when the template in this chapter initially was saved (Figure 7–8 on the previous page). Saving templates in the Templates folder rather than another folder is the standard procedure in the business world. If the YouBuild Computers Sales Analysis Template created in this chapter had been saved in the Templates folder, then the template would appear in the New dialog box after clicking My templates in the Available Templates list. The template then could have been selected to create a new workbook.

When you select a template from the New gallery or New dialog box to create a new workbook, Excel names the new workbook using the template name with an appended digit 1 (for example, Template1). This is similar to what Excel does when you first start Excel and it assigns the name Book1 to the workbook.

Excel provides additional workbook templates, which you can access by clicking the links in the Templates list shown in Figure 7–10. Additional workbook templates also are available on the Web. To access the templates on the Web, click the links in the Office.com Templates list.

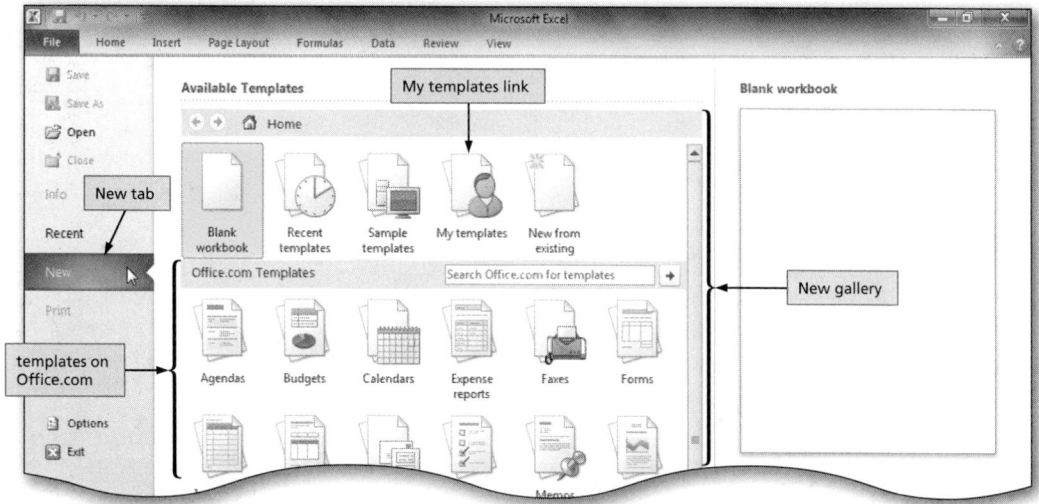

Figure 7–10

To Open a Template and Save It as a Workbook

The following steps open the YouBuild Computers Sales Analysis template and save it as a workbook.

1

- With Excel active, click File on the Ribbon to open the Backstage view.

- Click the Open command to display the Open dialog box.

- Navigate to the location of the file to be opened (in this case, the Excel folder on the USB flash drive).

- Click the YouBuild Computers Sales Analysis Template file to select it (Figure 7–11).

Figure 7–11

2

- Click the Open button (Open dialog box) to open the selected file.

- Click File on the Ribbon to open the Backstage view, and then click the Save As command to display the Save As dialog box.

- Type **YouBuild Computers Sales Analysis** in the File name box.

- Click the 'Save as type' box arrow and then click Excel Workbook to save the file as a workbook (Figure 7–12).

3

- Click the Save button (Save As dialog box) to save the workbook.

Q&A

How does Excel automatically select the file type and file name?

In a production environment in which templates are saved to the Templates folder, Excel automatically selects Excel Workbook as the file type when you attempt to save a template as a workbook. Excel also appends the digit 1 to the workbook name as described earlier.

Figure 7–12

External Data
Imported data that maintains a refreshable link to its external source is called external data. When you use external data, your worksheet will be updated whenever a change is made to the original file and the data in the worksheet is refreshed. You can choose when and how to refresh the data.

Importing Data

Data may be sent from a variety of sources and in a range of formats. Even though many users keep data in databases such as Microsoft Access, it is common to receive text files with fields of data separated by commas, especially from mainframe computer users. In addition, with the popularity of the World Wide Web, more companies are creating HTML files and posting data on the Web as a Web page. Word documents, especially those including tables of data, often are used in business as a source of data for workbooks. XML also is a very popular format for data exchange. Excel allows you to import data made available in many formats, including text files, Access tables, Web pages, Word documents, and XML files. Importing data into Excel can create a refreshable link that can be used to update data whenever the original file changes.

Plan Ahead

Analyze the existing workbook and the formats of the data to be imported.
Before importing data, become familiar with the layout of the data, so that you can anticipate how each data element will be arranged in the worksheet. In some cases, the data will need to be transposed, meaning that the rows and columns need to be switched. You also might need to format the data, move it, or convert it from or into a table.

Importing Text Files

A **text file** contains data with little or no formatting. Many programs, including Excel, offer an option to import data from a text file, also called an ASCII text file. **ASCII** stands for the American Standard Code for Information Interchange.

In text files, commas, tabs, or other characters often separate the fields. Alternately, the text file may have fields of equal length in columnar format. Each record usually exists on a separate line. A **delimited file** contains data fields separated by a selected character, such as a comma. Such a file is called a comma-delimited text file. A **fixed width file** contains data fields of equal length with spaces between the fields. In the case of a fixed width file, a special character need not separate the data fields. During the import process, Excel provides a preview to help identify the type of text file being imported.

To Import Data from a Text File into a Worksheet

The following steps import a comma-delimited text file into the YouBuild Computers Sales Analysis workbook using the Text Import Wizard. The text file on the Data Files for Students contains data about sales for the North region for 2012 and 2013 (Figure 7–1a on page EX 427).

1

- With the YouBuild Computers Sales Analysis worksheet active, if necessary, select cell A4.

- Click Data on the Ribbon to display the Data tab (Figure 7–13).

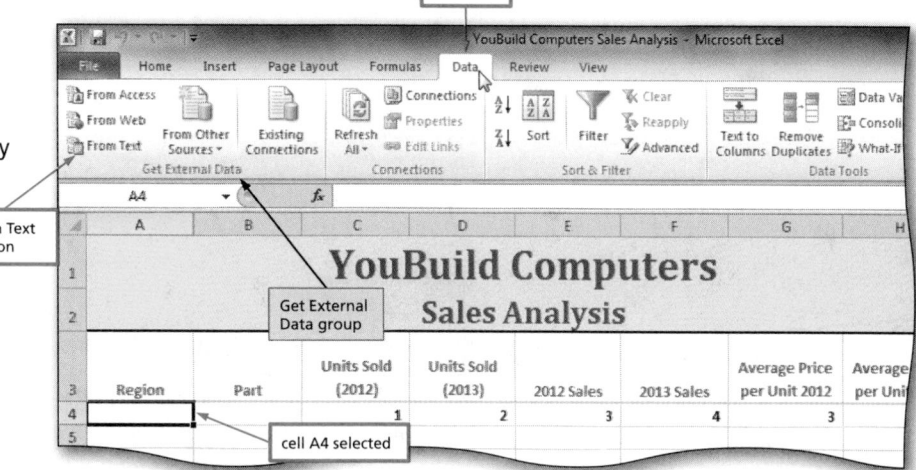

Figure 7–13

2

- Click the From Text button (Data tab | Get External Data group) to display the Import Text File dialog box.

- If necessary, navigate to the location of the file containing text to insert (in this case, the Excel folder on the USB flash drive) to display the Data Files (Figure 7–14).

Q&A

Why can I not find the From Text button?

If you have more than one Excel add-in installed, such as Solver, the From Text button may appear on a submenu that is displayed when you click the Get External Data button. The Get External Data group on the Ribbon may be collapsed to a single Get External Data button.

Figure 7–14

- Click the file name, YouBuild Computers North Sales 2013, to select it.

- Click the Import button (Import Text File dialog box) to start the Text Import Wizard and display the Text Import Wizard – Step 1 of 3 dialog box (Figure 7–15).

Q&A

What is the purpose of the Text Import Wizard?

The Text Import Wizard provides step-by-step instructions for importing data from a text file into an Excel worksheet. The Preview box shows that the text file contains one record per line and the fields are separated by commas. The Delimited option button is selected in the 'Original data type' area.

Figure 7–15

- Click the Next button (Text Import Wizard – Step 1 of 3 dialog box) to display the Text Import Wizard – Step 2 of 3 dialog box (Figure 7–16).

Figure 7–16

- Click Comma to place a check mark in the Comma check box and to display the data fields correctly in the Data preview area.

- Click Tab to remove the check mark from the Tab check box (Figure 7–17).

Figure 7–17

- Click the Next button (Text Import Wizard – Step 2 of 3 dialog box) to display the Text Import Wizard – Step 3 of 3 dialog box (Figure 7–18).

Q&A

What is shown in the Text Import Wizard – Step 3 of 3 dialog box?

Step 3 allows the format of each column of data to be selected. General is the default selection. The Data preview area shows the data separated based on the comma delimiter. The commas in the last two columns of numbers in the Data preview area (Figure 7–18) are not considered to be delimiters because each of these data values was surrounded by quotation marks in the text file.

Figure 7–18

7

- Click the Finish button (Text Import Wizard – Step 3 of 3 dialog box) to finish importing the selected text file and display the Import Data dialog box.

Q&A

What is shown in the Import Data dialog box when importing text?

The Import Data dialog box allows you to choose in which cell to import the text and to specify properties of the imported text.

- Click the Properties button (Import Data dialog box) to display the External Data Range Properties dialog box.

- Click 'Adjust column width' to remove the check mark from the 'Adjust column width' check box.

- Click the 'Overwrite existing cells with new data, clear unused cells' option button to select the option button (Figure 7–19).

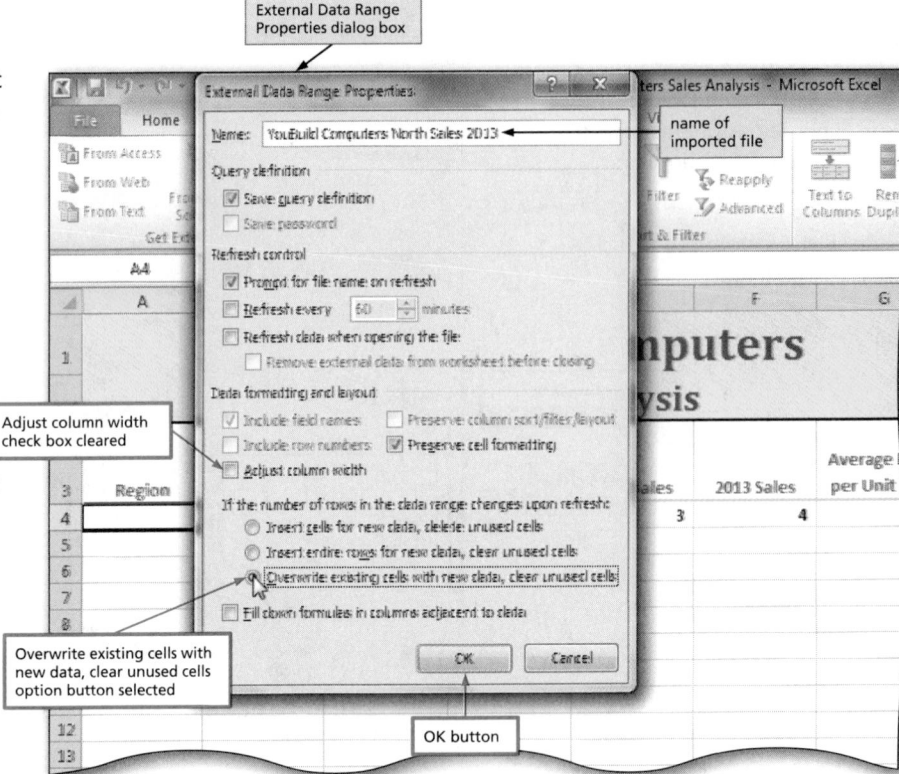

Figure 7–19

8

- Click the OK button (External Data Range Properties dialog box) to accept the settings and display the Import Data dialog box again.

- Click the OK button (Import Data dialog box) to import the data from the text file into the worksheet beginning at cell A4.

- Display the Home tab.

- Select the range C4:F4 to prepare for copying its formatting.

- Click the Format Painter button (Home tab | Clipboard group) and then drag though the range C5:F10 to copy the formatting to the range C5:F10 (Figure 7–20).

Q&A

What if the data in the text file is changed?

After the text file is imported, Excel can refresh, or update, the data whenever the original text file changes using the Refresh All button (Data tab | Connections group).

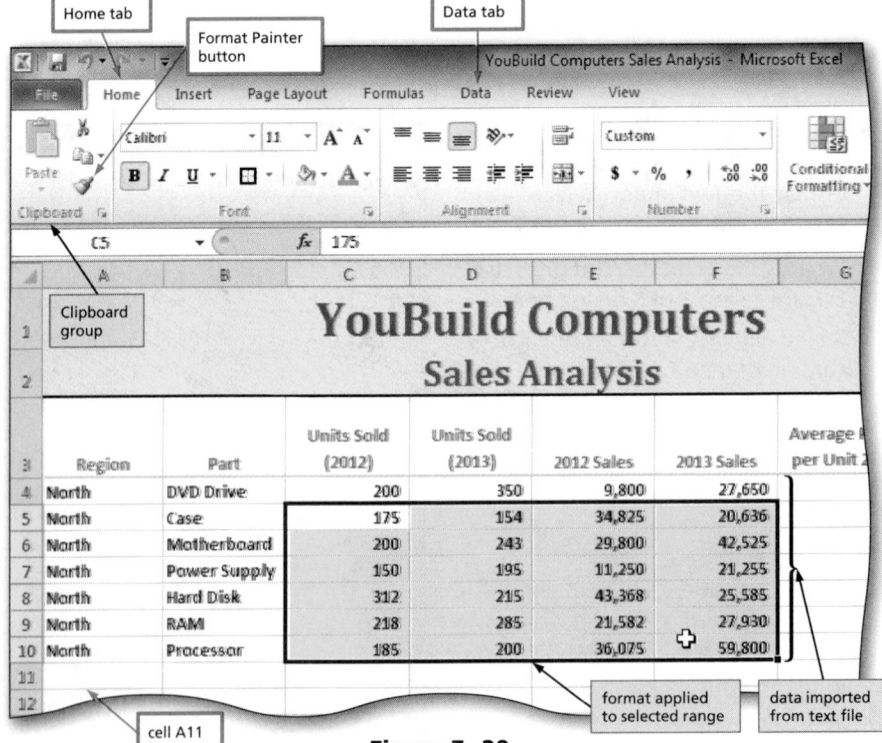

Figure 7–20

Other Ways

1. Select text, right-click selection, click Format Painter button on Mini toolbar

Importing Data from a Database

To import data from an Access database, the first step is to make a query of the data. A **query** is a way to qualify the data to import by specifying a matching condition or asking a question of a database. For example, a query can identify only those records that pass a certain test, such as records containing numeric fields greater than a specific amount or records containing text fields matching a specific value. When Excel imports a database table, the data is placed in a table. A table format is not desirable for the YouBuild Computers Sales Analysis worksheet, so the table must be converted to a range and the cells and should be reformatted after Excel imports the data.

BTW

Dragging and Dropping an Access File

If you have both Excel and Access open on your desktop, you can drag and drop an entire table or query from Access to Excel. In the Access window, select the table or query you want to transfer, and then drag it to the desired location in the worksheet.

To Import Data from an Access Table into a Worksheet

The following steps import an entire table from an Access database into an Excel table and then reformat the data to match the existing worksheet. The table in the Access database on the Data Files for Students contains data about sales revenue in the South region for 2012 and 2013 (Figure 7–1b on page EX 427).

1

- Select cell A11 so that the Access table is imported starting in cell A11.

- Click Data on the Ribbon to display the Data tab.

- Click the From Access button (Data tab | Get External Data group) to display the Select Data Source dialog box.

- Navigate to the location of the Access database file containing the table to insert (in this case, the Excel folder on the USB flash drive) (Figure 7–21).

Figure 7–21

2

- Click the file name, YouBuild Computers South Sales 2013, in the Name list to select the file.

- Click the Open button (Select Data Source dialog box) to display the Import Data dialog box (Figure 7–22).

What if the database contains more than one table?

If more than one table is in the database, then Excel allows you to choose which table to import.

Figure 7–22

3

- Click the OK button (Import Data dialog box) to import the data in the database to a table in the range A11:F18 (Figure 7–23).

Q&A What is shown in the Import Data dialog box when importing from an Access database?

The Import Data dialog box allows you to choose whether to import the data into a table, a PivotTable Report, or a PivotChart and associated PivotTable Report. You also can choose to import the data to an existing worksheet or a new worksheet.

Figure 7–23

Q&A What happened to the layout of the worksheet when Excel imported the data?

Excel created a table using the data in the only table in the database. The names of the fields in the Access database appear in row 11. The table is formatted with the default table style for the worksheet's theme. Excel also changed the widths of the columns in the worksheet.

Q&A How should I format the worksheet now?

The table in the range A11:F18 must be converted to a range. When the table is converted to a range, the cells in each column in the converted range should be formatted to match the data in the cells that were imported for the North region. The table headers in row 11 should be deleted by deleting the entire row.

4
- Right-click cell A11, point to Table on the shortcut menu, and then click Convert to Range to display the Microsoft Excel dialog box, which asks whether Excel should convert the table to a normal range.

- Click the OK button (Microsoft Excel dialog box) to convert the table to a range (Figure 7–24).

cell A11

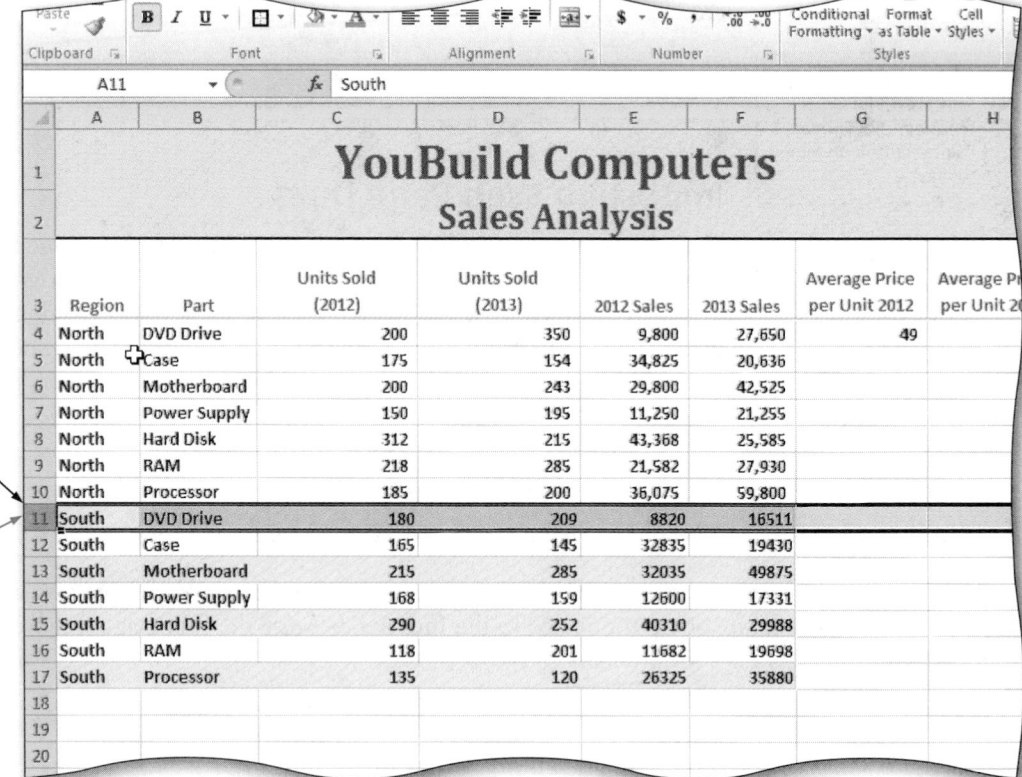

Region	Part	Units Sold (2012)	Units Sold (2013)	2012 Sales	2013 Sales	Average Price per Unit 2012	Average Pr per Unit 2(
North	DVD Drive	200	350	9,800	27,650	49	
North	Case	175	154	34,825	20,636		
North	Motherboard	200	243	29,800	42,525		
North	Power Supply	150	195	11,250	21,255		
North	Hard Disk	312	215	43,368	25,585		
North	RAM	218	285	21,582	27,930		
North	Processor	185	200	36,075	59,800		
Region	Part	Units Sold (2012)	Units Sold (2013)	2012 Sales	2013 Sales		
South	DVD Drive	180	209	8820	16511		
South	Case	165	145	32835	19430		
South	Motherboard	215	285	32035	49875		table converted to range
South	Power Supply	168	159	12600	17331		
South	Hard Disk	290	252	40310	29988		
South	RAM	118	201	11682	19698		
South	Processor	135	120	26325	35880		

Figure 7–24

5
- Right-click the row heading for row 11 to display the shortcut menu.

- Click Delete on the shortcut menu to delete row 11 (Figure 7–25).

row 11 deleted

row heading for row 11

YouBuild Computers
Sales Analysis

Region	Part	Units Sold (2012)	Units Sold (2013)	2012 Sales	2013 Sales	Average Price per Unit 2012	Average Pr per Unit 2(
North	DVD Drive	200	350	9,800	27,650	49	
North	Case	175	154	34,825	20,636		
North	Motherboard	200	243	29,800	42,525		
North	Power Supply	150	195	11,250	21,255		
North	Hard Disk	312	215	43,368	25,585		
North	RAM	218	285	21,582	27,930		
North	Processor	185	200	36,075	59,800		
South	DVD Drive	180	209	8820	16511		
South	Case	165	145	32835	19430		
South	Motherboard	215	285	32035	49875		
South	Power Supply	168	159	12600	17331		
South	Hard Disk	290	252	40310	29988		
South	RAM	118	201	11682	19698		
South	Processor	135	120	26325	35880		

Figure 7–25

6

- If necessary, display the Home tab.

- Select the range A7:F7 to prepare for copying the formatting.

- Click the Format Painter button (Home tab | Clipboard group), and then drag though the range A11:F17 to copy the formats of the selected range to the range A11:F17.

- Click cell A18 to deselect the range and prepare for importing other data (Figure 7–26).

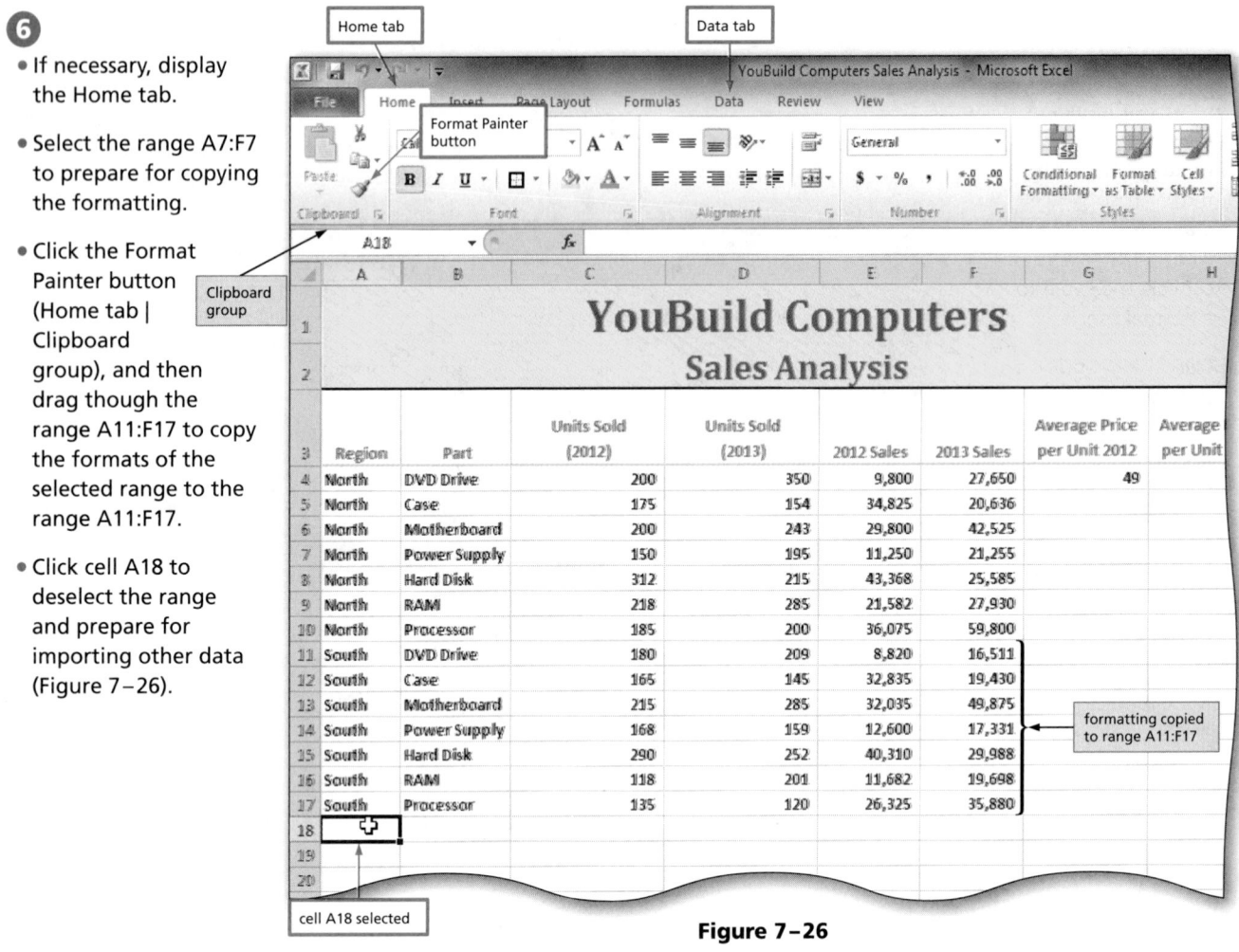

Figure 7–26

Importing Web Page Data

Web pages use a file format called HTML. HTML stands for Hypertext Markup Language, which is a language that Web browsers can interpret. Excel can import data from a Web page into preformatted areas of the worksheet using a Web query. A **Web query** selects data from the Internet to add to the Excel worksheet. The Web Query dialog box includes options to specify which parts of the Web page to import and how much of the HTML formatting to keep.

To Import Data from a Web Page into a Worksheet

The following steps create a new Web query and import data from a Web page into a worksheet. Performing these steps does not require being connected to the Internet, because the Web page (Figure 7–1c on page EX 427) is available with the Data Files for Students.

1

- With cell A18 selected, display the Data tab.

- Click the From Web button (Data tab | Get External Data group) to display the New Web Query dialog box.

- Type **F:\CIS 101\Excel\ YouBuild Computers West Sales 2013.htm** in the Address bar and then click the Go button (New Web Query dialog box) to display the Web page in the preview area (Figure 7–27).

Q&A Why does file:/// appear at the beginning of the address in the Address bar?

Excel appends file:/// to the beginning of the address to indicate that the address points to a file saved on disk.

Q&A What should I do if my Data Files on are on a different drive?

Substitute the name of your drive (such as E:) for F: in the address.

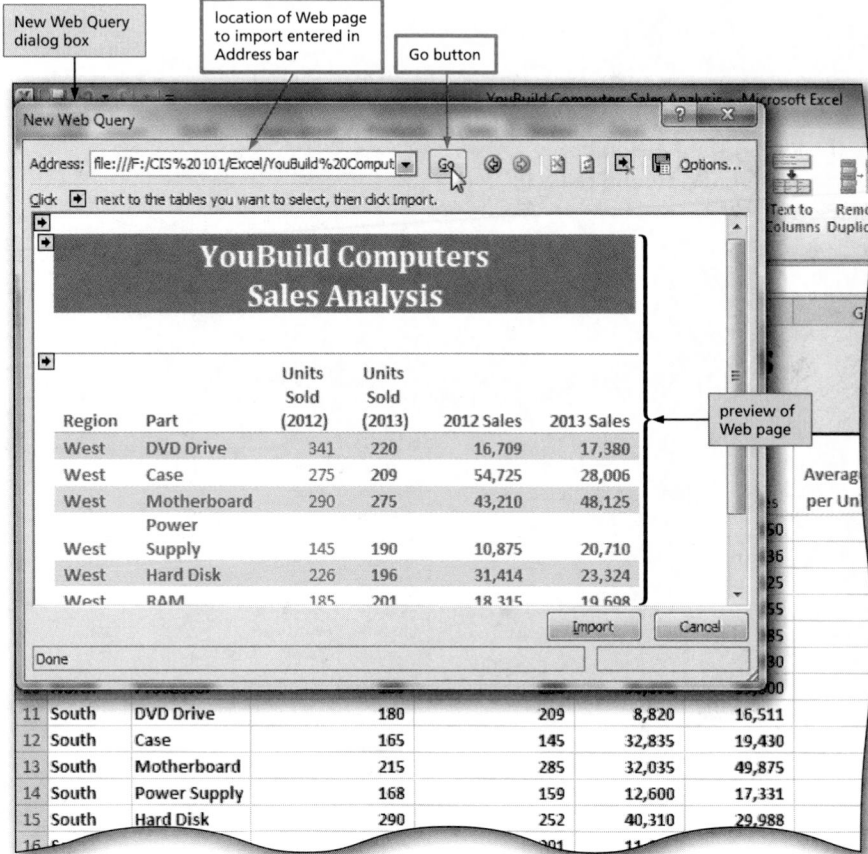

Figure 7–27

2

- Click the second 'Click to select this table' arrow to select the HTML table containing the West region sales report (Figure 7–28).

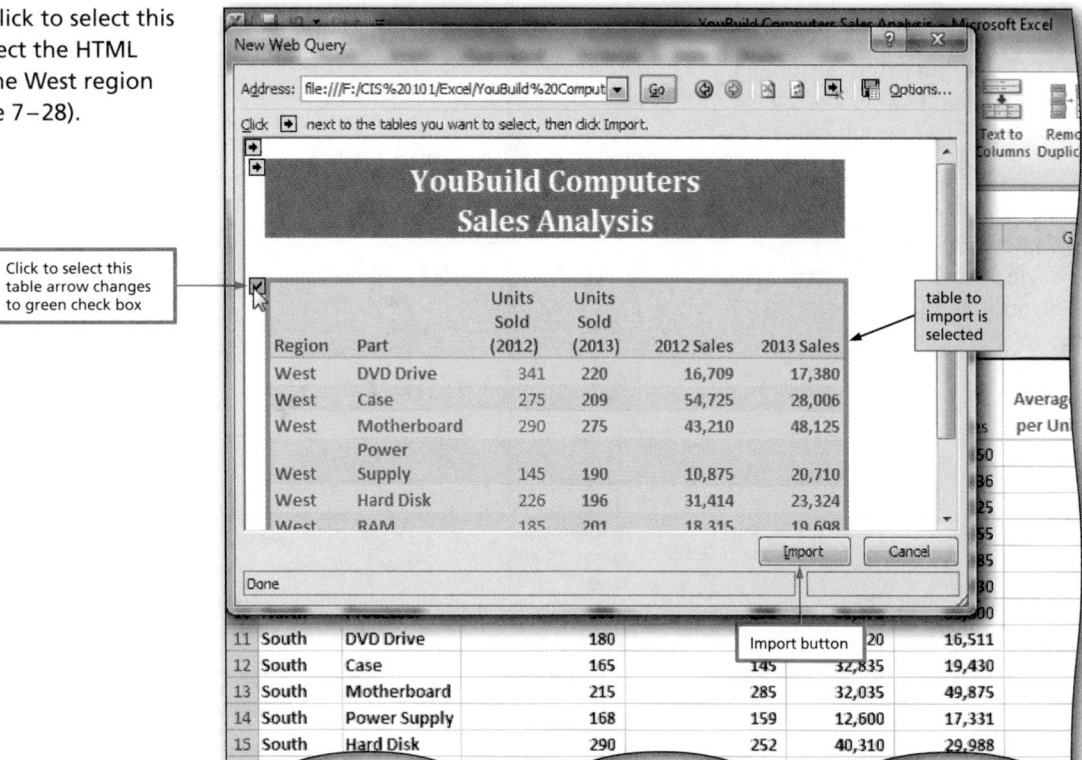

Figure 7–28

❸

• Click the Import button (New Web Query dialog box) to display the Import Data dialog box and a marquee around cell A18 (Figure 7–29).

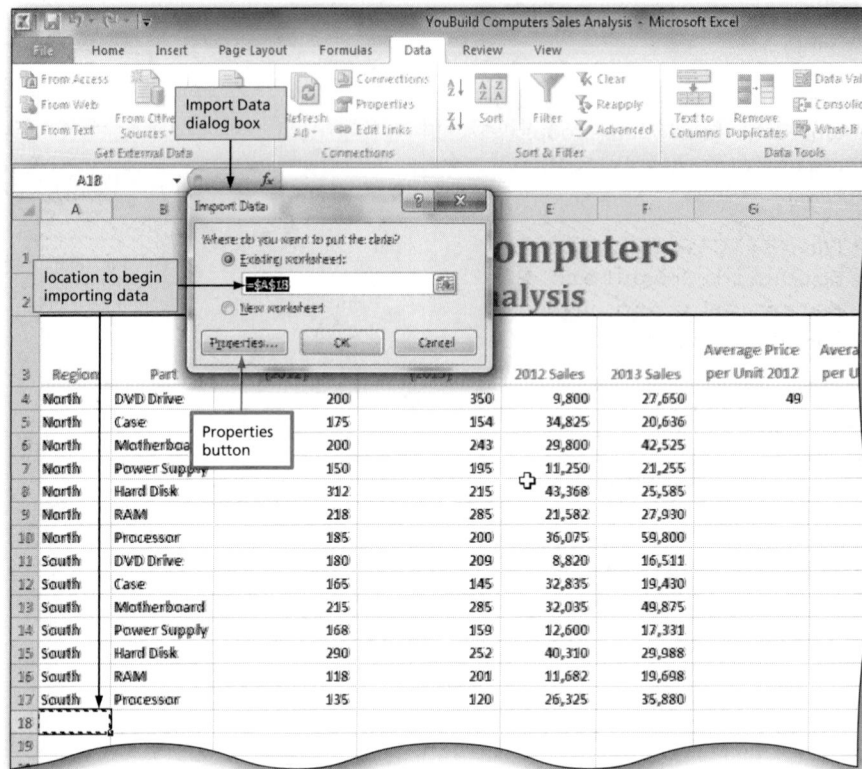

Figure 7–29

❹

• Click the Properties button (Import Data dialog box) to display the External Data Range Properties dialog box.

• Click 'Adjust column width' to remove the check mark from the 'Adjust column width' check box (Figure 7–30).

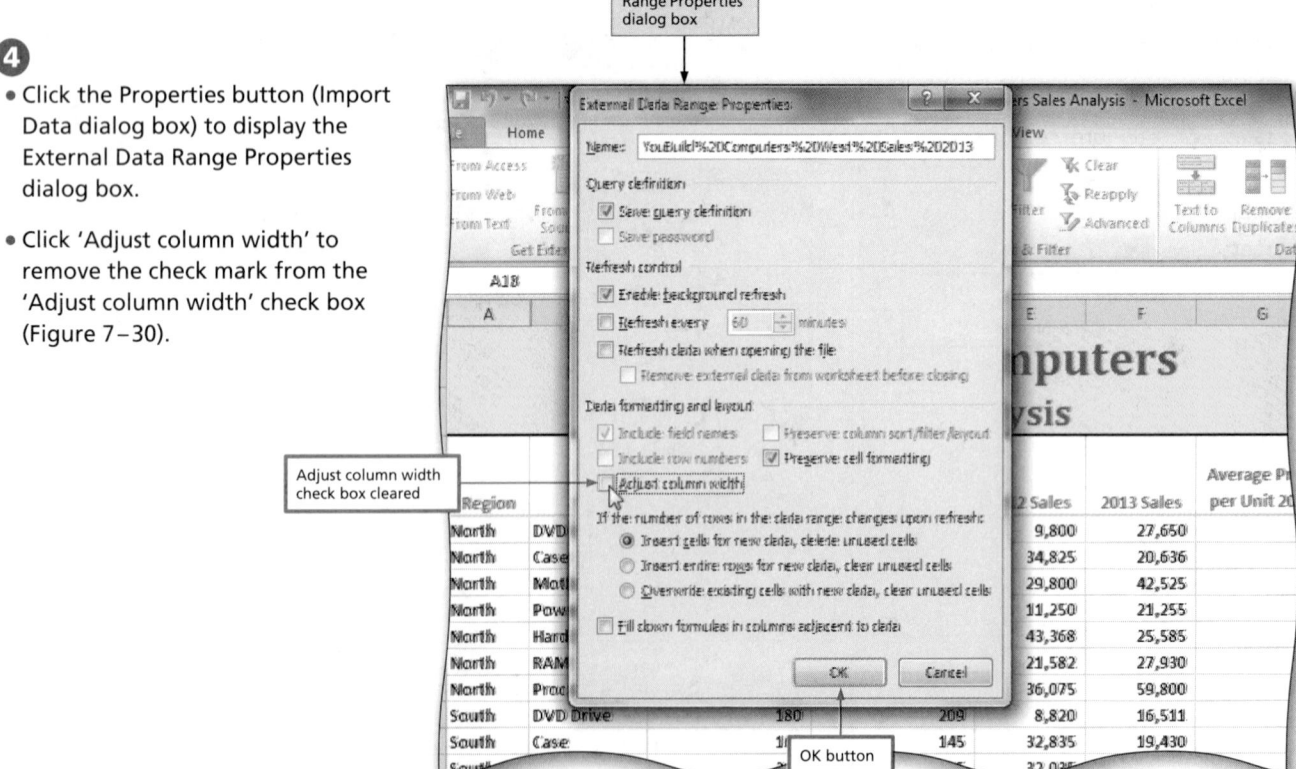

Figure 7–30

5

- Click the OK button (External Data Range Properties dialog box) to close the dialog box, instruct Excel not to adjust the column widths when the data is imported, and display the Import Data dialog box again.

- Click the OK button (Import Data dialog box) to import the data from the Web page into the worksheet beginning at cell A18 (Figure 7–31).

Q&A

Why is the data imported starting in cell A18?

By default, the cell that is active when the Web query is performed will become the upper-left cell of the imported range. To import the data to a different location, change the location in the Import Data dialog box.

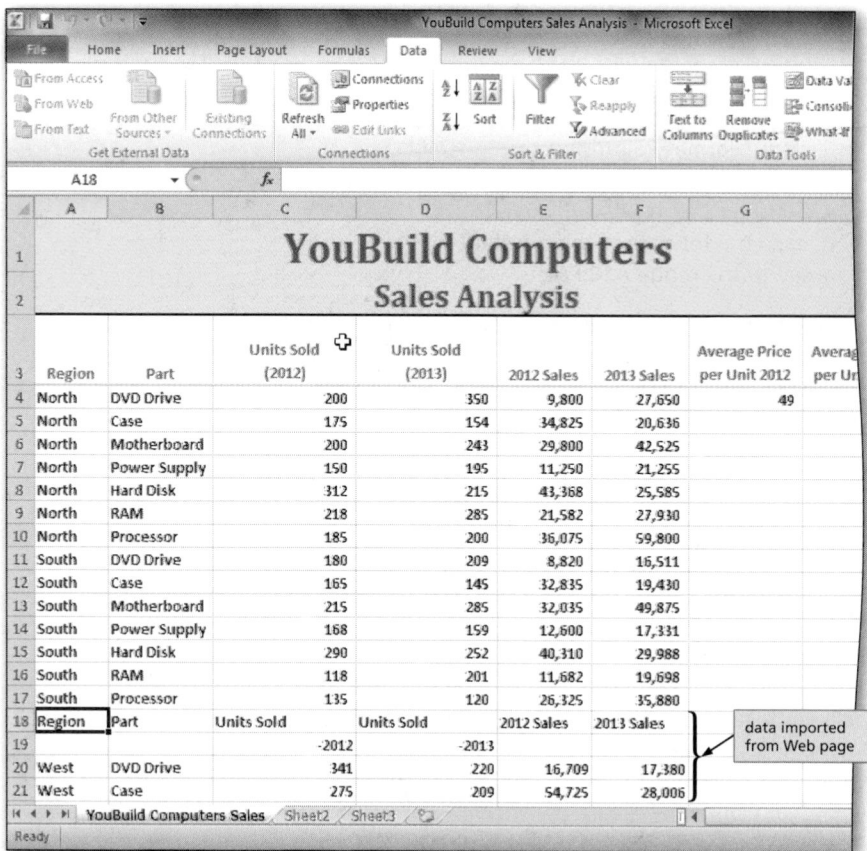

Figure 7–31

6

- Drag through the row headings in rows 18 and 19 to select the rows.

- Right-click the selected rows, and then click Delete on the shortcut menu to delete rows 18 and 19, which contained the column headings from the Web page (Figure 7–32).

Q&A

Why are the column headings repeated in row 18?

Because the column headings appeared in the Web page, they are imported with the other data and are displayed in rows 18 and 19. The extra column headings must be deleted from the imported Web page table.

	A	B	C	D	E	F	G
4	North	DVD Drive	200	350	9,800	27,650	49
5	North	Case	175	154	34,825	20,636	
6	North	Motherboard	200	243	29,800	42,525	
7	North	Power Supply	150	195	11,250	21,255	
8	North	Hard Disk	312	215	43,368	25,585	
9	North	RAM	218	285	21,582	27,930	
10	North	Processor	185	200	36,075	59,800	
11	South	DVD Drive	180	209	8,820	16,511	
12	South	Case	165	145	32,835	19,430	
13	South	Motherboard	215	285	32,035	49,875	
14	South	Power Supply	168	159	12,600	17,331	
15	South	Hard Disk	290	252	40,310	29,988	
16	South	RAM	118	201	11,682	19,698	
17	South	Processor	135	120	26,325	35,880	
18	West	DVD Drive	341	220	16,709	17,380	
19	West	Case	275	209	54,725	28,006	
20	West	Motherboard	290	275	43,210	48,125	
21	West	Power Supply	145	190	10,875	20,710	
22	West	Hard Disk	226	196	31,414	23,324	
23	West	RAM	185	201	18,315	19,698	
24	West	Processor	279	350	54,405	104,650	
25							
26							
27							
28							

row headings 18 and 19

rows 18 and 19 deleted

Figure 7–32

7

- Display the Home tab.

- Select the range A17:F17 to prepare for copying its formatting.

- Click the Format Painter button (Home tab | Clipboard group), and then drag though the range A18:F24 to copy the formats of the selected range to the range A18:F24.

- Select cell A34 to deselect the range and prepare for importing other data (Figure 7–33).

Q&A

Why should I use a Web query instead of copying and pasting from a Web page?

Using a Web query has advantages over other methods of importing data from a Web page. For example, copying data from Web pages to the Office Clipboard and then pasting it into Excel does not maintain all of the Web page formatting. In addition, copying only the desired data from a Web page can be tedious. Finally, copying and pasting does not create a link to the Web page for future updating.

Figure 7–33

Other Ways

1. Select text, right-click selection, click Format Painter button on Mini toolbar

---

BTW

Copying
To copy the contents of a cell to the cell directly below it, click in the target cell and press CTRL+D.

Importing Word Data

A Word document often contains data stored in a table. You can use the Office Clipboard and Copy and Paste commands to copy the data in the table to an Excel worksheet. On some occasions, imported data requires a great deal of manipulation once you import it into Excel. For example, the imported data may be easier to work with if the rows and columns were switched, or **transposed**. In other situations, you may find that an imported column of data should be split into two columns.

To Copy and Transpose Data from a Word Document to a Worksheet

The Word document that contains the East region's sales data (Figure 7–1d on page EX 427) includes a table in which the rows and columns are switched when compared with the YouBuild Computers Sales worksheet. The first column of data also includes data for both the region and the part type. The following steps copy and transpose the data from the Word document to the YouBuild Computers Sales worksheet.

- With cell A34 selected, start Word and then open the Word document named, YouBuild Computers East Sales 2013, from the Data Files for Students.

- In Word, if necessary, display the Home tab.

- Drag through all of the cells in the second through last columns in the table in the Word document to select the table cells.

Region, Part	East, DVD Drive	East, Case	East, Motherboard	East, Power Supply	East, Hard Disk	East, Ram	East, Processor
Units Sold (2012)	350	201	196	190	275	209	220
Units Sold (2013)	279	185	226	145	290	275	341
2012 Sales	17,150	39,999	29,204	14,250	38,225	20,691	42,900
2013 Sales	22,041	24,790	39,550	15,805	34,510	26,950	101,959

Figure 7–34

- Click the Copy button (Home tab | Clipboard group) to copy the contents of the table to the Office Clipboard (Figure 7–34).

- Quit Word and, if necessary, click the YouBuild Computers Sales Analysis workbook taskbar button to make Excel the active window.

- Click the Paste button arrow (Home tab | Clipboard group) to display the Paste options (Figure 7–35).

				226	196	31,414	23,324
22	West	Hard Disk					
23	West	RAM		185	201	18,315	19,698

Figure 7–35

- Click Paste Special on the Paste menu to display the Paste Special dialog box.

- Click Text in the As list (Figure 7–36).

Q&A

Why do I select Text in the As list?

If a different format is selected, then formatting and other information may be pasted with the data. Importing the data as text provides greater flexibility for manipulating and formatting the data in Excel.

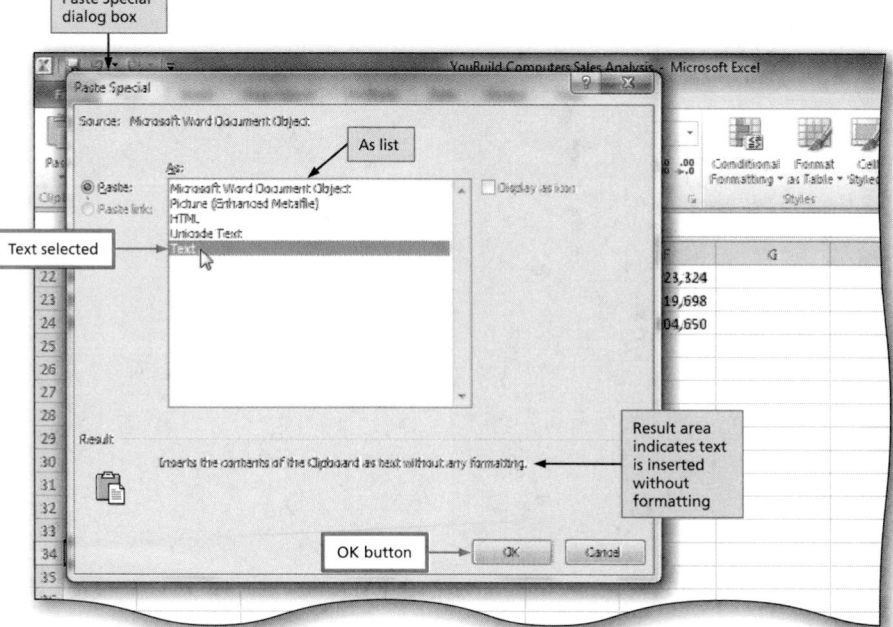

Paste Special

Source: Microsoft Word Document Object

As:
Microsoft Word Document Object
Picture (Enhanced Metafile)
HTML
Unicode Text
Text

Result
Inserts the contents of the Clipboard as text without any formatting.

22		23,324
23		19,698
24		04,650

Figure 7–36

4

- Click the OK button (Paste Special dialog box) to paste the contents of the Office Clipboard to the range A34:G38 (Figure 7–37).

Q&A

Why is the data pasted to the range A34:G38?

Excel's Transpose command requires that the source of the transposed data be different from the destination. In this case, the source is the range A34:G38 and the destination will be the range A25:E31.

Figure 7–37

5

- Click the Copy button (Home tab | Clipboard group) to copy the range A34:G38 to the Office Clipboard.

- Select cell A25 to prepare for pasting the copied data to the range beginning with cell A25.

- Click the Paste button arrow (Home tab | Clipboard group) and then point to Transpose on the Paste menu (Figure 7–38).

Figure 7–38

6

- Click Transpose on the Paste menu to transpose and paste the copied cells to the range beginning with cell A25 (Figure 7–39).

Q&A

What happens when the range is copied and transposed?

When the range is transposed, the first row of the selected range becomes the first column of the destination range, and so on. For example, row 34 (A34:G38) in the source range becomes column A (A25:E31) in the destination range.

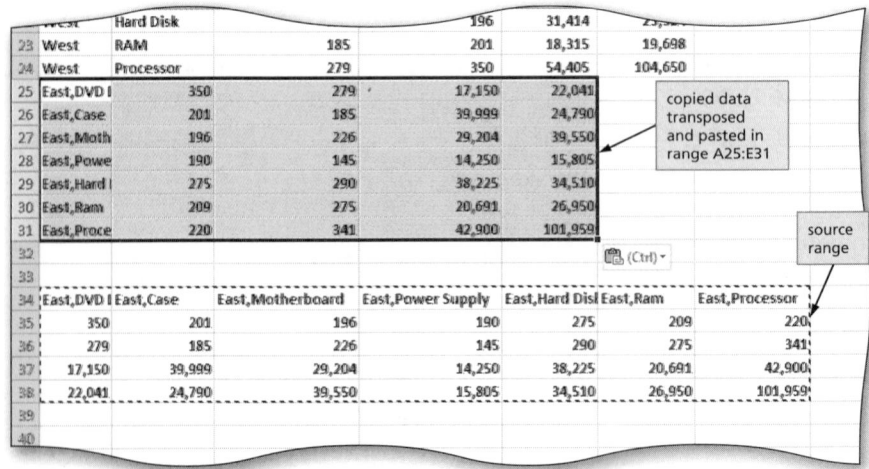

Figure 7–39

To Convert Text to Columns

As stated earlier and shown in Figure 7–33 on page EX 450, column A of the imported East data includes both the region and part data. The data must be separated using Excel's Convert Text to Columns command so that the shop type information is in column B. Before doing so, the source range for the data (A34:G38) should be deleted because it no longer is needed. Also, the cells in the range B25:E31 must be shifted one column to the right to accommodate the part data.

The following steps clear the range A34:G38, move the range B25:E31 one column to the right, and move the part data in column A to column B.

1

- If necessary, display the Home tab.

- Select the range A34:G38 and then press the DELETE key to delete the range.

- Select the range B25:E31 and then click the Cut button (Home tab | Clipboard group) to delete the range from the worksheet and copy it to the Office Clipboard (Figure 7–40).

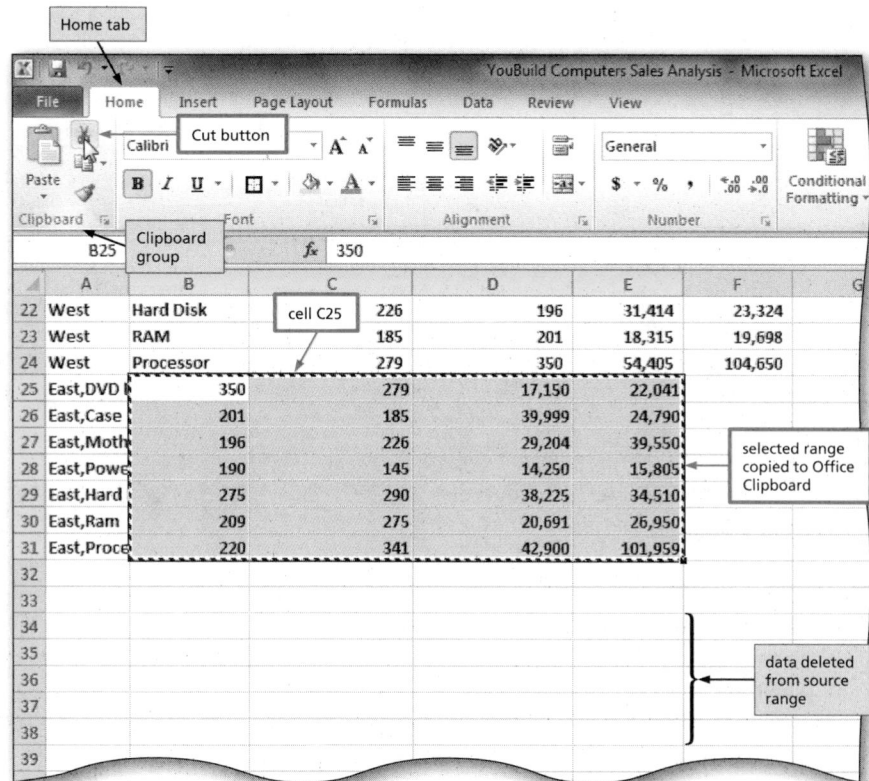

Figure 7–40

2

- Select cell C25 and then click the Paste button (Home tab | Clipboard group) to paste the source data beginning in cell C25 (Figure 7–41).

Q&A

Why does the range B25:E31 need to be cut and pasted to the new range?

The data in the range B25:E31 contains the part information that needs to be placed in the range C25:F31. Moving the range B25:E31 one column to the right will accommodate the part information.

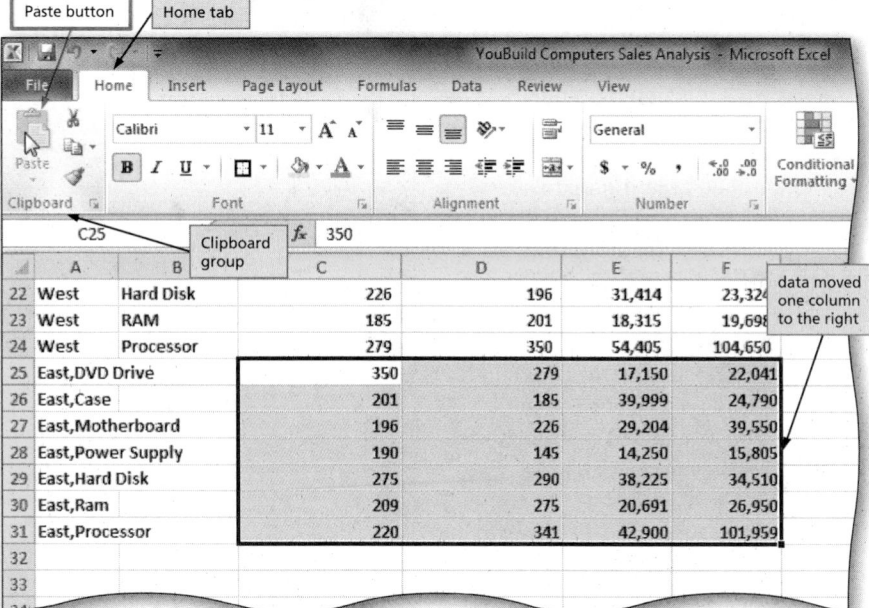

Figure 7–41

3

- Select the range A23:F23 and then click the Format Painter button (Home tab | Clipboard group) to copy the formatting of the selected cells.

- Select the range A25:F31 to copy the formats from range A23:F23 to the range A25:F31 (Figure 7–42).

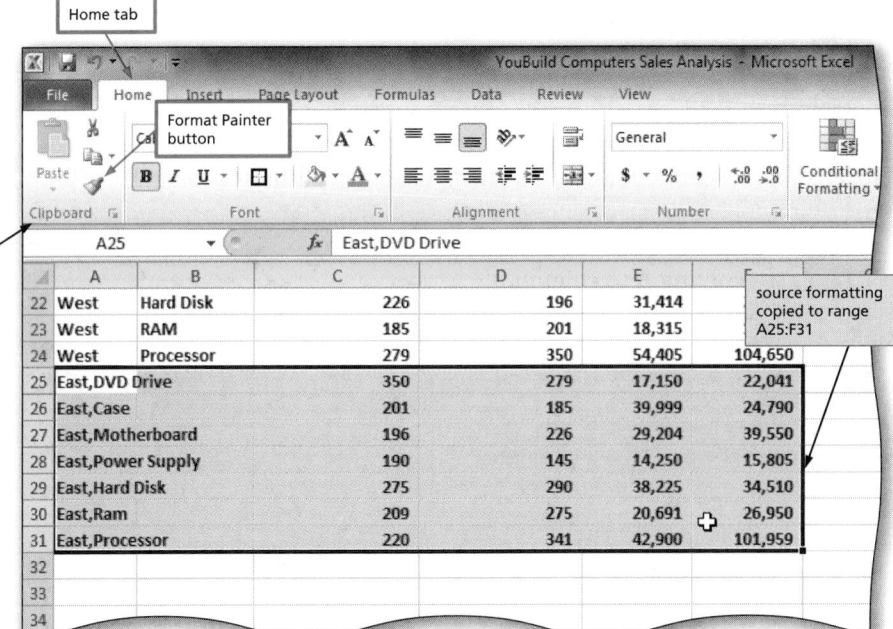

Figure 7–42

4

- Select the range A25:A31 to prepare for converting the text to columns.

- Display the Data tab.

- Click the Text to Columns button (Data tab | Data Tools group) to display the Convert Text to Columns Wizard – Step 1 of 3 dialog box (Figure 7–43).

Q&A

What other tasks can be accomplished using the Convert Text to Columns Wizard?

The wizard can be used only when a range that includes a single column is selected. The Convert Text to Columns Wizard is a powerful tool for manipulating text data in columns, such as splitting first and last names into separate columns. Most often, however, you will use the wizard to manipulate imported data. For example, survey data may be imported in one column as a series of Y and N characters, indicating answers to questions on the survey (e.g., YNNYYN). You can split the answers into separate columns by specifying fixed width fields of one character each.

Figure 7–43

- Click the Next button (Convert Text to Columns Wizard – Step 1 of 3 dialog box) to accept Delimited as the file type of the data and to display the Convert Text to Columns Wizard – Step 2 of 3 dialog box.

- Click Comma to insert a check mark in the Comma check box and to display the data fields correctly in the Data preview area.

- Click Tab to remove the check mark from the Tab check box (Figure 7–44).

Figure 7–44

- Click the Finish button (Convert Text to Columns Wizard – Step 2 of 3 dialog box) to close the dialog box and separate the data in column A into two columns.

- Display the Home tab to prepare for the next task (Figure 7–45).

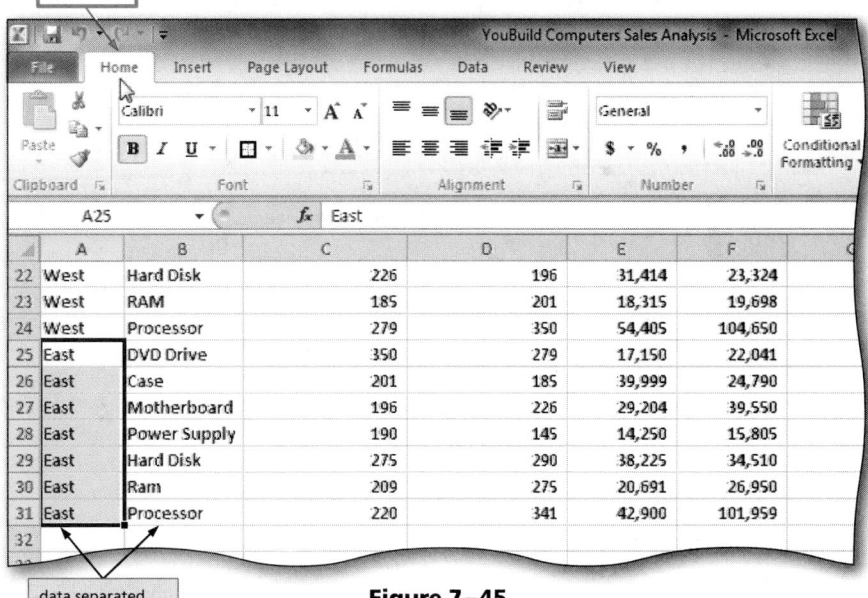

Figure 7–45

Other Ways

1. Select text, right-click selection, click Format Painter button on Mini toolbar

Replicating Formulas after Importing

The workbook opened at the beginning of this project contained a worksheet title, headings for each column, and formulas in cells G4 and H4 to calculate the average price per unit for 2012 and 2013. The formulas must be copied, or replicated, through row 31 to complete the calculations for the remaining rows in the worksheet. Some spreadsheet specialists refer to copying formulas as **replication**. You often replicate formulas after completing an import because the total number of records to be imported usually is unknown.

BTW

Selecting a Range of Cells

You can select any range of cells with entries surrounded by blank cells by clicking a cell in the range and pressing CTRL+SHIFT+ASTERISK (*).

To Replicate Formulas

The following steps use the fill handle to replicate the formulas.

1

• Select the range G4:H4 to prepare for copying the formulas in the range (Figure 7–46).

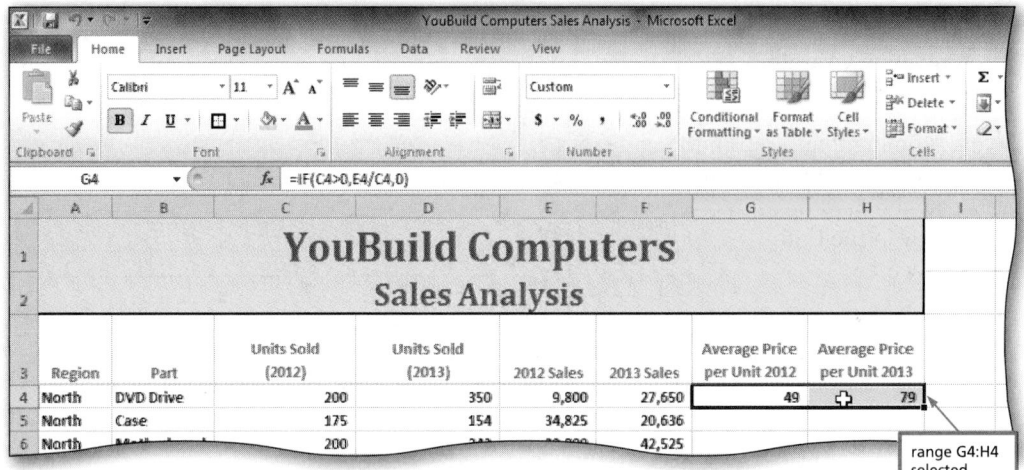

Figure 7–46

2

• Drag the fill handle down through row 31 to copy the two formulas to the range G5:H31 and display the new values for the Average Price per Unit 2012 and Average Price per Unit 2013 columns (Figure 7–47).

Q&A

What if I just want to copy formulas rather than replicate them?

Replicating a formula causes Excel to adjust the cell references so that the new formulas contain references corresponding to the new locations. Excel then performs calculations using the appropriate values. To create an exact copy without replication, hold down the CTRL key while dragging the fill handle. Holding down the SHIFT key while dragging the fill handle inserts new cells, rather than overwriting existing data.

Figure 7–47

3

• Click Cell H32 to deselect the range G5:H31.

• Click the Save button on the Quick Access Toolbar to save the workbook using the same file name, YouBuild Computers Sales Analysis.

Other Ways

1. Click Copy button on Quick Access Toolbar, click Paste button on Quick Access Toolbar

2. Press CTRL+C, press CTRL+V

3. Click Copy on shortcut menu, click Paste on shortcut menu

Break Point: If you wish to take a break, this is a good place to do so. You can quit Excel now. To resume at a later time, start Excel, open the file called YouBuild Computers Sales Analysis, and continue following the steps from this location forward.

Using the Find and Replace Commands

BTW

The Find Command
If you want to search only a specified range of a worksheet, select the range before using the Find command. The range can consist of adjacent cells or nonadjacent cells.

A **string** can be a single character, a word, or a phrase in a cell on a worksheet. To locate a string in a worksheet, you can use the Find command on the Find & Select menu. Display the Find & Select menu by clicking the Find & Select button on the Home tab. To locate one string and then replace it with another string, use the Replace command on the Find & Select menu. The Find and Replace commands are not available for a chart sheet.

Selecting the Find or Replace command displays the Find and Replace dialog box. The Find and Replace dialog box has two variations. One version displays minimal options, while the other version displays all of the available options. When you select the Find or Replace command, Excel displays the dialog box variation that was used the last time either command was selected.

Plan Ahead

Determine whether data you import needs to be standardized.
Before importing files from various sources, examine the data to determine whether it fits in with the other data. For example, the author of one source might refer to a DVD drive, while the author of another source might refer to the same item as an optical disc drive. Determine which terminology you want to use in your spreadsheet, and use the appropriate commands to standardize all wording.

To Find a String

The following steps show how to locate the string, Motherboard. The Find and Replace dialog box that displays all the options will be used to customize the search by using the Match case and 'Match entire cell contents' options. Match case means that the search is case sensitive and the cell contents must match the word exactly the way it is typed. 'Match entire cell contents' means that the string cannot be part of another word or phrase and must be unique in the cell. If you have a cell range selected, the Find and Replace commands search only the range; otherwise, the Find and Replace commands begin at cell A1, regardless of the location of the active cell.

1
• Click the Find & Select button (Home tab | Editing group) to display the Find & Select menu (Figure 7–48).

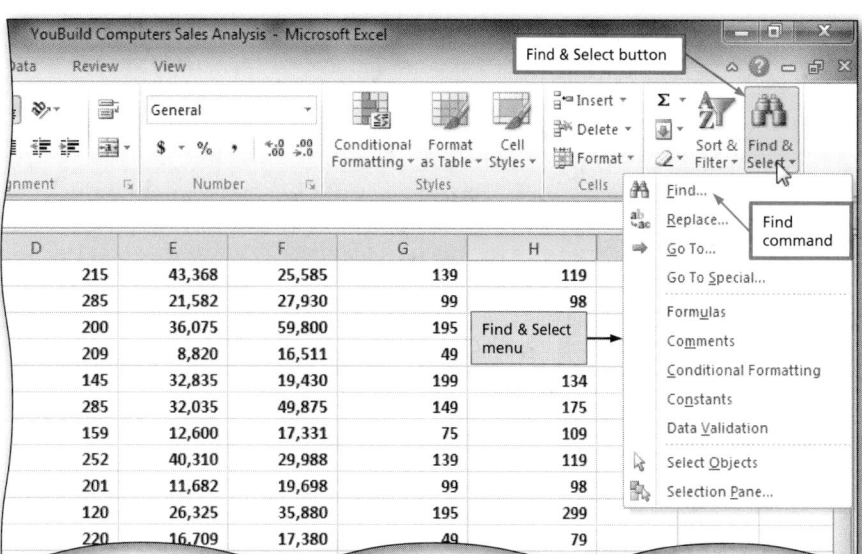

Figure 7–48

2

- Click Find to display the Find and Replace dialog box.

- Click the Options button (Find and Replace dialog box) to expand the dialog box so that it appears as shown in Figure 7–49.

- Type **Motherboard** in the Find what box to enter the search text.

- Click Match case and then click 'Match entire cell contents' to insert check marks in those check boxes (Figure 7–49).

Figure 7–49

Q&A
Why does the appearance of the Options button change?

The two less than signs pointing to the left on the Options button indicate that the more comprehensive Find and Replace dialog box is active.

3

- Click the Find Next button (Find and Replace dialog box) to cause Excel to begin the search at cell A1 on the YouBuild Computers Sales worksheet and make cell B6 the active cell (Figure 7–50).

Q&A
Why is cell B6 the active cell after completing Step 3?

Cell B6 is the first cell to match the search string.

Figure 7–50

4

- Continue clicking the Find Next button (Find and Replace dialog box) to find the string, Motherboard, in three other cells on the worksheet.

- Click the Close button (Find and Replace dialog box) to stop searching and close the Find and Replace dialog box.

Q&A
What if Excel does not find the search string?

If the Find command does not find the string for which you are searching, Excel displays a dialog box indicating it searched the selected worksheets and cannot find the search string.

Other Ways

1. Press CTRL+F

Working with the Find and Replace Dialog Box

The Format button in the Find and Replace dialog box in Figure 7–50 allows you to fine-tune the search by adding formats, such as bold, font style, and font size, to the string. The Within box options include Sheet and Workbook. The Search box indicates whether Excel will search vertically through rows or horizontally across columns. The Look in box allows you to select Values, Formulas, or Comments. If you select Values, Excel will look for the search string only in cells that do not have formulas. If you select Formulas, Excel will look in all cells. If you select Comments, Excel will look only in comments. If you select the Match case check box, Excel will locate only cells in which the string is in the same case. For example, ram is not the same as RAM. If you select the 'Match entire cell contents' check box, Excel will locate only the cells that contain the string and no other characters. For example, Excel will find a cell entry of RAM, but not DVD RAM.

To Replace a String with Another String

Use the Replace command to replace the found search string with a new string. You can use the Find Next and Replace buttons to find and replace a string one occurrence at a time, or you can use the Replace All button to replace the string in all locations at once. The following steps show how to use the Replace All button to replace the string, DVD Drive, with the string, Optical Disc Drive.

- Click the Find & Select button (Home tab | Editing group) to display the Find & Select menu.

- Click Replace on the Find & Select menu to display the Find and Replace dialog box.

- Type `DVD Drive` in the Find what box and `Optical Disc Drive` in the Replace with box to specify the text to find and to replace.

- If necessary, click Match case and then click 'Match entire cell contents' to insert check marks in those check boxes (Figure 7–51).

Figure 7–51

- Click the Replace All button (Find and Replace dialog box) to replace the string (Figure 7–52).

- Click the OK button (Microsoft Office Excel dialog box).

- Click the Close button (Find and Replace dialog box).

Q&A | What happens when Excel replaces the string?

Excel replaces the string, DVD Drive, with the replacement string, Optical Disc Drive, throughout the entire worksheet. If other worksheets contain matching cells, Excel replaces those cells as well. Excel displays the Microsoft Excel dialog box indicating four replacements were made.

Figure 7–52

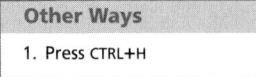

Other Ways
1. Press CTRL+H

Inserting a Clustered Cone Chart

The requirements document shown in Figure 7–2 on page EX 429 specifies that the workbook should include a Clustered Cone chart. The Clustered Cone chart is similar to a 3-D Bar chart in that it can show trends or illustrate comparisons among items.

Plan Ahead

> **Plan the layout and location of the required chart.**
> The Clustered Cone chart in Figure 7–53, for example, compares the average price per unit for 2013 of the different parts for the North region. The chart should be placed on a separate worksheet. WordArt is used to draw the reflected chart title, Price Analysis, in an eye-catching and professional format.

Figure 7–53

To Insert the Clustered Cone Chart

The following steps add a Clustered Cone chart to a new sheet and then change the layout of the chart to rotate it, remove the series label, and add a title to the horizontal axis.

1

- Select the range B4:B10 to select the first set of data to include in the chart.

- Hold down the CTRL key and then select the range H4:H10 to select the second set of data for the chart.

- Click Insert on the Ribbon to display the Insert tab.

- Click the Column button (Insert tab | Charts group) and then click Clustered Cone (column 1, row 4) in the Column gallery to insert a Clustered Cone chart (Figure 7–54).

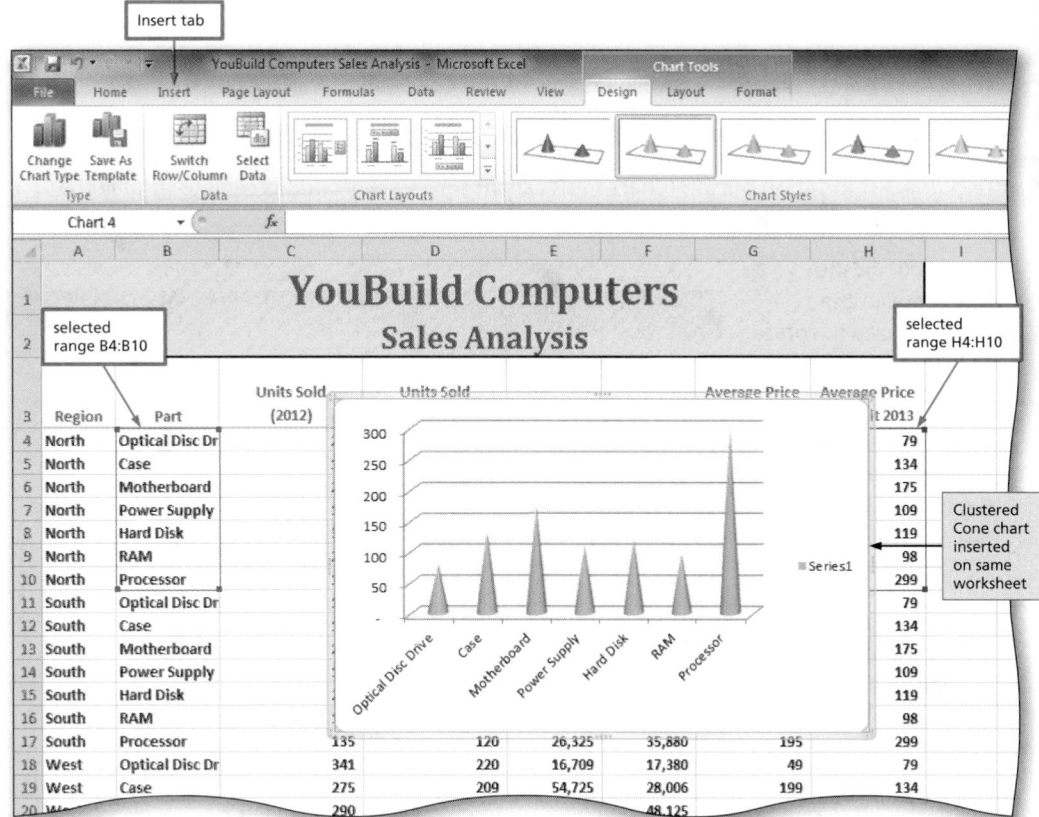

Figure 7–54

2

- Click the Move Chart button (Chart Tools Design tab | Location group) to display the Move Chart dialog box.

- Click the New sheet option button and then type **Clustered Cone Chart** as the sheet name in the New sheet text box.

- Click the OK button (Move Chart dialog box) to move the chart to the new sheet (Figure 7–55).

Figure 7–55

- Right-click the Clustered Cone Chart sheet tab, point to Tab Color on the shortcut menu, and then click Green in the Standard Colors row of the Color palette to change the tab color.

- Click Layout on the Ribbon to display the Chart Tools Layout tab.

- Click the 3-D Rotation button (Chart Tools Layout tab | Background group) to display the Format Chart Area dialog box.

- Type **7 0** in the X text box in the Rotation area to rotate the chart 70 degrees along the x-axis.

- Type **3 0** in the Y text box in the Rotation area to rotate the chart 30 degrees along the y-axis.

- Click the Close button (Format Chart Area dialog box) to finish formatting the chart (Figure 7–56).

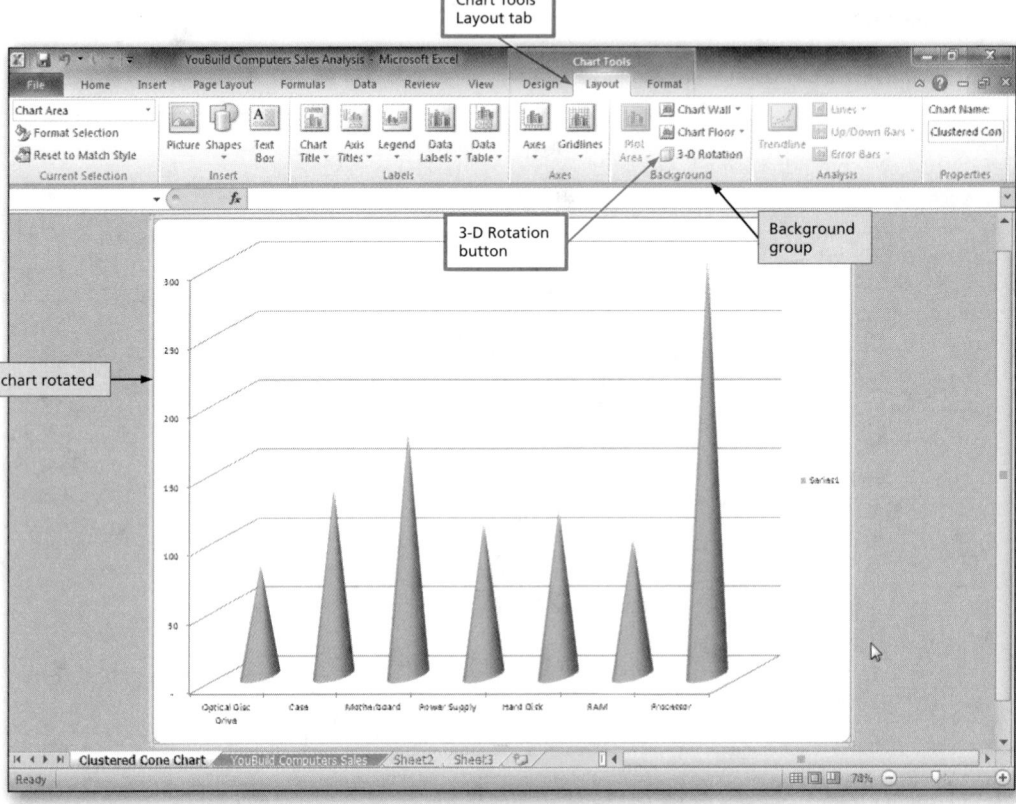

Figure 7–56

Experiment

- Try entering different values in the X and Y text boxes to see how changing the values affects the rotation of the chart. When you are finished, return the values to those specified in Step 3.

- Click the Legend button (Chart Tools Layout tab | Labels group) and then click None to remove the legend from the right side of the chart (Figure 7–57).

Figure 7–57

5

- Click the Axis Titles button (Chart Tools Layout tab | Labels group) to display the Axis Titles menu.

- Point to Primary Horizontal Axis Title on the Axis Titles menu and then click Title Below Axis in the Primary Horizontal Axis Title gallery to add a title to the horizontal axis.

- Select the Axis Title text and then type **North Region** as the new title (Figure 7–58).

Q&A

What does the chart show?

The Clustered Cone chart compares the prices of the seven different computer parts. You can see from the chart that, of the parts sold, the processor is the most expensive, and the optical disc drive is the least expensive.

Other Ways

1. Select range, click chart type button (Insert tab | Charts group), click chart type in gallery

2. Select range, press F11

Figure 7–58

To Add a Chart Title Using the WordArt Tool

Earlier, you learned how to add a chart title by using the Chart Title button on the Chart Tools Layout tab, and how to format it using the Home tab. You also can create a chart title using the WordArt tool. The WordArt tool allows you to create shadowed, skewed, rotated, and stretched text on a chart sheet or worksheet and apply other special text formatting effects. The WordArt text added to a worksheet is called an object. The following steps show how to add a chart title using the WordArt tool.

1

- With the Clustered Cone Chart sheet active, click anywhere on the chart.

- Display the Insert tab.

- Click the WordArt button (Insert tab | Text group) to display the WordArt gallery.

- Point to the Gradient Fill – Turquoise, Accent 4, Reflection (column 5, row 4) selection in the WordArt gallery to highlight that color and effect (Figure 7–59).

Figure 7–59

2
- Click the Gradient Fill – Turquoise, Accent 4, Reflection selection in the WordArt gallery to insert a new WordArt object.

- Type **Price Analysis** as the title of the Clustered Cone chart (Figure 7–60).

Figure 7–60

3
- Select the text in the WordArt object to display the Mini toolbar (Figure 7–61).

Figure 7–61

4
- Click the Font Size box arrow on the Mini toolbar and then click 44 in the Font Size list to change the font size of the WordArt object to 44 points (Figure 7–62).

Figure 7–62

5

- Drag the top edge of the WordArt object so that the object is positioned in the upper-middle part of the chart (as shown in Figure 7–63).

position of WordArt object changed

PRICE ANALYSIS

Figure 7–63

6

- Click outside the chart area to deselect the WordArt object (Figure 7–64).

7

- Click the Save button on the Quick Access Toolbar to save the workbook using the file name, YouBuild Computers Sales Analysis.

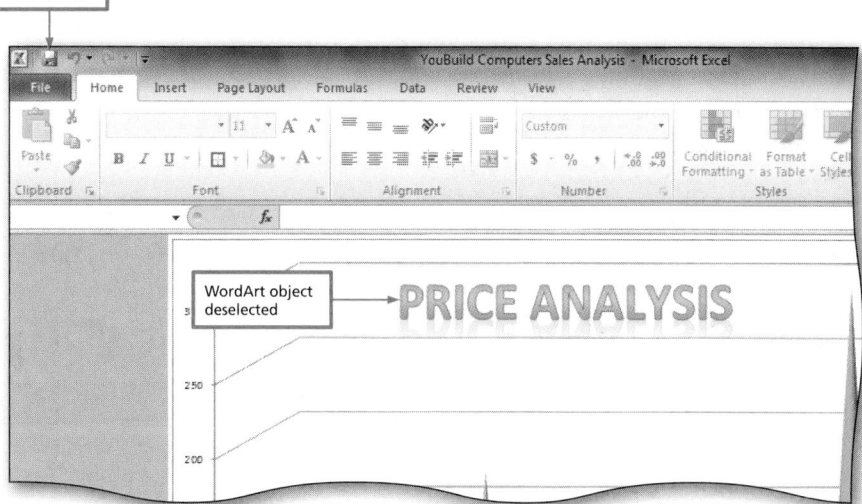

Save button

WordArt object deselected

PRICE ANALYSIS

Figure 7–64

Other Ways

1. Click WordArt, change font size in Font box (Home tab | Font group)

Working with SmartArt Graphics

A SmartArt graphic is a customizable diagram that you use to pictorially present lists, processes, and relationships. For example, you can use a SmartArt graphic to illustrate the manufacturing process to produce an item. Excel includes nine types of SmartArt graphics: List, Process, Cycle, Hierarchy, Relationship, Matrix, Pyramid, Picture, and Office.com. Each type of graphic includes several layouts, or templates, from which to choose. After selecting a SmartArt graphic type and layout, you customize the graphic to meet your needs and present your information and ideas in a compelling manner.

Choose the type of SmartArt graphics to add.
Consider what you want to illustrate in the SmartArt graphic. For example, if you are showing nonsequential or grouped blocks of information, select a SmartArt graphic in the List category. To show progression or sequential steps in a process or task, select a Process diagram. After inserting a SmartArt graphic, increase its visual appeal by formatting the graphic, for example, with 3-D effects and coordinated colors.

Plan Ahead

To Insert a Picture Strips SmartArt Graphic

Excel allows you to insert SmartArt graphics that can contain pictures. To illustrate the type of computer parts YouBuild Computers sells, you decide to use a Picture Strips SmartArt graphic. The following steps insert a Picture Strips SmartArt graphic.

1

• Click the Sheet2 tab to make Sheet2 the active worksheet.

• Rename the worksheet **Computer Parts** to provide a descriptive name for the worksheet.

• Change the color of the tab to blue to distinguish it from other sheets.

• Click View on the Ribbon to display the View tab.

• Click the Gridlines check box (View tab | Show group) to turn off gridlines on the worksheet (Figure 7–65).

 Why should I turn off gridlines?

Although useful during the process of creating a worksheet, many spreadsheet specialists remove the gridlines to reduce the clutter on the screen. This is especially true when working with graphics and images on a worksheet.

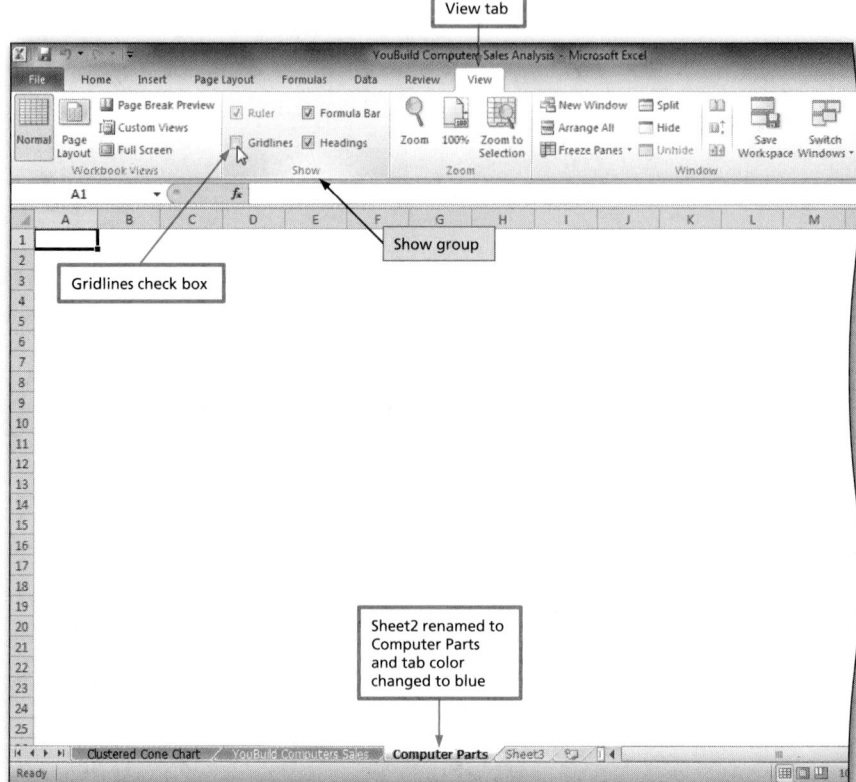

Figure 7–65

2

• Display the Insert tab.

• Click the SmartArt button (Insert tab | Illustrations group) to display the Choose a SmartArt Graphic dialog box (Figure 7–66).

Figure 7–66

3

- Click Picture in the Type list in the left pane of the Choose a SmartArt Graphic dialog box.

Q&A

What do the middle and right panes of the dialog box display?

The middle pane of the dialog box (the layout list) displays a gallery of picture charts, and the right pane (the preview area) displays a preview of the selected SmartArt graphic.

- Click Picture Strips (column 2, row 4) in the layout list to see a preview of the chart in the preview area (Figure 7–67).

Figure 7–67

Experiment

- Click the various SmartArt graphics to see a preview of each in the preview area. When you are finished, click Picture Strips in the layout list.

4

- Click the OK button (Choose a SmartArt Graphic dialog box) to insert a Picture Strips SmartArt graphic in the worksheet.

- If necessary, click the Text Pane button (SmartArt Tools Design tab | Create Graphic group) to display the Text pane (Figure 7–68).

Figure 7–68

• While holding down the ALT key, click and drag the top of the SmartArt graphic so that the upper-left corner is over cell G1 (Figure 7–69).

Figure 7–69

• Click the middle sizing handle on the right edge of the SmartArt graphic, hold down the ALT key, and then drag the sizing handle until the right edge of the SmartArt graphic is aligned with the right edge of column O.

• Release the ALT key, point to the middle sizing handle on the bottom edge of the chart, hold down the ALT key, and then drag the sizing handle until the bottom edge of the chart is aligned with the bottom edge of row 25 (Figure 7–70).

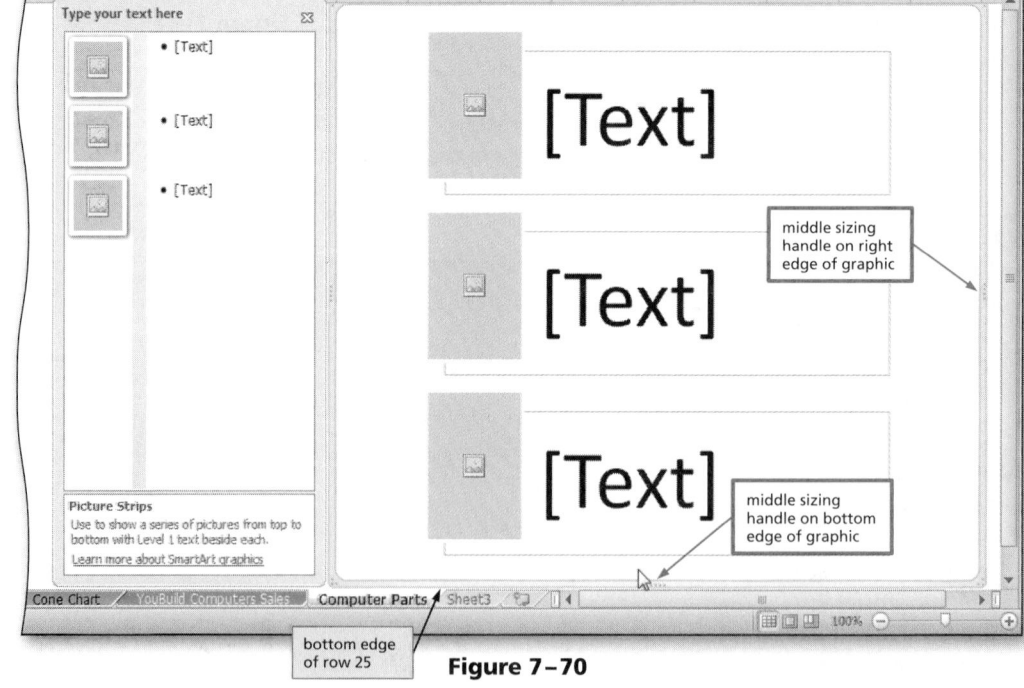

Figure 7–70

Other Ways

1. To display or hide Text pane, right-click SmartArt, click Show Text Pane or Hide Text Pane

2. To display Text pane, click expand button on SmartArt tab

To Add Shapes in the Picture Strips SmartArt Graphic

The default Picture Strips SmartArt graphic layout includes three shapes. You need six shapes to show the six computer parts that must be installed in a computer's case when building a computer. The following steps add three new shapes to the Picture Strips SmartArt graphic.

- Right-click the top shape in the Picture Strips SmartArt graphic to display the shortcut menu.

- Point to Add Shape on the shortcut menu to display the Add Shape submenu (Figure 7–71).

Figure 7–71

- Click Add Shape Before to add a new shape to the Picture Strips SmartArt graphic (Figure 7–72).

Q&A

Why does Excel change the layout of the chart?

When you add a new shape to a SmartArt graphic, Excel rearranges the shapes in the graphic to fit in the same area. As shown in Figure 7–72, Excel reduces the size of each shape and the font size of the text to accommodate the added shape.

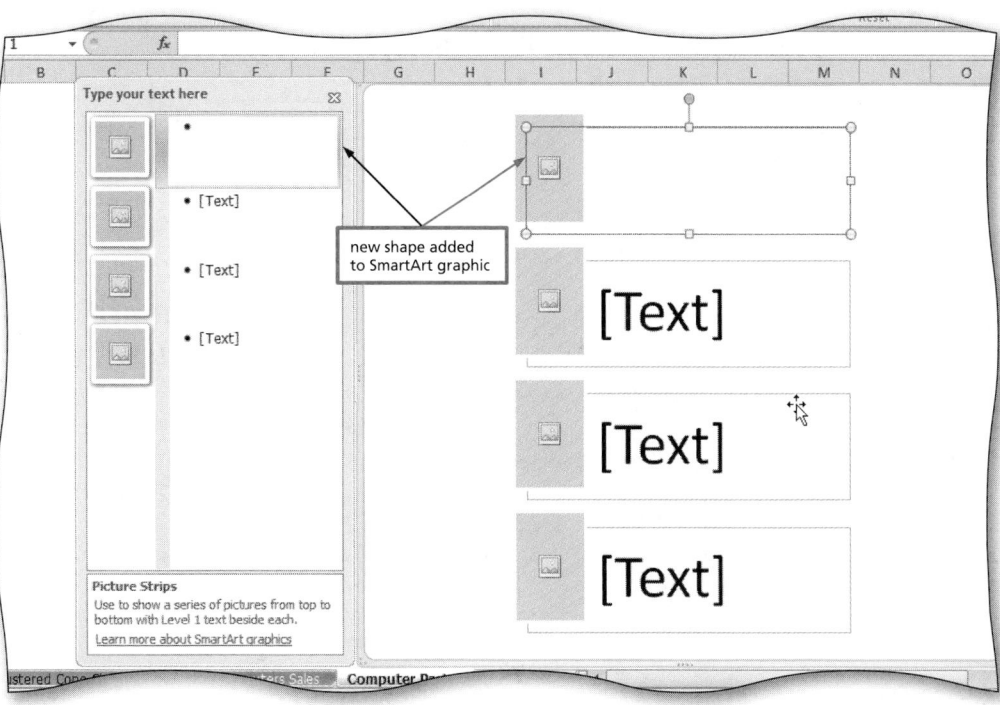

Figure 7–72

3

- If necessary, click the first shape of the chart to select it.

- If necessary, display the SmartArt Tools Design tab.

- Click the Add Shape button arrow (SmartArt Tools Design tab | Create Graphic group) to display the Add Shape menu.

- Click Add Shape After on the Add Shape menu to add a new shape below the first shape.

- Repeat these steps to insert a third additional shape to the Picture Strips SmartArt graphic (Figure 7–73).

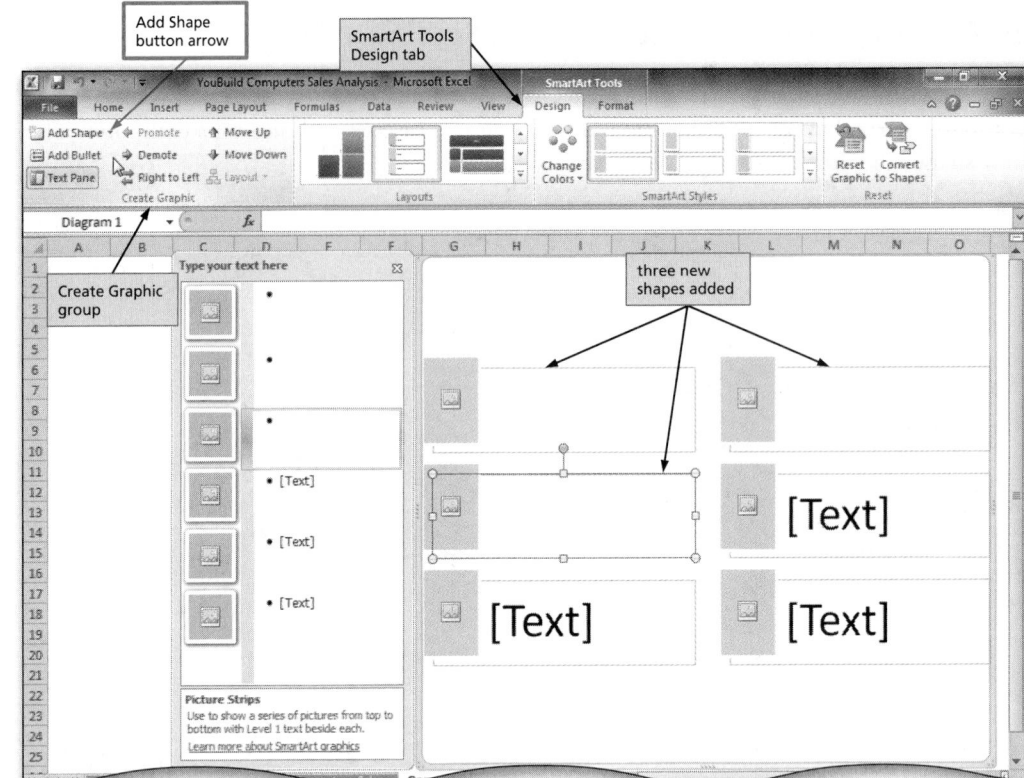

Figure 7–73

To Add Text to Shapes in the Picture Strips SmartArt Graphic

The following steps add text to the Picture Strips SmartArt graphic.

1

- Click the first shape's text box and then type **Motherboard** to add text to the shape (Figure 7–74).

Q&A

Why does Excel add the same text to the Text pane?

As you change the text in the chart, the Text pane reflects those changes in an outline. You can type text in the shapes or type text in the Text pane, as shown in the following step.

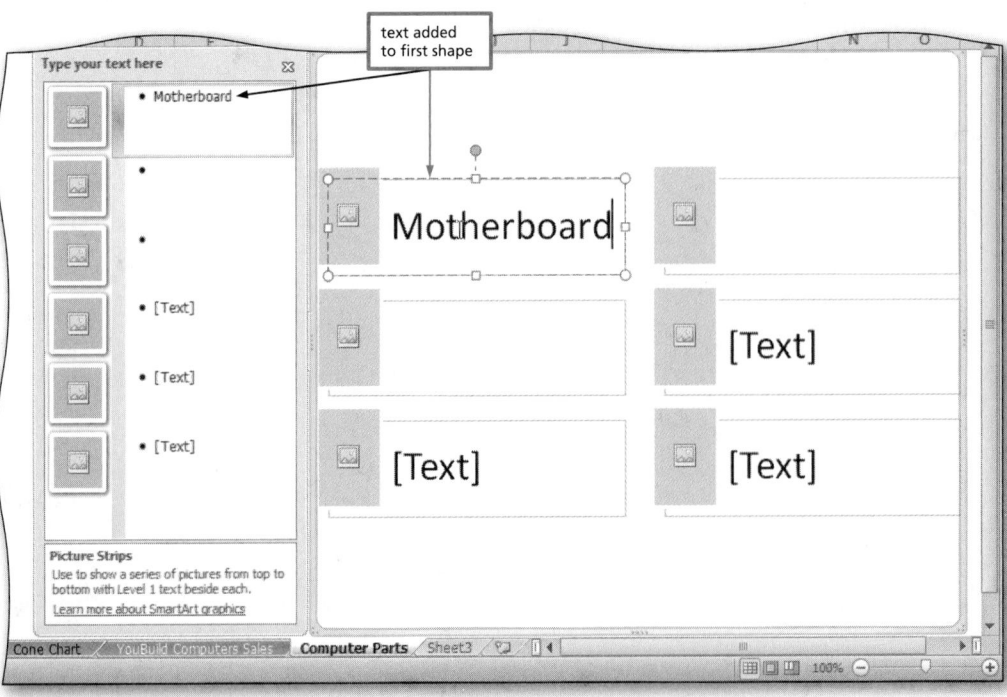

Figure 7–74

2

- Click the entry under Motherboard in the Text pane to select it.

- Type **Power Supply** in the second line of the Text pane to change the text in the second shape (Figure 7–75).

Figure 7–75

3

- Repeat Step 2 for each of the remaining shapes in the Picture Strips SmartArt graphic and enter text in each shape as shown in Figure 7–76.

Figure 7–76

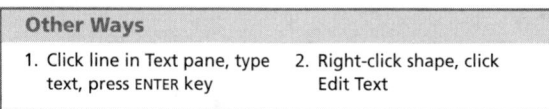

Other Ways	
1. Click line in Text pane, type text, press ENTER key	2. Right-click shape, click Edit Text

To Add Pictures to Shapes in the Picture Strips SmartArt Graphic

The following steps add pictures to the Picture Strips SmartArt graphic. The pictures to add are provided with the Data Files for Students and each has the same name as the computer part it displays.

- Click the upper-left shape's Insert Picture icon to display the Insert Picture dialog box.

- Navigate to the location of the picture to insert (in this case, the Excel folder on the USB flash drive) and click the Motherboard file to select the picture (Figure 7–77).

Figure 7–77

- Click the Insert button (Insert Picture dialog box) to insert the picture in the first shape (Figure 7–78).

Q&A

Could I also use the Insert Picture icon in the Text pane?

Yes, as with the text, you can add a picture from either the Text pane or the shape itself.

Figure 7–78

- Repeat Steps 1 and 2 for each of the remaining shapes in the picture strips and enter the picture in each shape (as shown in Figure 7–79).

Figure 7–79

To Add an Effect to the Picture Strips SmartArt Graphic

Excel allows you to change the style of your SmartArt graphic to create different effects. The following steps change the style of the Picture Strips SmartArt graphic for added emphasis.

- If necessary, display the SmartArt Tools Design tab.

- Click the SmartArt Styles More button (SmartArt Tools Design tab | SmartArt Styles group) to display the SmartArt Styles gallery.

- Point to the Intense Effect SmartArt style (column 2, row 2) in the Best Match for Document section to display a preview of the style in the worksheet (Figure 7–80).

Figure 7–80

- Click the Intense Effect SmartArt style to apply the style to the SmartArt graphic.

- Click cell A1 to deselect the Picture Strips SmartArt graphic.

- Click the Save button on the Quick Access Toolbar to save your work.

Using Images on a Worksheet

Besides adding images to SmartArt, Excel allows you to insert images on a worksheet and then modify the image by changing its shape and size or adding borders and effects. You can enhance a worksheet by including an image such as a corporate logo, photograph, diagram, or map. To use an image, the image must be stored digitally in a file.

BTW

Quick Reference
For a table that lists how to complete the tasks covered in this book using the mouse, Ribbon, shortcut menu, and keyboard, see the Quick Reference Summary at the back of this book, or visit the Excel 2010 Quick Reference Web page (scsite.com/ex2010/qr).

Obtain the images to be used in the worksheet.
Before inserting an image in a workbook, make sure you have permission to use the image. Although you might not need to pay for images available on Web sites, you most likely still need to request and receive permission to duplicate and use the images according to copyright law. Only images that are in the public domain are free for anyone to use without permission, although you still should credit the source of the image, even if the image creator is not specifically named. For example, include a credit line such as "Courtesy of NPS" if you use a public-domain photo from the National Park Service.

Plan Ahead

To Insert and Modify an Image in the Worksheet

The following steps insert an image of a computer case with all the parts installed, position and resize the image, and add an effect to the image.

1

- Display the Insert tab.

- Click the Insert Picture from File button (Insert tab | Illustrations group) to display the Insert Picture dialog box.

- Navigate to the location of the picture to insert (in this case, the Excel folder on the USB flash drive) and then click the Completed Case file to select the picture (Figure 7–81).

Figure 7–81

2

- Click the Insert button (Insert Picture dialog box) to insert the picture in the worksheet (Figure 7–82).

Q&A

How does Excel determine where to insert the image?

Excel inserts the image so that the upper-left corner of the image is located at the upper-left corner of the selected cell, which is cell A1 in this case.

Figure 7–82

3

- Click anywhere in the image, hold down the ALT key, drag the image so that the upper-left corner is aligned with the upper-left corner of cell B7, and then release the ALT key.

- Drag the lower-right sizing handle of the image to the lower-right corner of cell E19 (Figure 7–83).

Figure 7–83

④
- If necessary, click Format on the Ribbon to display the Picture Tools Format tab.

- Click the Picture Styles More button (Format tab | Picture Styles group) to display the Picture Styles gallery.

- Point to the Reflected Rounded Rectangle picture style (column 5, row 1) to see a preview of the style in the worksheet (Figure 7–84).

 Experiment

- Point to the various picture styles to see a preview of each style in the worksheet.

⑤
- Click the Reflected Rounded Rectangle picture style to apply the style to the image.

- Click the Save button on the Quick Access Toolbar to save the workbook.

Figure 7–84

Using Screen Shots on a Worksheet

Excel allows you to take a screen shot of any open window and add it to a workbook. Using the screen shot feature, you can capture whole windows or only part of a window. For example, if your company has a Web page, you can take a screen shot of the page and insert it into a workbook before presenting the workbook at a meeting. In addition, you can capture a screen clipping to include in your Excel workbook. A **screen clipping** is a portion, usually of one object or section of a window, of the screen.

BTW

Rotating Illustrations
To rotate pictures in Excel, select the image to be rotated, click the Rotate button (Picture Tools Format tab | Arrange group). You can select 90 degree left and right rotations from the menu, or select More Rotation Options from the menu and then specify the degree of rotation desired in the Format Picture dialog box.

To Insert a Screen Shot on a Worksheet

The staff at YouBuild Computers often share helpful sites that contain instructions about building computers. In anticipation of an upcoming meeting where the sales analysis will be reviewed, the CEO requests a screen shot of a popular Web site that provides instructions about building a computer. The steps on the next pages add a screen shot to a worksheet.

1

- Click the Internet Explorer button on the taskbar to start Internet Explorer.

- Type `http://electronics.howstuffworks.com/how-to-tech/build-a-computer.htm` in the Address bar and press the ENTER key to display the Web page (Figure 7–85).

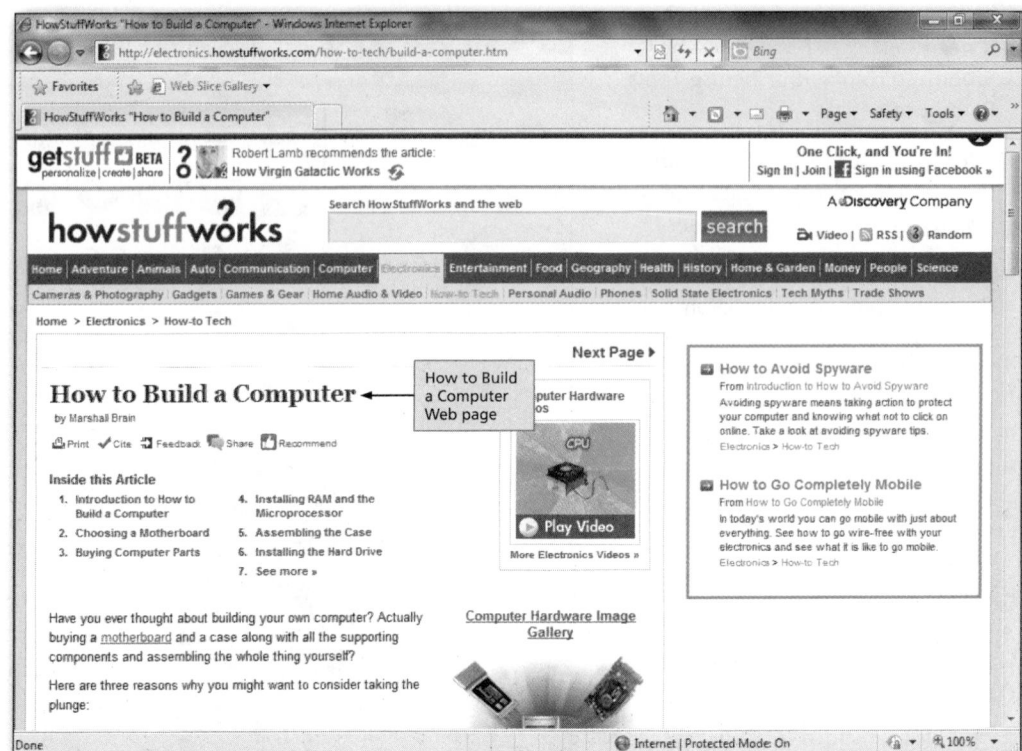

Figure 7–85

2

- Make the Excel window the active window.

- Click the Sheet3 tab to make it the active worksheet.

- Rename the worksheet to **Screenshot** and color the tab yellow to distinguish it from other worksheets.

- Display the View tab.

- Click the Gridlines check box (View tab | Show group) to turn off gridlines on the worksheet.

- If necessary, click cell A1 to make it the active cell (Figure 7–86).

Figure 7–86

- Display the Insert tab.

- Click the Screenshot button (Insert tab | Illustrations group) to display the Screenshot menu (Figure 7–87).

Figure 7–87

- Click the 'HowStuffWorks "How to Build a Computer" – Windows Internet Explorer' live preview to insert a screen shot of the 'HowStuffWorks "How to Build a Computer" – Windows Internet Explorer' window (Figure 7–88).

- Click the Save button on the Quick Access Toolbar to save your work.

- Close Internet Explorer.

Q&A How do you insert a screen clipping?

To insert a screen clipping instead of a screen shot, click the Screenshots button (Insert tab | Illustrations group) to display the Screenshots gallery, click Screen Clipping, and then draw a rectangle over the portion of the screen you want to insert into the Excel workbook.

Figure 7–88

To Quit Excel

The project is complete. Thus, the following step quits Excel.

❶ Click the Close button on the right side of the title bar to quit Excel.

Chapter Summary

In this chapter, you have learned how to create a template, import data, insert WordArt on a chart, insert SmartArt, insert images, and add a screen shot on a worksheet. The items listed below include all the new Excel skills you have learned in this chapter.

1. Save the Template (EX 435)
2. Open a Template and Save It as a Workbook (EX 437)
3. Import Data from a Text File into a Worksheet (EX 439)
4. Import Data from an Access Table into a Worksheet (EX 443)
5. Import Data from a Web Page into a Worksheet (EX 446)
6. Copy and Transpose Data from a Word Document to a Worksheet (EX 450)
7. Convert Text to Columns (EX 453)
8. Replicate Formulas (EX 456)
9. Find a String (EX 457)
10. Replace a String with Another String (EX 459)
11. Insert the Clustered Cone Chart (EX 460)
12. Add a Chart Title Using the WordArt Tool (EX 463)
13. Insert a Picture Strips SmartArt Graphic (EX 466)
14. Add Shapes in the Picture Strips SmartArt Graphic (EX 469)
15. Add Text to Shapes in the Picture Strips SmartArt Graphic (EX 470)
16. Add Pictures to Shapes in the Picture Strips SmartArt Graphic (EX 471)
17. Add an Effect to the Picture Strips SmartArt Graphic (EX 473)
18. Insert and Modify an Image on the Worksheet (EX 474)
19. Insert a Screen Shot on a Worksheet (EX 475)

If you have a SAM 2010 user profile, your instructor may have assigned an autogradable version of this assignment. If so, log into the SAM 2010 Web site at www.cengage.com/sam2010 to download the instruction and start files.

Learn It Online

Test your knowledge of chapter content and key terms.

Instructions: To complete the Learn It Online exercises, start your browser, click the Address bar, and then enter the Web address `scsite.com/ex2010/learn`. When the Excel 2010 Learn It Online page is displayed, click the link for the exercise you want to complete and then read the instructions.

Chapter Reinforcement TF, MC, and SA
A series of true/false, multiple choice, and short answer questions that test your knowledge of the chapter content.

Flash Cards
An interactive learning environment where you identify chapter key terms associated with displayed definitions.

Practice Test
A series of multiple choice questions that test your knowledge of chapter content and key terms.

Who Wants To Be a Computer Genius?
An interactive game that challenges your knowledge of chapter content in the style of a television quiz show.

Wheel of Terms
An interactive game that challenges your knowledge of chapter key terms in the style of the television show *Wheel of Fortune*.

Crossword Puzzle Challenge
A crossword puzzle that challenges your knowledge of key terms presented in the chapter.

Apply Your Knowledge

Reinforce the skills and apply the concepts you learned in this chapter.

Importing Data into an Excel Worksheet

Note: To complete this assignment, you will be required to use the Data Files for Students. See the inside back cover of this book for instructions on downloading the Data Files for Students, or contact your instructor for information about accessing the required files.

Instructions: Start Excel. Open the workbook Apply 7-1 Hinkley's Bazaar from the Data Files for Students, and then save the workbook as Apply 7-1 Hinkley's Bazaar Complete. In this workbook, you are to consolidate information about quarterly sales from four sources. Figure 7–89 shows the completed Quarterly Sales worksheet.

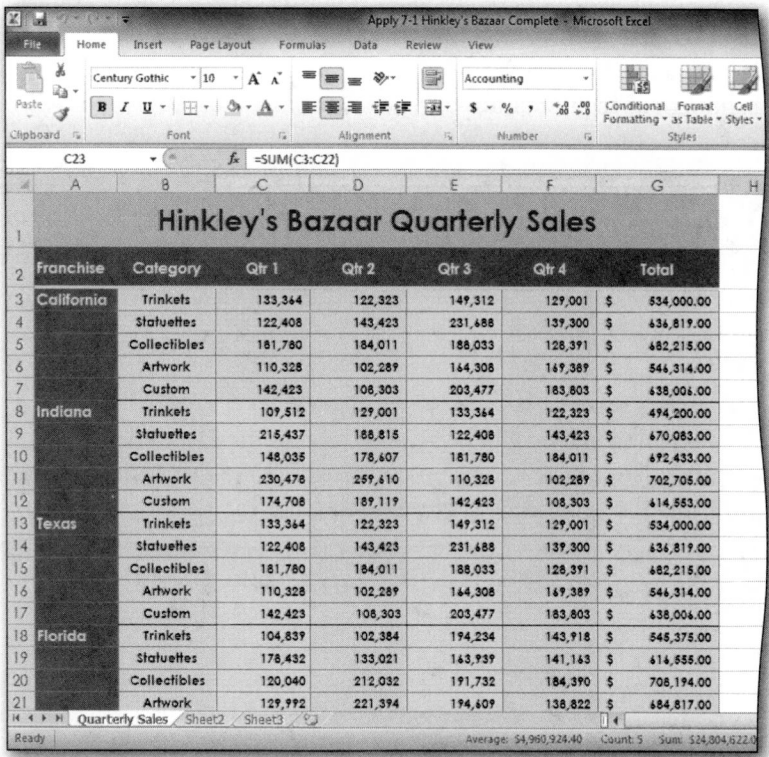

Figure 7–89

Perform the following tasks:

1. Select cell A3, and then enter the text **California**. Select cell A9, and then enter the text **Indiana**. Select cell A14, and then enter the text **Texas**. Select cell A20 and then enter the text **Florida**.

2. Select cell B3. Import the comma-delimited text file, Apply 7-1 California, from the Data Files for Students. In the Text Import Wizard - Step 2 of 3 dialog box, use Comma delimiters, not Tab delimiters; otherwise accept the default settings. In the Import Data dialog box, click the Properties button. In the External Data Range Properties dialog box, do not adjust the column width. Import the text data to cell B3 of the worksheet.

3. Select cell B8. Import the Access database file, Apply 7-1 Indiana, from the Data Files for Students. Choose to view the data as a table, and insert the data starting in cell B8 in the existing workbook. Accept all of the default settings to import the data. Right-click any cell in the table, point to Table, and then click Convert to Range. Click the OK button to permanently remove the connection to the query. Delete row 8.

Continued >

Apply Your Knowledge *continued*

4. Start Microsoft Word, and then open the Word file, Apply 7-1 Texas, from the Data Files for Students. Copy all of the data in the table except for the first row. Switch to Excel. Select cell B13, and then use the Paste Special command to paste the data as text into the Quarterly Sales worksheet. Close Word without saving any changes. Adjust the column widths as necessary to display all of the data.

5. Select cell B18. Import the Web page, Apply 7-1 Florida.htm, from the Data Files for Students. Select the HTML table containing the Florida sales data. In the Import Data dialog box, click the Properties button. In the External Data Range Properties dialog box, do not adjust the column width. Import the text data to cell B18 of the existing worksheet. Delete row 18.

6. Select cell G3 and then total the row. Copy the formula to cells G4:G23.

7. Select cell C23 and then total the column. Copy the formula to cells D23:F23.

8. Format the range C3:F22 in the Comma style with no decimal places. Format the ranges G3:G23 and C23:F23 in the Accounting Number format with two decimal places. Adjust the column widths as necessary to display all of the data.

9. Change the document properties as requested by your instructor. Change the worksheet header to include your name, course number, and other information as specified by your instructor.

10. Print the worksheet, and then save the workbook.

11. Submit the assignment as requested by your instructor.

Extend Your Knowledge

Extend the skills you learned in this chapter and experiment with new skills. You may need to use Help to complete the assignment.

Inserting a SmartArt Organization Chart and Image on a Worksheet

Note: To complete this assignment, you will be required to use the Data Files for Students. See the inside back cover of this book for instructions on downloading the Data Files for Students, or contact your instructor for information about accessing the required files.

Instructions: Start Excel. Open the workbook Extend 7-1 BCIA Medical from the Data Files for Students and then save the workbook as Extend 7-1 BCIA Medical Complete. You will add a SmartArt graphic and an image to the workbook and then format both graphics as shown in Figure 7–90.

Perform the following tasks:

1. In cell A12, insert a SmartArt graphic using the Hierarchy type and the Organization Chart layout (column 1, row 1).

2. Using the Add Shape shortcut menu, add an Assistant shape to the first shape.

3. Using the Add Shape shortcut menu, add a shape after the last shape in the third row.

Figure 7–90

4. Change the text in the first shape to read Jill Van Kirk. Change the text in the middle row to read Juan Aguilara in the left shape and Elise Hammermill in the right shape. Change the text in the third row to read, from left to right, Rose Kennedy, Mark Allen, Karen Franklin, and Lance Marion.

5. Change the color scheme of the hierarchy chart to Colored Fill – Accent 2 (column 2, row 4) in the Change Colors gallery.

6. Change the font size of the text in the shapes to 14 points.

7. Use the Shape Effect gallery to change the effects on the SmartArt shapes to Preset 4 in the Preset gallery.

8. Close the Text pane, if necessary, and then move the SmartArt graphic so the upper-left corner of the graphic is in the upper-left corner of cell A12.

9. In cell E1, insert the Extend 7-1 LobbyFlowers image file from the Data Files for Students on the worksheet.

10. Move and resize the image so that the upper-left corner of the image is aligned with the upper-left corner of cell E1 and the lower-right corner of the image is in cell I11.

11. Format the image to use the Soft Edge Rectangle style (column 6, row 1) in the Picture Styles Gallery.

12. Change the document properties as specified by your instructor. Change the worksheet header so that it contains your name, course number, and other information as specified by your instructor. Save the workbook. Submit the assignment as requested by your instructor.

Make It Right

Analyze a workbook and correct all errors and/or improve the design.

Manipulating SmartArt and Using Find & Replace

Note: To complete this assignment, you will be required to use the Data Files for Students. See the inside back cover of this book for instructions on downloading the Data Files for Students, or contact your instructor for information about accessing the required files.

Instructions: Start Excel. Open the workbook Make It Right 7-1 GreenFirst Services and then save the workbook as Make It Right 7-1 GreenFirst Services Complete. The Site List worksheet contains design flaws and other errors. Correct the problems so that the Site List sheet appears as shown in Figure 7–91.

Perform the following tasks:

1. Edit the shape on the left of the cycle chart so that it says Reduce.

2. Add a new shape after the Recycle shape. Insert the text Reuse in the new shape.

3. Find all occurrences of Kenway Rd and replace them with Charles Ave (without any punctuation).

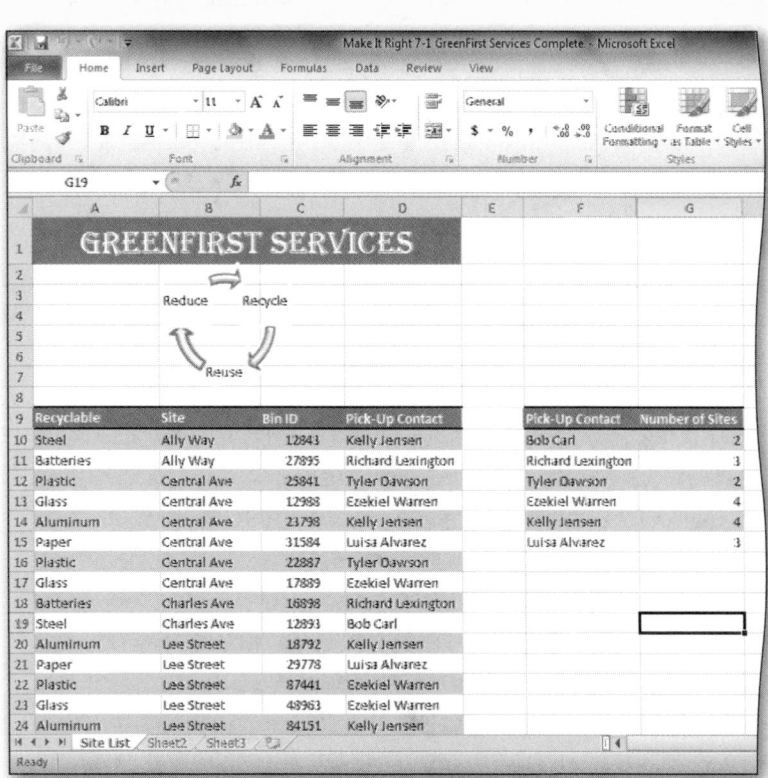

Figure 7–91

Continued >

Make It Right *continued*

4. Find all occurrences of Kelly Montag and replace them with Kelly Jensen (without any punctuation).

5. Use the Find All button in the Find and Replace dialog box to find and list all occurrences of Bob Carl in the range A9:D27. Be sure not to include the range F9:G15 in the search. Enter the number of the occurrences in G10.

6. Use the same technique to find and list all occurrences of the text and enter the number of occurrences as shown in Table 7–1.

7. Change the document properties as specified by your instructor. Change the worksheet headers to include your name, course number, and other information as specified by your instructor.

8. Save the workbook, and submit the revised workbook as requested by your instructor.

Table 7–1 Text to Find and Count

Find All Occurrences of:	Enter Number of Occurrences in Cell:
Richard Lexington	G11
Tyler Dawson	G12
Ezekiel Warren	G13
Kelly Jensen	G14
Luisa Alvarez	G15

In the Lab

Create or modify workbooks using the guidelines, concepts, and skills presented in this chapter. Labs are listed in order of increasing difficulty.

Lab 1: Using a Template to Create a Multiple-Sheet Workbook

Note: To complete this assignment, you will be required to use the Data Files for Students. See the inside back cover of this book for instructions on downloading the Data Files for Students, or contact your instructor for information about accessing the required files.

Problem: Natalee's Organic is a company that specializes in all organic products. The company has stores in Washington, Tampa, Cincinnati, Boston, and Atlanta, and a corporate office in Orlando. All of the five stores sell their products online, in the store, and through mail order. Every year, the corporate officers in Orlando use a template to create a year-end sales analysis workbook. The workbook contains four sheets, one for each of the three sales types, or channels (online, in-store, and mail), and one sheet to consolidate data and determine the company totals. Figure 7–92 shows the Consolidated sheet.

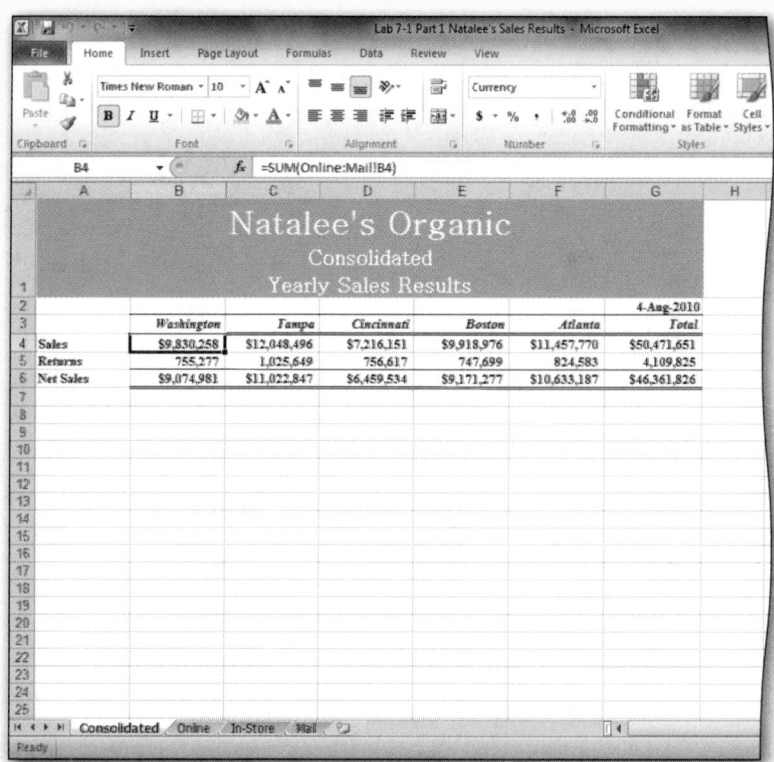

Figure 7–92

The template you need to create the sales analysis workbook is part of the Data Files for Students. Alice Stewart, the company's accountant, has asked you to use the template to create the sales analysis workbook.

Instructions Part 1:   Perform the following tasks:

1. Open the template Lab 7-1 Natalee's Organic Template from the Data Files for Students. Save the template as a workbook using the file name, Lab 7-1 Part 1 Natalee's Sales Results. Make sure Excel Workbook is selected in the 'Save as type' list when you save the workbook.
2. Add a worksheet to the workbook between Sheet1 and Sheet2, copy the contents of Sheet1, and then paste it to the three empty sheets.
3. From left to right, rename the sheet tabs Consolidated, Online, In-Store, and Mail. Color the tabs from left to right as purple, green, red, and blue. On each of the three sales channel sheets, double-click cell A1 and change the "Location" subtitle to match the tab name. Use the title, Consolidated, in cell A1 of the Consolidated worksheet. Change the fill color for each title area in the range A1:G1 to match its tab color. Enter the data in Table 7–2 into the three sales channel sheets.

Table 7–2 Natalee's Organic Yearly Sales Data by Store and Sales Channel				
		Online	In-Store	Mail
Washington	Sales	4589123	1950125	3291010
	Returns	275375	451002	28900
Tampa	Sales	5789632	2101054	4157810
	Returns	500250	62198	463201
Cincinnati	Sales	3698741	1258473	2258937
	Returns	352677	105520	298420
Boston	Sales	2587471	3100500	4231005
	Returns	250500	435001	62198
Atlanta	Sales	6541280	1975200	2941290
	Returns	137980	612453	74150

4. On the Consolidated worksheet, use the SUM function, 3-D references, and copy-and-paste capabilities of Excel to total the corresponding cells on the three sales channel sheets. First, compute the sum in cell B4 and then compute the sum in cell B5. Copy the range B4:B5 to the range C4:F5. The Consolidated sheet should resemble Figure 7–92.
5. Change the document properties as specified by your instructor. Select all four sheets. Add a worksheet header with your name, course number, and other information as specified by your instructor. Add the page number and total number of pages to the footer. Change the left and right margins to 0.5.
6. With the four sheets selected, preview and then print the workbook in landscape orientation and use the Black and white option.
7. Save the workbook with the new page setup characteristics. Close the workbook.
8. Submit the assignment as requested by your instructor.

Instructions Part 2:   Perform the following tasks:

1. Start Excel. Open the workbook Lab 7-1 Part 1 Natalee's Sales Results and then save the workbook using the file name, Lab 7-1 Part 2 Natalee's Sales Results.
2. Create an embedded Clustered Cylinder chart in the range A8:H25 on the Consolidated worksheet by charting the range A3:F5.
3. Move the chart to a separate sheet using the Move Chart button on the Design tab. Name the sheet Chart and color the sheet tab yellow. Drag the Chart sheet tab to the far right.

Continued >

In the Lab continued

4. Increase the font size of the labels on both axes to 12-point bold. Increase the font size of the legends on the right side of the chart to 16 points.
5. Change the chart style to Style 8 using the Chart Styles gallery on the Chart Tools Design tab.
6. Use the WordArt button on the Insert tab to add the chart title Annual Sales and Returns. Select Fill – Orange, Accent 6, Gradient Outline – Accent 6 (column 2, row 3) from the WordArt gallery. Figure 7–93 shows the completed chart.
7. Preview and print all five sheets at one time. Save the workbook and then close the workbook.
8. Submit the assignment as requested by your instructor.

Figure 7–93

Instructions Part 3: Perform the following tasks:
1. Start Excel. Open the workbook Lab 7-1 Part 2 Natalee's Sales Results. Do not save the workbook with a different name in this part of the exercise.
2. Select cell A1 on the Consolidated worksheet. Select all the worksheets except for the Chart sheet.
3. Use the Find & Select button on the Home tab to list all occurrences of the word, Sales, in the workbook. Use the Find All button in the Find and Replace dialog box. Write down the number of occurrences and the cell locations of the word Sales.
4. Repeat Step 3, but find only cells that exactly match the word Sales. If necessary, click the Options button to display the desired check box. Use the Find & Select button to find all occurrences of the word Sales. Write down the number of occurrences and the cell locations that exactly match the word Sales.
5. Use the Find & Select button to find all occurrences of the word, Sales, in bold white font. For this find operation, clear the check mark from the Match entire cell contents check box.
6. Use the Replace command to replace the word, Sales, with the word, Revenue, on all four sheets. Print the four sheets. Close the workbook without saving changes.
7. Submit the assignment as requested by your instructor.

In the Lab

Lab 2: Inserting a Balance Chart and Image on a Worksheet

Note: To complete this assignment, you will be required to use the Data Files for Students. See the inside back cover of this book for instructions on downloading the Data Files for Students, or contact your instructor for information about accessing the required files.

Problem: Pattierson Artist, your company, is considering having a mural painted on the side of their building. You have been asked to create a worksheet with a high-level overview of the pros and cons regarding the mural. The finished worksheet should look like Figure 7–94.

Figure 7–94

Perform the following tasks:

1. Open the workbook Lab 7-2 Pattierson Artists from the Data Files for Students. Save it as Lab 7-2 Pattierson Artists Complete.
2. Insert the Pattierson Mural image file from the Data Files for Students on the worksheet.
3. Move and resize the image so that its upper-left corner is aligned with the upper-left corner of cell A4 and the lower-right corner of the image is aligned with the lower-right corner of cell F19.
4. Select the image. On the Picture Tools Format tab, click the Picture Effects button, point to Shadow in the Picture Effects gallery, and then select Perspective Diagonal Upper Right (column 2, row 8).
5. Click the Picture Effects button, point to Bevel in the Picture Effects gallery, and then select Art Deco (column 4, row 4) in the Bevel gallery.
6. Deselect the image, and then insert a SmartArt graphic using the Relationship type and the Balance layout (column 1, row 1).
7. Move and resize the SmartArt graphic so that its upper-left corner is aligned with the upper-left corner of H4 and the lower-right corner of the graphic is aligned with the lower-right corner of cell M19.

Continued >

In the Lab *continued*

8. Use the Text pane to enter the text for the balance chart as shown in Table 7–3, making certain that the Pros column appears on the left of the chart. Be sure to delete the unused shape on the right side of the balance chart by right-clicking the shape and then clicking Cut on the shortcut menu. The upper-left shape in the chart should read Pros, and the upper-right shape in the chart should read Cons. Note that the direction of the tilt of the balance changes when more pros than cons are entered in the chart.

Table 7–3 Pros and Cons	
Pros	**Cons**
Beautifies Neighborhood	Difficult to Replace
Promotes Marketing	Costly
Shows Off Talent	

9. Change the color scheme of the Balance chart to Colored Fill – Accent 3 (column 2, row 5) in the Change Colors gallery.

10. Apply the Subtle Effect SmartArt style (column 3, row 1) to the Balance chart.

11. Change the document properties as specified by your instructor. Add a worksheet header with your name, course number, and other information as specified by your instructor. Save the workbook. Submit the assignment as requested by your instructor.

In the Lab

Lab 3: Using a Template and Importing Data

Note: To complete this assignment, you will be required to use the Data Files for Students. See the inside back cover of this book for instructions on downloading the Data Files for Students, or contact your instructor for information about accessing the required files.

Problem: You work as a teacher at a private school. You teach every subject to the four students in your gifted class except for art, computers, and physical education. To help you in determining a student's grade for a semester, you ask the art, computers, and physical education instructors to send you grades for your four students, although each data set is in a different format. The art teacher sends you a Web page from the school's Web system. The computer teacher, who uses an Access database to maintain data, queried the database to create a table for you. The physical education teacher typed all the information in a Word table. At the conclusion of the instructions, the Grades Summary worksheet should appear as shown in Figure 7–95.

Figure 7–95

Perform the following tasks:

1. Open the template Lab 7-3 Alistarr Academy Template from the Data Files for Students. Save the template as a workbook using the file name, Lab 7-3 Alistarr Academy Complete. Make sure Excel Workbook is selected in the 'Save as type' list when you save the workbook.

2. Select cell B4. Import the Web page, Lab 7-3 Art.htm, from the Data Files for Students. Select the HTML table containing the art grades. In the Import Data dialog box, click the Properties button. In the External Data Range Properties dialog box, do not adjust the column width. Import the text data to cell B4 of the existing worksheet. Delete row 4.

3. Select cell B8. Import the Access database file, Lab 7-3 Computer, from the Data Files for Students. Choose to view the data as a table, and insert the data starting in cell B8 in the existing workbook. Accept all of the default settings to import the data. Right-click any cell in the table, point to Table, and then click Convert to Range. Click the OK button to permanently remove the connection to the query. Delete row 8. Copy the format from B7:D7 to B8:D11.

4. Start Microsoft Word, and then open the Word file, Lab 7-3 Physical Education, from the Data Files for Students. Copy all except the first column of data in the table. Switch to Excel. Select cell B18, and then use the Paste Special command to paste only the text into the Grades Summary worksheet. Close Word without saving any changes. Copy the range B18:E20. Select cell B12, and then use the Paste Special command to paste and transpose the data. Adjust the column widths as necessary to display all of the data.

5. Delete the range B18:E20, and then delete row 16. Copy the formatting of cells C11:D11 and apply the formatting to the range C12:D15. Copy the formula in cell E11 to the range E12:E15.

6. Change the document properties as requested by your instructor. Change the worksheet header to include your name, course number, and other information as specified by your instructor.

7. Print the worksheet, and then save the workbook.

8. Submit the assignment as requested by your instructor.

Cases and Places

Apply your creative thinking and problem solving skills to design and implement a solution.

Note: To complete these assignments, you may be required to use the Data Files for Students. See the inside back cover of this book for instructions on downloading the Data Files for Students, or contact your instructor for information about accessing the required files.

1: Create a Cover Sheet

Academic

You are competing to design a cover sheet for your school's department to include in their workbooks when they send out school statistics. Open your Web browser and view the Web page for a department at your school. Create a workbook and turn off the viewing of gridlines for the first sheet. Insert a screen shot of the department Web page and size it appropriately. Insert a SmartArt bulleted list to highlight three or four of the best qualities of your department. Below the bulleted list, add a screen clipping of the school's logo. Finally, next to the logo add your name and format it so that it appears as a title. Below your name, in a smaller font, insert the course name.

2: Create a SmartArt Graphic with Photos

Personal

You decide to create a workbook with pictures to chronicle your favorite activity, such as skiing or cooking. Find five digital photos that convey your experience in your favorite activity. Create an Excel workbook. Insert a Titled Picture Blocks SmartArt in a worksheet. Add your five photos and enter a title for each one as well as a caption that describes the photo.

3: Import and Analyze Sales Data

Professional

Open the template Case 7-3 SecurityEnablers Template. Save the template as a workbook named Case 7-3 SecurityEnablers. Import the data from the Sales table in the Case 7-3 SecurityEnablers database to a table starting in cell A4. Import the data from the text file Case 7-3 Security Enablers Text starting in cell H5. Cut and paste the data in H5:L12 to A17:E24. Fix the formulas in F17:F24, if necessary. Replace all instances of NorthCentral with Central. If necessary, copy the formula in cell F4 to the range F5:F24, and format the data appropriately. Update the totals in the range C25:F25, if necessary.

8 Working with Trendlines, PivotTable Reports, PivotChart Reports, and Slicers

Objectives

You will have mastered the material in this chapter when you can:

- Analyze worksheet data using a trendline
- Create a PivotTable report
- Format a PivotTable report
- Apply filters to a PivotTable report
- Create a PivotChart report
- Format a PivotChart report

- Apply filters to a PivotChart report
- Analyze worksheet data using PivotTable and PivotChart reports
- Create slicers to filter PivotTable and PivotChart reports
- Format slicers
- Analyze PivotTable and PivotChart reports using slicers

8 | Working with Trendlines, PivotTable Reports, PivotChart Reports, and Slicers

Introduction

In both academic and business environments, people are presented with large amounts of data that need to be analyzed and interpreted. Data are increasingly available from a wide variety of sources, and gathered with much more ease. Analysis of data and interpretation of the results of the analysis are important skills to acquire. Questions can be asked that identify patterns in data, providing businesses and individuals with information that can be used for making decisions about business situations.

Project Planning Guidelines

> The process of developing a worksheet that communicates specific information requires careful analysis and planning. As a starting point, establish why the worksheet is needed. Once the purpose is determined, analyze the intended users of the worksheet and their unique needs. Then, gather information about the topic and decide what to include in the worksheet. Finally, determine the worksheet design and style that will be most successful at delivering the message. Details of these guidelines are provided in Appendix A. In addition, each project developed in this book provides practical applications of these planning considerations.

Project — Eckart Pet Supplies Sales Analysis

Eckart Pet Supplies is a regional pet shop chain serving the southwest area of the United States. The company provides pet supplies to stores in five states. Originally located in central business districts, the chain has expanded into malls over the past decade, and now has 20 stores throughout the southwest. The stores are managed by five Eckart managers, who are each responsible for stores in more than one state. The owner of Eckart Pet Supplies is interested in reviewing sales figures for the past six years to look for sales trends during this period. The company owner also has requested that you compare the sales figures for the last two years to examine performance by managers and by state, controlling for location. In this chapter, you will learn how to use the trendline charting feature in Excel to examine data for trends, and to analyze sales data for Eckart Pet Supplies using PivotTable and PivotChart reports. The results of this analysis are shown in Figure 8–1.

A **trendline** (Figure 8–1a on page EX 491) is a visual way to show how two variables relate to each other. Trendlines often are used to represent changes in one set of data over time, but also can represent changes in one set of data with changes in another. Excel can overlay a trendline on certain types of charts.

PivotTable reports, PivotChart reports, and trendlines provide methods to manipulate and visualize data. A **PivotTable report** (Figure 8–1b on page EX 491) is an interactive view of worksheet data that gives users the ability to summarize the data

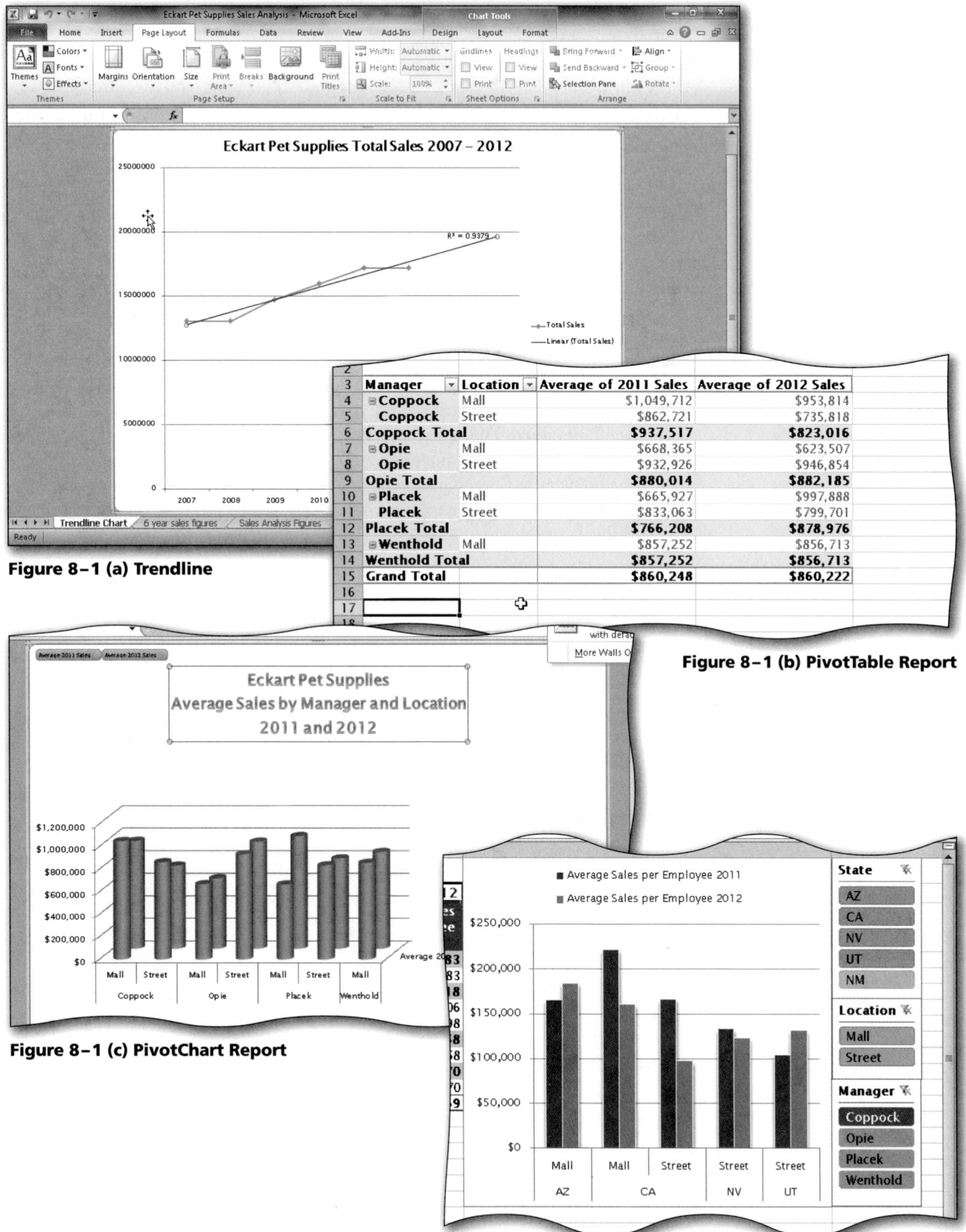

Figure 8–1 (a) Trendline

Figure 8–1 (b) PivotTable Report

Figure 8–1 (c) PivotChart Report

Figure 8–1 (d) Slicers

by selecting categories in which to group their data. When using a PivotTable report, you can quickly change selected categories, without needing to manipulate the worksheet itself. You can examine and analyze several complex organizations of the data, and may spot relationships you might not otherwise see. For example, you can look at total sales for each manager, broken down by store location, and then look at the store location data again, organized by state, without having to do complex reorganizations of the data.

A **PivotChart report** (Figure 8–1c on page EX 491) is an interactive chart that allows users to change the groupings that graphically present data. For example, if Eckart Pet Supplies wanted to view a pie chart showing percentages of total sales from each state, a PivotChart could show that percentage categorized by several different options, such as mall versus street locations or number of employees, without having to rebuild the chart from scratch for each view. PivotChart reports are visual representations of PivotTables. When you create a PivotChart report, Excel creates and associates a PivotTable with that PivotChart report.

Slicers (Figure 8–1d on page EX 491) are graphic objects that contain buttons you click to filter the data in PivotTables and PivotCharts. Each button clearly identifies the filter it applies, making it easy to interpret the data displayed in the PivotTable report.

Using trendlines, PivotTables, PivotCharts, and slicers, a user with little knowledge of formulas, functions, and ranges can complete powerful what-if analyses of a set of data.

Figure 8–2 illustrates the requirements document for the Eckart Pet Supplies Sales Analysis worksheet. It includes the needs, source of data, calculations, and other facts about the worksheet's development.

REQUEST FOR NEW WORKBOOK

Date Submitted:	September 12, 2012
Submitted By:	Gareth Davies
Worksheet Title:	Eckart Pet Supplies Sales Analysis
Needs:	Evaluate two different sets of sales data: 1. Total Sales data for 2007 – 2012. Provide a visual representation of Sales over the past 6 years, and a forecast for the next 2 years based on the current trend. 2. Sales data for 2011 and 2012 for all stores, with details identifying State, physical location (mall vs. street), Manager, number of full-time employees. For this data, use PivotTables and PivotCharts to look for patterns and anomalies in the sales data, based on different breakouts. Management is interested in comparing performance across managers and performance across states to help inform strategies for expansion and marketing campaigns moving forward. There is also interest in evaluating performance in mall locations versus street locations, again with an eye to marketing strategies. Finally, management would like to identify any underperforming mall stores in 2012. Underperformance is noted as total sales of less than seven hundred and fifty thousand dollars.
Source of Data:	Data is available in the spreadsheet Eckart Pet Supplies Data.xlsx, which can be found in my research directory on the server.
Calculations:	In addition to total sales for the various grouping, management would like to see comparisons of average sales for those groupings. They would also like to see an evaluation of average sales per employee.
Special Requirements:	None

Approvals

Approval Status:	X	Approved
		Rejected
Approved By:	Kelly Weston	
Date:	September 19, 2012	
Assigned To:	M. Jones, Spreadsheet Specialist	

Figure 8–2

Overview

As you read this chapter, you will learn how to produce the workbook shown in Figure 8–1 by performing these general tasks:

- Analyze worksheet data using a trendline.
- Create and work with PivotTable reports.
- Create and work with PivotChart reports.
- Format PivotTable and PivotChart reports.

Plan
Ahead

General Project Guidelines

When working with an Excel worksheet, you need to make several decisions that will determine the appearance and characteristics of the finished worksheet. As you create workbooks with trendlines, PivotTables, and PivotCharts such as those shown in Figure 8–1, you should follow these general guidelines:

1. **Identify the trend or trends to analyze with a trendline.** Consider what trend you want to analyze. You typically analyze a trend in data over a period of time. Consider which data to analyze and which period to consider. You also should consider if the trendline should forecast the trend into the future and if so, how far into the future is reasonable for the forecast.

2. **Determine the type of trendline to add.** You add a trendline to a chart to show trends in current or future data. Select one of six types of trendlines to add to a chart. The type of data you have determines the type of trendline to use.

3. **Identify the types of questions to ask of your data.** You can create PivotTable and PivotChart reports in almost any configuration of your existing data. Because PivotTable and PivotChart reports answer questions about your data, especially when comparing subtotals and totals in different categories, you need to create these reports with questions in mind.

4. **Visualize your workbook in various PivotTable and PivotChart layouts.** PivotTables and PivotCharts provide a great deal of flexibility in how data is summarized. You should consider the types of comparisons and summary functions that you may want to make. Often, sketches of a few ideas will help you in planning effective PivotTables and PivotCharts.

5. **Consider using slicers to filter a PivotTable.** When you need to analyze the data presented in PivotTables and PivotCharts, use a slicer to select the data to display and summarize. Slicers offer significant advantages over filtered PivotTables and PivotCharts.

When necessary, more specific details concerning the above guidelines are presented at appropriate points in the chapter. The chapter also will identify the actions you perform and decisions made regarding these guidelines during the modification of the worksheets shown in Figure 8–1 on page EX 491.

With a good understanding of the requirements document and an understanding of the necessary decisions, the next step is to use Excel to learn about the existing worksheet and solve the problem.

To Start Excel and Open a Workbook

To begin this project, you will open a file located on the Data Files for Students. See the inside back cover of this book for instructions on downloading the Data Files for Students, or contact your instructor for more information about accessing the required files. If you are using a computer to step through the project in this chapter and you want your screens to match the figures in this book, you should change your screen's resolution to 1024 × 768.

The following steps start Excel, open a file, and then save it with a new file name.

1 Start Excel. If necessary, maximize the Excel window.

2 Open the workbook, Eckart Pet Supplies Sales Data, located on the Data Files for Students.

3 Save the workbook using the file name, Eckart Pet Supplies Sales Analysis.

4 If the worksheet window in Excel is not maximized, click the Maximize button next to the Close Window button on the Ribbon to maximize the worksheet within Excel (Figure 8–3).

Figure 8–3

BTW

The Ribbon and Screen Resolution
Excel may change how the groups and buttons within the groups appear on the Ribbon, depending on the computer's screen resolution. Thus, your Ribbon may look different from the ones in this book if you are using a screen resolution other than 1024 × 768.

BTW

BTWs
For a complete list of the BTWs found in the margins of this book, visit the Excel 2010 BTW Web page (scsite.com/ex2010/btw).

Adding a Trendline to a Chart

Using a trendline on certain Excel charts allows you to illustrate an underlying tendency of how one set of data is changing in relation to another set of data. Trends are most often thought about in terms of how a value changes over time, but trends can also describe the relationship between two variables, such as height and weight. In Excel, you add a trendline to an existing Excel chart. However, not all types of Excel charts can have a trendline added to them. Chart types that do not examine the relationship between two variables, such as Pie and Donut charts, which examine the contribution of different parts to a whole, cannot include trendlines. Excel allows you to add trendlines to several types of charts, such as Unstacked 2-D Area, Bar, Column, Line, Stock, XY (Scatter), and Bubble charts.

Plan Ahead

Identify the trend or trends to analyze with a trendline.
Before you add a trendline to a chart, you need to determine the data series to analyze. If the chart uses only one data series, Excel uses it automatically. If the chart involves more than one data series, you select the one you want to use as you add a trendline. You then can analyze current or future trends.

- To analyze a current trend, make sure you have enough data available for the period you want to analyze. For example, two years of annual sales totals might not provide enough data to analyze sales performance. Five years of annual sales totals or two years of monthly sales totals are more likely to present a trend.

(Continued)

(Continued)

Plan Ahead

- To analyze a future trend, you use a trendline to project data beyond the values of the data set. This process is called forecasting. **Forecasting** helps predict data values that are outside of a data set. For example, if a data set is for a 10-year period and the data shows a trend in that 10-year period, Excel can predict values beyond that period or estimate what the values may have been before that period.

When you add a trendline to a chart, you can set the number of periods to forecast forward or backward in time. For example, if you have six years of sales data, you can forecast two periods forward to show the trend for eight years: six years of current data and two years of projected data. You also can display information about the trendline on the chart to help guide your analysis. For example, you can display the equation used to calculate the trend and show the **R-squared value**, which is a number from 0 to 1 that measures the strength of the trend. An R-squared value of 1 means the estimated values in the trendline correspond exactly to the actual data.

Determine the type of trendline to add.
You can add one of six types of trendlines to a chart. The linear trendline is most commonly used. Both linear and moving average trendlines assume a linear relationship in the data. Logarithmic, polynomial, power, and exponential trendlines reflect curvilinear relationships. You can use any type of trendline with any data, but you should select the type that best fits your data and can reveal a significant trend.

Plan Ahead

To Create a 2-D Line Chart

A trendline must be added to an existing chart. The following steps create a 2-D line chart of the Eckart Pet Supplies sales data. You will add a trendline to the chart shortly.

1

- If necessary, make '6 year sales figures' the active sheet.

- Select cells A4:G5 to select the range to be charted (Figure 8–4).

Figure 8–4

- Click Insert on the Ribbon to display the Insert tab.

- Click the Line button (Insert tab | Charts group) to display the Line gallery (Figure 8–5).

Figure 8–5

- Click the Line with Markers chart type in the 2-D Line area of the Line gallery to insert a 2-D line chart with data markers (Figure 8–6).

Q&A

What are data markers?

A data marker is the symbol in a chart that represents a single value from a worksheet cell. In this case, the data markers are diamonds that represent the six sales figures.

Figure 8–6

- Click the Move Chart button (Chart Tools Design tab | Location group) to display the Move Chart dialog box.

- Click the New sheet option button (Move Chart dialog box) to select it.

- If necessary, double-click the default text in the New sheet text box to select the text.

- Type **Trendline Chart** to enter a name for the new chart sheet (Figure 8–7).

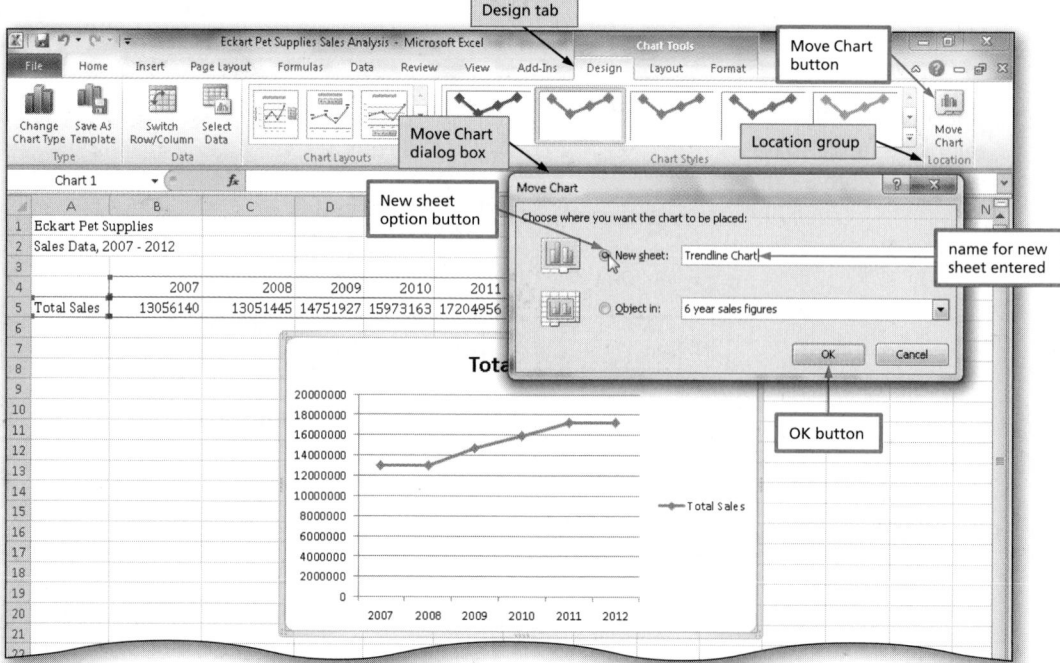

Figure 8–7

5

- Click the OK button (Move Chart dialog box) to move the chart to a new sheet named Trendline Chart.

- Click the default Total Sales chart title to select it.

- Type **Eckart Pet Supplies Total Sales 2007 – 2012** and then press the ENTER key to enter the new chart title.

- Click outside of the chart area to deselect the chart (Figure 8–8).

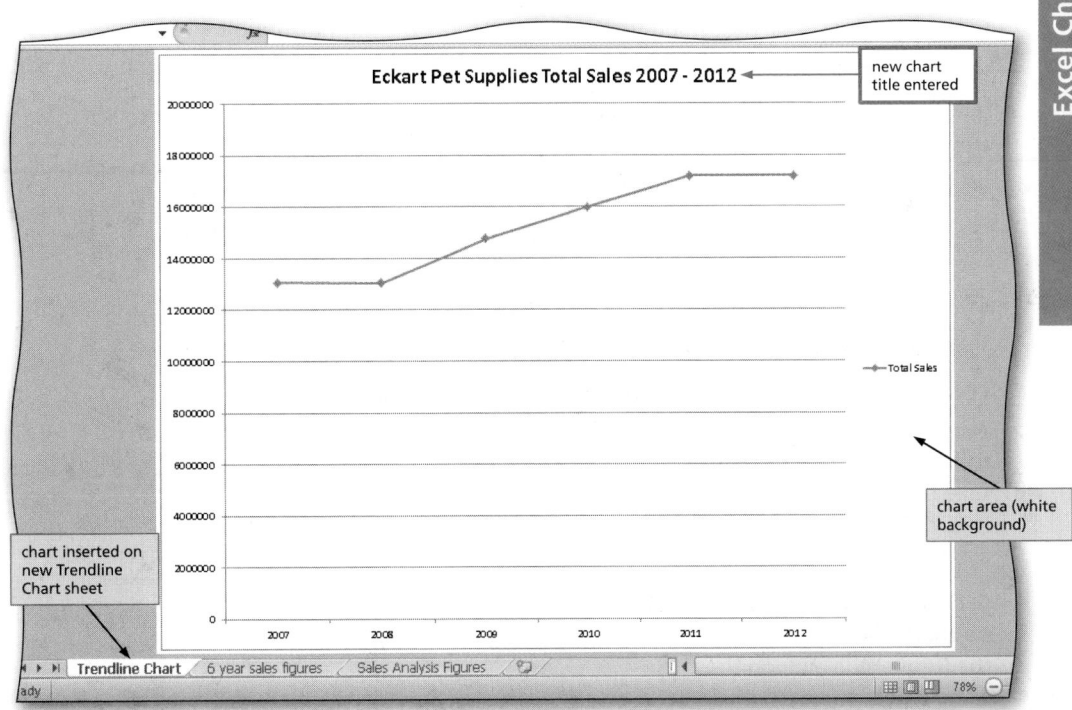

Figure 8–8

Other Ways

1. ALT+N, N

To Add a Trendline to a Chart

The following steps add a trendline to the Eckart Pet Supplies Total Sales 2007 – 2012 chart and predict the total sales two years beyond the data set in the 6 year sales figures worksheet.

1

- Click the chart to select it.

- Click Layout on the Ribbon to display the Chart Tools Layout tab.

- Click the Trendline button (Chart Tools Layout tab | Analysis group) to display the Trendline menu (Figure 8–9).

Figure 8–9

- Click the More Trendline Options command to display the Format Trendline dialog box.
- If necessary, click the Trendline Options category in the left pane (Format Trendline dialog box).
- If necessary, click the Linear option button in the Trend/Regression Type area to select a linear trendline type.

Q&A Why should I select the Linear option button in this case?

The 2-D line chart you created is a basic straight line, so it is appropriate for a linear trendline, which shows values that are increasing or decreasing at a steady rate.

- Drag to select the default value in the Forward text box in the Forecast area.
- Type **2.0** to add a trendline to the chart with a two-period forward forecast.

Q&A What does it mean to enter a two-period forward forecast?

A two-period forward forecast estimates the total sales for the two time periods (in this case, years) that follow the sales data you used to create the line chart.

- Click the 'Display R-squared value on chart' check box to display the R-squared value on the chart to help determine its reliability (Figure 8–10).

Q&A What is the effect of selecting the 'Display R-squared value on chart' check box?

Selecting this check box displays the R-squared value on the chart. The R-squared value is a measure of how well the trendline describes the relationship between total sales and time. The closer the value is to 1, the more accurate the trendline.

Figure 8–10

- Click the Close button (Format Trendline dialog box) to add the trendline with the selected options.
- Click Page Layout on the Ribbon to display the Page Layout tab.
- Apply the Concourse theme (Page Layout tab | Themes group) to the workbook (Figure 8–11).

Other Ways

1. Click Trendline button (Chart Tools Layout tab | Analysis group), click Linear Trendline

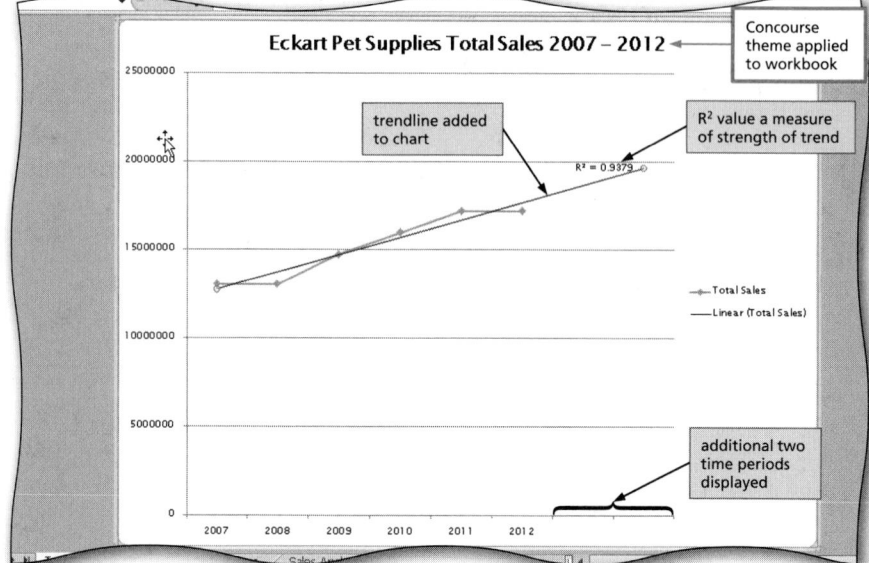

Figure 8–11

More about Trendlines

It is important to take note of the axes when looking at trendlines. Charts with trendlines are often reformatted to start the vertical axis at a number other than zero, particularly when the values on the vertical axis are high. When interpreting a trendline, you should look at the vertical axis to see if it starts at zero. If it does not, be aware that trends represented by the trendline may appear exaggerated. Figure 8–12 shows a chart with a trendline that uses the same data as the chart in Figure 8–11. The difference between the two charts is in the vertical axis, which starts at zero in Figure 8–11 and at 13,000,000 in Figure 8–12. The difference between the projected values for 2013 and 2014 appears much larger in Figure 8–12 where the axis starts at 13,000,000. When analyzing, always check the axes to be sure that the differences shown in the chart are not being visually overstated.

BTW

Q&As
For a complete list of the Q&As found in many of the step-by-step sequences in this book, visit the Excel 2010 Q&A Web page (scsite.com/ex2010/qa).

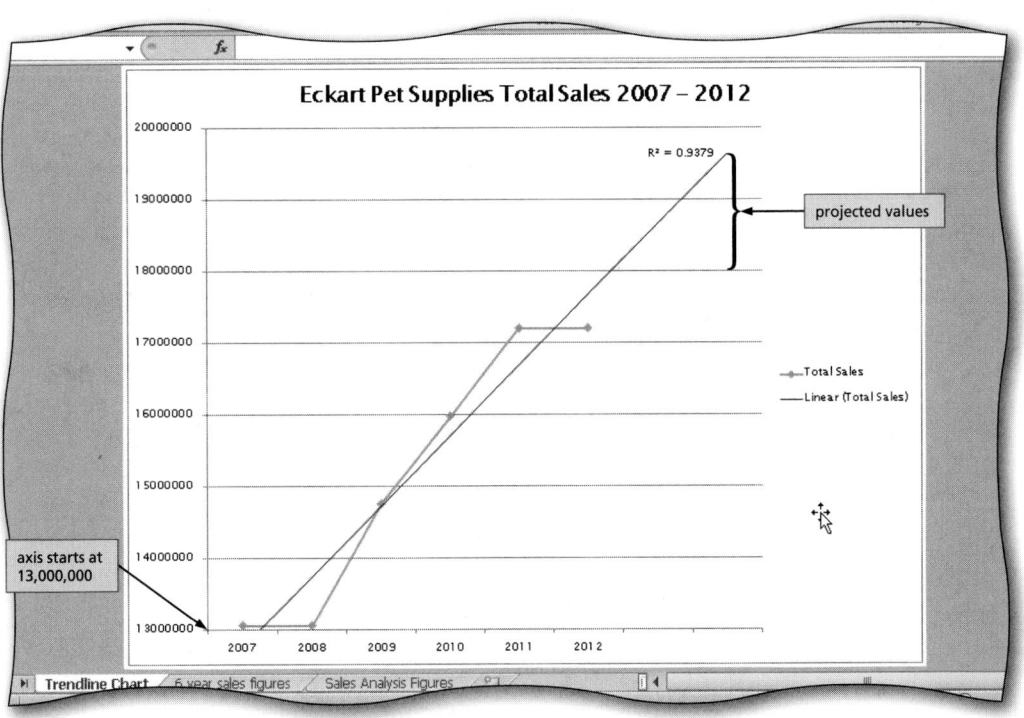

Figure 8–12

Creating and Formatting PivotTable and PivotChart Reports

A PivotTable report is an interactive tool that summarizes worksheet data. When working with data tables or lists of data, each different organization of the data requires a new table or list. In contrast, you can reorganize data and examine summaries in a PivotTable report with a few clicks of a mouse. PivotTable reports allow you to view different summaries of the data quickly and easily, using just a single table.

When creating a PivotTable report, you can use categories in the data to summarize different groups or totals. PivotTable **fields** are drawn from columns in the worksheet data. Fields can be one of two types: data, which contains values that the PivotTable will summarize, and category, which describes the data by categorizing it. Category fields correspond to columns in the original data, and data fields correspond to summary values of original data across categories. You can change row and column groupings quickly to summarize the data in different ways to ask new questions. Reorganizing the table reveals different levels of detail and allows you to analyze specific subgroups.

BTW

PivotTable and PivotChart Reports in Compatibility Mode
Some features of PivotTables and PivotCharts are disabled when a workbook is in compatibility mode. Make sure to save workbooks in the latest version of Excel before creating PivotTable and PivotChart reports so you can take full advantage of the features available.

You can create PivotTable reports either on the same worksheet as the data to be analyzed, or on a new sheet in the same workbook as the sheet containing the data. When you create a PivotTable report, you also can create a PivotChart report. PivotChart reports are interactive charts that also allow you to change the way that data is organized and displayed. PivotCharts are always based on a PivotTable. In fact, they are visual representations of the PivotTable that forms their base.

Plan Ahead

Identify the types of questions to ask of your data.
You can create PivotTable and PivotChart reports in almost any configuration of your existing data. To use this powerful tool effectively, you need to create these reports with questions in mind. Look at the categories you can use to describe your data and think about how the various categories can interact. Common questions relate to how the data changes over time, and how the data varies in geographical locations, such as states or regions, different functional groups within an organization, and demographic groupings such as age and gender.

One PivotTable created in this project is shown in Figure 8–13. It summarizes the Eckart Pet Supplies data to show the total sales and average sales in 2011 and 2012 for each manager by location (street or mall). The filter button in cell A3 filters the results by manager, and the filter button in cell B3 filters the results by location. Columns C and D show the values for the average of sales in 2011 and 2012, and columns E and F show the values for the total sales in 2011 and 2012.

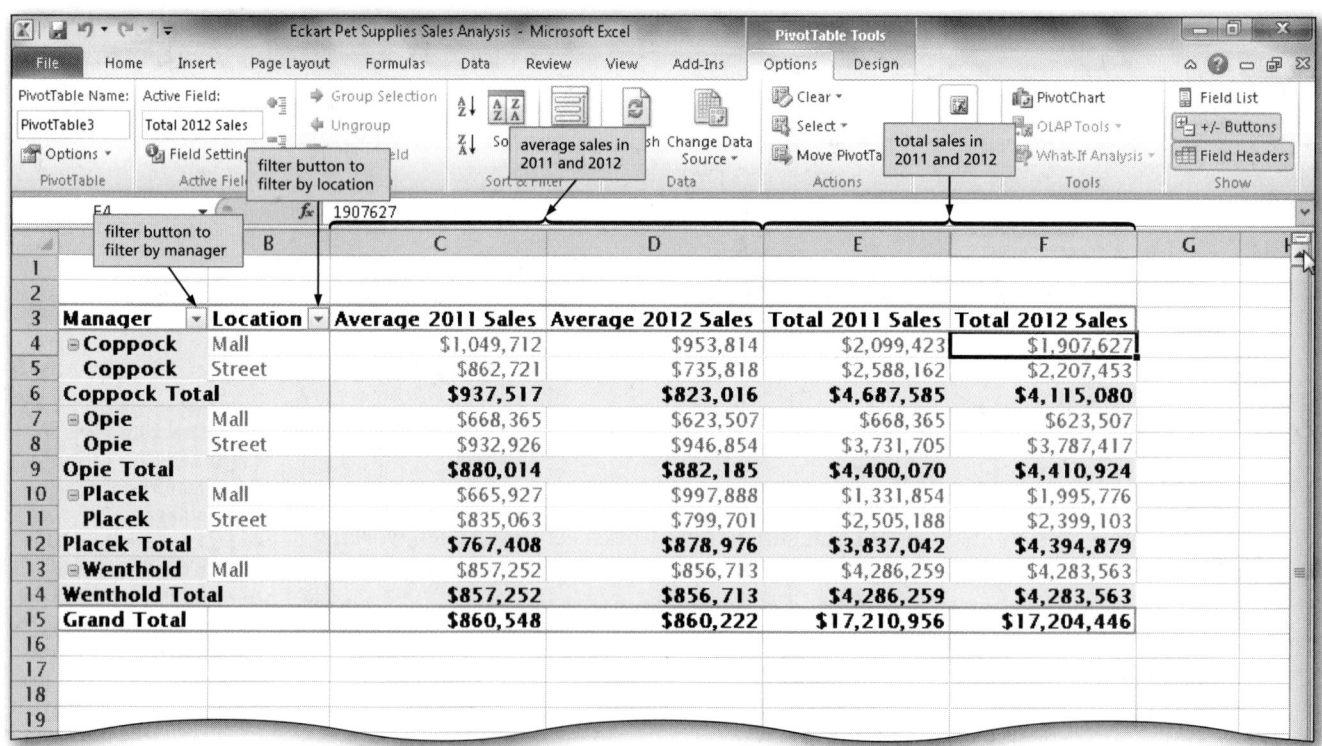

Figure 8–13

To Create a Blank PivotTable Report

The following steps create a blank PivotTable report using the Create PivotTable dialog box.

1

• Click the Sales Analysis Figures sheet tab to make the Sales Analysis Figures sheet active.

• Click cell A3 to select a cell containing data for the PivotTable.

• Click Insert on the Ribbon to display the Insert tab.

Q&A
Do I have to click the first cell with values to be used in the PivotTable?

You can click anywhere in the range that contains the data that will be used in the PivotTable.

• Click the PivotTable button arrow (Insert tab | Tables group) to display the PivotTable menu (Figure 8–14).

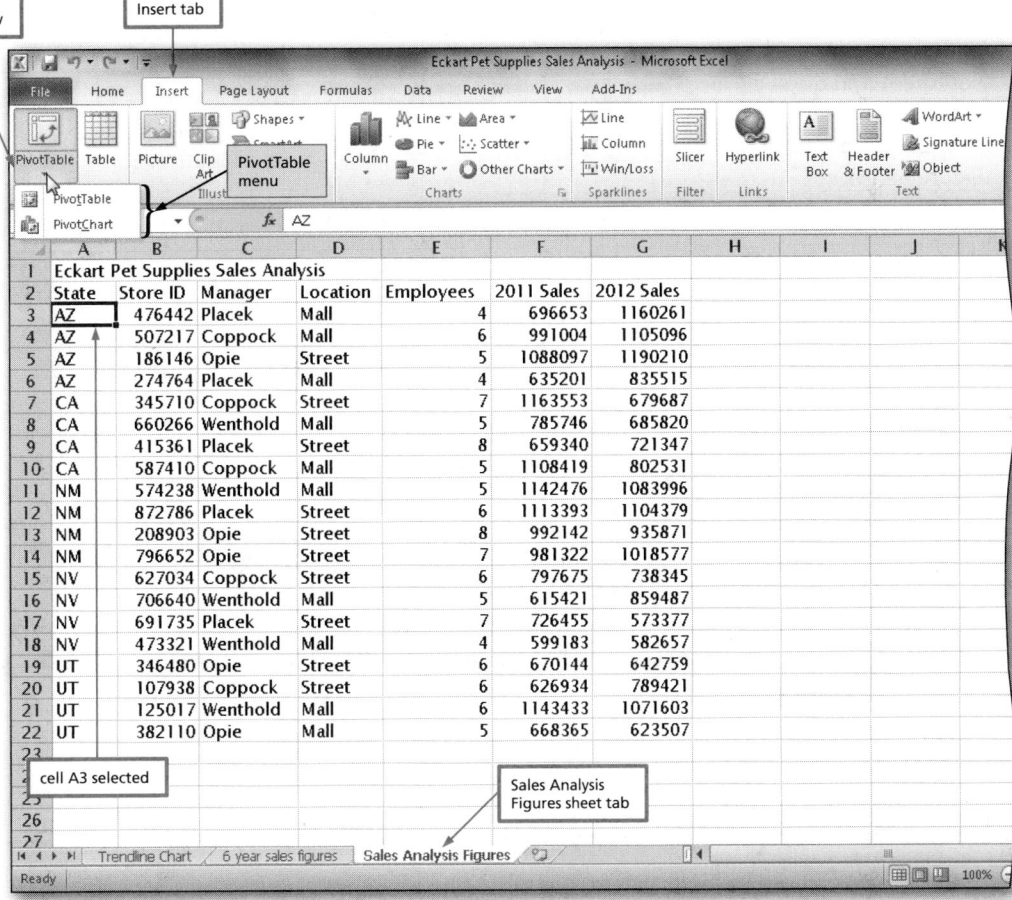

Figure 8–14

2

• Click PivotTable to display the Create PivotTable dialog box (Figure 8–15).

Figure 8–15

● Click the OK button
(Create PivotTable
dialog box) to create
a blank PivotTable
report on a new
worksheet and display
the PivotTable
Field List pane
(Figure 8–16).

Q&A

Why is the PivotTable
blank?

When you create a
PivotTable, you first
insert the structure.
The resulting
PivotTable is blank
until you add content
to it, which you do in
the next set of steps.

Q&A

My field list just
disappeared. What
happened?

If you click outside of
the PivotTable or
PivotChart, the field list will no longer be displayed. To redisplay
the field list, click in the PivotTable or PivotChart report.

Figure 8–16

Other Ways

1. Click PivotTable button
   (Insert tab | Tables group)

To Add Data to the PivotTable

The next step in creating the PivotTable report as shown in Figure 8–13 on page EX 500 is to add data
by selecting fields in the PivotTable Field List pane. Add data by selecting check boxes in the PivotTable Field
List pane or by dragging fields from the 'Choose fields to add to report' area to the 'Drag fields between areas
below' areas. Fields added to the Values area must contain summary numeric data. Fields added to the Column
Labels area also should contain summary numeric data. As shown in Figure 8–13, the rows show locations by
managers. The columns include the two data fields, 2011 Sales and 2012 Sales. The following step adds data to
the PivotTable.

1

- Drag the Location field from the 'Choose fields to add to report' list to the Row Labels area to add the Location field to the PivotTable report.

- Click the Manager check box in the 'Choose fields to add to report' list to add the Manager field to the Row Labels area below the Location field.

Q&A | How did the Manager field end up in the Row Labels area?

Excel places a checked field in the group it determines is correct for that field. You can drag the field to a different group if you choose.

- Drag the 2011 Sales field to the Values area to add the field to column B of the PivotTable.

- Drag the 2012 Sales field to the Values area to add the field to column C of the PivotTable (Figure 8–17).

Q&A | What is shown in the PivotTable report?

Excel displays the Location and Manager fields as Row Labels in the PivotTable. The 2011 Sales and 2012 Sales are totaled for each manager within each location.

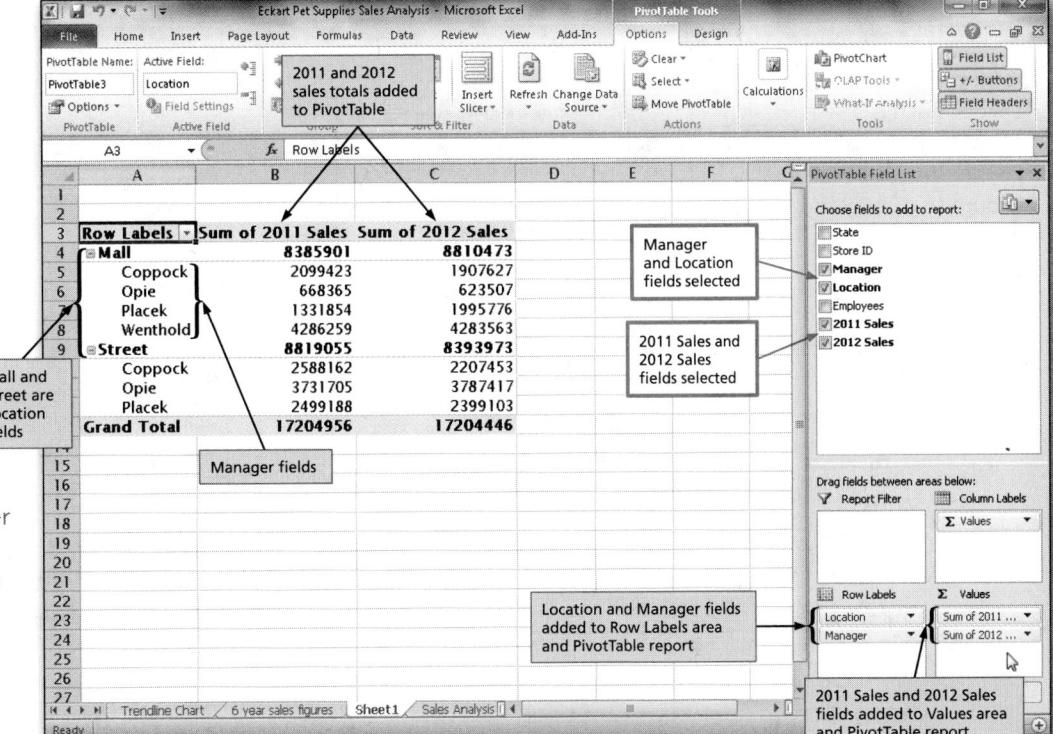

Figure 8–17

Other Ways
1. Click check box for each field name

More about PivotTable Reports

PivotTable reports can be based on information stored in one or more worksheets or in external data sources such as Microsoft Access databases. The contents of a PivotTable report are not refreshed when the data from which they are created change. This means you must manually refresh the PivotTable report when underlying data change. If you add rows to the source data, a new PivotTable must be created to incorporate the new data. The exception to this are PivotTable reports that are built on data tables. A PivotTable built on a data table that has new rows added to the bottom of the table will automatically incorporate those new rows when you refresh the PivotTable report.

To Change the Layout of a PivotTable Report

You can display a PivotTable report in one of three layouts. By default, PivotTable reports are presented in a compact layout. When using multiple row labels, a different layout can make identifying the groups and subgroups easier for the reader. The following steps change the layout of the PivotTable report to the tabular layout, and then add item labels to all rows.

1

• Click Design on the Ribbon to display the PivotTable Tools Design tab.

• Click the Report Layout button (PivotTable Tools Design tab | Layout group) to display the Report Layout menu (Figure 8–18).

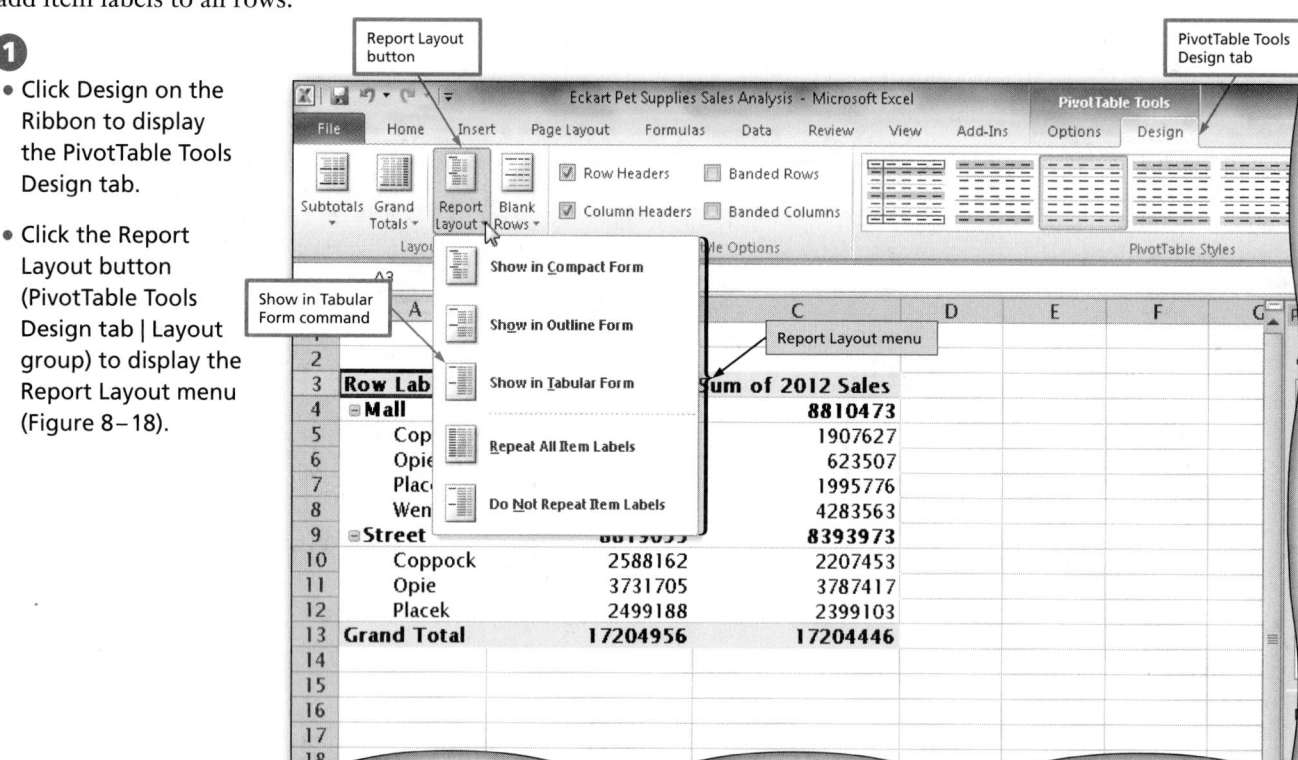

Figure 8–18

2

• Click the Show in Tabular Form command to display the PivotTable report in a tabular format (Figure 8–19).

Figure 8–19

3

- Click the Report Layout button (PivotTable Tools Design tab | Layout group) to display the Report Layout menu.

- Click Repeat All Item Labels to display item (Location) labels for all manager entries (Figure 8–20).

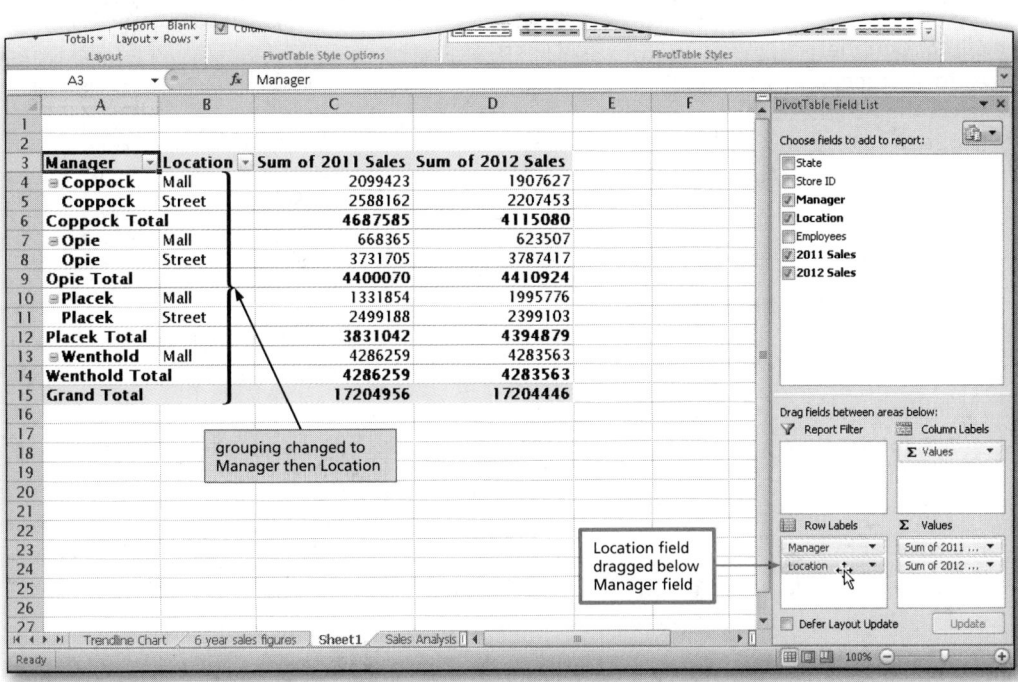

Figure 8–20

To Change the View of a PivotTable Report

The PivotTable report in the Eckart Pet Supplies Sales Analysis workbook currently shows the sum of revenue for each year by location and manager (Figure 8–20). You can change the view of this data depending on what you want to analyze. If you use the sort and summary features in Excel, comparing sales in all locations for each manager would require many steps. With PivotTable reports, this comparison is accomplished quickly. The following step changes the view of the PivotTable to show total sales by location for each manager.

1

- Click and drag the Location button in the Row Labels area of the PivotTable Field List pane below the Manager button to group revenue by the Manager field rather than by the Location field (Figure 8–21).

Figure 8–21

Other Ways

1. Click Location button arrow, click Move Down

To Filter a PivotTable Report Using a Report Filter

In a PivotTable report, you can add detail by further categorizing the data to look at specific subgroups. For example, you could examine the relationship between location and manager by reviewing the data for a single state or group of states. You can use the State field to select specific states for which to view total sales. Viewing a PivotTable report only for a subset that meets a selection criterion is known as **filtering**. The following steps add a report filter to change the view of the PivotTable and then filter the PivotTable by state.

- Drag the State field from the 'Choose fields to add to report' area to the Report Filter area in the PivotTable Field List pane to create a new report filter in the PivotTable (Figure 8–22).

Figure 8–22

2

- Click the State AutoFilter button in cell B1 to display the AutoFilter menu.

- Click AZ on the AutoFilter menu to select the AZ criterion (Figure 8–23).

Figure 8–23

3

- Click the OK button to display totals for Arizona stores only (Figure 8–24).

Q&A

What is shown now in the PivotTable report?

Now the PivotTable shows total sales for each manager in mall and street stores in Arizona only.

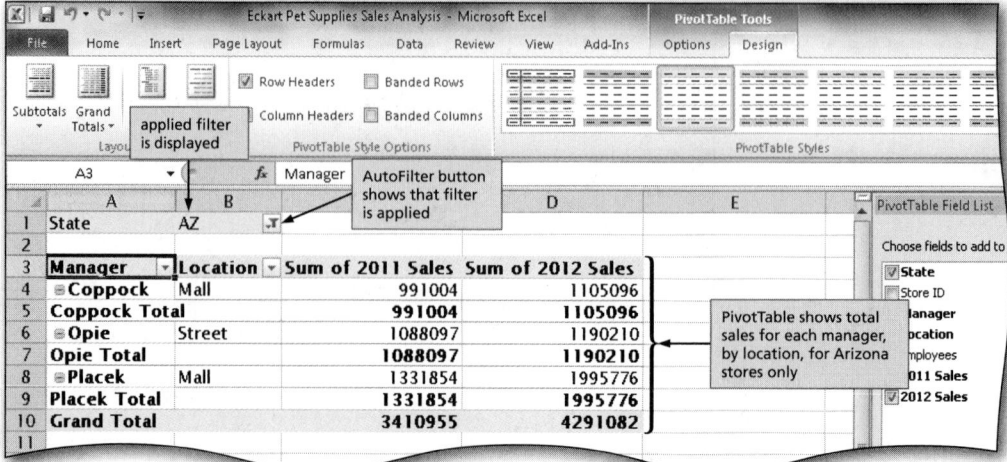

Figure 8–24

To Filter a PivotTable Report Using Multiple Selection Criteria

You may want to identify a subset that is defined by more than one filter criterion. The following steps add a criterion to a report filter.

- Click the AutoFilter button in cell B1 to display the AutoFilter menu for the State field.

- Click the Select Multiple Items check box to prepare for adding a criterion.

- Click the CA check box on the AutoFilter menu to select the CA criterion (Figure 8–25).

Figure 8–25

- Click the OK button to display sales totals for Arizona and California stores (Figure 8–26).

Q&A

How does adding a criterion change the PivotTable report?

Now the PivotTable shows total sales for each manager in mall and street stores in Arizona and California.

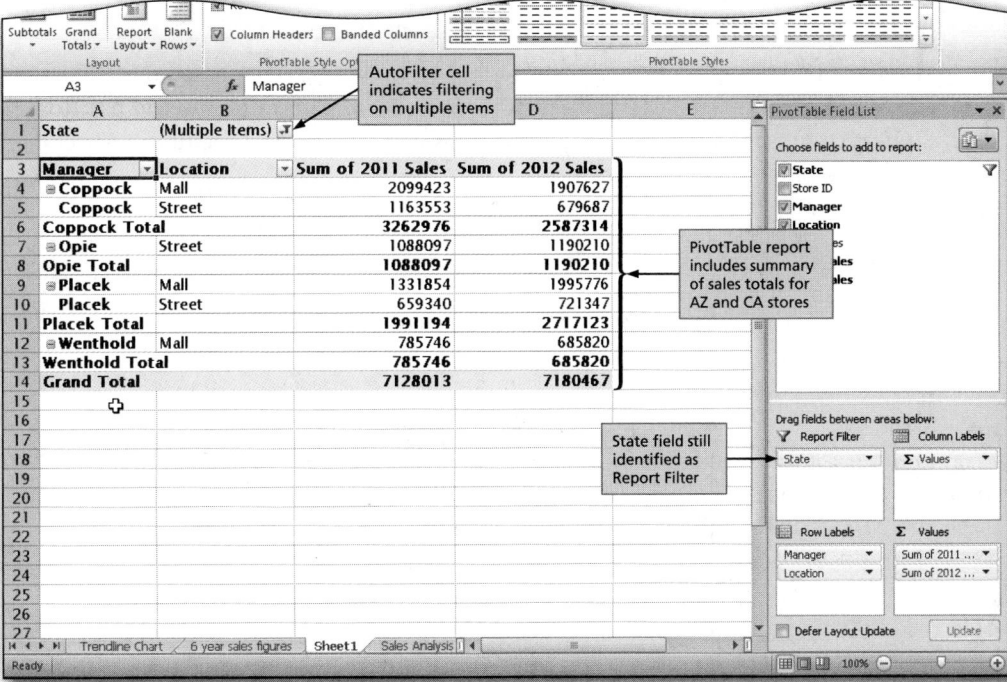

Figure 8–26

To Remove a Report Filter from a PivotTable Report

When you no longer need to display filtered data in a PivotTable report, you can easily remove the filter. The following step removes the State report filter from the PivotTable report.

1

• Click and drag the State button from the Report Filter area in the PivotTable Field List pane to outside of the PivotTable Field List pane to remove the report filter from the PivotTable report (Figure 8–27).

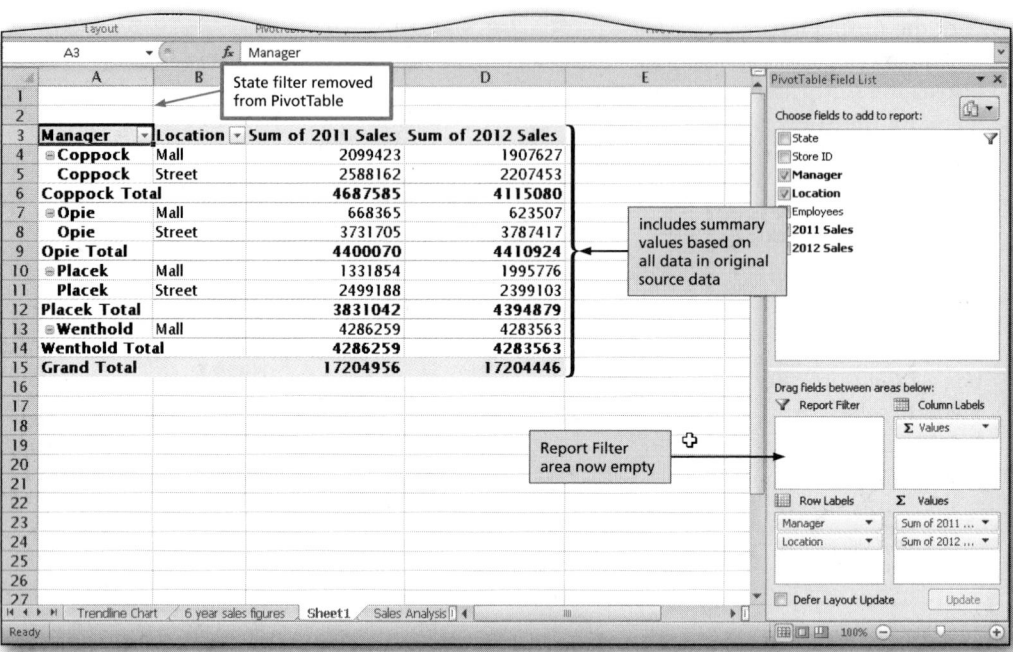

Figure 8–27

To Filter a PivotTable Report Using the Row Label Filter

In a PivotTable report, you may want to look at a subset of data based on fields that are already in use. For example, you could review the data for pet stores located in malls only. You can use Row Label menus in PivotTable reports to view a subset of data. The following steps use a Row Label menu to restrict data in the PivotTable report to mall locations only.

1

• Click the Location AutoFilter button in cell B3 to display the Location AutoFilter menu (Figure 8–28).

Q&A

I do not have a Location AutoFilter button in cell B3. How do I access the menu?

The AutoFilter buttons may be hidden. Click the Field Headers button (PivotTable Tools Options tab | Show group) to turn the field headers on and make the AutoFilter buttons visible.

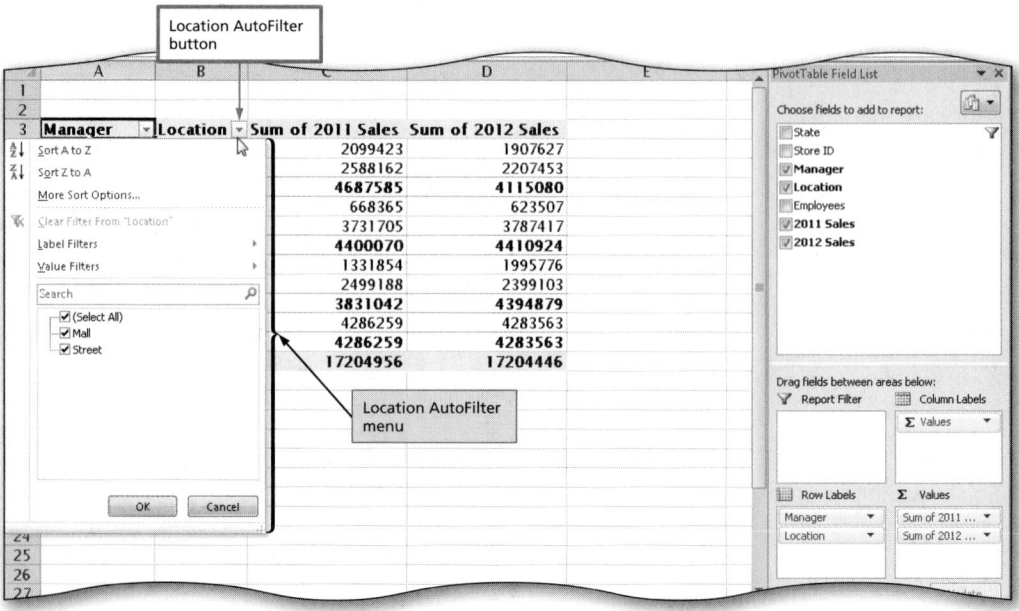

Figure 8–28

2
- Click the Street check box on the Location AutoFilter menu to deselect Street and leave only the Mall location selected (Figure 8–29).

Figure 8–29

3
- Click the OK button to display total sales figures for mall stores only, categorized by manager (Figure 8–30).

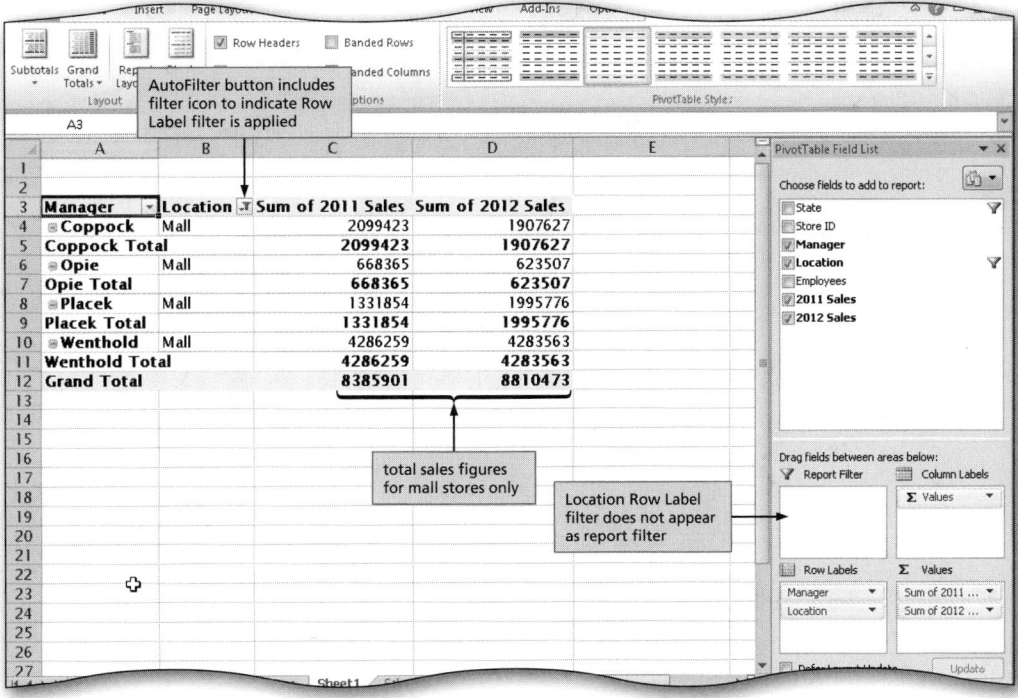

Figure 8–30

To Remove a Row Label Filter from a PivotTable Report

The following steps remove a Row Label filter from a PivotTable report.

1

- Click the Location AutoFilter button in cell B3 to display the Location AutoFilter menu (Figure 8–31).

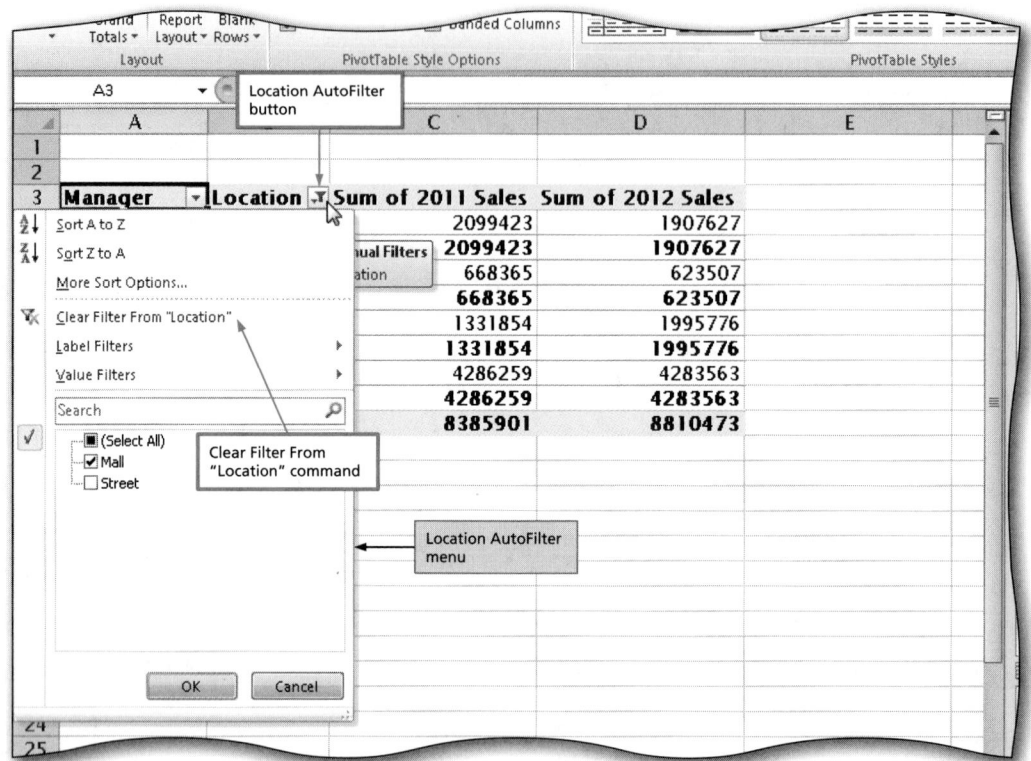

Figure 8–31

2

- Click Clear Filter From "Location" on the Location AutoFilter menu to display total sales figures for stores in all locations (Figure 8–32).

Figure 8–32

Formatting PivotTable Reports

You can use several formatting options to enhance the appearance of PivotTable reports and make the content easier to read. Excel includes a number of preset PivotTable report styles to simplify this task. These styles function in a similar fashion to Excel's table styles. Care should be taken when formatting PivotTable reports, however, because formatting techniques that work for regular tables of data do not behave in the same fashion in PivotTable reports. PivotTable report formatting requires the use of PivotTable styles and field settings.

Visualize your workbook in various PivotTable and PivotChart layouts.
When you plan PivotTables and PivotCharts, consider what information you want to display in each report. As you are developing a report, review the galleries of PivotTable and PivotChart styles to find the best one to display your data. For example, some PivotTable styles include banded rows and columns, which can make it easier to scan and interpret the report.

Plan Ahead

To Format a PivotTable Report

The following steps format a PivotTable by applying a PivotTable style and specifying number formats for the fields.

1

• Double-click the Sheet1 tab to select the name, type **Sales PivotTable Report**, and then press the ENTER key to rename the sheet tab.

• Right-click the Sales PivotTable Report tab, and then point to Tab Color on the shortcut menu to prepare for changing the color of the sheet tab.

• Click Turquoise, Accent 1 (column 5, row 1) in the Theme Colors area to apply the color to the sheet tab.

• Click cell A4 to select a cell in the PivotTable.

• If necessary, click Design on the Ribbon to display the PivotTable Tools Design tab (Figure 8–33).

Figure 8–33

• Click the More button in the PivotTable Styles gallery (PivotTable Tools Design tab | PivotTable Styles group) to expand the gallery.

• Point to the Pivot Style Light 9 PivotTable style (column 3, row 2) in the PivotTable Styles gallery to display a preview of the style in the PivotTable (Figure 8–34).

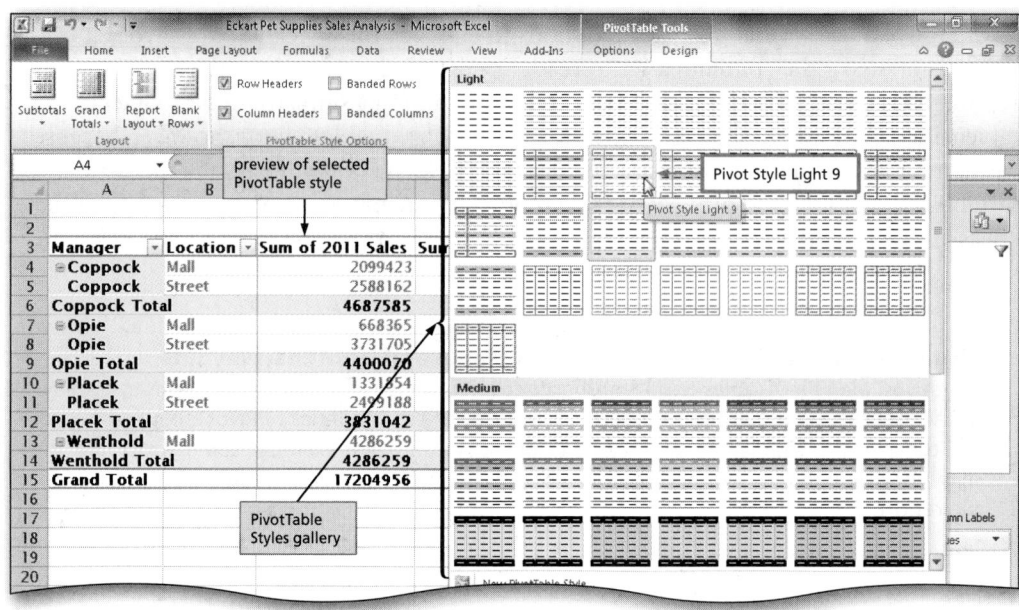

Figure 8–34

3

• Click the Pivot Style Light 9 PivotTable style to apply the style to the PivotTable report (Figure 8–35).

Figure 8–35

4

• Right-click cell C4 and then click Number Format on the shortcut menu to display the Format Cells dialog box.

• Click Currency in the Category list to select the Currency number format.

• Type 0 in the Decimal places box to specify no decimal places (Figure 8–36).

Figure 8–36

5

- Click the OK button (Format Cells dialog box) to apply the Currency style to all 2011 Sales values in the PivotTable report.

Q&A Why does the number format change apply to all 2011 Sales values?

When formatting is applied to a PivotTable field, all field entries are updated to reflect that formatting.

Q&A Why is the dollar currency symbol displayed for the 2011 Sales values?

The dollar currency symbol is included by default.

- Right-click cell D4 to display the shortcut menu and prepare for formatting the 2012 Sales values.

- Click Number Format on the shortcut menu to display the Format Cells dialog box.

- When Excel displays the Format Cells dialog box, click Currency in the Category list to select the Currency number format.

- Type 0 in the Decimal places box to specify no decimal places.

- Click the OK button (Format Cells dialog box) to apply the Currency style to all 2012 Sales values in the PivotTable report.

Q&A Could I just apply the currency format to the range of cells?

In a PivotTable report, formats applied to individual cells or groups of cells only last as long as the report lasts in the current format. Once the table is rearranged, the individual cell formatting is lost. To have the formatting remain with the PivotTable report through report manipulations, apply PivotTable styles or change field settings.

- Click cell A17 to deselect the PivotTable report.

- Click the Save button on the Quick Access toolbar to save the workbook (Figure 8–37).

Figure 8–37

To Switch Summary Functions in a PivotTable

In addition to analyzing total sales per year for various groupings, you are also interested in looking at average sales per year for those same groupings. In PivotTable reports, you can easily change the function used to summarize data from the original table. Currently the PivotTable report for Eckart Pet Supplies displays the sum of the sales for each manager by location. However, these results can be difficult to interpret. An average of sales per employee might be a better measure for comparing the sales of each manager in each location. The following steps show how to switch summary functions in a PivotTable.

1

- Right-click cell C4 to display the shortcut menu and prepare for changing the summary function for the 2011 Sales values.

- Point to Summarize Values By on the shortcut menu to display the Summarize Values By menu (Figure 8–38).

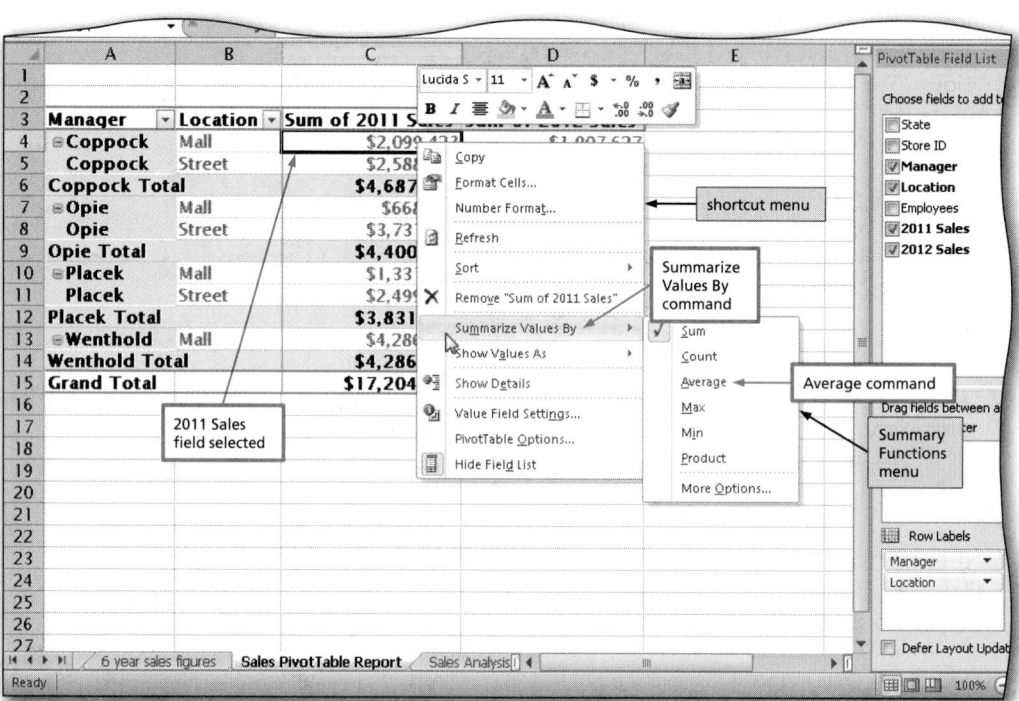

Figure 8–38

2

- Click Average on the Summarize Values By menu to change the summary function from Sum to Average (Figure 8–39).

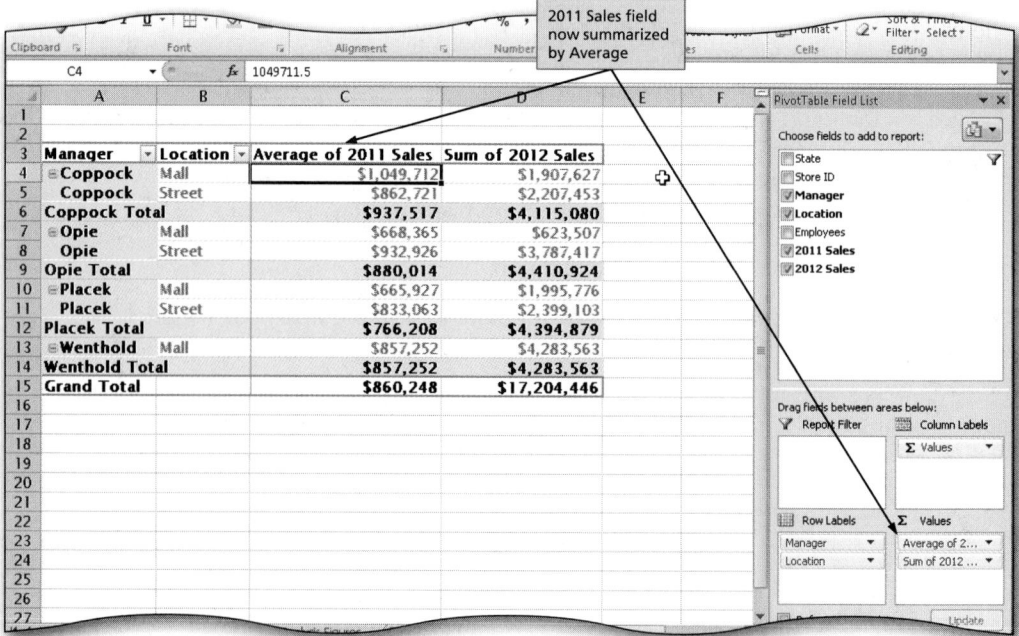

Figure 8–39

3

- Repeat Steps 1 and 2 to change the summary function used in column D from Sum to Average.

- Click cell A17 to deselect the PivotTable and close the PivotTable Field List pane (Figure 8–40).

Figure 8–40

More on Summary Functions for PivotCharts and PivotTables

Table 8–1 lists the summary functions Excel provides for analysis of data in PivotChart and PivotTable reports. Summary functions can be selected from the shortcut menu of a cell in the PivotTable report, as was just illustrated when changing the Summary function from Sum to Average. Some summary functions do not appear directly on the shortcut menu, but rather are accessed by clicking More Options on the shortcut menu. Summary functions can also be selected by using the Calculations button in the

Table 8–1 Summary Functions for PivotChart Report and PivotTable Report Data Analysis	
Summary Function	**Description**
Sum	Sum of the values (default function for numeric source data)
Count	Number of data values
Average	Average of the values
Max	Largest value
Min	Smallest value
Product	Product of the values
Count Nums	Number of data values that contain numeric data
StdDev	Estimate of the standard deviation of all of the data to be summarized, used when data is a sample of a larger population of interest
StdDevp	Standard deviation of all of the data to be summarized, used when data is the population of interest
Var	Estimate of the variance of all of the data to be summarized, used when data is a sample of a larger population of interest
Varp	Variance of the data to be summarized, used when data is the population of interest

Actions group on the PivotTable Tools Options tab (Figure 8–41a) or by using the field button arrow in the Values area of the PivotTable Field List (Figure 8–41b) to access the Value Field Settings command and the Value Field Settings dialog box.

Figure 8–41 (a) Summarize Values By Menu

Figure 8–41 (b) Value Field Settings Dialog Box

To Filter a PivotTable Report Using Multiple Criteria

In a PivotTable report, you may want to look at a subset of data defined by more than one condition. For example, you might be interested in reviewing the data for pet stores located in malls with sales of less than $750,000. You can use Row Label menus in PivotTable reports to view a more restricted subset of data. The following steps use a Row Label menu to restrict data in the PivotTable report to mall locations with sales of less than $750,000.

1

- Click the Location AutoFilter button in cell B3 to display the Location AutoFilter menu.

- Click the (Select All) check box on the Location AutoFilter menu to deselect all locations.

- Click the Mall check box to specify total sales figures for mall stores only.

- Point to the Value Filters command to display the Value Filters menu (Figure 8–42).

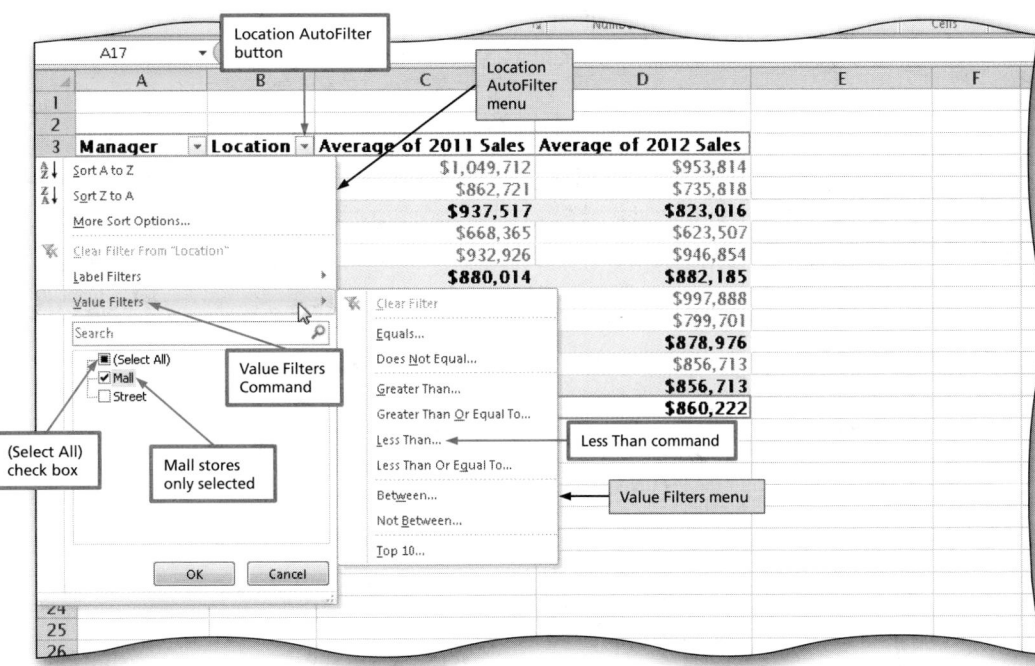

Figure 8–42

2

- Click Less Than to display the Value Filter (Location) dialog box.

- Click the first arrow button, and then click Average of 2012 Sales to select the first part of the condition.

- If necessary, click the second arrow button, and then click 'is less than' to select the second part of the condition.

- Click the third text box, and then type 750000 to set the filter to select Manager records where 2012 sales are less than 750,000 dollars (Figure 8–43).

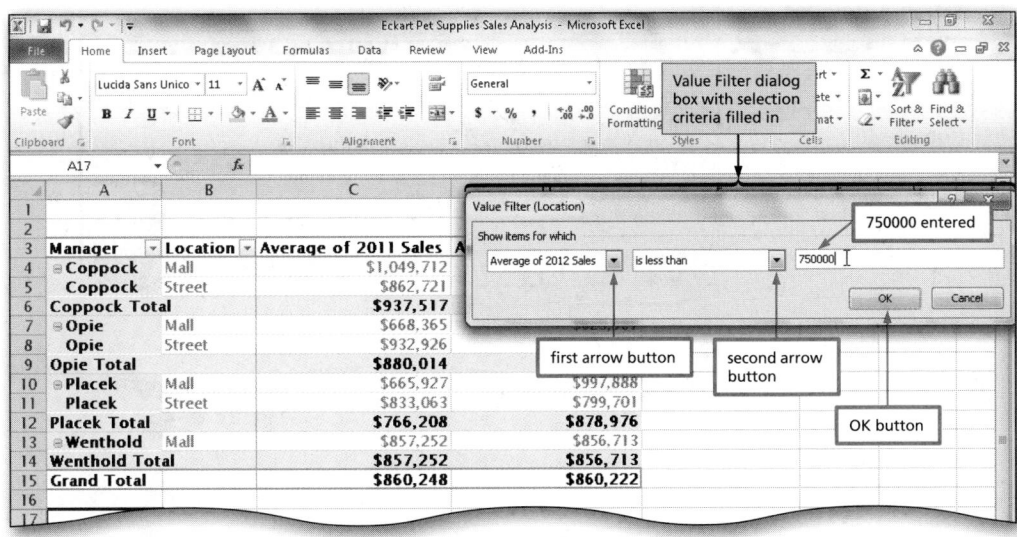

Figure 8–43

3

- Click the OK button (Value Filter (Location) dialog box) to apply the filter to the PivotTable report (Figure 8–44).

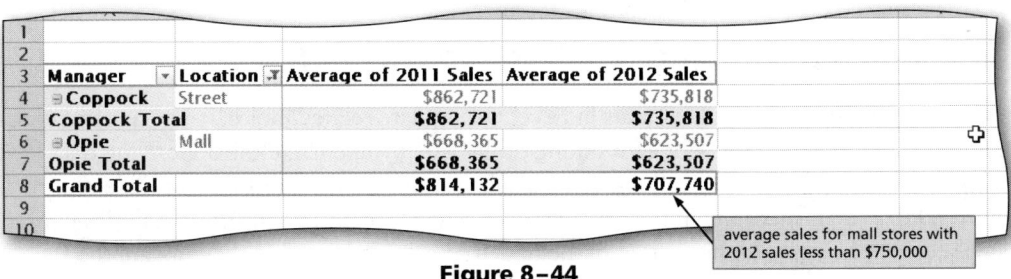

Figure 8–44

To Remove Multiple Filter Criteria from a PivotTable Report

The following steps remove multiple filter criteria from a PivotTable report.

1

• Click the Location AutoFilter button in cell B3 to display the Location AutoFilter menu (Figure 8–45).

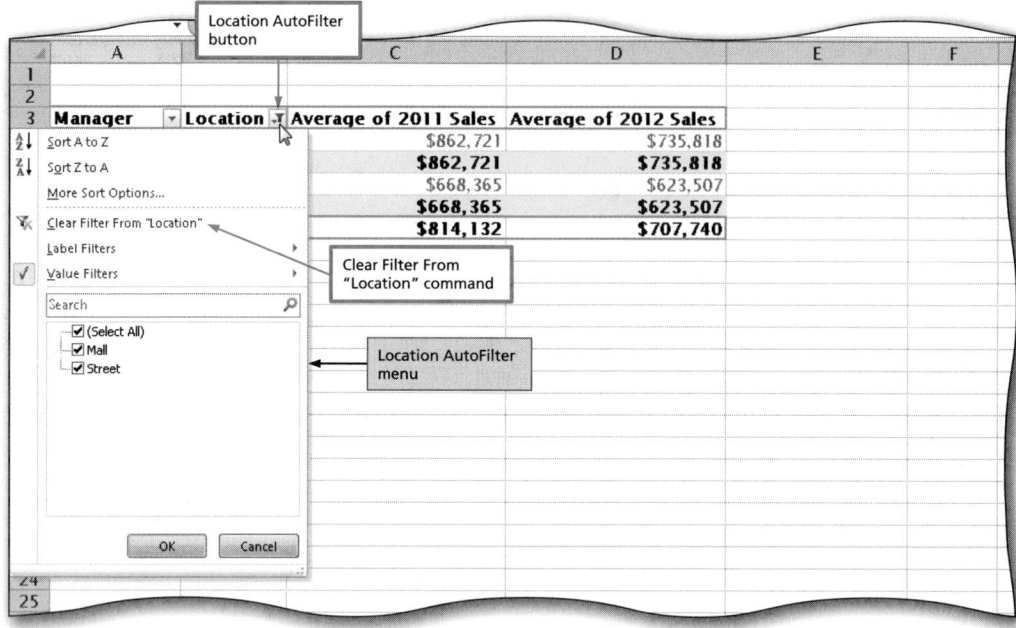

Figure 8–45

2

• Click Clear Filter From "Location" on the Location AutoFilter menu to display total sales figures for stores at all locations (Figure 8–46).

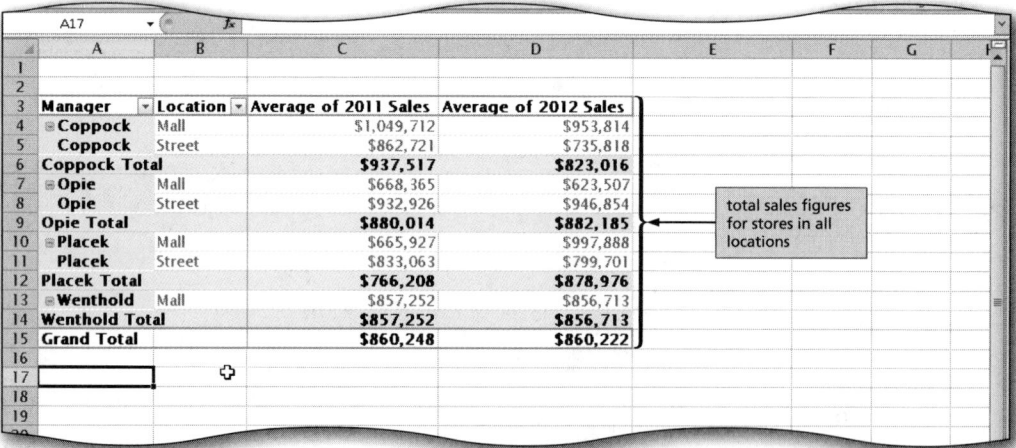

Figure 8–46

Break Point: If you wish to take a break, this is a good place to do so. You can quit Excel now. To resume at a later time, start Excel, open the file called Eckart Pet Supplies Sales Analysis, and continue following the steps from this location forward.

To Update the Contents of a PivotTable Report

When you update cell contents in Excel, you update related tables, formula calculations, and charts in Excel. However, PivotTables do not update automatically when you change the underlying data for the PivotTable report. You must manually update the PivotTable to recalculate summary data in the PivotTable report. The sales figure for 2011 for store ID 872786 is incorrect in the original sheet. The correct value for the 2011 sales figure is 1,119,393. The following steps correct the typographical error in the underlying worksheet, and then update the PivotTable report.

1

- Click the Sales Analysis Figures sheet tab to make it the active sheet.

- Click cell F12, type **1119393**, and then press the ENTER key to change the contents of the cell (Figure 8–47).

Q&A

What data will this change affect in the PivotTable?

The changed value is for Placek's sales in street stores. This value is displayed in cell C11 in the Sales PivotTable Report worksheet.

	A	B	C	D	E	F	G	H	I	J	K
1	Eckart Pet Supplies Sales Analysis										
2	State	Store ID	Manager	Location	Employees	2011 Sales	2012 Sales				
3	AZ	476442	Placek	Mall	4	696653	1160261				
4	AZ	507217	Coppock	Mall	6	991004	1105096				
5	AZ	186146	Opie	Street	5	1088097	1190210				
6	AZ	274764	Placek	Mall	4	635201	835515				
7	CA	345710	Coppock	Street	7	1163553	679687				
8	CA	660266	Wenthold	Mall	5	785746	685820				
9	CA	415361	Placek	Street	8	659340	721347				
10	CA	587410	Coppock	Mall	5	1108419	802531				
11	NM	574238	Wenthold	Mall	5	1142476	1083996				
12	NM	872786	Placek	Street	6	1119393	1104379				
13	NM	208903	Opie	Street	8	992142	935871				
14	NM	796652	Opie	Street	7	981322	1018577				
15	NV	627034	Coppock	Street	6	797675	738345				
16	NV	706640	Wenthold	Mall	5	615421	859487				
17	NV	691735	Placek	Street	7	726455	573377				
18	NV	473321	Wenthold	Mall	4	599183	582657				
19	UT	346480	Opie	Street	6	670144	642759				
20	UT	107938	Coppock	Street	6	626934	789421				
21	UT	125017	Wenthold	Mall	6	1143433	1071603				
22	UT	382110	Opie	Mall	5	668365	623507				
23											
24											
25											

change made in source data; PivotTable not refreshed

Figure 8–47

2

- Click the Sales PivotTable Report tab to make it the active sheet.

- If necessary, click inside the PivotTable report to make it active.

- Click Options on the Ribbon to display the PivotTable Tools Options tab.

- Click the Refresh button (PivotTable Tools Options tab | Data group) to update the PivotTable Report to reflect the change to the underlying data (Figure 8–48).

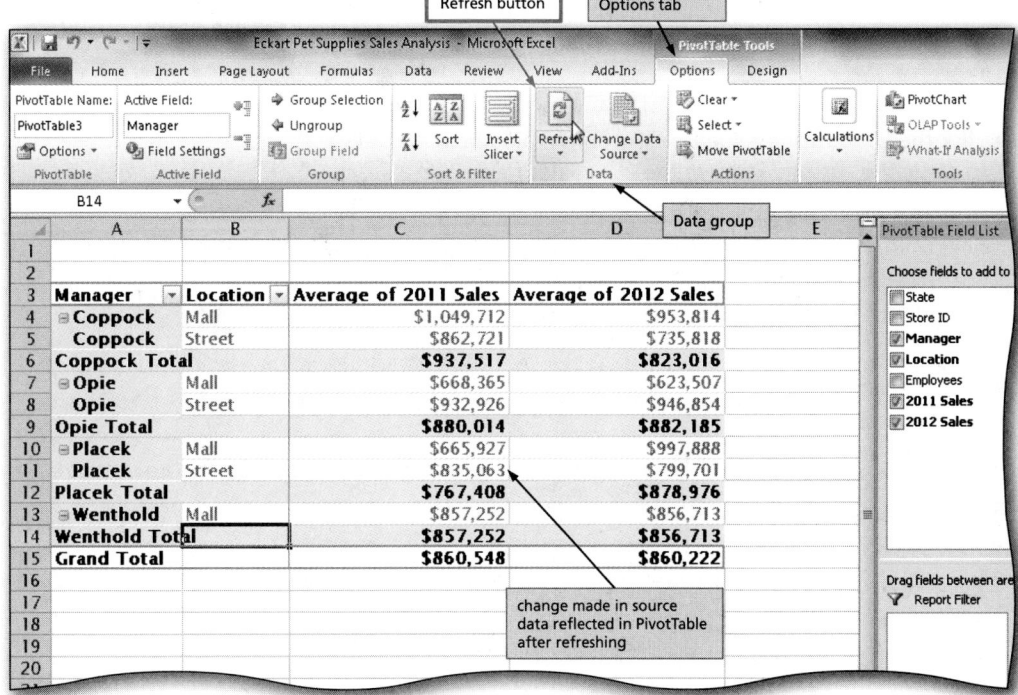

Refresh button

PivotTable Tools Options tab

Data group

change made in source data reflected in PivotTable after refreshing

Figure 8–48

To Add a Second Value Calculation to a PivotTable Report

In addition to updating data, you may need to add new fields to analyze additional or more complex questions. You have been asked to review average sales for 2011 and 2012 in addition to total sales. You will need to add value fields and change the summary function to meet this request. The following steps add a second value calculation for each of the two years and use these fields in the PivotTable report.

1

- In the PivotTable Field List pane, drag the 2011 Sales field to the Values area to add the field to column E of the PivotTable.

- In the Values area, click the Sum of 2011 Sales button, and then click Value Field Settings to display the Value Field Settings dialog box.

- Enter `Total 2011 Sales` in the Custom Name text box to rename the value field (Figure 8–49).

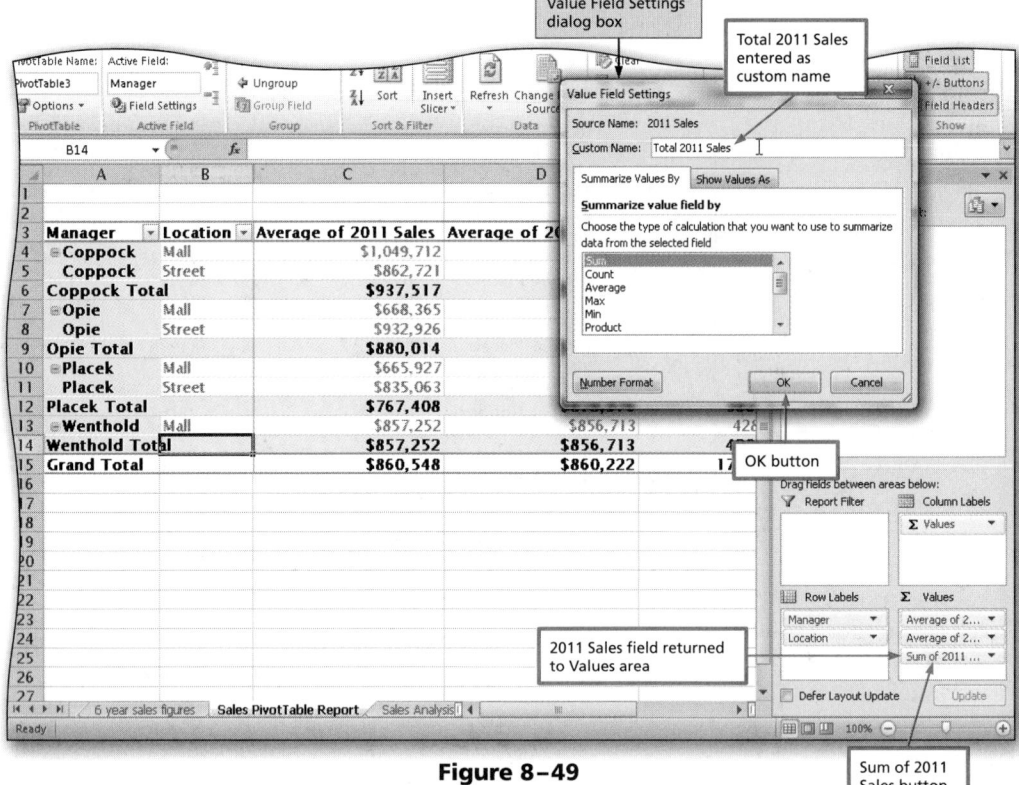

Figure 8–49

2

- Click the OK button (Value Field Settings dialog box) to apply the custom name to the 2011 Sales field.

- Drag the 2012 Sales field to the Values area to add the field to column F of the PivotTable.

- Click the Sum of 2012 Sales button, and then click Value Field Settings to display the Value Field Settings dialog box.

- Enter `Total 2012 Sales` in the Custom Name text box to rename the value field.

- Click the OK button (Value Field Settings dialog box) to apply the custom name.

- Use the Value Field Settings dialog box to customize the names as shown in cells C3 and D3 (Figure 8–50).

Figure 8–50

3

- Format the values in columns E and then F to the Currency category, 0 decimal places, and the $ symbol.

- Click the Save button on the Quick Access toolbar to save the workbook (Figure 8–51).

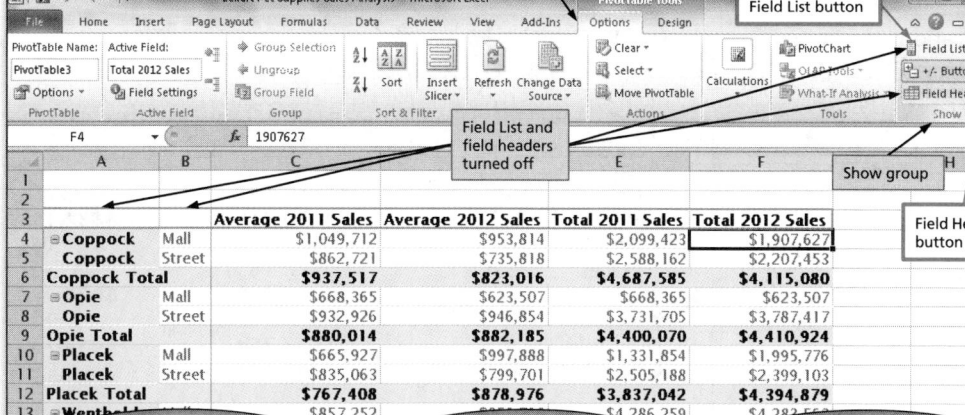

Figure 8–51

To Customize the Display of the Field List and Field Headers in the PivotTable Report

After adding the two calculated fields, the worksheet is becoming quite full. You can choose which supporting items you display in the PivotTable report and on the worksheet containing the report. You can display or hide the PivotTable Field List pane, field headers, and buttons. You can also turn off the autofitting of column widths to further customize the columns of the report. The following steps remove the PivotTable Field List pane and field headers from the report and worksheet, and turn off the column autofitting.

1

- Click the Field List button (PivotTable Tools Options tab | Show group) to hide the PivotTable Field List pane.

- Click the Field Headers button (PivotTable Tools Options tab | Show group) to hide the field headers (Figure 8–52).

Q&A How can I display the PivotTable Field List pane and field headers after hiding them?

The Field List, +/– Buttons, and Field Header buttons are toggle buttons. You need to click them again to turn the display back on.

Figure 8–52

- Click the Options button (PivotTable Tools Options tab | PivotTable group) to display the PivotTable Options dialog box.

- Click the 'Autofit column widths on update' check box to remove the check mark (Figure 8–53).

- Click the OK button (PivotTable Options dialog box) to turn off the autofitting of column widths.

Figure 8–53

To Customize the Display of the +/– Buttons in the PivotTable Report

The +/– buttons expand and collapse across categories, reducing the amount of detail visible in the report without removing the field from the report. In some instances, you may decide that the report will be more visually appealing without the +/– buttons in the report. The following steps illustrate expanding and collapsing categories using the buttons and shortcut menus, and then suppressing the display of the +/– buttons in the report.

1

- Click the collapse button in cell A4 to collapse the Coppock location information (Figure 8–54).

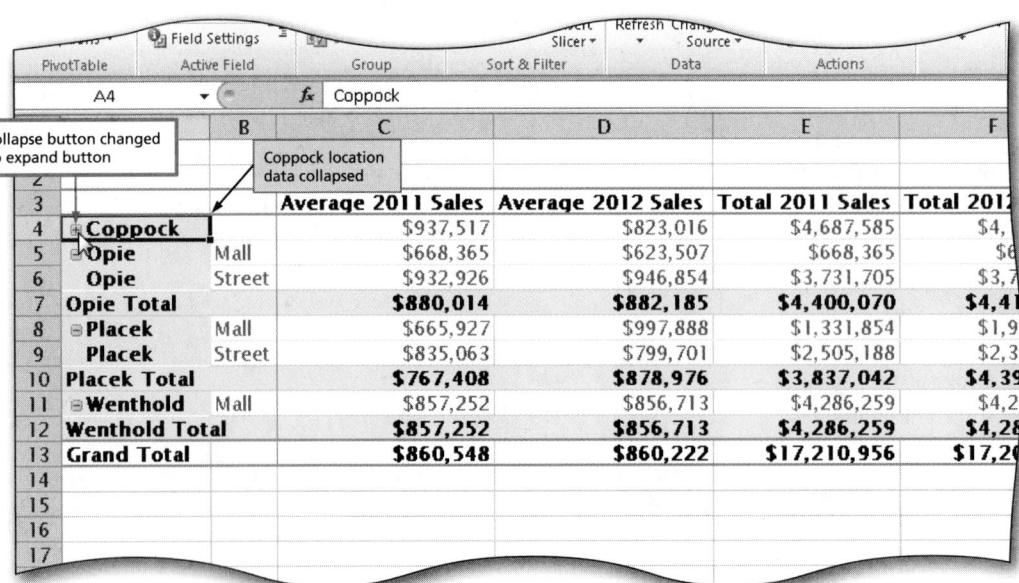

Figure 8–54

2

- Right-click cell A11 to display the shortcut menu, and then point to Expand/Collapse to display the Expand/Collapse menu (Figure 8–55).

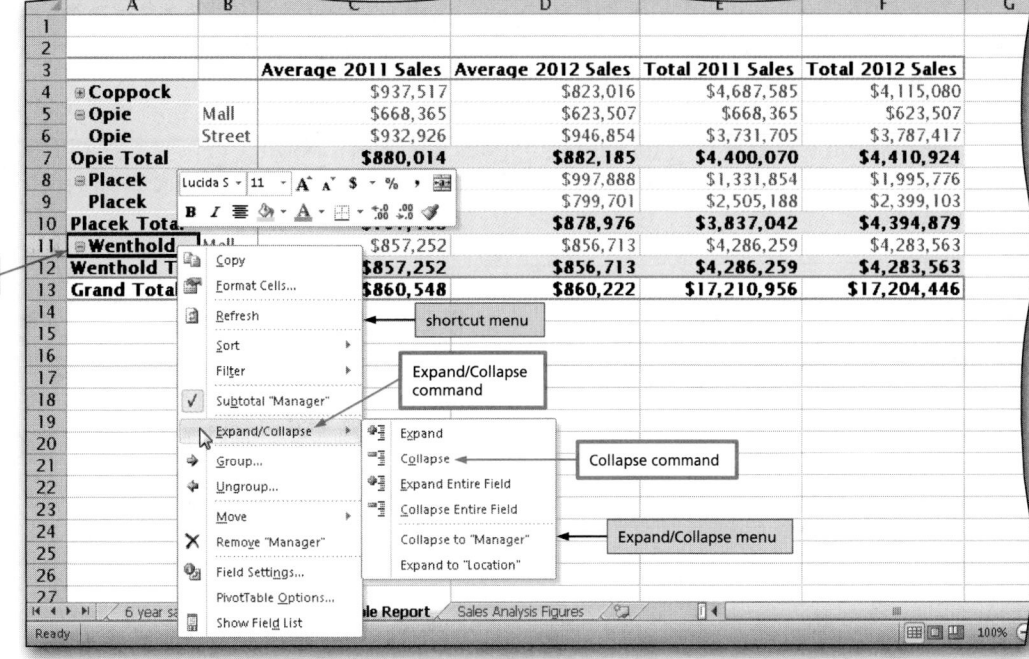

Figure 8–55

3

- Click Collapse to collapse the Wenthold location data.

- Click the +/– Buttons button (PivotTable Tools Options tab | Show group) to hide the expand and collapse buttons in the PivotTable (Figure 8–56).

Figure 8–56

4

- Right-click cell A4, and then point to Expand/Collapse on the shortcut menu to display the Expand/Collapse menu.

- Click Expand Entire Field to expand the Location field.

- In cell A1, enter the title **Eckart Pet Supplies Sales Report**, and in cell A2, enter the subtitle **2011 and 2012**.

- Merge and center the text across A1:F1 and A2:F2. Apply the Title style to cell A1. Apply the fill color Light Turquoise, Background 2, Darker 25% to cells A1:A2 (Figure 8–57).

Figure 8–57

To Create a PivotChart Report from an Existing PivotTable Report

A PivotChart report must always be associated with a PivotTable report. The association is created in one of two ways. You can create a PivotChart report directly from data using the PivotChart command on the PivotTable menu as shown in Figure 8–14 on page EX 501, which automatically creates an associated PivotTable report. If you have already created a PivotTable report, you can create a PivotChart report for that PivotTable report using the PivotChart button on the PivotTable Tools Options tab. The following steps create a PivotChart report from the existing PivotTable report, formatting it as a 3-D Clustered Column chart that shows the two-year data for average sales side by side.

- If necessary, click cell A4 to select it in the PivotTable report.
- Click the Field List button (PivotTable Tools Options tab | Show group) to display the PivotTable Field List pane.
- Click the PivotChart button (PivotTable Tools Options tab | Tools group) to display the Insert Chart dialog box.
- Click 3-D Clustered Column (column 4, row 1) in the 'Column chart type' gallery to select the chart type (Figure 8–58).

Figure 8–58

2
- Click the OK button (Insert Chart dialog box) to add the chart to the Sales PivotTable Report worksheet (Figure 8–59).

Figure 8–59

To Change the Location of a PivotChart Report and Delete Total Sales Data

By default, a PivotChart report will be created on the same page as the associated PivotTable report. The following steps move the PivotChart report to a separate sheet, and change the tab color to match the tab color of the PivotTable report tab.

❶

• With the 3-D Clustered Column chart selected, click the Move Chart button (PivotChart Tools Design tab | Location group) to display the Move Chart dialog box.

• Click the New sheet option button (Move Chart dialog box) to select it.

• Type **Average Sales PivotChart Report** in the New sheet text box to name the new worksheet (Figure 8–60).

Figure 8–60

❷

• Click the OK button (Move Chart dialog box) to move the 3-D Clustered Column chart to the new Average Sales PivotChart Report sheet.

• Right-click the new sheet tab and then point to Tab Color on the shortcut menu to prepare for formatting the sheet tab.

• Click Red, Accent 2 (column 6, row 1) to change the color of the sheet tab.

• In the PivotTable Field List pane, drag Total 2011 Sales and Total 2012 Sales out of the Values area to remove the total sales data from the PivotChart report and PivotTable report (Figure 8–61).

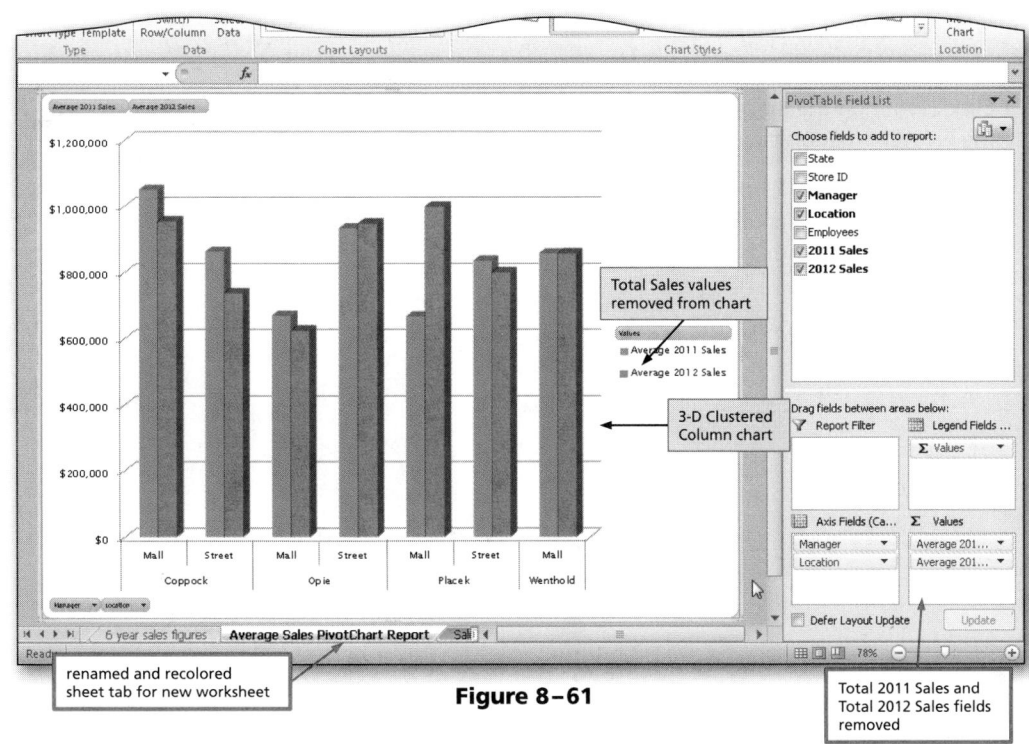

Figure 8–61

1

• Click the Clear Filter button on the State slicer and the Location slicer to remove the filters and return the PivotTable and PivotCharts to their unfiltered states.

• Click Wenthold in the Manager slicer to see the aggregate data for the stores that Wenthold manages, broken down by State and Location (Figure 8–91).

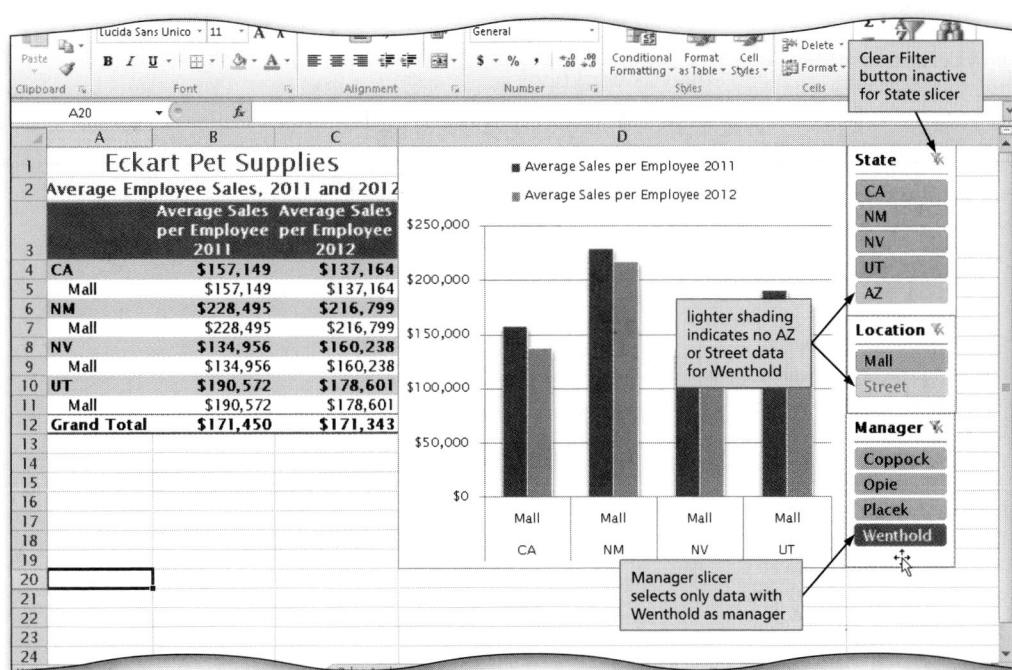

Figure 8–91

2

🔍 **Experiment**

• Click different managers and combination of managers to see how the aggregate data changes.

• Click Coppock in the Manager slicer to see the aggregate data for the stores that Coppock manages, broken down by State and Location (Figure 8–92).

Q&A

How can I save a particular PivotTable setup?

PivotTables are dynamic by nature. To save a particular configuration, make a copy of the sheet, and use the Protect sheet command to keep changes from being made to the worksheet copy. You can continue to use the PivotTable on the original sheet to analyze the data.

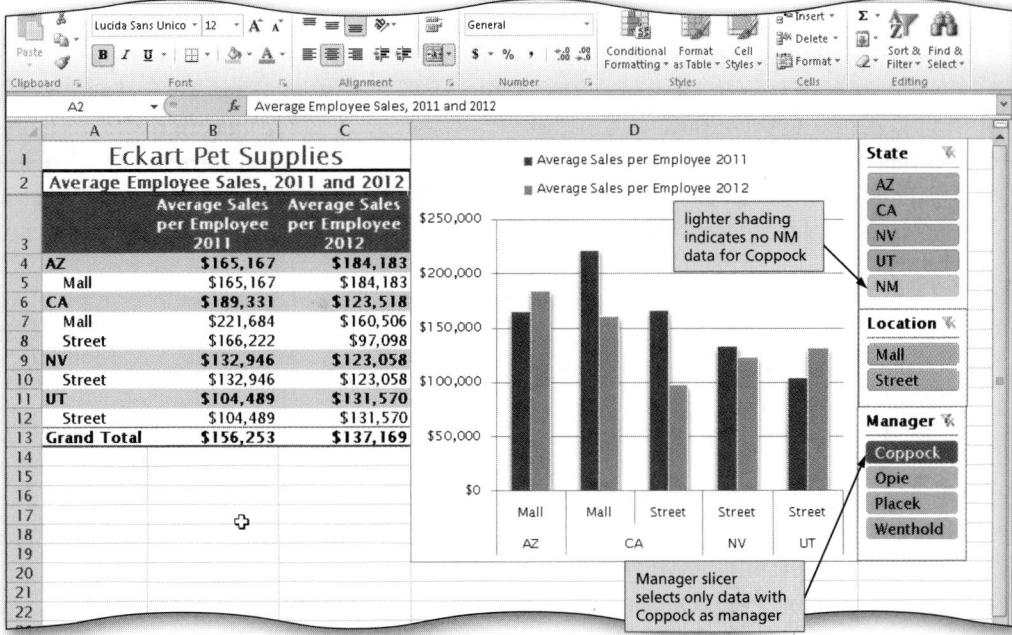

Figure 8–92

3

• Save the workbook.

BTW

Certification
The Microsoft Office Specialist (MOS) program provides an opportunity for you to obtain a valuable industry credential — proof that you have the Excel 2010 skills required by employers. For more information, visit the Excel 2010 Certification Web page (scsite.com/ex2010/cert).

BTW

Quick Reference
For a table that lists how to complete the tasks covered in this book using the mouse, Ribbon, shortcut menu, and keyboard, see the Quick Reference Summary at the back of this book, or visit the Excel 2010 Quick Reference Web page (scsite.com/ex2010/qr).

To Close the Workbook

The project is complete. The following steps close the Eckart Pet Supplies Sales Analysis workbook.

1 Click the workbook Close button.

2 If Excel displays the Microsoft Office Excel dialog box, click the Yes button.

To Quit Excel

The following steps quit Excel.

1 Click the Close button on the right side of the title bar.

2 If Excel displays the Microsoft Office Excel dialog box, click the No button.

Chapter Summary

In this chapter, you learned how to create a trendline on a chart, and create, format, filter, and analyze interactive PivotTables and PivotCharts. The items listed below include all the new Excel skills you have learned in this chapter.

1. Create a 2-D Line Chart (EX 495)
2. Add a Trendline to a Chart (EX 497)
3. Create a Blank PivotTable Report (EX 500)
4. Add Data to the PivotTable (EX 502)
5. Change the Layout of a PivotTable Report (EX 503)
6. Change the View of a PivotTable Report (EX 505)
7. Filter a PivotTable Report Using a Report Filter (EX 506)
8. Filter a PivotTable Report Using Multiple Selection Criteria (EX 507)
9. Remove a Report Filter from a PivotTable Report (EX 508)
10. Filter a PivotTable Report Using the Row Label Filter (EX 508)
11. Remove a Row Label Filter from a PivotTable Report (EX 509)
12. Format a PivotTable Report (EX 511)
13. Switch Summary Functions in a PivotTable (EX 514)
14. Filter a PivotTable Report Using Multiple Criteria (EX 516)
15. Remove Multiple Filter Criteria from a PivotTable Report (EX 518)
16. Update the Contents of a PivotTable Report (EX 518)
17. Add a Second Value Calculation to a PivotTable Report (EX 519)
18. Customize the Display of the Field List and Field Headers in the PivotTable Report (EX 521)
19. Customize the Display of the +/- Buttons in the PivotTable Report (EX 522)
20. Create a PivotChart Report from an Existing PivotTable report (EX 524)
21. Change the Location of a PivotChart Report and Delete Total Sales Data (EX 525)
22. Change the PivotChart Type and Format the Chart (EX 526)
23. Change the View of a PivotChart (EX 529)
24. Create a PivotChart Report Directly from Data (EX 530)
25. Add a Calculated Field to a PivotTable Report (EX 532)
26. Format the PivotTable and PivotChart (EX 533)
27. Add Slicers to the Worksheet (EX 537)
28. Format Slicers (EX 538)
29. Use the Slicers to Review Groups in the PivotTable (EX 540)
30. Use the Slicers to Review Groups Not in the PivotTable (EX 540)

Learn It Online

Test your knowledge of chapter content and key terms.

Instructions: To complete the Learn It Online exercises, start your browser, click the Address bar, and then enter the Web address `scsite.com/ex2010/learn`. When the Excel 2010 Learn It Online page is displayed, click the link for the exercise you want to complete and then read the instructions.

Chapter Reinforcement TF, MC, and SA
A series of true/false, multiple choice, and short answer questions that test your knowledge of the chapter content.

Flash Cards
An interactive learning environment where you identify chapter key terms associated with displayed definitions.

Practice Test
A series of multiple choice questions that test your knowledge of chapter content and key terms.

Who Wants To Be a Computer Genius?
An interactive game that challenges your knowledge of chapter content in the style of a television quiz show.

Wheel of Terms
An interactive game that challenges your knowledge of chapter key terms in the style of the television show *Wheel of Fortune*.

Crossword Puzzle Challenge
A crossword puzzle that challenges your knowledge of key terms presented in the chapter.

Apply Your Knowledge

Reinforce the skills and apply the concepts you learned in this chapter.

Creating a PivotTable
Note: To complete this assignment, you will be required to use the Data Files for Students. See the inside back cover of this book for instructions on downloading the Data Files for Students, or contact your instructor for information about accessing the required files.

Instructions: Start Excel. Open the document, Apply 8-1 Javier's Used Autos, from the Data Files for Students, and then save the workbook as Apply 8-1 Javier's Used Autos Complete.

The owner of Javier's Used Autos wants you to create a PivotTable from the current inventory and then manipulate it to display different totals. Figure 8–93 on the next page shows the completed Inventory PivotTable worksheet.

Continued >

Apply Your Knowledge *continued*

Figure 8–93

Perform the following tasks.

1. Select cell A3, and then click the PivotTable button (Insert tab | Tables group) to display the Create PivotTable dialog box. Make sure New Worksheet is selected and then click OK.

2. Drag the Make field from the 'Choose fields to add to report' list to the Row Labels area to add the Make field to the PivotTable. Repeat this step for the Model, Color, and Category fields.

3. Drag the Price field from the 'Choose fields to add to report' list to the Values list to add the sum of the Price field to the PivotTable.

4. Write down the totals for each make of auto and the grand total.

5. Click the Row Labels AutoFilter button in cell A3 to display the Row Labels AutoFilter menu. Select only Dodge and Subaru and then click OK. Write down the totals for the makes and the grand total.

6. Click the Undo button on the Quick Access toolbar to display the data for all makes.

7. Drag the Category button in the Row Labels area to the Report Filter area in the PivotTable Field List pane to create a new field. Click the Category AutoFilter button, click Sport, and then click OK. Write down the totals for the makes and the grand total.

8. Click cell A4, click the PivotTable Styles More button on the PivotTable Tools Design tab, and then click Pivot Style Medium 2 to apply the style to the PivotTable.

9. Name the sheet Inventory PivotTable. Save the workbook with the PivotTable, and then close the workbook.

10. Submit the assignment as requested by your instructor.

Extend Your Knowledge

Extend the skills you learned in this chapter and experiment with new skills. You may need to use Help to complete the assignment.

Grouping Content in PivotTables

Note: To complete this assignment, you will be required to use the Data Files for Students. See the inside back cover of this book for instructions on downloading the Data Files for Students, or contact your instructor for information about accessing the required files.

To Change the PivotChart Type and Format the Chart

The default chart type for a PivotChart is a Clustered Column chart. PivotCharts can support most chart types, except XY (Scatter), Stock, and Bubble. The following steps change the PivotChart type to 3-D Cylinder, add a title to the PivotChart report, and apply formatting options to the chart.

1

- Click the Change Chart Type button (PivotChart Tools Design tab | Type group) to display the Change Chart Type dialog box.

- Click the 3-D Cylinder chart type (row 2, column 4) to select it (Figure 8–62).

Figure 8–62

2

- Click the OK button (Change Chart Type dialog box) to change the chart type to 3-D Cylinder.

- Click Layout on the Ribbon to display the PivotChart Tools Layout tab.

- Click the Chart Title button (PivotChart Tools Layout tab | Labels group) to display the Chart Title menu (Figure 8–63).

Figure 8–63

- Click Above Chart on the Chart Title menu to insert a Chart Title placeholder above the chart.

- Drag to select the title text in the chart title placeholder.

- Type **Eckart Pet Supplies** as the first line in the chart title, and then press the SHIFT+ENTER keys to move to a new line.

- Type **Average Sales by Manager and Location** as the second line in the chart title, and then press the SHIFT+ENTER keys to move to a new line.

- Type **2011 and 2012** as the third line in the chart title, and then click anywhere on the chart to add the title to the chart (Figure 8–64).

Figure 8–64

- Click the chart title to select it.

- Click Format on the Ribbon to display the PivotChart Tools Format tab.

- Click the More button (PivotChart Tools Format tab | WordArt Styles group) to display the WordArt gallery.

- Click the Gradient Fill – Turquoise, Accent 1 WordArt style (column 4, row 3) to apply it to the chart title (Figure 8–65).

Figure 8–65

- Click Layout on the Ribbon to display the PivotChart Tools Layout tab.
- Click the Chart Wall button (PivotChart Tools Layout tab | Background group) to display the Chart Wall menu (Figure 8–66).

Figure 8–66

- Click the More Walls Options command to display the Format Walls dialog box.
- If necessary, click Fill in the left pane (Format Walls dialog box) to display the Fill options.
- Click the Gradient fill option button (Format Walls dialog box) to select a gradient fill for the walls area of the chart.
- Select the following Fill options: Type: Linear; Direction: Linear up; Color: Light Turquoise, Background 2, Darker 25% (column 3, row 3) (Figure 8–67).

Figure 8–67

- Click the Close button (Format Walls dialog box) to apply the Fill formatting to the background of the PivotChart (Figure 8–68).

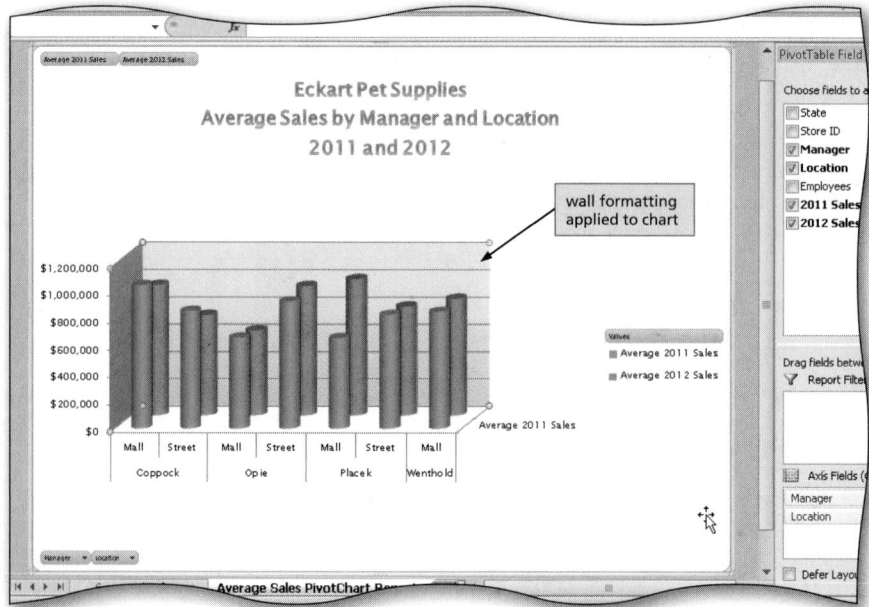

Figure 8–68

To Change the View of a PivotChart

As with regular charts, when the data in a PivotTable report is changed, any PivotChart reports built upon that PivotTable report update to reflect those changes. Unique to PivotCharts, however, is that changes made to the view of the PivotChart are automatically reflected in the view of the PivotTable. The following steps change the view of the PivotChart report and then show how the change in the PivotChart causes a corresponding change in the view of its PivotTable report.

1

- Click Analyze on the Ribbon to display the PivotChart Tools Analyze tab.

- If necessary, click the Field List button (PivotChart Tools Analyze tab | Show/Hide group) to display the PivotTable Field List pane.

- Click the Manager check box to deselect the Manager field.

- Click the State check box to select the State field and add it to the Axis Fields area.

- Click and drag the Location button in the Axis Fields area so it is below the State button to display the data first by state and then by location (Figure 8–69).

Figure 8–69

2

- Click the Sales PivotTable Report sheet tab to view the changes in the corresponding PivotTable report (Figure 8–70).

Q&A

What happens when the view of the PivotChart report changes?

Changes in the PivotChart report are automatically reflected in the PivotTable report. Changes to category (x-axis) fields, such as Manager in this case, are correspondingly made to **row fields** in the PivotTable report. Similarly, changes to series (y-axis) fields in a PivotChart report appear as changes to **column fields** in the PivotTable report.

Figure 8–70

- In the PivotTable report, delete the State field and replace it with the Manager field in the Row Labels area.

- If necessary, change the order of the row labels to display the data first by manager and then by location.

- Click the Average Sales PivotChart Report tab to make it the active tab (Figure 8–71).

- Click the Save button on the Quick Access toolbar to save the workbook.

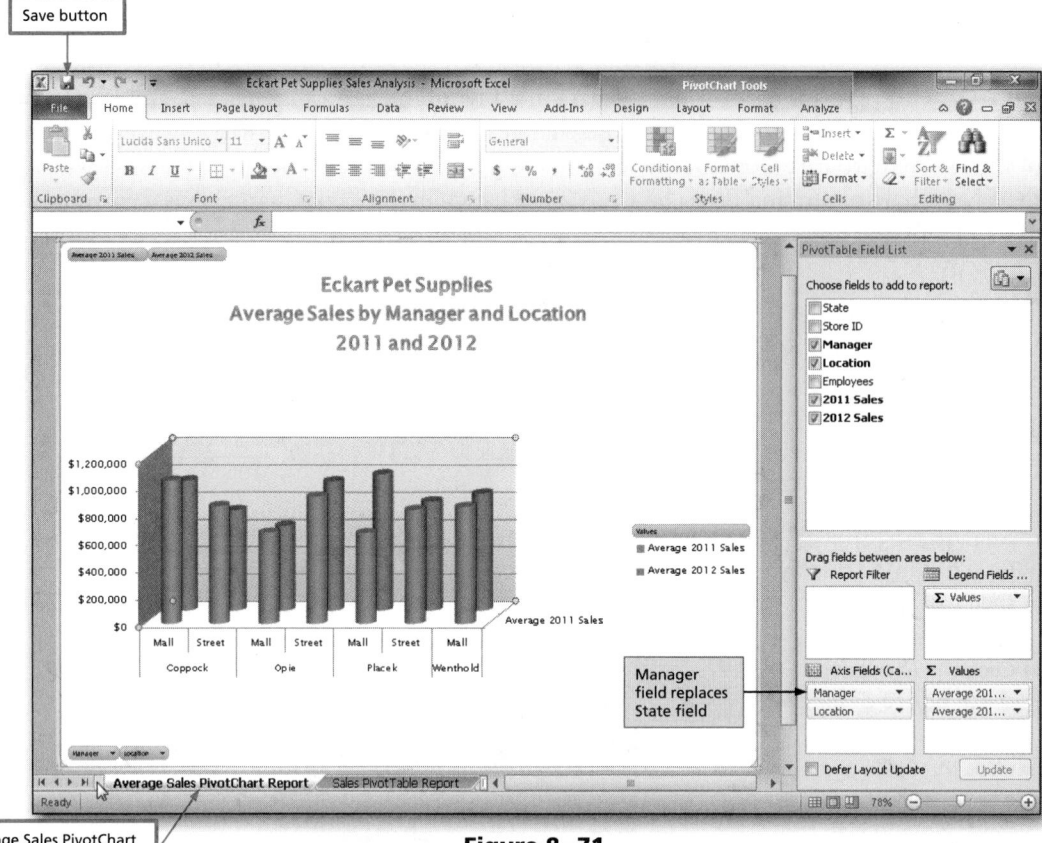

Figure 8–71

Break Point: If you wish to take a break, this is a good place to do so. You can quit Excel now. To resume at a later time, start Excel, open the file called Eckart Pet Supplies Sales Analysis, and continue following the steps from this location forward.

To Create a PivotChart Report Directly from Data

The requirements document included a request to create a second PivotChart and PivotTable that examine the average sales per employee, controlling for different variables. As noted earlier, PivotChart reports are created in Excel either based on an existing PivotTable report, or directly from data. The following steps create a PivotChart report and its associated PivotTable report directly from available data.

1

- Click the Sales Analysis Figures tab to display the worksheet.

- Click Insert on the Ribbon to display the Insert tab.

- Click cell A3 to select a cell displaying sales data.

- Click the PivotTable button arrow (Insert tab | Tables group) to display the PivotTable menu (Figure 8–72).

Figure 8–72

2

- Click the PivotChart command to display the Create PivotTable with PivotChart dialog box.

- If necessary, click the New Worksheet option button (Create PivotTable with PivotChart dialog box) (Figure 8–73).

Figure 8–73

3

- Click the OK button (Create PivotTable with PivotChart dialog box) to add a new worksheet containing a blank PivotTable and blank PivotChart (Figure 8–74).

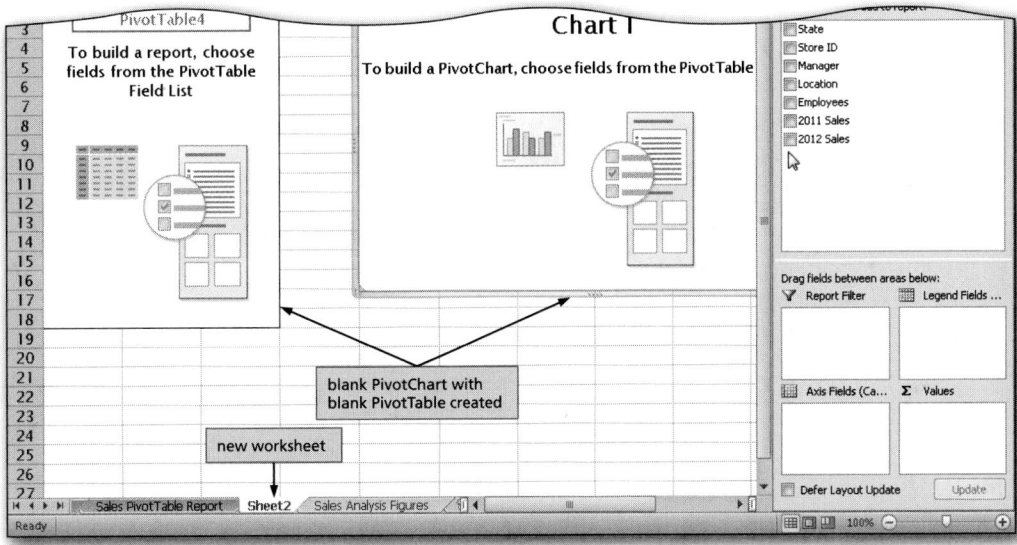

Figure 8–74

4

- Add the State and Location fields to the Axis Fields area.

- Add the 2011 Sales and 2012 Sales fields to the Values area (Figure 8–75).

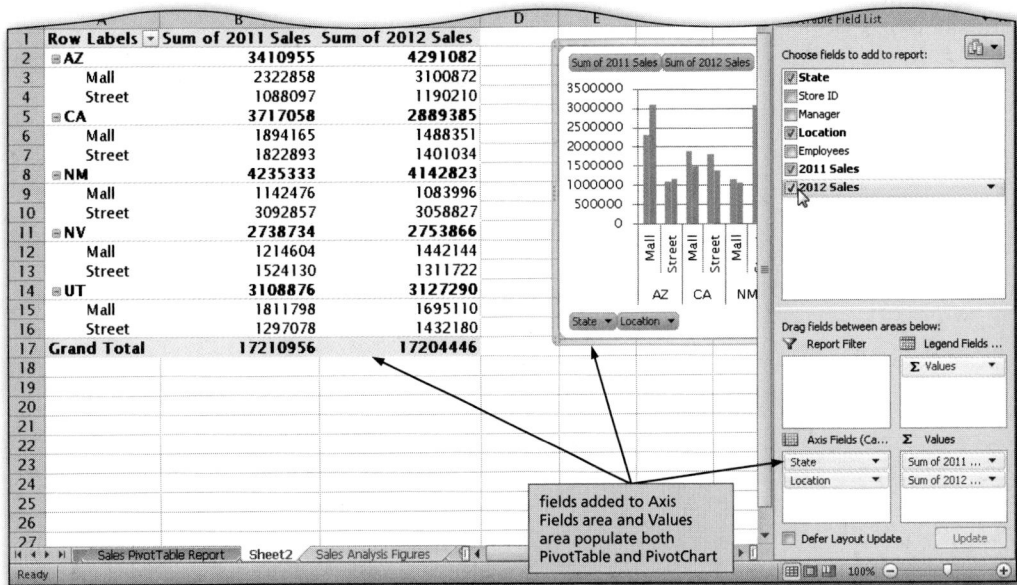

Figure 8–75

To Add a Calculated Field to a PivotTable Report

In addition to updating data, you may need to create new fields based on data in the underlying table. You have been asked to review average sales per employee for 2011 and 2012, but this information is not currently part of the data set with which you are working. You can, however, calculate the values you need through the use of a calculated field. A **calculated field** is a field with values not entered as data, but determined by computation involving data in other fields. In this case, Average 2011 Sales per Employee and Average 2012 Sales per Employee are new calculated fields, based on the existing values of the 2011 Sales, 2012 Sales, and Employees fields. The following steps create calculated fields that use the existing data, and then use these calculated fields in the PivotTable and PivotChart reports.

- Rename the new sheet to Average Sales per Employee.

- Click the Close button to close the PivotTable Field List pane.

- If necessary, click the PivotTable to make it active.

- Click Options on the Ribbon to display the PivotTable Tools Options tab.

- Click the Calculations button (PivotTable Tools Options tab | Calculations group) to display the Calculations menu.

- Click the Fields, Items, & Sets command on the Calculations menu to display the Fields, Items, & Sets menu (Figure 8–76).

Figure 8–76

- Click the Calculated Field command on the Fields, Items, & Sets menu to display the Insert Calculated Field dialog box (Figure 8–77).

Figure 8–77

- In the Name text box, type **Average 2011 Sales per Employee**.

- In the Formula text box, delete the value to the right of the equal sign, in this case, 0.

- Double-click the 2011 Sales entry in the Fields list to select it, type /, and then double-click the Employees entry in the Fields list to complete the formula, which should read = '2011 Sales'/Employees.

- Click the Add button (Insert Calculated Field dialog box) to add the calculated field to the Fields list (Figure 8–78).

Figure 8–78

- Repeat Step 3 to create a calculated field named Average 2012 Sales per Employee, calculated using 2012 Sales data rather than 2011 Sales data.

- Click the OK button (Insert Calculated Field dialog box) to close the dialog box (Figure 8–79).

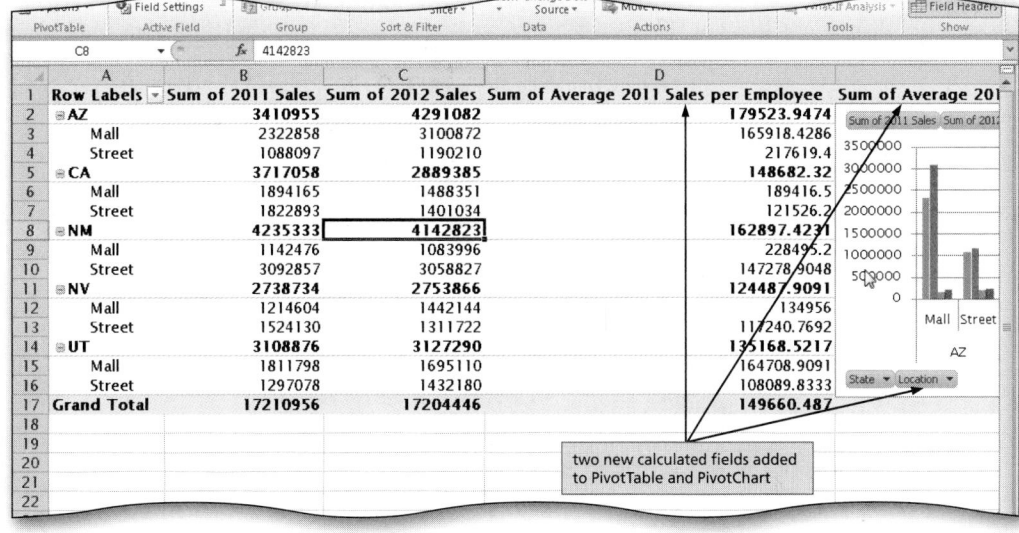

Figure 8–79

To Format the PivotTable and PivotChart

Now that you have added a calculated field, you can format the PivotTable and PivotChart so they look professional and are easy to interpret. The following steps format the PivotTable and PivotChart reports.

1 If necessary, click the Field List button (PivotTable Tools Options tab | Show group) to display the PivotTable Field List pane, and then click the 2011 Sales check box and the 2012 Sales check box to remove these fields from the PivotTable report and the PivotChart report.

2 If necessary, click cell A3, click Design on the Ribbon to display the PivotTable Tools Design tab, and then apply Pivot Style Medium 10 to the PivotTable.

③ Insert two blank rows above the PivotTable. In cell A1, enter the title `Eckart Pet Supplies`. In cell A2, enter the subtitle `Average Employee Sales, 2011 and 2012`. Merge and center the text across A1:C1 and A2:C2. Apply the Title style to cell A1 and the Heading 2 style to cell A2.

④ Change the field name in cell B3 to Average Sales per Employee 2011. Change the field name in cell C3 to Average Sales per Employee 2012.

⑤ Change the column widths for columns B and C to 15.00.

⑥ Wrap and center the field names in cells B3 and C3.

⑦ Change the column width for column D to 50.

⑧ Apply the Currency number format with zero decimal places and the $ symbol to the Average Sales per Employee 2011 and Average Sales per Employee 2012 fields.

⑨ Use the Field List button, the +/- Buttons button, and the Field Headers button (PivotTable Tools Options tab | Show group) to hide the field list, the collapse buttons, and the field headers (Figure 8–80).

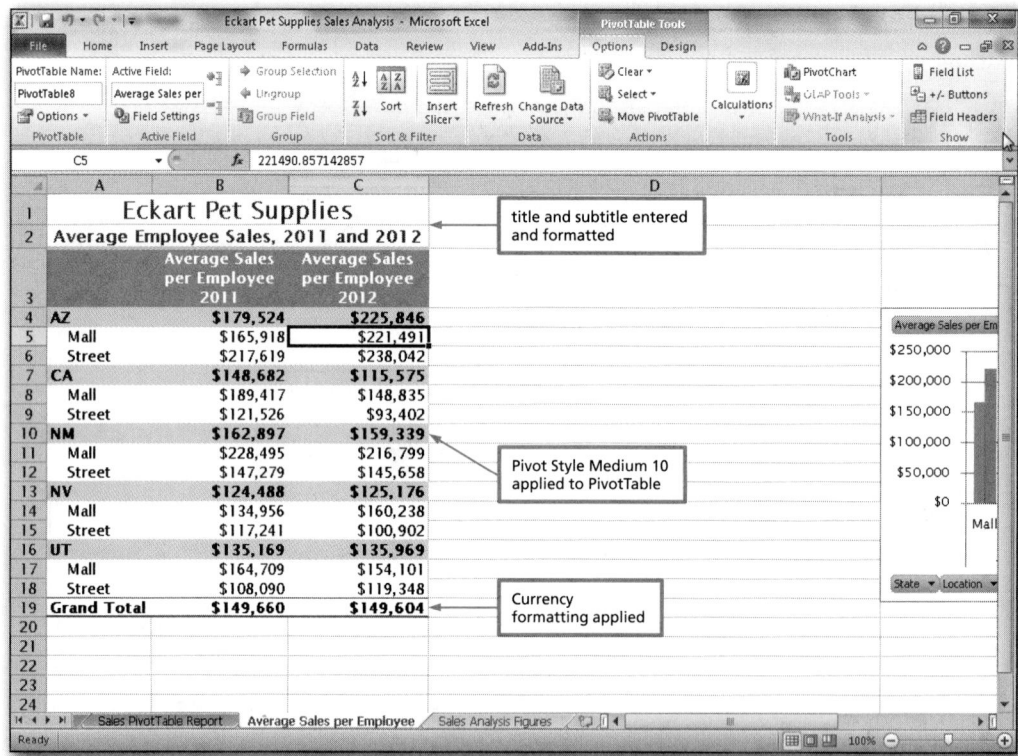

Figure 8–80

⑩ Select the PivotChart and then apply Style 2 in the Chart Styles gallery. Use the Legend button (PivotChart Tools Layout tab | Labels group) to position the legend at the top of the PivotChart report.

⑪ Click the Field Buttons button (PivotChart Tools Analyze tab | Show/Hide group) to hide the field buttons.

⑫ If necessary, click in the PivotChart report to select it. Resize the PivotChart report so that it fills the range D1:D19. Click cell A20 to deselect the PivotChart report.

⑬ Save the workbook (Figure 8–81).

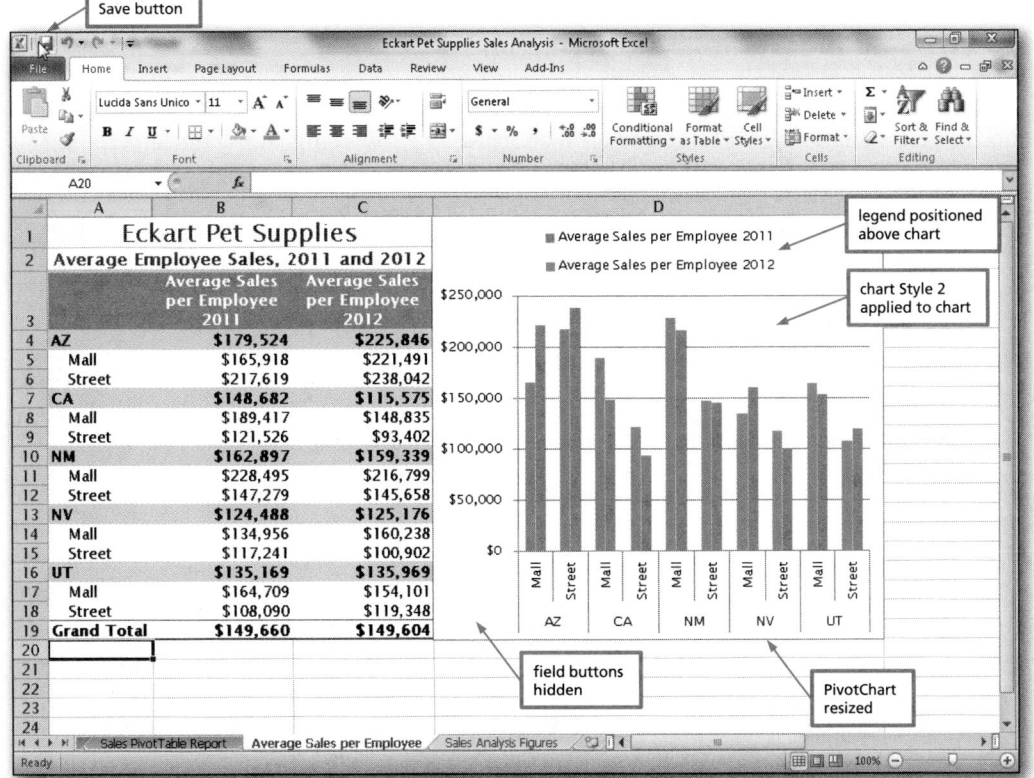

Figure 8–81

Working with Slicers

One of the strengths of PivotTables is that you can ask questions of the data by using filters. Being able to identify and examine subgroups is a useful analytical tool. Slicers are a visual filter used to make PivotCharts and PivotTables easier to interpret. When using filters and autofilters, the user cannot always tell which subgroups the filters and autofilters have selected, without clicking filter buttons to see the subgroups selected. With Slicers, the subgroups are immediately identifiable, and can be changed with a click of a button or buttons.

Consider using slicers to filter a PivotTable.

One effective way to analyze PivotTable data is to use slicers to filter the data in more than one field. Slicers let you refine the display of data in a PivotTable. They offer the following advantages over filtering directly in a PivotTable:

- In a PivotTable, you use the AutoFilter button to specify how to filter the data, which involves a few steps. After you create a slicer, you can perform this same filtering task in one step.

- You can filter only one PivotTable at a time, whereas you can connect slicers to more than one PivotTable to filter data.

- Excel treats slicers as graphic objects, which means you can move, resize, and format them as you can any other graphic object. As graphic objects, they invite interaction.

Plan Ahead

The owner of Eckart Pet Supplies asked you to examine the sales data to identify underperforming stores and managers. You can use slicers to complete this task efficiently.

To Copy a PivotTable and PivotChart

To analyze sales data and find underperforming stores and managers, you first need to create a new PivotTable and a PivotChart. The following steps copy an existing PivotTable and PivotChart, format the PivotTable, and rename the sheet.

1 Create a copy of the Average Sales per Employee worksheet, and locate the copy before the Sales Analysis Figures worksheet.

2 Rename the new sheet `Slicers`.

3 Apply the Pivot Style Medium 13 style to the PivotTable.

4 Set the column widths of columns B and C to 14.00. If necessary, wrap the text in cells B3 and C3 and then center it. Set the font size in cell A2 to 12 point.

5 If necessary, turn off the display of field headers and +/– buttons (Figure 8–82).

Figure 8–82

To Format the PivotChart

The following steps format the PivotChart.

1 If necessary, close the PivotTable Field List pane to provide more room to format the PivotChart.

2 Apply chart Style 15 to the PivotChart to format the PivotChart.

3 If necessary, resize the PivotChart so that it fills the range D1:D19 (Figure 8–83).

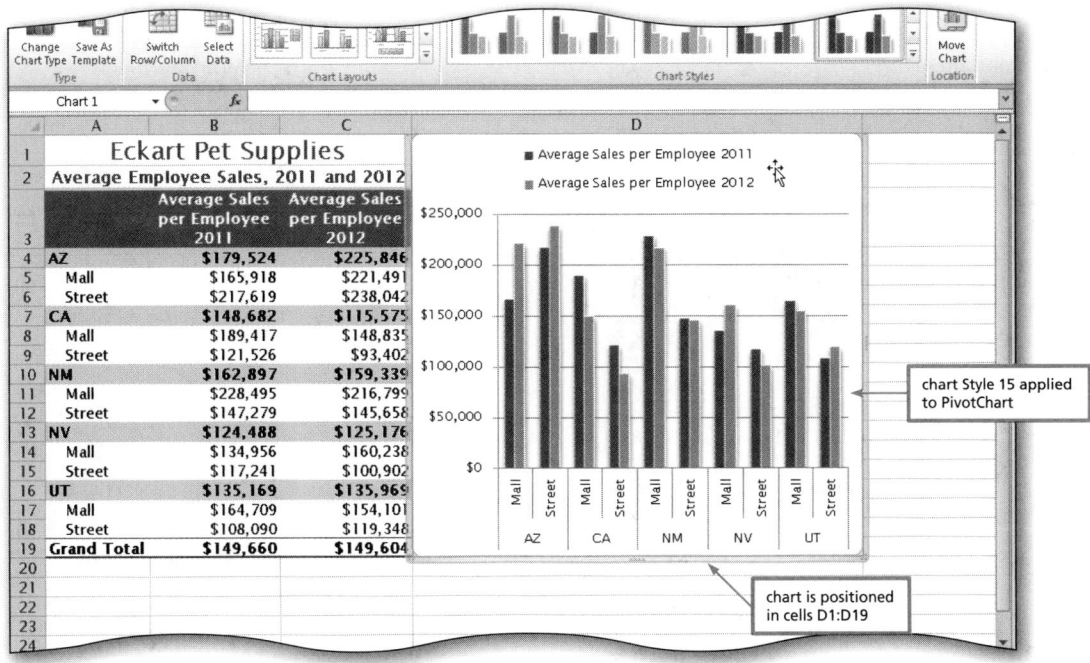

Figure 8–83

To Add Slicers to the Worksheet

To analyze sales data and find underperforming stores and managers, you can use slicers instead of PivotTable filters. The following steps show how to add a slicer that provides an easier way to filter the new PivotTable and PivotChart.

- If necessary, click to make the PivotChart active.

- Click Analyze on the Ribbon to display the PivotChart Tools Analyze tab.

- Click the Insert Slicer button arrow (PivotChart Tools Analyze tab | Data group) to display the Insert Slicer menu (Figure 8–84).

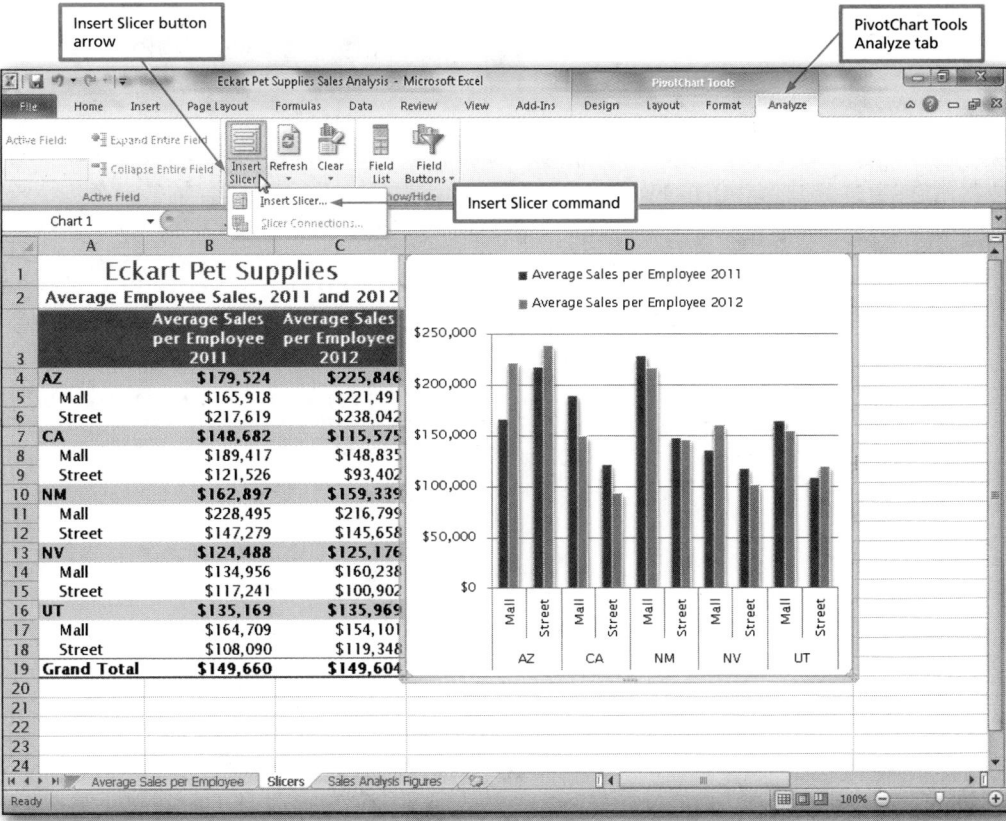

Figure 8–84

2

- Click the Insert Slicer command to display the Insert Slicers dialog box.

- Click the State, Manager, and Location check boxes (Figure 8–85).

Figure 8–85

3

- Click the OK button (Insert Slicer dialog box) to display the selected slicers on the worksheet (Figure 8–86).

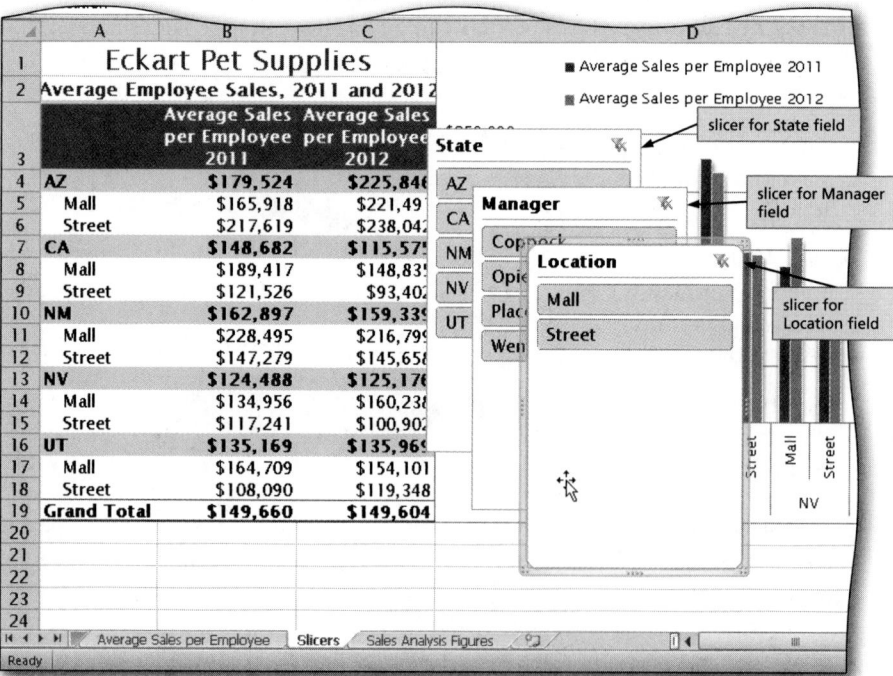

Figure 8–86

To Format Slicers

The slicers are now added to the PivotTable report. They need to be moved so that they do not obscure the PivotTable or PivotChart. Formatting them will make them easier to read and use. The following steps move the slicers to the right of the PivotChart, and format them to fit in with the PivotTable and PivotChart styles.

1

- Click the title bar of the State slicer, and then drag the State slicer to column E.
- Use the resize handles to adjust the length of the slicer so that it ends at the bottom of row 6.
- Click and drag the Location slicer to column E, locating the top of the Location slicer against the bottom of the State slicer.
- Use the resize handles to change the length of the Location slicer so that it ends at the bottom of row 11.
- Click and drag the Manager slicer to column E, locating the top of the slicer against the bottom of the Location slicer.
- Use the resize handles to adjust the length of the Manager slicer so that it ends at the bottom of row 19.
- Hold down the CTRL key and then click to select all three slicers.
- Click the Height text box (Slicer Tools Options tab | Buttons group) and then set the button height to 0.23.
- Click the Width text box (Slicer Tools Options tab | Buttons group) and then set the button width to 0.98.
- Click the Width text box (Slicer Tools Options tab | Size group) and then set the slicer width to 1.17 (Figure 8–87).

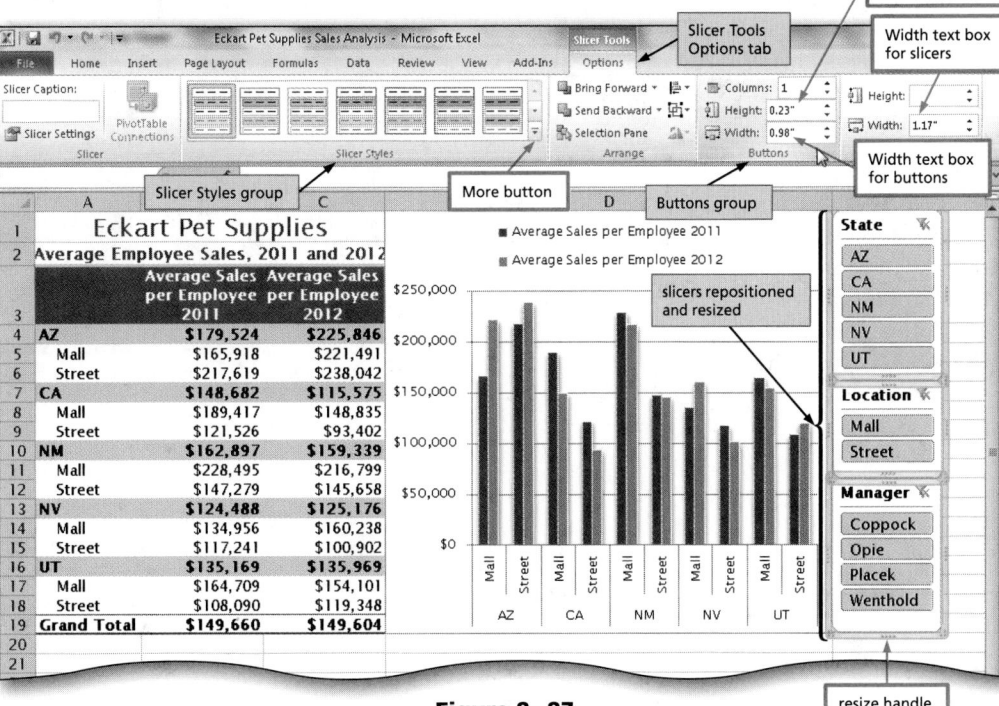

Figure 8–87

2

- Click cell A20 to deselect the three slicers, and then click the State slicer to select it.
- Click the More button (Slicer Tools Options tab | Slicer Styles group) to display the Slicer Styles gallery.
- Click the Slicer Style Other 1 style to apply it to the State slicer.
- Click the Location slicer to select it, and then apply the Slicer Style Light 5 style to the Location slicer.
- Click the Manager slicer, and then apply the Slicer Style Dark 5 style to the Manager slicer.
- Click cell A20 to deselect the slicer (Figure 8–88).

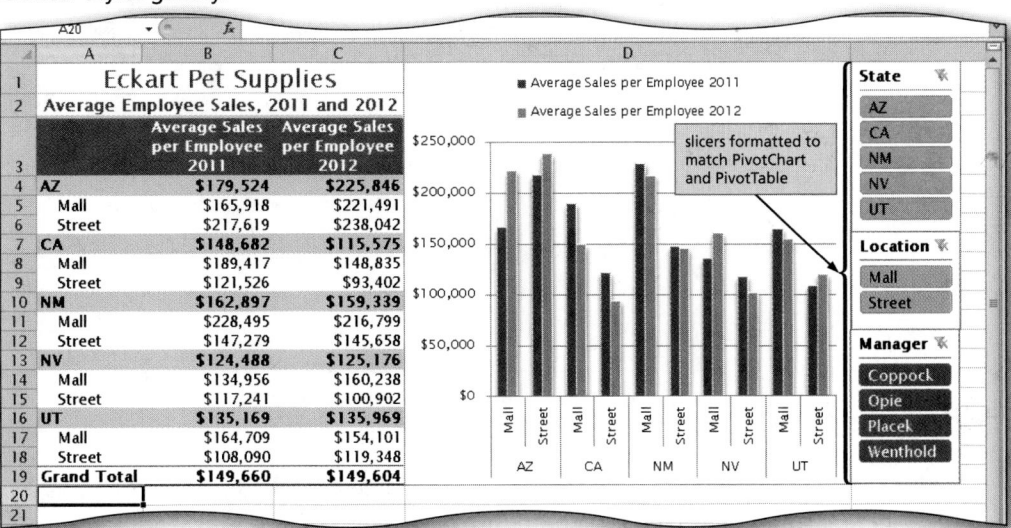

Figure 8–88

To Use the Slicers to Review Groups in the PivotTable

Slicers provide you with a visual means of filtering data. You do not need knowledge of Excel to use slicers. Instead, you click the subgroups of interest. Slicers based on Row Label fields provide the same results as AutoFilters in a PivotTable. They narrow the table down to a visible subgroup or subgroups. The following steps use slicers to review average sales for different combinations of state and location. In particular, you have been asked to look at the effect AZ sales are having on overall figures, and to provide a snapshot of sales figures with AZ excluded.

1

● Hold down the CTRL key and then click AZ in the State slicer to remove the AZ data from the PivotTable and PivotChart calculations.

● Release the CTRL key, and then click Mall in the Location slicer to display the data for mall stores only for California, Nevada, New Mexico, and Utah (Figure 8–89).

Figure 8–89

2

● Click Street in the Location slicer to see the data for Street stores only for California, Nevada, New Mexico, and Utah (Figure 8–90).

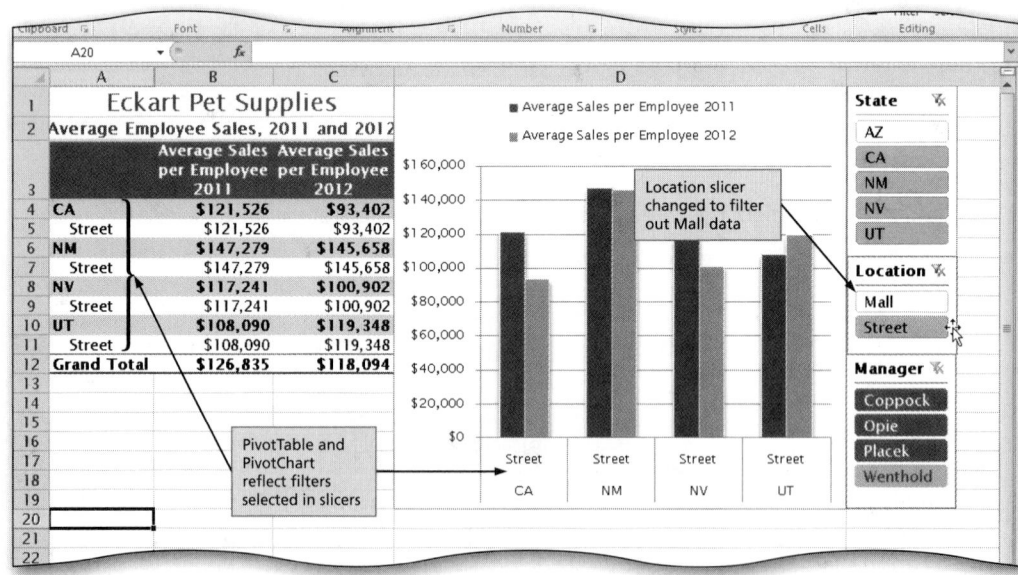

Figure 8–90

To Use the Slicers to Review Groups Not in the PivotTable

Slicers based on fields not included in the PivotTable provide the same results as report filters. They regroup and narrow the PivotTable content to groups not visible in the PivotTable. You can use slicers to analyze influences other than those recorded in the PivotTable as possible explanations for patterns. The following steps show how to use slicers to review groups not currently included in the PivotTable.

Instructions: Start Excel. Open the workbook Extend 8-1 Tylorstown Food Carts from the Data Files for Students, and then save the workbook using the file name, Extend 8-1 Tylorstown Food Carts Complete.

Create a PivotTable and PivotChart for Tylorstown Food Carts that analyzes a year's worth of sales data. Figure 8–94 shows the completed Income Review worksheet.

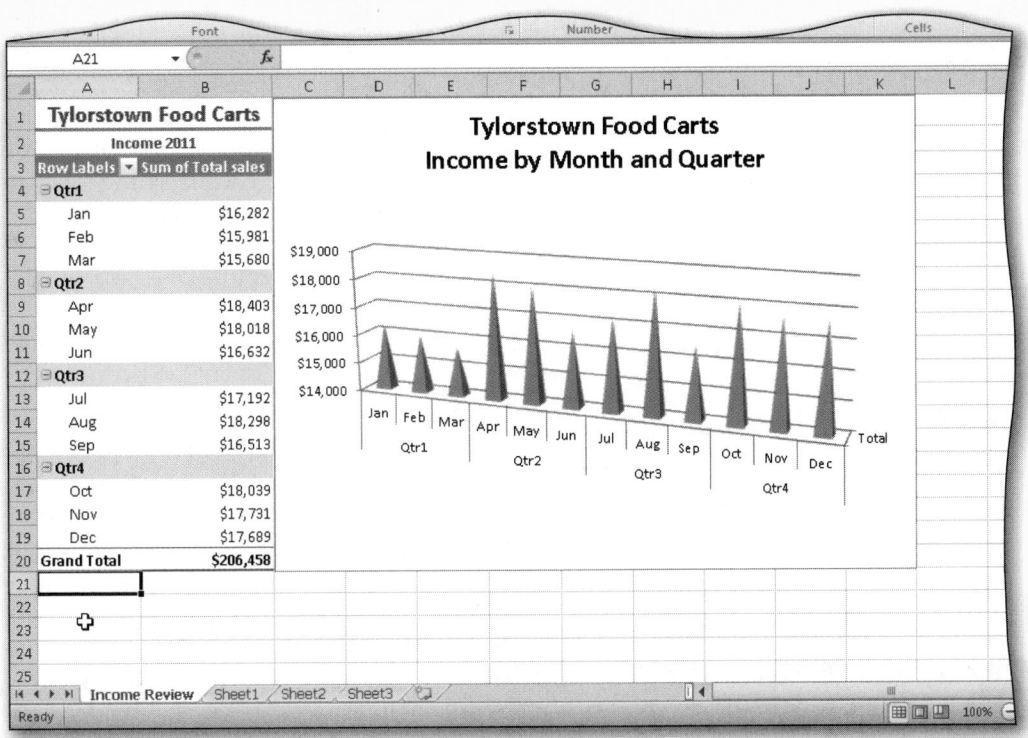

Figure 8–94

Perform the following tasks.

1. Create a PivotTable based on the sales data in Sheet1. Use Date as the Row Label and use Total sales as the Values field. Name the new sheet containing the PivotTable **Income Review**. Change the PivotTable style to Pivot Style Medium 9. Add a title and subtitle to the PivotTable as shown in Figure 8–94, formatting cell A1 using the Heading 1 cell style and A2 using the Heading 2 cell style. Format the Sum of Total Sales column with the Currency number format.

2. Use the Group Field command (PivotTable Tools Options tab | Group group) to group the daily sales figures by months and quarters. Format the Total sales values as Currency with no decimal places.

3. Create a PivotChart, and locate it on the same sheet as the PivotTable. Use the 3-D Pyramid chart type, and set up the chart to have no legend. Hide the field buttons. Edit the chart title to match the title and resize the PivotChart shown in Figure 8–94. Change the document properties as specified by your instructor. Add a worksheet header with your name, course number, and other information as specified by your instructor.

4. Preview and then print the PivotTable sheet in landscape orientation and use the Black and white option.

5. Save the workbook with the new page setup characteristics.

6. Submit the assignment as requested by your instructor.

Make It Right

Analyze a workbook and correct all errors and/or improve the design.

Manipulating a Chart and Adding a Trendline

Note: To complete this assignment, you will be required to use the Data Files for Students. See the inside back cover of this book for instructions on downloading the Data Files for Students, or contact your instructor for information about accessing the required files.

Instructions: Start Excel. Open the workbook Make It Right 8-1 Livingston Emporium and then save the workbook as Make It Right 8-1 Livingston Emporium Complete. Correct the following design and formula problems so that the Sales Totals sheet appears with an embedded chart as shown in Figure 8–95.

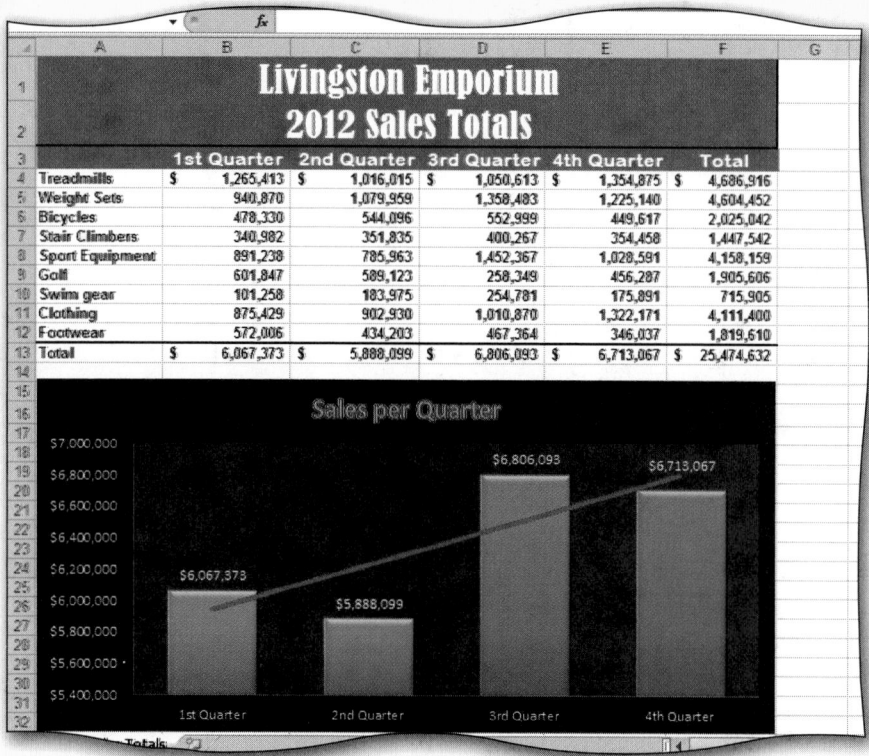

Figure 8–95

Perform the following tasks:

1. Click the Chart sheet tab to display the Bar of Pie chart and then click the chart.

2. Click the Chart Tools Design tab and then complete the following chart tasks:

   a. Change the Bar of Pie chart to a Clustered Column chart (column 1, row 1 in the Column area).

   b. Change the chart layout to Layout 4. Delete the Series 1 legend below the chart.

   c. Apply chart Style 43 (column 3, row 6 in the Chart gallery).

   d. Add a linear trendline to the chart. Format the trend line to 3 point, dark red. Click the value above the 4th Quarter column and drag it above the trendline.

   e. Add a chart title above the chart using the text Sales per Quarter, and then apply the Fill – Red, Accent 2, Double Outline – Accent 2 (column 5, row 3) WordArt style. Move the Sales chart title above the chart. If necessary, change the font size of the chart title to 18.

   f. With the PivotChart selected, click the Select Data button (Chart Tools Design tab | Data group) and change the selected data to include the ranges B3:E3 and B13:E13.

   g. Click the Plot Area of the chart, and then drag the top middle sizing handle down to make room for the title. Move the chart to the Sales Totals sheet. Drag the chart to the range A15:F32. Make any necessary adjustments so that the chart appears as shown in Figure 8–95.

3. Change the document properties as specified by your instructor. Change the worksheet header to include your name, course number, and other information as specified by your instructor.

4. Save the workbook, and submit the revised workbook as requested by your instructor.

In the Lab

Create a workbook using the guidelines, concepts, and skills presented in this chapter. Labs are listed in order of increasing difficulty.

Lab 1: Creating a PivotTable Report and PivotChart Report

Note: To complete this assignment, you will be required to use the Data Files for Students. See the inside back cover of this book for instructions on downloading the Data Files for Students, or contact your instructor for information about accessing the required files.

Problem: You work for RealQuick Connect and help the financial director prepare and analyze revenue and expenses. He has asked you to create two PivotTables and corresponding PivotCharts based on sales data. One PivotTable and PivotChart summarize the sales by Supplier (Figure 8–96a). The other PivotTable and PivotChart summarize the computer sales by month for the top computer supplier (Figure 8–96b).

Instructions: Perform the following tasks.

1. Open the workbook Lab 8-1 RealQuick Connect from the Data Files for Students, and then save the workbook using the file name, Lab 8-1 RealQuick Connect Complete.

2. Using the data in the Sales Results worksheet, create the PivotTable and associated PivotChart shown in Figure 8–96a in a separate sheet in the workbook. Name the worksheet Sales By Supplier.

3. If necessary, add two blank lines above the PivotTable, and then change the contents of cell A4 to Supplier and cell B3 to Stores. Apply the Pivot Style Dark 3 style to the PivotTable. Format the values as Currency values with a dollar sign and no decimal places. Apply the chart Style 28 to the PivotChart. Resize the PivotChart to cover the range A20:G37 and then hide the field buttons.

4. Create a second PivotTable and associated PivotChart as shown in Figure 8–96b in a separate sheet in the workbook. Name the worksheet Computer Sales By Month.

5. Change the contents of cell A4 to Month and cell B3 to Store. Apply the Pivot Style Dark 3 style to the PivotTable. Format the values as Currency values with a dollar sign and no decimal places. Turn off the legend for the chart.

6. Filter the category by Computer. Filter the store to Green Spring Club.

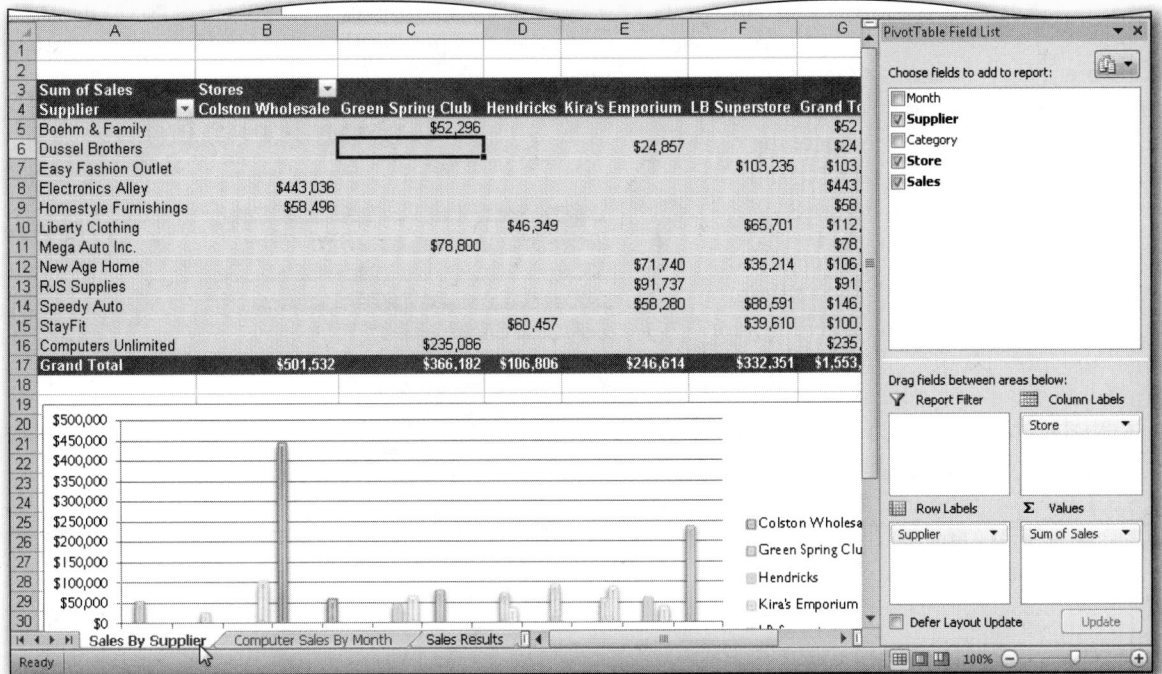

Continued >

Figure 8–96 (a)

In the Lab *continued*

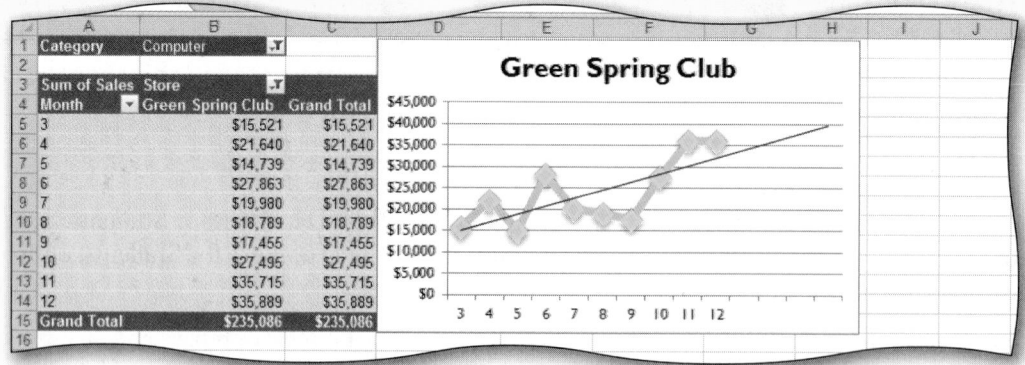

Figure 8–96 (b)

7. Change the chart type to Line and then add a linear trendline that forecasts the trend for four more months. Apply the Chart Style 28 to the PivotChart, and hide the field buttons.

8. Change the document properties as specified by your instructor. Change the Computer Sales By Month worksheet header to include your name, course number, and other information as specified by your instructor.

9. Print the worksheet. Change the Sales By Supplier worksheet header to include your name, course number, and other information as specified by your instructor. Print the worksheet, and then save the workbook.

10. Submit the assignment as requested by your instructor.

In the Lab

Lab 2: Creating Charts for a Sports Department

Note: To complete this assignment, you will be required to use the Data Files for Students. See the inside back cover of this book for instructions on downloading the Data Files for Students, or contact your instructor for information about accessing the required files.

Problem: You volunteer with the Branton High School sports department. The basketball coach has asked you to create charts using last year's statistics so that he can present them to the advisory committee. He wants a chart to show game results, a chart to compare field goals made and attempted, and a chart to compare the points earned by player. The table and charts appear as shown in Figure 8–97.

Instructions: *Perform the following tasks.*

1. Open the workbook Lab 8-2 Branton High School from the Data Files for Students, and then save the workbook using the file name, Lab 8-2 Branton High School Complete.

2. Click the Schedule sheet tab. Create a Clustered Horizontal Cylinder chart using Our Score and Opp. Score data. Move the chart to its own sheet. Name the sheet Game Results. Change the chart layout to

Figure 8–97 (a)

Layout 2. Change the chart style to Style 4. Replace the chart title with WordArt as shown in Figure 8–97a. Use the Gradient Fill – Indigo, Accent 1 WordArt style. Change font size to 40.

3. Click the Season Results tab. Create a 3-D Line chart using Player, FGM, and FGA data. Move the chart to its own sheet. Name the sheet Made vs Attempted. Change the chart layout to Layout 9. Change the chart style to Style 4. Replace the chart title with WordArt as shown in Figure 8–97b. Use the Gradient Fill – Indigo, Accent 1 WordArt style. Change the font size to 40.

Figure 8–97 (b)

4. Click the Season Results tab. Create a PivotTable based on the data in the range A5:K16. Insert the PivotTable on a new worksheet named FG analysis. Add Player as a Row Label. Add the following fields as Values: FGA, FGM, 3FGA, and 3FGM. Create two calculated fields: %FGM (calculated as FGM/FGA) and %3FGM (calculated as 3FGM/3FGA). Change the value field settings to provide custom names as shown in Figure 8-97c. Format the %FGM and %3FGM fields using the Percentage number format with zero decimal places. Apply a filter to select players with a %FG Made value of less than 60% (0.60). Create a PivotChart for the filtered data on the same sheet as the PivotTable. Add a title, subtitle, and chart title, and format the PivotTable and PivotChart as shown in Figure 8–97c.

5. Change the document properties as specified by your instructor. Select all three chart sheets. Add a worksheet header with your name, course number, and other information as specified by your instructor.

Figure 8–97 (c)

In the Lab

Lab 3: Manipulating PivotTables and PivotCharts

Note: To complete this assignment, you will be required to use the Data Files for Students. See the inside back cover of this book for instructions on downloading the Data Files for Students, or contact your instructor for information about accessing the required files.

Problem: The Cyber Consultants finance officer has asked you to analyze the current week's billing sheet using PivotTables and PivotCharts. She wants you to create them for three scenarios: a) the payment amount totals for hours billed, b) the averages of the hours per region, and c) the cost of the miscellaneous hours if they had been billable. The PivotTables and PivotCharts should appear as shown in Figure 8–98.

Figure 8–98 (a)

Instructions: *Perform the following tasks.*

1. Open the workbook Lab 8-3 Cyber Consultants from the Data Files for Students, and then save the workbook using the file name, Lab 8-2 Cyber Consultants Complete.

2. Create the PivotTable shown in Figure 8–98a based on the data in the range A4:F29 in the Billing worksheet. Add a calculated field called Payment Amount that multiplies the hours billed by 50. The results should include totals of 1749.3 and 87465. Create the PivotChart shown in Figure 8–98a. Name the worksheet Payment Amounts. Change the contents of cell A3 to Regions. Apply the Pivot Style Medium Style 12 to the PivotTable. Format the Payment values as Currency values with a dollar sign and no decimal places. Format the Hours Billed as Number. Apply the chart Style 22 to the PivotChart.

3. Create the PivotTable and PivotChart shown in Figure 8–98b. Change the calculations to averages. The results should include totals of 69.972, 7.98, and 77.952. Name the worksheet Average Hours. Change the contents of cell A3 to Regions. Apply the Pivot Style Medium Style 12 to the PivotTable. Format all value fields as Number with no decimal places. Apply the Chart Style 22 to the PivotChart.

4. Create the PivotTable shown in Figure 8–98c. Add a calculated field called Potential Payment that multiplies the miscellaneous hours by 50. The results should include a total of 9975. Create the PivotChart shown in Figure 8–98c. Name the worksheet Potential Payments. Change cell

Figure 8–98 (b)

A3 to Regions. Apply the Pivot Style Medium Style 12 to the PivotTable. Format the Potential Payment values as Currency values with a dollar sign and no decimal places. Apply the chart Style 22 to the PivotChart. Remove the legend. Hide the field headers, expand/collapse buttons, and the PivotTable Field List pane. Add a Region slicer. Apply the Slicer Style Light 4 to the slicer. Set button widths to 1" and button heights to .25". Set slicer size to 1.19" wide and 1.60" high. Position the slicer as shown in Figure 8–98c. Use the slicer to display potential payments for the eastern region only.

5. Change the document properties as specified by your instructor. Select all three PivotTable sheets. Add a worksheet header with your name, course number, and other information as specified by your instructor. With the three sheets selected, preview and then print the sheets. Save the workbook with the new page setup characteristics. Submit the assignment as requested by your instructor.

Figure 8–98 (c)

Cases and Places

Apply your creative thinking and problem solving skills to design and implement a solution.

Note: To complete these assignments, you may be required to use the Data Files for Students. See the inside back cover of this book for instructions on downloading the Data Files for Students, or contact your instructor for information about accessing the required files.

1: Identifying Student Grade Totals

Academic

Central City College's math department has compiled its faculty grades into a worksheet. They want to use a PivotTable to filter the data and analyze the results. Your task is to help the department by creating the PivotTable and then calculating the results.

Open the workbook Case 8-1 Math Department Grades from the Data Files for Students and then save the workbook using the file name, Case 8-1 Math Department Grades Complete. Create a PivotTable using Professor and Course as Row lablels, and grade as 3 columns (summarize them using the Min, Max, and Average functions). Format the Grades as Number with no decimal places.

The totals for Min, Max, and Average should be 40, 100, and 75. Move Course to the Report Filter. Filter the courses for the two beginning classes MTH1101 and MTH1102. The totals should be 40, 99, and 73. Filter the courses for MTH2143. The totals should be 40, 100, and 75. Filter the courses for MTH2450. The totals should be 53, 97, and 82. Rename the PivotTable sheet to Grade Analysis. Print the worksheets and save the workbook. Submit the assignment as requested by your instructor.

2: Analyzing a Home Budget

Personal

You have created a table that shows your household income and expenses. You would now like to create charts to help you analyze your budget. Part of this includes identifying a trend in your spending habits. Open the workbook Case 8-2 Household Budget Analysis from the Data Files for Students and then save the workbook using the file name, Case 8-2 Household Budget Analysis Complete.

Create a Clustered Cone chart using the expenses from the budget. Move the chart to its own sheet. Use WordArt to add a chart title of Household Expenses to the chart using Gradient Fill – Blue, Accent 1. Create a Clustered Column chart using the Cash flow data from the budget. Move the chart to its own sheet. Use WordArt to add a chart title of Cash Flow Trend to the chart using Gradient Fill – Blue, Accent 1. Add a trendline to the chart that shows trends for the next four months. Rename the chart sheets as appropriate to match their contents. Print the worksheets and save the workbook. Submit the assignment as requested by your instructor.

3: Comparing Health Care Plans

Professional

Allied Professionals have given you a worksheet that tracks the monthly cost of various health plans for last year and the current year. You are to create a PivotTable and PivotChart to analyze the data that you have been given. Open the workbook Case 8-3 Health Care Plan Comparison from the Data Files for Students and then save the workbook using the file name, Case 8-3 Health Care Plan Comparison Complete. Create a PivotTable and PivotChart that compares the costs showing the min, max, and average for each company for both years. Print the worksheets and save the workbook. Submit the assignment as requested by your instructor.

9 | Formula Auditing, Data Validation, and Complex Problem Solving

Objectives

You will have mastered the material in this chapter when you can:

- Use formula auditing techniques to analyze a worksheet

- Trace precedents and dependents

- Add data validation rules to cells

- Use Error Checking to identify and correct errors

- Use trial and error to solve a problem on a worksheet

- Use goal seeking to solve a problem

- Circle invalid data on a worksheet

- Use Solver to solve a complex problem

- Use the Scenario Manager to record and save sets of what-if assumptions

- Create a Scenario Summary report

- Create a Scenario PivotTable report

- Save a workbook for use in a previous version of Excel

9 | Formula Auditing, Data Validation, and Complex Problem Solving

Introduction

This chapter introduces you to auditing the formulas in a worksheet, validating data, and solving complex problems. **Formula auditing** allows you to examine formulas to determine which cells are referenced by those formulas, and examine cells to determine which formulas are built upon those cells. Auditing the formulas in a worksheet can give you insight into how a worksheet is structured and how cells are related to each other. Formula auditing is especially helpful when presented with a workbook created by someone else.

    Data validation allows you to set cells so that the values they accept are restricted in terms of type and range of data. This feature, introduced in Chapter 4, can be set up to display prompts and error messages when users select a cell or enter invalid data. You can also use data validation to circle cells containing data that does not meet the criteria you specified.

    When trying to solve some problems, you can make an educated guess if you are familiar with the data and the structure of the workbook. This process is called **trial and error**. For simpler problems, you may find a solution using this process. For more complex problems, you might need to use software such as Excel to find a satisfactory solution.

    One of the tools that Excel provides to solve complex problems is **Solver,** which allows you to specify up to 200 cells that can be adjusted to find a solution to a problem. Solver also lets you place limits or constraints on allowable values for some or all of those cells. A **constraint** is a limitation on the possible values that a cell can contain. Solver will try many possible solutions to find one that solves the problem subject to the constraints placed on the data.

Project — River's Edge Handweavers Show Inventory Worksheet

In previous chapters, simple what-if analyses have shown the effect of changing one value on another value of interest. This chapter introduces you to Excel tools used to solve complex problems. The worksheet in Figure 9–1a on page EX 556 was created to assist River's Edge Handweavers in determining if they can weave enough products to appear in the juried shows to which they have been invited.

    River's Edge Handweavers produce various hand-loomed goods, including cotton, wool, and luxury wraps, or shawls. Their main income source is a standing contract with a supplier to boutique home goods stores. In addition to this contract, the group sells at a series of high-end holiday fairs each year. These are juried shows, requiring an invitation to vend. Contracts for the juried shows require a certain inventory level. In addition, booth fees at these fairs are high, so vendors must have and sell enough products to make the fairs worthwhile. This year, River's Edge Handweavers has received new fair invitations that require higher inventory levels than in previous years. River's Edge Handweavers operates with three looms, two automated and one equipped with a fly shuttle. The three looms have differing output capacities. Looms 1, 2, and 3 can produce three, four, and six shawls per hour, respectively. The worksheet in Figure 9–1a shows the details of the materials requirements for the three looms, taking into account these differing output capacities. The worksheet includes a loom cost per day, based on daily wages and overhead costs. The worksheet also lists materials costs for the three different types of wraps.

An eight-hour workday is broken down into two parts: four hours of weaving time and four hours dedicated to finishing the woven goods and redressing the looms. Figure 9–1b shows the details of the inventory requirements. Columns B, C, and D each refer to one of the three looms in production. Rows 4 and 5 contain information on the number of wraps produced per day for each loom, and the loom cost per day. Rows 8 through 10 represent the number of wraps per loom that should be produced to achieve needed totals. Highlighted cells represent wrap types that cannot be produced on a certain loom. For instance, Loom 2 cannot be used to produce cotton wraps. Row 13 shows total days needed to produce a specific quantity of wraps. Row 14 shows total materials costs for the number of wraps produced. Row 15 shows the total loom cost for the number of wraps produced, and Row 16 gives a total cost for materials and loom. Updating the numbers for each wrap in rows 8 through 10 results in changes in the values in rows 13 through 16.

In Figure 9–1a, the initial figures reflect allocating wraps exclusively to particular looms. Cotton, luxury, and wool wraps are allocated to Looms 1, 2, and 3, respectively. The objective is to maximize the total number of wraps (cell E11) while producing the needed types of wraps within certain time constraints. All the looms are run at the same time for a particular job. The constraints for the current order under consideration are entered in the range B19:B22.

In Figure 9–1b, Solver has modified the values of cells in the range B8:D10 to find the best combination of wraps to weave on each loom to maximize the total number and meet the show inventory needs. After applying a different set of order constraints, Solver determines a new solution. When Solver finishes solving a problem, you can instruct it to create an Answer Report. An **Answer Report** (Figure 9–1c on page EX 556) shows the answer that Solver found, which constraints were in place, and which values in the worksheet Solver manipulated in order to solve the problem within those constraints.

Excel's **Scenario Manager** is a what-if analysis tool that allows you to record and save different sets of what-if assumptions used to forecast the outcome of a worksheet model. This chapter shows you how to use Scenario Manager to manage the two sets of Solver data for two scenarios involving the inventory of handwoven wraps. Scenario Manager also allows you to create reports that summarize the scenarios on your worksheet. Figure 9–1d on page EX 557 shows a Scenario Summary report and Figure 9–1e on page EX 557 shows a Scenario PivotTable that each concisely report the differences in the two inventory scenarios.

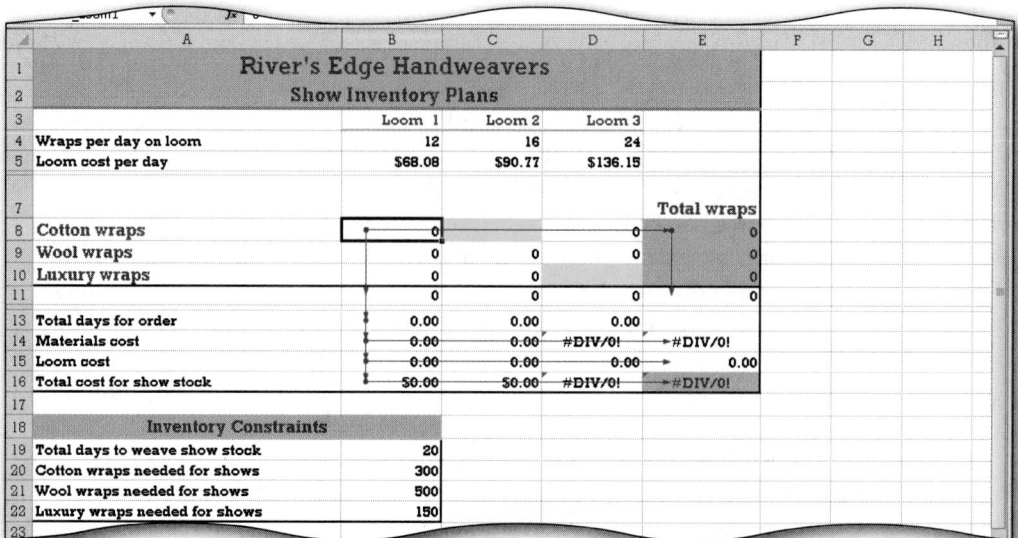

Figure 9–1 (a) Tracing Cells in Original Data

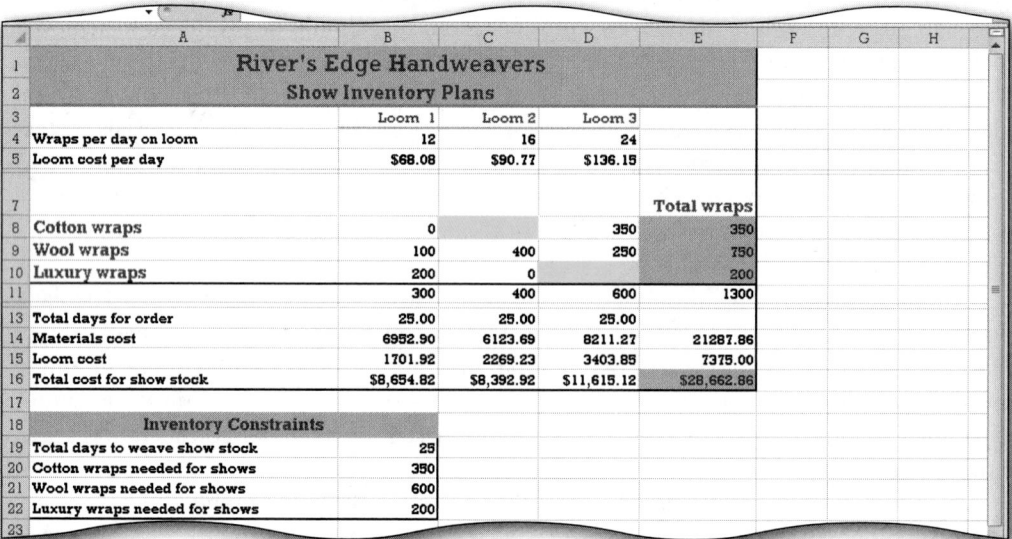

Figure 9–1 (b) First Solution Found by Solver

Figure 9–1 (c) Answer Report

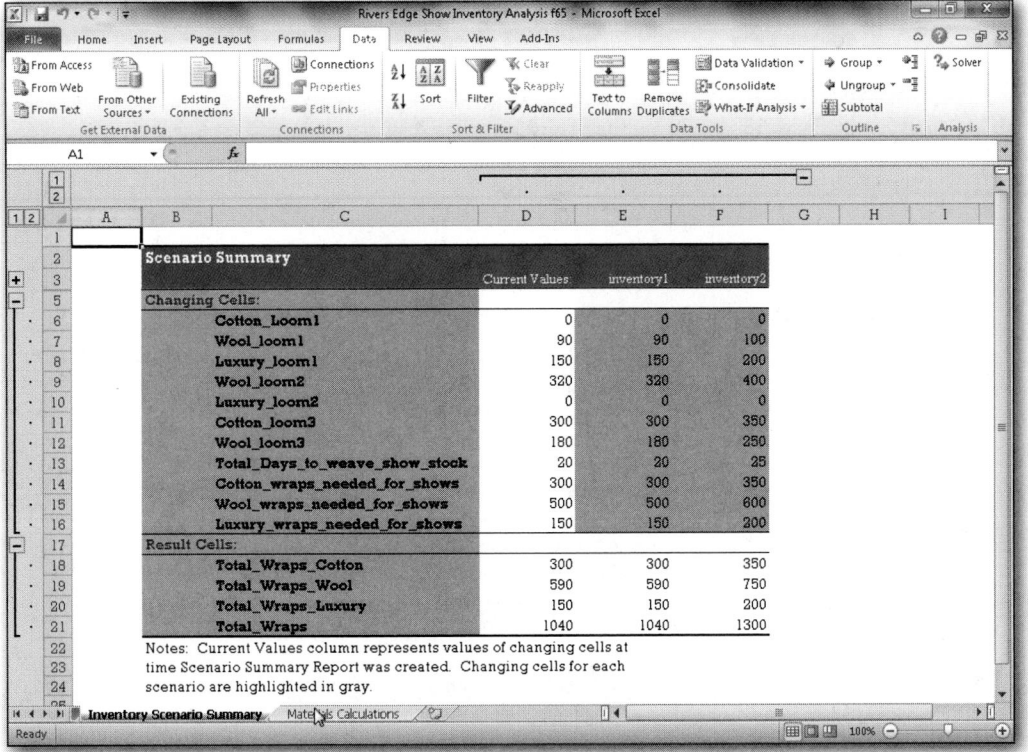

Figure 9–1 (d) Scenario Summary

Figure 9–1 (e) Scenario PivotTable

Figure 9–2 illustrates the requirements document for the River's Edge Handweavers Show Inventory worksheet. It includes the needs, source of data, data for two scenarios, and other facts about its development.

REQUEST FOR NEW WORKBOOK

Date Submitted:	September 10, 2012
Submitted By:	Susan Bell
Worksheet Title:	River's Edge Handweavers Show Inventory Plans
Needs:	River's Edge Handweavers needs to plan production to meet the inventory needs of the upcoming holiday fairs. Inventory required to meet contractual requirements for the fairs includes a minimum of 300 cotton wraps, 500 wool wraps, and 150 luxury wraps. Looms can be taken off our standing order production for 20 days to produce the holiday fair inventory. You need to determine the optimal use of the three looms in order to produce the maximum number of wraps during the 20 days, while meeting the inventory requirements for each of the wrap types.
	A second analysis is needed, that evaluates a second scenario with an expanded holiday fair presence. In this second case, contractual requirements would include a minimum of 350 cotton wraps, 600 wool wraps, and 200 luxury wraps, with looms being available for production for 25 days. Again, optimal use would maximize the total number of wraps while meeting the inventory requirements for each of the wrap types.
	Reports should be generated that illustrate that the constraints of time and wrap type have been met, for each of the two holiday fair inventory requirements.
	Finally, the workbook should be made available in the Excel 97-2003 format. Any private data should be removed from the workbook.
Source of Data:	The workbook shown in Figure 9-1a is available with the Data Files for Students with the file name, Rivers Edge Show Inventory Data. The workbook contains the worksheet shown in Figure 9-1a, and a second worksheet containing detailed calculations of materials needs and costs.
Calculations:	Analyze the Rivers Edge Show Inventory Data worksheet and any related worksheets to understand the calculations involved in the worksheets.
Web Requirements:	None.

Approvals

Approval Status:	X	Approved
		Rejected
Approved By:	Margaret Olin	
Date:	September 10, 2012	
Contracted To:	M. Jones, Spreadsheet Specialist	

Figure 9–2

Overview

As you read this chapter, you will learn how to modify the existing workbook as shown in Figure 9–1 by performing these general tasks:

- Use formula auditing techniques to analyze a worksheet.
- Add data validation rules to cells.
- Use Solver to solve a complex problem and produce reports to summarize the solution.
- Use Scenario Manager to record and save two solutions and use reports to compare the scenarios.
- Prepare a workbook for distribution.

Plan
Ahead

General Project Guidelines

While working with an Excel worksheet, you need to make several decisions that will determine the appearance and characteristics of the finished worksheet. As you update an existing worksheet to meet the requirements shown in Figure 9–2, you should follow these general guidelines:

1. **Analyze the formulas in the workbook to learn about the workbook.** Excel provides several commands to use when analyzing, or auditing, a workbook. Tracing precedents and dependents allows you quickly to learn how cells in a worksheet are related.

2. **Establish data validation rules for changing cells.** Data validation commands in Excel allow you to place rules on cells that restrict a user to entering only particular values in cells. For example, the requirements document in Figure 9–2 implies that cells in the ranges B8:B10, C9:C10, and D8:D9 must be nonnegative whole numbers. Data validation rules should be applied to those cells to restrict a user from entering invalid data.

3. **Propose strategies for solving a complex problem.** Excel provides many methods for solving complex problems. Strategies should be tested from the least complex method to the most complex method.

4. **Consider which cells in the worksheet constitute a scenario.** An Excel scenario needs to recall only the values in those cells that change, or have an impact on, the solution. In essence, a scenario recalls cell values that serve as input data for the problem solved by a worksheet.

5. **Evaluate the steps to take in finalizing a workbook.** Before sending a workbook to colleagues and co-workers, several steps should be taken to ensure that the workbook is finalized and saved in a proper format. The steps you take to perform this task depend on several factors that are discussed later in this chapter.

   When necessary, more specific details concerning the above guidelines are presented at appropriate points in the chapter. The chapter also will identify the actions you perform and decisions made regarding these guidelines during the modification of the worksheets shown in Figure 9–1 on pages EX 556 and EX 557.

With a good understanding of the requirements document and an understanding of the necessary decisions, the next step is to use Excel to learn about the existing worksheet and solve the problem.

To Start Excel and Open a Workbook

To begin this project, you will open a file located on the Data Files for Students. See the inside back cover of this book for instructions on downloading the Data Files for Students, or contact your instructor for more information about accessing the required files. If you are using a computer to step through the project in this chapter and you want your screens to match the figures in this book, you should change your screen's resolution to 1024×768.

The following steps start Excel, open a file, and then save it with a new file name.

① Start Excel. If necessary, maximize the Excel window.

② Open the workbook, Rivers Edge Show Inventory Data, located on the Data Files for Students.

② Save the workbook using the file name, Rivers Edge Show Inventory Analysis.

④ If the worksheet window in Excel is not maximized, click the Maximize button next to the Close Window button on the Ribbon to maximize the worksheet within Excel (Figure 9–3).

BTW

The Ribbon and Screen Resolution
Excel may change how the groups and buttons within the groups appear on the Ribbon, depending on the computer's screen resolution. Thus, your Ribbon may look different from the ones in this book if you are using a screen resolution other than 1024 × 768.

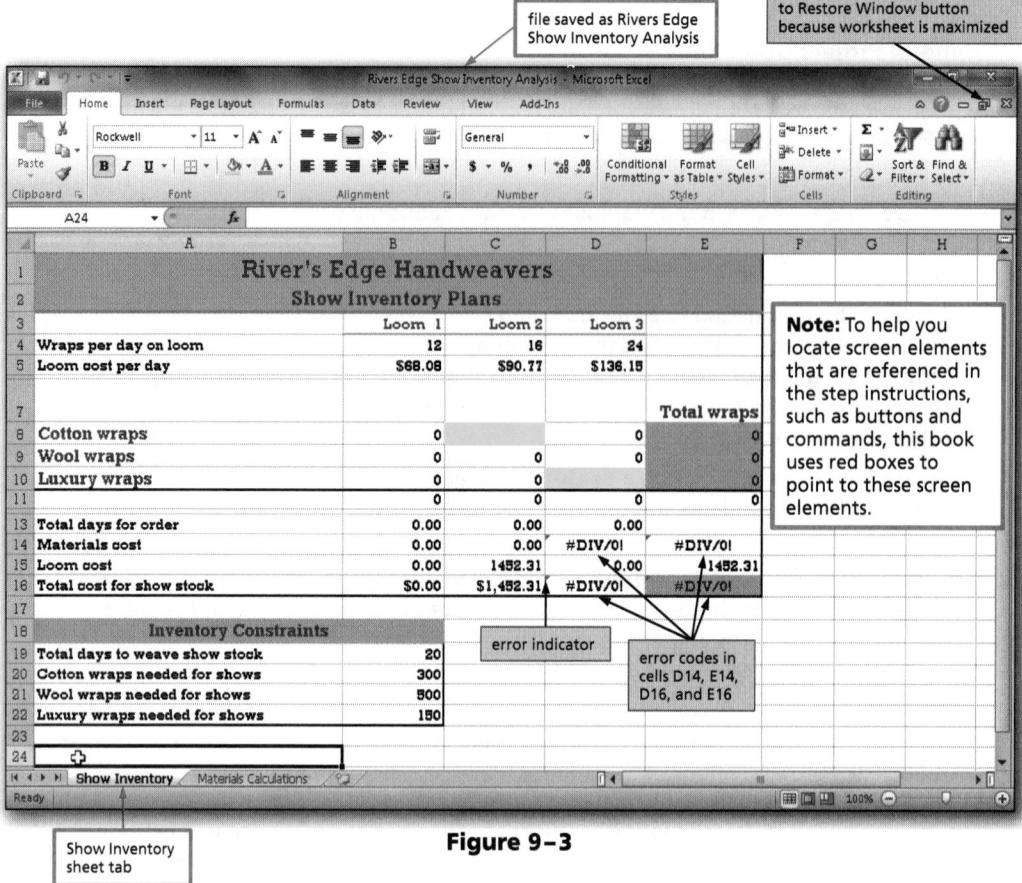

Figure 9–3

BTW

BTWs
For a complete list of the BTWs found in the margins of this book, visit the Excel 2010 BTW Web page (scsite.com/ex2010/btw).

About the Show Inventory Worksheet

The Show Inventory worksheet shown in Figure 9–1a provides information for three looms and three types of wraps. Rows 4 and 5 show the daily output and loom cost for each of the three looms. The range B8:D10 contains the optimal combination of wraps produced on each machine for a particular inventory mix, which is the information that needs to be determined in this chapter. The empty cells — cells C8 and D10 — indicate that a particular loom cannot produce a certain type of wrap. Rows 13 through 16 show the total days and cost for each loom, based on the quantities listed in the range B8:D10. As cells in the range B8:D10 change, the values in the range B13:D16 are updated. The total number of wraps is calculated in cells E8:E11, and the total cost for the holiday show inventory is calculated and shown in cell E16. The goals of the project in this chapter are (1) to keep the total number of wraps produced for the holiday show inventory (range E8:E10) equal to or greater than the constraints in the range B19:B22 and (2) to maximize the number of wraps produced, calculated in cell E11, without using each loom more than the number of days shown in cell B19.

The current worksheet displays inventory constraints for the first inventory scenario in the range B19:B22. As outlined in the requirements document in Figure 9–2 on page EX 558, a second inventory, reflecting a more aggressive holiday show participation, must also be analyzed. The information in the range B19:B22 thus will be modified later in the chapter to reflect the constraints associated with the more aggressive holiday show participation.

Formula Auditing

Errors can be introduced into a worksheet in formulas. Formula auditing is the process of reviewing formulas for errors. Errors can be obvious, with results that indicate that a formula is incorrect. In Figure 9–3, cells D14, E14, D16, and E16 display error codes. These errors are flagged by both the error code #/DIV0! and the error indicator, a green triangle, in the upper-left corner of those cells. Errors can be less obvious, introduced through formulas which, while technically correct, introduce unintended results to the worksheet. A complex worksheet should be reviewed to correct obvious errors and to correct formulas that do not produce error indicators, but still do not produce the intended results. You also can use formula auditing to review the formulas in a worksheet.

Analyze the formulas in the workbook to learn about the workbook.
Tracing precedents and dependents reveals how formulas and values are related. Use Excel tools to examine the structure of the worksheet and identify where the source of an identified error is located, and to review and confirm the logic of the relationships between formulas and values. You should check to find the source of errors and to make sure that formulas have been constructed correctly. This requires a basic understanding of the necessary calculations in the worksheet.

Plan Ahead

The Formula Auditing group on the Formulas tab supplies several tools that you can use to analyze the formulas in a worksheet. Some tools, such as the Error Checking command, deal with identified errors. You also can use other auditing tools that provide visual cues to identify how cells in a worksheet are related to each other. For example, related cells can be joined by arrows called tracer arrows. **Tracer arrows** are drawn from one cell to another, identifying cells that are related to other cells through use in a formula. A tracer arrow can be drawn from a cell that appears in a formula in another cell, or from a cell that contains a formula with cell references. Red tracer arrows indicate that one of the referenced cells contains an error. The Watch Window button opens a separate window that displays values and formulas for specific cells that you choose to monitor. This allows you to keep an eye on cells that you have identified as being related, so you can observe changes to the cells even when viewing a different worksheet or workbook.

A cell containing a formula that references other cells is said to have precedents. Each cell referenced in the formula is a **precedent** of the cell containing the formula. For example, in the formula C24 = C23/$B$1, cells C23 and B1 are precedents of cell C24. Cells C23 and B1 can also have precedents, and these cells would also be precedents of cell C24. Tracing precedents in Excel allows you to see upon which cells a particular cell is based, not only directly by the formula in the cell, but indirectly via precedents for the precedent cells. Tracing precedents can highlight where a formula may be incorrect. Tracing precedents in Excel is accomplished by clicking the Trace Precedents button in the Formula Auditing group on the Formulas tab on the Ribbon.

To Trace Precedents

The following steps show how to trace the precedent cells for cell E15, which displays the total loom cost for producing the holiday show inventory of woven wraps.

1

- If necessary, make Show Inventory the active sheet to trace precedents in the Show Inventory worksheet.

- Click Formulas on the Ribbon to display the Formulas tab.

- Click cell E15 to make it the active cell.

- Click the Trace Precedents button (Formula Auditing group | Formulas tab) to draw a tracer arrow across precedents of the selected cell (Figure 9–4).

Q&A How do I interpret the precedent arrows?

The arrows in Figure 9–4 and Figure 9–5 have arrowheads on traced cells and dots on cells that are direct precedents of the cells with arrowheads. Cells B15 through D15 are precedents of cell E15. Cell D15, which is assigned the formula =D13*loom_cost_24, has precedents in cells D13 and D5. Clicking the Trace Precedents button a second time displays the next level of precedents for the traced cell. A heavier blue line through a range of cells indicates that all cells in the range are precedents. For example, in Figure 9–4, the heavier blue line through the range B15:D15 indicates that these cells are precedents of cell E15.

2

- Click the Trace Precedents button (Formula Auditing group | Formulas tab) again to draw arrows indicating precedents of cells B15:D15 (Figure 9–5).

Q&A How do precedent arrows help troubleshooting?

The arrows in Figure 9–5 indicate why cell C15 contains 1452.31, when it should be 0. Cells B15 and D15 have precedent cells in rows 13 and 5. However, cells C5 and C4 should be precedents to cell C15. This inconsistency, along with the nonzero value in C15, suggests that the formula in cell C15 is incorrect.

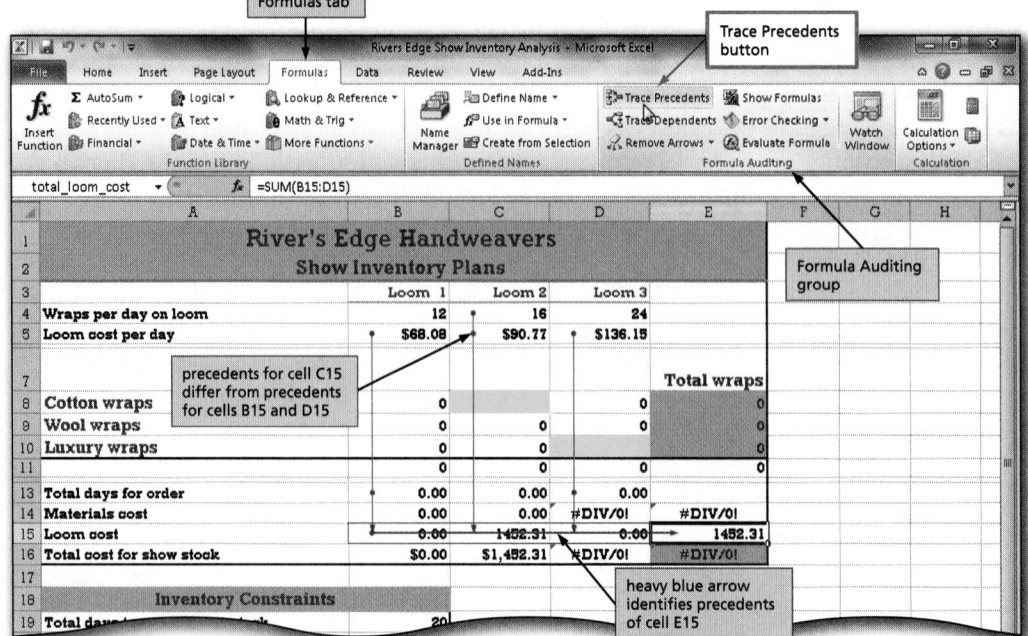

Figure 9–4

Figure 9–5

3

• Click the Trace Precedents button (Formula Auditing group | Formulas tab) once more to identify another level of precedent cells (Figure 9–6).

Figure 9–6

To Review Precedents on a Different Worksheet

Precedents can be located on different worksheets in the same workbook, or in different workbooks. In Figure 9–6, the dashed precedent arrows and worksheet icons identify precedents on another worksheet. The following steps review the precedents located on a different sheet.

1

• Double-click the dashed arrow pointing to the dot in cell C5 to display the Go To dialog box (Figure 9–7).

Figure 9–7

2

- Select the sheet and cell reference, '[Rivers Edge Show Inventory Analysis.xlsx]Materials Calculations'!$M$5, to prepare for reviewing the precedent on the Materials Calculations sheet.

- Click the OK button (Go To dialog box) to switch to the Materials Calculations worksheet with cell M5 as the active cell (Figure 9–8).

Q&A

What does it mean that cell M5 in the Materials Calculations worksheet is a precedent cell for cell C5?

In this case, it means that cell C5 contains a formula that refers to cell M5.

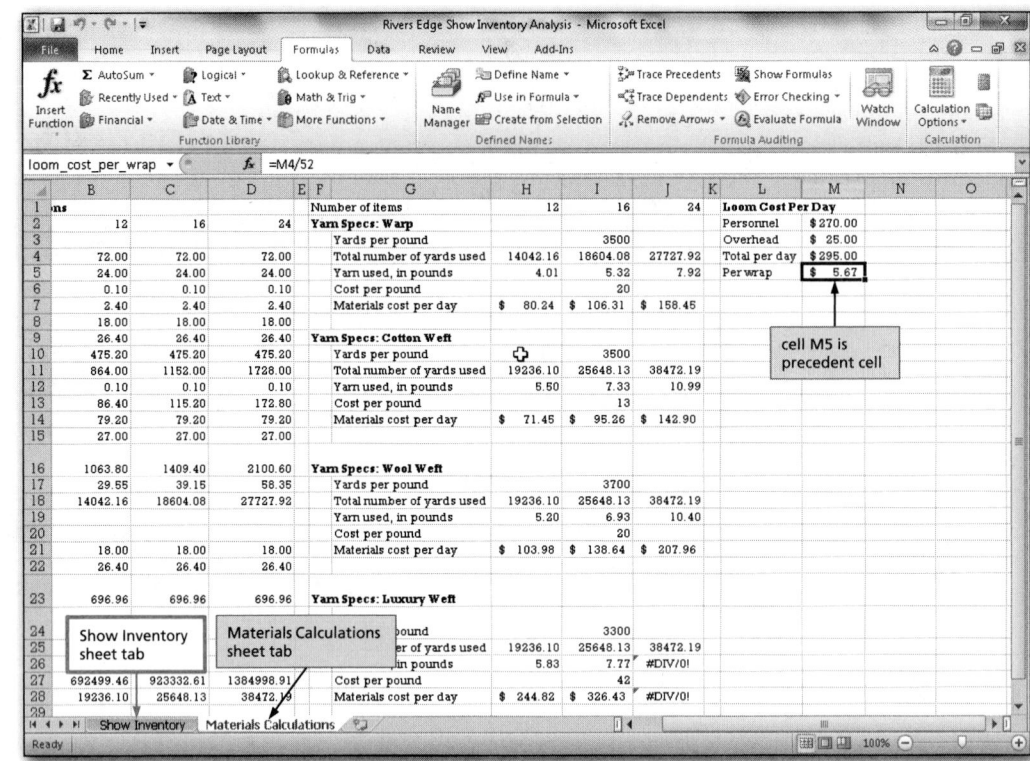

Figure 9–8

To Remove the Precedent Arrows

After reviewing the precedents of cell E15, you determine that cell C15 needs to be changed to calculate the total loom cost correctly for Loom 2. The following steps show how to remove the precedent arrows level by level and then correct the formula in cell C15.

1

- Click the Show Inventory sheet tab to make the Show Inventory worksheet the active worksheet.

- Click the Remove Arrows button arrow (Formulas tab | Formula Auditing group) to display the Remove Arrows menu (Figure 9–9).

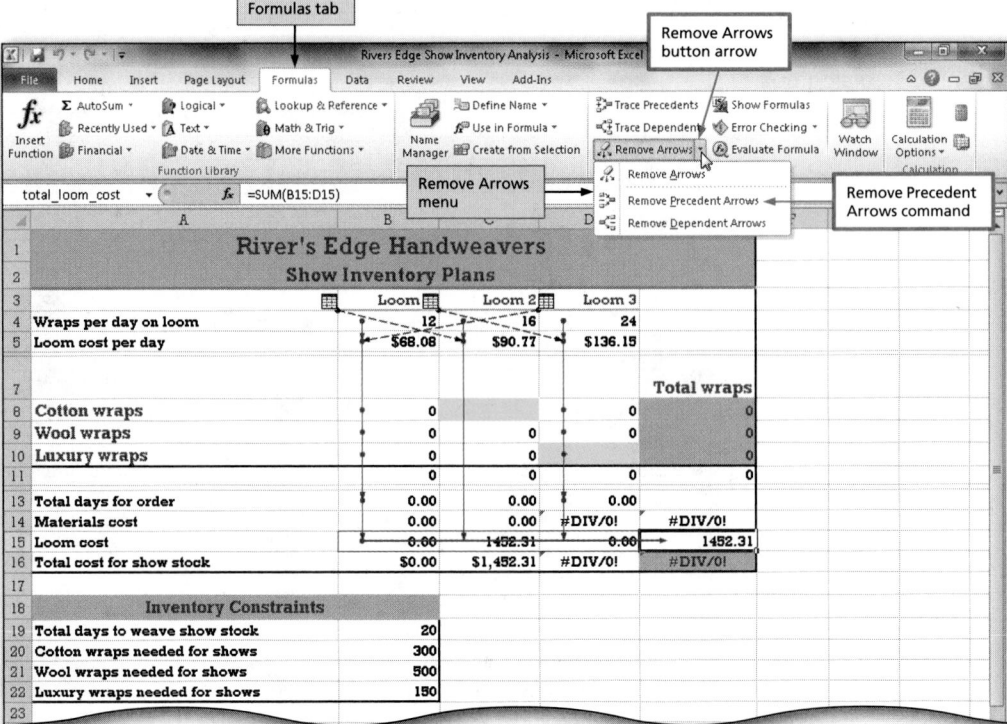

Figure 9–9

2

- Click Remove Precedent Arrows to remove precedent arrows linking to the Materials Calculations sheet.

- Click the Remove Arrows button arrow (Formulas tab | Formula Auditing group) again to display the Remove Arrows menu.

- Click Remove Arrows to remove the remaining tracer arrows.

- Edit cell C15 to read =C13*C5 to correct the error (Figure 9–10).

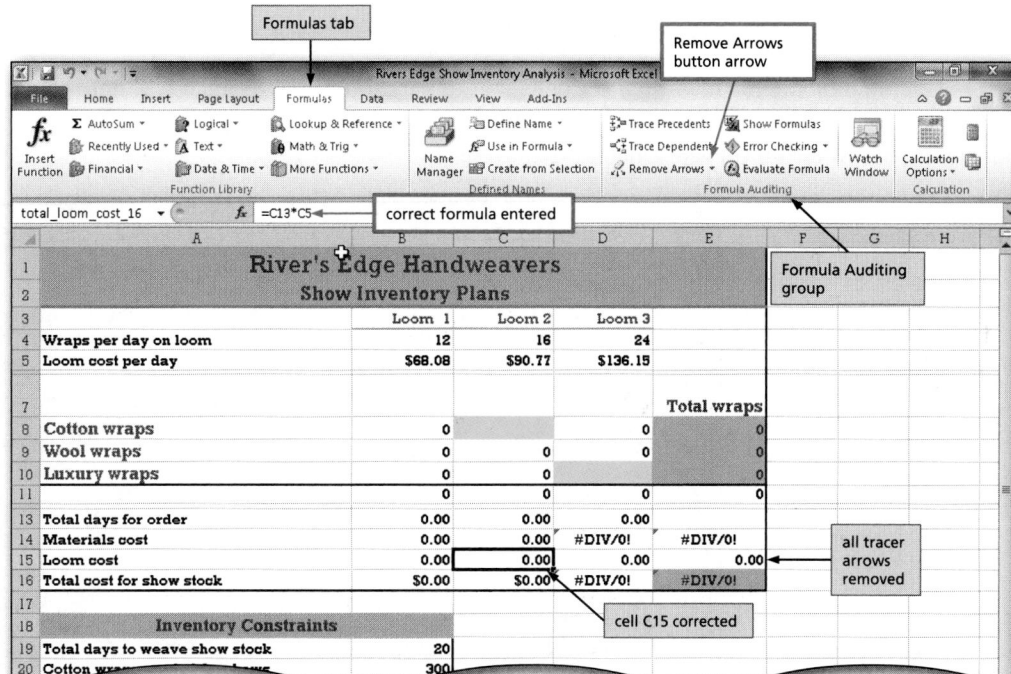

Figure 9–10

Q&A Do I have to remove the precedent arrows level by level?

No. If you click the Remove Arrows button, you remove all arrows at once.

To Trace Dependents

A cell that references another cell is said to be a **dependent** of that referenced cell. If cell A3 contained the formula =B2/B4, cell A3 would be a dependent of cells B2 and B4. Changing the value in cell B2 or cell B4 also changes the result in the dependent cell A3. Identifying dependents highlights where changes will occur in the worksheet as a result of changing the value in the cell you are identifying as a referenced cell. The following step traces the dependents of cell B8, which eventually will show the optimal number of cotton wraps to weave on Loom 1.

1

- Click cell B8 to make it the active cell.

- Click the Trace Dependents button (Formulas tab | Formula Auditing group) to draw arrows to dependent cells B11, B13, B14, and E8.

- Click the Trace Dependents button two more times to draw arrows indicating the remaining dependents of cell B8 (Figure 9–11).

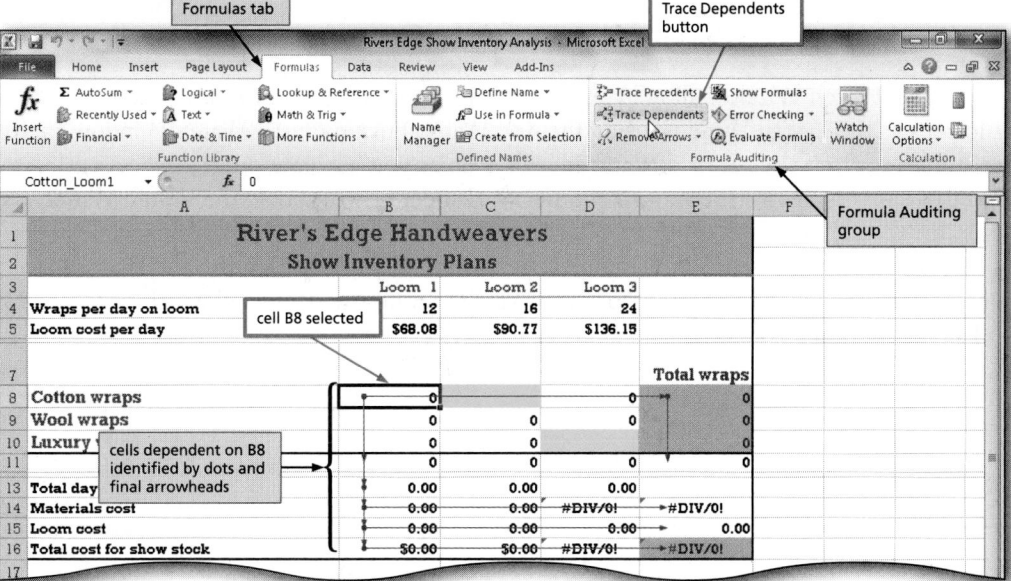

Figure 9–11

Q&A What is the meaning of the dependent arrows?

Figure 9–11 indicates that cells B11, B13, B14, and E8 depend on cell B8. Cell B8 must have a value entered before any of its dependents can have a value other than zero.

To Remove the Dependent Arrows

Tracing dependents identified the cells that depend on cell B8, which will help to correct the #DIV/0! errors, so you are finished auditing the worksheet with formula auditing. The following step shows how to clear the dependent arrows from the worksheet.

1

- Click the Remove Arrows button (Formula Auditing group | Formulas tab) to remove all of the dependent arrows (Figure 9–12).

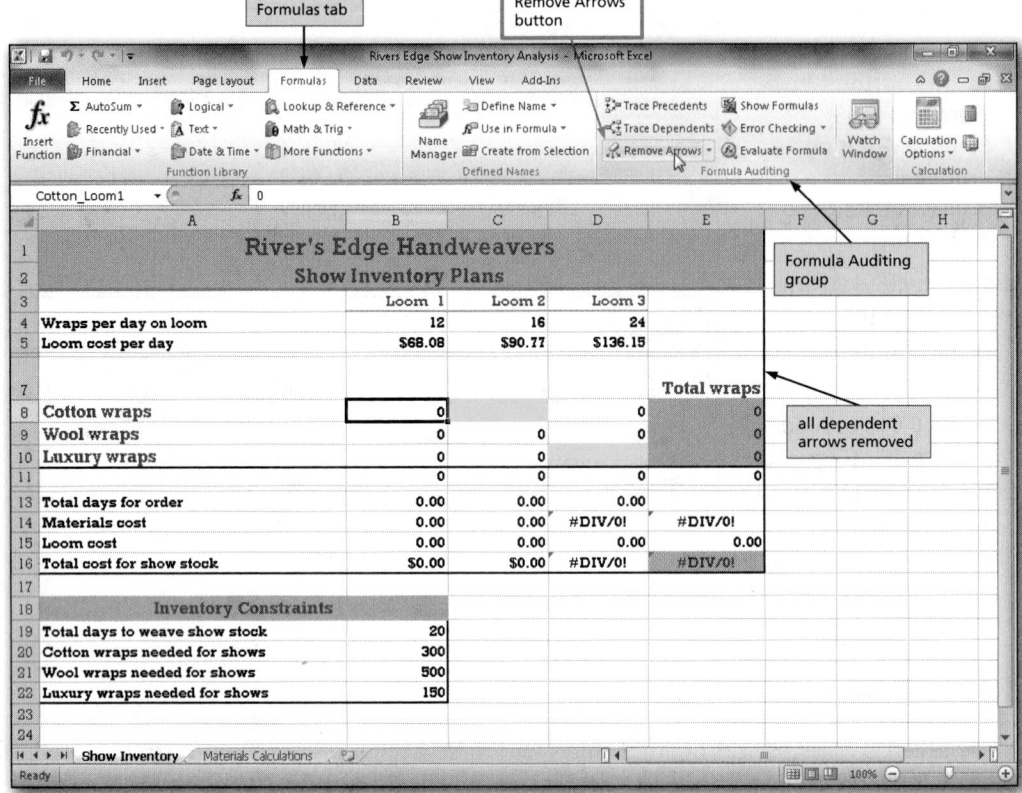

Figure 9–12

To Open the Watch Window and Add Cell Watches

The Watch Window allows you to monitor the values and formulas in cells as you work on a worksheet. You add cells to the Watch Window using the Add Watch button on the Watch Window toolbar. The Watch Window continues to show the values of watched cells even as you navigate the worksheet and the cells are no longer in view. Similarly, if you change the view to another worksheet or workbook, the Watch Window allows you to continue to monitor the cell values.

Based on the results of tracing precedents earlier, you can identify cells that you want to keep under observation. The following steps open the Watch Window and add cell watches to cells D14, D16, E14, and E16, the cells that contain error codes.

1

- If necessary, click Formulas on the Ribbon to display the Formulas tab.

- Click the Watch Window button (Formulas tab | Formula Auditing group) to open the Watch Window.

- If necessary, move the Watch Window to the location shown in Figure 9–13 so it does not cover cells with data.

Q&A

What is displayed in each column of the Watch Window?

The Watch Window displays six columns of information for each cell: the workbook that contains the cell (Book), the worksheet that contains the cell (Sheet), the cell name (Name), the cell reference (Cell), the current value in the cell (Value), and the formula for the cell (Formula).

Figure 9–13

2

- Click the Add Watch button on the Watch Window toolbar to display the Add Watch dialog box (Figure 9–14).

Figure 9–14

• If necessary, move the Add Watch dialog box so that rows 14 through 16 of columns D and E are not hidden.

• Select cell D14 to include it as the first cell in the Add Watch dialog box.

• Hold down the CTRL key and then select the cells D16, E14, and E16 to include them as additional cells in the Add Watch dialog box (Figure 9–15).

Figure 9–15

• Click the Add button (Add Watch dialog box) to add the selected cells to the Watch Window.

• If necessary, expand the Name column in the Watch Window to view the complete cell names.

• Reduce the width of the Value column to match Figure 9–16.

Q&A

How should I use the Watch Window?

You continue to display the Watch Window while you make adjustments to the structure of a worksheet or while you modify other values in the worksheet. To remove a watch, select the watched cell in the Watch Window and then click the Delete Watch button on the Watch Window toolbar.

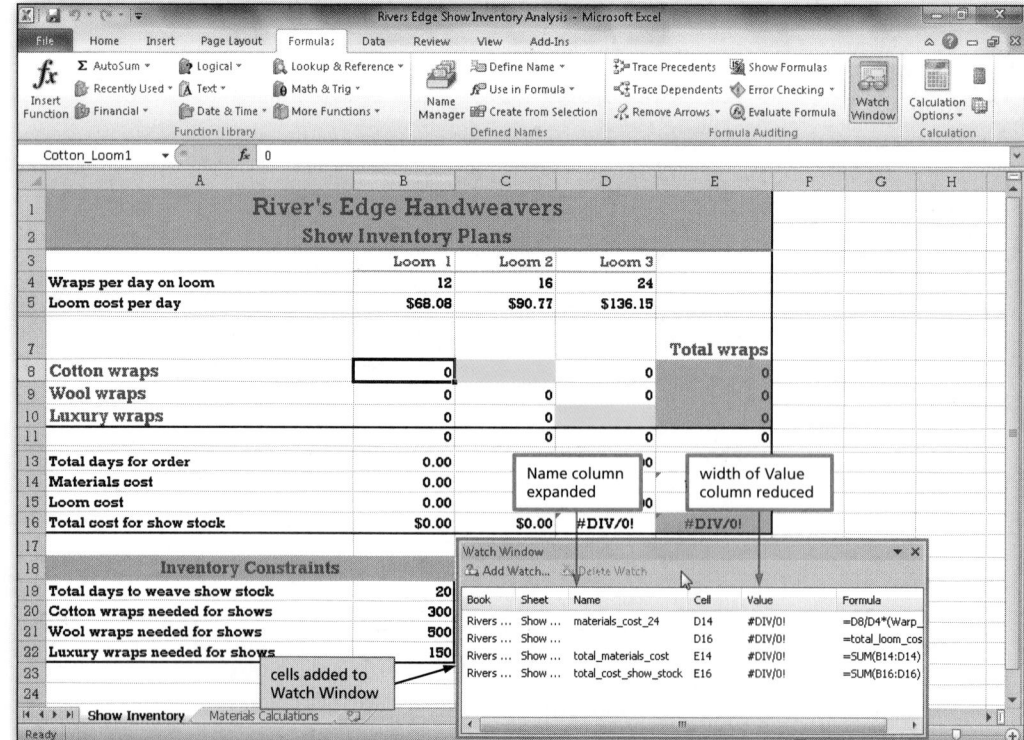

Figure 9–16

To Use Error Checking to Correct Errors

Cells D14:E14 and D16:E16 all contain error codes. Their contents indicate that these cells are in error because the formulas they contain attempt to divide a number by zero. The following steps use Error Checking features to find the source of these errors and correct them.

1

• Click cell E16 to select it.

• Click the Trace Precedents button (Formulas tab | Formula Auditing group) three times to identify the precedents of cell E16 (Figure 9–17).

Figure 9–17

 2

• Double-click the dashed arrow pointing to the dot in cell D14 to display the Go To dialog box.

• Select the sheet and cell reference, '[Rivers Edge Show Inventory Analysis.xlsx]Materials Calculations'!$J$28 (the last cell reference in the Go to list) (Figure 9–18).

Figure 9–18

3

- Click the OK button (Go To dialog box) to switch to the Materials Calculations worksheet with cell J28 as the active cell displaying a #DIV/0! error code.

- Move the Watch Window to the upper-left corner of the worksheet.

- Click the Error Checking button (Formulas tab | Formula Auditing group) to display the Error Checking dialog box (Figure 9–19).

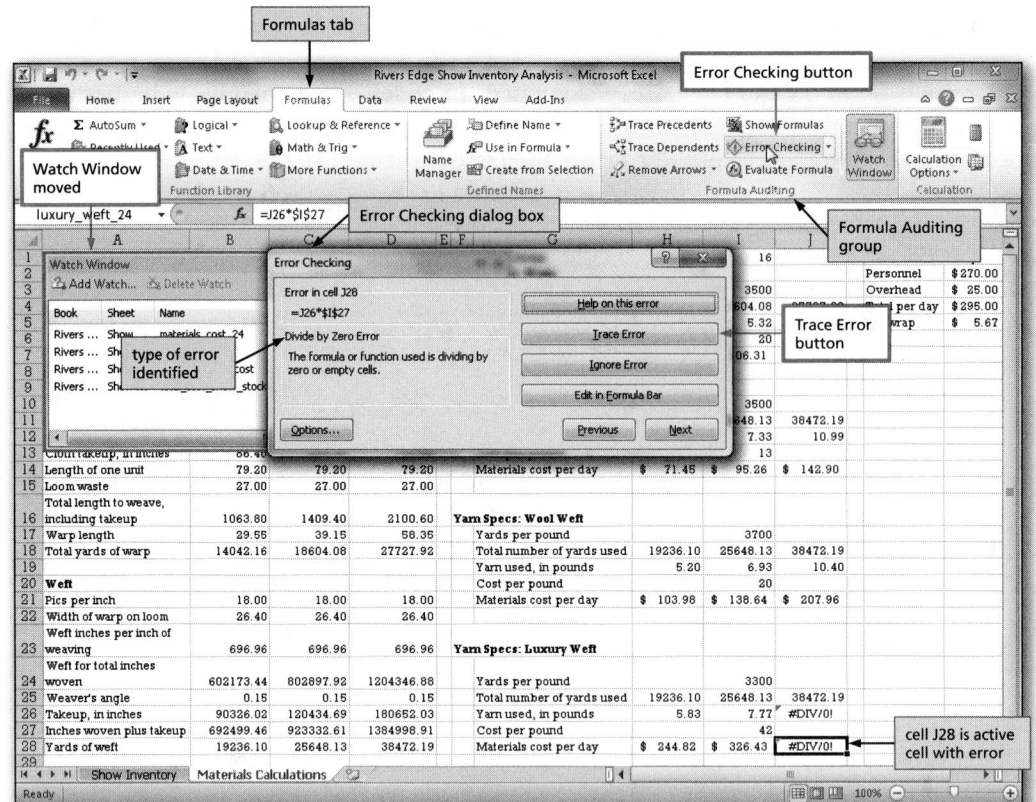

Figure 9–19

4

- Click the Trace Error button (Error Checking dialog box) to highlight the precedent of the active cell, which also contains an error code.

- Click cell J26 to make it the active cell, noting that the formula it contains is =J25/J24.

- Edit cell J26 to read =J25/$I$24 (Figure 9–20).

Q&A

Why did editing the formula in cell J26 correct the error?

Cell J26 should contain the amount of yarn used in pounds, which can be calculated by dividing the number of yards used in cell J25 by the number of yards per pound in cell I24. Originally, this cell contained the formula =J25/J24. Because cell J24 does not contain a value, Excel displayed a #DIV/0! error code in cell J26. Correcting this error also corrects the error in cell J28 because cell J26 is a precedent cell for cell J28. The Watch Window now contains 0.00 and $0.00 in the Value column, meaning that cells D14:E14 and D16:E16 no longer contain #DIV/0 errors.

Figure 9–20

5

- Click the Resume button (Error Checking dialog box) to resume checking errors.

- Click the OK button (Microsoft Excel dialog box) to close the dialog box.

- Move the Watch Window to the lower-right corner of the Excel window.

- Click the Show Inventory sheet tab to make Show Inventory the active sheet.

- If necessary, click the Remove Arrows button (Formula Auditing group | Formulas tab) to remove all of the dependent arrows (Figure 9–21).

Figure 9–21

Q&A Why are all of the #DIV/0! errors corrected in the Show Inventory worksheet?

Cell J28 on the Materials Calculations worksheet is a precedent cell of cell D14. Correcting the error in cell J28 corrected the error in D14. D14 is a precedent of cells E14 and D16, so the correction in cell D14 also corrected the errors in cells E14 and D16. Finally, cell D16 is a precedent cell of E16, so the correction to D16 corrects the error in cell E16. Correcting one error can have a waterfall effect throughout a worksheet.

6

- Click the Close button on the Watch Window title bar to close the Watch Window.

More about the Formula Auditing Group

Figure 9–22 shows the buttons in the Formula Auditing group on the Formulas tab. You have already used the Trace Precedents, Trace Dependents, and Remove Arrows buttons, which provide insight into the structure of the worksheet. You can use four other buttons when auditing formulas.

The Error Checking button provides you with an error check for the entire worksheet. Click the Error Checking button to display a message that the worksheet contains no errors, or to display the Error Checking dialog box, which highlights each error in the sheet in sequence and displays options for correcting it. When you select a cell containing an error and then click the Error Checking button arrow, you have two additional options. The Trace Error command highlights with red arrows the precedents of the selected cell with the error, which may point out the source of the error. The second option, Circular References, is available only when the error in the cell is a **circular reference**. When a cell contains a circular reference, it means that one of its defining values is itself. For example, if you type =B2/A2 in cell B2, you have created a circular reference. Excel displays an error message when you create a circular reference, and provides you with access to the appropriate Help topic. In complex worksheets with multiple precedent levels, these errors are not uncommon.

Table 9–1 lists common error codes identified in Excel.

BTW

Setting Iterative Calculation Options
In certain situations, you will want Excel to recalculate a formula that contains a circular reference, to enable Excel to converge upon an acceptable solution. Changing the Iterative Calculation option allows Excel to recalculate a formula a specified number of times after the initial circular reference error message is dismissed. To allow Excel to recalculate a formula, open the Excel Options dialog box, and click the Formulas button. In the Calculation Options section, click to select Enable Iterative Calculation. You can specify the maximum number of iterations, and the smallest amount of change acceptable between iterations. Be aware that turning this option on will slow down the worksheet due to the additional computations.

Table 9–1 Common Excel Error Codes	
Error Code	**Description**
#DIV/0!	Indicates that you have created a formula that divides a number by zero
#N/A!	Indicates that a value is not available to a formula or function
#NAME?	Indicates use of an invalid function name
#NULL!	Indicates no common cells in two ranges a formula identifies as having an intersection
#NUM!	Indicates that you used an invalid argument in a formula
#REF!	Indicates that a cell reference in a formula is not valid; it may be pointing to an empty cell, for instance
#VALUE!	Indicates that you have included nonnumeric data in a calculation

The Evaluate Formula button allows you to move through a formula step by step, which can be a useful tool when working with long, complex formulas.

Two other buttons in the group provide you with display options for viewing the worksheet and keeping an eye on cells of interest. The Show Formulas button displays the formulas instead of values in the active worksheet. The Watch Window button opens a separate window that displays values and formulas for specific cells that you choose to monitor.

Figure 9–22

Data Validation

When calculating formulas, some values used in calculations might not have any useful meaning for the problem at hand. For example, cells B8 and D8 in the Show Inventory worksheet display the number of cotton wraps produced. Because you cannot create a negative number of wraps, only values greater than or equal to zero should be entered in cells B8 and D8. In other words, only values greater than or equal to zero are valid in cells B8 and D8. Excel provides you with tools to restrict the values that can be placed in cells to valid values. You can place restrictions on values, provide a message to the user when a cell with restrictions is selected, and create an error message that is displayed when a restricted, or invalid, value is entered.

Excel's data validation rules apply only when you enter data into the cell manually. Excel does not check the validation rules if a cell is calculated by a formula or set in a way other than direct input by the user.

Plan Ahead

> **Establish data validation rules for changing cells.**
> When considering which cells to assign data validation rules, review the changing cells and determine which, if any, need restriction. Formulas in a cell may be mathematically possible for any values entered, but may not make sense for a range of data. In this case, validation rules need to be set to ensure that any numbers entered meet the criteria specified in the requirements document.

The types of data validation criteria you can use include any specified value, whole numbers, a value in a list (such as a text value), dates, and custom values. When using the Custom validation type, you can use a formula that evaluates to either true or false. If the value is false, users may not enter data in the cell. Suppose, for example, you have a cell that contains an employee's salary. If the salary is zero, which indicates the employee no longer is with the company, you may want to prohibit a user from entering a percentage in another cell that contains the employee's raise for the year.

To Add Data Validation to Cells

In the Show Inventory worksheet, the number of wraps produced on each loom, for each fiber type, must be nonnegative whole numbers. The cells that need to be restricted are cells B8:B10, C9:C10, and D8:D9 because they display the number of wraps produced. You can use data validation to apply these conditions and restrictions to the cells. The following steps add data validation to cells in the ranges B8:B10, C9:C10, and D8:D9.

- Select cells B8 and D8 to prepare for adding data validation rules to them.
- Click Data on the Ribbon to display the Data tab.
- Click the Data Validation button (Data tab | Data Tools group) to display the Data Validation dialog box.
- In the Validation criteria area (Data Validation dialog box), click the Allow box arrow to display a list of validation criteria types.
- Click Whole number in the Allow list to select it as the validation criteria type.
- Click the Data box arrow and then click 'greater than or equal to' in the Data list to select it.
- Type 0 in the Minimum box to specify that the values in the selected cells must be whole numbers greater than or equal to zero (Figure 9–23).

Q&A

What is the purpose of the Ignore blank check box?

The Ignore blank check box should be cleared if you want to require that the user enter data in the cell.

Figure 9–23

By leaving the Ignore blank check box selected, Excel allows the user to select the cell and then deselect the cell without entering data.

2

- Click the Input Message tab (Data Validation dialog box) to display the Input Message options.

- Type **Number of Cotton Wraps** in the Title text box to enter a title for the message displayed when cell B8 or D8 is selected.

- Type **Enter the number of cotton wraps to weave on this loom. The number must be a whole number that is greater than or equal to zero.** in the Input message box to enter the text for the message (Figure 9–24).

Figure 9–24

 Q&A

How else can I validate data?

Excel allows several types of validation to be set in the Validation criteria area shown in Figure 9–23. Each selection in the Validation criteria area changes the type of value that Excel allows a user to enter in the cell. In the Allow list, the Any value selection allows you to enter any value, but still allows you to specify an input message for the cell. The Whole number, Decimal, Date, and Time selections permit only values of those types to be entered in the cell. The List selection allows you to specify a range that contains a list of valid values for the cell. The Text length selection allows only a certain length of text string to be entered in the cell. The Custom selection allows you to specify a formula that validates the data entered by the user.

3

- Click the Error Alert tab (Data Validation dialog box) to display the Error Alert options.

- If necessary, click the Style arrow button and then click Stop to select the Stop error style.

- Type **Input Error** in the Title text box to enter a title for the error message displayed if invalid data is entered in cell B8 or D8.

- Type **You must enter a whole number that is greater than or equal to zero.** in the Error message box to enter the text for the error message (Figure 9–25).

Figure 9–25

Q&A What does the Stop error style mean?

You can select one of three types of error styles. Stop prevents users from entering invalid data in a cell. Warning displays a message that the data is invalid, and lets users accept the invalid entry, edit it, or remove it. Information displays a message that the data is invalid, but still allows users to enter it.

- Click the OK button (Data Validation dialog box) to accept the data validation settings for cells B8 and D8.

- Repeat Steps 1 through 3 twice, once for wool wraps in cells B9:D9, and once for luxury wraps in cells B10:C10. Click the OK button after completing Step 3 each time. Use the same constraints for the values that can be entered in the cells, and make the appropriate changes for cell addresses and the text in the input message.

- Select cell A24 to make it the active cell.

Q&A What is the result of the validation rules just created?

If a user selects one of the cells in the ranges B8:B10, C9:C10, or D8:D9, Excel displays the input message defined in Figure 9–24. If the user enters a value that either is less than zero or is not a whole number in cells in the ranges B8:B10, C9:C10, and D8:D9, Excel displays the error message defined in Figure 9–25 and forces the user to change the value to a valid number before deselecting the cell.

Solving Complex Problems

In the Rivers Edge Show Inventory Analysis workbook, the problem of determining how to produce the number of wraps needed within the constraints provided is not straightforward, due to the number of variables involved. You can attempt to solve the problem manually, through trial and error, or you can use an Excel tool to automate some or all of the solution. To solve the problem manually, you could try adjusting cells in the ranges B8:B10, C9:C10, and D8:D9 until the criteria for the order are met. Because there are many possible combinations that could meet the criteria, you could hold one or more of the variables constant that fall within the constraints, and make adjustments to the other variables to attempt to meet the rest of the criteria.

BTW

Copying Validation Rules
You can copy validation rules from one cell to other cells using the Paste Special command. Select the cell that contains the validation rules you need to copy, select the cell or cells to which you want to apply the validation rules, click the Paste button arrow, and then click Paste Special. In the Paste Special dialog box, under Paste, select Validation, and then click OK.

**Plan
Ahead**

Propose strategies for solving a complex problem.
When considering an approach to a complex problem in Excel, start with the least complex method of attempting to solve the problem. In general, the following methods can be useful in the order shown:

1. **Use trial and error** to modify the input, or changing, values in the worksheet. Use a common sense approach and keep in mind the range of acceptable answers to your problem. For example, the number of wraps produced on a loom in this chapter should not be a negative number.

2. **Use Excel's Goal Seek feature** to have Excel automatically modify a cell's value in a worksheet in an attempt to reach a certain goal in a dependent cell.

3. **Use Excel's Solver feature** to provide Excel with all of the known rules, or constraints, of your problem as well as the goal you are seeking. Allow Solver to attempt as many different solutions to your problem as possible.

To Use Trial and Error to Attempt to Solve a Complex Problem

Trial and error is not making blind guesses. Because you understand how the spreadsheet is set up and how the various variables interact, you can use this knowledge and logic to inform each subsequent trial following the first trial. In the first trial for the Rivers Edge Show Inventory Analysis workbook, you will set up the production so all the wraps are produced on Loom 1, and then make some adjustments based on the results. The following steps illustrate the process of using trial and error to attempt to solve a complex problem.

1

- Click cell B8 to make it the active cell and display the Number of Cotton Wraps input message.

- Type 300.5 and then press the ENTER key to enter the number of cotton wraps to weave on Loom 1 and display the Input Error dialog box (Figure 9–26).

Q&A

Why does the Input Error dialog box appear after entering 300.5 in cell B8?

You set a data validation rule in cell B8 that accepts only whole numbers greater than or equal to zero. Because 300.5 is not a whole number, Excel displays the Input Error dialog box with the title and error message you specified when you set the data validation rule.

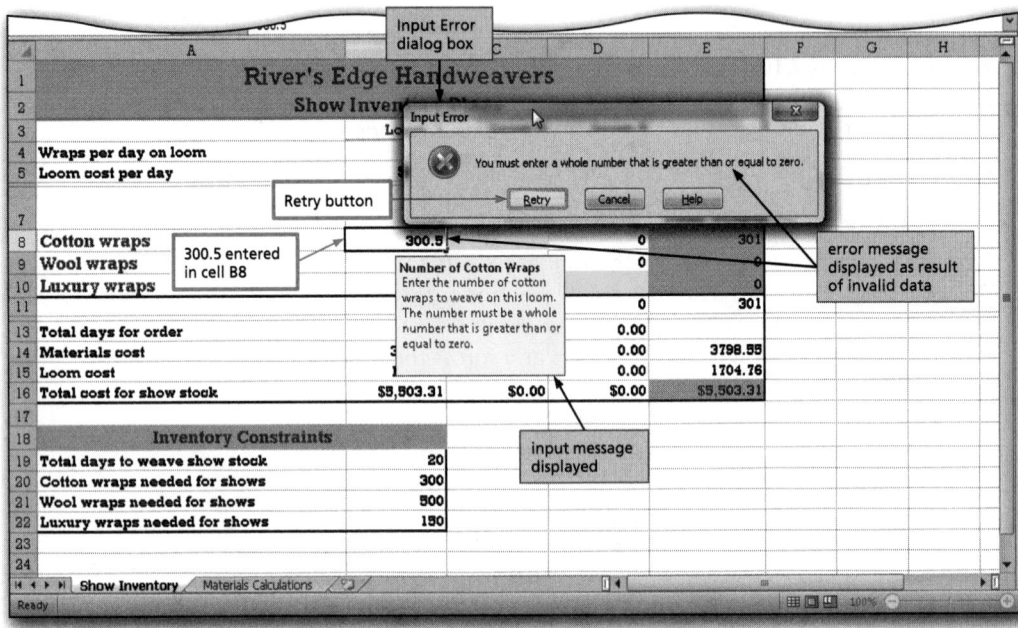

Figure 9–26

2

- Click the Retry button (Input Error dialog box) to enter a valid value in cell B8.

- Enter 300 in cell B8 as the number of cotton wraps to weave on Loom 1.

- Enter 500 in cell B9 as the number of wool wraps to weave on Loom 1.

- Enter 150 in cell B10 as the number of luxury wraps to weave on Loom 1.

- If necessary, press the ENTER key to update the totals in the range B13:D16 and column E (Figure 9–27).

Q&A

Do the values entered in Step 2 solve the problem for Loom 1?

No. Cell B19 indicates that the wraps must be woven in 20 days or less. The values entered in Step 2 mean that the wool wraps will be woven in 79.17 days on Loom 1.

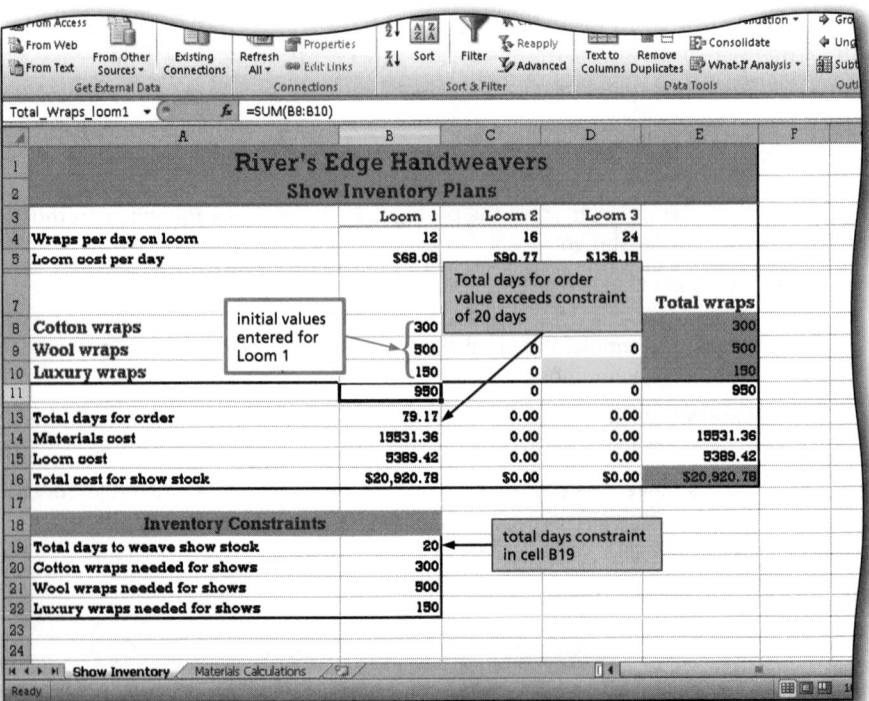

Figure 9–27

3

- Click cell D9 to make it the active cell.

- Type **500** and then press the ENTER key to enter the number of wool wraps to weave on Loom 3 (Figure 9–28).

Q&A Does the value entered in Step 3 solve the problem for Loom 3?

No. The value entered in Step 3 means that the wool wraps will be woven in 20.83 days on Loom 3, which is greater than the 20-day constraint shown in cell B19.

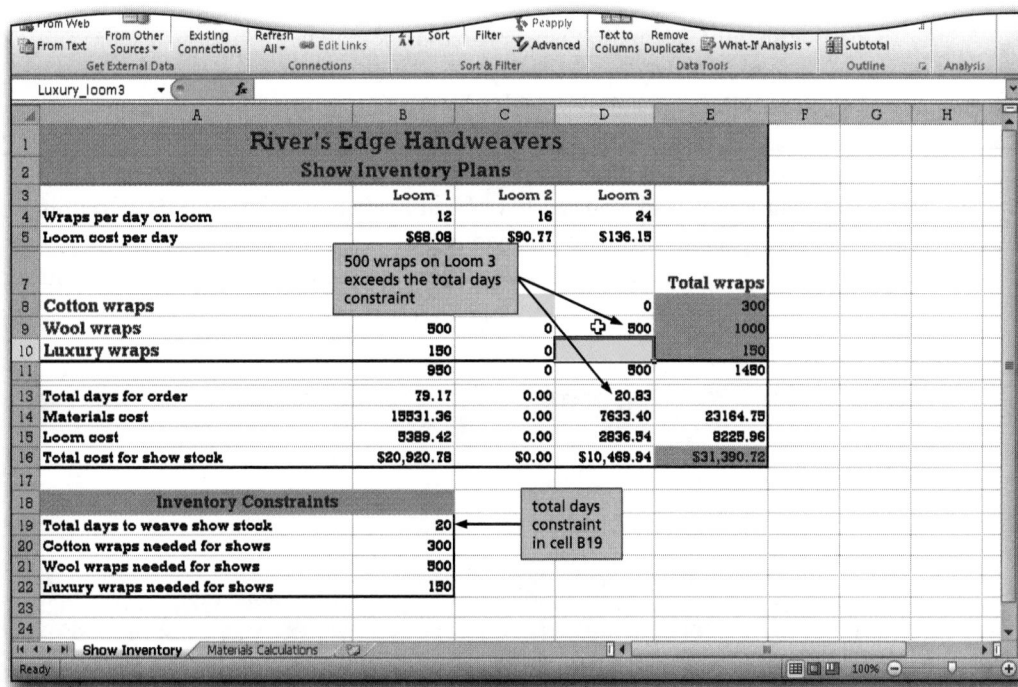

Figure 9–28

4

- Click cell B9 to make it the active cell.

- Enter **0** as the number of wool wraps to weave on Loom 1.

- Enter **100** in cell C9 as the number of wool wraps to weave on Loom 2.

- Enter **400** in cell D9 as the number of wool wraps to weave on Loom 3 (Figure 9–29).

Q&A Do the values entered in Step 4 solve the problem for all looms?

No. Although the values entered in Step 4 mean that the

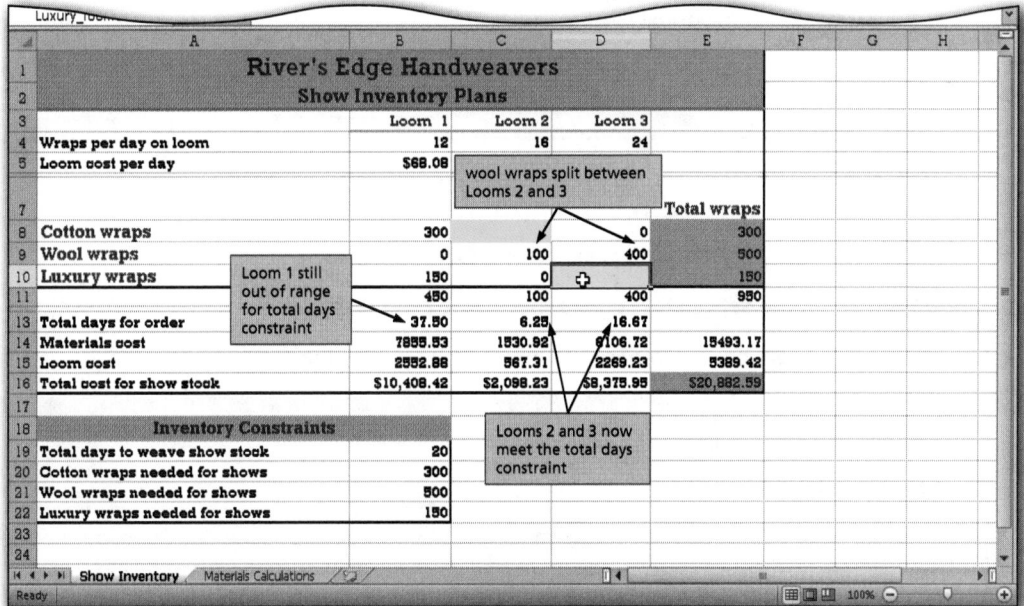

Figure 9–29

wool wraps will be woven in less than 20 days on Looms 2 and 3, weaving the cotton and luxury wraps on Loom 1 still requires more than 20 days.

Q&A What are some problems with using trial and error?

While trial and error can be used on simple problems, it has many limitations when used to solve complex problems. The Show Inventory worksheet has seven cells (B8, B9, B10, C9, C10, D8, and D9) that can be adjusted to solve the problem. There are endless combinations of values that could be entered in those seven cells to try to come up with a solution. Using trial and error, it is difficult to determine if a solution you reach satisfies the goal of maximizing the number of wraps produced, subject to the constraints.

To Use the Goal Seek Command to Attempt to Solve a Complex Problem

Figure 9–29 illustrates a situation where Goal Seek may help you to solve a complex problem. You know that cell B13 needs to be less than or equal to 20 days. The formula in cell B13 is =(B8+B9+B10)/B4, which means that B13 depends on cells B8:B10 and cell B4. With Goal Seek, you can manipulate one of these precedent cells to find a solution for cell B13 that meets the 20-day constraint. Goal seeking will change the value of a cell until a single criterion is met in another cell. You cannot reduce the value in cell B8 because doing so would result in cell D13 becoming greater than 20. Instead, you can have Goal Seek manipulate cell B10. In doing this, you hope that the other constraints of the problem also are satisfied.

The following steps show how Goal Seek can be used to change the number of luxury wraps on Loom 1 to keep the total days for Loom 1 at less than or equal to 20.

1

- If necessary, click Data on the Ribbon to display the Data tab.

- Click the What-If Analysis button (Data tab | Data Tools group) to display the What-If Analysis menu (Figure 9–30).

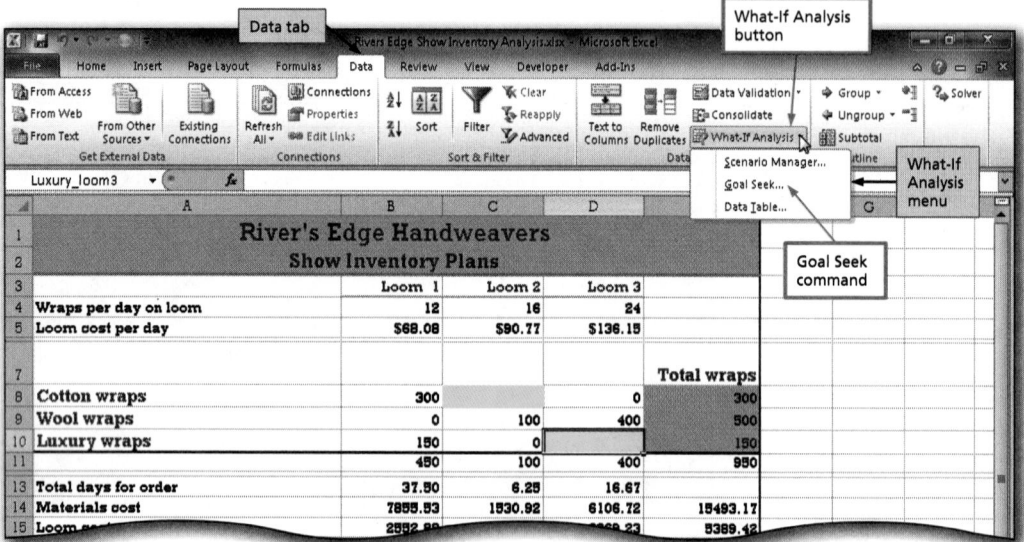

Figure 9–30

2

- Click Goal Seek to display the Goal Seek dialog box.

- Type **$B$13** in the Set cell text box to specify the cell that should contain the goal value.

- Click the To value text box to prepare for entering the goal value.

- Type **20** as the goal value.

- Click the 'By changing cell' text box to prepare for entering the cell containing the value to change.

- If necessary, move the Goal Seek dialog box so that cell B10 is visible on the worksheet and then click cell B10 to enter its reference in the 'By changing cell' text box (Figure 9–31).

Figure 9–31

3

- Click the OK button (Goal Seek dialog box) to seek the goal of 20 days in cell B13 and display the Goal Seek Status dialog box, which indicates that goal seeking found a solution.

- Click the OK button (Goal Seek Status dialog box) to close the dialog box and display the updated worksheet.

- Click cell A24 to deselect any other cell (Figure 9–32).

Figure 9–32

Q&A

How can cell B10 contain a negative number when data validation rules only allow numbers greater than or equal to zero?

Data validation rules are applied only to data that is entered into a cell. Entries that are the result of calculations will not produce a data validation error.

To Circle Invalid Data and Clear Validation Circles

Goal Seek does have some characteristics that require that you stay vigilant when using it. The previous set of steps illustrates that the data validation rules set up earlier apply only to data directly entered into a cell, not to the results of features such as Goal Seek. In this case, Goal Seek found a solution that satisfied the criteria specified for the goal, but that same solution violated the conditions specified for data validation. To check for invalid data entered as the result of a formula or automated tool such as Goal Seek, use the Circle Invalid Data command. It is good practice to check your worksheet for invalid data periodically through use of the Circle Invalid Data command. The following steps check for and circle any invalid data on the Show Inventory worksheet and then clear the validation circles.

1

- Click the Data Validation button arrow (Data tab | Data Tools group) to display the Data Validation menu (Figure 9–33).

Figure 9–33

2

- Click Circle Invalid Data on the Data Validation menu to place a red validation circle around cell B10 (Figure 9–34).

Q&A

What are some limitations of using goal seeking?

Goal seeking allows you to manipulate only one cell in order to reach a goal. In this example, to change the total number of days on Loom 1 to 20, the number of luxury wraps is changed to –60. Goal Seek can produce a result that is acceptable mathematically, but not logically, as is the case here.

Q&A

Has the problem been solved?

No. At this point, all looms are meeting the 20-day constraint, but there are no luxury wraps being produced. Even if all holiday show inventory constraints were met, you still have no way of knowing whether the goal to maximize production (cell E11) has been achieved.

Figure 9–34

3

- Click the Data Validation button arrow (Data tab | Data Tools group) to display the Data Validation menu.

- Click Clear Validation Circles on the Data Validation menu to remove the red validation circle.

- If necessary, select cell A24 to deselect any other cell.

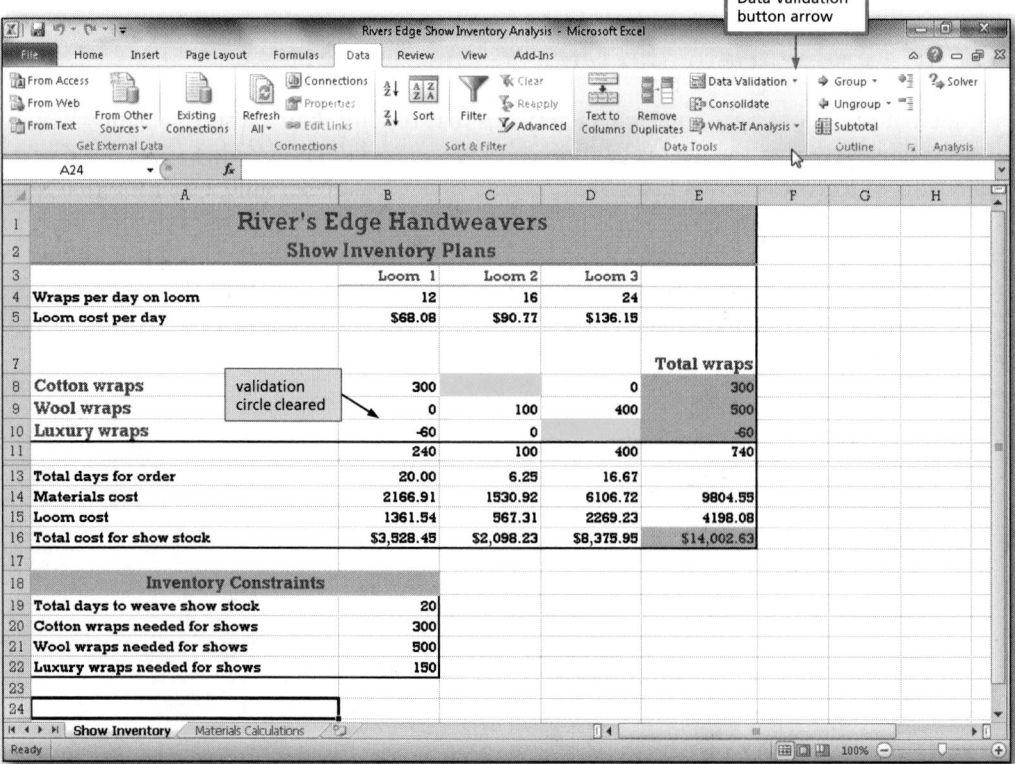

Figure 9–35

Using Solver to Solve Complex Problems

Solver allows you to solve complex problems where a number of variables can be changed in a worksheet in order to meet a goal in a particular cell. Unlike Goal Seek, Solver is not constrained to changing one cell at a time, and can efficiently evaluate many combinations for a solution.

The technique Solver uses to solve a problem depends on the model that the user selects as best representing the data. There are three techniques available. For the current workbook, Solver will use a technique called linear programming to solve problems. **Linear programming** is a complex mathematical process used to solve problems that include multiple variables and the minimizing or maximizing of result values. Solver essentially tries as many possible combinations of solutions as it can. On each attempt to solve the problem, Solver checks to see if it has found a solution. The other two techniques are beyond the scope of this chapter.

Figure 9–36a shows the result of using Solver on the Show Inventory worksheet. Cells in the ranges B8:B10, C9:C10, and D8:D9 are the changing cells. **Changing cells**, or **adjustable cells**, are the cells modified by Solver to solve the problem. The total number of wraps in cell E11 is identified as the **target cell**. Solver will attempt to maximize the value of this cell by varying the values in the other changing cells, within the constraints you set. Constraints are the requirements that have been placed on certain values in the problem, as listed in the requirements document. For example, no loom should be in production for more than 20 days. You have also been provided with a minimum mix of wraps that needs to be produced in the 20-day period.

BTW

Solver Requirements
Regardless of the technique Solver uses to solve a problem, it requires three different types of input from the user: the objective, or the result you need for the target cell; variable cells, the values that can change; and constraints, the conditions that the solution has to meet.

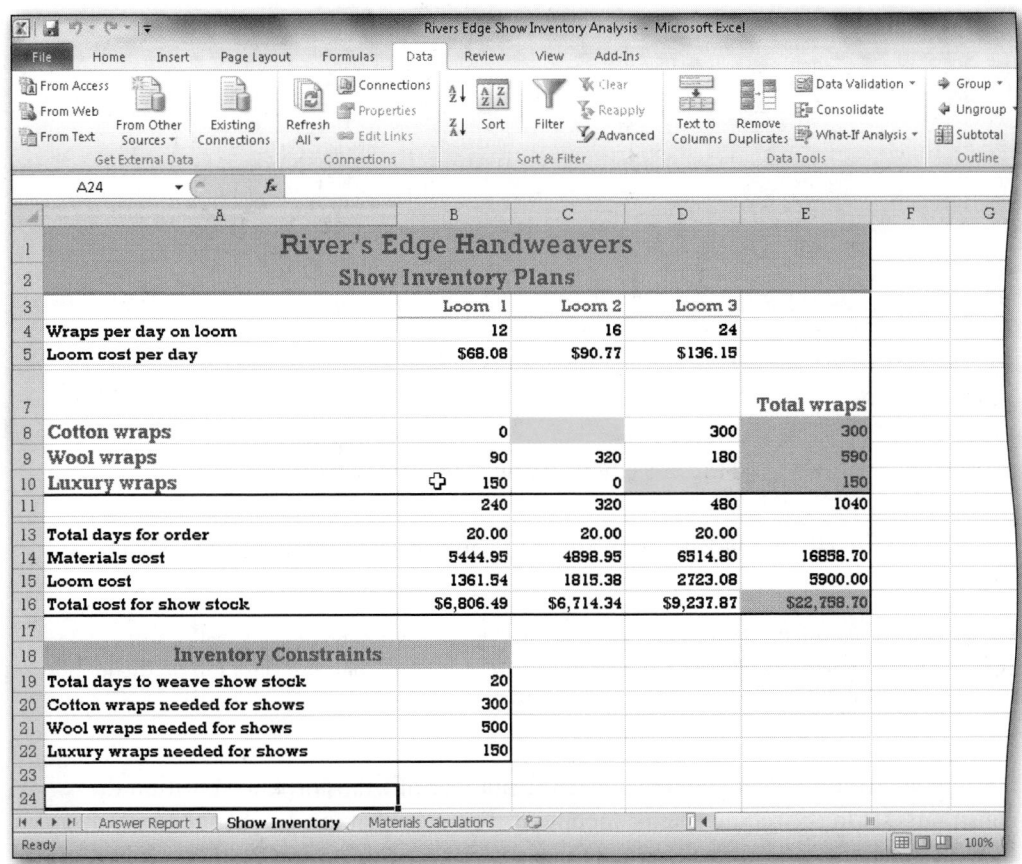

Figure 9–36 (a) Result of Using Solver

Figure 9–36b shows a Solver Answer Report. As previously discussed, an Answer Report is a worksheet summarizing a Solver calculation. It shows the answer for the target cell, the values used in the changing cells to arrive at that answer, and the constraints that were applied to the calculation. The report satisfies the requirement to document the results of the show inventory calculation, as shown in Figure 9–2 on page EX 558.

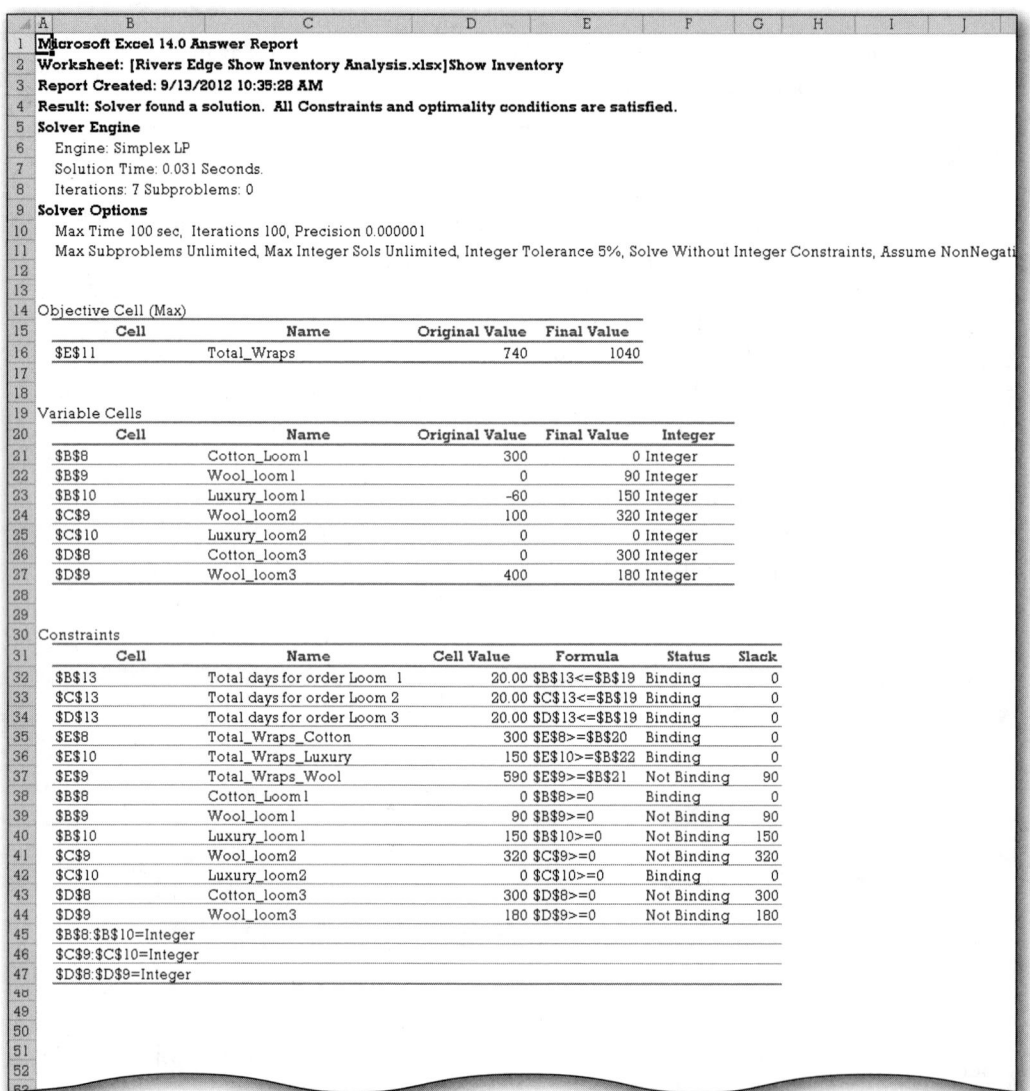

Figure 9–36 (b) Solver Answer Report

The Data tab on the Ribbon includes the Solver button, which starts Solver.

Note: If the Solver button does not appear on the Data tab, then you must use the Add-Ins page in the Excel Options dialog box to add it. If other Add-Ins, such as the Analysis ToolPak, are selected on your computer, then the Data tab on the Ribbon may appear differently than shown in this book.

The goal for Solver is to maximize the number of wraps produced, within the constraints set in the requirements document. The cells that can be changed by Solver to accomplish this goal are cells in the ranges B8:B10, C9:C10, and D8:D9, which contain the number of wraps to weave on each loom. The constraints are summarized in Table 9–2.

Table 9–2 Constraints for Solver

Cell or Range	Operator	Constraint
$B$8:$B$10	>=	0
$B$8:$B$10	int	integer
$C$9:$C$10	>=	0
$C$9:$C$10	int	integer
$D$8:$D$9	>=	0
$D$8:$D$9	int	integer
$E$8	>=	$B$20
$E$9	>=	$B$21
$E$10	>=	$B$22
$B$13	<=	$B$19
$C$13	<=	$B$19
$D$13	<=	$B$19

To Use Solver to Find the Optimal Solution to a Complex Problem

The following steps show how to use Solver to find the optimal solution to solve the problem in the Show Inventory worksheet within the given constraints.

- Click the Solver button (Data tab | Analysis group) to display the Solver Parameters dialog box.

- Click the Collapse Dialog button in the Set Objective text box to collapse the Solver Parameters dialog box.

- Click cell E11 to set the target cell.

- Click the Expand Dialog button on the right side of the collapsed Solver Parameters dialog box to expand the dialog box.

- If necessary, click the Max option button to specify that the value of the target cell should be as large as possible.

- Click the Collapse Dialog button in the By Changing Variable Cells text box to collapse the Solver Parameters dialog box.

- Select the range B8:B10 to enter the cells containing the first set of values to adjust.

- Hold down the CTRL key and then select the ranges C9:C10 and D8:D9 to add the cells to the By Changing Variable Cells text box.

- Click the Expand Dialog button on the right side of the collapsed Solver Parameters dialog box to expand the dialog box (Figure 9–37).

Figure 9–37

2

• Click the Add button to display the Add Constraint dialog box.

• If necessary, move the Add Constraint dialog box so that the range B8:B10 is visible.

• Select the range B8:B10 to set the value of the Cell Reference box.

• Click the middle box arrow and then select >= in the list.

• Type 0 in the Constraint box to set the constraint on the cells in the range B8:B10 to be greater than or equal to 0 (Figure 9–38).

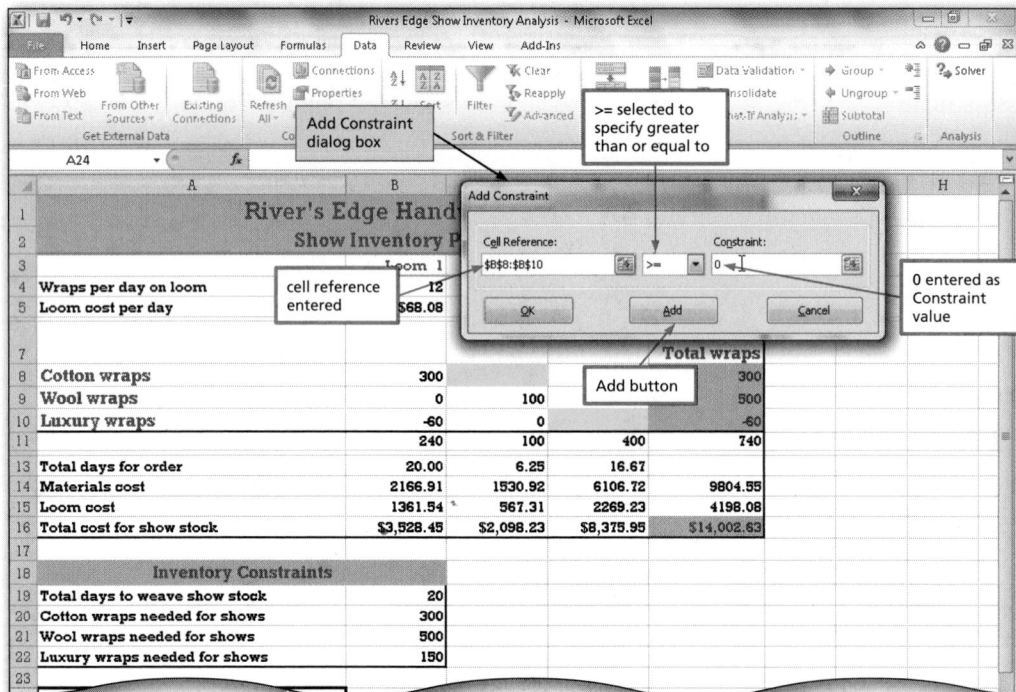

Figure 9–38

Q&A How is the Constraint box used?

When adding constraints, as shown in Figure 9–38, Solver allows you to enter a cell reference followed by an operator. If the operator is <=, >=, or =, then you enter the constraint value in the Constraint box. The constraint can be a value or a cell reference. Other valid operators are **int**, for an integer value, or **bin**, for cells that contain only one of two values, such as yes/no or true/false.

Q&A What do the entries in the Add Constraint dialog box in Figure 9–38 mean?

The entries limit the number of wraps on Loom 1 (cells B8:B10) to a number greater than or equal to zero.

3

• Click the Add button (Add Constraint dialog box) to add a second constraint.

• Select the range B8:B10 to set the value of the Cell Reference box.

• Click the middle box arrow and then select int in the list to set a constraint on the cells in the range B8:B10 to be assigned only integer values (Figure 9–39).

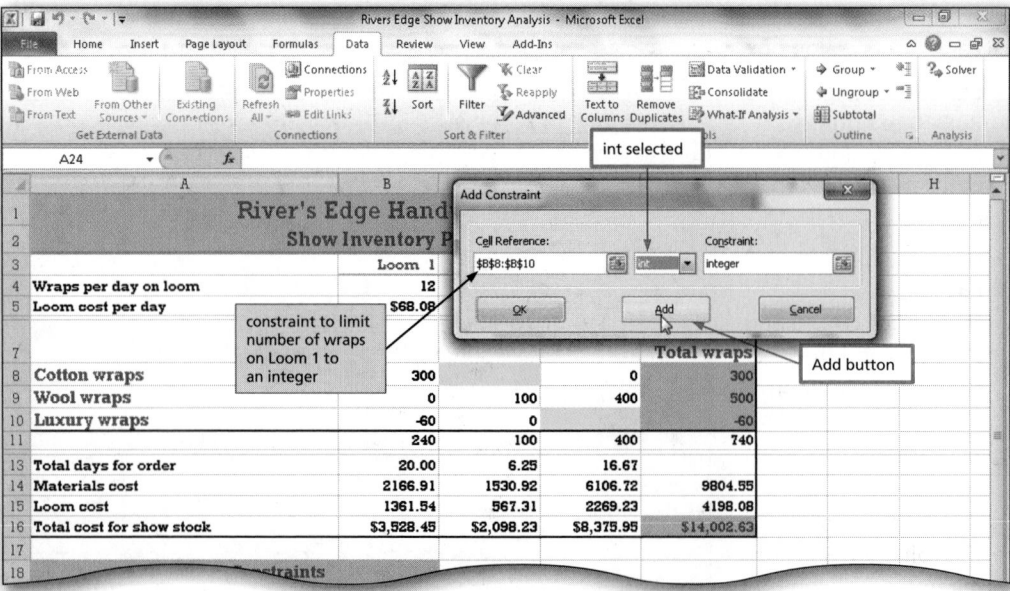

Figure 9–39

4

- Click the Add button (Add Constraint dialog box) to add a third constraint.

- Click cell E8 to set the value of the Cell Reference box.

- Click the middle box arrow and then select >= in the list.

- Click the Constraint box and then click cell B20 to add a constraint to cell E8 indicating that its value must be greater than or equal to the value in cell B20 (Figure 9–40).

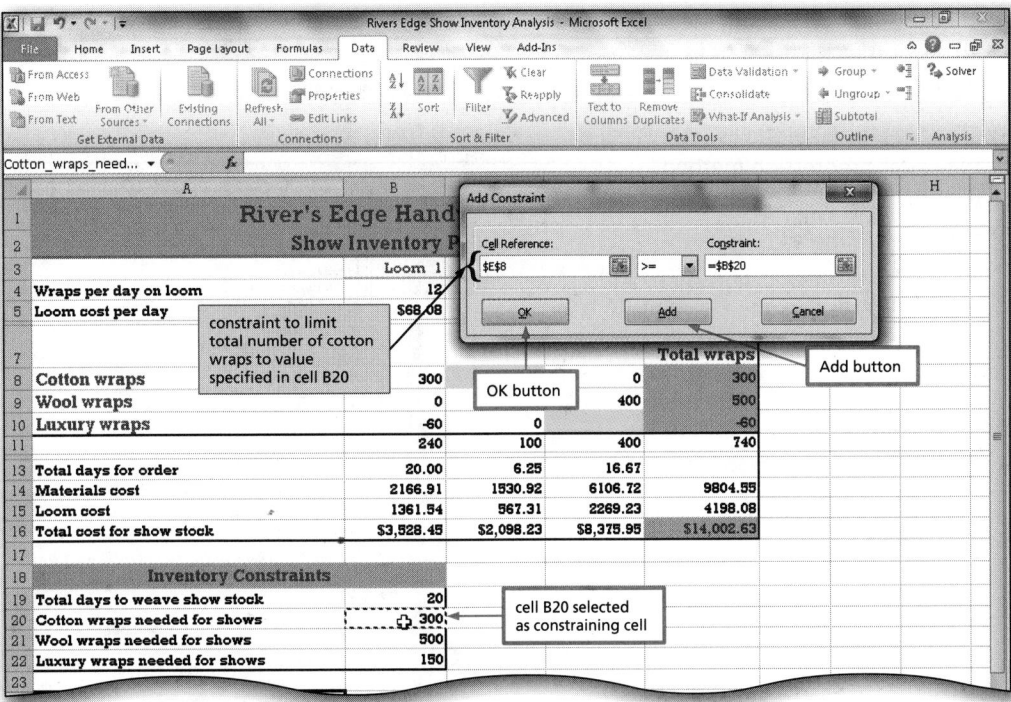

Figure 9–40

5

- Click the Add button (Add Constraint dialog box) to add a fourth constraint.

- Enter the remaining constraints shown in Table 9–2 on page EX 583, beginning with the constraints for the range C9:C10.

- When finished with the final constraint, click the OK button (Add Constraint dialog box) to close the dialog box and display the Solver Parameters dialog box (Figure 9–41).

Q&A What should I do if a constraint does not match the ones shown in Figure 9–41?

Select the constraint, click the Change button, and then enter the constraints as shown in Table 9–2 on page EX 583.

Figure 9–41

6

- Click the Select a Solving Method arrow button to display a list of solving methods.

- Click Simplex LP in the list to select the linear progression method (Figure 9–42).

Q&A | What does Simplex LP mean?

LP stands for linear progression, and Simplex refers to the basic problem solving method used to solve linear problems.

Figure 9–42

7

- Click the Solve button (Solver Parameters dialog box) to display the Solver Results dialog box, indicating that Solver found a solution to the problem (Figure 9–43).

Figure 9–43

8

- Click Answer in the Reports list to select the type of report to generate (Figure 9–44).

Figure 9–44

9

- Click the OK button (Solver Results dialog box) to display the values found by Solver and the newly recalculated totals (Figure 9–45).

Q&A

What is the result of using Solver?

Figure 9–45 shows that all of the constraints in the problem have been satisfied. The total number of wraps is 1040, which is 90 more than the number needed for show inventory. This solution both meets the constraints and maximizes the number of wraps produced.

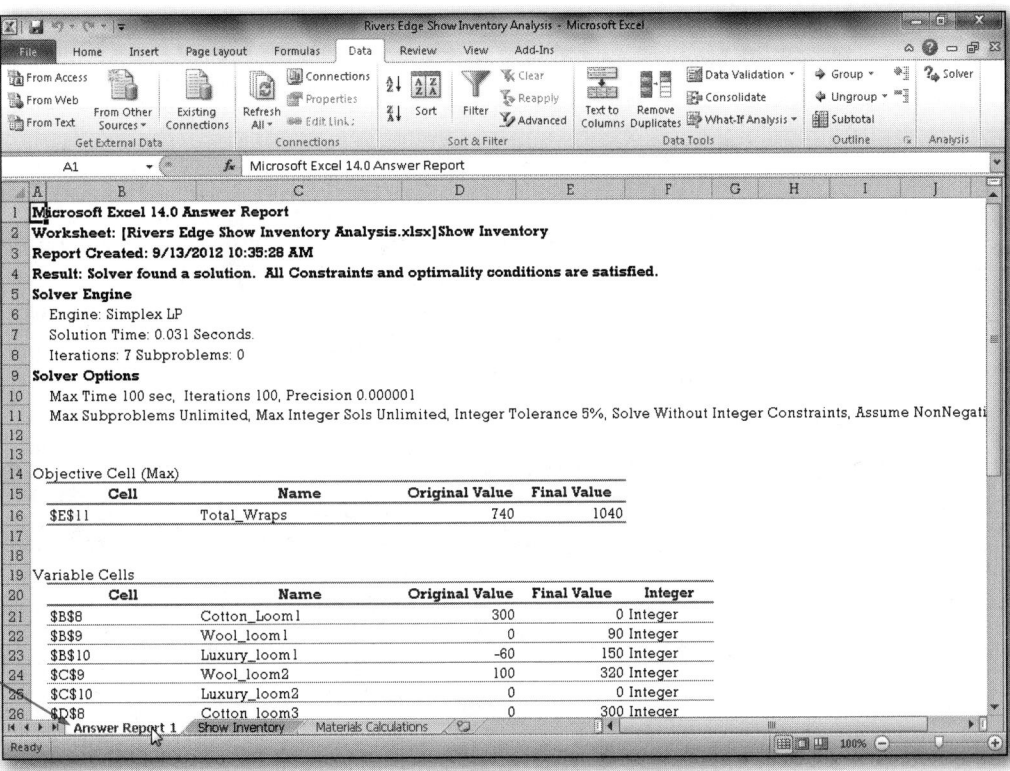

Figure 9–45

To View the Solver Answer Report

As shown in Figure 9–46, Solver creates the requested Answer Report on a separate worksheet after it finds a solution. The Solver Answer Report summarizes the problem that you have presented to Solver. It shows the original and final values of the target cell along with the original and final values of the changing cells (adjustable cells) that Solver adjusted to find the answer. Additionally, it lists all of the constraints that you imposed on Solver.

The Answer Report documents that a particular problem has been solved correctly. Because it lists all of the relevant information in a concise format, you can use the Answer Report to make certain that you have entered all of the constraints and allowed Solver to vary all the cells necessary to solve the problem. You also can use the report to reconstruct the Solver model in the future.

The following steps view the Solver Answer Report.

1

- Click the Answer Report 1 sheet tab to display the Solver Answer Report (Figure 9–46).

Figure 9–46

2

- Drag the Answer Report 1 sheet tab to the right of the Show Inventory sheet tab to move the worksheet in the workbook.

- Double-click the Answer Report 1 sheet tab to select the name.

- Type **Show Inventory Answer Report1** to rename the worksheet.

- Change the color of the sheet tab to Green, Accent 1.

- Scroll down to view the remaining cells of the Answer Report (Figure 9–47).

	A	B	C	D	E	F	G	H	I
22		$B$9	Wool_loom1	0		90 Integer			
23		$B$10	Luxury_loom1	-60		150 Integer			
24		$C$9	Wool_loom2	100		320 Integer			
25		$C$10	Luxury_loom2	0		0 Integer			
26		$D$8	Cotton_loom3	0		300 Integer			
27		$D$9	Wool_loom3	400		180 Integer			
28									
29									
30	Constraints								

Cell	Name	Cell Value	Formula	Status	Slack
$B$13	Total days for order Loom 1	20.00	$B$13<=$B$19	Binding	0
$C$13	Total days for order Loom 2	20.00	$C$13<=$B$19	Binding	0
$D$13	Total days for order Loom 3	20.00	$D$13<=$B$19	Binding	0
$E$8	Total_Wraps_Cotton	300	$E$8>=$B$20	Binding	0
$E$10	Total_Wraps_Luxury	150	$E$10>=$B$22	Binding	0
$E$9	Total_Wraps_Wool	590	$E$9>=$B$21	Not Binding	90
$B$8	Cotton_Loom1	0	$B$8>=0	Binding	0
$B$9	Wool_loom1	90	$B$9>=0	Not Binding	90
$B$10	Luxury_loom1	150	$B$10>=0	Not Binding	150
$C$9	Wool_loom2	320	$C$9>=0	Not Binding	320
$C$10	Luxury_loom2	0	$C$10>=0	Binding	0
$D$8	Cotton_loom3	300	$D$8>=0	Not Binding	300
$D$9	Wool_loom3	180	$D$9>=0	Not Binding	180
$B$8:$B$10=Integer					
$C$9:$C$10=Integer					
$D$8:$D$9=Integer					

modified sheet tab

Show Inventory | **Show Inventory Answer Report1** | Materials Calculations

Figure 9–47

Q&A

What is shown in the Answer Report?

Figure 9–47 shows additional information about the constraints that you placed on the problem and how the constraints were used to solve the problem. Column F, the **Status column**, indicates whether the constraint was binding or not. A constraint that is **binding** is one that limited the final solution in some way. For example, the total number of wraps in cell E11 in the Show Inventory worksheet is binding because the solution found the maximum number required by the constraints, which is 1,040 wraps. No more wraps could be produced given the constraints. A constraint that is **not binding** is one that was not a limiting factor in the solution that Solver provided.

BTW

Viewing Other Solutions
If you want to view solutions other than the one Solver identifies as optimal, select the Show Iteration Results check box in the Solver Parameters dialog box. After each iteration, the Show Trial Solution dialog box will be displayed, and you will have the option of saving that scenario and then stopping Solver or continuing on to the next solution.

Working with Solver Methods and Options

When you selected the Simplex LP method of solving the inventory problem in the Solver Parameters dialog box shown in Figure 9–42, you selected a linear programming method that assumes the problem to solve is a linear one. After selecting the Solving method, you can select various options to further configure the inner workings of Solver. Discussion of many of these parameters is beyond the scope of this book. Table 9–3 presents some of the more commonly used Solver options.

Table 9–3 Commonly Used Solver Parameters in the Solver Options Dialog Box

Parameter	Meaning
Max Time	The total time that Solver should spend trying different solutions, expressed in seconds
Iterations	The number of possible answer value combinations that Solver should try
Constraint Precision	Instructs Solver how close it must come to the target value in order to consider the problem to be solved. For example, if the target value is 100 and the Tolerance is 5%, then 95 is an acceptable answer.
Use Automatic Scaling	Selected by default, specifies that Solver should internally rescale values of variables, restraints, and the objective to reduce the effect of outlying values

Excel saves the most recently used Solver parameters and options. When using Solver, three other issues must be kept in mind. First, some problems do not have solutions. The constraints may be constructed in such a way that an answer that satisfies all of the constraints cannot be found. Second, sometimes multiple answers solve the same problem. Solver does not indicate when this is the case, and you will have to use your own judgment to determine if you should continue seeking another solution. As long as you are confident that you have given Solver all of the constraints for a problem, however, all answers should be equally valid. Finally, Solver may require more time or iterations to solve the problem if it fails to find a solution.

Break Point: If you wish to take a break, this is a good place to do so. You can quit Excel now. To resume at a later time, start Excel, open the file called Rivers Edge Show Inventory Analysis, and continue following the steps from this location forward.

Using Scenarios and Scenario Manager to Analyze Data

Scenarios are named combinations of values that are assigned to variables in a model. These values are what-if assumptions for a model. In this chapter, each different show inventory option being analyzed can be considered a scenario. For example, a show inventory option requiring 300 cotton wraps, 500 wool wraps, and 150 luxury wraps produced in 20 days would be a scenario named inventory1. Changing the number of wraps in any or all categories creates a new scenario. Each set of values in these examples represents a what-if assumption. You use the Scenario Manager to keep track of various scenarios, and produce a report detailing the what-if assumptions and results for each scenario.

The primary uses of Scenario Manager are to:

1. Create different scenarios with multiple sets of changing cells.
2. Build summary worksheets that contain the different scenarios.
3. View the results of each scenario on your worksheet.

Consider which cells in the worksheet constitute a scenario.
When considering which cells to save in a scenario, you should plan to save as few cells in a scenario as possible. Rule out cells with the following three characteristics:

1. **Cells that contain sheet title, row heading, or column heading text**. These cells are static cells.

2. **Cells that include formulas**. These cells change when their precedents change.

3. **Cells that remain constant across scenarios**. In the Show Inventory worksheet, the number of wraps that can be produced per day for each loom is a constant, determined by the equipment.

   You should include cells that are input cells for your model. In this example, the total number of each type of wrap could change from scenario to scenario. The number of each type of wrap produced on each loom and the number of days available to produce them could also change from scenario to scenario. Therefore, the changing cells would be B8:B10, B19:B22, C9:C10, and D8:D9.

Plan Ahead

The next section in this chapter shows how to use Scenario Manager for each of the three uses listed earlier. After you create the scenarios, you can instruct Excel to build the summary worksheets, including a Scenario Summary worksheet and a Scenario PivotTable worksheet.

To Save the Current Data as a Scenario

The current data on the Show Inventory worksheet consists of constraints and the values that correctly solve the inventory problem. These values can be saved as a scenario named inventory1 that can be accessed later or compared to other scenarios. The following steps save the current data for the inventory1 scenario using the Scenario Manager dialog box.

- Click the Show Inventory sheet tab to make Show Inventory the active sheet.

- Click the What-If Analysis button (Data tab | Data Tools group) to display the What-If Analysis menu (Figure 9–48).

Figure 9–48

- Click Scenario Manager on the What-If Analysis menu to display the Scenario Manager dialog box, which indicates that no scenarios are defined (Figure 9–49).

Figure 9–49

- Click the Add button (Scenario Manager dialog box) to prepare for adding a scenario to the workbook.

- When Excel displays the Add Scenario dialog box, type **inventory1** in the Scenario name text box to provide a name for the scenario (Figure 9–50).

Figure 9–50

- Click the Collapse Dialog button (Add Scenario dialog box) to collapse the dialog box.

- Select the range B8:B10, hold down the CTRL key, and then select the ranges C9:C10, D8:D9, and B19:B22 to select the cells for the scenario.

- Release the CTRL key to display a marquee around the selected cells and assign the cells to the Changing cells text box (Figure 9–51).

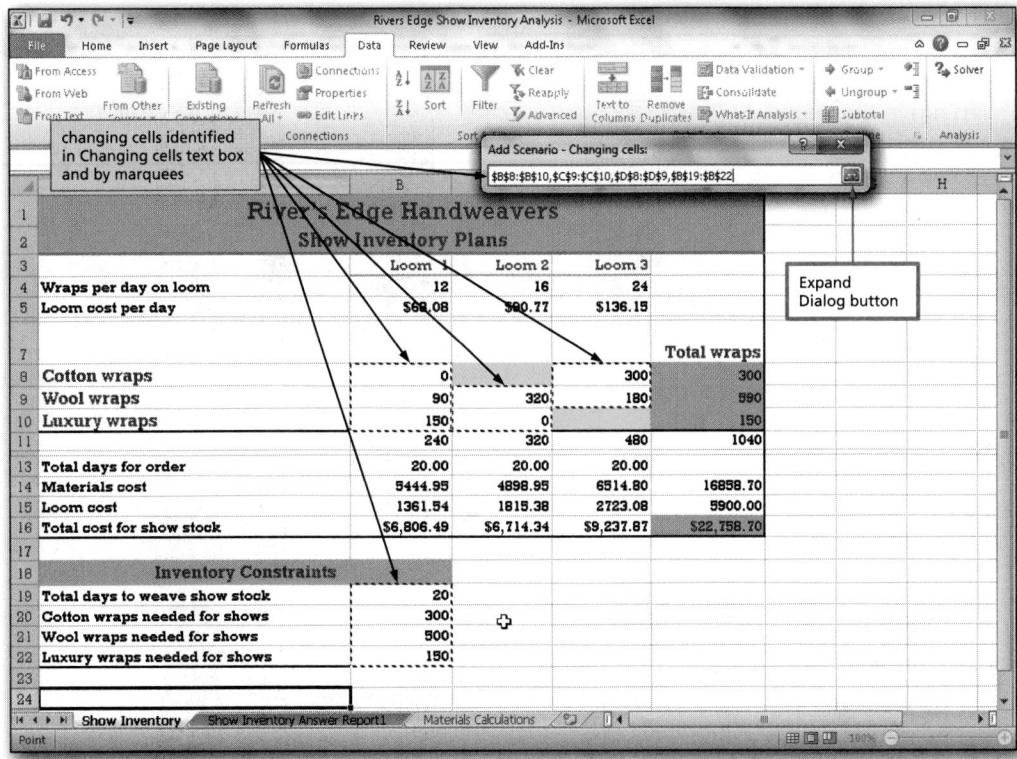

Figure 9–51

⑤

- Click the Expand Dialog button (Add Scenario — Changing cells dialog box) to change the Add Scenario dialog box to the Edit Scenario dialog box (Figure 9–52).

Figure 9–52

6

● Click the OK button (Edit Scenario dialog box) to accept the settings in the dialog box and display the Scenario Values dialog box (Figure 9–53).

Q&A

What does Excel display in the list of changing cells in the Scenario Values dialog box?

Excel displays the cells identified as changing cells in a numbered list with their current values (Figure 9–53). Names were assigned to these cells when the worksheet was created, and these are used rather than cell references in the numbered list. The names make it easier to determine which variables are included.

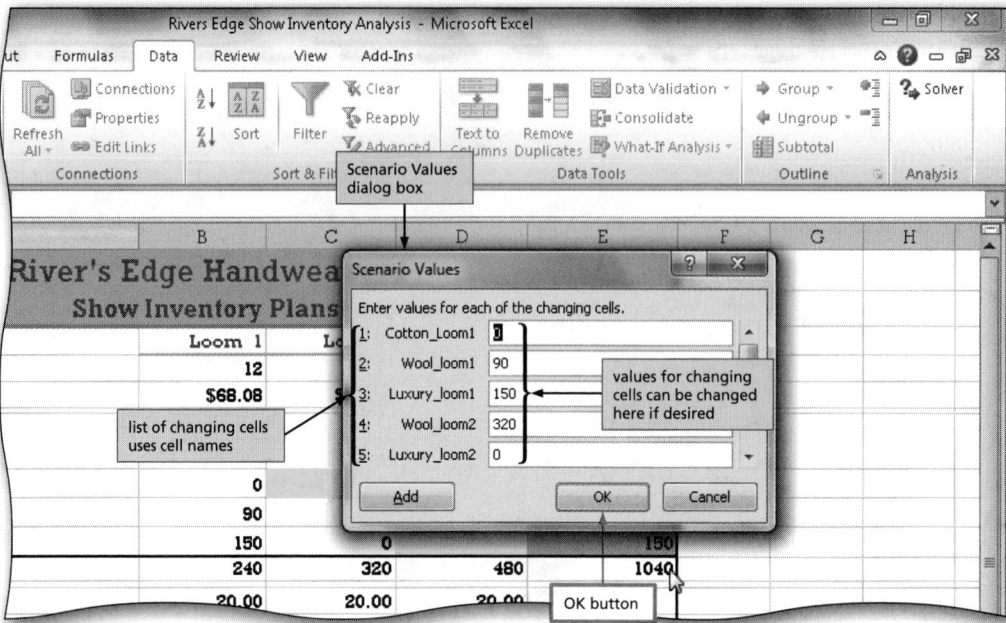

Figure 9–53

Q&A

What can I do with the scenario?

After the scenario has been saved, you can recall it at any time using Scenario Manager. In Figure 9–53, the values of the changing cells in the Scenario Values dialog box default to the current values in the worksheet. By changing the text boxes next to the cell names, you can save the scenario using values different from the current values.

7

● Click the OK button (Scenario Values dialog box) to display the Scenario Manager dialog box with the inventory1 scenario selected in the Scenarios list (Figure 9–54).

8

● Click the Close button in the Scenario Manager dialog box to save the inventory1 scenario in the workbook.

Figure 9–54

Adding Data for a New Scenario

After saving the inventory1 scenario, you can enter the data for the inventory2 scenario directly in the worksheet and then use Solver to solve the inventory2 scenario (Figure 9–55a) in the same way that you solved the inventory1 scenario. Because both scenarios are based on the same model, you do not need to reenter the constraints. The Answer Report (Figure 9–55b) meets the requirement that you create supporting documentation for your answer.

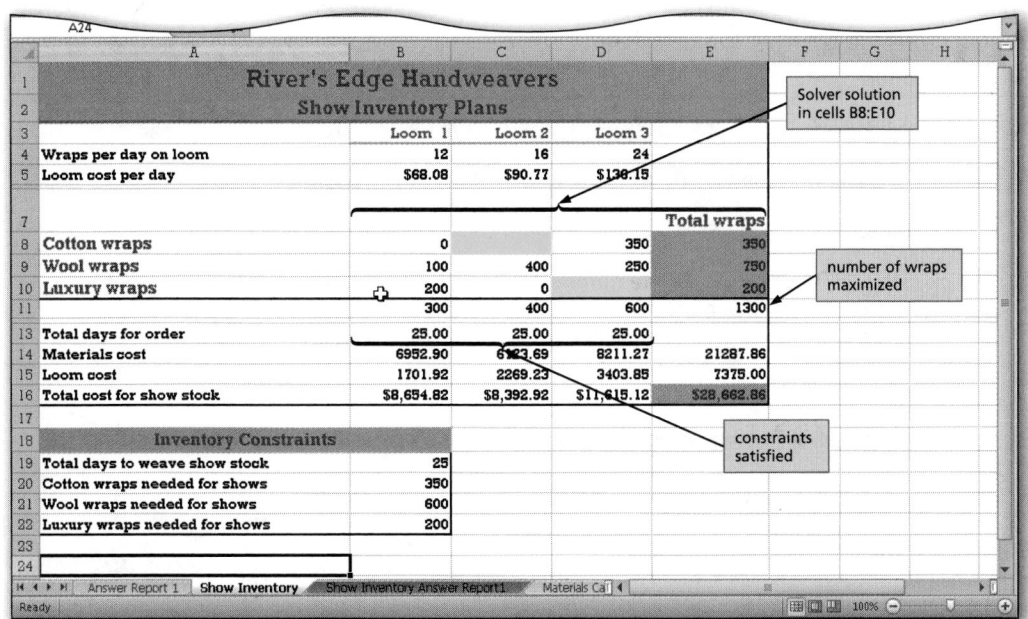

Figure 9–55 (a) Results of Using Solver with Second Scenario

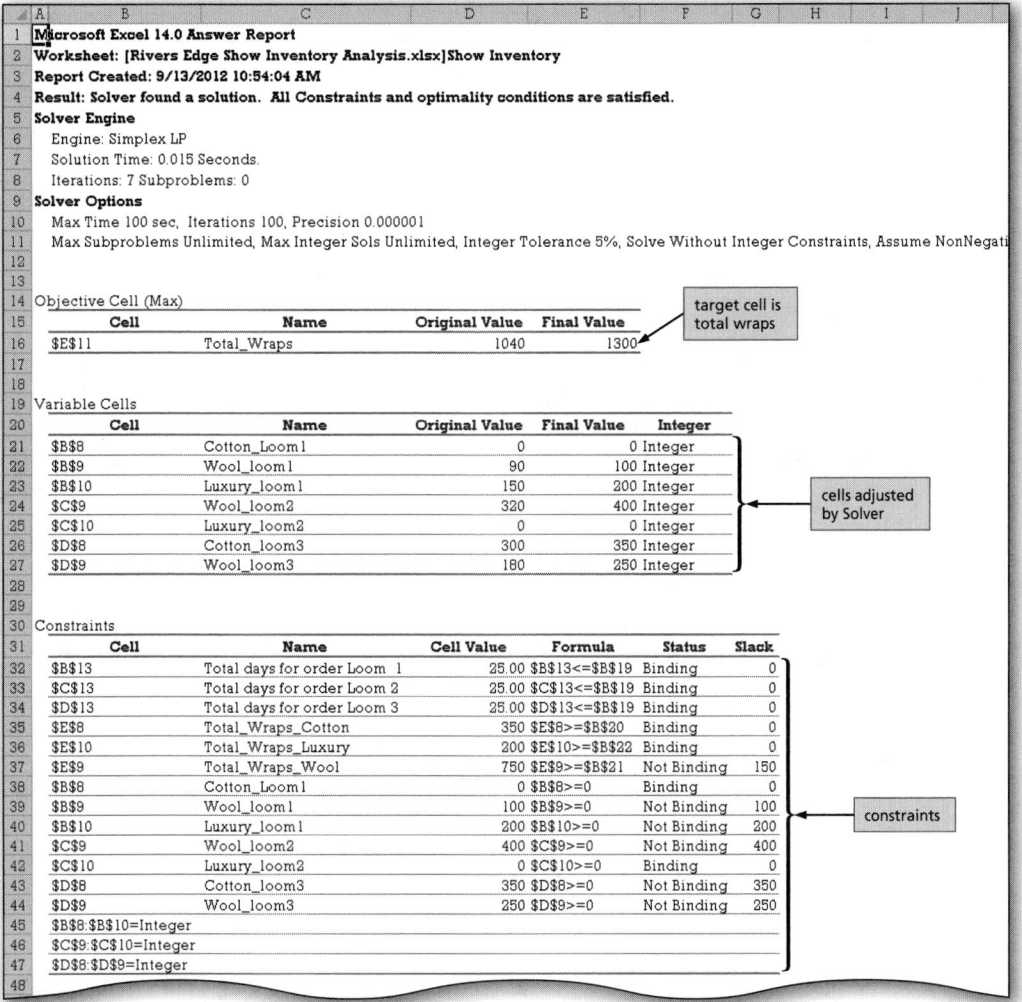

Figure 9–55 (b) Solver Answer Report for Second Scenario

BTW

Baseline Scenarios
For each model, it is helpful to define a baseline scenario that represents the starting assumptions. Even if the results of the baseline scenario do not figure prominently in the final analysis, they represent the starting point and should be saved.

BTW

Naming Cell Ranges
Naming ranges for use with input variables is helpful when dealing with multiple input variables. Name ranges for all input variables before creating your first scenario. Named ranges will make scenario reports easier to understand and interpret.

To Add the Data for a New Scenario

The constraints for the inventory2 scenario require that at least 350 cotton wraps, 600 wool wraps, and 200 luxury wraps be produced in 25 workdays. These values must be entered into the appropriate cells before you can use Solver.

The following steps add the data for a new scenario.

1 Click cell B19 and type **25** as the maximum days for the order.

2 Click cell B20 and type **350** as the number of cotton wraps.

3 Click cell B21 and type **600** as the number of wool wraps.

4 Click cell B22, type **200** as the number of luxury wraps, and then click cell A24 to deselect cell B22 (Figure 9–56).

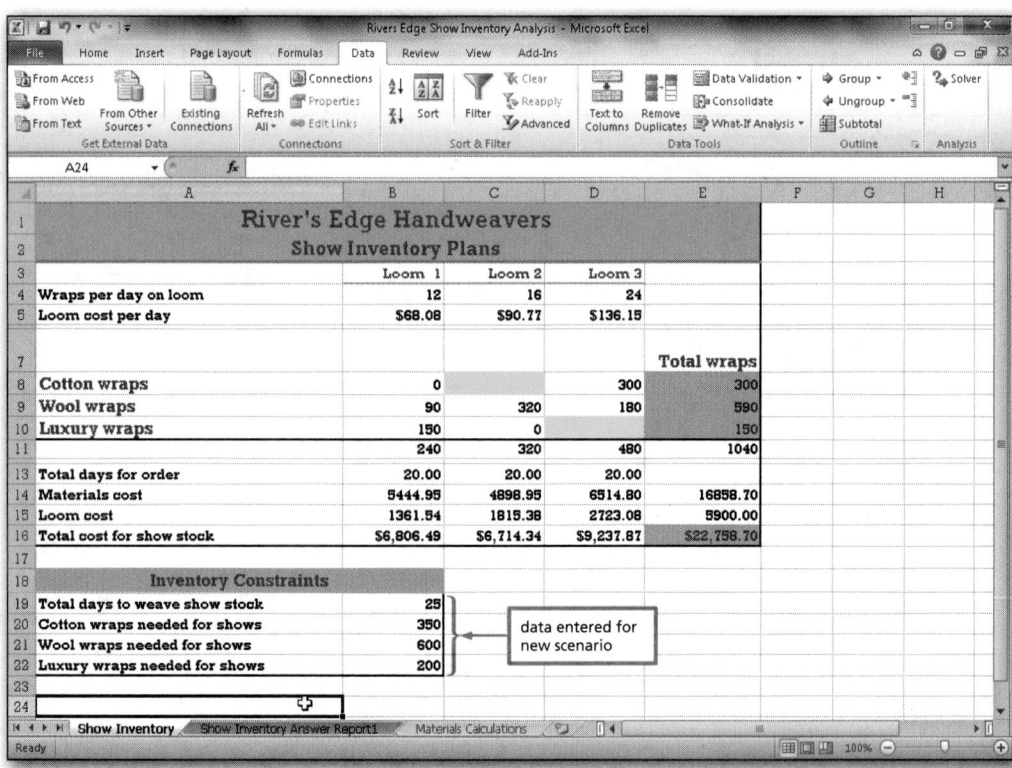

Figure 9–56

To Use Solver to Find a New Solution

After entering the new values, it is clear that the total number of wraps shown in cells E8:E10 does not satisfy the inventory constraints for the inventory2 scenario. You must now use Solver to determine if there is a solution for the constraints of inventory2. The following steps use Solver to seek a solution.

1

- Click the Solver button (Data tab | Analysis group) to display the Solver Parameters dialog box with the target cell, changing cells, and constraints used with the previous scenario (Figure 9–57).

Q&A

Why am I not updating the constraints?

When you set up the constraints in Solver for inventory1, you used cell references rather than actual numbers for the minimum number of each type of wrap. Entering the new figures in cells B19:B22 automatically updates the constraints.

Figure 9–57

2

- Click the Solve button (Solver Parameters dialog box) to solve the problem using Solver and the constraints just entered and display the Solver Results dialog box.

- Click Answer in the Reports list to select a report type (Figure 9–58).

Figure 9–58

3

- Click the OK button (Solver Results dialog box) to display the values found by Solver (Figure 9–59).

Q&A

What did Solver accomplish?

As shown in Figure 9–59, Solver found a solution that satisfies all of the constraints and maximizes the number of wraps produced. In this new scenario, inventory will be 1300 total wraps (cell E11), 350 cotton (cell E8), 750 wool (cell E9), and 200 luxury (cell E10).

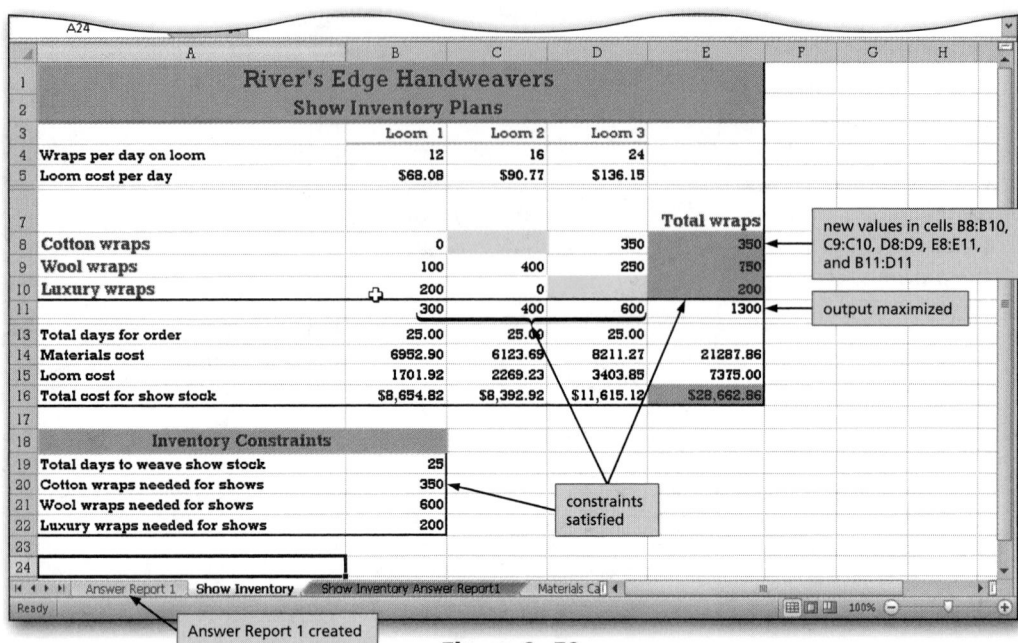

Figure 9–59

Q&A

My number of wraps differs slightly. Why?

The answers shown for the number of the various types of wraps for inventory2 may vary slightly on your computer depending on a number of factors that affect how Solver finds a solution. The maximum number of wraps, 1300, should not vary.

To View the Solver Answer Report for the Inventory2 Solution

The next step is to view the Answer Report for the inventory2 solution.

1

- Click and drag the Answer Report 1 tab to the right of the Show Inventory Answer Report1 tab to move the worksheet in the workbook.

- Rename the Answer Report 1 worksheet to **Show Inventory Answer Report2** to provide a descriptive name for the sheet tab.

- Change the tab color to Blue.

- Scroll down to view the remaining cells of the inventory2 Answer Report (Figure 9–60).

Figure 9–60

To Save the Second Solver Solution as a Scenario

With a second scenario created, you can begin to take advantage of the Scenario Manager. Scenario Manager allows you to compare multiple scenarios side by side. In order to use Scenario Manager for this, you must first save the second Solver solution as a scenario.

The following steps save the second Solver solution as a scenario.

1

• Click the Show Inventory sheet tab to make Show Inventory the active worksheet.

• Click the What-If Analysis button (Data tab | Data Tools group) to display the What-If Analysis menu (Figure 9–61).

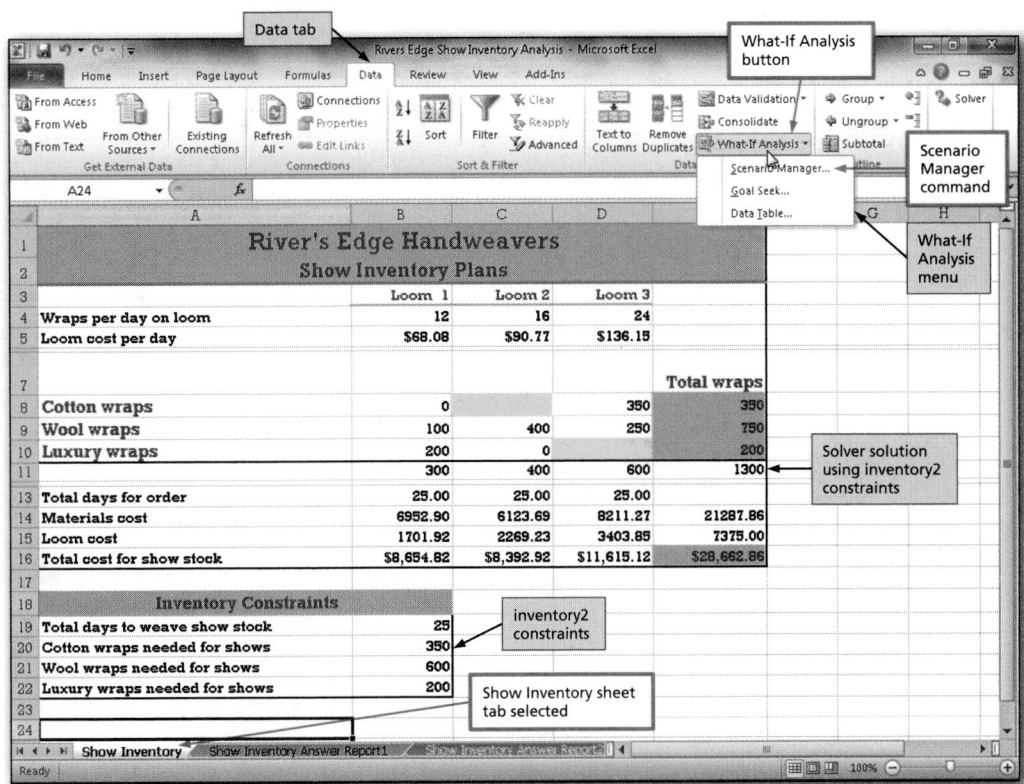

Figure 9–61

2

• Click Scenario Manager on the What-If Analysis menu to display the Scenario Manager dialog box (Figure 9–62).

Figure 9–62

• Click the Add button (Scenario Manager dialog box) to display the Add Scenario dialog box.

• Type **inventory2** in the Scenario name text box to name the new scenario (Figure 9–63).

Figure 9–63

• Click the OK button (Add Scenario dialog box) to display the Scenario Values dialog box with the current values from the worksheet (Figure 9–64).

Figure 9–64

5

• Click the OK button (Scenario Values dialog box) to display the updated Scenarios list in the Scenario Manager dialog box (Figure 9–65).

6

• Click the Close button (Scenario Manager dialog box) to save the inventory2 scenario and close the dialog box.

Figure 9–65

To Show a Saved Scenario

To display any scenario in the workbook, use the Show button in the Scenario Manager dialog box. The following steps display the inventory1 scenario created earlier.

1

• Click the What-If Analysis button (Data tab | Data Tools group) to display the What-If Analysis menu (Figure 9–66).

Figure 9–66

2

• Click Scenario Manager on the What-If Analysis menu to display the Scenario Manager dialog box.

• Select inventory1 in the Scenarios list (Figure 9–67).

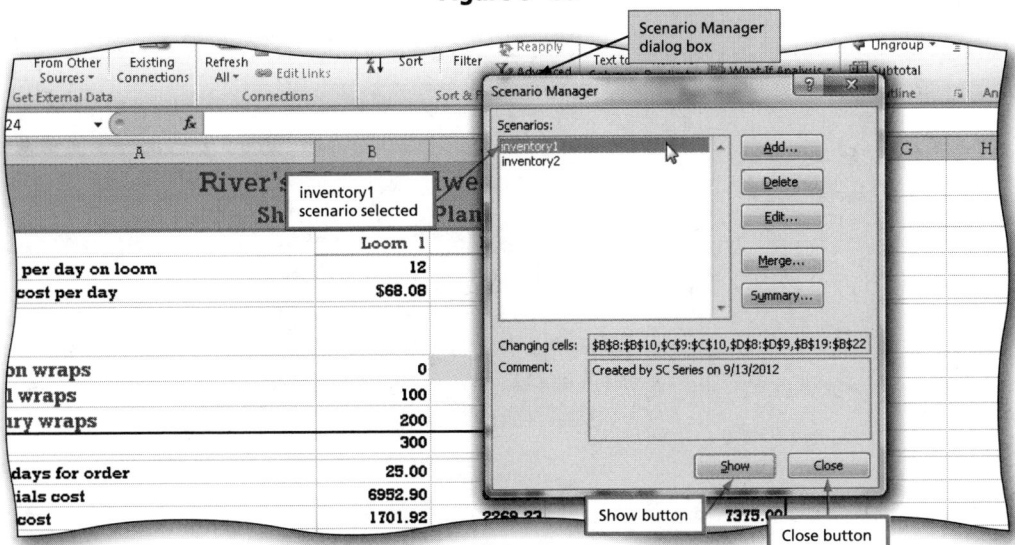

Figure 9–67

3

- Click the Show button (Scenario Manager dialog box) to display the data for the selected scenario in the worksheet.

- Click the Close button (Scenario Manager dialog box) to close the dialog box (Figure 9–68).

Q&A

Do I have to use Scenario Manager to switch between scenarios?

Once you have viewed two or more scenarios in a row, you can use the Undo and Redo commands to switch between them, as an alternative to using the Scenario Manager.

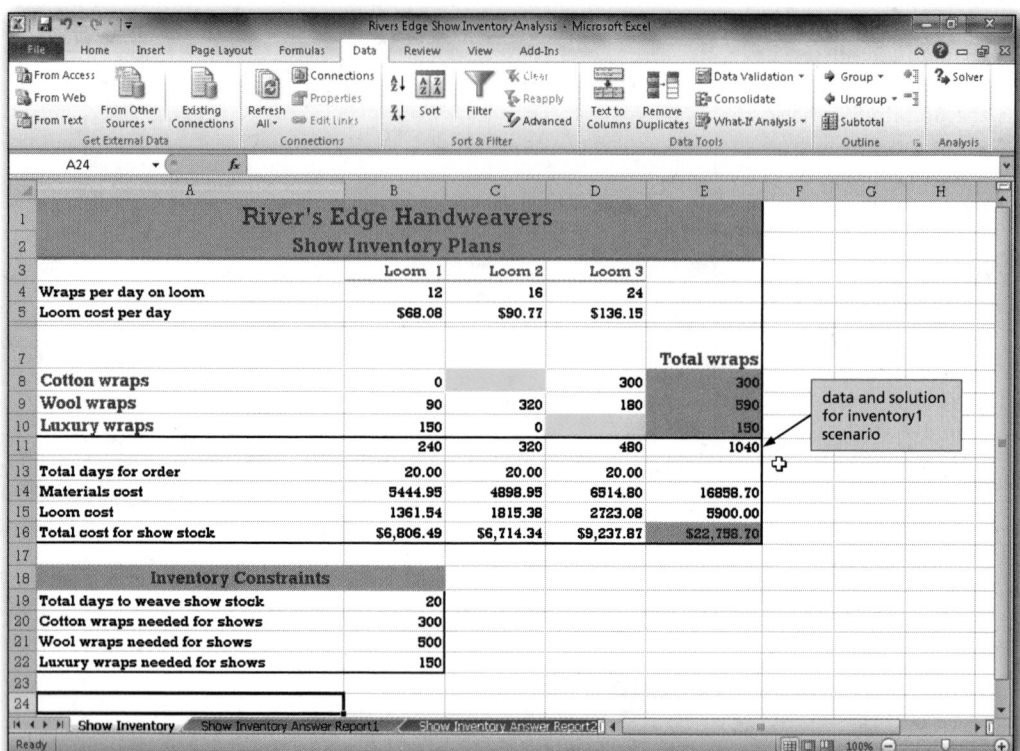

Figure 9–68

Summarizing Scenarios

You can create a Scenario Summary worksheet or a Scenario PivotTable worksheet to review and analyze various what-if scenarios when making decisions. A **Scenario Summary worksheet** generated by the Scenario Manager actually is a worksheet in outline format (Figure 9–69a) that you can print and manipulate just like any other worksheet. Chapter 5 presented skills that you can use to manipulate outline features for information presentation.

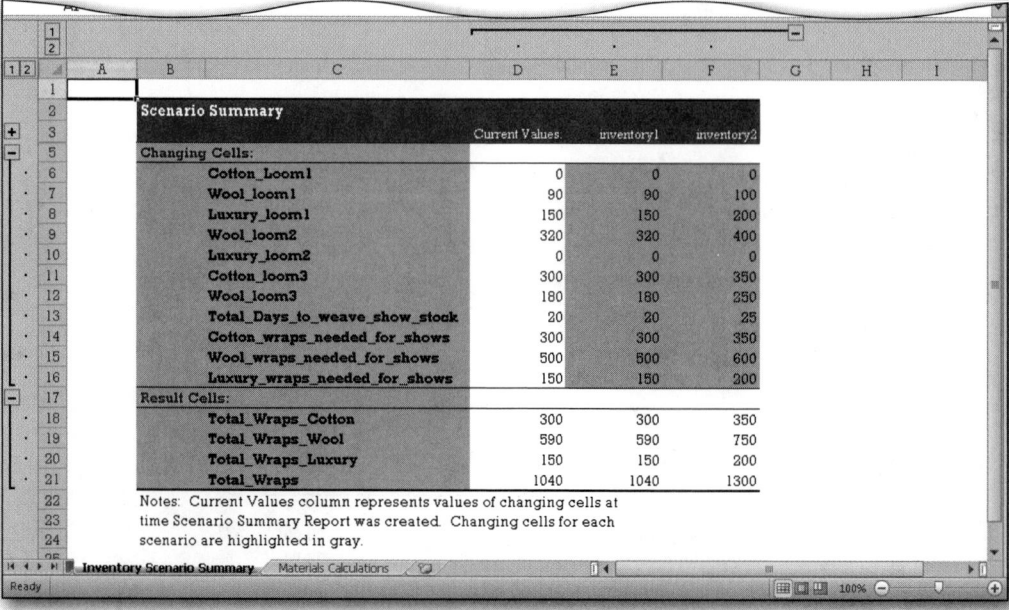

Figure 9–69 (a) Scenario Summary Worksheet

The **Scenario PivotTable worksheet** (Figure 9–69b) generated by the Scenario Manager also is a worksheet that you can print and manipulate like other worksheets. PivotTables summarize large amounts of data, and can be rearranged and regrouped to show the data in various forms. Chapter 8 presented skills that can be used to analyze summary data using PivotTables. The Scenario PivotTable worksheet allows you to compare the results of scenarios.

Figure 9–69 (b) Scenario PivotTable

To Create a Scenario Summary Worksheet

The Scenario Summary worksheet in Figure 9–69a shows the number of each type of wrap produced, and total number of wraps produced for the current worksheet values and the inventory1 and inventory2 scenarios. The optimal number of each type of wrap to produce on each loom calculated by Solver is shown for both show inventories.

The following steps create a Scenario Summary worksheet.

1
- Select cells E8:E11 to identify the result cells to summarize.

- Click the What-If Analysis button (Data tab | Data Tools group) to display the What-If Analysis menu (Figure 9–70).

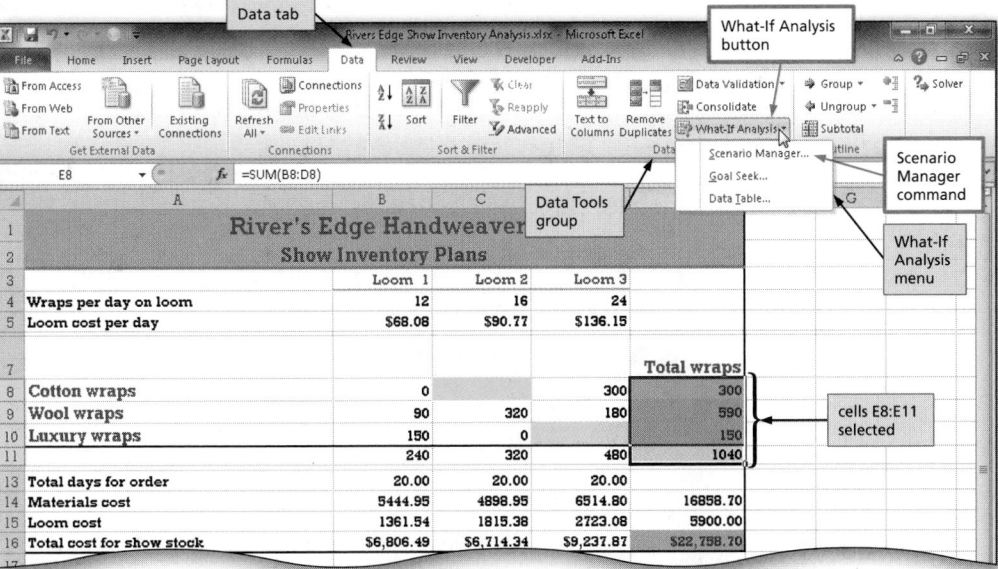

Figure 9–70

2

● Click Scenario Manager on the What-If Analysis menu to display the Scenario Manager dialog box (Figure 9–71).

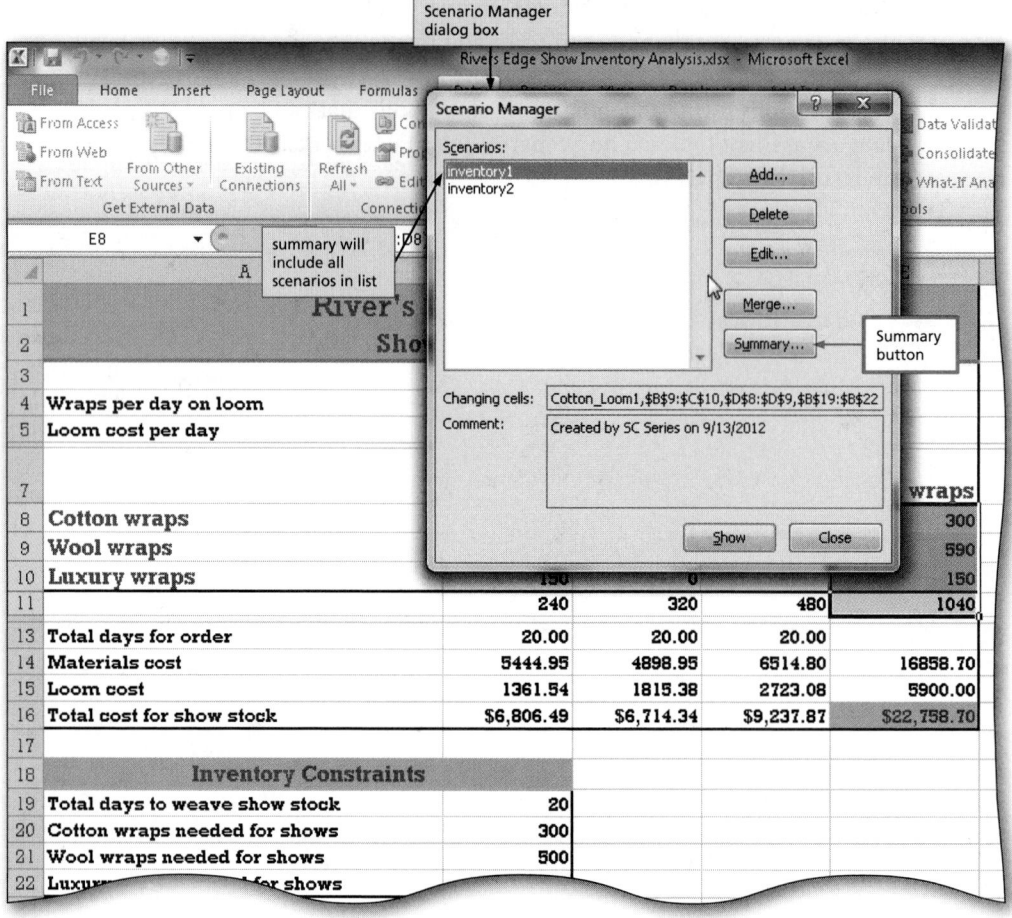

Figure 9–71

3

● Click the Summary button to display the Scenario Summary dialog box (Figure 9–72).

Figure 9–72

4

- Click the OK button (Scenario Summary dialog box) to generate a Scenario Summary report.

- Rename the Scenario Summary worksheet to **Inventory Scenario Summary** to provide a descriptive name for the sheet.

- Change the tab color to Black, Text 1.

- Drag the Inventory Scenario Summary tab to the right of the Show Inventory Answer Report2 tab to move the worksheet in the workbook (Figure 9–73).

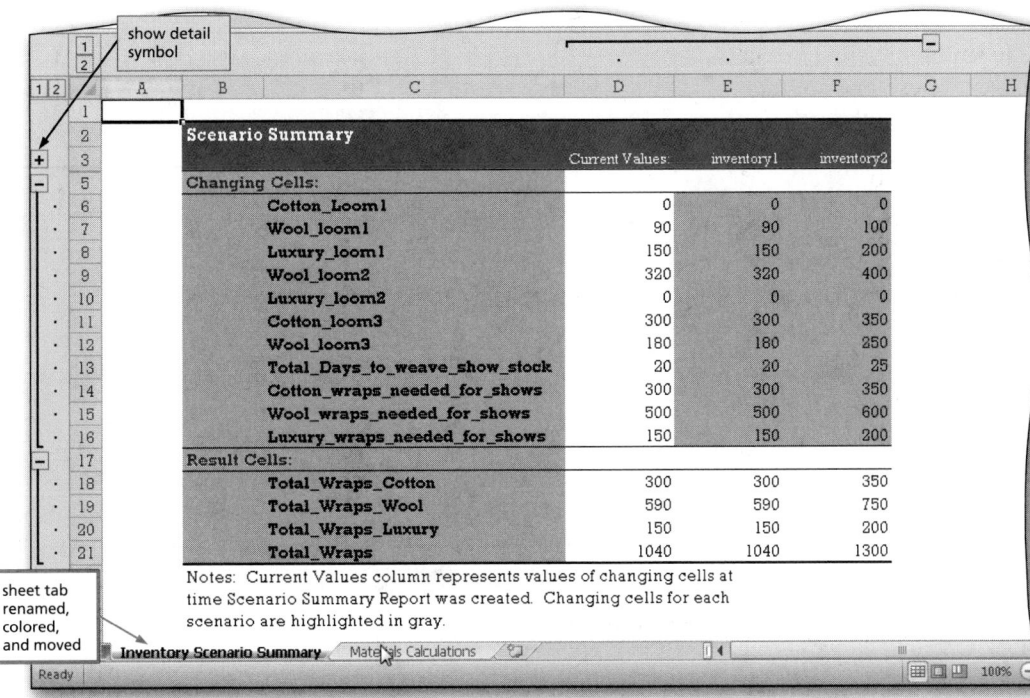

Figure 9–73

Q&A What is shown in the Inventory Scenario Summary worksheet?

The Inventory Scenario Summary worksheet shows the results of the current values in the Show Inventory worksheet and the results of any scenarios you have created. In Figure 9–73, current value results are shown in column D, and results for scenarios inventory1 and inventory2 are shown in columns E and F, respectively.

Working with an Outlined Worksheet

As shown in Figure 9–73, Excel automatically outlines the Scenario Summary worksheet. The outline symbols for expanding and collapsing appear above and to the left of the worksheet. Chapter 5 provided instruction on working with outlined worksheets. You can hide or display levels of detail by using the hide detail and show detail symbols. You can also use the row and column level symbols to collapse or expand rows and columns.

The outline feature is especially useful when working with very large worksheets. With smaller worksheets, the feature may not provide any real benefits. You can remove an outline by clicking the Ungroup button arrow in the Outline group on the Data tab and then clicking Clear Outline.

BTW

Scenario Summary Details
Clicking Show Detail on the Scenario Summary worksheet will display any information entered in the Comments box of the Scenario Manager dialog box, along with creation and modification information.

To Create a Scenario PivotTable Worksheet

Excel also can create a Scenario PivotTable Report worksheet to help analyze and compare the results of multiple scenarios. A Scenario PivotTable Report worksheet gives you the ability to summarize the scenario data and reorganize the rows and columns to obtain different views of the summarized data. Manipulation and interpretation of PivotTable reports was covered in some detail in Chapter 8. The Scenario PivotTable worksheet to be created in this chapter is shown in Figure 9–69b on page EX 601. The PivotTable summarizes the inventory1 and inventory2 scenarios and shows the result cells for the two scenarios for easy comparison.

The following steps create the Scenario PivotTable worksheet shown in Figure 9–69b.

1
- Click the Show Inventory sheet tab to make Show Inventory the active worksheet.
- Click the What-If Analysis button (Data tab | Data Tools group) to display the What-If Analysis menu.
- Click Scenario Manager to display the Scenario Manager dialog box (Figure 9–74).

Figure 9–74

2
- Click the Summary button (Scenario Manager dialog box) to display the Scenario Summary dialog box.
- In the Scenario Summary dialog box, click the Scenario PivotTable report option button in the Report type area (Figure 9–75).

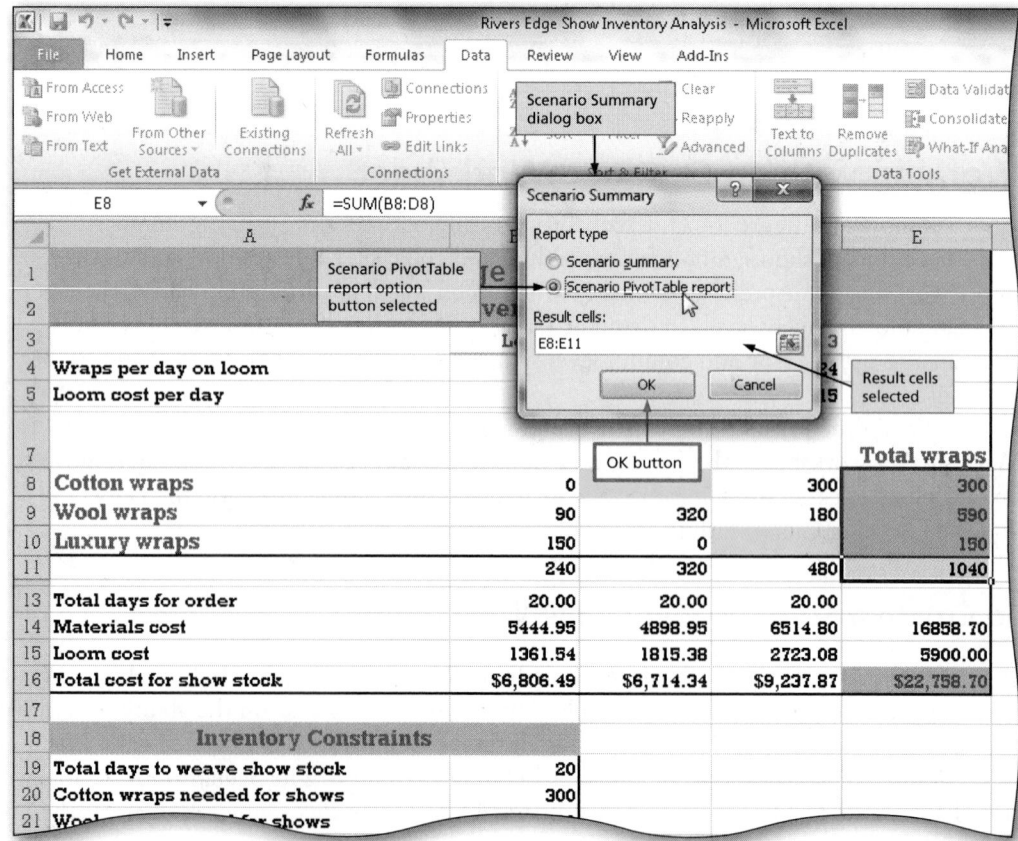

Figure 9–75

3

- Click the OK button (Scenario Summary dialog box) to display the Scenario PivotTable (Figure 9–76).

Figure 9–76

4

- Rename the Scenario PivotTable worksheet to **Inventory Scenario PivotTable** to provide a descriptive name for the worksheet.

- Change the tab color for the Inventory Scenario PivotTable worksheet to Rose, Accent 6.

- Drag the Inventory Scenario PivotTable tab to the right of the Inventory Scenario Summary tab to move the worksheet in the workbook.

- Reduce the width of column A so that columns A through E are all visible (Figure 9–77).

Figure 9–77

Q&A

How can I use the PivotTable?

After the PivotTable is created, you can treat it like any other worksheet. Thus, you can print or chart a PivotTable. If you update the data in one of the scenarios, click the Refresh All button on the Data tab on the Ribbon to update the PivotTable. If you show a scenario and merely change values on the scenario worksheet, it is not the same as changing the scenario. If you want to change the data in a scenario, you must use Scenario Manager.

- Click the Save button on the Quick Access toolbar to save the workbook.

Break Point: If you wish to take a break, this is a good place to do so. You can quit Excel now. To resume at a later time, start Excel, open the file called Rivers Edge Show Inventory Analysis, and continue following the steps from this location forward.

BTW

Certification
The Microsoft Office Specialist (MOS) program provides an opportunity for you to obtain a valuable industry credential — proof that you have the Excel 2010 skills required by employers. For more information, visit the Excel 2010 Certification Web page (scsite.com/ex2010/cert).

Preparing a Workbook for Distribution

Excel provides several methods to protect your privacy or data that you may not want to share with others. Before distributing your workbook to others, you should consider what type of hidden information may be in your document. In previous chapters, you have learned to hide rows and columns, protect cells, protect worksheets, and protect workbooks. Other types of information may be hidden in a workbook. Excel provides a tool called the Document Inspector to inspect and report such information. You then easily can remove the hidden information or choose to leave the information in the document.

When distributing a workbook, you also should consider whether the intended recipients have the most recent version of Excel. If this is not the case, Excel allows you to save a workbook for use in previous versions of Excel, such as Excel 97-2003. When you save a workbook in the Excel 97-2003 Workbook file format, Excel will invoke the Compatibility Checker, which notifies you if any of the content of your workbook cannot be saved in that format. Additionally, the Compatibility Checker will inform you if any content will not appear the same, such as cell or chart formatting.

To Inspect a Document for Hidden and Personal Information

The Document Inspector should be used before sharing a workbook publicly or when you suspect extraneous information remains in hidden rows and columns, hidden worksheets, document properties, headers and footers, or worksheet comments.

The following steps inspect the Rivers Edge Show Inventory Analysis workbook for hidden and personal information.

- Save the workbook with the name Rivers Edge Show Inventory Analysis2.

- Click the Show Inventory sheet tab to make Show Inventory the active worksheet.

- Click File on the Ribbon to open the Backstage view.

- If necessary, click the Info tab in the Backstage view to display the Info gallery (Figure 9–78).

Q&A

Why am I saving this workbook under a different name?

When preparing a workbook for distribution, you may decide to use the Document Inspector to make changes to the document. Saving the workbook with a different name ensures that you will not lose information, and that you will have a copy of the workbook with all information for your records.

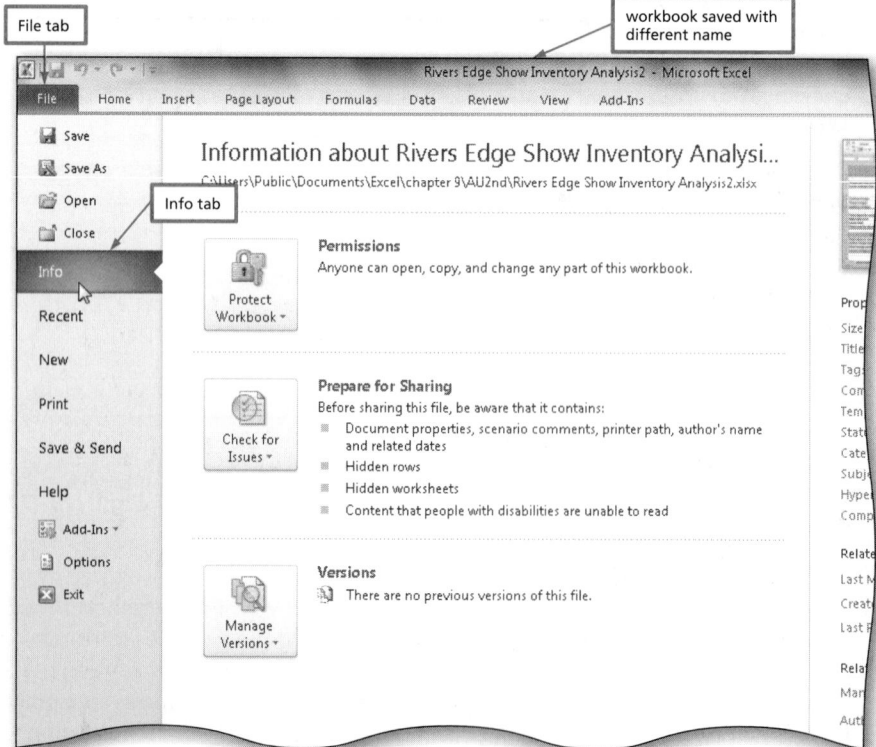

Figure 9–78

2

• Click the Check for Issues button in the Info gallery to display the Check for Issues menu (Figure 9–79).

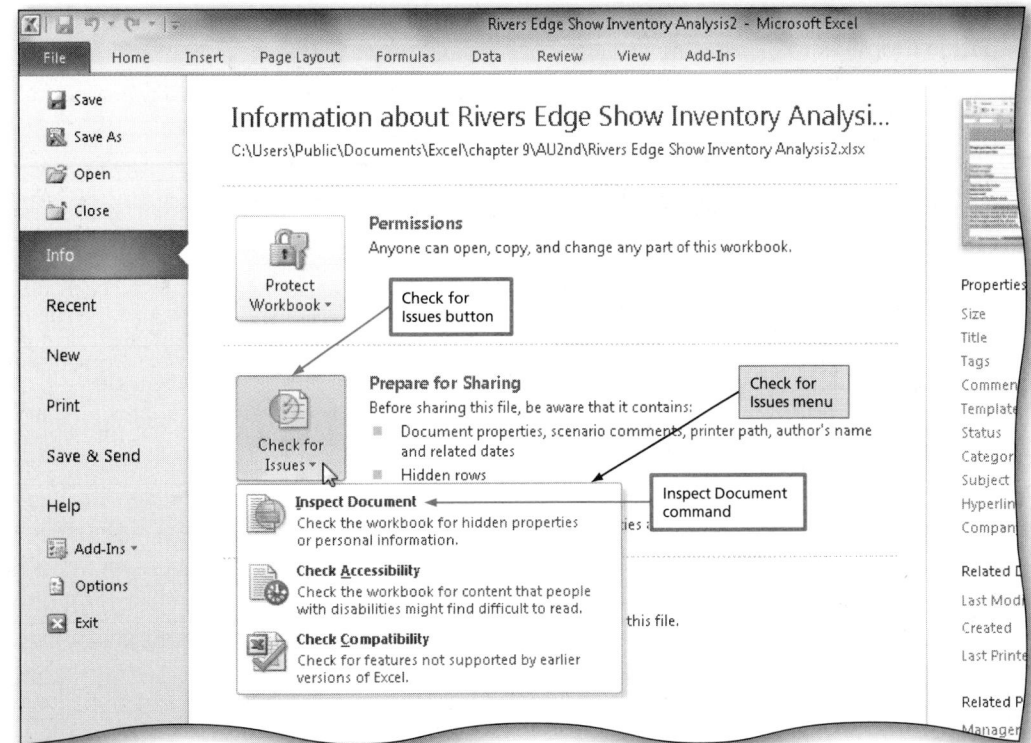

Figure 9–79

3

• Click Inspect Document to display the Document Inspector dialog box (Figure 9–80).

What is shown in the Document Inspector dialog box?

The Document Inspector dialog box allows you to choose which types of content to inspect. Unless you are comfortable with some items not being checked, you typically should leave all of the items selected. In Figure 9–80, the Document Inspector will search the document properties, which may contain your name. You purposefully want your name or other personal information in the document properties, so you may remove the check mark from the Document Properties and Personal Information check box.

Figure 9–80

4

- Click the Inspect button (Document Inspector dialog box) to run the Document Inspector and display its results (Figure 9–81).

Q&A

What did the Document Inspector find?

The Document Inspector found document properties, comments in the scenarios created in this chapter, a hidden row in the Scenario PivotTable, and two hidden worksheets. The Remove All buttons in the dialog box allow you quickly to remove the items found. In many instances, you

Figure 9–81

may want to take notes of the results and then investigate and remedy each one separately. In the Rivers Edge Show Inventory Analysis2 workbook, all of these items found by the Document Inspector are expected and do not need to be remedied.

5

- Click the Close button (Document Inspector dialog box) to close the dialog box.

Information Rights Management

Information Rights Management (IRM) is a feature of Excel that allows you to restrict access to workbooks. With IRM, you can restrict who can view, modify, print, forward, and copy a workbook. The types of restrictions include a variety of options. For example, expiration dates for reading or modifying a workbook are available. Before using IRM, your computer first must be configured with IRM, as should the computers of anyone attempting to use a document that includes IRM features.

When IRM is installed properly on your computer, the Protect Workbook submenu in the Permissions group in the Backstage view includes several commands for limiting access to the workbook. You can limit who can access the workbook, and who can make changes to the workbook. For more information about IRM, search Excel Help for Information Rights Management.

To Check Compatibility and Save a Workbook Using the Excel 97-2003 Workbook File Format and Mark a Workbook as Final

You occasionally need to save a workbook for use in previous versions of Excel. Each version of Excel includes varying features, so you should use the Compatibility Checker to determine if the features you use in your workbook are compatible with earlier versions of Excel.

Before sharing a workbook with others, you can mark the workbook as being final. When another user of your workbook opens the workbook, he or she will be notified that you have marked the workbook as final. The workbook can still be edited, but only if the user clicks a button to indicate that they want to edit the workbook.

The following steps check the compatibility of the workbook while saving the workbook in the Excel 97-2003 Workbook file format.

1

- Click the Save As command (File tab) to display the Save As dialog box.

- Click the 'Save as type' button and then click Excel 97-2003 Workbook to select the file format (Figure 9–82).

Figure 9–82

2

- Click the Save button (Save As dialog box) to display the Microsoft Excel - Compatibility Checker dialog box.

- Drag an edge of the dialog box to resize it so it displays all the issues (Figure 9–83).

Q&A What is shown in the Microsoft Excel - Compatibility Checker dialog box?

The Summary column of the list of issues shows that both the PivotTable and the style used to format the PivotTable are not compatible with previous versions of Excel. While the workbook still will be saved in the Excel 97-2003 file format, the Inventory Scenario PivotTable will not be available as a PivotTable report. In addition, some cell formatting is unique to Excel 2010. These formats will be converted to the nearest approximation in the earlier version of Excel.

Figure 9–83

3

• Click the Continue button (Microsoft Excel - Compatibility Checker dialog box) to save the workbook in the Excel 97-2003 Workbook file format.

• Click File on the Ribbon to open the Backstage view.

• Click the Protect Workbook button to display the Protect Workbook menu (Figure 9–84).

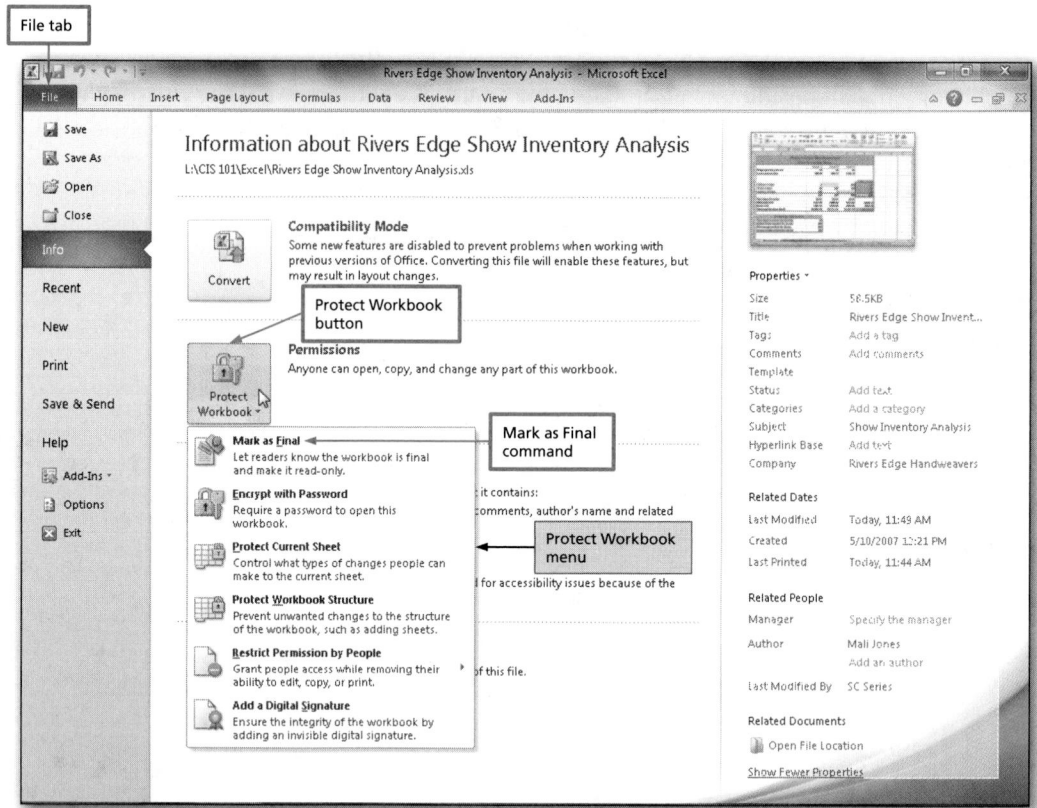

Figure 9–84

4

• Click Mark as Final to display the Microsoft Excel dialog box (Figure 9–85).

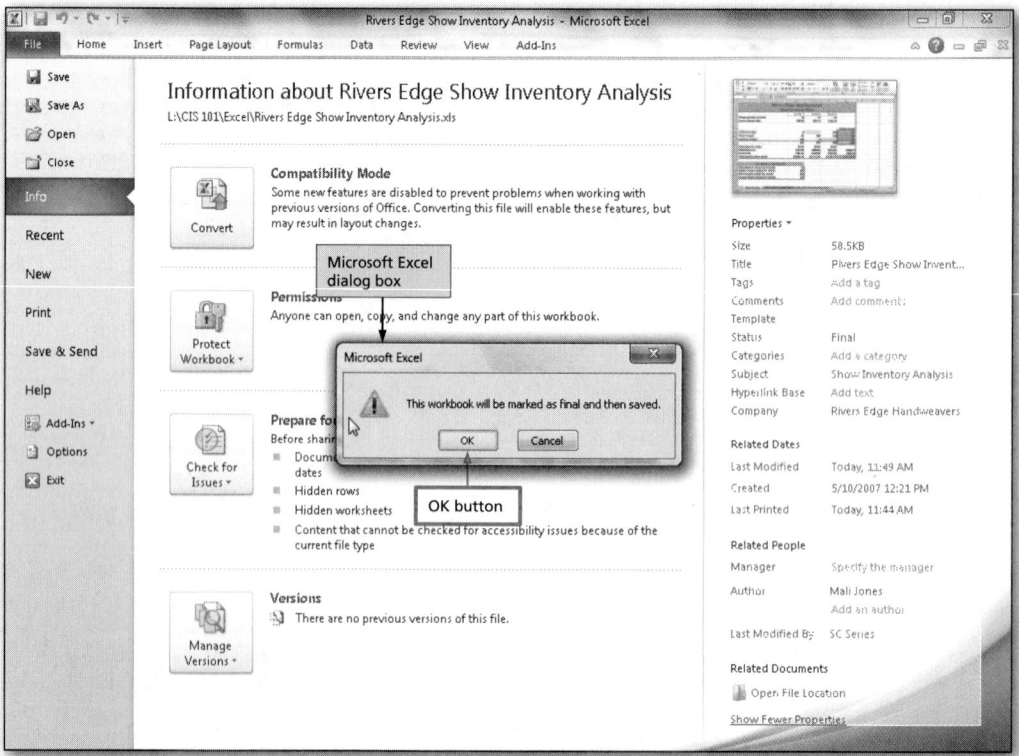

Figure 9–85

5

- Click the OK button (Microsoft Excel dialog box) to indicate you want to mark the workbook as final.

- If necessary, click the Continue button (Microsoft Excel - Compatibility Checker dialog box) to display the Microsoft Excel dialog box.

- Click the OK button to close the Microsoft Excel dialog box and mark the workbook as final (Figure 9–86).

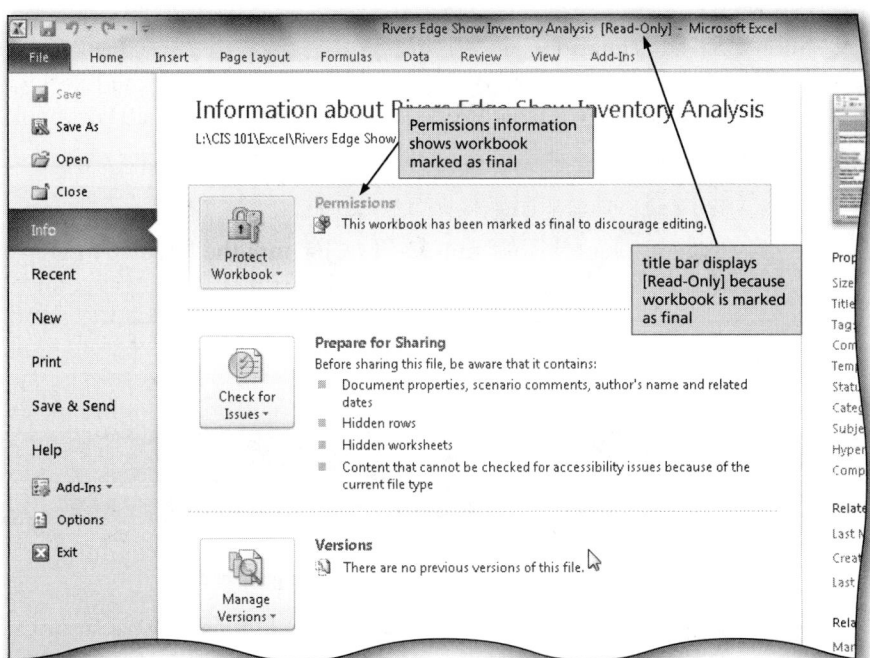

Figure 9–86

To Quit Excel

The following steps quit Excel.

1 Click the Close button on the right side of the title bar.

2 If Excel displays a Microsoft Excel dialog box, click the Don't Save button.

BTW

Quick Reference
For a table that lists how to complete the tasks covered in this book using the mouse, Ribbon, shortcut menu, and keyboard, see the Quick Reference Summary at the back of this book, or visit the Excel 2010 Quick Reference Web page (scsite.com/ex2010/qr).

Chapter Summary

In this chapter, you learned how to use a number of techniques to solve problems using Excel, including using trial and error, goal seeking, and Solver; analyze a worksheet using formula auditing techniques; use data validation on cells and inform a user about the validation rules; manage different problems on the same worksheet using Scenario Manager and then summarize the results of the scenarios with a Scenario Summary worksheet and a Scenario PivotTable worksheet; prepare a workbook for distribution; and save a workbook for use in a previous version of Excel. The items listed below include all the new Excel skills you have learned in this chapter.

1. Trace Precedents (EX 561)
2. Review Precedents on a Different Worksheet (EX 563)
3. Remove the Precedent Arrows (EX 564)
4. Trace Dependents (EX 565)
5. Remove the Dependent Arrows (EX 566)
6. Open the Watch Window and Add Cell Watches (EX 566)
7. Use Error Checking to Correct Errors (EX 569)
8. Add Data Validation to Cells (EX 573)
9. Use Trial and Error to Attempt to Solve a Complex Problem (EX 576)
10. Use the Goal Seek Command to Attempt to Solve a Complex Problem (EX 578)
11. Circle Invalid Data and Clear Validation Circles (EX 579)
12. Use Solver to Find the Optimal Solution to a Complex Problem (EX 583)
13. View the Solver Answer Report (EX 587)
14. Save the Current Data as a Scenario (EX 590)
15. Add the Data for a New Scenario (EX 594)
16. Use Solver to Find a New Solution (EX 594)
17. View the Solver Answer Report for the Inventory2 Solution (EX 596)

18. Save the Second Solver Solution as a Scenario (EX 597)
19. Show a Saved Scenario (EX 599)
20. Create a Scenario Summary Worksheet (EX 601)
21. Create a Scenario PivotTable Worksheet (EX 603)

22. Inspect a Document for Hidden and Personal Information (EX 606)
23. Check Compatibility and Save a Workbook Using the Excel 97-2003 Workbook File Format and Mark a Workbook as Final (EX 608)

If you have a SAM 2010 user profile, your instructor may have assigned an autogradable version of this assignment. If so, log into the SAM 2010 Web site at www.cengage.com/sam2010 to download the instruction and start files.

Learn It Online

Test your knowledge of chapter content and key terms.

Instructions: To complete the Learn It Online exercises, start your browser, click the Address bar, and then enter the Web address `scsite.com/ex2010/learn`. When the Excel 2010 Learn It Online page is displayed, click the link for the exercise you want to complete and then read the instructions.

Chapter Reinforcement TF, MC, and SA
A series of true/false, multiple choice, and short answer questions that test your knowledge of the chapter content.

Flash Cards
An interactive learning environment where you identify chapter key terms associated with displayed definitions.

Practice Test
A series of multiple choice questions that test your knowledge of chapter content and key terms.

Who Wants To Be a Computer Genius?
An interactive game that challenges your knowledge of chapter content in the style of a television quiz show.

Wheel of Terms
An interactive game that challenges your knowledge of chapter key terms in the style of the television show *Wheel of Fortune*.

Crossword Puzzle Challenge
A crossword puzzle that challenges your knowledge of key terms presented in the chapter.

Apply Your Knowledge

Reinforce the skills and apply the concepts you learned in this chapter.

Calculating the Units for a Shipment
Note: To complete this assignment, you will be required to use the Data Files for Students. See the inside back cover of this book for instructions on downloading the Data Files for Students, or contact your instructor for information about accessing the required files.

Instructions: Start Excel. Open the workbook Apply 9-1 CareFree Fruit Company from the Data Files for Students, and then save the workbook as Apply 9-1 CareFree Fruit Company Complete.

You work for CareFree Fruit Company, which ships three kinds of fruit baskets to gift shops. You need to use Solver to find the optimal mix of baskets so that each shipment includes at least 12 baskets. The company has up to 40 units of Basket 1, 25 units of Basket 2, and 15 units of Basket 3 available for shipping at any one time. Maximize total profit for the shipment. Figure 9–87 shows the completed Costs and Shipping worksheet.

Figure 9–87

Perform the following tasks.

1. Use Solver to find a solution to the problem so that the total profit on the shipment (cell E12) is maximized. Allow Solver to change cells B9, C9, and D9. The total number of baskets should be greater than or equal to 12. The results in cells B9, C9, and D9 should be integer values. Add constraints to Solver to limit the number of baskets to no more than 40 of Basket 1, 25 of Basket 2, and 15 of Basket 3. Use the Simplex LP option in Solver.

2. Instruct Solver to create the Answer Report for your solution. Solver should find the answer as shown in Figure 9–87.

3. Trace precedents for cell E13 by clicking the Trace Precedents button (Formulas tab | Formula Auditing group) two times. Remove the precedent arrows. Trace dependents for cell C9 by clicking the Trace Dependents button (Formulas tab | Formula Auditing group) two times. Remove the dependent arrows.

4. Use the Watch Window to monitor cells E11:E13. Change values in the range B9:D9 and view changes in the Watch Window. Close the Watch Window. Use the Undo button on the Quick Access toolbar to change the values in the range B9:D9 to their original values.

5. Change the document properties as specified by your instructor. Add a worksheet header to the original worksheet with your name, course number, and other information as specified by your instructor.

6. Submit the assignment as requested by your instructor.

Extend Your Knowledge

Extend the skills you learned in this chapter and experiment with new skills. You may need to use Help to complete the assignment.

Working with Data Validation Rules

Note: To complete this assignment, you will be required to use the Data Files for Students. See the inside back cover of this book for instructions on downloading the Data Files for Students, or contact your instructor for information about accessing the required files.

Instructions: Start Excel. Open the workbook Extend 9-1 Car4You Calculator from the Data Files for Students, and then save the workbook as Extend 9-1 Car4You Calculator Complete.

You have been asked to create data validation rules in an Excel worksheet that calculates rental charges for Car4You Rentals, a company that rents cars in Southern California. Car4You Rentals rents four types of cars, each at a different daily rate for up to two weeks (14 days). They also provide extra services such as child seats for an additional daily rate and offer a 15% discount for customers who rent cars in the summer. Figure 9-88 shows the completed Rental Calculator worksheet.

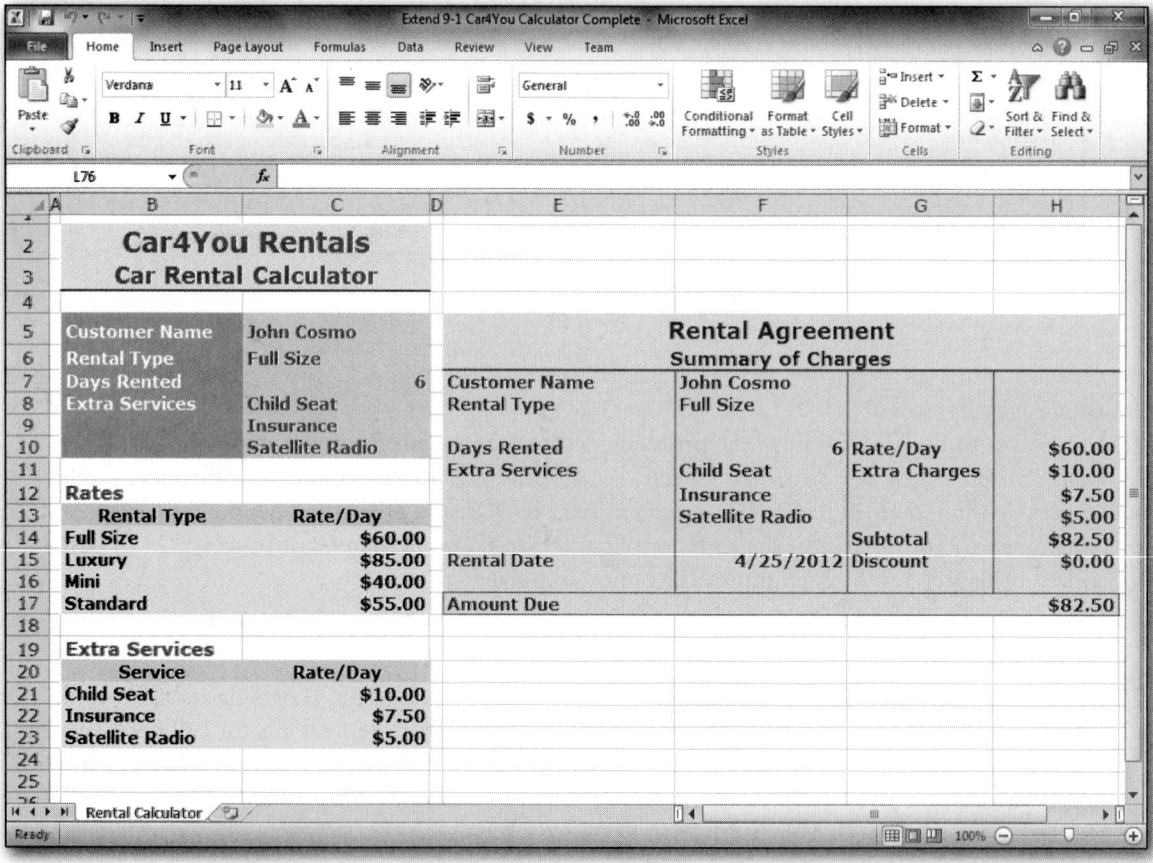

Figure 9-88

Perform the following tasks:
1. In cell C5 on the Rental Calculator worksheet, enter a data validation rule that allows users to enter any value. Use **Customer Name** as the input message title and **Please enter the customer's full name.** as the input message. Because entering the full name is not required, an error alert is not necessary. Remove the check mark from the 'Show error alert after invalid data is entered' check box.

2. In cell C6, enter a data validation rule that requires users to select a rental type from a list. Allow users to select the data from a list of rental types, which is contained in the range B14:B17. Do not allow users to leave cell C6 blank. Use **Rental Type** as the input message title and **Select the type of car the customer rented.** as the input message. Because entering the rental type is required, choose a Stop style of error alert. Use **Invalid Rental Type** as the error alert title and **Select Mini, Standard, Full Size, or Luxury from the list.** as the error message.

3. In cell C7, enter a data validation rule that requires users to enter a whole number from 1 to 14 for the number of days the customer rented a car. Do not allow users to leave cell C7 blank. Use **Days Rented** as the input message title and enter an input message that reminds users to enter the number of days the customer used the car. Choose an appropriate style of error alert. Use **Invalid Entry** as the error alert title and enter an error message that instructs users to enter a number from 1 to 14.

4. In cell C8, enter another data validation rule that allows users to select a valid entry from a list of extra services, which are included in cells B21:B23. These are optional services, so you can allow users to leave cell C8 blank. For the input message, use an appropriate title and display text that reminds users to enter the first extra service the customer used. Choose a style of error alert considering that if users enter a service, they must select one of the three services in the list. Enter an appropriate error alert title and an error message that instructs users to select a service from the list.

5. In cell C9, enter a data validation rule that uses the custom formula =AND(C9<>C8,C9<>C10) as its validation criteria to verify that the value entered in cell C9 is not the same as the value in cell C8 or C10. For the input message, use an appropriate title and display text that reminds users to enter the second service the customer used. Choose a style of error alert considering that if users enter a second service, they must enter one of the three services not already entered. Enter an appropriate error alert title and an error message.

6. In cell C10, enter a data validation rule that uses a custom formula similar to the one you entered for cell C9. This formula, however, should verify that the value entered in cell C10 is not the same as the value in cell C8 or C9. For the input message, use an appropriate title and display text that reminds users to enter the third service the customer used. Choose an appropriate style of error, error alert title, and error message.

7. In cell F15, enter a data validation rule that displays an informational message when users enter a date between 5/2/2012 and 8/28/2012. For the input message, use an appropriate title and display text that reminds users to enter the date the customer arrived. Choose the appropriate style of error alert, error alert title, and error message that reminds users the summer discount applies only from 5/2/2012 to 8/28/2012.

8. Test the data validation rules by entering the following values in the specified cells. If an error message appears, click the Retry button or the Cancel button and then enter valid data.
   C5: John Cosmo
   C6: Van
   C7: 16
   C8: Insurance
   C9: Child Seat
   C10: Limo Service
   F15: 6/25/2012

9. Change the document properties as specified by your instructor. Modify the sheet header to include your name, course number, and other information as specified by your instructor. Save the workbook.

10. Submit the assignment as requested by your instructor.

Make It Right

Analyze a workbook and correct all errors and/or improve the design.

Correcting Solver Parameters and Options

Note: To complete this assignment, you will be required to use the Data Files for Students. See the inside back cover of this book for instructions on downloading the Data Files for Students, or contact your instructor for information about accessing the required files.

Instructions: Start Excel. Open the workbook Make It Right 9–1 Berkley Financial from the Data Files for Students, and then save the workbook as Make It Right 9–1 Berkley Financial Complete. The workbook is used to forecast home savings for 35 years. In the situation shown in Figure 9–89, suppose a client has $1,500 to start saving, and that she wants to contribute to a savings account for 35 years. She estimates that from year 1 to year 20, she will earn 8% interest on the money in the account. After that, she will earn 6%. After her initial deposit in year 1, she will increase her contribution by $400. Starting in year 24, she will withdraw $10,000 per year. The workbook uses Solver to determine the minimum amount she can contribute to savings in year 1 to realize at least $850,000 in home savings in year 35.

Correct the following problems with formulas, Solver parameters, and Solver options to achieve the results shown in Figure 9–89.

Year	Starting Balance	Annual Contribution	Withdrawal	Return	Ending Balance
1	$ 1,500.00	$ 2,954.26	$ -	8%	$ 4,810.60
2	4,810.60	3,354.26	-	8%	8,818.05
3	8,818.05	3,754.26	-	8%	13,578.09
4	13,578.09	4,154.26	-	8%	19,150.94
5	19,150.94	4,554.26	-	8%	25,601.61
6	25,601.61	4,954.26	-	8%	33,000.34
7	33,000.34	5,354.26	-	8%	41,422.97
8	41,422.97	5,754.26	-	8%	50,951.41
9	50,951.41	6,154.26	-	8%	61,674.12
10	61,674.12	6,554.26	-	8%	73,686.65
11	73,686.65	6,954.26	-	8%	87,092.18
12	87,092.18	7,354.26	-	8%	102,002.16
13	102,002.16	7,754.26	-	8%	118,536.93
14	118,536.93	8,154.26	-	8%	136,826.48
15	136,826.48	8,554.26	-	8%	157,011.20
16	157,011.20	8,954.26	-	8%	179,242.70
17	179,242.70	9,354.26	-	8%	203,684.71
18	203,684.71	9,754.26	-	8%	230,514.09
19	230,514.09	10,154.26	-	8%	259,921.82
20	259,921.82	10,554.26	-	8%	292,114.16
21	292,114.16	10,954.26	-	6%	321,252.53
22	321,252.53	11,354.26	-	6%	352,563.19
23	352,563.19	11,754.26	-	6%	386,176.50
24	386,176.50	12,154.26	10,000.00	6%	411,630.60
25	411,630.60	12,554.26	10,000.00	6%	439,035.96
26	439,035.96	12,954.26	10,000.00	6%	468,509.63
27	468,509.63	13,354.26	10,000.00	6%	500,175.72
28	500,175.72	13,754.26	10,000.00	6%	534,165.78
29	534,165.78	14,154.26	10,000.00	6%	570,619.24
30	570,619.24	14,554.26	10,000.00	6%	609,683.91
31	609,683.91	14,954.26	10,000.00	6%	651,516.46
32	651,516.46	15,354.26	10,000.00	6%	696,282.96
33	696,282.96	15,754.26	10,000.00	6%	744,159.45
34	744,159.45	16,154.26	10,000.00	6%	795,332.53
35	795,332.53	16,554.26	10,000.00	6%	850,000.00

Berkley Financial Investments
Home Savings Evaluator

Answer Report 1 | **Home Savings**

Figure 9–89

Perform the following tasks:

1. The formula for the ending balance in column H does not properly include the annual return on investment listed in column G or any withdrawals. Update the formula in the column to correctly include the return and the withdrawals.

2. Start Solver to view the Solver parameters for the worksheet.

3. The Solver target is set to maximize the first annual contribution in cell E5. The value should be minimized rather than maximized. The changing cells should be set to change cell E5, rather than cell H5.

4. The constraints set for Solver include three constraints that are not necessary for cells F39, G39, and H39. Delete these three constraints.

5. The remaining constraint on cell H39 is incorrect. The value in this cell should be greater than or equal to $850,000.

6. The solving method should be Simplex LP. Click the Solve button in the Solver Parameters dialog box to run Solver. Create an answer report.

7. Change the document properties as specified by your instructor. Change the worksheet headers to include your name, course number, and other information as specified by your instructor.

8. Save the workbook, and submit the revised workbook as requested by your instructor.

In the Lab

Create a workbook using the guidelines, concepts, and skills presented in this chapter. Labs are listed in order of increasing difficulty.

Lab 1: Using Goal Seek to Create Scenarios for a Student Loan

Note: To complete this assignment, you will be required to use the Data Files for Students. See the inside back cover of this book for instructions on downloading the Data Files for Students, or contact your instructor for information about accessing the required files.

Problem: You want to select the best options for a student loan you will be getting. You have created a data table to examine the effects of interest rates from 4.5% to 7.5% for a loan. You want to use Goal Seek to figure out how many months it will take to pay off a loan of 35,000 with an interest rate of 5.5% using different monthly payment goals.

Instructions: *Perform the following tasks.*

1. Open the workbook Lab 9-1 Student Loan from the Data Files for Students, and then save the workbook as Lab 9-1 Student Loan Complete.

2. Enter a loan amount of 35,000 (cell H5), interest rate of 5.5% (cell H6), and months of 36 (cell H7) in the workbook (Figure 9–90).

Continued >

In the Lab *continued*

Figure 9–90

3. Select cell H8 and then display the Goal Seek dialog box by clicking the What-If Analysis button (Data tab | Data Tools group), and then clicking Goal Seek. Determine how many months you need to pay off the loan if you pay $300 per month by setting cell H8 to the value 300 and changing cell H7.

4. Use Goal Seek to determine how many months you need to pay off the loan if you pay $450 per month.

5. Change the document properties as specified by your instructor. Change the Student Loan Calculator worksheet header to include your name, course number, and other information as specified by your instructor.

6. Print the worksheet and then save the workbook.

7. Submit the assignment as requested by your instructor.

In the Lab

Lab 2: Finding the Optimal Production Combinations

Note: To complete this assignment, you will be required to use the Data Files for Students. See the inside back cover of this book for instructions on downloading the Data Files for Students, or contact your instructor for information about accessing the required files.

Problem: Witherson Furniture produces four types of custom shelving units. Each involves a certain amount of labor and materials to produce a unit. Your job is to determine the combination of units to produce based on the amount of available labor and materials for the first two weeks in June. Table 9–4 shows the assumptions for each type of unit manufactured during the first week of June.

Table 9–4 Custom Shelving Assumptions: June Week 1			
Unit Type	**Produce at Least**	**Produce at Most**	**Value Must Be**
3-shelf	1	30	Integer
4-shelf	1	30	Integer
4-shelf plus cabinet	1	55	Integer
Entertainment center	12	55	Integer

Instructions: *Perform the following tasks.*

1. Open the workbook Lab 9-2 Witherson Furniture from the Data Files for Students, and then save the workbook as Lab 9-2 Witherson Furniture Complete.

2. Use Solver to determine the mix of products that maximizes the number of units to manufacture in the first week of June. The total amount of labor hours available this week is 5,200 hours, and the total amount of materials is worth $55,000. Use the Simplex LP option in Solver. Instruct Solver to create an Answer Report if it can find a solution to the problem. Figure 9–91a shows the values Solver should find.

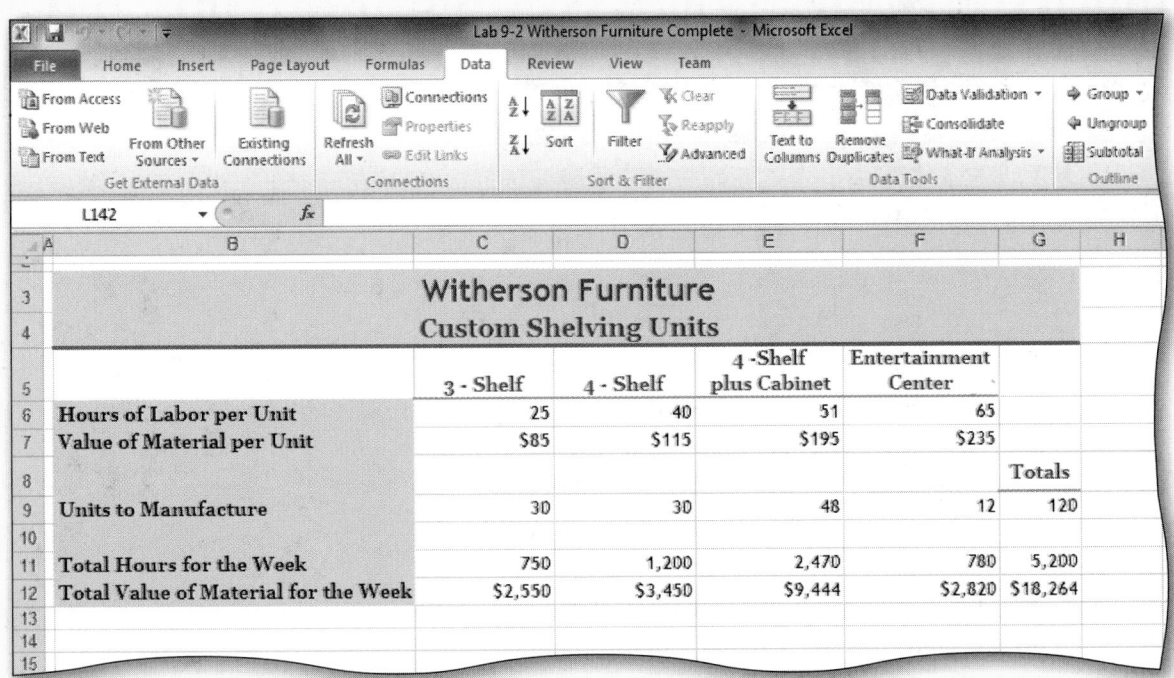

Figure 9–91 (a)

Continued >

STUDENT ASSIGNMENTS

In the Lab *continued*

3. You have been given new assumptions to use in the worksheet for the second week of June. The new assumptions are that 3-Shelf units take 30 labor hours to produce, 4-Shelf units take 48 labor hours to produce, 4-Shelf plus Cabinet units take 60 labor hours to produce, and Entertainment Center units take 72 labor hours to produce. Enter these new values in the Shelving Unit Planning worksheet.

4. Save the scenario as June Week 1. The changing cells are C9:F9. Rename the Answer Report containing the scenario as June Week 1.

5. Change the worksheet header to include your name, course number, and other information requested by your instructor. Print the Shelving Unit Planning worksheet and the June Week 1 worksheet.

6. Use Solver to find a solution to the problem of maximizing the number of units produced in one week, based on the new labor assumptions. Instruct Solver to create an Answer Report if it can find a solution to the problem. Solver should report that the optimal number of units of 3-Shelf units is 30, of 4-Shelf units is 30, of 4-Shelf with Cabinet units is 33, and of Entertainment Center units is 12.

7. Save the scenario as June Week 2. Rename the Answer Report worksheet containing the second scenario as June Week 2.

8. Create a Scenario Summary (Figure 9–91b) showing the two scenarios you saved in Scenario Manager. Change the Scenario Summary worksheet header to include your name, course number, and other information as specified by your instructor. Print the Scenario Summary worksheet.

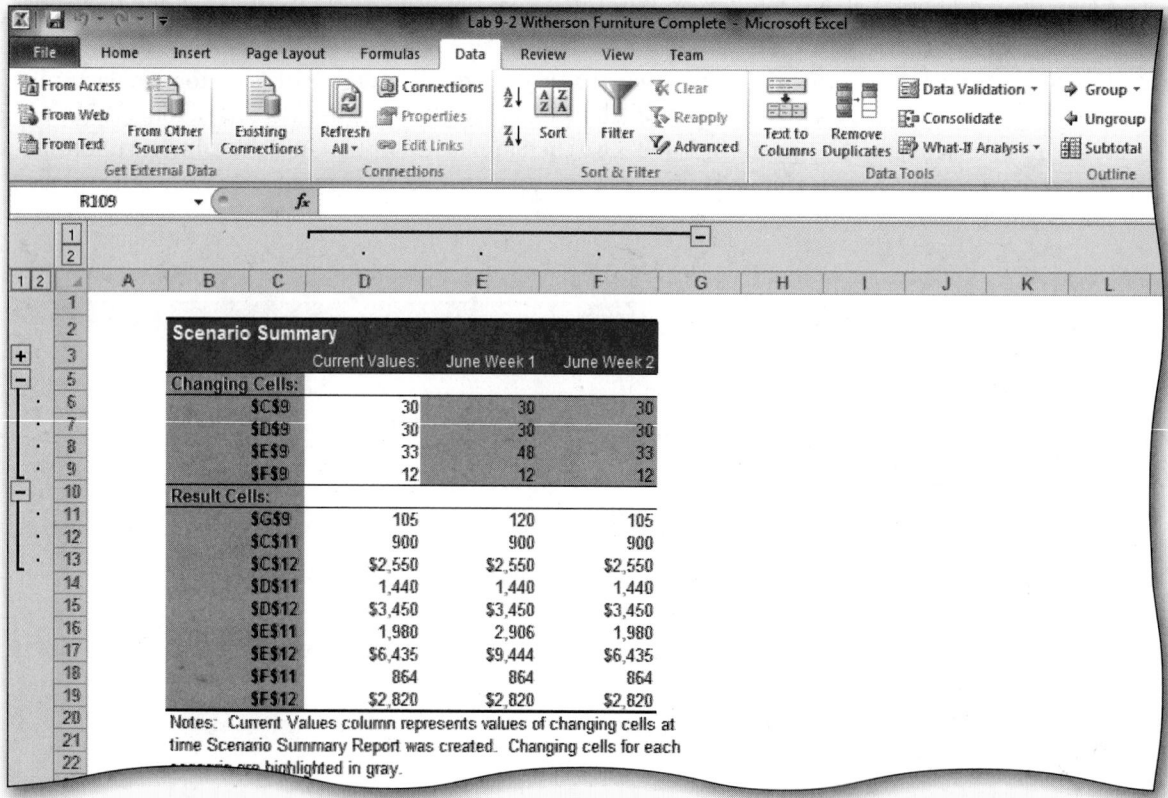

Figure 9–91 (b)

9. Change the document properties as specified by your instructor.

10. Submit the assignment as requested by your instructor.

In the Lab

Lab 3: Creating and Comparing Scenarios

Note: To complete this assignment, you will be required to use the Data Files for Students. See the inside back cover of this book for instructions on downloading the Data Files for Students, or contact your instructor for information about accessing the required files.

Problem: The owners of Creatican Resort, a timeshare resort island, want to determine the impact of raising commissions for their sales team from 4% to 8%. To accommodate the potential increase, the owners need to increase the markup at which they sell timeshares. Currently, the markup is 15%. When the owners increase price, they assume they will sell fewer timeshares. Create and compare three scenarios for the new commission rate and projected timeshare sales based on three potential price markups.

Instructions: *Perform the following tasks.*

1. Open the workbook Lab 9-3 Creatican Resort from the Data Files for Students, and then save the workbook as Lab 9-3 Creatican Resort Complete.

2. Create three new scenarios with the changing cells B4, B6, and B9. The first scenario, Markup 17, Timeshare 105 should include the number of timeshares sold as 105, markup as 17%, and the proposed commission rate of 8%. The second scenario, Markup 18, Timeshare 100 should include timeshares sold as 100, markup as 18%, and the proposed commission rate of 8%. The third scenario, Markup 19, Timeshare 94 should include timeshares sold as 94, markup as 19%, and the proposed commission rate of 8%.

3. Create a Scenario PivotTable report (Figure 9–92a) showing the three scenarios that you have saved in Scenario Manager. The result cells are B7, B8, and B10.

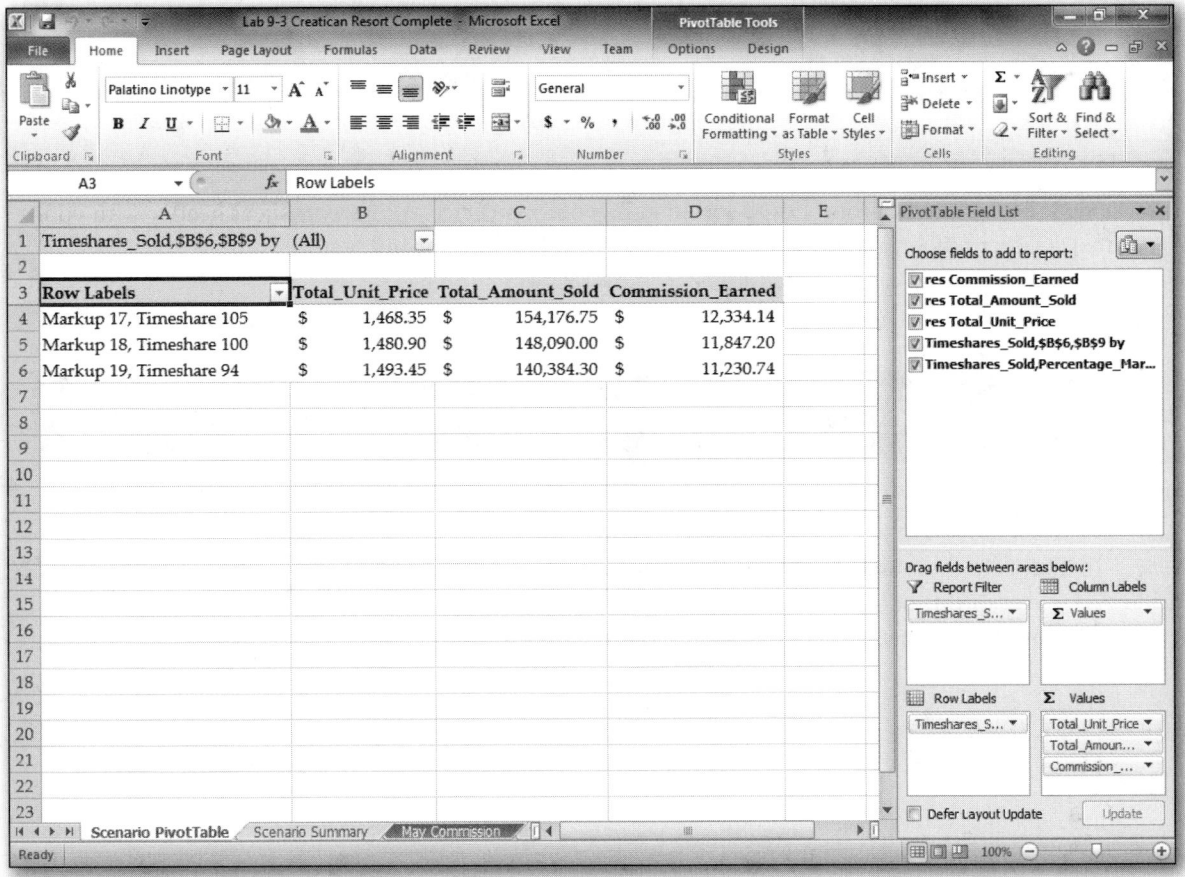

Figure 9–92 (a)

Continued >

In the Lab *continued*

4. Create a Scenario Summary report (Figure 9–92b) showing the three scenarios that you have saved in Scenario Manager. The result cells are B7, B8, and B10.

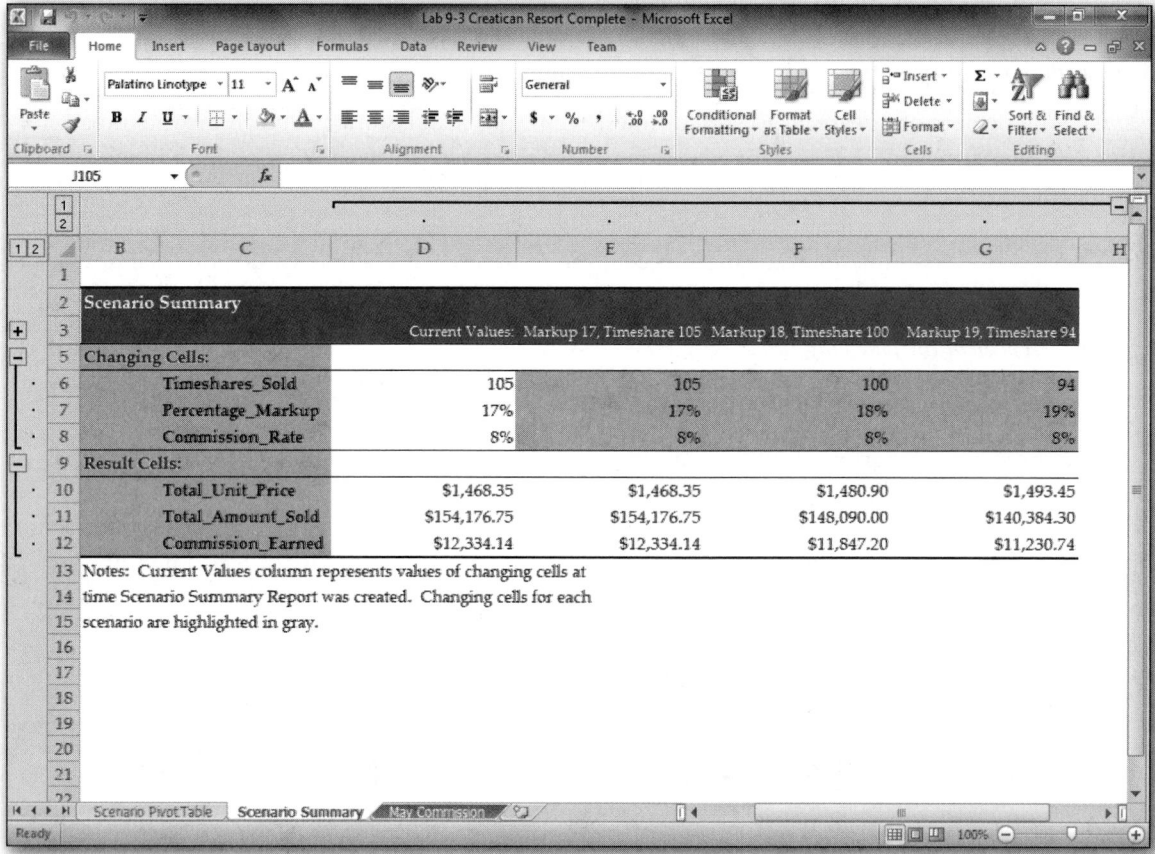

Figure 9–92 (b)

5. Change the document properties as specified by your instructor. Add a worksheet header with your name, course number, and other information as specified by your instructor.

6. Submit the assignment as requested by your instructor.

Cases and Places

Apply your creative thinking and problem solving skills to design and implement a solution.

Note: To complete these assignments, you may be required to use the Data Files for Students. See the inside back cover of this book for instructions on downloading the Data Files for Students, or contact your instructor for information about accessing the required files.

1: Using Solver to Find the Most Profitable Product Mix

Academic

BAU Supply is an on-campus store that sells supplies for students who want to purchase grocery and sundry items for their dorm rooms. You are in charge of ordering beverages for the store. Beverages are available in single cans, 6-packs, and 12-packs. The store is expanding to a new campus location where they have allocated 46 square feet of shelf space to beverages, and they want to be certain the most profitable combination of products is placed on the shelves. They want no more than 40 single cans, 20 6-packs, and 30 12-packs. Table 9–5 shows the three types of items, profitability per item, and how much shelf space each item requires. Create a worksheet with the necessary information and use Solver to determine the most profitable combination of items to place on the shelves. Create an Answer Report that shows that the constraints have been met. Print the worksheet and Answer Report.

Table 9–5 Beverage Item Information

Beverage Item	Profit per Item	Square Feet per Item
Single can	$0.08	0.2
6-pack	$0.51	1.2
12-pack	$0.91	2.1

2: Optimizing a Meal Plan

Personal

You are in charge of creating your family dinners. You have decided to create meal plans to follow the Let It Simmer diet-planning book you just bought. Your challenge is to find meals that meet certain nutritional requirements. Open the workbook Case 9–2 Let It Simmer from the Data Files for Students, and then save the workbook as Case 9–2 Let it Simmer Complete. Use Excel to find the optimal servings mix to comprise a meal with no more than 1,800 calories and 45 grams of fat. The meal must include at least one serving of each item and not more than four. You want to minimize the total fat grams while keeping the other constraints. You have priced options and have come up with three calorie/fat grams options as shown in Table 9–6. Create the three scenarios and generate a scenario summary worksheet.

Table 9–6 Values per Serving

Meal Option	Calories	Fats
Scenario 1		
Vegetarian	274	12
One-Pot Chicken	382	15
Beef Stew	556	18
Scenario 2		
Vegetarian	300	11
One-Pot Chicken	425	14
Beef Stew	645	20
Scenario 3		
Vegetarian	220	16
One-Pot Chicken	450	13
Beef Stew	600	14

Continued >

Cases and Places *continued*

3: Meeting Sales Goals

Professional

Open the workbook Case 9-3 YouSelfStore from the Data Files for Students, and then save the workbook as Case 9-3 YouSelfStore Complete. Use formula auditing to learn about the worksheet. Trace two levels of precedents for cell B22, the Total Rental Revenue. Print the worksheet with the arrows and submit it to your instructor. Use goal seeking to determine the number of rental units the company needs to meet their sales goal for each building. The company wants to generate $2,500 per month for the two types of small units and $3,000 per month for the two types of large units. Save the workbook. Note that the number of units for each unit type is not an integer value. Prepare an explanation of this fact and submit the explanation to your instructor.

10 | Using Macros and Visual Basic for Applications (VBA) with Excel

Objectives

You will have mastered the material in this chapter when you can:

- Use passwords to assign protected and unprotected status to a worksheet

- Use the macro recorder to create a macro

- Execute a macro and view and print code for a macro

- Customize the Quick Access Toolbar by adding a button

- Understand Visual Basic for Applications (VBA) code and explain event-driven programs

- Add controls, such as command buttons, options buttons, and check boxes to a worksheet

- Assign properties to controls

- Use VBA to write a procedure to automate data entry into a worksheet

- Review a digital signature on a workbook

10 | Using Macros and Visual Basic for Applications (VBA) with Excel

Introduction

Before a computer can take an action and produce a desired result, it must have a step-by-step description of the task to be accomplished. The step-by-step description is a series of precise instructions called a **procedure**. **Program** and **code** are other names for a procedure. The process of writing a procedure is called **computer programming**. Every Excel command and Ribbon button has a corresponding procedure that the computer executes, or carries out the step-by-step instructions, when you click the command or button.

Because Excel does not have a command or button for every possible worksheet task, Microsoft has included a powerful programming language called Visual Basic for Applications. **Visual Basic for Applications** (**VBA**) is a programming language that allows you to customize and extend the capabilities of Excel. You also can create a macro to group together commonly used combinations of tasks, which then can be reused later. Use macros to ensure consistency in calculations, formatting, and manipulation of nonnumerical data.

In this chapter, you will learn how to create macros using a code generator called a **macro recorder**. A **macro** is a procedure composed of VBA code. It is called a macro rather than a procedure, because it is created using the macro recorder. You also will learn how to add buttons to the Quick Access Toolbar and then associate these with macros. Finally, you will learn the basics of VBA, including creating a user interface, setting the properties, and writing the code.

Project — Green Valley Conservation Group

The project in the chapter follows proper design guidelines and uses Excel to create the worksheets shown in Figure 10–1 and Figure 10–2. Green Valley Conservation Group has grown from a small group of concerned neighbors to a regional group that tackles environmental educational causes. The group is planning a fundraiser and membership drive. Existing membership data needs some attention to ensure that all information is in a standard form as the group adds new members. The membership information was being maintained informally by one of the members in a previous version of Excel. Figure 10–1a shows the state of the existing membership information, and Figure 10–1b shows the final layout for the information. In addition, some of the membership information for existing members exists in hard copy only. The group needs to develop a way to enter this hard copy data uniformly. The group also needs an easy-to-use interface that will allow people at the membership drive and fundraiser to provide their contact information and other pertinent information themselves at one of several membership

(a) Initial Worksheet

(b) Final Layout

(c) Add Member Data Worksheet

```
'Add Data Button Procedure
' Date Created: 10/17/2012
' Run from:  Add Member Data sheet by clicking button labeled Add Member Data
'Function: When executed, this procedure accepts member data via input boxes and updates the member lis

Private Sub CommandButton1_Click()
    Range("Last_Name").Value = InputBox("Last Name?", "Enter", , 800, 6000)
    Range("First_Name").Value = InputBox("First Name?", "Enter", , 800, 6000)
    Range("Street_Address").Value = InputBox("Street Address?", "Enter", , 800, 6000)
    Range("City").Value = InputBox("City?", "Enter", , 800, 6000)
    Range("State").Value = InputBox("State?", "Enter", , 800, 6000)
    Range("Zip_Code").Value = InputBox("Zip Code?", "Enter", , 800, 6000)
    Range("A9:F9").Select
    Selection.Copy
    Sheets("All Members").Select
    Application.Goto Reference:="r1c1"
    Selection.End(xlDown).Select
    ActiveCell.Offset(1, 0).Range("A1").Select
    Selection.PasteSpecial Paste:=xlPasteValues, Operation:=xlNone, SkipBlanks _
        :=False, Transpose:=False
    Sheets("Add Member Data").Select
    Application.CutCopyMode = False
    ActiveCell.Select
    Range("A9:F9").Select
    Selection.ClearContents
    Range("A2").Activate
    ActiveWorkbook.Save
End Sub
```

(d) Procedure for Adding Existing Member Data

Figure 10–1

stations the group plans to set up at the event. The interface can assume some comfort with computers, but should not assume Excel knowledge. Figure 10–2 shows the user interface that will be used at the membership drive.

The membership information repository is created according to the following phases:

Phase 1 — Use the macro recorder to create macros that reformat the member names in the membership data worksheet so that the last name is in column A and first name in column B. This will require two macros. Both macros will be assigned to a key combination and one will be assigned to a button on the Quick Access Toolbar.

Phase 2 — Create an Add Member Data button on the worksheet as shown in Figure 10–1c, assign the button properties, and write an associated procedure (Figure 10–1d) that steps the user through entering the required membership data for existing members whose data did not transfer correctly.

Phase 3 — Create an area on a worksheet called New Member Signup (Figure 10–2) that allows a new member with no Excel knowledge to enter his or her name, address, and additional information using command buttons, check boxes, and option buttons.

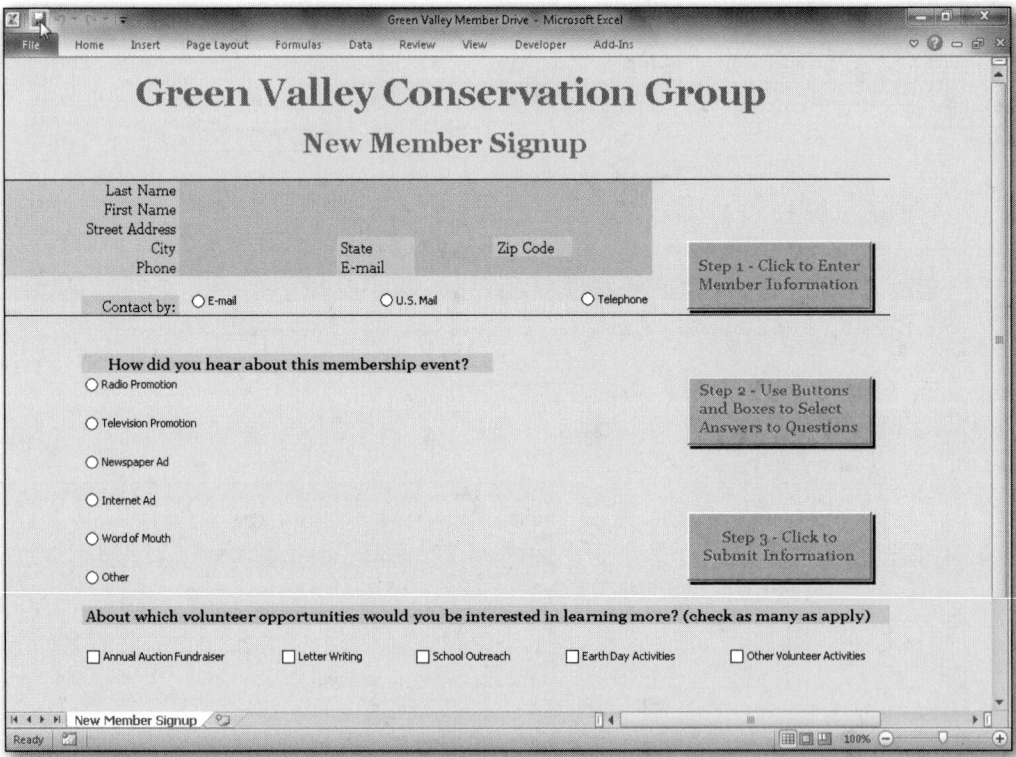

Figure 10–2

Figure 10–3 illustrates the requirements document for the Green Valley Conservation Group workbooks. It includes the needs, source of data, summary of format changes, and other facts about its development. The requirements document indicates that the development of the workbooks should be done in three phases, as outlined earlier.

REQUEST FOR NEW WORKBOOK

Date Submitted:	October 10, 2012
Submitted By:	Andrew Mendina
Worksheet Title:	Green Valley Membership and Green Valley Member Drive
Needs:	Create an easy-to-use interface for the organization's Membership activities as follows: Phase 1: Use the macro recorder to create macros that reformat the member names in the membership data worksheet so that the last name is in column A and first name in column B. This will require two macros. Both macros will be assigned to a key combination and one will be assigned to a button on the Quick Access Toolbar. Phase 2: Create an Add Member Data button on the worksheet as shown in Figure 10–1c, assign the button properties, and write an associated procedure (Figure 10–1d) that steps the user through entering the required membership data for existing members whose data did not transfer correctly. Phase 3: Create an area on a worksheet called New Member Signup (Figure 10–2) that allows a new member with no Excel knowledge to enter his or her name, address, and additional information using command buttons, check boxes, and option buttons.
Source of Data:	The workbook shown in Figures 10-1a and 10-1c is available in the Data Files for Students with the file name, Green Valley Data. The workbook containing the base information for the workbook shown in Figure 10-1b is available in the Data Files for Students, with the file name Member Drive Data.
Calculations:	None
Web Requirements:	None

Approvals

Approval Status:	X	Approved
		Rejected
Approved By:	Edward Arthurs	
Date:	October 10, 2012	
Contracted To:	M. Jones, Spreadsheet Specialist	

Figure 10–3

Overview

As you read this chapter, you will learn how to modify the existing Green Valley workbook as shown in Figure 10–1 and Figure 10–2 by performing these general tasks:

- Use passwords to protect and unprotect a worksheet.
- Use the macro recorder to create macros.
- Execute macros, view and print code for macros, and assign macros to key combinations and to a button on the Quick Access Toolbar.
- Use VBA to write a procedure to automate data entry into a worksheet.
- Add controls to a worksheet and assign properties to the controls.
- Test and validate incoming data.

General Project Guidelines

While working with an Excel worksheet, you need to make several decisions that will determine the appearance and characteristics of the finished worksheet. As you update an existing worksheet to meet the requirements shown in Figure 10–3, you should follow these general guidelines:

1. **Determine the actions you want to automate, and plan the steps to create a macro.** A macro is created by performing a set of steps and recording the steps as they are performed. The steps and their order should be determined and rehearsed before creating the macro.

2. **Create the first user interface.** In this chapter, two separate user interfaces are created that automate data entry for the membership list. Excel provides several types of controls, such as buttons, text boxes, and check boxes, that you can use in a user interface. Which controls you use for each task is determined by the type of data the control is used to enter.

3. **Determine properties for controls in the user interface.** Each type of control includes a different set of properties that you set as you design the user interface. For example, the size, color, and shape of a button are all properties of the button. The properties that you set give meaning and limitations to the user regarding the control's use.

4. **Establish the Visual Basic code needed for each control.** When a user interacts with a control, such as clicking a button, Visual Basic code that is associated with that action is executed. Which actions will require a response from Visual Basic code? What should that response from the Visual Basic code be? For example, what precise actions should occur on a worksheet when a button is clicked? As a worksheet developer, you design and write the Visual Basic code.

5. **Create the second user interface.** To suit the needs of the users and the purpose of the workbook, you use a wider range of form controls to create the second user interface than you used in the first user interface.

6. **Evaluate the completed user interface through testing.** The final step in creating a user interface is to test it to prove that the interface behaves as designed and as a user expects.

Creating a sketch of the worksheet can help you visualize its design. Figure 10–4 shows a sketch of the New Member Signup worksheet described in Phase 3 in the requirements document, to provide a visual representation of the more complex aspects of the requirements. The sketch for the Phase 3 New Member Signup worksheet includes check boxes, option buttons, and command buttons.

When necessary, more specific details concerning the above guidelines are presented at appropriate points in the chapter. The chapter also will identify the actions you perform and decisions made regarding these guidelines during the modification of the worksheet shown in Figure 10–1 on page EX 627 and Figure 10–2 on page EX 628.

With a good understanding of the requirements document, an understanding of the necessary decisions, and a sketch of the worksheet, the next step is to use Excel to open the existing Green Valley Conservation Group workbook.

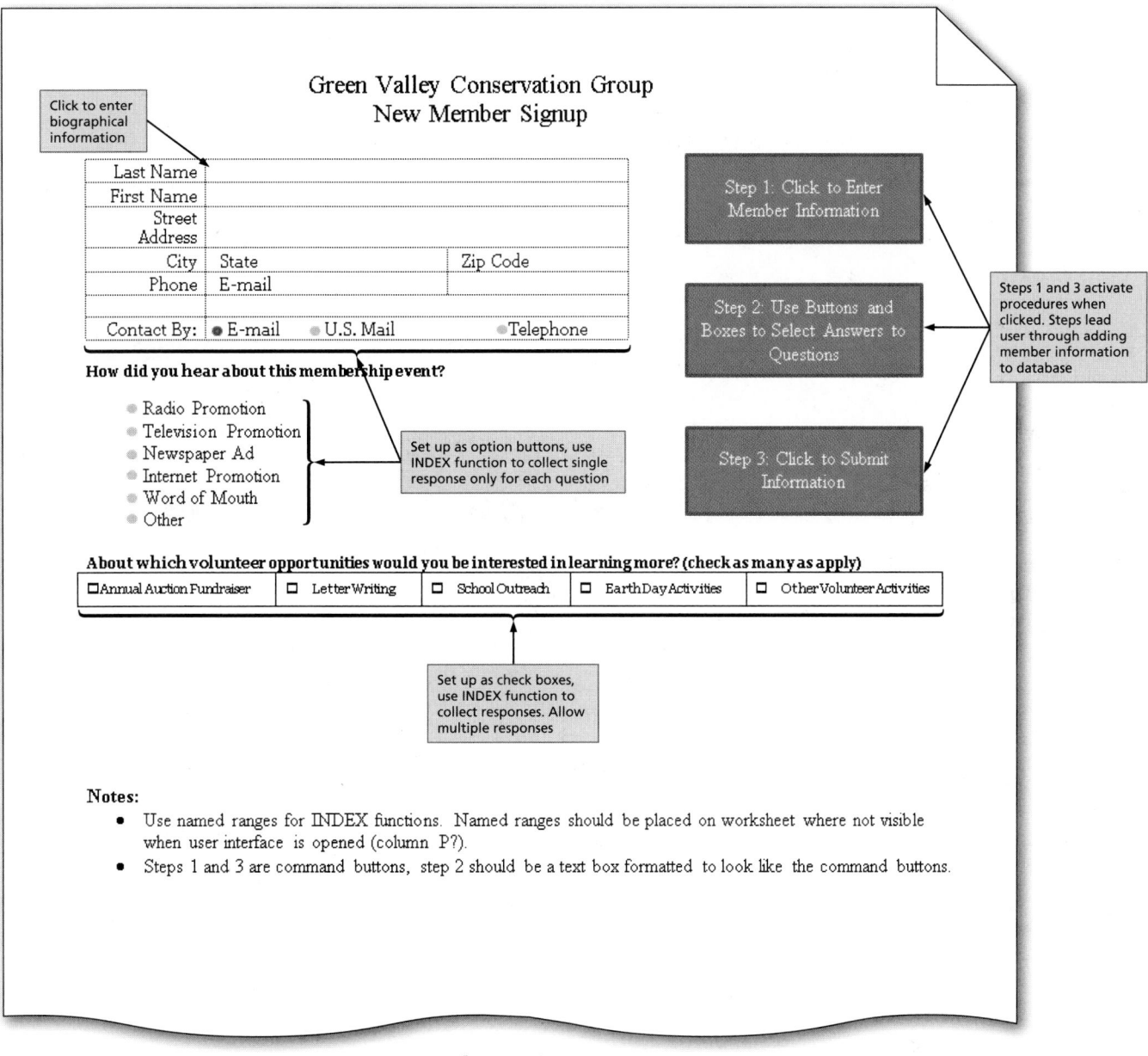

Figure 10–4

To Start Excel and Open a Workbook

To begin this project, you will open a file located in the Data Files for Students. See the inside back cover of this book for instructions on downloading the Data Files for Students, or contact your instructor for more information about accessing the required files. If you are using a computer to step through the project in this chapter and you want your screens to match the figures in this book, you should change your screen's resolution to 1024 × 768.

The following steps start Excel, open a file, and then save it with a new file name.

1 Start Excel. If necessary, maximize the Excel window.

2 Open the workbook, Green Valley Data, located on the Data Files for Students.

3 Save the workbook using the file name, Green Valley Membership.

4 If necessary, click the Add Member Data sheet tab to display the Add Member Data worksheet.

5 If the worksheet window in Excel is not maximized, click the Maximize button next to the Close Window button on the Ribbon to maximize the worksheet within Excel (Figure 10–5).

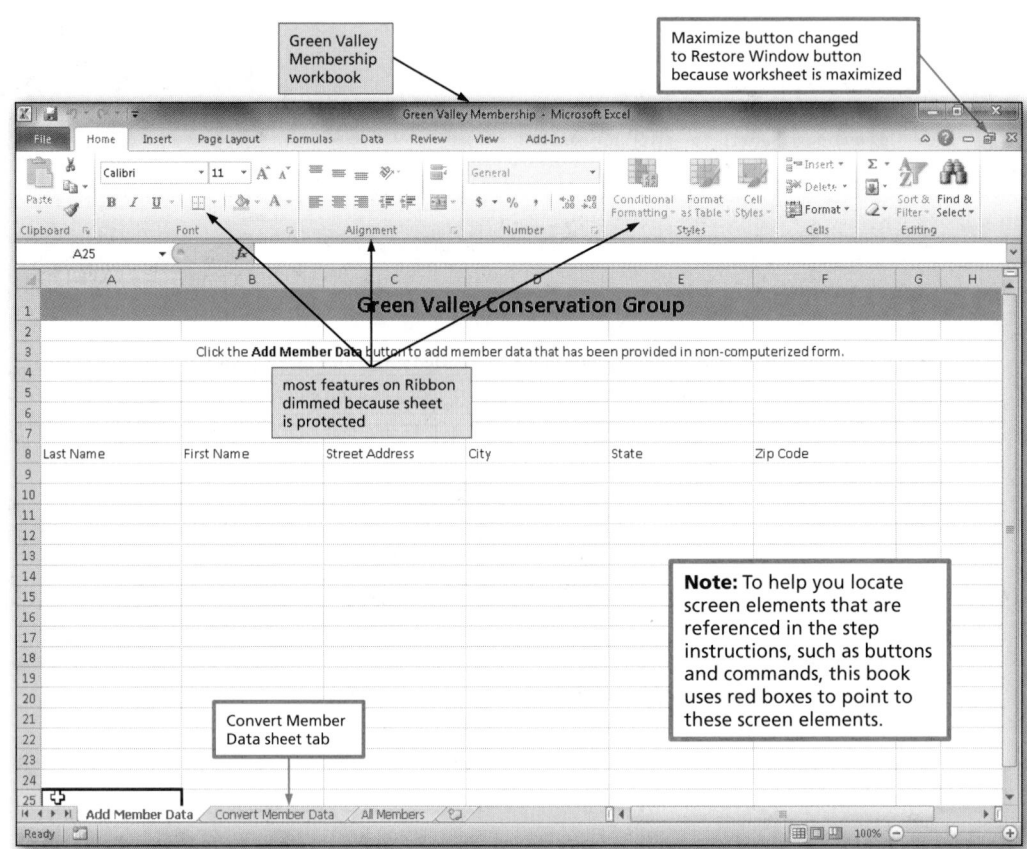

Figure 10–5

Learning about a Workbook Created by Someone Else

When you work with a workbook created by someone else, such as the Green Valley Membership workbook, you should review the content and structure of the workbook before you make changes to it. You can learn more about a workbook by doing as much of the following as possible to the worksheet:

1. Press CTRL+ACCENT MARK (`) to display any formulas to gain an understanding of what formulas and functions are used in the worksheet and which cells are referenced by the formulas and functions.

2. Use Range Finder or the auditing commands to show which cells are referenced in formulas and functions. You double-click a cell with a formula or function to activate Range Finder.

3. Check which cells are locked and which cells are unlocked. Usually all cells in a workbook are locked, except for those in which you enter data. For example, on the Add Member Data worksheet, only the cells in the range A9:F9 are unlocked.

4. Enter sample data and verify the results.

To Unprotect a Password-Protected Worksheet

The worksheets in the Green Valley Membership workbook are protected, which restricts the changes you can make to the worksheet to unlocked cells only. You cannot make changes to locked cells, or modify the worksheet itself. Before modifying the worksheet, you must unprotect it by entering the password assigned when it first was protected. A **password** ensures that users cannot unprotect the worksheet simply by clicking the Unprotect button. The password for the worksheets in this workbook is awareness.

The following steps unprotect the password-protected Convert Member Data worksheet.

1

• Click the Convert Member Data sheet tab to make it the active sheet.

• Click Review on the Ribbon to display the Review tab.

• Click the Unprotect Sheet button (Review tab | Changes group) to display the Unprotect Sheet dialog box.

• When the Unprotect Sheet dialog box appears, type **awareness** in the Password text box (Figure 10–6).

Figure 10–6

Are there rules for passwords?

Yes. Passwords in Excel can contain, in any combination, letters, numbers, spaces, and symbols, up to 15 characters long. Passwords are case sensitive. If you decide to password-protect a worksheet, make sure you write down the password and keep it in a secure place. If you lose the password, you cannot open or gain access to the password-protected worksheet.

2

- Click the OK button (Unprotect Sheet dialog box) to unprotect the Convert Member Data worksheet (Figure 10–7).

Q&A

Can I work with the entire worksheet now?

Yes. With the worksheet unprotected, you can modify the contents of cells regardless of whether they are locked or unlocked. Cells must both be locked and the worksheet protected to restrict what users can do to cell contents.

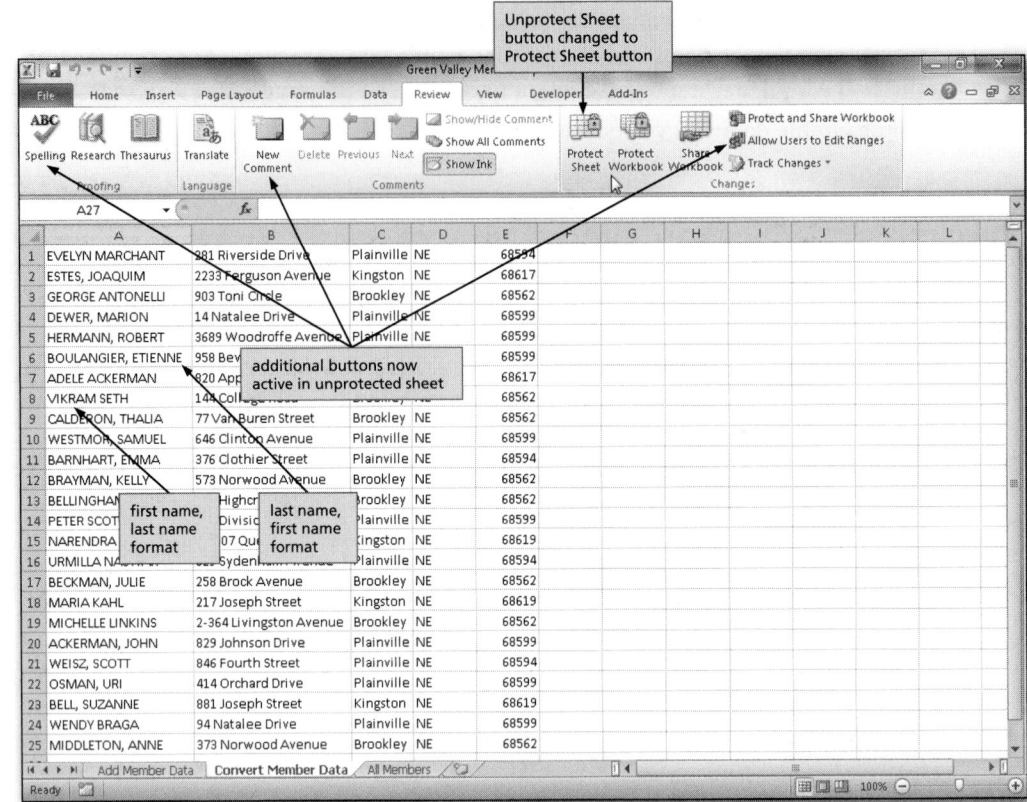

Figure 10–7

Phase 1 — Recording Macros and Assigning Them to a Toolbar Button and Keyboard Combination

BTW

Q&As
For a complete list of the Q&As found in many of the step-by-step sequences in this book, visit the Excel 2010 Q&A Web page (scsite.com/ex2010/qa).

The first phase of this project creates a macro to reformat the membership data so that it can be more easily sorted. Currently, the first and last names of the members appear in column A, in all uppercase. In some instances, the first name appears first, in others, the last name appears first (Figure 10–7). The planned macros will (1) change the case from uppercase to mixed case; (2) create new columns for text manipulation; (3) split the contents of column A, placing first names in one column and last names in another column; (4) delete the working columns; and (5) copy the contents of the worksheet to a separate worksheet.

The purpose of these macros is to automate editing tasks that would be repetitive and time-consuming if done for each entry separately. The macros save time, but they also ensure consistency in how the membership data is organized. After the macros are created, they will be assigned to a key combination or a button on the Quick Access Toolbar. When additional membership data is available that needs to be reformatted, it can be copied or imported into this workbook. The macros will ensure that the new membership data conforms to the format needed.

Excel includes a macro recorder that can record a series of actions and save them as a macro. The macro recorder can be turned on, during which time it records your activities, and then turned off to stop the recording. After recording a macro you can play it back, or **execute** it, as often as you want to repeat the steps you recorded with the macro recorder.

Three steps must be taken in preparation for working with macros in Excel. The Developer tab on the Ribbon includes commands used to work with macros. The Developer tab, which by default does not appear on the Ribbon, must be made available by changing an Excel option. Second, a security setting in Excel must be modified to enable macros whenever you use Excel. Finally, Excel requires a workbook that includes macros to be saved as an Excel Macro-Enabled Workbook file type.

To Display the Developer Tab, Enable Macros, and Save a Workbook as a Macro-Enabled Workbook

The following steps display the Developer tab on the Ribbon, enable macros, and save the workbook as a macro-enabled workbook.

- Click the File tab to display the Backstage view.

- Click the Options command to display the Excel Options dialog box.

- Click the Customize Ribbon tab (Excel Options dialog box) to display the Customize the Ribbon tools (Figure 10–8).

Figure 10–8

2

- Click the Developer check box in the Main Tabs list to select the Developer tab for display on the Ribbon (Figure 10–9).

Figure 10–9

3

- Click the OK button (Excel Options dialog box) to display the Developer tab on the Ribbon.

- Click the Developer tab to make it the active tab.

- Click the Macro Security button (Developer tab | Code group) to display the Trust Center dialog box.

- Click the 'Enable all macros' option button to select it (Figure 10–10).

Figure 10–10

4

- Click the OK button (Trust Center dialog box) to close the dialog box and enable macros.
- Click the File tab to display the Backstage view.
- Click the Save As command to display the Save As dialog box.
- When the Save As dialog box is displayed, click the 'Save as type' button to display a list of file types.
- Click Excel Macro-Enabled Workbook in the 'Save as type' list to select the appropriate file type (Figure 10–11).

Figure 10–11

5

- Click the Save button (Save As dialog box) to save the workbook as an Excel Macro-Enabled Workbook file.

To Convert Names to Proper Case and Add Extra Columns

Before creating the macros, you will prepare the worksheet by converting the names to proper case and creating extra columns.

1

- Insert a blank column to the left of column A to move the column containing the names to column B.
- Set the width of column A to 20.00 to resize the column.
- Click cell A1 to select it.
- Type **=PROPER(** and then click cell B1 to begin entering a formula with the PROPER function (Figure 10–12).

Figure 10–12

• Click the Enter box to complete the formula, convert the name to proper case, and display the result in A1.

• Copy cell A1 to the range A2:A25 to convert all the names to proper case.

• Insert four blank columns to the right of column B to prepare for adding data (Figure 10–13).

Figure 10–13

Recording Macros

A macro is created by performing a set of steps and recording the steps as they are performed. The steps and their order should be determined and rehearsed before creating the macro. When recording the macro, you perform the steps as they are recorded, and so you can confirm that the macro will do what you expect it to do.

Plan Ahead

> **Determine the actions you want to automate, and plan the steps to create a macro.**
>
> To create the macro to reformat the membership data for Green Valley Conservation, you will turn on the macro recorder and then complete the following tasks.
>
> 1. Select the first instance of membership data where the name is in the form of first name last name. Use the LEN function in column C to determine the total number of characters in the member name. The result of the LEN function should be displayed in column C.
>
> 2. Use the SEARCH function in column D to determine the position of the space that separates the first and last names. The result of the SEARCH function should be displayed in column D.
>
> 3. Use the RIGHT function to capture the last name. The result of the RIGHT function should be displayed in column E. Use the Paste Values command to replace the formula with a text value.
>
> 4. Use the LEFT function to capture the first name. The result of the LEFT function should be displayed in column F. Use the Paste Values command to replace the formula with a text value.
>
> 5. Stop the macro recorder.

When you create a macro, you assign a name to it. A **macro name** can be up to 255 characters long; it can contain numbers, letters, and underscores, but it cannot contain spaces and other punctuation. The name is used later to identify the macro when you want to execute it. Executing a macro causes Excel to step through all of the recorded steps just as they were recorded. The first macro name in this project is FirstName.

When planning your macro, you must determine if you are going to select any cells using keyboard navigation. Entering a cell reference always directs the macro to that specific cell. However, navigating to a cell using keyboard navigation requires the use of relative cell addressing. If you will be using keyboard navigation, you must ensure that the **Use Relative References button** in the Code group on the Developer tab is selected so that the macro works properly.

To Record a Macro to Reformat the Membership Data where First Name Appears First

The following steps record the FirstName macro to separate into two different columns the first name and last name for the entries that appear as FirstName, LastName in column A.

- If necessary, click Developer on the Ribbon to display the Developer tab.

- Click the Use Relative References button (Developer tab | Code group) so that the macro uses relative cell references when selecting cells.

- Select cell A1, the first instance of first name appearing first.

- Click the Record Macro button (Developer tab | Code group) to display the Record Macro dialog box.

- When the Record Macro dialog box is displayed, type **FirstName** in the Macro name text box.

- Type **f** in the Shortcut key text box to set the shortcut key for the macro to CTRL+F.

- Make sure the 'Store macro in' box displays This Workbook, and then type **Macro splits names for entries with first name appearing first.** in the Description text box (Figure 10-14).

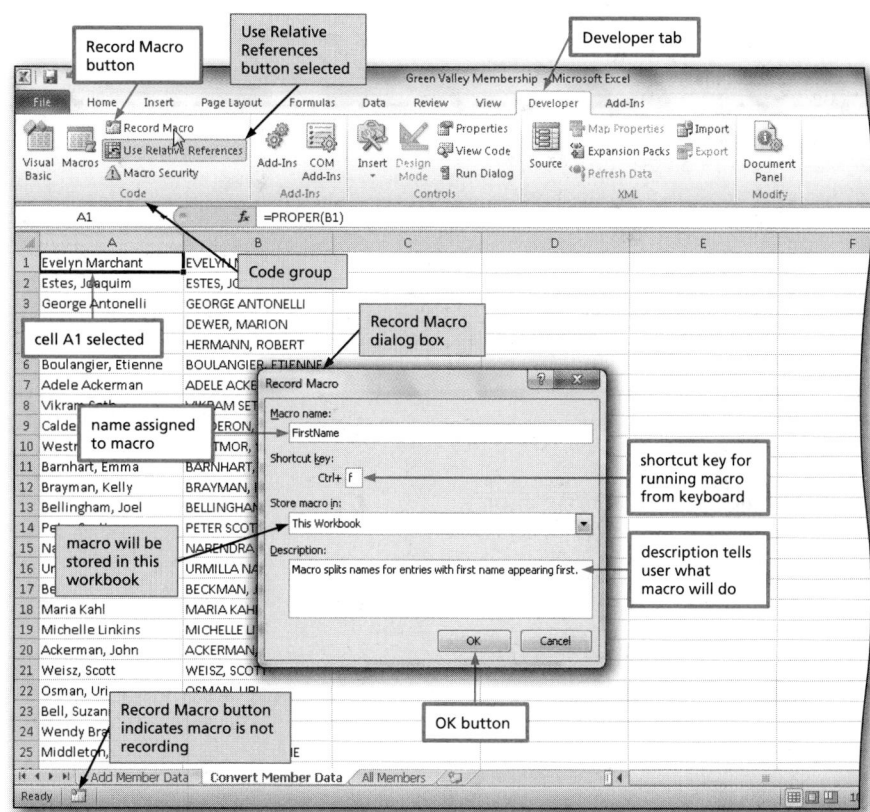

Figure 10-14

Q&A Where are macros stored?

In the Record Macro dialog box, you can select the location to store the macro in the 'Store macro in' box. If you want a macro to be available to use in any workbook whenever you use Microsoft Excel, select Personal Macro Workbook in the 'Store macro in' list. This selection causes the macro to be stored in the **Personal Macro Workbook**, which is part of Excel. If you click New Workbook in the 'Store macro in' list, then Excel stores the macro in a new workbook. Most macros created with the macro recorder are workbook-specific and thus are stored in the active workbook. Selecting This Workbook in the 'Store macro in' list, as specified in Step 1, stores the macro in the active workbook.

2

- Click the OK button (Record Macro dialog box) to begin recording the macro and to change the Record Macro button to the Stop Recording button.

Q&A What will be included in the macro?

Any task you perform in Excel will be part of the macro. When you are finished recording the macro, clicking the Stop Recording button on the Ribbon or on the status bar ends the recording.

Q&A What is the purpose of the Record Macro button on the status bar?

You can use the Record Macro button on the status bar to start or stop recording a macro. When you are not recording a macro, this button is displayed as the Record Macro button. If you click it to begin recording a macro, the button changes to become the Stop Recording button.

- Click Home on the Ribbon to display the Home tab.

- Click the RIGHT ARROW key twice to move to cell C1.

- Type **=LEN(** and then click cell A1 to begin entering a formula (Figure 10–15).

Figure 10–15

- Click the Enter box to compute the number of characters in cell A1.

- Press the RIGHT ARROW key once to move to cell D1.

- Type =SEARCH (" ", and then click cell A1 to begin entering a formula (Figure 10–16).

Figure 10–16

- Click the Enter box to compute the location of the space separating the first and last names in cell A1.

- Press the RIGHT ARROW key once to move to cell E1.

- Type =RIGHT(A1, C1-D1 and then click the Enter box to copy the last name to cell E1 (Figure 10–17).

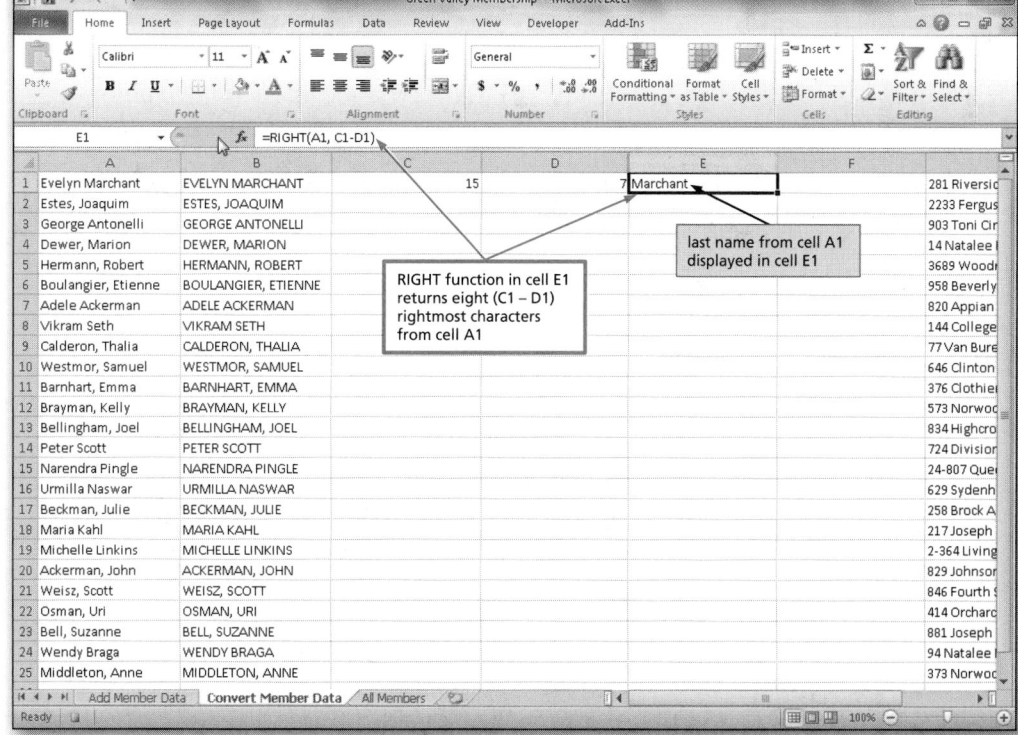

Figure 10–17

- Press CTRL+C to copy the cell contents.

- Click the Paste button arrow (Home tab | Clipboard group) to display a gallery of paste options.

- Click Values (V) in the Paste Values gallery to replace the RIGHT function with the text value (Figure 10–18).

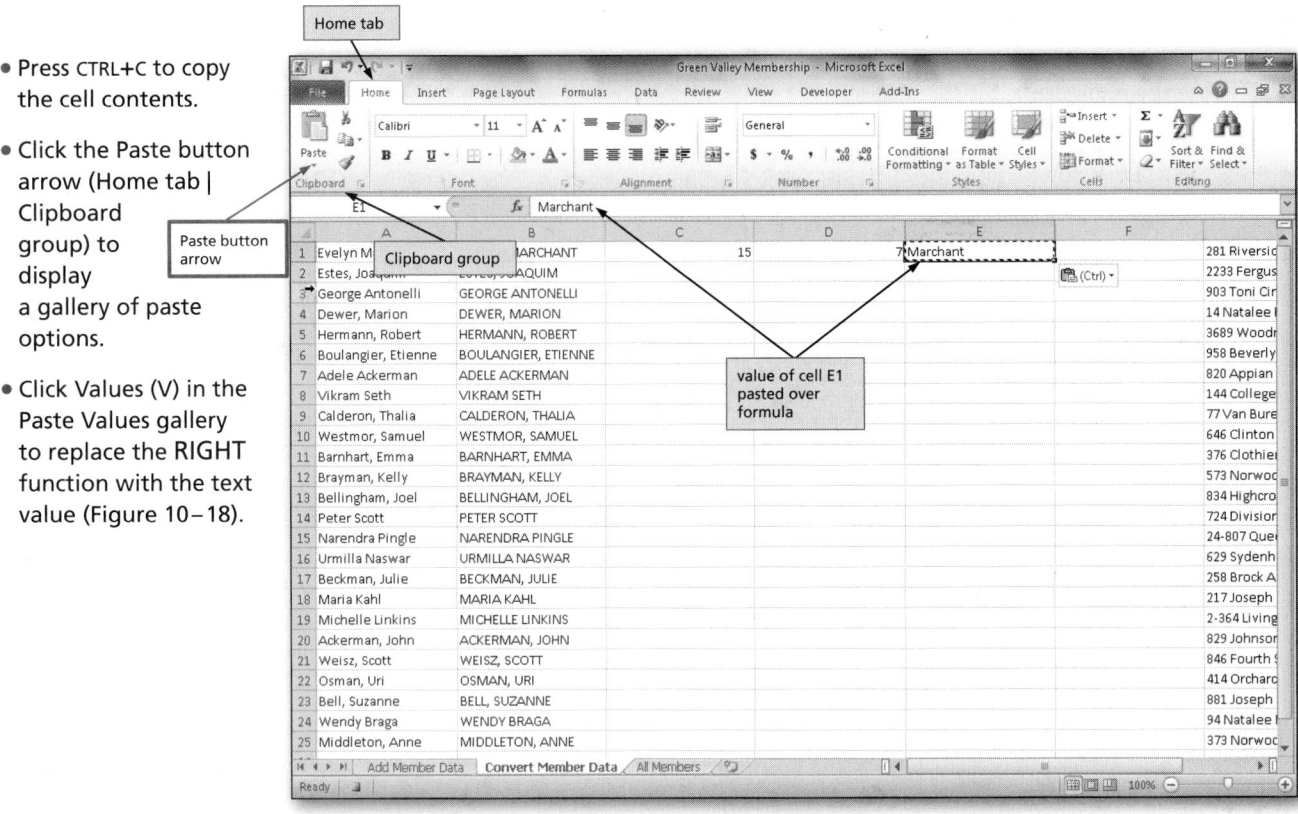

Figure 10–18

5

- Press the RIGHT ARROW key once to move to cell F1.

- Type =LEFT(A1, D1-1 and then click the Enter box to copy the first name to cell F1.

- Press CTRL+C to copy the cell contents.

- Click the Paste button arrow (Home tab | Clipboard group) to display a gallery of paste options.

- Click Values (V) in the Paste Values gallery to replace the LEFT function with the text value (Figure 10–19).

Figure 10–19

6

- Press the HOME key to make cell A1 the active cell (Figure 10–20).

Figure 10–20

7

- Press the ESC key to remove the marquee in cell F1.

- Click Developer on the Ribbon to display the Developer tab.

- Click the Stop Recording button (Developer tab | Code group) to stop recording the worksheet activities (Figure 10–21).

Q&A

What if I make a mistake while recording the macro?

If you make a mistake while recording a macro, delete the macro and record it again. You delete a macro by clicking the Macros button (Developer tab |

Figure 10–21

Code group), clicking the name of the macro in the Macro dialog box, and then clicking the Delete button. You can then record the macro again with the same macro name. When the Macro dialog box is displayed, click the name of the macro (FirstName, in this case) and then click the Delete button. Finally, record the macro again.

Other Ways

1. Click Developer tab, click Record Macro button

To Record a Macro to Reformat the Membership Data where Last Name Appears First

To create the macro to reformat the membership data for Green Valley Conservation when the last name appears first, you will turn on the macro recorder and then complete the following tasks.

1. Use the LEN function in column C to determine the total number of characters in the member name. The result of the LEN function should be displayed in column C.

2. Use the SEARCH function in column D to determine the position of the space that separates the first and last names. The result of the SEARCH function should be displayed in column D.

3. Use the LEFT function to capture the last name. The result of the LEFT function should be displayed in column E. Use the Paste Values command to replace the formula with a text value.

4. Use the RIGHT function to capture the first name. The result of the RIGHT function should be displayed in column F. Use the Paste Values command to replace the formula with a text value.

5. Stop the macro recorder.

The following steps record the LastName macro to separate into two different columns the first name and last name for the entries that appear as LastName, FirstName.

1 Select cell A2, the first instance of last name appearing first.

2 Start the Macro Recorder to record a macro named **LastName**, with a shortcut key of CTRL+L, and a Description of **Macro splits names for entries with Last Name first.**

3 Enter the formula **=LEN(A2)** in cell C2.

4 Enter the formula **=SEARCH(" ", A2)** in cell D2.

5 Enter the formula **=LEFT(A2, D2-2)** in cell E2. Replace the content of cell E2 with the text value, using the Paste Values command.

6 Enter the formula **=RIGHT(A2, C2-D2)** in cell F2. Replace the content of cell F2 with the text value, using the Paste Values command.

7 Press the ESC key to remove the selection marquee, make cell A2 the active cell, and then stop the Macro Recorder (Figure 10–22).

Figure 10–22

To Password-Protect the Worksheet, Save the Workbook, and Close the Workbook

The following steps protect the Convert Member Data worksheet, save the workbook using the file name Green Valley Membership, and then close the workbook.

1 Click the Developer tab on the Ribbon, and then click the Protect Sheet button (Developer tab | Changes group). When the Protect Sheet dialog box is displayed, type **awareness** in the 'Password to unprotect sheet' text box and then click the OK button (Protect Sheet dialog box). When the Confirm Password dialog box is displayed, type **awareness** and then click the OK button (Confirm Password dialog box).

2 Save the workbook.

3 Click the workbook's Close button on the right side of its menu bar to close the workbook and leave Excel active.

Changing the Macro Security Level

Macros provide you with an opportunity to make certain tasks much more efficient and accurate. However, macros introduce an element of risk to your work in the form of computer viruses. A **computer virus** is a potentially damaging computer program designed to affect, or infect, your computer negatively by altering the way it works without your knowledge or permission. The increased use of networks, the Internet, and e-mail have accelerated the spread of computer viruses.

Macros are known carriers of viruses because of the ease with which a person can add programming code to macros. To combat this menace, most computer users run antivirus programs that search for viruses and destroy them before they ever have a chance to infect the computer. In addition, Excel provides four levels of protection from macro viruses: Disable all macros without notification, Disable all macros with notification, Disable all macros except digitally signed macros, and Enable all macros. By default, the macro security level is set to Disable all macros with notification, meaning that only macros from trusted sources can be used. Trusted sources are discussed later in this chapter.

To Set the Macro Security Level to Medium

The following steps set the level of protection to Disable all macros with notification.

1

• Click Developer on the Ribbon to display the Developer tab.

• Click the Macro Security button (Developer tab | Code group) to display the Trust Center dialog box.

• Click the 'Disable all macros with notification' option button (Figure 10–23).

2

• Click the OK button (Trust Center dialog box) to close the dialog box.

Figure 10–23

Other Ways

1. Click File tab, Options, Trust Center, Trust Center Settings

Enabling Macros
Excel remembers your decision about enabling macros. If you've enabled macros in a worksheet, Excel will not ask you about enabling them the next time you open the worksheet, but will open the worksheet with macros enabled.

More About Macro Security

Each time you open a workbook with an associated macro and the macro security level is set to 'Disable all macros with notification', Excel displays a Security Warning bar with an Enable Content button. Clicking the Enable Content button enables the macros, which means that the code can be executed.

If you are confident of the source (author) of the workbook and macros, click the Enable Content button. If you are uncertain about the reliability of the source of the workbook and macros, you can work with the macros disabled, which means that the code is not executable.

To Open a Workbook with Macros and Execute a Macro

The following steps open the Green Valley Membership workbook and enable the macros in the workbook. The steps show how to execute the recorded macro LastName by using the shortcut keys CTRL+L established when the macro was created.

- With Excel active, open the Green Valley Membership workbook (Figure 10–24).

Figure 10–24

- Click the Enable Content button in the Security Warning bar to open the workbook with macros enabled.

- Click Review on the Ribbon to display the Review tab.

- Click the Unprotect Sheet button (Review tab | Changes group) to unprotect the Convert Member Data worksheet using the password **awareness**.

- In the Convert Member Data worksheet, click cell A4 to select it.

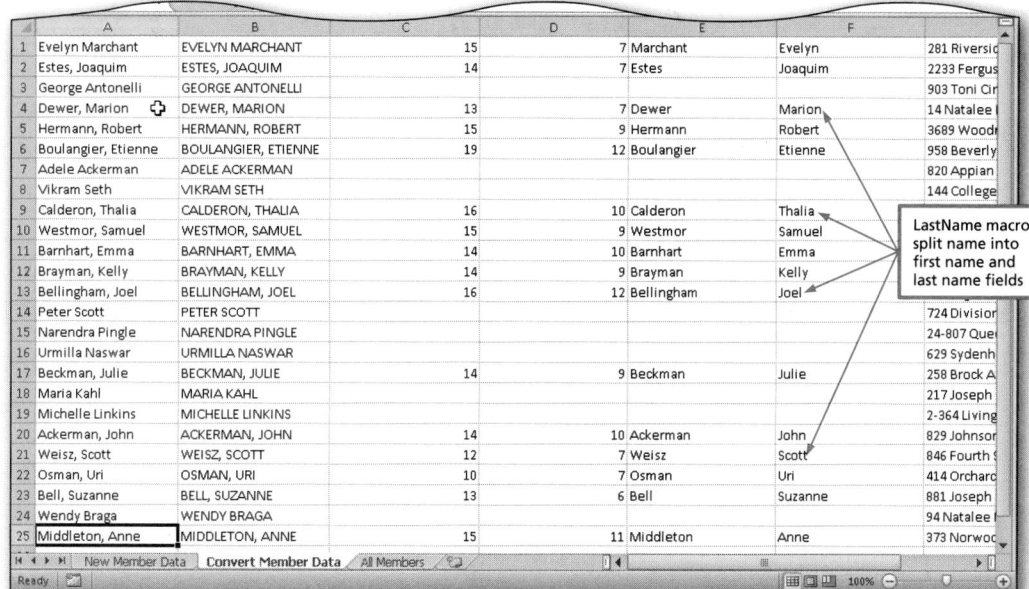

Figure 10–25

- Press CTRL+L to run the LastName macro.

- Click all cells in column A with names in the last name, first name format, and then run the LastName macro in each cell to format the name text in the desired format (Figure 10–25).

Q&A

Should I also run the FirstName macro?

Not yet. You will run the FirstName macro shortly.

Other Ways

1. On Developer tab, click Macros button, double-click macro name

To View and Print a Macro's VBA Code

As described earlier, a macro is composed of VBA code, which is created automatically by the macro recorder. Use the **Visual Basic Editor** to view and print the VBA code. The Visual Basic Editor is used by all Office applications to enter, modify, and view VBA code. The following steps view and print the FirstName macro's VBA code.

1

- If necessary, click Developer on the Ribbon to display the Developer tab.

- Click the Macros button (Developer tab | Code group) to display the Macro dialog box.

- When the Macro dialog box is displayed, click FirstName in the Macro name list (Figure 10–26).

Figure 10–26

2

- Click the Edit button (Macro dialog box) to display the Microsoft Visual Basic Editor.

- If necessary, click the Maximize button to maximize the Visual Basic Editor window (Figure 10–27).

Q&A

Can I edit the macro code?

Yes, you can edit the code in the Visual Basic Editor. For instance, if you had entered a period rather than a comma as the SEARCH argument when recording the macro, you could edit the code to modify the macro rather than re-recording the macro. After making the change in the code, closing the Visual Basic Editor will automatically save the changes you made.

Figure 10–27

3

- Examine the VBA code.

- When you are finished, click File on the menu bar to display the File menu (Figure 10–28).

4

- Click the Print command to display the Print - VBAProject dialog box.

- Click the OK button (Print - VBAProject dialog box) to print the macro code.

- Click the Microsoft Visual Basic Editor Close button on the right side of the title bar to close the Visual Basic Editor window.

Figure 10–28

To Add a Button to the Quick Access Toolbar, Assign the Button a Macro, and Use the Button

You can add as many buttons as you want to the Quick Access Toolbar. You also can select an icon for the buttons you add. The following steps add a button to the Quick Access Toolbar, change the button image, assign the FirstName macro to the button, and then use the button to reformat the membership data for Green Valley when the first name appears first.

1

- Right-click anywhere on the Quick Access Toolbar to display the shortcut menu (Figure 10–29).

Figure 10–29

2

- Click the Customize Quick Access Toolbar command on the shortcut menu to display the Customize the Quick Access Toolbar page of the Excel Options dialog box.

- Click the 'Choose commands from' box arrow to display a list of commands to add to the Quick Access Toolbar (Figure 10–30).

Figure 10–30

3

- Click Macros in the 'Choose commands from' list to display a list of macros.

- Click the FirstName macro to select it.

- Click the Add button (Excel Options dialog box) to add the FirstName macro to the Customize Quick Access Toolbar list (Figure 10–31).

Q&A

How can I delete the buttons that I add to the Quick Access Toolbar?

You can reset the Quick Access Toolbar to its installation default by clicking the Reset button on the Customize Quick Access Toolbar page of the Excel Options dialog box. If you share a computer with others, you should reset the Quick Access Toolbar before you quit Excel.

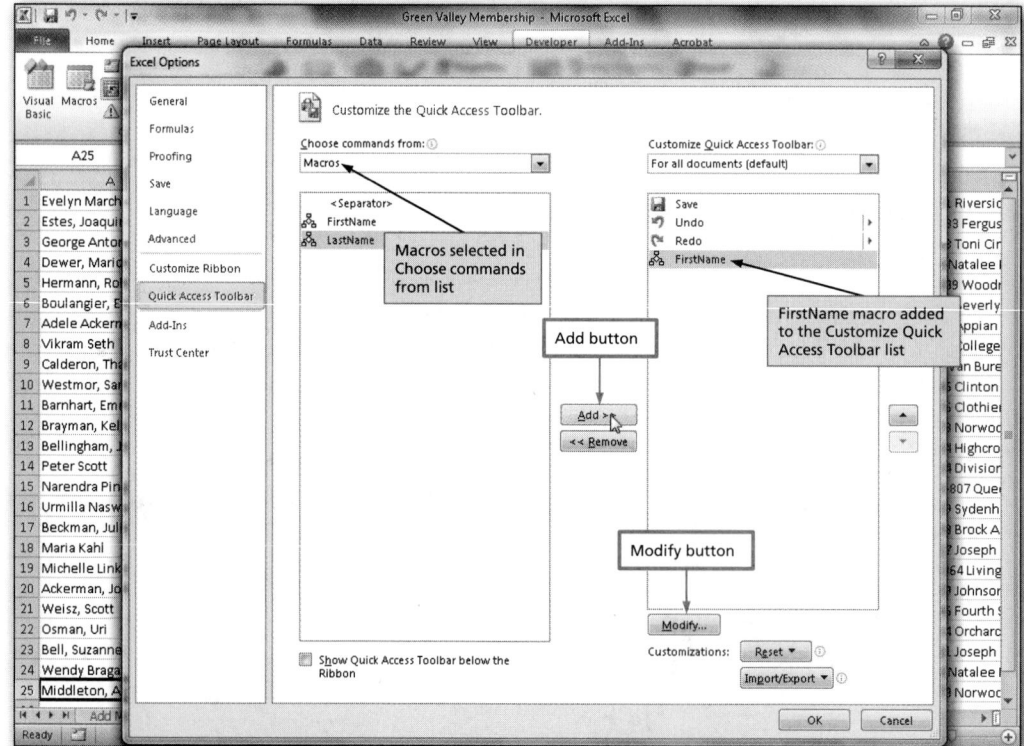

Figure 10–31

4

- Click the Modify button to display the Modify Button dialog box.

- Click the left arrow icon (column 12, row 2) in the Symbol list to select it (Figure 10–32).

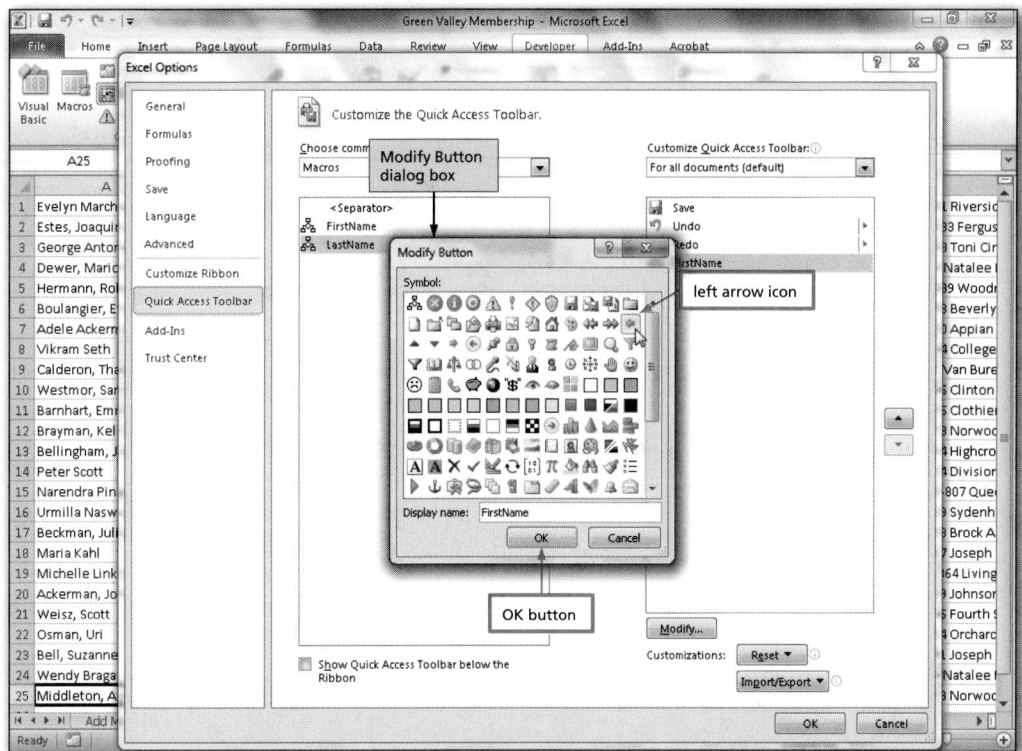

Figure 10–32

5

- Click the OK button (Modify Button dialog box) to assign the left arrow icon to the new command and to close the dialog box.

- Click the OK button (Excel Options dialog box) to close the dialog box.

- Point to the FirstName button on the Quick Access Toolbar to display the ScreenTip for the button (Figure 10–33).

Figure 10–33

6

- Select cell A3 and then click the FirstName button on the Quick Access Toolbar to run the FirstName macro.

- Click each remaining entry in column A with the first name appearing first and click the FirstName button to run the macro.

- Delete columns A through D, and then select cell A1 (Figure 10–34).

7

- Select the range A1:F25, and then press the CTRL+C keys to copy the contents of the range.

- Click the All Members sheet tab to make it the active sheet.

- Select cell A3 and then press the CTRL+V keys to paste the converted member data into the All Members sheet.

- Save the workbook.

Figure 10–34

Break Point: If you wish to take a break, this is a good place to do so. You can quit Excel now. To resume at a later time, start Excel, open the file called Green Valley Membership, and continue following the steps from this location forward.

Phase 2 — Creating a Procedure to Automate Existing Member Data Entry

The Green Valley Membership workbook up to now has been concerned with working with data that has already been entered. Macros were used to edit the existing data consistently. Member records stored on hard copy need to be entered manually. A novice user in an office driven by volunteers, however, might not know what cells to select or how to navigate the worksheet. To facilitate entering existing member records, Phase 2 calls for creating a Command Button control (Figure 10–35a) and an associated procedure (Figure 10–35b) that steps the user through entering data using dialog boxes.

A Command Button control is different from a toolbar button in that it is an object you draw on the worksheet. In this chapter, after a user triggers the event by clicking the Add Member Data Command Button control, the instructions in the associated procedure guide the user through entering the required member information, and then the procedure copies the result of each entry to a master list of members. The Command Button control also serves as the user interface. The user interface can be as simple as a button or as complex as a series of windows that accept data and display results. The **user interface**, together with the procedure, is called an **application**.

(a) Worksheet with Add Member Data Button

(b) Procedure Associated with Add Member Data Button

Figure 10–35

Create the first user interface.

The most common way to execute a procedure in Excel is to create a Command Button control. To create the control, click the Command Button button (Developer tab | Controls group). Next, use the mouse to locate and size the control in the same way you locate and size an embedded chart. You then can assign properties and the procedure to the Command Button control while Excel is in Design mode.

Plan Ahead

Two modes of Visual Basic for Applications exist within Excel: Design mode and Run mode. In **Design mode**, you can resize controls, assign properties to controls, and enter VBA code. All controls are active in **Run mode** and thus cannot be changed. If you click a control in Run mode, it triggers the event, and Excel executes the procedure associated with the control.

If you step through the procedure (Figure 10–35b) beginning at the line directly below Private Sub CommandButton1_Click(), you can see how a procedure methodically steps the user through entering the data in the range A9:G9, as outlined in the following list. Cell names that have been assigned to the cells in the range are used in the code to make the code more readable.

1. The first six lines present the user with dialog boxes prompting for specific information, and then record the user responses in named cells.

2. Lines 7 and 8 select the entered data and copy it to the Clipboard.

3. Lines 9 through 14 paste the data in the All Members sheet, after the last row of data.

4. Lines 15 through 21 return control to the Add Member Data worksheet. The entry that was just copied to the All Members sheet is erased from the Add Member Data worksheet, A2 is made the active cell, and the workbook is saved.

Visual Basic applications are built using the three-step process shown in Figure 10–36: (1) create the user interface; (2) set the properties; and (3) write the VBA code.

Step 1 — Create the User Interface

(a) Worksheet with the Add Member Data Button

Step 2 — Set the Properties

(b) Properties Window for Add Member Data Button

Step 3 — Write the VBA Code

```
Private Sub CommandButton1_Click()
    Range("Last_Name").Value = InputBox("Last Name?", "Enter", , 800, 6000)
    Range("First_Name").Value = InputBox("First Name?", "Enter", , 800, 6000)
    Range("Street_Address").Value = InputBox("Street Address?", "Enter", , 800, 6000)
    Range("City").Value = InputBox("City?", "Enter", , 800, 6000)
    Range("State").Value = InputBox("State?", "Enter", , 800, 6000)
    Range("Zip_Code").Value = InputBox("Zip Code?", "Enter", , 800, 6000)
    Range("A9:F9").Select
    Selection.Copy
    Sheets("All Members").Select
    Application.Goto Reference:="r1c1"
    Selection.End(xlDown).Select
    ActiveCell.Offset(1, 0).Range("A1").Select
    Selection.PasteSpecial Paste:=xlPasteValues, Operation:=xlNone, SkipBlanks _
        :=False, Transpose:=False
    Sheets("Add Member Data").Select
    Application.CutCopyMode = False
    ActiveCell.Select
    Range("A9:F9").Select
    Selection.ClearContents
    Range("A2").Activate
    ActiveWorkbook.Save
End Sub
```

(c) VBA Code Associated with Button

Figure 10–36

To Unprotect a Password-Protected Worksheet

1 With the Green Valley Membership workbook open, click the Add Member Data sheet tab to make the worksheet active, click Review on the Ribbon to display the Review tab, and then click the Unprotect Sheet button (Review tab | Changes group).

2 When the Unprotect Sheet dialog box is displayed, type **awareness** as the password and then click the OK button to unprotect the worksheet.

To Add a Command Button Control to the Worksheet

The following steps add a Command Button control to the worksheet. Before you can create the user interface, the Add Member Data worksheet in the Green Valley Membership workbook must be unprotected. The following steps unprotect the worksheet.

1

- Click Developer on the Ribbon to display the Developer tab.

- Click the Insert button (Developer tab | Controls group) to display the Controls gallery (Figure 10–37).

Figure 10–37

2

- Click the Command Button button in the ActiveX Controls area of the Controls gallery (column 1, row 1 of ActiveX area) to switch to Design mode.

- Move the mouse pointer (a crosshair) to the upper-left corner of cell C5.

- Drag the mouse pointer through the lower-right corner of cell D6 and hold down the mouse button (Figure 10–38).

Figure 10–38

3

• Release the mouse
button to add the
Command Button
control with the
default caption
CommandButton1
(Figure 10–39).

Figure 10–39

Other Ways

1. Click Design Mode
   button on Developer tab

Setting Control Properties

Each control available in the Controls gallery has many **properties**, or
characteristics, that can be set to determine the control's appearance and behavior.
You set these properties using the Properties window while working in Design mode.

Plan
Ahead

Determine properties for controls in the user interface.
As shown in the Properties window in Figure 10–36b on page EX 654, a Command Button
control has 25 different properties, such as caption (the words on the face of the button),
background color, foreground color, height, width, and font. After you add a Command
Button control to a worksheet, you can change any one of the 25 properties to improve the
control's appearance and modify how it works. For the Add Member Data worksheet, the
control's caption should read Add Member Data to reflect the purpose of the button.
The color of the caption's font should be changed to a color that is consistent with the
worksheet.

To Set the Command Button Control Properties

The following steps change the Command Button control's caption, the font size of the caption, and the color of the caption.

1

- With the Command Button control selected and Excel in Design mode, click the Properties button (Developer tab | Controls group) to open the Properties window for the Command Button control.

- If necessary, when the Properties window opens, click the Alphabetic tab.

- Click Caption in the Properties list, double-click the entry in the Caption box, and then type **Add Member Data** as the caption.

- Click ForeColor in the Properties list, click the ForeColor arrow, and then click the Palette tab to display a palette of colors to apply to the button text (Figure 10–40).

Figure 10–40

2

- Click green (column 5, row 5) on the ForeColor palette to select the font color.

- Click Font in the Properties list and then click the ellipsis button to display the Font dialog box.

- When the Font dialog box appears, click Bold in the Font style list and 14 in the Size list to select the font format (Figure 10–41).

Figure 10–41

3

- Click the OK button (Font dialog box) to display the Command Button control.

- If necessary, drag an edge of the Properties window to resize the window and display all of the properties in the window (Figure 10–42).

Figure 10–42

Writing Code for a Command Button

Using the Controls gallery to insert a Command Button control into a worksheet inserts an object only. To have the button take action when a user clicks it, you must write VBA code that directs the events in the worksheet after the command button is clicked.

Plan Ahead

Establish the Visual Basic code needed for each control.
The next step is to write and then enter the procedure that will execute when the user clicks the Add Member Data button.

- When you trigger the event that executes a procedure, such as clicking a button, Excel steps through the Visual Basic statements one at a time, beginning at the top of the procedure. The statements should reflect the steps you want Excel to take, in the exact order in which they should occur. An **event-driven program** includes procedures that are executed when the specific actions taken by the user or other events occur.

- After you determine what you want the procedure to do, write the VBA code on paper, creating a table similar to Table 10–1. Test the code before you enter it in the Visual Basic Editor, by stepping through the instructions one at a time yourself. As you do so, think about how the procedure affects the worksheet. This process is called **desk checking,** and it is an important part of the development process.

- Use comments to document each procedure. This will help you remember its purpose at a later date or help somebody else understand its purpose. In Table 10–1, the first five lines are comments. **Comments** begin with the word Rem (short for Remark) or an apostrophe ('). Comments have no effect on the execution of a procedure; they simply provide information about the procedure, such as name, creation date, and function. Comments can be placed at the beginning before the Sub statement, in between lines of code or at the end of a line of code, as long as each comment begins with an apostrophe ('). It is good practice to place comments containing overall documentation and information at the beginning, before the Sub statement.

Table 10–1 Add Member Data Button Procedure

Line	Statement
1	' Add Data Button Procedure
2	' Date Created: 10/17/2012
3	' Run from: Add Member Data sheet by clicking button labeled Add Member Data
4	' Function: When executed, this procedure accepts member data via input box and updates the member list
5	'
6	Private Sub CommandButton1_Click()
7	Range("Last_Name").Value = InputBox("Last Name?", "Enter", , 800, 6000)
8	Range("First_Name").Value = InputBox("First Name?", "Enter", , 800, 6000)
9	Range("Street_Address").Value = InputBox("Street Address?", "Enter", , 800, 6000)
10	Range("City").Value = InputBox("City?", "Enter", , 800, 6000)
11	Range("State").Value = InputBox("State?", "Enter", , 800, 6000)
12	Range("Zip_Code").Value = InputBox("Zip Code?", "Enter", , 800, 6000)
13	Range("A9:F9").Select
14	Selection.Copy
15	Sheets("All Members").Select
16	Application.Goto Reference:="r1c1"
17	Selection.End(xlDown).Select
18	ActiveCell.Offset(1, 0).Range("A1").Select
19	Selection.PasteSpecial Paste:=xlPasteValues, Operation:=xlNone, SkipBlanks _
20	:=False, Transpose:=False
21	Sheets("Add Member Data").Select
22	Application.CutCopyMode = False
23	ActiveCell.Select
24	Range("A9:F9").Select
25	Selection.ClearContents
26	Range("A2").Activate
27	ActiveWorkbook.Save
28	End Sub

About the Command Button Control Code

A procedure begins with a Sub statement and ends with an End Sub statement (lines 6 and 28 in Table 10–1). The **Sub statement** includes the keyword Private or Public followed by the name of the procedure, which Excel determines from the name of the control (in this case, CommandButton1) and the event that causes the procedure to execute (in this case, Click). **Private** means that the procedure can be executed only from this workbook. **Public** means that it can be executed from other workbooks or programs. The name of the Command Button control procedure is CommandButton1_Click().

The parentheses following the keyword Click in the Sub statement in line 6 are required. They indicate that arguments can be passed from one procedure to another. Passing arguments is beyond the scope of this chapter, but the parentheses still are required. The **End Sub statement** in line 17 signifies the end of the procedure and returns Excel to Ready mode.

The first executable statement in Table 10–1 is line 7, which presents the user with a dialog box in which to enter the last name, and copies the entry to the named cell Last_Name. One at a time, lines 8 through 12 accept the balance of the member data from the user and assign the data to other named cells. The named cells are found in the range A9:F9. The code uses the cell name to make the code more readable. Each one of these five statements handles one cell. To the right of the equal sign in lines 7 through 12 is the InputBox function. A **function** returns a value to the program. In this case, the **InputBox function** displays a dialog box and returns the value entered by the user. For example, in line 7, the InputBox function displays a dialog box with the message, "Last Name?" When the user responds and enters a name, the InputBox function returns the value entered to the program and assigns it to the cell named Last_Name, which is cell A9.

To Enter the New Data Button Procedure Using the Visual Basic Editor

To enter a procedure, you use the Visual Basic Editor. To activate the Visual Basic Editor, Excel must be in Design mode. To activate the Visual Basic Editor, select a control to switch Excel to Design mode and then click the View Code button (Developer tab | Controls group).

The Visual Basic Editor is a full-screen editor, which allows you to enter a procedure by typing the lines of VBA code as if you were using word processing software. At the end of each line, you press the ENTER key or use the DOWN ARROW key to move to the next line. If you make a mistake in a statement, you can use the arrow keys and the DELETE or BACKSPACE key to correct it. You also can move the insertion point to previous lines to make corrections.

The following steps activate the Visual Basic Editor and create the procedure for the Add Member Data button.

1

- Double-click the Add Member Data button to display the Microsoft Visual Basic Editor.

- When the Microsoft Visual Basic Editor starts, if the Project Explorer window appears on the left, click its Close button.

- If necessary, double-click the title bar of the Microsoft Visual Basic window to maximize it (Figure 10–43).

Figure 10–43

Why is there already code in the Microsoft Visual Basic Editor window?

The Visual Basic Editor automatically inserts the Sub and End Sub statements and positions the insertion point between the two statements when you double-click an ActiveX control with no code associated with it.

2

- Click to the left of the letter P in the word Private on the first line and press the ENTER key to add a blank line before the Sub statement.

- Move the insertion point to the blank line and then type the five comment statements (lines 1 through 5) in Table 10–1 on page EX 659, making sure you enter an apostrophe (') at the beginning of each comment line.

- Press the ENTER key to start a new line.

- Position the insertion point on the blank line between the Sub and End Sub statements (Figure 10–44).

Q&A Why does the code appear in different colors?

Excel automatically displays the comment lines in green. Keywords, such as Private and Sub, appear in blue. Other code appears with a black font color.

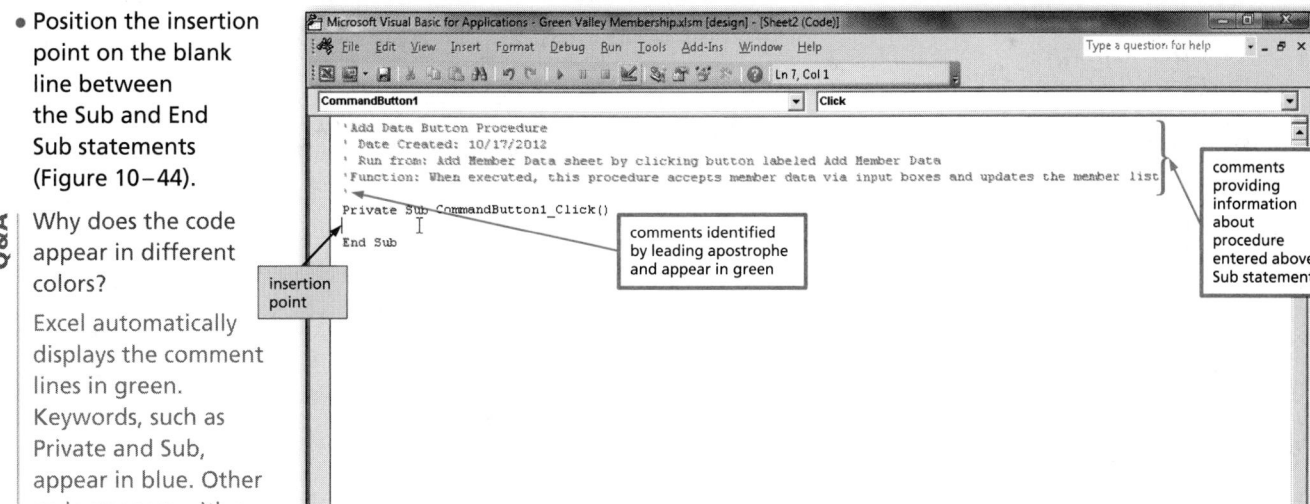

Figure 10–44

3

- Enter lines 7 through 27 in Table 10–1, using the spacebar to indent all lines between the Sub statement and End Sub statement by two spaces for clarity (Figure 10–45).

Q&A How should I exit the Visual Basic Editor and return to Excel?

Excel provides two ways to return control from the Visual Basic Editor to the worksheet. The Close button on the title bar (Figure 10–45) closes the Visual Basic Editor

Figure 10–45

and returns control to the worksheet. The View Microsoft Excel button on the Standard toolbar (Figure 10–45) also returns control to Excel, but only minimizes the Visual Basic Editor window. If you plan to switch between Excel and the Visual Basic Editor, then use the View Microsoft Excel button; if you want to close the Visual Basic Editor and return to Excel, use the Close button.

- Click the Close button on the right side of the Microsoft Visual Basic title bar to return to the worksheet. (Figure 10–46).

- Click the Design Mode button (Developer tab | Controls group) to return to Run mode.

Q&A

What is the result of clicking the Design Mode button?

Excel returns to Run mode, which means if you click the Add Member Data button, Excel will execute the associated procedure.

Figure 10–46

Other Ways

1. Click Visual Basic button on Ribbon

2. In Design mode, right-click control, click View Code on shortcut menu

More about Visual Basic for Applications

Visual Basic for Applications includes many more statements than those presented here. Even this simple procedure, however, can help you understand the basic composition of a Visual Basic statement. For example, each of the statements within the procedure shown in Figure 10–45 includes a period. The entry on the left side of the period identifies the object you want to affect. An **object** can be a cell, a range, a chart, a worksheet, a workbook, a button, or any other control you create on a worksheet. Objects also can be other applications in Windows or parts of other applications. The entry on the right side of the period identifies what you want to do to the object. You can place a method or property on the right side of the period. For example, the following statement:

```
Range("A9:F9").Select
```

selects the range A9:F9. The next statement:

```
Selection.ClearContents
```

clears the contents of the range A9:F9. You could combine the two statements into one:

```
Range("A9:F9").ClearContents
```

You use a method, such as ClearContents, to change an object's behavior. In this case, the method ClearContents is changing the behavior of the range by clearing its contents.

You previously were shown how to change an object's procedure using the Microsoft Visual Basic Editor window (Figure 10 – 45 on page EX 661). The following example shows that you also can change an object's properties during execution of a procedure. The object in this case is a Command Button control.

```
CommandButton1.Caption = "Add Member Data"
```

This statement changes the value of the Caption property of the button to Add Member Data during execution of the procedure.

Several of the statements in the procedure include equal signs. An equal sign instructs Excel to make an assignment to a cell. For example, when executed as part of the procedure, as in the following example:

```
Range("Last_Name").Value = InputBox("Last Name?",
"Enter", , 800, 6000)
```

the equal sign instructs Excel to display a dialog box called Enter with the prompt message, Last Name? The statement then assigns the value entered by the user in response to the dialog box to cell A9, which is named Last_Name. The numbers 800, 6000 instruct Excel where to display the dialog box.

To Add Member Data Using the Add Member Data Button

Before attempting to enter data using the Add Member Data button, be sure you exit Design mode and return Excel to Run mode, as illustrated in Step 5 in the previous set of steps. The following steps enter member data as follows: Last Name — Cross; First Name — Jane; Address — 24 Park Avenue; City — Brookley; State — NE; and Zip Code — 68562.

1

- Click the Add Member Data button to display the first Enter dialog box with the prompt message, Last Name?.

- Type **Cross** in the text box (Figure 10–47).

Figure 10–47

- Click the OK button (Enter dialog box) or press the ENTER key to provide a last name and close the dialog box.

- Enter the data as requested by Excel for each of the subsequent dialog boxes, clicking OK or pressing the ENTER key until you enter the zip code in the dialog box (Figure 10–48).

Figure 10–48

- Click the OK button to enter the zip code and close the dialog box.

Q&A

What happens when the OK button is clicked?

Excel copies the contents of the range A9:F9, switches to the All Members worksheet, navigates to the first blank row, and then pastes the member information into that row. Excel then saves the workbook and returns to the Add Member Data worksheet.

- Repeat Steps 1 and 2 for member Jason Webber, 438 Leonard Drive, Plainville, NE, 68599.

- Click the OK button (Enter dialog box) to complete the entry for Jason Webber.

- Click the All Members sheet tab to make the worksheet active (Figure 10–49).

Figure 10–49

To Protect a Worksheet and Save the Workbook

With Phase 2 of this project complete, the final step is to protect the worksheet and save the workbook.

1 Click Review on the Ribbon to display the Review tab, and then click the Protect Sheet button (Review tab | Changes group) to open the Protect Sheet dialog box.

2 When the Protect Sheet dialog box is displayed, type `awareness` in the 'Password to unprotect sheet' text box and then click the OK button. When the Confirm Password dialog box is displayed, type `awareness` and then click the OK button.

3 Save the workbook.

4 Click the Close Window button on the right side of the Ribbon to close the Green Valley Membership workbook but leave Excel open.

Break Point: If you wish to take a break, this is a good place to do so. You can quit Excel now. To resume at a later time, start Excel, and continue following the steps from this location forward.

Phase 3 — Creating a New Member Drive Data Entry Screen Automating the New Member Data Entry

The final phase of this project requires that the Green Valley Member Drive workbook be edited to automate the new member data entry. In Phase 2, clicking the Add Member Data button on the Add Member Data sheet in the Green Valley Membership workbook triggered Excel to display a series of input dialog boxes. Phase 3 uses this approach for entering some of the new member data. The remaining data (preferred method of communication, source of information about event, and volunteer opportunities) is entered using check boxes and option buttons to help reduce input errors that can be caused by mistyped data. By having all data entry done through controls and input dialog boxes, protecting the workbook before using it to gather data will limit user interaction to those controls and dialog boxes.

Figure 10–50 shows how the New Member Signup worksheet will look when complete. When you click the Step 1 – Click to Enter Member Information button, Excel displays input dialog boxes to accept the member information for the information in rows 4 through 8.

Below the member information are check boxes and option buttons that collect information about preferred method of contact, source of information about the group, and volunteer interests. Multiple check boxes can be selected for volunteer interests. Users are restricted to one preferred method of contact and one source of information through the use of option buttons.

BTW

Certification
The Microsoft Office Specialist (MOS) program provides an opportunity for you to obtain a valuable industry credential — proof that you have the Excel 2010 skills required by employers. For more information, visit the Excel 2010 Certification Web page (scsite.com/ex2010/cert).

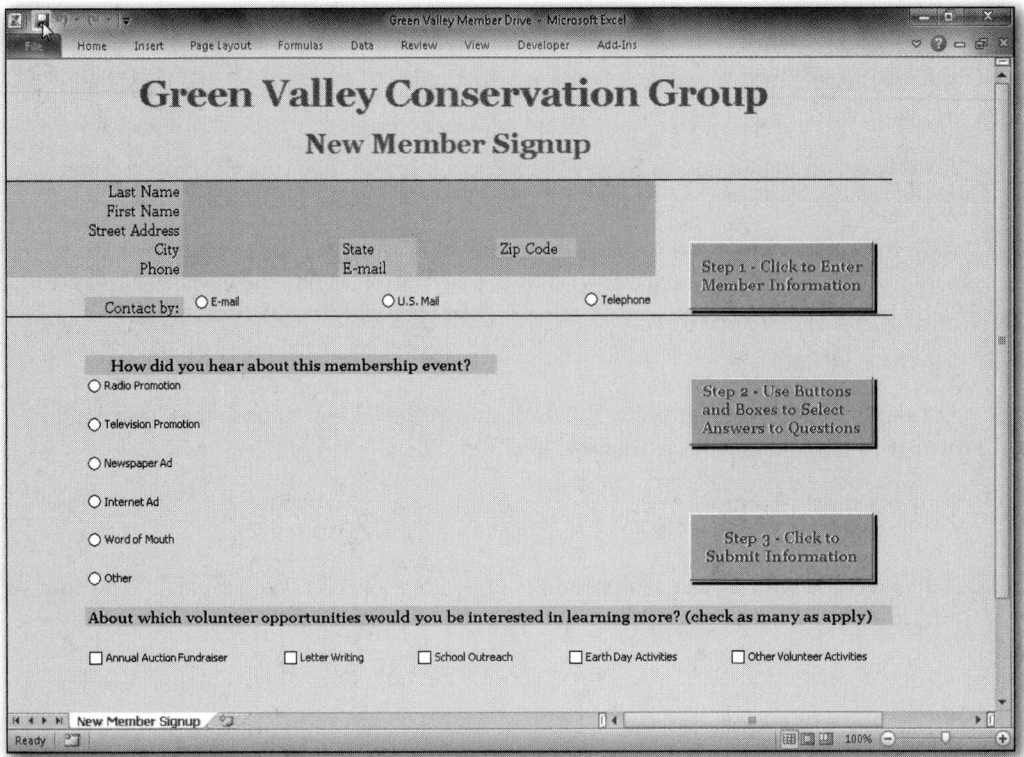

Figure 10–50

Plan Ahead	**Create the second user interface.**
	In Phase 3, the first step is to create the New Member Signup user interface shown in Figure 10–50. After creating the gray background for the New Member Signup worksheet, the following controls must be added:
	• Nine option button form controls
	• Five Check Box form controls
	• Two Control button ActiveX controls
	• One Text Box ActiveX control
	When you first create a user interface, you position the controls as close as you can to their final location on the screen, and then you finalize the locations of the controls, after setting the properties.

Figure 10–51 shows the Controls gallery and where the above referenced controls can be found in the gallery.

Figure 10–51

More on Form Controls and ActiveX Controls

Form controls and ActiveX controls look identical in the gallery. However, they do have functional differences that can help determine which one is the best choice for an object. Form controls require no knowledge of VBA to use. You can assign an Excel macro directly to a form control, allowing the macro to be run with a simple click. Form controls also allow you to easily reference cells and use Excel functions and expressions to manipulate data. You can customize their appearance at a rudimentary level.

ActiveX controls provide great flexibility in terms of their design. They have extensive properties that can be used to customize their appearance. ActiveX controls cannot be assigned an Excel macro directly. The macro code must be part of the VBA code for the control.

In this project, you will use form controls for the Check Box and Option Button controls, because of their ease of use and the ability to use Excel functions with no additional code. You will use ActiveX controls for the Command Button and Text Box controls to provide a more visually appealing interface than would be possible using form controls.

The Option Button controls will be used with the Excel INDEX function to record the single selections for two entries: the member preferred method of contact and how members heard about the fundraiser. The control itself returns a number indicating which option button was selected. The INDEX function matches that selection to a list, and returns the entry in the list. This allows the workbook to contain entries such as "Telephone", "E-Mail", and "U.S. Mail", rather than values that the control returns such as 1, 2, and 3.

To Open a Workbook and Unprotect a Worksheet

The following steps open the workbook Member Drive Data, apply the Civic theme, and save the workbook using the file name Green Valley Member Drive.

1 Open the Member Drive Data workbook from the Data Files for Students.

2 Unprotect the worksheet using the password awareness.

3 Apply the Civic theme to the workbook.

4 Save the workbook using the name Green Valley Member Drive.

To Enter Name and Address Fields

The following steps format the title, subtitle, name, and address fields.

1 Merge and center the ranges A1:K1 and A2:K2.

2 Format the title in cell A1 to 28 point, bold, and format the subtitle in cell A2 to 20 point, bold.

3 Set the height of row 1 to 50.25, and the height of row 2 to 25.50. Middle-align the text in rows 1 and 2.

4 Set the text color in rows 1 and 2 to Blue-Grey, Text 2.

5 Set column B to a width of 10.44, and right-align the contents of cells B4:B10.

6 Merge and center the range B13:F13, and apply bold to the cells.

7 Merge the range B26:K26, and apply bold to the cells.

⑧ Apply the Teal, Accent 3, Lighter 80% fill color to the entire worksheet.

⑨ Apply the Teal, Accent 3, Lighter 60% fill color to cells A4:B8, B10, E7:E8, G7, B13, and B26.

⑩ Merge ranges C4:H4, C5:H5, C6:H6, C7:D7, C8:D8, and F8:H8.

⑪ Apply the Ice Blue, Background 2 fill color to C4:C6, C7:C8, F7, H7, and F8.

⑫ Apply a bottom border to ranges A3:K3 and A10:K10 (Figure 10–52).

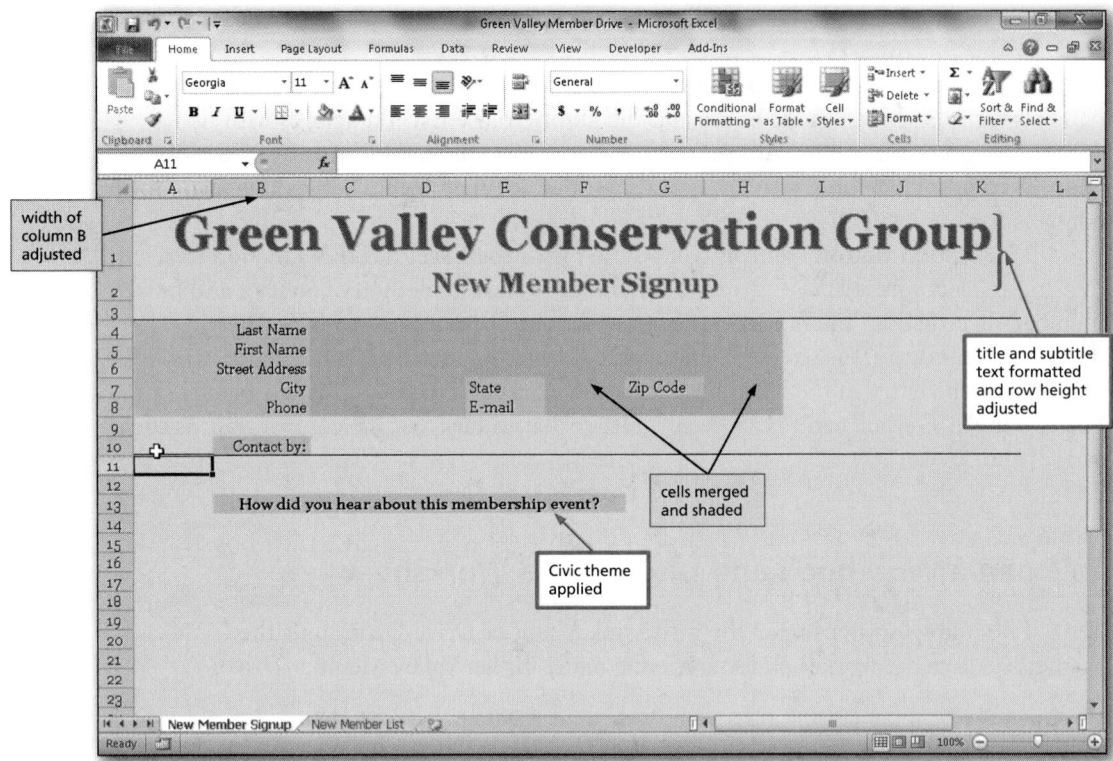

Figure 10–52

To Add Form Controls to a User Interface

The following steps create the form controls, but do not position them exactly in the locations shown in Figure 10–50.

- Click Developer on the Ribbon to display the Developer tab.
- Click the Insert button (Developer tab | Controls group) to display the Controls gallery (Figure 10–53).

Figure 10–53

2

- Click the Option Button button in the Form Controls area in the Controls gallery.

- Drag the mouse pointer so the control is displayed as shown in Figure 10–54.

Q&A The option button I added looks different. It uses the same Civic theme font as used in the rest of the worksheet. What should I do?

You probably selected the Option Button control in the ActiveX Controls area of the Controls gallery. Click the Option Button control, press the DELETE key, and then repeat Steps 1 and 2.

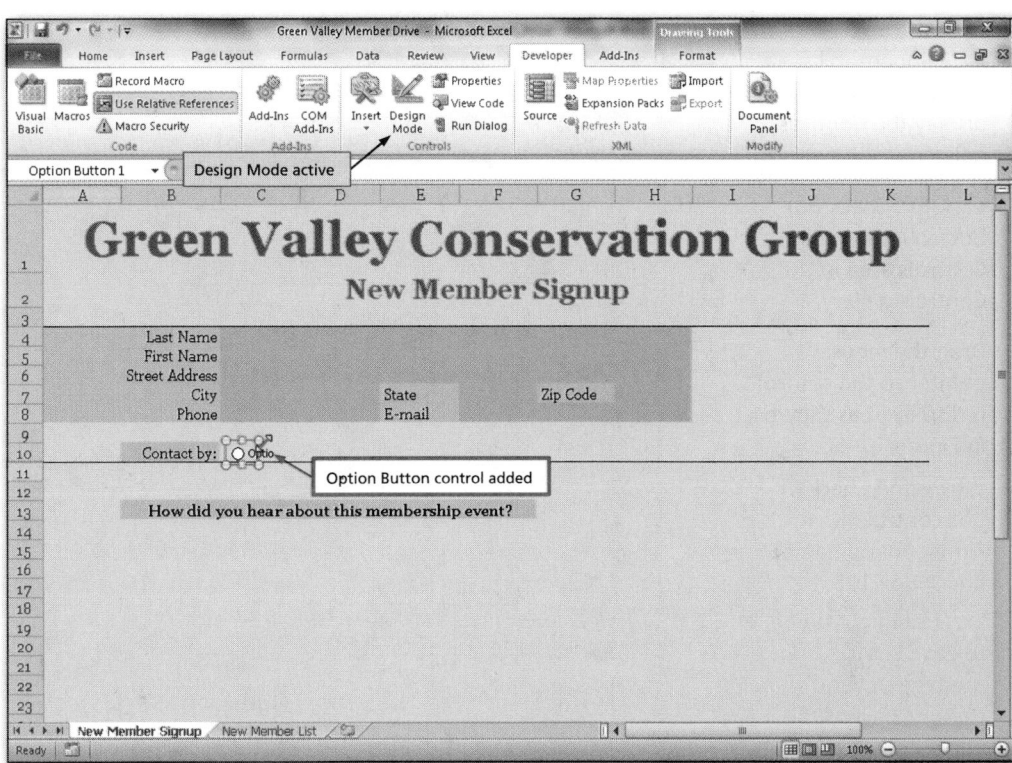

Figure 10–54

3

- Repeat Step 2 to place eight additional option buttons as shown in Figure 10–55.

Q&A What if I add a control in error?

You can delete a control by selecting the control while in Design mode, and then pressing the DELETE key.

Figure 10–55

- Click the Insert button (Developer tab | Controls group) to display the Controls gallery.

- Click the Check Box button in the Form Controls area in the Controls gallery.

- Drag the mouse pointer so the control is displayed as shown in Figure 10–56.

Q&A

Why is the Check Box control in Figure 10–56 named Check Box 10?

Excel assigns a name to each control, using the type of control as the first part of the

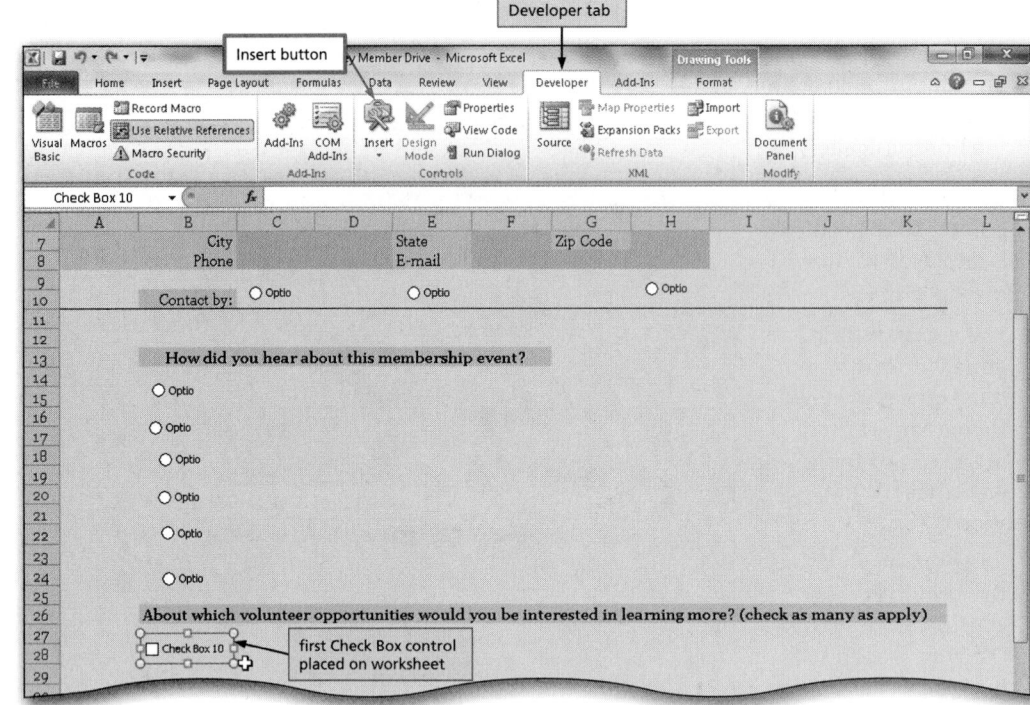

Figure 10–56

name and an incremented number as the second part. The first Check Box control added to a workbook is typically Check Box 1, but if other Check Box controls have been added, the name uses a different number in sequence.

- Repeat Step 4 to place four additional check box buttons as shown in Figure 10–57.

Q&A

What if I placed the control incorrectly?

If you want to reposition a control, select the control while in Design mode and then drag it to its new location.

Q&A

The check box is not the size I need it to be. What can I do?

Check boxes are easily resized. The check boxes here will be resized after the captions are changed later in this chapter.

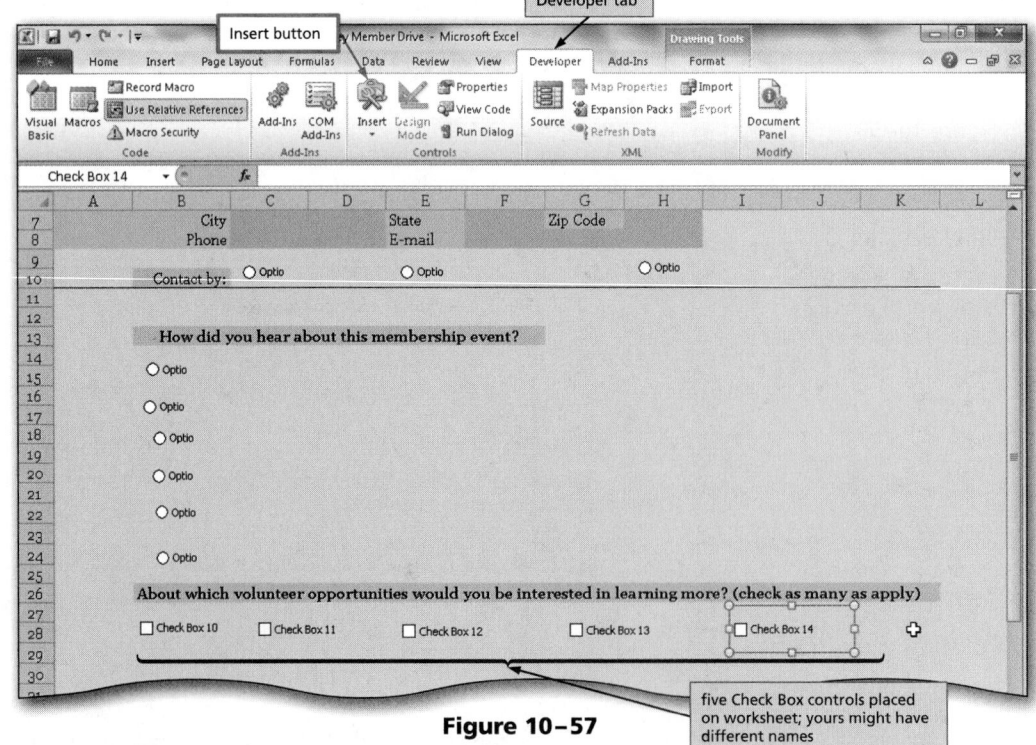

Figure 10–57

Other Ways

1. Select control, click Copy button (Home tab | Clipboard group), click Paste button

   (Home tab | Clipboard group)

2. Right-click control, click Copy on shortcut menu, right-click

   worksheet, click Paste on shortcut menu

3. Select control, press CTRL+C to copy, press CTRL+V to paste

To Group Option Buttons in a User Interface

With form controls, only one of the option buttons on the form can be selected as the form is set up now. Use the Group Box form control to group one set of the option buttons together. The following steps create the Group Box form control, and group option buttons inside it.

1

- Click the Insert button (Developer tab | Controls group) to display the Controls gallery (Figure 10–58).

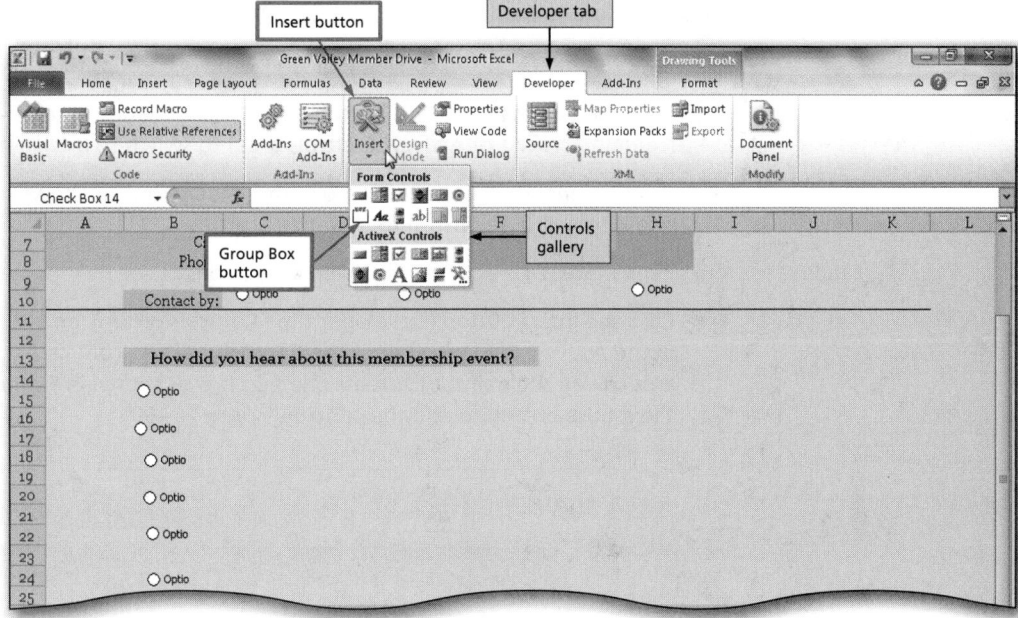

Figure 10–58

2

- Click the Group Box button in the Form Controls area in the Controls gallery.

- Drag the mouse pointer so the Group Box control is displayed as shown in Figure 10–59.

Q&A How accurate does the group box have to be?

The Option Button controls need to be completely enclosed in the Group Box control in order for it to work correctly.

Q&A I do not like the outline of the box around the option buttons. What can I do?

You can make the box outline invisible using VBA code. You add this later, when you associate code with the control.

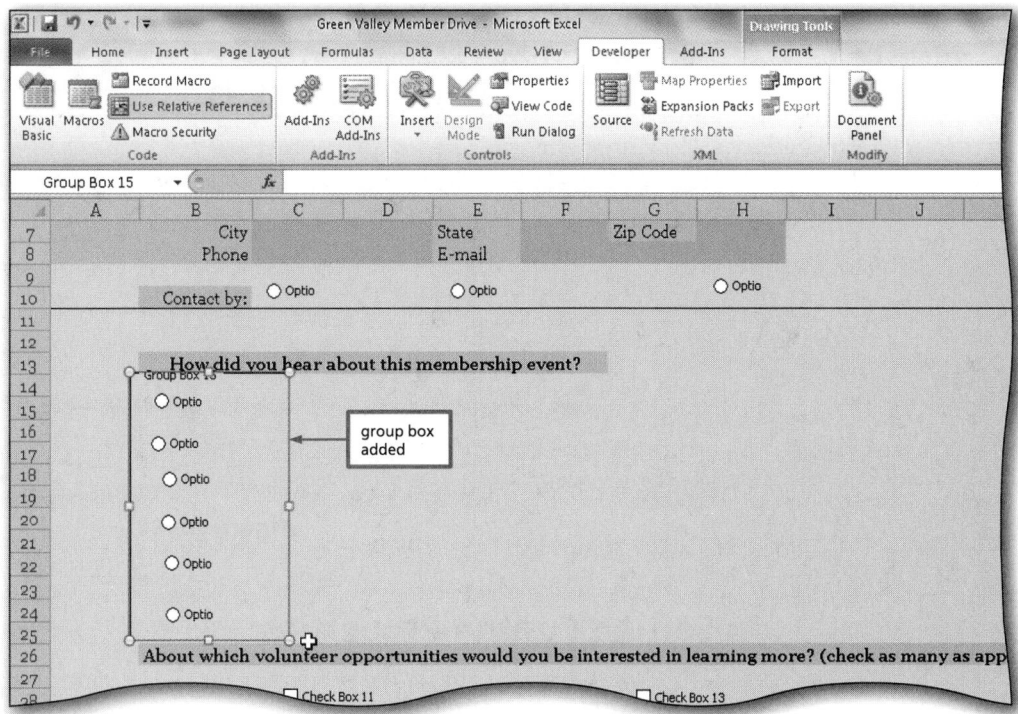

Figure 10–59

To Add Command Buttons and a Text Box Control in a User Interface

When possible, reuse code to save time and effort. The code created in Phase 2 to enter member data will be reused, with edits, to enter new member data, and to save new member data to a different worksheet. The following steps create the Command buttons.

1 Click the Insert button (Developer tab | Controls group) to display the Controls gallery.

2 Click the Command Button button in the ActiveX Controls area of the Controls gallery (column 1, row 1 of ActiveX Controls area) to switch to Design mode.

3 Drag the mouse pointer to create CommandButton1 as shown in Figure 10–60, and then release the mouse button to add the control.

4 Repeat Steps 1 – 3 to create CommandButton2.

5 Click the Insert button (Developer tab | Controls group), and then click the Text Box button in the ActiveX Controls area of the Controls gallery (column 5, row 1 of ActiveX Controls area). Drag the pointer to create the text box as shown in Figure 10–60, and then release the mouse button to add the control (Figure 10–60).

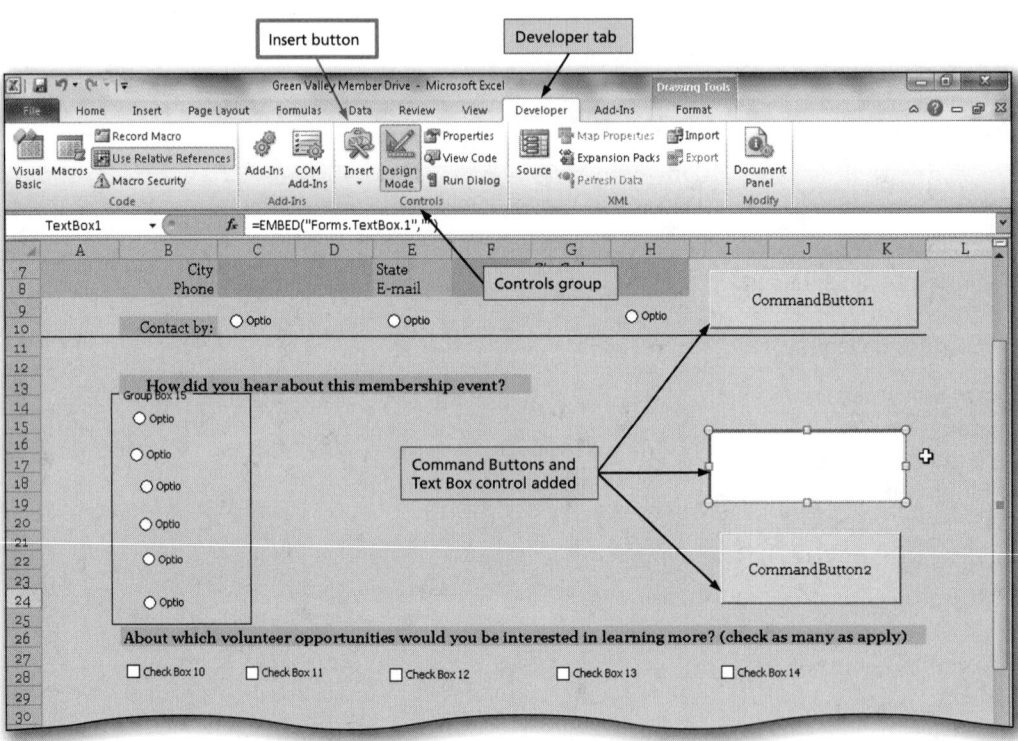

Figure 10–60

Setting Control Properties

The next step is to set the properties for the 16 controls that make up the user interface. The 16 controls best can be seen by referring to Figure 10–50 and counting the option buttons, check boxes, and command buttons. The properties will be set as follows:

1. **Option buttons** — Set the captions to match those in Figure 10–50. Resize the controls so that the entire caption shows. Align and horizontally distribute the Contact by: controls. Align and vertically distribute the option buttons inside the Group box. Link the first Contact by: option button to the named range,

contact, and link the first option button in the Group box to the named range information_source.

2. **Group box** — Hide the group box border.

3. **Check boxes** — Set the captions to match those in Figure 10–50. Resize the controls so that the entire caption shows. Align and horizontally distribute the check box controls. Link the Check box controls to the appropriate named ranges.

4. **Command buttons and text box** — Set the captions to match those in Figure 10–50. Resize the controls so that the entire caption is displayed.

To Format the Option Button Controls for Contact Method

The following steps change the text associated with the Option Button controls, resize the controls, and align and distribute the controls.

- With Excel in Design mode, right-click the first option button control in the Contact by area to select it.

- Click the control to close the shortcut menu.

- Use the sizing handles to enlarge the control so the text is completely visible.

- Right-click the control to display the shortcut menu (Figure 10–61).

Figure 10–61

- Click Edit Text on the shortcut menu so you can edit the control text.

- Delete the text in the control and type **E-mail** to replace the text.

- Resize the control so that it just encloses the new text (Figure 10–62).

Figure 10–62

- Repeat Steps 1 and 2 to resize and rename the other two contact controls, naming them as shown in Figure 10–63.

- Click the Telephone control to select it.

- Hold down the ALT key and drag the control until the right edge is aligned with the right edge of column H (Figure 10–63).

Figure 10–63

- Hold down the CTRL key, and then click the other two controls to select all three Option Button controls.

- Click Format on the Ribbon to display the Drawing Tools Format tab.

- Click the Align button (Drawing Tools Format tab | Arrange group) to display the alignment options.

- Click Align Bottom to align the three controls along their bottom borders.

- Click the Align button again to display the alignment options.

- Click Distribute Horizontally to space the three controls evenly between columns A and H (Figure 10–64).

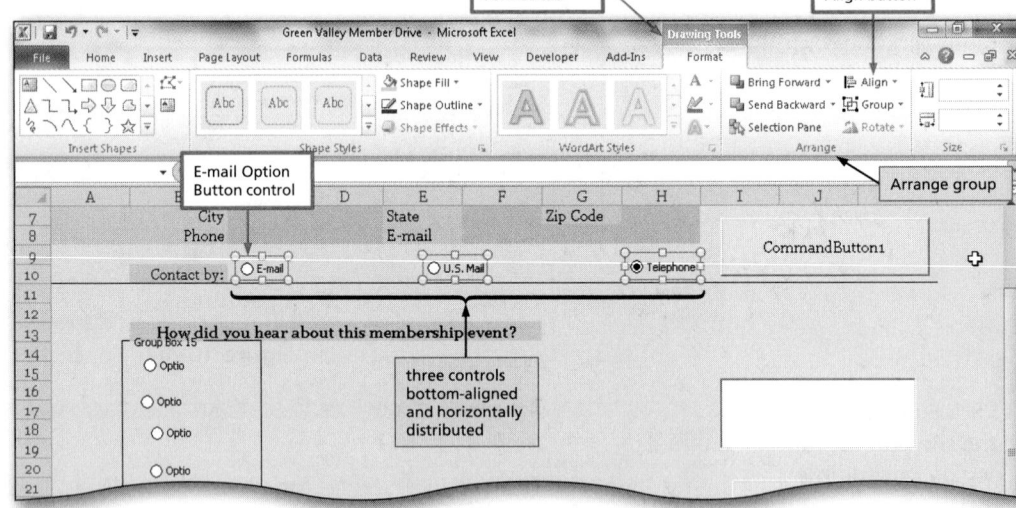

Figure 10–64

Q&A Is there a way to make the controls stand out more?

You can format the controls with borders and fill colors to make them stand out from the background. Choose Format Object on the shortcut menu and use the Color and Lines tab in the Format Object dialog box to apply colors and patterns.

Q&A Can I make the controls a specific size?

Size and placement of controls can also be set using the Format Control command on the shortcut menu.

To Record User Input for Contact Method to Another Location on the Worksheet

The following steps record the user input for contact information at another place on the worksheet.

1

- Click the worksheet to deselect the controls.

- Right-click the E-mail Option Button control to display the shortcut menu.

- Click Format Control to display the Format Control dialog box.

- If necessary, click the Control tab to display the Control settings.

- Enter `$I$40` in the Cell link box to enter the identity of the option button selected in cell I40 (Figure 10–65).

Figure 10–65

2

- Click the OK button (Format Control dialog box) to close the dialog box.

- Click cell I39 to make it the active cell.

- Enter `=INDEX (contact,$I$40)` to return text rather than numbers in row 39 (Figure 10–66).

How does the INDEX function work here?

You were introduced to the INDEX function in Chapter 6. In this instance, the INDEX function looks at the value in cell I40, which identifies which Option Button was selected, and returns the entry associated with that value from the named range contact. The named range contact is found in column P in this worksheet.

Figure 10–66

To Record User Input for the Group Box Controls

The following steps format the option buttons in the Group Box control, and record the user input in another place on the worksheet.

1 Select each of the six option buttons in the group box in turn and edit the text to match the text in Figure 10–67.

2 Move the top option button so that its upper-left corner aligns with the upper-left corner of cell B14, and move the bottom option button so that its lower-left corner aligns with the lower-left corner of cell B24.

3 Select all six controls, and using the Align button, apply the Align Left and Distribute Vertically formats to the group.

4 Right-click the Radio Promotion Option Button control and then click Format Control. In the Format Control dialog box, enter `$J$40` in the Cell link box.

5 Make cell J39 the active cell. Enter `=INDEX(information_source,$J$40)` to return text from the named range information_source rather than numbers in row 39 (Figure 10–67).

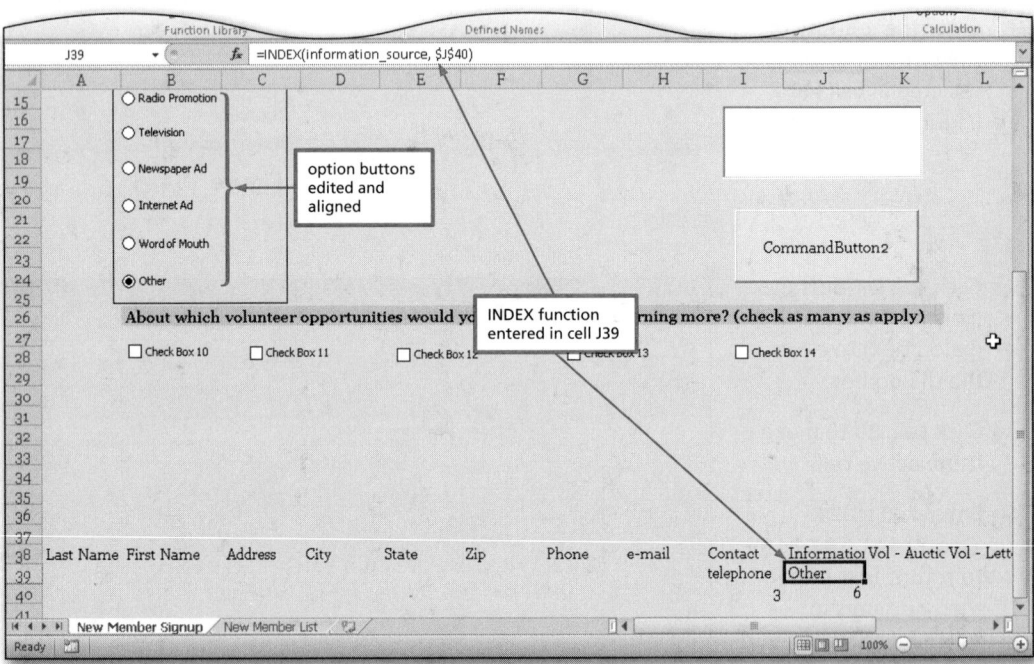

Figure 10–67

To Format the Check Box Controls

The Check Box controls are formatted in the same fashion as the Option Button controls. The following steps format and align the Check Box controls.

1 Select each of the five check box buttons in turn and edit the text to match the text in Figure 10–68.

2 Move the far-left check box button so that its upper-left corner aligns with the upper-left corner of cell B28, and move the far-right check box button so that its upper-right corner aligns with the upper-right corner of cell K28.

3 Select all five controls, and using the Align button, apply the Align Bottom and Distribute Horizontally formats to the group (Figure 10–68).

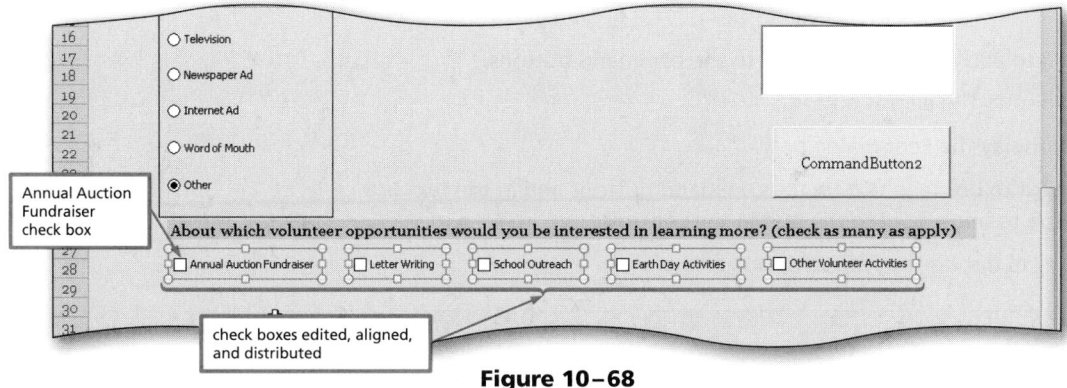

Figure 10–68

To Record User Input for the Check Box Controls

The following steps record the user input for the check boxes at another place on the worksheet.

1 Select the Annual Auction Fundraiser Check Box control. Use the shortcut menu to display the Format Control dialog box. In the Cell link box (Format Control dialog box, Control tab), enter the cell address $K$39 to record user input.

2 Repeat Step 1 for each of the remaining four check box controls, using cells L39 through O39 for the cell links.

To Format the Command Button and Text Box Controls

The Command Button and Text Box controls are formatted using the Properties window. The following steps set the properties for the Command Button and Text Box controls.

1

- Select the two Command Button controls and the Text Box control to prepare for setting their properties.

- Click the Properties button (Developer tab | Controls group) to open the Properties window.

- Click the BackColor property to display the BackColor box arrow.

- Click the BackColor box arrow to display two palettes of colors.

- Click the Palette tab to display the colors on that tab (Figure 10–69).

Figure 10–69

2

- Click gray (column 1, row 3) to add a gray background to the command buttons.

- Click the Font property to display the ellipsis button.

- Click the ellipsis button to display the Font dialog box.

- Click Bold in the Font style list to bold the text on the command buttons and in the text box, and then click the OK button to apply bold to the text in the controls.

- Click the ForeColor property to display the ForeColor box arrow.

- Click the ForeColor box arrow to display two palettes of colors.

- Click the Palette tab to display the colors on that tab.

- Click purple (column 8, row 5) change the font color to purple.

- Set the WordWrap and Shadow properties to True.

- Set Height to 50.25 and Width to 140.25.

- Use the Align button to apply the Align Right and Distribute Vertically formats to the group (Figure 10–70).

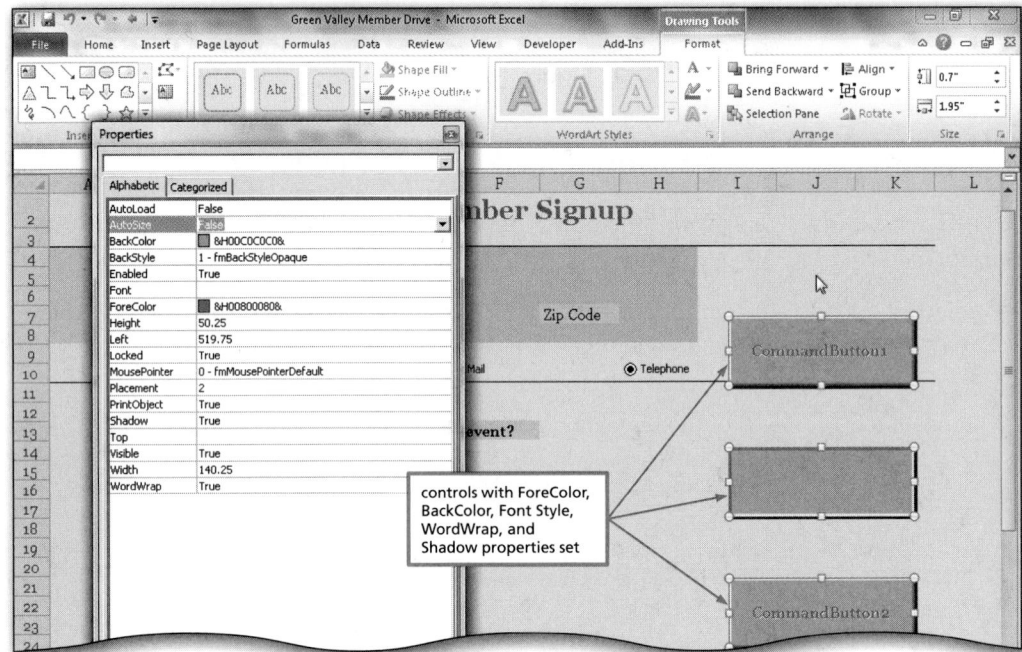

Figure 10–70

3

- Select the Command Button controls individually, and set the Caption for each one to the text shown in Figure 10–71.

- Select the text box to prepare for entering properties for the control.

- Set the Multiline property to True so that users can enter more than one line of text.

- Set Special Effect to 1 – fmSpecialEffect Raised to format the control.

- Set Text to the text shown in the text box in Figure 10–71.

4

- Close the Properties Window.

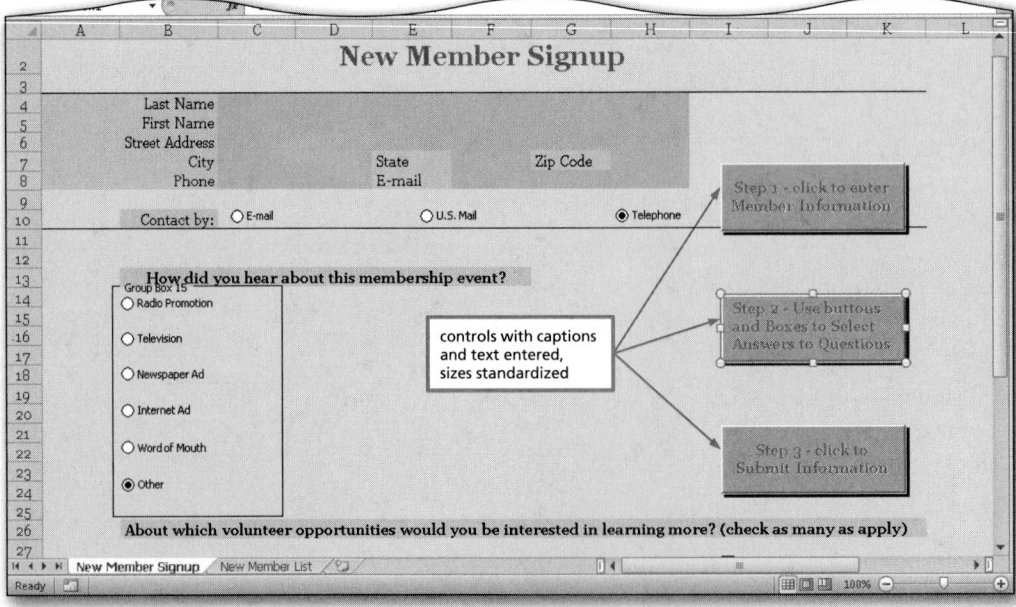

Figure 10–71

To Assign Names to Cells

The VBA code in Tables 10–4 and 10–5 requires that some cells be named, and that some cells contain references to other cells. The following steps assign names to cells and enter necessary references. The list of cell names and references are found in Tables 10–2 and 10–3.

Table 10–2 Cell Names	
Cell	**Name**
A39	Last_Name
B39	First_Name
C39	Street_Address
D39	City
E39	State
F39	Zip_Code
G39	Telephone
H39	Email_Address

Table 10–3 Cell References	
Cell	**Name**
C4	=A39
C5	=B39
C6	=C39
C7	=D39
F7	=E39
H7	=F39
C8	=G39
F8	=H39

1
- Click Formulas on the Ribbon to display the Formulas tab.

- Click the Name Manager button (Formulas tab | Defined Names group) to open the Name Manager dialog box (Figure 10–72).

Figure 10–72

- Click the New button (Name Manager dialog box) to open the New Name dialog box.

- Enter **Last_Name** in the Name text box.

- Delete any contents in the Refers to text box, and then click cell A39 to enter the sheet and cell reference for that cell (Figure 10–73).

Figure 10–73

- Click the OK button (New Name dialog box) to enter the cell name.

- Repeat Step 2 for each entry in Table 10–2, clicking OK after completing each entry (Figure 10–74).

- Click the Close button (Name Manager dialog box) to close the dialog box once all names are entered.

- Enter the cell references listed in Table 10–3 into the appropriate cells.

Figure 10–74

To Enter the Command Button Procedures Using the Visual Basic Editor

The following steps activate the Visual Basic Editor and create the procedure for the Step 1 button.

- With the Step 1 button selected and Excel in Design mode, click the View Code button (Developer tab | Controls group) to display the Microsoft Visual Basic Editor.

Q&A

Do I need to maximize the Microsoft Visual Basic Editor window?

Yes. If necessary, double-click the title bar to maximize the Microsoft Visual Basic Editor window.

- Click the Object box arrow at the top of the window and then click CommandButton1 in the alphabetical list.

- Enter the VBA code shown in Table 10–4 (Figure 10–75).

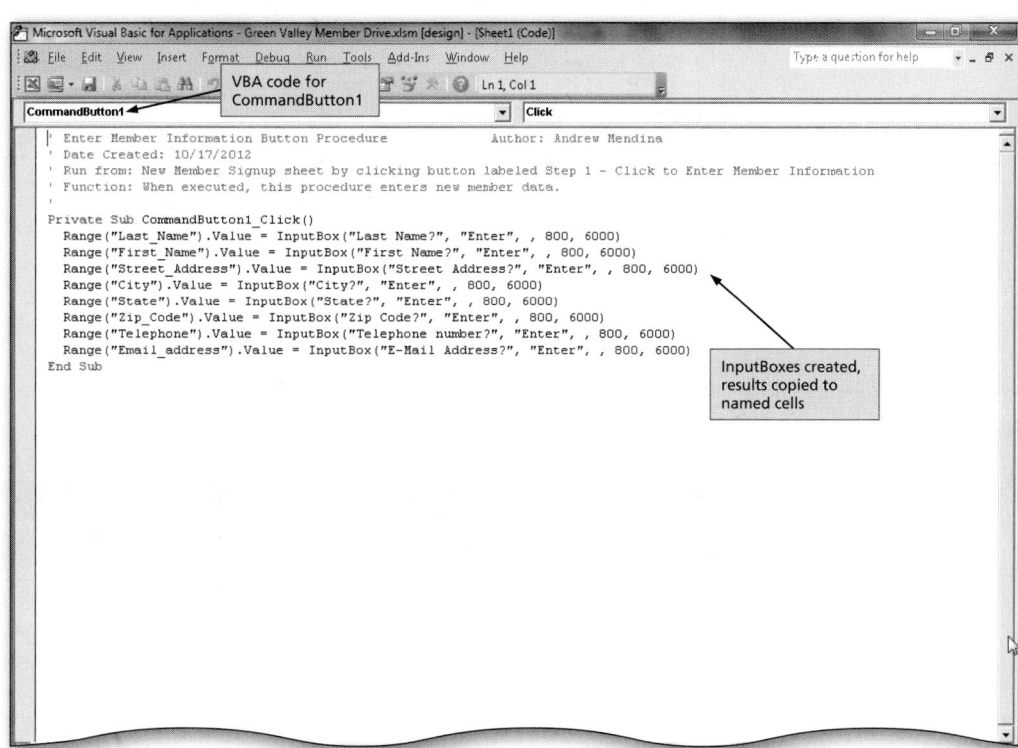

Figure 10–75

Line	Statement
	Table 10–4 Enter Member Information Button Procedure
1	' Enter Member Information Button Procedure Author: Andrew Mendina
2	' Date Created: 10/17/2012
3	' Run from: New Member Signup sheet by clicking button labeled Step 1 — Click to Enter Member Information
4	' Function: When executed, this procedure enters new member data.
5	'
6	Private Sub CommandButton1_Click()
7	Range("Last_Name").Value = InputBox("Last Name?", "Enter", , 800, 6000)
8	Range("First_Name").Value = InputBox("First Name?", "Enter", , 800, 6000)
9	Range("Street_Address").Value = InputBox("Street Address?", "Enter", , 800, 6000)
10	Range("City").Value = InputBox("City?", "Enter", , 800, 6000)
11	Range("State").Value = InputBox("State?", "Enter", , 800, 6000)
12	Range("Zip_Code").Value = InputBox("Zip Code?", "Enter", , 800, 6000)
13	Range("Telephone").Value = InputBox("Telephone number?", "Enter", , 800, 6000)
14	Range("Email_address").Value = InputBox("E-Mail Address?", "Enter", , 800, 6000)
15	End Sub

BTW

Printing VBA Code
Some people find it easier to review and edit code by working with a printout. To print out VBA code while using the Visual Basic Editor, click File on the menu bar and then click Print.

2

• Repeat Step 1 for the Step 3 button (CommandButton2), using the VBA code shown in Table 10–5 (Figure 10–76).

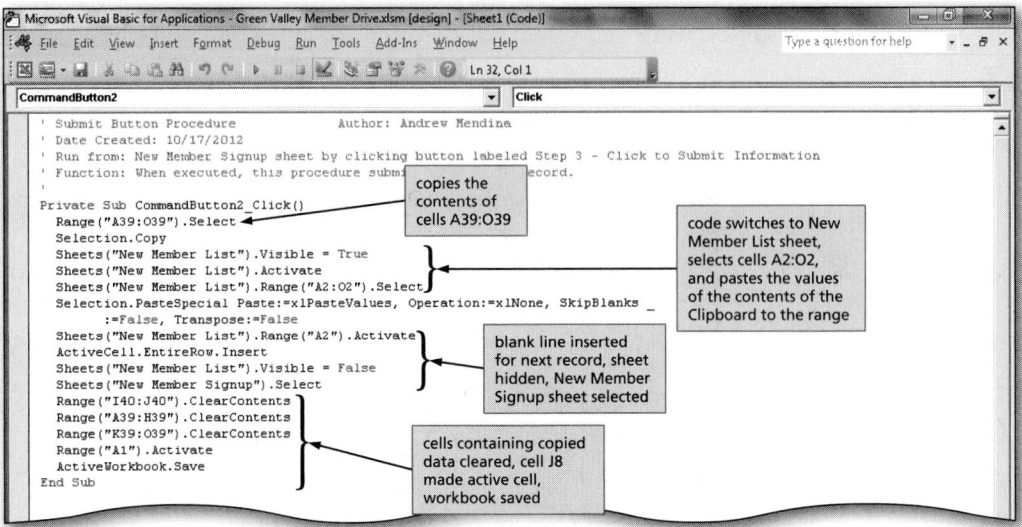

Figure 10–76

Line	Statement
	Table 10–5 Submit Button Procedure
1	' Submit Button Procedure Author: Andrew Mendina
2	' Date Created: 10/17/2012
3	' Run from: New Member Signup sheet by clicking button labeled Step 3 — Click to Submit Information
4	' Function: When executed, this procedure submits new member record.
5	'
6	Private Sub CommandButton2_Click()
7	Range("A39:O39").Select
8	Selection.Copy
9	Sheets("New Member List").Visible = True
10	Sheets("New Member List").Activate
11	Sheets("New Member List").Range("A2:O2").Select
12	Selection.PasteSpecial Paste:=xlPasteValues, Operation:=xlNone, SkipBlanks _
13	:=False, Transpose:=False
14	Sheets("New Member List").Range("A2").Activate
15	ActiveCell.EntireRow.Insert
16	Sheets("New Member List").Visible = False
17	Sheets("New Member Signup").Select
18	Range("I40:J40").ClearContents
19	Range("A39:H39").ClearContents
20	Range("K39:O39").ClearContents
21	Range("A1").Activate
22	ActiveWorkbook.Save
23	End Sub

To Remove the Outline from the Group Control

Removing the outline requires a line of VBA code. You will enter this in the Immediate window in the VBE. The Immediate window is often used for debugging and executing statements during design. The following step removes the outline from the group control.

1

- Switch to the Visual Basic Editor.

- Press the CTRL+G keys to open the Immediate window.

- Type **activesheet .groupboxes .visible = false** and press ENTER to remove the box from around the group control (Figure 10–77).

```
Private Sub CommandButton2_Click()
    Range("A39:O39").Select
    Selection.Copy
    Sheets("New Member List").Visible = True
    Sheets("New Member List").Activate
    Sheets("New Member List").Range("A2:O2").Select
    Selection.PasteSpecial Paste:=xlPasteValues, Operation:=xlNone, SkipBlanks _
        :=False, Transpose:=False
    Sheets("New Member List").Range("A2").Activate
    ActiveCell.EntireRow.Insert
    Sheets("New Member List").Visible = False
    Sheets("New Member Signup").Select
    Range("I40:J40").ClearContents
    Range("A39:H39").ClearContents
    Range("K39:O39").ClearContents
    Range("A1").Activate
    ActiveWorkbook.Save
End Sub
```

Immediate

```
activesheet.groupboxes.visible = false
```

group box outline made invisible

Figure 10–77

To Prepare and Protect the Worksheet and Save the Workbook

The VBA code is complete. Before closing the Visual Basic Editor, you should verify your code by comparing it again with the content of Tables 10–4 and 10–5 on pages EX 681–682. The following steps close the Visual Basic Editor, quit Design mode, prepare and protect the worksheet, and save the workbook.

1

- Close the Visual Basic Editor.

- When the Excel window is visible, click the Design Mode button (Developer tab | Controls group) to exit Design mode.

- Click File on the Ribbon to open the Backstage view.

- Click Options to display the Excel Options dialog box.

- Click Advanced in the left pane to display the advanced options.

- Click the Show page breaks and 'Show a zero in cells that have zero value' check boxes to deselect them (Figure 10–78).

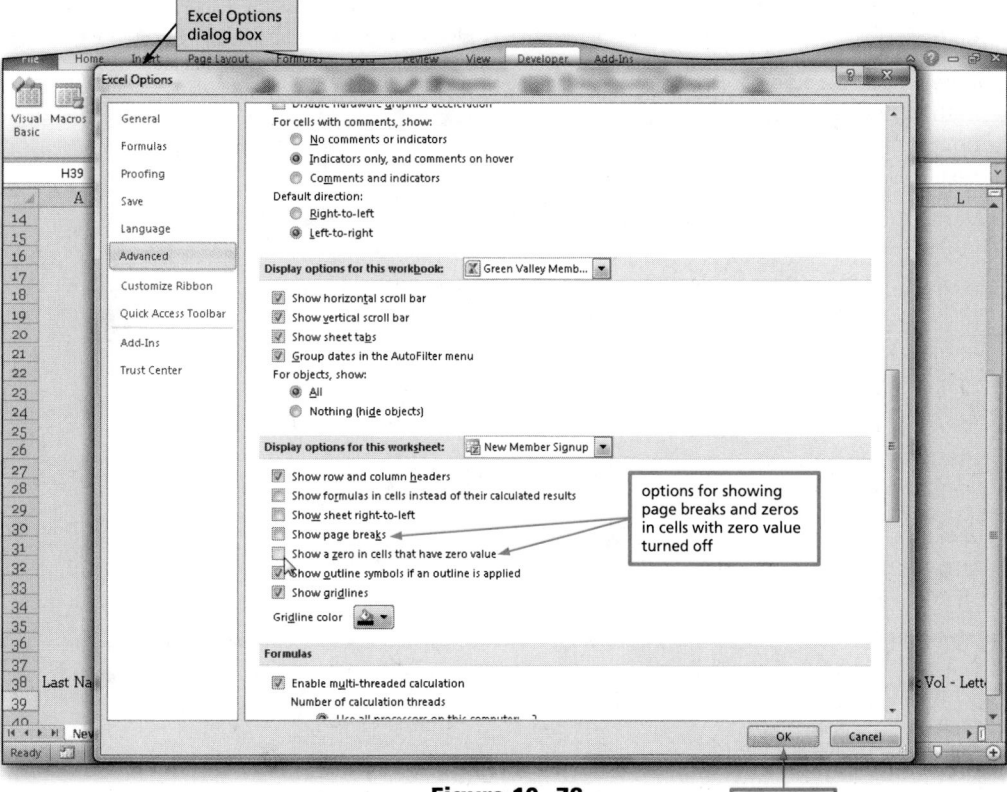

Excel Options dialog box

options for showing page breaks and zeros in cells with zero value turned off

OK button

Figure 10–78

2

- Click the OK button (Excel Options dialog box) to close the dialog box.

- Click View on the Ribbon to display the View tab.

- Click the Gridlines, Formula Bar, and Headings check boxes (View tab | Show group) to deselect them.

- Click the Minimize the Ribbon button on the title bar to minimize the Ribbon (Figure 10–79).

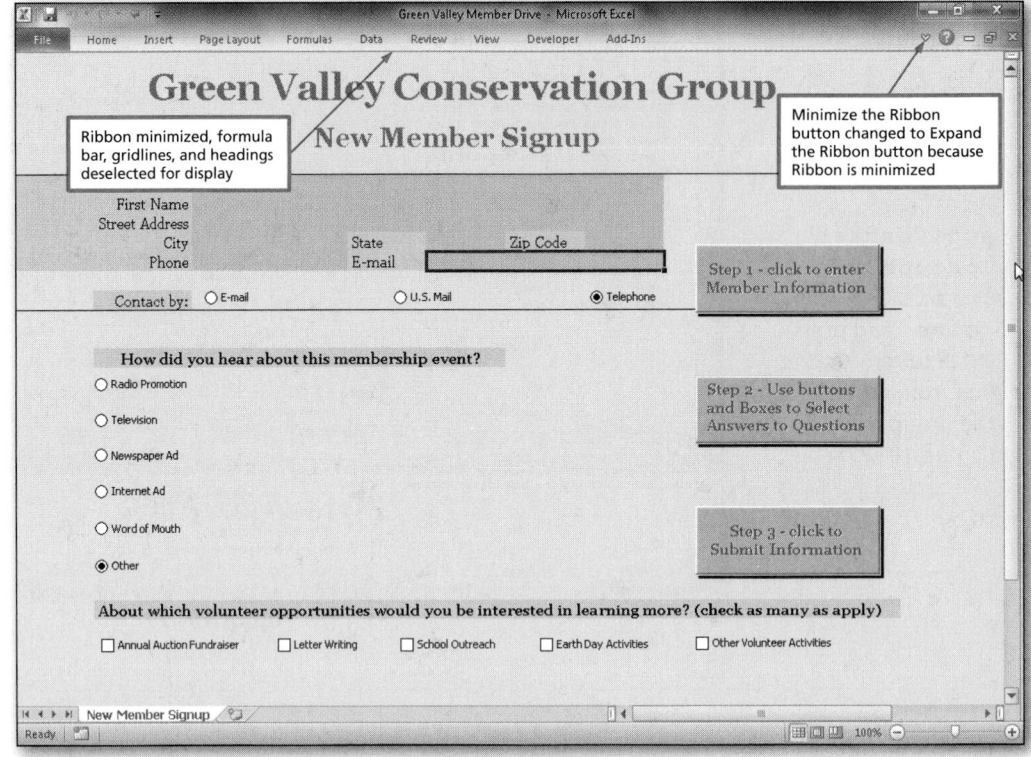

Figure 10–79

3

- If necessary, right-click the New Member List sheet tab to display a shortcut menu.

- Click Hide Sheet to hide the New Member List worksheet.

- Click Review on the Ribbon to display the Review tab.

- Click the Protect Sheet button (Review tab | Changes group) to display the Protect Sheet dialog box.

- Type **awareness** in the 'Password to unprotect sheet' text box.

- Verify the password when prompted.

- Click the OK button (Protect Sheet dialog box) to close the dialog box.

- Press the F5 key to display the Go To dialog box.

- Enter **J8** and press ENTER to make cell J8 the active cell.

- Click the Save button on the Quick Access Toolbar to save the workbook (Figure 10–80).

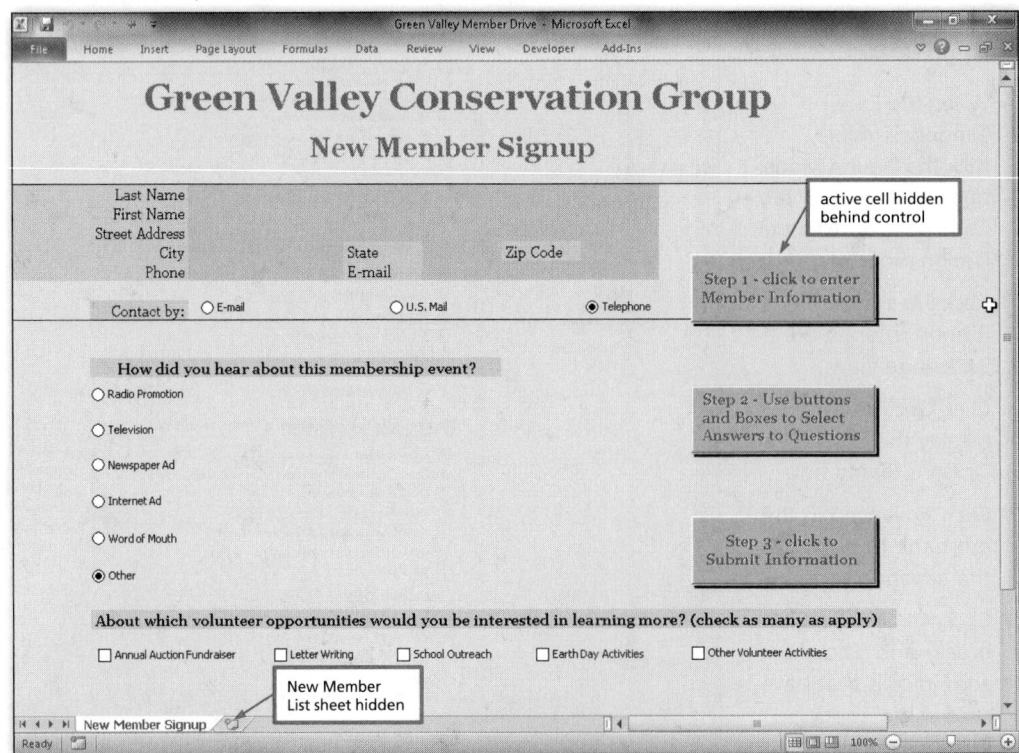

Figure 10–80

To Test the Controls in the New Member Signup Sheet

The final step is to test the controls in the New Member Signup sheet. To test the controls, use the following test data:

Cross, Jane, 24 Park Avenue, Brookley, NE, 68562, 555-555-1212, jcrossne@scseries.com, Telephone, Word of Mouth, Letter Writing

Webber, Jason, 438 Leonard Drive, Plainville, NE, 68599, 555-555-1313, jwebber@scseries.com, E-Mail, Internet Ad, Earth Day Activities, School Outreach.

1 For each of the records above, using the command buttons, enter the data, following prompts, and submit the data.

2 Unhide the New Member List sheet, and confirm that the records copied correctly (Figure 10–81).

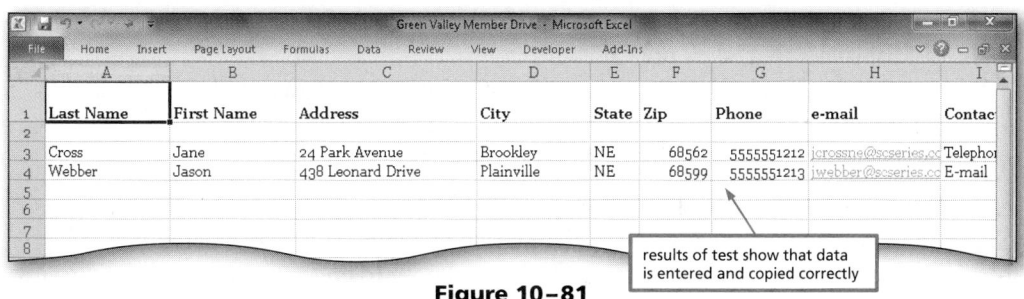

Figure 10–81

To Reset the Quick Access Toolbar and Ribbon and Quit Excel

The following steps reset the Quick Access Toolbar in order to remove the FirstName button, remove the Developer tab from the Ribbon, and quit Excel.

1 Right-click anywhere on the Quick Access Toolbar and then click Customize Quick Access Toolbar on the shortcut menu.

2 When the Excel Options dialog box is displayed, click the Reset button and then click Reset all customizations on the Reset menu. Click the Yes button in the Microsoft Office dialog box, and then click the OK button to close the Excel Options dialog box.

3 Click the Close button on the right side of the title bar.

4 If the Microsoft Excel dialog box is displayed, click the Don't Save button.

Digital Signatures

Some users prefer to attach a digital signature to verify the authenticity of a document. A **digital signature** is an electronic, encrypted, and secure stamp of authentication on a document. This signature confirms that the file originated from the signer (file developer) and that it has not been altered.

A digital signature may be visible or invisible. In either case, the digital signature references a digital certificate. A **digital certificate** is an attachment to a file or e-mail message that vouches for its authenticity, provides secure encryption, or supplies a verifiable signature. Many users who receive files enable the macros based on whether they are digitally signed by a developer on the user's list of trusted sources.

You can obtain a digital certificate from a commercial **certificate authority**, from your network administrator, or you can create a digital signature yourself. A digital certificate you create yourself is not issued by a formal certification authority. Thus, signed macros using such a certificate are referred to as **self-signed projects**. Certificates you create yourself are considered unauthenticated and still will generate a warning when opened if the security level is set to very high, high, or medium. Many users, however, consider self-signed projects safer to open than those with no certificates at all.

TO ADD A DIGITAL SIGNATURE TO A WORKBOOK

After adding a digital signature, Excel will display the digital signature whenever the document is opened. If you wanted to add a digital signature to an Excel workbook, you would perform the following steps.

1. Open the Green Valley Member Drive workbook and then unprotect the worksheet using the password of awareness.
2. Click the Insert tab on the Ribbon and then click the Signature Line button on the Ribbon. If the Microsoft Excel dialog box appears, click the OK button.
3. When the Signature Setup dialog box appears, type your name in the Suggested signer text box and then click the OK button (Figure 10–82).
4. When Excel adds the signature box to the workbook, right-click anywhere in the signature box and then click Sign on the shortcut menu. If the Microsoft Excel dialog box is displayed, then click the OK button.
5. When the Sign dialog box appears, type your name in the signature box or click the Select Image link to select a file that contains an image of your signature.
6. Click the Sign button to digitally sign the document.

If you do not have any digital certificates on your computer when you click the Sign command in Step 3, you will be prompted in the Microsoft Excel dialog box to obtain or create a new digital certificate. You can choose to create a certificate online with a service provider recommended by Microsoft by clicking the Signature Services from the Office Marketplace button. By doing so, other users can authenticate the signature on your workbooks because the certificate is available online. This alternative, however, may require payment. You also can click the Create your own Digital ID button to create a digital certificate that is valid only on your computer, but is free of charge.

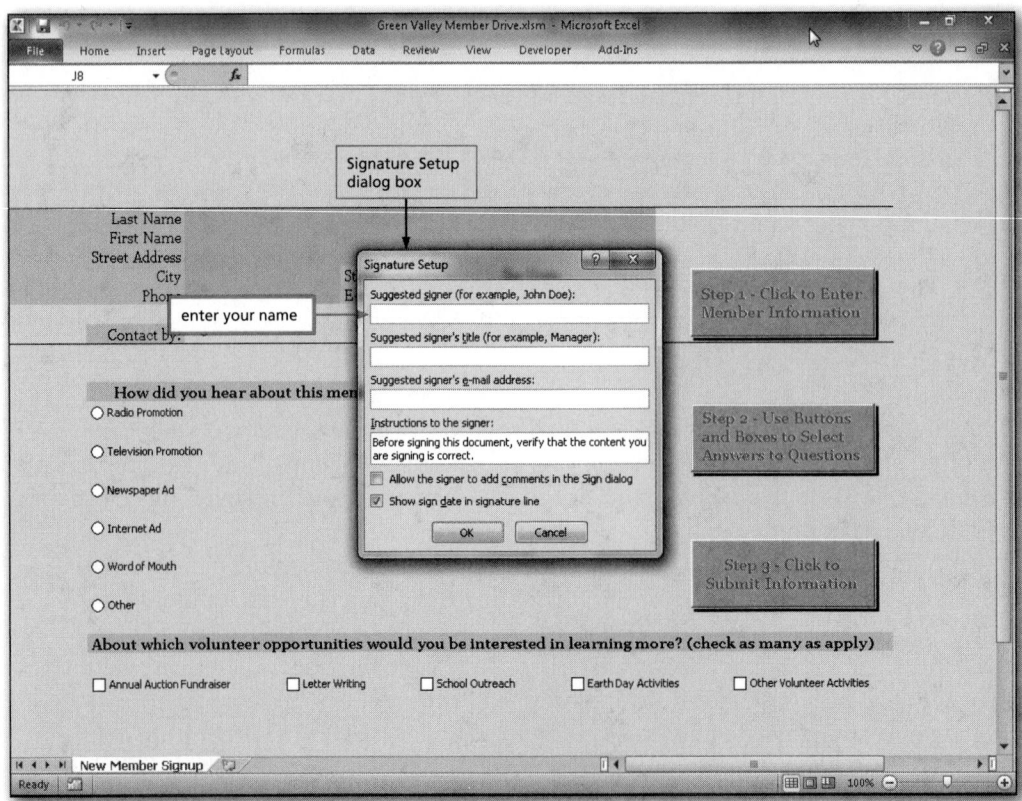

Figure 10–82

To Review a Digital Signature on a Workbook

A **file digital signature** is a digital signature that is displayed when you e-mail a document from Excel. Excel will display the digital signature whenever the document is opened. When you open a digitally signed document, Excel displays a message announcing the signature on the status bar while the file opens. After the file is opened, Excel displays a certification icon on the status bar. You can click the icon to find out who digitally signed the document. The word, (Signed), also appears on the title bar in parentheses, indicating the document is signed digitally. If you wanted to review a digital signature on an Excel workbook, you would perform the following steps.

1. Click the File tab to open the Backstage view. Click the Info tab, and then click View Signatures to open the Signatures pane.

2. Select a name from the Valid signature list in the signature pane and then click the button arrow next to the name. When the shortcut menu appears, click Signature Details.

3. When you are finished reviewing the certificate, click the Close button in the Signature Details dialog box and then close the workbook without saving it.

BTW

Quick Reference
For a table that lists how to complete the tasks covered in this book using the mouse, Ribbon, shortcut menu, and keyboard, see the Quick Reference Summary at the back of this book, or visit the Excel 2010 Quick Reference Web page (scsite.com/ex2010/qr).

Chapter Summary

In this chapter, you learned how to unprotect and protect a worksheet and workbook using a password. In Phase 1, you learned how to record a macro and assign it to a button on the Quick Access Toolbar. In Phase 2, you learned how to create a Command Button control, assign it properties, and write Visual Basic for Applications (VBA) code that executes when you click the button. In Phase 3, you learned how to create a user interface made up of Command Button controls, Check Box controls, and Option Button controls, set properties for those controls using the Properties window, write VBA code for the controls, and add and review a digital signature on a workbook. The items listed below include all the new Excel skills you have learned in this chapter.

1. Unprotect a Password-Protected Worksheet (EX 633)
2. Display the Developer Tab, Enable Macros, and Save a Workbook as a Macro-Enabled Workbook (EX 635)
3. Convert Names to Proper Case and Add Extra Columns (EX 637)
4. Record a Macro to Reformat the Membership Data where First Name Appears First (EX 639)
5. Record a Macro to Reformat the Membership Data where Last Name Appears First (EX 644)
6. Password-Protect the Worksheet, Save the Workbook, and Close the Workbook (EX 645)
7. Set the Macro Security Level to Medium (EX 646)
8. Open a Workbook with Macros and Execute a Macro (EX 647)
9. View and Print a Macro's VBA Code (EX 648)
10. Add a Button to the Quick Access Toolbar, Assign the Button a Macro, and Use the Button (EX 649)
11. Add a Command Button Control to the Worksheet (EX 655)
12. Set the Command Button Control Properties (EX 657)
13. Enter the New Data Button Procedure Using the Visual Basic Editor (EX 660)
14. Add Member Data Using the Add Member Data Button (EX 663)
15. Enter Name and Address Fields (EX 667)
16. Add Form Controls to a User Interface (EX 668)
17. Group Option Buttons in a User Interface (EX 671)
18. Add Command Buttons and a Text Box Control in a User Interface (EX 672)
19. Format the Option Button Controls for Contact Method (EX 673)
20. Record User Input for Contact Method to Another Location on the Worksheet (EX 675)
21. Record User Input for the Group Box Controls (EX 676)
22. Format the Check Box Controls (EX 676)
23. Record User Input for the Check Box Controls (EX 677)
24. Format the Command Button Controls (EX 677)
25. Assign Names to Cells (EX 679)
26. Enter the Command Button Procedures Using the Visual Basic Editor (EX 681)

25. Remove the Outline from the Group Control (EX 682)

26. Test the Controls in the New Member Signup Sheet (EX 685)

27. Reset the Quick Access Toolbar and Ribbon and Quit Excel (EX 685)

28. Add a Digital Signature to a Workbook (EX 686)

29. Review a Digital Signature on a Workbook (EX 687)

 If you have a SAM 2010 user profile, your instructor may have assigned an autogradable version of this assignment. If so, log into the SAM 2010 Web site at www.cengage.com/sam2010 to download the instruction and start files.

Learn It Online

Test your knowledge of chapter content and key terms.

Instructions: To complete the Learn It Online exercises, start your browser, click the Address bar, and then enter the Web address **scsite.com/ex2010/learn**. When the Excel 2010 Learn It Online page is displayed, click the link for the exercise you want to complete and then read the instructions.

Chapter Reinforcement TF, MC, and SA
A series of true/false, multiple choice, and short answer questions that test your knowledge of the chapter content.

Flash Cards
An interactive learning environment where you identify chapter key terms associated with displayed definitions.

Practice Test
A series of multiple choice questions that test your knowledge of chapter content and key terms.

Who Wants To Be a Computer Genius?
An interactive game that challenges your knowledge of chapter content in the style of a television quiz show.

Wheel of Terms
An interactive game that challenges your knowledge of chapter key terms in the style of the television show *Wheel of Fortune*.

Crossword Puzzle Challenge
A crossword puzzle that challenges your knowledge of key terms presented in the chapter.

Apply Your Knowledge

Reinforce the skills and apply the concepts you learned in this chapter.

Creating a Macro and Assigning It to a Button
Note: To complete this assignment, you will be required to use the Data Files for Students. See the inside back cover of this book for instructions on downloading the Data Files for Students, or contact your instructor for information about accessing the required files.

Instructions: Start Excel. Open the workbook Apply 10 – 1 Finkle Trinkets (Figure 10–83) from the Data Files for Students and then save the workbook using the file name, Apply 10–1 Finkle Trinkets Complete, saving the workbook as an Excel Macro-Enabled Workbook file type.

In the following steps, you open a workbook, create a macro to add a column to a worksheet, assign the macro to a button on the Quick Access Toolbar, and then execute the macro.

Figure 10-83

Perform the following tasks:

1. If the Developer tab is not displayed on the Ribbon, click the File tab, click the Options button, click Customize Ribbon, click the Developer check box in the Customize the Ribbon area, and then click OK.

2. Change the document properties as specified by your instructor. Add a worksheet header with your name, course number, and other information as specified by your instructor.

3. Create a macro that adds a column before the Totals column by doing the following:

   a. Click the Record Macro button (Developer tab | Code group).

   b. When the Record Macro dialog box appears, name the macro **AddColumn,** assign the shortcut key CTRL+N, store the macro in this workbook, enter your name in the Description box, and then click the OK button to start the macro recording process.

   c. Select cell C3, click Insert Sheet Columns (Home tab | Cells group | Insert button arrow), select cell C6 and sum the cell range C4:C5, set the column width to 15, and then click the Stop Recording button (Developer tab | Code group).

4. In the newly added column, enter **Necklaces** in C3, **14,279** in C4, and **14,350** in C5.

5. Click the Macros button (Developer tab | Code group) to display the Macro dialog box. Run the AddColumn macro to add a column. Enter the following data: **Earrings, 15,765,** and **18,110**. Click the Macros button again, select AddColumn macro, and then click the Edit button (Macro dialog box). When the Visual Basic Editor displays the macro, click File on the menu bar and then click Print. Close the Visual Basic Editor.

6. Right-click the Quick Access Toolbar and then click Customize Quick Access Toolbar. When the Excel Options dialog box is displayed, click the 'Choose commands from' box arrow and choose Macros. Click AddColumn, click the Add button, and then click the OK button to close the Excel Options dialog box.

Continued >

STUDENT ASSIGNMENTS

Apply Your Knowledge *continued*

7. Run the macro as follows: (a) click the AddColumn button on the Quick Access Toolbar, and enter **Bracelets, 12,320,** and **14,250** for the column values; and (b) press CTRL+N, and enter **Charms, 13,115,** and **17,500** for the column values.

8. Protect the worksheet using the password, **sheltered**.

9. Right-click the Quick Access Toolbar and then click Customize Quick Access Toolbar. Remove the AddColumn button and then click the OK button.

10. Save the workbook and then quit Excel.

11. Submit the assignment as requested by your instructor.

Extend Your Knowledge

Extend the skills you learned in this chapter and experiment with new skills. You may need to use Help to complete the assignment.

Creating and Using a Custom Function

Note: To complete this assignment, you will be required to use the Data Files for Students. See the inside back cover of this book for instructions on downloading the Data Files for Students, or contact your instructor for information about accessing the required files.

Instructions: Start Excel. Open the workbook Extend 10-1 Carlie Auto from the Data Files for Students and then save the workbook using the file name Extend 10-1 Carlie Auto Complete, saving the workbook as an Excel Macro-Enabled Workbook file type.

Create a macro that runs when the workbook is opened. The macro sorts the sales representatives by last name, and first name, and then formats sales amounts greater than 75,000 (Figure 10–84).

Figure 10–84

Perform the following tasks:

1. Start Excel. If the Developer tab is not displayed on the Ribbon, click the File tab, click the Options button, click Customize Ribbon, click the Developer check box in the Customize the Ribbon area, and then click OK.

2. Create a macro that sorts the sales representatives by last name and first name, and highlights sales values greater than 75,000 by doing the following:

   a. Click the Record Macro button (Developer tab | Code group).

   b. When the Record Macro dialog box is displayed, name the macro `Auto_Open,` store the macro in this workbook, enter your name in the Description box, and then click the OK button to start the macro recording process.

   c. Select cell range A3:C10, sort by Last Name and then by First Name, select cell range C4:C10, apply conditional formatting to highlight cells with sales values greater than 75,000, and then click the Stop Recording button (Developer tab | Code group).

3. Undo the changes to the workbook to return it to unsorted, unhighlighted columns. Save the workbook. Close the workbook.

4. Open the Extend 10-1 Carlie Auto Complete workbook. If necessary, enable content so that the macro runs to produce the results shown in Figure 10–84. Save the workbook.

5. Change the document properties as specified by your instructor. Add a worksheet header with your name, course number, and other information as specified by your instructor.

6. Print both the worksheet and VBA custom function code. Print the formulas version of the worksheet.

7. Save the workbook and then quit Excel.

8. Submit the assignment as requested by your instructor.

Make It Right

Analyze a workbook and correct all errors and/or improve the design.

Changing Properties and Correcting Visual Basic Code

Note: To complete this assignment, you will be required to use the Data Files for Students. See the inside back cover of this book for instructions on downloading the Data Files for Students, or contact your instructor for information about accessing the required files.

Instructions: Start Excel. Open the workbook Make It Right 10-1 Monthly Payment Calculator workbook from the Data Files for Students and then save the workbook using the file name, Make It Right 10-1 Monthly Payment Calculator Complete, saving the workbook as an Excel Macro-Enabled Workbook file type. In the workbook, correct the problems in a macro assigned to a button.

Perform the following tasks:

1. If the Developer tab is not displayed on the Ribbon, click the File tab, click the Options button, click Customize Ribbon, click the Developer check box in the Customize the Ribbon area, and then click OK.

2. Click the Design Mode button (Developer tab | Controls group).

3. Change the caption of the button to `New Payment`. Change the foreground color of the button to Green and move the button from column B to column C (Figure 10–85a).

4. Click the View Code button (Developer tab | Controls group) and make the following adjustments to the procedure shown in Figure 10–85b:

Continued >

Make It Right *continued*

(a)

(b)

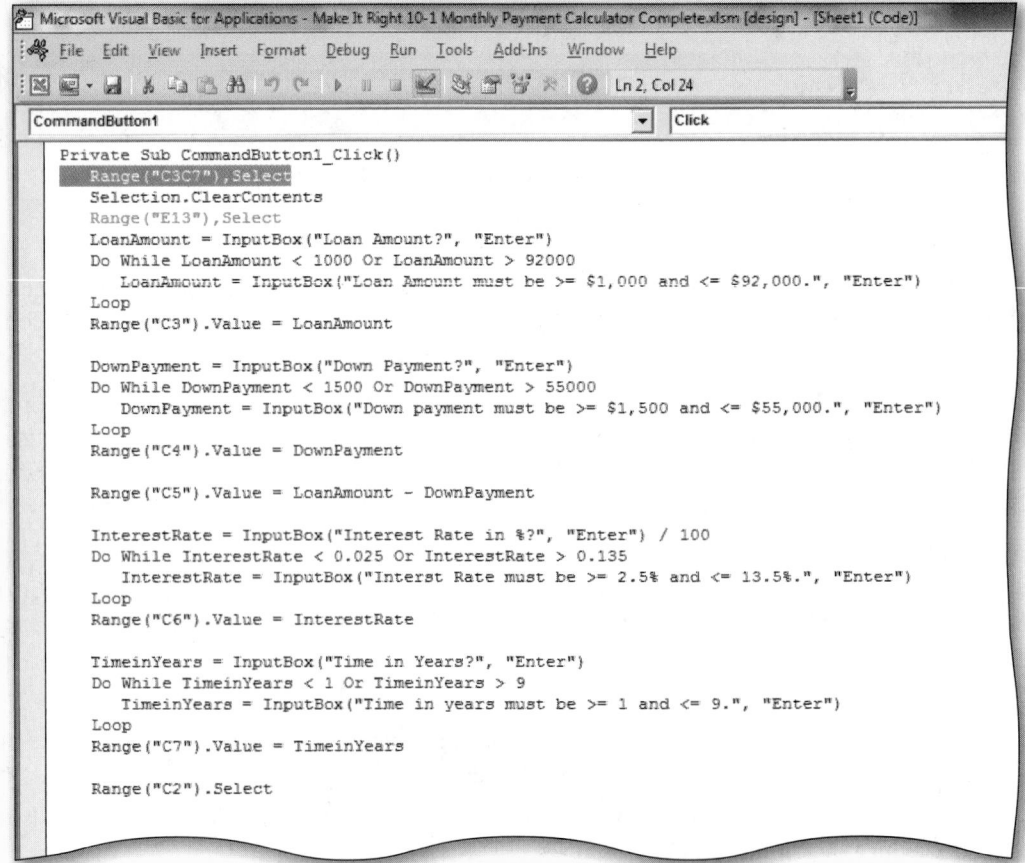

Figure 10–85

a. Add comments before the first line of code. Include a procedure title, your name, date, and the purpose of the procedure.

b. Add End Sub at the end of the macro.

c. Fix the first line of the function. The range should be C3:C7. Also change the comma before the Select to a period.

d. In the Second Select, change the comma before the Select to a period.

e. Select cell B14 before exiting the procedure.

f. Add comments to explain what is happening before each calculation.

5. Click the View Microsoft Excel button on the Standard toolbar to exit Microsoft Visual Basic and return to Excel.

6. Click the Design Mode button (Developer tab | Controls group) to exit Design mode.

7. Click the New Payment button and enter the following loan data: Loan Amount = $45,000; Down Payment = $2,750; Interest Rate = 7.5%; Years = 6. The monthly payment in cell C8 should equal $730.51. Enter additional data that tests the limits of acceptable loan data.

8. To disable macros, click the Macro Security button (Developer tab | Code group). When the Trust Center dialog box is displayed, click 'Disable all macros with notification' and then click the OK button.

9. Change the document properties as specified by your instructor. Add a worksheet header with your name, course number, and other information as specified by your instructor.

10. Print both the worksheet and Visual Basic code.

11. Save the workbook and then quit Excel.

12. Submit the assignment as requested by your instructor.

In the Lab

Create a workbook using the guidelines, concepts, and skills presented in this chapter. Labs are listed in order of increasing difficulty.

Lab 1: Automating a Credit Card Calculator

Note: To complete this assignment, you will be required to use the Data Files for Students. See the inside back cover of this book for instructions on downloading the Data Files for Students, or contact your instructor for information about accessing the required files.

Problem: HTFE Financial advises customers on how to manage their credit card debt by using a credit card calculator. The calculator shows how much can be paid off during a 24-month time period, given the minimum payment for the particular card. The chief financial officer, Jane Seifer, has asked you to automate the entry of financing data into the calculator.

Part 1 Instructions: Perform the following tasks:

1. Start Excel. If the Developer tab is not displayed on the Ribbon, click the File tab, click the Options button, click Customize Ribbon, click the Developer check box in the Customize the Ribbon area, and then click OK.

2. To enable macros, click the Macro Security button (Developer tab | Code group). When the Trust Center dialog box is displayed, click 'Enable all macros' and then click the OK button.

Continued >

In the Lab *continued*

3. Open the Lab 10-1 HTFE Financial workbook from the Data Files for Students and then save the workbook using the file name, Lab 10-1 Part 1 HTFE Financial Complete, saving the workbook as an Excel Macro-Enabled Workbook file type.

4. Draw a Thick Box Border around the range E5:F10 and color the background Black, Text 1, Lighter 50% (column 2, row 2 on the Fill Color palette).

5. Click the Developer tab on the Ribbon. Click the Insert button (Developer tab | Controls group) and then click Command Button (column 1, row 1) in the ActiveX Controls area. Draw the button within the range E6:F6 in the location shown in Figure 10–86a.

6. With the Command Button control selected, click the Properties button (Developer tab | Controls group). If necessary, change the following properties: (a) Caption = Enter Data; (b) Font = Arial, Bold, 14 pt.; and (c) PrintObject = False. Close the Properties window.

7. With the Command Button control selected, right-click the button and select View Code. Enter the procedure shown in Figure 10–86b. Check your code carefully.

(a)

(b)

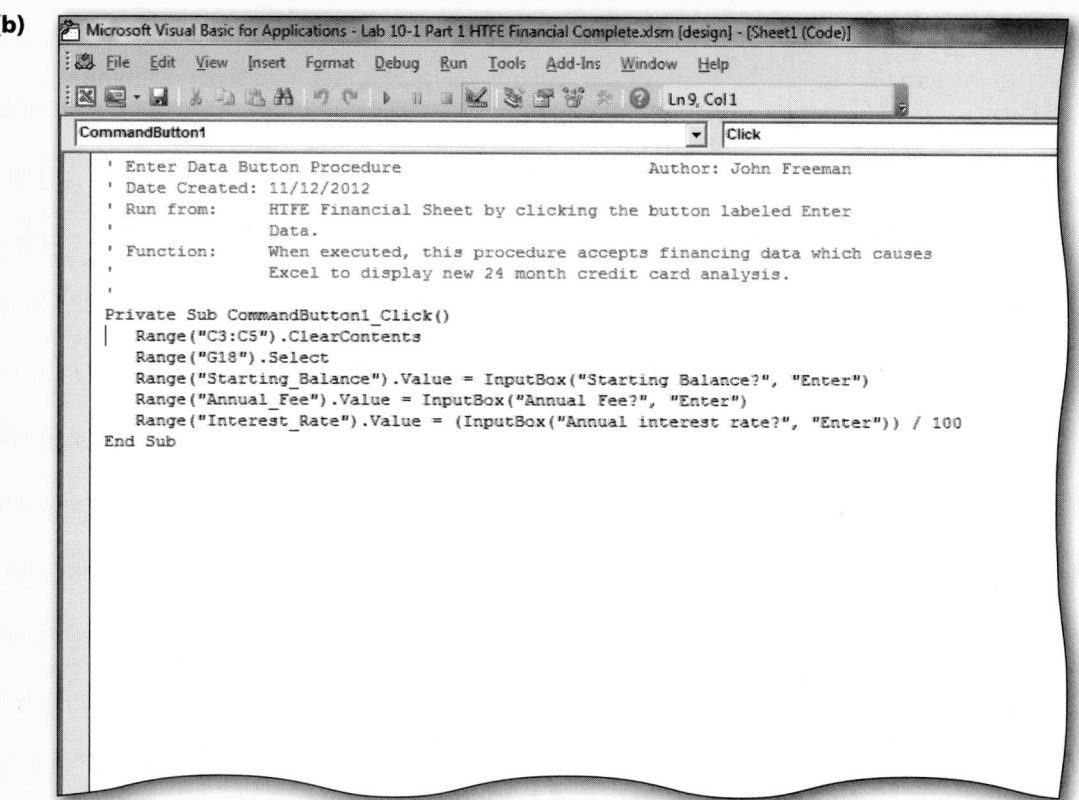

```
Microsoft Visual Basic for Applications - Lab 10-1 Part 1 HTFE Financial Complete.xlsm [design] - [Sheet1 (Code)]

 File   Edit   View   Insert   Format   Debug   Run   Tools   Add-Ins   Window   Help

                                                              Ln 9, Col 1

CommandButton1                                        ▼   Click

' Enter Data Button Procedure                    Author: John Freeman
' Date Created: 11/12/2012
' Run from:       HTFE Financial Sheet by clicking the button labeled Enter
'                 Data.
' Function:       When executed, this procedure accepts financing data which causes
'                 Excel to display new 24 month credit card analysis.
'
Private Sub CommandButton1_Click()
    Range("C3:C5").ClearContents
    Range("G18").Select
    Range("Starting_Balance").Value = InputBox("Starting Balance?", "Enter")
    Range("Annual_Fee").Value = InputBox("Annual Fee?", "Enter")
    Range("Interest_Rate").Value = (InputBox("Annual interest rate?", "Enter")) / 100
End Sub
```

Figure 10–86

8. Close the Visual Basic Editor window. Click the Design Mode button (Developer tab | Controls group) to return to the workbook.

9. Change the document properties as specified by your instructor. Add a worksheet header with your name, course number, and other information as specified by your instructor.

10. Use the newly created button to display the credit card analysis for the following financing data and then print the worksheet for each data set: (a) Starting Balance = $2,500; Annual Fee = $35; Rate = 18.75%; (b) Starting Balance = $5,000; Annual Fee = $0; Rate = 15.75.

11. Print the worksheet and then print the Visual Basic code.

12. To disable macros, click the Macro Security button (Developer tab | Code group). When the Trust Center dialog box is displayed, click 'Disable all macros with notification' and then click the OK button.

13. Protect the worksheet using the password, **HTFE**. Save the workbook and then quit Excel.

14. Submit the assignment as requested by your instructor.

Part 2 Instructions: Perform the following tasks to add a macro to the workbook and add a button to the Quick Access Toolbar that executes the macro:

1. Open the workbook Lab 10-1 Part 1 HTFE Financial Complete and then save the workbook using the file name Lab 10-1 Part 2 HTFE Financial Complete and saving the workbook as an Excel Macro-Enabled Workbook file type.

2. Unprotect the worksheet using the password, **HTFE**.

Continued >

In the Lab *continued*

3. Create a macro that copies the credit card calculator values to a new worksheet by doing the following:

 a. Click the Record Macro button (Developer tab | Code group). When the Record Macro dialog box is displayed, name the macro `CopyCalculator,` assign the shortcut key CTRL+V, add your name in the Description box, and store the macro in this workbook. Click the OK button to start the macro recording process.

 b. Copy the cell range B3:D30; insert a new worksheet; paste the values and source formatting to the cell range A3:C30; resize the columns so all data shows; and click the Stop Recording button (Developer tab | Code group).

5. Click the Insert button (Developer tab | Controls group), and then click Command Button (column 1, row 1) in the Form Controls area. Draw the button below the Enter Data button as shown in Figure 10–87. Assign the macro CopyCalculator to the button.

6. Right-click the button and edit the text, changing the text to `Copy Results`. Change the font size to 14 and bold the text.

7. Test the Copy Results button. Print the created worksheet.

8. To disable macros, click the Macro Security button (Developer tab | Code group). When the Trust Center dialog box is displayed, click 'Disable all macros with notification' and then click the OK button.

9. Protect the worksheet using the password, `HTFE`. Save the workbook and then quit Excel.

10. Submit the assignment as requested by your instructor.

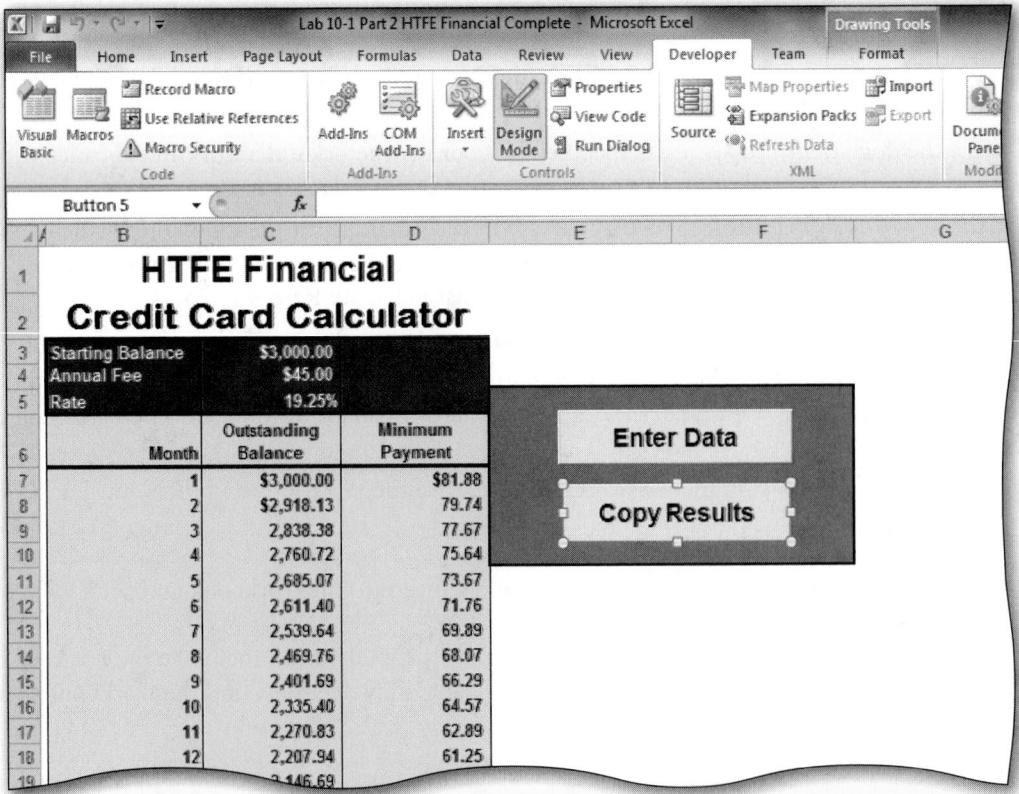

Figure 10–87

In the Lab

Lab 2: Automating a Forecast Workbook

Note: To complete this assignment, you will be required to use the Data Files for Students. See the inside back cover of this book for instructions on downloading the Data Files for Students, or contact your instructor for information about accessing the required files.

Problem: As an intern at Compbest Watches, you have been asked to use your Visual Basic for Applications skills to complete the task of automating the Forecast workbook as shown in Figure 10–88. The person working on the project left the company unexpectedly, and you have been asked to step in and finish the project. The objective is to simplify data entry for the company's financial analysts. This worksheet projects financial information for a seven-year period based on the previous year's sales and additional data. The user interface on the right side of the screen accepts the assumptions in the range K19:K23. The numbers in the range B5:H18 are based on these assumptions. The person working on this project had completed the outline of the user interface, including placing the controls, but had not yet formatted the controls, inputted the VBA code for the controls, or tested the interface. You have not worked with some of these controls before, but have been assured that given the knowledge you have about other controls, and the Help feature of Excel, you will be able to complete this project.

The user interface in the range J2:K16 has two command buttons, one spin button, and three scroll bars. The Reset Assumptions command button resets the assumptions as follows: (a) cell K19 = 3,000; (b) cell K20 = $300.00; (c) K21 = 14.5%; (d) K22 = 3%; and (e) K23 = 52%. The Units Sold in 2010 Command Button accepts and ensures the units sold figure in 2010 is greater than zero and then assigns it to cell K19. The Unit Cost spin button changes the unit cost in cell K20. The Annual Sales Growth scroll bar changes the annual sales growth in cell K21. The Annual Price Decrease scroll bar changes the annual price decrease in cell K22. The Margin scroll bar changes the margin in cell K23. The interface is using ActiveX controls.

Instructions: *Perform the following tasks:*
1. Start Excel. If the Developer tab is not displayed on the Ribbon, click the File tab, click the Options button, click Customize Ribbon, click the Developer check box in the Customize the Ribbon area, and then click OK. To enable macros, click the Macro Security button (Developer tab | Code group). When the Trust Center dialog box is displayed, click 'Enable all macros' and then click the OK button.

2. Open the Lab 10-2 Compbest Watches from the Data Files for Students and then save the workbook using the file name, Lab 10-2 Compbest Watches Complete, saving the workbook as an Excel Macro-Enabled Workbook file type.

3. Unprotect the Financial Statement worksheet using the password, **watches**.

4. Set the background color of the range J2:K16 to White, Background 1 Darker 25% (column 1, row 4 on the Fill Color palette). Draw a thick box border around the range J2:K16.

5. Click the Design Mode button (Developer tab | Controls group). Use the concepts and techniques developed in this project to set the properties for the 17 controls shown in Figure 10–88. The controls' properties are described in Table 10–6.

Continued >

In the Lab *continued*

Figure 10–88

6. One at a time, click the buttons, scroll bars, and spin button listed below and enter the corresponding procedures. Click the View Code button (Developer tab | Controls group) to display the Visual Basic window after selecting a button, scroll bar, or spin button. Click the View Microsoft Excel button on the Standard toolbar to display the workbook after you finish entering a procedure.

a. Enter the Reset Assumptions Button procedure, which resets the assumptions as follows:

```
Range("K19").Value = 3000

spnUnitCost = 30000

scrAnnualSalesGrowth = 1450

scrAnnualPriceDecrease = 300

scrMargin = 5200

Range("A22").Select
```

b. Enter the Units Sold in 2010 Button procedure, which accepts and validates the number of devices sold in 2010 in cell K19 as follows:

```
UnitsSold = InputBox("Units Sold in 2010?", "Enter")

Do While UnitsSold <= 0

UnitsSold = InputBox("Units Sold in 2010 must be > zero.",
"Please Reenter")

Loop

Range("K19").Value = UnitsSold
```

c. Enter the Unit Cost Spin Button procedure, which enters the unit cost in the Unit Cost Spin Button Label control and in cell K20 as follows:

```
lblUnitCost = Format$(spnUnitCost.Value / 100, "currency")
Range("K20").Value = spnUnitCost.Value / 100
```

The Format$ function in the first line formats the result that will be displayed in the Unit Cost Spin Button Label control to include a floating dollar sign and two decimal positions to the right of the decimal.

d. Enter the Annual Sales Growth Scroll Bar procedure, which changes the annual sales growth in cell K21 as follows:

```
Range("K21").Value = scrAnnualSalesGrowth.Value / 10000
```

e. Enter the Annual Price Decrease Scroll Bar procedure and the Margin Scroll Bar procedure (Figure 10–89). These procedures work in a fashion similar to the procedure for the Annual Sales Growth scroll bar, except that they assign values to cells K22 and K23, respectively.

Figure 10–89

Continued >

In the Lab *continued*

Table 10–6 Controls and Properties

Control	Name	Caption	Back Color	Font	Text Align	Special Effect	Max	Min	Small Chg	Large Chg
Reset Assumptions Button	btnReset	Reset Assumptions		8-point bold						
Units Sold in 2010 Button	btnUnitsSold	Units Sold in 2010		8-point bold						
Unit Cost Label	Unit Cost		Gray	8-point bold	Right					
Unit Cost Spin Button	spnUnitCost						100000	0	100	
Unit Cost Spin Button Label	lblUnitCost	$325.00		10-point bold	Right	Sunken				
All three 0 Labels		0	Gray	8-point bold	Center					
All three 100 Labels		100	Gray	8-point bold	Center					
Annual Sales Growth Label		Annual Sales Growth	Gray	8-point bold	Center					
Annual Sales Growth Scroll Bar	scrAnnualSalesGrowth						10000	0	25	100
Annual Price Decrease Label		Annual Price Decrease	Gray	8-point bold	Center					
Annual Price Decrease Scroll Bar	scrAnnualPriceDecrease						10000	0	25	100
Margin Label		Margin	Gray	8-point bold	Center					
Margin Scroll Bar	scrMargin						10000	0	25	100

7. Click the Design Mode button (Developer tab | Controls group) to turn off Design mode.

8. Use the newly designed interface to determine the five-year projections based on the following assumptions and then print the worksheet for each data set: (a) Devices Sold in 2010 = 4,750; Unit Cost = $257.00; Annual Sales Growth = 16%; Annual Price Decrease = 7%; and Margin = 55%; (b) Devices Sold in 2010 = 5,000; Unit Cost = $325.00; Annual Sales Growth = 9%; Annual Price Decrease = 4%; and Margin = 45%. The Net Income for the year 2017 in cell H18 for (a) is $374,759 and for (b) is $140,074.

9. Change the document properties as specified by your instructor. Add a worksheet header with your name, course number, and other information as specified by your instructor.

10. Print the worksheet and the procedures.

11. Protect the worksheet using the password, `watches`. Save the workbook.

12. To disable macros, click the Macro Security button (Developer tab | Code group). When the Trust Center dialog box is displayed, click 'Disable all macros with notification' and then click the OK button. Quit Excel.

13. Submit the assignment as requested by your instructor.

In the Lab

Lab 3: Automating Workbook Formatting

Note: To complete this assignment, you will be required to use the Data Files for Students. See the inside back cover of this book for instructions on downloading the Data Files for Students, or contact your instructor for information about accessing the required files.

Problem: As sales manager at City Sports, you have been asked to use your Visual Basic for Applications skills to automate the formatting of the workbook as shown in Figure 10–90. The objective is to simplify formatting by making macros to set up the header and footer, run conditional formatting, change the page layout, change the font size, apply a theme, undo all changes, and print the worksheet.

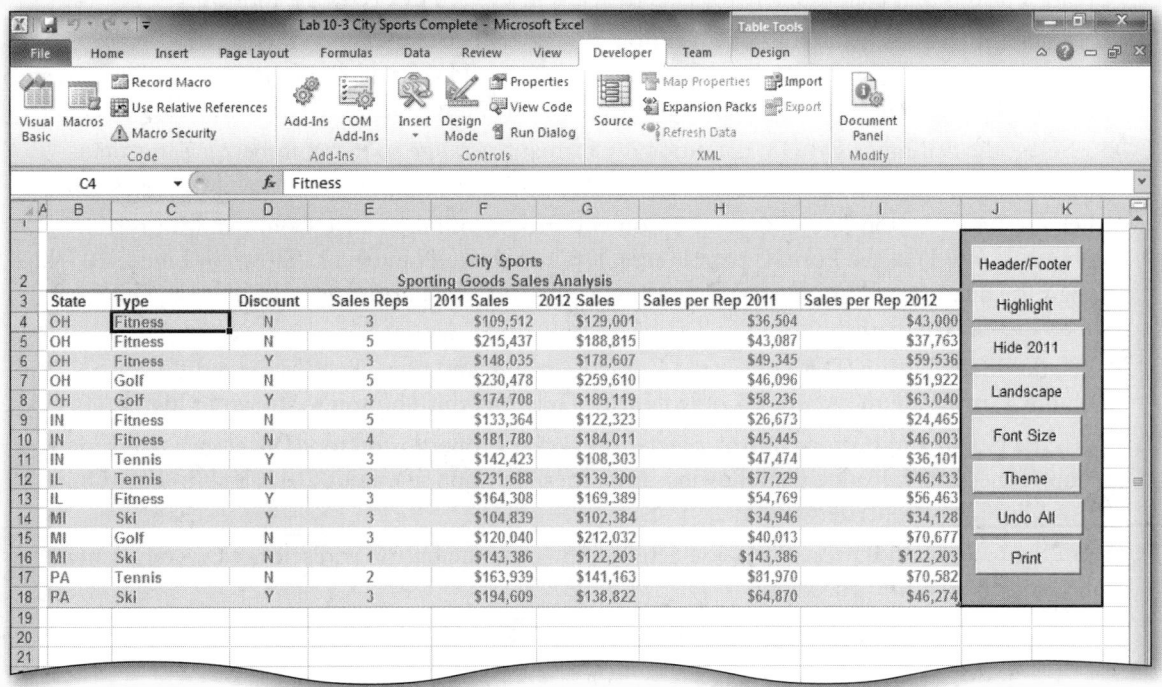

Figure 10–90

Instructions: Perform the following tasks:

1. Start Excel. If the Developer tab is not displayed on the Ribbon, click the File tab, click the Options button, click Customize Ribbon, click the Developer check box in the Customize the Ribbon area, and then click OK. To enable macros, click the Macro Security button (Developer tab | Code group). When the Trust Center dialog box is displayed, click 'Enable all macros' and then click the OK button.

2. Open the Lab 10-3 City Sports from the Data Files for Students and then save the workbook using the file name, Lab 10-3 City Sports Complete, saving the workbook as an Excel Macro-Enabled Workbook file type.

3. Set the background color of the range J2:K18 to White, Background 1 Darker 25% (column 1, row 4 on the Fill Color palette). Draw a thick box border around the range J2:K18.

4. Click the Developer tab on the Ribbon. Click the Insert button (Developer tab | Controls group) and then click Command Button (column 1, row 1) in the ActiveX Controls area. Draw the first button as shown in Figure 10–90.

Continued >

In the Lab *continued*

5. With the Command Button control selected, click the Properties button (Developer tab | Controls group). If necessary, change the following properties: (a) Caption = Header/Footer; and (b) PrintObject = False. Close the Properties window.

6. With the Command Button control selected, right-click the button and select View Code. Enter the following code in the procedure:

```
newHeader = InputBox("Please Enter the Header", "Enter")
ActiveSheet.PageSetup.CenterHeader = newHeader
newFooter = InputBox("Please Enter the Footer", "Enter")
ActiveSheet.PageSetup.CenterFooter = newFooter
```

7. Create a macro that conditionally formats the cells in H4:I18 by doing the following:

    a. Click the Record Macro button (Developer tab | Code group). When the Record Macro dialog box is displayed, name the macro **CondFormat,** add your name in the Description box, and store the macro in this workbook. Click the OK button to start the macro recording process.

    b. Select the cell range H4:I18; conditionally format the range so that numbers greater than 80,000 are highlighted; and click the Stop Recording button (Developer tab | Code group).

8. Click the Insert button (Developer tab | Controls group) and then click Command Button (column 1, row 1) in the Form Controls area. Draw the second button as shown in Figure 10–90. Assign the macro CondFormat to the button. Right-click the button and edit the text, changing the text to **Highlight.**

9. Click the Insert button (Developer tab | Controls group) and then click Command Button (column 1, row 1) in the ActiveX Controls area. Draw the third button as shown in Figure 10–90.

10. With the Command Button control selected, click the Properties button (Developer tab | Controls group). If necessary, change the following properties: (a) Caption = Hide 2011; and (b) PrintObject = False. Close the Properties window.

11. With the Command Button control selected, right-click the button and select view code. Enter the following code in the procedure:

```
Range("F:F,H:H").Select
Range("H1").Activate
Selection.EntireColumn.Hidden = True
```

12. Create a macro that changes the page layout to landscape by doing the following:

    a. Click the Record Macro button (Developer tab | Code group). When the Record Macro dialog box is displayed, name the macro **ChangeLayout,** add your name in the Description box, and store the macro in this workbook. Click the OK button to start the macro recording process.

    b. Change the page layout to landscape; and then click the Stop Recording button (Developer tab | Code group).

13. Click the Insert button (Developer tab | Controls group) and then click Command Button (column 1, row 1) in the Form Controls area. Draw the fourth button as shown in Figure 10–90. Assign the macro Change Layout to the button. Right-click the button and edit the text, changing the text to **Landscape.**

14. Click the Insert button (Developer tab | Controls group) and then click Command Button (column 1, row 1) in the ActiveX Controls area. Draw the fifth button as shown in Figure 10–90.

15. With the Command Button control selected, click the Properties button (Developer tab | Controls group). If necessary, change the following properties: (a) Caption = Font Size; and (b) PrintObject = False. Close the Properties window.

16. With the Command Button control selected, right-click the button and select View Code. Enter the following code in the procedure:

```
newSize = InputBox("Please Enter a Font Size", "Enter")
Cells.Select
Selection.Font.Size = newSize
```

17. Create a macro that changes the theme to Foundry by doing the following:

    a. Click the Record Macro button (Developer tab | Code group). When the Record Macro dialog box appears, name the macro `ChangeTheme,` add your name in the Description box, and store the macro in this workbook. Click the OK button to start the macro recording process.

    b. Change the theme to Foundry; and then click the Stop Recording button (Developer tab | Code group).

18. Click the Insert button (Developer tab | Controls group) and then click Command Button (column 1, row 1) in the Form Controls area. Draw the sixth button as shown in Figure 10–90. Assign the macro ChangeTheme to the button. Right-click the button and edit the text, changing the text to `Theme`.

19. Create a macro that undoes the changes done by the other buttons by doing the following:

    a. Click the Record Macro button (Developer tab | Code group). When the Record Macro dialog box is displayed, name the macro `UndoChanges,` add your name in the Description box, and store the macro in this workbook. Click the OK button to start the macro recording process.

    b. Remove the header and footer; unhide columns between F and H; clear conditional formatting from range H4:I18; change page layout to portrait; change font size for worksheet to 10; change theme to Technic; and then click the Stop Recording button (Developer tab | Code group).

20. Click the Insert button (Developer tab | Controls group) and then click Command Button (column 1, row 1) in the Form Controls area. Draw the seventh button as shown in Figure 10–90. Assign the macro UndoChanges to the button. Right-click the button and edit the text, changing the text to `Undo All`.

21. Create a macro that prints the worksheet by doing the following:

    a. Click the Record Macro button (Developer tab | Code group). When the Record Macro dialog box is displayed, name the macro `PrintWorkSheet,` add your name in the Description box, and store the macro in this workbook. Click the OK button to start the macro recording process.

    b. Hide columns J and K; print the worksheet; unhide columns J and K; and then click the Stop Recording button (Developer tab | Code group).

22. Click the Insert button (Developer tab | Controls group) and then click Command Button (column 1, row 1) in the Form Controls area. Draw the eighth button as shown in Figure 10–90. Assign the macro PrintWorksheet to the button. Right-click the button and edit the text, changing the text to `Print`.

23. Change the document properties as specified by your instructor.

24. Print the worksheet and the procedures.

25. To disable macros, click the Macro Security button (Developer tab | Code group). When the Trust Center dialog box is displayed, click 'Disable all macros with notification' and then click the OK button. Quit Excel.

26. Submit the assignment as requested by your instructor.

Cases and Places

Apply your creative thinking and problem solving skills to design and implement a solution.

Note: To complete these assignments, you may be required to use the Data Files for Students. See the inside back cover of this book for instructions on downloading the Data Files for Students, or contact your instructor for information about accessing the required files.

1: Automating Printing Tasks

Academic

You are interning at the school bookstore. Open the workbook Case 10-1 HTEU Bookstore from the Data Files for Students and then save the workbook using the file name, Case 10-1 HTEU Bookstore Complete, saving the workbook as an Excel Macro-Enabled Workbook file type. Create a macro that prints the formulas version of the Forecast worksheet in landscape orientation using the Fit to option. Make sure that the macro resets the Page Setup options before terminating. Execute the macro. Print the worksheet and macro. Save the workbook. Submit the assignment as requested by your instructor.

2: Calculating Auto Loans

Personal

Consider the next automobile that you want to purchase and determine possible models, their current sales prices including tax, and other information regarding the financing of an auto loan. Open the workbook Case 10-2 My Loan Calculator from the Data Files for Students and then save the workbook using the file name, Case 10-2 My Loan Calculator Complete, saving the workbook as an Excel Macro-Enabled Workbook file type. Add a New Auto Loan button that accepts the values in the cells C3, C4, C5, C7, and C8. The procedure associated with the New Auto Loan button on the worksheet should validate the price, down payment, interest rate, and years as follows: (a) the price must be between $3,000 and $50,000 inclusive; (b) the down payment must be between $500 and $25,000 inclusive; (c) the interest rate must be between 3% and 19% inclusive; and (d) the years must be between 1 and 6 inclusive. Print the procedure. Create and enter two sets of valid test data based on your personal preference for an auto and your financial information. Print the worksheet for each set. Save the workbook. Submit the assignment as requested by your instructor.

3: Creating a Well-Balanced User Interface

Professional

Open the workbook Case 10-3 Midleton Expo Center from the Data Files for Students and then save the workbook using the file name, Case 10-3 Midleton Expo Center Complete, saving the workbook as an Excel Macro-Enabled Workbook file type. Create a well-balanced user interface made up of a Reset button and five scroll bars, one for each of the cells in the range B23:B27. Have the Reset button set the five assumptions to 35%, 7%, 32%, 4%, and 3%, respectively. The scroll bars should range from 0% to 100% and increment by 0.25% (scroll arrows) and 1% (scroll bars). Use the titles in the Assumptions box in the range A23:A27 for the names of the scroll bars. Print the worksheet and the Reset button control procedure. Create and enter two sets of data to test the user interface. Print the worksheet for each set. Save the workbook. Submit the assignment as requested by your instructor.

11 | Collaboration Features for Workbooks

Objectives

You will have mastered the material in this chapter when you can:

- Explain sharing and collaboration techniques
- Insert, edit, and delete a comment
- Review all comments in a workbook
- Track changes and share a workbook
- Accept and reject tracked changes made to a workbook
- Turn off tracked changes
- Distribute a workbook through e-mail

- Add and edit hyperlinks in a worksheet
- Distribute a workbook using Windows Live SkyDrive
- Save a workbook as a PDF file
- Compare and merge workbooks
- Save a custom view of a worksheet and format a worksheet background

11 | Collaboration Features for Workbooks

Introduction

In today's business environment, colleagues are as likely to be in the next state as in the next office. In this chapter, you will learn how to use the collaboration features in Excel to gather input from multiple users, by a variety of methods, to update and enhance an Excel workbook. Excel allows you to share and collaborate with others through a variety of features, depending on your resources and preferences and the resources and preferences of those with whom you are collaborating.

To allow several people to view and change a workbook at the same time, a user can **share** the workbook. Excel also has the capability to **track changes** to a workbook by marking who changed what data, in which cell, and when. **Comments**, or descriptions, which do not regularly appear as part of the worksheet data, can be added to the workbook to alert the recipients to special information and then later can be edited or deleted. Workbooks that have been saved and copied to others also can be compared and merged. **Comparing** workbooks allows users to view and scroll worksheets side by side and visually search the worksheets for differences. **Merging** allows users to bring together copies of workbooks that others have worked on independently. You also will learn how to save a **custom view** of a worksheet, which enables each user to view the worksheet in a familiar manner, even if other users alter the appearance or layout of a worksheet.

Project — Spinning Around Bicycles Sales Analysis

Spinning Around Bicycles is a family-run business that has recently expanded. The business has shops in three states. The main products sold are road, mountain, and hybrid bikes. The shops all carry the same basic inventory, but bike sales reflect the demographics of the three areas. The expansion to three shops occurred two years ago, and the family has decided to review the results thus far. In order to decide which detailed questions to ask about sales, the group has decided to review annual sales data first. Rather than incurring travel expenses, the business will use the collaborative features in Excel to exchange and update data. The initial worksheet shared among the owners contains queries about initial sales data provided (Figure 11–1a). The final version of that worksheet reflects a series of decisions by the owners about content and presentation, and corrections to the data (Figure 11–1b). A final version of the sponsorship worksheet includes a background image and hyperlinks (Figure 11–1c).

(a) Initial Worksheet with Queries

(b) Final with Corrections

(c) Sponsorship sheet with Background Image and Hyperlinks

Figure 11–1

Figure 11–2 illustrates the requirements document for Spinning Around Bicycles Sales Analysis worksheet. It includes the needs, source of data, calculations, and other facts about the worksheet's development.

REQUEST FOR NEW WORKBOOK

Date Submitted:	January 11, 2013
Submitted By:	Marty Fields
Worksheet Title:	Spinning Around Analysis, and Spinning Around Sponsorship
Needs:	Update sales data from 2011 and 2012 to provide a base spreadsheet the business can use to determine which detailed analyses to pursue. For this initial evaluation, all work will be done using collaboration features of Excel, to allow managers to provide and review information without traveling for meetings.
	There are some data gaps that the shops need to fill in. Managers should make use of comment features whenever possible to query and explain.
	The sales analysis worksheet should be set up for sharing via e-mail. It should be sent out to all three stores in a form that will allow for merging of edits to a single workbook. It is important that it can be determined who made the individual changes, in case any changes raise questions.
	The sponsorship data also need to be reviewed, and the sheet prepared for sharing with interested parties outside of the company. We are hoping to find a sponsorship partner moving forward. We would like to see incorporation of a graphic to add visual interest. The sponsorship worksheet should also include a link to the USA Cycling Organization Web site, and a link that can be used to send an e-mail message to our sponsorship coordinator. The sponsorship data should be saved to Windows Live SkyDrive, to a sponsorship folder. The folder should be set up to restrict access to only e-mail addresses listed.
Source of Data:	The workbooks used as a base for the workbooks shown in Figures 11-1a and 11-1b are available in the Data Files for Students with the file names Spinning Around Data and Spinning Around Sponsorship.
Calculations:	None.
Special Requirements:	Windows Live SkyDrive will be used to save a Sponsorship workbook.

Approvals

Approval Status:	X	Approved
		Rejected
Approved By:	Arthur Fields	
Date:	January 16, 2013	
Contracted To:	M. Jones, Spreadsheet Specialist	

Figure 11–2

Overview

As you read this chapter, you will learn how to modify the existing workbook as shown in Figure 11–1 by performing these general tasks:

- Insert, edit, and delete comments.
- Track changes and share a workbook.
- Compare and merge shared workbooks.
- Add and edit hyperlinks.
- Save custom views.

General Project Guidelines

While working with an Excel worksheet, you need to make several decisions that will determine the appearance and characteristics of the finished worksheet. As you update an existing worksheet to meet the requirements shown in Figure 11–2, you should follow these general guidelines:

Plan
Ahead

1. **Determine the needs of the people with whom you will be collaborating.** Excel provides several methods to work with others on a workbook. You need to determine how they will be working with the workbook, what software they have available, and whether they have access to network resources.

2. **Evaluate the various options Excel provides for collaboration.** Excel provides several methods to work with others on a workbook. In some cases, you may send the workbook to a group of people all at once and then consolidate their changes and suggestions. In other cases, you may want to send a workbook to one person at a time and allow each person to add to the changes and suggestions that others have made.

3. **Determine what types of changes you want your collaborators to be able to make.** How much editing your collaborators should be able to do can determine the tools you use to collaborate.

4. **If merging workbooks, gather workbooks to be merged and then assess any differences in the workbooks that are in disagreement.** In the case of the Spinning Around Sponsorship worksheets noted in the requirements document (Figure 11–2 on page EX 708), several people will be providing changes to a workbook. Before merging the workbooks, ensure that you have all of the workbooks from the individuals. When merging the workbooks, conflicts in changes to cells may arise, at which point you must make decisions to resolve the conflicts.

When necessary, more specific details concerning the above guidelines are presented at appropriate points in the chapter. The chapter also will identify the actions you perform and decisions made regarding these guidelines during the modification of the worksheet shown in Figure 11–1 on page EX 707.

With a good understanding of the requirements document and an understanding of the necessary decisions, the next step is to use Excel to learn about the existing worksheet and solve the problem.

To Start Excel and Open a Workbook

To begin this project, you will open a file located on the Data Files for Students. See the inside back cover of this book for instructions on downloading the Data Files for Students, or contact your instructor for more information about accessing the required files. If you are using a computer to step through the project in this chapter and you want your screens to match the figures in this book, you should change your screen's resolution to 1024 × 768.

The following steps start Excel, open a file, and then save it with a new file name.

1 Start Excel. If necessary, maximize the Excel window.

2 Open the workbook, Spinning Around Data, located on the Data Files for Students.

3 Save the workbook using the file name, Spinning Around Analysis.

4 If the worksheet window in Excel is not maximized, click the Maximize button next to the Close Window button on the Ribbon to maximize the worksheet within Excel (Figure 11–3).

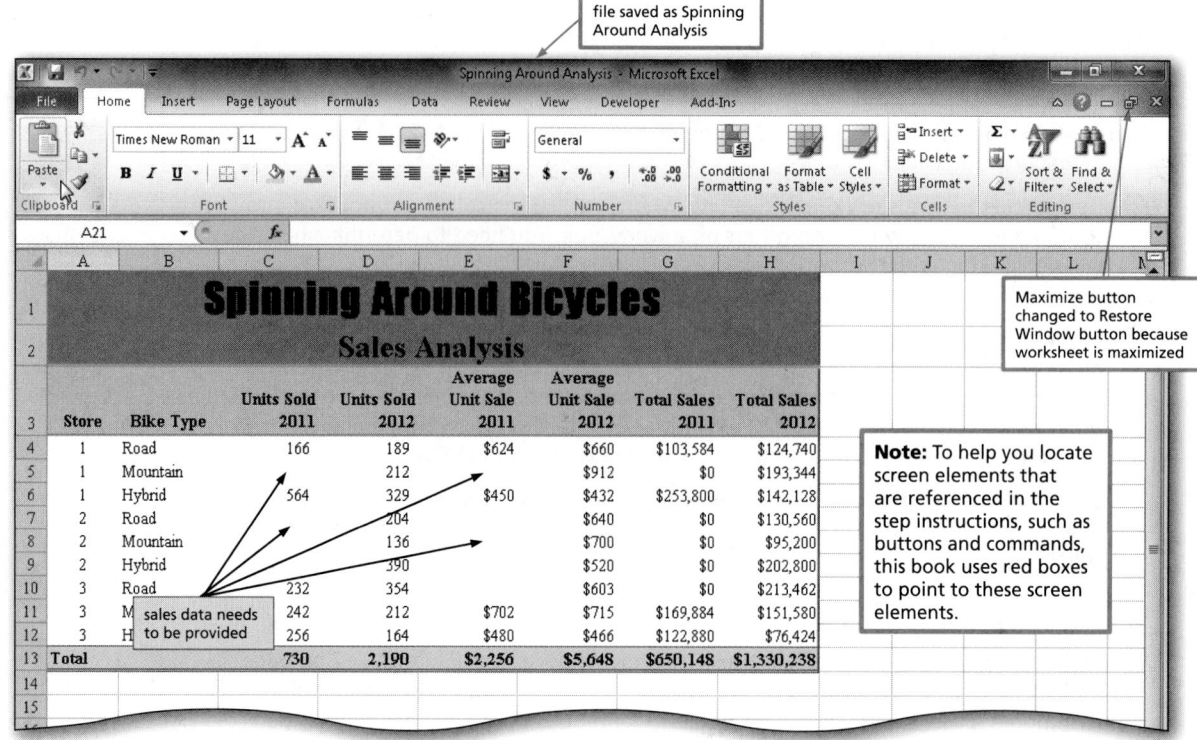

Figure 11–3

BTW

The Ribbon and Screen Resolution
Excel may change how the groups and buttons within the groups appear on the Ribbon, depending on the computer's screen resolution. Thus, your Ribbon may look different from the ones in this book if you are using a screen resolution other than 1024 × 768.

BTW

BTWs
For a complete list of the BTWs found in the margins of this book, visit the Excel 2010 BTW Web page (scsite.com/ex2010/btw).

About the Spinning Around Analysis Worksheet

As shown in Figure 11–3, the Spinning Around Analysis worksheet is incomplete in terms of data. Before sending this worksheet out to gather data, you will add comments to the worksheet specifying what you need from people.

Gathering Feedback Using Comments

Comments are the electronic version of sticky notes or annotations in the margin. They can request additional information or clarification of existing information. Comments can provide direction to the reader about how to interpret content or describe what type of content to add. You can add comments to a cell in a worksheet. Once added, you can edit, format, move, copy, or resize them. You can choose to show comments in a worksheet, to display only a comment indicator, or to hide comments. Comments work well when multiple people are collaborating and commenting on a worksheet. Comments added by each user are identified by a name in the comment, set by the user.

Plan Ahead

Determine the needs of the people with whom you will be collaborating. The needs of the people with whom you will be collaborating are determined by the resources they have available to them. People with Excel available to them will have different needs than those without Excel available. Different versions of the software necessitate a different approach to providing content for collaboration.

Depending on the nature of the comments, you may decide to delete some or all comments after reading them and making edits to the worksheet, if appropriate.

To Add Comments to a Worksheet

The Sales Analysis worksheet in the Spinning Around Analysis workbook has some missing data. You can add comments to serve as reminders to gather and then enter the data. The following steps add comments to the worksheet in cells A4, A7, and A10.

1

- Click cell A4 to make it the active cell.

- Right-click cell A4 to display the shortcut menu (Figure 11–4).

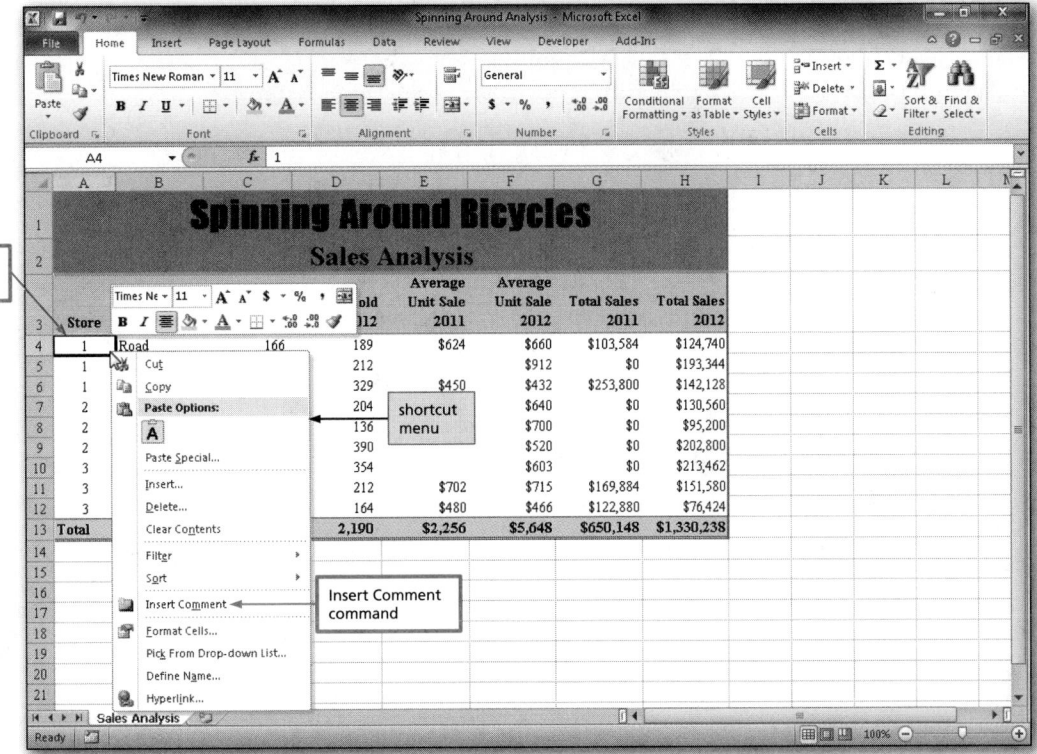

Figure 11–4

2

- Click Insert Comment on the shortcut menu to open a comment box next to the selected cell and display a comment indicator in the cell (Figure 11–5).

Figure 11–5

3

• Enter the text
Note to self -
supply units
sold and
average unit
sales figures
for 2011. in
the comment box
(Figure 11–6).

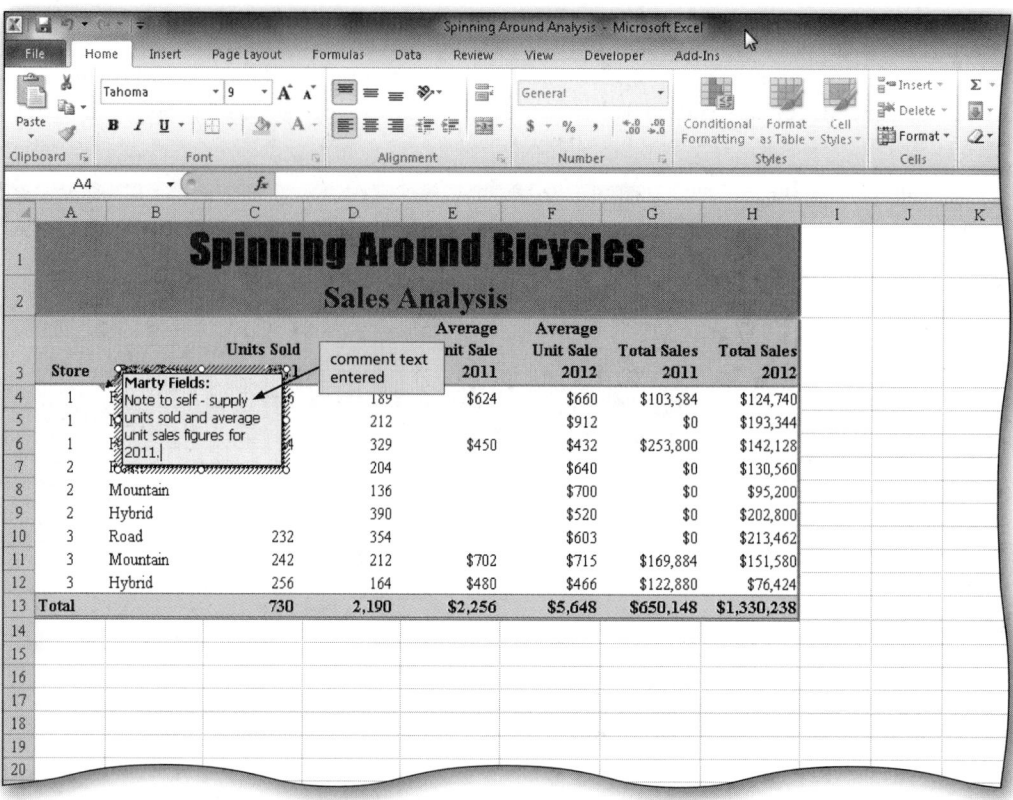

Figure 11–6

4

• Click outside the
comment box to close
the comment box and
display only the red
comment indicator in
cell A4 (Figure 11–7).

Figure 11–7

5

- Enter a comment in cell A7 with the text `Note to self - supply units sold and average unit sales figures for 2011.`

- Click outside the comment box to close the comment box and display only the red comment indicator in cell A7.

- Enter a comment in cell A10 with the text `Please supply average unit sales, Road bikes for 2011.`

- Click outside the comment box to close the comment box and display only the red comment indicator in cell A10.

- Click the Save button on the Quick Access Toolbar to save the workbook (Figure 11–8).

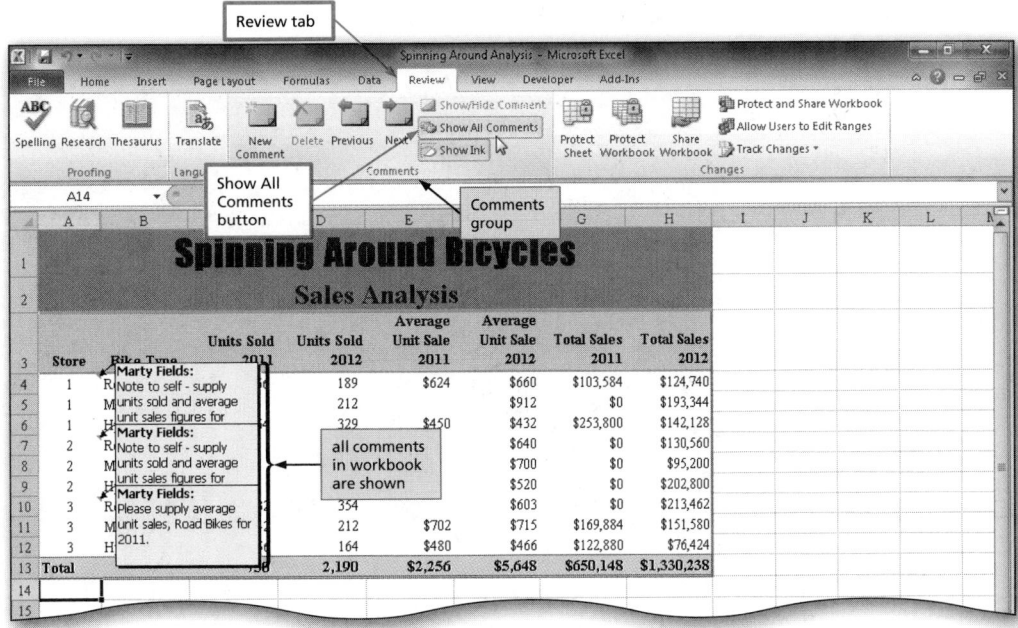

Save button

comments entered in cells A4, A7, and A10

Figure 11–8

Other Ways

1. Click New Comment button (Review tab | Comments group)

2. Press SHIFT+F2

To Display All Comments on a Worksheet

The comments are currently hidden. You can make some or all of the comments visible. The following step makes all comments visible.

1

- Click Review on the Ribbon to display the Review tab.

- Click the Show All Comments button (Review tab | Comments group) to show all comments in the workbook (Figure 11–9).

Q&A

What if I want to hide all comments?

The Show All Comments button is a toggle switch. Clicking it once shows all comments, clicking it a second time hides all comments.

Review tab

Show All Comments button

Comments group

all comments in workbook are shown

Marty Fields: Note to self - supply units sold and average unit sales figures for

Marty Fields: Note to self - supply units sold and average unit sales figures for

Marty Fields: Please supply average unit sales, Road Bikes for 2011.

Figure 11–9

To Edit Comments on a Worksheet

After adding comments to a worksheet, you can edit them to add or change information. The following steps edit the comment in cell A4.

1
- Click cell A4 to make active the cell containing the comment to edit.
- Right-click cell A4 to display the shortcut menu (Figure 11–10).

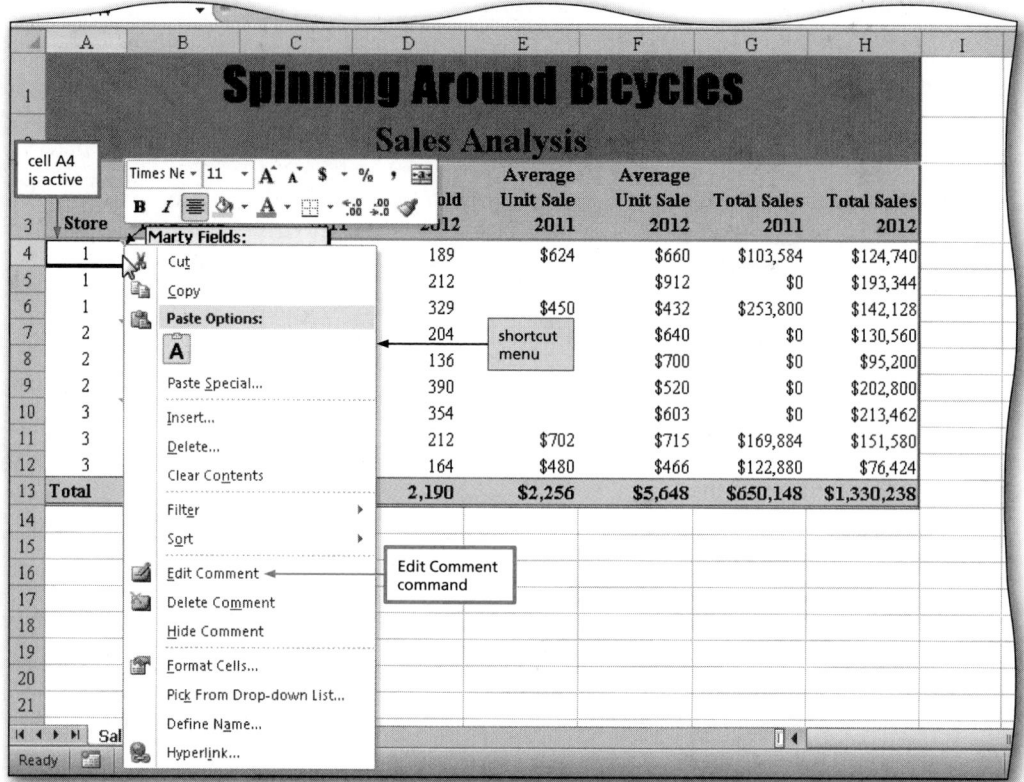

Figure 11–10

2
- Click Edit Comment on the shortcut menu to open the comment for editing (Figure 11–11).

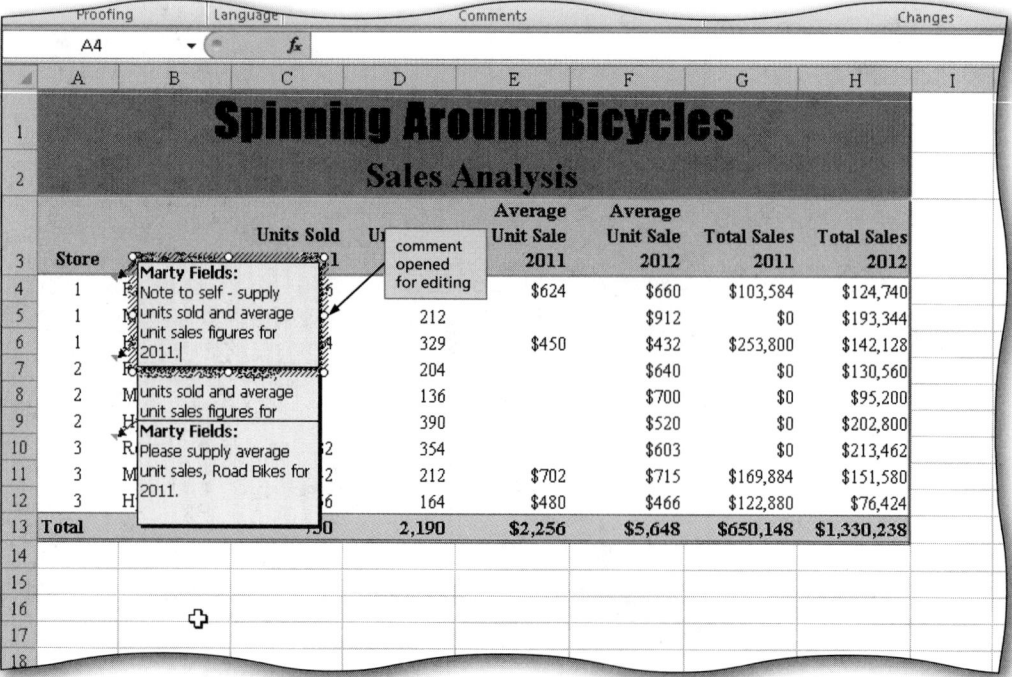

Figure 11–11

3

- Change the comment text to read `Note to self - supply units sold and average unit sales figures for 2011, Mountain Bikes.` (Figure 11–12).

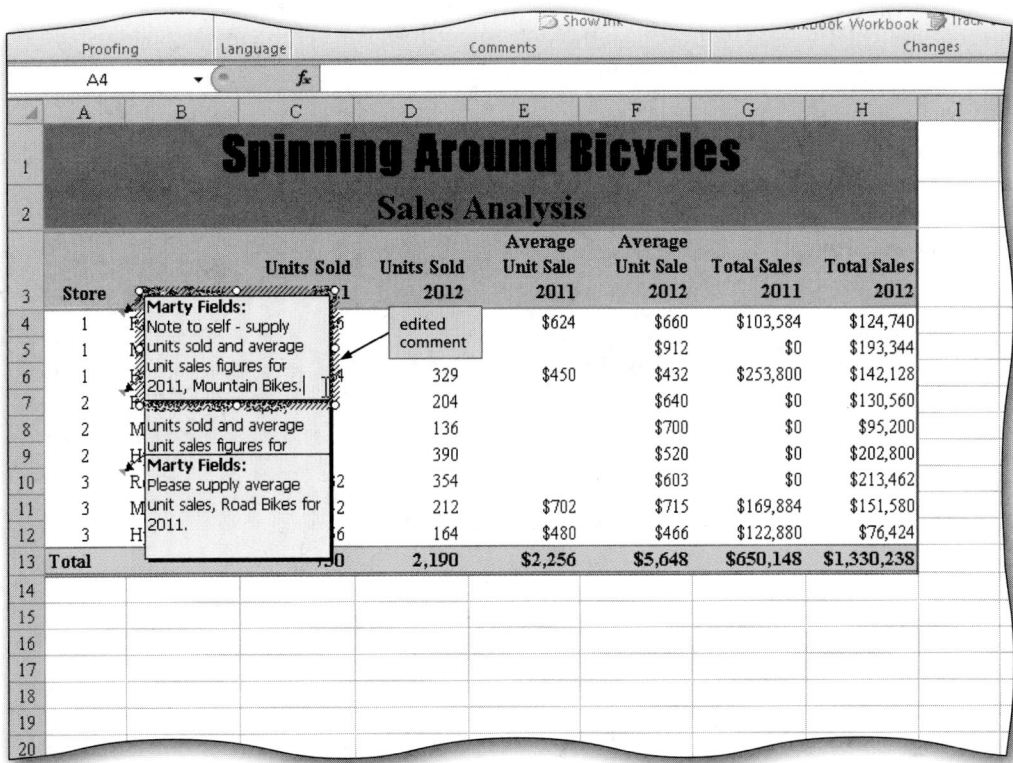

Figure 11–12

4

- Click cell A14 to complete the editing. Click the Show All Comments button (Review tab | Comments group) to hide all comments in the workbook (Figure 11–13).

Q&A How can I quickly read a hidden comment in a worksheet?

Point to a comment indicator to display the related comment.

Q&A Can I edit a hidden comment?

Yes. The Edit Comment command can be accessed whether the comment is hidden or visible.

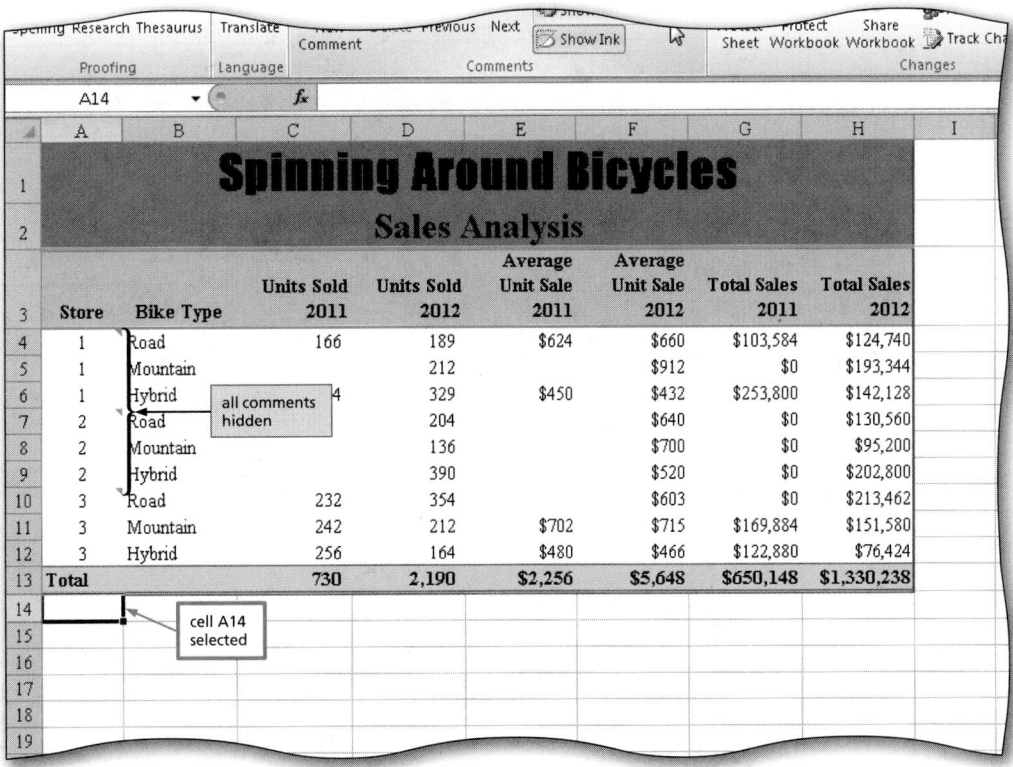

Figure 11–13

To Format Comments on a Worksheet

You may want to change the appearance of a particular comment to make it stand out from other comments. The following steps format the comment text in cell A4.

1

- Click cell A4 to make active the cell containing the comment to format.

- Click the Edit Comment button (Review tab | Comments group) to open the comment for editing (Figure 11–14).

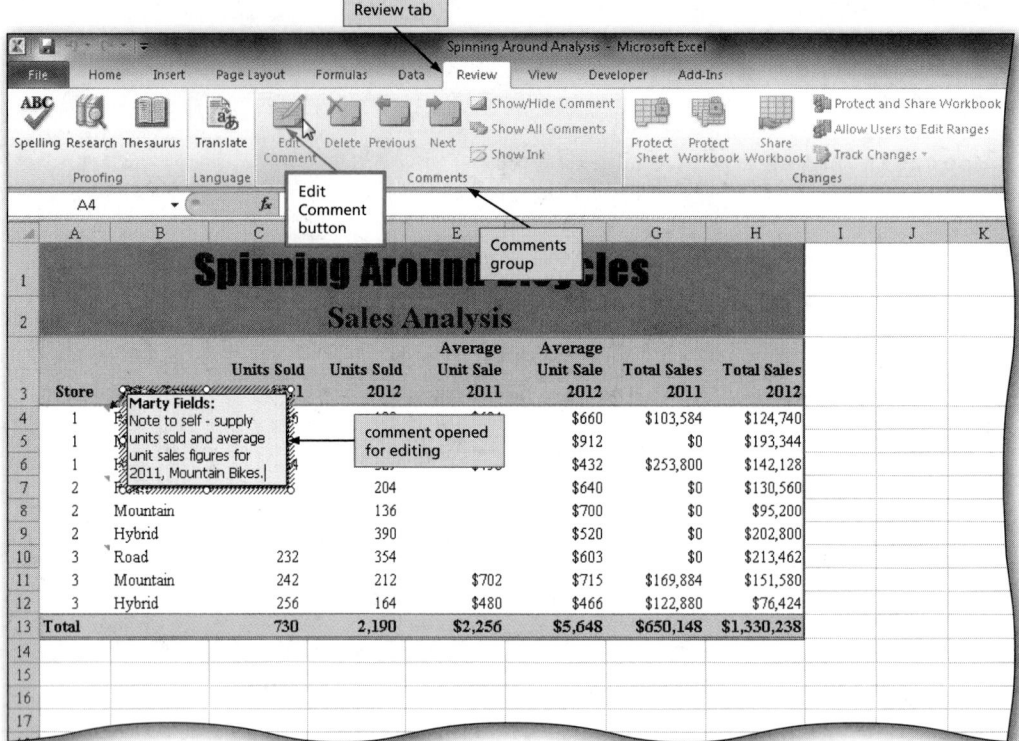

Figure 11–14

2

- Drag to select the comment text to prepare for formatting it.

- Right-click the text and then click Format Comment on the shortcut menu to display the Format Comment dialog box.

- Change the comment text to red and bold (Figure 11–15).

Figure 11–15

3

- Click the OK button (Format Cells dialog box) to apply the selected formatting to the comment text.

- Click cell A4 to deselect the comment text, and then point to cell A4 to display the formatted comment (Figure 11–16).

Q&A

Can I print comments?

Yes. You can print comments where they appear on the sheet by displaying all comments and then printing the sheet. You can print a list of comments separately by selecting the 'At end of sheet' option in the comments list on the Sheet tab of the Page Setup Dialog box (Page Layout tab | Page Setup Dialog Box Launcher).

Figure 11–16

Collaborating and Tracking Changes on a Workbook

The next steps in the project are to share the workbook and then turn on features to track changes.

If others need to edit a workbook or suggest changes, Excel provides three ways to collaborate. **Collaborating** means working together in cooperation on a document with other Excel users.

The first option is to **distribute** the workbook to others, physically on a disk through e-mail using the Save & Send command in the Backstage view, or via Windows Live SkyDrive. With the Save & Send command, the document can be embedded as part of the e-mail message or the file can be sent as an e-mail attachment, which allows recipients of the e-mail message to open the file if Excel is installed on their system.

A second option is to collaborate by **sharing** the workbook. Sharing involves more than simply giving another user a copy of a file; it allows multiple people to work independently on the same workbook at the same time if they are in a networked environment. Sharing a workbook puts restrictions on the types of edits a user can make, which provides a degree of control over the editing process that distributing the workbook does not. If users are not in a networked environment, workbook sharing allows them to work on the workbook in turn, while keeping track of who was responsible for the various edits. In a non-networked environment, having several people work consecutively on a shared workbook provides the original user with the control over what types of edits can be performed.

A third option is to collaborate interactively with other people through discussion threads or online meetings. The use of SharePoint Services with Microsoft Office 2010 allows people at different sites to share and exchange files.

BTW

Q&As
For a complete list of the Q&As found in many of the step-by-step sequences in this book, visit the Excel 2010 Q&A Web page (scsite.com/ex2010/qa).

BTW

Copying Comments
You can copy comments from one cell to other cells using the Paste Special command. Select the cell that contains the comment you need to copy, select the cell or cells to which you want to apply the comment, click the Paste button arrow, and then click Paste Special. In the Paste Special dialog box, under Paste, select Comments, and then click OK.

Plan Ahead	**Evaluate the various options Excel provides for collaboration.** The option you choose will reflect the needs of the project. You can take into account the need for reviewer privacy, the required turnaround for the collaborative feedback, and the resources available to the people who are providing you with feedback.

BTW

Passwords and Workbook Sharing
Excel keeps a change history of 30 days by default for a shared workbook. You can use passwords with a shared workbook to protect the change history. Use the Protect Shared Workbook button (Review tab | Changes group). The workbook cannot be shared at the time the password is added.

Sharing can be turned on for a workbook using the Share Workbook button on the Review tab. When workbook sharing is enabled, a number of Excel features — merging cells, deleting worksheets, changing or removing passwords, using scenarios, creating data tables, modifying macros, using data validation, and creating PivotTables — are disabled for the workbook. For this reason, the time when a workbook is shared should be limited; further, sharing should be used only for the purpose of reviewing and modifying the contents of worksheet data.

When a workbook is shared with other users, changes made and saved by the other users are visible only when you attempt to save changes. When Excel recognizes that another user has modified a shared workbook, Excel displays a dialog box indicating that the workbook has been updated with changes saved by other users; you then can review and accept or reject their work. If both you and another user change the same cell, Excel displays a Resolve Conflicts dialog box when the workbook is saved. The dialog box lists the conflicting changes and provides options to choose which change to accept in the workbook.

To Share and Collaborate on a Workbook

The following steps turn on sharing for the Spinning Around Analysis workbook and then allow collaboration with another user in a networked environment to make changes to the workbook.

1
- Click the Share Workbook button (Review tab | Changes group) to display the Share Workbook dialog box.

- When Excel displays the Share Workbook dialog box, click the 'Allow changes by more than one user at the same time' check box to insert a check mark (Figure 11–17).

Q&A

What is shown in the Share Workbook dialog box?

The 'Allow changes by more than one user at the same time' check box is selected, indicating that the workbook should be shared. The 'Who has this workbook open now' list in the Share Workbook dialog box lists all users who currently have a copy of the workbook open.

Figure 11–17

2

- Click the OK button (Share Workbook dialog box) to share the workbook with other users.

- When Excel displays the Microsoft Excel dialog box, click the OK button to share the workbook (Figure 11–18).

Q&A

How do I know when the workbook is being shared?

The text "[Shared]" appears on the title bar next to the file name, indicating that the workbook is being shared.

Figure 11–18

3

- If possible, have a classmate open a second copy of the workbook.

- With a second copy of the workbook open, click the Share Workbook button (Review tab | Changes group) to display the Share Workbook dialog box, which lists all users who currently have the workbook open (Figure 11–19).

Figure 11–19

4

- Click the OK button (Share Workbook dialog box) to close the dialog box.

- Ask the second workbook user to click cell C7, enter 183 as the new value, and then save the workbook.

- In your copy of the workbook, click the Save button on the Quick Access Toolbar to display the Microsoft Excel dialog box indicating that the workbook has been updated with changes saved by another user (Figure 11–20).

Figure 11–20

Q&A

Must I save the workbook before I am notified of another user's changes?

Yes. Until the workbook is saved, Excel provides no indication that another user has changed the shared workbook. To prohibit another user from saving additional updates to the workbook, click the user name in the Share Workbook dialog box and then click the Remove User button.

5

- Click the OK button (Microsoft Excel dialog box) to close the dialog box.

- Point to the triangle in cell C7 to display the comment indicating the other user's changes (Figure 11–21).

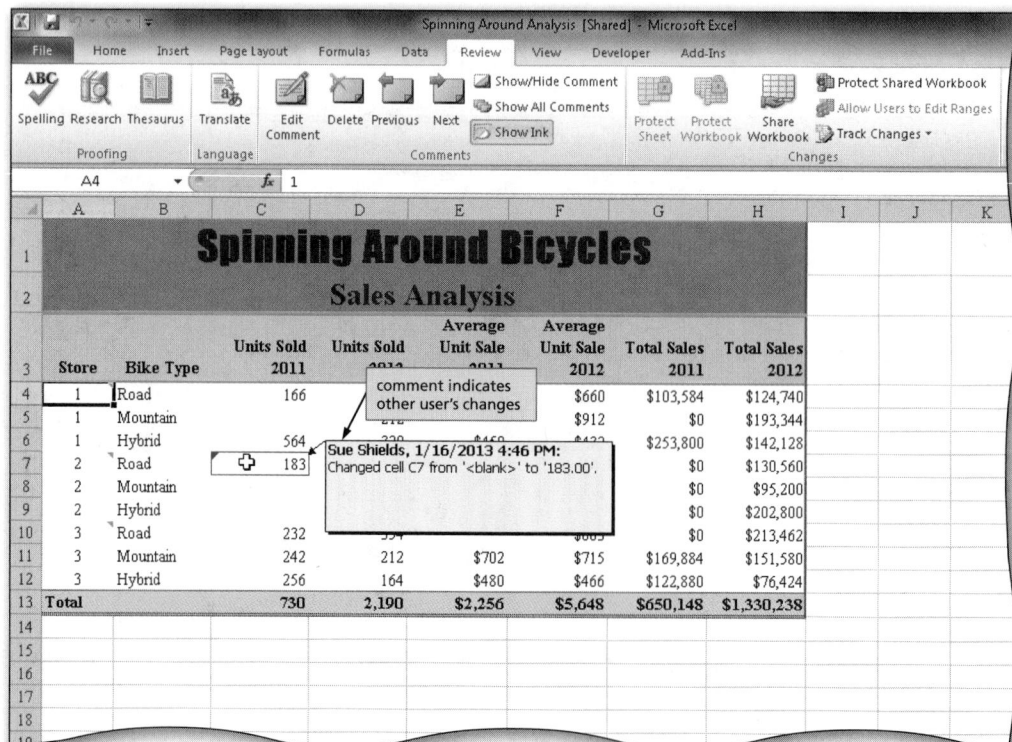

Figure 11–21

6

- Ask the second user of the workbook to close the workbook.

- Click the Share Workbook button (Review tab | Changes group) to display the Share Workbook dialog box.

- When Excel displays the Share Workbook dialog box, click the 'Allow changes by more than one user at the same time' check box to remove the check mark (Figure 11–22).

Figure 11–22

7

- Click the OK button (Share Workbook dialog box) to stop sharing the workbook (Figure 11–23).

8

- If Excel displays the Microsoft Excel dialog box asking whether the workbook should be removed from shared use, click the Yes button.

Figure 11–23

To Turn On Track Changes

When working collaboratively, keeping track of the changes that others make to a workbook is important. Tracking changes means that Excel, through the Track Changes command, will display the edited cells with a comment indicating who made the change, when the change was made, and what the original value was of the cell that was changed. Tracking and sharing work together. If either tracking or sharing is enabled, Excel enables the other by default. The following steps turn on track changes.

1

- Click the Track Changes button (Review tab | Changes group) to display the Track Changes menu (Figure 11–24).

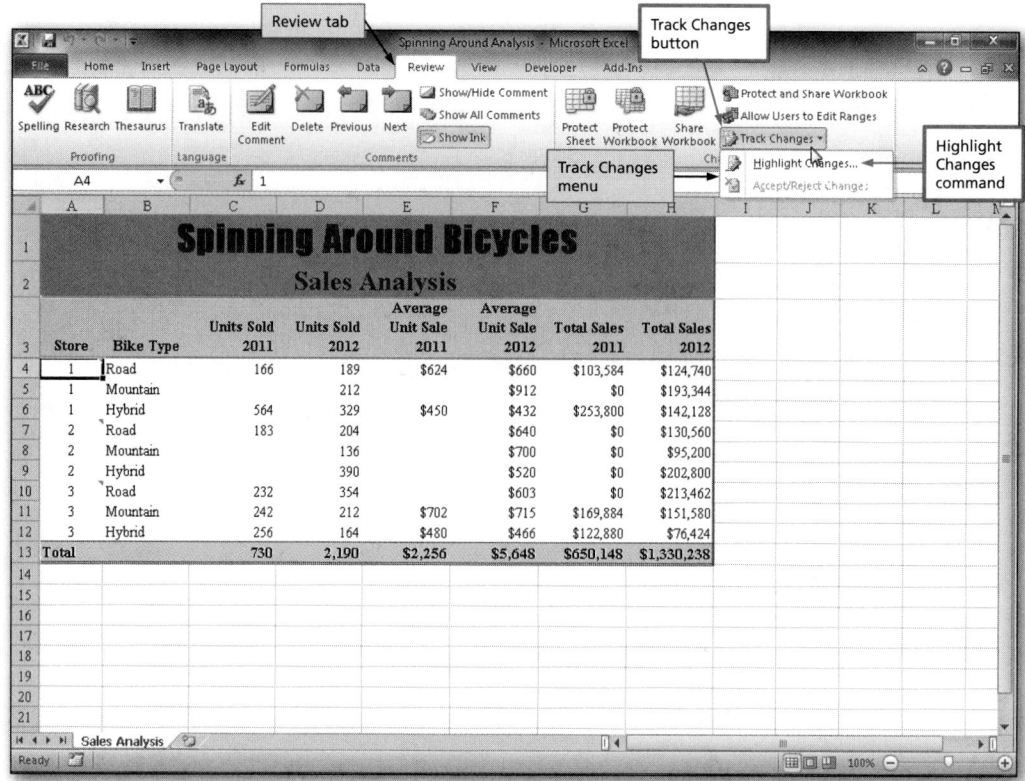

Figure 11–24

2

- Click Highlight Changes on the Track Changes menu to display the Highlight Changes dialog box.

- Click the 'Track changes while editing' check box to insert a check mark.

- If necessary, click all of the check boxes in the 'Highlight which changes' area to clear them (Figure 11–25).

Q&A

What is the purpose of clearing the check marks?

Clicking the 'Track changes while editing' check box enables track changes and shares the workbook. The When, Who, and Where check boxes and list boxes play no role when track changes first is enabled.

Figure 11–25

3

- Click the OK button (Highlight Changes dialog box) to close the dialog box and display the Microsoft Excel dialog box.

- Click the OK button (Microsoft Excel dialog box) to share and track changes in the workbook (Figure 11–26).

Q&A

What is the change history and how can it be protected?

Excel keeps a change history with each shared workbook. In the case of a shared workbook in which changes should be tracked, Excel provides a way for users to make data entry changes, but does not allow them to modify the change history. To protect the change history associated with a shared workbook, click the Protect Shared Workbook button (Review tab | Changes group). When Excel displays the Protect Shared Workbook dialog box, click 'Sharing with track changes' to select it and then click the OK button. After a shared workbook is protected, no one can unprotect or change it except the owner.

workbook is shared because Track Changes is turned on

Spinning Around Bicycles
Sales Analysis

Store	Bike Type	Units Sold 2011	Units Sold 2012	Average Unit Sale 2011	Average Unit Sale 2012	Total Sales 2011	Total Sales 2012
1	Road	166	189	$624	$660	$103,584	$124,740
1	Mountain		212		$912	$0	$193,344
1	Hybrid	564	329	$450	$432	$253,800	$142,128
2	Road	183	204		$640	$0	$130,560
2	Mountain		136		$700	$0	$95,200
2	Hybrid		390		$520	$0	$202,800
3	Road	232	354		$603	$0	$213,462
3	Mountain	242	212	$702	$715	$169,884	$151,580
3	Hybrid	256	164	$480	$466	$122,880	$76,424
Total		730	2,190	$2,256	$5,648	$650,148	$1,330,238

Figure 11–26

To Distribute a Workbook by E-Mail

You may need to have a workbook reviewed by someone who does not share network access with you. You can send a shared workbook using e-mail. The recipient can make changes, and then send the workbook back to you for review. The following steps save the workbook and send it by e-mail.

1

- With Excel active, click File on the Ribbon to open the Backstage view.

- Click the Save & Send tab to display the Save & Send pane (Figure 11–27).

Figure 11–27

- If necessary, click Send Using E-mail to display the Send Using E-mail options in the right pane.

- Click the Send as Attachment button to open an e-mail message with the workbook as an attachment (Figure 11–28).

- Fill in the To: line, add any message you want to send, and then click the Send button to send the message with attached workbook.

- Close the Spinning Around Analysis workbook.

Figure 11–28

Reviewing Tracked Changes

Instead of writing suggestions and changes on a printed draft copy and sending it to the person in charge of a workbook, Excel's track changes feature allows users to enter suggested changes directly in the workbook. The owner of the workbook then looks through each change and makes a decision about whether to accept it.

Plan Ahead

Determine what types of changes you want your collaborators to be able to make. Evaluate the content on which you are seeking collaboration, and select your tools accordingly. Sharing a workbook provides you with the most restrictions on types of edits. In situations where you are looking for input on how to evaluate data, sharing would not be a suitable tool. In situations where a particular evaluative framework must be used, the limitations of sharing a workbook would be welcome.

To Open a Workbook and Review Tracked Changes

After a workbook has been reviewed by others, it usually is returned to the owner. When track changes is enabled for a workbook, the file, when returned to the owner, will contain other users' changes, corrections, and comments. The owner of the workbook then can review those changes and make decisions about whether to accept the changes. A workbook named Spinning Around Analysis1, which includes tracked changes from other users to the Spinning Around Analysis workbook, is saved on the Data Files for Students. The following steps use this workbook to illustrate reviewing tracked changes.

1

- With Excel active, open the file, Spinning Around Analysis1, from the Data Files for Students.

- If necessary, click the Enable Editing button on the Protected View bar to open the workbook for editing.

- Click Review on the Ribbon to display the Review tab.

- Click the Track Changes button (Review tab | Changes group) to display the Track Changes menu (Figure 11–29).

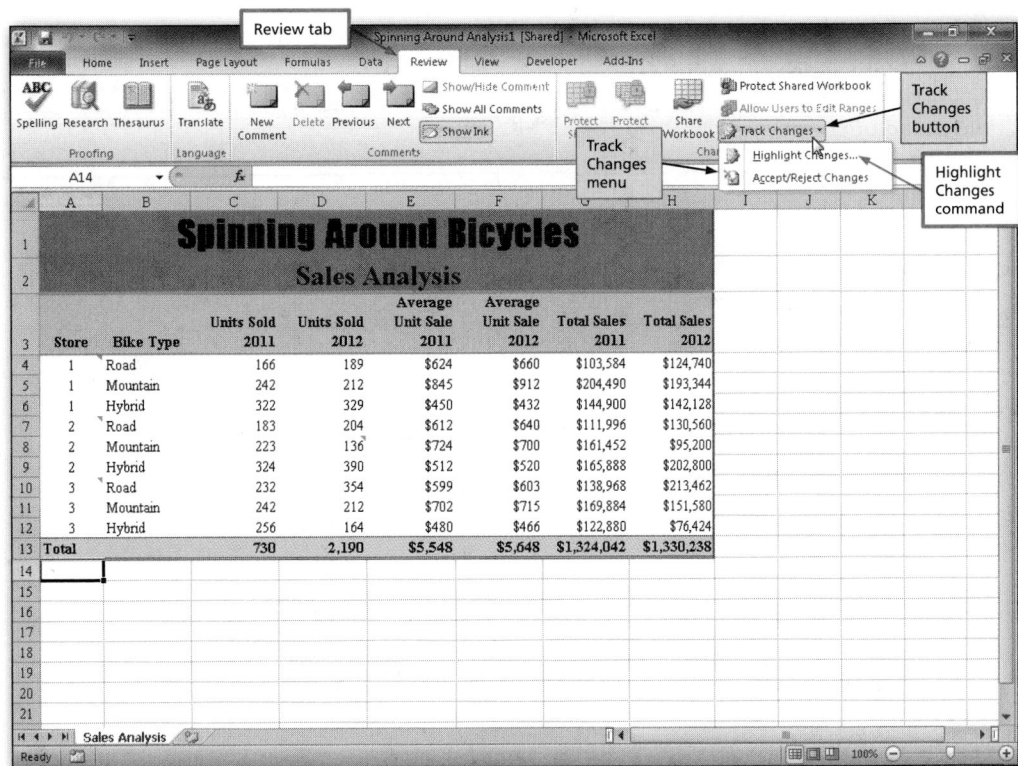

Figure 11–29

2

- Click Highlight Changes on the Track Changes menu to display the Highlight Changes dialog box.

- When Excel displays the Highlight Changes dialog box, click the When check box to remove the check mark and have Excel highlight all changes (Figure 11–30).

Q&A

When would I insert check marks in the When, Who, and Where check boxes?

You would select these check boxes when you want to highlight only some changes, such as those made since you last saved or those made by everyone except you.

Figure 11–30

3

- Click the OK button (Highlight Changes dialog box) to close the dialog box.

- Point to cell C8 to display a comment box with information about the change made to the cell C8 (Figure 11–31).

Figure 11–31

4

- Click the Track Changes button (Review tab | Changes group) to display the Track Changes menu (Figure 11–32).

Figure 11–32

⑤

- Click Accept/Reject Changes on the Track Changes menu to display the Select Changes to Accept or Reject dialog box.

- If necessary, click all check boxes to clear them, indicating that all changes in the change history file should be reviewed (Figure 11–33).

Q&A

What is the purpose of clearing the check mark?

Clearing the check mark from the When check box indicates that all changes in the change history should be available for review. Excel can track three categories of changes in the change history.
The When check box allows you to specify the time from which you want to review changes.
The Who check box allows you to specify individual users from whom to review changes. The Where check box allows you to specify a range of cells to check for changes.

Figure 11–33

⑥

- Click the OK button (Select Changes to Accept or Reject dialog box) to display the first tracked change (Figure 11–34).

Figure 11–34

7

- Click the Accept button (Accept or Reject Changes dialog box) to accept the change to the cell.

- As Excel displays each change in the Accept or Reject Changes dialog box, click the Accept button until the dialog box closes (Figure 11–35).

Could I click the Accept All button to accept all remaining changes?

Yes, though you cannot review changes when you click the Accept All button.

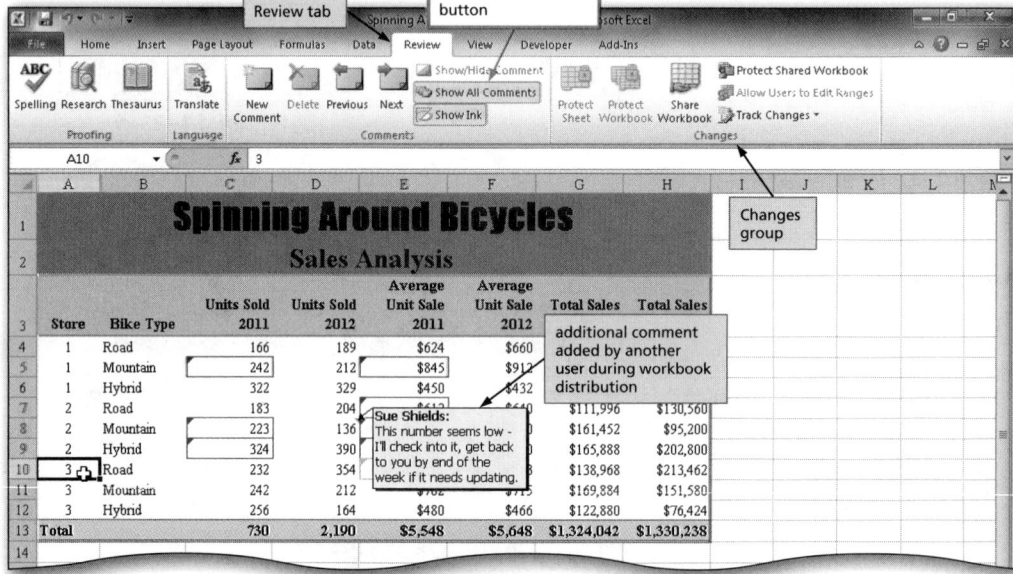

Figure 11–35

8

- Click the Show All Comments button (Review tab | Comments group) to display all comments in the worksheet.

- Right-click cell A4 and then click Delete Comment on the shortcut menu to delete the comment.

- Right-click cell A7 and then click Delete Comment on the shortcut menu to delete the comment.

- Right-click cell A10 and then click Delete Comment on the shortcut menu to delete the comment (Figure 11–36).

Figure 11–36

- Click the Show All Comments button (Review tab | Comments group) to hide the remaining comment.

Other Ways

1. Click Delete Comment button (Review tab | Comments group)

To Save the Workbook with a New File Name

1 Click File on the Ribbon to display the Backstage view, and then click Save As to display the Save As dialog box.

2 Type **Spinning Around Analysis2** in the File name text box.

3 Click the Save button (Save As dialog box) to save the workbook with the new file name.

To Turn Off Track Changes

When workbook sharing is enabled, Excel denies access to a number of features. Turning off track changes, which also turns off sharing and saves the workbook, provides access to those features again. The workbook is saved as an **exclusive workbook,** one which is not shared and can be opened only by a single user. The following steps turn off track changes and make the workbook exclusive.

1

- Click the Track Changes button (Review tab | Changes group) to display the Track Changes menu.

- Click Highlight Changes on the Track Changes menu to display the Highlight Changes dialog box.

- Click the 'Track changes while editing' check box to remove the check mark.

- Click the OK button (Highlight Changes dialog box) to close the dialog box, turn off track changes, and display the Microsoft Excel dialog box asking if the workbook should be made exclusive.

Figure 11–37

- Click the Yes button to make the workbook exclusive (Figure 11–37).

What happens when track changes is disabled?

When track changes is disabled, sharing is disabled as well. At the same time, Excel erases the change history. The workbook automatically is resaved as an exclusive workbook, which is not shared and can be opened only by a single user.

How do I know that the workbook is an exclusive workbook?

The text "[Shared]" is no longer displayed in the title bar.

2

- Close all open workbooks, but keep Excel open.

Break Point: If you wish to take a break, this is a good place to do so. You can quit Excel now. To resume at a later time, start Excel, and continue following the steps from this location forward.

Comparing and Merging Workbooks

Excel provides you with two commands when working with multiple versions of a workbook. You can open multiple copies of the same workbook and move through the workbooks in a synchronized manner so that the same area of each workbook is always in view. For example, as a user scrolls down a worksheet, Excel automatically updates the view of the second worksheet to show the same rows as the first worksheet. This functionality allows for a side-by-side, visual comparison of two workbooks.

<table>
<tr>
<td>Plan
Ahead</td>
<td>**If merging workbooks, gather workbooks to be merged and then assess any differences in the workbooks that are in disagreement.** When working with multiple copies of the same workbook, you can be faced with a situation where the same cell can contain different values in the various copies of the workbook. Careful review and evaluation is necessary to ensure that the correct value for cells in question is retained in the final workbook.</td>
</tr>
</table>

In the case of multiple copies of a workbook, Excel provides the ability to merge multiple copies into a single workbook. This feature requires you to do some setup. To merge the changes from one or more workbooks into another, all workbooks must satisfy the following requirements:

- The original workbook must be shared before making copies, and each workbook must be a copy of the same workbook.
- When copies of the workbook are made, track changes or sharing must be enabled, so that the change history of the workbook is kept.
- Clicking the Share Workbook button on the Review tab displays a dialog box with a tab for recording the number of days to record the change history. Shared workbooks must be merged within that time period.
- If the workbooks have been assigned passwords, all workbooks involved in the merge must have the same password.
- Each copy of the workbook must have a different file name.

When all of the copies of the workbook are available on your hard disk or USB drive, you can use the Compare and Merge Workbooks command to merge the workbooks. When Excel merges the workbooks, both data and comments are merged, so that if comments are recorded, they appear one after another in a given cell's comment box. If Excel cannot merge the workbooks, information from one workbook still can be incorporated into another by copying and pasting the information from one workbook to another.

BTW

Merging and the Change History
If there is any question about how long it will take to get all copies of a workbook back, err on the side of caution and set a high number of days for recording the change history.

To Compare Workbooks

Spinning Around Bicycles sponsors teams in local road races. The company maintains sponsorship expense information in a workbook that has been shared and copied to two other members of the staff for review. Because two different users — Mary and Robert — modified the separate workbooks, the workbooks must be merged. Before merging the workbooks, they should be compared visually to note the changes. The following steps open the Spinning Around Sponsorship and Spinning Around Sponsorship Mary workbooks and compare the workbooks side by side.

1

- Open the file, Spinning Around Sponsorship, from the Data Files for Students.

- If the file opens in a maximized state, click the workbook's Restore Window button to resize the window.

- Open the file, Spinning Around Sponsorship Mary, from the Data Files for Students.

- If the file opens in a maximized state, click the workbook's Restore Window button to resize the window.

- Click View on the Ribbon to display the View tab (Figure 11–38).

Figure 11–38

2

- Click the View Side by Side button (View tab | Window group) to display the workbooks side by side.

Q&A

How should the workbooks be arranged after clicking the View Side by Side button?

Depending on how previous Excel windows were arranged on your computer, the workbooks may appear next to each other left-to-right, or with one window above the other.

- Use the scroll bar in the top window to scroll the Spinning Around Sponsorship Mary worksheet (Figure 11–39).

Figure 11–39

Q&A

What happens when I scroll the workbook?

Because the Synchronous Scrolling button is selected, both workbooks scroll at the same time so that you can make a visual comparison of the workbooks.

3

- Click the View Side by Side button (View tab | Window group) again to display the windows separately and turn off synchronous scrolling.

- Click the workbook's Close Window button to close the Spinning Around Sponsorship Mary workbook.

- If Excel displays the Microsoft Office Excel dialog box, click the No button.

- Click the Maximize button in the Spinning Around Sponsorship window to maximize the window.

To Merge Workbooks

After the initial review, the next step is to merge the two workbooks changed by Mary and Robert into the original Spinning Around Sponsorship workbook. All three of the workbooks are shared. The following steps merge the workbooks containing changes from Mary and Robert with the original workbook, Spinning Around Sponsorship.

1

- Click the Customize Quick Access Toolbar button arrow next to the Quick Access Toolbar and then click More Commands on the Customize Quick Access Toolbar menu to open the Excel Options dialog box.

- Select All Commands in the 'Choose commands from' list.

- Scroll to the Compare and Merge Workbooks command in the list on the left and then select it.

- Click the Add button (Excel Options dialog box) to add the Compare and Merge Workbooks button to the list on the right side of the dialog box (Figure 11–40).

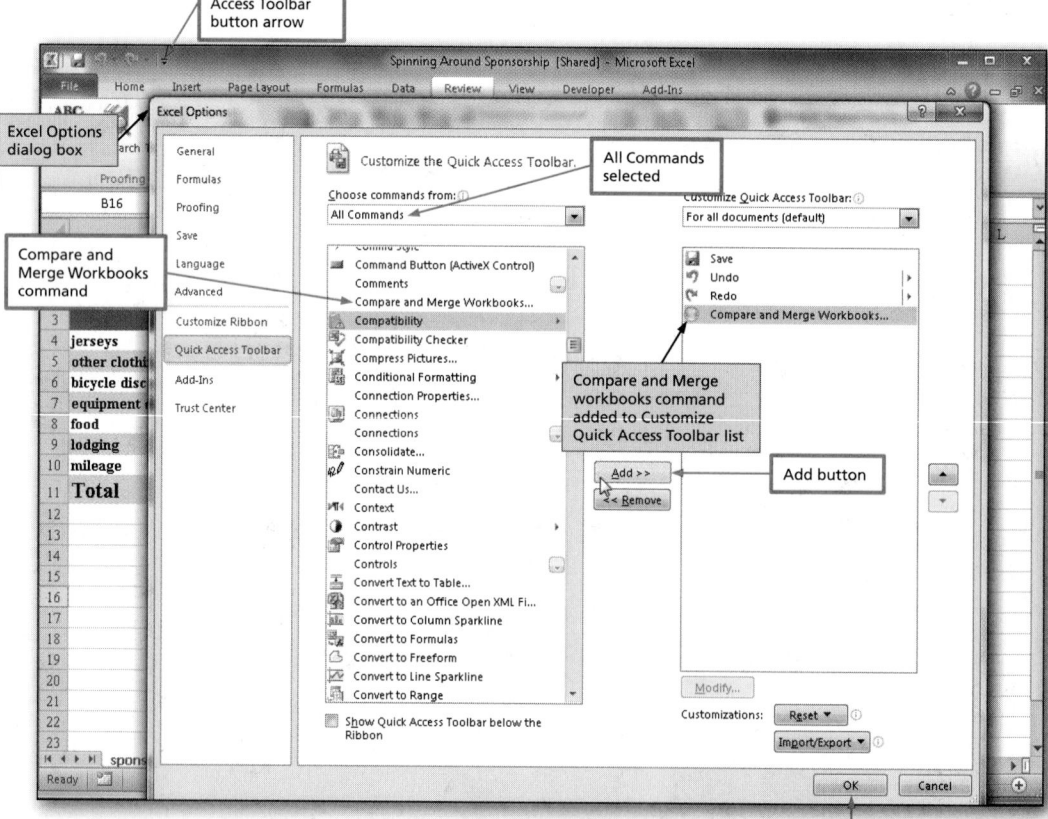

Figure 11–40

2

● Click the OK button to add the Compare and Merge Workbooks button to the Quick Access Toolbar.

● Click the Compare and Merge Workbooks button on the Quick Access Toolbar to display the Select Files to Merge Into Current Workbook dialog box.

● Navigate to the save location of the files (in this case, the Excel folder in the CIS 101 folder [or your class folder] on the USB flash drive).

● Click Spinning Around Sponsorship Mary, hold down the SHIFT key, and then click Spinning Around Sponsorship Robert to select both files (Figure 11–41).

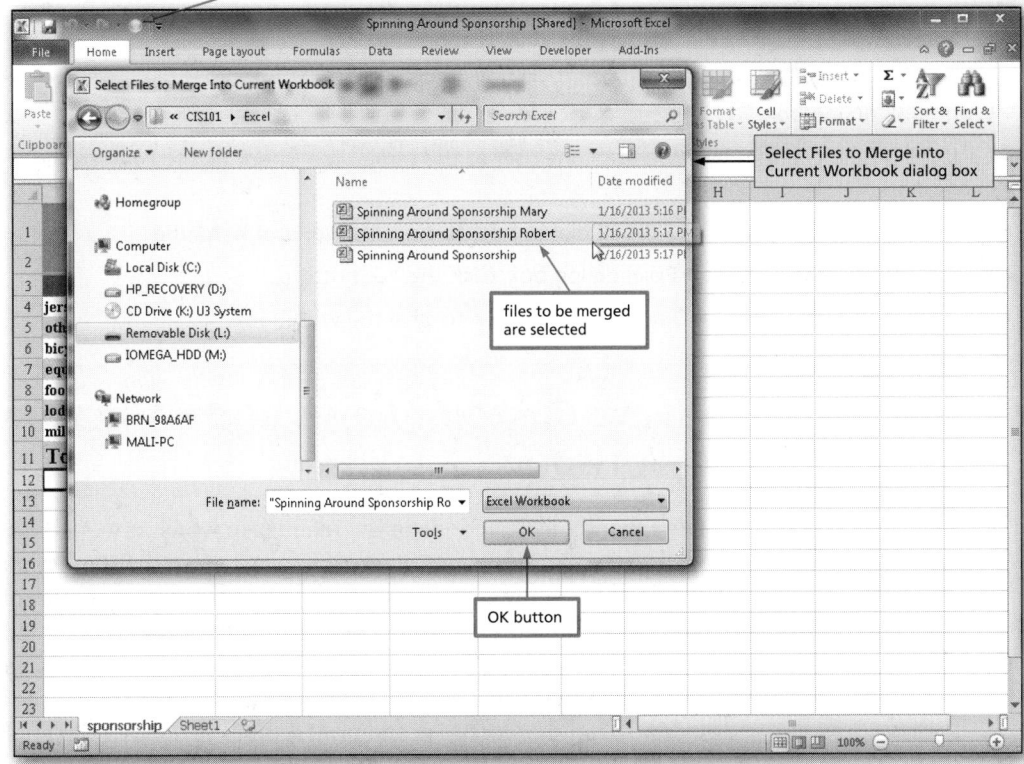

Figure 11–41

3

● Click the OK button (Select Files to Merge Into Current Workbook dialog box) to merge the workbooks (Figure 11–42).

Q&A

What is the result of the merge?

The workbooks have been merged, and the Spinning Around Sponsorship worksheet reflects the changes from Mary and Robert. If Mary and Robert had changed a common cell with different values, Excel would have displayed a prompt, asking which change to keep in the merged workbook.

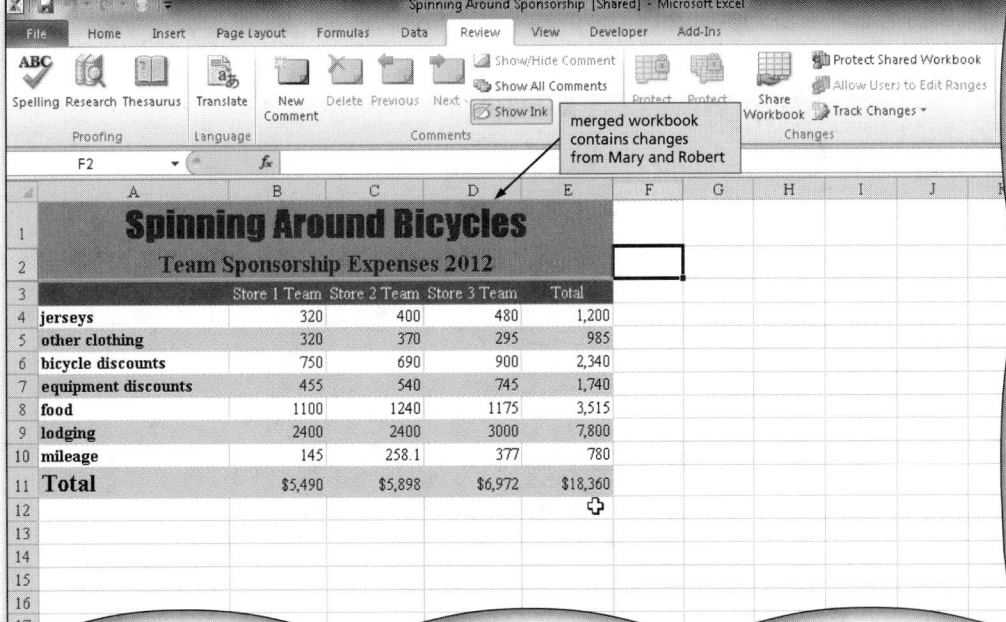

Figure 11–42

To Turn Off Workbook Sharing and Save the Workbook

The next step is to turn off workbook sharing so that the data can be manipulated.

- Click Review on the Ribbon to display the Review tab.
- Click the Share Workbook button (Review tab | Changes group) to display the Share Workbook dialog box.
- Click the 'Allow changes by more than one user at the same time' check box to remove the check mark.
- Click the OK button (Share Workbook dialog box) to turn off workbook sharing.
- If Excel displays the Microsoft Excel dialog box, click the Yes button.
- Click the Save button on the Quick Access Toolbar to save the workbook.

Saving Custom Views and Formatting a Worksheet Background

After a workbook functions in the manner in which it was designed, final touches can be added to the worksheets in the workbook to make them more attractive and easy to use. Custom views allow certain layout and printing characteristics of a workbook to be saved and then used later. **Worksheet backgrounds** allow an image to be specified for use as a background image, or watermark, behind the data in cells of a worksheet.

When a custom view of a workbook is saved, Excel stores information about the window size of the workbook and print settings that have been applied to the workbook at the time it is saved. Because of this, the workbook should be changed to have the desired layout and print settings before saving a custom view of a workbook. Each custom view that is created includes a name. The Custom Views button on the View tab is used to save, delete, and show custom views. When a user saves a view, Excel also stores the name of the current worksheet. When a user shows a view by clicking the Show button in the Custom Views dialog box, Excel switches to the worksheet that was active in the workbook when the workbook view was saved.

To Save a Custom View of a Workbook

The following steps create and save a custom view of the Spinning Around Sponsorship workbook.

1
- Resize the Spinning Around Sponsorship workbook window as shown in Figure 11–43.

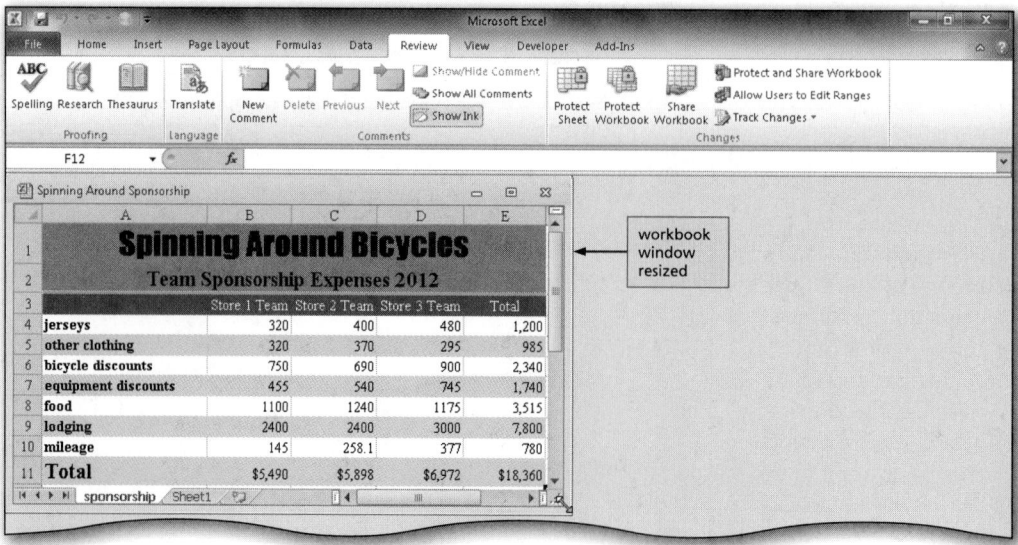

Figure 11–43

2

- Click View on the Ribbon to display the View tab.

- Click the Custom Views button (View tab | Workbook Views group) to display the Custom Views dialog box (Figure 11–44).

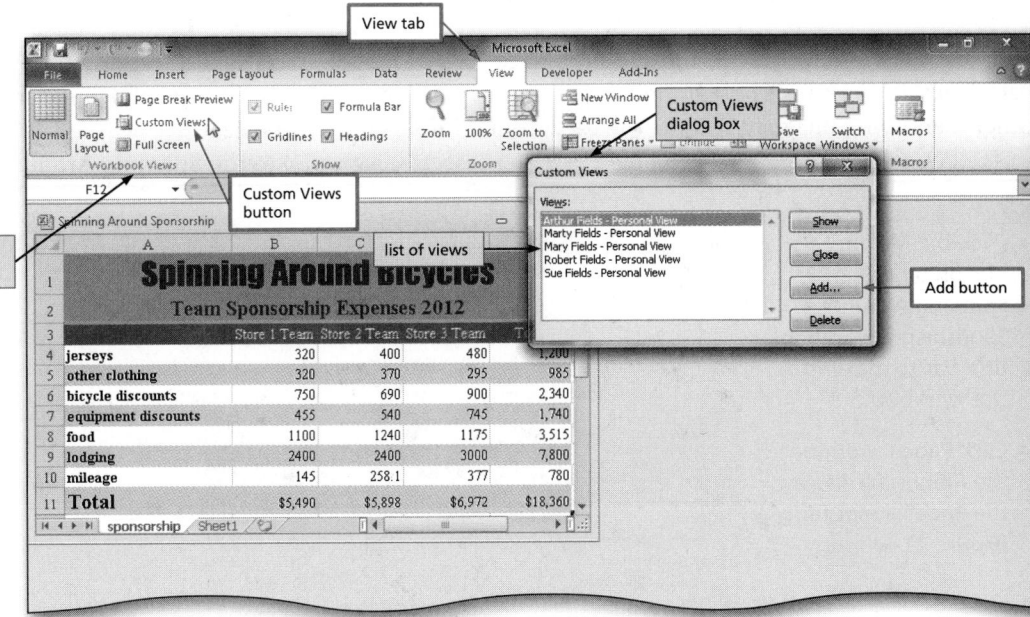

Figure 11–44

3

- Click the Add button (Custom Views dialog box) to display the Add View dialog box.

- Type **Sponsorship Expenses** in the Name text box to provide a name for the custom view (Figure 11–45).

4

- Click the OK button (Add View dialog box) to close the dialog box.

Figure 11–45

- Click the Maximize button on the Spinning Around Sponsorship workbook title bar to maximize the workbook.

- Click the Custom Views button (View tab | Workbook Views group) to display the Custom Views dialog box.

- Click Sponsorship Expenses in the Views list and then click the Show button (Custom Views dialog box) to display the Sponsorship Expenses view, which includes a resized workbook.

Q&A

Can I delete a view?

Yes. To delete views, use the Delete button in the Custom Views dialog box shown in Figure 11–44.

To Format a Worksheet Background

Besides adding color to the background of cells or ranges, Excel also allows an image to be used as a worksheet background. Worksheet backgrounds can provide visual appeal to a worksheet, allowing for a corporate logo or other identifying image to serve as the background for an entire worksheet.

The following steps add an image as a worksheet background to the Spinning Around Sponsorship worksheet.

1
- Click the Maximize button on the Spinning Around Sponsorship workbook title bar to maximize the workbook.

- Click Page Layout on the Ribbon to display the Page Layout tab (Figure 11–46).

Figure 11–46

2
- Click the Background button (Page Layout tab | Page Setup group) to display the Sheet Background dialog box.

- Navigate to the location of the Data Files for Students, and select the Sponsor image file (Figure 11–47).

Figure 11–47

- Click the Insert button (Sheet Background dialog box) to display the image as the worksheet background.

- Click View on the Ribbon to display the View tab.

- Click the Gridlines check box (View tab | Show group) to turn off gridlines (Figure 11–48).

4

- Save the workbook.

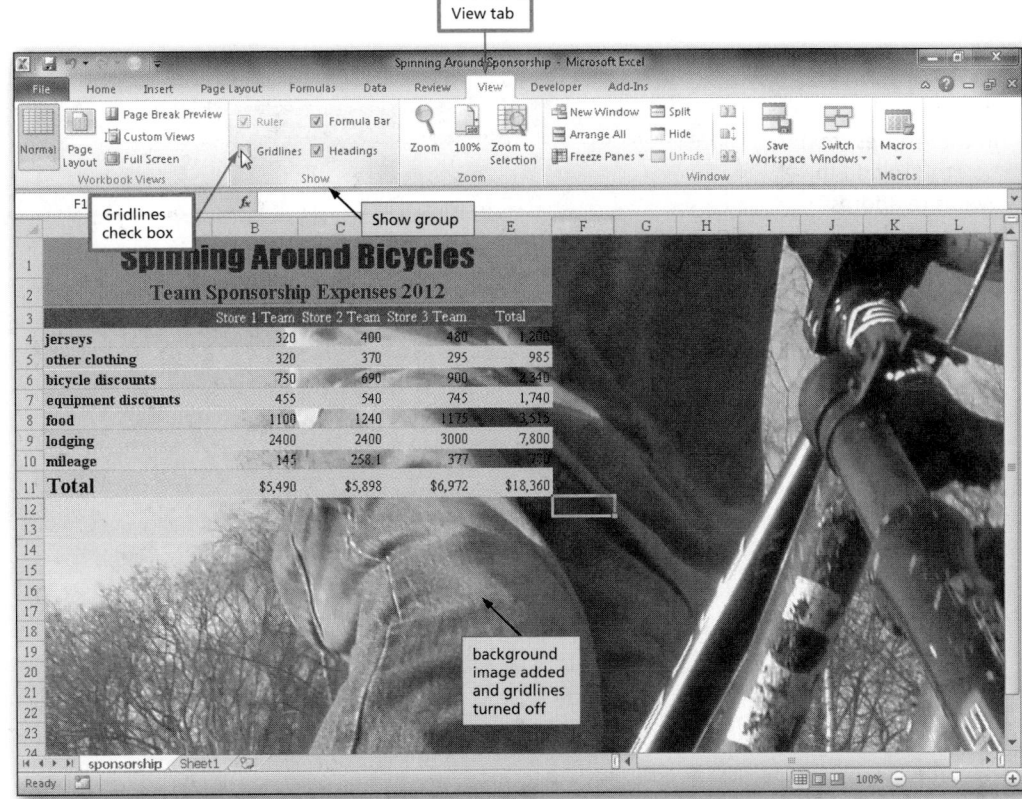

Figure 11–48

To Add a Hyperlink to a Web Page

You need to add a hyperlink that will take readers to the USA Cycling Web site, where they can review upcoming races and results from races the teams have entered. The following steps add a hyperlink to a cell in the worksheet.

1

- Click cell A13 to make it the active cell.

- Right-click cell A13 and then click Hyperlink on the shortcut menu to display the Insert Hyperlink dialog box (Figure 11–49).

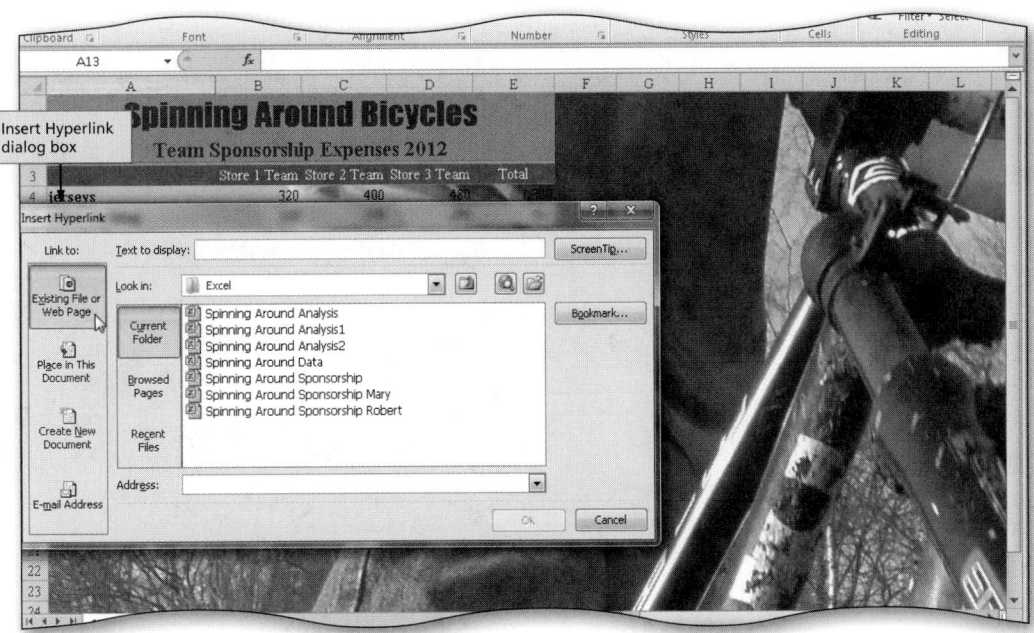

Figure 11–49

2

- Type **http://www. usacycling.org** in the Address text box to provide the Web site address.

- Click in the 'Text to display' text box, and then type **USA Cycling Web site** to provide display text for the hyperlink (Figure 11–50).

Figure 11–50

3

- Click the ScreenTip button (Insert Hyperlink dialog box) to display the Set Hyperlink ScreenTip dialog box.

- Type **Click to go to USA Cycling Web site** in the ScreenTip text text box to provide a ScreenTip (Figure 11–51).

Figure 11–51

4

- Click the OK button (Set Hyperlink ScreenTip dialog box) to close the dialog box.

- Click the OK button (Insert Hyperlink dialog box) to close the dialog box and display the hyperlink in the worksheet (Figure 11–52).

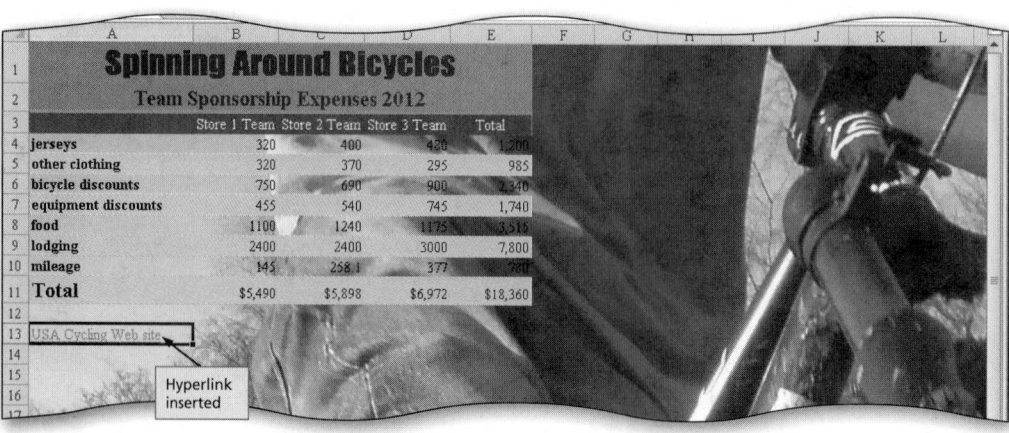

Figure 11–52

5

- Click the link to ensure that it is working.

- Close the browser window.

Other Ways

1. Click Hyperlink button (Insert tab | Links group)
2. Press CTRL+K

To Add a Hyperlink to an E-Mail Address

You need to add a hyperlink that allows readers to contact the team sponsorship coordinator by e-mail. The following steps add a hyperlink to an e-mail address.

1

- Click cell A15 to make it the active cell.

- Right-click cell A15 and then click Hyperlink on the shortcut menu to display the Insert Hyperlink dialog box.

- Click E-mail Address in the Link to list to update the Insert Hyperlink dialog box with fields related to e-mail.

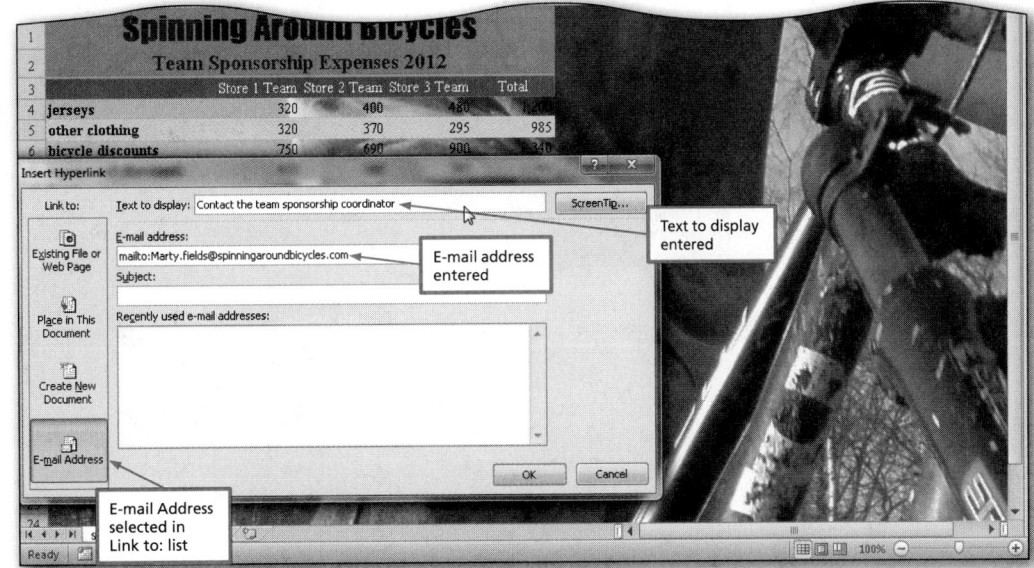

Figure 11–53

- Type `Marty.Fields@spinningaroundbicycles.com` in the E-mail address text box to enter an e-mail address.

- Drag to select the text in the 'Text to display' text box, and then type `Contact the team sponsorship coordinator` to provide the display text (Figure 11–53).

 Q&A

Why not fill in the Subject text box?

Any text entered in the Subject text box will automatically appear in the subject line of any e-mail messages initiated using this link. You do not have to fill this text box in. Leaving this blank allows the user to determine the subject of their e-mail message.

2

- Click the ScreenTip button (Insert Hyperlink dialog box) to open the Set Hyperlink ScreenTip dialog box.

- Type `Click to contact the team sponsorship coordinator` as the ScreenTip text (Figure 11–54).

Figure 11–54

- Click the OK button (Set Hyperlink ScreenTip dialog box) to close the dialog box.

- Click the OK button (Insert Hyperlink dialog box) to close the dialog box and display the e-mail hyperlink in the worksheet.

- Merge cells A15:B15 so that the text for the hyperlink is completely enclosed in one cell (Figure 11–55).

Figure 11–55

To Format the Hyperlinks

You can change the formatting of the hyperlinks and their cells to match the look of your worksheet. The following steps change the formatting of the hyperlinks.

- Click the Cell Styles button (Home tab | Styles group) to display the Cell Styles gallery.

- Right-click the Hyperlink cell style to display the shortcut menu (Figure 11–56).

Figure 11–56

- Click Modify on the shortcut menu to display the Style dialog box.

- Click the Format button (Style dialog box) to display the Format Cells dialog box.

- Click the Font tab, click the Color arrow button, and then click Dark Red, Accent 1, Darker 25% (column 5, row 5) in the color gallery.

- Click the Fill tab and then click the salmon color (column 5, row 2) in the Background Color gallery (Figure 11–57).

Figure 11–57

- Click the OK button (Format Cells dialog box) to close the dialog box.

- Click the OK button (Style dialog box) to apply the hyperlink style to the hyperlinks (Figure 11–58).

Q&A

Why is only the second hyperlink formatted?

You tested the first hyperlink in a previous step, so it is now formatted with the Followed Hyperlink style.

Figure 11–58

4

- Repeat Steps 1 through 3 for the Followed Hyperlink style in the Cell Styles gallery (Figure 11–59).

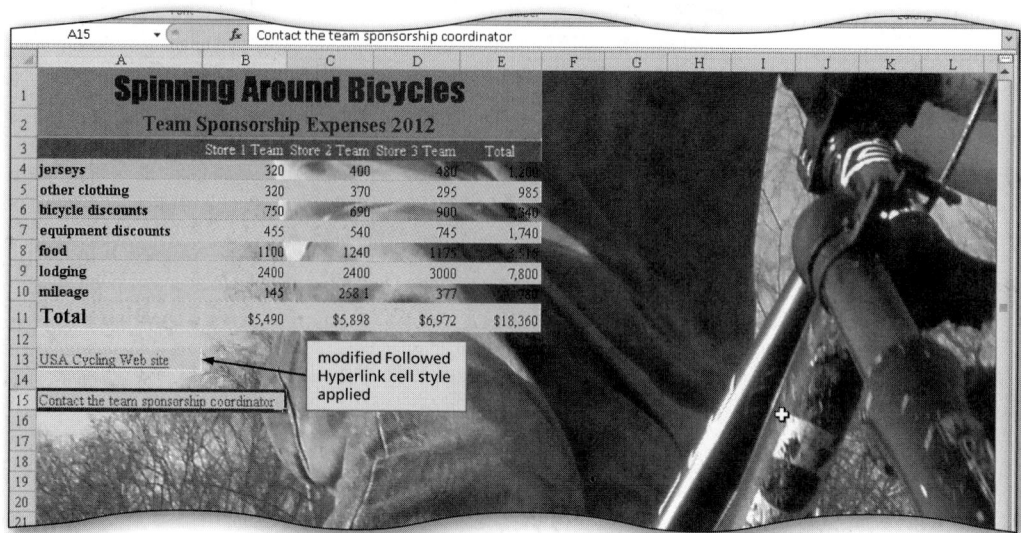

Figure 11–59

To Edit the Hyperlinks

You can edit hyperlinks after they have been inserted in a worksheet. You decide to change the e-mail address to the coordinator address. The following steps edit the e-mail address in the hyperlink.

1

- Right-click cell A15 and then click Edit Hyperlink on the shortcut menu to display the Edit Hyperlink dialog box.

- Change the E-mail address entry in the dialog box to `mailto: coordinator @spinning aroundbicycles .com` (Figure 11–60).

Q&A

Why does the E-mail address entry now include "mailto:"?

The mailto: prefix is a standard prefix for e-mail hyperlinks, which Excel adds automatically.

Figure 11–60

2

- Click the OK button (Edit Hyperlink dialog box) to save the hyperlink with the new e-mail address.

Q&A

What if I want to delete a hyperlink rather than editing it?

You can delete a hyperlink by right-clicking the cell containing the hyperlink and selecting Remove Hyperlink on the shortcut menu. You can also remove the hyperlink from the Edit Hyperlink dialog box by using the Remove Hyperlink button.

To Create a Shared Folder and Save a File on Windows Live SkyDrive

Another option for distributing workbooks is to use Windows Live SkyDrive. This option is useful when you need to distribute a file to someone not on your network who cannot accept e-mail with attachments, or if you need to distribute a file that exceeds the maximum size for e-mail attachments. The following steps show you how to create a folder on Windows Live SkyDrive, restrict access to the contents of the folder, and save a copy of the Spinning Around Sponsorship workbook.

1

- Click File on the Ribbon to display the Backstage view.

- Click the Save & Send tab to display the Save & Send pane (Figure 11–61).

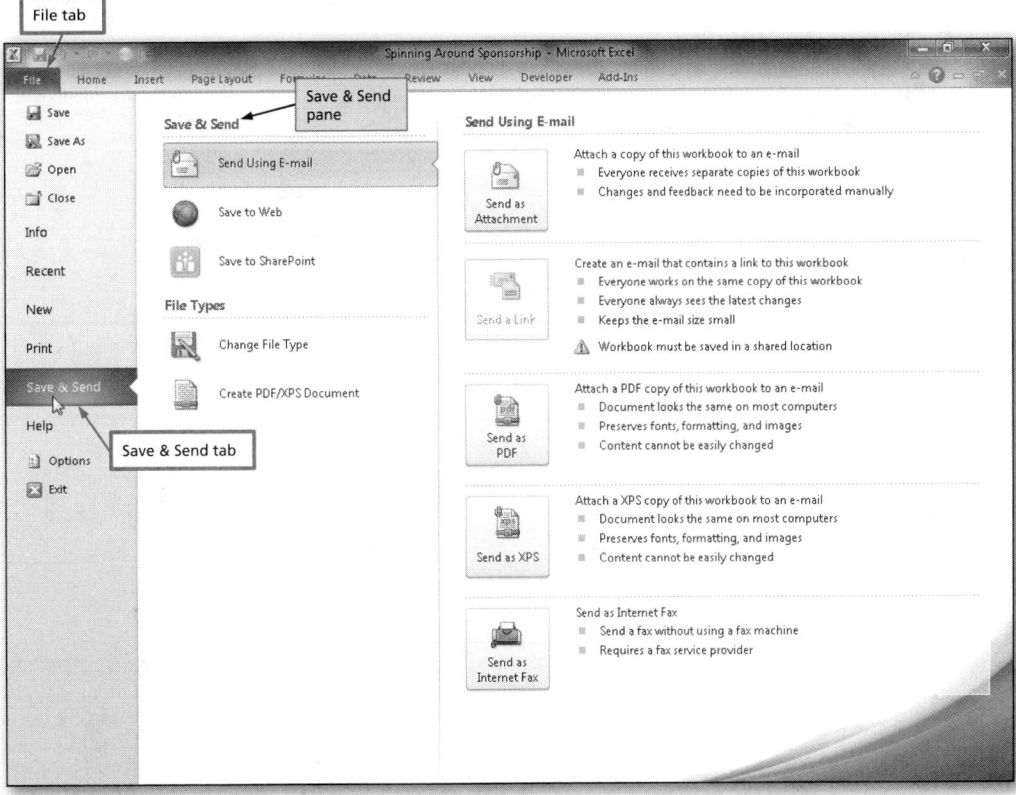

Figure 11–61

2

• Click Save to Web in the Save & Send pane to display information about saving a file to the Web (Figure 11–62).

Figure 11–62

3

• If necessary, click the Sign In button to display a Windows Live login dialog box that requests your e-mail address and password (Figure 11–63).

Q&A

Instead of the Sign In button, a Save As button is displayed in the right pane of my window. What should I do?

Read but do not perform Steps 3 and 4. Continue by performing Step 5.

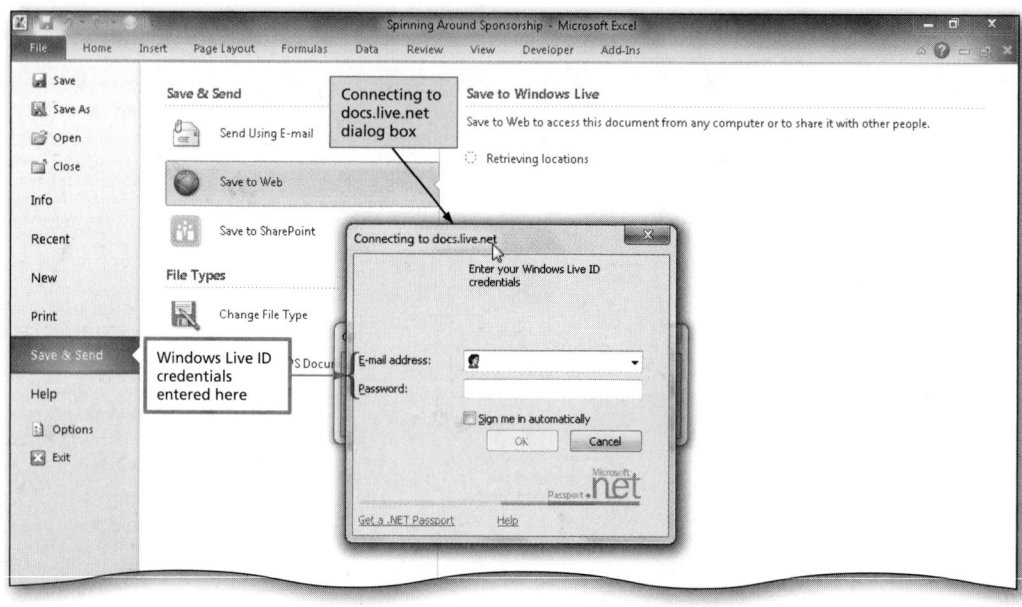

Figure 11–63

4

• Enter your Windows Live e-mail address and password, and then click OK to sign into Windows Live and display the contents of your Windows Live SkyDrive in the Save to Windows Live SkyDrive pane (Figure 11–64).

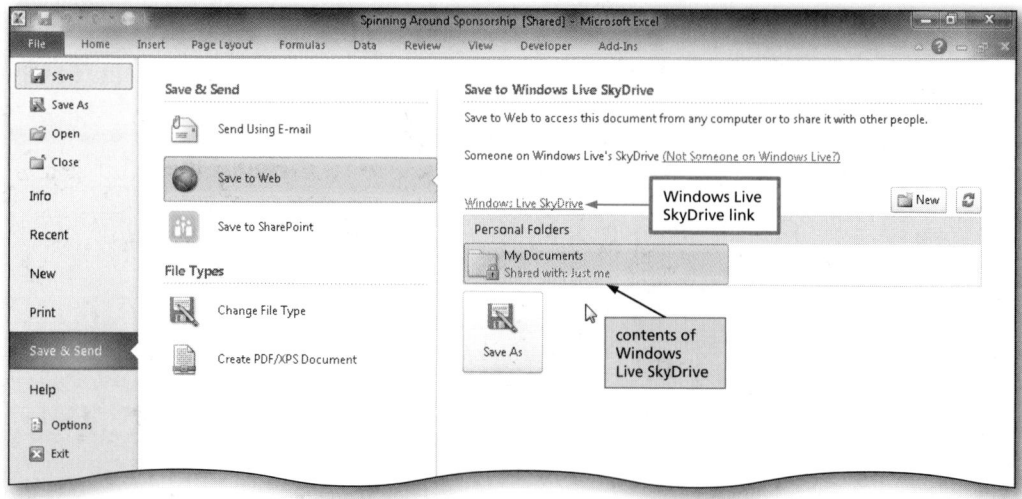

Figure 11–64

5

- Click the Windows Live SkyDrive link to open a browser session and switch to Windows Live SkyDrive.

- If necessary, maximize the browser window.

- Click the Sign In button and sign in using your Windows Live ID and display the All documents page (Figure 11–65).

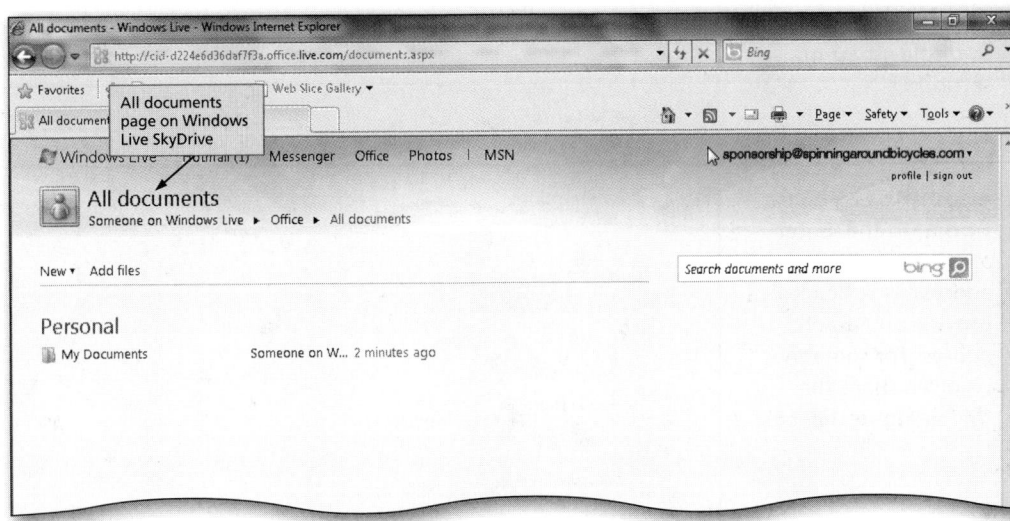

Figure 11–65

6

- Click the New arrow button to display the New menu (Figure 11–66).

Figure 11–66

7

- Click Folder to display the Create a folder page.

- Enter **Sponsorship** as the name of the new folder (Figure 11–67).

Figure 11–67

8
- Click the Change link to display sharing settings.

- Enter `mary@spinning aroundbicycles .com` in the 'Enter a name or an email address' text box to provide an e-mail address for someone who can share the folder (Figure 11–68).

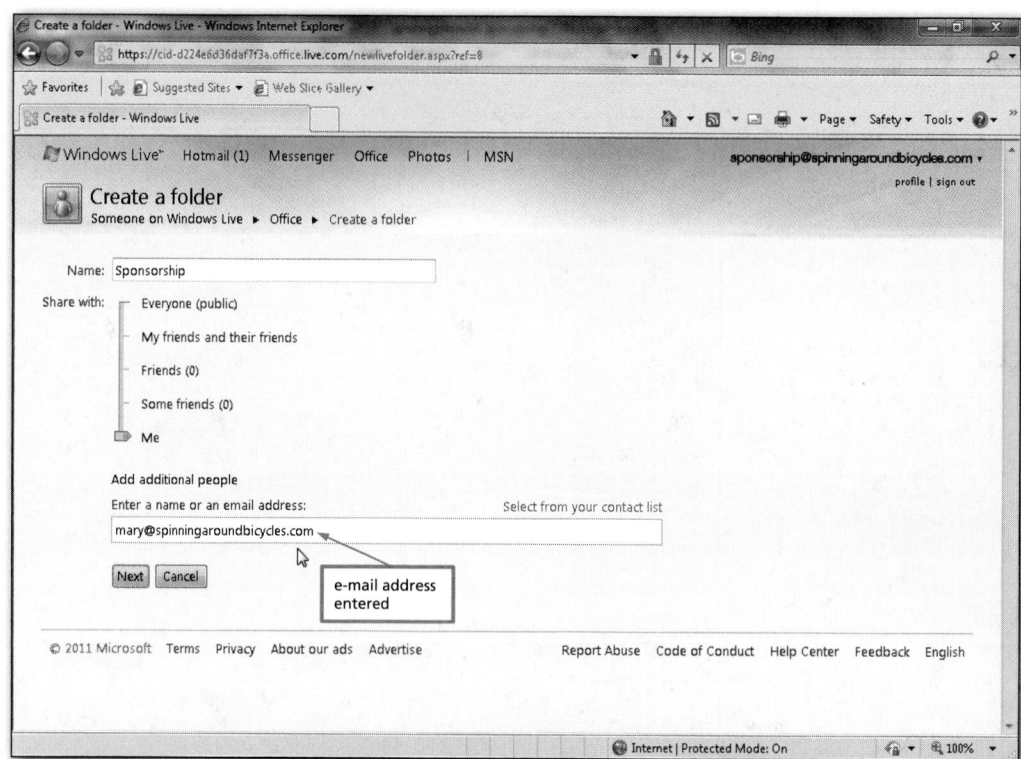

Figure 11–68

9
- Press the ENTER key to add the e-mail address to a list of those who can access the new folder.

- Enter `robert @spinning aroundbicycles .com` in the 'Enter a name or an email address' text box, and then press the ENTER key to add the e-mail address to a list of those who can access the new folder (Figure 11–69).

Figure 11–69

- Click the Next button to display the Sponsorship folder page.

- Click the Share link and then click 'Get a link' to display the Get a link page.

- Click the Copy link to copy the link to the Sponsorship folder (Figure 11–70).

Q&A

An Internet Explorer dialog box is displayed when I click the Copy link, asking if I want to allow access to my Clipboard. What should I do?

Click the Allow access button. You are copying a link for a folder you created, so you can safely copy the link to your Clipboard.

Figure 11–70

- Click the sign out link below your account name to sign out of Windows Live and return to Excel.

Q&A

My browser remains open. Should I close it?

Yes. Close your browser window before continuing.

- Click the Refresh Folder List button in the Save to Windows Live SkyDrive pane to display the folder you just created (Figure 11–71).

Figure 11–71

• If necessary, click the Sponsorship folder to select it.

• Click the Save As button to display the Save As dialog box (Figure 11–72).

Figure 11–72

• Type **Spinning Around Sponsorship Web** in the File name text box to enter the file name.

• Click the Save button (Save As dialog box) to save the file to Windows Live SkyDrive (Figure 11–73).

Figure 11–73

14
- Save the file locally as Spinning Around Sponsorship1 (Figure 11–74).

Q&A

What do I do with the link I copied?

Send the link to the people you listed as being allowed to edit files in the specified folder. Include instructions for editing the file. The permissions you gave allow them to access, edit, and then save a new version of the file to the folder you set up. They will not have access to any other part of your SkyDrive, unless you specifically set permissions for other folders on your SkyDrive.

Figure 11–74

Collaborating with Users Who Do Not Use Excel 2010

It is not unusual to need to collaborate with others who are using different versions of a software program, or a different software program, to do their work. It is not unheard of to find different versions of software being used within the same company. When collaborating with others, be sure to spend time evaluating how your collaborators will be working with the workbooks you create. The results of this evaluation will inform decisions you make about how to save files and distribute them.

In instances where people are working with earlier versions of software, or different software, you need to provide them with the workbook in a format that they can use.

To Save a Workbook in an Earlier Version of Excel

If someone is using an earlier version of Excel, you can save the workbook in that earlier format. You should be aware that some features in Excel 2010 are not compatible with earlier versions of the software. In cases where you have used one of these features, Excel will use the most compatible features of the earlier version of the software whenever possible. The following steps save the workbook in an earlier version of Excel.

1 Click the File tab to display the Backstage view.

2 Click the Save As command to display the Save As dialog box.

3 Click the 'Save as type' button to display a list of file types.

4 Click Excel 97-2003 Workbook in the 'Save as type' list to select the appropriate file type (Figure 11–75).

⑤ Click the Save button (Save As dialog box) to save the workbook as an earlier version of Excel.

⑥ If the Microsoft Excel — Compatibility Checker dialog box is displayed, click the Continue button to continue saving the workbook.

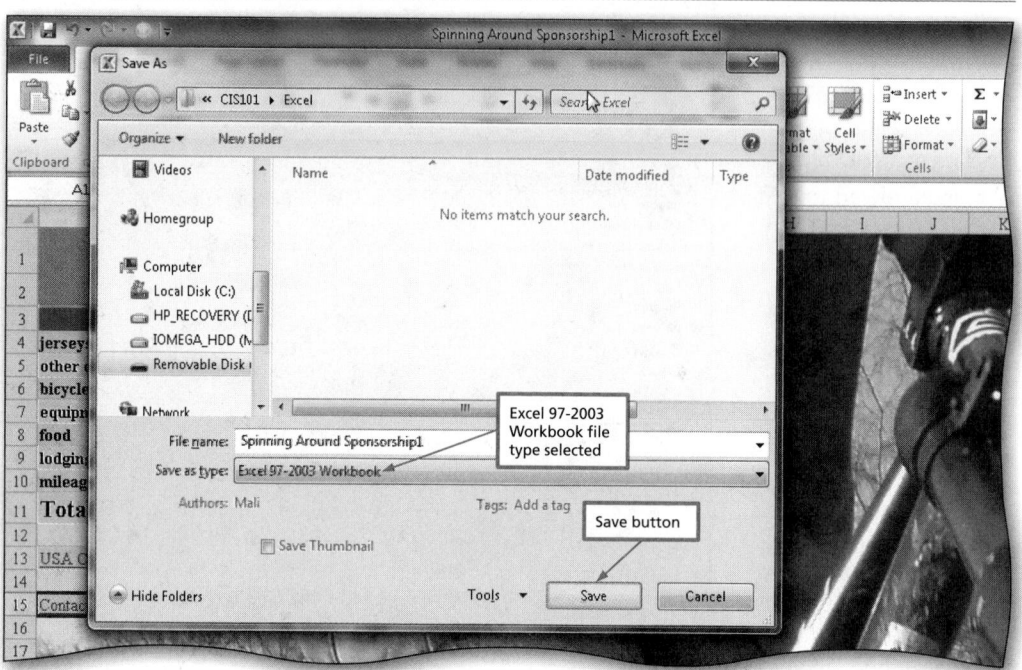

Figure 11–75

To Save a Workbook as a PDF File

Some people prefer not to work in Excel when giving feedback. One option is to provide them with a PDF file, which they can either mark up electronically, or print out and mark up a hard copy to return to you. The following steps save the workbook as a PDF file in preparation for distribution.

- Click the File tab to display the Backstage view.
- Click the Save As command to display the Save As dialog box.
- Click the 'Save as type' button to display a list of file types.
- Click PDF in the 'Save as type' list to select the appropriate file type (Figure 11–76).

- Click the Save button (Save As dialog box) to save the workbook as a PDF file.
- If necessary, close Adobe Reader or Adobe Acrobat.

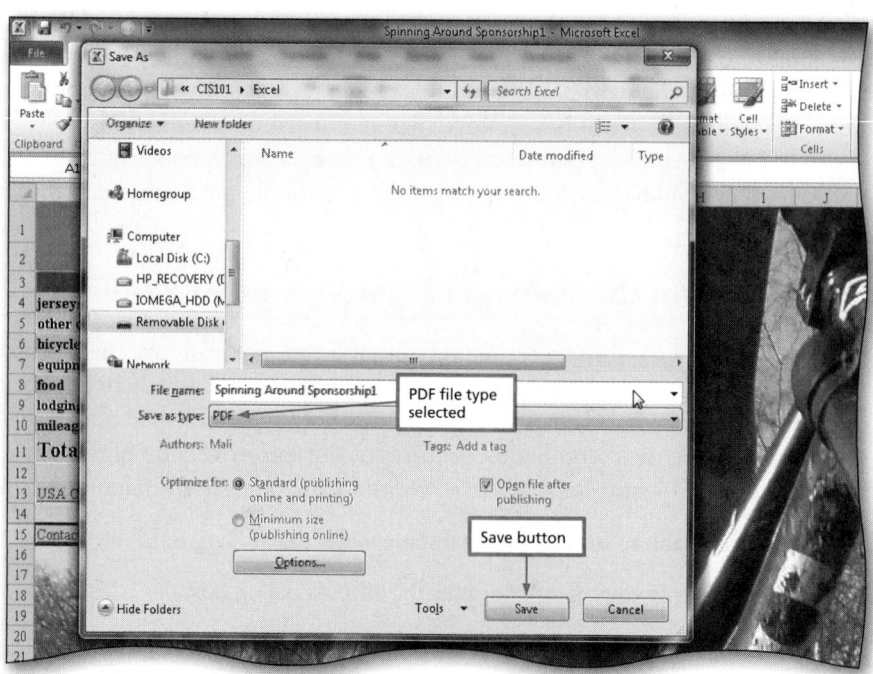

Figure 11–76

Importing and Exporting XML Data for Collaboration

XML is an increasingly popular format for sharing data. **XML** stands for **Extensible Markup Language**, which is a language that is used to encapsulate data and a description of the data in a single text file, or **XML file**. **Tags** are used in XML files to describe data items, which are called **elements**. XML files typically have a file extension of xml. Industry organizations and companies create standard XML file layouts and tags to describe commonly used types of data.

Excel is capable of importing and exporting XML in a variety of layouts, as long as the XML file is described by a schema. A **schema** is a special type of XML file used to describe the layout of data in other XML files. A schema describes what information an XML file should contain, the order in which the elements should appear, the values allowed for each element, and a variety of other information. A schema file typically is sent from a technical source, such as a programmer or a person in a company's information technology department.

Before importing XML data into a worksheet or exporting XML data from a worksheet, the schema file that describes the format of the XML file to import must be added to a workbook. When a schema is added to a workbook, the schema is called an **XML map** in Excel.

With an XML map, an import area can be created on a worksheet by dragging elements from the XML map to cells in a worksheet. When the XML data is imported, it is imported as a table. To attach an XML map to a workbook, you first must display the Developer tab on the Ribbon as described in Chapter 10 on page EX 635. The XML group is displayed on the Developer tab. Click the Source button (Developer tab | XML group) to display the XML Source task pane. Click the XML Maps button and then click the Add button (XML Maps dialog box). You then can navigate to the location of the schema file that was provided to you and drag and drop XML elements to your worksheet to create the XML map. When your XML map is complete, click the Import button (Developer tab | XML group) to begin the process of importing an XML file. After importing the XML data, you often may need to convert the table to a range because, as stated earlier, XML data always is imported as a table.

BTW

Certification
The Microsoft Office Specialist (MOS) program provides an opportunity for you to obtain a valuable industry credential — proof that you have the Excel 2010 skills required by employers. For more information, visit the Excel 2010 Certification Web page (scsite.com/ex2010/cert).

BTW

Quick Reference
For a table that lists how to complete the tasks covered in this book using the mouse, Ribbon, shortcut menu, and keyboard, see the Quick Reference Summary at the back of this book, or visit the Excel 2010 Quick Reference Web page (scsite.com/ex2010/qr).

To Quit Excel

The following steps restore the Quick Access Toolbar to its original state and quit Excel.

1. Remove the Compare and Merge Workbooks button from the Quick Access Toolbar.

2. Click the Close button on the right side of the title bar.

3. If Excel displays the Microsoft Excel dialog box, click the No button.

Chapter Summary

In this chapter, you learned how to use comments to give feedback, edit, format and delete comments, share workbooks and track changes, distribute workbooks by e-mail and Windows Live SkyDrive, compare and merge workbooks, save a custom view of a workbook, format a worksheet background, and save a file to different formats to facilitate collaboration. The items listed below include all the new Excel skills you have learned in this chapter.

1. Add Comments to a Worksheet (EX 711)
2. Display All Comments on a Worksheet (EX 713)
3. Edit Comments on a Worksheet (EX 714)
4. Format Comments on a Worksheet (EX 716)
5. Share and Collaborate on a Workbook (EX 718)
6. Turn On Track Changes (EX 721)
7. Distribute a Workbook by E-Mail (EX 723)
8. Open a Workbook and Review Tracked Changes (EX 724)
9. Turn Off Track Changes (EX 729)
10. Compare Workbooks (EX 730)
11. Merge Workbooks (EX 732)
12. Turn Off Workbook Sharing and Save the Workbook (EX 734)
13. Save a Custom View of a Workbook (EX 734)
14. Format a Worksheet Background (EX 736)
15. Add a Hyperlink to a Web Page (EX 737)
16. Add a Hyperlink to an E-Mail Address (EX 739)
17. Format the Hyperlinks (EX 740)
18. Edit the Hyperlinks (EX 742)
19. Create a Shared Folder and Save a File on Windows Live SkyDrive (EX 743)
20. Save a Workbook in an Earlier Version of Excel (EX 749)
21. Save a Workbook as a PDF File (EX 750)

If you have a SAM 2010 user profile, your instructor may have assigned an autogradable version of this assignment. If so, log into the SAM 2010 Web site at www.cengage.com/sam2010 to download the instruction and start files.

Learn It Online

Test your knowledge of chapter content and key terms.

Instructions: To complete the Learn It Online exercises, start your browser, click the Address bar, and then enter the Web address `scsite.com/ex2010/learn`. When the Excel 2010 Learn It Online page is displayed, click the link for the exercise you want to complete and then read the instructions.

Chapter Reinforcement TF, MC, and SA
A series of true/false, multiple choice, and short answer questions that test your knowledge of the chapter content.

Flash Cards
An interactive learning environment where you identify chapter key terms associated with displayed definitions.

Practice Test
A series of multiple choice questions that test your knowledge of chapter content and key terms.

Who Wants To Be a Computer Genius?
An interactive game that challenges your knowledge of chapter content in the style of a television quiz show.

Wheel of Terms
An interactive game that challenges your knowledge of chapter key terms in the style of the television show *Wheel of Fortune*.

Crossword Puzzle Challenge
A crossword puzzle that challenges your knowledge of key terms presented in the chapter.

Apply Your Knowledge

Reinforce the skills and apply the concepts you learned in this chapter.

Working with Comments and Tracked Changes

Note: To complete this assignment, you will be required to use the Data Files for Students. See the inside back cover of this book for instructions on downloading the Data Files for Students, or contact your instructor for information about accessing the required files.

Instructions: Start Excel. Open the workbook Apply 11-1 Q.L. Spark Speaker Expenses from the Data Files for Students, and then save the workbook as Apply 11-1 Q.L. Spark Speaker Expenses Complete.

Figure 11–77 shows the initial workbook. You need to make changes based on comments, create a worksheet showing the history of tracked changes, and accept/reject tracked changes.

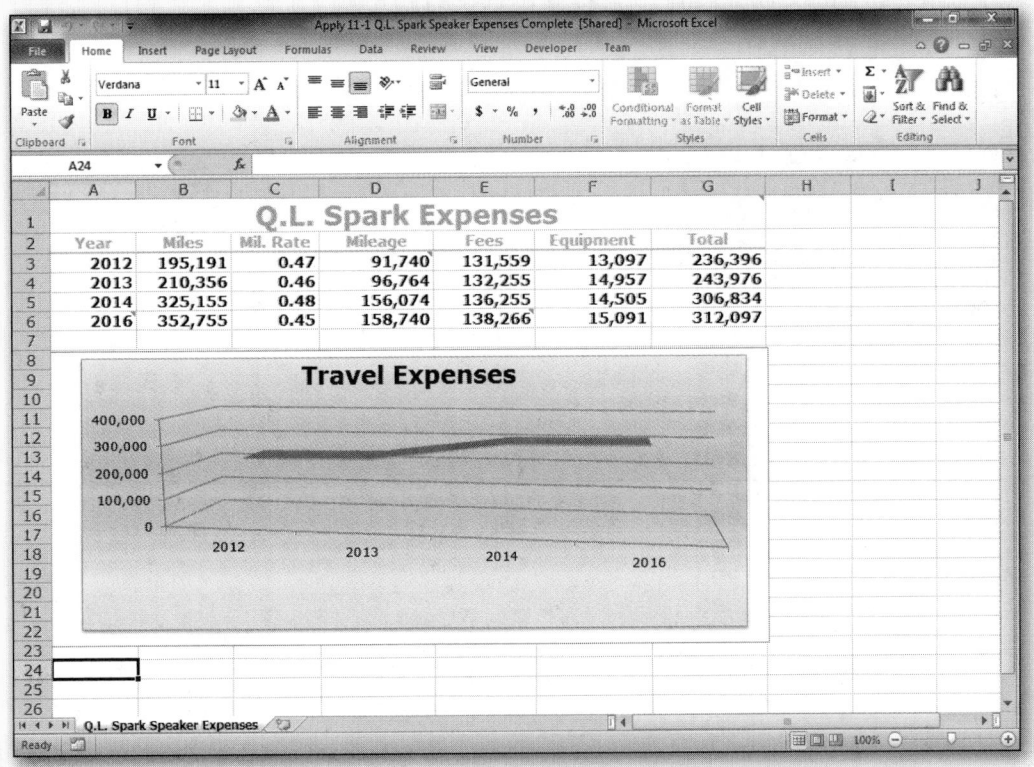

Figure 11–77

Perform the following tasks:

1. Change the document properties as specified by your instructor. Add a worksheet header with your name, course number, and other information as specified by your instructor.

2. Click the Track Changes button (Review tab | Changes group), and then click Highlight Changes on the Track Changes menu. Clear the three check boxes in the 'Highlight which changes' area. Click the 'List changes on a new sheet' check box. Click OK. Print the History worksheet.

3. In the Q.L. Spark Speaker Expenses worksheet, click the Track Changes button (Review tab | Changes group), and then click Accept/Reject Changes on the Track Changes menu. Clear the When check box, and then click OK. Reject the change to cell C2. Accept all other changes.

4. Click the Show All Comments button (Review tab | Comments group). Make the changes as indicated in the comments. Print the worksheet.

5. Save the workbook and then quit Excel.

6. Submit the assignment as requested by your instructor.

Extend Your Knowledge

Extend the skills you learned in this chapter and experiment with new skills. You may need to use Help to complete the assignment.

Consolidating Worksheets by Category

Note: To complete this assignment, you will be required to use the Data Files for Students. See the inside back cover of this book for instructions on downloading the Data Files for Students, or contact your instructor for information about accessing the required files.

Instructions: Start Excel. Open the workbook Extend 11-1 IPA Publishing from the Data Files for Students, and then save the workbook as Extend 11-1 IPA Publishing Complete.

Modify the workbook so that it consolidates data from existing worksheets. The data in the worksheets have the same column and row labels (Figure 11–78).

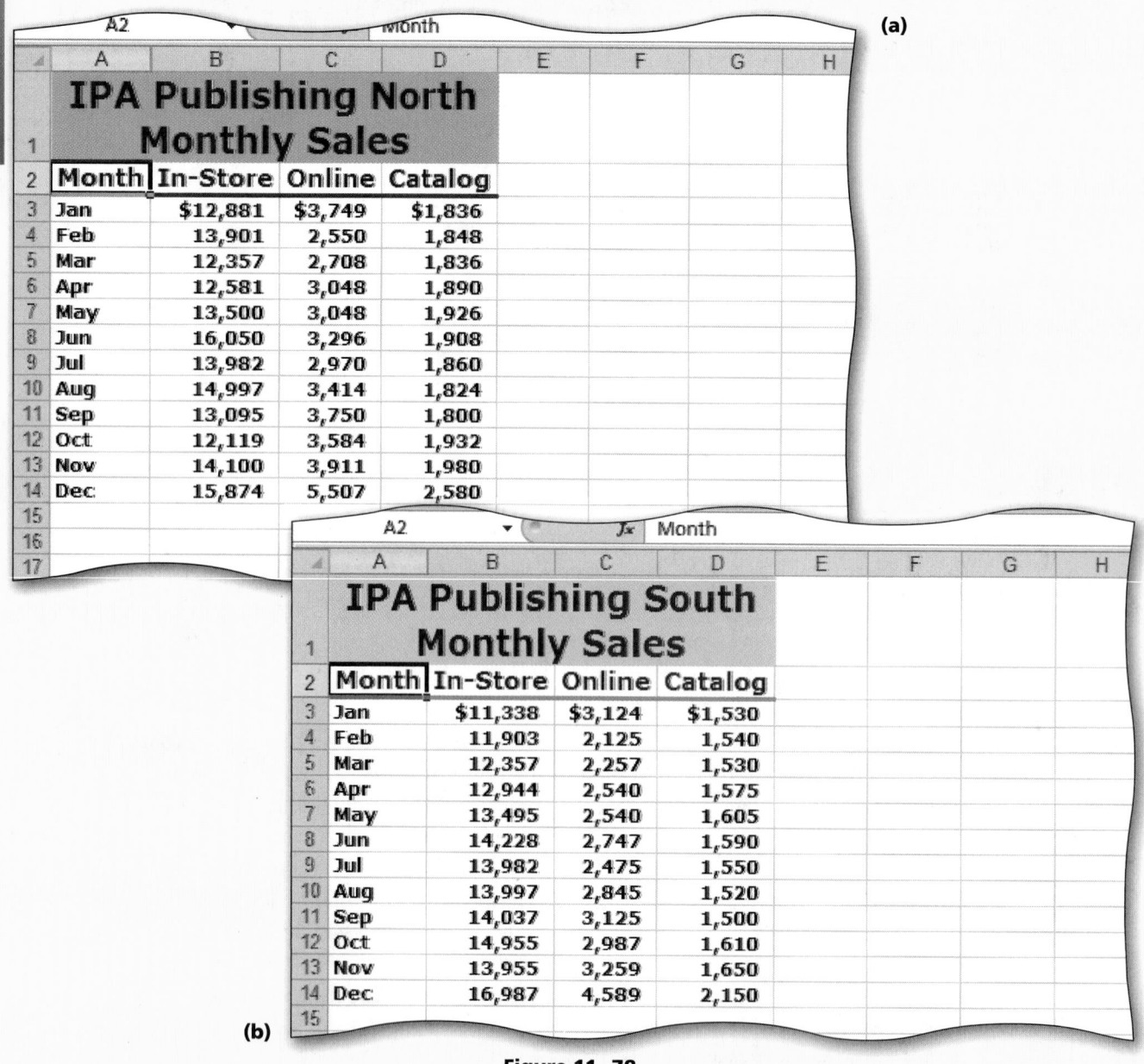

(a)

| A2 | | Month | | | | | |

IPA Publishing North Monthly Sales

Month	In-Store	Online	Catalog
Jan	$12,881	$3,749	$1,836
Feb	13,901	2,550	1,848
Mar	12,357	2,708	1,836
Apr	12,581	3,048	1,890
May	13,500	3,048	1,926
Jun	16,050	3,296	1,908
Jul	13,982	2,970	1,860
Aug	14,997	3,414	1,824
Sep	13,095	3,750	1,800
Oct	12,119	3,584	1,932
Nov	14,100	3,911	1,980
Dec	15,874	5,507	2,580

| A2 | | fx | Month |

IPA Publishing South Monthly Sales

Month	In-Store	Online	Catalog
Jan	$11,338	$3,124	$1,530
Feb	11,903	2,125	1,540
Mar	12,357	2,257	1,530
Apr	12,944	2,540	1,575
May	13,495	2,540	1,605
Jun	14,228	2,747	1,590
Jul	13,982	2,475	1,550
Aug	13,997	2,845	1,520
Sep	14,037	3,125	1,500
Oct	14,955	2,987	1,610
Nov	13,955	3,259	1,650
Dec	16,987	4,589	2,150

(b)

Figure 11–78

Perform the following tasks.

1. Select the IPA Publishing South worksheet. Select the range A2:D14 and name the range `South`.

2. Select the IPA Publishing North worksheet. Select the range A2:D14 and name the range `North`.

3. Insert a blank worksheet. Name the worksheet `Consolidated` and color the tab Blue. Copy the cell range A1:D1 from the IPA Publishing North worksheet, and paste it to the range A1:D1 on the Consolidated worksheet. Change the background color of the range to Light Blue. Change IPA Publishing North Monthly Sales in cell A1 to `IPA Publishing`.

4. Select cell A2. Click the Consolidate button (Data tab | Data Tools group). In the Consolidate dialog box, type `South` in the Reference text box, and then click Add. Type `North` in the Reference text box, and then click Add. Click the 'Top row' and 'Left column' check boxes to insert check marks. Click OK to consolidate the worksheets.

5. Change the document properties as specified by your instructor. Add a worksheet header with your name, course number, and other information as specified by your instructor.

6. Print the consolidated worksheet.

7. Save the workbook and then quit Excel. Submit the assignment as requested by your instructor.

Make It Right

Analyze a workbook and correct all errors and/or improve the design.

Preparing and Sharing a Workbook

Note: To complete this assignment, you will be required to use the Data Files for Students. See the inside back cover of this book for instructions on downloading the Data Files for Students, or contact your instructor for information about accessing the required files.

Instructions: Start Excel. Open the workbook Make It Right 11-1 QuickSell Booths from the Data Files for Students, and then save the workbook as Make It Right 11-1 QuickSell Booths Complete.

The workbook is going to be shared among team members; however, several editing and formatting items have to be resolved before sharing as the changes cannot be made after the file is shared. After making the changes, you will share the workbook. The completed Booth Sales worksheet is shown in Figure 11–79.

Figure 11–79

Continued >

Make It Right *continued*

Perform the following tasks:

1. Click cell A3 in the data table. Click the Convert to Range button (Table Tools Design tab | Tools group) to convert the table to a range.
2. Merge and center the cell range A1:D1.
3. Delete Sheet2 and Sheet3 from the workbook.
4. Change the document properties as specified by your instructor. Add a worksheet header with your name, course number, and other information as specified by your instructor.
5. Click Protect Workbook (Review tab | Changes group). Set the password to **boothsales** for the workbook.
6. Click Share Workbook (Review tab | Changes group). Click the 'Allow changes by more than one user at the same time' check box. Click OK to share the workbook.
7. Print the worksheet.
8. Save the workbook and then quit Excel.
9. Submit the assignment as requested by your instructor.

In the Lab

Create a workbook using the guidelines, concepts, and skills presented in this chapter. Labs are listed in order of increasing difficulty.

Lab 1: Routing Workbooks, Tracking Changes, and Inserting Comments

Note: To complete this assignment, you will be required to use the Data Files for Students. See the inside back cover of this book for instructions on downloading the Data Files for Students, or contact your instructor for information about accessing the required files.

Problem: You are a teaching assistant for a professor who is teaching an IT Capstone class. You have been asked to verify the project grades for student projects. Three graduate students function as project leaders for the projects and provide grades for each student's project performance (Figure 11–80).

	IT Capstone Project Evaluations				
Student Name	Group	Project Supervisor	Project Score	Project Grade	Participation Bonus
John Casado	1	Richards	92	A	5%
Tim Agrado	1	Richards	89	A	3%
Yin Hu	2	Kahn	76	B	2%
Susan Glassman	3	Velazquez	84	B	1%
Leslie Schwarz	1	Richards	93	A	2%
Wanda Newberry	2	Kahn	74	C	5%
Carl Hopsman	2	Kahn	82	B	3%
Andrew McKenzie	3	Velazquez	87	A	2%
Rick Sloan	2	Kahn	68	C	1%
Charlotte Alvarez	3	Velazquez	90	A	2%
Allen Brown	3	Velazquez	83	B	4%
Dana Lowenstein	1	Richards	78	B	2%

Figure 11–80

Part 1 Instructions: Start Excel and perform the following tasks.

1. Open the Lab 11-1 IT Capstone Project workbook from the Data Files for Students and then save the workbook using the file name, Lab 11-1 IT Capstone Project Complete.

2. Add a comment to cell D5. Enter `I entered an 89 for this project score. Can you verify this score?` for the comment text.

3. Track changes to the workbook. Click the Track Changes button (Review tab | Changes group), and then click Highlight Changes on the Track Changes menu. Click the 'Track changes while editing' check box and then clear the three check boxes in the 'Highlight which changes' area.

4. Send the workbook to two classmates by clicking the Save & Send tab (File tab), clicking Send Using E-mail, and then clicking Send as Attachment. Select the e-mail addresses of two classmates and enter `IT Capstone Project Verification` in the Subject text box. Enter appropriate message text in the Message text box, requesting that each classmate add comments to at least one cell and change the contents of two cells. Click the Send button.

5. Ask a classmate to send the workbook to you as well. When you receive the e-mail, print it. Add a comment to at least one cell and change the contents of at least three cells before sending the workbook to the next recipient.

6. When you receive your workbook after it has been sent to all recipients, click the Track Changes button (Review tab | Changes group), and then click Accept/Reject Changes on the Track Changes menu. Reject two changes and accept all the others.

7. In the Comments group on the Review tab, click the Show All Comments button.

8. Change the document properties as specified by your instructor. Change the worksheet header to include your name, course number, and other information as specified by your instructor. Print the worksheet in landscape orientation. Save the workbook.

9. Submit the assignment as requested by your instructor.

In the Lab

Lab 2: Consolidating Revenue Data

Note: To complete this assignment, you will be required to use the Data Files for Students. See the inside back cover of this book for instructions on downloading the Data Files for Students, or contact your instructor for information about accessing the required files.

Problem: You work for Rittmer Motorcycle Rentals. You have been asked to consolidate revenue data from the three sectors where the motorcycles are rented. After you have consolidated the data, you will save a version in a previous format for sharing with your supervisor who has Excel 2003.

Part 1 Instructions: Perform the following tasks.

1. Start Excel. Open the Lab 11-2 Rittmer Motorcycle Rentals workbook from the Data Files for Students and then save the workbook using the file name, Lab 11-2 Rittmer Motorcycle Rentals Complete.

2. Select the Sector 1 worksheet. Select the range A2:E7 and name the range `Sector1`.

3. Repeat Step 2 for the Sector 2 worksheet, except name the range `Sector2`. Repeat Step 2 for the Sector 3 worksheet, except name the range `Sector3`.

4. Insert a blank worksheet. Name the worksheet `Revenue Results` and color the tab Green. Copy the cell range A1:E1 from the Sector 1 worksheet, and paste it to the range A1:E1 on the Revenue Results worksheet. Change the background color of the range to green. Change Sector 1 in the cell to `Companywide`.

5. Select cell A2. Click the Consolidate button (Data tab | Data Tools group). Type `Sector1` in the Reference text box, and then click Add. Next, add `Sector2` and `Sector3`. If necessary, click the 'Top row' and 'Left column' check boxes to select them. Click OK to consolidate the worksheets. If necessary, type Vehicle Type in cell A2. Format the cells similar to the format of Sector 1 except use green for the color of the range A1:E1, as well as the border between rows 2 and 3. Resize the columns as necessary (Figure 11 – 81).

Continued >

In the Lab *continued*

	A	B	C	D	E
1	Rittmer Motorcycle Rentals Companywide				
2	Vehicle Type	Rental Revenue	Equipment Sales	Clothing Sales	Totals
3	Harley-Davidson	10,538.00	460.00	1,565.00	12,563.00
4	Honda	5,450.00	389.00	471.00	6,310.00
5	Piaggio	5,202.50	156.00	275.00	5,633.50
6	Suzuki	7,446.00	575.00	520.00	8,541.00
7	Kawasaki	12,078.75	350.00	265.00	12,693.75
8					
9					
10					
11					
12					
13					
14					

Figure 11–81

6. Change the document properties as specified by your instructor. Add a worksheet header with your name, course number, and other information as specified by your instructor.

7. Print the Revenue Results worksheet. Save the workbook.

8. Submit the assignment as requested by your instructor.

Instructions Part 2: Perform the following tasks to save the workbook in Excel 2003 format.

1. If necessary, open Lab 11-2 Rittmer Motorcycle Rentals Complete.

2. Click Save As (File tab). Change the file name to Lab 11-2 Rittmer Motorcycle Rentals Complete 2003. Change the file type to Excel 97-2003 Workbook. Click Save. After reviewing Compatibility Checker results, click Continue to save the workbook.

3. Exit Excel. Submit the assignment as requested by your instructor.

In the Lab

Lab 3: Merging Workbooks

Note: To complete this assignment, you will be required to use the Data Files for Students. See the inside back cover of this book for instructions on downloading the Data Files for Students, or contact your instructor for information about accessing the required files.

Problem: As the collegewide lab director, you have created a workbook using the time sheets from the lab assistants and have shared the workbook with the lab managers who made their own copies. They have sent their copies back with their changes to the timesheet data for the various lab assistants from the West, East, and Central locations of Eastbrook Cole University, as shown in Figure 11–82. Juan, Carla, and Robert are floating lab managers who oversee the three labs. You now need to merge their changes into one workbook.

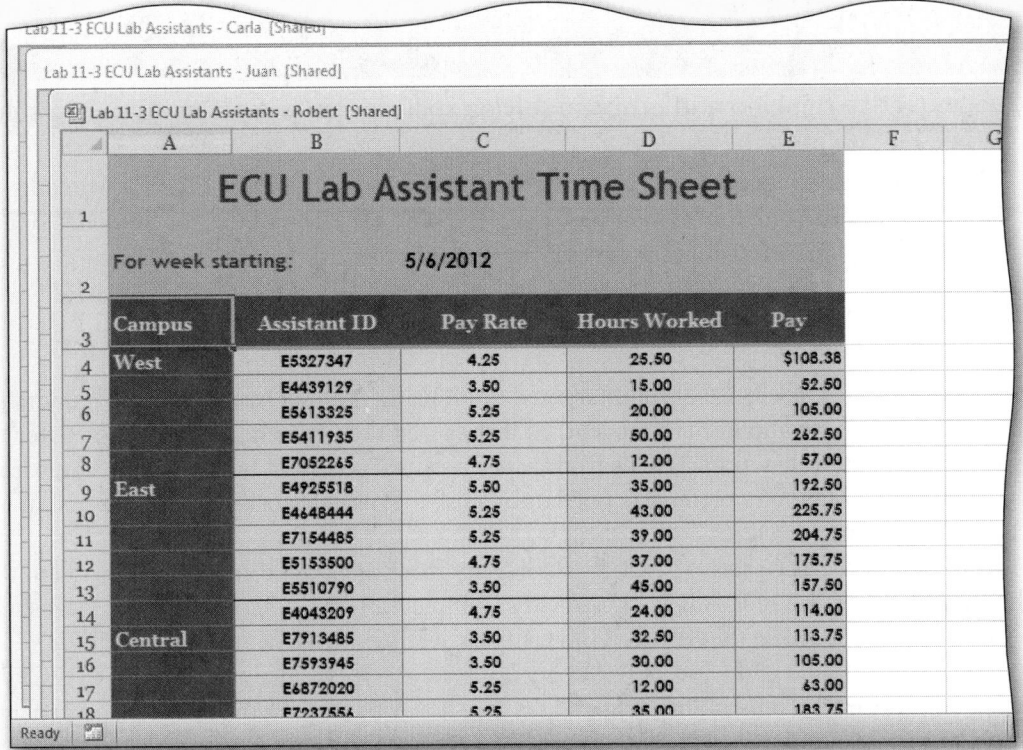

Figure 11–82

Instructions: Start Excel. Perform the following tasks:

1. Open the workbook Lab 11-3 ECU Lab Assistants from the Data Files for Students and then save the workbook using the file name, Lab 11-3 ECU Lab Assistants Complete.

2. If necessary, add the Compare and Merge Workbooks button to the Quick Access Toolbar. Use the Compare and Merge Workbooks command to merge the workbooks Lab 11-3 ECU Lab Assistants – Carla, Lab 11-3 ECU Lab Assistants – Juan, and Lab 11-3 ECU Lab Assistants – Robert into Lab 11-3 ECU Lab Assistants Complete.

3. In the Lab 11-3 ECU Lab Assistants Complete workbook, click the Track Changes button (Review tab | Changes group), and then click Accept/Reject Changes on the Track Changes menu. Clear the When check box, if necessary. For cell D5, accept Carla's change. For cell C8, accept Robert's changes. For cell C18, accept Juan's change. Accept all other changes.

4. Turn off sharing so that the workbook is exclusive.

5. Change the document properties as specified by your instructor. Add a worksheet header with your name, course number, and other information as specified by your instructor.

6. Print the worksheet. Save the workbook.

7. Submit the assignment as requested by your instructor.

Cases and Places

Apply your creative thinking and problem solving skills to design and implement a solution.

Note: To complete these assignments, you may be required to use the Data Files for Students. See the inside back cover of this book for instructions on downloading the Data Files for Students, or contact your instructor for information about accessing the required files.

1: Merging Workbooks and Reviewing Changes

Academic

AllCity University Art Gallery has several targeted fundraising drives. During the April fundraising drive at the university, a computer error occurred that caused the file to become corrupt. After reconstructing the latest donation records from paper receipts, you have been asked to compare the two worksheets containing reconstructed data against the master worksheet to ensure that all information has been updated.

Open the workbook Case 11-1 AllCity University from the Data Files for Students and then save the workbook as Case 11-1 AllCity University Complete. Review the Fundraising worksheet, which lists donations made to the AllCity University Art Gallery fund. Merge the workbooks Case 11-1 AllCity University – Laura and Case 11-1 AllCity University – Jorge into the Case 11-1 AllCity University Complete workbook. Highlight and review the changes that your fundraising managers Laura and Jorge made to the workbook. Accept all the changes and then turn off sharing so that the workbook is exclusive. In cell D13, insert the label Subtotals. In cell E13, calculate the sum of the donations made to date. Format the label and results using the Total cell style. Print the worksheet and save the workbook. Submit the assignment as requested by your instructor.

2: Commenting and Sharing a Fitness Schedule

Personal

Open the workbook Case 11-2 Family Fitness from the Data Files for Students and then save the workbook using the file name, Case 11-2 Family Fitness Complete. For a fitness goal, you and your family have joined a local gym. Using e-mailed information about your family's hours spent at the gym in four categories, you have created a workbook. You now want to add comments and then share the workbook and send it to your family. Add a comment asking what they think of the title of the worksheet. For your mother, father, and siblings (Betty, Lee, and Tony), add comments asking them to review the hours and adjust them accordingly. Share the workbook. Save the workbook. Submit the assignment as requested by your instructor.

3: Consolidating Employee Hours Data

Professional

Open the workbook Case 11-3 CarryFast Shipping from the Data Files for Students and then save the workbook using the file name, Case 11-3 CarryFast Shipping Complete. You work for the CarryFast Shipping home office and are tasked with consolidating employee hour projections from the South and North branches. Insert a new worksheet and name it Employee Hours. Copy the first three rows from the South worksheet. Replace the South subtitle with Employee Hours Analysis. Also copy the range A4:A10 to the Employee Hours worksheet. Name the range B4:E10 as **Hours1** on the South worksheet and **Hours2** on the North worksheet. Consolidate the data by position in the Employee Hours worksheet. Print the worksheet. Save the workbook. Submit the assignment as requested by your instructor.

NOTES

NOTES

NOTES

NOTES

Appendix A

Project Planning Guidelines

Using Project Planning Guidelines

The process of communicating specific information to others is a learned, rational skill. Computers and software, especially Microsoft Office 2010, can help you develop ideas and present detailed information to a particular audience.

Using Microsoft Office 2010, you can create projects such as Word documents, PowerPoint presentations, Excel spreadsheets, and Access databases. Productivity software such as Microsoft Office 2010 minimizes much of the laborious work of drafting and revising projects. Some communicators handwrite ideas in notebooks, others compose directly on the computer, and others have developed unique strategies that work for their own particular thinking and writing styles.

No matter what method you use to plan a project, follow specific guidelines to arrive at a final product that presents information correctly and effectively (Figure A–1). Use some aspects of these guidelines every time you undertake a project, and others as needed in specific instances. For example, in determining content for a project, you may decide that a chart communicates trends more effectively than a paragraph of text. If so, you would create this graphical element and insert it in an Excel spreadsheet, a Word document, or a PowerPoint slide.

Determine the Project's Purpose

Begin by clearly defining why you are undertaking this assignment. For example, you may want to track monetary donations collected for your club's fund-raising drive. Alternatively, you may be urging students to vote for a particular candidate in the next election. Once you clearly understand the purpose of your task, begin to draft ideas of how best to communicate this information.

Analyze Your Audience

Learn about the people who will read, analyze, or view your work. Where are they employed? What are their educational backgrounds? What are their expectations? What questions do they have?

PROJECT PLANNING GUIDELINES

1. DETERMINE THE PROJECT'S PURPOSE
Why are you undertaking the project?

2. ANALYZE YOUR AUDIENCE
Who are the people who will use your work?

3. GATHER POSSIBLE CONTENT
What information exists, and in what forms?

4. DETERMINE WHAT CONTENT TO PRESENT TO YOUR AUDIENCE
What information will best communicate the project's purpose to your audience?

Figure A–1

Design experts suggest drawing a mental picture of these people or finding photos of people who fit this profile so that you can develop a project with the audience in mind.

By knowing your audience members, you can tailor a project to meet their interests and needs. You will not present them with information they already possess, and you will not omit the information they need to know.

Example: Your assignment is to raise the profile of your college's nursing program in the community. How much do they know about your college and the nursing curriculum? What are the admission requirements? How many of the applicants admitted complete the program? What percent pass the state board exams?

Gather Possible Content

Rarely are you in a position to develop all the material for a project. Typically, you would begin by gathering existing information that may reside in spreadsheets or databases. Web sites, pamphlets, magazine and newspaper articles, and books could provide insights of how others have approached your topic. Personal interviews often provide perspectives not available by any other means. Consider video and audio clips as potential sources for material that might complement or support the factual data you uncover.

Determine What Content to Present to Your Audience

Experienced designers recommend writing three or four major ideas you want an audience member to remember after reading or viewing your project. It also is helpful to envision your project's endpoint, the key fact you wish to emphasize. All project elements should lead to this ending point.

As you make content decisions, you also need to think about other factors. Presentation of the project content is an important consideration. For example, will your brochure be printed on thick, colored paper or posted on the Web? Will your PowerPoint presentation be viewed in a classroom with excellent lighting and a bright projector, or will it be viewed on a notebook computer monitor? Determine relevant time factors, such as the length of time to develop the project, how long readers will spend reviewing your project, or the amount of time allocated for your speaking engagement. Your project will need to accommodate all of these constraints.

Decide whether a graph, photo, or artistic element can express or emphasize a particular concept. The right hemisphere of the brain processes images by attaching an emotion to them, so audience members are more apt to recall these graphics long term rather than just reading text.

As you select content, be mindful of the order in which you plan to present information. Readers and audience members generally remember the first and last pieces of information they see and hear, so you should place the most important information at the top or bottom of the page.

Summary

When creating a project, it is beneficial to follow some basic guidelines from the outset. By taking some time at the beginning of the process to determine the project's purpose, analyze the audience, gather possible content, and determine what content to present to the audience, you can produce a project that is informative, relevant, and effective.

Appendix B

Publishing Office 2010 Web Pages Online

With Office 2010 programs, you use the Save As command in the Backstage view to save a Web page to a Web site, network location, or FTP site. **File Transfer Protocol (FTP)** is an Internet standard that allows computers to exchange files with other computers on the Internet.

You should contact your network system administrator or technical support staff at your Internet access provider to determine if their Web server supports Web folders, FTP, or both, and to obtain necessary permissions to access the Web server.

Using an Office Program to Publish Office 2010 Web Pages

When publishing online, someone first must assign the necessary permissions for you to publish the Web page. If you are granted access to publish online, you must obtain the Web address of the Web server, a user name, and possibly a password that allows you to connect to the Web server. The steps in this appendix assume that you have access to an online location to which you can publish a Web page.

TO CONNECT TO AN ONLINE LOCATION

To publish a Web page online, you first must connect to the online location. To connect to an online location using Windows 7, you would perform the following steps.

1. Click the Start button on the Windows 7 taskbar to display the Start menu.
2. Click Computer in the right pane of the Start menu to open the Computer window.
3. Click the 'Map network drive' button on the toolbar to display the Map Network Drive dialog box. (If the 'Map network drive' button is not visible on the toolbar, click the 'Display additional commands' button on the toolbar and then click 'Map network drive' in the list to display the Map Network Drive dialog box.)
4. Click the 'Connect to a Web site that you can use to store your documents and pictures' link (Map Network Drive dialog box) to start the Add Network Location wizard.
5. Click the Next button (Add Network Location dialog box).
6. Click 'Choose a custom network location' and then click the Next button.
7. Type the Internet or network address specified by your network or system administrator in the text box and then click the Next button.
8. Click 'Log on anonymously' to deselect the check box, type your user name in the User name text box, and then click the Next button.
9. If necessary, enter the name you want to assign to this online location and then click the Next button.
10. Click to deselect the Open this network location when I click Finish check box, and then click the Finish button.

11. Click the Cancel button to close the Map Network Drive dialog box.

12. Close the Computer window.

TO SAVE A WEB PAGE TO AN ONLINE LOCATION

The online location now can be accessed easily from Windows programs, including Microsoft Office programs. After creating a Microsoft Office file you wish to save as a Web page, you must save the file to the online location to which you connected in the previous steps. To save a Microsoft Word document as a Web page, for example, and publish it to the online location, you would perform the following steps.

1. Click File on the Ribbon to display the Backstage view and then click Save As in the Backstage view to display the Save As dialog box.

2. Type the Web page file name in the File name text box (Save As dialog box). Do not press the ENTER key because you do not want to close the dialog box at this time.

3. Click the 'Save as type' box arrow and then click Web Page to select the Web Page format.

4. If necessary, scroll to display the name of the online location in the navigation pane.

5. Double-click the online location name in the navigation pane to select that location as the new save location and display its contents in the right pane.

6. If a dialog box appears prompting you for a user name and password, type the user name and password in the respective text boxes and then click the Log On button.

7. Click the Save button (Save As dialog box).

The Web page now has been published online. To view the Web page using a Web browser, contact your network or system administrator for the Web address you should use to connect to the Web page.

Appendix C

Saving to the Web Using Windows Live SkyDrive

Introduction

Windows Live SkyDrive, also referred to as **SkyDrive**, is a free service that allows users to save files to the Web, such as documents, spreadsheets, databases, presentations, videos, and photos. Using SkyDrive, you also can save files in folders, providing for greater organization. You then can retrieve those files from any computer connected to the Internet. Some Office 2010 programs including Word, PowerPoint, and Excel can save files directly to an Internet location such as SkyDrive. SkyDrive also facilitates collaboration by allowing users to share files with other SkyDrive users (Figure C–1).

Windows Live SkyDrive

Figure C–1

Note: An Internet connection is required to perform the steps in this Appendix.

To Save a File to Windows Live SkyDrive

You can save files directly to SkyDrive from within Word, PowerPoint, and Excel using the Backstage view. The following steps save an open Excel spreadsheet (Brain Busters, in this case) to SkyDrive. These steps require you to have a Windows Live account. Contact your instructor if you do not have a Windows Live account.

1

• Start Excel and the open a workbook you want to save to the Web (in this case, the Brain Busters workbook).

• Click File on the Ribbon to display the Backstage view (Figure C–2).

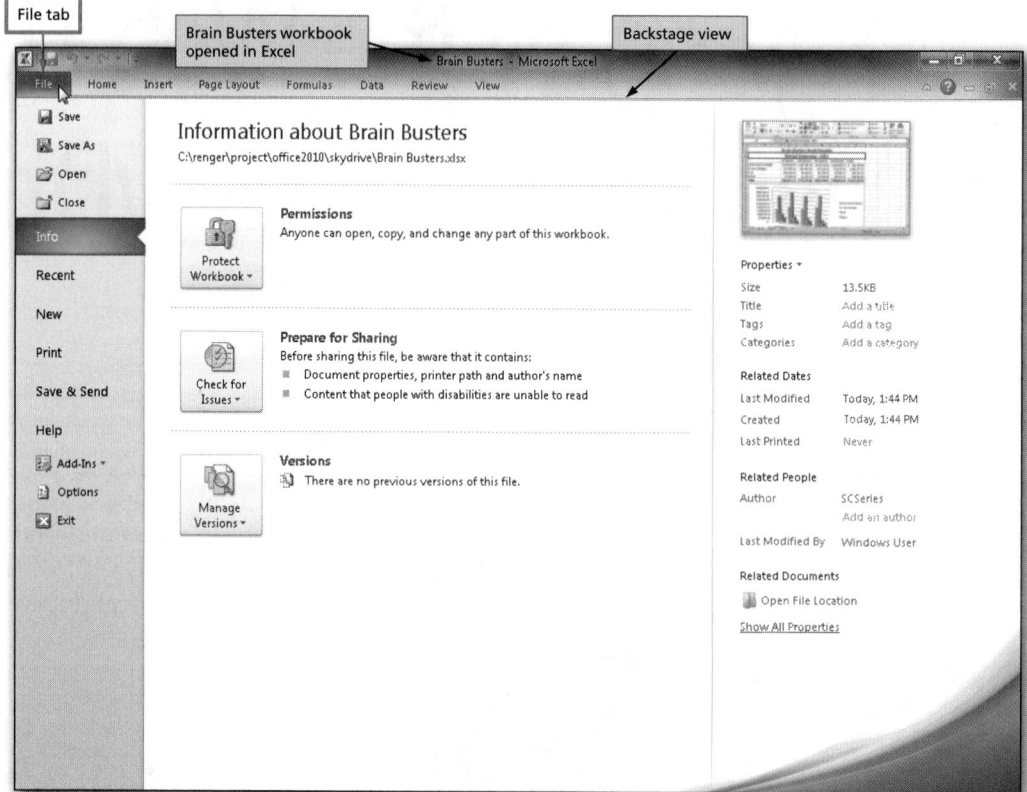

Figure C–2

2

• Click the Save & Send tab to display the Save & Send gallery (Figure C–3).

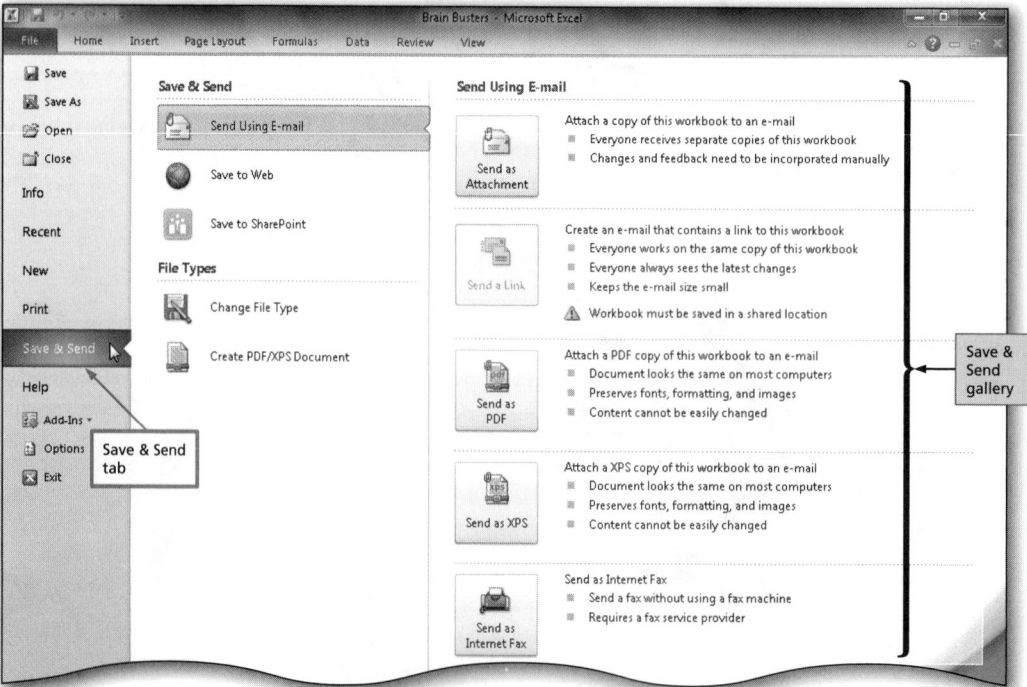

Figure C–3

3

- Click Save to Web in the Save & Send gallery to display information about saving a file to the Web (Figure C–4).

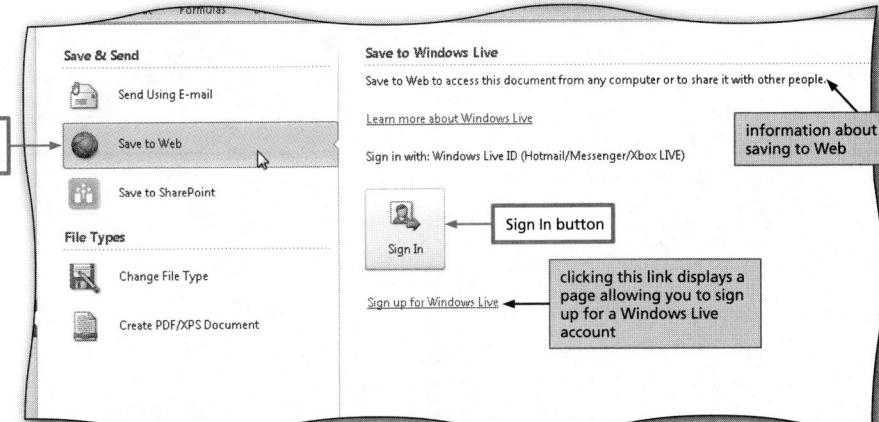

Figure C–4

4

- Click the Sign In button to display a Windows Live login dialog box that requests your e-mail address and password (Figure C–5).

Q&A What if the Sign In button does not appear?

If you already are signed into Windows Live, the Sign In button will not be displayed. Instead, the contents of your Windows Live SkyDrive will be displayed. If you already are signed into Windows Live, proceed to Step 6.

Figure C–5

5

- Enter your Windows Live e-mail address in the E-mail address text box (Windows Live login dialog box).
- Enter your Windows Live password in the Password text box.
- Click the OK button to sign into Windows Live and display the contents of your Windows Live SkyDrive in right pane of the Save & Send gallery.
- If necessary, click the My Documents folder to set the save location for the document (Figure C–6).

Q&A What if the My Documents folder does not exist?

Click another folder to select it as the save location. Record the name of this folder so that you can locate and retrieve the file later in this appendix.

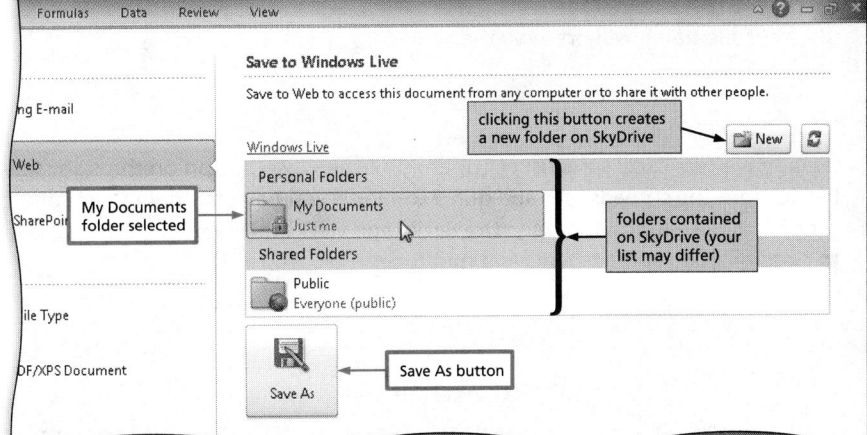

Figure C–6

Q&A What is the difference between the personal folders and the shared folders?

Personal folders are private and are not shared with anyone. Shared folders can be viewed by SkyDrive users to whom you have assigned the necessary permissions.

6

- Click the Save As button in the right pane of the Save & Send gallery to contact the SkyDrive server (which may take some time, depending on the speed of your Internet connection) and then display the Save As dialog box (Figure C–7).

Figure C–7

7

- Type **Brain Busters Web** in the File name text box to enter the file name and then click the Save button (Save As dialog box) to save the file to Windows Live SkyDrive (Figure C–8).

Q&A

Is it necessary to rename the file?

It is good practice to rename the file. If you download the file from SkyDrive to your computer, having a different file name will preserve the original file.

Figure C–8

8

- If you have one Excel spreadsheet open, click the Close button on the right side of the title bar to close the spreadsheet and quit Excel; or if you have multiple Excel spreadsheets open, click File on the Ribbon to open the Backstage view and then click Exit in the Backstage view to close all open spreadsheets and quit Excel.

Web Apps

Microsoft has created a scaled-down, Web-based version of its Microsoft Office suite, called **Microsoft Office Web Apps,** or **Web Apps**. Web Apps contains Web-based versions of Word, PowerPoint, Excel, and OneNote that can be used to view and edit files that are saved to SkyDrive. Web Apps allows users to continue working with their files even while they are not using a computer with Microsoft Office installed. In addition to working with files located on SkyDrive, Web Apps also enables users to create new Word documents, PowerPoint presentations, Excel spreadsheets, and OneNote notebooks. After returning to a computer with the Microsoft Office suite, some users choose to download files from SkyDrive and edit them using the associated Microsoft Office program.

To Open a File from Windows Live SkyDrive

Files saved to SkyDrive can be opened from a Web browser using any computer with an Internet connection. The following steps open the Brain Busters Web file using a Web browser.

1

• Click the Internet Explorer program button pinned on the Windows 7 taskbar to start Internet Explorer.

• Type **skydrive.live.com** in the Address bar and then press the ENTER key to display a SkyDrive Web page requesting you sign in to your Windows Live account (Figure C–9).

Q&A

Why does the Web address change after I enter it in the Address bar?

The Web address changes because you are being redirected to sign into Windows Live before you can access SkyDrive.

Q&A

Can I open the file from Microsoft Excel instead of using the Web browser?

If you are opening the file on the same computer from which you saved it to the SkyDrive, click File on the Ribbon to open the Backstage view. Click the Recent tab and then click the desired file name (Brain Busters Web, in this case) in the Recent Workbooks list, or click Open and then navigate to the location of the saved file (for a detailed example of this procedure, refer to the Office 2010 and Windows 7 chapter at the beginning of this book).

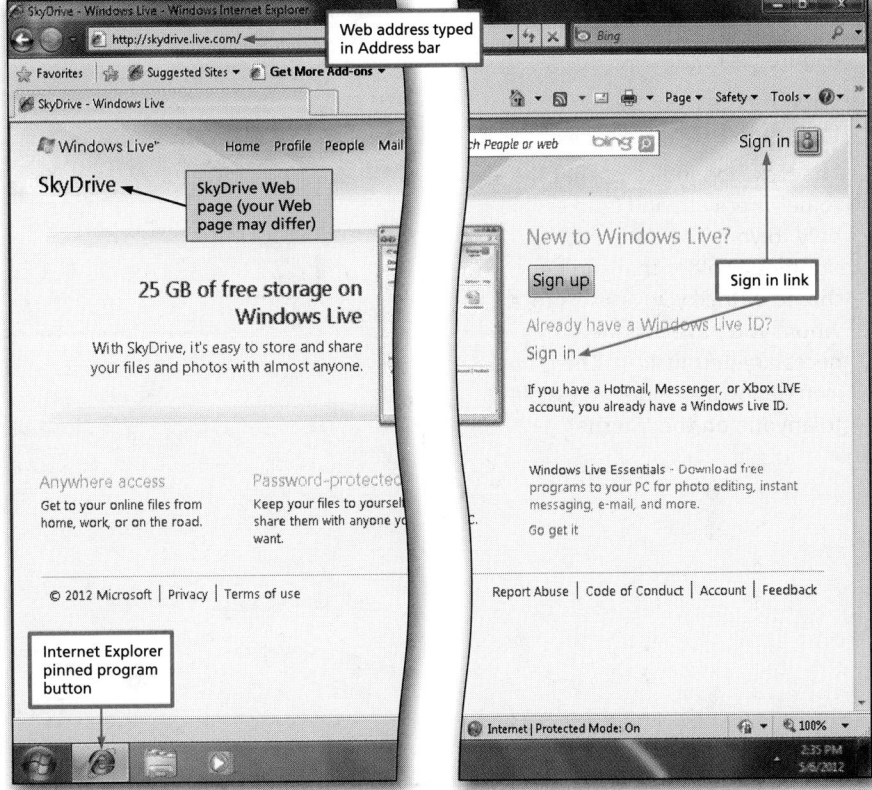

Figure C–9

2

• Click the Sign in link to display the Windows Live ID and Password text boxes (Figure C–10).

Q&A

Why can I not locate the Sign in link?

If your computer remembers your Windows Live sign in credentials from a previous session, your e-mail address already may be displayed on the SkyDrive Web page. In this case, point to your e-mail address to display the Sign in button, click the Sign in button, and then proceed to Step 3. If you cannot locate your e-mail address or Sign in link, click the Sign in with a different Windows Live ID link and then proceed to Step 3.

Figure C–10

- If necessary, enter your Windows Live ID and password in the appropriate text boxes and then click the Sign in button to sign into Windows Live and display the contents of your SkyDrive (Figure C–11).

Q&A

What do the icons beside the folders mean?

The lock icon indicates that the folder is private and is accessible only to you. The people icon signifies a folder that can be shared with SkyDrive users to whom you have assigned the necessary permissions. The globe icon denotes a folder accessible to anyone on the Internet.

Figure C–11

- Click the My Documents folder, or the folder containing the file you wish to open, to select the folder and display its contents (Figure C–12).

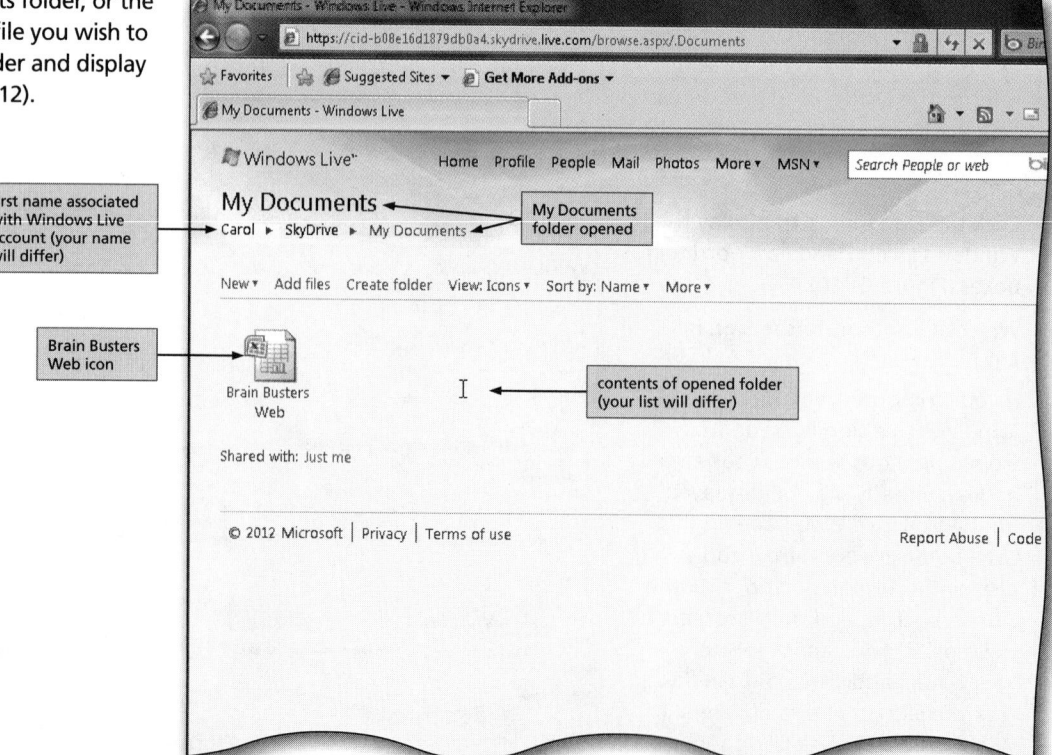

Figure C–12

5

• Click the Brain Busters Web file to select the file and display information about it (Figure C–13).

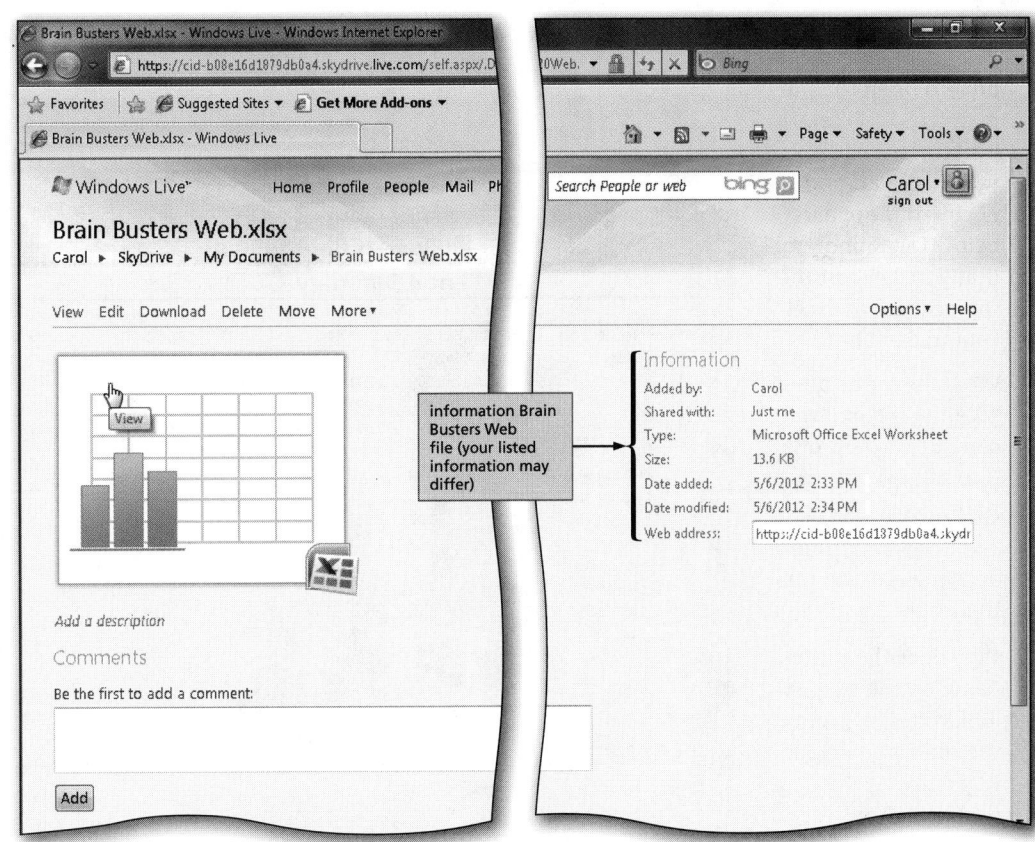

Figure C–13

6

• Click the Download link to display the File Download dialog box (Figure C–14).

Figure C–14

• Click the Open button (File Download dialog box) to open the file in Microsoft Excel. If necessary, click the Enable Editing button if it appears below the Ribbon so that you can edit the spreadsheet in Excel (Figure C–15).

Q&A

What if I want to save the file on my computer's hard disk?

Refer to the Office 2010 and Windows 7 chapter at the beginning of this book.

Q&A

Why does the file name on the title bar look different from the file name I typed when saving the document?

Because you are opening the file directly from SkyDrive

Figure C–15

without first saving it to your computer, the file name may differ slightly. For example, spaces may be replaced with "%20" and a number in parentheses at the end of the file name may indicate you are opening a copy of the original file that is stored online.

Collaboration

In today's workplace, it is common to work with others on projects. Collaborating with the members of your team often requires sharing files. It also can involve multiple people editing and working with a certain set of files simultaneously. Placing files on SkyDrive in a public or shared folder enables others to view or modify the files. The members of the team then can view and edit the files simultaneously using Web Apps, enabling the team to work from one set of files. Collaboration using Web Apps not only enables multiple people to work together, it also can reduce the amount of time required to complete a project.

Appendix D

Microsoft Office 2010 Specialist and Expert Certifications

What Are Microsoft Office Specialist and Expert Certifications?

Microsoft Corporation has developed a set of standardized, performance-based examinations that you can take to demonstrate your overall expertise with Microsoft Office 2010 programs, including Microsoft Word 2010, Microsoft PowerPoint 2010, Microsoft Excel 2010, Microsoft Access 2010, and Microsoft Outlook 2010. When you successfully complete an examination for one of these Office programs, you will have earned the designation as a specialist or as an expert in that particular Office program.

These examinations collectively are called the Microsoft Office 2010 Specialist and Microsoft Office 2010 Expert certification exams. The information in Table D–1 identifies each of these examinations.

Table D–1 Microsoft Office Specialist and Expert Certifications

Certification Exam	Description	Requirement	Credential Earned
Microsoft Word 2010 Specialist	Indicates you have proficiency in using at least 80 percent of the features and capabilities of Word 2010	Successfully complete Exam 77-881	Microsoft Office Specialist: Microsoft Word 2010
Microsoft Word 2010 Expert	Indicates you have proficiency in using Word 2010 at the feature and functionality levels, together with advanced features of Word 2010	Successfully complete Exam 77-887	Microsoft Office Specialist: Microsoft Word 2010 Expert
Microsoft PowerPoint 2010 Specialist	Indicates you have proficiency in using PowerPoint 2010 by creating complex slide shows using sophisticated data presented in visual formats	Successfully complete Exam 77-883	Microsoft Office Specialist: Microsoft PowerPoint 2010

Table D–1 Microsoft Office Specialist and Expert Certifications (*continued*)			
Certification Exam	Description	Requirement	Credential Earned
Microsoft Excel 2010 Specialist	Indicates you have proficiency in using at least 80 percent of the features and capabilities of Excel 2010	Successfully complete Exam 77-882	Microsoft Office Specialist: Microsoft Excel 2010
Microsoft Excel 2010 Expert	Indicates you have proficiency in using Excel 2010 at the feature and functionality levels, together with advanced features of Excel 2010	Successfully complete Exam 77-888	Microsoft Office Specialist: Microsoft Excel 2010 Expert
Microsoft Access 2010	Indicates you have proficiency in using Access 2010 by creating, modifying, and extending functionality of basic database objects	Successfully complete Exam 77-885	Microsoft Office Specialist: Microsoft Access 2010
Microsoft Outlook 2010	Indicates you have proficiency in using Outlook 2010 by formatting message content, creating contact records and appointments, scheduling meetings, and sharing schedules	Successfully complete Exam 77-884	Microsoft Office Specialist: Microsoft Outlook 2010

You will notice in Table D–1 that Word and Excel have an Expert certification. The other programs do not.

Microsoft provides one other level of Office certification: 2010 Microsoft Office Master certification. To be certified as a 2010 Microsoft Office Master, you must successfully complete the following exams:

- 77-887: Word 2010 Expert
- 77-888: Excel 2010 Expert
- 77-883: PowerPoint 2010

and either

- 77-885: Access 2010

or

- 77-884: Outlook 2010

Why Should You Be Certified?

Microsoft Office 2010 certification provides a number of benefits for both you and your potential employer. The benefits for you include the following:

- You can differentiate yourself in the employment marketplace from those who are not Microsoft Office Specialist or Expert certified.
- You have proved your skills and expertise when using Microsoft Office 2010.
- You will be able to perform at a higher skill level in your job.
- You will be working at a higher professional level than those who are not certified.
- You will broaden your employment opportunities and advance your career more rapidly.

For employers, Microsoft Office 2010 certification offers the following advantages:

- When hiring or promoting employees, employers have immediate verification of employees' skills.
- Companies can maximize their productivity and efficiency by employing Microsoft Office 2010 certified individuals.

Taking the Microsoft Office 2010 Certification Exams

The Certiport Company administers the Microsoft Office 2010 Specialist and Expert certification exams. You can contact Certiport at 888-999-9830 x138 or at the Web site, http://www.certiport.com. On the Web site, click the Microsoft Office 2010 Specialist link. Be sure to explore the links on these Certiport pages to obtain a thorough understanding of the Microsoft Office 2010 certification exams.

To take an exam, you must register and pay a fee. The fee varies depending on the test and the testing center. Each exam requires that you complete specified tasks using the program on which you are being tested, that is, tasks you would perform while at work. Remember — these are performance-based exams, so you will be using the software, not answering questions about the software.

You can find testing centers by following the links on the Certiport Web site and then clicking Find a Testing Center.

How Do I Prepare for the Microsoft Office 2010 Specialist Exam?

The Shelly Cashman Series offers Microsoft-approved textbooks for the certification exams listed in Table D–1 on pages APP 13 and APP 14. These textbooks can be found by visiting the Web site, www.cengagebrain.com, and then entering the search topic, Shelly. Using any of the approved textbooks will prepare you to take and pass the indicated Microsoft Office 2010 Specialist or Expert exam. For a list of skill sets specific to this book, see Table D–2 on pages APP 16 through APP 20 and Table D–3 on pages APP 20 through APP 21. The use of all appropriate Shelly Cashman Series Office 2010 textbooks will prepare you for the 2010 Microsoft Office Master certification.

For further information from Microsoft regarding Microsoft Office 2010 certification, please visit www.microsoft.com/learning/en/us/certification/mos.aspx and www.office.microsoft.com/en-us/word-help/should-you-become-a-microsoft-office-specialist-HA001211101.aspx.

Table D–2 Specialist-Level Skill Sets and Locations in Book for Microsoft Excel 2010	
Skill Set	**Page Number(s)**
Managing the Worksheet Environment	
Navigate through a worksheet	
Use hot keys	EX 35
Use the Name box	EX 7, EX 34–35
Print a worksheet or workbook	
Print only selected worksheets	EX 46–47, EX 118
Print an entire workbook	EX 118
Construct headers and footers	EX 114–116, EX 397–399
Apply printing options	
Scale	EX 195
Print titles	EX 268
Page setup	EX 119–120, EX 267, EX 268
Print area	EX 268
Gridlines	EX 268, EX 466
Personalize the environment by using Backstage	
Manipulate the Quick Access Toolbar	EX 649–652, EX 732–733
Customize the Ribbon	
Tabs	EX 635–636
Groups	APP 22–24
Manipulate Excel default settings (Excel Options)	EX 45, EX 149, EX 278
Manipulate workbook properties (document panel)	EX 43–44
Manipulate workbook files and folders	
Manage versions	EX 48
AutoSave	EX 20
Creating Cell Data	
Construct cell data	EX 8–9
Use Paste Special	
Formats	EX 82, EX 153
Formulas	EX 82, EX 153
Values	EX 82, EX 153
Preview icons	EX 152–153, EX 394–395
Transpose rows	EX 452
Transpose columns	EX 452
Operations	
Add	APP 24
Divide	APP 25
Comments	EX 717
Validation	EX 575
Paste as a link	EX 153
Cut	EX 50, EX 154
Move	EX 153–154
Select cell data	EX 35, EX 50, EX 51

Table D–2 Specialist-Level Skill Sets and Locations in Book for Microsoft Excel 2010 (*continued*)

Skill Set	Page Number(s)
Apply Auto Fill	
Copy data	EX 148
Fill a series	EX 147, EX 148
Preserve cell format	EX 148
Apply and manipulate hyperlinks	
Create a hyperlink in a cell	EX 737–740
Modify hyperlinks	EX 742–743
Modify hyperlinked cell attributes	EX 740–742
Remove a hyperlink	EX 743
Formatting Cells and Worksheets	
Apply and modify cell formats	
Align cell content	EX 30, EX 231, EX 237
Apply a number format	EX 31–33
Wrap text in a cell	EX 72
Use Format Painter	EX 178–179
Merge or split cells	
Use Merge & Center	EX 28–29
Merge across	EX 304
Merge cells	EX 667
Unmerge cells	EX 29
Create row and column titles	
Print row and column headings	EX 268
Print rows to repeat with titles	EX 268
Print columns to repeat with titles	EX 268
Configure titles to print only on odd or even pages	EX 117
Configure titles to skip the first worksheet page	EX 117
Hide or unhide rows and columns	
Hide or unhide a column	EX 107, EX 108, EX 354
Hide or unhide a row	EX 107, EX 111, EX 282
Hide a series of columns	EX 107, EX 354
Hide a series of rows	EX 107, EX 282
Manipulate Page Setup options for worksheets	
Configure page orientation	EX 46
Manage page scaling	EX 119–121
Configure page margins	EX 114–115
Change header and footer size	EX 114–115
Create and apply cell styles	
Apply cell styles	EX 23
Construct new cell styles	EX 380

Table D–2 Specialist-Level Skill Sets and Locations in Book for Microsoft Excel 2010 (*continued*)	
Skill Set	**Page Number(s)**
Managing Worksheets and Workbooks	
Create and format worksheets	
Insert worksheets	
Single	EX 384
Multiple	EX 384
Delete worksheets	
Single	EX 304
Multiple	EX 304
Reposition worksheets	EX 194
Copy worksheets	EX 194
Move worksheets	EX 194
Rename worksheets	EX 42, EX 193
Group worksheets	EX 385
Apply color to worksheet tabs	EX 193
Hide worksheet tabs	EX 276
Unhide worksheet tabs	EX 276
Manipulate window views	
Split window views	EX 198–199
Arrange window views	EX 406
Open a new window with contents from the current worksheet	EX 199
Manipulate workbook views	
Use Normal workbook view	EX 118
Use Page Layout workbook view	EX 114
Use Page Break workbook view	EX 402
Create custom views	EX 734–735
Applying Formulas and Functions	
Create formulas	
Use basic operators	EX 75
Revise formulas	EX 50, EX 51, EX 77
Enforce precedence	
Order of evaluation	EX 77
Precedence using parentheses	EX 77
Precedence of operators for percent vs exponentiation	EX 77
Apply cell references in formulas	
Relative and absolute references	EX 78–80, EX 162–164
Apply conditional logic in a formula	
Create a formula with values that match conditions	EX 338–340
Edit defined conditions in a formula	EX 316, EX 351
Use a series of conditional logic values in a formula	EX 164–166
Apply named ranges in formulas	
Define ranges in formulas	EX 234, EX 238–239
Edit ranges in formulas	EX 335
Rename a named range	EX 239, EX 335
Apply cell ranges in formulas	
Enter a cell range definition in the formula bar	EX 85
Define a cell range	EX 86, EX 238–239

Table D–2 Specialist-Level Skill Sets and Locations in Book for Microsoft Excel 2010 (*continued*)

Skill Set	Page Number(s)
Presenting Data Visually	
Create charts based on worksheet data	EX 38–41
Apply and manipulate illustrations	
Insert	EX 474
Position	EX 474
Size	EX 474
Rotate	EX 475
Modify clip art SmartArt	EX 468–470
Modify shape	EX 469–472
Modify screenshots	EX 476–477
Create and modify images by using the Image Editor	
Make corrections to an image	
Sharpen or soften an image	APP 26
Change brightness	APP 26
Change contrast	APP 26
Use picture color tools	APP 26
Change artistic effects on an image	APP 26
Apply sparklines	
Use Line chart types	EX 170–171
Use Column chart types	EX 170
Use Win/Loss chart types	EX 170
Create a Sparkline chart	EX 170–171
Customize a sparkline	EX 173
Format a sparkline	EX 172
Show or hide data markers	EX 173
Sharing Worksheet Data with Other Users	
Share spreadsheets by using Backstage	
Send a worksheet via e-mail or SkyDrive	EX 723–724
Change the file type to a different version of Excel	EX 749–750
Save as PDF or XPS	EX 750
Manage comments	
Insert	EX 711–713
View	EX 713
Edit	EX 714–715
Delete comments	EX 728
Analyzing and Organizing Data	
Filter data	
Define a filter	EX 327, EX 332
Apply a filter	EX 328, EX 332
Remove a filter	EX 329
Filter lists using AutoFilter	EX 327–328
Sort data	
Use sort options	
Values	EX 322–324
Font color	EX 327
Cell color	EX 327

Table D–2 Specialist-Level Skill Sets and Locations in Book for Microsoft Excel 2010 (*continued*)

Skill Set	Page Number(s)
Apply conditional formatting	
Apply conditional formatting to cells	EX 104–106
Use the Rule Manager to apply conditional formats	EX 105
Use the IF function to apply conditional formatting	EX 316
Clear rules	EX 703
Use icon sets	EX 317–318
Use data bars	EX 316, EX 350

Table D–3 Expert-Level Skill Sets and Locations in Book for Microsoft Excel 2010

Skill Set	Page Number(s)
Sharing and Maintaining Workbooks	
Apply workbook settings, properties, and data options	
Set advanced properties	EX 45, EX 149, EX 237, EX 401
Save a workbook as a template	EX 435–436
Import and export XML data	EX 751
Apply protection and sharing properties to workbooks and worksheets	
Protect the current sheet	EX 272–274
Protect the workbook structure	EX 610–611
Restrict permissions	EX 275
Require a password to open a workbook	EX 645
Maintain shared workbooks	
Merge workbooks	EX 730–733
Set Track Changes options	EX 721–723
Applying Formulas and Functions	
Audit formulas	
Trace formula precedents	EX 562–563
Trace dependents	EX 565
Trace errors	EX 569–571
Locate invalid data	EX 569–571
Locate invalid formulas	EX 569–571
Correct errors in formulas	EX 570
Manipulate formula options	
Set iterative calculation options	EX 571
Enable or disable automatic workbook calculation	EX 37
Perform data summary tasks	
Use an array formula	APP 27
Use a SUMIFS function	EX 338–339
Apply functions in formulas	
Find and correct errors in functions	EX 278–280, EX 569–572
Applying arrays to functions	APP 27
Use Statistical functions	EX 84–85
Use Date functions	EX 160
Use Time functions	EX 160
Use Financial functions	EX 242–243
Use Text functions	EX 637–638
Cube functions	APP 28

Table D–3 Expert-Level Skill Sets and Locations in Book for Microsoft Excel 2010 (*continued*)

Skill Set	Page Number(s)
Presenting Data Visually	
Apply advanced chart features	
Use trendlines	EX 497–498
Use dual axes	EX 37
Use chart templates	EX 38–39, EX 181
Use sparklines	EX 170–172
Apply data analysis	
Use automated analysis tools	EX 177, EX 200–202
Perform What-If analysis	EX 200–202
Apply and manipulate PivotTables	
Manipulate PivotTable data	EX 503, EX 506–510
Use the slicer to filter and segment your PivotTable data in multiple layers	EX 537–538, EX 540–541
Apply and manipulate PivotCharts	
Create a PivotChart	EX 524, EX 530–531
Manipulate PivotChart data	EX 525
Analyze PivotChart data	EX 532–533
Demonstrate how to use the slicer	
Choose data sets from external data connections	EX 539–541
Working with Macros and Forms	
Create and manipulate macros	
Run a macro	EX 647
Run a macro when a workbook is opened	EX 647
Run a macro when a button is clicked	EX 649–652
Record an action macro	EX 639–643
Assign a macro to a command button	EX 667
Create a custom macro button on the Quick Access Toolbar	EX 649–652
Apply modifications to a macro	EX 648, EX 650–652
Insert and manipulate form controls	
Insert form controls	EX 668–670
Set form properties	EX 677–678

The chapters in this book have covered most of the topics necessary for the Excel certification; however, you need to know about a few more to be ready for the certification exam.

Customizing the Ribbon

You may find that you use certain commands regularly, and would find it helpful to have these commands on a single tab, or in a single group on a tab. You can customize the Ribbon in Excel to add new tabs, and add groups on existing or new tabs to increase your efficiency when using Excel.

To Add Tabs and Groups to the Ribbon

The following steps create a new tab on the Ribbon with a single group containing three commands.

- Click the File tab to display the Backstage view.

- Click the Options command to display the Excel Options dialog box.

- Click the Customize Ribbon tab (Excel Options dialog box) to display the Customize the Ribbon tools.

- Click the New Tab button (Excel Options dialog box) to add a new tab containing a new group (Figure D–1).

Figure D–1

- Click the Rename button (Excel Options dialog box) to display the Rename dialog box.

- Type **Setup** in the Display name text box to rename the new group (Figure D–2).

Figure D–2

3

- Click the OK button (Rename dialog box) to rename the group to Setup.

- Click New Tab (Custom) in the Main Tabs list to select the new tab for renaming.

- Click the Rename button (Excel Options dialog box) to display the Rename dialog box.

- Type **Report Creation** in the Display name text box to rename the new tab.

- Click the OK button (Rename dialog box) to rename the tab to Report Creation (Figure D–3).

Figure D–3

4

- Click the Move Down button (Excel Options dialog box) until the Report Creation tab appears below the View tab in the Main Tabs list.

- Click Setup (Custom) to make the Setup group active.

- Add the Calculate Now, Delete Sheet Columns, and Delete Sheet Rows commands to the Setup group (Figure D–4).

Figure D–4

- Click the OK button (Excel Options dialog box) to display the new Report Creation tab.

- Make Report Creation the active tab (Figure D–5).

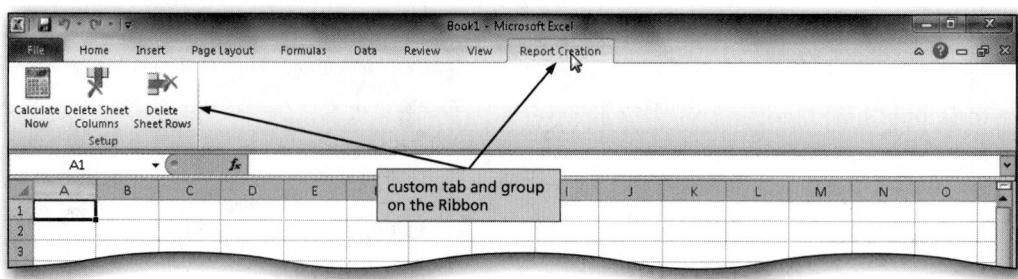

Figure D–5

Using Paste Special for Mathematical Operations

In addition to pasting certain attributes of cells to new locations, Paste Special can be used to perform mathematical operations when pasting numerical data into cells that already contain data. Figure D–6 shows the Paste Special dialog box, accessed either from the Paste menu or the shortcut menu.

Figure D–6

You can use the Operations options of the Paste Special command to add, subtract, multiply, or divide the contents of the copied cells and the destination cells and then store the results in the destination cells.

TO ADD CELL CONTENTS USING PASTE SPECIAL

If you wanted to add the contents of a copied cell or range to a destination cell or range, replacing the original values in the destination cells with the results of the addition, you would perform the following steps.

1. Select the cells you want to copy and press CTRL+C to copy the contents to the Clipboard.

2. Select the destination cells.

3. Click the Paste button arrow (Home tab | Clipboard group) to display the Paste menu. Click Paste Special on the menu to display the Paste Special dialog box.

4. Click Add in the Operation group (Paste Special dialog box) to indicate the mathematical operation you want to perform.

Q&A Do the copied cells and the destination cells need to be the same size?

The copied cells either need to be the same size as the destination range, resulting in a 1:1 match, or a single copied cell can be used. When a single copied cell is used, each of the destination cells is subject to the selected mathematical operation using the contents of the single copied cell.

5. Click the OK button (Paste Special dialog box) to replace the contents of the destination cells with the results of adding the contents of the copied cells to the contents of the destination cells.

TO DIVIDE CELL CONTENTS USING PASTE SPECIAL

If you wanted to divide the contents of a copied cell or range by the value in a destination cell or range, replacing the original values in the destination cells with the results of the division, you would perform the following steps.

1. Select the cell containing the divisor and press CTRL+C to copy the contents to the Clipboard.
2. Select the destination cells.
3. Click the Paste button arrow (Home tab | Clipboard group) to display the Paste menu. Click Paste Special on the menu to display the Paste Special dialog box.
4. Click Divide in the Operation group (Paste Special dialog box) to indicate the desired mathematical operation.
5. Click the OK button (Paste Special dialog box) to replace the contents of the destination cells with the results of dividing the contents of the destination cells by the content of the copied cell.

Modifying Images

Excel provides an image editor for basic image modifications. You can sharpen or soften an image, change brightness and contrast, use picture color tools, and apply artistic effects to an image. You access image editing tools from one of three galleries in the Adjust group on the Picture Tools Format tab. These galleries are shown in Figure D–7.

Figure D–7(a)   **Figure D–7(b)**

Figure D–7a shows the Corrections gallery, which is used for adjusting sharpness, brightness, and contrast of an image. Figure D–7b shows the Color gallery, used to adjust the saturation and tone of an image and to apply recoloring effects. Figure D–7c shows the Artistic Effects gallery, used to apply artistic effects to an image.

Figure D–7(c)

To Make Corrections to an Image

To adjust the brightness, contrast, and sharpness of an image, you would perform the following steps.

1. Click anywhere in the image on the worksheet to make the image active and display the Picture Tools Format tab.

2. Click the Corrections button (Picture Tools Format tab | Adjust group) to display the Corrections gallery.

3. In the Brightness and Contrast section, click to select the desired brightness and contrast of the picture.

4. Click the Corrections button (Picture Tools Format tab | Adjust group) again, and in the Sharpness section of the gallery, click the desired sharpness level to sharpen the picture.

To Use Color Picture Tools

You can adjust the saturation or color tone of an image, or recolor the image for a particular effect. To change the saturation of an image, you would perform the following steps.

1. If necessary, click the image to make the Picture Tools Format tab the active tab. Click the Color button (Picture Tools Format tab | Adjust group) to display the Color gallery.

2. Click the desired saturation level in the gallery to change the saturation.

To Change Artistic Effects on an Image

You can use artistic effects in Excel to add interest to an image. To apply an artistic effect, you would perform the following steps.

1. If necessary, click the image to make the Picture Tools Format tab the active tab. Click the Artistic Effects button (Picture Tools Format tab | Adjust group) to display the Artistic Effects gallery.

2. Click the desired artistic effect to apply the effect to the image.

Using Arrays in Excel

When working with large, complex worksheets, you should determine whether arrays could make your worksheet more efficient. An **array** is a collection of items. In Excel, these items are cell entries that can be organized in a row (a one-dimensional horizontal array), a column (a one-dimensional vertical array), or a group of rows and columns (a two-dimensional array), as illustrated in Figure D–8. **Array formulas** permit multiple calculations on one or more items in an array. Using arrays, you can replace many instances of a formula copied into cells with a single array formula that references all those cells. You can also use arrays with functions to replace many instances of a formula with a single instance.

Array formulas are indicated by curly brackets placed around the formula, as shown in Figure D–8. You do not need to type the curly brackets directly because Excel inserts them when you press CTRL+SHIFT+ENTER rather than ENTER to finish entering the formula. To edit an array formula, you must select the entire array and then edit the formula in the formula bar. If you select a single cell in the array and attempt to edit the formula, you will get an error message.

Arrays produce more efficient worksheets. In the vertical array in Figure D–8, the one array formula would need to be replaced by eight formulas if each of the cells in D2:D9 were calculated separately.

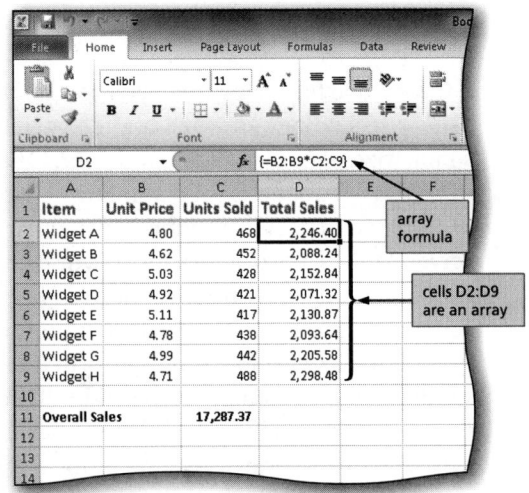

Figure D–8

Arrays can also reduce the potential for error. In very large worksheets with columns of calculations where the formula is copied down a column of cells, rows at the top or bottom of the range could be missed when the formula is updated. With an array formula, once an array is identified, it must be treated as a single unit, thereby removing the possibility that one of its items would be missed in an update.

To Use an Array Formula

To create an array formula that multiplies the contents of one array (B2:B9) by the contents of another array (C2:C9) and stores the results in a third array (D2:D9), as illustrated in Figure D–8, you would perform the following steps.

1. Select the range D2:D9 to specify the location for the array formula.

2. Type `=B2:B9*C2:C9` and then press CTRL+SHIFT+ENTER to enter the formula as an array formula.

Q&A Why does Excel insert curly brackets when I press CTRL+SHIFT+ENTER?

Excel inserts the curly brackets to indicate that the formula is an array formula.

To Apply an Array to a Function

You can use arrays with functions with the same savings in efficiency and error reduction. In the previous set of steps, you learned how to multiply one array by another and record the results in a third array. If you wanted to know the sum of those products, you can use a function with an array to accomplish the multiplication and summation using a single formula, as illustrated in Figure D–8. To accomplish this, you would perform the following steps.

1. Select cell C11 to specify the location for the array formula that will calculate the total of the products.

2. Type `=SUM(B2:B9*C2:C9)` and then press CTRL+SHIFT+ENTER to enter the formula as an array formula.

Cube Functions

Excel's Cube functions allow you to analyze vast amounts of data on remote servers using a technology known as online analytical processing (OLAP). OLAP analyzes and summarizes data on a database server. OLAP technology is used because of its great speed in processing requests for summarized data. Excel's Cube functions work with a Microsoft SQL Server database. A **cube** is a summary of data from a database and is stored on a server. Unlike a two-dimensional worksheet of rows and columns, a cube can summarize data in multiple dimensions. For example, revenue for a company's products may be summarized in a cube by product, region, state, city, quarter, weight, and production cost.

Excel's Cube functions perform queries on cubes. While the functions display the resulting data in a range, each cell in the result range contains a function that queries the cube for a specific value. When querying a cube, you must first know where the cube exists. A cube is located on a server by a value known as a connection. Table D–4 shows several terms used to describe some types of data that a cube may contain.

Table D–4 Types of Data in a Cube	
Data Type	**Description**
Dimension	The primary means of organizing data in a cube, such as region, state, city, or quarter.
Member	An item in a dimension in a cube. For example, if one dimension in a cube is quarter, then the dimension's members might be First, Second, Third, and Fourth.
Tuple	An intersection of one or more members from multiple dimensions. For example, if two dimensions in a cube of product revenue are quarter and region, then a tuple might be for the fourth quarter product revenue for the Midwest region.
Set	A group of tuples, each of which consists of the members from the same dimensions. For example, if two dimensions in a cube of product revenue are quarter and region, then a set might be a tuple for the fourth quarter product revenue for the Midwest region and a tuple for the fourth quarter product revenue for the East region.
Key Performance Indicator (KPI)	A value used by an organization to measure a critical aspect of its performance. Key performance indicators allow management quickly to see whether the organization is meeting its goals. For example, a key performance indicator might be that weekly product revenue for each city must always be 10% greater than similar sales for the same week in the previous year. If the target is not being met, a manager quickly can determine the cause of the shortfall and decide if action is necessary to correct the shortfall. Key performances indicators are created and exist with a cube on a server.

Table D–5 shows the Cube functions available in Microsoft Excel 2010.

Table D–5 Microsoft Excel 2010 Cube Functions	
Function	**Description**
CUBEKPIMEMBER(connection, kpi_name, kpi_property, [caption])	Returns a Key Performance Indicator (KPI) property and displays the KPI name in the cell
CUBEMEMBER(connection, member_expression, [caption])	Returns a member or tuple from the cube; the member_expression parameter that evaluates to a unique member or tuple in a cube
CUBEMEMBERPROPERTY(connection, member_expression, property)	Returns the value of a member property from the cube
CUBERANKEDMEMBER(connection, set_expression, rank, [caption])	Returns the nth, or ranked, member in a set; the set_expression parameter indicates the set to rank
CUBESET(connection, set_expression, [caption], [sort_order], [sort_by])	Defines a calculated set of members or tuples by sending a set expression to the cube on the server, which creates the set, and then returns that set to Excel
CUBESETCOUNT(set)	Returns the number of items in a set
CUBEVALUE(connection, [member_expression1], [member_expression2], …)	Returns an aggregated value from the cube

Index

Quick Reference Summary

Microsoft Excel 2010 Quick Reference Summary

Task	Page Number	Mouse	Ribbon	Shortcut Menu	Keyboard Shortcut
2-D Line Chart, Create	EX 495		Line button (Insert tab | Charts group), chart in 2-D Line area		
3-D Chart, Rotate	EX 462		3-D Rotation button (Chart Tools Layout tab | Background group), change rotation (Format Chart Area dialog box)		
3-D Reference, Enter	EX 392	Start entering formula, click sheet tab, click cell			
Accept or Reject Tracked Change	EX 721		Track Changes button (Review tab | Changes group), Accept/Reject Changes, OK		
Access Data, Import	EX 443		From Access button (Data tab | Get External Data group), double-click file (Select Data Source dialog box)		
Accounting Number Format, Apply	EX 100		Accounting Number Format button (Home tab | Number group)		
Add Calculated Field to PivotTable Report	EX 532		Calculations button (PivotTable Tools Options tab | Calculations group), Fields, Items, & Sets, Calculated Field		
Add Cells to Watch in Watch Window	EX 567	Click Add Watch button on Watch Window toolbar			
Add Check Box to Worksheet	EX 670		Insert button (Developer tab | Controls group), Check Box in Form Controls area, drag to draw control		
Add Command Button to Worksheet	EX 655		Insert button (Developer tab | Controls group), Command Button in ActiveX Controls area, drag to draw button		
Add Comment to Cell	EX 711		New Comment button (Review tab | Comments group)	Cell, Insert Comment	SHIFT+F2

Microsoft Excel 2010 Quick Reference Summary *(continued)*

Task	Page Number	Mouse	Ribbon	Shortcut Menu	Keyboard Shortcut
Add Data Validation to Cell	EX 573		Data Validation button (Data tab | Data Tools group)		
Add Group Box to Worksheet	EX 671		Insert button (Developer tab | Controls group), Check Box in Form Controls area, drag to draw control		
Add Multiple (*n*) Worksheets to Workbook	EX 384		Select *n* worksheet tabs, Insert Cells button arrow (Home tab | Cells group), Insert Sheet	Select *n* worksheet tabs, Insert	Select *n* worksheet tabs, SHIFT+F11
Add Option Button to Worksheet	EX 668		Insert button (Developer tab | Controls group), Option Button in Form Controls area, drag to draw control		
Add Slicers to Worksheet	EX 537		Insert Slicer button arrow (PivotChart Tools Analyze tab | Data group), Insert Slicer		
Add Text Box to Worksheet	EX 672		Insert button (Developer tab | Controls group), Text Box in ActiveX Controls area, drag to draw control		
Add Trendline to Chart	EX 497		Trendline button (Chart Tools Layout tab | Analysis group), trendline type *or* Trendline button (Chart Tools Layout tab | Analysis group), More Trendline Options, Trend/Regression Type option button, Close		
Add VBA Code to Control	EX 660	Double-click control	Visual Basic button (Developer tab | Code group)	Control (in Design mode), View Code	
Add Worksheet to Workbook	EX 384	Click Insert Worksheet tab	Insert Cells button arrow (Home tab | Cells group), Insert Sheet	Insert	SHIFT+F11
Advanced Filter, Apply	EX 332		Advanced button (Data tab | Sort & Filter group)		
All Data in a Cell, Select	EX 51	Double-click if there are no spaces in data			
Answer Report, Generate	EX 586		Solver button (Data tab | Analysis group), Solve button, Answer		
Arrange Multiple Workbooks	EX 406		Arrange All button (View tab | Window group), click Arrange option (Arrange Windows dialog box)		
Assign Name to Cell	EX 679			Name Manager button (Formulas tab | Defined Names group), New button	

Microsoft Excel 2010 Quick Reference Summary *(continued)*

Task	Page Number	Mouse	Ribbon	Shortcut Menu	Keyboard Shortcut
Auto Fill	EX 18	Drag fill handle	Fill button (Home tab | Editing group)		
AutoCalculate	EX 48	Select range, right-click AutoCalculate area, click calculation			
AutoFilter buttons, Display in PivotTable Report	EX 508		Field Headers button (PivotTable Tools Options tab | Show group)		
AutoFilter Data in Table	EX 324	Click AutoFilter button arrow, click filter option *or* click AutoFilter button arrow, type in Search box, click OK			
Autofit PivotTable Report Columns on Update	EX 522		Options button (PivotTable Tools Options tab | PivotTable group), 'Autofit column widths on update' check box		
Average Function	EX 84	Click Insert Function box in formula bar, click AVERAGE in Select a function list, click OK, select range, click OK	Sum button arrow (Home tab | Editing group) or Sum button arrow (Formulas tab | Function Library)		Type =av, DOWN ARROW, ENTER
Background Color, Change	EX 96		Format Cells Dialog Box Launcher (Home tab | Font group), Fill tab, color option, OK	Format Cells, Fill tab (Format Cells dialog box)	CTRL+1
Best Fit	EX 107	Select columns, point to boundary until arrow is split double arrow, double-click			
Bold	EX 25	Click Bold button on Mini toolbar	Bold button (Home tab | Font group)	Format Cells, Font tab (Format Cells dialog box), Bold	CTRL+B
Borders, Add Custom	EX 234		Borders button arrow (Home tab | Font group), More Borders	Format Cells, Border tab (Format Cells dialog box)	
Button, Add to Quick Access Toolbar	EX 649			Quick Access Toolbar, Customize Quick Access Toolbar, click command, click Add button	
Calculated Field, Add to PivotTable Report	EX 532		Calculations button (PivotTable Tools Options tab | Calculations group), Fields, Items, & Sets, Calculated Field		
Cell Entries, Clear Selected	EX 52	Drag fill handle from empty cell through cells with entries	Clear button (Home tab | Editing group) | Clear Contents	Clear Contents	DELETE
Cell Names, Create Based on Row Titles	EX 238		Create from Selection button (Formulas tab | Defined Names group)		

Microsoft Excel 2010 Quick Reference Summary (continued)

Task	Page Number	Mouse	Ribbon	Shortcut Menu	Keyboard Shortcut
Cell Names, Enter	EX 239	Click Name box, type name	Define Name button (Formulas tab | Defined Names group)		
Cell Reference, Add	EX 78	Click cell			
Cell Style, Apply	EX 382		Cell Styles button (Home tab | Styles group), click style		
Cell Style, Change	EX 52		Cell Styles button (Home tab | Styles group)		
Cell Style, Create	EX 380		Cell Styles button (Home tab | Styles group), New Cell Style		
Cell, Highlight	EX 19	Drag mouse pointer			
Cell, Select	EX 34	Click cell or click Name box, type cell reference, press ENTER			Use arrow keys
Cells, Merge and Center	EX 28	Click Merge & Center button on Mini toolbar	Merge & Center button (Home tab | Alignment group)	Format Cells, Alignment tab (Format Cells dialog box)	
Change Chart Type for PivotChart	EX 526		Change Chart Type button (PivotChart Tools Design tab | Type group), chart type		
Change Margins	EX 397	In the Backstage view, click Normal Margins button (Print tab | Settings area)	Page Setup Dialog Box Launcher (Page Layout tab | Page Setup group), Margins tab (Page Setup dialog box)		
Change Slicer Style	EX 539		More button (Slicer Tools Options tab | Slicer Styles group), select style		
Change Summary Functions in PivotTable Report	EX 514			Field cell, Summarize Values By, function	
Change View in PivotChart Report	EX 529	Drag row labels or column labels in PivotTable Fields List pane to a new location or Click field button arrow, click Move Up or Move Down			
Characters to Left of Insertion Point, Delete	EX 50				BACKSPACE
Characters to Right of Insertion Point, Delete	EX 50				DELETE
Characters, Highlight	EX 51	Drag through adjacent characters			SHIFT+RIGHT ARROW or SHIFT+LEFT ARROW
Chart Wall, Format in PivotChart	EX 528		Chart Wall button (PivotChart Tools Layout tab | Background group)		
Chart, Add	EX 38		Charts group | Insert tab		

Microsoft Excel 2010 Quick Reference Summary *(continued)*

Task	Page Number	Mouse	Ribbon	Shortcut Menu	Keyboard Shortcut
Chart, Move	EX 461		Move Chart button (Chart Tools Design tab | Location group), select option (Move Chart dialog box)		
Chart, Remove Legend	EX 462		Legend button (Chart Tools Layout tab | Labels group), None		
Chart Template, Create	EX 181		Save as Template button (Chart Tools Design tab | Type group)		
Check Box, Add to Worksheet	EX 670		Insert button (Developer tab | Controls group), Check Box in Form Controls area, drag to draw control		
Check Errors in Worksheet	EX 570		Error Checking button (Formulas tab | Formula Auditing group), Trace Error button		
Circle Invalid Data	EX 579		Data Validation button arrow (Data tab | Data Tools group), Circle Invalid Data		
Clear Filter in Slicer	EX 541	Click Clear Filter button			
Clear Validation Circles	EX 580		Data Validation button arrow (Data tab | Data Tools group), Clear Validation Circles		
Color Tab	EX 42			Tab Color	
Color Text	EX 27	Click Font Color button on Mini toolbar	Font Color button arrow (Home tab | Font group)		
Column Width	EX 33	Drag column heading boundary		Column Width	
Comma Style Format, Apply	EX 100		Comma Style button (Home tab | Number group)		
Comma-Delimited Text File, Import	EX 439		From Text button (Data tab | Get External Data group), double-click file (Import File dialog box), complete wizard		
Command Button, Add to Worksheet	EX 655		Insert button (Developer tab | Controls group), Command Button in ActiveX Controls area, drag to draw button		
Comment, Add to Cell	EX 711		New Comment button (Review tab | Comments group)	Cell, Insert Comment	SHIFT+F2
Comment, Delete	EX 728		Delete Comment button (Review tab | Comments group)	Comment, Delete Comment	
Comment, Edit	EX 714		Edit Comment button (Review tab | Comments group)	Cell, Edit Comment	SHIFT+F2
Comment, Format	EX 716		Edit Comment button (Review tab | Comments group), right-click text, Format Comment	Cell, Edit Comment, right-click text, Format Comment	

Microsoft Excel 2010 Quick Reference Summary *(continued)*

Task	Page Number	Mouse	Ribbon	Shortcut Menu	Keyboard Shortcut
Comments, Copy	EX 575		Copy cell containing comment, Paste Options button (Home tab | Clipboard group) Paste Special, Comments, OK		
Comments, Show All	EX 713		Show All Comments button (Review tab | Comments group)		
Compatibility, Check in Excel 97-2003 Workbook as	EX 609	Save button, 'Save as type' box arrow, Excel 97-2003 Workbook			CTRL+S, 'Save as type' box arrow, Excel 97-2003 Workbook
Complete an Entry	EX 8	Click Enter box			ENTER
Conditional Formatting	EX 104		Conditional Formatting button (Home tab | Styles group)		
Conditional Formatting with IF Function	EX 316		Conditional Formatting button (Home tab | Styles group), New Rule, 'Use a formula to determine which cells to format' check box, enter IF function		
Conditional Formatting Rule, Add with Icon Set	EX 317		Conditional Formatting button (Home tab | Styles group), New Rule, Format Style box arrow (New Formatting Rule dialog box), Icon Sets, enter condition		
Constraint, Add to Solver	EX 583		Solver button (Data tab | Analysis group), Add button		
Control, Add VBA Code to	EX 660	Double-click control	Visual Basic button (Developer tab | Code group)	Control (in Design mode), View Code	
Control, Edit Text	EX 673			Control (Design mode), Edit Text	
Control, Record User Input	EX 676			Control (Design mode), Format Control, Control tab	
Control, Resize	EX 673	Drag edge or corner			
Control, Select Properties for	EX 657		Properties button (Developer tab | Controls group)	Control (in Design mode), Properties	
Convert Table to Range	EX 312			Table, Convert to Range	
Copy Data to Multiple Worksheets	EX 385		Copy button (Home tab | Clipboard group), select worksheets, Paste button (Home tab | Clipboard group)	Copy, select worksheets, Paste	CTRL+C, select worksheets, CTRL+V
Copy Range of Cells	EX 80	Select range, drag fill handle	Copy button (Home tab | Clipboard group)	Copy	CTRL+C

Microsoft Excel 2010 Quick Reference Summary *(continued)*

Task	Page Number	Mouse	Ribbon	Shortcut Menu	Keyboard Shortcut
Create 2-D Line Chart	EX 495		Line button (Insert tab | Charts group), chart in 2-D Line area		
Create Blank PivotTable Report	EX 501		PivotTable button arrow (Insert tab | Tables group), PivotTable, OK		
Create Cell Style	EX 380		Cell Styles button (Home tab | Styles group), New Cell Style		
Create PivotChart Directly from Data	EX 530		PivotTable button arrow (Insert tab | Tables group), PivotChart, select location		
Create PivotChart Report	EX 524		PivotChart button (PivotTable Tools Options tab | Tools group), chart type		
Create Scenario PivotTable Worksheet	EX 604		What-If Analysis button (Data tab | Data Tools group), Scenario Manager, Summary button, Scenario PivotTable report		
Create Scenario Summary Worksheet	EX 601		What-If Analysis button (Data tab | Data Tools group), Scenario Manager, scenario name, Summary button, Scenario summary		
Create Workspace File	EX 407		Save Workspace button (View tab | Window group)		
Currency Style Format, Apply	EX 100		Format Cells: Number Dialog Box Launcher (Home tab | Number group)		CTRL+1 OR CTRL+SHIFT+DOLLAR SIGN ($)
Custom Filter, Apply to Numeric Data	EX 329	Click AutoFilter arrow, point to Number Filters, click Custom Filter			
Custom Format, Create	EX 378			Format Cells, Number tab (Format Cells dialog box), Custom category	
Custom Name, Set for PivotTable Report Field	EX 520	Click field button in PivotTable Field List pane, click Value Field Settings, enter name			
Custom Page Header, First Page	EX 117		Page Setup Dialog Box Launcher (Page Layout tab | Page Setup group), Header/Footer tab, Different first page check box		
Custom Page Header, Odd and Even Pages	EX 117		Page Setup Dialog Box Launcher (Page Layout tab | Page Setup group), Header/Footer tab, 'Different odd and even pages' check box		

Microsoft Excel 2010 Quick Reference Summary *(continued)*

Task	Page Number	Mouse	Ribbon	Shortcut Menu	Keyboard Shortcut
Custom Sort, Apply to Table	EX 325		Sort & Filter button (Home tab | Editing group), click Custom Sort	Sort, click Custom Sort	
Custom View, Display	EX 735		Custom Views button (View tab | Workbook Views group), click custom view		
Custom View, Save	EX 734		Custom Views button (View tab | Workbook Views group), Add button, enter name		
Data Validation, Add to Cell	EX 573		Data Validation button (Data tab | Data Tools group)		
Data, Add to PivotTable Report	EX 502	Drag fields to PivotTable areas in PivotTable Fields List pane *or* Click check box for field name			
Data, Copy to Multiple Worksheets	EX 386		Copy button (Home tab | Clipboard group), select worksheets, Paste button (Home tab | Clipboard group)	Copy, select worksheets, Paste	CTRL+C, select worksheets, CTRL+V
Data, Enter on Multiple Worksheets at the Same Time	EX 387	Select worksheets, enter data			
Date, Format	EX 98		Format Cells: Number Dialog Box Launcher (Home tab | Number group)	Format Cells, Number tab (Format Cells dialog box)	
Define Range as Data Table	EX 249		What-If Analysis button (Data tab | Data Tools group), Data Table		
Delete Comment	EX 728		Delete Comment button (Review tab | Comments group)	Comment, Delete Comment	
Dependent Arrows, Remove	EX 566		Remove Arrows button (Formulas tab | Formula Auditing group)		
Dependents, Trace	EX 565		Trace Dependents button (Formulas tab | Formula Auditing group)		
Design Mode, Switch to	EX 656		Design Mode button (Developer tab | Controls group)		
Design, Change for PivotTable Report	EX 504		Report Layout button (PivotTable Tools Design tab | Layout group), option on Report Layout menu		
Developer Tab, Display	EX 636		Options command (File tab), Customize Ribbon category (Excel Options dialog box), Developer check box		

Microsoft Excel 2010 Quick Reference Summary *(continued)*

Task	Page Number	Mouse	Ribbon	Shortcut Menu	Keyboard Shortcut
Display Custom View	EX 735		Custom Views button (View tab | Workbook Views group), click custom view		
Display Developer Tab	EX 636		Options command (File tab), Customize Ribbon category (Excel Options dialog box), Developer check box		
Display Error Alert in Cell	EX 574		Data Validation button (Data tab | Data Tools group), Error Alert tab		
Display Hidden Workbook	EX 277		Unhide button (View tab | Window group), click workbook name (Unhide dialog box)		
Display Hidden Worksheet	EX 276			Unhide, click worksheet name (Unhide dialog box)	
Display Input Message in Cell	EX 574		Data Validation button (Data tab | Data Tools group), Input Message tab		
Document Properties, Change	EX 43		Properties button (File tab | Info tab)		
Document Properties, Print	EX 45		File tab | Print tab, first box arrow (Settings area)		
Document Properties, Set or View	EX 43		File tab | Info tab		
Document, Inspect	EX 606		Check for Issues button (File tab | Info tab), Inspect Document, Inspect button		
Drill Data through Worksheets	EX 387	Select worksheets, enter data			
Edit Comment, Edit	EX 714		Edit Comment button (Review tab | Comments group)	Cell, Edit Comment	SHIFT+F2
Edit Control Text	EX 673			Control (Design mode), Edit Text	
Edit Macro	EX 648		Macros button (Developer tab | Code group), Edit button		
E-mail Workbook	EX 723		Send Using E-mail (File tab | Save & Send tab), Send as Attachment button		
Enable All Macros	EX 636		Macro Security button (Developer tab | Code group), Enable all macros option button		
Entry, Complete	EX 8	Click Enter box			ENTER
Error Alert, Display in Cell	EX 574		Data Validation button (Data tab | Data Tools group), Error Alert tab		

Microsoft Excel 2010 Quick Reference Summary *(continued)*

Task	Page Number	Mouse	Ribbon	Shortcut Menu	Keyboard Shortcut
Errors, Check in Worksheet	EX 570		Error Checking button arrow (Formulas tab | Formula Auditing group), Trace Error button		
Excel 97-2003 File Type, Save Workbook as	EX 609	Save button, 'Save as type' box arrow, Excel 97-2003 Workbook			CTRL+S, 'Save as type' box arrow, Excel 97-2003 Workbook
Excel Macro-Enabled Workbook, Save as	EX 635	Save button, 'Save as type' box arrow, Excel Macro-Enabled Workbook			CTRL+S, 'Save as type' box arrow, Excel Macro-Enabled Workbook
Expand/Collapse Buttons, Hide in PivotTable Report	EX 523		+/− Buttons button (PivotTable Tools Options tab | Show group)		
Expand/Collapse Buttons, Show in PivotTable Report	EX 523		+/− Buttons button (PivotTable Tools Options tab | Show group)		
Field Entries, Format in PivotTable Report	EX 513			Field cell, Number Format	
Field Headers, Hide in PivotTable	EX 521		Field Headers button (PivotTable Tools Options tab | Show group)		
Field Headers, Show in PivotTable	EX 521		Field Headers button (PivotTable Tools Options tab | Show group)		
Fill Handle, Create Series with	EX 247	Select range, drag fill handle	Fill button (Home tab | Editing group), click option	Right-drag fill handle, click Fill Series	
Filter PivotTable Report	EX 506–EX 507	Click field AutoFilter button in report, click value(s)			
Filter PivotTable Report Using Multiple Criteria	EX 517	Click field AutoFilter button in report, click Select All, click value(s)			
Filter Values in PivotTable Report	EX 517	Click field AutoFilter button in report, click value(s), point to Value Filters, click command, select criteria			
Filter, Remove from PivotTable Report	EX 508	Drag field from filter area			
Find and Replace Text	EX 459		Find & Select button (Home tab | Editing group), Replace		CTRL+H
Find Text	EX 457		Find & Select button (Home tab | Editing group), Find		CTRL+F
Font Color	EX 27	Click Font Color box arrow on Mini toolbar	Font Color button arrow (Home tab | Font group)	Format Cells, Font tab (Format Cells dialog box)	
Font Size, Decrease	EX 26	Click Font Size box arrow on Mini toolbar	Decrease Font Size button (Home tab | Font group)	Format Cells, Font tab	

Microsoft Excel 2010 Quick Reference Summary (continued)

Task	Page Number	Mouse	Ribbon	Shortcut Menu	Keyboard Shortcut
Font Size, Increase	EX 26	Click Font Size box arrow on Mini toolbar	Increase Font Size button (Home tab | Font group)	Format Cells, Font tab (Format Cells dialog box)	
Font Type	EX 24	Click Font box arrow on Mini toolbar	Font box arrow (Home tab | Font group)	Format Cells, Font tab (Format Cells dialog box)	
Font, Change	EX 24	Click Font box arrow on Mini toolbar	Font box arrow (Home tab | Font group)	Format Cells, Font tab (Format Cells dialog box)	
Footer, Add	EX 398	Click Page Layout button in status bar, click Footer box			
Footer, Insert Page Number in	EX 398	In Page Layout view, click Footer box, type & [Page]	Page Number button (Header & Footer Tools Design tab | Header & Footer Elements group)		
Format Comment	EX 716		Edit Comment button (Review tab | Comments group), right-click text, Format Comment	Cell, Edit Comment, right-click text, Format Comment	
Format Field Entries in PivotTable Report	EX 513			Field cell, Number Format	
Format PivotTable Report	EX 512		More button in PivotTable Styles gallery (PivotTable Tools Design tab | PivotTable Styles group), style		
Format Range as Table	EX 305		Format as Table button (Home tab | Styles group), click table style		
Format Worksheet Background with Picture	EX 736		Background button (Page Layout tab | Page Setup group), navigate to picture file, Insert button (Sheet Background dialog box)		
Formulas Version	EX 119				CTRL+ACCENT MARK (`)
Generate Answer Report	EX 586		Solver button (Data tab | Analysis group), Solve button, Answer		
Generate Solution Using Solver	EX 586		Solver button (Data tab | Analysis group), Solve button		
Goal Seek, Start	EX 578		What-If Analysis button (Data tab | Data Tools group), Goal Seek		
Group Box, Add to Worksheet	EX 671		Insert button (Developer tab | Controls group), Group Box in Form Controls area, drag to draw control		
Gridlines, Show or Hide	EX 466		Gridlines check box (View tab | Show group)		
Header, Add	EX 397	Click Page Layout button in status bar, click Header box			

Microsoft Excel 2010 Quick Reference Summary *(continued)*

Task	Page Number	Mouse	Ribbon	Shortcut Menu	Keyboard Shortcut
Header, Insert Current Date in	EX 398	In Page Layout view, click Header box, type & [Date]	Current Date button (Header & Footer Tools Design tab | Header & Footer Elements group)		
Header, Insert Current Time in	EX 398	In Page Layout view, click Header box, type & [Time]	Current Time button (Header & Footer Tools Design tab | Header & Footer Elements group)		
Height, Set for Slicer Height	EX 539		Height text box (Slicer Tools Options tab | Buttons group), enter height		
Hide PivotTable Field Headers	EX 521		Field Headers button (PivotTable Tools Options tab | Show group)		
Hide PivotTable Field List Pane	EX 521		Field List button (PivotTable Tools Options tab | Show group)		
Hide Workbook	EX 277		Hide button (View tab | Window group)		
Hide Worksheet	EX 276			Hide	
Highlight Cells	EX 28	Drag mouse pointer			SHIFT+ARROW KEY
Icon Set, Use in Conditional Formatting Rule	EX 317		Conditional Formatting button (Home tab | Styles group), New Rule, Format Style box arrow (New Formatting Rule dialog box), Icon Sets, enter condition		
Icon, Modify for Button on Quick Access Toolbar	EX 651			Quick Access Toolbar, Customize Quick Access Toolbar, click command, click Modify button, click icon	
Image, Add to Worksheet	EX 474		Insert Picture from File button (Insert tab | Illustrations group), double-click file		
Image, Adjust Color	APP 26		Color button (Picture Tools Format tab | Adjust group)		
Image, Apply Style to	EX 475		Picture Styles More button (Picture Tools Format tab | Picture Styles group), click style		
Image, Make Corrections	APP 26		Corrections button (Picture Tools Format tab | Adjust group), select desired corrections		
Image, Rotate	EX 475		Rotate button (Picture Tools Format tab | Arrange group)		

Microsoft Excel 2010 Quick Reference Summary *(continued)*

Task	Page Number	Mouse	Ribbon	Shortcut Menu	Keyboard Shortcut
Import Access Data	EX 443		From Access button (Data tab | Get External Data group), double-click file (Select Data Source dialog box)		
Import Comma-Delimited Text File	EX 439		From Text button (Data tab | Get External Data group), double-click file (Import Text File dialog box), complete wizard		
Import Web Page Data	EX 447		From Web button (Data tab | Get External Data group), enter address (New Web Query dialog box), select table, click Import		
In-Cell Editing	EX 50	Double-click cell			F2
Input Message, Display in Cell	EX 574		Data Validation button (Data tab | Data Tools group), Input Message tab		
Inspect Document	EX 606		Check for Issues button (File tab | Info tab), Inspect Document, Inspect button		
Insert and Overtype modes, Toggle between	EX 50				INSERT
Insert Page Break	EX 402		Breaks button (Page Layout tab | Page Setup group), Insert Page Break		
Insertion Point, Move	EX 8	Click			Use arrow keys
Insertion Point, Move to Beginning of Data in Cell	EX 51	Point to left of first character and click			HOME
Insertion Point, Move to Ending of Data in Cell	EX 51	Point to right of last character and click			END
Invalid Data, Circle	EX 579		Data Validation button arrow (Data tab | Data Tools group), Circle Invalid Data		
Iterative Calculation, Enable	EX 571		Formulas button (File tab | Options tab) Enable Iterative Calculation		
Layout, Change for PivotTable Report	EX 504		Report Layout button (PivotTable Tools Design tab | Layout group), option on Report Layout menu		
Legend, Remove from Chart	EX 462		Legend button (Chart Tools Layout tab | Labels group), None		
Line Chart, Create 2-D	EX 495		Line button (Insert tab | Charts group), chart in 2-D Line area		
Macro Security, Set Level	EX 636		Macro Security button (Developer tab | Code group), click option button		
Macro, Edit	EX 648		Macros button (Developer tab | Code group), Edit button		

Microsoft Excel 2010 Quick Reference Summary *(continued)*

Task	Page Number	Mouse	Ribbon	Shortcut Menu	Keyboard Shortcut
Macro, Record	EX 639	Record Macro button in status bar	Record Macro button (Developer tab | Code group), enter macro name		
Macro, Run	EX 647		Macros button (Developer tab | Code group), macro name		CTRL+SHORTCUT KEY
Macro, Stop Recording	EX 640	Stop Recording Macro button in status bar	Stop Recording button (Developer tab | Code group)		
Macros, Enable All	EX 636		Macro Security button (Developer tab | Code group), Enable all macros option button		
Margins, Change	EX 114	Click Page Layout button on status bar, click Page Layout tab, click Margins button	Page Setup Dialog Box Launcher (Page Layout tab | Page Setup group), Margins tab		
Mark Workbook as Final	EX 610		Protect Workbook button (File tab | Info tab), Mark as Final		
Max Function	EX 86	Click Insert Function box in formula bar, click MAX in Select a function list, click OK, select range, click OK	Sum button arrow (Home tab | Editing group) or Sum button arrow (Formulas tab | Function Library group)		
Min Function	EX 87	Click Insert Function box in formula bar, click MIN in Select a function list, click OK, select range, click OK	Sum button arrow (Home tab | Editing group) or Sum button arrow (Formulas tab | Sum group), Margins tab		
Modify Icon for Button on Quick Access Toolbar	EX 651			Quick Access Toolbar, Customize Quick Access Toolbar, click command, click Modify button, click icon	
Modify Table Quick Style	EX 307		Format as Table button (Home tab | Styles group), right-click table style, click Duplicate, type style name, set formatting options		
Move Chart	EX 461		Move Chart button (Chart Tools Design tab | Location group), select option (Move Chart dialog box)		
Multiple Criteria, Filter PivotTable Report Using	EX 517	Click field AutoFilter button in report, click Select All, click value(s)			
Multiple Workbooks, Arrange	EX 406		Arrange All button (View tab | Window group), click Arrange option (Arrange Windows dialog box)		
Name Cells	EX 238	Click Name box, type name	Define Name button (Formulas tab | Defined Names group)		
Name, Assign to Cell	EX 679		Name Manager button (Formulas tab | Defined Names group), New button		

Microsoft Excel 2010 Quick Reference Summary *(continued)*

Task	Page Number	Mouse	Ribbon	Shortcut Menu	Keyboard Shortcut
Name, Customize for PivotTable Report Field	EX 520	Click field button in PivotTable Field List pane, click Value Field Settings, enter name			
New Line in Cell, Start	EX 71				ALT+ENTER
Numbers, Format	EX 31	Click Accounting Number Format, Percent Style, or Comma Style button on Mini toolbar	Cell Styles button (Home tab | Styles group) or Accounting Number Format, Percent Style, or Comma Style button (Home tab | Number group), or Format Cells: Number Dialog Box Launcher | Accounting, or Percentage or Number Format list arrow | Accounting or Percentage		
Open Watch Window	EX 567		Watch Window button (Formulas tab | Formula Auditing group)		
Open Workbook	EX 48		Open or Recent (File tab)		CTRL+O
Option Button, Add to Worksheet	EX 669		Insert button (Developer tab | Controls group), Option Button in Form Controls area, drag to draw control		
Outline Worksheet	EX 345		Group button (Data tab | Outline group)		
Outline, Remove from Group Box Control	EX 683		View Code button (Developer tab | Controls group), press CTRL+G, type `activesheet .groupboxes.visible = false`		
Page Break, Hide	EX 403		File tab, Options button, Advanced button (Excel Options dialog box), 'Show page breaks' check box		
Page Break, Insert	EX 402		Breaks button (Page Layout tab | Page Setup group), Insert Page Break		
Page Break, Remove	EX 402		Breaks button (Page Layout tab | Page Setup group), Remove Page Break		
Password-Protect Worksheet	EX 645		Protect Sheet button (Review tab | Changes group), enter password		
PDF, Save Worksheet as	EX 750		Save As (File tab), 'Save as type' button, PDF		
Percent Series, Create with Fill Handle	EX 247	Select range, drag fill handle	Fill button (Home tab | Editing group), click option	Right-drag fill handle, click Fill Series	
Percent Style Format	EX 103		Percent Style button (Home tab | Number group)	Format Cells, Number tab (Format Cells dialog box), Percentage	CTRL+SHIFT+ percent sign (%)

Microsoft Excel 2010 Quick Reference Summary *(continued)*

Task	Page Number	Mouse	Ribbon	Shortcut Menu	Keyboard Shortcut
Picture, Display as Worksheet Background	EX 736		Background button (Page Layout tab | Page Setup group), navigate to picture file, Insert button (Sheet Background dialog box)		
PivotChart Report, Change View	EX 529	Drag row labels or column labels in PivotTable Fields List pane to a new location *or* Click field button arrow, click Move Up or Move Down			
PivotChart Report, Create	EX 524		PivotChart button (PivotTable Tools Options tab | Tools group), chart type		
PivotChart, Add Title to	EX 526		Chart Title button (PivotChart Tools Layout tab | Labels group)		
PivotChart, Change Type	EX 526		Change Chart Type button (PivotChart Tools Design tab | Type group), chart type		
PivotChart, Create Directly from Data	EX 530		PivotTable button arrow (Insert tab | Tables group), PivotChart, select location		
PivotChart, Format Chart Wall	EX 528		Chart Wall button (PivotChart Tools Layout tab | Background group)		
PivotTable Field Headers, Hide	EX 521		Field Headers button (PivotTable Tools Options tab | Show group)		
PivotTable Field Headers, Show	EX 521		Field Headers button (PivotTable Tools Options tab | Show group)		
PivotTable Field List Pane, Hide	EX 521		Field List button (PivotTable Tools Options tab | Show group)		
PivotTable Field List Pane, Show	EX 521		Field List button (PivotTable Tools Options tab | Show group)		
PivotTable Report Columns, Autofit on Update	EX 522		Options button (PivotTable Tools Options tab | PivotTable group), 'Autofit column widths on update' check box		
PivotTable Report Columns, Turn Off Autofit on Update	EX 522		Options button (PivotTable Tools Options tab | PivotTable group), 'Autofit column widths on update' check box		
PivotTable Report Field, Set Custom Name for	EX 520	Click field button in PivotTable Field List pane, click Value Field Settings, enter name			

Microsoft Excel 2010 Quick Reference Summary *(continued)*

Task	Page Number	Mouse	Ribbon	Shortcut Menu	Keyboard Shortcut
PivotTable Report, Add Calculated Field to	EX 532		Calculations button (PivotTable Tools Options tab | Calculations group), Fields, Items, & Sets, Calculated Field		
PivotTable Report, Add Data to	EX 502	Drag fields to PivotTable areas in PivotTable Fields List pane *or* Click check box for field name			
PivotTable Report, Change Design of	EX 504		Report Layout button (PivotTable Tools Design tab | Layout group), option on Report Layout menu		
PivotTable Report, Change Summary Functions in	EX 514			Field cell, Summarize Values By, function	
PivotTable Report, Change View	EX 505	Drag row labels or column labels in PivotTable Fields List pane to a new location *or* Click field button arrow, click Move Up or Move Down			
PivotTable Report, Create Blank	EX 501		PivotTable button arrow (Insert tab | Tables group), PivotTable, OK		
PivotTable Report, Display AutoFilter buttons in	EX 508		Field Headers button (PivotTable Tools Options tab | Show group)		
PivotTable Report, Filter	EX 506–EX 507	Click field AutoFilter button in report, click value(s)			
PivotTable Report, Filter Using Multiple Criteria	EX 517	Click field AutoFilter button in report, click Select All, click value(s)			
PivotTable Report, Filter Values	EX 517	Click field AutoFilter button in report, click value(s), point to Value Filters, click command, select criteria			
PivotTable Report, Format	EX 512		More button in PivotTable Styles gallery (PivotTable Tools Design tab | PivotTable Styles group), style		
PivotTable Report, Format Field Entries in	EX 513			Field cell, Number Format	
PivotTable Report, Hide Expand/Collapse Buttons	EX 523		+/− Buttons button (PivotTable Tools Options tab | Show group)		
PivotTable Report, Refresh	EX 519		Refresh button (PivotTable Tools Options tab | Data group)		

Microsoft Excel 2010 Quick Reference Summary *(continued)*

Task	Page Number	Mouse	Ribbon	Shortcut Menu	Keyboard Shortcut
PivotTable Report, Remove Filter	EX 508	Drag field from filter area			
PivotTable Report, Show Expand/Collapse Buttons	EX 523		+/− Buttons button (PivotTable Tools Options tab | Show group)		
Precedent Arrows, Remove	EX 564		Remove Arrows button arrow (Formulas tab | Formula Auditing group)		
Precedents, Review on Different Worksheet	EX 563	Double-click dashed arrow, click sheet and cell reference			
Precedents, Trace	EX 562		Trace Precedents button (Formulas tab | Formula Auditing group)		
Print Area, Set	EX 268		Print Area button (Page Layout tab | Page Setup group), Set Print Area		
Print Scaling Option	EX 120		Page Setup Dialog Box Launcher (Page Layout tab | Page Setup group)		
Print Section of Worksheet	EX 118		Print Active Sheets (File | Print tab) or Print Area button (Page Layout tab | Page Setup group)		
Print Worksheet	EX 46		File tab | Print tab		CTRL+P
Properties, Select for Control	EX 657		Properties button (Developer tab | Controls group)	Control (in Design mode), Properties	
Protect Worksheet	EX 274, EX 645		Protect Sheet button (Review tab | Changes group)		
Quick Access Toolbar, Add Button to	EX 649			Quick Access Toolbar, Customize Quick Access Toolbar, click command, click Add button	
Quick Access Toolbar, Modify Icon for Button	EX 651			Quick Access Toolbar, Customize Quick Access Toolbar, click command, click Modify button, click icon	
Quit Excel	EX 47	Click Close button on right side of title bar	Exit (File tab)		
Range Finder	EX 91	Double-click cell			
Range, Deselect	EX 19	Click outside range			
Range, Format as Table	EX 305		Format as Table button (Home tab | Styles group), click table style		
Range, Select	EX 28	Drag fill handle through range			

Microsoft Excel 2010 Quick Reference Summary (continued)

Task	Page Number	Mouse	Ribbon	Shortcut Menu	Keyboard Shortcut
Record Macro	EX 639	Record Macro button in status bar	Record Macro button (Developer tab | Code group), enter macro name		
Record Macro Using Relative References	EX 639		Use Relative References button (Developer tab | Code group)		
Redo	EX 51	Click Redo button on Quick Access Toolbar			CTRL+Y
Refresh PivotTable Report	EX 519		Refresh button (PivotTable Tools Options tab | Data group)		
Relative References, Record in Macro	EX 639		Use Relative References button (Developer tab | Code group)		
Remove Dependent Arrows	EX 566		Remove Arrows button (Formulas tab | Formula Auditing group)		
Remove Outline from Group Box Control	EX 683		View Code button (Developer tab | Controls group), press CTRL+G, type activesheet. groupboxes.visible = false		
Remove Page Break	EX 402		Breaks button (Page Layout tab | Page Setup group), Remove Page Break		
Remove Precedent Arrows	EX 564		Remove Arrows button arrow (Formulas tab | Formula Auditing group)		
Review Precedents on Different Worksheet	EX 563	Double-click dashed arrow, click sheet and cell reference			
Review Tracked Changes	EX 722		Track Changes button (Review tab | Changes group), Highlight Changes		
Rotate 3-D Chart	EX 462		3-D Rotation button (Chart Tools Layout tab | Background group), change rotation (Format Chart Area dialog box)		
Row Height	EX 110	Drag row heading boundary		Row Height	
Row Label Filter, Remove from PivotTable Report	EX 510	Click field AutoFilter button in report, click Clear Filter From *field*			
Row, Add to Table	EX 156	Drag table sizing handle	Insert button arrow (Home tab | Cells group), Insert Table Rows Above or Insert Table Row Below	Insert, Table Rows Above or Table Row Below	TAB (in last cell)
Run Macro	EX 647		Macros button (Developer tab | Code group), macro name		CTRL+SHORTCUT KEY
Run Mode, Switch to	EX 662		Design Mode button (Developer tab | Controls group)		

Microsoft Excel 2010 Quick Reference Summary *(continued)*

Task	Page Number	Mouse	Ribbon	Shortcut Menu	Keyboard Shortcut
Save Custom View	EX 734		Custom Views button (View tab | Workbook Views group), Add button, enter name		
Save Data as Scenario	EX 590		What-If Analysis button (Data tab | Data Tools group), Scenario Manager, Add button, enter name		
Save Workbook	EX 20	Click Save button on Quick Access Toolbar	Save button (File tab)		CTRL+S
Save Workbook as Excel Macro-Enabled Workbook	EX 635	Save button, 'Save as type' box arrow, Excel Macro-Enabled Workbook			CTRL+S, 'Save as type' box arrow, Excel Macro-Enabled Workbook
Save Workbook, New Name	EX 20		Save As button (File tab)		
Save Workbook, Same Name	EX 20	Click Save button on Quick Access Toolbar	Save button (File tab)		CTRL+S
Save Worksheet as PDF	EX 750		Save As button (File tab), 'Save as type' button, PDF		
Save Worksheet to Web	EX 744		Save to Web (File tab | Save & Send tab)		
Scenario PivotTable Worksheet, Create	EX 604		What-If Analysis button (Data tab | Data Tools group), Scenario Manager, Summary button, Scenario PivotTable report		
Scenario Summary Worksheet, Create	EX 601		What-If Analysis button (Data tab | Data Tools group), Scenario Manager, scenario name, Summary button		
Scenario, Create from Data	EX 590		What-If Analysis button (Data tab | Data Tools group), Scenario Manager, Add button, enter name		
Scenario, Show Saved	EX 599		What-If Analysis button (Data tab | Data Tools group), Scenario Manager, scenario name, Show button		
Screen Shot, Add to Worksheet	EX 477		Screenshot button (Insert tab | Illustrations group), click screen image		
Select Cell	EX 7	Click cell or click Name box, type cell reference, press ENTER			Use arrow keys
Select Entire Worksheet	EX 52	Click Select All button			CTRL+A
Select Nonadjacent Cells	EX 100	Select first cell, hold down CTRL key while selecting second cell			
Select Solving Method in Solver	EX 586		Solver button (Data tab | Analysis group), Select a Solving Method box arrow		

Microsoft Excel 2010 Quick Reference Summary *(continued)*

Task	Page Number	Mouse	Ribbon	Shortcut Menu	Keyboard Shortcut
Selected Characters, Delete	EX 50		Cut button (Home tab | Clipboard group)		DELETE
Selected Chart, Delete	EX 53				DELETE
Send Workbook Using E-mail	EX 723		Send Using E-mail (File tab | Save & Send tab), Send as Attachment button		
Set Macro Security Level	EX 636		Macro Security button (Developer tab | Code group), click option button		
Set Print Area	EX 268		Print Area button (Page Layout tab | Page Setup group), Set Print Area		
Set Up Worksheet to Print	EX 267		Page Setup Dialog Box Launcher (Page Layout tab | Page Setup group)		
Share Workbook	EX 718		Share Workbook button (Review tab | Changes group), 'Allow changes by more than one user at the same time' check box		
Sheet Name, Change	EX 42	Double-click sheet name		Rename	
Show All Comments	EX 728		Show All Comments button (Review tab | Comments group)		
Show PivotTable Field Headers	EX 521		Field Headers button (PivotTable Tools Options tab | Show group)		
Show PivotTable Field List Pane	EX 521		Field List button (PivotTable Tools Options tab | Show group)		
Show Saved Scenario	EX 599		What-If Analysis button (Data tab | Data Tools group), Scenario Manager, scenario name, Show button		
Slicer, Change Style	EX 539		More button (Slicer Tools Options tab | Slicer Styles group), select style		
Slicer, Clear Filter in	EX 541	Click Clear Filter button			
Slicer, Set Height	EX 539		Height text box (Slicer Tools Options tab | Buttons group), enter height		
Slicer, Set Width	EX 539		Width text box (Slicer Tools Options tab | Buttons group), enter width		
Slicer, Use	EX 540	Click slicer button			
Slicers, Add to Worksheet	EX 537		Insert Slicer button arrow (PivotChart Tools Analyze tab | Data group), Insert Slicer		
SmartArt, Add Effect to	EX 473		SmartArt Styles More button (SmartArt Tools Design tab | SmartArt Styles group), click style		

Microsoft Excel 2010 Quick Reference Summary *(continued)*

Task	Page Number	Mouse	Ribbon	Shortcut Menu	Keyboard Shortcut
SmartArt, Add Picture to	EX 472	Click Insert Picture icon, double-click file			
SmartArt, Add Shape to	EX 469			Add Shape, add shape option	
SmartArt, Add to Worksheet	EX 466		SmartArt button (Insert tab | Illustrations group), click type (Choose a SmartArt Graphic dialog box), click layout		
Solver Answer Report, Generate	EX 586		Solver button (Data tab | Analysis group), Solve button, Answer		
Solver, Add Constraint to	EX 583		Solver button (Data tab | Analysis group), Add button		
Solver, Generate Solution	EX 586		Solver button (Data tab | Analysis group), Solve button		
Solver, Select Solving Method in	EX 586		Solver button (Data tab | Analysis group), Select a Solving Method box arrow		
Solver, Start	EX 583		Solver button (Data tab | Analysis group)		
Solving Method, Select in Solver	EX 586		Solver button (Data tab | Analysis group), Select a Solving Method box arrow		
Sort Table	EX 322		Sort & Filter button (Home tab | Editing group), click sort option	Sort, click sort option	
Sparkline Chart, Customize	EX 173		Any check box(es) (Sparkline Tools Design tab | Show group)		
Sparkline Chart, Format	EX 173		More button (Sparkline Tools Design tab | Style group)		
Sparkline Chart, Insert	EX 173		Insert Line/Column/Win/Loss Sparkline button (Insert tab | Sparklines group)		
Spelling	EX 112		Spelling button (Review tab | Proofing group)		F7
Start Goal Seek	EX 578		What-If Analysis button (Data tab | Data Tools group), Goal Seek		
Start Solver	EX 583		Solver button (Data tab | Analysis group)		
Stop Recording Macro	EX 640	Stop Recording Macro button in status bar	Stop Recording button (Developer tab | Code group)		
Style, Change for Slicer	EX 539		More button (Slicer Tools Options tab | Slicer Styles group), select style		
Subtotals, Display in Table	EX 342		Convert table to range, click Subtotal button (Data tab | Outline group)	Table, Convert to Range, click Yes (Microsoft Excel dialog box), click Subtotal button (Data tab | Outline group)	

Microsoft Excel 2010 Quick Reference Summary *(continued)*

Task	Page Number	Mouse	Ribbon	Shortcut Menu	Keyboard Shortcut
Subtotals, Remove	EX 345		Subtotal button (Data tab | Outline group), Remove All button (Subtotal dialog box)		
Sum	EX 15	Click Insert Function button in formula bar, click SUM in Select a function list, click OK, select range, click OK	Sum button (Home tab | Editing group)		ALT+EQUAL SIGN (=) twice
Summary Functions, Change in PivotTable Report	EX 514			Field cell, Summarize Values By, function	
Switch to Other Open Workbook	EX 405		Switch Windows button (View tab | Window group), click open workbook		
Table Quick Style, Modify	EX 307		Format as Table button (Home tab | Styles group), right-click table style, click Duplicate, type style name, set formatting options		
Table, Add Row to	EX 156	Drag table sizing handle	Insert button arrow (Home tab | Cells group), Insert Table Rows Above *or* Insert Table Row Below	Insert, Table Rows Above *or* Table Row Below	TAB (in last cell)
Table, Add Total Row to	EX 319		Total Row check box (Table Tools Design tab | Table Style Options group)	Table, Totals Row	
Table, Apply Custom Sort	EX 325		Sort & Filter button (Home tab | Editing group), click Custom Sort	Sort, click Custom Sort	
Table, Convert to Range	EX 312			Table, Convert to Range	
Table, Sort	EX 322		Sort & Filter button (Home tab | Editing group), click sort option	Sort, click sort option	
Template, Create from Workbook	EX 435	Click Save button, click 'Save as type' box arrow, click Excel Template			CTRL+S, 'Save as type' box arrow, Excel Template
Template, Save as Workbook	EX 438		Save As button (File tab), 'Save as type' box arrow, Excel Workbook		
Text Box, Add to Worksheet	EX 672		Insert button (Developer tab | Controls group), Text Box in ActiveX Controls area, drag to draw control		
Text, Convert to Columns	EX 454		Text to Columns button (Data tab | Data Tools group), complete wizard		
Text, Delete After Typing (but before pressing the ENTER key)	EX 8	Click Cancel box in formula bar			ESC
Text, Delete While Typing	EX 8				BACKSPACE
Title, Add to PivotChart	EX 526		Chart Title button (PivotChart Tools Layout tab | Labels group)		

Microsoft Excel 2010 Quick Reference Summary *(continued)*

Task	Page Number	Mouse	Ribbon	Shortcut Menu	Keyboard Shortcut
Total Row, Add to Table	EX 319		Total Row check box (Table Tools Design tab | Table Style Options group)	Table, Totals Row	
Trace Dependents	EX 565		Trace Dependents button (Formulas tab | Formula Auditing group)		
Trace Errors in Worksheet	EX 570		Error Checking button arrow (Formulas tab | Formula Auditing group), Trace Error button		
Trace Precedents	EX 562		Trace Precedents button (Formulas tab | Formula Auditing group)		
Track Changes, Turn Off	EX 729		Track Changes button (Review tab | Changes group), Highlight Changes, 'Track changes while editing' check box		
Track Changes, Turn On	EX 725		Track Changes button (Review tab | Changes group), Highlight Changes, 'Track changes while editing' check box		
Tracked Change, Accept or Reject	EX 727		Track Changes button (Review tab | Changes group), Accept/Reject Changes, OK		
Tracked Changes, Review	EX 722		Track Changes button (Review tab | Changes group), Highlight Changes		
Transpose Copied Word Data	EX 451		Paste button arrow (Home tab | Clipboard group), Transpose		
Trendline, Add to Chart	EX 497		Trendline button (Chart Tools Layout tab | Analysis group), trendline type *or* Trendline button (Chart Tools Layout tab | Analysis group), More Trendline Options, Trend/Regression Type option button, Close		
Turn Off Track Changes	EX 729		Track Changes button (Review tab | Changes group), Highlight Changes, 'Track changes while editing' check box		
Turn Off Workbook Sharing	EX 721		Share Workbook button (Review tab | Changes group), 'Allow changes by more than one user at the same time' check box		

Microsoft Excel 2010 Quick Reference Summary (continued)

Task	Page Number	Mouse	Ribbon	Shortcut Menu	Keyboard Shortcut
Turn On Track Changes	EX 725		Track Changes button (Review tab | Changes group), Highlight Changes, 'Track changes while editing' check box		
Undo	EX 51	Click Undo button on Quick Access Toolbar			CTRL+Z
Unlock Cells	EX 273			Format Cells, Protection tab (Format Cells dialog box), Locked check box	
Unprotect Worksheet	EX 275		Unprotect Sheet button (Review tab | Changes group), enter password		
Use Slicer	EX 540	Click slicer button			
User Input, Record for Control	EX 675			Control (Design mode), Format Control, Control tab	
Validate Cell Data	EX 573		Data Validation button (Data tab | Data Tools group)		
Validation Circles, Clear	EX 580		Data Validation button arrow (Data tab | Data Tools group), Clear Validation Circles		
Validation Rules, Copy	EX 575		Copy cell contain validation rule, Paste Options button (Home tab | Clipboard group) Paste Special, Validation, OK		
VBA Code, Add to Control	EX 661	Double-click control	Visual Basic button (Developer tab | Code group)	Control (in Design mode), View Code	
Versions, Manage	EX 48		Manage Versions button (File tab | Info Tab)		
View Workbooks Side by Side	EX 731		View Side by Side button (View tab | Window group)		
View, Change for PivotTable Report	EX 505	Drag row labels or column labels in PivotTable Fields List pane to a new location or Click field button arrow, click Move Up or Move Down			
Watch Window, Add Cells to Watch	EX 567	Click Add Watch button on Watch Window toolbar			
Watch Window, Open	EX 567		Watch Window button (Formulas tab | Formula Auditing group)		

Microsoft Excel 2010 Quick Reference Summary *(continued)*

Task	Page Number	Mouse	Ribbon	Shortcut Menu	Keyboard Shortcut
Web Page Data, Import	EX 447		From Web button (Data tab | Get External Data group), enter address (New Web Query dialog box), select table, click Import		
Web, Save Worksheet to	EX 744		Save to Web (File tab | Save & Send tab)		
Width, Set for Slicer	EX 539		Width text box (Slicer Tools Options tab | Buttons group), enter width		
Word Data, Transpose When Pasted	EX 451		Paste button arrow (Home tab | Clipboard group), Transpose		
WordArt, Add to Worksheet	EX 463		WordArt button (Insert tab | Text group), click WordArt		
Workbook Sharing, Turn Off	EX 721		Share Workbook button (Review tab | Changes group), 'Allow changes by more than one user at the same time' check box		
Workbook Theme, Change	EX 94		Themes button (Page Layout tab | Themes group)		
Workbook, Display Hidden	EX 277		Unhide button (View tab | Window group), click workbook name (Unhide dialog box)		
Workbook, Hide	EX 277		Hide button (View tab | Window group)		
Workbook, Mark as Final	EX 610		Protect Workbook button (File tab | Info tab), Mark as Final		
Workbook, Open Copy	EX 199		New Window button (View tab | Windows group)		
Workbook, Save as Excel 97-2003 File Type	EX 609	Click Save button, 'Save as type' box arrow, Excel 97-2003 Workbook			CTRL+S, 'Save as type' box arrow, Excel 97-2003 Workbook
Workbook, Save as Template	EX 436	Click Save button, click 'Save as type' box arrow, click Excel Template			CTRL+S, 'Save as type' box arrow, Excel Template
Workbook, Send Using E-mail	EX 723		Send Using E-mail (File tab | Save & Send tab), Send as Attachment button		
Workbook, Share	EX 718		Share Workbook button (Review tab | Changes group), 'Allow changes by more than one user at the same time' check box		
Workbook, Switch to Other Open	EX 405		Switch Windows button (View tab | Window group), click open workbook		
Workbooks, View Side by Side	EX 731		View Side by Side button (View tab | Window group)		

Microsoft Excel 2010 Quick Reference Summary *(continued)*

Task	Page Number	Mouse	Ribbon	Shortcut Menu	Keyboard Shortcut
Worksheet Background, Format with Picture	EX 736		Background button (Page Layout tab | Page Setup group), navigate to picture file, Insert button (Sheet Background dialog box)		
Worksheet Name, Change	EX 42	Double-click sheet tab, type name		Rename	
Worksheet, Add to Workbook	EX 384	Click Insert Worksheet tab	Insert Cells button arrow (Home tab | Cells group), Insert Sheet	Insert	SHIFT+F11
Worksheet, Clear	EX 52		Select All button, Clear button (Home tab | Editing group)		CTRL+A, DELETE
Worksheet, Display Hidden	EX 276			Unhide, click worksheet name (Unhide dialog box)	
Worksheet, Hide	EX 276			Hide	
Worksheet, Outline	EX 345		Group button (Data tab | Outline group)		
Worksheet, Prepare to Print	EX 267		Page Setup Dialog Box Launcher (Page Layout tab | Page Setup group)		
Worksheet, Preview	EX 46		File tab | Print tab		CTRL+P
Worksheet, Protect	EX 274		Protect Sheet button (Review tab | Changes group)		
Worksheet, Save to Web	EX 744		Save to Web (File tab | Save & Send tab)		
Worksheet, Unprotect	EX 275, EX 633		Unprotect Sheet button (Review tab | Changes group), enter password		
Workspace File, Create	EX 407		Save Workspace button (View tab | Window group)		

Credits

Excel Chapter 7: Images in Figure 7-1, Figures 7–78 – 7-84: Courtesy of Seagate Technology; © Wm. Baker / GhostWorx Images / Alamy; © JUPITERIMAGES/ Thinkstock / Alamy; Courtesy of Intel Corporation; Courtesy of Hewlett-Packard Company; © Andrew Howe /iStockphoto; © Jaroslaw Wojcik/iStockphoto; Courtesy of Intel Corporation; Courtesy of Kingston Technology.